The Reign of King Henry VI
The Exercise of Royal Authority
1422–1461

Ralph A. Griffiths

Reader in History, University College of Swansea

The Reign of King Henry VI

The exercise of royal authority,
1422–1461

UNIVERSITY OF CALIFORNIA PRESS
Berkeley and Los Angeles

University of California Press
Berkeley and Los Angeles, California

© Ralph A. Griffiths 1981

Typeset in Great Britain by Elanders Ltd, Inverness, Scotland
Printed and bound in the United States of America

ISBN 0–520–04372–3
Library of Congress Catalog Card Number: 80:53771

For Margaret Sharp and Charles Ross who first
introduced me to Henry VI and those
in the University College of Swansea with whom
I have studied him since

Preface

This book began as a study of the structure of politics during Lancastrian England. It ended as a study of the exercise of royal authority during the reign of Henry VI. The reason for the lowering of sights and the change of direction was an early realization that many basic questions relating to Henry's reign required resolution – more than were evident at first sight. This fact, combined with the lack of a reliable, up-to-date general account of events between 1422 and 1461, modified my original intention. Many of the outstanding problems concerned the nature of the government conducted by King Henry or in his name, and its impact on the king's subjects, the provinces of the realm, and neighbouring countries. The fact that Henry VI reigned for at least fourteen years before he began to rule, and then, in 1453, collapsed so completely that the realm's government fell into the hands of others, dictated a tripartite arrangement for the volume. That being so, neither a biographical study of Henry himself (if that were possible), nor a straightforward chronological discussion of the politics of the reign, seemed quite appropriate to my purpose. The result is an exceptionally long book.

My debts, incurred over several years of investigation, are just as prodigious. As a result of grants from the British Academy, the Leverhulme Trust, the Twenty-seven Foundation, and the Council of the University College of Swansea, I visited a number of record repositories which would otherwise have been beyond my reach. I record with gratitude the co-operation and courtesy which made my archival perambulations in the United Kingdom, France, and the United States such a pleasure. Access to the private muniments at Belvoir Castle, Eton College, and Longleat was made possible by the generosity, respectively, of His Grace the Duke of Rutland, the Librarian of Eton (Dr P. Strong) and Mrs F. Strong, and the Marquess of Bath. It was a privilege to be able to read a number of unpublished theses and dissertations; they contain much that is valuable and it is heartening to observe a century that was once the 'Cinderella' of English history now attracting such well-directed attention. Indeed, Dr C. F. Richmond and Professor C. D. Ross kindly brought to my notice several outstanding undergraduate dissertations which bore on my theme; they form a notable contribution to the study of the reign. I have long found students of fifteenth-century England to be a congenial and helpful band, and my enquiries of them (and others) were, without exception, answered readily and fully; some even offered me material unsolicitedly. In this connection, I am especially indebted to Miss P. Black, Miss M. Condon, Dr R. W. Dunning, Mr D. A. L. Morgan, Dr J. E. Law, Miss J. D. Lee (of the Henry VI Society), Dr C. F. Richmond, Mr I. W. Rowlands, Professor R. L. Storey, and Dr B. Waller. In a different category are Mr J. G. Reid and Dr R. S. Thomas, who placed their notes on fifteenth-century archives at my disposal; periodic acknowledgement in the footnotes hardly does justice to their kindness.

A special word of thanks is due to Dr R. W. Dunning, Mr T. H. Lloyd, Professor J. W. McKenna, Professor A. C. Reeves, and Professor C. D. Ross, who read various parts of this book in manuscript; I trust I have used their valued comments properly and sensibly. The Librarian and his staff at the University College of Swansea showed me their customary patience and forbearance; in particular, Dr F. G. Cowley and Miss M. K. Dale tolerated what must, I think, have been unreasonable demands on their time and knowledge. To produce a final manuscript would have been impossible without the swift and tireless work of my mother, Mrs M. L. Griffiths, who typed most of the book, supplemented by the efforts of the several secretaries of the department of history at Swansea. Mr R. Davies kindly produced many of the plates, and Mr G. B. Lewis the maps. To all go my sincere thanks. Finally, no author has had a more sympathetic publisher: the patience of John Collis over several years is matched only by the wisdom of his comments on earlier drafts of all the chapters; the suggestions of his colleague Charles Allen were also much appreciated.

University College
Swansea
April 1980

Ralph A. Griffiths

Contents

Illustrations and maps

Abbreviations

Unless otherwise stated, the place of publication is London.

Add. Ch.	British Library, additional charter
Add. MS	British Library, additional manuscript
AHC	*Annuarium historiae conciliorum*
AJ	*Archaeological journal*
Amunde-sham	J. Amundesham, *Annales monasterii S. Albani,* ed. H. T. Riley (2 vols., RS, 1870–71).
AN	Archives Nationales, Paris
Arch. Camb.	*Archaeologia Cambrensis*
Arch. Cant.	*Archaeologia Cantiana* (Kent archaeological society)
Bain	J. Bain (ed.), *Calendar of documents relating to Scotland preserved in the Public Record Office, London* (4 vols., Edinburgh, 1881–84)
Basin	C. Samaran (ed.), *T. Basin, Histoire de Charles VII* (2 vols., Paris, 1933, 1944)
BBCS	*Bulletin of the board of celtic studies*
Bekynton Corr.	G. Williams (ed.), *Official correspondence of Thomas Bekynton* (2 vols., RS,1872)
Belvoir	Muniments of the duke of Rutland, Belvoir castle
'Benet's Chron.'	'John Benet's chronicle for the years 1400 to 1462', ed. G. L. and M. A. Harriss, in *Camden Miscellany,* vol. XXIV (Camden soc., 4th ser., IX, 1972), 151–233
BIHR	*Bulletin of the institute of historical research*
BirmPL	Birmingham public library, manuscripts department
BJRL	*Bulletin of the John Rylands library*
BL	British Library
BM	British Museum
BN	Bibliothèque Nationale, Paris
Bodl.	Bodleian Library, Oxford
BristRO	City of Bristol record office
Brut	F. W. D. Brie (ed.), *The Brut, or the chronicles of England,* vol. II (EETS, CXXXVI, 1908)
C	Public Record Office, Chancery
CAD	*Calendar of ancient deeds*

Cal. Ormond Deeds	Calendar of Ormond Deeds
CardiffCL	Cardiff central library
CCR	*Calendar of the close rolls*
CChR	*Calendar of the charter rolls*
CFR	*Calendar of the fine rolls*
Chartier	A. Vallet de Viriville (ed.), *J. Chartier, Chronique* (3 vols., Paris, 1858)
Chastellain, Chroniques	K. de Lettenhove (ed.), *Georges Chastellain, Oeuvres* (7 vols., Brussels, 1863–65)
CheshRO	Cheshire record office, Chester
Chester RO	City of Chester record office
ChichRO	West Sussex record office, Chichester
CHJ	*Cambridge historical journal* (later *Historical journal)*
Chron. of London	N. H. Nicolas and E. Tyrell (eds.) *A chronicle of London, 1189–1483* (1827)
CMH	C. W. Previté-Orton and Z. N. Brooke (eds.), *The Cambridge mediaeval history,* vol. VIII (Cambridge, 1926)
CMilP	A. B. Hinds (ed.), *Calendar of state papers, Milan,* vol. I (1912)
CP	Public record office, common pleas
CPapReg.	*Calendar of entries in the papal registers relating to Great Britain and Ireland*
CPR	*Calendar of the patent rolls*
Croyland Chron.	H. T. Riley (ed.), *Ingulph's chronicle of the abbey of Croyland* (1854)
CVenP	R. Brown (ed.), *Calendar of state papers and manuscripts, Venice,* vol. I (1864)
DevonRO	Devon record office, Exeter
DerbsRO	Derbyshire record office, Matlock
Dict.Biog. Franc.	*Dictionnaire de biographie française* (Paris, in progress, 1933–)
DKR	*Reports of the deputy keeper of the public records*
DL	Public record office, duchy of Lancaster
DNB	*The dictionary of national biography* (63 vols., 1885–1900)
DorsetRO	Dorset record office, Dorchester
E	Public record office, exchequer
EconHR	*Economic history review*
EETS	Early English texts society
Eg.Ch.	British Library, Egerton charter
EHD	A. R. Myers (ed.), *English historical documents,* vol. IV, *1327–1485* (1969)
EHL	C. L. Kingsford, *English historical literature in the fifteenth century* (Oxford, 1913)
EHR	*English historical review*
Emden, Cambridge	A. B. Emden, *A biographical register of the University of Cambridge to* A.D.*1500* (Cambridge, 1963)

Emden, Oxford	A. B. Emden, *A biographical register of the University of Oxford to* A.D.*1500* (3 vols., Oxford, 1957–59)
English Chron.	J. S. Davies (ed.), *An English Chronicle of the reigns of Richard II, Henry IV, Henry V, and Henry VI* (Camden society, old series, LXIV, 1856)
English trade	E. E. Power and M. M. Postan (eds.), *Studies in English trade in the fifteenth century* (1933)
D'Escouchy	G. du Fresne de Beaucourt (ed.), *Mathieu d'Escouchy, Chronique* (3 vols., Paris, 1863–64)
Fabyan's Chron.	H. Ellis (ed.), *The new chronicles of England and France, by Robert Fabyan* (1811)
f.fr.	Bibliothèque Nationale, fonds français
Flenley	R. Flenley (ed.), *Six town chronicles* (Oxford, 1911)
Foedera	T. Rymer (ed.), *Foedera, conventiones, literae . . .* (3rd ed., 10 vols., The Hague, 1739–45)
Gairdner, *PL*	J. Gairdner (ed.), *The Paston letters* (6 vols., 1904).
Gascoigne	J. E. T. Rogers (ed.), *Thomas Gascoigne, Loci e libro veritatum* (Oxford, 1881)
GCH	T. B. Pugh (ed.), *Glamorgan county history*, vol. III: *The middle ages* (Cardiff, 1971)
GEC	V. Gibbs *et al.* (eds.), G. E. Cokayne, *The complete peerage of England, Scotland, Ireland, Great Britain and the United Kingdom, . . .* (12 vols., 1910–59)
Giles	J. A. Giles (ed.), *Incerti scriptores chronicon Angliae . . .*, part 4 (1848)
'Gregory's Chron.'	J. Gairdner (ed.), *The historical collections of a citizen of London in the fifteenth century* (Camden society, new series, XVII, 1876)
Great Chron.	A. H. Thomas and I. D. Thornley (eds.), *The great chronicle of London* (1938)
Grey Friars' Chron.	J. G. Nichols (ed.), *The chronicle of the Grey Friars of London* (Camden society, old series, LIII, 1852)
GuildhallRO	City of London record office, Guildhall
HBC	F. M. Powicke and E. B. Fryde (eds.), *The handbook of British chronology* (2nd ed., 1961)
HJ	*Historical journal* (formerly *Cambridge historical journal*)
HL	Henry E. Huntington library, San Marino
HLQ	*Huntington library quarterly*
HMC	*Historical manuscripts commission*
IHS	*Irish historical studies*
JBAA	*Journal of the British archaeological association*
JEccH	*Journal of ecclesiastical history*
JMH	*Journal of mediaeval history*
JRL	John Rylands library, Manchester
JRSAI	*Journal of the royal society of antiquaries of Ireland*

JSA	*Journal of the society of archivists*
JWCI	*Journal of the Warburg and Courtauld institutes*
KentRO	Kent record office, Maidstone
KB	Public record office, king's bench
King's	H. M. Colvin (ed.), *The history of the king's works:*
works	*the middle ages* (2 vols., 1 box, 1963)
LeedsRO	City of Leeds record office
LeicsRO	Leicestershire record office, Leicester
Le Neve	J. M. Horn *et al.* (eds.), John le Neve, *Fasti ecclesiae*
	Anglicanae, 1300–1541 (12 vols., 1962–67)
Letter-book	R. R. Sharp (ed.), *Calendar of letter-books preserved*
K	*among the archives of the corporation of the city*
	of London: letter-book K (1911)
LichRO	Lichfield joint record office
LincsRO	Lincolnshire record office, Lincoln
Lit.Cant.	J. B. Sheppard (ed.), *Literae Cantuarienses* (3 vols.,
	RS, 1887–89).
London	C. L. Kingsford (ed.), *The chronicles of London*
Chrons.	(1905)
Longleat	Manuscripts of the marquess of Bath, Longleat
LQR	*Law quarterly review*
MedSt	*Mediaeval studies*
MLR	*Modern language review*
Mod.	*Modern Philology*
Philol.	
n.a.fr.	Nouvelle acquisition française
NLWJ	*National library of Wales journal*
Norf. Arch.	*Norfolk archaeology*
NorthantsRO	Northamptonshire record office, Northampton
Nott. Med. St.	*Nottingham mediaeval studies*
PBA	*Proceedings of the British academy*
PCC	Public record office, prerogative court of
	Canterbury
PL	N. Davis (ed.), *Paston letters and papers of the*
	fifteenth century (2 vols., Oxford, 1971–76)
PMLAA	*Proceedings of the modern language association of*
	America
PP	*Past and present*
PPC	N. H. Nicolas (ed.), *Proceedings and ordinances of the*
	privy council (7 vols., Record commission, 1834–37)
PRIA	*Proceedings of the royal Irish academy*
PRO	Public record office, London
PSO	Public record office, privy seal office
RC	Record commission
RDP	*Reports from the Lord's committee.... touching the*
	dignity of a peer (5 vols., 1820–29)

Reg. *Chichele*	E. F. Jacob (ed.), *The register of Henry Chichele, archbishop of Canterbury, 1414–43* (4 vols., Canterbury and York society, 1938–47)
Reg.Lacy	G. R. Dunstan (ed.), *Register of Edmund Lacy, bishop of Exeter, 1420–1455* (5 vols., 1963–72)
Reg.Whet- *hamstede*	H. T. Riley (ed.), *Registrum abbatiae Johannis Whethamstede* (2 vols., RS, 1872–73)
RP	*Rotuli parliamentorum* (6 vols., 1767; index vol., 1832)
RS	Rolls series
SalopRO	Shropshire record office, Shrewsbury
SC	Public record office, special collections
ScotHR	*Scottish historical review*
ShakesBT	Shakespeare birthplace trust, Stratford
SomsRO	Somerset record office, Taunton
SR	*Statutes of the realm* (11 vols., 1810–28)
Stevenson	J. Stevenson (ed.), *Letters and papers illustrative of the wars of the English in France during the reign of Henry the sixth, etc.* (RS, 2 vols. in 3, 1861–64), including the pseudo-William Worcester annals
Sussex Arch. Coll.	*Sussex archaeological collections*
TBGAS	*Transactions of the Bristol and Gloucestershire archaeological society*
TCWAAS	*Transactions of the Cumberland and Westmorland archaeological society*
TDA	*Transactions of the Devonshire association*
Three Chrons.	J. Gairdner (ed.), *Three fifteenth-century chronicles . . . .* (Camden society, 3rd series, XXVIII, 1880)
TRHS	*Transactions of the royal historical society*
UBHJ	*University of Birmingham historical journal*
VCH	*Victoria history of the counties of England*
WA	Westminster abbey manuscripts
WarwsRO	Warwickshire record office, Warwick
Waurin	W. and E. L. C. P. Hardy (eds.), *Jehan de Waurin, Recueil des croniques et anchiennes istories de la Grant Bretaigne* (5 vols., RS, 1864–91)
Wedgwood, *Biographies*	J. C. Wedgwood (ed.) *History of Parliament: biographies of the members of the commons house, 1439–1509* (1936)
Wedgwood, *Register*	J. C. Wedgwood (ed.), *History of parliament: register of the ministers and of the members of both houses, 1439–1509* (1938)
WHR	*Welsh history review*
WiltsRO	Wiltshire record office, Trowbridge
WorcsRO	Worcestershire record office, Worcester

The Reign of King Henry VI

Wright   T. Wright (ed.), *A collection of political poems and songs relating to English history, from the accession of Edward III to the reign of Henry VIII* (2 vols., RS, 1859–61)

Note on quotations

Extracts from original sources in foreign languages have been translated into modern English. Those in contemporary English are given in the original in most cases so as to convey something of the flavour of the period.

Some Important Dates

1420	22 May	Treaty of Troyes, followed (2 June) by Henry V's marriage to Katherine of Valois
1421	6 December	Henry VI born
1422	31 August	Henry V died
	21 October	Charles VI of France died; accession of Charles VII
	5 December	Bedford and Gloucester appointed protector and defender of England, followed (9 December) by formal appointment of councillors
1423	17 April	Treaty of Amiens between England, Brittany, and Burgundy
	31 July	Anglo-Burgundian victory at Cravant
1424	17 August	English victory at Verneuil
	16 October	Gloucester left for his campaign in the Low Countries
1425	30 October	Riots in London against Bishop Beaufort
1426	12 March	Reconciliation of Beaufort and Gloucester
1427	25 March	Beaufort made cardinal
	5 September	French victory at Montargis
1428	7 October	English siege of Orléans began, during which Salisbury was killed (3 November)
1429	23 February	Joan of Arc met Charles VII at Chinon
	8 May	English siege of Orléans abandoned
	18 June	French victory at Patay
	17 July	Charles VII crowned at Reims
	6 November	Henry VI crowned at Westminster, followed by ending of the protectorate (15 November)
1430	23 April	Henry VI left for France
	23 May	Joan of Arc captured
1431	17 May	Gloucester suppressed lollard rising
	30 May	Joan of Arc burned
	16 December	Henry VI crowned in Paris
1432	29 January	Henry VI returned to England
1435	5 August	Congress of Arras began, followed by Franco-Burgundian treaty (21 September)

	15 September	Bedford died
	28 October	French captured Dieppe
1436	13 April	French captured Pontoise, followed (17 April) by fall of Paris
	28 July	Henry VI first showed personal initiative in politics
	30 July	Burgundian siege of Calais abandoned
	15 August	Scottish siege of Roxburgh abandoned
1437	3 January	Queen Katherine died
	21 February	James I of Scotland murdered
	12 November	Formal re-establishment of personal rule
1439	30 April	Warwick died at Rouen
	July–September	Anglo-French conference at Oye
	28 September	English truce with Burgundy
1440	2 July	Release of duke of Orléans agreed
	12 September	Henry VI founded Eton College
1441	12 February	Henry VI founded King's College, Cambridge
	19 September	French take Pontoise
	23 October	Eleanor Cobham condemned
1443	30 March	Somerset appointed captain-general of France and Gascony
	12 April	Archbishop Chichele died
1444	24 May	Henry VI and Margaret of Anjou betrothed, followed (28 May) by truce of Tours
1445	19 April	Margaret of Anjou arrived in England, followed (23 April) by marriage
	22 December	Undertaking to surrender Maine to the French
1447	23 February	Gloucester died
	11 April	Beaufort died
	9 December	York appointed lieutenant of Ireland
1448	16 March	English surrendered Le Mans
1449	24 March	English attacked Fougères
	29 October	English surrendered Rouen
1450	9 January	Bishop Moleyns murdered
	26 January	Suffolk's impeachment began, followed (31 January) by resignation of chancellor, Archbishop Stafford
	15 April	French victory at Formigny
	2 May	Suffolk murdered
	June–July	Cade's rebellion, followed (12 July) by Cade's death
	12 August	French captured Cherbourg
	c. 8 September	York returned from Ireland
1451	12 June	French captured Bordeaux, followed (12 August) by surrender of Bayonne

1452	2 March	York submitted at Dartford
	23 October	English recovered Bordeaux
1453	17 July	French victory at Castillon; Shrewsbury killed
	c. 1 August	Henry VI collapsed
	24 August	Percy–Neville clash at Heworth
	13 October	Prince Edward born
1454	22 March	Cardinal Kemp died
	27 March	York appointed protector and defender of England, followed (2 April) by Salisbury's appointment as chancellor
	11 October/ 1 November	Percy–Neville clash at Stamford Bridge
1454	c. 25 December	Henry VI recovered
1455	22 May	First battle of St Albans; Somerset and Northumberland killed
	19 November	York appointed protector and defender of England
1456	25 February	York resigned as protector and defender
	late August	Court travelled to Coventry and the midlands
1457	28 August	French attacked Sandwich
	4 December	Public recantation of Bishop Pecock
1458	25 March	Reconciliation of the English nobility
1459	23 September	Battle of Blore Heath
	12 October	Battle of Ludford Bridge
	20 November	Parliament opened at Coventry
1460	26 June	Yorkists landed in England
	10 July	Battle of Northampton; Buckingham and Shrewsbury killed
	3 August	James II of Scotland died
	September	York returned from Ireland
	31 October	York acknowledged as heir to the throne
	30 December	Battle of Wakefield; York, Salisbury, and Rutland killed
1461	2/3 February	Battle of Mortimer's Cross
	17 February	Second battle of St Albans
	4 March	Edward IV assumes the crown
	29 March	Battle of Towton; Northumberland killed
	28 June	Edward IV crowned
	22 July	Charles VII of France died; accession of Louis XI

Acknowledgements

Plates 13, 29, and 30 are reproduced by gracious permission of Her Majesty The Queen.

Plates 16 and 17, from the Public Record Office, are reproduced by permission of the Controller of Her Majesty's Stationery Office (PRO, KB27/797 and PRO, KB27/798).

Thanks are also due to the following:
Alinari, Florence: Plate 32
Mr J. Auld and the Museum of London: Plate 19
Musée des Arts Décoratifs, Paris: Plate 8
Bibliothèque Municipale, Arras and Giraudon, Paris: Plate 27
Bibliothèque Nationale, Paris: Plates 5, 25 (BN, MS.Lat.1158 f.27)
City of Bristol Record Office: Plate 11
The British Library: Plates 1 (BL, Royal MS.15E VI f.3), 9 (BL, Royal MS.16F.ii.f.73), 10 (BL, Add.MS.48976), 12 (BL, Add.MS.48976), 18 (BL, Harleian MS.4826 f.1*), 21 (BL, Royal MS.15E VI f.2), 23 (BL, Add.MS.18850 f.256v), 24 (BL, Harleian MS.2900 f.55), 39 (BL, Harleian MS.6298 f.148)
Dean and Chapter, Canterbury Cathedral: Plate 33
Courtauld Institute of Art and Mr M.H. Ridgway: Plate 31
Dean and Chapter, Ely Cathedral: Plate 34
Giraudon, Paris: Plate 37
The Principal and Fellows of Jesus College, Oxford: 22 (Jesus College MS. 124 (R))
Musée du Louvre, Paris: Plates 6, 7
The Vicar of St Catherine's Church, Ludham: Plate 38
The National Portrait Gallery: Plates 2, 14, 15
The Marquess of Northampton: Plate 26
Mr M.H. Ridgway: Plate 35
Mr Lawrence Stone: Plate 36
The Earl of Verulam (from the Gorhambury Collection): Plate 28
The Victoria and Albert Museum: Plate 4
The National Museum of Wales: Plate 20
Dean and Chapter, Westminster Abbey: Plate 3

Introduction: the Making of
a Reputation

The third and last Lancastrian king of England has the singular distinction of being the only medieval English king to rate a leader in *The Times*. During August 1972 one feature article, one leader article, and no less than ten letters were published in *The Times* on the subject of Henry VI's qualifications for sainthood. The chairman of the Henry VI Society and several Roman Catholic priests and historians boldly asserted their faith in the miracles attributed to Henry after his death; and in authoritative circles the canonization campaign is once again regarded as 'eminently viable'. The editor of *The Times* provided a not uncommon – certainly a more sceptical – assessment of the monarch: 'In a canonised king one is entitled to expect an exemplar of kingship, and to feel disappointed ... if one finds instead a full display of the monkish virtues'. Neither view quite grasps the man who wore the crown.

Yet Henry VI and his reign are no less remarkable on a more mundane and realistic level. He was, by a considerable margin, the youngest monarch ever to have ascended the English throne: Henry was less than nine months old when his father, Henry V, died in France on 31 August 1422. There was no time in his conscious early life, therefore, when he was not king of England. He had had none of the wide and varied experience that Henry IV, Edward IV, Richard III, even that Henry V or Henry VII gained as the scions of great English aristocratic houses; and he had never been able to observe another king of England at work.[1] Secondly, Henry VI personally undertook the cares of kingship and brought his minority effectively to an end at an earlier age than did all other young English kings after 1066. Henry III had begun his personal rule in 1227 at the age of nineteen, King Edward III when he was eighteen; and Richard II, much as he strove to avoid it, lived under conciliar control until he was well-nigh twenty years of age. By contrast, Henry VI was just sixteen years old in November 1437 when he expressly asserted his royal prerogatives and virtually declared his minority ended; indeed, he had begun to take a positive part in government at least a year before that.[2] Whatever the supposed capabilities of teenagers then or now, by any standard this was a very youthful introduction to effective kingship. Henry, too, was the only English king to be acknowledged by French authorities as rightfully king

1

of France, to preside over a dual monarchy created as a consequence of the treaty of Troyes in 1420. As such, he was the only English king to receive solemn coronation in France – at Notre Dame in Paris on 16 December 1431. The responsibilities of this dual kingship were shouldered by no other English king, and were far heavier and more complex than the demands placed on a primarily military conqueror like Edward III or Henry V.[3]

Moreover, Henry's was the third longest reign to date since the Norman conquest – lasting almost thirty-nine years; if he had abilities or defects as a king, such a passage of time would give them ample and relentless opportunity to display themselves unmistakably. In fact, Henry's reign saw the beginning of the most extensive and debilitating civil war in England since the reign of Stephen. It ended in 1461 with only the second instance of dynastic revolution in which the acknowledged heir was passed over in favour of another claimant; and in the political upheaval that followed, Henry is noteworthy as being the only king to date to have had two separate reigns, for he was temporarily restored to the throne in 1470-71.[4] An assessment of Henry's life, character, and personality is crucial to an appraisal of his and his councillors' statecraft and to an understanding of why the dynastic disaster of 1461 occurred.

A civil war like the 'Wars of the Roses' places peculiar and formidable historiographical difficulties in the path of the historian: the written statements of contemporaries on the subject of kings and their achievements are almost inevitably distorted by partisan considerations, private fears, or personal obsequiousnesses. If one searches for an authentic contemporary assessment of Henry VI and his rule, one is immediately handicapped by the fact that Henry was deposed and attainted in 1461 and then succeeded by his rival's son, Edward of York; commentators writing after that event needed to be most circumspect – preferably disparaging – when talking about the deposed monarch. To one English chronicler, commenting in the mid-1460s, the state of England in 1459 seemed thus:

> In this same tyme, the reame of Englonde was oute of alle good gouernaunce, as it had be meny dayes before, for the kyng was simple and lad by couetous counseylle, and owed more then he was worthe. His dettes encreased dayly, but payment was there none; alle the possessyons and lordeshyppes that perteyned to the croune the kyng had yeue awey, some to lordes and some to other simple persones, so that he had almoste noughte to lefe onne . . . For these mysgouernaunces, and for many other, the hertes of the peple were turned away from thayme that had the londe in gouernance, and theyre blyssyng was turnyd in to cursyng.

To this anonymous writer, then, Henry was simple, ill-advised, and a poor ruler.[5] According to official Yorkist ideology, the root of his disastrous reign went even deeper into the very moral fibre of Lancastrian rule. The 'unrest, inward werre and trouble, unrightwisnes, shedyng and effusion of innocent blode, abusion of the Lawes, partialte, riotte, extorcion, murdre, rape and viciouse lyvyng' of Henry's reign were condign punishment for the seizure of the crown by his grandfather in 1399, the subsequent murder of Richard II, and the diversion of the true line of kings.[6] And this myth was of such force that it determined the course of fifteenth-century historiography for long after.

When Henry VI died in 1471, the writers of Yorkist England felt able to make more generous reference to the late king. Moreover, the sheer embarrassment to the Yorkists of the timing and manner of his death in the Tower of London – immediately after his recapture by the newly-returned Edward IV, and at a time when no less a person than King Edward's brother, Richard, duke of Gloucester, was in the building – seems to have made them anxious to allay any suspicion that he had been done away with. They therefore allowed Henry VI a few redeeming features, though suitably innocuous or negative ones. John Warkworth, writing soon after 1474, maintained that:

> . . . myscheves peple that were aboute the Kynge, were so covetouse towarde them selff, and dyde no force of the Kynges honour, ne of his wele, ne of the comone wele of the londe, where Kynge Herry trusted to them that thei schuld do, and labour in tyme of innocence, evere for the comone wele, whiche thei dyde contrary to his wille; . . . And these were the causes, withe other, that made the peple to gruge ageyns hym, and alle bycause of his fals lordes, and nevere of hym; . . .

According to this writer, Henry's rule was indeed disastrous, although the king himself was guiltless and well-meaning.[7]

Later views of Henry were partly determined by Richard III's action in August 1484 in ostentatiously transferring the body of the last Lancastrian king from its obscure grave in Chertsey abbey to a new shrine in St George's chapel, Windsor. It was a symbolic act of reconciliation that recalls Henry V's translation of Richard II's corpse to Westminster abbey in 1413. It also seemed wiser to harness, rather than suppress or ignore, the popular veneration of the dead monarch and the miracle-working in his name which had been reported in recent years.[8] This purposeful rehabilitation of Henry VI's reputation may even have given John Blacman courage to pen his short eulogy entitled 'A compilation of the meakness and good life of King Henry VI', before Blacman died in January 1485. He was able to draw on his own recollection of Henry, for Blacman had been a fellow of Eton (from 1443) and warden of King's Hall, Cambridge (1452–57), two foundations that were close to the king's heart. He had also consulted one of the king's confessors, perhaps Bishop Aiscough who was murdered in 1450,

3

and several other royal servants and attendants, including William Waynflete, who as provost of Eton from 1442 knew Blacman well; perhaps too Thomas, Lord Stanley, the king's chamberlain from 1455; and certainly Sir Richard Tunstall, who was chamberlain by 1459 and again in 1470. In short, Blacman's information came from sources spread over more than a generation and from a range of informants who had known the king, some before and some after his physical and mental collapse in 1453, some before and some after his deposition and flight in 1461, and even some who had encountered him as a captive after 1464.[9] Such circumstances make it difficult to measure the myopia in Blacman's portrait of a king whom he himself had known when he served as his chaplain perhaps as much as forty years earlier. To Blacman, Henry was simple but also God-fearing, just, lacking in deceit and craft; in truth, his name seemed worthy to be entered in 'the register' of the saints of Heaven.

> He was . . . a man simple and upright, altogether fearing the Lord God, and departing from evil. He was a simple man, without any crook of craft or untruth, as is plain to all. With none did he deal craftily, nor ever would say an untrue word to any, but framed his speech always to speak truth. He was both upright and just, always keeping to the straight line of justice in his acts. Upon none would he willingly inflict any injustice. To God and the Almighty he rendered most faithfully that which was His.[10]

That this was the prevailing opinion at Richard's court is reflected in the so-called *Croyland Chronicle*, penned most probably in his retirement in 1486 by John Russell, bishop of Lincoln and chancellor of England when Richard III ordered the dead king's body to be brought to Windsor castle.

> How great his deserts were, by reason of his innocence of life, his love of God and of the Church, his patience in adversity, and his other remarkable virtues, is abundantly testified by the miracles which God has wrought in favour of those who have, with devout hearts, implored his intercession.[11]

Henry's rehabilitation reached its highest point at Henry VII's hands. As the destroyer of Yorkist monarchy and the self-announced heir of the house of Lancaster, this king was the son of Henry VI's half-brother, Edmund Tudor, and of Henry's cousin, Margaret Beaufort. He unsuccessfully petitioned a succession of popes to canonize his uncle and he proposed to dig up his body a second time and re-inter it in the magnificent chapel then being built in Westminster abbey. A natural accompaniment of all this was a book of miracles allegedly worked by the dead king, written first in English after the body was transferred to Windsor and then in Latin soon after 1500.[12] The veneration of the king was now widespread in late-fifteenth-century England, and the growing stream of pilgrims to his tomb is attested by scores of pilgrim badges dedicated to his sanctity and by the wrought-iron collecting-box for offerings which may still be seen at Windsor.[13] Is it surprising that in the *Anglica historia*, composed early in the sixteenth century by Polydore Vergil, Henry VI finally appeared with the stylized qualities of sainthood?

> King Henry was a man of milde and plaine-dealing disposition, who preferred peace before warres, quietnes before troubles, honestie before utilitie, and leysure before busines; and, to be short, there was not in this world a more pure, more honest, and more holye creature. There was in him honest shamfastnes, modestie, innocencie, and perfect patience, taking all humane chances, miseries, and all afflictions of this life in so good part as though he had justly by some his offence deserved the same. He ruled his owne affections that he might more easily rule his owne subjectes; he gaped not after riches, nor thirsted for honor and worldly estimation, but was careful onely for his soules health; such things as tended to the salvation thereof he onely esteemed for good; and that very wisely; such againe as procured the losse thereof he only accompted evill.

And again:

> He dyd of his owne naturall inclynation abhorre all vices both of body and mynde, by reason wherof he was of honest conversation eaven from a chylde, pure and clene, partaken of none evell, ready to conceave all that was good, a contemner of all those thinges whiche commonly corrupt the myndes of men, so patient also in suffering of injuryes, receavyd now and then, as that he covetyd in his hart no revenge, but for the very same gave God Almighty most humble thankes, because therby he thowght his sinnes to be wasshed away; yea, what shalle we say, that this good, gratious, holy, sober, and wyse man, wold affirme all these myseryes to have happenyd unto him both for his owne and his ancestors manyfold offences; wherfor he dyd not muche account what dignitie, what honor, what state of lyfe, what soone, what frinds he had lost, nor made muche dole for the same, but yf in any thing he had offendyd God, that had he regard of, that dyd he morne for, that was he sorry for.[14]

Tudor writers and their masters might adapt for their own purposes the Yorkist view that the civil strife had originated in the deposition of a king in 1399, but more immediately they laid 'the troublous season of King Henry the Sixth' (to quote Edward Hall's book printed in 1548) and the degradation of his line at the door of aristocratic dissension (Shakespeare's 'viperous worm, That gnaws the bowels of the commonwealth'), dynastic ambition, and the malign influence of two French women, Joan of Arc and Margaret of Anjou, Henry's own queen. Henry himself, the virtuous and the saintly, seemed to Tudor eyes the ill-starred victim of these malignancies and as such he stands aside from – and ultimately above – the action of Shakespeare's civil-war play in three parts, *Henry VI*.[15] One might be forgiven for suspecting that a veil has been drawn over the real Henry, and the true character of his reign obscured, by his successors' propaganda.

Not even the surviving portraits of the king allow one to see the real man: the hands clasped in customary ecclesiastical fashion, the cross dangling from the distinctive Lancastrian chain about his neck, a modest cap and unostentatious gown – all are the pictorial equivalent of Henry VI as 'the saintly muff' (to quote J. R. Lander); though Henry, in fact, spent freely every year on fine new gowns and hats for himself, and greeted the French envoys in 1445 richly robed in cloth of gold. The opaque, gormless face of the portraits of young Henry, with the small, rose-bud of a mouth, or the care-worn suffering visage of the older Henry – both are part and parcel of the saintly legend, for no known royal portrait of any worth pre-dates those early Tudor workshops which were commissioned to turn out a score of saintly Henries.[16] Nor can the prayers or the *Sanctus* which Henry is supposed to have composed be dated to his lifetime and are more likely the product of late-fifteenth- and early-sixteenth-century hagiography.[17] Thus, in the space of thirty politically topsy-turvy years, Henry VI had been transformed, by a remarkable exercise in posthumous propaganda, from an incompetent innocent into a guileless saint. In order to uncover the real Henry and the nature of his rule, one needs to penetrate beneath these cosmetic layers so expertly applied.

Notes

1 Henry Tudor's experiences in the household of Lord Herbert and as an exile with his uncle Jasper were different from those of other fifteenth-century monarchs, but arguably not without value to a prospective king (S. B. Chrimes, *Henry VII* [1972], pp. 15-49).

2 S. B. Chrimes and A. L. Brown (eds.), *Select documents of English constitutional history, 1307–1485* (1961), pp. 275-6; R. L. Storey, *The end of the house of Lancaster* (1966), p. 31.

3 J. Shirley (ed.), *A Parisian journal* (Oxford, 1968), pp. 182-3, 250, 268-73; C. T. Allmand, 'The Lancastrian land settlement in Normandy, 1417–50', *EconHR*, 2nd ser., XXI (1968), 461-79. Anglo-Breton and Anglo-Norman government in the mid-fourteenth century was of a more modest order (M. Jones, *Ducal Brittany, 1364–99* [Oxford, 1970], chs. I, II, VI; J. H. Le Patourel, 'Edward III and the kingdom of France', *History*, XLIII [1958], 182-4, 187-8).

4 His second reign is not examined here because its significance more properly belongs to the reign of Edward IV.

5 *English Chron.*, p. 79. Cf. John Hardyng's harsh judgement in the second,

Yorkist, version of his chronicle, completed in the mid-1460s (C. L. Kingsford, 'The first version of Hardyng's chronicle', *EHR*, XXVII [1912], 465-6, 475).

6 *RP*, V, 464, partially quoted in Storey, *End of Lancaster*, p. 2.

7 P. Grosjean, *Henrici VI Angliae regis miracula postuma* (Brussels, 1935), pp. 129*-51* (an assemblage of references to Henry VI's death); J. O. Halliwell (ed.), *Warkworth's chronicle* (Camden Soc., 1839), pp. 11-12. Cf. William Caxton's *Chronicles*, printed in 1480 and cited in *EHL*, p. 122; and even 'Gregory's Chron.', p. 208 (probably written in mid-1470, when Henry was still in prison).

8 The first precisely dated miracle occurred in 1481, but the veneration of Henry in London and York had probably begun by 1472–73 (Grosjean, op. cit., p. 17; J. W. McKenna, 'Piety and propaganda: the cult of King Henry VI', in B. Rowland [ed.], *Chaucer and middle English studies in honour of R. H. Robbins* [1974], pp. 74-5; B. Spencer, 'King Henry of Windsor and the London pilgrim', in J. Bird, H. Chapman, and J. Clark [eds.], *Collectanea Londiniensia* [London and Middsx. Arch. Soc., 1978], pp. 240-1). Henry VI's statue on the rood screen (*c.* 1455–60) of York minster was removed by 1479 to prevent its veneration; it was restored after 1485 but finally removed at the Reformation (G. E. Aylmer and R. Cant [eds.], *A History of York minster* [Oxford, 1977], pp. 108, 181-5).

9 M. R. James (ed.), *John Blacman's Henry the Sixth* (Cambridge, 1919), pp. 26-43. He referred to a great lord who had been chamberlain (for Stanley, see below, p. 302), and a prelate who had served as the king's confessor for 10 years (for Aiscough, below, p. 644). The informants mentioned by name included Waynflete, Tunstall, Dr William Towne, a foundation fellow of King's College, Cambridge, and John Bedon and Thomas Mannyng, Henry's secretary in 1455-60, both of whom had been captured with the king in 1465 (see below, p. 888; Emden, *Oxford*, III, 1889–90; I, 147; II, 1216–17). Blacman's account now survives only in a printed edition of 1510, reprinted in 1732, with both collated in James's edition.

10 R. Knox and S. Leslie (eds.), *The miracles of King Henry VI* (Cambridge, 1923), pp. 1-16; Grosjean, op. cit., pp. 11-14; Blacman, op. cit., pp. 25-6. Blacman entered the Carthusian order, to which Henry was an especially generous patron, about 1459 and spent the rest of his life at the Charterhouses in London and Witham (Somerset) (ibid., pp. xv-xvi; Emden, *Oxford*, I, 194-5; idem, *Cambridge*, pp. 670-1).

11 H. T. Riley (ed.), *Ingulph's chronicle of the abbey of Croyland* (1854), p. 468 (*s.a.* 1471). Cf. the sentiments in a roll-chronicle compiled after Henry VI's reburial at Windsor but before the death of Richard III: 'he was good, pious and devoted to God; caring little about warlike matters, he left them all to his councillors' (JRL, Latin MS 113).

12 McKenna, in *Chaucer and middle English studies*, pp. 77-84. The process to secure canonization had begun by October 1494, when Pope Alexander VI instituted an inquiry. The move to Westminster was never in fact made. The book of miracles is now BL, Royal MS 13 C. VIII, from which BL, Harl. MS 423 was copied in the early sixteenth century and Grosjean, op. cit., pp. 1-305, produced his edition in 1935 (above n. 7). See also E. Ettlinger, 'Notes on a woodcut depicting King Henry VI being invoked as a saint', *Folklore*, LXXXIV (1973), 115-19 (from Bodl. MS 277 f. 376*v*).

13 Spencer in *Collectanea Londiniensia*, pp. 235-64; even Henry VIII made

7

a pilgrimage to the tomb in 1529. For surviving pre-Reformation paintings and carvings of the king in English country churches, see *A fifteenth-century pilgrimage* (published by *The Henry VI Society*).

14 H. Ellis (ed.), *Three books of Polydore Vergil's English history* (Camden Soc., 1844), pp. 70-1, 156-7; Grosjean, op. cit., pp. 152*-233*. Cf. John Rous's comment of 1486, in T. Hearne (ed.), *Historia regum Angliae* (Oxford, 1745), p. 210; *Brut*, p. 527 (written at the end of the fifteenth century); *London Chrons.*, p. 184 (written soon after 1496); and James Ryman's poem, 'A remembrance of Henry VI' (written in 1492), in R. H. Robbins (ed.), *Historical poems of the XIVth and XVth centuries* (New York, 1959), pp. 199-201.

15 *Henry VI*, part I, act III, scene i. For the role of Queen Margaret, see Vergil, op. cit., pp. 70-1; and for York's ambition and the consequent dissension, ibid., pp. 84, 86-7, 93-4. See also E. M. W. Tillyard, *Shakespeare's history plays* (1969 ed.), pp. 167-204; S. C. Gupta, 'The substance of Shakespeare's "Histories"', in W. A. Armstrong (ed.), *Shakespeare's histories* (1972), pp. 60-91; J. P. Brockbank, 'The frame of disorder – Henry VI', in ibid., pp. 92-122; E. Jones, '"Henry VI" and the spectre of strife', *Listener*, 7 July 1977, pp. 13-14. Shakespeare's debt to the Tudor writers E. Hall and R. Holinshed is well established (Tillyard, op. cit., pp. 47-60).

16 J. R. Lander, *Conflict and stability in fifteenth century England* (1969 ed.), p. 68; PRO, E101/409/9 f. 37r; /11 f. 37r; /16 f. 33r; Stevenson, I, 103, 157; R. Strong, *Tudor and Jacobean portraits* (2 vols., 1969), I, 146-8; II, pl. 283, 284, 288; although R. Strong postulates 'an original *ad vivum* likeness' behind the portrait in the royal collection at Windsor. See J. Fletcher, 'Tree ring dates from some panel paintings in England', *Burlington Magazine*, CXVI (1974), especially p. 257.

17 For prayers inspired by Henry VI, see Blacman, op. cit., pp. xii-xiii, 50-1; Knox and Leslie, op. cit., pp. 7-15; McKenna, in *Chaucer and middle English studies*, p. 86 n. 24; Bodl., Jones MS 46 f. 108-17; Gough, liturg. 19 f. 32v; 7 f. 118v; Don. e. 120 f. 1-4 (datable before the body was moved to Windsor; see J. Raine, 'The Pudsays of Barford', *Archaeologia Aeliana*, new ser., II (1858), 175-6, and Grosjean, op. cit., pp. 237-9); Latin MS liturg. q. 5 pp. 217-19. For those prayers supposedly composed by the king himself, see Blacman, op. cit., pp. xiv-xv. *The Henry VI Society* has recently (1979) published a liturgical oddity, a Book of Hours containing hymns and prayers written in the king's honour. J. Mescal, *Henry VI* (1980), is the most recent plea for Henry's canonization.

1
COLLECTIVE RULE
1422–1436

1 The King's Accession

Henry V's death in 1422 was unexpected by all save those personal companions who witnessed his last illness, and it had an unusually bewildering impact on people living on both sides of the English channel. Most demoralizing for the English was the fact that Henry was barely thirty-five years old when he died at Vincennes, 8 miles south-east of Paris, between 2 and 3 o'clock in the morning of Monday, 31 August.[1] Hardly less dispiriting was the fact that no king of England had reigned for so short a time – nine and a half years – since the twelfth century. As a result, Henry's only son and heir, born at Windsor on 6 December 1421, six months after the king had left for France for the last time, became England's youngest monarch. Moreover, not since his forebear, Richard the Lionheart, was slain at Châlus in 1199 had a king of England died outside his realm. All these circumstances combined to nonplus King Henry's friends, subjects, and enemies alike, and complicated and delayed their adjustment to his death.

It is remarkable how widespread was the grief felt at Henry's passing. To read the panegyrics of an English chronicler like John Strecche or the memorial verses of a prolific poet like John Lydgate should cause no surprise. But similar laments flowed from the pen of Enguerrand de Monstrelet and other Burgundian writers, though admittedly their master, the duke of Burgundy, had been King Henry's ally. Most surprising to the contemporary English observer were the tributes offered by some of Henry's deadliest foes, followers of Charles, dauphin of France. The sense of loss was therefore widespread and unmistakably profound.[2] After all, Henry was not only in the prime of life in 1422, but also at the height of his achievement and reputation in France. Two years earlier at Troyes he had been formally acknowledged by King Charles VI as heir to the French throne and regent of France during Charles's lifetime, thereby disinheriting the dauphin. He had conquered all Normandy and extensive areas around the duchy which the conquerors appropriately named the *pays de conquête*. One of the most powerful of the French princes, Duke Philip the Bold of Burgundy, was his ally, so that the conquest of all France seemed possible. The glowing reputation of this monarch at home was thus matched by the awe and fear in which he was held abroad.

No authoritative measures affecting the government of the English territories across the channel, the prosecution of the war in France, or the exercise of the regency there could be taken after Henry V's death independently of the important decisions pending in England. News travelled more slowly in the fifteenth century than it does today, and information was judged immediate only in so far as it could be brought by a devoted messenger riding his horse hard. The bearing of news from France to England also had to contend with the unpredictable weather and turbulent tides of the channel. Hence, the shattering news from the Bois de Vincennes took about a week to reach the centre of government at Westminster and the household of the new king at Windsor. It was a topic of discussion in Flanders by 7 September and probably spread through the south-east of England to London at about the same time. The abbot of the Lincolnshire monastery of Neubo could seal a charter in his chapter house on 5 September and still date it by Henry V's regnal year, unaware that what he was doing was technically invalid. But five days later, a messenger sent northward from London with the tidings of the king's death had reached Biggleswade in Bedfordshire.[3] Yet Bishop Philip Morgan of Worcester, an experienced and respected politician who was now summoned to Windsor, was still at the Dominican friary in Gloucester on 20 September. Even the chancellor of England, Bishop Thomas Langley of Durham, was at York as late as 22 September, presiding over a meeting of convocation, though it is difficult to believe that at that stage he was still oblivious of the dreadful news current further south.[4]

Such delays, coupled with the fact that the new king was a baby, made immediate decisions impossible and a rapid transfer of power more difficult than was usual at the accession of a king. Yet it should not be thought that confusion reigned at Westminster or at Windsor castle, where the new king lay in his cradle.[5] The circumstances were extraordinary, but as far as possible customary procedures were followed. It had long been accepted in England that kingship was dynastic and that succession to the throne was normally vested in the king's eldest son, even if he were an infant. This had been demonstrated in 1216 and again in 1377; if the revolution of 1399 had damaged the principle in any way, king and parliament together had reaffirmed it in 1406 by a statute which devolved the crown upon, in turn, Henry IV and the heirs of his body.[6] In 1422 no one questioned Henry of Windsor's lineage or his accession; baby or not, there would be no dispute about the succession and no interregnum. The main difficulty was a practical one, since in implementing customary procedures there was no effective king to take the initiative or to be counselled into doing so, and the bulk of Henry V's advisers were abroad.

When Henry V died, his young wife Katherine of Valois was staying with her parents, the king and queen of France, at Senlis some twenty-five miles north of Paris. Although she did not visit the dying king, she remained in France and travelled with his body back to England. Even if she had not been a twenty-one-year-old woman, inexperienced in politics and with little acquaintance with England, she was not immediately available to take a guiding role beside her little son.[7] This responsibility fell in the first instance on the dead king's younger surviving brother, thirty-two-year-old Duke Humphrey of Gloucester, who had been designated keeper of the realm in May 1422 while Henry V was in France. Early in September 1422 he was probably at or near Westminster, directly in touch with the government departments. The late king's uncle, Henry Beaufort, bishop of Winchester, was also in the country: a wealthy, able, and knowledgeable man, he was nearly fifty years of age and much versed in the government, politics, and diplomacy of Henry IV's reign as well as of Henry V's. He frequently resided at the Southwark residence of the bishops of Winchester, and can be imagined speeding hot-foot to Windsor when news of his nephew's death arrived – if, indeed, he were not already there. Despite the presence of these two men and of the sixty-year-old archbishop of Canterbury, Henry Chichele (who, if he were at Canterbury or his palace at Lambeth, would have been one of the first in England to hear of King Henry's death), little of formal importance could be done without Henry V's chancellor, Bishop Langley, who was in Yorkshire with the great seal. If Gloucester, Beaufort, and Chichele considered immediately the steps necessary for the inauguration of the new reign, it was only when Langley arrived with the great seal that formal dispositions could be made. In any case, Langley's personal qualities and unrivalled experience in Lancastrian service going back beyond 1399 would be of inestimable value in the new circumstances.

Langley took no more than six days to return to Windsor from York by 28 September, which was no mean feat for a man of about sixty-two.[8] On that day, a small group of the most important men of rank available among the English magnates and bishops met in the king's chamber at Windsor. Henry V had been dead fully four weeks, but it is difficult to see how such a meeting could have been arranged sooner. Until it was held, not even the most pressing, routine matters necessary to the basic functioning of government in the short term could be properly settled. As was explained to parliament in November, the meeting's foremost concern was 'the immediate need of governing the realm, both for the preservation of peace and display of justice and for the exercise of the king's offices', for the latter's commissions had automatically lapsed when Henry V died. In most urgent need of affirmation was the authority of the crown's judicial officers, on whose shoulders rested responsibility for maintaining peace and order throughout the realm.[9]

With these things in mind, those at the meeting first of all acknowledged the underlying continuity of English kingship, and the fact that a new king was reigning, by performing homage and swearing fealty to Henry of Windsor as King Henry VI. Langley then surrendered the late king's great gold seal to Simon Gaunstede, keeper of the chancery rolls, who knew what to do with it since he had had custody of it before when the chancellor was abroad. For the shortest of periods,

Gaunstede exemplified the continuity of government from one reign to the next. He took the seal to the chancery in London for safe keeping until Bishop Langley was reappointed on 16 November to become Henry VI's first chancellor. Next day, 29 September, in the Star Chamber of the palace of Westminster, in the supporting presence of Langley and several other lords, Gaunstede sealed a number of patents renewing the appointment of certain key officers, particularly those at the head of the exchequer and the law courts.[10] As far as possible, due procedures were being followed so that, in the short term at least, the normal conduct of English government could be maintained.

All this had been achieved by an astonishingly small, makeshift assembly. It was natural that three of the most powerful men in the kingdom should be there – they, after all, had presumably decided to summon the meeting in the first place. And no doubt the attendance of Henry V's three chief officers was required: Langley as chancellor; John Stafford, dean of St Martin-le-Grand and keeper of the privy seal; and William Kinwolmersh, the treasurer, who may have been too ill to attend and in fact died on 18 December.[11] Others present included Bishop Morgan of Worcester, who had an unrivalled knowledge of diplomacy and of English government in France, for he had recently been chancellor of Normandy.[12] The remaining six at the meeting were representative of the nobility of the realm; but there are strong signs that they were called to Windsor hurriedly and for no other reason than that they happened to be close at hand. Richard Fleming, the scholarly bishop of Lincoln, barely had time to shake the dust from his feet after landing from the latest of his diplomatic missions abroad; he had just arrived at Sandwich (probably already apprised of Henry V's death) and reached London only a day before the Windsor conclave.[13] Bishop Edmund Lacy of Exeter, the scholar-friend of Henry V, had been in London since the end of June; after attending this and other meetings at the beginning of the new reign, he returned to his diocese on 4 December and never left it again for reasons of state.[14] John, Lord Talbot and James Butler, earl of Ormond probably found it a great strain to sit together in the same room, even if it were the royal chamber: they were fast becoming bitter enemies and in September 1422 were in the middle of denouncing one another for activities in Ireland, where Talbot had once held the lieutenancy (1414–20) which in 1422 Ormond occupied. It is unlikely that in normal circumstances they would have deliberated together willingly.[15] Both Lord Clinton and Lord Poynings were presumably conveniently to hand like the rest, though as middle-aged men they were not without experience of war or politics. The atmosphere of the meeting was hardly conducive to smooth discussion or a constructive conclusion: not only were Talbot and Ormond at loggerheads, but relations between Gloucester, Chichele, and Henry Beaufort had been soured some years before.

There were other reasons for the modest attendance at this meeting. When Henry V crossed to France in June 1421, he took with him an impressive array of English noblemen and bishops to join others who were already there; a further contingent accompanied Queen Katherine and John, duke of Bedford when they journeyed to France in May 1422. By the time of the king's death, Bedford, the elder of his brothers, headed the noblemen and the small group of able English bishops who were the English establishment in northern France. Thomas Beaufort, the duke of Exeter, younger brother of Bishop Beaufort and Henry V's uncle, was also there; and so was the earl of March, a man of impressive lineage but limited ability, along with the earls of Salisbury, Suffolk, Warwick, and Stafford. Bishop John Kemp of London and John Wakering, bishop of Norwich, were capable men – Wakering having served John of Gaunt and the duchy of Lancaster – and they too were in Henry V's entourage.[16] Nearly one-quarter of the lords were in France in August 1422 – indeed, as many as one-half of the earls and dukes.

They left back in England a depleted company of temporal and spiritual lords to take part in the important discussions of September – October. Of these, a few were physically inaccessible: the earls of Westmorland and Northumberland appear to have been in the north of England, taking care of their estates or guarding the Scottish border. The rest of the earls and dukes at least were too young to count: York, Devon, and Oxford (who nevertheless was in France) were mere teenagers. As for the remaining bishops (fifteen in all), hardly any were of significance in temporal affairs in 1422. One great figure of the past, Nicholas Bubwith of Bath and Wells, was old and had long retired to his diocese; another, Henry Bowet of York, was an invalid. Polton of Chichester was on one of his many visits to the papal court in Rome, and Chaundler of Salisbury was seriously ill. So too was John Fordham of Ely, whose survival this long (he had been a bishop since 1381) must have astonished his contemporaries. Bishop Heyworth of Coventry and Lichfield took no part in public affairs, and the four Welsh bishops rarely merited serious consideration when it came to offering secular advice or political support.[17]

However, those who were at Windsor on the 28th were mostly elderly men of experience and this proved crucial. The meeting dealt with its immediate business expeditiously, and the government of the realm was tided over without panic or partisanship. It was conscious of the fact that such a small group of men could do little more than accomplish the practical transfer of power, and therefore resolved to summon parliament at the earliest possible moment.[18] It may be assumed that these lords – and others too – were discussing the long-term problem of how to govern England during the king's inevitably long minority. But decisions on such an important matter could not be taken without parliament.

It was not clear in 1422 who precisely should settle the future government of England. Experience gained now was to provide a precedent later when Henry VI was ill and, again, when the boy Edward V succeeded in 1483, and it enabled a constitutional principle to be laid down for the guidance of future generations. No such example was available in 1422. Rather did the temporal and spiritual lords, led by the king's relatives, take the initiative, with parliament summoned at the earliest opportunity. Two sets of guidelines were available to them. One had been provided by Henry V himself, who drew up a will at Dover on 10 June 1421, just before he embarked for France. This was supplemented by death-bed dispositions made late in August 1422. The other set could be distilled from the experience of 1377, when Richard II became king at the age of ten, and 1216, when the nine-year-old Henry III succeeded as the first royal minor since the Norman conquest. Both precedents were carefully examined by the men of 1422. Neither was entirely appropriate to meet the political circumstances and personal ambitions of that year and, as a result, neither was followed to the letter. In the event, an arrangement was made which, however successfully it regularized the rule of England and English France in 1422, could not eliminate the possibility of personal and political strains during the minority ahead.

In composing a new will in 1421, on the eve of another expedition to France, Henry V was following his own prudent example of 1415 and 1417. A copy of this third will has recently come to light at Eton College, but, as is the nature of personal wills, it does not treat of the unique problems associated with the government of England and France in the event of Henry's death.[19] Yet these problems are certain to have occupied the warrior king in 1421, if only because the dynastic situation had changed dramatically since 1417. For one thing, the eldest of his brothers and heir presumptive to his throne, Thomas, duke of Clarence, was slain on 22 March 1421 in one of those rash sorties – this time at Baugé – for which the duke was renowned. The news reached Henry in England round about 11 April.[20] The next heir was his second brother, John, duke of Bedford, who was left in charge of England as keeper of the realm when Henry set sail for France. By then, Henry was aware that Queen Katherine, whom contemporaries imply he had married for love as well as for politics, was pregnant. The treaty of Troyes was another circumstance that demanded careful consideration.[21] In 1420 Henry had become heir and regent of France during the lifetime of the elderly and insane King Charles VI. If Henry wished to provide for the government of England and France in the event of his own death before his child reached maturity, new arrangements were essential. But there was one circumstance which Henry does not seem to have foreseen – that he would predecease Charles VI, who was eighteen years his senior. The treaty of Troyes had assumed that Henry would in due course become king of France; it contained no provision for an alternative regent should he fail to do so, and Henry V may not have thought to repair the omission in 1421. His arrangements, therefore, were only of partial help to the politicians of 1422.

Whatever dispositions Henry made in June 1421 were obviously relevant to the situation in August 1422. But those concerning France may have been less than adequate since Charles VI still lived, Normandy therefore remained separate from the French realm (according to the treaty of Troyes), and the English were committed by the treaty to provide, in agreement with Burgundy and other French nobles, a guardian for King Charles who was either French-born or French-speaking. Supplementary dispositions had therefore to be made by Henry V before he died. While on his death-bed at Vincennes, on 26 August he dictated several codicils to his last will which at least made clear his wishes as to the upbringing of his baby son.[22] At the same time, he drew certain of his companions closer to him and uttered his final political instructions to supersede those of 1421. From Gloucester's statements and the reaction of his brother Bedford and the lords to them, it is clear that Henry V nominated his younger brother to take charge of England.[23] The Burgundian chronicler, Monstrelet, was surely mistaken in recording Henry's charge to the duke of Exeter to take on the rule of England, for which (Monstrelet made the king declare) he was well prepared and which should keep him permanently in England.[24] Gloucester strenuously upheld his brother's last wish and some lords initially supported him; even when they recanted, Exeter's claims were never mentioned as their justification for doing so.

It would be strange indeed if the rule of France were not intended for Bedford, the elder of Henry's brothers and the more experienced in warfare and dependable in a crisis. But no such simple arrangement was possible in August 1422. Realizing that Charles VI would survive him – and the implications that flowed from that – Henry appears to have committed independent Normandy to the care of Bedford and the rule of France to Burgundy. This need only last until Charles's death, which, to judge by his state of health, might not be long delayed. When it happened, Henry VI would become king of France (and require a regent), Normandy would be reunited with the French realm, and any guardian of King Charles would lose his power. Monstrelet reported that Henry asked Bedford to take on the regency of France only if Burgundy refused it, and this interpretation has been echoed by historians ever since, even though it implies that Bedford might have little independent authority in France after Charles's demise and none at all in England. Such a view may be a later, telescoped rationalization of a rapid sequence of events between the end of August and late October 1422. What Henry did on his death-bed may simply have been to delay Bedford's accession to the regency of France until Charles VI died.[25]

After Henry V's death the problem of the French regency was sorted out at meetings between Bedford, Burgundy, the French council, and the late king's advisers. The settlement of Troyes was reaffirmed and, in accordance with it, Bedford was made keeper of Normandy; Burgundy probably became regent of the king and kingdom of France.[26] When Charles died at 7 a.m. on 21 October, Bedford may have been a little uncertain as to whether or not Burgundy would relinquish his authority; hence Bedford's anxiety, in a letter to the city of London five days later, to express his disquiet at certain provisions of 'the ordonnance or wil' of Henry V and to advertise his own claim to a special position in England, based on 'lawes and ancien usage and custume' and his close blood relationship to Henry VI. Bedford had no real desire to contradict Henry V's wishes, but if Burgundy were to deprive him of France, he may have felt it prudent to set forth his claims in England, 'which we fully trust was not his [i.e., Henry V's] intent to harm or prejudice'. Bedford was still referring to himself as *gubernator Normannie* on 1 November, six days after his letter was despatched to England. But in the event, he soon emerged as French regent for his young nephew who, as Henry VI, was king of a France reunited with Normandy.[27] On 19 November, Bedford presided as regent in the parlement of Paris and dedicated himself to work for the good of France; the treaty of Troyes was confirmed once again. The duke was content: he never again questioned the settlement of England and was in no hurry to travel home; he did so finally in December 1425 only in response to an urgent appeal from Bishop Beaufort. Philip of Burgundy could hardly afford to resist English wishes, for he depended on English support after the murder of his father in 1419 by the henchmen of the dauphin (now Charles VII).

Henry V's arrangements had contained one fatal flaw: not until the last few days of his life had he conceived of the possibility that he might predecease King Charles. Moreover, the treaty of Troyes had restricted Henry's freedom of action on his death-bed. The arrangements he now hastily made for France's government were intended to cover both the short term (up to Charles's death) and the long term (when Henry VI would be monarch of both realms). It is a reflection of Burgundy's dependence on England and the steadfastness of the English commanders in France (despite Bedford's alarm on 26 October) that Charles's death did not weaken the English hold on northern France or disrupt the Anglo-Burgundian alliance. If Henry V's aim had been to ensure Bedford's regency of France, it was eventually fulfilled. Yet, the famous king could not have died at a less opportune moment. His death put his achievements and his arrangements for the future at risk. For Burgundy, events may have been frustrating, even humiliating, for he was in no position to flout Henry's ultimate design. Committed as he was to the realities and the letter of the treaty of Troyes, he acknowledged Bedford as regent. This does not mean that he liked doing so, and he absented himself from the obsequies of both Henry V and Charles VI. Monstrelet, the Burgundian, is the only contemporary to claim that Burgundy willingly stepped down from the regency in order to let Bedford have it, and in saying this he may have been providing his patron with a face-saving device.[28] Monstrelet's testimony has been relied on with more confidence than it deserves. It arouses suspicion by claiming to record the last words of the dying Henry V, whilst the content of this speech makes the chronicle even more suspect. It directed a gratuitous insult at Gloucester and further maintained that Henry had ceded the government of England to the duke of Exeter; no one present, certainly not Exeter, is known to have maintained later that this was so. The chronicle was written after Gloucester's invasion of the Low Countries in 1425, which provoked Burgundy's hostility, and after Gloucester had repulsed Duke Philip's attack on Calais in 1436. These circumstances could explain the distortion of fact in Henry's supposed speech as far as Duke Humphrey is concerned. Monstrelet's overall intention was to heighten the self-esteem of Burgundy and, in particular, to explain why Burgundy did not continue as regent of France in 1422: Monstrelet claimed that he was offered the title (as Henry V was said to have instructed), but declined it.

Historians have quoted Thomas Walsingham's statements in support of Monstrelet's interpretation, and, true enough, the St Albans chronicler did not record that Burgundy was made regent and that Bedford was assigned Normandy. But his chronicle ends on 31 August 1422, shows no interest in Charles VI's death six weeks later and, therefore, records nothing of the changed circumstances in France thereafter. Walsingham could not record Bedford's eventual nomination as regent because his chronicle had already ended.[29]

Henry V's committal of England to Gloucester was comprehensible. But the powers he intended his brother to enjoy aroused bitter argument. On 7 November, the day of the solemn interment of Henry's corpse in Westminster abbey, there was a formal reading of the will, with its attached codicils, by Bishop Langley in the presence of Archbishop Chichele, Bishop Beaufort, and the dukes of Gloucester and Exeter, all of whom studied it carefully.[30] At first, the authority of the dead king's wishes was sufficient to elicit agreement from some lords – at least according to Gloucester who, since he was reminding these same lords of their initial attitude, would hardly have misrepresented it. But once the full implications of Henry's directions were apparent, objections were raised: first, by Bedford on 26 October, when he may still have been unsure of his future in France. Others were perhaps apprehensive of Gloucester's youth and unsteady reputation. As a result, many lords expressed serious misgivings about the scope of the powers bestowed on Gloucester by the codicil of 1422. Henry's talk of the *tutela* or wardship of the king and his affairs after the manner of Roman law and French regencies of the fourteenth century was repugnant to the English mind, no matter how closely it reflected Henry V's inclinations towards authoritarian rule and ways French. Those who accompanied the late king's body back to England early in November 1422 may have carried Bedford's reservations with them. Whatever the reason, the lords' attitude to Gloucester's claim was clearly changing.[31]

Both Gloucester and the lords resorted to an alternative set of guidelines to help them resolve the conflict between them – precedent.

The Lancastrians had realized the importance of precedent and history in securing what they wanted in 1399. Duke Humphrey shared the family skill in searching records and drawing historical comparisons. If he studied the events of 1377, he would have deduced little of value to his cause, for his grandfather, John of Gaunt, had been accorded no special position in the governing councils of Richard II's minority. But 1216, when the first minority since the Norman conquest began, provided more promising material in the status and powers of William the Marshal, *rector* of the king and realm under Henry III. In stressing this precedent, Gloucester could also pose as the conciliator, offering to forego wardship of the young king in order to secure wardship of the kingdom. This would enable him to uphold the wishes of Henry V and at the same time appear to offer a concession.[32]

The lords did not view history in quite the same light. 1216 seemed less appropriate (certainly further in the past) than 1377, but they reserved their fiercest attack for the will itself, safe in the knowledge that Bedford, heir to the throne, was equally unhappy about one of the codicils. They denied that Henry V had any right to determine the government of England after his death, for contemporaries were inclined to distinguish between arranging the inheritance of property by will and disposing of kingdoms and royal prerogatives in the same way.[33] Moreover, the language of the will was foreign to English ears and leaned too heavily on Roman law. Much as Gloucester might remonstrate and proclaim the rights of birth, he had no alternative but to agree to a further compromise. This was the famous protectorate under which England was to be governed for the first seven years of Henry VI's reign, the first constitutional experiment in formal protection in English history.

Henry V's last wishes had therefore proved inadequate to meet the situation created by his death. They failed to provide for the uncontentious rule of France in the immediate future, and their arrangements for England were not acceptable to important Englishmen, including the new king's heir. Relations between Bedford, Gloucester, and the lords were vitiated by the controversy over the will and its codicils and the struggle for power in England to which it gave rise. This struggle poisoned relations between those whose co-operation was essential if a long minority were to be weathered successfully. Henry's death-bed dispositions for France eventually proved adequate to the occasion, though they strained relations with the duke of Burgundy on whom the English position in France was partly founded. All in all, the death of Henry V was a severe shock to Englishmen at home and abroad, not least because it came at a most unpropitious juncture. It was the most consequential event in the history of the Lancastrian monarchy between 1399 and 1461, and was not without significance in moulding constitutional custom in England long after.

The protectorate of England was inaugurated by Henry VI's first parliament on 5 December 1422. For more than two months, suggestions had been floated, arguments advanced, and bargains proposed. Bedford, unlike his younger brother Gloucester and his Beaufort uncles, played no direct part in it all and remained in France. But several of his wartime companions accompanied Henry V's funeral cortège to England; amongst them were magnates and members of the late king's household, executors of Henry's will, and witnesses of the dying king's last pronouncements. Some of them doubtless shared Bedford's attitudes and conveyed his wishes to England. They arrived in London on 5 November. A full meeting of lords was held in the council chamber at Westminster that day. Bedford's letter had arrived a few days earlier and could now be amplified by the returning lords. This meeting was consequently wary of Gloucester's claims. Of those who had been present on 28 September, Ormond (the lieutenant of Ireland) and John Stafford, keeper of the privy seal, were now absent. But the duke of Exeter, the earl of Warwick, Bishop Wakering of Norwich, Lords FitzHugh and Cromwell had just returned from France and attended, along with others called from their estates in England – John Langdon who, before becoming bishop of Rochester, had been with Henry V in France, the earls of Norfolk and Northumberland, Lords Ferrers, Botreaux, Audley, and Berkeley – to form a 'more fully and representatively attended' conference of prelates and nobles, though none of lesser status.[34] They provided an injection of youth into discussions hitherto conducted by a rather elderly group. All but one of the additional lords were under the age of forty and six were barely thirty. Whether they reflected a 'representative' view among the baronage of England may be doubted. Five of them were newly returned from France bearing, one might suppose, the opinions of the duke of Bedford. Four may be regarded as forming a Beaufort circle, for both Northumberland and Norfolk had married daughters of Joan Beaufort, countess of Westmorland, who was the sister of Exeter and Bishop Beaufort. If, as John Hardyng recorded, the latter was firmly opposed to Gloucester's pretensions in 1422, he could count on influential allies from this quarter.[35]

On 5 November, there was a foretaste of the coming rift between Gloucester and other lords: should the duke be allowed to open and close the forthcoming parliament (which was due to assemble on 9 November)? A decision on this would be relevant to the wider question of minority rule in England. The meeting, whether in deference to Bedford's reservations or swayed by Bishop Beaufort's hostility, or counselled by their own estimate of Gloucester's capacity, affirmed that the duke's keepership of the realm had been terminated by Henry V's death and announced that he might open and close parliament only with the council's assent.[36] It was a hard blow for Gloucester, who unsuccessfully challenged the ruling, aware that his wider claims were being prejudiced.

The signs were made even clearer on the first day of parliament when, in the absence of a chancellor, Archbishop Chichele delivered the sermon.[37] Just as Moses, *duc* or leader of the Israelites, was advised to seek the support of others, so suitable persons from each 'estate' in society should play a role in the government of England. The purport of this text was unmistakable. The crunch came during parliament's meeting, prompted perhaps by a request from the commons that they be told who was to govern the realm. After a long discussion among the lords and careful investigation of law and precedent, Gloucester's demand to be given the powers of a regent was rejected on 5 December: claims based on his birth, the will, and on precedents quoted by him were found wanting. He was offered instead the title of 'Defensor of this Reme and chief counseiller of the kyng', which entailed the specific duty of defending the kingdom and acting as the king's chief councillor. His title 'emporteth a personall duetee of entendance to the actuell defense of the land as well against thenemys utward, yf cas required, as ayenst Rebelles inward, yf any were'; but no 'name of Tutour, Lieutinent, Governour, nor of Regent, nor no name that shuld emporte auctorite of governaunce of the lond' was implied (so the lords explained later in 1428). Gloucester was allowed a special position whenever his brother, Bedford, was abroad, but this hardly met the duke's pretensions. Moreover, the lords determined that these arrangements should not necessarily last until the king came of age, but only 'as long as it liked the Kyng', and to this the commons agreed.[38]

The position of Bedford as heir to the throne was safeguarded by the provision that whenever he was in the realm he should take Gloucester's place as protector, defender, and chief councillor. The lords in parliament were also concerned to ensure that no matter how limited the special powers of Bedford and Gloucester, they should not exercise them unless they were in England; the suspicion of Henry V's 'dual monarchy' which had been aroused immediately after the sealing of the treaty of Troyes was still fresh in the mind.[39] The protector's rights were strictly limited and his patronage did not extend beyond appointments to certain minor offices and benefices. The powers of the new council established in parliament were correspondingly enormous. For its membership, this council relied heavily on those who had borne the brunt of the discussions during the previous two months. Setting aside the three officers of state, four of the councillors had been at the initial meeting on 28 September: Gloucester, Chichele, Beaufort, and Bishop Morgan. Seven others had been at the 5 November meeting (Bishop Wakering, Lords FitzHugh and Cromwell, the earls of Norfolk, Northumberland, and Warwick, and the duke of Exeter). The council, therefore, was well aware of the problems of personality and principle which had arisen and was probably hostile to Gloucester's ambition. Three others were added who were recently home from France and were likely to be aware of Bedford's views (Bishop Kemp of London, who was the retiring chancellor of Normandy, the earl of March, and Sir Walter Hungerford). As many as ten of the seventeen councillors were either supervisors or executors of Henry V's will and would therefore provide continuity of interest and thinking (except on the question of Gloucester's role) between the two reigns. F. M. Powicke's judgement on the council of 1216, whose core was King John's executors, is appropriate to the circumstances of 1422: 'The need was for men who would link the will of the dead with the interests of the new king'.[40] Furthermore, the non-official members of the council were well representative of the governing society of England: its five senior ecclesiastics (Canterbury, Winchester, London, Worcester, and Norwich) were vigorous, knowledgeable men. The two dukes (Gloucester and Exeter) and five earls (Westmorland, Northumberland, Norfolk, March, and Warwick) were important figures. The three barons (FitzHugh, Tiptoft, and Cromwell) were loyal supporters of the house of Lancaster, and the two knights (Walter Hungerford and Walter Beauchamp) had been close to Henry V. They represented, too, a cross-section of generations: although at least six of them were over fifty in 1422, five were below the age of thirty. There is no doubting the experience in government, diplomacy, and war, of the group as a whole. There was no lord, ecclesiastic or secular, alive who had been an officer of state or of the royal household since 1399 who was not present on this council. Four former officers of state were there, and two former principal officers of the king's household, as well as two former chancellors of Normandy. It is difficult to conceive of a more capable, experienced, or vigorous group of men to exercise the royal authority at the opening of a long minority.[41] The only reservation about their choice – the presence of personal tensions and rivalries arising from the circumstances of 1422 – was eventually to prove disastrous.

To assist its deliberations and ensure efficiency, regulations were drawn up for the conduct of conciliar business. The council's powers specifically included all shire and port appointments and the disposal of the king's feudal patronage, his wardships and marriages. Such patronage should be equitable and impartial, the resources of the king's treasury kept confidential, and a careful record noted of attendance and decisions at council meetings. A quorum was fixed of at least four councillors (apart from the officers of state), provided that the majority was present if truly important matters were to be decided; the protector had to be consulted on those matters which, in normal circumstances, would be referred to the king. It was a sensible and flexible framework within which to conduct business, though in the event it proved rather too flexible and imprecise to control the personal predilections of certain of the councillors.[42]

These councillors undertook their duties as from 9 December 1422, although a council had for all practical purposes been in existence since 28 September and had been referred to as such.[43] Now, however, it was established formally in parliament, at the request of the commons. The lords alone assented to its details, and the list of councillors and the schedule of their powers were taken by a delegation of lords to the commons, who expressed themselves satisfied with the arrangements. As in 1377 such matters were considered inappropriate for discussion by the commons, who simply received the lords' decisions.[44] Straight after parliament was dissolved on 18 December, Bishop Kemp wrote to his agent in Rome that England was at 'tranquil peace'.[45]

Notes

1 *Foedera*, IV, iv, 80, ends the minor controversy about the time of death. Henry V's last months are described in J. H. Wylie and W. T. Waugh, *The reign of Henry V* (3 vols., 1914–29), III, 418.

2 V. J. Scattergood, *Politics and poetry in the fifteenth century* (1972), p. 135; F. Taylor, 'The chronicle of John Strecche for the reign of Henry V (1414–1422)', *BJRL*, XVI (1932), 53; L. Douet d'Arcq (ed.), *La chronique d'Enguerran de Monstrelet... 1400–1444* (6 vols., Paris, 1857–62), IV, 140-1; T. Walsingham, *Historia anglicana, 1272–1422*, ed. H. T. Riley (2 vols., RS, 1863–64), II, 345. See Wylie and Waugh, op. cit., III, 418, 423-5.

3 ibid., 418; LeicsRO, 26 D 53/47; *RP*, IV, 194.

4 WorcsRO, Reg. Morgan, pp. 96-7; R. L. Storey, *Thomas Langley and the bishopric of Durham, 1406–1437* (1961), p. 44. The journey between London and York took five or six days later in the century (C. A. J. Armstrong, 'Some examples of the distribution and speed of news in England at the time of the wars of the roses', in R. W. Hunt, W. A. Pantin, and R. W. Southern [eds.], *Essays in medieval history presented to F. M. Powicke* [Oxford, 1948], pp. 46-7).

5 Henry of Windsor's reign as King Henry VI was regarded as beginning on 1 September, the day after the day on which Henry V was alive and dead. This had been the practice (with exceptions in 1327 and 1399) since Edward I's death; before that the king's coronation was regarded as the formal beginning of a reign. Cf. E. H. Kantorowicz, *The king's two bodies* (Princeton, NJ, 1957), pp. 328-30. Oddly enough, the anniversary of Henry V's death was kept at Westminster abbey on 30 August, though he had died early next day (*RP*, VI, 187; above n. 1).

6 *SR*, II, 151, reproduced in Chrimes and Brown, op. cit., pp. 225-6.

7 Wylie and Waugh, op. cit., III, 416. Before her husband's death, Katherine had been in England for a total of only fifteen months, from 1 February 1421 to early May 1422 (ibid., pp. 267, 402).

8 Storey, *Thomas Langley*, pp. 44-5, 236. Chichele was certainly at Lambeth on 25 September when he ordered prayers for Henry V's soul and for the health and prosperity of Henry VI (WorcsRO, Reg. Morgan, pp. 98-9).

9 *RP*, IV, 170. J.S. Roskell, 'The office and dignity of protector of England, with special reference to its origins', *EHR*, LXVIII (1953), 193-233, is a careful study of the constitutional significance of the events of 1422.

10 *RP*, IV, 170; *HBC*, p. 85; *CCR, 1422–29*, pp. 26, 47. For Gaunstede, see Wylie and Waugh, op. cit., III, 22. A new great seal and signet were made at Windsor by a London goldsmith before 18 October; Henry V's privy seal simply had its legend altered (PRO, E403/664 m.1).

11 *RP*, IV, 170; *CCR, 1422–29*, p. 46.

12 Emden, *Oxford*, II, 1312–13, supplemented by R. G. Davies, 'The episcopate of England and Wales, 1378–1443' (Manchester PhD thesis, 1974), III, cci-ccv, and M. L. Bull, 'Philip Morgan (d. 1435): ecclesiastic and statesman' (Wales MA dissertation, 1977).

13 R. G. Davies, thesis, III, cxx; Emden, *Oxford*, II, 697-9 (which wrongly states that he returned on 27 October); PRO, E101/321/40.

14 Emden, *Oxford*, II, 1081-3; R. G. Davies, thesis, III, clvii-clix; G. R. Dunstan (ed.), *The register of Edmund Lacy, bishop of Exeter, 1420–1455* (5 vols., Cant. and York Soc., 1963-72), V, ix.

15 A. J. Otway-Ruthven, *A history of medieval Ireland* (1968), pp. 354ff. Ormond was not an English peer and did not receive a summons to parliament; this fact fortifies the impression that the meeting was hurriedly arranged. Talbot was in England following the death of his wife on 31 May 1422.

16 Wylie and Waugh, op. cit., III, 402, 406-7; Roskell, *EHR*, LXVIII (1953), 194-5, 200.

17 Biographical notes on all these bishops are in Emden, *Oxford*, I-III, or R. G. Davies, thesis, III; for the lay peers, see *GEC*. The earls of Huntingdon and Somerset had been captured at Baugé (1421) and were still prisoners (Wylie and Waugh, op. cit., III, 306).

18 *RP*, IV, 170.

19 I am grateful to Dr and Mrs P. Strong for informing me of the document's discovery and allowing me to consult it at Eton. They have since edited it (as Eton College records 59) in *EHR*, XCVI (1981), 79-102.

20 Wylie and Waugh, op. cit., III, 299-310; Thomas de Elmham, *Vita et Gesta Henrici Quinti Anglorum Regis*, ed. T. Hearne (Oxford, 1727), pp. 304-7.

21 *Foedera*, IV, iii, 179-80, and *EHD*, IV, 225-6. For Henry's feelings towards Katherine, see Waurin, II, 286.

22 *RP*, IV, 280-2; Walsingham, op. cit., II, 343; Eton Coll. MS; below, p. 51.

23 Cf. Roskell, *EHR*, LXVIII (1953), 203ff.

24 Monstrelet, op. cit., IV, 404-5.

25 As he lay dying, Henry urged Burgundy, through his envoy, to uphold earlier undertakings and alliances with the English (L. M. E. Dupont [ed.], *Mémoires de Pierre de Fenin... 1407–27* [Paris, 1837], pp. 185-6). Cf. Roskell, *EHR*, LXVIII (1953), 200 n. 3, whose speculations on the significance of Henry's death before that of Charles VI deserve greater prominence than historians have accorded them.

26 ibid., 204-5, 207-8; Walsingham, op. cit., II, 345 (whose chronicle ends with Henry V's death and shows no interest in the consequences of Charles VI's demise); Fenin, op. cit., p. 187. Charles VI solemnly confirmed the treaty of Troyes when he heard of Henry's death, and Bedford, Burgundy, and Exeter, along with other French and English lords, also swore to maintain it (Walsingham, op. cit., II, 344; Monstrelet, op. cit., IV, 407). Mandates were issued in Normandy by Bedford as governor of the duchy in September–October 1422 (BN, n. a. f. 1482 nos. 13-20; f. f. 25766 no. 816).

27 R. R. Sharpe, *London and the Kingdom* (3 vols., 1894–95), III, 367-8, reprinted in Chrimes and Brown, op. cit., p. 245; Roskell, *EHR*, LXVIII (1953), 216, 220; *EHD*, IV, 225-6; BN, f. f. 25766 no. 816; C. de Fauquembergue, *Journal*, ed. A. Tuetey and H. Lacaille (3 vols., Paris,

1903-13), II, 59, 72-5. On 6 October, Bedford had contemplated a visit to England (ibid., 146). On 7 November, after Charles's death, Burgundy once again pledged himself to maintain the treaties with the English and put himself at the disposal of the French council (ibid., 68-70).

28 Monstrelet, op. cit., IV, 404-5, 415; V, 2-6; Shirley, op. cit., pp. 178-83; Walsingham, op. cit., II, 345. If Burgundy was thrust aside by Bedford (C. A. J. Armstrong, 'La double monarchie France – Angleterre et la maison de Bourgogne [1420–1435]: le déclin d'une alliance', *Annales de Bourgogne*, XXXVII (1963), 82-3), why did he conclude a contract with Bedford on 12 December 1422 for the latter to marry Anne of Burgundy? idem, 'La politique matrimoniale des ducs de Bourgogne de la maison de Valois', ibid., XL (1968), 13. See also B.-A. Pocquet du Haut-Jussé, 'Anne de Bourgogne et le testament de Bedford (1429)', *Bibl. de l'école des Chartes*, XCV (1934), 296-306.

29 Above, n. 26.

30 Roskell, *EHR*, LXVIII (1953), 203; *RP*, IV, 299-300.

31 The change is made clear in Gloucester's memorandum sometime in November (S. B. Chrimes, 'The pretensions of the duke of Gloucester in 1422', *EHR*, XLV [1930], 102-3, reprinted in Chrimes and Brown, op. cit., pp. 248-9). For the concept of *tutela* in France and the principle, established by edict in 1407, that the care of king and kingdom during a royal minority or incapacity should rest with a *régence*, see P. Dupuy, *Traité de la majorité de nos rois, et des régences du royaume* (Paris, 1655), pp. 15-16, 87-92, 205-17.

32 Chrimes and Brown, op. cit., pp. 248-9. In practice, William the Marshal assigned the wardship of Henry III to the bishop of Winchester (below, p. 51). For the situation in 1377, see T. F. Tout, *Chapters in the administrative history of mediaeval England* (6 vols., Manchester, 1920–33), III, 323, 326. The year 1327, when Edward III succeeded at the age of fourteen, was less relevant; power had then been seized by the queen-mother and her lover, Roger Mortimer. The question of separating the government of king and kingdom came up again in 1547, after Edward VI's accession; the discussions of 1422 were quoted in evidence (L. B. Campbell, 'Humphrey, duke of Gloucester and Elianor Cobham his wife in the "Mirror for Magistrates"', *HLQ*, V [1934], 120-1).

33 *RP*, IV, 326-7, with full commentary by Roskell, *EHR*, LXVIII (1953), 210-18. Cf. Kantorowicz, op. cit., p. 370. Gloucester's memorandum (cited above, n. 31) represents a stage in the argument. In 1216, King John does not seem to have left directions in his will for other than the disposal of his property (G. J. Turner, 'The minority of Henry III, Part I', *TRHS*, n. s., XVIII [1904], 283).

34 *PPC*, III, 6-7; Roskell, *EHR*, LXVIII (1953), 197-9.

35 H. Ellis (ed.), *John Hardyng's Chronicle* (1812), pp. 390-1.

36 *RP*, IV, 169, though the context in which the council's assent would operate was far from clear. One document, however, did refer to Gloucester as *custos Angliae* when he opened the parliament (PRO, E101/407/13 f. 23).

37 *RP*, IV, 169; Roskell, *EHR*, LXVIII (1953), 207-10.

38 *RP*, IV, 326-7; Chrimes and Brown, op. cit., pp. 248-9. It is possible, as Gloucester himself claimed, that the commons preferred the title of 'gouernour'. For Gloucester's consciousness of his position as 'son,

brother and uncle of kings', see his style in LeicsRO, DE 221/10/5/24, 23 (writs of 7 July 1436 and 20 January 1437).

39 Chrimes and Brown, op. cit., pp. 242-3.

40 *RP*, IV, 175-6; F. M. Powicke, *The Thirteenth Century* (Oxford, 1953), pp. 2-3. Roskell, *EHR*, LXVIII (1953), 233, gives the full range of overseers, administrators, and executors of Henry V's will.

41 Nor was this council shackled, as the October council of 1377 had been, by affixing a precise time-limit (one year) to its existence and disqualifying its members from future councils for the next two years (A. Steel, *Richard II* [Cambridge, 1940], p. 45).

42 *RP*, IV, 175-6; below, pp. 29ff.

43 e.g., *CPR, 1422-29*, pp. 1, 3-4.

44 A. Tuck, *Richard II and the English nobility* (1973), pp. 38-9. It was useful, though possibly fortuitous, that three of the councillors had acted as speaker of the commons in the past: Lord Tiptoft (1406), Sir Walter Hungerford (1414), and Sir Walter Beauchamp (1416).

45 BL, Cotton MS, Cleopatra C IV f. 172r.

2 The King's Councillors

The new council

From the day of his accession, the prerogatives of kingship and the powers of government reposed in Henry VI. These prerogatives and powers were usually exercised by – or with – a council, and the same was true after 1422, even though the king was a baby. The authority of his council sprang from Henry himself, not from the will of his father (as Duke Humphrey had implied) or from the lords of parliament. That this was so is apparent from the lords' retort to Gloucester's complaint about the restrictions placed on him on 5 November 1422, when he was authorized to open and close parliament.[1] They declared that they were unable to dispose of the royal authority without the king's full knowledge (which at his age could not be secured) and denied that Humphrey could do so either. This principle underlay the political settlement of 1422, though it was only given tangible and literal expression after a period of practical experience and challenge, especially by Gloucester.

The formal appointment of councillors on 9 December 1422 took place in parliament on the king's authority so that the appointees would *assist* in the government of the realm.[2] The collective responsibility of the lords, 'the whiche duryng the tendre age aforseide of the Kyng, Governe and Reule undre hym, and by his auctoritee', was later challenged by both Bedford and Gloucester, with the result that in January 1427 this responsibility was defined more precisely.[3] On that occasion, the lords declared unequivocally that authority to govern resided in the king alone, even though he was a minor; because he was at present unable to exercise it personally, this authority reposed temporarily in the lords assembled in parliament or council, and especially (for the sake of convenience) in the lords of the council. Definition was forced on them by the long minority and by the demand for one-man rule that the duke of Gloucester expressed.

In short, the undeniably convenient fiction of the 'undying king' was being publicized; and by doing so, the lords might be able to deter the ambitious and the unscrupulous from assaulting what was declared to be the royal authority. It did not, in fact, stop Gloucester; indeed, it enabled him to defy his fellow councillors in 1427, when he stated that he was answerable to no one but the king and that such answerability was only feasible when Henry VI came of age.[4] The paradox in the idea of the undying king when the monarch was himself incapable of ruling could not therefore be completely reconciled; nor could the responsibility of any one councillor to his fellows or even to the king be rigorously enforced so long as the king were a boy. The situation was the more uncertain because two of the councillors were successively the king's next heirs.

The practical responsibilities of the councillors were defined on occasion during the 1420s, either in response to requests from the commons or under pressure of circumstance, and as time passed they were minuted with greater care and precision. At the first formal appointment of councillors in December 1422, only details essential for the conduct of business were recorded by the parliamentary clerks.[5] A modest quorum of four councillors out of a total of sixteen (excluding the three officers of state) was required to be present for the transaction of business, but when important matters were being discussed, a majority of the councillors was felt necessary; and either Bedford or Gloucester as chief councillor should be consulted in those cases where the king would ordinarily have played a part. There was rarely any difficulty in attaining a quorum of four, and hardly any decisions were taken with fewer councillors present.[6]

The councillor's oath urged such laudable sentiments as impartiality, honesty, and confidentiality, the fundamental principles which all good committees, whether of an executive or an advisory nature, observe. They were sound principles, but they left several things unsaid which time and experience would bring to the fore and require modification of the 1422 arrangements.

In other respects, the regulations worked less well. What, for instance, were the important matters that required the advice of the majority of councillors, and was it practicable to assemble them often enough to deal with these questions? With three further additions to the sworn councillors on 26 January 1423, the majority was now ten, and it would have been optimistic to say the least to expect that number to assemble regularly. Apart from three weeks in February 1423 and a similar period from the end of the following April, this rule was rarely adhered to until the parliamentary session began in February 1424. Well attended meetings of the council, which had been recognized as of value by the politicians of 1422, proved unattainable: whereas ten councillors and two officers of state discussed a pension for the king's chambermaid and laundress on 27 April 1423, only six councillors and three officers made arrangements on 6 March 1423 for the mission of the earl of Northumberland to the Council of Pavia.[7]

By the time the second parliament of the reign met on 23 October 1423, there were loop-holes in the way England was being governed that required attention; in particular, recent experience indicated that more detailed guidelines were desirable. Accordingly, just before the end of the session (28 February 1424), eight new articles were approved.

Henceforth, bills presented to the council for consideration would normally be read on a Wednesday and answered briskly on the following Friday. On the other hand, the difficulty of ensuring large attendances at councils was met simply by abandoning the intentions of 1422: the majority authorizing a decision would now be a majority of those present during the discussion, and during 1424 and 1425 a clear majority of councillors seems never to have assembled on a single occasion. When decisions were made by at least four (excluding the officers), they would have their assent recorded by their own hand, and these signatures appear on conciliar warrants from at least July 1424, though not on all of them.[8] Questions affecting the royal prerogative or the king's resources were not to be resolved until the justices had been consulted and their opinion recorded. But only one instance is known during 1424–25 when a law officer is specifically recorded as participating in a decision; on 3 March 1425 the chief baron of the exchequer attended a discussion about repaying crown loans.[9] The clerk of the council was expected, when drawing up the order of business, to give priority to poor men's bills and to do so free of charge. Other articles were intended to prevent the council from being so deluged with business during the minority that care, efficiency, and speed would be prejudiced: hence, common law suits ought to be referred to the appropriate court unless Henry's own interests were directly affected, as, for example, by quarrels that threatened the king's peace.[10]

The most serious threat to the council's effectiveness was the undermining of its corporate will. In view of the disagreements of 1422, it was probably inevitable that the councillors should dissolve into factions, each holding opinions that sometimes dictated contradictory courses of action. This may account for the rule devised in February 1424 that no councillor, not even the duke of Gloucester, should make a grant alone, without the other councillors being informed. The occasions had been few when only one councillor (apart from an officer) had concluded business, but on 14 January 1423 Gloucester, from his own home, had licensed St Mary's abbey, York, to proceed to the election of an abbot; Bishop Beaufort, Bishop Morgan, and the earl of Warwick had similarly acted alone.[11] Nor should any councillor communicate personally with a foreign power against the policy of the council as a whole; this was a constraint probably prompted by Gloucester's precipitate decision to campaign in the Low Countries on behalf of his wife, Jacqueline of Hainault. These specifications of February 1424 enabled the council (which was again formally nominated in parliament at the request of the commons, with six additions, two resignations, and one change of officer) to proceed with a renewed collective purpose and greater expedition.

However, by the middle of 1425, by which time England had not seen its protector for six months, increasing disorder and aristocratic squabbles were penetrating the council. Further safeguards were therefore needed to ensure its proper functioning, and these were provided in the parliament which met on 30 April 1425.[12] An attempt was made to emphasize the collective responsibility of the councillors, and it was even felt desirable that they should swear an amended oath to maintain peace and order in the realm, and to promote good government during Henry VI's minority.

Yet the most thorough overhaul of the framework of conciliar rule was undertaken after the bitter struggle between Gloucester and Beaufort in the winter of 1425–26, and the delicate compromise devised later at the Leicester parliament. In any case, there had been some considerable changes of personnel on the council since the beginning of 1425.[13] Now, on 24 November 1426, renewed stress was laid on improving the formal procedures for the conduct of conciliar business; but the recurrent difficulty of confining quarrelsome councillors to frank but peaceful argument had become more formidable.[14] Although it was perhaps implicit in his oath that an individual councillor should not be present when matters affecting him were under review (and Exeter had been absent from such a discussion on 4 March 1423, even though he attended another council discussion on the same day), this principle was now stated in black and white: it might help to promote open and frank discussion without fear or favour. Gloucester himself had taken part when a petition from his own lordship of Tenby was considered on 2 March 1423, but after this formal change of procedure, Beaufort, as a cardinal, absented himself when relations between England and the Roman church were being discussed in December 1429.[15] As a further aid, the essential confidentiality of conciliar proceedings was reiterated.

The emphasis of these revised regulations on impartiality is unmistakable; a corollary was that a formal record of decisions should be kept and (as had been recommended in 1424) of the names of those who subscribed to them. This latter practice had in fact become customary by 1426, so that few warrants authorized by the council did not carry the signatures of those present; if any were unhappy about a particular decision, they appear to have been allowed to withhold their signature.[16] Evenhanded government would be further promoted if councillors assembled at the agreed meeting-place and not elsewhere; *ad hoc*, surreptitious, unrecorded meetings of small groups in the name of the whole council would thereby be prevented. Although most meetings were already being held at Westminster palace or some other authorized place (such as Leicester, when parliament was meeting there), a few had been arranged elsewhere, with a small number present. Gloucester, in particular, had been prone to do this early in 1423 and again in October 1425.[17] Furthermore, only exceptional or urgent matters should henceforward be dealt with outside the normal council terms when, presumably, a substantial number of councillors would be difficult to contact and less readily assembled. If there was any suggestion of deviating from the good practices of the past four years, these regulations of 1426 nipped it in the bud.

At the same time, the council's control over the king's patronage was reinforced. It was proposed in 1426 that this patronage should be directed more towards rewarding loyal personal servants of the three Lancastrian kings, implying presumably that councillors and others had been trying to secure grants of offices, benefices, lands, and fees in their own or their servants' favour. The grip of both Bedford and Gloucester on Henry's patronage was weakened: they could delay a grant for one day if they found themselves in a minority, but thereafter the opinion of the majority would carry the day. This provision may account for Gloucester's occasional refusal to signify his assent to a conciliar decision.[18] The concern expressed in 1425 about personal disputes intruding in the council was still strongly felt at the end of 1426, and a firm ban was therefore placed on councillors or their servants maintaining criminals or in other ways undermining the law; the collective responsibility of the council (including the king's uncles) to preserve law and order was accordingly stressed anew. The principle that each councillor should give exclusive service to the king alone was a similar attempt to bring councillors to a clear appreciation of their fundamental responsibilities during the minority.

This code of behaviour guided the council for the remaining three years of the protectorate. When Duke Humphrey was discharged in the parliament of 1429–30 and the protectorate came to an end, these rules were reissued substantially unchanged as far as the council was concerned.[19] That no further changes were necessary reflects the success with which the role of protector had been limited in the 1420s and deprived of any independent authority which Gloucester especially may have envisaged for it. Political dominance during the remaining years of the king's minority would only be achieved by less direct methods, by influence and the persuasion of individuals. This, it seems likely, is what Duke Humphrey attempted after 1429.

The protector and his colleagues

From 1422 to 1429 England may be described institutionally as a protectorate, just like Oliver Cromwell's England in the mid-seventeenth century – but with the cardinal difference that in the fifteenth century England was still a monarchy and not a republic. During the first seven years of Henry VI's minority, his realm was administered by three principal officers of state, chancellor, treasurer, and keeper of the privy seal. They did so in conjunction with a nominated council which, during the protectorate, was never less than twelve in number and could even rise to eighteen on occasion. The protector was also the king's chief councillor and he probably presided over this council whenever he was present. For most of the time, Humphrey, duke of Gloucester was protector and defender of England, although when his elder brother, the duke of Bedford, was in the realm Gloucester temporarily lost his pre-eminence. This council had advisory, executive, and judicial responsibilities, and during a minority it took vital decisions and executed them.

During the 1420s, it was very unusual for a council to meet which did not have at least two of the permanent officers present, sometimes all three, for their expertise could be placed at the government's disposal full-time. On the other hand, these officers almost never met alone as a council.[20] Nevertheless, it misinterprets the nature of the council to conclude that the additional, nominated councillors were expected to supervise or restrain the permanent officers of state.[21] The desirability of seeking widespread (or, in contemporary language, substantial) advice in the conduct of affairs was fully appreciated by contemporaries and hence the care taken to ensure that the officers were always accompanied in council by other reliable advisers. For this reason, too, a quorum of councillors was insisted upon in the regulations of 1422 and seldom was this provision ignored.[22]

For the first twenty months of the new reign, Bishop Langley's vast experience of politics, government, and foreign relations was placed at the disposal of Henry VI. His formal reappointment as chancellor of England on 16 November 1422 ensured continuity with the previous reign and a sound appreciation of the acknowledged priorities of English government. William Kinwolmersh, treasurer of England under Henry V, was confirmed in office as soon as possible on 30 September, so that crucial financial questions raised by Henry V's demise could be dealt with speedily. Likewise, the keeper of Henry V's privy seal, John Stafford, stayed in office under the new monarch.[23] The virtues of continuity and experience which these three officers embodied were unfortunately undermined almost immediately by Kinwolmersh's death, but the adjustments that had to be made as a result were minor and hardly altered the principles guiding the new régime. John Stafford was quickly transferred to the treasury, and a suitable bishopric was found for him at an early opportunity – though not as speedily as Stafford himself expected.[24] As for the privy seal office, William Alnwick was promptly placed at its head; as Henry V's secretary during the last year of the king's life, he was one of a number of clerks who moved from this post to the privy seal office, capitalizing on the intimate experience gained of the king's personal affairs.[25] The three ecclesiastics, Langley, Stafford, and Alnwick, together directed the country's administration until July 1424.

The councillors associated with them were nominated publicly and formally in parliament on 5 December 1422.[26] Their complement of fifteen was soon afterwards augmented by the appointment of three others in January 1423 : Sir Walter Hungerford, Sir Ralph Botiller, and Sir Lewis Robessart (commonly known as Lord Bourgchier since his marriage to Elizabeth, Lady Bourgchier in 1421).[27] The addition of these three did not alter the essential character of the council, except in so

33

far as they reinforced its non-magnate element. After all, they had each been close to Henry V and loyal to the house of Lancaster, and all of them had military experience which would prove valuable in conciliar discussions about France and the war. Sir Walter Hungerford's family had been in Lancastrian service since Edward II's day, and his father had been John of Gaunt's chief steward. At forty-four, Hungerford had already been an MP four times and had acted as the commons' speaker in 1414. His diplomatic and military activities had been manifold under Henry V, with whom his relations were exceptionally close, not least when he was steward of the royal household and constable of Windsor castle; in 1421 Sir Walter was named an executor of the king's will. Nor was he a stranger to the council table, for he had been summoned to it in 1417 and was a good friend of one of the present councillors, Sir John Tiptoft.[28] Sir Ralph Botiller was a younger man (at twenty-eight), but he too was a soldier and he enjoyed the confidence of the duke of Bedford. His mother was related to the Beauchamps of Powick and to the earl of Warwick, another councillor. Moreover, Botiller had useful London connections as a result of his marriage to the widow of Sir John Hende, whose Essex and London property was thereby added to his own west midlands estates.[29] Robessart was a soldier of even greater distinction. A Hainaulter by birth, he became a denizen of England and entered the personal service of Henry V. Like Hungerford, he was an executor of the king's will and served as his standard-bearer on campaign.[30] This enlarged group of eighteen councillors remained virtually unchanged for a further year. Like the chief officers, they offered continuity and stability of service, and an unshakeable devotion to the family of the late king; at the same time, they supervised the baby monarch's personal household by filling its principal offices and overseeing his upbringing.[31] Their responsibilities enveloped both king and realm.

To judge by the names of those who were present at council meetings, some of the knights played an insignificant role as councillors, however close they might have stood about the king. Sir Walter Beauchamp and Sir Ralph Botiller rarely attended, whilst Hungerford was out of England for much of the second half of 1423.[32] Only Robessart put in an occasional appearance, but then his influence, along with that of the other knights, was felt more directly in the king's household, where they were important officials. On the other hand, there was little done by the council without the abiding presence of Gloucester, the chief councillor. He, together with Lord Cromwell and the earl of Warwick, were present at most meetings, and so were the duke of Exeter and Sir John Tiptoft (at least until the end of May 1423, when Exeter journeyed to France).[34] The other lay councillors – the earls of March, Northumberland, Westmorland, and Norfolk, and Lord FitzHugh – were much less regular attenders.[34] In fact, the ecclesiastical councillors played a markedly more important and regular part in the council's affairs; they probably found it easier to resist other demands on their time – most notably diocesan duties – than did the lay aristocracy, who were also required to fight in France as well as manage their estates at home. Thus, Archbishop Chichele and Bishop Morgan were almost as regular attenders at the council as Gloucester and Beaufort, while John Kemp, bishop of London, was usually present up until the end of May 1423, when he was seconded for six months to advise Bedford in France.[35] The decline in lay attendance and the consequent dependence on bishops may have prompted the – albeit modest – reinforcement of the council which took place early in 1424.

On 25 January two esquires, William Allington and Thomas Chaucer, took the councillor's oath while parliament was in session.[36] Whereas lay representation on the council (particularly of non-magnates) did need strengthening by this time, the commons may also have been eager to press some of their own kind on the council. Both Allington and Chaucer fitted the bill on both counts and were acceptable to some of the existing councillors. They had once been respected members of the commons and Chaucer had been speaker on no less than five occasions. Both were loyal and valued servants of Henry V, and had close connections with Bishop Beaufort. Allington was over fifty by 1424: he brought to the council wide experience of government, especially on its financial side as a former treasurer of Calais in 1398 and of Ireland from 1403; he had served in the household of both Richard II and Henry IV, but his closest association had been with Thomas, duke of Clarence, who appointed him his executor. More recently, he had been engaged in France, particularly as treasurer and receiver-general of Normandy from 1419. His nomination to the council, while no doubt approved by the commons, may have been sponsored by Beaufort and Lord Cromwell, for all three men were feoffees of Clarence's estates.[37]

Thomas Chaucer's intimate relationship with Beaufort and the duke of Exeter is beyond question. His mother was a sister of John of Gaunt's mistress (and later wife), Catherine Swynford, by whom Gaunt had had several children, including Beaufort and Exeter. Chaucer, who was at least as old as Allington in 1424, entered Gaunt's service in 1386 and continued to serve the duchy of Lancaster thereafter. In 1402 he was appointed chief butler of England for life, an office which was confirmed to him by the new king on 5 December 1422. In 1406 he became constable of his cousin's castle of Taunton and surveyor of the bishop's Somerset estates. He was equally favoured by his kinsman, Henry V, and between 1414 and 1420 engaged in the same military and diplomatic work abroad as did many another loyal servant. His relations with some of the magnates are noteworthy, especially with the earl of Warwick and the earl of Salisbury, whose father-in-law Chaucer had become by 1421.[38] Continuity between the old reign and the new was evidently an important consideration in the appointment of Allington and Chaucer, although their presence also altered the political complexion of the council a mite in favour of Beaufort's friends. This fact, together with an injection of commoner blood in the highest counsels of the realm, may have been responsible for the compensatory inclusion among the councillors of Sir John Scrope a month later; he secured his attainted brother's forfeited barony of Masham in the Leicester parliament of 1426 and soon proved a warm supporter of Duke Humphrey. Scrope's presence may therefore have done something to maintain the balance of political, personal, and social interests among the councillors of Henry VI.[39]

Bishop Langley was now an old man of about sixty-four, and on 16 July 1424 he was finally replaced after a spell in office that made him the longest serving chancellor since the middle of Edward III's reign. His successor was Bishop Beaufort, a man of great prestige, experience, and royal lineage who had been chancellor once before in 1403–05. The choice of Beaufort probably reflects the strength of opinion in his favour in a council which included (whatever the frequency of their attendance) such well-wishers as his brother Exeter, his brothers-in-law Westmorland and Northumberland, the earl of Warwick, Lord Cromwell, Sir Walter Hungerford, Sir Walter Beauchamp, and the two esquires, Allington and Chaucer.[40] It may also be seen as a stern attempt by the council to curb Gloucester's territorial ambitions in Hainault which, following his marriage to the Duchess Jacqueline early in 1423, threatened to endanger England's alliance with Burgundy; Beaufort was one of the few Englishmen with the strength of personality and the confidence arising from his Lancastrian blood to undertake this task.[41] Although in the circumstances there was little alternative to Beaufort's appointment, it proved fateful in the event, for it seriously endangered the stability of the council and led to a major political explosion when Gloucester returned from the Low Countries in April 1425.[42]

This was the most severe domestic crisis of the protectorate. The collision between Beaufort and Gloucester led to even more drastic changes within the council at the end of the first session of the Leicester parliament in March 1426. These materially modified the political complexion of the council and transformed the personnel of the great offices of state. Natural causes had already taken their toll of the king's advisers during 1425. Several who had served Henry V, and provided that crucial element of continuity and stability which made the transition to a minority régime a peaceful one, passed away. In the middle of winter, on 11 January 1425, died the renowned soldier Lord FitzHugh who was well into his seventies. He had not been a conspicuous attender at the council for about two years past, but with his death disappeared a steadfast Lancastrian of outstanding gifts.[43] A week later the earl of March died of plague in Ireland, where he had been sent as the king's lieutenant the year before. Never an able or distinguished councillor, his noble status and venerable lineage had nevertheless been great assets of the Lancastrian régime in recent years.[44] On 9 April, Bishop Wakering of Norwich expired; an intermittent participant in conciliar discussions, he had been one of Henry V's trusty diplomatists.[45] Finally, on 21 October 1425 Ralph, earl of Westmorland died. He, too, had been nominated to the council at the very beginning of the reign, but his age (he was born about 1352), and his duties in the north and on the Scottish border, rarely enabled him to attend; nevertheless, he was an outstanding figure in early Lancastrian England and a brother-in-law of the Beauforts. Whereas the earlier deaths had done little to weaken Beaufort's influence in the council, Westmorland's demise came at a time when the hostility between the chancellor and the protector was about to erupt in public conflict.[46] Moreover, his death reduced yet further the lay element on the council, for in the early summer of 1425 Thomas Chaucer ceased to attend, so that by the autumn of 1425 the number of councillors available to tender advice and take decisions was smaller than at any time since 1422.[47] This fact alone, aside from the imminence of strife in London, made some afforcement of the council (if not a change of officers) urgent.

The parliament which assembled at Leicester on 18 February 1426 attempted to reconstruct the government of England. As part of the reconciliation between Gloucester and Beaufort, the latter was replaced as chancellor on 13 March by John Kemp, archbishop of York since July 1425. The new treasurer, appointed the same day, was Sir Walter Hungerford, who had just been raised to the peerage; he replaced Bishop Stafford. Alnwick stayed on as keeper of the privy seal and, indeed, was provided to John Wakering's vacant see of Norwich soon after the parliament opened.[48] The new appointments drastically diminished Beaufort's influence, but they did not involve a complete revolution in politics, for Hungerford's sympathies were likely to remain with the bishop. In fact, four days later, two new councillors were nominated who would sustain the Beaufort interest. On 20 March 1426 the earls of Huntingdon and Stafford joined the council and regularly attended discussions during the next two years.[49] Later in 1426 two further highly respected persons were added to their number: in November the earl of Salisbury, perhaps England's most outstanding soldier, who served intermittently during the following two years; and, in October, William Gray, the scholar-bishop of London, who attended often during the next three years.[50] Yet, from Beaufort's point of view, they were hardly a sufficient substitute for his brother Exeter, who died on the last day of the year; though ill and, to judge by his handwriting, increasingly feeble in the last year or so of his life, he had attended the council to within a fortnight of his death, and his removal, therefore, seriously diminished his brother's political influence.[51]

By the time Bedford and Beaufort left England together in mid-March 1427, the councillors and officers of state had changed their collective character. The chastening effect of the Gloucester – Beaufort struggle and the personal inclinations of Bedford were the significant causes. Wartime demands, especially the need to launch frequent expeditions, had early on deprived the king of the regular services of some of his advisers; recently, a few of the soldier-councillors had been brought into political discussions more frequently, particularly when extra cash had to be raised in response to unaccustomed reverses. But by increasing the number of lay councillors, together with the appointment of Hungerford as treasurer in 1426, new personal rivalries were introduced to the council chamber; the earlier effort to bring in a few non-magnate councillors had borne little fruit, since they rarely attended the meetings. Yet it should not be thought that the changes of 1425–27 reflected the disgrace of Bishop Beaufort (who was shortly to be raised to the cardinalate and to receive his long-coveted red hat from Bedford at Calais) or the extinction of his influence at Westminster. Moreover, surviving all the changes was a solid core of devoted servants of Henry V who continued to protect the fortunes of his young son: on the clerical side, Archbishop Chichele, Bishop Morgan, Bishop Stafford (despite his replacement as treasurer), Archbishop Kemp, and Bishop Alnwick, with Bishop Langley as a stalwart of the dynasty until at least 1426 and Bishop Gray taking his place thereafter. Of the laymen, Exeter (until the end of 1426), Warwick, and Lords Cromwell, Tiptoft, Scrope (from 1424), and Hungerford were dependable men, with Lord Bourgchier and the earls of Salisbury, Huntingdon, and Stafford attending the council frequently in the last three years of the protectorate. Continuity with the preceding reign was a guiding principle throughout, but the strains of conflicting personal ambitions, disputed foreign ventures and, in 1428–29, a shattering military defeat in France produced such a crisis in government that the protectorate was brought to an end in November 1429.

The conciliar régime, 1429–36

The ending of the protectorate on 15 November 1429 had few immediate or momentous consequences for the basic structure of English government, but it had significant ones for the duke of Gloucester. The respective roles of Bedford and his younger brother remained unaltered in certain essential respects, for they were still the king's chief councillors. It is true that they lost the title of protector and defender of the realm once Henry VI had taken his coronation oath on 6 November and assumed the protective responsibilities of kingship himself.[52] But detailed regulations which were probably drawn up before parliament was dissolved on 23 February 1430 were primarily a reiteration of the principles underpinning the government since 1422.[53]

Nor was there any immediate change made in the personnel of the young king's council, over which Gloucester (or Bedford, if he were in the country) presided. Its duties and personnel were unaltered; those who had served as councillors in the 1420s continued to offer advice now. In fact, there could be no precipitate change, for no councillor or major officer could be removed without the assent of the entire council, and when King Henry was abroad in 1430–32, no additions could be made without the agreement of all the councillors in England and France.[54] With few exceptions, the individual changes that did occur during the next seven or eight years were minor ones and usually resulted from death or personal inclination. Actual attendance at the council was more variable than hitherto, as councillors withdrew temporarily or turned up more regularly, and in some cases this was determined by political or military considerations.

Moreover, the three principal officers of state stayed in office after the coronation: Archbishop Kemp as chancellor, Bishop Alnwick as keeper of the privy seal, and Lord Hungerford as treasurer. These three were the pillars of the council, along with Gloucester as chief councillor and the archbishop of Canterbury. William Gray, bishop of London, and Bishop Langdon of Rochester strengthened the ecclesiastical representation, whereas only Lord Cromwell was at all influential among the lay councillors. These eight men, five of them clerics, virtually governed England under Gloucester's chairmanship while the king was in France. It was an entirely aristocratic gathering of undoubted ability and experience, and only when other individuals began to return from France was it significantly enlarged.

Gloucester can hardly have welcomed the change in his status and title in 1429, not least because it temporarily weakened his position *vis-à-vis* Cardinal Beaufort. He found, too, that his salary as chief councillor was correspondingly reduced to 2,000 marks *per annum*, and when the bishopric of Carlisle was filled in December 1429, his opposition to the proposal that Beaufort's client, Marmaduke Lumley, should be provided to the see was unavailing. A sense of pique may have led the duke to refuse his assent to several decisions of the council in December.[55] His influence was even more seriously shaken on 18 December, when his attempt to ban Beaufort from the council because he was now a cardinal was resisted by parliament. There was admittedly no precedent for combining both positions in one person, but Beaufort's royal blood and his services to church and state weighed heavily in his favour (not to speak of his advocates on the council); the only restriction placed on him was that he should absent himself from any discussion of Anglo-papal relations.[56] The duke was doubtless glad to see his uncle leave for France in the following spring of 1430. Beaufort was a reluctant traveller, and he only agreed to go provided the English commanders who were to accompany him did not quarrel amongst themselves. Gloucester, on the other hand, was anxious to keep him out of the country for as long as possible and hence Beaufort was told that he should not return within three months unless specific permission were granted.[57] With the cardinal gone and the king himself on his way to France, on 21 April 1430 Gloucester was formally appointed the king's lieutenant, with authority to hold councils and parliaments during the king's absence and to govern with the advice of the other councillors.[58]

Henry VI's visit to his French realm during 1430–32, and the need to enlarge his council there at a time of military difficulty, caused a temporary redistribution of the king's advisers and a change in

Gloucester's status (though not in his powers) which the duke must have welcomed. The king was accompanied at various times in France by Cardinal Beaufort, Bishops Morgan of Ely and Stafford of Bath and Wells, by the duke of Norfolk and the earls of Warwick, Stafford, and Huntingdon, as well as by Lords Tiptoft, Bourgchier, and Cromwell. Quite naturally laymen were the more numerous in a royal entourage journeying to a war-torn country.[59] It is surprising, therefore, that only two new councillors were appointed in England: William de la Pole, earl of Suffolk, who was consulted on occasion from the end of 1430, and Bishop Langdon of Rochester, whose talents lay in the diplomatic field and in the pursuit of heretics.[60] Although great figures like Northumberland, Bishop Langley, and Lord Scrope attended infrequently or when other preoccupations allowed, there was really no substantial change in the ranks of those who governed England between 1426 and February 1432.

Gloucester's practical powers during the king's absence were scarcely different from those he had enjoyed as protector and defender before 1429; some of his opponents, especially Cardinal Beaufort, were in France. Nevertheless, others were not prepared to allow him his own way. The council was still the balanced group of men whom Bedford left behind him in 1427, as Gloucester discovered when he tried to increase his salary in November 1431. It was clear by then that the king would soon return to England and that Gloucester's dignity (and remuneration) would be reduced once more. On 28 November the treasurer, with the caution expected of a financial official, proposed an extra 2,000 marks annually while the king was abroad and the normal salary of 4,000 marks after his return.[61] Lord Scrope, Gloucester's firm ally, suggested a more generous figure – 5,000 marks after the king's return and 6,000 marks in the meantime – and this proposal presumably reflected the lieutenant's own wish. There was a wide measure of support for Scrope's proposal, but also significant dissent from the ageing archbishop of Canterbury and Beaufort's protégé, Bishop Lumley of Carlisle, as well as from several lay lords. After some discussion and, perhaps, the application of pressure, all seven dissentients were brought to agree to the Scrope suggestion. Gloucester's inclination in this and other matters was to persist until he got his own way; equally, there were still elements in the council prepared to resist him as long as they dared. The embarrassing dispute may have been one of the reasons why, on 28 January 1432, the conciliar regulation that at least four councillors and one officer should be present when decisions were taken was eased so that should the officer refuse his assent, the matter could still pass if the remaining councillors were a majority – provided always that matters affecting either the chancellor or the treasurer were discussed in the presence of one or other of these officers. Stubbornness of the kind shown by Lord Hungerford in the recent argument could henceforward be ignored, and the tedium of persuading an officer to the majority point of view avoided.[62]

Gloucester took advantage of his lieutenancy in other ways: to avail himself of the king's patronage and to embarrass Cardinal Beaufort as often as he could. The duke presided over parliament in January 1431, seated on the throne, and it was he who celebrated St George's day at Windsor in 1430 and 1431 in the king's place.[63] Meanwhile, Beaufort had, somewhat provocatively, returned unheralded from France in November 1430; within a year Gloucester had resurrected the delicate question of his cardinalate.[64] On this occasion, the propriety of his continuing to hold the bishopric of Winchester was investigated, and Bishop Morgan was brought to admit that Beaufort had induced the pope to exempt him from the jurisdiction of the archbishop of Canterbury. It is probable that Gloucester would have taken the matter further had not Bishop Lumley objected to doing so in the cardinal's absence; so a damaging accusation under the statute of *praemunire* was deferred until Beaufort could appear in person. The council contented itself with authorizing a further investigation of the matter and an ominous consultation with the king's justices.

The joyous return of Henry VI to England in February 1432 precipitated a reshaping of the council, now that all its members were at last available to give their assent. Within days of Henry's triumphant entry into London on 21 February, important and sweeping changes were announced. A new chancellor was appointed in place of Kemp: John Stafford, bishop of Bath and Wells, who had been keeper of the privy seal and then treasurer earlier in the reign and had been replaced in 1426 when Bedford was in England; more recently, he had been with the king in France, and after his return at the end of 1430 he served regularly on the council. William Lyndwood was chosen as the new keeper of the privy seal. He had already worked in the privy seal office as second-in-command, but he too had been in France with the young king. The new treasurer was an out-and-out partisan of Duke Humphrey, John, Lord Scrope of Masham.[65] Sir William Philip, the last treasurer of Henry V's household, was newly recruited to the council in May 1432, while the dismissed officers, along with Lord Bourgchier, withdrew from its meetings. At about the same time, in late February and early March, the leading officers of Henry VI's household were replaced, although not without some blunt speaking particularly from Lord Cromwell, who found himself ousted by Sir William Philip as chamberlain without (he claimed later) prior consultation.[66]

It is difficult to escape the conclusion that Gloucester set out to strengthen his grip on the government of the realm and his influence over the upbringing of the king now that his lieutenancy was at an end. By 13 May 1432 Humphrey could well afford to reassure parliament that he would do nothing without the assent of the lords and decide nothing in defiance of the majority of the councillors. That said, he confidently invited parliament to offer him its ready co-operation and aid in governing the realm.[67] Gloucester's *coup* (for so it may be regarded) of February–March 1432 made him even bolder in his treatment of his arch-rival. A large quantity of Cardinal Beaufort's jewels had already been seized at Sandwich as they were being brought ashore in stout chests; the cardinal held them as security for loans he had earlier advanced to the crown.[68] These pledged jewels were the occasion of further charges against Beaufort when parliament met in May. Gloucester urged both lords and commons to dispose of their business quickly, perhaps because he had it in mind to level accusations of treason against Beaufort. The basis of the charges seems to have been the cardinal's readiness to obey papal mandates in preference to a royal command to go to France; but he defended himself vigorously and with some effect for he was soon assured in writing that no such accusations would be formally made. Nevertheless, the incident served one crucial purpose which was probably in Gloucester's mind from the start. Beaufort was induced to lend a further £6,000 to the crown as an earnest of his loyalty and in order to recover the jewels – unless (so the imperious caveat ran) Gloucester should wish to claim any of them for himself! In this parliament, too, Lord Cromwell received short shrift when, on 3 July, he complained about his dismissal as chamberlain of the royal household; he was informed peremptorily that Gloucester's and the lords' fiat was sufficient explanation of his removal. This was stern treatment indeed, although Beaufort at least salvaged one crumb from his predicament: he was granted immunity from any charge of breaking the statute of provisors (though not the more formidable statute of *praemunire*) and the statute which banned the reception of unauthorized papal bulls in the realm.[69]

Duke Humphrey's position seemed unchallenged: he held council meetings in his own house, whether at London or Greenwich, and in November 1432 he secured an attractive lease of the late duke of Norfolk's estates during the heir's minority.[70] He continued to dig deep into the king's store of patronage during the following months, when he was also extending his personal estate at Greenwich, constructing a brand new tower there, and embattling other buildings.[71] Beaufort's influence was obviously pared, and when he wished to travel to the Council of Basle in February 1433 he was so apprehensive of what Gloucester might do in his absence that he secured from the king an assurance that he would not be taken to court by the crown during the next two years for anything he had done in the past.[72] He need not have worried, for relief was at hand – in the person of John, duke of Bedford.

The arrival of Duke John in England in June 1433 meant that at one stroke Gloucester lost his pre-eminent position and his status as the king's chief councillor. The chancellor and the keeper of the privy seal stayed in office for some considerable time after 1432 (in Stafford's case for eighteen years, in Lyndwood's for fourteen) – eloquent testimony to their sound choice as royal advisers. But the bitter hostility between Gloucester and Beaufort meant that the duke found it very difficult to sustain his confrère Scrope in the office of treasurer, now that Bedford was able to reinforce the cardinal's influence. In fact, Scrope was replaced on 11 August 1433 and he withdrew increasingly from the council from about the same time. Sir William Philip, who had also joined the councillors in 1432, ceased to attend by the summer of 1433.[73] Bishop FitzHugh of London, who became a councillor when the king was abroad, had already attended his last council on 28 January 1433; thereafter, he busied himself with the English mission to the Council of Basle. Bishop Langdon, who had likewise been relied upon quite heavily during the king's absence, also redirected his energies to the Basle discussions.[74] By contrast, the earl of Northumberland started to attend the council once again after Bedford's return.[75] Lord Cromwell was appointed treasurer of England on 11 August, and William de la Pole, earl of Suffolk became steward of Henry VI's household three days later.[76]

The return of Bedford to England in June 1433 curbed Gloucester's ambitions; once again, considerations affecting the dual monarchy had imposed significant changes on the government of England. For one thing, a bitter dispute broke out between the brothers, during which accusations of mishandling the war effort were flung at Bedford. Rumours of such criticism had already reached Duke John in France (perhaps during a joint meeting of the king's advisers held recently at Calais), and the duke was anxious to counter it by returning to England; at the same time he would be able to make peace between Beaufort and Gloucester.[77]

On 13 July a discussion was initiated in parliament on Bedford's forthright rejection of the accusations made against him, and this public debate elicited from Duke Humphrey and the other councillors an assurance that no suggestion of negligence had been intended. Nevertheless, the sharp exchange had not endeared Gloucester to the hard-pressed French lieutenant. So indignant was Bedford that, after the summer holiday, the speaker of the commons went out of his way to pay tribute to John's exertions in France on behalf of the dual monarchy, and even praised his calming influence in England; the speaker, Roger Hunt, pleaded with him to remain in the realm for a while longer so that the recent squabbles might be terminated. A few days later, on 26 November, after the lords and the council had reinforced the speaker's pleadings, Bedford agreed to stay and at the more modest fee of £1,000 *per annum*. A reluctant Gloucester was induced to accept grudgingly the same payment on 28 November.[78] The terms under which Bedford undertook to prolong his visit to England underline his determination to act as an energetic chief councillor, without whose advice little of importance could be done, and to neutralize his younger brother's influence. At the same time, an attempt was made formally to publicize the names of the king's councillors, perhaps to encourage fuller attendance at meetings, though some, like the aged Langley, were excused. Parliament acceded to Bedford's wishes on 18 December.[79]

The tensions between the two royal brothers were not likely to be removed by these arrangements. Gloucester's personality alone would ensure that, and ominous events in France inevitably brought them to the surface again in 1434. In April and early May of that year, Gloucester was busily occupied in spreading further rumours about the way the war was being conducted, suggesting that he could do better.[80] But when he offered to serve in France, serious doubts were expressed about the feasibility of raising the £48,000–£50,000 that was considered necessary for his expedition. His speech to the council on 24 April raised a number of eyebrows and caused deep offence to Bedford, who demanded a copy of it and quickly replied in equally belligerent tones. The argument looked like getting out of hand among a welter of mutual recriminations, which would seriously undermine the government's effectiveness and confidence in its own war effort. The young king, himself now twelve years old, was prompted to intervene personally and with a child's innocence he begged his two uncles to compose their differences and become friends again. These events were a prelude to Bedford's return to France, the preparations for which were vitiated by the same bitter disputes. Before he left, he not unnaturally presented to the council his conditions for further service, and on 15 June these were accepted.[81] They guaranteed him a substantial revenue from the duchy of Lancaster estates with which to raise an army, and also command of Calais and its marches in order that their resources could be diverted to the Norman campaign. Accordingly, on 12 July 1434 Bedford was appointed lieutenant of Calais and captain of its supporting castles, which were now regarded as a vital, though subsidiary, buttress of the main thrust further south.[82] This was not a view likely to commend itself to those (including Gloucester) who shared the opinions expressed a little later in the *Libelle of Englysche Polycye*.

With Bedford's departure for France in July 1434, Gloucester once again became the king's chief councillor. Beaufort's plans to set out on a pilgrimage probably pleased him even more, and they were formally approved by the king on 15 June.[83] But Duke Humphrey does not seem to have presided over council meetings during the remainder of 1434 or early in 1435. Two events occurred in the course of 1435 which changed his prospects. One was the failure of the congress of Arras in August (and Beaufort's peace mission on behalf of the dual monarchy), and the other was the death of Bedford at Rouen in September. No longer would Gloucester have to tolerate his brother's chidings and reproofs, while for the moment the policies of his uncle were discredited.[84] On the contrary, the looming threat from Charles VII and Philip the Good put Gloucester in an unusually advantageous position at home. On 1 November he succeeded his brother as lieutenant of Calais, and two days earlier the town and castle of Calais, and its outlying fortresses, had been placed in his charge for a period of nine years.[85] He received, too, a pardon on 3 November for all enfeoffments that had been made by him and his wife in the past without royal licence and which had made him financially vulnerable when Bedford was ruling; should he die without heirs, his wife was given the singular privilege of enjoying all his properties for life, with ultimate reversion to the king, his blood heir.[86]

In repelling the Burgundian forces before Calais in August 1436, and harrying the Flemish immediately afterwards, Gloucester received further expressions of favour. In preparation for this expedition, he was appointed lieutenant-general of the king's army on 27 July, and three days later was granted hereditary lordship over the county of Flanders, for in English eyes it was a fief of Henry VI's French crown, regardless of the sovereignty of Charles VII and the seignorial rights of the duke of Burgundy.[87] On his return from Flanders, Gloucester was widely acclaimed. On 23 November he secured the islands of Guernsey and Jersey, which Bedford had held at his death, and thereby extended his naval authority as warden of the Cinque ports and constable of Dover castle.[88] The entire defence of the channel, the Low Countries and the coastline of southern and eastern England now rested squarely on his shoulders. Gloucester's stock had never been so high nor his practical powers so extensive. Parliament met at his beckoning early in 1437. He knelt before his king on 25 February and argued strongly that arrangements should be made for him to discharge his duty effectively as captain of Calais, and that wages should be paid to his soldiers to avoid desertion; he emphasized his point by declaring that neither he nor his soldiers could be held responsible for the consequences if such arrangements were not made, no matter how loyal they or he might be.[89] It took a little while to discuss the duke's demands, but a month later the unusual step was taken to set aside part of the wool subsidy for the men's wages, and the treasurer was authorized by parliament to make up the difference. A few days after that, on 27 March, Gloucester was fulsomely complimented by parliament for his defence of Calais and for resisting the treacherous duke of Burgundy so successfully.[90] So besotted was the kingdom with Gloucester's military accomplishments that in mid-May he was not only pardoned an embarrassing £1,272 which he had been overpaid as chief councillor, but was granted a further 2,000 marks.[91] It all speaks volumes for Gloucester's continuing popularity and influence in the year following the siege of Calais. Yet Cardinal Beaufort was not without his influence, too. The commons which had praised Gloucester thanked the cardinal, along with the officers and certain of the lords, for aiding the cause of justice in the realm, and on 13 April Beaufort was denied permission by the council to embark on a pilgrimage abroad because he was needed for possible peace negotiations.[92] His position was probably less secure than Gloucester's. He was evidently thinking of going abroad, and on 16 July 1437 he thought it advisable to secure a pardon for holding on to some of the crown jewels as security for loans which had still not been paid: ten days later be obtained a general pardon.[93]

At this very time, the episcopal representation on the council was seriously reduced by death and other causes. Bishop Morgan of Ely, a stalwart of the régime for decades, followed Bedford to the grave in October 1435; early in the new year, two other councillors passed away, Bishop FitzHugh in January and Bishop William Gray in February. Archbishop Chichele was getting on in years and his attendances had been declining gradually since 1434 until in 1436 he was almost never there. The bishop of Durham had played little regular part in state affairs since the 1420s and had ceased to attend the council completely by 1435. On the other hand, by May 1435 Gloucester had begun to turn up more frequently and was usually present at council meetings during the remainder of the year and in 1436. But so also were several magnates – especially Northumberland, Suffolk, and Lord Hungerford – whose interests over the years had been identified with those of the cardinal.[94] Only Bishop Brouns of Rochester was added to the council, in July 1436; his links with Chichele and Langdon, his service in Normandy under Henry V, and his reputation as a lollard persecutor would commend themselves to Duke Humphrey, who was probably responsible for recruiting him to the council. To some extent, therefore, English policy, in the wake of the disastrous Arras conference and with war in prospect with both Charles VII and the duke of Burgundy, was falling into the hands of a more secular section of the king's advisers by the time that Henry VI began to take a hand himself in politics and to exert his own influence by the end of 1436. It was a smaller council, too, more so than at any time since the king's coronation, and hence more occasions arose when the regulation requiring a quorum of at least four councillors and one officer was not fulfilled. Yet the strengthening of the lay element in these years cannot be taken as an indisputable sign that Gloucester's influence in the inner counsels of the realm was paramount, for all the popular enthusiasm generated by his exploits in Flanders.

Notes

1 *PPC*, III, 6.
2 *RP*, IV, 175-6, with a more accurate version of the warrant in ibid., V, 404-5.
3 ibid., 406-7; *PPC*, III, 174-7, 237-42.
4 ibid., III, 237-42. These enunciations of principle may have been a consequence of the council's attempt in November 1426 to make all the councillors (including Bedford and Gloucester) collectively responsible for conciliar acts.
5 *RP*, IV, 175-6; *PPC*, III, 17-18.
6 Less than 3 per cent.
7 PRO, E28/40/19; 39/78. Nor did the regulations explain how the council should reach its decisions.
8 PRO, E28/45, 46.
9 *PPC*, III, 168.
10 See below, p. 128.
11 *PPC*, III, 19, 20; PRO, E28/39; 41/115.

12 Below, p. 135.
13 Below, pp. 73ff.
14 *RP*, V, 407; *PPC*, III, 213-21.
15 PRO, E28/39/56-8, 41; *RP*, IV, 338.
16 PRO, E28/48/6, 9. Too few warrants survive from 1425 to enable one to view precisely the development by which signatures, from being appended to about half the warrants during July–November 1424, were added to almost all by 1426 (ibid., 47-8).
17 *PPC*, III, 19, 178-9; PRO, E28/39/77.
18 ibid., 50/25, 29, 45, 48 (February 1428).
19 *RP*, IV, 343-7. There is a slight suggestion (e.g., in clause 17) that the special responsibility laid on Bedford and Gloucester in 1426 to ensure that councillors were not corrupted was removed now that the protectorate was ended.
20 The few exceptions were on 27 June 1426 (when the chancellor and treasurer alone signed a warrant) and 6 December 1426 (when the three officers signed) (PRO, E28/47/37; 48/64-5).
21 As B. Wilkinson hints in 'The duke of Gloucester and the Council, 1422-8', *BIHR*, XXI (1958), 20.
22 Above, p. 29. Conclusions on the attendance of councillors are mainly based on *PPC*, III, and PRO, E28.
23 *CPR, 1422-29*, pp. 1, 109; *RP*, IV, 171.
24 Apart from the poor sees of Bangor and Llandaff, and the archdiocese of York (which could hardly be filled by anyone other than a bishop of some repute), Carlisle was the first see to become vacant in the new reign, in February 1423. It does not seem to have been considered wealthy or convenient enough for Stafford, who waited until October 1424, when the next see, Bath and Wells, fell vacant; his earlier intrigues at Rome for something better came to nothing. E. F. Jacob, *Essays in later mediaeval history* (Manchester, 1968), pp. 40-2.
25 A. J. Otway-Ruthven, *The king's secretary and the signet office in the XV century* (Cambridge, 1939), esp. p. 88. There is unnecessary confusion about the date of Stafford's and Alnwick's appointment. *PPC*, III, 8, makes it clear that Kinwolmersh died within three days of 16 December and that the reappointments followed immediately, probably on 18 December to judge from *CPR, 1422–29*, p. 80; though Alnwick was in fact paid from 20 December (PRO, E404/39/721).
26 Above, pp. 22ff.
27 Hungerford and Botiller were admitted to the council at a meeting held at the Dominican friary in London on 26 January (*PPC*, III, 22-3). Robessart began attending on 20 January (ibid., 20).
28 J. L. Kirby, 'The Hungerford family in the later middle ages' (London MA thesis, 1939), pp. 13-37, 173-4; *GEC*, VI, 613-16.
29 ibid., XII, i, 419-21; R. Kretschmer, 'Ralph Botiller, Lord Sudeley' (Keele BA dissertation, 1973), pp. 2-6, 64-72.
30 *GEC*, II, 247-8; XI, 40-1.
31 Below, p. 54.
32 He sailed for Cherbourg on 2 July (PRO, E403/661 m. 11).
33 Exeter's departure was delayed by illness until at least the end of May (PRO, E28/41/75).

34 Norfolk was one of the leaders of the French expedition in the second half of 1423 (PRO, E28/39/82; *CPR, 1422–29*, p. 78).

35 PRO, E28/41/75; 43/40. Kemp accompanied Exeter's expeditionary force. See J. A. Nigota, 'John Kempe: a political prelate of the fifteenth century' (Emory PhD thesis, 1973), ch. 3, and M. Witchell, 'John Kemp (d. 1454): an ecclesiastic as statesman' (Wales MA thesis, 1979).

36 *PPC*, III, 265-7.

37 J. S. Roskell, *The commons and their speakers in English parliaments, 1376–1523* (Manchester, 1965), pp. 197-9. Allington became speaker also in 1429–30.

38 ibid., pp. 149-53, 160, 173; J. S. Roskell, *The commons in the parliament of 1422* (Manchester, 1954), pp. 165-7. See M. B. Ruud, *Thomas Chaucer* (Minneapolis, 1926).

39 *GEC*, XI, 566-8; C. D. Ross, 'The Yorkshire baronage, 1399–1435' (Oxford DPhil thesis, 1951), pp. 208-13. Scrope was designated a councillor on 27 February 1424, though he had attended six days earlier (*PPC*, III, 143, 265-7).

40 Hungerford would be one of Exeter's executors in 1426 (ibid., 250-1).

41 Efforts at arbitration between Gloucester and Jacqueline's first husband, Duke John of Brabant, had broken down towards the end of June 1424 (K. H. Vickers, *Humphrey, duke of Gloucester* [1907], pp. 27-37).

42 Below, pp. 73ff.

43 Ross, thesis, pp. 245-55.

44 *GEC*, VIII, 450-3.

45 R. G. Davies, thesis, pp. ccxciv – ccxcvi.

46 *GEC*, XII, ii, 544-7; Ross, thesis, pp. 9ff.

47 Neither Norfolk nor Northumberland was anything more than an occasional attender after 1422.

48 *HBC*, pp. 85, 92, 102, 243, 265.

49 Stafford was paid as a councillor from 20 March 1426, though he may have been present at meetings a little earlier (PRO, E364/69 m. N 2; *PPC*, III, 187, 190).

50 *GEC*, XI, 393-5; Emden, *Oxford*, II, 809-14.

51 *GEC*, V, 200-4. For his shaky handwriting, see PRO, E28/47/105 (8 May 1426). He seems to have died at Greenwich and was buried at Bury St Edmunds (PRO, E101/514/22).

52 *RP*, IV, 336-7. When Gloucester surrendered the protectorship on 15 November, he did so without prejudice to Bedford's attitude.

53 ibid., 343-4.

54 *PPC*, IV, 36-9 (16 April 1430).

55 *PPC*, IV, 12, 8-9; PRO, E28/51/5, 11, 8, 12, 14 (6-14 December 1429). The speaker of the 1429-30 parliament was none other than Beaufort's partisan, William Allington (Roskell, *Speakers*, pp. 197-9; above, p. 35).

56 *RP*, IV, 338. Be it noted that on 1 May 1429 Beaufort had granted hefty life pensions to four prominent councillors, Northumberland, Salisbury, Bourgchier, and Hungerford (J. Greatrex [ed.], *The register of the common seal of the priory of St Swithin, Winchester, 1345–1497* [Hants. Rec. Ser., II, 1978], nos. 208-10).

57 *PPC*, IV, 35-9, 33-4.

58 ibid., 40-4; *CPR, 1429-36*, p. 55.

59 *PPC*, IV, 28-30, 76, 84; V, 415-18; PRO, E404/50/343; 47/189; E403/707 m. 11.
60 PRO, E28/53/13 (Suffolk). Langdon began to attend on 16 April 1430 (ibid., 51/82).
61 *PPC*, IV, 103-5. It should also be noted that Kemp's estrangement from Gloucester began at this time (Nigota, thesis, pp. 254ff).
62 *RP*, V, 433.
63 ibid., IV, 367; PRO, E403/695 m. 8; 699 m. 1.
64 *CPR, 1429-36*, p. 99; *PPC*, IV, 100-1, 103-5. See L. B. Radford, *Henry Beaufort* (1908), ch. IX.
65 Jacob, *Essays in later mediaeval history*, pp. 35ff; Emden, *Oxford*, II, 1191-3; above, p. 36.
66 Below, p. 58.
67 *RP*, IV, 389.
68 ibid., 390-2; PRO, E159/208, *adhuc communia*, E. m. 2.
69 *RP*, IV, 392.
70 *PPC*, IV, 132, 139, 159.
71 ibid., 138. These works continued during the 1430s (ibid., pp. 466, 498-9; *CPR, 1429-36*, p. 240; ibid., *1436–41*, p. 74 [1433, 1437]).
72 ibid., *1429–36*, p. 254 (16 February).
73 Philip is last known to have attended on 24 May 1433 (*PPC*, IV, 163).
74 R. G. Davies, thesis, pp. cxvi-cxviii, clxi-clxiv; Emden, *Oxford*, II, 689-90, 1093-4. FitzHugh died in January 1436 and Langdon at Basle in September 1434.
75 Northumberland's first attendance in 1433 was on 26 July (*PPC*, IV, 174). It seems that the marriage of Northumberland's heir in 1434 to Lord Poynings's granddaughter was arranged by Beaufort (Bodl. Roll 5).
76 Suffolk is first recorded as steward on 14 August (*Foedera*, IV, iv, 197); the evidence attributing his appointment to 21 April (i.e., before Bedford's return) is slight (R. L. Storey, 'English officers of state, 1399–1485', *BIHR*, XXXI [1958], 89). He married Cardinal Beaufort's kinswoman, Alice Chaucer, widow of the earl of Salisbury (d. 1428), in about 1430 (C. A. Metcalfe, 'Alice Chaucer, duchess of Suffolk, *c.* 1404–1475' [Keele BA dissertation, 1970], p. 6, quoting the marriage settlement in BL, Harl. Ch. 54. 1. 9).
77 *RP*, IV, 420.
78 *PPC*, IV, 185-6, 218-21; *RP*, IV, 424-5. The revised fee was backdated to 24 May 1433. Bedford may have been anxious to stay for the time being, especially since a public invitation from parliament and council would strengthen his position. The reduced salary may have been his *quid pro quo.*
79 ibid., 424, 455-7.
80 *PPC*, IV, 210-16.
81 ibid., 222-6, 243-7; *RP*, V, 435-8. Cardinal Beaufort now offered two loans totalling 13,000 marks for the war (*PPC*, IV, 232-9, 243-54; *CPR, 1429-36*, pp. 346, 414).
82 *DKR*, XLVIII, 300.
83 *CPR, 1429–36*, p. 414.
84 For unease at the undue influence (probably Gloucester's) being exerted on the king at this time, see below, p. 60.
85 *DKR*, XLVIII, 306; *Foedera*, V, i, 23; *RP*, V, 483-4.

86 *CPR, 1429–36*, pp. 503-6. Despite an exemption from paying fines for charters or other instruments, which had been granted on 21 March 1433, he had paid 9,000 marks by mid-1435 (*PPC*, IV, 156-7; *CCR, 1429–35*, p. 359).
87 *DKR*, XLVIII, 314; *Foedera*, V, i, 33-4.
88 *PPC*, V, 5. The formal patent was dated 9 April 1437 (*DKR*, XLVIII, 317).
89 *RP*, IV, 496-7.
90 ibid., 499, 502.
91 *CPR, 1436–41*, pp. 54, 70. In return, he surrendered his patent granting him 5,000 marks as an annual salary.
92 *RP*, IV, 502-3; *PPC*, V, 9-13.
93 ibid., 33-4; *CPR, 1436–41*, p. 70; *Foedera*, V, i, 40-1.
94 Above n. 56, 76. Huntingdon and Stafford attended more often in 1435 and 1436, and Tiptoft was rarely absent by 1436; none of these was a staunch ally of Gloucester.

3   The King and his Household

Henry's early upbringing

The influence which a baby king could exert on events was negligible; and care needs to be taken lest the influence of those who had charge of him be exaggerated. From September 1422 until November 1429, the royal prerogative was in commission, at the disposal of a protector and, above all, a specially nominated council. During these years, the significance of the king's personal actions hardly extended beyond the nursery or the occasional formal ceremonial; the importance of his guardians and entourage was correspondingly limited. However, for the future these years were vital ones in the upbringing of the king, for elements in his character were established and at least a few of his attitudes formed. But it would be foolish to suppose that after five centuries the historian can do more than guess what these elements and attitudes were or from whom he acquired them.

Henry's earliest years were spent in the shadow of his famous father. On his death-bed Henry V committed his only heir to the keeping of Thomas Beaufort, duke of Exeter, who was designated the prince's guardian; Sir Walter Hungerford and Lord FitzHugh were given special responsibility in his household. As in the years following 1216 and 1377, the care of the king was separated from the government of the realm after 1422.[1] Although Exeter seems to have acted as guardian only formally, Hungerford and FitzHugh played a prominent role in the royal household, along with several other servants and friends of the late king. A number of these – Warwick, Babthorp, Robessart, Porter, and Walter Beauchamp – had been Henry V's companions in arms and executors of his will. They had spent a lifetime – and most of them were middle-aged in 1422 – in Lancastrian service and could be expected to guard the new king vigilantly and advise him with the sound sense born of long experience of royal affairs. The queen, too, had her part to play in her son's upbringing, so that Henry VI was nurtured in the traditions of Lancastrianism and the newer significance of the dual monarchy.

As a baby, Henry VI needed only a modest household to cater for his needs. From birth he was swaddled by a small group of nurses who devoted themselves to his service during his early years and were well rewarded for doing so. His chief nurse was Joan Asteley, whose husband Thomas was also in royal service and as such went with Henry to France in 1430. She received a £20 annuity right from the king's birth, and this was doubled in January 1424 when her worth was proved.[2] A day-nurse and two chamberwomen completed the permanent nursing staff; they naturally received more modest rewards, which had to be increased in December 1427 because all three were finding it difficult to fulfil their duties properly while at the same time maintain a standard of living appropriate to the king's household. The services of these women were so valued that in May 1428 they (apart from Asteley) were admitted to the confraternity of St Albans abbey, which was patronized by the royal family and the nobility; there they joined a company that included the most high-born ladies in the land.[3]

As the king emerged from infancy, he needed more imaginative care, albeit still from experienced womenfolk. When he was rather more than two, Dame Alice Botiller, a suitably wise and expert person in matters of 'courtesy and nurture', was appointed to attend on the king, to teach him what was appropriate for his boyish years, and, if necessary, to chastise him without fear of the consequences. Alice was the daughter of Sir John Beauchamp of Powick (and hence a kinswoman of Sir Walter Beauchamp and the earl of Warwick), and she had married Thomas Botiller, co-heir to the Sudeley estates in Gloucestershire; her son Ralph was closely associated with Henry V as one of his companions in France, and in 1423 he became a councillor of the new monarch.[4] Alice's role was evidently greater than that of a nurse, for she often advised on how the funds of Henry's household should be spent. She gathered her reward of £40 *per annum* from May 1423 and a further 40 marks from March 1426.[5]

Other aspects of the upbringing of a king could only be supervised by a man. A conception of the duties of a monarch of two realms, one of which was in a permanent state of war, could best be conveyed by an experienced and distinguished nobleman, and there was no better choice than Richard Beauchamp, earl of Warwick, 'the best-nurtured man' in England.[6] He was formally appointed by a great council on 1 June 1428 to serve as the young king's guardian, to teach him 'good manners, letters, languages, nurture and courtesy', and especially to bring him up as a virtuous, God-fearing lad. For this portentous charge he was to receive 250 marks each year. Like Dame Alice before him, the earl was careful to ensure that he could correct and punish Henry without running the risk of future reprisals.[7] Warwick had a reputation for courtesy and chivalrous conduct, his own accomplishments in education and artistic patronage were notable, and his distinction in arms beside the king's father would ensure the best possible protection for Henry, second only to that of Bedford and Gloucester.

There is no reason to suppose that Henry, having been brought up by such persons as these, was anything but normal, healthy, and well educated in an orthodox fashion. In May 1423 it was reported to Uncle Bedford in France that he was in perfect health; neither his appearance nor his demeanour caused anyone at this juncture to attribute to him the qualities of a saint.[8]

By March 1428, the six-year-old boy could be described as 'so gone and grown in person, in wit and understanding' that it may be concluded that Dame Alice had done her work well. It was estimated that Henry would be able to exercise his prerogative personally within a few years, though admittedly in saying this the council was more anxious to resist Gloucester's power-seeking demands than to comment accurately on the king's abilities.[9] Indeed, the commission to Warwick six months later was probably intended partly to insulate the king from the political rivalries that had been rocking the council for some time past.

Little is known of the details of Henry's education, but a *primer* (or religious manual) was certainly bought for his use in May 1427 and by March of the following year he was able to recite some of the services. If he had any musical talent, it was catered for by a pair of organs purchased for him that same month.[10] The physical trappings of knighthood were introduced to the king at this early age by the earl of Warwick and others. Two 'lytill cote armurs' were made for Henry when he was seven years old and he was given a long-bladed sword (a doubtful toy this!) 'for to lerne the kyng to play in his tendre age'.[11] The presents he was given on New Year's Day and on other occasions were usually in the form of jewels. Attractive though these may have been, they can hardly have kept his interest for long, and a ruby that Bedford gave him at Christmas 1425 was passed on to Queen Katherine on New Year's Day two years later. His generosity with such possessions extended even beyond his own property, for in 1428, much to the council's embarrassment, he snatched a gold collar from the earl of Oxford (to whom he had earlier given it) with his own hand and presented it to a Polish knight who was visiting the court.[12] He may have valued rather more highly a heavy silver-gilt ship on four wheels which was bought for him from the duke of Exeter's executors early in 1427; this he could run along the floor as an absorbing toy.[13]

The royal chapel and Henry's religious devotions were ordered in conventional, orthodox fashion. Apart from George Arthurton, his confessor, several clerks were responsible for organizing the religious routine.[14] They doubtless accompanied Henry on his pilgrimages – to Waltham abbey and Bury St Edmunds (where the king's visit is commemorated by John Lydgate's colourful illuminations in his life of St Edmund and St Fremund which was subsequently presented to the king).[15] And if the royal chapel retained any of the character imparted to it by Henry IV and Henry V, its music was outstanding in its liveliness and simplicity.[16]

On the secular side, the household was entertained by troupes of minstrels and players, who amused the king and his entourage at Windsor and on their travels through south-eastern England. More essential were the pages and grooms who waited on the assemblage of people gathered about the household, although during Henry's early years they were chronically short of pay and were said (at least by themselves) to be verging on destitution. In May 1426 they came near to resigning in a body.[17]

The king was not the only youngster to be brought up in this environment, for several of his noble subjects were with him in the household as his wards. They were his companions and friends while their estates and other resources became part of the patronage at the disposal of his advisers. Thomas, Lord Roos (who was born in 1406) was one young heir who spent part of the 1420s with the king. After the death of the earl of Westmorland in 1425, the countess and her ward, Richard, duke of York (born in 1411), also lived in the royal household. The council facilitated such arrangements when, in June 1425, it decreed that lordly heirs who were the king's wards should reside in the royal household, each with a master paid by the king himself.[18] Henry even had royal company in the person of James I, king of the Scots; until 1424 he was a prisoner at the English court, though he and Henry had little in common apart from their royal status since James was born in 1394.[19]

The household in which the king grew up was staffed by a small group of capable servants. Out of respect for the dead king's wishes and in accordance with the queen's inclinations, most of those who managed his affairs were experienced members of Henry V's household or close friends of his who could be trusted absolutely. Four of them were councillors, who thereby provided a valuable link between the king's entourage and his government. One was Sir Walter Hungerford, who had been enjoined by the dying Henry V to attend personally on the new king. A staunch servant of the house of Lancaster in peacetime and in war, he had been steward of the household in 1415–21; after an interval during which Sir Robert Babthorp served both Henry V and Henry VI, Hungerford was reappointed on 24 April 1424.[20] His successor on 18 March 1426, John, Lord Tiptoft, came from the same mould.[21] Another middle-aged soldier devoted to the Lancastrians, he was the first layman ever to become treasurer of the household (in 1406) and in 1408 he became treasurer of England. His military, diplomatic, and administrative service to two kings made him an obvious choice as a councillor in 1422 and secured him a peerage shortly before he came to head Henry VI's household. Both Hungerford and Tiptoft would feel entirely at home in the company of the elderly Lord FitzHugh who, before serving as the young king's chamberlain until July 1423, had been treasurer of England during 1416-21 and Henry V's own chamberlain.[22] In his mid-sixties by 1422, he was soon succeeded as chamberlain by Sir Lewis Robessart, the courageous Hainaulter who was Henry V's standard-bearer; recognized as Lord Bourgchier after his marriage to Elizabeth Bourgchier (by 1421), he remained the king's chamberlain for the remainder of the protectorate.[23]

To minister to Henry's ailments, John Somerset, the Oxford- and Cambridge-trained scholar who was also an experienced doctor, joined the household at Eastertide 1427 from the duke of Exeter's service. John's intellectual powers and medical training were put to good use at court when he became one of the king's teachers; from 1429 he was sometimes known as 'the king's master'.[24] These men headed Henry's personal and private household establishment. They were constantly on hand (unless, like Hungerford in 1423, their absence was specially authorized), and they accompanied the king on his short journeys about the country.[25]

After the years of babyhood, Henry's household increased in size and changed its character. If any single interest can be said to have dominated it and to have influenced the king's upbringing, it is that of the Beauchamps. By Christmas 1427, and especially after the appointment of Warwick as guardian in 1428, there was recruited to the household a circle of youngish men who were engaged to wait on the royal person. Two ushers of the chamber, John Hampton, a former protégé of the earl of Stafford, and Gilbert Parr, were there by Christmas.[26] In the following May four esquires of the king's body – his personal bodyguard – were taken on to Warwick's staff and each was given 50 marks to sharpen his vigilance and fortify his personal service to the king. John Chetwynd, who came from a family with deep Warwickshire roots and whose loyalties lay staunchly with the Beauchamps, was one of them.[27] Three weeks later, four knights were assigned to the royal household, headed by one of Warwick's own relatives, Sir Walter Beauchamp. He and the others – Sir William Philip, Sir Ralph Rocheford, and Sir William Porter – were specifically detailed to look after the young king, and in return they received generous provision for their expenses and comfort at court.[28] Beauchamp had joined Henry IV's household, had fought in France with Henry V, and had displayed his organizational talents as, successively, treasurer of the king's household in 1420–21 and steward of Queen Katherine's household. Philip had been treasurer of Henry V's household in France at the time of the king's death.[29] Rocheford, too, was a soldier, and his experience as constable of Hammes castle in Picardy would be useful in protecting the young king.[30]

This increase in the number of the king's personal attendants meant a rise in the cost of maintaining the royal household, through its department of the wardrobe under a keeper (who was also known appropriately as the treasurer of the household). After the initial expense of setting up a household for the baby king in 1422, its cost to the exchequer was relatively restrained (standing at about £660 *per annum* in 1423–25); but thereafter the expenses rose substantially until in 1427–28 an annual income of more than £1,000 was required from the exchequer.[31] A Hertfordshire lawyer, John Hotoft, had charge of budgeting from 1 March 1423 and, with the exception of 1423–25 when he had inadequate funds at his disposal, he skilfully managed to balance the books, though perhaps at the expense of some of the household's employees. Hotoft, after all, had considerable financial expertise at his command.[32] As long ago as 1411, he had been controller of Henry V's household as prince of Wales, and since then his legal training had been consolidated in the court of common pleas.

As Henry V had insisted before he died, Queen Katherine lived with the new king in his household, and although this inflated the size and cost of the establishment, she was expected to meet the daily expenses of herself and her entourage. In 1427–28 her contribution amounted to more than £2,500 at a rate of £7 per day, and this helped to put the finances of the royal household on a satisfactory basis.[33]

Katherine's presence at court meant that her influence on her young son was direct and immediate, and she played an important role in bringing up her son. Indeed, some of those who joined the king's service did so with the queen's commendation. Dame Alice Botiller had served Katherine when Henry V was alive, and this partly explains the size of her annuity in 1423. The king's confessor by 1424, George Arthurton (who was hardly overtaxed by a three-year-old conscience), was clerk of the queen's closet a year or so earlier.[34] Sir Walter Beauchamp, too, was the queen's man, for he had become her chief steward in 1421.[35] These men reflect the queen's influence on her son and enabled her to maintain it throughout the 1420s.

Despite this close association between mother and son, Katherine had her own domestic suite, which was financed from the substantial estates and cash granted her as dower on 9 November 1422, and from French revenues amounting to 20,000 francs *per annum* which were guaranteed to her in widowhood by the treaty of Troyes. She was worth in England and Wales alone more than £6,000, of which £2,300 was due from the exchequer each year.[36] The latter at least was regularly received by her receiver-general, who was able to meet the expenses incurred while she lived with the king.[37] From 1 October 1422 Katherine's receiver-general and attorney-general was Thomas Rokes, who was one of her most constant advisers.[38] He managed the queen's financial affairs and supervised her extensive estates, which stretched from Anglesey to Kent and from Devon to Yorkshire, aside from those in northern France; the most valuable blocks were in Anglesey (worth £425 *per annum*), Flintshire (£238), Leicester (£332) and Knaresborough (£385). They included convenient residences to which the king sometimes travelled during his childhood – especially those at Leicester, Hertford, Wallingford, and Waltham.[39] There Katherine kept queenly state in her own household.[40]

Henry and his court spent almost the entire decade of the 1420s in the Thames valley, moving between favoured royal residences, such as Windsor and Eltham, and the seat of government at Westminster, where even a young king's presence was sometimes required, particularly when parliament was assembling. His frequent visits to some of his mother's castles were specially timed to coincide with the great festivals of Christmas and Easter. St George's day almost always found him appropriately at Windsor. The furthest Henry ever travelled in these years was to Leicester and Kenilworth at the time of the 1426 parliament; in 1425 he visited Woodstock (Oxfordshire), the country house beloved of Edward III.[41]

Henry's boyhood public appearances were few, and were confined to ceremonial acts. He is known to have been present at the opening of all the early parliaments of the reign, with the single exception of the first in November 1422; but after the presentation of the commons' speaker he withdrew from the sessions. The Londoners were able to view their young king in 1425 and 1428, when Henry led a procession through the city, and again at his coronation late in November 1429. Apart from these occasions, however, he spent most of his time in a relatively small sector of his realm and in comparative seclusion.[42]

The visit to France, 1430–32

Those who ordered King Henry's life and supervised his upbringing before the coronation continued to do so after the ceremony. Lord Tiptoft, the steward of the royal household, and Lord Bourgchier, the chamberlain, headed the imposing contingent that accompanied the king to France in April 1430, while the earl of Warwick continued his guardianship of the boy and led the army that embarked at the same time.[43] The king's knightly bodyguard maintained its vigilance about his person, with the exception of Sir Walter Beauchamp; when he died, he was replaced on 16 February 1430 by another Beauchamp kinsman, Sir Ralph Botiller.[44] This escort was reinforced by four further knights, who were appointed king's carvers in the royal chamber on 6 February. Again, the prominence of Warwick's associates is striking, for these new recruits were Sir Robert Roos, Sir Edmund Hungerford, Sir Thomas and Sir William Beauchamp.[45] These eight knights were to a man included in the king's retinue when he sailed for Calais two months later.

Thus, most of those who surrounded the young king during his French visit were known to him and he continued to live in a familiar environment. After all, his entourage included his governess's son, Sir Ralph Botiller, and although it is not known whether Dame Alice travelled to France as well, she certainly remained in household employ throughout the minority.[46] John Somerset, Henry's mentor and physician, was with him, and so was Thomas Asteley, the husband of his head nurse. Yet, no matter how well cared for the king was, his absence in France for well-nigh two years meant that for long periods his household was isolated from those left in England to govern the realm. It is true that before the king left, it had been agreed that no major officer or councillor should be dismissed or appointed without the consent of the entire body of councillors in England and France; nevertheless, some important changes were made abroad and not always with the full approval of the council in England.[47] For example, on 1 February 1431,

John Hotoft resigned as treasurer of the household. For the time being, one of the king's more experienced household knights, Sir William Philip, stepped into the breach and undertook duties which were familiar to him from Henry V's later years.[48] After a few months, John Tyrell succeeded him as treasurer on 25 May. In fact, Tyrell had been nominated in March to join the councillors in France and he left England with a retinue in May, presumably in the knowledge that he was to be the new treasurer. He was one of Gloucester's long-standing retainers and had quite recently acted as speaker in the parliament which the duke opened in January 1431.[49] The lieutenant of the realm had evidently utilized his right to advise on this important appointment, which carried responsibility for the king's personal finances.

Such consultation probably did not take place when a new chamberlain was nominated. Lord Bourgchier was killed in action at Amiens on 26 November 1431, and a replacement was immediately required for this vital household office. The choice fell on Ralph, Lord Cromwell and, to judge by Gloucester's reaction, there was no communication with England beforehand – perhaps because the king's return to his realm was imminent. Indeed, it seems likely that the king's French residence required a household-in-transit of officials with designated duties; and they could doubtless be augmented from time to time during the visit.

Politics and the royal household, 1432–36

The king's return to England meant that this household-in-transit would be absorbed into the customary household establishment in England. This raised some delicate problems and a series of changes in household personnel (as well as of the officers of state), which not only upset some of those who were dismissed, but unnerved the king's guardian, Warwick. Lord Cromwell was removed from the chamberlainship on 1 March 1432, after barely three months in office; in parliament a few months later, he complained bitterly of his treatment, claiming that Gloucester had acted improperly in not consulting the entire council first. The complaint was swept aside on 3 July. Cromwell's successor, Sir William Philip, was the king's knight who had so commended himself to Henry V that he had been made treasurer of the late king's household by the time of his death – and, of course, had briefly held the office while the king was in France in 1431.[50] On the same 1 March, Lord Tiptoft was replaced as steward of the household by Sir Robert Babthorp, another who had been trusted by Henry V as an executor of his will and as his household steward from 1421 (in which post he was retained until April 1424).[51] Care was also taken to remove some of the household clerks who were most likely to influence an impressionable boy. These included a bachelor in theology, Master William Hayton, who had been appointed the king's secretary by October 1430; and John de la Bere, another clerk who had crossed to France in the retinue of the king's master of horse, Sir John Styward, and had become the king's almoner by November 1431. Both men were removed on the fateful 1 March. The new almoner was Master Robert Felton, one of Archbishop Chichele's servants;[52] Hayton, however, was not replaced, presumably because it was not anticipated that Henry would need a secretary in England to take charge of his signet seal for some years yet. At the same time, Master Robert Gilbert, dean of the royal chapel for fifteen years and more, was succeeded by Master Richard Praty, a royal chaplain who would prove a 'large-hearted, benevolent and business-like prelate' later on; the king's confessor, Dr John Walden, had already given way to John Lowe a week earlier.[53]

When these numerous changes are assessed in relation to simultaneous changes in the offices of state, it becomes clear that Gloucester was determined to reassert at the earliest opportunity his control over the government of the realm and the king's household, now that Henry had returned to England and his own lieutenancy was at an end. When he came to make the new appointments, the duke resolved that the king should be brought up in a staunchly orthodox religious environment, insulated from the whiffs of heresy that were currently swirling round the land. Felton, Praty, Lowe, and the new keeper of the privy seal, William Lyndwood, were notable heretic-hunters, a diversion to which Gloucester had recently shown himself to be addicted.[54]

Later in 1432, Warwick had cause to feel uneasy about certain pressures and influences upon the young king. He was anxious about his own role now that the eleven-year-old Henry was 'growen in yeers in stature of his persone and also in conceyte and knoweleche of his hiegh and royale auctoritee and estate', and was beginning to grumble at Warwick's periodic chastising. The earl was equally concerned about those who distracted the king from his studies and improperly influenced his mind when Warwick or the household knights were not present. On 29 November 1432 the earl received specific guidelines for the king's future upbringing which would safeguard Warwick's own position and ensure that the king was suitably protected; at least one of the king's knights should always be present at interviews with the king. Nevertheless, Warwick's guardianship was in practice subject to the final scrutiny of the king's uncles, Bedford and Gloucester; and that meant Gloucester's scrutiny so long as Bedford remained in France.[55] For example, Warwick could not remove any of the more important personal servants of the king, and he could not add to the knights and esquires of the body (as perhaps he had done in the case of Sir Ralph Botiller and the carvers in 1430) without the advice of the council and of either Bedford or Gloucester. But the earl was still the king's guardian, and a number of his protégés continued to staff the household. Moreover, by August 1433 Sir Robert Babthorp was replaced as steward by a man who had close family ties with the Beaufort family and later became the cardinal's political heir: William de la Pole, earl of Suffolk, whose wife was Alice Chaucer.[56]

Bedford's visit to England in 1433–34 restored for a short while some balance to the competing interests of the king's mentors. And as his visit drew to its close in July 1434, the council took the precaution of confirming the powers of Warwick, Suffolk, and the other household officials to organize the king's movements as seemed appropriate.[57] This step was well-advised, for the council was aware that the 'mocions and sturynges' of which Warwick had complained in 1432 might re-emerge once Bedford had left the realm. Hence, in November 1434, it was pointed out to the king that, despite 'grete understandyng and felyng, as evere thei [the councillors] sawe or knewe in any Prince, or other persone of his age', he was not yet sufficiently experienced in matters of government to dispense with his council; he was advised not to change his officers or policies without consulting the councillors, and to be wary of those who might urge him to do so. Fear of a repetition of what had happened in 1432 gripped them once again; and it is noteworthy that while Cardinal Beaufort was present at this council meeting, Gloucester was not.[58] By May 1436, Warwick had reached the limit of his patience at the situation in the household. Using the pretext that he needed to devote more time to his own affairs than had been possible in recent years, on 19 May he resigned as King Henry's guardian and no successor was appointed. Warwick's links with the Beauforts were strong and this too may have made his position less tenable after the failure of the congress of Arras.[59] A major rival to Gloucester's influence over the king was thereby removed.

The queens–dowager

At about this time, two other prominent members of the royal family receded into the background. Queen Katherine was a young and active figure during the minority; she travelled widely and naturally had a crucial role to play in her son's upbringing. At Henry's coronation on 6 November 1429, she had sat near the king; and she continued to live in his household (and to contribute to its upkeep) until at least the end of 1430.[60] It is possible that she accompanied her son to France for at least part of his stay there, for she was the most convincing symbol of the treaty of Troyes.[61] But she does not appear to have lived in the household after the king's return, except on ceremonial occasions or at special festivals. Rather was she the focus of her own household, dividing her time between her favoured residences, especially Waltham manor (Essex) and Hertford castle.[62]

It is likely that she was already (1431–32) secretly married to the Welsh esquire Owen Tudor. The pot-pourri of myth, romanticism, tradition, and later anti-Tudor propaganda surrounding this match can rarely be substantiated with historical fact. We do not know how or where this unlikely pair met: whether at a ball during which Owen was so unsteady on his feet that he fell into the queen-dowager's lap, or after a river swim during which Katherine had played the part of a 'peeping Tom', or in Henry V's household, or through Owen's possible role in managing the queen's dower estates in Wales.[63] Despite the mystery, no contemporary cast doubt on the fact that this extraordinary marriage actually took place (though no queen had contracted a morganatic union in England since the Norman period), or on the legitimacy of the three sons and a daughter which it produced. The precise date of the marriage is not known, and the public at large (chroniclers included) were probably not aware of it until after the queen died. Katherine had lived in the king's household until 1430 and it is unlikely that she married Owen then. On the other hand, four children were born to the queen before her death on 3 January 1437, none of whom was ever claimed to be a bastard; hence the marriage may have taken place round about 1431–32. The marriage of a queen-dowager was a matter of signal importance to the council, especially because the king was still so young and might fall under the influence of a stepfather. Moreover, Katherine, to quote a brutally frank contemporary, was scarcely able to control her passions – after all, she was still only thirty in 1431.[64] On one occasion in the 1420s she had been courted by Edmund Beaufort, the bishop's nephew, but the hostility of Gloucester and others on the council to such a match can be imagined. The proposal doubtless worsened relations between the duke and the bishop and may well have prompted the statutory prohibition on anyone marrying an English queen without the council's assent.[65] The existence of the statute passed in the 1427–28 parliament explains the secrecy of the Tudor match.[66]

Katherine's connection with the Beauforts seems to have flourished, despite her clandestine marriage to Owen, rather than Edmund Beaufort. The cardinal was with her at Waltham soon after Christmas 1430, and at some stage she granted the stewardship of her Oxfordshire, Bedfordshire, and Berkshire lands to Thomas Chaucer and the earl of Suffolk in survivorship; soon after her death her children were placed in the care of the abbess of Barking (Essex), Katherine de la Pole, who was Suffolk's sister.[67] For a time, also, she continued her public activities, having discussions with the treasurer of England, Lord Hungerford, at Waltham on 30 November 1431 and attending the king's New Year festivities at Gloucester in 1435. And she successfully negotiated a readjustment of her dower grant in the parliament of July 1433.[68] But some while before her death, Katherine entered Bermondsey abbey either in disgrace or to secure better treatment for the illness which, at the time she drew up her will on 1 January 1437, was described as a 'long, grievous malady, in the which I have been long, and yet am, troubled and vexed by the visitation of God'.[69] Her illness proved fatal, and before the end came she may have been seriously deranged; she lost command of her wits sufficiently for several of her servants to secure favourable bequests from her which had to be annulled shortly afterwards.[70] Katherine died on 3 January 1437, no more than thirty-six years of age. In death, a semblance of queenly dignity remained: the

61

supervisors of her will were no lesser persons than Cardinal Beaufort, the duke of Gloucester, and Bishop Alnwick of Lincoln. King Henry himself was appointed her executor, though the melancholy details were attended to by his household servants.[71]

With Katherine in her tomb in Westminster abbey, her Welsh spouse could be given his deserts. Owen was summoned before the council; but rightly fearing for his safety, he sought sanctuary at Westminster. He was eventually persuaded to come out in order to disprove the hostile stories (which were presumably related to his marriage) that were being told about him to the king. He was soon arrested and immured in Newgate gaol, despite a safe-conduct from the duke of Gloucester who, to absolve himself from the deceit which the imprisonment implied, secured an indemnity for his action in July 1437.[72] Neither Gloucester nor the council could be sure of the king's future attitude to his stepfather and to those who had ill-treated him after Katherine's death; and by July 1437, Henry was already demonstrating that he had a will of his own. In the event, Owen Tudor was allowed to live in honourable, if modest, circumstances for the next twenty years; while his two eldest sons by Queen Katherine were eventually raised to the peerage by their royal half-brother.[73]

The queen's death had removed Henry's closest relative, even if she had rather withdrawn from public life in her last years. The extent of her influence on the king is difficult to gauge. Certainly, she was often in his company in the years up to her second marriage, and it is possible that she maintained her contacts with Cardinal Beaufort and his family. But in the 1430s these links (which Gloucester did not relish) and her marriage to the Welsh esquire may have led to her seclusion and reduced the frequency of her contacts with the king.

By contrast, the king's step-grandmother, Joan of Navarre, Henry IV's queen (and second wife), played no significant part in the affairs of the realm during her latter years. The disgrace into which she had fallen because of her dabblings in witchcraft had been forgiven her in 1421, but she carried no political weight thereafter as she entered her sixties.[74] She spent most of her time at her manor house of Langley in the Thames valley; not even the fire which destroyed several rooms on 25 March 1431, as a result of the carelessness of a minstrel, seems to have disrupted her life there.[75] She died six months after Queen Katherine, on 18 July 1437 at Havering atte Bower in Essex, one of her dower manors; the solemn obsequies at Canterbury cathedral, where she was interred on 11 August beside her dead husband, were organized by Gloucester and the council.[76] Joan's modest estates, which had been allowed to her by Henry V in an act of reconciliation towards the end of his reign, were organized by faithful servants, some of whom were confirmed in office by the king as her death approached.[77]

Joan's interest in politics was probably satisfied merely by the occasional chat with a visitor or by the receipt of news from those with something to impart. She could learn of her young step-grandson, for example, from the earl of Warwick, who was in her service in October 1433.[78] More significant, perhaps, was the fact that several of her officials were also in the employ of Cardinal Beaufort: John Foxholes, her treasurer and receiver-general in 1423–25, was one and Lewis John, the émigré Welshman who was steward of her manor of Havering from 1424 until her death, was another. Beaufort's kinsman, Thomas Chaucer, and even his nephew, Edmund Beaufort, had close links with the queen in the 1420s and 1430s and provided a direct link with the bishop's household.[79] Through these men Beaufort may have been able to cultivate the favour of the older queen (for what it was worth) at the same time as he was assured of access to Katherine of Valois's apartments. Even so, Joan's death in July 1437 was not likely to affect the king's upbringing, except to the extent of removing one further member of an already small family of the blood royal. There is no sign that she ever attracted the king's affection or, indeed, that he ever visited her (or she him) while he was a child. Perhaps the only personal link between them was Gilles of Brittany, Joan's grandson who, after he first arrived in England in 1432, became the king's firm friend.[80]

Notes

1 These arrangements are in the codicils drawn up at Vincennes on 26 August; they contain the only known reference to Henry of Windsor as prince of Wales, though he had not been formally created such (Eton Coll. MS). See also Wylie and Waugh, op. cit., III, 417. Hungerford would be one of Exeter's executors (*PPC*, III, 250-1). Bishop Beaufort and the earl of Warwick are mentioned by some writers as being involved in the king's guardianship (Roskell, *EHR*, LXVIII [1953], 201-2, 204-5). Cf. Powicke, op. cit., p. 2 (1216), and Tout, *Chapters*, III, 345 (1377).
2 PRO, E28/40/20; E101/408/11; *CPR, 1422–29*, pp. 84, 179; *PPC*, III, 131. For *gentiles femmes* in the household, see PRO, E404/42/306 (1426).
3 The three were Maud (or Matilda) Fosbroke (day-nurse), and Margaret Brotherman and Agnes Jakeman (*lotrices*) (PRO, E28/40/18, 19; *CPR, 1422–29*, pp. 84, 452, 455, 531; *Amundesham*, I, 21).
4 *PPC*, III, 143; Kretschmer, dissertation, pp. 2-3.
5 PRO, E28/44/64; /50/22, 23; /41/46; *PPC*, III, 143, 284-6, 190-1.
6 *Brut*, p. 564.
7 *CPR, 1422–29*, pp. 491-2; *Foedera*, IV, iv, 137; *RP*, V, 411. Warwick was referred to as the king's master on 8 May 1428 (*PPC*, III, 294-5). For his reputation, see T. B. Pugh (ed.), *Glamorgan county history*, III (Cardiff, 1973), 187-91; for his household, C. D. Ross, *The estates and finances of Richard Beauchamp, earl of Warwick* (Dugdale occasional papers, XII, 1956).
8 *PPC*, III, 86-8. But ct. *EHD*, IV, 233-4.
9 *RP*, IV, 326-7.
10 PRO, E403/681 m. 1, 4; E404/44/334; G. A. Holmes, 'Cardinal Beaufort and

the crusade against the Hussites', *EHR*, LXXXVIII (1973), 729. The organs were portable and travelled with the court in 1427–28.

11 *CPR, 1452-61*, p. 247. The king had been formally knighted by Bedford in 1426 (below, p. 80).

12 *PPC*, III, 282, 284-6; PRO, E28/50/23; E403/684 m. 18.

13 ibid., 678 m. 16; E404/43/295. For other purchases from Exeter's executors which Henry then gave away, see PRO, E403/686 m. 9.

14 John Kyngman, clerk of the chapel (PRO, E28/49/4) and Thomas Yonge, sergeant of its vestibule (E101/408/5 m. 7).

15 BL, Harleian MS 2278, with representations of the king as a boy on f. 6, 4v. For the king's gifts to Waltham abbey, not far from the queen's estates at Waltham (Essex), and his alms at a requiem mass in memory of John of Gaunt, see PRO, E28/50/22.

16 *Sotheby & co. catalogue*, 9 July 1973, pp. 24-30.

17 PRO, E403/681 m. 3 (Richard Geffrey, the king's minstrel, October 1424); E101/408/11 (clerks and minstrels in the household, 1430–31); E404/44/334 (London companies at Eltham, Christmas 1425); E28/50/22 (heralds, clerks, and minstrels travelling from Abingdon to Hertford, 1427); *PPC*, III, 294 (French players and dancers at Windsor, 1428). See PRO, E28/47/105-6 and E403/684 m. 1 for the financial plight of the grooms and pages in 1426–27.

18 *PPC*, III, 170, 292-3 (York); PRO, E28/46 (15 November 1424), 47/6, 50/22 (Roos).

19 R. Nicholson, *Scotland: the later middle ages* (Edinburgh, 1974), pp. 226-7, 258-60; below, p. 155.

20 *PPC*, III, 37-8; *HBC*, p. 75. See Kirby, thesis, pp. 21-37, and *GEC*, VI, 613-17. Babthorp was one of Henry V's executors.

21 *PPC*, III, 286. Hungerford resigned to become treasurer of England (*HBC*, p. 102). For Tiptoft, see Roskell, *Speakers*, pp. 147-9, 367-8; *GEC*, XII, i, 746-9.

22 PRO, E28/42/34 (15 June 1423); *GEC*, V, 421-5.

23 *CPR, 1422-29*, p. 128 (11 July 1423); *GEC*, II, 247-8; XI, 40-1. He was still chamberlain on 24 May 1431 (PRO, E101/408/9 m. 3).

24 *CPR, 1422-29*, p. 460; *PPC*, III, 287-8; PRO, E101/408/10 m. 7. For a biography, see Wedgwood, *Biographies*, pp. 780-1; Emden, *Oxford*, III, 1727-8; Wylie and Waugh, op. cit., III, 432-3. For a possible book of his, containing medical and other treatises, see Bodl, Ashmole 1827.

25 From 1417 Hungerford was constable of Windsor castle, one of Henry's principal residences in the 1420s (S. Bond, 'The medieval constables of Windsor castle', *EHR*, LXXXII [1967], 248). Robessart was travelling with the king during 1423 (*CPR, 1422-29*, p. 128).

26 PRO, E28/50/22; Wedgwood, *Biographies*, pp. 415-17 (Hampton).

27 *PPC*, III, 294-5; *CPR, 1422–29*, p. 531. Philip Chetwynd was a servant of the earl at court in 1428, while Rose Chetwynd was engaged on the king's service in February 1429 (ibid., p. 525; PRO, E28/50/22).

28 Each had his own esquire and two valets, as well as provisions for his chamber and an annual grant of 100 marks (*PPC*, III, 294-5). Like Warwick these knights were assigned their duties some weeks (31 May) before their formal appointment on 11 June 1428 (PRO, E403/689, m. 3, 4).

29 Roskell, *Speakers*, pp. 348-50; *HBC*, p. 79.

30 PRO, E28/44/16. For his close connection with Lord Cromwell, see R. L.

Friedrichs, 'The career and influence of Ralph, Lord Cromwell, 1393–1456' (Columbia PhD thesis, 1974) p. 148.

31 The finances of the household in 1422–29 can be studied in PRO, E101/407/13, 16; 408/3, 5.

32 *HBC*, p. 79; Roskell, *1422*, p. 191. John Hotoft's appointment as treasurer was resolved by the council on 8 February 1423 (*PPC*, III, 24). For underpaid household servants, see below, p. 111. Other financial officers included the keeper of the king's jewels (John Newton in 1426 and John Merston from 1427), and the clerk of the great wardrobe (Robert Rolleston throughout the minority).

33 Eton Coll. MS; PRO, E101/408/6. Katherine and the king travelled from her castle at Hertford to St Albans and Windsor between Easter (4 April) and St George's day (23 April) 1428 (*Amundesham*, I, 21); A. Crawford, 'The king's burden? – the consequences of royal marriage in fifteenth-century England', in R. A. Griffiths (ed.), *Patronage, the crown and the provinces in later medieval England* (Gloucester, 1981), ch. 2, is a comparative study of the queens.

34 PRO, E28/41/46 (Botiller); *CPR, 1422–29*, p. 233; *CCR, 1422–30*, p. 53 (Arthurton).

35 Above, p. 55. See also Sir Robert Babthorp, steward of the household of Henry V and Henry VI in 1421–24, and steward of Katherine's Leics. estates (and others) by 1423 (LeicsRO, DG5/857); and Giles Thorndon, the queen's carver by 1424 and a servant in the king's household two years later (R. A. Griffiths, *The principality of Wales in the later middle ages*, vol. I: *South Wales, 1277–1536* [Cardiff, 1972], 216-18). Lewis Robessart, now Lord Bourgchier and since 1423 the king's chamberlain, had attended Katherine at Troyes in 1420 (Wylie and Waugh, op. cit., III, 200).

36 *RP*, IV, 183-4; *Foedera*, IV, iii, 179-80. The dower grant was slightly amended in 1423 (*RP*, IV, 202-6; *CPR, 1422–29*, p. 17). On his deathbed, Henry V had been careful to guarantee dower to his queen (Eton Coll. MS).

37 In the seven years 1422–29, about £16,100 was due to the queen from the exchequer; she received about £15,600 in tallies of assignment, and only £108 of this proved difficult to collect. PRO, E403/658-91.

38 PRO, E159/199 *communia*, Hil, m. 2. He was still serving in 1429 (ibid., E101/408/6).

39 *RP*, IV, 183-9, 202-6.

40 ibid., 314-15. For other of the queen's servants in England, see *CPR, 1422–29*, p. 287; *Amundesham*, I, 65, 21; Stevenson, II, 263-82.

41 The king's itinerary has been plotted by M. E. Christie, *Henry VI* (1922), pp. 375ff.

42 For parliaments, see *RP*, IV, 261, 262, 296, 316; *Brut*, p. 452; *Three Chrons.*, p. 58; *Great Chron.*, p. 128. The London procession is in ibid., p. 132.

43 PRO, E403/691 m. 22-28; E404/46.

44 PRO, E28/51/58. The others were Philip, Rocheford, and Porter (above, p. 55).

45 PRO, E403/691 m. 17. Sir William Beauchamp was Gloucester's chamberlain by January 1428 (WA MS 12161). By 20 October 1432, Sir John Beauchamp had replaced Sir Thomas Beauchamp, and the annual salary of

the carvers had been raised from 40 marks to £40 (*PPC*, IV, 128; *CPR*, *1429–36*, p. 267).

46 PRO, E101/408/24 f. 43-44 (1437–38).

47 *PPC*, IV, 36-9.

48 Roskell, *1422*, p. 191; *PPC*, IV, 77.

49 PRO, E101/408/13; Roskell, *1422*, pp. 226-9; above, p. 41.

50 *PPC*, IV 109-11; *RP*, IV, 392; above, p. 58.

51 *PPC*, IV, 109-11; above, p. 54.

52 *Reg. Chichele*, I, lxxvi; Otway-Ruthven, *King's secretary*, pp. 33-4, 154, 169. Hayton may be identified with Henry V's secretary in 1419–20; despite A. J. Otway-Ruthven's tentative suggestion (ibid., pp. 91-8) that the Frenchman Lawrence Calot succeeded Hayton in 1432, the group of French secretaries active in England and France in 1431–37 was probably exclusively concerned with relations between the two Lancastrian kingdoms.

53 Emden, *Oxford*, II, 766-7, 1168-9; III, 1514; R. G. Davies, thesis, III; *Reg. Chichele*, III, 126-30. Cromwell, Tiptoft, and Robert Gilbert were close friends of Archbishop Kemp, who was dismissed as chancellor at this time (above, p. 41; Nigota, thesis, pp. 264-5).

54 Below, p. 140.

55 *PPC*, IV, 133-4; *RP*, V, 433-4.

56 Above, p. 43.

57 *PPC*, IV, 259-61.

58 ibid, pp. 287-9; *RP*, IV, 438.

59 *CPR, 1429–36*, p. 589. Warwick's daughter, the widowed Lady Roos, had married Edmund Beaufort, count of Mortain, before about April 1435; the king stood as godfather for their son early in 1436 (PRO, E28/56/26; *GEC*, XII, i, 53-4).

60 Above, p. 56; PRO, E101/408/6; /9 m. 2.

61 She seems to have been at Rouen with her son, and several of her servants were in the king's household in February 1431 (PRO, E28/57/96; *PPC*, IV, 77). For John Lydgate's portrayal of Katherine as a symbol of unity between England and France, see W. F. Schirmer, *John Lydgate* (1961), pp. 106-7, 131-3.

62 *Amundesham*, I, 56; *PPC*, IV, 108-9 (Waltham, 1430–31); Stevenson, II, i, 273, 276, 282 (Hertford, 1434, 1436). Two of Katherine's sons by Owen Tudor were born in Hertfordshire: Edmund at Much Hadham, Bishop Morgan of Ely's house, and Jasper at Bishop's Hatfield, Bishop FitzHugh of London's residence (R. S. Thomas, 'The political career, estates and "connection" of Jasper Tudor, earl of Pembroke and duke of Bedford (d. 1495)' [Wales PhD thesis, 1971], pp. 20-1).

63 For a sober examination of these stories, and much else, see R. S. Thomas, thesis, ch. I. The first reference to Owen as a servant in the queen's chamber appears to be JRL, Latin MS 113 (c. 1484).

64 Giles, p. 17.

65 R. A. Griffiths, 'Queen Katherine of Valois and a missing statute of the realm', *LQR*, XCIII (1977), 248-58, with a correction in one particular by G. Hand, 'The King's widow and the King's widows', ibid., 506-7, and a further comment by G. O. Sayles, 'The royal marriages act, 1428', ibid., XCIV (1978), 188-92.

66 Griffiths, *LQR*, XCIII (1977), 257-8, for a contemporary copy of the statute in LeicsRO, BR II/3/3.

67 *Amundesham*, I, 56; *CPR, 1436-41*, p. 14; R. S. Thomas, thesis, p. 26. See below n. 72 for Owen Tudor in the custody of Suffolk and Edmund Beaufort in 1438.

68 PRO, E28/57/96; *RP*, IV, 459-60.

69 ibid., V, 505-6; A. Strickland, *Lives of the queens of England*, II (1857), 153-4 (which is the only study of the queen).

70 *Foedera*, IV, i, 37.

71 *RP*, V, 505-6 (26 March 1437). Her Book of Hours, which includes (f. 17) prayers specifically for her use and perhaps in her own hand, is Bodl, Lat. liturg. f. 9; see N. Denholm-Young, *Handwriting in England and Wales* (Cardiff, 1954), pl. 21, for an illustration of f. 39.

72 *PPC*, V, 46-50; R. S. Thomas, thesis, pp. 21-6; Chrimes, *Henry VII*, pp. 325-6. After escaping early in 1438, Owen was placed in the custody of the earl of Suffolk at Wallingford, a castle Owen knew well, for it had been Katherine's; a few months later he was transferred to Windsor, where the new constable was Edmund Beaufort.

73 R. S. Thomas, thesis, pp. 26-8; below, p. 358.

74 A. R. Myers, 'The captivity of a royal witch: the household accounts of Queen Joan of Navarre, 1419-21', *BJRL*, XXIV (1940), 263-84; XXVI (1941), 82-100. A further account for her last months of confinement in Leeds castle (Kent), from 8 March to 24 July 1422, is noted in *Sotheby and co. catalogue*, 26 June 1974, p. 88 (with facing illustrations); this is the hitherto 'lost' account noted by Strickland, op. cit., II, 99.

75 e.g., *PPC*, V, 61-4; *CPR, 1429-36*, pp. 196, 244, 266-7; ibid., *1436-41*, p. 57. For the fire, see *Amundesham*, I, 61-2.

76 *PPC*, V, 56.

77 e.g., *CPR, 1436-41*, pp. 58, 68, 71. Her imminent death is indicated by several royal grants of her properties in the week before 18 July, to take effect from her death (ibid., p. 77; *CFR, 1429-37*, p. 339).

78 *CPR, 1429-36*, p. 328. He had been her champion at her coronation in 1403 (J. L. Kirby, *Henry IV of England* [1970], p. 151).

79 PRO, E159/199 *communia*, E. m. 2; E403/661 m. 6; 669 m. 7; 671 m. 8 (Foxholes); KB9/224 m. 14; *CPR, 1436-41*, p. 68 (John); A. J. Elder, 'A study of the Beauforts and their estates, 1399-1450' (Bryn Mawr PhD thesis, 1964), p. 39 n. 46; Ruud, op. cit., pp. 8, 93. For their association with Beaufort, see PRO, E403/661 m. 1; 664 m.1 (Foxholes); *CPR, 1429-36*, p. 114; *CCR, 1436-41*, pp. 67-8 (John). See A. D. Carr, 'Sir Lewis John – a medieval London Welshman', *BBCS*, XXII (1967), 260-70.

80 Above, p. 61. For the king's New Year gift to Joan in 1437, see *PPC*, V, 61-4, and for Gilles, below, p. 207.

4 Clients, Patrons, and Politics, 1422–1429

The new establishment

The accent of England's governance after the death of Henry V lay on continuity and reliability. As was to be expected from experienced men of proven loyalty to the dynasty, the main concern of those lords who undertook the management of the kingdom's affairs in 1422 was to appoint sheriffs, castle-constables, and other royal agents in England and Wales who were loyal and dependable like themselves. Thus, on 28 September 1422 they renewed the commissions of appointment of Henry V's administrators and officers because these had automatically lapsed at the king's demise. As soon as parliament met, their action was confirmed.[1] Few sheriffs were changed in the opening weeks of the new reign, some indeed not until November 1423.[2] Within the king's private duchy of Lancaster, the chancellor who had been in office since 1413, the notably successful civil servant John Wodehouse, was retained; the recently appointed sheriff of Lancashire, Sir Richard Radcliffe, was also re-engaged.[3] Most of the key royal castles retained their constables, some of whom, like Sir Walter Hungerford at Windsor and Sir William Philip at Norwich, were soon to become important figures in the new régime.[4]

Even when there was an opportunity to consider new appointments or promotions, men who had sharpened their experience in Henry V's service at home or abroad – or, indeed, in that of his father or grandfather – were generally preferred. Nor is this surprising. Domestic security and defence at the beginning of a minority, and the need to raise and support armies for France and Ireland, and to provide for the routine administration of shire and lordship, these were the new council's foremost concerns. Known and reliable knights and esquires, preferably recommended by one or more of the councillors themselves, would fit the bill best. During the course of 1423, all twenty-five shrievalties in England (excluding those in the palatine counties of Chester, Lancaster, and Durham) were filled in either February or November. The most significant qualifications of the new appointees – influential connections and a tradition of service, frequently on campaign – perpetuated the character of Henry V's shrievalties into the reign of his son. Sir Thomas Waweton (sheriff of Bedfordshire–Buckinghamshire from Michaelmas 1422) was a cousin of Sir John

Tiptoft, one of the more conscientious among the new king's council-lors, and he was also attached to the earl of March, another councillor. Sir William Bonville (sheriff of Devon in February 1423) and Sir John Cockayne (in Nottinghamshire–Derbyshire from the same time) had fought valiantly at the side of the ill-fated duke of Clarence.[5] Others were both well-known to the English magnates and respected for their war service in France: William Allington (sheriff of Cambridgeshire–Huntingdonshire) had been in his time a protégé of both Clarence and Bishop Beaufort, as well as a valued administrator in the government of Calais, Ireland, and English Normandy; he joined the council himself in 1424.[6] Take another personality, Sir William Mountford, whose territorial interests, family service, and military adventures brought him into the circle of another king's councillor, the earl of Warwick; in November 1423 he became sheriff of Worcestershire, where the shrievalty was virtually a Beauchamp preserve.[7] A similar pattern emerges in the private franchise of the duchy of Lancaster. Geoffrey Lowther, the duchy's new receiver-general and attorney-general from 1 February 1423, was a lawyer who had entered Gloucester's service in France and became his lieutenant as constable of Dover castle and warden of the Cinque ports; Sir William Talbot, steward of Monmouth lordship from 19 May 1423, was a kinsman of Lord Talbot who, for all his Irish antics, had played an important role in the critical initial weeks of the new reign.[8] In the other royal duchy, Cornwall, one of Bishop Beaufort's acquaintances, the Welsh esquire Lewis John, was ap-pointed receiver-general of the duchy and steward of Devon on 8 February 1423.[9] Men of similar character and experience were relied upon for security purposes. On 18 November 1423, Sir Ralph Cromwell, the young friend of Henry V and a councillor of his son, took custody of Somerton castle (Somerset) for a ten-year period; away to the north, in Yorkshire, Scarborough castle was put in the hands of Thomas Burgh, one of Gloucester's esquires, in July 1423, whilst in Northamp-tonshire Sir Thomas Burton, a knight entrusted with the custody of several distinguished French prisoners, had become constable of Fotheringhay.[10]

The bishops played a central part in this nexus of patronage on which both secular and ecclesiastical government depended, and the way in which their elections were conducted reflects the assumptions by which the council ruled England. In the earliest years of the reign, the translation of these assumptions into practice was hindered, and sometimes deflected, by Pope Martin V's determination to assert his own right to provide to English and Welsh bishoprics. The translation of Bishop Barrow from Bangor to Carlisle in April 1423 represented only a modest advancement of the bishop's career, and for that reason it was uneventful and devoid of political significance; so too was the election of his successor, John Cliderow, a cleric of illegitimate gentry birth in Kent who had commended himself to the pope and several English bishops during residence at the papal curia.[11] By contrast, the long-expected death of Archbishop Bowet of York on 20 October 1423 'provided a catalyst' for 'the intrigues simmering in ecclesiastical circles'; and these intrigues had important implications for the establishment of the new régime.[12] Towards the end of 1423, one of the most prominent and capable of the royal councillors, Philip Morgan, bishop of Worcester, was proposed as Bowet's successor and the council assented to what was a deserved promotion of one of their number. The treasurer of England, John Stafford, merited a bishopric by virtue of his services to the state and it was fully intended that he should follow Morgan to Worcester; Stafford did his utmost to further this plan by energetic canvassing of his own in Rome. But the English council had not bargained with the strong-willed pope, who was not only anxious to secure the York plum for his own agent, Richard Fleming, at present bishop of Lincoln ('a man of greater ambitions than political sense'), but was in no mood to submit to dictation on so high a matter.[13] Pope Martin accordingly provided Fleming to York on 14 February 1424, much to the disgust of a council which did not view this new archbishop in quite the same political light as it did Morgan; such an appointment would amount to the waste of a valuable archbishopric. The impasse was only ended in July 1425 with John Kemp's promotion to York, which he himself had eagerly urged in Rome.[14]

Conscious of their responsibilities and of the difficulties confronting them during a minority, the councillors appear at first to have shown little partisanship or personal favour towards the clients of any particular group or individual on the council. A protégé of Gloucester could be pricked as sheriff of Essex–Hertfordshire (John Tyrell) alongside William Allington, one of Beaufort's associates, or John Lancastre who, as sheriff of Norfolk–Suffolk, had predictable Mowbray links, or Sir Rowland Lenthale (sheriff of Herefordshire), a servant of the earl of March.[15] Likewise, on the king's personal estates, the advancement of Geoffrey Lowther, Duke Humphrey's lieutenant, took place at the same time as that of Lewis John, a Beaufort client, whilst Bishop Morgan's elevation to York would probably have been acceptable to the council as a whole, and not least to Archbishop Chichele, to whom he was closely attached.[16] The fatal flaw of faction had not yet begun to mar the practice of government at Westminster or in the provinces: the example of Henry V was still strong and in order to avoid divisive partisanship it must continue to be followed.

The appearance of faction, 1424–26

Signs of a change in attitude became apparent when both Bedford and Gloucester were out of the country, and England was therefore without an effective protector, from October 1424 to April 1425. The elder of the king's uncles was still in France and he remained there until December 1425; Gloucester, meanwhile, had sailed to Hainault in an attempt to recover his duchess's county from the duke of Brabant, who had Burgundian support.[17] During these months, Beaufort was the dominant personality at Westminster, and there is no doubt that he was able to impose his will on the other councillors and officers, especially after he became chancellor of England in July 1424. As a result, partisan rule became so pronounced that Gloucester found its consequences intolerable when he returned to England.[18] For example, among the sheriffs newly appointed in November 1424 were at least six of the bishop's associates, and the relationship between Beaufort and at least some of them was more than that of a generous lord and an intermittent client or well-wisher. Sir Edward Stradling, the new sheriff of Somerset–Dorset, was married to Beaufort's bastard daughter, Jane, and benefited materially as a consequence.[19] Sir Richard Vernon (in Nottinghamshire–Derbyshire) seems also to have developed an association with the bishop by this stage, while John Golafre, who was appointed sheriff of Oxfordshire–Berkshire, was a friend of Beaufort's cousin, Thomas Chaucer, and others of his circle.[20] Indeed, this group of Oxfordshire landowners gave Beaufort a strong and steady grip on the local shrievalty in the 1420s; it included Thomas Stonor, who was pricked sheriff of Oxfordshire–Berkshire in 1424. The neighbouring counties of Bedfordshire and Buckinghamshire were presented with Richard Wyot, shortly to be Beaufort's steward, as their sheriff. Further north, Sir John Langton (appointed for Yorkshire) had family connections with the Nevilles and Harringtons which also implied Beaufort sympathies.[21] Sir Walter Hungerford, who became chamberlain of the duchy of Lancaster on 12 February 1425, acted as executor of the duke of Exeter's will, so he too was probably looked upon favourably by the bishop.[22] Moreover, although Sir John Scrope of Masham, himself a councillor by this time and one of Gloucester's supporters a little later, secured the stewardship of Pickering on 29 January 1425, the very next day the companion Yorkshire stewardship of Pontefract (together with the constableship of its castle) was awarded to Sir Richard Neville, son of the earl of Westmorland and his countess, Joan Beaufort.[23]

Beaufort's role is less clear in bishop-making during 1424–25 than in other spheres; he may have been more restrained out of respect for the person and prerogatives of Pope Martin, who was well disposed towards him.[24] Several sees fell vacant while Beaufort was chancellor and Gloucester was out of the country, and Bedford, who as regent of France was engaged in his own discussions with Martin V, brought these English bishoprics into his negotiations. Despite his absence, then, Duke John took an eager interest in episcopal appointments in England.[25] On 27 October 1424 Bishop Bubwith of Bath and Wells died; his successor, John Stafford, had been but a step from the episcopal bench since the beginning of the year, and his position as treasurer of England merited a notable see. Although his elevation was therefore likely to be generally acceptable in the council, Beaufort may have been particularly satisfied at the advancement of a Stafford and indeed he himself consecrated the new bishop at Blackfriars on Whitsunday 1425.[26] General approbation may also have greeted William Alnwick's election as bishop of Norwich early in 1426, in succession to John Wakering, who had died in April 1425; keeper of the privy seal since 1422 and (though hardly in anything more than a formal sense) the king's confessor and, perhaps, secretary by 1424, Alnwick's promotion had been postulated some time earlier.[27] The delay in finding a new bishop of Norwich was matched by the delay in providing York with a new archbishop, though it did not cause anything like as much bitterness.

These and other episcopal appointments reflect the part played by the duke of Bedford in shaping relations with the papacy. It was Bedford's intervention which resolved the dispute over York in July 1425 in favour of John Kemp who, like Stafford and Alnwick, appears to have attracted the support of all parties, including Beaufort and Gloucester.[28] Martin V promptly replaced him at London on 30 July 1425 with William Gray – a man of north-country baronial origins whose brother had married into the Beaufort clan. More significant than this was his dedicated work at the Council of Pavia-Siena, his contacts with the pope himself, and his friendship with Archbishop Kemp.[29] There was some delay, from the English side on this occasion, in confirming Gray's provision; and it was only the arrival of Bedford in the realm in late December 1425, and the opening of a parliament at Leicester in February 1426, that precipitated a decision. The log-jam in episcopal patronage was thereupon released. By early April 1426, Gray had been accepted by the English council as bishop of London, Kemp had been finally elected archbishop of York by the chapter there, Bishop Morgan had been translated to Ely (where the aged John Fordham had died on 19 November 1425), Thomas Polton had moved from Chichester to Worcester, and John Rickinghale, Bedford's own confessor, was straightway installed at Chichester.[30] Alnwick's move to Norwich was finalized, Bishop Cliderow received the Bangor temporalities, Wells's long-delayed succession to Llandaff was achieved after his return from Rome, and the imprudent Fleming ignominiously returned to Lincoln in August 1426.[31] If these tergiversations reveal anything, it is the difficulties experienced by a minority council in England, headed for a time by a bishop-chancellor and gradually riven by dissensions, and which at the same time was engaged in a contest with an energetic pope. Only Bedford, who was conducting his own negotiations with Martin V over episcopal appointments in Normandy, was able to strike a bargain with the pope and re-establish a workable relationship.[32]

Most fateful of all the council's appointments during Gloucester's absence was that of Richard Woodville as custodian of the Tower of London on 26 February 1425.[33] The situation in the capital was sufficiently unstable to warrant the employment of a man of military experience and, as the duke of Bedford's chamberlain, political importance. He was seconded from the duke's service in France for this particular purpose and provided with a substantial garrison, eighty-strong. However justifiable this appointment was, it affronted Gloucester when, on his return to England, he was refused entry to the fortress, even though he was specifically charged with the protection and defence of the realm.[34] There can be no doubt that Bedford was fully aware of the appointment of one of his personal servants, especially since it meant leaving the duke's presence and returning to England. This, together with Bedford's intimate involvement in the discussions that preceded John Kemp's translation to York in July 1425, suggests that the duke was prepared to intervene in English politics from abroad while his brother Gloucester was away.[35] When Duke Humphrey came home, relations with the chancellor deteriorated sharply. Gloucester's resentment at his brother's attitude towards the recent expedition to Hainault was intensified by Bedford's tacit support of the English council's actions, under the direction of Bishop Beaufort. When the hostility resulted in civil disorder in October 1425, it was to Bedford that Beaufort appealed.

The months of crisis, 1425–26

The twenty-ninth of October was traditionally the day on which a newly elected mayor of London rode to Westminster to take his oath of office. In 1425 it proved to be a day of chronic unrest in the city. The new mayor, John Coventry, a mercer, returned from the customary journey to find himself at the centre of what proved to be the most serious domestic threat to the stability of Henry VI's government.[36] A dangerous dispute arose from the increasingly strained relations between Bishop Beaufort and the protector, relations which had deteriorated seriously while Gloucester was in Hainault and the bishop attempted to mould the personnel and policies of the government in his own interests. The new mayor barely had time to sit down to his election feast when messengers arrived from Duke Humphrey summoning him, along with the aldermen of the city and other commoners, to a meeting.[37] John Coventry was told to take immediate measures to ensure the peace of the city during the coming night in view of the large force which Beaufort had assembled at his inn near the Southwark end of London bridge.[38] The bishop's men-at-arms and archers included Lancashiremen and Cheshiremen, and he had drawn from Windsor castle certain of the king's household servants and from the inns of court some of the law apprentices; they all came armed and ready for a fight.[39] Beaufort also sent for the mayor and aldermen of London, but his recent arrest of a number of citizens made the city officials reluctant to offer their support to the bishop.[40]

Acting on the orders of the mayor and Gloucester, the gates of London bridge were manned throughout 30 October in order to prevent the bishop's men from crossing into the city or – what was perhaps equally likely – to deter the angry Londoners from swarming across to Southwark. By 8 a.m. the city was awake and up in arms. Many flocked down to the Thames with the intention of crossing over and attacking the bishop's residence.[41] An hour or so later, Beaufort's men drew the chains across the stulps (or pillars) at the southern end of the bridge; they dragged barricades into place, and stationed themselves – knights, esquires, and countless others – so that the stulps themselves seemed embattled and the windows and other vantage points were strongly defended. In the city itself shops hurriedly closed, and everyone congregated near the bridge to defend their city against the bishop's men.[42] The two armed, but ill-disciplined, forces confronted each other. The astute observer would have realized that this was no sudden, unpremeditated eruption of violence. London had been in a state of excitement for some time, and the popular attitude towards Bishop Beaufort had been growing daily more hostile. Had the Londoners crossed the bridge that day, the bishop, his men, and his inn would very likely have been destroyed. As it was, the action of the mayor (at Gloucester's prompting) in holding the bridge not only protected the city from a dangerous incursion, but also prevented a clash on the bridge itself.[43]

The particular cause of Gloucester's exasperation with Beaufort concerned the Tower of London and Richard Woodville. The 'certain urgent causes' which had prompted the latter's appointment as the fortress's custodian as from 26 February 1425 were serious anti-alien outbursts which alarmed Bishop Beaufort. On 13 February anonymous bills hostile to the Flemings were being distributed in the city and its suburbs, and some were nailed to Beaufort's door. Such 'seditious and odiouse billes and langage' (to use Beaufort's venomous description of them) caused foreigners to flee from the city, and they so perturbed the bishop that he took immediate steps to strengthen the Tower and install the new custodian, Richard Woodville.[44] He was despatched to the Tower the very next day with a substantial force. The council on 26 February was therefore authorizing a change of custody which had already taken place on the chancellor's initiative – a change which can hardly have been sustained without Bedford's approval.[45] Beaufort also arrested several citizens. A number of Londoners had been accused (wrongly, so it was widely believed) of treason by a malicious appealer in Beaufort's pay.[46] Suspicion of the bishop was therefore strong in the city, not least because he was thought to favour the alien merchants. It was commonly believed that, despite his position as chancellor, he connived at breaching one of the conditions of the grant of tunnage and poundage conceded in the parliament which met in April 1425, namely, that aliens should be hosted with Englishmen while they were trading in the realm. As a result, this parliament was said to have had 'an evylle faryng ende' on 14 July.[47] During the session, there was a huge demonstration against Beaufort at Wine Crane's wharf, a short distance up-river from his inn and on the opposite bank; 'billes and langage off slaundre and manasse' included the Londoners' threat that they would throw the bishop into the Thames to teach him 'to swim with wings'.[48]

Reports of the unrest in London doubtless caused Duke John some unease, especially since to begin with neither he nor his younger brother was in the realm to protect and defend it, according to their sworn charge. The attacks on the Flemish merchants were an embarrassment to the duke, for he was desperately trying to repair the alliance with Duke Philip of Burgundy (who was also count of Flanders) after it had been undermined by Gloucester's invasion of Hainault. Woodville, then, was well chosen for the task of occupying the Tower. He had had close – even friendly – relations with almost every member of the Lancastrian royal family since 1399; more recently, he had secured prominent military and administrative commands in Normandy under Henry V, and was captain of Caen and other fortresses, and he acted as treasurer-general of the duchy under Bedford.[49] When Gloucester, after his return from the continent, attempted to gain entrance to the Tower, ostensibly to lodge there as protector and defender of the realm, Richard Woodville refused him access and was supported in his decision by Bishop Beaufort.[50]

These annoyances made London the scene of serious civil strife simply because they brought to flash-point the fierce personal animosity that existed between Beaufort and Gloucester, who was a popular figure in London and highly sensitive about his position as protector and defender of the realm. Contemporary commentators on these events are unanimous that London gave Gloucester its full support on 29-30 October. Not only did the city officials respond to his call for defensive measures on the evening of the 29th, but the mass of citizenry clamoured along the Thames embankment just as much in his cause as to protect their shops and premises from a possible Beaufort attack.[51] His residence at Baynard's Castle within the city made him a Londoner.[52]

The outraged pride of the imperious Gloucester may be imagined. He had suffered rebuffs from Beaufort and the council before; to be denied entry to the oldest royal fortress in the land, one which dominated the capital, was the residence of kings and housed the royal wardrobe, the armoury, and valuable prisoners, was insupportable and, in his eyes, against his 'state and worship'. The Woodville appointment rankled in the months that followed, and Beaufort later claimed that Humphrey played on the apprehensions of the Londoners at the presence of a strong garrison in the Tower and exaggerated its threat to London.[53] Gloucester had an additional reason to be angry at Woodville's stubbornness. Immured in the Tower was a prisoner in whom the duke was particularly interested: the infamous Friar Randolf, who had been implicated in 1419 in the magical pastimes of Queen Joan, and had been imprisoned for his indiscretions. Gloucester's fascination with necromancy, witchcraft, and magic is well known, and so, again pitting his authority as protector against that of the council, he ordered

Woodville's lieutenant, Robert Scot, to surrender the friar to him. So worried was Scot by this conflict of authority that he consulted the chancellor, Bishop Beaufort. It was this dispute, and Gloucester's bid to override conciliar authority, that caused the bishop to consolidate the Tower's garrison and to support Woodville in his refusal to allow the duke into the fortress without a proper warrant from the council.[54]

According to his own testimony, Duke Humphrey was equally affronted by a plan which would have effectively insulated Henry VI from his uncle's influence. Gloucester's absence in Hainault had done just that for six months already. On his return, it seemed to the duke that Bishop Beaufort was determined to 'putte hym [Henry VI] in suche governaunce as hym lyst' without any authorization from the protector or the council.[55] Compared with the Tower dispute, there is little direct evidence to substantiate Gloucester's accusation or Beaufort's denial, but that such charges were voiced reflects Gloucester's sensitivity about his position as protector and Beaufort's deep distrust of him. At the beginning of the reign, Gloucester had not been assigned the guardianship of the king, and this may still have rankled, for in 1426 he claimed that control of Henry was his right before that of any other man. The fortification of the gate of London bridge by Beaufort's men was thought to be an attempt to prevent Gloucester from hastening to Eltham in order to foil the bishop's plan. Beaufort's denial of the charge was immediate and he explained the gathering of a force by his own need for protection from Gloucester and the Londoners. This can hardly be denied; nevertheless, it does seem likely that Beaufort had taken the initiative in raising forces in Southwark. One chronicler noted that they were partly composed of men from the king's household at Windsor, so it is possible that Gloucester's fears that the bishop was about to transport the king from Eltham to Windsor castle had some foundation.[56] To secure control of the king himself would, after all, give the bishop surest protection.

Gloucester had never been satisfied with the political settlement of 1422. His dissatisfaction was turned into suspicion and apprehension when he returned to England in mid-April 1425 to discover how Beaufort, as chancellor, had strengthened his influence and fortified the council's authority – and seemed to be planning to continue to do so. The struggle of October 1425 is, therefore, readily comprehensible. The council had summoned additional spiritual and temporal lords to London by 20 October, but a last-minute attempt to compose the differences between Beaufort and Gloucester eight days later was inconclusive.[57] The violence broke out next day.

Such a fundamental problem of authority in the kingdom could not be solved overnight: the most that could be done was to remove the immediate threat to public order in London and to soothe the worst extremes of resentment felt by Beaufort and Gloucester. This was achieved through the tireless efforts of Archbishop Chichele, the earl of Stafford, and especially of Pedro, the Portuguese duke of Coimbra, who was Gloucester's first cousin and had just arrived in London; he lodged in the bishop of London's palace on 28 October, only a day before the worst unrest occurred.[58] During 30 October these mediators rode between the contending parties no less than eight times. Eventually, the mayor and aldermen were able to disperse the Londoners, but the 'prive wrath' between duke and bishop was scarcely diminished. They remained, to quote the understatement of the decade, 'not goode frendys'.[59]

Beaufort had good reason to believe that the matter was far from settled. Next day, 31 October, he wrote to Bedford, who had taken an intermittent interest in the deterioration of public order in London and in the acrimonious relations between his brother and uncle. If Bedford were to return to England, it would immediately place Gloucester at a disadvantage, for his authority as protector and defender on which Humphrey had staked his position would thereby be superseded. In great haste, therefore, Beaufort wrote to his nephew in France to induce him to visit England:

> Right high and mighty prince, and my right noble after one [i.e., the king] levest lord. I recommend me unto you with all my heart and service. And as you desire the welfare of the king our sovereign lord and of his realms of England and of France, and your own weal and ours also, haste you hither; for by my troth if you tarry, we shall put this land in adventure with a field [i.e., a battle]. Such a brother you have here. God make him a good man.
> For your wisdom knows well that the prosperity of France stands in the welfare of England.[60]

This letter, whose contents became known to Gloucester, only served to prolong the bitterness. Gloucester denounced it as full of malicious lies, especially the implication that he was about to precipitate a battle. To judge by Beaufort's response, the duke accused the bishop himself of planning a breach of the peace. It is a measure of Beaufort's insecurity that when challenged about the letter, he modified its forthrightness by claiming limply that he simply meant that Gloucester had not done all he could to suppress a rising of London craftsmen and labourers for higher wages.[61]

It was not until Bedford at last arrived in England two months later that the fragile truce achieved by the mediators on 30 October had any hope of being converted into a more formal and more permanent reconciliation. This was achieved at a parliament at Leicester, a good distance away from the disturbed city of London. The writs of summons were sent out on 7 January, almost as soon as Bedford set foot in England, and the interval between summons and assembly (barely six weeks) was one of the shortest in recent memory. Bedford was concerned first and foremost with the maintenance of public order, and to some extent he shared Beaufort's distrust of London. When he and his duchess entered the city on 10 January, they were accompanied by the bishop, much to the dismay and distaste of the citizens. The latter's feelings were controlled in Bedford's presence, and accordingly the cavalcade was met by the mayor; after a brief stop at the bishop of Durham's inn near Charing Cross, it was escorted to the royal palace at Westminster, with Beaufort stopping off at the nearby abbey. The handsome presents offered by the city to Bedford did little to assuage the duke's temper, and he responded with 'but little thanks'.[62]

Parliament opened at Leicester on 18 February 1426. The commons took an unusually long time to elect a speaker; only on 28 February was Sir Richard Vernon eventually presented to the king. The reason for the delay may have been the fact that a great council had already urged spiritual and temporal lords, along with certain knights and esquires, to meet the king beforehand at St Albans on 21 February to discuss the extraordinary problems facing the assembled parliament. The meeting was abortive because Gloucester, then at his Devizes estate (Wiltshire), refused to attend; it was therefore adjourned to Northampton, further along the king's route to Leicester. The duke had even seemed likely to absent himself from parliament until a peremptory royal letter a week before 18 February overcame his stubbornness.[63] Thus displaced by his elder brother as protector and royal lieutenant in parliament, Gloucester's pride made it very difficult for him to travel to Leicester as one among many peers, still less to submit himself to judgement. According to the official roll of the parliament, the dissension between Beaufort and Gloucester was the first and most urgent matter to be discussed, though any course of action required careful deliberation and, probably, an element of bargaining and compromise. Meanwhile, the commons grew anxious for a decision and deputed a prominent lawyer, Roger Hunt (rather than their speaker), to lead a deputation to Bedford to emphasize the dangers of magnate discord. In reply, Bedford and the other lords issued a declaration on 4 March which outlined their proposals for dealing with the quarrel – and to do so impartially, confidentially, and with the twin aims of preserving domestic peace and bringing both parties to a just agreement. To strengthen the chances of success, it was proposed that the lords in this 'remarkably full assembly' should publicly and solemnly bind themselves to uphold any settlement that was reached. A delegation returned to the commons to explain this plan of action, and sheriffs throughout the country were specifically enjoined to keep the peace.[64]

Three days later, on 7 March, Gloucester and Beaufort agreed, at Bedford's request, to submit their quarrel to a panel of arbitrators who would announce a decision to which the two parties would adhere. These arbitrators included Archbishop Chichele, Bishops Langley of Durham, Morgan of Worcester, and Stafford of Bath and Wells (the treasurer), the duke of Exeter, the earl of Stafford, Lord Cromwell, and William Alnwick (keeper of the privy seal). In other words, it was a meeting of the council shorn of Gloucester, Beaufort, and one or two secular lords who rarely attended anyway; but it was not termed a council because the parties involved were themselves councillors. The judgement required each side to forgive and forget anything said or done against the other before 7 March. Gloucester would then undertake to be a 'good lorde' to the bishop, who in turn would declare his affection for Gloucester and undertake to serve him as he should. Similarly, each would be a 'goode lorde' to the followers of the other and adopt an attitude of forgiveness for things past. The bishop thereupon swore an oath of loyalty to the king before the entire assembly of lords and commons, in the presence of Henry VI and Bedford, and he formally denied the charges laid against him. On the lords' advice, Beaufort was declared a true and loyal subject of the king and this was so enacted formally in parliament. The entire procedure was a public humiliation for Beaufort; it was made worse by the arbitrators' insistence that he apologize personally and publicly to Gloucester. A fair balance between the two men was hardly struck when Gloucester was merely requested to express himself willing to receive Beaufort's expressions of affection and good will. The two contestants took each other by the hand in token of their mutual 'love and accorde' in the presence of the king and his parliament. An observer at the scene might be pardoned for concluding that Beaufort was conceding much and that Gloucester's dignity remained unimpaired – perhaps even enhanced by these proceedings. Whatever the attitude of Bedford and Beaufort to London and the apparent sympathy of Duke John for Beaufort's position, it proved difficult to humble Duke Humphrey even in a parliament which met far away from his London friends in the territory of Queen Katherine. It may have been recognized, even by those who had no love for Gloucester, that Beaufort had recently exceeded the bounds of propriety in the provocative promotion of his dependants, whereas Humphrey stood close to the throne itself and would become protector of England again once Bedford had returned to France. It was perhaps inevitable that Beaufort who had seized much should lose most at Leicester.

Beaufort resigned the chancellorship of England a few days later on 16 March; at the same time, Bishop Stafford vacated the office of treasurer. They were replaced by respected and experienced men in whom most of the councillors had confidence: Archbishop Kemp took the great seal and Sir Walter Hungerford the treasurership. Already, before parliament met, the delayed appointments to the offices of sheriff and escheator had been made, with a distinct attempt to avoid those who moved in the Beaufort circle, and to favour instead men who, to judge by their careers, may have been circumspectly chosen by Bedford.[65] On 14 May, Beaufort was given permission to undertake a pilgrimage overseas, probably to Rome.[66]

This Leicester parliament came to be known as the 'Parliament of Bats', a sobriquet which conveys something of the tense atmosphere in which it met. Because of the recent unrest in London and the blistering attacks directed by Gloucester and Beaufort at one another – not to speak of other magnate rivalries which had been simmering for years – all those who congregated at Leicester, whether they were members of the parliament or their followers, were instructed to leave swords, bucklers, bows, and arrows at their inns. But fifteenth-century men were reluctant to venture abroad unarmed, and so they hid bats 'in their neckys'. These could be just as offensive as more conventional weapons, and next day they too were ordered to be left at home. The retainers of the lords finally resorted to carrying large stones in the voluminous folds and sleeves of their attire as they crowded near the parliament chamber.[67]

Not only did the Gloucester–Beaufort quarrel strain men's loyalties at this parliament and threaten the edifice of the law in the country at large. Bedford also found himself having to reconcile as best he could the long-standing rivalry between Lord Talbot and the earl of Ormond, for both were present at Leicester. Moreover, the Earl Marshal and the earl of Warwick may still have been in dispute over questions of precedence which had been discussed in the parliament of 1425. The material from which quarrels and violence among seignorial retinues could arise was undoubtedly in the mind of those who banned the carrying of weapons in Leicester.[68] Strenuous efforts were made to achieve a settlement of the most serious of all the disputes, and in the short term at least they had some success. The Talbot–Ormond quarrel was just as intractable and perhaps more violent; events over the next twenty years indicate that no real solution to it was found at Leicester. The problem of precedence had been formally solved in 1425; now, to soothe his offended dignity and quieten the discord, Norfolk was elevated to a dukedom.[69] In fact, the creation of Norfolk and the young earl of Cambridge as dukes, together with the elevation of relatively large numbers to the rank of knighthood (about thirty-six in all), may be regarded as an attempt to gratify the aristocracy, reward a number of soldiers who had distinguished themselves in France, fortify the knightly obligations of well-born young men at a time of intensive warfare, and promote the unity and loyalty of the king's most influential subjects by a ceremonial act that enhanced the monarch's own honour.[70] The four-year-old king was himself knighted by Bedford on 19 May 1426, during the parliamentary session. In view of the unsteady political situation, it may have appeared desirable to emphasize the king's position in this way, especially since it was a customary preliminary to coronation, which had not yet taken place but may have been in the mind of some even at this juncture.[71] The knighting ceremony had been arranged a fortnight before: on 4 May twenty-four men of largely aristocratic birth were summoned to receive the honour, and a week later messengers were sent to at least five shires bidding certain other esquires to join them. At the same time, several lords who had not yet attended the parliament were again requested to do so, presumably to witness the event and enhance its dignity. After his own knighting, King

Henry then proceeded to dub the heirs of several magnates (including Norfolk, Northumberland, and – by a skilful stroke – Ormond and Talbot), several young magnates (York, Oxford, Westmorland, Roos, Mautravers, Fauconberg, Latimer, Welles, and Berkeley), as well as distinguished war commanders like Sir Edmund Hungerford, Sir William ap Thomas, Sir Richard Woodville, and Sir Ralph Botiller, who could expect favours from the hands of the French regent they had served. Hardly any of these was younger than the king himself; a number of the aristocrats had reached the customary age of fifteen, and many of the soldiers were youngish men.

A delicate political balance, 1427–29

Bedford's sojourn in England until March 1427 acted as a solvent of the acrimony between the Beaufort and Gloucester factions which was threatening the effectiveness of the king's government. In his relations with the pope and in the appointment of bishops, Duke John had largely succeeded in restoring normality by early April 1426. In secular affairs, too, he attempted a modest improvement, though it should be remembered that his sympathies lay more with Beaufort than with his brother Gloucester.

It was unusual for the annual appointment of new sheriffs to be delayed much beyond the beginning of December, but on this occasion it was 15 January 1426, three weeks after the arrival of Bedford in the realm, before the council issued the necessary commissions for the coming year. Servants of both Bishop Beaufort and Gloucester seem to have been excluded as far as possible. Instead, in Gloucestershire, John Greville, Bedford's receiver-general, was pricked, and in Surrey–Sussex a kinsman of Archbishop Kemp, Sir Thomas Lewkenore.[72] An utterly reliable Lancastrian servant, John Merbury, became sheriff of Herefordshire, while Sir William Palton (in Devon) was closely connected with Lord Botreaux and, to some extent, Lord Tiptoft.[73] Even in the traditionally Beaufort-dominated shrievalty of Oxfordshire –Berkshire, a more neutral sheriff was installed, Sir Richard Walkestede, chamberlain of north Wales since 1423 and a former servant of Henry V. Sir Richard Hastings, appointed in Yorkshire, had also seen service in France under the great Harry and had been constable of Knaresborough castle since 1422; his connections were with the Percies. Likewise in Staffordshire, the new sheriff, Sir John Bagot, had served the Lancastrians in wartime, in his case since John of Gaunt's day.[74] Some attempt at healing and settling was probably being made. Beaufort's replacement as chancellor by Archbishop Kemp and Hungerford's appointment as treasurer pointed in the same direction.[75]

One may even see the election of Simon Sydenham as bishop of Salisbury in September 1426 in the same light. The new bishop would later nominate Lord Hungerford as a supervisor of his will, and the relationship between the two men may have been formed as early as 1414, when both went on embassy to Germany.[76] Martin V, who was campaigning more vigorously than ever for a revision of the statute of provisors that limited his powers of provision to English and Welsh sees, withheld his assent to Sydenham's election. Much of the pope's anger was directed against Archbishop Chichele, though some he reserved for Gloucester and Archbishop Kemp. Bedford meanwhile returned to France. Only Bishop Beaufort was considered friendly, though his usefulness to Martin V was curtailed by his absence on crusade in Germany. Nevertheless, the pope resolved to provide Beaufort's nephew, Robert Neville, to Salisbury on 9 July 1427, thereby quashing the election of Sydenham. It looks as if Neville's candidacy had been accepted by the council itself after Bishop Chaundler's death in July 1426, but the chapter at Salisbury intervened to elect Sydenham; after the return of Bedford to France the council lacked the will to stand by its earlier decision (or else the withdrawal of Bedford and Beaufort weakened Neville's position) and it allowed Sydenham to pursue his election – in vain. It was Beaufort's support for his nephew, communicated to Martin by letter from Malines (in Brabant), which proved crucial.[77] The political rivalries in England were therefore demonstrably in danger of paralysing English government and allowing political decisions to be warped by factional – even external – influences.

Beaufort's resignation as chancellor in March 1426 did not mean that his influence was entirely negated; it certainly did not mean that his rival, Gloucester, could enjoy unfettered power so long as Bedford remained in the kingdom (until 19 March 1427). Hence, among the sheriffs elected in December 1426 was (in Oxfordshire–Berkshire) Sir Thomas Wykeham, one of the bishop's 'connection'; in November 1427, after Bedford had returned to France and Beaufort had embarked on crusade, William Allington, Sir Richard Vernon, and Thomas Stonor were pricked.[78] Nor should Bishop Neville's provision to Salisbury be overlooked as evidence of Beaufort's continuing influence in the realm. Nevertheless, after March 1427 Gloucester doubtless savoured a rare taste of freedom from the irksome presence of his brother and his uncle, for Beaufort did not return until 1 September 1428 and Bedford not before the protectorate came to an end. Beaufort's influence revived when he (a newly-created cardinal) landed back in England and the likelihood of a renewed confrontation between duke and bishop grew strong again. In November 1428 at least three of Beaufort's circle became sheriffs. They were friends of John Golafre, a member of the Chaucer circle which was devoted to the bishop's interest: Sir Walter de la Pole (in Cambridgeshire–Huntingdonshire); his brother-in-law, Robert James (in Oxfordshire–Berkshire, where Chaucerian influence was almost beyond challenge); and William Brocas (in Hampshire).[79]

At the same time, the role of Richard Beauchamp, earl of Warwick was becoming more conspicuous, not least because of his appointment as the king's guardian on 1 June 1428. To some extent, he was able to step into Bedford's shoes as a steadying and moderating influence in politics. Among the sheriffs appointed later in 1428 were three of his servants: Robert Andrew (in Gloucestershire), Philip Chetwynd (in Staffordshire), and John Nanfan (in Cornwall).[80] Care was also taken to include among the new sheriffs at least two royal servants who were closely connected with the king's government: John Hotoft (pricked for Essex–Hertfordshire) was treasurer of the king's household, and Sir John Cockayne (in Nottinghamshire–Derbyshire) was another long-standing Lancastrian servant.[81] Nevertheless, it may have been Beaufort's presence that helped to determine who should succeed Bishop Rickinghale at Chichester early in July 1429. Although Thomas Brouns, Archbishop Chichele's chancellor, was elected by the cathedral chapter and received the king's assent, Pope Martin preferred Simon Sydenham, the unsuccessful candidate for Salisbury in 1426–27, and his choice probably received Beaufort's support.[82] In the duchy of Lancaster, too, the cardinal's influence over appointments seems to have revived after his return to England. Sir William Harrington, who was connected by marriage to the late duke of Exeter, was made chief steward of Lancashire on 5 October 1429 and secured the shrievalty of Yorkshire a month later.[83]

John, duke of Bedford had momentarily succeeded in calming the political storms that raged about Beaufort and Gloucester during the autumn and winter of 1425; his continued presence in England until 1427, and Beaufort's own absence abroad, helped to restore normal political life in the country. Beaufort's return did not mean an immediate recurrence of violent or blatant partisanship, but political stability in the country was made a whit more precarious and the council's conduct of government would henceforward have to be more finely balanced.

Disposing of the king's patronage, 1422–29

The crown's material resources were considerable and were constantly, if fortuitously, replenished. The death of a well-endowed tenant-in-chief when his heir was still young, or the forfeiture of a substantial estate as a result of rebellion, provided the crown with resources of patronage which, if circumspectly awarded, could satisfy the aspirations of individuals, ensure social stability throughout the realm, and augment the monarchy's financial reserves. During Henry VI's minority, it was the council's duty, in accordance with its commission of December 1422, to supervise these resources and bestow this patronage; the principles which it adopted for its guidance shed light on the nature of conciliar government itself.[84]

The estates of a ward of the crown were likely to bring profit to their custodian, even if they were enjoyed for only a short time and despite the customary obligation to maintain the property and its buildings in a satisfactory state of repair. Moreover, an estate supported servants, officers, and annuitants with whom it was useful for a custodian to establish a co-operative relationship that might well outlast his temporary tenure of the estate. For the crown to bestow such properties on its own servants, supporters, or councillors was an economical method of financial reward. The marriage of an heiress, although initially it might prove an expensive purchase for what could be (to quote a comment about Richard II's first queen) 'a small bit of body', offered even greater advantage to the recipient.[85] And the same can be said of that growing regiment of wealthy widows whom English land law often left endowed with extensive estates. To have a dazzling marriage at one's disposal opened up the prospect of forging links with wealthy families that might transcend a generation and more. The forfeited estates of attainted rebels were also at the crown's disposal, and if they were not restored when memories grew dim or politics interceded, they might become a permanent acquisition for the fortunate recipient of the king's bounty.[86]

The crown was the fulcrum of this scheme of patronage. At first, it was the circumspect intention of the council, formally announced in parliament in December 1422, that its disposal of such 'casualties' should be dictated solely by the financial interests of the king: wardships, marriages, and properties would be bestowed at the most profitable rates and without partiality, favour, or fraud.[87] In practice this ideal was observed more in the breach than in its fulfilment. In February 1423 the council imposed one temporary restraint upon itself. It was agreed (presumably at the request of the lords concerned, three of whom were themselves councillors) that if any of the lords, led by Exeter, Norfolk, Willoughby, and Sir Walter Hungerford, should die during the expedition on which they were about to embark, and leave a minor as his heir, the latter's wardship would be granted to the lord's widow or to his executors or nominees. It is true that in return the guardian would be expected to pay an annual sum, but there is no doubt that this privilege, extended to the country's military leaders, limited the council's exercise of royal patronage.[88] Its powers were more profoundly modified by the practical political needs of the 1420s. For example, on 15 May 1423, a week before the closing date by which bids were to be received, special arrangements were made for the sheriff of Oxfordshire–Berkshire, William Lisle, to name any suitable farm or other reward which, it was conceded, he could have at an unusually low price.[89] Furthermore, it was impossible to avoid the habits of centuries: those who secured the royal favour would enjoy the royal bounty, and during Henry VI's minority it was influence in the council that directed the flow of patronage. All but the most modest of decisions were collective ones after 1422, and not those of any single individual, even if he were the protector; but there were a host of ways of reaching a collective decision.[90]

Henry VI's councillors wove a pattern of patronage whose main strands were apparent even before 1422. Some of the greatest favours had then been extended to the Beaufort family and its 'connection'. For example, the lands of the young earl of Oxford, John de Vere, had been placed in the custody of the duke of Exeter after the death of the earl's father in 1417, and these properties Exeter continued to manage to his own profit after Henry V's demise. He advised his young charge in the choice of a wife, and by September 1425 John de Vere had married Elizabeth, daughter of Sir John Howard, a knight in the service of the queen-dowager, Joan of Navarre; this was in despite of the council, which had planned to deploy his marriage as security for loans made to the crown by individual councillors.[91] Thomas Courtenay, who was only eight years old when his father, the earl of Devon, died in June 1422, may also have been in Beaufort care when Henry V died, for he married Margaret, a daughter of John Beaufort, the late earl of Somerset, and a niece of both Henry Beaufort and the duke of Exeter.[92] Their nephew, Sir Richard Neville, had custody of the property and marriage of the heir of Richard, Lord Scrope of Bolton, from September 1420, and soon afterwards he successfully resisted a challenge to his rights from the young scholar Marmaduke Lumley, whom Scrope had patronized.[93] This favour, with the social influence and economic benefit which it implied, continued to be enjoyed by the Beauforts and their relatives after 1422. It strengthened a position among the English nobility, particularly in the north country, whereby Beaufort blood coursed through the veins of a number of lordly families. The daughters of Joan Beaufort by the earl of Westmorland married Stafford, Despenser, Northumberland, Norfolk, and Greystoke; their son Richard wedded Alice, heiress of the earl of Salisbury. And if Joan's kinship with the royal house facilitated these *coups*, the military services of Exeter secured further favours, whilst Bishop Beaufort's wealth inveigled other patronage from the Lancastrian monarchs for himself and his relatives.

Both Westmorland and Exeter were distinguished members of the council and important figures in the opening years of Henry's reign. They also cornered some of the most valuable items of royal patronage – and within a year of the proclamation inviting open bidding. On 13 December 1423 the custody of the twelve-year-old Richard, duke of York was granted to the earl of Westmorland, and the boy was henceforward brought up in the Neville–Beaufort household; within a year he had married Cecily, one of the earl's daughters by Joan Beaufort. When Earl Ralph died in October 1425, Duke Richard was placed in the countess's custody. At first she took 200 marks annually from his Dorset and Suffolk estates to pay for his upbringing, but this was increased by a further 100 marks on 20 May 1426, after the duke had been knighted.[94] Parts of Duke Richard's estates that were inherited from his uncle, the earl of March, who died in Ireland in January 1425, were granted to Exeter, who enjoyed the East Anglian estates (including the honour of Clare) from 1 May 1425 until his death at the end of 1426.[95] The fact that Bishop Beaufort was chancellor of England at this juncture doubtless assisted the claims of his relatives to the York estates and their heir. Significantly, two of Beaufort's closest associates among the gentry benefited from royal patronage at about the same time and probably for the self-same reason. In May 1425 Sir Edward Stradling, his son-in-law, received joint custody of certain estates of the earldom of March in south-west Wales, while on 26 February 1426, three weeks before Beaufort's removal from the chancery, Thomas Chaucer, his kinsman and servant, secured custody of Joan, daughter and heiress of Sir John Drayton, for 100 marks.[96] Beaufort's decided inclination to reserve at least the marriages of widows for selected individuals may not have escaped the commons' attention, for at Leicester early in 1426 they complained that as chancellor he had been refusing to license widows' remarriage in return for the usual fine.[97]

The Beauforts were not alone in capitalizing on their influential position on the council, for others were able to benefit handsomely from the crown's patronage in the 1420s. Not least among them was the protector himself. Although Exeter had secured part of the earldom of March, Gloucester received the bulk of it. Furthermore, his own enormous salary as protector of 8,000 marks was partly secured on the wardship lands (up to 1,000 marks) of Thomas, Lord Roos, who spent his teenage years at the king's court, and partly (up to 800 marks) on those of Ralph, second earl of Westmorland.[98] The duke of Bedford's access to the crown's resources was inevitably more restricted, but his stay in England during 1425–27 enabled him to acquire some items, most notably the de Vere estates of the earl of Oxford after the death of Exeter in December 1426.[99]

Few of the persons and properties that fell into the crown's custody during the protectorate were in fact retained by it; most of them were quickly disposed of to influential persons. Not even the bulk of the Roos properties were retained for long, though their heir lived with the king in his household.[100] Admittedly, these particular estates were much reduced in value by the claims of two dowagers; but nevertheless, in June 1425 the remainder was farmed to Lord Cromwell and a Roos family retainer, Robert Hutton, for a £500 annual payment.[101] The crown capitalized on the opportunities afforded by the wardship of Thomas himself, for in December 1423, when he was seventeen, he was licensed to marry whom he wished in return for 1,000 marks; in the event, a daughter of the earl of Warwick became his wife in about 1427, just before the earl was appointed King Henry's guardian.[102]

The crown's practical control over these resources was further limited by its need to discharge certain debts and responsibilities. This is graphically illustrated by the case of Sir John Radcliffe, seneschal of Aquitaine from 1423 to 1436. His extensive military service in northern France and Aquitaine had placed the government massively in his debt for both his own wages and those of the retinues he engaged. As a result, one valuable wardship and two marriages were assigned to him in part-payment: on 24 July 1425 he was granted the wardship and marriage of John, son and heir of Sir Henry Beaumont, for £600; in the following year, he received the 200 marks which Elizabeth, widow of Sir John Clifford, had to pay to secure her freedom to marry whom she wished. Then, in the same year, the marriage of the young earl of Westmorland was given to Radcliffe to help defray unpaid wages as seneschal of Aquitaine of 2,000 marks, but this he seems to have sold (no doubt profitably) soon afterwards to the eager earl of Northumberland; eventually, in the autumn of 1426 Earl Ralph was married off to Northumberland's widowed sister, Elizabeth.[103] Finally, in February 1428 Radcliffe's petition for £200 worth of the lands of Sir Andrew Bagney was conceded by the council.[104]

Rarely in these years do wardships and marriages appear to have been granted in return for an annual farm which would bring in a steady, though hardly spectacular, income for the crown. More often were they bestowed in return for a single initial payment, which produced ready cash in the short term but would not enable the government to exploit these resources for as long as the heir remained a minor. The greatest benefit frequently accrued to the individual magnate, especially if he was of the Beaufort 'connection'.

Several marriages slipped through the fingers of the crown's agents and were only registered by commissioners appointed periodically to establish if any of the crown's feudal rights – wardships, marriages, reliefs, or payments for alienating land – were being concealed. After all, not even the king's council could control the dictates of love or determine the private machinations of families. But when such things were revealed by commissioners, those involved were made to pay for their indiscretion or presumption. John Holand, earl of Huntingdon, married the widow of the earl of March without securing a royal licence; he found the large fine of 1,200 marks so crushing that he was allowed to pay half of it within three years and the rest after the king came of age – which was far in the future.[105] No less painful was the £1,000 fine imposed in March 1423 on Margery, widow of John, Lord Roos, for marrying without authorization Roger Wentworth, a mere Yorkshire squire.[106]

However, such vigilance did not characterize the government between 1424 and 1427. Indeed, in November 1426, Nicholas Thorley and Alice, formerly the earl of Oxford's wife, were freely pardoned for marrying without royal permission, and those of Alice's dower lands which had been seized for their offence were now returned. Thorley had meantime been pardoned in February 1424 in return for one year's income from his wife's estates, and in December 1424 they were both fined a further £100; but the exchequer's proposal to impose further sanctions in 1426 was ignored by the government.[107] Beaufort as chancellor and Bedford during his period as protector proved strangely insensitive to the potential profit from the king's feudal rights –

strangely, in view of Beaufort's sharp financial acumen in advancing his own interests. Licences allowing widows to marry seem to have been granted rarely in the years after 1423, so rarely in fact that the commons in the 1426 parliament became restive about the chancellor's apparent refusal to issue them; they also drew attention to his failure to license alienations of land (also in return for a fine) by tenants-in-chief to the church and other institutions.[108] But these complaints went largely unheeded for the moment, and only after Bedford had left for France in March 1427 was administrative action taken. Thereafter, a spate of investigations was launched in all parts of the country into feudal rights of the crown which had been concealed. The most comprehensive was that initiated on 20 July 1427, only four months after Bedford set sail.[109]

The council, under Beaufort's direction and then Bedford's, was somewhat careless of the crown's fuedal resources, their financial value, and the political and social purposes to which they could be put. When they were disposed of, it was frequently in a way calculated to further the factional interests and partisan influence of the Beauforts. This in 1424–27 was a consequence of the widening divisions within the government and the serious clash between the bishop and Duke Humphrey. In the few remaining years of the protectorate, a modest effort was made to remedy a situation which had already concerned parliament in 1426.

Notes

1 *RP*, IV, 170. Justices, sheriffs, and escheators were specifically mentioned.

2 *List of sheriffs for England and Wales* (PRO, Lists and Indexes, IX, 1898) has details of appointment.

3 Roskell, *1422*, pp. 238-9; R. Somerville, *History of the duchy of Lancaster*, I (1956), 389, 462.

4 Below, pp. 33, 55.

5 Roskell, *1422*, pp. 233-5, 153-5, 167-9. Bonville had married a daughter of Lord Grey of Ruthin in 1414, and his brother, Thomas, a daughter of Lord St John. Cockayne was a duchy of Lancaster annuitant and the nephew of John Cockayne, justice of the common bench from 1406 to 1429.

6 Roskell, *Speakers*, pp. 197-9.

7 Roskell, *1422*, pp. 204-5; below, p. 97. Mountford was related to the Beauchamps and to Lord Clinton.

8 Roskell, *1422*, pp. 201-3; Somerville, op. cit., pp. 398, 647.

9 Carr, *BBCS*, XXII (1967), 260-70. John was a protégé of Thomas Chaucer, Beaufort's cousin, and he joined the bishop's retinue on the 1431 expedition; in 1413 he had married the earl of Oxford's daughter.

10 PRO, E28/43/10; E. Price, 'Ralph, Lord Cromwell and his household' (London MA thesis, 1948), pp. 23ff; above, p. 21 (Cromwell); *CPR, 1422–29*, p. 116; PRO, E403/661 m. 12 (Burgh); *PPC*, III, 118-21, 37-8, 85 (Burton). Burton should be distinguished from Thomas Burton, treasurer

of Cardinal Beaufort's household in February 1429 (PRO, E403/688 m. 11).

11 R. G. Davies, thesis, I, 336-8; III, xxii-xxiii, xcii-xciv; Emden, *Oxford*, I, 118-19, 444. Both appointments originated with Martin V and probably for that reason Bishop Cliderow did not have the temporalities of his see restored to him for some years. Similarly, the papal provision of John Wells, a friar, to Llandaff in July 1423 was not immediately followed by the restoration of the see's temporalities. Below, p. 72.
12 R. G. Davies, thesis, I, 326.
13 ibid., 341-51; Jacob, *Essays in later medieval history*, pp. 40-1; above, p. 14.
14 R. G. Davies, thesis, I, 343, 353; below, p. 72.
15 Roskell, *1422*, pp. 226-9 (Tyrell), 194-6 (Lancastre, who seems to have died not long after his appointment in November 1423); above, p. 35 (Allington); PRO, E28/48/3 (Lenthale). Lenthale also served Queen Katherine (*Amundesham*, I, 65).
16 Above, p. 69; R. G. Davies, thesis, I, 327.
17 Below, p. 179.
18 For comparable effects of his absence on law and order, see below, p. 138.
19 R. A. Griffiths, 'The rise of the Stradlings of St Donat's', *Trans. Glamorgan Hist. Soc.*, VII (1963), 22-30. The marriage had taken place before 1423.
20 J. S. Roskell, 'Sir Richard Vernon of Haddon, speaker in the parliament of Leicester, 1426', *Derbs. Arch. Journal*, LXXXII (1962), 43-53; Roskell, *1422*, pp. 231-3 (Vernon), 184-6 (Golafre). For the Chaucer circle, see Ruud, op. cit., pp. 5-20, and Lydgate's celebratory verses in H. N. MacCracken (ed.), *The minor poems of John Lydgate*, part 2 (EETS, 192, 1934), pp. 657-9.
21 C. L. Kingsford (ed.), *The Stonor letters and papers, 1290–1483*, I (Camden Soc., 3rd series, XXIX, 1919), xix-xxi (Stonor); PRO, KB9/222/2/50; 1046/51 (Wyot, 1427, 1430); A. Gooder (ed.), *The parliamentary representation of the county of York, 1258–1832*, I (Yorks. Arch. Soc., XCI, 1935), 179-80 (Langton).
22 Somerville, op. cit., p. 417; *PPC*, III, 250-1; above, p. 34.
23 Somerville, op. cit., pp. 533, 513, 515; above, p. 36.
24 The cardinalate was offered to Beaufort twice (in 1418 and 1426) by Martin V, who was shortly to provide Robert Neville to Salisbury 'moved solely by the cardinal's prayer'. R. G. Davies, thesis, I, 376-8.
25 C. T. Allmand, 'The relations between the English government, the higher clergy and the papacy in Normandy, 1417–50' (Oxford DPhil thesis, 1963), ch. V, VI.
26 R. G. Davies, thesis, I, 351-2; Jacob, *Essays in later medieval history*, p. 42. The chapters of Bath and Wells, the council, and the pope appear to have concurred in this appointment with unusual speed (R. G. Davies, thesis, III, cclxvi). Cf. L. R. Betcherman, 'The making of bishops in the Lancastrian period', *Speculum*, XLI (1966), 409 n. 172, who regards Stafford as more friendly to Gloucester than to Beaufort.
27 R. G. Davies, thesis, I, 351-2, 357-8; III, vi; Emden, *Cambridge*, p. 11. For his influential connections, see *Amundesham*, I, 300.
28 R. G. Davies, thesis, I, 354. See Nigota, thesis, pp. 173-203, for Kemp's machinations on his own behalf.
29 R. G. Davies, thesis, III, cxxxiii-cxxxv; Emden, *Oxford*, II, 808-9.
30 R. G. Davies, thesis, I, 357-64.

31 Fleming's unedifying experience during 1424–26 may have chastened him to such a degree that his health had deteriorated by 1428 and in 1431 he died, still only in his forties (ibid., III, cxxi).

32 Allmand, thesis, ch. V; Betcherman, *Speculum*, XLI (1966), 409.

33 PRO, E159/202 *brevia directa baronibus*, E. m. 1. The constable of the Tower was John Holand, earl of Huntingdon.

34 Below, p. 74.

35 Above, p. 72.

36 The fullest accounts are in *Brut*, p. 432, and 'Gregory's Chron.', p. 159, though the latter misdates the events by one month to September. See Vickers, op. cit., ch. V.

37 'Gregory's Chron.', p. 159; *Great Chron.*, pp. 136-7.

38 'Gregory's Chron.', p. 159; *London Chrons.*, p. 76.

39 ibid., p. 130; *English Chron.*, pp. 53-4; *Chron. of London*, p. 114; *Great Chron.*, p. 136; *Brut*, p. 432; 'Gregory's Chron.', p. 158. Beaufort accused Gloucester too of recruiting from the inns (*Great Chron.*, p. 142; *London Chrons.*, pp. 76-84).

40 'Gregory's Chron.', p. 158; *Great Chron.*, p. 136.

41 *English Chron.*, pp. 53-4; *Brut*, p. 432; 'Gregory's Chron.', p. 159. Beaufort claimed that Gloucester urged the mayor and aldermen to assemble 300 horsemen on 30 October (*Great Chron.*, p. 142; *London Chrons.*, pp. 76-84).

42 'Gregory's Chron.', p. 159; *London Chrons.*, pp. 76-84; *Great Chron.*, p. 139.

43 *English Chron.*, pp. 53-4; *Brut*, p. 432.

44 'Gregory's Chron.', p. 158; *Great Chron.*, p. 136. Cf. Beaufort's justification for the appointment of a new custodian in ibid., p. 140, and *London Chrons.*, pp. 76-84.

45 'Gregory's Chron.', p. 158; *Great Chron.*, p. 136. The councillors who authorized the appointment on 26 February included Chichele, Beaufort (chancellor), Bishops Kemp of London, Morgan of Worcester, Stafford of Bath and Wells (treasurer), Lords Scrope, Tiptoft, and Hungerford, Sir John Cornwall, and William Alnwick (keeper of the privy seal) (PRO, E159/202 *brevia directa baronibus*, E. m. 1). Woodville had 30 men-at-arms and 50 archers under his command for three weeks, and 20 men-at-arms and 40 archers thereafter until the end of October 1425 (PRO, E403/669 m. 14).

46 The appealer also incriminated men from other towns, including Canterbury, Leicester, Exeter, Bristol, Coventry, York, and Chester, in an extravagant outburst (*Great Chron.*, p. 136; 'Gregory's Chron.', p. 158).

47 ibid., pp. 157-8; *RP*, IV, 275-6. Beaufort claimed that he had even been warned not to attend the parliament at Westminster (*London Chrons.*, pp. 76-84; *Great Chron.*, p. 141).

48 ibid., p. 141; *London Chrons.*, pp. 76-84.

49 *GEC*, XI, 17-18; R. A. Newhall, *The English Conquest of Normandy, 1416–1424* (New Haven, 1924), pp. 171, 178, 205, 217, 220, 222, 241, 290.

50 *Great Chron.*, pp. 138-43; *London Chrons.*, pp. 76-84.

51 *Three Chrons.*, p. 59; *London Chrons.*, p. 76; *Brut*, pp. 567, 499.

52 ibid., p. 567.

53 *London Chrons.*, pp. 76-84; *Great Chron.*, p. 141.

54 Moreover, major repairs were authorized for the Tower on 12 May 1425

(*CPR, 1422-29*, p. 304). For Friar Randolf and his contacts with Gloucester, see Myers, *BJRL*, XXIV (1940), 4-5; Vickers, op. cit., pp. 181-3, 276-7.

55 *London Chrons.*, pp. 76-84; *Great Chron.*, p. 138. In the sixteenth century Edward Hall (*Chronicle*, ed. H. Ellis [1809], p. 131) stated that the bishop's plan was to take Henry VI from Eltham to Windsor.

56 'Gregory's Chron.', p. 158; *Great Chron.*, p. 136. In the event, Henry was brought from Eltham to London on 5 November by Gloucester and all the available lords ('Gregory's Chron.', p. 160).

57 PRO, E403/673 m. 1; *London Chrons.*, p. 82; *Great Chron.*, p. 137. The council appears to have been urged to take this eleventh-hour step by emissaries from the duke of Bedford who included Sir Ralph Botiller and 'Master Lewis'.

58 Giles, pp. 7-8; *Brut*, p. 432; 'Gregory's Chron.', p. 159; *Great Chron.*, p. 136. Coimbra was the son of King John I of Portugal and Philippa, John of Gaunt's daughter. He appears to have been in England earlier in the year, when he was made a knight of the garter (*Brut*, pp.156-7).

59 'Gregory's Chron.', p. 159.

60 *London Chrons.*, p. 84; *Great Chron.*, p. 137.

61 ibid.

62 *Brut*, pp. 433, 453; *Great Chron.*, pp. 137-8; 'Gregory's Chron.', p. 160.

63 ibid.; *Great Chron.*, p. 138; PRO, E403/673 m. 13.

64 *RP*, IV, 296; PRO, E403/673 m. 13 (4 March); J. S. Roskell, 'The problem of attendance of the lords in medieval parliaments', *BIHR*, XXIX (1956), 184 (for the quotation). The list of lords recorded in *London Chrons.*, p. 88, as swearing the oath numbered 33 (including Oxford and Roos, who were under age, but excluding Grey of Rougemont, Grey of Ruthin, FitzWalter, and Berkeley, the abbots of St Mary's, York, and St Albans, and the bishop of Hereford, who were not present). The list in *Great Chron.*, pp. 149-50, included the above temporal lords. For Hunt, who had ties with Tiptoft and Norfolk, see Roskell, *Speakers*, pp. 207-8.

65 Above, p. 37. *Brut*, p. 568, noted that many new officers were appointed in this parliament.

66 *Foedera*, IV, iv, 121.

67 'Gregory's Chron.', p. 160; *Great Chron.*, pp. 138-44.

68 *Brut*, p. 433; Giles, pp. 7, 8-9; above, p. 79.

69 Above, p. 14; Giles, pp. 8-9.

70 Although 24 were summoned to Leicester to be knighted, most chroniclers agree that about 36 were actually dubbed (*Foedera*, IV, iv, 121 [23 and the king]; *Brut*, pp. 499 [38], 568 [24]; *London Chrons.*, pp. 95 [36], 130-1 [38]; 'Gregory's Chron.', p. 160 [35]; *Three Chrons.*, p. 59 [34]; *Amundesham*, I, 16 [37]; *Great Chron.*, pp. 149-50 [36]). See F. H. Winkler, 'The making of king's knights in England, 1399–1461' (Yale PhD thesis, 1943), pp. 78-92.

71 *Great Chron.*, p. 149.

72 Roskell, *1422*, pp. 187-8, 197-9.

73 Griffiths, *Principality of Wales*, pp. 132-4; Roskell, *1422*, pp. 207-8. Neither Palton nor Lewkenore had strong political commitments, which may have commended them to the council in the over-heated atmosphere of 1425–26.

74 R. A. Griffiths, 'Patronage, politics and the principality of Wales, 1413–1461', in H. Hearder and H. R. Loyn (ed.), *British government and*

administration: studies presented to S. B. Chrimes (Cardiff, 1974), p. 80; Somerville, op. cit., p. 525; Gooder, op. cit., pp. 183-5 (Hastings); J. C. Wedgwood, 'Staffordshire parliamentary history', *William Salt Soc.*, 1917, pp. 149-50 (Bagot).

75 Above, p. 37.

76 R. G. Davies, thesis, III, cclxxxi.

77 ibid., I, 368-71; 375-9; above, p. 71. Beaufort was on his way to fight the Hussites (Holmes, *EHR*, LXXXVIII [1973], 722).

78 Roskell, *1422*, pp. 239-41. For the Beaufort sympathies of Allington, Vernon, and Stonor, see above, pp. 35, 71.

79 Roskell, *1422*, pp. 172-4, 193-4, 156-7.

80 ibid., p. 147; above, p. 64; Wedgwood, *Biographies*, pp. 621-2.

81 Roskell, *1422*, pp. 191, 167-9.

82 R. G. Davies, thesis, I, 380; III, lxii; Emden, *Oxford*, III, 1838. The English government announced its approval of Sydenham's appointment early in January 1431.

83 Somerville, op. cit., p. 492; J. S. Roskell, *The knights of the shire for the county palatine of Lancaster, 1377-1460* (Chetham Soc., n.s., XCVI, 1937), pp. 16, 179.

84 *RP*, IV, 175-6.

85 McKisack, *The fourteenth century, 1307–1399* (Oxford, 1959), p. 427 n. 1.

86 Most of the estates of the attainted Henry, Lord Scrope of Masham (d. 1415) were farmed or granted outright to Henry, Lord FitzHugh, and for a time he enjoyed undisputed possession of them. But from 1423 onwards, Scrope's brother and heir, John, campaigned for their recovery by legal and illegal means; not until 1442 was the dispute settled by a bargain which deprived FitzHugh's heir of at least part of what had been granted to his father. Ross, thesis, pp. 197, 201-2, 208-15.

87 *RP*, IV, 175-6. A proclamation of 4 March 1423 tried to put this into effect by inviting prospective purchasers of wardships and marriages to appear before the treasurer of England by 23 May, when preference would be given to the highest bidder (*CCR, 1422–30*, p. 67).

88 *PPC*, III, 38. In fact, none of the lords died on this expedition to France.

89 ibid., 86. The council may not yet have abandoned its declared policy, for a month after the closing date for bids, on 27 June 1423, Sir John Cornwall was assigned 500 marks a year out of the wardship lands of Sir John Arundel, to recompense him for surrendering a French prisoner, but only if the next parliament agreed (ibid., 108-10).

90 *RP*, IV, 175.

91 *GEC*, X, 236-8; *CPR, 1422–29*, p. 271. The king had already been given £1,000 for the marriage (which presumably had to be returned) and de Vere was eventually pardoned for his effrontery only in return for a £2,000 fine (ibid., p. 543). On 19 May 1423 Exeter was allowed £100 *per annum* for his expenses in taking charge of Oxford during his minority (*PPC*, III, 93; PRO, E28/41/101). For Sir John Howard, see Roskell, *1422*, pp. 191-3.

92 *GEC*, IV, 326-7. The Courtenay estates (apart from the dower properties) were delivered to the Countess Anne and Lord Talbot on 1 May 1424 during the earl's minority and in return for 700 marks *per annum*. As a mark of special favour, on 20 February 1433 (not 1423, as in ibid, and *HBC*, p. 425) the eighteen-year-old Earl Thomas, who was already a father, was granted the 700 marks and other revenues from the estates, and was enabled to enter

his inheritance without demonstrating proof of age when he became 21; he paid a fine of 1,000 marks for this privilege (*CPR, 1429–36*, p. 271).

93 Ross, thesis, pp. 240-1; R. L. Storey, 'Marmaduke Lumley, bishop of Carlisle, 1430–1450', *TCWAAS*, n.s., LV (1955), 115. The young Lord Scrope, Henry, was the son of Margaret Neville; hence, Sir Richard was his uncle (*GEC*, XI, 543).

94 ibid., XII, ii, 905-6; *CPR, 1422–29*, p. 343. York's first guardian had been the venerable Lancastrian knight Sir Robert Waterton. McFarlane, *The nobility of later mediaeval England* (Oxford, 1973), p. 87, concludes that at 3,000 marks Westmorland had a bargain.

95 *CPR, 1422–29*, pp. 395, 518.

96 *CFR, 1422–30*, p. 100 (though the Stradling grant was revoked on 15 June 1426, after Beaufort's resignation as chancellor [*CPR, 1422–29*, pp. 322, 342]; ibid., p. 330.

97 *RP*, IV, 306-7; above, p. 36.

98 *CPR, 1422–29*, p. 518; *CFR, 1422–30*, pp. 103-4; *PPC*, III, 26-7; above, p. 54. Of the remainder, 4,000 marks came from the duchy of Lancaster and 1,700 marks from the exchequer itself.

99 *PPC*, III, 177-8, 246-7; PRO, E28/41/101 (24 February 1427).

100 On 18 May 1423, 100 marks *per annum* were paid to Thomas, Lord Roos from his estates for his support while he was at court, together with arrears of £40 *per annum* originally granted him by Henry V (*PPC*, III, 88-9).

101 Ross, thesis, pp. 155-6, 158-61. This was not a good bargain for the farmers, for the remainder of the estate was only worth about £500 *per annum*; and if Bedford had not returned in December 1425 to supersede Gloucester as protector, part of whose salary was taken from the Roos income, it would have been worth even less (above, p. 86).

102 *PPC*, III, 129-30; *CPR, 1422–29*, pp. 200-1.

103 ibid., pp. 264, 350; *PPC*, III, 204; PRO, E28/47/52; *GEC*, XII, ii, 549-50.

104 PRO, E28/50/53.

105 *PPC*, III, 252-3 (6 March 1427).

106 ibid., 49, 130; *CPR, 1422–29*, p. 183; *GEC*, XI, 104. Margery, who enjoyed dower rights in the Roos estates, was a Despenser (Ross, thesis, pp. 155-6; above, p. 86). For other examples, see *PPC*, III, 164 (Margaret, Lady Scrope of Bolton, £100); *CPR, 1422–29*, p. 180 (Margaret, Lady Hoo, £200).

107 ibid., p. 422; *PPC*, III, 145-6; PRO, E28/48/39. The marriage had taken place in Henry V's reign.

108 *RP*, IV, 306-7. The government made a negative response. Beaufort may have controlled the marriage of widows in his own interest, rather as he did other aspects of crown patronage (above, p. 86).

109 It may have been as a result of such an inquiry that John Darcy's marriage to Joan, daughter of Lord Greystoke, incurred a 200-mark fine in March 1424 (*CPR, 1422–29*, pp. 406, 464; PRO, E28/50/43). For these commissions up to 1429, about 20 in all, of which 16 were issued from May 1426 onwards and as many as 13 from July 1427, see *CPR, 1422–29*, passim. The new treasurer, Lord Hungerford, may have been more vigorous in this respect than his predecessor.

5   Clients, Patrons, and Politics, 1429–1436

Partisanship and patronage, 1429–33

Despite the king's coronation in November 1429, and the consequential ending of the protectorate, the council continued to reach its decisions about appointments to office and the disposal of royal patronage according to guidelines formulated after the duke of Bedford's return to France in March 1427.[1] Gloucester was disinclined (or unable) to control the granting of wardships, marriages, and offices as tightly as his brother and uncle had done in 1425–27. As the king's chief councillor normally resident in the realm, he may have felt it unnecessary, though it is more likely that his conciliar colleagues were not prepared to allow him such freedom of action. One wonders, too, if Gloucester shared the single-minded determination of his uncle to subject the means of government to his own interests. In fact, the regulations for the conduct of council business that were reaffirmed in February 1430 made it very difficult for any single councillor to make significant decisions alone, and after the king went to France in 1430 it was almost impossible for Gloucester, who was appointed keeper of the realm on 21 April, to do so.[2] Nor does the duke appear to have had many staunch well-wishers among the councillors, with the transparent exception of Lord Scrope of Masham. On several occasions, Scrope's support alone proved too flimsy a means by which Duke Humphrey could persuade the council to his point of view.[3] By contrast, neither Cardinal Beaufort nor the duke of Bedford spent much time in England between 1429 and 1433. Beaufort spent a total of almost three years on a series of missions to France and Burgundy, whilst Bedford did not set foot in England again until late in June 1433. Nevertheless, Beaufort's relatives and clients among the aristocracy and gentry formed a circle that was powerful enough to protect his interests during his absence, and Bedford, as heir to the Lancastrian throne, retained his adherents. During these years, therefore, the king's patronage was open to vigorous personal lobbying and constant political influence; but it did not consistently benefit any one faction, still less Gloucester. Indeed, there is some indication that the Beauforts and their satellites were still able to harvest a number of plums from the disposable resources of the crown, despite the cardinal's foreign travels. Conversely, there is surprisingly little sign that

94

Gloucester availed himself of the opportunity to mulct the crown of rich pickings.

Of the four major estates that came into the crown's hands between 1429 and 1433, three were quickly disposed of to influential persons. William de Moleyns had died at Orléans on 8 May 1429 and at first two-thirds of his lands (apart from his widow's dower) were assigned to his mother and widow jointly, provided they agreed a suitable rate of payment with the treasurer of England. This they failed to do within the required time-limit and so, on 3 November 1431, most of the Moleyns property, together with the marriage of William's daughter and heiress, Eleanor, was transferred to Beaufort's ambitious kinsman, Thomas Chaucer. He was required to pay, not an annual farm that would assure the exchequer a regular income, but 400 marks then and there, and 100 marks later on; moreover, should the Moleyns women die before Eleanor came of age, Chaucer would receive the remaining third of the Moleyns estate.[4] This was a worthwhile windfall.

One of the councillors, Lord Tiptoft, benefited from another arrangement, made on 14 July 1431, whereby the estate of Thomas, Lord Roos and the wardship of his three-year-old heir were made over to him in return for £800. This might prove an equally valuable acquisition, although its worth was temporarily much reduced because the bulk of the Roos lands were in the possession of two dowagers.[5] The FitzWalter estate passed into the custody of a man to whom the government was heavily indebted and who was probably patronized by Gloucester. Sir John Radcliffe's military and administrative exertions in Gascony had left him massively out of pocket, and the government had already tried to discharge its debt to him by a number of grants. Now, on 24 May 1433, he became custodian of the estates of Walter, Lord FitzWalter and of the marriage of his daughter and heiress, Elizabeth; in return, he was required to pay £533 6s. 8d.[6] The inheritance was retained by the Radcliffe family because Sir John astutely arranged that Elizabeth should marry his eldest son, though for a time the Dowager Lady FitzWalter kept some of the East Anglian estates as her dower.

To its modest credit, the council did not dispose of quite all of the crown's prerogative resources. Perhaps the most prodigious of them in this period was the Mowbray estate of the duke of Norfolk.[7] Duke John died on 19 October 1432 and his heir was declared of age, and received his inheritance, as from 13 September 1436; in the meantime, he was the king's ward and the Mowbray lands appear to have been kept in crown hands, to be administered by the exchequer for the direct benefit of the king at a time when his government was in need of extra cash. It might be said with justice that the council showed commendable responsibility in thus harbouring the crown's resources even before Lord Cromwell took over at the exchequer in August 1433. Further evidence of this prudence is provided by the council's treatment of widows and heiresses who were royal wards and wished to marry at will and were prepared to pay for a licence to do so (or because they had already done so without one!). Such licences were readily forthcoming in return for substantial fines. John Botreaux paid no less than £200 on 5 November 1432 in order to marry Anne, dowager countess of Devon, whilst the dowager countess of Arundel's new husband, the earl of Stafford, had to find 200 marks on 20 January 1433.[8] At the same time, the much-sought-after privilege of regulating the marriage of a high-born lady was put up for sale like an acre of property, and sometimes at a fat price. It is true that one of the councillors, Lord Cromwell, secured one such concession for only £20 on 12 February 1433, but Lewis John, the Welsh retainer of Queen Katherine and Cardinal Beaufort, paid as much as £200 on the following 14 March, and the earl of Stafford 400 marks for another on 20 July 1433.[9] Moreover, when the earl of Devon petitioned to be allowed to occupy his estates two years before coming of age, he was required to pay a 1,000-mark fine for the privilege (partly as compensation to the crown) on 20 February 1433.[10] This was hard-headed business, and insistent pressure for money to finance the French war must surely account for it. Those who received these grants concluded that a lump sum down would be amply recompensed if a ward and her property could be kept in the family by a judicious marriage, or disposed of to a friend or client whose alliance might prove valuable in the future.

Investigations of those who concealed such royal rights as wardships, forfeitures, and marriages had been frequent from 1427 and continued to be widespread and assiduous. In addition to a wide-ranging commission of inquiry on 20 July 1430 in counties along the south and east coasts and in the west country (which also, incidentally, dealt with other offences whose punishment could be financially profitable to the crown), a number of local commissions into concealments (eight in all) were set up in various corners of the land between 1429 and 1433.[11]

The absorbing events of the 1429 parliament – the king's coronation, preparations for his visit to France, the end of the protectorate, and the confirmation of the council's authority – somewhat delayed more routine business, including the appointment of sheriffs which should have taken place in November 1429. Instead, the new appointees were not nominated for the English shires until 10 February 1430.[12] Considerations which had weighed heavily with the council since 1427 were still uppermost in its collective mind: loyalty and proven service to the Lancastrians, a recommendation from a councillor or other magnate, a determination to avoid favouring one faction above others, especially if it were Gloucester's. As a result, even after the king had departed for France, there is little sign that Duke Humphrey was able or inclined to bend the crown's patronage of office to his private purposes. On 5 November 1430, for example, Sir Thomas Wykeham was pricked as sheriff for Oxfordshire–Berkshire, two counties that usually had a Beaufort client as sheriff in the 1420s; Wykeham, in fact, was married to a daughter of William Willicotes, a former MP for

Oxfordshire, whilst his son had served in the retinues of Cardinal Beaufort and his nephew, Edmund.[13] The influence of the king's guardian, Warwick, remained strong, especially in those counties where he was the dominant landowner. John Throckmorton was one of the earl's bureaucrats and a trustee of his will; he became sheriff of Worcestershire in November 1430. Sir William Mountford, the new sheriff of Warwickshire–Leicestershire, also had a Beauchamp connection and had been sheriff of the county once before in 1423.[14]

A similar pattern is discernible a year later. In Essex–Hertfordshire, Sir Nicholas Thorley, who was appointed sheriff on 26 November 1431, came from a local family that had served Queen Joan, some of whose estates lay in the vicinity.[15] That same year, Sir John Scudamore became sheriff of Herefordshire. He was in dispute with Edmund Beaufort over the estates of Owain Glyndŵr which Scudamore had occupied as the husband of Owain's daughter, even though John Beaufort, earl of Somerset had been granted all the rebel leader's estates in 1400.[16] Fortunately, Scudamore had powerful aristocratic protection, for he was Lord Audley's deputy as justiciar of south Wales, was a feoffee of the earl of Ormond, had a tradition of Lancastrian service at his back and a connection with Anne, countess of Stafford. But when the cardinal's influence reached its height during the duke of Bedford's visit to England in 1433–34, Scudamore found himself fatally vulnerable. He became a victim of Henry IV's harsh legislation directed against anyone marrying into Welsh stock (particularly Glyndŵr's) and was promptly sacked from all his administrative posts. In Oxfordshire–Berkshire, it causes no surprise to discover that in November 1431 a member of the Chaucer–Golafre circle of local landowners, William Fyndern, was pricked as sheriff; whereas Sir Robert Roos, one of the king's knights and a household carver from 1430, secured the post in Lincolnshire.[17]

The two main factors governing high ecclesiastical patronage during the protectorate continued to operate after 1429: one was the relative influence of individuals or groups in the royal council; the other was the relationship between council and pope. Conflict between these two factors was more easily avoided when Beaufort was in the country, for as a cardinal he was anxious to avoid offending strong-willed popes like Martin V and Eugenius IV. He was therefore a useful papal ally and his intervention could make the appointment of a bishop less divisive than it might otherwise be. Immediately after the coronation in November 1429, Beaufort's influence was considerable, and his periodic returns to England simply reinforced the opposition to Gloucester's control of this important segment of royal patronage.[18] As a result, there was a degree of Anglo-papal co-operation during 1429–31, and Gloucester's influence is scarcely discernible. The only occasion when the pope would not agree to an English proposal was the first. After the death of John Rickinghale in summer 1429, the council supported the election to Chichester of one of Henry V's servants, Thomas Brouns; Martin preferred Simon Sydenham, a man in his late fifties who was known to the pope and probably had at least one friend on the council, Lord Hungerford, who later acted as supervisor of Sydenham's will.[19] At first, the indignant council refused to change its mind; so did Martin, with the result that on 24 January 1431 Beaufort announced in parliament that Sydenham was acceptable after all. The pope's views had doubtless weighed heavily with the cardinal and presumably induced him to support Sydenham.

Three other appointments were made with the ready assent of both council and pope: Marmaduke Lumley's promotion to Carlisle in December 1429, William Gray's translation from London to Lincoln in April 1431, and Robert FitzHugh's nomination to London that same month.[20] All three elections were probably acceptable to Beaufort as well as to a majority of the council. Lumley, indeed, had strong links with the Nevilles, was a protégé of Queen Katherine, and became the cardinal's friend. Gloucester's keen disappointment at this particular appointment was ill-concealed and at a council on 3 December 1429 the duke and Lord Scrope denounced it vigorously – but to no avail. Gray had been bishop of London since 1425, when he was associated with Archbishop Kemp; but his links with the Nevilles were just as strong as Lumley's, even though Gray's nephew would later marry Gloucester's illegitimate daughter, the evocatively named Antigone. FitzHugh's attachment to Beaufort is less clear; but his father was a man of distinction and Robert seems to have won the trust of Queen Katherine later on, for it was at one of his manor houses (Much Hadham) that her eldest son by Owen Tudor, Edmund, was born. These three clerics had much in common: they were of the same generation and sprang of noble stock from the north of England, where the Grays and FitzHughs were closely related. Thus, even when Gloucester was the king's chief councillor and keeper of the realm during Henry's absence in France, ecclesiastical patronage did not fall into his grasp any more readily than did the other resources of the crown.

Bedford in England, 1433–34

The arrival of Bedford and Beaufort from France in the last week of June 1433 enabled them to marshal their friends and associates, and to concentrate their influence so as to reward their supporters and servants and insinuate them in positions of authority. Henry VI had returned to England early in 1432; now with the duke of Bedford to hand as well, there was no question of the council having to refer matters of patronage to the councillors at Rouen. Hence, as in 1425–27, the period from July 1433 witnessed a deliberate attempt on the part of Bedford and his uncle to extend their own power in the realm by gratifying the ambitions of their clients.

In the sphere of wardships and marriages the opportunity to do so was strictly limited because no substantial estate or attractive ward came into the king's hands at this juncture.[21] However, the annual appointment of sheriffs tells a plainer story. As in the past, Beaufort and Bedford set about manipulating the shrieval appointments to ensure that those with status and authority in the shires, who organized parliamentary elections and maintained order, should be their dependants. They deliberately indulged in the necessary intrigue and persuasion in the council in order to achieve their end. At least seven of the twenty-three sheriffs appointed in November 1433 were of their 'connection'. Roger Hunt, in Cambridgeshire–Huntingdonshire, had links with the duke of Norfolk before his death in 1432 and more recently with Lord Tiptoft; he had been speaker of the commons in 1433 and may not have been well disposed towards Gloucester.[22] Richard Waller in Surrey–Sussex had strong links with Beaufort, most notably as master of his household.[23] The dependence of some of the new sheriffs on Bedford is even more obvious. In Essex–Hertfordshire, Robert Whittingham had been Bedford's receiver-general since 1427, while in Kent his chamberlain, Sir Richard Woodville, was appointed.[24] Thomas Darcy, whose kinsman Robert was one of Bedford's servants at the time of the duke's death, filled the vacancy in Lincolnshire, and Thomas Woodville, a kinsman of Sir Richard, acquired the Northamptonshire shrievalty.[25]

At the same time, important offices in the duchy of Lancaster were filled with carefully selected men. At Pontefract and Pickering (Yorkshire) a new receiver was appointed on 28 July 1433 – Robert Constable, who served as chancellor and receiver-general of Bishop Robert Neville at Durham and, when he drew up his will years later, left a bequest to the earl of Salisbury. More striking was the successful attempt by Edmund Beaufort, count of Mortain, to engineer the destruction of Sir John Scudamore's landed power and his removal from significant offices which Edmund promptly filled. Thus, on 8 August 1433 he was dismissed from the stewardships of Kidwelly, Monmouth, and the Three Castles, and from the constableship of Carmarthen castle; Edmund immediately took his place.[26] It is difficult to imagine a more overt deployment of influence for partisan motives at a time when Bedford and Beaufort were in temporary control of the council.

Paradoxically, Gloucester's modest influence on ecclesiastical promotions is most clearly evident at this time; the only two occasions when clerics who were very likely his protégés were elevated to the episcopal bench occurred within weeks of Bedford's arrival in England in June 1433. But they involved two of the least desirable sees in the entire provinces of Canterbury and York, and may therefore represent a sop to Gloucester by his brother and uncle. On 17 August 1433, John Lowe, the Augustinian friar who had been made Henry's confessor by Duke Humphrey in February 1432, was provided to the small see of St Asaph; whilst in October, Thomas Rudbourne, one of Henry V's chaplains, acquired St David's.[27] Both were probably men after Gloucester's own heart, for they had pretensions to scholarly and humanistic interests: Lowe was a noted bibliophile, while Rudbourne may have been the author of the *Life* of Henry V commissioned by Gloucester after the king's death. For these unimportant sees, papal and conciliar approval came easily and no alternative candidates were proposed.

This was not so with the far wealthier see of Worcester, when it required a replacement for Bishop Morgan later in 1433.[28] Thomas Bourgchier, an astonishing choice in view of his uncanonical age (he was twenty-two), was championed by Beaufort, Bedford, Archbishop Kemp, and a number of secular lords, while Chichele and other bishops eventually acquiesced in the choice. Bourgchier's aristocratic blood, and especially his links with the Stafford family, were his main commendation, though his candidacy was said by contemporaries to be justified by his kinsmen, his 'connyng and vertues'. Pope Eugenius, who may seriously have doubted the rectitude of appointing such a young man, refused to accept Bourgchier and provided instead Thomas Brouns, the disappointed candidate urged by the council for Chichester in 1429. It was only when the see of Rochester became vacant in 1435 that Brouns could be accommodated without either pope or council losing face. In Bourgchier's case, Eugenius eventually relented, after lobbying at the *curia* by letter and in person by one of Beaufort's clients, Adam Moleyns. To prefer the young Bourgchier so stubbornly against the council's own candidate of four years previously reeks of faction. Moreover, the dispute upset Anglo-papal relations for some little time, until Rochester became vacant. In 1434 Eugenius IV was reluctant to proceed to the election for this minor see without knowing the government's opinion; in fact, he waited until the late autumn for its view to be communicated to him. The government's support for Brouns at this late stage, and Eugenius's willingness to accept him, represent a determined effort by both sides to forget the differences of 1429 and 1433, and to re-establish their amicable relationship.

With the exception of the blatantly partisan choice of Lumley and Bourgchier, those clerics provided to English and Welsh sees after 1429 were well versed in the church's administration or in the service of Henry V. From those available with such qualifications, care was taken to appoint to the greater sees those who were acceptable to the council and the pope, and that meant to Cardinal Beaufort, the one English prelate who was most likely to be able to sustain the spirit of co-operation between Westminster and Rome. In this he had the solid backing of the duke of Bedford, who had his own reasons in Normandy for desiring the pope's friendship.

Conciliar patronage, 1434–36

Bedford left England for the last time in July 1434. This event, together with the collapse of Beaufort's cherished plans for an agreement with

Charles VII in the summer of 1435, severely tested the influence which the Beaufort circle had recently cultivated in England. To some extent, Gloucester found his authority enhanced – after all, he was chief councillor again – but it was the council as a body which governed and directed the king's patronage. One of the most prominent councillors and the nephew of another (neither of whom was sympathetic towards Duke Humphrey) benefited substantially from their position. On 18 November 1435, Lord Hungerford headed a group of people who acquired the wardship and marriage of Sir John Arundel's heir in return for 1,000 marks.[29] A few months later, on 20 February 1436, Edmund Beaufort received the wardship and marriage of Robert, son and heir of Thomas, Lord Morley, who had died in the preceding December.[30] He paid 800 marks for this prize, and subsequently arranged for Robert to marry Elizabeth, daughter of William, Lord Roos, who herself was a ward in Lord Tiptoft's custody. Tiptoft's connection with the Beaufort family was an enduring one, and this marriage could be expected eventually to unite two magnate estates whose new lord could be helpful to Beaufort interests.

Nevertheless, as in 1432, the largest estate of all to come the crown's way in these years was maintained largely intact for the time being. This was the superlative inheritance of the heir to the throne, the duke of Bedford, who died in September 1435 without legitimate offspring; his extensive estates thereupon passed to Henry VI.[31] Their income was used to underpin the unsteady financial position of the crown, and in particular to discharge a part of its burgeoning debt. Five thousand marks from the Bedford inheritance was accordingly assigned to various royal creditors and so, on 2 December 1435, was the income from the Arundel lands; unfortunately, the latter had already been assigned a fortnight earlier to Hungerford and his associates. It is true that portions of the Bedford estate were later disposed of – for example, the forest of Dean went to the earl of Warwick for seven years on 23 January 1437 – but the bulk of it was wisely kept in crown hands at least for a while.[32] Lord Cromwell, the treasurer, is likely to have supported such action after undertaking his review of the royal finances; but, to be fair to the other councillors, it was a policy that had been inaugurated even before his appointment.[33]

Variable though they might be, it had become a habit to rely on the king's prerogative rights as a financial asset, as the earl of Oxford discovered when, ostensibly because of dire poverty, he tried to obtain a pardon for the last £300 of a 3,000-mark fine imposed on him in 1425 for marrying without royal permission.[34] On 22 March 1437 he was informed that the government was relying on the fine to honour some of its assignments and the only arrangement that could be made was to grant him in the future a wardship or other source of income as compensation; even so, the government was only prepared to release him for £200. It is striking, too, how the marriage fine imposed on Jacquetta of Luxembourg, Bedford's widow, and her new husband,

Richard Woodville, the son of Bedford's chamberlain (one need hardly wonder how or where they met!), was quickly increased from the £500 imposed by parliament on 23 March 1437 to the £1,000 that was in fact demanded of them.[35] Though it cannot be ruled out that Gloucester was prepared to mulct two people with whom his past relations had been far from cordial, the financial straits of the government were responsible for this step. Likewise, the months between July 1435 and May 1436 saw a renewed interest shown by the council in royal rights that were being concealed; five commissions were issued in ten English counties. And at the same time, an investigation of customs evasion was ordered through a veritable spate of commissions, perhaps at the instance of English merchants and staplers whose loans to the crown were now so vital.[36]

Bedford's return to France in June 1434 seems to have allowed the initiative in appointing sheriffs to revert almost wholly to the councillors as a group. In both November 1434 and November 1435, local gentlemen were nominated who had influential aristocratic connections but did not belong to an identifiable faction or a single partisan circle. Both John Hampden (in Bedfordshire–Buckinghamshire in 1434) and William Brocas (Hampshire in 1435) had personal links with Thomas Chaucer's confederates, but few of the others can be regarded as dependants of Cardinal Beaufort.[37] The aged John Merbury, pricked for Herefordshire in 1434, had great experience of provincial administration and was a loyal Lancastrian servant to his fingertips; so was Sir John Cockayne (in Nottinghamshire–Derbyshire, 1434) who, although he had withdrawn from public life in recent years, had once been a retainer of the late duke of Clarence.[38] Sir John Bertram was a good choice for Northumberland (1434) because he was well acquainted with border problems and the dispiriting negotiations with Scottish envoys.[39] Other councillors' clients included Thomas Hugford, appointed to Worcestershire in 1435 and therefore closely connected with the earl of Warwick, and Thomas Fetiplace, who was pricked for Oxfordshire–Berkshire in the same year and had personal ties with Lord Talbot's family.[40] No actual dependants of Duke Humphrey can be identified among these sheriffs.

Despite the failure of the papal mediators to bring about an Anglo-French settlement at Arras in August 1435, the partnership between the pope and the council in the appointment of bishops continued. During 1435–37, when six dioceses had to be provided with a spiritual pastor, their good relations held firm; the only exception was a major dispute into which Eugenius IV was drawn unwittingly by disputes among the aristocratic councillors. As the papal collector in England, Piero da Monte, put it early in 1436:

> Of the higher benefices, four cathedral churches are vacant, viz. Ely, Bangor, London, and Lincoln, and there has been much questioning here for a long time about the provision to be made to them by Your

Holiness; not that there is any doubt amongst the important people here about the right of provision, but rather about the persons to be elected. They have, however, arrived at unanimity at last...[41]

Da Monte was too optimistic. The independent influence which Gloucester exerted was as muted here as elsewhere, despite the fact that Beaufort had been somewhat discredited by his futile attempts to secure peace with France. On 5 March 1436, Duke Humphrey's confessor was promoted to Bangor, but the poverty and insignificance of this north Wales see was such that the appointment can in no way be regarded as a triumph for the duke; and Thomas Cheriton, the Dominican appointee, was 'the most obscure bishop of the period'.[42] Indeed, it is likely that Gloucester, as chief councillor, led those who campaigned for the translation of Thomas Rudbourne, bishop of St David's and a former chaplain in Henry V's service, to Ely early in 1436.[43] After the death of Bishop Morgan on 25 October 1435, the council decided that Robert FitzHugh should be translated from London to replace him, but their choice died unexpectedly on 15 January before the procedures could be completed. The strength of personal attitudes among the councillors – and the vital importance of the episcopal bench in politics – is well indicated by the private efforts of Lord Tiptoft, who was no supporter of Gloucester, to persuade the monks at Ely cathedral to elect the young bishop of Worcester, Thomas Bourgchier. Hoping to avoid a repetition of the unseemly squabble over Bourgchier in 1433–35, the pope agreed; unfortunately, Eugenius had been misled. Bourgchier was not the agreed choice of the council, which in fact resisted Tiptoft's proposal. Eugenius found himself drawn into the centre of a dispute which sprang from the factional manoeuvres of certain councillors and which dragged on until September 1437.

In every other case, the pope fell in with the council's wishes: the translation of William Alnwick from Norwich to Lincoln in May 1436, the appointment of John Gilbert to London in February 1436, and the promotion of Thomas Brouns from Rochester to Norwich the following September.[44] Each of these bishops was a man of unwavering Lancastrian sympathies who had served Henry V in a personal capacity in England and France and supported his young son during his minority. For these reasons, they may well have been acceptable to Gloucester, though their promotion now hardly represents an attempt by the duke to insinuate his supporters on to the bench of bishops. Alnwick, indeed, had catholic aristocratic connections, including Lord Cromwell, whose relations with Gloucester were not good. The English council seems to have acknowledged the pope's co-operation by readily accepting Eugenius's choice for Rochester in September 1436, William Wells.[45] A highly-strung Benedictine monk, his appointment owed most to his service at Rome and Basle, and his good personal relations with the pope's representative in England, Piero da Monte. Thus, the episcopal appointments during the years when Gloucester was the king's next heir and sole chief councillor added to the hierarchy several experienced clerics who were generally well qualified and not bound to narrow factional interests. There were notable pursuers of heretics among them and both Alnwick and Brouns, who now occupied two of the richest sees, were noted for their vigorous orthodoxy during the recent lollard scare. This reputation probably weighed heavily with Gloucester and led him to acquiesce willingly in their appointment even if, for other reasons, he was less enthusiastic about some of the new bishops.

During Henry VI's minority, the means of government – in particular the king's patronage – had been deployed by a council whose leadership had been somewhat unstable. The explanation for this must take account of the French war, which so absorbed the energies of the king's heir, Bedford, that he spent only short periods in England in 1425–27 and 1433–34, and the personal incompatibility of Bedford and Gloucester and their uncle Beaufort. Gloucester was less inclined to indulge in intrigue and power-seeking than Bedford and Beaufort, partly because his position as protector, lieutenant, or chief councillor was ultimately assured. Beaufort, on the other hand, realized that he must use whatever means were available to him, as chancellor, councillor, cardinal, and financier, if he were to achieve political dominance. Bedford, who in any case had distrusted his younger brother since 1422, was prepared to co-operate with Beaufort. By the end of 1436, no single faction controlled English government, certainly not Gloucester's and not even Beaufort's. The aristocratic council still ruled collectively, though this state of affairs would shortly be brought to an end when the king himself was introduced to the art of ruling.

Notes

1 Above, p. 82.
2 Above, p. 38; *PPC*, IV, 36-9, 59-66; *CPR, 1429–36*, pp. 40-4.
3 Above, p. 36; *PPC*, IV, 104.
4 *GEC*, IX, 42; *CPR, 1429–36*, p. 156. By 1440 Eleanor Moleyns was married to Robert, grandson of Lord Hungerford who, as treasurer, had recommended the grant to Chaucer.
5 ibid., p. 145; *GEC*, XI, 105.
6 Above, p. 86; *CPR, 1429–36*, p. 263; *GEC*, V, 484-5.
7 *CPR, 1429–36*, pp. 242, 369, 445, 603.
8 ibid., p. 250. Cf. Beaufort's attitude to this matter in the 1420s (above, p. 86).
9 *CPR, 1429–36*, pp. 253, 263, 261, 284.
10 ibid., p. 271.
11 ibid., passim (p. 94 for the commission of July 1430).
12 PRO, *Lists and Indexes*, IX.
13 Roskell, *1422*, pp. 239-41.
14 Wedgwood, *Biographies*, pp. 851, 604; Roskell, *1422*, pp. 204-5; above, p.

69. Throckmorton had been the earl's steward, a lawyer on his council, and an annuitant in the 1420s (WarwsRO, 899/102; 98 m. 1; 95/5/92; 95/6/96; 95/1/15 m. 2; Ross, *Richard Beauchamp*, p. 11).

15 Robert Thorley had been her receiver-general in 1419–20, and John Thorley was a clerk in her household by March 1431; the queen died at her Essex manor of Havering atte Bower in 1437 (PRO, SC6/1051/17 m. 1; *CPR, 1429–36*, p. 196; *PPC*, V, 56).

16 Griffiths, *Principality of Wales*, I, 139-41.

17 Fyndern was a feoffee of John Golafre and Lord Hungerford (Roskell, *1422*, pp. 182-3); for Roos, see above, p. 57.

18 Beaufort was abroad in February 1430, April–December 1430, spring 1431–April 1432 (R. G. Davies, thesis, III, xxvii-xxviii; Radford, op. cit., pp. 178-83).

19 R. G. Davies, thesis, I, 380; III, *s. n.*

20 ibid., I, 382-6; III, *s. n.* See C. W. Smith, 'The register of Robert FitzHugh, bishop of London, 1431–36' (Ohio MA dissertation, 1979); Storey, *TCWAAS*, LV, n. s. (1955), 112-31.

21 For the grant of the marriage of James, son and heir of John Luttrell of Dunster (Somerset), to the earl of Stafford for 400 marks on 20 July 1433, see *CPR, 1429–36*, p. 284; above, p. 38.

22 Roskell, *1422*, p. 193; idem, *Speakers*, pp. 207-9. Hunt, very unusually, served as sheriff for two years running.

23 Wedgwood, *Biographies*, pp. 915-16; *DNB*, LIX, 130-1.

24 PRO, E403/681 m. 8.

25 Roskell, *1422*, p. 172.

26 Griffiths, *Principality of Wales*, I, 139-41, 201, 411; above, p. 97. Scudamore died two years later.

27 R. G. Davies, thesis, I, 387-8; III, *s. n.*

28 ibid., I, 389-94; III, *s. n.* For Bourgchier's expenditure on gifts for Beaufort's servants and his retention of Moleyns at Rome, see WorcsRO, 009.1/175/92475 (which records a prodigious expenditure by his receiver-general in 1435–36).

29 *CPR, 1429–36*, p. 497.

30 ibid., p. 510; *GEC*, IX, 219. Salisbury paid 4,700 marks to marry his daughter to Warwick's heir in 1434 (McFarlane, *Nobility*, p. 87).

31 *CPR, 1429–36*, p. 498.

32 *CFR, 1430–35*, p. 314.

33 Above, p. 95.

34 *RP*, IV, 499; *CPR, 1436–41*, p. 71. Oxford claimed to be oblivious of the fact that his guardian, the duke of Exeter, had not obtained the necessary licence.

35 *RP*, IV, 498; *CPR, 1436–41*, p. 53. The duchess had recently (6 February 1436) been granted dower provided she did not remarry without royal permission (WA MS 12164).

36 *CPR, 1436–41*, passim. Gloucester may have been sympathetic to any importuning they may have attempted.

37 Wedgwood, *Biographies*, pp. 414-15; Roskell, *1422*, pp. 156-7.

38 Griffiths, *Principality of Wales*, I, 132-4; Roskell, *1422*, pp. 168-9.

39 ibid., pp. 151-2.

40 Wedgwood, *Biographies*, pp. 479, 321; Ross, *Richard Beauchamp*, p. 8.

41 Quoted in F. R. H. Du Boulay, 'The fifteenth century', in C. H. Lawrence

(ed.), *The English church and the papacy in the middle ages* (New York, 1965), p. 226; cf. A. N. E. D. Schofield, 'England and the council of Basel', *AHC*, V, no. 1 (1973), 91-2.

42 R. G. Davies, thesis, I, 397; III, *s. n.*

43 ibid., I, 397-402; III, *s. n.*

44 ibid., I, 402-5; III, *s. n.* For earlier, unsuccessful efforts to promote Brouns, see E. F. Jacob, 'Thomas Brouns, bishop of Norwich, 1436–45', in H. R. Trevor-Roper (ed.), *Essays in British history presented to Sir K. Feiling* (1964), pp. 67-9; above, pp. 97-8.

45 R. G. Davies, thesis, I, 406; III, *s. n.*

6   Financial Resources

Income and expenditure

In 1433 the new treasurer of England, Lord Cromwell, laid before parliament a comprehensive statement of the income and expenditure of the kingdom prepared for him by the exchequer.[1] The intention was to inform parliament of the possibilities in policy-making in relation to the obligations of government and the resources available. This 'balance-sheet' is well-nigh unique in its scope, thoroughness, and detail so far as the fifteenth century is concerned, but as a statement of the current financial situation in time of parliament it may not have been unusual.[1] In most parliaments during the minority, the government was enabled to borrow money on the security of parliamentary taxation. The large sums involved – £20,000 in 1425 and double that in 1426 – would hardly have been authorized without an explanatory statement from the king's ministers. Indeed, at Leicester in 1426 a full exposition of the royal finances was presented to parliament by Lord Hungerford; for this purpose, rolls and memoranda were transported from London to Leicester during May.[3] Three years later, in January 1429, Hungerford informed the council plainly that the kingdom's expenditure was likely to exceed its income by at least 20,000 marks, and that the gap was expected to widen.[4] It is difficult to imagine a treasurer of England coming to such a conclusion without a comprehensive analysis of financial resources before him.

Aside from the exceptional value of Cromwell's statement as an appraisal of the realm's financial health in 1433, its picture of the various demands placed on government during Henry VI's minority is a vivid one. Cromwell's statement was based on figures relating to the years 1429–32 and it is possible that he affected a certain pessimism when facing parliament. Nevertheless, although the king's household was doubtless a lighter burden during the 1420s than it was in 1433, the expectation was that its financial needs would gradually increase as the king approached manhood. Again, the customs and subsidies collected at the ports had been markedly more profitable at the beginning of the reign (in excess of £40,000), but strained relations with Burgundy after Gloucester's invasion in 1424 seriously disrupted wool exports.[5] The ancient revenues of the crown, particularly the county farms collected by sheriffs and the town farms returned by urban officials, were often based on outdated assessments, as the petitions from individual sheriffs and towns demonstrated.[6] Population migration and contraction, economic decline and reorientation, not to speak of more natural phenomena such as floods and coastal changes, all tended to divorce ancient assessment from current value in some cases. All in all, one may conclude that the financial resources of the English crown (including the customs) barely sufficed to finance the normal domestic needs of government (including defence) during the minority.[7] Permanent commitments in Ireland, Gascony, and especially Calais threw them massively into deficit (by about £15,892).

Resources	Income	Expenditure	Profit (Deficit)
shire, town, and other farms	£ 9,290	£ 6,751	£ 2,539
feudal revenues	4,698	159	4,539
administrative	3,131	23,009	(19,878)
duchy of Cornwall	2,789	2,638	151
principality of Wales	2,238	1,176	1,062
Chester	765	720	45
duchy of Lancaster	4,953	2,544	2,409
miscellaneous	208	—	208
Scottish border	—	4,817	(4,817)
royal household	—	14,035	(14,035)
customs and subsidies	30,722	3,756	26,966
Total	58,794	59,605	(811)
Ireland	2,340	5,026	(2,686)
Gascony	808	4,138	(3,330)
Calais	2,866	11,931	(9,065)
Grand Total	64,808	80,700	(15,892)

Neither parliament nor the convocations of Canterbury and York were generous with direct taxes during the protectorate, and evidently the government was expected to manage on its regular income, using such assets as the crown jewels as additional security for loans. Only after the dramatic reverses in France in the late 1420s was a more realistic attitude adopted to commitments in France and at sea which now began to grow rapidly. Even so, parliamentary and clerical taxes were not all they seemed. The assessment of the lay subsidy of a tenth and fifteenth had been drawn up as long ago as 1334 and was no longer assessed on individuals but rather on each township and borough, whose capacity to pay might well have altered considerably in the interval. The estimated £37,000 expected from a subsidy in Henry VI's reign may not, therefore, have been easy to realize and indeed from 1433 a reduction of £4,000 was conceded in view of the poverty of certain towns and villages.[8] The clerical tenths granted by the convocations of Canterbury and York suffered from the same problem of squaring a traditional assessment with the present pattern of prosperity; moreover, the poverty of parishes in the north enabled York to offer only £1,400 per subsidy compared with Canterbury's £12,000. These serious drawbacks of traditional direct taxes were partly responsible for the occasional resort to special taxation. Not since the unfortunate experience of Richard II's early years (when the Peasants' Revolt had brought such experiments to an abrupt end) had the government introduced a special tax on individual wealth; but between 1428 and 1436 it imposed three to supplement more conventional imposts. Their very nature made the financial return unpredictable and they were greeted with resistance, fraud, and even administrative mismanagement, so that the 1431 expedient had to be abandoned altogether.[9] Moreover, the declared purpose of these taxes was the defence of the realm (for which all were considered to have an obligation) and the safety of the seas.[10] After Charles VI's death, King Henry theoretically commanded resources in France which could appropriately be spent on completing the conquests of his father and administering the conquered provinces. Limitations on the use of English cash for these purposes were therefore enunciated by parliament; even so, it was a moot point whether England's defence was not best served by protecting Normandy and the other French territories, and the government seems to have been persuaded by the argument.

Much of the crown's income, particularly the subsidies and customs, were not realizable immediately and their collection was inevitably somewhat leisurely. That being so, it was inevitable that the government should resort to borrowing, both to meet the extraordinary obligations which it incurred from time to time and to provide liquid capital for routine administration. The willingness of the king's wealthy subjects to advance him large sums of ready cash on the security of taxation was therefore a central feature of English government finance. Just as parliament had an overriding interest in granting taxes, so it had a close interest in the level of the crown's borrowing; if the relationship between them became unbalanced, then unpaid debts would climb and bankruptcy result. Parliament had begun formally to guarantee loan repayments from the taxes it granted in 1416, in response to Henry V's projected campaigns in France.[11] During the minority it was the practice for almost every parliament to do so and, for the first time, to specify a maximum borrowing level: this had the merit of encouraging lenders to part with their money and at the same time acknowledged parliamentary oversight of its grants. The 1422 parliament guaranteed loans up to 20,000 marks in order to meet Henry V's outstanding debts to Bishop Beaufort and other creditors; the demands of the French war in the decade that followed caused this figure to be raised until in 1429–30 loans amounting to £50,000 were being contemplated.[12] But for much of the 1420s parliament failed to match this anticipated expenditure with grants of direct taxation. Moreover, the loans, when they materialized, were frequently granted for specific purposes which seemed worthwhile to the lenders.[13]

Direct taxation, 1422–36

Tax	Total	1422–28 p.a.	1428–36 p.a.
Lay subsidies:			
10th and 15th at £37,000 to 1432, £33,000 from 1433	207,821	—	25,978
Clerical subsidies:			
10th Canterbury at £12,000	81,000	2,000	8,625
10th York at £ 1,400	2,450	117	219
Other taxes:			
1428	c. 3,000	500	
1431			cancelled
1436	c. 9,000		1,125
		2,617	35,947
Authorized borrowing level		12,222	33,333

The danger of engaging in enterprises for which the resources were not available was painfully apparent to Lord Cromwell by 1433. When he presented his statement to parliament, he drew attention to the fact that the government's debt (£168,437) was more than two and a half times the current year's income. Some of this had accumulated during the minority, when direct taxation had been meagre; but even in 1422 Henry VI found himself saddled with substantial debts incurred by his father.

If a 'budget' were compiled when John Stafford became treasurer in December 1422, it would have recorded a daunting list of liabilities arising from the war in France and the provisions of Henry V's will. The late king had borrowed massively to finance his campaigns, and a number of his loans had not been repaid by the time of his death. The prior of St John of Jerusalem in England was owed 2,000 marks, though he held certain jewels as security, half of which had been returned to the king without the debt ever being reduced.[14] The city of London was another creditor – and to an even larger sum exceeding 5,000 marks; whilst Henry V's greatest single debt was to Bishop Beaufort, who was owed £14,000 for one loan and an overall total of more than £20,000 by 31 August 1422.[15]

Other liabilities included the wages, salaries, and expenses of Henry V's officers and servants. The exchequer clerk and poet Thomas Hoccleve had lamented his unpaid wages in pointed verse, but his experience was shared by others, some of whom had greater cause to complain.[16] Nor were they entirely successful in securing repayment from the new government, though influential creditors like Beaufort and the wardens of the Scottish marches had less difficulty than some in obtaining replacements for warrants voided by the king's death.[17] In the middle of a major war, there were inevitably some commanders and retinues who had not had their indentures honoured. The first parliament of the new reign resolved to pay arrears of this sort (with, of course, appropriate deductions for any war gains or ransoms secured by the soldiers themselves), especially if any of the crown jewels were being held as security.[17] Nevertheless, in February 1424 Lord Talbot was on the point of refusing to help the besieged fortress of Crotoy because his arrears of £244 as constable of Montgomery castle were still unpaid.[19]

The largest single obligation which Henry VI inherited was created by his father's will. After 1422, large sums of money would be required to fulfil the provisions of Henry V's last will and testament, and there was still a 19,000-mark debt outstanding from the will of Henry IV (d. 1413). Consequently, in the parliament of 1423 Henry V's surviving executors were instructed to fulfil the terms of both wills by drawing on 40,000 marks that had been made available by parliament for this purpose the year before. But these good intentions were slow to bear fruit, for when the commons in 1425 urged that outstanding royal debts should be cleared, the demand was answered somewhat evasively by the government.[20]

The crown's creditors, 1422–29

The most prolific lender to the Lancastrian kings – remarkably so – was their kinsman, Bishop Beaufort. The extent of his wealth defies calculation, but there is no doubt that he was an exceedingly rich prelate by Henry VI's reign. His diocese was the richest in England, with temporalities worth perhaps £4,000 a year net; he acquired wardships, marriages, and estates from all three Lancastrian monarchs; the jewels, plate, and property which came his way in the course of financial dealings enhanced his worth; and his large interest in the customs administration offered further opportunities for gain.[21] To Beaufort, crown loans were both politically expedient and a financial investment: £9,333 in March 1424 and yet another £1,000 later in the same year (13 December) which was specifically intended to meet Northumberland's wages as warden of the east march. Others too were induced to lend, including the duchy of Lancaster's feoffees who controlled large parts of the duchy estates for the purpose of implementing Henry V's will; they provided £1,000 in February 1424 for the relief of Crotoy.[22]

The council also enjoyed the goodwill of English and foreign merchants.[23] But from 1426, by which time the reputation of the government had suffered some damage, not least from the rivalry between Gloucester and Beaufort, some of this goodwill gradually evaporated. Beaufort was abroad for much of the following two years and his surrender of the great seal discouraged him from lending further. Thus, although he lent large sums between March 1424 and May 1425 (at least £18,250), nothing was forthcoming for the remainder of the protectorate.[24] Even London, which was prepared to lend £3,000 for the realm's defence in June 1425, raised very little afterwards until two loans worth a total of £4,000 in March and June 1428, when the news from France was grim.[25]

In these circumstances, the government capitalized on the obligation of all the king's subjects, which had been acknowledged since Edward I's day, to help him in his urgent necessity. On 23 July 1426 commissioners were appointed to raise loans quickly from 'the better sort of the laity' throughout the realm; they would be repaid within a year from the customs and tunnage and poundage granted to the king in the recent Leicester parliament. Commissioners were even assigned in independent palatinates like Chester. But this traditional mode of pleading necessity and expecting every subject to respond was a conspicuous failure. Excuses, ingeniously plausible, were offered to the royal agents so that only a modest sum was raised – certainly nothing to compare with the great loans of individuals or groups.[26] The country's religious may have been unforthcoming too, for in the diocese of Worcester fourteen religious houses mustered only £295 between them.[27] Towns and cities were solicited as well as the merchant communities.[28]

The government's good credit had declined by the beginning of 1427. In that year no loans of any consequence are recorded, whilst in 1428 only the merchants of London, Bristol, and the Calais staple produced anything of any size – and then only the comparatively modest total of £9,000.[29] Although Beaufort had been able to establish a 'close personal grip' on at least the customs revenue in return for substantial loans earlier in the reign, others were not so lucky.[30] He successfully claimed preferential treatment in the repayment of his loans, and on 1 March 1424 had been allowed to sell those crown jewels (said to be worth £4,000) which he had received from Henry V as part-security for a £14,000 loan.[31] It is small wonder that the council soon became anxious to recover all crown jewels that had been pledged as security in this way; yet Beaufort kept those he had acquired in 1424 and they remained in his possession until the end of his life.[32] The priority given to repaying his loans from the customs meant that others had to take their turn before receiving payment of their, admittedly smaller, loans. As long ago as July 1417 Beaufort had acquired the right to nominate one of the collectors at Southampton, so that he could be certain that the customs assigned to him would reach his deep pockets. This valuable 'long commission' was extended to every port in the realm in February 1423, and even though Henry V's debts to the bishop were paid by the end of May 1425, the privilege was confirmed a month later. At the same time, he was allowed first call on the wardship revenues of the crown, a step which could only consolidate Beaufort influence over the king's patronage.[33] There is a strong suspicion, therefore, that Beaufort, especially when he was chancellor, ruthlessly exploited the crown's indebtedness to him and it has not been entirely dispelled by recent examination.[34]

It was in the more difficult military and financial situation of 1428 that the government, for the first time since 1381, explored the feasibility of a special tax on the country's wealthy, and requested further loans as an expression of the subject's obligation to aid a needy king. On 25 March parliament authorized a tax on householders, parish by parish, graduated so that poorer and more sparsely populated areas would pay less. The results were disappointing, for no more than £3,000 seems to have been collected and there was resistance in some quarters to such a novel expedient.[35] This first attempt at direct taxation in Henry VI's reign must therefore be counted a failure. A sense of realism had not yet penetrated either the commons in parliament or the noble and merchant houses of the kingdom.

As far as loans are concerned, the net was cast as widely as in 1426 for cash was needed to relieve Orléans. Commissioners were appointed in mid-May to negotiate a loan by 20 June. In addition, the Calais staplers offered 5,000 marks, London £4,000, and Bristol 200 marks; appeals had even gone to royal territories like Cheshire, the lordship of Chirk, and the principality of Wales in February 1428.[36]

The need for cash culminated in the loans required to finance the king's personal expedition to France in 1430. Even before parliament met in December 1429, large-scale borrowing was authorized on the security of customs which, it was anticipated, the commons would shortly grant to Henry VI.[37] The city of London provided £5,333 in May – June 1429.[38] But the growing reluctance to lend is reflected in the terms under which loans were formally authorized when parliament met. For the first time, it was specifically stated that no loan should be forcibly extracted and no enforced obligation should be entered into with the king; reluctant subjects should not be compelled to meet their obligations.[39]

The consequences of failing to prevent the gap between expenditure and income from widening may be seen in the government's difficulty in paying some of its important agents, notably the wardens of the Scottish marches. Northumberland had been astute enough to seek insurance against the fortuitous annulment of his assignments; in 1424 it was agreed that should his tallies be voided by the death or removal of a royal official, new tallies would be cut forthwith. As a result, an abnormal number of his tallies was cancelled and replaced in the 1420s – which was an inconvenience, to say the least.[40] Sir John Tiptoft, seneschal of Aquitaine in 1415–23, fared no better: when he left office, he was owed £11,100, and three-and-a-half years later only £692 of this had been paid. His patience understandably ran thin and in December 1426 he received extensive Gascon estates to help defray the debt.[41] One of the government's biggest creditors was Sir John Radcliffe, Tiptoft's successor in Aquitaine. By June 1429, he was owed £6,620 and arrangements were made for him to take £1,000 annually from the customs of Melcombe and Redcliff (Dorset) until it was all paid.[42] Three weeks later, the treasurer, threatened by a mounting debt and growing commitments, ordered a temporary suspension of all payments in cash or by assignment for any purpose other than to clear the debts of the royal household. Without substantial taxation, bankruptcy was imminent.[43]

The signs of the time can be read elsewhere in the record of more minor transactions. As early as March 1423, the council had decided to sell some of the ships built by Henry V. There were wealthy merchants prepared to purchase them for their commercial enterprises, but care was taken that no foreigner (unless he were the subject of an English ally) should buy any of them.[44] Much more valuable were the crown jewels, which were used as security for loans. The council became uneasy at the dispersal of the jewels and periodically tried to recover them. In 1422 parliament had resolved to pay the war-wages of those who held them as security, while in July 1426 further efforts were made to recover them.[45] The gold crown which Beaufort still held was ordered to be produced at a council meeting in February 1427, but other jewels in his possession were not surrendered; Gloucester and the earl of Salisbury successfully petitioned in the 1427 parliament to be allowed to keep certain jewels because wages owing to them had not been paid.[46] The recovery of this treasure would be a welcome windfall for a government wishing to negotiate loans from an increasingly resistant community.

France and a question of priorities

The greater direct English involvement in France that was heralded by the coronation in November 1429 implied an increased financial commitment by England to the dual monarchy. Moreover, the reverses on the French mainland raised unaccustomed problems of sea-keeping and coastal defence that led the council to argue that the best means of providing security for England was to finance expeditions to France.

The financial problems of the 1430s, though they were apparent to the council and the treasurer, were not always appreciated by parliament or convocation. At first, the council confronted the financial implications of the Valois advances by reassuring Englishmen that Normandy would continue to finance the war and its own administration.[47] Moreover, future campaigns should be paid for by granting French estates to the conquerors, with an explicit obligation to defend them. But faced with a deteriorating military situation, these principles were not easily implemented. Lord Hungerford and Lord Cromwell realized the unpalatable truth that all the king's obligations could not be discharged with the resources available: faced with paying for Salisbury's expedition to France in March 1431, Hungerford pleaded for the establishment of clear priorities so that the requisite cash could be devoted to the campaign.[48]

The situation had worsened by the time that Cromwell took office in August 1433.[49] In his opinion, the royal household, wardrobe, and essential works should be the first priority, for when parliament met in July, there had been no money in the treasury for the household or the king's personal needs, let alone for other aspects of government.[50] The council was reluctant to take decisive action, and in desperation the exchequer was authorized on 11 July to pay at its discretion the multifarious claimants on its resources, including the household, government officials, and creditors.[51] When Cromwell took office a month later, he was determined that parliament should adequately provide for the household and wardrobe as well as for the government of the realm, its defence, and its debts. But without clear guidance and firm support, he could not do his job properly. An obscure but conscientious official, William Burgh, made his own assessment of the ills from which the exchequer suffered. His pessimistic conclusion was that payments and assignments were inadequately supervised and that abuses went undetected; his recommendation was that the treasurer himself should exercise greater control over the exchequer and the treasury. Even if Cromwell did not read Burgh's paper, he came to hold a very similar view.[52]

Two days after his appointment, he suspended payment of all assignments in excess of £2,000, unless they were for the household or were intended to repay loans, the life-blood of the régime.[53] He then insisted on informing parliament of the precise state of the king's finances; he did so not least because neither lords nor commons had hitherto heeded warnings. His famous statement was compiled from the exchequer's own records, which were laid open for inspection, and it was enrolled formally and in full on the official parliament roll.[54] A number of the exchequer's officials were retired soon after Cromwell's appointment and replaced by men who had served him in a private capacity and whom he therefore felt could be trusted.[55] Bedford, who had recently returned to England with expensive French plans, probably supported the treasurer whose appointment he had advocated. Cromwell set about his task not a month too soon, and urgently recommended that parliament itself should assume responsibility for the apportionment of the kingdom's available resources, subjecting all future grants of lands, rents, wardships, and marriages to the treasurer's scrutiny. It is likely to have been on his initiative that a precise order of priorities for the honouring of crown debts was at last drawn up.[56] As a result of this thorough and forthright review, the council was able to tell Gloucester in May 1434 that it had no idea where the £48,000 – £50,000 required to fund his proposed French expedition might come from.[57] Without adequate parliamentary taxation to provide the necessary security, borrowing on a large scale was not feasible and, therefore, little extraordinary expenditure ought to be incurred.

It was Henry VI's journey to France in April 1430, and the need for several expeditions to accompany him and reinforce the Lancastrian régime there, that finally prompted parliament in 1429–30 and 1431 to grant taxation and at a substantial level. In 1429–30 the commons offered two tenths and fifteenths, the first to be paid by 14 January 1430 and the second by Christmas.[58] This unusual grant took some people's breath away, and to one chronicler at least it seemed a heavy burden for the king's subjects to bear.[59] Beaufort had been instrumental in persuading the commons to be liberal, though they could not refrain from expressing the hope that good government would ensue from those lords whom they trusted. By contrast, the commercial grants of tunnage and poundage and the wool subsidies were modest. Tunnage and poundage were renewed until the next parliament, but they were not imposed on foreign merchants. The wool subsidy, which was granted at the urging of the lords, was more equitable: whereas English merchants were expected to pay at the rate of 33s. 6d. a sack, 43s. 4d. was demanded from aliens, and the grant was to last for two years from 12 November 1431. All of these grants were specifically made for the defence of the realm and the keeping of the seas, but it was easy to justify the king's expedition in these terms because of Henry's participation.

When parliament reassembled in January 1431, the king was still in France and for this reason the grants were again liberal.[60] The treasurer, Hungerford, spoke strongly of the needs of the English armies in France. Accordingly, one and one-third subsidies were granted and payment was envisaged within a year. To a grateful government this grant seemed 'as great a sum as has heretofore been levied in like case', and care was taken that no one should slip through its net unless, as with the drowning town of Mablethorpe (Lincolnshire), an official exemption had been issued.[61] At the same time, tunnage and poundage were extended for a further two years until November 1434 and, as far as English merchants were concerned, at the same rate as 1429; but on this occasion, aliens were not exempt and were saddled with a higher rate of 6s. per tun of wine and 1s.6d. per pound of merchandise. The wool subsidy, too, was extended until November 1434, although, perhaps in compensation for the higher tunnage and poundage rate, the rate for aliens was reduced to that for English merchants (i.e., 33s.6d). Yet the crown's prodigious need for cash is graphically reflected in the novel supplementary tax imposed by this parliament on men and women holding knights' fees worth at least £1, or enjoying an annual landed income of £20. It was to be paid on 24 June 1431, a mere three months after parliament ended; it was therefore an urgent expedient.[62] The difficulties involved in imposing such a tax had been experienced in 1428, but now an attempt was made to remove hostility by nominating local people as assessors and collectors, excluding MPs (who had had a hand in granting the tax), and expressing a readiness to hear appeals. Unfortunately, the government did not anticipate reactions carefully enough: the tax proved unworkable because (it was claimed in 1432) of the doubts and confusions to which it gave rise.[63] It was therefore abandoned when the next parliament met.

Convocations of Canterbury and York showed a similar willingness to provide money for the king in France. There was still, in the early fifteenth century, a correlation between the timing of meetings of parliament and the Canterbury convocation, and also in the scale of taxation which they offered.[64] Thus, Canterbury's convocation met in December 1429 and was persuaded by a delegation of councillors to supersede an earlier grant of half a tenth by one-and-a-half tenths; this was in line with parliament's liberality in the months before Henry VI embarked.[65] This clerical grant, like its lay counterpart, was specifically intended for the defence of the realm and the church, though there is no doubt that the money it produced helped to finance the king's French venture. Indeed, the Canterbury convocation of February 1431 voted a further tenth whilst parliament was sitting.[66] The York convocation granted a single tenth in 1430, and there were so many exemptions made for poor religious houses and benefices in the three most northerly counties that it can hardly have been of much real value to the government.[67]

Once the king was back in England, parliament's willingness to make grants evaporated, despite the gloomy revelations about the nation's finances by Hungerford and Cromwell. In 1432 parliament offered only half a subsidy, to be collected over a year and a half, and specified no guaranteed borrowing level. As a result, the treasurer, Lord Scrope, was unable to raise a loan for the earl of Huntingdon's expedition to France and in April he demanded renewed provision for borrowing.[68] Not only were the tenths and fifteenths granted in 1432–35 payable over a longer period, but their size was substantially reduced: only half a subsidy in 1432, and in 1433 and 1435 a full one reduced by over 10 per cent (£4,000) because of the poverty of certain towns and parishes.[69] Convocations followed suit. None of the assemblies of 1432 and 1433 was at all forthcoming; indeed, during Canterbury's convocation in November–December 1433, Archbishop Chichele was unable to secure unanimous agreement to a grant of three-quarters of a tenth and had to rest content with a grudging majority vote.[70] Tunnage and poundage rates changed only slightly, though the wool customs payable by foreign

117

merchants tended to rise a little in the early 1430s.[71] At least the government was assured of a steady income from these commercial sources in the immediate future and that gave a measure of confidence to the crown's creditors.

The diplomatic débâcle at Arras and military advances by Valois armies enabled the government to appeal to parliament in October 1435 with greater conviction. The commons accordingly conceded another supplementary expedient in the form of a graduated income tax, to be collected speedily by late April 1436; it was to be imposed on all freehold lands and offices worth more than £5 a year. Nevertheless, no more than £9,000 was realized because of significant underassessment of certain landed income. Though more productive than those of 1428 and 1431, this expedient cannot be counted a success either.[72] Instead, the parliament of 1437, encouraged by Gloucester's success in Calais and Flanders in August 1436, offered one tenth (minus the £4,000 relief) and with a somewhat shorter period of payment.[73] The convocation of Canterbury likewise granted a whole tenth, something which it had not done since 1431.[74] The archdiocese of York had already made its diminutive contribution in June 1436 when, after lengthy discussions and the personal intervention of Archbishop Kemp, a half-tenth (£700) was granted to relieve the king's pressing needs; it was voted especially for the defence of the Scottish marches, which was naturally the first concern of the northern clergy.[75]

Thus, grants of direct taxation by parliament and convocations were at a far higher level from 1429 than during the protectorate.[76] Faced with a deteriorating situation in France which required a lengthy visit by the king and his coronation at Notre Dame, and with overwhelming evidence that the crown's income in England could not sustain its permanent commitments in France, let alone cope with crises or emergencies that demanded military action, the king's subjects voted relatively substantial grants for the defence of the king, the realm, the seas, and the church. Their yield fell short of expectations, partly because of outdated assessments and partly because of resistance to novelties; the bases of wealth in the kingdom had changed considerably since the early fourteenth century, but newer, more realistic imposts were obstructed or ineffectively implemented.[77] The need may have been recognized but the will to respond was lacking.

Loans in the 1430s

At the same time as it granted more taxes, parliament raised the threshold of borrowing on guaranteed security to an annual average rate during 1428–36 that was almost three times that in 1422–28.[78] It has been calculated, too, that the total loans to the crown in the decade 1432–42 were higher than at any comparable period in the century between 1377 and 1485 – and were double the level of 1422–32.[79] But a combination of parliamentary niggardliness in the past and enlarged obligations more recently had done serious damage to the realm's finances which the reduction in taxation after 1432 simply accentuated. A growing regiment of government creditors found their tallies of assignment uncashable. Once again, bankruptcy was imminent.[80]

Some prominent lenders[81]

Lender	1422–28		1428–36	
Bishop Beaufort	£15,066:	2,511 *p.a.*	61,151:	7,644 *p.a.*
London	7,477:	1,246	56,776:	7,097
Calais merchants	4,000:	667	12,059:	1,507
Total		4,424		16,248

King Henry's expedition was the occasion for the announcement of a major loan. On 6 March 1430 it was resolved to assemble men in all counties, towns, and cities to persuade them to disgorge money in the declared hope that it would end the war (and therefore the borrowing).[82] The two tenths and fifteenths voted in the recent parliament would act as security. By mid-May loans worth more than £24,000 had been negotiated in this way, including 10,000 marks from the city of London, £3,029 from the duchy of Lancaster's feoffees, and (the largest single loan of all) almost £10,000 from the affluent Beaufort. It was a not inconsiderable achievement and a demonstration of goodwill towards the king.[83]

Although the government had recently reaffirmed its view that Normandy should finance its own defence and administration, assistance from English sources was inevitable as the king's stay in France lengthened. It was not always easy to raise money in England for purposes not directly connected with the realm's defence, but at Calais, in the presence of the king, the staplers could hardly refuse a loan for the avowed purpose of defending Lancastrian France. On 12 July 1430 they lent £2,333 on security provided not by parliament but by five prominent councillors.[84] The opportunity had been seized to induce some of the king's wealthiest subjects to lend, without appearing to divert English resources to an exclusively French purpose.

Henry's absence was probably longer than had been foreseen, and hence on 9 October 1430 a great council recommended further borrowing.[85] The parliament of January 1431 provided the necessary security and Beaufort offered the largest sum of all, £15,674.[86] A more systematic campaign was launched as soon as parliament was dissolved. On 26 March new commissioners were appointed to negotiate with knights, esquires, gentlemen, townsmen, and clergy in every county of the realm, and to overcome any resistance of principle, it was carefully stated that financial support for the king in France was, in reality, an aid to the defence of England itself.[87] In Norfolk and Suffolk, it was the earl of Suffolk who persuaded local notables to contribute £1,500; in Yorkshire, Lord Greystoke was less successful (£400).[88] Norwich offered its contribution well before time and was suitably commended in the king's name.[89] The result of these and other efforts was that £33,322 was delivered to the king's wardrobe in France between Michaelmas 1429 and 24 May 1431, when John Tyrell took over as treasurer of the wars and the household.[90]

Pleas of defence seemed hollower with the king safely back in England, though the fundamental disparity between income and expenditure remained. As a result, taxation declined and so, therefore, did loans: according to A. B. Steel, the annual average total of loans to the crown between Easter 1432 and Easter 1435 was barely more than half the yearly average during Michaelmas 1429 – Easter 1432.[91] In fact, no general loan was sought for two years and wealthy individuals were wooed instead. In February 1433 the duchy of Lancaster feoffees lent £3,000 to raise an army, the loan to be repaid from the customs of Southampton, where they already named one of the collectors. In June 1434, these same feoffees agreed that their entire income should be handed over to Henry VI, with the result that in February 1435 £6,000 was transferred to the chancellor of France for purely French needs.[92] More questionable means were used to force Cardinal Beaufort to provide more cash. In February 1432 Gloucester seized his treasure and jewels at Sandwich, and when parliament met in July, Beaufort was induced to pay £6,000 to recover them and to advance loans of £6,000 and £8,667, probably to avoid a charge of *praemunire* or even treason.[93]

The government optimistically sought a new general loan on 26 February 1434. This time repayment was guaranteed not only on the security provided by direct taxation (which in any case was hardly adequate), but also on the customs, the crown jewels, and the king's regular income.[94] A certain amount of resistance was encountered and the response was very disappointing indeed. In the following year, on 15 May, another series of loans was contracted, amounting in all to about £14,200; this time repayment was not pledged on direct taxation, which was by now woefully inadequate. Were it not for £7,167 subscribed by Beaufort, £3,091 by the duchy of Lancaster feoffees and £2,667 by London, the return would have been quite insubstantial.[95]

The crisis year of 1436 loosened Englishmen's purse-strings. On 14 February, magnates, clerics, cities, towns, and others were requested to support an army that was being assembled under Richard, duke of York. Taxation was once again available as security and the king is said to have raised 100,000 marks; if this is an exaggeration, it at least reflects contemporaries' awareness that the French and Burgundian threats had galvanized Englishmen to support their king to an unusual degree. London contributed 5,000 marks and the staplers £5,393; but once again it was Beaufort who made the appeal successful, for between February and August 1436 he produced more than £28,000.[96] Loans received by the exchequer in the Michaelmas term of 1435–36 are said to have reached one of the highest figures of the century.[97] Yet, if the contributions of Beaufort, London, and the duchy's feoffees are subtracted, the financial investment of the king's subjects as a whole in his enterprises appears small.

In the 1430s the gap between the crown's resources and its commitments, both permanent and exceptional, widened alarmingly. Parliament was prepared to acknowledge this reluctantly by authorizing increased borrowing, but its grants of direct taxation were inadequate security. By the autumn of 1433, Cromwell had discovered that at least four tenths and fifteenths (double the largest single grant by any parliament during the minority) were immediately required simply to clear the crown's accumulated debt of £164,000; yet without greater awareness of the seriousness of the situation, there was little hope that the deterioration in the crown's financial position would be arrested. Generous loans depended on good credit, but from the 1420s this had been conspicuously lacking. Prominent men (and potential lenders) had learned this while in the king's service; in the first two years of his term as lieutenant of Ireland from May 1431, Sir Thomas Stanley was only assigned £888 and tallies issued to him from 1433 proved increasingly difficult to translate into cash.[98] Little reached the earl of Northumberland on the east march in the early 1430s and uncashed tallies had been cluttering his coffers for a decade. Salisbury was no better off on the west march, for his faulty tallies increased in number from 1431. If such men developed doubts about the soundness of Lancastrian finances, it is not surprising that others should have been reluctant to invest their cash in its causes. When new loans were mooted in April 1437, some wanted to discuss the matter with the treasurer of England, presumably in order to gain exemption or make sure of repayment or reduce their quota; counties like Suffolk agreed to lend only if other communities were doing so; and Lord Tiptoft, from whom the government might have expected better, tried to ensure that he would have a cast-iron guarantee of repayment.[99]

Over-reliance on a dominant financier like Beaufort was itself fraught with risks: not only did his massive loans virtually monopolize the best sources of repayment, but there was a distinct danger that he would combine financial power with unchallengeable political authority.[100] To expect London and the merchants to disgorge a proportion of their wealth regularly depended on the government's reputation and the effectiveness of its policies; if either failed, then so might financial support from these quarters. The crown was still able to call on substantial reserves in 1436, but their base was worryingly narrow: where were the well-disposed knights, gentry, clergy, and burgesses?[101]

In financial terms, the situation had deteriorated unnoticed by all save a few in the 1420s; the decade of the 1430s, with its series of foreign crises, was the pivot of the reign.

Notes

1 *RP*, IV, 432-9, tabulated in Chrimes and Brown, op. cit., pp. 270-4. See J. L. Kirby, 'The issues of the Lancastrian exchequer and Lord Cromwell's estimates of 1433', *BIHR*, XXIV (1951), 121-51. Cromwell was appointed treasurer on 11 August; parliament sat from July to December.

2 Cf. T. F. Tout and D. M. Broome, 'A national balance sheet for 1362–3 . . .', *EHR*, XXXIX (1924), 404-19.

3 PRO, E403/675 m. 3. This statement, like that of 1433, followed the appointment of a new treasurer; Hungerford took up his duties on 16 March 1426. Cf. William Kinwolmersh's financial survey in May 1421, only a couple of months after he became treasurer (*Foedera*, IV, iv, 26-27).

4 *PPC*, III, 322-3.

5 Above, p. 55; J. H. Ramsay, *Lancaster and York* (2 vols., 1892), II, 266.

6 PRO, SC8/6083/122 (sheriff of Lincs., 1437); 4477/90 (Andover, 1435); M. A. Rose, 'Petitions in parliament under the Lancastrians from, or relating to, towns' (London MA thesis, 1926), p. 58 (Lincoln). See J. G. Edwards, *The second century of the English parliament* (Oxford, 1979), p. 25; below, p. 117.

7 As far as the southern part of the principality of Wales goes, Cromwell's estimates are confirmed by a detailed study of its finances in the 1420s and 1430s (R. A. Griffiths, 'Royal government in the southern counties of the principality of Wales, 1422–85' [Bristol PhD thesis, 1962], pp. 592-3).

8 Edwards, op. cit., p. 25; below, p. 117.

9 Edwards, op. cit., pp. 27-30; below, p. 117; Kirby, *BIHR*, XXIV (1951), 157, believes the actual yield of a Canterbury tenth to be nearer £10,000; this to some extent is confirmed by the return in 1374–75, though further sums may have come in a little later (G. A. Holmes, *The good parliament* [Oxford, 1975], p. 70.

10 *RP*, IV, 318.

11 ibid., 95-6. This precedent was followed in 2 of Henry V's 4 remaining parliaments (ibid., 117, 130).

12 ibid., 210-11, 277 (1425, £20,000), 300 (1426, £40,000), 339-40 (1429–30, £50,000). Repayment of these loans was to be made from the crown's regular resources, including its treasure and jewels and the customs. The creditors were allowed to nominate those financial officials whose resources they wished to earmark for repayment by a stated date (which was usually within a year).

13 In July 1429 a loan from the city of London was intended for the realm's defence and to resist French rebels (*CPR, 1422–29*, pp. 518-19). Another, in February 1424, was for an expedition to relieve Crotoy (*PPC*, III, 135).

14 The council took steps to repay him on 21 February 1424 (PRO, E28/44/55).

15 The London loan was repaid by 15 February 1424 (*PPC*, III, 116-17, 142). For Beaufort's debt, see K. B. McFarlane, 'At the death-bed of Cardinal

Beaufort', in R. W. Hunt, W. A. Pantin, and R. W. Southern (eds.), *Studies in mediaeval history presented to F. M. Powicke* (Oxford, 1948), p. 412; it was repaid by 1425.

16 J. Mitchell, *Thomas Hoccleve* (Chicago, 1968), pp. 2-4, 132-3.

17 Kirby, *BIHR*, XXIV (1951), 129. Northumberland was owed £6,543 as warden of the east march, but in February 1423 he was assigned the customs of Newcastle-upon-Tyne, Boston, and Hull until the debt was discharged (PRO, E28/39/40). Warrants for payment made void by the king's death were often renewed after 1422, especially if prominent persons were involved (G. L. Harriss, 'Fictitious loans', *EconHR*, 2nd ser., VIII [1955-56], 189-93).

18 *RP*, IV, 178. For an example, see *PPC*, III, 124-5.

19 ibid., 138.

20 *RP*, IV, 178,206-8, 289-90; Eton Coll. MS; below, p. 112.

21 McFarlane, 'At the death-bed of Beaufort', pp. 405-28; Elder, thesis, pp. 101ff.

22 McFarlane, 'At the death-bed of Beaufort', p. 414; *PPC*, III, 125. In March 1425 several other loans were arranged from bishops, lords, and knights, almost all of whom were councillors; they produced 4,600 marks. The loans were to be repaid by Michaelmas 1425 from the proceeds of the marriage of the earl of Oxford (which, however, was soon to be granted away) or, failing that, from the estates of Lord Roos (of which 1,000 marks were already in Gloucester's hands)(*CPR, 1422–29*, p. 271; *PPC*, III, 167-8). See also *CPR, 1422–29*, p. 293, and *PPC*, III, 167-8, for a further £4,400 from Bishops Stafford and Beaufort in July 1425.

23 Loans from foreign merchants were not large at this time: e.g., in June 1425 the Venetians contributed 500 marks and the Florentines £500 (*CPR, 1422–29*, p. 286).

24 McFarlane, 'At the death-bed of Beaufort', pp. 414-15.

25 Apart from £650 in August 1426 (*CPR, 1422–29*, pp. 293, 318-19; PRO, E403/686 m.1, 7). See C. M. Barron, 'The government of London and its relations with the crown, 1400–1450' (London PhD thesis, 1970), pp. 619-21.

26 *CPR, 1422–29*, pp. 353-6. For the commission in even the palatinates of Lancs. and Cheshire, see PRO, E28/47/36; the reactions (and excuses) of Essex, Leics., Norfolk, Suffolk, Dorset, and Herts. are in ibid., m.14-17, 20, 43. For such commissions in general, see G. L. Harriss, 'Aids, Loans and Benevolences', *HJ*, VI (1963), 1-19.

27 WorcsRO, Reg.Polton, p. 13. For receipts from other religious houses at the beginning of October 1426, see PRO, E403/678 m. 1.

28 PRO, E403/675 m. 13-15.

29 ibid., 686, m.1, 7, 8; E28/50/10. For London's £4,000, see Barron, thesis, p. 621.

30 The phrase is taken from G. L. Harriss, 'Cardinal Beaufort – Patriot or Usurer', *TRHS*, 5th ser., XX (1970), 136-7, where accusations of usury against Beaufort are treated sceptically, though the political influence his loans gave him can hardly be refuted (142-6).

31 A further 4,000-marks worth of jewels were given him in February 1424 as security for another loan (*PPC*, III, 144, 146-7). In June 1425 he was even allowed to keep a gold crown (given to him by Henry V) and a gold, bejewelled collar (given early in Henry VI's reign) until yet another loan was repaid.

32 McFarlane, 'At the death-bed of Beaufort', p. 412. The quip of the traitor Sir John Mortimer, that he 'would play with his [Beaufort's] money', may reflect popular resentment at the bishop's financial dealings (ibid., p. 415 n.3).

33 ibid., pp. 414-15; *RP*, IV, 278-80; above, p. 86. He also had first call on clerical and parliamentary subsidies that would be granted after 1 May 1425.

34 McFarlane, 'At the death-bed of Beaufort', p. 413; ct. G. L. Harriss's doubts in *TRHS*, 5th ser., XX (1970), 129-48.

35 *RP*, IV, 368. For resistance in New Romney, see KentRO, NR/FAc 2 f. 108.

36 PRO, E28/50/10, 15; E403/686 m. 1, 7, 8; *CPR, 1422–29*, 480-2; *PPC*, III, 295; Griffiths, thesis, pp. 374, 397.

37 *PPC*, III, 328.

38 *CPR, 1422–29*, 534, 518-19; Barron, thesis, pp. 621-2; PRO, E403/689 m. 13. A group of ecclesiastics offered loans too (ibid., m. 10).

39 *RP*, IV, 317-18; Harriss, *HJ*, VI (1963), 1-19.

40 Kirby, *BIHR*, XXIV (1951), 139; Harriss, *EconHR*, 2nd ser., VIII (1955-56), 195. It was Northumberland, too, who complained in 1428 that certain sources of revenue were overassigned – something from which he presumably suffered (ibid., 196).

41 PRO, E28/48/50. A 1,000-mark payment was authorized for him at the same time. Ormond, as lieutenant of Ireland in 1425–26, was only able to secure £367 of his debt in December 1427 by foregoing £183 (PRO, E403/684 m. 9). This method of payment was a consequence of bargaining (Harriss, *BIHR*, XXX [1957], 20-1).

42 *PPC*, III, 339.

43 ibid., 348.

44 Henry V seems to have approved of the sale before his death, though not to foreigners (Eton Coll. MS). The sale appears to have taken place at Southampton (PRO, E28/42/75; *CCR, 1422–29*, p. 58; *CPR, 1422–29*, p. 57; *PPC*, III, 53-3). See B. C. Turner, 'Southampton as a naval centre, 1414-1458', in J. B. Morgan and P. Peberdy (eds.), *Collected essays on Southampton* (Southampton, 1958), pp. 46-7.

45 Above, p. 111; *CPR, 1422–29*, p. 345; PRO, E28/47/42.

46 *PPC*, III, 250; *RP*, IV, 320-1.

47 *RP*, IV, 415-19.

48 *PPC*, IV, 79-80.

49 *RP*, IV, 432. See Price, thesis, and Friedrichs, thesis, esp. ch. 4.

50 In May 1432 the commons said that the clerks of Henry V's chapel were still unpaid and that Henry VI's officers had not received any cash since 1422 (*RP*, IV, 393-4; *CPR, 1429–36*, p. 205). In February 1433 money earmarked for Henry V's former servants was diverted to the war (*PPC*, IV, 141-2).

51 *RP*, IV, 420-1; PRO, E404/49/169.

52 WA MS 12234. Burgh was a teller of the exchequer in 1431–32 and his paper was written during Cromwell's term, perhaps about the time Sir John Radcliffe's debts were dealt with (1434) (PRO, E404/48/141-42; below, p. 206).

53 *RP*, IV, 420-1.

54 Chrimes and Brown, op. cit., pp. 271-4. A day after Cromwell's

appointment, customs collectors were ordered to bring their records for inspection to the exchequer on 30 September; in the meantime, they were forbidden to make any further payments (*PPC*, IV, 175-6).

55 They included his receiver-general, William Stanlowe, and other estate officials (Friedrichs, thesis, pp. 96-8). Cromwell insisted on service in person and not by deputy (*PPC*, IV, 175-6).

56 *PPC*, IV, 339-40; his own unpaid war-wages, dating from Henry V's reign, could now be honoured too (Friedrichs, thesis, pp. 15-16, quoting PRO, E101/50/9). Cf. new controls imposed on John Merston as keeper of the king's jewels in February 1434 (*PPC*, IV, 201).

57 ibid., 213-16.

58 *RP*, IV, 337-8, 341-2; *CFR, 1422–30*, pp. 290-7. Indeed the payment date of the first grant was brought forward to 19 November and the second to early October (*RP*, IV, 342-3; *CFR, 1422–30*, pp. 328-33).

59 *Amundesham*, I, 55.

60 *RP*, IV, 368-9.

61 *CFR, 1430–37*, pp. 65-7; *RP*, IV, 285; Kirby, thesis, p. 41.

62 *RP*, IV, 369. For the yield of taxation in 1428–36, see table, p.110.

63 *RP*, IV, 409-10. The 1428 tax is said to have produced more than £12,000 by Kirby, *BIHR*, XXIV (1951), 137; but Ramsay, op. cit., I, 259, puts the figure at about £2,500. The former may be referring to the anticipated yield.

64 *Reg. Chichele*, I, cxxiv-cxxviii.

65 ibid., III, 524-6; *CFR, 1422–30*, pp. 306-9. The same convocation authorized a graduated tax on priests' stipends.

66 *CFR, 1430–37*, pp. 62-4; *Reg. Chichele*, III, 524-6.

67 *CFR, 1430–37*, pp. 23-4; table, p. 110.

68 *RP*, IV, 389; *PPC*, IV, 157-9.

69 *RP*, IV, 389 (July 1432), 425-6 (December 1433), 487-8 (December 1435). This reduction replaced temporary reliefs as a result of individual petitions (Rose, thesis, pp. 47ff; above, p. 108). A tenth and fifteenth was henceforth assessed at about £33,000 (table, p. 110).

70 *Reg. Chichele*, I, cxxviii; III, 524-6; *CFR, 1430–37*, pp. 159-61, 180-2. Canterbury voted a half-tenth in 1430 and three-quarters of a tenth in 1433; York a mere quarter-tenth in 1433.

71 *RP*, IV, 389-90, 426, 488.

72 *RP*, IV, 486-7; *CFR, 1430–37*, pp. 267-9, 257-62; PRO, E404/47/123; *PPC*, IV, 343. See H. L. Gray, 'Incomes from land in England in 1436', *EHR*, XLIX (1934), 607-39; C. D. Ross and T. B. Pugh, 'The English baronage and the income tax of 1436', *BIHR*, XXV (1953), 1-28. Cheshire alone was assessed at 10,000 marks, though there was resistance and it had to be acknowledged that the imposition on a semi-independent franchise would not be construed as a precedent (PRO, E28/56/5 [18 March 1436]).

73 *RP*, IV, 503-4 (by November 1438).

74 *Reg. Chichele*, III, 524-6.

75 *CFR, 1430–37*, pp. 309-10.

76 See table, p. 110.

77 C. Phythian-Adams, *Desolation of a city* (Cambridge, 1979), pp. 16-19.

78 Table p. 110. It rose from £50,000 in 1429 to £100,000 by 1435 (*RP*, IV, 339 [1429], 374-5 [£50,000, 1431], 426-7 [100,000 marks, 1433], 482 [1435]).

79 A. Steel, *The receipt of the exchequer, 1377–1485* (Cambridge, 1954), p.

242, and tables on pp. 455-64. For these loans in general, see Harriss, *HJ*, VI (1963), 1-19; and K. B. McFarlane, 'Loans to the Lancastrian kings; a problem of inducement', *CHJ*, IX (1947–49), 57-61.

80 For the increase of 'bad' uncashable tallies, especially from 1432, see Steel, op. cit., p. 242; below, p. 121.

81 Based on Barron, thesis, pp. 611, 619-24; McFarlane, 'At the death-bed of Beaufort', passim.

82 *CPR, 1429–36*, pp. 49-51; PRO, E403/695 m. 8 (commissioners sent to Bristol, Dorset, and Soms.). Repayment was authorized for 1 July (PRO, E404/52/400). The royal prerogative was also employed in February 1430 to justify £40 fines for distraint of knighthood, and these were collected in the autumn (*CCR, 1429–35*, p. 67; *PPC*, IV, 54; Steel, op. cit., p. 175).

83 London produced £4,820 within 6 weeks of being asked and Beaufort £8,833 by mid-May (*CPR, 1429–36*, pp. 60-2; PRO, E403/695 passim). On 4 December 1430 the duchy's feoffees were allowed to nominate a customs collector at Southampton to facilitate repayment from the port's revenue; but their loan had still not been paid in its entirety by May 1436 (*CPR, 1429–36*, p. 104; PRO, E403/ 716 m. 7).

84 On 23 November 1430 security was also provided by the recent clerical tenth from Canterbury (PRO, E404/47/149; *CPR, 1429–36*, p. 111).

85 *Amundesham*, I, 55; Steel, op. cit., p. 175.

86 *Amundesham*, I, 58; Steel, op. cit., pp. 174-5; *PPC*, IV, 79; PRO E403/696. Receipts for £2,567 advanced by Beaufort in France to the treasurer of the king's household between July 1431 and January 1432 are Bodl, MS Ch. England, 19-22.

87 *CPR, 1429–36*, pp. 124-7.

88 *CPR, 1429–36*, p. 111; PRO, E404/48/108. East Anglia was one of England's most prosperous regions and perhaps more susceptible than most to central control. For the Herts. commissioners, led by Bishop Morgan of Ely, who held a meeting at Hertford priory on 22 May, see *Amundesham*, I, 64.

89 PRO, E404/47/337, 191. Likewise, London disgorged another 5,000 marks, though twice as much had been asked for (E. J. Davies and M. I. Peake in 'Loans from the city of London to Henry VI, 1431–1449', *BIHR*, IV [1926–27], 168-9).

90 PRO, E101/408/9. Normandy produced £13,772 for the king's wardrobe in 1429–31.

91 Steel, op. cit., pp. 459-60.

92 *CPR, 1429–36*, pp. 260-1; PRO, E28/54/66-67; *PPC*, IV, 289-91. Cf. duchy loans for the garrisons of French fortresses in February 1434 (*PPC*, IV, 294-7). The net value of the enfeoffed lands was £5,503 in 1431–32 (Somerville, op. cit., p. 202).

93 PRO, E159/208, *adhuc communia*, E. m. 2; *PPC*, IV, 236-9; *Foedera*, IV, i, 10; *RP*, IV, 392; above, p. 42. These loans were intended for the defence of the realm against the king's rebels in France, a significant conjunction of the theoretical and the real.

94 *CPR, 1429–36*, pp. 353-5; Steel, op. cit., pp. 205-6; PRO, E403/716 passim; *PPC*, IV, 202-3, 214.

95 ibid., 207; *CPR, 1429–36*, pp. 466-7; Davies and Peake, *BIHR*, IV (1926–27), 168-9.

96 *Brut*, p. 468; *PPC*, IV, 316-29, 352; *CPR, 1429–36*, pp. 328-30; PRO, E28/ 56/41, 51. On 16 May 1436 an attempt was made to recover crown jewels

from those who held them as security *(CPR, 1429–36,* p. 517; PRO, E404/52/410).

97 Steel, op. cit., pp. 208-9. The duchy's feoffees lent £2,180 on 8 May. But for advantageous conditions extracted by merchant-lenders, see *PPC,* IV, 291-3; McFarlane, *CHJ,* IX (1947–49), 53 n. 10.

98 The following sentences are based on PRO, E403/699-727 passim; and Steel, op. cit., pp. 175ff, 258-9; see below, p. 167.

99 *PPC,* V, 6-7, 313, 13-14. Out of £21,000 received between Easter and Michaelmas 1437, Beaufort and the staplers contributed £20,116 (Steel, op. cit., p. 210).

100 ibid., pp. 210, 251, and passim; PRO, E403/691-727 passim. J. L. Kirby calculated that between 1422 and 1432, 1½ per cent of Beaufort's tallies had to be renewed before payment, compared with 41½ per cent of those of the wardens of the Scottish marches (*BIHR,* XXIV [1951], 139).

101 Steel, op. cit., pp. 259-61, 269.

7   Lawlessness and Violence

The first priority in the autumn of 1422 was to preserve social stability; in the longer term, it was to safeguard the peace of the realm on behalf of the king. It was in this spirit that the Windsor meeting was held on 28 September: its particular purpose was to guarantee peace and justice to all the king's subjects and to defend England from enemies within as well as without. Parliament saw its duty in almost identical terms when it met six weeks later; and when the king's uncles were assigned their special responsibilities, the obligation to protect and defend the realm received prime emphasis.[1] The maintenance of the law and the preservation of order, with an assurance of peace and justice to all, were fundamental elements of this obligation. In practical terms, it meant the impartial control of crime, especially violent crime.

Fifteenth-century men found it well nigh impossible to chart statistically the rise and fall of criminal activity, and the task is scarcely easier for the historian. As a result, conclusions about the prevalence of crime during Henry VI's early years must remain impressionistic and provisional for the time being, though a few important studies have been made of the operation of the royal courts during the fifteenth century.[2] Crime was normally dealt with by the common law courts, especially by the justices of the peace in their quarterly sessions in each county and by the central court of king's bench at Westminster.[3] Beyond this routine, petition could be made to the council, especially by those living in franchises like Lancashire or the Welsh marcher lordships, and in any case, it quickly turned its attention to particularly dangerous unrest; occasionally, cases were referred to it by parliament.[4] Parliament itself offered a similar forum, which responded to petitions from, or sponsored by, its MPs.[5] Meanwhile, the chancellor of England was developing his equitable jurisdiction to supplement the normal processes of common law by his 'conscience, reason, equity [and] good faith'.[6] The records produced by each of these courts varied in the degree of accuracy and bias with which they recounted the facts of cases heard. Indictments before JPs or in king's bench were couched in formalized language that included supposititious rather than actual details: attacks on property and persons, for example, seem to have taken place *vi et armis* and at night with surprising frequency.[7] Likewise, petitions to the council or to parliament might involve special pleading or exaggeration to ensure swift or favourable remedy. On the other hand, commissions of oyer and terminer for specialized purposes were expressly intended to seek the truth and punish actual law-breaking; their indictments and proceedings carry, therefore, somewhat greater authority.[8] Moreover, the eloquent speeches and lengthy petitions of MPs could be readily checked against the experience of their colleagues. If wrongful arrests were made or unwarranted punishments imposed, avenues of complaint and redress were available. Moreover, chroniclers occasionally witnessed crimes (or reported them second-hand), even if they were often blind to the issues involved.[9] All in all, a controlled scepticism must be applied by the historian to the surviving materials, without taking the virtues of criticism to a fault.

The nature of crime during the protectorate

Treason, felony, trespass, and lollardy encompassed practically every crime committed in England in the early fifteenth century. Although several trespasses (for example, extortion and the use of fraudulent weights and measures) stopped short of physical violence towards property or persons, there were few crimes which did not resort to (or result in) violence at some stage in their story. Crime was endemic, and a régime's success in controlling it may be gauged by the ability to curb its violent forms.[10]

Property – its acquisition and protection – was one of the most frequent causes of dispute and lawlessness in a society that placed a high premium on landownership as the foundation of social position, wealth, and political influence. Attacks on property, therefore, were as likely to involve magnates as well as lesser mortals. What William, Lord Ferrers suffered at his house at Smethwick (Staffordshire) on 6 May 1426, when Sir William Bermingham came from Coventry with a band of men and reportedly stole goods and killed two of Ferrers's servants, was mirrored by the experience of John de Fursdon, whose more modest property in Cornwall was ravaged and his family terrorized by an armed gang in 1424.[11] Within a landowner's estate, the instinctive friction between landowner and tenant (particularly the unfree tenant) often caused economic disruption and endangered public order. Much of the unrest was focussed on ecclesiastical landowners (abbots, priors, and bishops), against whom the anticlericalism of the age was also directed. There were several reports in the 1420s of tenants resisting the performance of time-honoured labouring services by a series of well co-ordinated plots. In the autumn of 1423 the abbot of Waltham's bondmen in Essex refused to do their customary services and organized a rising against the abbot. The torrential rain and high winds that destroyed the harvest that year had doubtless shortened their tempers.[12] Such organized action was aimed at lay landlords too, as Richard

129

Knyghtly of Fawsley (Northamptonshire) could testify in 1425; while the park at Woking (Surrey) of the widowed duchess of Clarence was invaded during the night of 5 January 1425 by a large band of armed men. The parks of the wealthy, with their herds of deer and other game, were an attractive quarry and easier to attack than more compact properties.[13] Social distinctions evidently had a violent dimension, and this was equally apparent in the Severn valley, where cut-throats from the forest of Dean threatened river traders who conveyed goods by boat for lords and ladies.[14]

Such landed lawlessness arose from strictly local causes – exasperation with the complexities of the land law, jealousy of the rights or property of others, the ambition to acquire more land, the desire for greater local influence, or 'the will to power' – so that the bane of a landowner's life was more likely than not to be his neighbours or his tenants. The dispute in Newcastle-upon-Tyne between the experienced soldier Sir William Elmeden and the influential Northumberland knight Sir Robert Ogle was so sensitive that it merited the nomination of a panel of arbitrators on 9 June 1425; if they failed to compose the quarrel, then three locally prominent umpires (the earl of Northumberland, Sir Robert Umfraville, and John, Lord Greystoke) would try to reach a settlement.[15] Thomas, Lord Dacre's animosity towards his wife's half-brother, Sir Richard Neville, in Yorkshire was calmed on 15 September 1429 when each concluded a bond worth £2,000 to keep the peace towards one another.[16] The locality where such incidents occurred was seemingly too small to contain all its ambitious landowners in peaceful proximity. Unmistakably a struggle for authority and power, though on a wider scale, was the confrontation between the duke of Gloucester and Bishop Beaufort in October 1425; and the jealousy and bitter rivalry in Ireland between Lord Talbot and the earl of Ormond was of a similar order.[17]

The prospect of financial gain tempted others to break the law and threaten the king's peace. No one succumbed more readily than the unscrupulous office-holder who was prepared to abuse his authority. A minor local official like the bailiff of Market Harborough (Leicestershire) could be accused of extortion and abuse of office in July 1425.[18] And the greater the office, the greater the temptation. Sheriffs so often failed to resist it that a common distrust of sheriffs had sprung up by the fifteenth century. Financial corruption was a frequent accusation levelled against them, and in Northumberland their blatant extortions assumed the mantle of custom. In the parliament of 1425 the community of the shire, probably through its MPs, clamoured for the abolition of what had become a regular form of taxation whereby 'headpennies' were exacted illegally to the value of £51 every third year and £5 every fourth; as a result, the most practised extortioners in the county were said to be manoeuvring for the shrievalty in these most profitable years.[19]

Heresy, which was usually of the lollard variety in the early fifteenth century, was normally dealt with by the diocesan courts. But occasionally lollards were suspected of trespass, felony, or even treason: some were militant, others no more than enthusiastic preachers bent on winning converts. They presented the greatest danger in 1414–17, when Sir John Oldcastle was at their head; but in 1431, too, uprisings in London and the midlands had a lollard tinge to them. In the intervening years, the threat was muted, although lollard communities kept in contact with one another and individual lollards were dealt with as criminals as well as heretics.[20] Coventry was a major centre of the movement, and in December 1424 a popular, seditious, and heretic preacher had such success among the people there that riots broke out while the local sheriff was supine.[21] Next to Oldcastle and 'Jack Sharp', the most notorious lawbreaker to whom contemporaries attributed heretical proclivities was William Wawe, though he displayed greater zeal in robbing ecclesiastics, nunneries, travellers, and merchants than in embracing eccentric religious beliefs. His followers resembled the retinue of a lawless layman, but during 1427 a number of them were arrested and hanged, along with (on 16 July) Wawe himself.[22] To 'lollardize' known criminals like Wawe would ensure their punishment in the king's courts.

Symptomatic of the inability of normal law enforcement agencies to protect the king's subjects adequately was the appearance of protection rackets and the practice of ransoming. The most celebrated instance of the first occurred in the countryside around Cambridge. In 1429 Irish students at the university – and a few from Wales and Scotland too – distributed bills to rich local gentlemen threatening them with arson unless substantial sums of money were handed over.[23] Equally reprehensible were the activities of Lord Talbot and his retinue, who used Goodrich castle (Herefordshire) as a dungeon in which unfortunates were held to ransom as if in wartime. His men so terrorized the nearby hundred of Wormelowe that a petition presented in parliament in 1423, doubtless by MPs from the distraught shire, was adopted by the commons as a whole. So serious was the situation that a mass rising in Herefordshire was feared and the council appointed a special commission of oyer and terminer.[24]

Every part of the realm could muster its quota of criminals and violent crime, but the periphery of England posed special problems. The Scottish borderland, Yorkshire, the principality of Wales, the marcher lordships, and the south-west peninsula proved less easy to control than counties nearer London or in easier communication with the seat of government. Violence seems to have been especially common in Herefordshire, which abutted several marcher lordships, to whose varied and distinctive jurisdictions criminals could flee with reasonable hope of avoiding repatriation and ultimate justice; there, too, the criminally inclined could recruit their retinues and gangs. One of the first acts of Henry VI's government (3 October 1422) was to proclaim the new king's peace in the border English counties and the adjacent marches, though in relying on the Talbot and Ferrers families to supervise operations it was setting poachers to act as gamekeepers.[25] The district of Archenfield and the forest of Dean were notorious for their tenuous links with the regular peace-keeping agencies at Hereford and Gloucester. In 1429 it was brought to parliament's attention by the burgesses of Tewkesbury that providence was tempted – and one's neck risked – by trading on the river Severn. Armed robbers were certain to emerge from the forest and the nearby hundreds of Bledisloe and Westbury (Gloucestershire), which were infected (so contemporaries believed) by the lawless air of Wales.[26]

Yorkshire distinguished itself criminally for different reasons. It was a large county for peace-keeping officers to supervise, despite its triple division into ridings. Even more significant was the presence in Yorkshire of an unusually large number of magnate and gentry families consumed with mutual jealousies that frequently erupted in feuding and violence. Henry, Lord FitzHugh and his kinsfolk were both victims and perpetrators of such crimes. Soon after Henry's Yorkshire estates were forcibly broken into late in 1424, 200 of his men, led by his brother George and his son and heir William, were accused of seizing Clifton manor near Ripon on 11 January 1425, even though it was in royal custody.[27] Dacre, Neville, FitzHugh, Percy, Mortimer, Greystoke, and others, including the king himself, jostled each other as landowners in the county and thereby laid the foundation for personal rivalries and family disputes galore. This area, too, supported some of the largest and wealthiest monasteries in England, and a number of them, both near York and in the dales, attracted the same sort of tenant hostility that was apparent elsewhere.[28] Further north the shires along the Scottish border suffered from periodic Scottish raids and were kept on permanent alert. Not only did this habituate northerners to a life of violence to some degree, but for reasons of defence the wardens of the marches, sheriffs, and other local officers were given unusual latitude in discharging their responsibilities – with the possibility of abuse becoming an occasional reality. In Northumberland, therefore, Scottish devastation was matched by shrieval extortion.[29]

It was geographical isolation that hindered the law and hampered the crown's officers in Devon and Cornwall. Communication across Dartmoor with the rest of the kingdom was difficult. By contrast, the sea-passage from the peninsula to the nearest non-English coastline – that of Brittany – was so direct that Breton privateers were able to descend on Cornish and Devon fishing villages with relative impunity. The sense of isolation and the obstacles to law enforcement by commissions from Westminster encouraged the attacks on property, terrorizing of the subject, highway robberies, and pirate raids which induced Henry VI's council to initiate urgent inquiries into crime in the area.[30]

Elsewhere in England and Wales, franchises and liberties, royal and private alike, were a law unto themselves – or, more precisely, unto their lords – even though the common law of England or, as in the case of the Welsh marches, an adaptation of it was generally in operation. Apart from the fact that these franchises were situated near the borders of the realm, with all the impediments to communication with the capital which that implied, their extraordinary judicial privileges made it difficult for outside authorities to penetrate them. Witness the reluctance to apply the statute of livery in the palatinate of Lancaster in 1427.[31] Moreover, local loyalties and a sense of separateness meant inevitable delays in apprehending criminals who fled from one franchise to another. It was not that procedures to cope with these circumstances had not been devised, for the royal council was ultimately available; but the obstacles could not be overcome with ease. This was frustratingly apparent to the prior of Goldcliff (Gwent) in 1424. In August of that year, his grange at Goldcliff was attacked by a Welshman from Netherwent, John ap Philip Morgan, who happened to be constable of Berkeley castle, across the estuary in Gloucestershire. A large herd of cattle was rustled and taken by him to Berkeley; two weeks later, the priory itself was attacked with such ferocity that the prior and monks fled. In seeking a remedy, the prior faced the uniquely independent privileges of the marcher lords, in this case of Edmund Mortimer, earl of March. The king's writ could achieve little in the earl's lordship of Caerleon, but neither, it transpired, could a suit introduced in the court of the lordship itself. Frustrated and helpless, in mid-November the prior appealed directly to the council.[32]

The methods of violence employed varied from the crude to the sophisticated. Direct assault, even to the point of death, was not uncommon. Lord Talbot's gang was capable of extreme violence in Herefordshire, and so was Sir William Bermingham's in Coventry; even a lowly bailiff of the bishop of London at Braintree (Essex) had his life threatened in court in June 1424 in the very presence of the bishop's steward.[33] More organized and more subtle were conspiracies with violent intent. The attacks by bond tenants on many landowners were apparently carefully planned with the aid of oaths of association.[34] Equally skilful was the use of maintenance by influential men to bend the legal process in their favour and, perhaps, to ensure for themselves immunity from the consequences of their deeds. In the 1420s complaint was continually voiced in the commons about such maintenance, and even royal councillors could be observed indulging in it. In 1429, therefore, it was resolved that councillors should not harbour criminals, nor favour a case in response to a gift or grant, nor maintain an officer, judge, or juryman by taking him into service or presenting him with livery. And these rules were to apply to the friends, neighbours, and servants of councillors too. The plea for impartial jurors was echoed in a variety of contexts in those same parliaments.[35]

One notorious maintainer of other men's quarrels was John de Langedon, whose lawless affinity committed depredations in Lancashire in 1426 and uttered threats of worse to come. Little hope of remedy was placed in the palatinate's own institutions or in arbitration, for by May 1426 the matter had been referred to the king's council.[36] Even known fugitives and felons were being maintained; when Thomas Sygeswick of Cheshire escaped from the Tower of London in July 1422, he was fed, armed, and abetted by other Cheshiremen living in Middlesex, and as a result he was able to continue his career as a thief.[37]

For those of gentle or noble rank, maintenance took the form of offering livery to men who might engage in crime with or without the knowledge of their lord or maintainer. William FitzHugh found himself the victim of such practices in 1425, when he attempted to recover his dead father's estates: the liveried *familia* of his enemies staffed the inquiry *post mortem*, whilst the sheriff and coroners were allegedly part of the same affinity and hence could delay proceedings and pack the juries.[38] More general protests were voiced in parliament in 1427 and 1429 at the uncontrolled bestowal of livery and its abuse by those who wore and granted it. The renewed attempt to prevent knights and lesser folk from granting their livery to other than their household servants, officers, and lawyers, and to extend this prohibition to the royal palatinates of Chester and Lancaster, tackled only part of the problem, for the aristocracy was equally deserving of censure. The council was reluctant to tamper fundamentally with laws that had been long on the statute book, even if they were ineffective. But a firm reiteration in 1429 (taking care that the assembly of retinues for war was in no way prejudiced) eventually received the government's approval: to grant livery for the purpose of maintenance would henceforward incur a fine and a prison sentence of one year.[39]

There was one further aid available to the criminal. Since the late fourteenth century, necromancy, sorcery, witchcraft, soothsaying, and magic were thought to promise much, though when Sir Ralph Botiller employed practitioners of these 'black' arts to bring about the death of William, Lord Botreaux (or so the latter claimed) in 1426, the results proved disappointing.[40]

Crime was not the prerogative of any one sex, age-group, or rank in society. It was to be expected from the habitually unruly: those who swung from trees on to unsuspecting travellers on the king's highway, or who retreated for safety to the woods and forests of England, were nothing more than common robbers and outlaws.[41] More remarkable (at least in the eyes of one chronicler) was the murder in June 1429 of a suspected Breton spy (who had battered to death and dismembered a London widow) by a crowd of bloodthirsty women.[42] As a group, the Irish immigrant community was far from law-abiding; whether as students or inhabitants of the seaports or larger towns, Irishmen had a distinctive contribution to make to crime in England. In the countryside around Oxford, disturbances in the 1420s were laid at the door of 'wylde Irisshmen', even though some of those responsible were not born in Ireland. They threatened the bailiffs of Oxford so that no arrests were made. Exasperation was such that it was decreed in parliament in 1422 that all Irishmen should leave the realm within six weeks unless they had visible means of support and a recognized occupation. In the event, close control of Irishmen entering England and (especially undergraduates) once they were in the realm was insisted upon, though it took a little time for the council to make the arrangements for sureties and declarations of loyalty work properly.[43] Even so, the violence involving Irishmen did not abate. At Rochester (Kent), there was unrest in May 1429 in which an Irishman was involved, whilst the tailor 'Long John of Ireland' caused an outburst at Hounslow (Middlesex).[44]

Far more serious was the threat to law and order posed by those people who might reasonably be regarded as the more stable elements of society – magnates and gentry (especially their young sons), tenantry and soldiery. When they were involved in crime, the prospect of upholding the law and ensuring impartial justice was in grievous danger. Not even the king's councillors stopped short of crime, though collectively they were prepared to curb it in others. Prominent knights resorted to violence in their quarrels and to illegalities in pursuit of their ambitions. Good intentions were frequently proclaimed, as in July 1424 when, in the interests of social peace, the protector and the lords agreed that disputes between them should be brought before them *ensemble* in order to prevent open violence.[45] Such declarations were not always effective, as the 'inveterate feud' in Bedfordshire between John Holand, earl of Huntingdon and John Mowbray, duke of Norfolk illustrated in 1428. Both magnates were removed from the Bedfordshire commission of the peace in July 1428, and JPs were temporarily forbidden to hold sessions in the shire, presumably while Gloucester himself investigated.[46] Huntingdon appears to have been a high-handed individual by nature, for when parliament met in September 1429, he crossed swords with his brother-in-law, Humphrey, earl of Stafford, and both men arrived at Westminster armed to the teeth. According to one chronicler interested in Huntingdon's activities, this altercation induced parliament to ban the carrying of weapons by a magnate's servant in the palace of Westminster while parliament was sitting.[47] The potential lawlessness of magnates had already caused the commons in 1425 to intervene in the dispute over precedence between Norfolk and the veteran soldier and royal councillor Richard Beauchamp, earl of Warwick. Precedence lay at the heart of a magnate's personal dignity, honour, and worthiness in society and for this reason was the more likely to produce heated argument when it was challenged. The presence at this parliament of the earl of March with a large liveried retinue demonstrated how fragile public order could be when responsibility for its maintenance rested in the main on people who were determined to display their power and assert their position – and in March's case perhaps his lineage too. At Salisbury inn, the London residence near Fleet Street of the bishop of Salisbury, March offered open house to all who would eat at his table. Such provocation caused serious tension between March and other lords, especially Gloucester who regarded himself as the greatest magnate then present in the realm. One contemporary concluded that March's despatch to Ireland as the king's lieutenant was adopted as a solution.[48] But the forebodings of the commons and the aristocratic flaw in the maintenance of law and order reappeared a few months later in the frenetic discord between Gloucester himself and Bishop Beaufort. If there had been any doubt before, this episode made it clear that responsible aristocratic behaviour was the key to domestic peace.

No lord was more blatant in his flouting of the law and the king's justice than John, Lord Talbot. He was, perhaps, habituated to warfare by his service in France, and more inclined to use force than argument because of his experiences in Ireland, where he became locked in conflict with the earl of Ormond. In 1423 Talbot and a retinue fifty-strong were responsible for killings and disturbances in Hereford-shire; his old partner-in-crime and former receiver-general, John Abrahall, had recently fallen out with Talbot and roamed the area with an armed gang that was not much smaller, ruthlessly extorting payments from innocent bystanders. Parliament in 1423 and 1425 could extract little more than promises of future good behaviour and, to judge by events in 1426, these were lightly given. In that year, Talbot, with his brother-in-law, Sir Hugh Cockesay, quarrelled violently with Joan Beauchamp, Lady Abergavenny, and as a result William Talbot, John's brother, was killed. The duke of Bedford himself had to intervene to bring the two parties to arbitration, and in November 1426 each concluded a bond of £1,000 to keep the peace towards the other.[49]

The power of example was strong in a hierarchical society, and inevitably the tenantry of landowners resorted to the kind of violence to which their superiors were addicted in order to settle their quarrels and relieve their grievances.[50] Soldiers of the king, assembled to fight in France, often fell into disorder as a result of frustration at the delays in paying their wages, taking musters, and preparing troop ships. Coastal areas like Kent and Sussex suffered in particular and com-plained loudly. The need to provision the waiting soldiery led (as in 1424, when Gloucester's expedition to Hainault was in preparation) to oppression and enforced purveyance without the courtesy of offering payment or seeking consent. Four years later, when the king's own journey to Calais was in prospect, Kentish and Sussex villagers exploded with a resentment that had been accumulating since Henry V's day; now specific proposals were placed before parliament to control the soldiers' behaviour and compensate local people for their losses. Yet it was no simple matter. The council was reluctant to impose irksome restrictions on soldiers who were recruited, assembled, and pacified only with difficulty.[51] Too many conflicting interests were at work to make the execution of the law and the preservation of order as straightforward a matter as it might seem.

Crime and law enforcement, 1422–29

The effectiveness of law enforcement in fifteenth-century England is difficult to assess; it is easier to detect when and how it was undermined. One notable way in which the law was brought into disrepute was through the activities of appealers. By 1422, the reliability of an appealer as an accuser had become seriously suspect because he was not above maligning otherwise innocent men, sometimes with revenge in mind, sometimes to divert attention from his own misdeeds. There is no doubting his poor reputation by this time. The commons denounced him on several occasions in the 1420s, and if such people had had any merit in the past in detecting crime and bringing lawbreakers to court, it had now disappeared, though the government was still reluctant to tamper fundamentally with the law of indictment and placed its faith rather in more thorough examination and investigation.[52]

The record of pleas in king's bench gives the decided impression that many serious crimes were never brought to a conclusion, let alone led to the punishment of the guilty.[53] Nor could the common practice of resorting with official blessing to arbitrators or an umpire to compose quarrels (especially between influential persons) out of court inspire confidence in the judicial process.[54] Moreover, parliament, council, and chancellor frequently preferred to seek mere promises of good behaviour, fortified by monetary sureties or recognisances, instead of following the legal process relentlessly to its end.[55]

The personnel of judicial offices did not help either. In the farflung parts of the kingdom, such as Cheshire and in the principality of Wales, justice was administered by local men deputizing for their absent superiors, and such men were among the most prominent lawbreakers of the area. By May 1423 a multitude of feuds had sprung up among the local Cheshire gentry (for example, between the Egertons and Breretons) who filled the principal offices in the palatinate. In 1426 the council had to order the justiciar of Chester, the duke of Exeter, to arrest several Cheshire squires who were scions of influential local families. In Ireland justice was feeble even when a magnate or the king's lieutenant was present. Talbot's ruthless reputation was widespread, but Ormond too was reported in 1429 as being on the rampage with Lord Dudley.[56] In the shires of the south-east and midlands, where justice was administered mainly by the JPs now that the king's bench no longer perambulated the country, those who enforced the law were not above indulging in criminal activity themselves.[57] The crown was beyond devising 'a substitute for a system of law maintenance based very largely on the unpaid assistance of gentlemen and noble amateurs, yet there was a great need to do so since much of the crime originated in the misdeeds of those same classes'.[58] Nor was the problem solved once the lawless had been arrested. There was growing concern about the security of English prisons, especially when political criminals were incarcerated in them. Sir John Mortimer's escape from the Tower of

London in 1423 inspired a statute whereby the escape of a suspected traitor would of itself incur a charge of treason. So unsatisfactory had conditions of imprisonment become that keepers of prisons, especially of the Tower, were afraid of their own prisoners.[59]

For all the frailties of English justice, the reign of Henry V saw the level of crime in England kept successfully under control; not even the frequent absence of the king in France from 1417 caused a deterioration comparable with that of earlier royal absences.[60] Indeed, this state of affairs was maintained during the first two years of Henry VI's reign, when it might be expected that disorder would increase. There was a genuine determination by protector, councillors, and parliament alike to enforce the law and meet the challenge of a long minority. But in mid-October 1424 Duke Humphrey went on his expedition to Hainault, and with Bedford still in Normandy, England was without an effective protector and defender. The presence of the royal *alter ego*, in default of the king himself, had a deterrent effect upon criminals and lawless localities, as the visit of Gloucester to Bedfordshire demonstrated in 1428.[61] When neither was available, judicial effectiveness was undermined.

Moreover, after Gloucester's return to England in mid-April 1425, his quarrel with Bishop Beaufort rose to such a pitch that it endangered the peace of the realm.[62] The spectacle of such turmoil among the rulers of the kingdom could hardly have a salutary effect on the violently, let alone criminally, inclined. To judge from the cases which came before king's bench and council, and the attempts by the government to inquire into and quell unrest in the kingdom, the years 1425 and, more especially, 1426 saw a marked increase in lawlessness and violent crime. Among the noble classes, Sir Ralph Botiller plotted the murder of Lord Botreaux, Sir William Elmeden and Sir Robert Ogle were at odds in Newcastle-upon-Tyne, Sir William Bermingham attacked Lord Ferrers's estates, the FitzHughs were embroiled in disputes in Yorkshire, Lord Talbot was marauding the Welsh borderland, and the earl of March cocked a snook at authority in London itself. Speaking generally, serious crime was at a much higher level in the years 1425–29 than it had been in the previous three years. The number of special commissions appointed to deal with it in 1426–29 (and they were especially numerous in 1428–29) was five times as great as in the period 1422–25, and they paid particular attention to violent unrest in the Welsh borderland, the south-west, and the north. Furthermore, measures to uphold law and order occupied a considerable amount of parliament's time during the sessions of 1429.[63] As the protectorate drew to its close, the task of maintaining justice, domestic tranquillity, and respect for law and the government appeared more formidable than in 1422.

The lollard rising of 1431

During the king's absence in France there occurred the most serious outbreak of lollard violence since 1414.[64] The government regarded it as a grave heretical threat which required the whole panoply of the law to suppress – even the personal presence of the lieutenant of the realm at some of the executions. Lollard scares were commonplace in early fifteenth-century England, and when the chancellor opened parliament in September 1429, he reminded the assembly of the presence of heresy and religious error in England. The occasional burning of heretics was nothing new either, and in 1430 several had taken place in London and the south-east.[65] The link with felony and treason which a nervous government made was probably responsible in 1430 for the investigation into the activities of the former lollard gentlemen Sir John and Thomas Cheyne, whilst the seven women who were clapped in the Fleet prison at Christmas 1430 for plotting the king's death may also have been suspected lollards.[66] Official awareness that the situation was deteriorating by the spring of 1431 led to the organization of a show-trial in London of the elderly Essex priest Thomas Bagley, who was a lapsed heretic. On or about 10 March 1431, he was solemnly burned at St Paul's cross with the maximum publicity in the presence of Gloucester and thousands of Londoners; beforehand, Archbishop Chichele, supported by no less than ten of his suffragans, had declaimed the formal sentence against all lollards and heretics.[67] It was a gruesome spectacle which failed, if it was intended to deter other dissidents who had been active in the city in recent weeks.

The programme of the leaders of the 1431 rising (and its widespread occurrence throughout southern England suggests a carefully co-ordinated plot) was reminiscent of the disendowment proposals of Henry IV's reign. But there were also flashes of treasonable social revolution in the ideas to do away with the king, his lords, and the ecclesiastical hierarchy, and to distribute the loot, along with the titles, to other (and unsuspecting, as far as one knows) individuals in London and elsewhere.[68] One London observer believed that the 'revolutionaries' themselves wanted to choose a crop of new dukes, earls, and barons.[69] Lollard propaganda was often voluminous and highly sophisticated. It employed the traditional art of preaching, but also capitalized on the spread of literacy and the rapid development of English as a written language, and it more than likely employed the itinerant artisans of the textile industry as distributors. The 1431 proposals were cast widely in the form of bills, and the government's realization of the crucial importance of written propaganda to the spread of these ideas is reflected in its own proclamation of 13 May against 'bille casters and keppers', and against those who read the defamatory and seditious bills which were skilfully concocted from plausible, if rather superficial, material. The government's finger pointed directly at the heart of the

139

lollard offensive, but its response merely amounted to repression of the propaganda's authors, disseminators, and readers.[70]

The leaders of the movement were Jack Sharp (*alias* William Maundreuil or William Perkyns), an Oxfordshire weaver from Abingdon who may have hailed originally from Wigmore on the Welsh border, and John Russell, a man with a record of criminal and heretical activities going back fifteen years.[71] Their rising in 1431 began in St Giles's parish, London, on 3 March and lasted for over two months, during which time it transferred its centre to Abingdon, but radiated to other towns such as Coventry, Oxford, Salisbury, Northampton, and Frome, where lollard sympathies had remained strong, and continued to rumble in the capital.[72] At last, the ringleaders and several of their acolytes were apprehended and severely dealt with. Sharp and five companions were captured at Oxford on 19 May, quickly condemned before Duke Humphrey himself, and beheaded (which was appropriate for traitors) at Abingdon three days later; the leader's head was despatched to London bridge for display as a grisly warning.[73] Russell was taken two months later, condemned in king's bench, and accorded a more ignominious death by hanging (as befitted a convicted thief) on about 12 July.[74] Other assorted conspirators, women among them, were rounded up elsewhere and summarily executed.[75] As a further precaution, on 19 June the arrest was ordered of the erstwhile lollard knight John Cheyne; the books and archives found in his Buckinghamshire home were to be scrutinized and a report made to the king's council.[76]

Gloucester's reputation was enhanced by these events. The vigour and despatch he showed in May 1431 was to be compared later with his behaviour in 1436, when he again caught the imagination of contemporaries and gave expression to a deeply-felt sentiment in Englishmen's make-up. In 1436 it was their patriotism; in 1431 their orthodoxy and fear of revolution.[77] He was well rewarded for his pains in galloping with his retinue from his country house at Greenwich to Oxfordshire to try some of the rebels, and his reward was a handsome life-annuity.[78] In fact, the sums granted to him were so large – 6,000 marks *per annum* so long as he remained lieutenant of the realm and 5,000 marks even after the king returned – that it must be wondered whether the duke took advantage of the alarm caused by the 1431 rising to equip himself with a substantial retinue and an equally substantial source of income. But to judge from the extensive coverage given to this rising by contemporary chroniclers, particularly in London, and the prompt and resolute reaction of Gloucester, there can be little doubt that the government was thoroughly alarmed at such a turn of events when the king was out of the country. Fears lingered on, but further precautions and prosecutions in the autumn of 1431 appear to have put paid once and for all to lollardy as a dangerous political and social force capable of widespread national rebellion.[79] Needless to say, the anti-clericalism on which it fed survived undimmed.[80]

Continuing disorder

Many of the king's subjects, aside from the insurrectionists of 1431, might have wished the death or disappearance of some of England's aristocracy. A number of magnates had engaged in lawlessness during the 1420s, or had supported those who were, and they continued to do so in the following decade. But it seems likely that magnates and lesser nobles were personally involved in violent crime against one another or their less influential neighbours on fewer occasions in the 1430s. It may be that the involvement of some of the more petulant magnates in the French war temporarily removed a disorderly element from the English countryside, fully justifying the belief held in 1474–75 that Edward IV's expedition would promote the peacefulness of English society.[81] Of those magnates who had been directly involved in violence before 1430, a good half – including the earls of Ormond, Huntingdon, and Stafford, the duke of Norfolk, Sir Ralph Botiller, and Cardinal Beaufort – accompanied Henry VI across the channel in April 1430. Perhaps, too, the gravity of the situation on the Norman frontier absorbed the attention of those who had estates in France. Moreover, the council's determined effort to direct magnate disputes towards the council board may have achieved a modicum of success. Once again, in April 1430, its responsibility to stop dissension among the lords was emphasized, and Beaufort was quite adamant that he would sail for France in 1430 only if the lay nobles in the expedition would refrain from quarrelling with one another.[82] In particular, the cardinal induced the duke of Norfolk and the earls of Huntingdon and Warwick to swear in Gloucester's presence that they would take to the council any dispute that might arise between them, their families, or their servants, whether in England or in France. When the king's company eventually returned to England in February 1432, the parliament which met in May tried to maintain the momentum for domestic peace, especially in view of the strong feelings roused by the changes of personnel in government and household. A number of the more prominent magnates – Norfolk, Suffolk, Huntingdon, Stafford, Northumberland, and Salisbury – were requested to leave any unusual retinue at home and to attend the session accompanied only by their customary *familia*.[83]

Nevertheless, there were bound to be some outbursts of aristocratic violence. In February 1435, for instance, local political interests in East Anglia were upset by servants of the duke of Norfolk and the earl of Suffolk, who became embroiled in a feud which resulted in the death of one of Suffolk's men.[84] Two years later, violence broke out between two Bedfordshire magnates for reasons that were not dissimilar. On this occasion, they came to blows over which of them had the greater ability to dominate the local justices' sessions. At Silsoe, a fight occurred between Lord Fanhope and Lord Grey of Ruthin when sessions were about to meet under the presidency of the one (Fanhope) in order to investigate the activities of tenants of the other; in fact, the sessions had to be abandoned.[85] This was undeniably a defeat for the recognized forces of law and order at the hands of noblemen who rated their own local position, reputation, and retinue higher than public order; and it was a sorry tale that was to be repeated in the provinces of the kingdom many times over in Henry VI's reign. No answer was yet forthcoming to the dilemma by which countrywide peace depended on influential magnates who were prepared to abuse their trust.

Perhaps the most serious of these incidents in the 1430s concerned that 'second Jezebel', Joan Beauchamp, Lady Abergavenny. She was still engaged in the private warfare that had preoccupied her in earlier years. Nor was she entirely the blameless party, even though Sir Edmund Ferrers led a large gang a thousand-strong against her and her servants at Birmingham in 1431. She was certainly capable of replying in kind, and it was claimed in the 1432 parliament that three years earlier she had even encouraged mass murder. She fought vigorously to obtain verdicts in her favour, even to reverse judgements already given against her; and she was sufficiently tenacious in pressing her suits to prevent parliament from deciding the issues between herself and her opponents.[86]

Apart from their willingness to disregard the law when their own interests were concerned, the aristocracy were also fair game for attacks by tenants and jealous neighbours. And in the 1430s there is some slight sign that political differences at Westminster were beginning to disturb the peace of the countryside as well. Occasionally, attacks were launched against members of the king's council or of his government. Thus, on 5 May 1430, one of the Leicestershire manors of the earl of Stafford, a councillor, was raided, while in March 1433 Sir Robert Babthorp, who had recently been appointed steward of the household, was among those robbed by a small gang of men.[87] A month later, another of Gloucester's appointees of February 1432, Lord Scrope of Masham, had one of his enclosures broken into by a veritable army of Yorkshiremen.[88] Lord Poynings, while on his way to a great council at Westminster on 23 April 1436, stopped overnight at the Crown inn in Rochester; there he was attacked by a large number of men, though the casualties – a stolen dog and a head-sore servant – are reminiscent more of a drunken brawl than of anything more serious.[89] Unpopular gentry were similarly treated, whether it be the case of Sir Lawrence Warenne, whose relations with his tenants and servants were tense by May 1433; or Sir William Mountford, on whom Oxford students descended in 1436 to burn his house and rob his estate; or the suffragan bishop of Coventry and Lichfield, whose house was broken into by more than seventy Coventry men in 1435.[90]

Irish and Welsh residents in England stood out from the mass of the king's subjects by their language, habits, and historical associations. For this reason, they were not only distrusted by many Englishmen, but felt themselves to be in an alien environment to which they often reacted with hostility and lawlessness – though the Welsh at least enjoyed greater legal protection than undoubted aliens like the Dutch and Germans.[91] Despite the protectorate's decision to expel unruly Irishmen involved in criminal activity, they continued to cause the authorities concern. Student unrest from this quarter seems to have been muted after the arson and attempted blackmail of 1429, but Irish craftsmen, labourers, and shiftless soldiers could still be found stealing and brawling in the streets of London and its suburbs.[92] Bristol, which had well-oiled links with the Irish ports, also suffered from disorderly Irish visitors and residents. In January 1437, for instance, men from Cork and Roscommon stole a cross and other precious ornaments from Keynsham parish church and disposed of them to a Bristol goldsmith who, along with several other Bristol merchants, had planned the theft.[93] Such incidents were commonest early in the 1430s and were responsible for a further proclamation hounding footloose Irishmen out of the country, ostensibly to defend their island against invasion.[94] Those members of the professional, commercial, and religious classes who were allowed to stay needed a licence to do so. This order was reissued twice in rapid succession, in September 1431 and October 1432, in years when Irishmen were proving a nuisance to the law-keeping agencies, particularly in London.[95] This campaign seems to have had the desired effect for, with the exception of the Bristol theft in 1437, the Irish community caused little trouble in the years immediately following.

If the Irish contribution to English crime was on the whole successfully reduced, the Welsh to some extent adopted their mantle as the instigators of crime and perpetrators of lawlessness in the 1430s. Of those who had gone home to Wales during the Glyndŵr revolt, few seem to have returned to England once the rebellion was over; perhaps, too, it was unwise for a Welshman to travel at large outside his country for a decade or more after Glyndŵr disappeared from public view. At all events, it was not until the 1430s that English judicial records began once again to throw up instances of disorderliness by Welshmen in England. Not unexpectedly, much of it occurred in and around the capital, which was a mecca for all kinds of migrants to the realm. A Welshman from Bangor, newly returned from the wars, was arrested on suspicion of felony in Middlesex in July 1431; another, a labourer from Laugharne (Carmarthenshire), was involved in a theft at Enfield four years later.[96] Welsh gentlemen were accused of similar behaviour and sometimes even took to brawling amongst themselves. Two living in Southall fought to the death in October 1435, whilst another gentleman, originally from Cardiff, was locked in the Marshalsea prison for theft in May 1437.[97] But if London and the home counties witnessed a degree of Welsh violence, towns near the border were equally afflicted. In Bristol in 1429, a professional scrivener (or text-writer) from Powys stole some vestments of Italian work from the church of Holy Trinity, Westbury-on-Trym, and he was harboured in the city by a Welsh girl, Juliana ap Hywel (who had adopted the English surname of Orchard).[98] In Shrewsbury, a number of Powis 'knaves' were enlisted as accomplices by Alice Mutton, a Shrewsbury widow whose family was rapidly becoming prominent in the town, for the purpose of murdering William Hord and his son Thomas.[99] Along the river Severn, the depredations of Welsh forest-dwellers on the river traffic continued and a weary parliament took yet further measures to combat it in 1431 – and probably with the same lack of success as earlier assemblies.[100]

Parliamentary remedy, 1429–37

The commons in parliament showed themselves as concerned as any about the prevailing disorder in the realm and the disrespect shown for the law by all sections of the community. The parliament of 1429 met in the knowledge that Henry VI was preparing to visit France for his coronation. Measures had to be taken to deal with the disquieting level of crime of the past few years before he left England with his household, some of his councillors, and a substantial proportion of his magnates. This was precisely what the parliament attempted to do, and with some success.[101] During 1430 and 1431, the momentum was maintained by Gloucester, particularly in Yorkshire (where the estates and officers of Archbishop Kemp, chancellor of England, invited attack), Lincolnshire, East Anglia, Cornwall, and Cardiganshire – all counties situated a considerable distance from the centre of government.[102] To judge by the recorded prosecutions, the level of serious crime seems to have been markedly lower in these few years than in those immediately preceding them; in particular, there were very few instances of aristocratic lawlessness in 1430–32 by those who had been responsible for it in the 1420s.[103] The one really serious disturbance in these years was the lollard rising, in which the infection of heresy was linked with the treasonable acts of several gangs. Gloucester, as lieutenant of the realm, acted swiftly, personally, and vigorously to suppress the rising once and for all.[104]

After the return of the king and his companions in February 1432, there appears to have been a significant increase in the incidence of serious crime, and not solely involving the aristocracy and royal officials. Although Cornwall, Devon, and north Wales predictably suffered, the renewed disturbances were more widespread and extended to a city like Bristol (by February 1432), counties like Hampshire, Somerset, and Berkshire (where the riots were more frequent than usual), and even to London.[105] This was the situation that faced Bedford when he visited England in 1433 and presided over the parliament that met on 8 July.

This assembly showed a singular preoccupation with order and justice throughout the realm. The critical state of affairs was brought home to the MPs on 13 August, when the assembly was prematurely adjourned; the principal reason for this, according to the government, was the disorder rife in the realm and the fact that full information about the disturbances was not yet available to parliament.[106] Three weeks after it reassembled on 13 October, an extraordinary measure was proposed which reflects MPs' grave concern with unrest and the inability of the common law to respond adequately. Counties distant from the capital were causing the most trouble – Salop and Herefordshire, Yorkshire, Nottinghamshire, and Derbyshire – although apprehension in the capital itself may have caused parliament to list Sussex too among the more lawless areas. The proposal which the commons put before the government was resurrected from the records of Edward II's reign: in manifest default of mortal agencies, spiritual assistance should be enlisted in the form of excommunication. If implemented, this would have been a reciprocal service for the statute of 1401, which had placed the secular arm at the disposal of the church in cases of heresy.

The suggestion was carefully discussed by Bedford, Gloucester, Beaufort, the chancellor, and the rest of the council, though understandably they were unwilling to admit that the situation was so grave as to warrant consigning themselves to the hands of the Almighty rather than to the common law of England. The speaker responded helpfully with a further suggestion that the more prominent of the king's subjects – the councillors, magnates, and prelates – should formally and publicly commit themselves to the preservation of peace and the advancement of sound, efficient government by re-swearing the oath they had taken in 1429. If fainter hearts required a pretext for repeating this solemn procedure, it lay in the fact that Bedford had not then been in the realm and consequently had never sworn the oath. A reaffirmation of principles might be a decisive example to all. This plan was acceptable to the government and the arrangements were made. On 3 November 1433 all the lords present swore the oath, and those who were absent did so shortly afterwards – for instance, Lord Scrope, who was seriously ill, did so at home on 5 December. Later in the day, the commons as a body also agreed to swear, and ten days after that Bedford received their oaths in person in the commons' house. Indeed, the duke seems to have been the moving spirit behind the implementation of the commons' suggestion, for he was determined to restore domestic peace, now that he was in the country, as a necessary preliminary to renewing the campaign in France with single-minded vigour.

The oath of 1429 and 1433 pinpointed the more grievous ills from which the country suffered. Those who swore it undertook not to maintain criminals or those indicted of crimes; nor would they support other men's quarrels, overawe jurors, officers, or judges, nor would they give livery to them nor take them into their private service. What was concerning parliament in 1433 was the abuse of the judicial system by powerful and influential persons; its intention was to free royal justice from the cancer of influence, corruption, bribery, and threats.[107] At the same time – and this was a crucial step – the lords undertook to

145

ensure that others in their localities would follow their example, a classic reflection of the territorial power which magnates still enjoyed in those areas where their estates or residences were located. The commons were anxious that no one of significance should frustrate the oath's intentions. Before parliament ended towards the end of December, it was agreed that not only should absent lords take the oath before the council as soon as possible, but that the parliamentary knights should inform the chancery who, in their opinion, would be most appropriate to swear in the shires during the following three months. Moreover, the realm's territorial franchises were to be treated in exactly the same way, and so were Wales and Cheshire, where 'love days' could be organized for the swearing ceremony. As a result, few socially prominent or politically powerful men were likely to escape their obligations, and the government's determination would be communicated to every corner of the land.[108]

This entire procedure was unusual, to say the least, but to induce the king's important subjects to reaffirm their allegiance to his peace and to the common law was founded on the most fundamental obligation of the subject. By 1 May 1434 the names of those required to swear had been given to the chancellor, so that before Bedford left England in July, he could feel satisfied that resolute and wide-ranging efforts were under way to ensure the peace of the realm and to eliminate (as far as a formal, public undertaking could do so) the worst examples of lawlessness.[109] With some justice, a contemporary chronicler concluded that Bedford, whilst he was in England, embarked on the punishment of rebels and the establishment of unity and peace throughout the kingdom.[110]

The commons joined wholeheartedly in his campaign. In 1433 they were preoccupied with questions of law and order to an extent beyond that of any other parliament of the minority, with the possible exception of that of 1429. Not only were they prepared to discuss extraordinary proposals for extending true justice to the king's subjects, but they also enacted new law on the subject.[111] Corruption and partisanship by sheriffs, particularly those in Herefordshire who had been notorious for decades, were tackled boldly. Care was taken to close the loophole in the law which allowed unfinished cases to be terminated by a change of JPs. On a more localized level, the keepers of the stews on the south bank of the Thames, which had an evil reputation as dens of vice, were prohibited from serving as jurors; and attacks on MPs while parliament was sitting were henceforward to be referred to the court of king's bench. Where existing law was relevant to impartial justice, it was unequivocally affirmed. In such cases, the common law as it stood was considered adequate, but it required re-emphasis by parliament and a clear declaration from the government that it would implement it. This Bedford and the parliament of 1433 provided.

The efforts of this parliament seem to have been rewarded, for to judge by the publicly expressed concern for law and order, the remaining years of the minority saw detected crime fall to a level that was adequately controlled by the normal peace-keeping agencies. The parliament of 1435 was less concerned with public order and justice; and commissions of inquiry into disorder, lawlessness, and treason in the realm were fewer in 1434–36 and concentrated on local disturbances.[112] But by 1437 the foundations of stability were cracking once more, for abroad there was military uncertainty and at home anti-alienism was reaching a new pitch, whilst the imminent ending of the king's minority may also have unnerved important Englishmen. Some of the increasing disorder of 1436–37 which can be detected in the records may be attributable to the unsettled times in which men lived.

When parliament opened on 21 January 1437, the chancellor, Bishop Stafford of Bath and Wells, made no bones about one of the main reasons for summoning the assembly: it was to re-establish peace and justice among the king's subjects.[113] In the following June, the quarrel between Lord Grey and Lord Fanhope broke out in Bedfordshire; not only did it escalate into an armed affray, but it disrupted the king's sessions.[114] A month later, arbitrators were required to compose the differences that had arisen between landowners in the midlands.[115] And in the city of Norwich truly serious riots occurred about the same time and caused the council to intervene dramatically. The root of these particular disturbances lay in the complex relationships within the city between merchants and craftsmen, citizens and clergy, and Norwich's reputation for misgovernment went back some years.[116] In 1437 it was feared that the dissensions and alignments among the citizenry would come to a head at the mayoral election scheduled for 1 May. The prospect of serious unrest filled the government with foreboding. On 26 April the council nominated one of its number, Bishop Lumley of Carlisle, and a royal justice, John Cotesmore, to hurry to Norwich by 30 April to supervise the election next day. They were authorized to punish any rioters and, if necessary, to threaten the city with the withdrawal of its liberties and direct rule from Westminster.[117] The election did not pass off peacefully and on 8 May a hospital in the city was attacked.[118] Certain Norwich men were thereupon brought before the council on 18 June to explain themselves and the situation in their city; their explanations and subsequent behaviour were far from satisfactory, because a month later, on 12 July, the fateful step was taken to revoke the liberties of Norwich.[119] A warden was appointed by the crown to rule the city, together with two sheriffs, and justices were also nominated.[120] The man lighted upon to represent King Henry in Norwich was an inspired choice. John Welles, a grocer and alderman of London since 1420, had been born in Norwich and therefore had local knowledge that would stand him in good stead in discharging his ticklish commission; at the same time, he was sufficiently removed from the factiousness of the city's politics to bring an independent will to bear on its problems.[121] Full powers of government were vested in this small group of men, though whether the stern initiative taken was in any way successful may be doubted: Norwich would

147

prove a threat to the stability of East Anglia once again a few years later.[122]

Notes

1 *RP*, IV, 170, 169, 174-5. Cf. the proclamation of 1 October 1422 which announced the new government's determination to establish peace even on the western border of the realm (*CCR, 1422–30*, p. 41; *Foedera*, IV, iv, 81-2).

2 For Herefs. crime in 1413–61, as reflected in the king's bench plea rolls, see A. Herbert (*née* Wright), 'Public order and private violence in Herefordshire, 1413–61' (Wales MA thesis, 1978); idem, 'Herefordshire, 1413-61: some aspects of society and public order', in Griffiths, *Patronage, the crown and the provinces*, ch. 5. Extracts relating to Staffs. from the plea rolls of Henry VI's reign have been printed by G. Wrottesley, *William Salt Arch. Soc.*, XVII (1896), 87-153; n.s., III (1900), 123-9. See the comprehensive analysis of the court of chancery by M. E. Avery, 'Proceedings in the court of chancery up to c. 1460' (London MA thesis, 1978), and more briefly in 'The history of the equitable jurisdiction of chancery before 1460', *BIHR*, XLII (1969), 129-44; of king's bench, in M. Blatcher, *The court of king's bench, 1450–1550* (1978), and in C. H. Williams, 'Fifteenth century *coram rege* rolls', *BIHR*, I (1923–24), 69-72; and of local commissions in J. B. Avrutick, 'Commissions of oyer and terminer in fifteenth-century England' (London M Phil thesis, 1967).

3 JPs are studied by B. H. Putman (ed.), *Proceedings before the justices of the peace in the fourteenth and fifteenth centuries, Edward III to Richard III* (1938), and their surviving records by E. G. Kimball, 'A bibliography of the printed records of the justices of the peace for counties', *University of Toronto Law Journal*, VI (1945–46), 401-13; one consequence of the settling of king's bench in London by 1421 was that these records were no longer centrally preserved and few survive for subsequent years.

4 Below, p. 133 (for a marcher lordship); *PPC*, III, 327 (Lancs.). See *RP*, IV, 289-90, for a reference from parliament, and in general, I. S. Leadam and J. F. Baldwin (eds.), *Select cases before the king's council, 1243–1482* (Selden Soc., XXXV, 1918).

5 Below, pp. 144ff. For parliament's interest in a franchise like Cheshire, see *CCR, 1422–30*, pp. 352-3.

6 W. P. Baildon (ed.), *Select cases in chancery* (Selden Soc., X, 1896), pp. xxx-xxxi. See Avery, thesis, and *BIHR*, XLII (1969), 129-44.

7 Below, pp. 129ff.

8 *CPR, 1422–29*, contains several such commissions. See Avrutick, thesis.

9 See *Amundesham*, I, 25, 42-3, for the quarrels between the earl of Huntingdon, on the one hand, and the duke of Norfolk and the earl of Stafford, on the other.

10 J. G. Bellamy, *Crime and public order* (1973), especially pp. 3, 33-6, 65-6.

11 PRO, KB9/935/15; *CPR, 1422–29*, p. 229. The Bermingham–Ferrers feud was well under way by 1423, when Sir Edmund Ferrers and a grand retinue (including an abbot, a prior, 5 esquires, and 3 gentlemen) attacked Sir William's manor (PRO, KB9/203 m. 19; E28/39/37; *William Salt Arch. Soc.*,

n.s. III [1900], 124). For the prevalence of forcible entries, see *RP*, IV, 352-3.

12 *CPR, 1422–29*, p. 174; *PPC*, III, 88-90; for the weather, see *London Chrons.*, p. 165, and *Great Chron.*, p. 128. Cf. *CPR, 1422–29*, pp. 327-8 (St Mary's, York), 402 (Bridlington priory); PRO, E28/45/69 (Osney abbey); below n. 85 (Launceston priory).

13 *CPR, 1422–29*, p. 300; PRO, KB9/221/1/30. Cf. ibid., 221/1/40 (an invasion of Sir Walter FitzWalter's park at Hanley [Sussex] in 1424); 223/2/70 (the countess of Stafford's park near Thaksted [Essex] in 1425), and *William Salt Arch. Soc.*, XVII (1896), 102 (a royal park entered in 1425 and robbed).

14 *RP*, IV, 345-6. Cf. below, p. 144.

15 *CCR, 1422–30*, p. 210. For Elmeden and Ogle (a high-ranking servant of Bishop Langley of Durham), see Roskell, *1422*, pp. 151-2, 175-6; Storey, *Langley*, pp. 81-2, 142-3.

16 *CCR, 1422–30*, p. 448. (*rectius* John, Lord Dacre). Cf. the attack by the west-country knight Sir William Bonville on Sir Thomas Broke's property at Axminster (Soms.) early in 1427 (ibid., p. 403).

17 Above, pp. 73ff.

18 PRO, KB9/221/1/24-26.

19 WA MS 12389 (a possible parliamentary petition of 1426 or 1432); *RP*, IV, 289-90. Cf. corrupt sheriffs in ibid., pp. 306 (1426), 352-3 (1429), and, in general, Bellamy, *Crime and public order*, pp. 13-14.

20 J. A. F. Thomson, *The later lollards, 1414–1520* (Oxford, 1965), esp. ch. I; C. A. Robertson, 'The tithe-heresy of Friar William Russell', *Albion*, VIII, no.1 (1976), 1-16; C. Kightly, 'The early lollards: a survey of popular lollard activity in England, 1382–1428' (York PhD thesis, 1975).

21 Thomson, op. cit., pp. 100-1; *CPR, 1422–29*, p. 275; *CCR, 1422–30*, p. 204.

22 R. A. Griffiths, 'William Wawe and his gang, 1427,' *Trans. Hants. Field Club and Arch. Soc.*, XXXIII (1977), 89-93. For probable examples of lollardy being used to blacken a reputation, see Thomson, op. cit., pp. 194, 196.

23 *RP*, IV, 349, 358; *Amundesham*, I, 45. Such arson was declared to be treason in 1429.

24 *RP*, IV, 253-60.

25 *CPR, 1422–29*, p. 35; *Foedera*, IV, iv, 81; below, pp. 136, 142. For Herefs. violence in 1423, see PRO, KB9/203 m. 30. For the recruitment of Welshmen by William FitzWaryn and Sir Richard Laken for an attack on Whittington castle (Salop) in November 1422, see *RP*, IV, 192. In 1424 the imprisoned traitor Sir John Mortimer was thought to be planning to raise 40,000 men in Wales and the marches to overturn the government (*Great Chron.*, pp. 130-1; *London Chrons.*, pp. 282-3).

26 *RP*, IV, 345-6.

27 *CPR, 1422–29*, p. 278; PRO, KB9/221/1/1-2. For the alleged attempt by Henry's enemies in 1425 to deny the FitzHugh inheritance to his son and heir, see *RP*, IV, 288-9.

28 *CPR, 1422–29*, pp. 327-8, 402. For riots in Pontefract in 1426, see PRO, E28/48/35.

29 *CCR, 1422–30*, p. 437; PRO, E159/199 *brevia directa baronibus*, M, m.19; above, p. 130.

30 *CPR, 1422–29*, pp. 229–30, 328, 468. The Isle of Wight was also open to attack by Bretons (ibid., p. 327 [1426]).
31 It was finally introduced there in 1429 (*RP*, IV, 329-30, 348-9).
32 PRO, E28/46/18. Cases from the palatinate of Lancaster and Chester were also heard by the council (*PPC*, III, 327, 345-7; below, p. 137).
33 Below, p. 136; PRO, E28/45/3. For similar attacks on jurors in Staffs. in 1423, see *William Salt Arch. Soc.*, XVII (1896), 99.
34 *CPR, 1422–29*, pp. 300, 402. Oaths were sworn in the attack on the Cornishman John de Fursdon in 1424 (ibid., p. 229; above, p. 129).
35 *RP*, IV, 343-7. The complaints are in ibid., pp. 288-9, 306, 327-8, 329-30, 348-9, 352-3.
36 PRO, E28/46/84.
37 PRO, KB9/219/2/17. Sygeswyk was still at large in June 1426 (PRO, E159/202 *Communia*, T, m. 9).
38 *RP*, IV, 288-9; William appealed to parliament in 1425. For comparable maintenance of the escheator of Soms.–Dorset and 12 jurors in 1430–31 by Margaret, Lady Luttrell for the purpose of packing an inquiry about her dower, see SomsRO, DD L Box 1/17 [3] m. 8.
39 *RP*, IV, 329-30, 348-9. For an esquire brought to court in 1424 for giving livery to a yeoman who was not in his household or his officer, see *William Salt Arch. Soc.*, n.s., III (1900), 124-5. See McFarlane, *Nobility*, ch. 6.
40 *CPR, 1422–29*, p. 363.
41 ibid., p. 468 (Devon); PRO, E28/46/84 (Lancs.); *RP*, IV, 356.
42 R. A. Griffiths, 'Un espion breton à Londres, 1425–29', *Annales de Bretagne et de l'Ouest*, LXXXVI (1979), 399-403.
43 *RP*, IV, 190-1, 253-60; *CCR, 1422–30*, p. 78; PRO, E28/41/44; 42/54, 90, 92.
44 ibid., 220/1, 12. For an attack on an Irish labourer in Paddington (Middlesex) about 1424, see PRO, KB9/218/2/36; and other examples of crime committed by Irishmen in ibid., 222/2/1-2 (Bucks, 1424), 4 (Surrey, 1427); 224 m. 239 (Middlesex, 1428). See also above, n. 21.
45 *PPC*, III, 148-52.
46 ibid., 302; *Amundesham*, I, 25; *CPR, 1422–29*, p. 559.
47 *Amundesham*, I, 42-3.
48 Giles, p. 6; *RP*, IV, 262-75. For disputes over precedence, see J. E. Powell and K. Wallis, *The house of lords in the middle ages* (1968), pp. 453-5, 463-5.
49 *RP*, IV, 253-60, 275; *CCR, 1422–30*, pp. 317-18; Herbert, thesis, pp. 45, 54-8; above, p. 80. For the Talbot–Ormond feud in Ireland, see Otway-Ruthven, *Medieval Ireland*, ch. XI; below, pp. 163ff. A valuable study of this theme is now C. Carpenter, 'The Beauchamp affinity: a study of bastard feudalism at work', *EHR*, XCV (1980), 515-32.
50 The council stressed the importance of good example in 1429 (*RP*, IV, 343-7).
51 ibid., 291-92, 351-52.
52 ibid., 289-90 (1425), 305 (1426), 353-4 (1429).
53 See Bellamy, *Crime and public order*, pp. 157-8, for the low percentage of felons convicted.
54 e.g., *CPR, 1422–29*, p. 265; *CCR, 1422–30*, p. 470; above, p. 136.
55 *RP*, IV, 253-60, 275; *PPC*, III, 345-7. The council could not decree death,

mutilation, or deprivation of livelihood; but oaths, sureties, and recognisances would appeal at least to councillors who were sometimes connected with the lawbreakers (A. Harding, *The Law Courts of Medieval England* [1973], pp. 105-6; Baldwin, *Select Cases before Council*, p. xlv).

56 *PPC*, III, 345-7; PRO, E28/41/53; /47/15, 19; /48/58. For Ireland, see *Amundesham*, I, 43-4; Otway-Ruthven, *Medieval Ireland*, ch. XI; below, pp. 163ff.

57 *RP*, IV, 288-9; *PPC*, III, 302.

58 Bellamy, *Crime and public order*, p. 2; cf. ibid., pp. 201-2.

59 *RP*, IV, 189-90, 260; for the escape from the Marshalsea of the infamous William Wawe, who was subsequently recaptured and hanged as a traitor, see above n. 22. Cf. generally R. B. Pugh, *Imprisonment in Medieval England* (Cambridge, 1968), ch. X, XI.

60 Bellamy, *Crime and public order*, pp. 8, 10 n. 22.

61 ibid., p. 11; above, p. 135.

62 For the alarm of the commons, see *RP*, IV, 296; above, pp. 73ff.

63 There was need, too, for renewed suppression of lollardy by convocation from 1428 onwards (Thomson, op. cit., pp. 223-5).

64 ibid., especially pp. 58-60; M. E. Aston, 'Lollardy and sedition, 1381–1431', *Past and Present*, XVII (1960), 24-30.

65 *RP*, IV, 335; *Amundesham*, I, 46, 50: Thomson, op. cit., pp. 123-4.

66 *Amundesham*, I, 56-7; *CPR, 1429–36*, pp. 75-181. See K. B. McFarlane, *Lancastrian kings and lollard knights* (Oxford, 1972), pp. 139ff.

67 Bagley's burning was widely reported with varying degrees of accuracy (*Amundesham*, I, 59, 61; *Brut*, pp. 456, 501; Giles, p. 12; 'Gregory's Chron.', p. 171; *CCR, 1429–35*, p. 142).

68 Aston, *Past and Present*, XVII (1960), 27-8; PRO, KB9/225/2-4, 22; *Amundesham*, I, 453.

69 'Gregory's Chron.', p. 172; cf. 'English Chron.', p. 54.

70 'Gregory's Chron.', p. 171; *Amundesham*, I, 63-4 (where bill-writers are mentioned); *PPC*, IV, 107-8; PRO, KB9/225/2-4, 22; 227/2/23, 26; *CCR, 1429–35*, p. 123.

71 'Gregory's Chron.', p. 171; Aston, *Past and Present*, XVII (1960), 25-6. Russell had also been imprisoned for theft in 1423 (PRO, KB9/225/21). Apart from a possible origin in Herefs., there is nothing to connect Sharp with the Mortimer claim to Henry VI's throne; in any case, the Welsh borderland was a noted refuge of lollards. Cf. Aston, *Past and Present*, XVII (1960), 44 n. 122. See J. F. Davis, 'Lollard survival and the textile industry in the south-east of England', *Studies in Church History*, III (1960), 191-201.

72 *Amundesham*, I, 63-4; 'Gregory's Chron.', p. 172; *London Chrons.*, pp. 96-7; PRO, KB9/225/2-4, 21, 22; 227/2/1A, 1B, 23, 26; *PPC*, IV, 89, 107-8.

73 'Gregory's Chron.', pp. 171-2; *English Chron.*, p. 54; *Brut*, p. 457; *London Chrons.*, pp. 96-7. He was betrayed by a lollard apprehended at Salisbury (*PPC*, IV, 99-100, 107-8; PRO, E404/48/125). Aston, *Past and Present*, XVII (1960), 28, says that Sharp was burned (a heretic's death).

74 Various dates in July are given for his death ('Gregory's Chron.', p. 172; *Brut*, p. 457; *London Chrons.*, pp, 97, 134), but that in PRO, KB9/225/2-4 22, is preferred here.

75 'Gregory's Chron.', p. 172 (Coventry); *PPC*, IV, 89 (near London).

76 Inquiry was also made into alleged riots and thefts by Sir John and his

kinsman, Thomas, but the latter was released on 4 August so presumably the allegations were not substantiated (*CPR, 1429–36*, pp. 153, 75, 181; PRO, KB9/225/41, 72; *CCR, 1429–35*, p. 89).

77 Below, p. 205. It was on Gloucester's direct orders that a justice of king's bench was sent to Kenilworth on 12 June to try more rebels (*PPC*, IV, 89; PRO, E404/49/324). For his subsequent reputation as defender of the church, see Bodl, Tanner 196 f. 53*v* (1430s).

78 *London Chrons.*, pp. 96-7; *Great Chron.*, pp. 155-6; *Amundesham*, I, 63-4. A grant on 28 November was to provide him with a bodyguard and to support his dignity (*CPR, 1429–36*, pp. 184-5; *PPC*, IV, 105-6). He also had his expenses paid, 500 marks on 11 May and further sums soon afterwards (ibid., pp. 88-9, 91; PRO, E404/47/316, 333 [before 16 July]). In addition, he and his wife were given gifts by a grateful Coventry (Aston, *Past and Present*, XVII [1960], 24-5).

79 ibid., 28-9; J. A. F. Thomson, 'A Lollard rising in Kent: 1431 or 1438?', *BIHR*, XXXVII (1964), 100-2. For the sparse and isolated nature of later lollard activity, see Thomson, op. cit., passim.

80 e.g., *RP*, IV, 458-9 (against St Mary's, York, 1432–33); *CPR, 1429–36*, p. 527 (disruption of a priest's induction, 1436); ibid., *1436–41*, p. 84 (against the dean and chapter of Lichfield, 1437).

81 *RP*, VI, 88-9.

82 ibid., IV, 415-18.

83 *PPC*, IV, 112-13. Lord Cromwell, who had just been dismissed as chamberlain of the household, was similarly instructed.

84 ibid., 298-301. Cf. accusations that the earl of Suffolk was a 'heavy lord' to the abbot of Bury and the prior of Walsingham in November 1431 (*CCR, 1454–61*, p. 77).

85 *PPC*, IV, 298-30; V, 38-9, 57-9; *CPR, 1436–41*, p. 87. Cf. 'the grete wranges extorsions and grevans' suffered by Launceston priory (Corn.) at the hands of William, Lord Boṭreaux and others in the 1430s (Bodl, Tanner 196 f. 53-54).

86 PRO, KB9/225/34; *RP*, IV, 410-13; *CPR, 1429–36*, p. 295. For Adam of Usk's description of her, see McFarlane, *Nobility*, p. 63.

87 PRO, KB9/938/73; 226/26.

88 ibid.

89 ibid., 228/2/13.

90 *CCR, 1429–35*, p. 283 (Warenne); PRO, KB9/228/1; 940/80 (Mountford); 227/2/87; 1/31 (the bishop).

91 Below, p. 168.

92 Above, p. 134; PRO, KB9/938/36; 1047/45; 1048/63; 226/20, 145, 112, 21.

93 ibid., 946/17; 939/1.

94 *CCR, 1429–35*, p. 42 (4 March 1430). The projected journey of the king to France may have been behind this precautionary move, both to remove troublesome Irish and to defend Ireland.

95 ibid., pp. 91-2; *CPR, 1429–36*, p. 266. For licences to stay, see ibid., pp. 64-5.

96 PRO, KB9/225/17; 227/1/29.

97 ibid., 225/18; 228/2/19.

98 ibid., 1049/14, 13.

99 ibid., 228/2/1.

100 *RP*, IV, 379; above, p. 130.

101 Above, pp. 57ff.
102 For commissions in these years, see *CPR, 1429–36*, passim; *CCR, 1429–35*, passim.
103 Above, p. 135.
104 Above, p. 140.
105 *CPR, 1429–36*, passim (pp. 199-200 for Bristol, p. 218 for Berks.).
106 *RP*, IV, 421-2.
107 ibid., 434-5. Efforts had been made to ensure good attendance at the second session of parliament (Powell and Wallis, op. cit., pp. 462-3).
108 *RP*, IV, 455-7. See J. W. Bennett, 'The mediaeval loveday', *Speculum*, XXXIII (1958), 351-70.
109 *CCR, 1429–35*, pp. 270-1; *CPR, 1429–36*, pp. 370-414.
110 Giles, p. 14.
111 *RP*, IV, 419-80 passim.
112 *RP*, IV, 481-94 passim; *CPR, 1429–36*, passim.
113 *RP*, IV, 495.
114 Above, p. 141.
115 *PPC*, V, 46.
116 *CPR, 1429–36*, p. 351; Storey, *End of Lancaster*, pp. 217-25; below, p. 566.
117 PRO, E28/58/79; *PPC*, V, 17-19; *CPR, 1436–41*, p. 86 (all dated 26 April 1437).
118 ibid., p. 87.
119 *PPC*, V, 34-5.
120 ibid, 45; *CPR, 1436–41*, p. 89.
121 ibid., p. 76; *CFR, 1430–37*, pp. 344-5; for Welles, see S. L. Thrupp, *The Merchant class of medieval London* (repr. Ann Arbor, 1962), p. 373.
122 Below, p. 566. There is a suggestion that royally-appointed aldermen were also sent to King's Lynn (Norfolk) and Canterbury at about the same time (*EHL*, p. 143).

8   Frontiers and Foreigners

The north

Within the British Isles, the English kingdom directly abutted another independent realm only in the north – Scotland. Elsewhere, the land of Wales was 'annexed and united' to the crown of England: the king (or his eldest son) directly ruled about half the country and was effective feudal superior of the remainder, and the integration of populations had made considerable headway despite the Glyndŵr uprising in Henry IV's reign. Further west, English rule in Ireland was far less secure, even though the king retained the formal style of 'lord of Ireland': the island had never been completely conquered, separatist tendencies were gathering strength, and social unrest was consequently endemic. Therefore, England had an unstable frontier in the far north and in Ireland; the political and social relationship between English shires and Welsh marcher lordships was of a different order.[1]

It was a prime concern of the government in the later middle ages to protect English communities close to the Scottish border and, by arrangements implemented by wardens and conservators of truces, to restrain cross-border depredations and provide facilities for the remedy of grievances voiced by both sides. Since Richard II's day, the wardenship of this marchland had been dominated by north-country magnates. From 1417 to 1424 the earl of Northumberland had charge of the east march (though not of Berwick castle until Bedford surrendered its custody in February 1427 before leaving for France), and between 1420 and 1435 Sir Richard Neville, son of the earl of Westmorland, was warden of the west march and constable of Carlisle castle.[2] It was equally the government's duty to protect the realm from invasion by the forces of the Scottish king; this was especially vital since his soldiers had been fighting in France against the English for some years past. The inherent difficulties experienced in discharging these obligations were accentuated in the fifteenth century by the need to pay the wardens promptly and equitably, and to support them resolutely when required. By the terms of his indenture, Neville could expect to be paid £1,250 in peace- or truce-time, and £2,500 a year should war break out; Northumberland was promised double these sums.[3] A government that failed to meet these obligations became vulnerable in the north to lawlessness and external danger.

England, with far-flung political and military preoccupations, could not risk a rupture with Scotland during the minority. At first the council, in its relations with the northern kingdom, possessed a cardinal asset, at least as far as maintaining public peace between the two realms and discouraging Scottish aid to the French were concerned: King James I had been a captive in English hands since 1406.[4] But if great hopes of peace and co-operation were pinned on James's marriage to an English lady and on the undertakings made by James before his release, they proved vain. Moreover, deep-seated hostility between England and Scotland ('there is nothing the Scots like better to hear than abuse of the English', commented the future Pope Pius II in 1435), and the unruliness of the border between them, created too large and too long-standing a problem to be overcome by the personal undertakings of a monarch – even if he were prepared to abide by his oath. The frustrations on the English side reached a new level of bitterness by the end of 1426, and neither a diplomatic marriage nor the presence of Bedford in England could alleviate them. Private feuds and localized warfare were seriously disruptive, and the activities of English border gentlemen were as troublesome as the elusive Scots; in 1424, for example, Sir Robert Tilliol, Sir Thomas Lucy, and men from Cumberland and Westmorland invaded Eskdale and later ravaged the earl of Douglas's estates.[5] At the same time, the patience of the English wardens was sorely tried by fruitless negotiations with the Scots and the exchequer's failure to supply them regularly with funds. By the time the protectorate came to an end in 1429, Anglo-Scottish relations were no more amicable than they had been in 1422, and in the meantime England had sacrificed its greatest asset, the person of James himself.

The prospective release of the Scottish king was of great significance for the English government; apart from the financial importance of his ransom, his marriage and future attitudes were likely to be crucial to the continuance of peaceful relations between the two kingdoms, the fostering of order along the border, and the withdrawal of Scottish aid to French armies. If James were to marry an English lady, great circumspection would need to be shown in the choice of the bride and in seeking cast-iron, sworn undertakings for the future. Whilst in England, James spent much of his time in the royal household, usually in the palace at Westminster; on his limited travels outside it he was accompanied by an entourage of clerks, valets, and pages. Henry V knighted him and took him to France on the expedition of 1421–22; he attended Henry's wedding at Troyes and mourned at his burial in Westminster abbey.[6] James was supported financially by the English exchequer, and during the year from February 1423 to January 1424 it provided him with £277 (apart from whatever he cost the household itself), including suitable clothing of cloth of gold for his wedding.[7] Once released, he could prove of considerable use to the council if his memories of England were pleasant and his sympathies warm. Negotiations for his release took place in 1423, and after the bishop of

Glasgow, chancellor of Scotland, visited him in June at the head of a strong mission, he travelled in person to Pontefract with the English commissioners.⁸ The discussions in Yorkshire were conducted principally by Bishop Langley, Bishop Philip Morgan, the experienced diplomat and councillor, and the earl of Northumberland as warden of the east march (so important were these talks felt to be). The agreement eventually reached at York on 10 September provided that James should marry a high-born English lady and, after his release, provide a ransom of 60,000 marks in annual instalments of 10,000 marks; these terms were reported to the commons in parliament on 21 November 1423, incorporated in protocols sealed in London on 4 December, and formally ratified by parliament on 28 January 1424.⁹

The lady chosen for James was Joan Beaufort, daughter of the earl of Somerset and a niece of Bishop Beaufort who, through his influence in the council, was able to engineer this family *coup*. The couple were married at the church of St Mary Overy in Southwark (now Southwark cathedral) on 2 February 1424 and adjourned to Beaufort's inn nearby for the wedding-breakfast.¹⁰ So far, so good: English influence would be exerted through the new Scottish queen and the exchequer stood to benefit handsomely. Details of the agreement affecting relations between the two states were to be worked out later, and for this reason in January 1424 new English envoys were nominated, led by Bishop Kemp, a skilled diplomat, and Langley who, as bishop of Durham, was singularly appropriate for this mission. They travelled towards the Scottish marches early in February, taking James and his queen with them. Their discussions took place in Durham cathedral in March, with the aim of concluding a treaty – or at least a truce – between the two states. The size and distinction of this embassy – it included the earls of Westmorland and Northumberland, Sir Richard Neville, the keeper of the privy seal, and Lords Dacre and Greystoke (who was constable of Roxburgh castle), and Sir Robert Umfraville¹¹ – are testimony to the importance attached to these negotiations. On 28 March a truce was sealed. As far as the captive king was concerned, the lines of the previous winter's agreement were followed, though with amplification on the subject of the total ransom (justified as repayment of expenses incurred while he was in England) and the surrender of hostages in the meanwhile to guarantee its payment. On wider matters, a truce to operate on land and sea was negotiated to last for seven years and neither side would assist the enemies of the other; presumably a full formal treaty had eluded the negotiators.¹² Northumberland and several northern knights were given the task of conducting the king and his new queen from Durham across the border into Scotland; it had been eighteen years since James had seen his native land.¹³ The hostages numbered more than twenty in all and included David, the son and heir of the earl of Athol, and the earls of Moray and Crawford, and they began arriving at the Tower of London from Yorkshire towards the end of May. They were well treated in England and were not placed in strict confinement; indeed, they appear to have been maintained in part at least at the exchequer's expense, and although some died of plague, others were allowed visits from their wives. Nor were individual hostages required to remain in captivity for the entire period during which the ransom was being paid; an elaborate exchange-scheme was authorized by parliament in 1425 to operate so long as James continued to be dilatory in meeting his financial obligations.[14]

The search for peace continued without conclusion. Bishop Langley, Sir John Scrope, and the keeper of the privy seal were at Berwick in August 1425 to discuss with the Scottish king violations of the recent truce, and disputes over the English practice of foraging outside Berwick and Roxburgh castles. In May of the following year, the dukes of Gloucester and Exeter, and the earls of Warwick, Northumberland, and Westmorland were among those who were commissioned to remedy similar grievances.[15] Such problems were admittedly localized ones, but they had wider implications for future good relations between the two countries; for this reason, the English wardens of the marches set up a committee of eight to advise them on the situation.[16] Such particular irritants were usually dealt with by the wardens themselves, assisted by conservators of the truce appointed specifically to negotiate with their opposite numbers in Scotland at traditional trysting places such as Reddenburn and Hawdenstank on designated 'love days' or 'days of the march'. The most hardworking conservator on the English side was undoubtedly Sir Robert Umfraville, who also served as deputy-warden of the east march; he spent much of his time at meetings trying to repair the truce, and when his term of office expired in the summer of 1426, he was urged to stay on until the end of Henry VI's minority, despite his own wish to retire.[17] These discussions were extraordinarily difficult and generally barren of lasting results. The Scots felt great hostility toward their adversary's wardens and their lieutenants, an attitude which was reciprocated on the English side; it was even difficult to induce the Scots to attend discussions, and it was doubtless frustration that prompted Umfraville to contemplate resigning.[18]

Without agreement on these minor, local issues, progress on a wider level was unlikely. It was therefore common prudence for the English to hold themselves in readiness to defend the border and throw back invasion. In March 1427 a commission of array was directed to all the northern counties of England, soon after major repairs, costing nearly £400, had been carried out at the border castles of Berwick, Roxburgh, and Carlisle.[19] At the same time, an envoy was sent by the impatient English government to tax James with the non-payment of his ransom (only 9,500 marks had so far been paid), and to raise the perennially vexatious question of breaches of the truce. Later in the year, in July 1427, another mission, led by Sir William Harrington and Bishop Gray of London, travelled to Scotland on the same errand.[20] English exasperation at the failure to pay the ransom on time was no doubt given sharper point by the growing difficulty experienced in paying the wages of the northern wardens. Although a serious effort was made to make appropriate revenue assignments available to the two wardens and the custodian of Roxburgh castle, to judge by those which had to be replaced, the government seriously defaulted from the summer of 1426 onwards – in Northumberland's case from February 1425. The situation became more precarious when payments owed to Northumberland and for the repair of the fortress at Berwick were ordered to be taken directly from the Scottish ransom; if that did not materialize, then the earl would have a real personal grievance against King James to exacerbate their already fragile relations on the border.[21]

Matters had advanced hardly at all by the last year of the protectorate, when a major offensive in search of peace was launched by Cardinal Beaufort himself. The wisdom of marrying James to Beaufort's niece in order to preserve strong English influence at the Scottish court could now be put to the test. Early in 1429 Beaufort was instructed to capitalize on his relationship with the Scots queen to secure an agreement from her husband at a personal meeting. The pretext for the discussions was the state of the Church Universal (including Beaufort's projected crusade against the Hussites), but quite clearly relations between the two realms were also on the agenda, as well as James's ransom and infractions of the truce; moreover, the alliance between Scotland and France was growing closer. Scottish forces had never ceased to aid the French in battle, despite the agreements of 1424, whilst in 1428 negotiations were finalized for the marriage of James's four-year-old daughter, Margaret, to the Dauphin Louis.[22] In this atmosphere, Beaufort travelled north to Berwick-on-Tweed in February with an imposing entourage one hundred-strong; he was probably accompanied by Bishop Langley, Northumberland, and the bishop of Carlisle, all of whose interests in the north were directly affected. Beaufort's meeting with King James and Queen Joan was most friendly, but of the negotiations that took place nothing is known.[23] Indeed, the situation actually deteriorated somewhat in the months that followed. For one thing, in April 1429 an attempt was made to intercept French ships which were thought to be conveying the Scottish princess to France, along with 6,000 marks for the French war effort. In the following month, the English government tried to apprehend James Stewart, who had fled to Ireland a few years before. As the younger surviving son and (after the execution of his father and elder brother by James I in 1426) ultimate heir of the late duke of Albany, he had been regarded by some as a possible heir to the king of Scots before the birth of a princess. Stewart's capture by the English authorities in Ireland would, therefore, not only remove a potential source of trouble in an already troublous island, but also place in the council's hands a Scottish nobleman whose pedigree might prove embarrassing to James I in the future.[24] The weary round of commissions that marked every period of truce with Scotland continued in July and October with further attempts to preserve order along the border and deal with complaints of truce violations.[25] By 1429 the release of James I must have seemed, on reflection, a major mistake to the English council. It had forfeited a great asset in dealing with the Scots, and even if Joan Beaufort had been endowed with the qualities of her uncle, her marriage to James did not bring the benefits to England that were anticipated. As the English envoy, Lord Scrope of Masham, reported in July 1430, the Scots king was free and he was a cunning man.[26] By employing delaying tactics with some skill and (if the English sources are to be believed) a lack of scruple, James succeeded in perpetuating the already interminable discussions so that confrontation with England was avoided until he decided otherwise. For their part, the English preferred agreement to conflict, and when, in 1436, James felt able to risk a passage of arms, it came at the worst possible time and could not be avoided.

Anglo-Scottish relations and life in the borderland were governed by the truce which was due to expire on 1 May 1431. Violations of its terms were committed by both sides: the Scots tried Englishmen's patience by their tardy negotiation of a renewal, their stubbornness in resisting payment of James's ransom, and by their apparent lack of seriousness in discussing the proposal to marry Henry VI to James's baby daughter. The English government was fully prepared to talk about all these matters; the only two caveats they made were that no peace treaty could be concluded while the king was a minor, and the question of his marriage would have to be referred to a meeting of the great council.[27] The danger in the situation was accurately divined by Lord Scrope when he made his report in the king's presence to his councillors at Calais on 9 July 1430.[28] The Franco-Scottish alliance was the greatest threat. The Scots favoured a truce on sea alone, which would allow them to transport men to France unhindered and, at the same time, would not oblige them to curb the border raids. As it was, the present truce was due to expire on 1 May 1431. If no agreement was reached by then, the English would find themselves in further difficulties. A renewal of war with Scotland at a time when France was absorbing all their energies would divert much-needed resources and prove very costly. Scrope's advice was sound: Henry VI's practice of negotiating monthly truces between the wardens of both sides could avoid the burden of a war on two fronts. Meanwhile, the English did not relax their vigilance in the north country, and as invasion scares arose so men were arrayed, beacons set up, and castles repaired.[29]

Accordingly, a strong panel of envoys was despatched north at Cardinal Beaufort's insistence in February 1430; it included the elderly bishop of Durham, the earls of Salisbury and Northumberland, the Yorkshire Lords Greystoke and Scrope of Masham, and Bishop Lumley, whose appointment to the see of Carlisle had been promoted by Beaufort. Very few Scottish negotiators came to the discussions, and the English envoys had to run something of a gauntlet while they were on Scottish soil. Still, they persisted in their mission, and Scrope and Master John Stokes, a professional diplomat, travelled northwards again in November.[30] This embassy achieved some success, and on 19 January 1431 a partial truce was announced on land and a general one at sea as from 1 May; it was to last for five years. It was not an entirely satisfactory outcome and could hardly remove English anxieties about the state of the frontier. But for the moment, the exchange of hostages confined in England after the release of King James was resumed, and an effort was made to recompense English merchants whose ships had been plundered by Scottish seamen.[31]

By the summer of 1433, this modest truce was showing signs of collapsing as old problems re-emerged. The exchange of hostages had again seemingly ceased, and breaches of the truce took on an aspect that was akin to open war. Parliament was informed in July that the poverty and destruction of the marches were now severe, though it was appreciated that without comparable remedial measures on the Scottish side, stiffer penalties for truce-breakers could only be partially effective and would cause resentment among northern Englishmen.[32] On 23 July new wardens and conservators of the truce were appointed in a vain effort to meet the Scots and organize mutual reparations; but there is no mistaking the English sense of frustration at what was regarded, not without justification, as the insincerity of the Scots. James I's complaints in January 1434 were blatantly provocative, for they directly criticized the disorder on the east march and the failure of the English commissioners to make amends and redress his subjects' grievances. It is difficult to acquit James of the charge of hypocrisy when it is recalled that his own agents had been less than co-operative in meeting the English representatives, and delays from the Scottish side had become a by-word with the English.[33]

From the Lancastrian point of view, the situation was such that peace discussions were advisable, even though the current truce had more than two years to run. On 1 February, Lord FitzHugh headed a commission charged with examining truce violations, although the mistrustful English were only prepared to consider mutual reparations; as far as the future was concerned, the envoys were instructed to discuss a firmer peace cemented by a royal marriage.[34] The parleys were predictably lengthy and inconclusive. Meanwhile, the English were careful to strengthen their fortresses along the border: the earl of Salisbury at Carlisle, Umfraville at Harbottle, and, in June 1434, Northumberland at Alnwick, where the charred and ruinous walls required speedy rebuilding.[35] These precautions culminated in July in the array of the northern shires, the extension of Salisbury's commission as warden of the west march to include the east as well, and the further fortification of Berwick. Salisbury, in fact, correctly identified the essential needs of northern defence: he insisted on adequate financial provision during his wardenship – something which Northumberland had not received – and the adequate repair and defence of Berwick.[36] He felt so strongly about these conditions that it was understood that if Berwick's reconstruction were not undertaken quickly by 11 November 1434, then the earl would be released from his responsibility; after the lapse of six months, during which he received only one-fifth of his annual peacetime salary of £2,500 as the eastern warden, he tendered his resignation and would not contemplate serving beyond a year. At the same time, in July 1435, and after fifteen years in an office that the Nevilles had come to regard as their own preserve, he decided to surrender the wardenship of the west march too, though his indenture still had a few months more to run (until 12 September). Salisbury's dramatic action may have been in the nature of a bluff designed to force the government at Westminster to take its commitments in the north more seriously; he can hardly have contemplated withdrawing from an official position that was so crucial to his family's interests in the region. Thus, Salisbury's resignation may have been the occasion when Sir Thomas Dacre submitted his attractive bid for the western wardenship, probably with Salisbury's blessing; for not only was Dacre a Cumberland landowner with long experience of border conditions, but two months earlier, on 22 April, he had become a retainer for life of the earl of Salisbury, 'in tyme of paix as of werre'. To a northern lord, a wardenship still represented a tempting opportunity to wield power with official authority, and Dacre (like Bishop Lumley soon afterwards) was prepared to accept a lower rate of pay than had been usual.[37] Yet for all its apparent attraction for the government, Dacre's offer was rejected (and Salisbury's bluff called). Instead, Salisbury was succeeded in both posts by the earls of Northumberland and Huntingdon jointly; the latter was an associate of Gloucester, who now dominated the council at Westminster.[38] This, and the fact that during the year or so when they presided over frontier affairs every effort was made to pay their salaries, probably reflect a determination by the council, under Gloucester's leadership, to strengthen England's defence at home as well as to pursue an energetic policy in France. Only thus could the worsening security position of the Lancastrians be improved.

In fact, the prospect of war in the north had moved distinctly closer by 1436. The earl of Dunbar, whose relations with James I had deteriorated sharply during 1435, came to England in the autumn, and his son led a raid into Scotland with English aid. These treasonable acts doubtless helped to decide James, after years of prevarication, to despatch his young daughter to France in March 1436 to marry the dauphin.[39] War began on 1 May, and by 7 June rumour had it that James was about to invade England along the coast; men from the northern counties and the palatinate of Durham were summoned to the border to assist the wardens.[40] The garrison at Berwick was alarmed and somewhat resentful at having to bear the brunt of hostilities yet again. After all, the soldiers had not been paid and after Northumberland's term as warden had ended, they believed that the prospect of payment had receded still further; numbers of them began to desert, leaving the mayor of Berwick, Thomas Elwyk, to hire watchmen at his own cost and to do his best to beg the soldiers to stay at their post.[41] Weapons were hurriedly carted north from London, and some hasty repairs undertaken at both Roxburgh and Berwick. Sir William Eure, a rough north-country landowner with a combative reputation, was put in charge of Berwick castle.[42] In the meantime, the Scottish king's siege of Roxburgh had begun early in August.

The danger receded as quickly as it came, with James's retreat from the fortress and his subsequent murder by a conspiracy among his own magnates. Efforts, albeit ineffectual, were resumed, in an atmosphere of frustration and periodic alarm, in order to remove the cause of truce disruptions. There even seems to have been some difficulty in finding new wardens to replace Huntingdon and Northumberland. Eventually, on 12 December 1436, the bishop of Carlisle was persuaded to assume responsibility for Carlisle and the west march, which directly affected his diocese's interests, though he was careful to secure specific safeguards for the protection of Carlisle itself. On these terms, he agreed to become warden for seven years, which was an unusually lengthy commitment by recent standards.[43] The young duke of Norfolk, John Mowbray, became warden of the east march as from Easter 1437 at the usual rates.[44] Both men seem to have been suitably supported with finance during the first months of their term, even though in Norfolk's case this amounted to as much as £5,000 *per annum* during the war which lasted until May 1438.[45] The English determination to defend the border was evidently strong in 1435–37.

There is no doubt that the Scottish frontier was a constant headache for the English council. The borderland was disorderly and the countryside was open to invasion, while Scottish aid to the French made it a sensitive diplomatic arena. The English, with other preoccupations and straitened finances, were generally anxious to conciliate the Scots, but any improvement in border conditions which stemmed from the truces did not last long. Raiding, mistrust, and recriminations, warlike commotions in the vicinity of Berwick, Roxburgh, and Carlisle, were the continuing themes of these years. England's alarm was greatest in 1435–36, when her difficulties elsewhere were most daunting. But on this occasion, Henry VI's government and the communities along the border were spared as a result of events in Scotland itself. It was an illusory relief: the two countries simply withdrew temporarily from the brink.

The Irish problem

Henry VI's advisers were fully aware of the difficulty of governing the king's lordship of Ireland right from the beginning of the reign – if only because Lord Talbot and James Butler, the 'white' earl of Ormond, who had been successively lieutenant of Ireland quite recently, were at Westminster on 28 September 1422.[46] The problems were borne in upon the council fairly relentlessly during the years that followed. Fundamentally, they arose out of the crucial question of whether English rule could in fact be firmly established, and then consolidated, in any part of Ireland outside the immediate environs of Dublin (the 'pale', as it was coming to be regarded).[47] 'The Gaelic or Irish reconquest' of Dublin had proceeded apace during the fourteenth century, and in 1422 the Irish 'enemies' were still a constant annoyance to the English establishment and its armies. During the 1420s complaints flooded to Dublin and Westminster of the rapine, arson, destruction, and devastation committed by them on a frontier-arc lying from 50 to about 70 miles from Dublin in cos. Meath, Kildare, Louth, and Dublin itself. Beyond this region, the embattled colonial communities of towns like Cork and Limerick could do little more than repair their gates and rebuild their walls under pressure from the Irish attackers.[48] Even some of the Anglo-Irish, descendants of colonists who had settled in Ireland during the interval since Henry II's expeditions there, were such a source of violent unrest that they were roundly condemned as 'rebels'; to the English authorities the 'Irish enemies and rebels' were a fearful combination which had hardened into a political concept.[49] The warlike prior of Kilmainham, Thomas Butler, who sprang (albeit illegitimately) from one of the greatest Anglo-Irish families, was fully capable of organizing armies of native Irish (as in 1417); and when they joined with another prominent Anglo-Irish nobleman, the unruly earl of Kildare, the serious threat to domestic order, and English rule itself, was unmistakable.[50]

Nor was this unhappy situation simply a threat to the king's authority in Ireland, for it also put St George's channel in hazard, thereby offering an opportunity to Scotsmen and others to cultivate their plots in the fertile field of Ireland. The spectre of Celtic collaboration against the English state had become a reality on more than one occasion during the previous century. Who could say that it would not do so again – even if the arrival of James Stewart in Ireland in 1425 was that of a Scottish exile fleeing from his wrathful king?[51] The state of Ireland was not improved by the action of some of the English establishment in Dublin, who were notorious for their corruption, extortion, oppression, and partisan persecution of rivals and enemies. Their factious divisions extended right to the top of the governing hierarchy and merely exacerbated the racial tension. The bitter hostility between Talbot and Ormond lasted for thirty years, and it led each to oppress the other when opportunity allowed and produced a battery of violent accusations which the council was powerless to assuage.[52] After six years as lieutenant, Talbot was replaced by Ormond in February 1420 for a two-year term, but Talbot's appointees among the officialdom stayed in office. His younger brother Richard, archbishop of Dublin (since 1417), was a thorn in Ormond's side throughout his lieutenancy, and after the latter's retirement the archbishop took temporary charge of the Irish administration as justiciar, only to become chancellor in May 1423 on the appointment of a new lieutenant. Meanwhile, Sir Lawrence

Merbury, a Herefordshire gentleman from Talbot country, was confirmed in office as chancellor on 4 October 1422.[53] Such rivalries enfeebled the English administration, more especially as they were absorbed into wider animosities among the Anglo-Irish, for not only were Talbot and Ormond themselves Irish landowners, but Kildare later became (by 1432) Ormond's father-in-law and the prior of Kilmainham was Ormond's bastard half-brother. According to the archbishop of Armagh, writing in 1428, Talbot and Ormond were

> the cause of the great harm that has been done to the king's liege people in this land. . . . When my Lord Talbot was in this country, there was great variance between him and my lord of Ormond, and yet they be not accorded. And some gentlemen of the country be well willed to my lord of Ormond; they hold with him and love him and help him and be not well willed to my Lord Talbot nor to none that love him. And they that love my Lord Talbot do in the same manner to my lord of Ormond. So all this land is severed.[54]

The native Irish would have been less than Irishmen if they had not taken advantage of such violent bickering and confusion to harry the frontiers of 'the land of peace'.[55]

To enable the English government to reassert its authority in Ireland, and to achieve permanent stability so that the western coasts of England and Wales would be secured, certain essential needs had to be met. Soldiers were needed from England in substantial numbers; a lieutenant of status and authority was required to reform the English establishment and its attitudes; and, above all, considerable sums of money were required to supplement the miserably inadequate resources of the Irish exchequer.[56]

The council's decision to appoint Edmund Mortimer, earl of March and lord of Ulster, as the king's lieutenant on 2 March 1423 was a step in the right direction; the detailed indentures of service were drawn up two months later on 9 May. Whatever the abilities of this earl (and they were not great), he was at least a man of distinguished lineage and dynastic dignity; moreover, his extensive Irish estates gave him a close vested interest in the re-establishment of orderly government and reconciled him to spending a period of time in Ireland itself. March's appointment was to run from 1 June 1423 for nine years, an unusually long term, to judge by recent practice; but perhaps it indicates a determination on the part of the council (perhaps, too, of the earl himself) to find a lasting solution to the Irish problem. He was provided with an army and financed by a stipend of 5,000 marks *per annum* so long as he remained in Ireland; almost all of this sum was quickly assigned to him by the English exchequer during the second half of 1423, any Irish contribution evidently proving negligible. Ships were duly assembled at Bristol and Liverpool to transport the earl and his retinue across the channel in the summer of 1423, though he did not in fact embark until the autumn of 1424.[57] Some adjustments were made to the administration in Ireland at about the same time. Archbishop Talbot had become chancellor on 19 May 1423, and a new treasurer, the clerk Hugh Bavent, replaced William Tynbegh in July 1424. Ormond, too, was brought into the government as March's deputy in the following summer, and disembarking with the new lieutenant and his company was none other than Lord Talbot. It was a tragic blow to this powerful and reconciliatory initiative that the earl of March died of plague on 18 January 1425.[58]

In the year following March's untimely death, both Talbot and Ormond appear to have worked for the submission of the Irish, particularly in the north towards Ulster. Talbot acted as justiciar for a few months while there was no royal lieutenant, but in April 1425 Ormond was appointed in March's stead for one year and he continued the task; when his term expired, he too temporarily became justiciar. To place such responsibilities in turn upon two men who were perpetually at one another's throat was hardly the most effective way of dealing with Ireland's problems.[59] Moreover, the government's will to provide the funds necessary for the re-establishment of peaceful rule weakened after March's demise, and Ormond was able to extract two-thirds of the £550 owing to him only by surrendering the remaining one-third in December 1427, nine months after his term as lieutenant came to an end.[60] Responsibility for this unsatisfactory state of affairs must rest squarely on the shoulders of Beaufort and the duke of Bedford, who presided over the council for much of this period.[61]

The appointment of Ormond's successor as royal lieutenant was decided upon in March 1427, and John, Lord Grey of Codnor assumed office on 21 May for three years; a considerable force of 600 men, together with 4,000 marks *per annum*, was placed at his disposal. If the introduction of another new face to the Irish scene, one with guaranteed resources and valuable experience of warfare in France, heralded a sensible initiative, the council's efforts proved vain. There was no noticeable improvement in the Irish situation, and Grey failed to serve his full term.[62] On 23 March 1428 Sir John Sutton replaced him for a term, dating from 30 April, which was more realistically fixed at two years.[63] The early replacement of Grey may have been prompted by the visit of a delegation of worried Irish bishops, led by the archbishop of Armagh, to the English council in March 1428, for Sutton's appointment was specially announced to them at Westminster on the 24th of the month. Provision was also made for the assembly of 525 men at Chester, to be transported across the channel in ships commandeered from the Bristol channel ports as soon as the new lieutenant was ready to embark. Substantial grants were made available to him by the English exchequer, amounting to 5,000 marks in his first year of office and 4,000 marks in the second; in fact, he received practically all of this by assignment, with scarcely any 'bad' tallies being cut in his favour.[64] To his credit, Sutton's efforts achieved some success against the Irish enemies before he returned to England late in 1429.[65]

During the protectorate the minority council had made modest attempts to cope with Ireland, but it accomplished little. Despite some not unsuccessful efforts to raise cash for the lieutenants, the impressment of commercial shipping (especially in the Bristol area) to transport retinues across St George's channel, and the appointment of royal lieutenants who were not members of the Talbot or Ormond factions, lasting improvement proved elusive. The appointment of the earl of March was the most promising, not to say decisive, action yet taken by the council, but his death dashed all the hopes to which it had given rise. The council's decision in March 1425, during Gloucester's absence in Hainault, to make Ormond lieutenant, while retaining Archbishop Talbot as chancellor, did nothing to abate the fatal rivalry between the two parties. Regardless of the efforts of Grey and Sutton, the English grip on Ireland was no firmer by 1429.[66]

The struggle to subdue the native Irish enemies and the Anglo-Irish rebels was perforce unremitting. The city of Waterford reported in July 1430 a series of attacks by Irish insurgents as well as roving Bretons, Scots, and Spaniards; they were so serious that the defences of the city had been much weakened over the previous three years, and many of the citizens were said to be fleeing to the comparative security of Wales. In the west, the walls of Limerick were in a similar condition of dangerous disrepair by 1433.[67] Little aid was forthcoming from some of the greater loyalist magnates – Ormond, Norfolk, and York among them – who had been allowed to absent themselves from their Irish estates while still drawing what revenues they could.[68] Nor did Ormond's absence mean that the internal rivalries among these Anglo-Irish magnates, in which his family had been enmeshed for more than a decade, were moderated. Complaints and counter-complaints so harried the lieutenant by 1435 that he concluded that Henry VI himself should visit Ireland.[69] The recent experience of the royal expedition to France should have alerted him to the limited good which such visits could achieve.

During Henry's absence in France, Gloucester's régime appointed a new Irish lieutenant on 29 January 1431, Sir Thomas Stanley, an energetic Cheshire gentleman; a few months later he was authorized to engage a retinue of 525 men for six years, and he was granted 5,000 marks for his first year of office and 4,000 marks annually thereafter to sustain him in Ireland. His powers were the customary ones, enabling him to replace all but the most senior officials of the Irish administration. Stanley sailed from Liverpool in August 1431, in ships hastily assembled from the ports lying between Bristol and Lancashire.[70] Although he appears to have paid more than one lengthy visit to Ireland, the hostile inroads in English-held territory continued. By 1435, the Irish council reported that 'the pale' had shrunk to little more than 30 miles in length and 20 miles in breadth, while Irish waters were dominated by the ubiquitous Bretons, Scots, and Spaniards. Failing a visit from the king, a lieutenant (preferably of royal blood) was required 'suche as the peple woll drede and be aferd of. . . and to be here before the begynyng of this somyr, or else the saide lande is like to be fynaly destrued'.[71] This forthright, melancholy, and despairing report had an immediate effect on an English government obsessed in 1435 with security. In that year and the next, steps were taken to ensure that Stanley's retinue was kept up to strength with suitably armed and hardy men-at-arms and archers. The thorough survey of his force which was ordered on 20 March 1436 may well be linked with the growing awareness of the vulnerability of England's shores to enemy attack, even from Ireland.[72] This concern for Stanley's army was complemented by more adequate financial provision for the lieutenant himself, for Ireland's own revenue was notoriously incapable of providing the necessary funds. During 1431–33 support from the Westminster exchequer was pitiful, and even by February 1434, when the matter was formally discussed, the initial 5,000 marks of Stanley's promised salary had still not been received, largely because he was competing with other insistent creditors.[73] The situation improved immediately afterwards, with a £3,000 payment on 24 February; yet this momentum could not be sustained without running the risk of issuing assignments that could not always be cashed easily. Only in March 1437 was another conscientious effort made (with an assignment of about £3,128) to provide adequate finance for Ireland.[74] In these circumstances, the English representatives could achieve little more than the preservation of their king's shaky lordship. 'Keeping the frontiers of the Pale safe was the essence of the military policy of most fifteenth-century governments'.[75]

Aliens in the realm

Aliens, whether they were long-term residents or short-term visitors, were identified as a separate community in fifteenth-century England and were treated as such. In the city of London, there were significant numbers of them, amounting to between 2 and 4 per cent of the population.[76] Elsewhere, aliens were present in Southampton, Sandwich, and other ports of the realm, where they played an important, though declining, role in the country's overseas trade; in border areas such as the Scottish and Welsh marches and the coastal towns facing Ireland; and in the University towns of Oxford and Cambridge. They were in England for a variety of reasons, but it may safely be accepted that the majority of them were engaged in commerce or its ancillary services of banking and exchange. A further number entered the service of noblemen and the royal family, or else joined the alien priories that were still open, or visited benefices which they had been granted in England.[77]

These foreigners were treated by the government differently from the king's subjects, although a law of naturalization did not yet exist to provide a clear distinction between denizen and alien. There was, too, an intermediate condition as far as the Irish and Welsh were concerned, for they did not always enjoy the rights and privileges of Englishmen in England (or indeed, in their own country), even though the king was their liege lord. The disorderliness of the Irish led to their mass expulsion from the realm after 1422 and the imposition of stringent controls on those who did not have a profession or peaceable occupation.[78] Nevertheless, it was dimly perceived that Irishmen were not entirely without a claim to rights in England, for when these ordinances of expulsion were reiterated in the early 1430s, the defence of Ireland was proclaimed as the justification, even though a determination to expel troublemakers may have been at least as compelling.[79] Again, the poll tax on aliens which was introduced in 1440 was at first extended to Irish people living in England, but after 1443 they were exempt from subsequent impositions.[80]

Correspondingly, fifteenth-century Welshmen were subject to the harsh provisions of the penal legislation passed by parliament early in the Glyndŵr rebellion. As a result, Welshmen were formally prevented from purchasing property not only in the Welsh boroughs, but also in England; they, and indeed Englishmen who married Welsh, could not henceforth hold office legally in Wales. But the king had statutory power to exempt whom he would from this last statute and the others too were gradually eroded almost before the ink was dry on the statute roll.[81] Nevertheless, the restrictions were still the law of the land in Henry VI's reign and, as Sir John Scudamore, the husband of one of Glyndŵr's daughters, discovered in 1433, they could be implemented with devastating consequences for prominent men.[82] Once the shock of rebellion was over, the government of Henry V and Henry VI was prepared to grant letters of denizenship to Welshmen anxious to be released from these disabilities and to have their status in the realm placed beyond doubt.[83] Welshmen, then, were in a somewhat vulnerable position compared with other subjects of Henry VI, though it may be that Queen Katherine's marriage to Owen Tudor, and his subsequent grant of denizenship in 1432, helped to remove the anomalies. Certainly, when the alien poll tax was imposed in 1440, Welshmen were specifically excluded from it.[84]

Henry VI's subjects as king of France – in practical terms, Gascons, Normans, Picards, and Flemings – were regarded as aliens in England in the 1420s and 1430s just like the Germans, Italians, and Catalans; but from time to time they were treated more considerately in deference to the ideal of the dual monarchy. A few, like the Norman Sir Ralph Sage in 1433, were made denizen, and complaints that French merchant ships were being attacked at sea by Englishmen were sympathetically heard.[85] In July 1428, it was declared to be the king's intention that Flemings should be treated as the king's French subjects and even allowed to trade freely in the king's two realms and especially in England. The same privilege was extended to Hollanders and Zeelanders, even though they were not Henry's subjects. The justification for this generosity was the belief that trade was necessary the world over for the public good.[86]

Like most societies, that of fifteenth-century England was deeply suspicious of aliens, and as the fortunes of the English in the French war began to decline in the 1430s, tension between Englishmen and the foreign visitor grew sharper. The strictures of the *Libelle of Englysche Polycye* were doubtless exaggerated for persuasive effect, but their force betrays the strength of patriotism and anti-alien sentiment in English opinion by 1436.[87] On a more mundane level, the disreputable stews (or brothels) situated on the south bank of the Thames in Southwark were exposed in 1437 as the haunts of Frenchmen, Flemings, and Picards, among whom were to be numbered spies, criminals, and other enemies. In fact, such hostility was more pronounced in London than elsewhere.[88]

The reasons for this instinctive anti-alien feeling are many, though fundamental is the distrust of society for the outsider and the foreigner. On top of this, there were factors peculiar to medieval England. Among these, commercial rivalry between English merchants and foreign factors and shippers was prominent, and the privileges which foreign merchants sometimes acquired in England caused greater resentment and distrust.[89] It was a short step for Englishmen to suspect that alien merchants manipulated the terms of trade to their own advantage and the loss of England. In parliament in 1429, it was reported that merchants from the Low Countries frequently deceived customs collectors and the Calais staple by hiding wool and hides underneath sea-coal and other commodities.[90] There was grave suspicion, too, of their banking activities, a facility for which the Florentines in particular were well suited in view of their contacts across the length and breadth of Europe. They were thought capable of manipulating the exchange regulations for their own purposes, though the government was wary of curbing international financial practices that were highly valued. Henry VI's first parliament listened to an attack on those aliens who acted as brokers in England for the way in which they dictated prices and indulged in commercial espionage; the same charges were made fourteen years later by the commons, who went so far as to demand that there should be no more alien brokers. On both occasions, the government declined to take action.[91] Allied to these accusations were fears that aliens were draining the country of its wealth in gold and silver. Parliament was accustomed to expressions of bullionist distrust, despite the existence of statutes that restrained the export of gold.[92]

Apart from the commercially inspired hostility to foreigners, there was a tradition of enmity towards the foreign servants of English kings and queens that went back to the twelfth century. Members of the households of Joan of Navarre and Katherine of Valois attracted the obloquy of Englishmen no less than had the Poitevins and Savoyards in Henry III's reign – and other aliens before that. Some, like the Italians in Gloucester's service, were welcomed for their skills in medicine and classical literature, but others were deeply distrusted. In the 1426 parliament, when relations with Brittany were deteriorating, an attempt was made to secure the expulsion from the realm of the alien servants of Queen Joan, who was also dowager duchess of Brittany.[93] As for the alien clergy, parliament was unhappy about their role too. Whereas at the Leicester assembly in 1426 the prior of the alien house of Holy Trinity, York, John de Costello, was able to secure a declaration that he and his convent were denizens, the commons took the opportunity to inveigh against aliens being presented to English benefices: it could mean neglect of services and loss of income to the realm. Although these complaints may not have gone unheeded, the government took no legislative action on the matter.[94]

The hostility towards foreigners expressed itself in a large number of ways, as far as merchants were concerned by restricting their operations. The tide of anti-alienism rose and fell partly in response to the government's policy and English fortunes in the Hundred Years War. Piracy and privateering, especially by the marauding seamen of the west country, were readily directed toward vessels from all countries, regardless of the government's wishes, and it would be impossible to distinguish rampant anti-foreignness in the make-up of Cornish seamen from lawlessness and greed, or revenge and retaliation for English ships captured by others.[95] Thus, some aliens were subjected to authorized reprisals by letters of marque if they were countrymen of a foreigner who had outraged an Englishman.[96] For example, in 1432 all German ships in English ports were arrested pending the release of a ship carrying English merchandise which had been captured at sea by German sailors; but soon afterwards the king ordered the East Anglians to desist from molesting Hanseatic merchants until a fuller inquiry had been made.[97]

Other measures against the aliens sprang from their foreign status. Although no national tax was imposed on them until 1440, some were unfortunate enough to be burdened with local imposts. When Dover's walls needed repairing by 1429, the necessary work was financed from a tax on alien merchandise entering the port.[98] Ever since the eleventh century, English governments had taken steps to restrict the movements and activities of aliens, particularly merchants, the largest group among them. More recent legislation in 1404 prevented them from exporting gold and silver from the country and attempted to limit their stay by insisting that they conduct their business within three months of arrival; it was further provided that within a fortnight they should be hosted in approved accommodation which was registered with the local authorities for purposes of supervision.[99] There is considerable doubt whether the hosting regulations were at all effective, especially in Southampton, and the absence of adequate machinery to enforce them was partly responsible.[100] Suggestions in parliament in 1433 that the controls should be even more stringent, with paid informers and investigators to ensure their enforcement, got nowhere; yet there can be no mistaking the increasing anti-alien attitude of the commons, with members of the merchant class vociferous amongst them.[101]

It is significant that the period of most intense anti-alien feeling early in Henry VI's reign occurred in the 1430s, following the resurgence of French power and the failure of the congress of Arras to bring at least a temporary respite. The commons in the parliaments of 1429 and 1433 showed themselves to be particularly critical of foreigners and eager to take legislative action against them, but the government itself shied away from endorsing their demands. Later on, it was driven to taking protective measures as feelings in the realm rose to a dangerous pitch in 1435–37 and foreigners seemed likely to be persecuted regardless of their origin, their length of residence in the country, or their own government's attitude towards England. Protection was offered in 1435 to friendly aliens who traded in fish and foodstuffs, but their friendliness was measured by the extent to which they were prepared in return to co-operate with the government when a ban was placed on trade with the hostile Flemings in September 1436.[102] Even loyal Flemings living in England were offered protection at the height of the invasion scares of 1436 and the rumours of an approaching siege of Calais later in the summer. Many of them, along with other Lowlanders, Frenchmen, Germans, and Danes to a number exceeding 1,800, came forward to swear loyalty to Henry VI so that they could continue to live in England unmolested at least by the government.[103] It was not in the government's interest to allow the wholesale disruption of that sector of English trade that was in alien hands, and as far as the Low Countrymen were concerned, there was a good expectation that their dependence on English wool would sooner or later wean them from the side of the duke of Burgundy. But to educate public opinion in these directions was no easy task. The dislike of English merchants for their competitors, the hatred shown by countryfolk from the coastal shires towards Burgundians (including Flemings) who, they had been informed, were the nation's enemies, did not discriminate between one foreigner and the next. The strength of feeling was apparent in London by June 1436, when efforts were made to disrupt beer-brewing by the Hollanders and Zeelanders on the grounds that 'such drink was poisonous and not fit to drink, and caused drunkenness'.[104] Propaganda fanned the latent xenophobia of the English, and after Arras renewed efforts in the war made them display their patriotism more vociferously than for many years past.

Notes

1 J. G. Edwards, *The principality of Wales, 1267–1967* (Caernarvon, 1969), pp. 38-9; R. R. Davies, *Lordship and society in the march of Wales, 1282–1400* (Oxford, 1978), ch. 12; J. F. Lydon, *Ireland in the later middle ages* (Dublin, 1973), ch. 5.

2 R. L. Storey, 'The wardens of the marches of England towards Scotland, 1377–1489', *EHR*, LXXII (1957), 604, 613.

3 Nicholson, op. cit., pp. 246-52; Storey, *EHR*, LXXII (1957), 604; J. M. W. Bean, *The estates of the Percy family, 1416–1537* (Oxford, 1958), p. 106. Roxburgh castle was in the custody of John, Lord Greystoke, another northern baron, from March 1421 until 1425, when he was replaced by Sir Robert Ogle; they could expect £1,000 *per annum* or £2,000 if war should occur (*GEC*, VI, 196-7; PRO, E403/658-91, passim).

4 He had been seized at sea in March 1406 when he was eleven years old; his father, Robert III, died three weeks later (Nicholson, op. cit., pp. 226-7; above, p. 54).

5 *PPC*, III, 353-4. See du Boulay, in Lawrence, *English church*, p. 236, for the future Pius's comment.

6 Nicholson, op. cit., pp. 250-2; *Brut*, p. 493; PRO, E28/40/7, 26; /42/80; E159/199 *brevia directa baronibus*, E. m. 9d. James accompanied Henry VI and his mother to Hertford for Christmas in 1423 (*Great Chron.*, p. 129).

7 PRO, E403/658-64; E28/43/63; *PPC*, III, 99-100, 133; *Foedera*, IV, iv, 94, 96, 107; *CPR, 1422–29*, pp. 112, 179.

8 PRO, E28/42/89; E403/661 m. 14; *PPC*, III, 116-17; *CPR, 1422–29*, p. 112; *Foedera*, IV, iv, 85, 93, 47.

9 *RP*, IV, 199, 211-12; PRO, E28/45/30: *Foedera*, IV, iv, 89-90, 99-101; Nicholson, op. cit., p. 259. The agreement was concluded at York between Bishop Langley, Bishop Morgan, Northumberland, and John Wodeham, on the English side, and Scots commissioners led by the bishop of Glasgow; in London, Bishop Morgan and three other councillors (the treasurer, the keeper of the privy seal, and Lord Cromwell) sealed the protocols (*Foedera*, IV, iv, 96-101). The English council had secretly been prepared to accept a 54,000-mark ransom (ibid., 96).

10 Nicholson, op. cit., p. 259; *Brut*, pp. 440, 497; Giles, p. 5; *Great Chron.*, p. 130. St Mary's was within Beaufort's jurisdiction as bishop of Winchester.

11 *RP*, IV, 211-12; *PPC*, III, 137, 139-42; PRO, E28/44/34, 5; *CPR, 1422–29*, p. 179.

12 *CCR, 1422–29*, p. 143; *Foedera*, IV, iv, 109-11. The Scottish king's oath to uphold the Durham agreement was being sought in July 1424 (PRO, E28/45/1).

13 *Foedera*, IV, iv, 111.

14 *CCR, 1422–29*, pp. 104-5, 182, 437-8; PRO, E28/45/22; 47/71; 50/53-54; E403/688 m. 12; *Foedera*, IV, iv, 101, 109, 111-18, 124-5; *RP*, IV, 276-7; *CPR, 1422–29*, pp. 279, 404; *PPC*, III, 259-65, 356-9. Hostages were still being held in England in the 1440s.

15 *Foedera*, IV, iv, 121.

16 *PPC*, III, 171-4; *Foedera*, IV, iv, 117 (the other commissioners appointed may not have attended).

17 PRO, E28/47/3, 32; E403/675 m.12; *PPC*, III, 171-4, 26.

18 ibid., 171-4; PRO, E28/47/43.

19 *CPR, 1422–29*, pp. 405-6; *Foedera*, IV, iv, 127; *PPC*, III, 221; PRO, E28/48/66.
20 *PPC*, III, 259-65, 356-9, 275; *Foedera*, IV, iv, 131. 10,000 marks of the 60,000-mark ransom had been deducted in place of Joan Beaufort's dowry (*Foedera*, IV, iv, 107).
21 PRO, E403/658-91; *Foedera*, IV, iv, 116, 140-1. Almost a third of the tallies issued to Northumberland in 1422–29 were replaced, and about 23 per cent of Neville's; the custodian of Roxburgh fared much better (4 per cent). The average annual amount of cash intended for all three was at least close to the sums agreed in their indentures: east march £3,000 (£2,500), west march £1,060 (£1,250), Roxburgh £780 (£1,000).
22 *PPC*, III, 318-19; *Foedera*, IV, iv, 141; PRO, E403/688 m. 11. Beaufort was paid £333 on 5 February 1429 as expenses for his journey northwards.
23 *PPC*, III, 328-9; *Foedera*, IV, iv, 143; PRO, E403/689 m. 11; Nicholson, op. cit., p. 289; *Amundesham*, I, 33-4.
24 *PPC*, III, 323-4, 327; Nicholson, op. cit., pp. 287, 322. Queen Joan eventually gave birth to twin sons in October 1430.
25 *Foedera*, IV, iv, 144, 148, 151. In July detailed procedures were agreed to this end by the commissioners of both sides. See in general N. A. T. Macdougall, 'Foreign relations: England and France', in J. M. Brown (ed.), *Scottish society in the fifteenth century* (1977), pp. 101-3.
26 *PPC*, IV, 73-5.
27 ibid., 19-27, 191-3, 346-50 (24 January 1430). In January 1430, a truce for ten years (by which time Henry would be eighteen) was authorized (ibid., 19-27).
28 ibid., 53, 73-5; C. Macrae, 'The English council and Scotland in 1430', *EHR*, LIV (1939), 415-26.
29 *CPR, 1429–36*, pp. 40 (5 October 1429), 71 (6 March 1430); PRO, E28/51/62 (25 February 1430).
30 *PPC*, IV, 68, 70-1; *CCR, 1429–35*, p. 118; Bain, IV, 213-14.
31 *PPC*, IV, 122; Bain, IV, 214; E. W. M. Balfour-Melville, *James I, king of Scots, 1406–1437* (1936), pp. 293-5. Scots envoys were well received in London and by parliament in March 1431 (*PPC*, IV, 78; 'Gregory's Chron.', p. 171).
32 *RP*, IV, 452; *PPC*, IV, 169-74.
33 ibid., IV, 350-2a. Even an English offer to hand over Berwick in October 1433 had been treated with suspicion by the Scots (Balfour-Melville, op. cit., pp. 208-13).
34 *PPC*, IV, 191-7; *Foedera*, IV, i, 12-13.
35 *CPR, 1429–36*, pp. 327-8, 345; *PPC*, IV, 217-18.
36 *CPR, 1429–36*, pp. 359-61; *PPC*, IV, 266-7. See Storey, *EHR*, LXXII (1957), 604.
37 R. W. Dunning, 'Thomas, Lord Dacre and the west march towards Scotland, 1435', *BIHR*, XLI (1968), 95-9. He also offered to pay his own expenses in meeting with Scottish representatives. For Dacre's indenture, see NorthantsRO, FitzWilliam MS 2049.
38 Storey, *EHR*, LXXII (1957), 604, 613; *PPC*, IV, 294-7; PRO, E404/53/351; 52/349. Sir Ralph Grey replaced Sir Robert Ogle as constable of Roxburgh on 24 June 1435 (ibid., 53/318, 147).
39 Bain, IV, 223; Balfour-Melville, op. cit., pp. 220-3, 226; L. A. Barbé, *Margaret of Scotland and the Dauphin Louis* (1917), ch. V-VII. The papal

envoy, Aeneas Silvius Piccolomini (later Pope Pius II), probably added his weight to the pressure on James to move closer to France (Balfour-Melville, op. cit., pp. 235-7).

40 *CCR, 1435–41*, p. 66.

41 PRO, E28/58/55; E404/53/131 (25 July 1436). See Storey, *EHR*, LXXII (1957), 605.

42 *CPR, 1429–36*, p. 611; PRO, E403/724 m. 3; Bain, IV, 225-6. Eure was appointed constable on 26 August 1436 and was paid on a weekly basis at 100 marks (PRO, E403/726 m. 6; E28/58/9).

43 ibid., 58/9; Storey, *EHR*, LXXII (1957), 605; Storey, *TCWAAS*, LV, new ser. (1955), 125. Instead of taking £2,500 during war and £1,250 in peacetime, Lumley settled for £1,050 *per annum* at all times. See *CPR, 1436–41*, p. 88; PRO, E28/58/53, 48, for a return to a regimen of inquiries and occasional arrays along the border in 1436–37.

44 PRO, E404/53/179. He was twenty-two years old.

45 Norfolk received £2,061 between 18 March and 11 July 1437 (PRO, E403/726-7). Lumley received £1,050 in two instalments on 21 November 1436 and 15 July 1437 (ibid.).

46 Above, p. 14. Talbot was the king's lieutenant during 1414–20 and Ormond during 1420–22 (Otway-Ruthven, *Medieval Ireland*, pp. 348, 387).

47 Lydon, *Later middle ages*, pp. 130-3.

48 *CPR, 1422–29*, pp. 105 (Cork, 1423), 391 (Limerick, 1427). See, in general, K. Nicholls, *Gaelic and Gaelicised Ireland in the middle ages* (Dublin, 1972), esp. pp. 17-20.

49 Otway-Ruthven, op. cit., pp. 348, 349, 353. For examples of the phrase 'Irish enemies and rebels', see *CPR, 1422–29*, pp. 104, 105, 391.

50 Otway-Ruthven, op. cit., pp. 353-4.

51 ibid., pp. 358-9; *PPC*, III, 327; above, p. 158.

52 Lydon, *Later middle ages*, pp. 135-9; Otway-Ruthven, op. cit., pp. 348ff. The fullest account of this feud is in M. C. Griffith, 'The Talbot–Ormond struggle for control of the Anglo-Irish government, 1414-47', *IHS*, II (1940–41), 376-97.

53 Otway-Ruthven, op. cit., pp. 358-9, 361; J. H. Bernard, 'Richard Talbot, archbishop and chancellor (1418–1449)', *PRIA*, XXXV, C (1918–20), 218-29. Merbury received a pension from Talbot in 1423 (A. J. Pollard, 'The family of Talbot, Lords Talbot and earls of Shrewsbury in the fifteenth century' [2 vols., Bristol PhD thesis, 1968]).

54 H. G. Richardson and G. O. Sayles, *The Irish parliament in the middle ages* (Philadelphia, 1952), p. 171, quoting from the archbishop's register.

55 Otway-Ruthven, op. cit., pp. 353-4, 361-2. For Ormond's second marriage to Elizabeth, daughter of Kildare, see *GEC*, X, 123-6.

56 For the financial problem, see Lydon, *Later middle ages*, pp. 37-8, 125-30.

57 *PPC*, III, 49, 67-9; *CPR, 1422–29*, pp. 122, 193; Otway-Ruthven, op. cit., p. 363; PRO, E403/661 m. 8, 13, 16; 664 m. 2, 5, 8, 9, 10. The lieutenant's stipend had been reduced drastically earlier in the century (Richardson and Sayles, op. cit., pp. 152-3).

58 *CPR, 1422–29*, pp. 103, 205; Otway-Ruthven, op. cit., p. 363. For the contemporary eulogy of Edmund 'the good' in the family chronicle of Wigmore, see W. Dugdale, *Monasticon anglicanum* (6 vols., 1817–30), VI, 355.

59 Otway-Ruthven, op. cit., pp. 363-4. Ormond seized his opportunity and in April 1426 replaced Archbishop Talbot as chancellor with his own supporter; this was short-lived, for in October Talbot returned to office (Griffith, *IHS*, II [1940–41], 382).

60 PRO, E403/684 m. 9. There is little sign that he received more of the 3,000 marks assigned him on his appointment (Richardson and Sayles, op. cit., p. 227).

61 Beaufort may have favoured Ormond's appointment in return for his support in resisting Gloucester's pretensions in 1422 (above, p. 14).

62 PRO, E403/681 m. 3, 7; 684 m. 5; Otway-Ruthven, op. cit., pp. 364-5. Grey received assignment tallies worth £1,353 during the second half of 1427 and a further £449 after he had ceased to be lieutenant. For his service in France under Henry V, see Wylie and Waugh, op. cit., II, 17; III, 319; *GEC*, VI, 129.

63 Otway-Ruthven, op. cit., p. 366; *CPR, 1422–29*, pp. 469, 493; PRO, E28/50.

64 PRO, E403/684 m. 18; 686 m. 10; 688 m. 13; 691 m. 10, 12, 18.

65 Otway-Ruthven, op. cit., p. 366; Richardson and Sayles, op. cit., p. 167.

66 As the archbishop of Armagh indicated in the autumn of 1428 (above, p. 164).

67 *CPR, 1429–36*, p. 68; PRO, E28/52/33; 54/43. See Otway-Ruthven, op. cit., pp. 367-8.

68 *CPR, 1429–36*, pp. 49, 66, 490, 493. For Ormond's absences during 1430–32 and from 1435, *Cal. Ormond Deeds*, III, passim.

69 Griffith, *IHS*, II (1940–41), 130-1.

70 *CPR, 1429–36*, pp. 105, 133, 153; PRO, E404/47/161.

71 Otway-Ruthven, op. cit., pp. 368-9.

72 *CPR, 1429–36*, pp. 471, 535.

73 *PPC*, IV, 198-200.

74 PRO, E403/695-727 passim.

75 Lydon, *Later middle ages*, p. 133.

76 S. L. Thrupp, 'Aliens in and around London in the fifteenth century', in A. E. J. Hollaender and W. Kellaway (eds.), *Studies in London history presented to P. E. Jones* (1969), p. 251.

77 idem, 'A survey of the alien population of England in 1440', *Speculum*, XXXII (1957), 262-73; this study does not include Italians, for whom see A. A. Ruddock, 'Alien merchants in Southampton in the later middle ages', *EHR*, LXI (1946), 1-17; idem, *Italian merchants and shipping in Southampton, 1270–1600* (Southampton, 1951), esp. ch. V.

78 Above, p. 135.

79 *CCR, 1430–35*, p. 42 (4 March 1430). Similar expulsion orders were issued in 1431 and 1432 (ibid., pp. 91-2; *CPR, 1429–36*, p. 266).

80 Thrupp, *Speculum*, XXXII (1957), 273. See G. J. Hand, 'Aspects of alien status in mediaeval English law, with special reference to Ireland', in D. Jenkins (ed.), *Legal history studies, 1972* (Cardiff, 1975), pp. 129-35.

81 I. Bowen (ed.), *Statutes of Wales* (1908), pp. 31-6.

82 *RP*, IV, 377-8, 440-1; above, p. 97.

83 The first such grant was made in 1413 to Rhys ap Thomas ap Dafydd, a loyal royal servant from west Wales (Griffiths, *Principality of Wales*, pp. 143-5; *RP*, IV, 6).

84 ibid., 415; M. S. Giuseppi, 'Alien merchants in England in the fifteenth

century', *TRHS*, new ser., IX (1895), 91-2; Thrupp, *Studies in London history*, p. 254. The occasional London Welshman was assessed, however.

85 *DKR*, XLVIII (1887), 294 (Sage); *PPC*, IV, 208-9.

86 ibid., 304-9; *Foedera*, IV, iv, 139.

87 G. Warner (ed.), *The libelle of Englysche polycye* (Oxford, 1926), pp. 1-58 passim.

88 *RP*, IV, 511; J. B. Post, 'A fifteenth-century customary of the Southwark stews', *JSA*, V (1977), 418-28. For greater harmony between local men and aliens in Southampton, compared with London, see Ruddock, *EHR*, LXI (1946), 1-17, and C. Platt, *Medieval Southampton* (1973), pp. 153-6.

89 In general, see A. Beardwood, *Alien merchants in England, 1350 to 1377* (Cambridge, Mass., 1931). Such privileges went back centuries and as far as foreign merchants went, the *Carta Mercatoria* of 1303 was the basis of them. The Hansards from Germany acquired more privileges than most (M. M. Postan, 'The economic and political relations of England and the Hanse from 1400 to 1475', in E. Power and M. M. Postan [eds.], *Studies in English trade in the fifteenth century* [1933], ch. III).

90 *RP*, IV, 359-60.

91 ibid., 192-6, 449; Warner, op. cit., pp. 18-23. For the Florentines, see G. A. Holmes, 'Florentine merchants in England, 1346–1436', *EconHR*, 2nd ser., XIII (1960), 193-208.

92 e.g., *RP*, IV, 250-1 (1423, to Bruges and the Low Countries), 360-1 (1429).

93 Joan's servants had been unpopular in her husband's reign (Kirby, *Henry IV*, pp. 166-7; *RP*, IV, 306 [with the government resisting the Bretons' ejection]). For grants of denizenship to some of Gloucester's Italians, see ibid., 473 (Jean de Signorellis of Ferrara, 1433), and *CPR, 1436–41*, p. 50 (Titus Livius Frulovisi, 1437).

94 *RP*, IV, 302, 304-5; *CPR, 1422–29*, p. 356. For the later provision of aliens to benefices, see *CPR, 1429–36*, p. 461; *PPC*, V, 27-8 (Louis of Luxembourg, bishop of Ely). For the long-standing hostility to the alien priories, see M. D. Knowles, *The religious orders in England*, II (Cambridge, 1957), 161-5.

95 The records abound with commissions to investigate English depredations against Flemish, Breton, Norman, Danish, Genoese, and German ships, usually in periods of truce. For the lawlessness of the west country, see above, p. 132.

96 e.g., *CPR, 1422–29*, p. 464.

97 *CCR, 1435–41*, pp. 145-6, 155-6.

98 *RP*, IV, 364.

99 *SR*, II, 150.

100 R. Flenley, 'London and foreign merchants in the reign of Henry VI', *EHR*, XXV (1910), 645. Henry IV's statute was reaffirmed in 1427 and 1432 (*RP*, IV, 328-9, 402). Aliens were also prohibited from direct trade with one another and from engaging in the retail trade; nor were they supposed to own houses, although as the death of a Spaniard in East Greenwich showed in 1424, these regulations were not rigidly enforced (*CCR, 1422–29*, p. 96).

101 A. A. Ruddock, 'Alien hosting in Southampton in the fifteenth century', *EconHR*, XIII (1946), 30-1; *RP*, IV, 453-4.

102 ibid., 492; *Foedera*, IV, i, 34; *CCR, 1435–41*, pp. 96-7.
103 ibid., p. 58; *Foedera*, IV, i, 27-8 (28 March); *CPR, 1429–36*, pp. 537-9, 541-88 (18 April); ibid., *1436–41*, pp. 36-7 (8 January 1437). In July 1436 the molesting of Flemings in London was forbidden (*Letter-book K*, p. 206).
104 ibid., p. 205.

9 England and the French Realm

England and France

The defence of the coast of southern England was a more complex military and diplomatic undertaking than either policing the Scottish border or subjugating the Irish. Coastal communities had suffered severe damage during the fourteenth century and required defending now that the French war had restarted. Furthermore, the trading arteries from England's ports, especially Sandwich, Southampton, and London, needed protection. And after 1417 there were English conquests in France to be maintained. These facts, coupled with the crown's traditional obligation to preserve English lordship in Gascony and (since 1347) Calais, presented the dual monarchy with intricate problems and formidable difficulties.

It was appreciated that by maintaining the conquered lands in northern France, England herself would be defended, thereby making naval protection of the channel a secondary line of defence; this was implicit in the loans and parliamentary taxes which were negotiated to support continental expeditions 'for the defence of the realm'.[1] Especially was this so after a degree of political stability had been established in northern France by the treaty of Troyes in 1420, the alliance between England, Burgundy, and Brittany in April 1423, and the continuing conquests of Henry V and the duke of Bedford towards the Loire.[2] The protection of Gascony, which was isolated on land and by sea from the other English territories, was best done in Gascony itself, with some military assistance from England and the goodwill of sympathetic southern French noblemen. Calais could be defended by its garrison and by the merchant community which used it as the staple port for the export of English wool to northern Europe. Normandy and the *pays de conquête* were protected by the regent Bedford, with aid from England. The only other sensitive sector of the channel seaboard was Brittany, whose political attitudes directly affected the south-west of England in particular and the Anglo-Gascon trade that passed in the lee of its rocky coast. Friendly relations had to be cultivated with this largely independent duchy, not least because its ruler's allegiance could give substance to the new dual monarchy of the Lancastrians. For his part, Duke Jean V's abiding aim was the preservation of his duchy's independence by means of amicable links not only with England and

Burgundy, but also with Charles VII. Such a delicate balancing-act could not be maintained indefinitely, for the English were campaigning close to his frontier against the Valois French. Relations between England and Brittany, therefore, slowly deteriorated from the summer of 1424 until, in January 1426, the government announced 'open war' against Brittany and took precautions against Breton raiders on the English coast.[3]

Relations with the other great French dukedom, Burgundy, were even more vital for the continuance of English dominion in France, and more immediately, the security of Calais depended on the goodwill and co-operation of the Burgundian duke, Philip the Good. Like Jean V, he too had long-term political ends in view which were not entirely compatible with continued English friendship. One of his greatest concerns was the consolidation of Burgundian influence in the Low Countries and especially the conquest of Holland. After Jacqueline, the heiress to Holland, Hainault, and Zeeland, had deserted her husband, John of Brabant, she sought refuge in England in 1421; when she married Humphrey, duke of Gloucester early in 1423, the spectre was raised of English intervention in the Low Countries to promote Jacqueline's claims. These directly conflicted with Philip's interests after 1424, when Jacqueline's uncle and rival, John of Bavaria, bishop of Liège, designated Philip as his heir. The outcome was Gloucester's disastrous expedition (to speak diplomatically as well as militarily) to Hainault in October 1424 and three years of desultory campaigning, accompanied by rumours of further English invasions and frantic efforts by Bedford to shore up the Anglo-Burgundian alliance on which his own power in northern France depended.[4]

Channel defence and coastal protection were not therefore of foremost concern to the Lancastrian government immediately after 1420. Indeed, the English fleet which had been assembled by Henry V was allowed to run down under his son; the office of keeper of the king's ships, which had been created by Henry, lost some of its importance; and ships which the great king had built or purchased were either sold during 1423–25 or allowed to rot in muddy dockyards.[5] England kept her admiral, whose responsibilities stretched round the entire coastline of England and Wales, but there was little for him to do at sea in the 1420s and slight wherewithal to do it. In any case, the duke of Exeter, who had been promoted admiral by Henry V and remained in office until his death in December 1426, hardly had any time to devote to naval activities.[6] Despite deteriorating relations with Brittany and Burgundy, the coastal towns, ports, and villages of England were reasonably safe for most of the protectorate. Rarely were their inhabitants threatened in these years, and only then when a Breton fleet attacked the south-west peninsula. Early in 1426 the Isle of Wight and the Devon coast became vulnerable and had to be protected by local militias; and in May 1427 a fleet was commissioned in Devon to strike back at the Bretons. The same thing occurred in June 1429.[7] Otherwise, the defence of England and its territorial and commercial interests on the continent was conducted in France itself.

Although every effort was made to induce Normandy to support the French war, Bedford relied heavily on England for military and financial aid. Significant numbers of English lords, headed by Bedford himself, crossed and recrossed the channel, expending time and energy in fighting on Normandy's frontiers. Even some of the king's councillors – Hungerford, Exeter, Norfolk, and Warwick among them – were periodically occupied abroad, thereby increasing the responsibility shouldered by the bishops who were councillors at home. Other Englishmen, too, were diverted from their normal occupations to serve in retinues, though in the 1420s the expeditionary armies were modest in size.[8] Those English knights and lords who had recently been granted or sold estates in northern France by Henry V or Bedford were required to perform their military duty there or face forfeiture.[9] This meant a constant human investment in operations which admittedly had a defensive purpose but drained manpower and wealth from England and inconvenienced her commerce. At least once a year during the minority merchants and shipowners had their vessels and crews impressed to convey soldiers and an even greater number of horses, stores, and weapons to Calais, Bordeaux, and the Norman ports. The burden fell especially heavily on those ports lying between the Thames estuary and the west country.[10] While they were mustering at Barham Down or Sandwich or Winchelsea, the soldiers were an affliction which the local population had to bear. Commissariat arrangements left much to be desired, and Kentishmen in particular complained bitterly of theft, depredations, and lawlessness.[11] The financial costs of channel protection and French defence were enormous, and the cash supplied by the exchequer was only part of it. Local revenue in Gascony, Calais, and Normandy was consumed immediately; and the soldiers' wages and army costs required substantial loans and the anticipation of regular revenue and direct taxation. In peacetime – let alone in wartime – the government's resources were hardly sufficient for the discharge of all its responsibilities; these additional commitments made them woefully inadequate and threatened the government's good credit.[12] If credit failed, royal enterprises would fail too.

Calais and Gascony during the protectorate

The crossing from Dover to Calais was the shortest and most direct route to the continent. This was a fact of great significance for the ports of the narrow strait and – which was more to the point in the 1420s – for the transport of reinforcements to France. Moreover, the commercial value of the port and fortress of Calais was unrivalled in northern Europe: wool shipments from England were taken to the warehouses of the staple merchants and the English garrison was there in large part to protect this profitable trade. Yet, the presence alongside the merchant community of soldiers who were sensitive about the regular payment of their wages did not always make for an easy relationship, and when it became strained, not only was the security of Calais threatened, but so also was the wool trade and the customs revenue it provided for the crown. On more than one occasion during the Hundred Years War, a failure to pay the garrison's wages led to the seizure by the soldiers of the wool packed on the quays at Calais. It happened in April 1423, with the result that the staplers lent £4,000 to the government so that the soldiers could be paid; the 'grete disese' of the garrison was temporarily alleviated.[13] Such crises demonstrated the decisive importance of the merchants to the defence of Calais and to the English government; in turn, they eagerly capitalized on their position to extort concessions and privileges from the government at Westminster. Although in the 1422 parliament the staplers' claim for judicial powers that would put Calais to some extent beyond the scope of the common law courts was rejected, in practice the government appointed special commissions which were directly answerable to the court of king's bench.[14]

The importance of Calais was reflected in its custodians and by the large sums of money devoted to its defence in the 1420s. The accomplished soldier Richard Beauchamp, earl of Warwick had been appointed captain of Calais by Henry V, and on 4 February 1423 the council renewed his appointment for a further two years; in fact, he stayed in office until he was replaced early in 1427 by Bedford, who was then about to return to France.[15] Several of the outlying fortresses of the Calais march were also in the charge of men trusted by Henry V and kept in office under his son.[16]

Regular payment of the garrisons and their captains was essential. The difficulties encountered in paying Warwick's men vitiated his entire period in office, and he agreed to his reappointment only if his men would accept a new wages assignment offered by the exchequer.[17] Such payment was a heavy charge on the government, far in excess of the commercial income of the port itself. In 1421, it had been estimated that in wartime Calais cost about £19,000 a year; by 1433, in peacetime, it was still as much as £12,000 with a revenue of barely £2,900. As the figures provided by the treasurer of England on both occasions show, unpaid debts were rising disturbingly.[18] At first, the protectorate took considerable care to meet its Calais obligations as promptly as possible, though by means of tallies of assignment rather than by cash; there is little evidence of delay in payment, and most of the assignments were eventually realized. It was advantageous to the soldiers to take annually a good proportion of the money owed to them from the revenue of the town and march of Calais, including the profits of the local mint, and from a subsidy of 13s. 4d. on each sack of wool transported to Calais from England.[19] Other sources assigned them were quite beyond their control: the principality of Wales, which was required to send £4,000 to Calais in May 1423; and the ransom of James I of Scotland (5,000 marks in February 1424, later increased in July 1426 as a result of the soldiers' demand for another 10,000 marks).[20] In fact, by the beginning of 1427 the garrison was again becoming restive, partly because there had been a marked drop (far below what was needed even for a peacetime establishment) since 1423 in the annual exchequer provision for soldiers' and captains' wages, some of which were unpaid from Henry V's reign, and partly because the sources of income assigned to the treasurer of Calais, Richard Buckland, had not lived up to expectations. Thus, the constable of Oye castle, Nicholas Horton, had gallantly stayed at his post without pay after his term ended, while the new custodian of Rysbank tower was required in November 1427 to serve at a wage that was 180 marks less than that received by his predecessor.[21] Buckland and soldiers' representatives crossed to England to attend the council on occasion (as in February 1427) to plead their case and demand better arrangements for the payment of their debts. They did so with some effect, because in 1427 and 1428 the financial provision at the exchequer was twice as large as it had been in the previous three years, though this was only possible by relying yet more heavily on the Scottish ransom (to the tune of 50,000 marks) and on the wool cargoes from England.[22] The dangers in this situation were obvious: James's failure to produce the bulk of his ransom exasperated the treasurer of Calais and those who relied on him; the heavier the Calais burden on the wool customs, the less likely was it that other crown creditors could recoup their debts from this source – especially when Bishop Beaufort had preferential claims on the customs; and when English commercial operations in the Low Countries were hampered by unsettled relations with Burgundy, the very source of this cash was imperilled.[23]

The protectorate, then, was generally aware of its responsibilities towards Calais, though occasionally it had to be reminded of them by the garrison. During Beaufort's ascendancy in 1424–26, finance was perhaps apportioned more niggardly than was required, but the return of Bedford to France in 1427, coupled with growing unrest in Calais, brought a quick remedy.[24] Only in that year did the exchequer provide funds which, when added to Calais's own income, were adequate for a peacetime military and administrative establishment. The colony's financial burden on the Lancastrian government was a weighty one, but the régime's good credit in the eyes of the soldiers was not yet seriously damaged, though the inherent weaknesses were apparent to the acute observer.

The duchy of Aquitaine (or Gascony) had relatively little direct relevance to the security of England. The crown's interest in it sprang rather from the traditional obligation to protect a province that had long belonged to the English king and the strong commercial links (particularly in the wine trade) that had been forged since the twelfth century.

The treaty of Troyes included no specific provision for the future absorption of Gascony into the French realm of an English-born king; the presumption was that it would remain a French province governed by representatives of English kings. After the death of Charles VI in 1422, it provided an ideal springboard from which to launch the conquest of those parts of France which did not yet acknowledge Henry VI as his successor.[25] Thus, the duty of Henry's council was to preserve English rule and English trade in Gascony, and to extend Lancastrian rule in south-western France so that the entire realm would one day accept Henry as its king – though without absorbing Gascony into its government any more than Brittany or Burgundy were.

The province was ill-equipped to achieve both purposes from its own resources. On 1 March 1423, the council was presented with a most depressing report on the state of Gascony; in particular, the fortress of Fronsac, which guarded the landward approach to Bordeaux in the Dordogne valley, was said to be in a pitiful plight.[26] Only by sending reinforcements and supplies on the long and hazardous sea journey from England could the situation be improved. Care was taken in May 1423 that Sir John Radcliffe's expedition to Gascony should be composed largely of English-born (and presumbly dependable) archers, and cargoes of wheat were sent the following year to sustain the citizens of Bordeaux.[27] Nevertheless, Radcliffe was so frustrated and dispirited as seneschal of Gascony that in May 1425 he tendered his resignation and requested that he be discharged of all responsibility for events there.[28]

Indeed, during the early years of the protectorate military aid from England was small. Apart from Radcliffe's expedition in May 1423 (only 200-strong), the duchy received nothing until 1428. Then, in July, Radcliffe, who had been persuaded to stay on as seneschal, was provided with a further 200 men, to serve for one year at the exchequer's expense (at £4,000).[29] But he fared no better than before in eliciting his own fees and the soldiers' wages from England. By July 1426, he had to be refunded 2,000 marks, and after another three years as much as £6,600 was owing to him as constable of Fronsac and seneschal.[30] Such a situation put large-scale offensive operations against Charles VII out of the question. On the other hand, the territorial integrity of Gascony itself was preserved. This was largely due to the recovery of the wine trade. Whereas in 1422 expenditure by the principal Gascon financial officer, the constable of Bordeaux, was well in excess of revenue, it was gradually brought under control; income from the wine trade rose during 1423–27 so that by the end of the protectorate the duchy's revenue actually exceeded its expenses.[31]

The security of Gascony was the responsibility of Englishmen, though the adverse report of March 1423 had led to some changes. The Lancastrian statesman Sir John Tiptoft remained seneschal of the southern region of the Landes (he had been in office since 1408), but surrendered the superior seneschalcy of all Gascony at the end of April

1423; his military and political duties elsewhere scarcely enabled him to take an active interest in his charge.[32] He was replaced on 1 May 1423 by Sir John Radcliffe, who had supervised the finances of Gascony since 1419; he proved an energetic and resident seneschal who suffered financially for his devotion and was driven to distraction by the meagre reinforcements sent from England.[33] Thomas Barneby, who already had a reputation for financial manipulation – though not always in the king's interest – succeeded Radcliffe as constable of Bordeaux on 18 May 1423.[34] Barneby died in March 1427 and Radcliffe sailed for England in the following September, but by then English authority in the duchy was secure enough and the financial situation healthy. Such confidence encouraged the government to appoint a native Gascon, Bernard Angevin, as the new constable of Bordeaux, and he also acted as regent and governor of the province while Radcliffe was away.[35]

Yet action against Valois France could only be contemplated via diplomacy, by inducing other French princes to harry the southern flank of Charles VII's dominion. Negotiations with the count of Foix and other noblemen in south-western France were resumed after Henry VI's accession, and in March 1423 envoys from Aragon and Foix visited England. But there was little positive achievement so long as Bedford was fully occupied in the north; and the count of Foix, at least, preferred inaction so long as he was courted by both the English and the French. Like Jean V of Brittany, he played a double game without risking the kind of punishment which Bedford could inflict on the Breton frontier. As a result, military operations against Charles VII from Gascony proved abortive by the end of 1425.[36]

The protectorate's record in Gascony was therefore one of modest achievement: solvency had been brought to the duchy in peacetime, even though the seneschal fared badly; the king's authority had been asserted and without crippling financial demands on the exchequer; and the wine trade had recovered, assisted no doubt by stabler relations with neighbouring French noblemen and the truce with Brittany. But it had been mainly an internal achievement, owing much to Sir John Radcliffe. Of the wider aim of recovering Valois lands in southern France for King Henry, little had been realized by diplomacy.

The war in northern France, 1422–29

The English occupation of Normandy and the *pays de conquête* was of very recent date in 1422. It offered the best possible protection for England's coastline, and the honour of England and her king demanded that these territories should be defended, supported, and, if possible, extended. The establishment of the dual monarchy had imposed newer obligations on Englishmen, namely, to complete the conquest of all France and punish the effrontery of the nineteen-year-old Charles VII. England's responsibilities could be conveniently discharged from the springboards of Calais and Gascony, in alliance with Brittany and Burgundy especially; they also demanded generous aid for Bedford and his commanders in Normandy.

Henry V died in mid-purpose, but his brother immediately resumed the task of completing the conquest of Normandy and defending it with castle garrisons. This he had accomplished by the summer of 1424, when his achievement was tested at the battle of Verneuil. Immediately after Henry V's death, the French, who in any case held the impregnable fortress of Mont St Michel, near the Breton frontier, had raided in lower Normandy. In Picardy to the north, the castle of Crotoy, at the mouth of the Somme, was in French hands.[37] Both sectors were invaded by English expeditions in aid of Bedford during 1423–24 with conspicuous success. In March 1423 an expedition to Normandy was planned under the leadership of the duke of Exeter, who was a very experienced commander; the force, mostly of archers, was about 1,600 strong. In the event, it put to sea without Exeter, who was ill and had to join it later. It arrived in Normandy in July under the earl of Norfolk, Sir Walter Hungerford, and Robert, Lord Willoughby. Beaufort lent 1,000 marks for the enterprise, whose intention was the 'protection and defence' of English France.[38] It fulfilled its brief well enough, for not only was most of Normandy cleared of the enemy, but some daring sorties were made south of the Loire in the vicinity of Bourges, Charles VII's capital.[39]

The expedition to Picardy in the following year had a more limited objective. William, earl of Suffolk, admiral of Normandy, had begun the attack on Crotoy late in June 1423, in association with a land force led by Sir Ralph Botiller. By October the besieged were ready to capitulate if no relief arrived by the following March. The appearance at Calais of 1,600 men from England in April–May delivered the *coup de grace*. This operation was planned by Bedford, and the expedition was commanded by the earl of Warwick, assisted by Lord Willoughby, Sir William Oldhall, and Lord Poynings, who had been retained for the purpose for half a year in March 1424. The feoffees of the duchy of Lancaster lent £1,000 for the venture.[40] After the fall of Crotoy, the northern flank of Normandy was secure. With Brittany's benevolence for the moment assured, and the duke of Burgundy bound by interest and (since October 1423) by blood to the English cause, Bedford could raise his eyes to horizons beyond the Norman frontier.

The strategy of the Lancastrians became more expansive as they swept up the Seine valley towards Paris and strengthened the western border with Brittany. The new departure was signalled by a council held by Bedford in Paris in June 1424. There the conquest of Anjou and Maine in the south and of Picardy in the north was planned, with crucial reliance placed on the Breton and Burgundian alliances.[41] The result was a great pitched battle at Verneuil, on the Normandy–Maine frontier, on 17 August 1424. On this battle depended the plans for future conquests by the English and the consolidation of Henry V's achievement in Normandy. It was a battle whose significance was well appreciated by those English writers who included detailed accounts of it in their chronicles and particularized the number of the dead. Verneuil proved to be a resounding victory for Bedford, assisted by the earls of Salisbury and Suffolk, as well as Willoughby, Oldhall, and Poynings, who had been in France since the siege of Crotoy. Exeter was suffering once again from the illness that afflicted him in later life, but nevertheless he contributed his retinue to the English lines. More than 10,000 of the French and their Scottish allies are said to have lain dead on the field when it was all over, to be counted up by the heralds.[42]

This notable victory opened before Bedford the prospect of extensive conquests in the French provinces around Normandy, especially those towards the Loire and the Valois strongholds beyond. Normandy was no longer in the front line. Some semblance of a civil administration could be introduced, and the regent Bedford made determined efforts to spare the Norman population the worst oppressions of a colonial régime; he also tried to convert the war outside Normandy into an enterprise which would engage the energies of the Normans themselves and encourage them to shoulder the inevitable financial burden. Such conquests would, after all, act as a defence for Normandy in the same way as the conquest of Normandy protected England; it was right, therefore, to expect the Normans to pay up – and they did so. Consequently, England's contribution to the war effort in 1425 was more modest than hitherto and seems to have been confined to transporting soldiers at the end of May and a quantity of bows and arrows in mid-July.[43] In Normandy direct taxation for war purposes was introduced in 1422–24, and men were assembled in the duchy for Bedford's armies. The Norman administration was concentrated in the hands of Bedford's servants: at first his chamberlain, Sir Richard Woodville, combined the offices of seneschal and treasurer-general, but in January 1423 the latter office was divided and a Norman, Pierre Sureau, became receiver-general; in November 1424 Sir William Oldhall was appointed seneschal, though his office was abolished one year later. Such close co-ordination had been desirable in wartime, but after Verneuil it seemed less appropriate for a more civil administration. Gradually from 1426 onwards, the organization of garrisons and field armies in Normandy passed under civilian control, through the treasurer and receiver-general.[44]

English colonization and settlement in Normandy proceeded apace. Since Henry V's day, estates in the conquered areas had been granted to Englishmen and submissive Normans, who thereby undertook military responsibilities that would assist in the duchy's security. Some of the strategically important channel ports and larger towns (such as Harfleur, Cherbourg, and Caen) had had colonies planted within their walls. These developments gathered speed in the comparatively stable conditions after Verneuil. Such were the brighter prospects for settlement from 1424 onwards that noble and non-noble alike from England began to purchase properties, though security needs dictated that the English-born should be the most favoured in the disposal of estates.[45]

It was unfortunate for the English commanders in France that at this juncture the diplomatic shelter under which stability and settlement were being fostered in Normandy began to fracture, and other problems, arising out of the very success of English arms, began to emerge. In the autumn of 1424, Gloucester's invasion of Hainault in support of his wife severely strained the Anglo-Burgundian accord. It required all Bedford's diplomatic skills to hold the two powers together and maintain Burgundian neutrality on the north-eastern flank of Normandy. Brittany, too, had become less enthusiastic about its English alliance by the autumn of 1424, and Duke Jean's intrigues with Burgundy and Charles VII were calculated to counter English military power on his eastern frontier.[46] The Scots continued to aid the French, and by 1428 Anglo-Scottish relations had deteriorated so seriously that Valois envoys (including the poet and chronicler Alain Chartier) were able successfully to negotiate an alliance on 30 October that provided for the eventual marriage of Charles's son, Louis, with James I's daughter, and further Scottish aid to the extent of 6,000 men-at-arms.[47] Furthermore, the financial demands placed on Normandy were growing heavier, and although they had been shouldered at first, their increasing weight bade fair to bleed the duchy white.[48]

The military command on the Norman frontier by the end of 1425 was the responsibility of three lieutenants under Bedford. To the east and south-east of Normandy stood the earl of Warwick, to the south Salisbury, and towards Brittany Suffolk.[49] In the absence of Bedford in England in 1425–27, some reorganization of the English command was necessary, and the extensive border of Normandy dictated a division like this; Warwick seems to have been the senior commander after his arrival some months later. The arrangements were vindicated by successes especially in the south, where Salisbury's capture of Le Mans and thirty-six other towns and castles was proudly recorded by more than one contemporary chronicler in England.[50]

Warwick sailed for France in July 1426, together with Sir Robert Hungerford, Sir Richard Stafford, and Sir John Passelawe.[51] The following year the elder Hungerford, Walter, went to relieve the threatened port of Cherbourg, of which he was constable.[52] But the main offensive did not take place until Bedford himself returned on 19 March 1427, and then English participation in the war became more vigorous than it had been of late. Preparations for the regent's embarkation were elaborate. He took with him an impressive company of English soldiers headed by Lord Roos, Lord Talbot, and Edmund Beaufort, the bishop's nephew; other Englishmen who held lands in France were summoned to attend him. The muster took place on Barham Down, just outside Dover.[53] They joined other forces in Normandy which were mainly composed of Englishmen resident in the duchy. The risk of relying on the hard-pressed Normans to supply men for armies of conquest in

Anjou and Maine was reflected from the autumn of 1427 onwards in the greater emphasis that was laid on recruiting English-born soldiers rather than local Frenchmen.[54] The culmination of these preparations was the siege of Orléans.

The Orléans campaign of 1428 involved England in once more raising and financing a major expeditionary force. The veteran Salisbury was put in charge of the siege itself and a new army was assembled on Barham Down, this time 2,400-strong under contract for half a year. A fleet of ships was assembled from the ports between the Thames estuary and the south-west, for the army required thousands of horses, as well as cannon, stores, carts, and arms for the besiegers. Many of the supplies were collected at Gravesend; the men sailed from Sandwich on the south coast at the end of June.[55]

The relief of Orléans by the French and the explosive impact of Joan of Arc, meant that an even greater burden would soon fall on England. To judge by the reports penned by English chroniclers, Salisbury's death at Orléans was a profound shock to English confidence, and contemporaries realized that the siege was a turning-point in the war with Charles VII.[56] The new situation was reported with gravity in Westminster on 15 April 1429, when Bedford argued that the coronation of the king in France was the sole propaganda weapon which might successfully counter the impact of the Maid and the proposed crowning of Charles VII in Rheims cathedral (which took place in the following July). Meanwhile, the regent's emergency measures included eliciting further aid from England in the wake of the Orléans disaster.[57] As a result, the army assembled by Beaufort for his crusade against the Hussite heretics in Bohemia was diverted at the last moment to serve in France. When Bedford outlined the situation to the great council in mid-April, he concluded that he needed an expedition of about 1,400 men for half a year. Beaufort's army was in process of being assembled during early summer, and the soldiers were quartered in Kent while they waited for transport ships. The council was understandably reluctant to see Beaufort go on a far-distant crusade with good fighting men who could be put to more immediate use in France. At first, on 18 June, it simply reminded the bishop that he should in no way denude France of soldiers while he was *en route* for Bohemia. But the defeat at Patay that same day raised the urgent possibility of actually diverting Beaufort's 2,750 men to Bedford's service for six months. Beaufort agreed at the beginning of July, when he was already in France, though with what degree of enthusiasm is not apparent; he realized that he was inviting the pope's wrath and consequently insisted on an assurance that his agreement to the change of plan would not be publicized lest his collusion be suspected. Beaufort was doubtless afraid lest his good credit with Martin V – perhaps even his ambitions in the church – be hopelessly compromised.[58] Events at Orléans brought to an end the Lancastrian advances to the south; the strength of the Norman military system would shortly be put to the test; and henceforward English

resources of men, supplies, and money would be required in considerable quantity.

Two coronations, 1429–32

Two of the most memorable events in Henry VI's life directly
concerned France. His English coronation at Westminster in November
1429 was in part a response to the fall of Orléans and the impact of Joan.
By the time his minority ended, his ministers had been forced to
undertake a fundamental reassessment of the Lancastrian position in
France and relations with the Low Countries. In the interval, Englishmen heard news of defeat, threats of invasion, and alarums such as they
had not heard for decades: the well-to-do were required to raise and lead
new armies to France, participate in negotiations, and contribute to
loans and taxes with increasing frequency; anti-alien attitudes were
roused in several parts of the realm; and within the royal family the
tensions and rivalries of the 1420s were exacerbated by disputes over
war strategy.

The Westminster crowning was the keystone of a bold plan devised
by the councillors in England and France. If one man was its moving
spirit, he was the duke of Bedford.[59] And the coronation was the prelude
to a lengthy visit to France by the king himself. Its timing was dictated
almost solely by the need for a striking English response to the revival
of French fortunes under the Maid's inspiration. There was certainly no
compelling reason in England for a coronation in 1429; it had been
delayed for seven years already, and there was no reason why it should
not wait until the king was older. But the Valois successes enabled
Charles VII to ride triumphantly to Rheims, the traditional altar of
consecration of French kings, and there, on 17 July 1429, he was
solemnly crowned king of France. It was an act of unusual symbolic
significance in the circumstances of the 1420s. Bedford was sufficiently
shaken by it to seek a meeting in Paris with the duke of Burgundy during
the first fortnight of October; the arrangements they made amounted to
a reappraisal of Lancastrian aims. On 13 October, the government of
Paris and the provinces adjacent to Normandy on the east and south was
assigned to Duke Philip so that Bedford could concentrate on
Normandy.[60] This decision effectively suspended the Lancastrian
campaign to conquer France by English-led armies. Yet the Valois
achievement also required a major counterstroke if King Henry's claim
to be ruler of France were to be recognized in the long term. His
coronation in France would fit the bill admirably, though it was
unthinkable that this should take place before his crowning in England;
Englishmen had already expressed fears lest their country be subordinated to an English régime in France. The presence of the Lancastrian
monarch in his second realm, with an imposing army at his back, would
also give heart to the English forces already there and fortify their

sympathizers and allies. Above all, it would give substance to the ideal of the dual monarchy. Its immediate, tactical aim was to relieve hard-pressed towns and cities like Paris and Rouen which, it was claimed in letters to Henry VI in December 1429, were in a desperate plight.[61] If successful, a royal expedition would even underpin the defence of England itself, as the government's agents carefully pointed out when taxes were imposed to cover its cost.[62]

On 5 November 1429, Henry VI was escorted to Westminster abbey for his coronation. He was barely eight years old. Whatever haste marked the arrangements, the ceremony was impressive and well-attended, and it stressed the king's dual heritage in England and France. Henry approached London by London bridge and lodged in the Tower, where he followed the eve-of-coronation ritual of creating a substantial number of knights, including the young earl of Devon, the earl of Warwick's son, and Lord Beaumont. Next day, the sixth, Warwick took his royal ward to Westminster abbey, where Cardinal Beaufort sat on the king's right and Queen Katherine nearby; an unexpected – though nonetheless welcome – guest was the king's cousin, Pedro, prince of Portugal, who arrived just in time. Indeed, the international flavour of the occasion emphasized the extraordinary significance of this coronation, for a French bishop was also in attendance and the son of the duke of Austria was one of the new knights. Even the king himself seems to have appreciated the importance of what was going on, for he looked round 'sadly and wisely' as Beaufort placed the heavy crown on his head. At the festivities that followed, the king's French heritage was stressed even on the elaborately designed jellies and pastries, whilst the memory of Henry V and his friendship with the Emperor Sigismund was conjured up in order to convey to all those present the Lancastrian *imperium* into which Henry VI was now entering.[63] No one who witnessed the spectacle could have mistaken its significance – unless he were among the bystanders crushed to death by the crowd or distracted by the London pickpockets.[64]

After the ceremony, final preparations were made for the expedition to France, which was a major exercise in logistics. Accompanying the king would be a substantial number of Englishmen, including some of his councillors. The exodus from the realm in April 1430 had, therefore, important implications for England and its government as well as for the Lancastrian leadership in France. As in Henry V's last months, the years 1430–32 saw a sizeable proportion of the English peerage in France at one time or another.[65] Eight dukes and earls went with the king, including Norfolk and York, Devon, Arundel, Warwick, Stafford, Huntingdon, and Ormond. About a dozen other lords also made the journey, among them Tiptoft, steward of the king's household, and Cromwell, his chamberlain. They headed the court which the king required on a lengthy sojourn, and they provided an experienced council for the political and military aspects of the visit. In all, more than 300 persons were in Henry's entourage, 182 of them menial servants from his household, of whom 137 were valets to cater for his court's daily needs. Five surgeons were ready to deal with its ailments, and John Somerset was there as the king's teacher and physician extraordinary. During the financial year 1430–31, the treasurer of the household spent all of £22,000 on food, materials, and other things – doubtless to the satisfaction of the craftsmen and shopkeepers of Calais, Rouen, and elsewhere.[66] The commissariat arrangements were herculean for what amounted to an itinerant community. Transporting the cavalcade to France was no mean task, involving as it did the assembly of countless weapons, hundreds of carts and carters, troops of horses and oxen, and household furniture suitable for a king on the move. Ships were assembled at Sandwich, though Henry himself sailed from Dover; his lords' retinues were marshalled on Barham Down, which frequently accommodated armies bound for the continent.[67] At Calais, which was only a modest-sized town, housing had to be specially prepared, and the nearby fortresses were alerted to protect this most important of visitors.[68] The king crossed to Calais in the last week of April. After a prolonged stay, which was probably dictated by detachments of French soldiers operating in the Seine basin, he made his way south to reach the capital of Normandy, Rouen, by the last week in July.[69] There the king resided for well over a year, for he did not visit Paris until December 1431.

By the beginning of 1431, Paris seemed reasonably secure, for several fortresses had been recovered by the English and, greatest boon of all, the seemingly invincible Maid had been captured in May 1430. In order that Henry could be taken safely from Rouen up the Seine, French domination of Champagne and the Oise valley had to be broken. By the spring of 1431, therefore, it had been decided to send reinforcements from England, both for Bedford's army and for the councillors in France who needed the concurrence of the royal advisers in England for any major initiative involving the person of the king. A new army was accordingly mustered in February and March 1431. It was to be led by Lords Audley and FitzWalter, with the actual command falling to Beaufort's nephews, Thomas, count of Perche, and Edmund, count of Mortain, who, as their titles suggest, possessed French estates which they were anxious to protect.[70] This army of more than 2,000 men crossed from Sandwich to Calais during the first part of March. It was followed in the summer by the retinues of Lord Clinton and Sir Thomas Tunstall (570 men), and by a further contingent (800 men) under Richard Neville, the new earl of Salisbury.[71] Squadrons of ships were commandeered in southern and south-eastern ports to ferry the soldiers and nearly 3,500 horses across from Sandwich and Southampton. Bows and arrows were purchased, some from Italian merchants in England, and shipped to Rouen for the use of the English archers.[72]

The ranks of the councillors in France were strengthened at about the same time by experienced and trusted officials; they were contracted for six months as from mid-March 1431.[73] Among them was Sir Richard

Woodville, a Norman administrator of some standing, The others were William Lyndwood, a clerical civil servant of distinction, and John Tyrell, a protégé of Gloucester who would soon be treasurer of the wars and the king's household. They joined several other councillors who were preparing to leave for France with Beaufort: Bishop Alnwick, and Lords Tiptoft and Cromwell.[74] Before their departure, they obtained from their fellow councillors views and opinions on current affairs to transmit to the king's advisers at Rouen. The council which was held at Canterbury on 1 May 1431 was understandably reluctant to be dogmatic about a military situation which changed more rapidly than fifteenth-century communications could accommodate, but they enunciated certain principles.[75] The king's French coronation was still the first priority, though the military danger was fully appreciated. Louviers and Rheims should therefore be captured first, for the councillors could imagine nothing worse than an ignominious, hole-in-the-corner coronation, or a royal expedition to Rheims which was denied entry to the city or, worst of all, was captured on the way. Secondly, the alliance with Burgundy was still vital to Lancastrian interests, although the terms under which it might continue should be carefully examined. Thirdly, financial support for the Lancastrian administration in France should still be provided locally rather than by England;[76] and the war would be made self-financing if estates and other property were distributed to those who captured them, a suggestion that was taken up by the councillors at Rouen in November 1431.[77]

This council also considered the question of how long the king should remain in France, and what should be done if Bedford (as seemed possible) declined to shoulder the responsibilities of regent for very much longer. In this connection, the councillors stressed the importance of establishing peace and order in France before Henry returned and indicated that at that point Bedford should be offered the lieutenancy in preference to anyone else. Some indication was also needed of the council's attitude to peace negotiations initiated by the papal envoy, Nicholas Albergati, cardinal of Santa Croce. The reaction was unenthusiastic: the councillors considered (and this was still the English view at Arras in 1435) that it was not possible to commit the king to a peace treaty with Charles VII during his minority; in any case, the treaty of Troyes had clearly stated that the three estates of both realms would have to agree to a peace settlement. As for the purely tactical problem of the future occupation of castles and towns at present in English hands, the council reluctantly authorized the surrender of those that could only be retained at great risk or high cost. These Canterbury discussions demonstrate that by May 1431 Henry VI's journey to France had not achieved its anticipated result: the financial strain was still acute; Burgundy's alliance was a mite less reliable after French successes north of Paris; and the dilemma of whether or not to engage in negotiations was being faced with reluctance and a marked lack of conviction. Perhaps the councillors could have advised in no other way

at this juncture. Although they reaffirmed certain fundamental principles, practical decisions were entrusted to those on the spot. Yet the
writing on the wall had been accurately read. The council was fully
aware of the financial problem, though the short-term solution of
distributing captured territory could only accentuate it in the long run
by reducing the crown's landed resources;[78] it entertained doubts as to
whether the king could be crowned in France after all; and it realized
that Lancastrian government in France after Henry's return would have
to be stabilized. In the meantime, England poured more men into the
breach.

The expeditions of 1431 enabled Bedford to clear the road up the
Seine valley to Paris, and at the beginning of December, Henry travelled
to St Denis, the hallowed burial place of French kings, *en route* to his
coronation at Notre Dame on 16 December. Once again, Beaufort
performed the actual crowning.[79] The reason why the coronation was so
long delayed must surely lie in the uncertain military situation in the
middle Seine valley. That this was so is indicated by Henry's subsequent
movements, which were unusually rapid and give the impression that
the ceremony was hurriedly fitted in before the king returned to
England. Despite the invitation to 'allx maner of nacyons' and lavish
banquets for those who came, this second coronation was mainly an
English affair dominated by Beaufort, some English bishops, and a
couple of Anglophile French ones. The occasion was marred by an
unseemly dispute between the canons of Notre Dame and some of the
English courtiers, an invasion of the banqueting hall by a number of
Parisians, and the failure of King Henry II to distribute the customary
largesse.[80] As soon as the ceremony was over, Henry was taken back
to Rouen and on to Calais during the first week in January 1432. The
royal entourage made the crossing to Dover on 29 January, and Henry
never set foot again in his French realm.

The impact of his coronation was significantly lessened by the
knowledge that three days earlier the duke of Burgundy had concluded
a general truce with Charles VII to last for six years.[81] During the next
three years, the Lancastrians strove to maintain their military commitment to the war whilst at the same time investigating a little more readily
the possibility of concluding their own truce with King Charles. Henry's
perfunctory visit to Paris had demonstrated that Lancastrian control
outside Normandy was weakening, not least because of Burgundy's
withdrawal from the fighting. This became more and more obvious
during 1432, when a series of French attacks was launched on Rouen,
Chartres, Lagny, and in Maine. At Lagny, indeed, Bedford collapsed
from exhaustion in August, and his disillusion with the campaign and
with Burgundy's alliance was deepened by the death of his devoted
wife, Anne, Philip the Good's sister, on 14 November. His second wife,
Jacquetta of Luxembourg, whom he married five months later, came
from a family that was greatly distrusted by Duke Philip.[82] Moreover,
the new army despatched from England in August 1432 had brought

little relief.[83] Ships had once again been impressed in the south-eastern ports and assembled at Winchelsea to transport about 1,200 men and 2,000 horses across the channel. The expedition was led by Lords Camoys and Hungerford, and substantial quantities of bows and arrows were bought for despatch to Bedford. They availed him little.

Calais and the war strategy, 1433–34

Faltering military fortunes led to serious differences of opinion on how the war should be conducted in the future. The vital consideration in Bedford's mind was the defence of Normandy, even at the expense of Paris and Calais. In October 1429, the regent had decided to withdraw to Rouen from Paris and recent events had given him no cause to regret his decision. Moreover, the possibility that Artois, the county which flanked Calais, might fall to his wife, as heiress of the duke of Burgundy, vanished in September 1430 when Philip the Good's son, Charles, was born; Bedford's personal interest in the north-east consequently declined.[84] Indeed, he was increasingly disillusioned with the war beyond Normandy's frontier, not least because his own health and determination were sapped by the campaigns of 1432. While in this frame of mind, he looked on Calais as a sentinel guarding Normandy's approaches, especially in view of Burgundy's unreliability. Gloucester, however, saw Calais in quite a different light. He had less direct interest in Normandy (where he had no wealthy estates, unlike Bedford) and he showed more concern for Calais, its merchants, and the bridgehead it provided towards the Low Countries and Philip of Burgundy, whom he regarded with suspicion. To Gloucester's way of thinking, Calais merited vigorous support in its own right and not simply as a strategic adjunct to Normandy. As the French pressed harder and more successfully on the English positions outside Normandy in the early 1430s, the differing attitudes of the two brothers came to a head, especially when it became increasingly doubtful that England's resources could stretch to the defence of both Calais and Normandy (let alone Gascony). This conflict of view added to the political strains within the council at home.

When Bedford and his advisers met Gloucester and several councillors from England at Calais in late April and May 1433, they failed to agree on the future conduct of the war. The delegation from England set out on 20 April and spent about four weeks in Calais, listening to Bedford's powerful advocacy. Gloucester was accompanied by Bishop Gray of Lincoln, Archbishop Kemp, and other councillors; Bedford was joined by Cardinal Beaufort and a number of French lords sympathetic to the Lancastrian cause. The urgency of the meeting is reflected in the meeting-place chosen, for Calais was still tense after a soldiers' mutiny. By his own testimony, Bedford did not secure a sympathetic hearing, and hence his journey to England a month later.[85]

His attitude to Calais was probably reiterated on this occasion. But it was Gloucester's views, which are likely to have reflected those of the staplers, that prevailed at Calais; that he and the commercial interest saw eye to eye is indicated by the staplers' loan to Gloucester on 25 April to finance an expedition to France under the earl of Huntingdon.[86] If such expeditions could still be launched, then the argument about the need to subordinate Calais to a Norman scheme of defence lost some of its force. But one loan would not win a war, and Huntingdon's expedition scarcely met the duke of Bedford's requirements.[87]

The rebuff which Bedford's plans received may have been partly responsible for his harsh treatment of the mutineers at Calais after Gloucester returned to England on 22 May. The Calais garrison may have had advance notice of Bedford's ideas on the future role of the port; it certainly became restive when the government failed to pay its wages before the end of 1432.[88] The mutiny began, therefore, with a dispute between the soldiers and Bedford's deputy in the town, Sir William Oldhall, a former seneschal of Normandy.[89] An inquiry was ordered on 21 February and entrusted *inter alia* to one of Gloucester's adherents, John Tyrell, treasurer of the king's household. But the soldiers were so exasperated that they seized the wool on Calais's wharves and thrust Oldhall out of the town, leaving his wife behind. The humiliated captain sped straight to Rouen to report to Bedford, who vowed he would be a 'hevy lord' to the mutineers.[90] He had already planned a visit to the Low Countries for his marriage to Jacquetta of Luxembourg. On the way and in the company of Oldhall and Louis of Luxembourg, chancellor of France and bishop of Thérouanne, he stayed at Balinghem castle, a few miles south of Calais; there a conference was held with Richard Buckland, treasurer of Calais, and the captain of Balinghem. A temporary agreement was negotiated with the mutineers, who were promised payment from the customs collected at Calais; relying on this, they allowed Bedford and his companions into the town on 3 April. The duke was well received by the burgesses and merchants, and even by the soldiery, who accompanied the visitors as far as Calais castle.[91]

Bedford the soldier had no intention of tolerating such behaviour from an English garrison and was determined to punish the mutineers. The day after his arrival, he sent for the keepers of the town gates and despatched serjeants to arrest some of the soldiers and their commanders, who were forthwith incarcerated in the castle; the number arrested was so great that some had to be taken to the marshal's prison in the town. The customs obligations which had just been promised to the soldiers were withdrawn. This done, Bedford and his entourage left for Picardy later in the week and at Thérouanne on 20 April 1433 he was married in the bishop's palace. On his return to Calais, the meeting with Gloucester took place. Its results so embittered Bedford that he set about making an example of the imprisoned soldiers. He ordered the mayor of the staple, Richard Vere, to adjudge four of them to death *pour encourager les autres*, and such action understandably caused great resentment towards the duke. He went to the town hall and sat with the mayor, before whom the soldiers were brought, disarmed and humiliated: 110 of them were banished, in addition to 120 who had already been ejected from the town. They included not only those billeted in Calais, who thereby lost all claim to their wages, but also those who lived in the town and who now lost all right to debts owed them. The angry Bedford then left for Rouen. Relations between the garrison and the duke were extremely bad, and it is hardly to be wondered that Bedford henceforward harboured a distrust of Calais and a scepticism as to its independent value to England and the dual monarchy. A chronicler based in London noted with some satisfaction that the duke enjoyed poor health thereafter until he died in September 1435.[92] Parliament proved less vindictive on 18 July 1433, when soldiers living in Calais had their wages, lands, and rents restored; but Bedford's presence was enough to ensure that they would not be allowed to live in the town ever again.[93]

The dispute over strategy between Gloucester and Bedford grew more bitter during Bedford's stay in England in 1433–34. He prefaced his arguments with a lengthy justification of his conduct of the war, while Gloucester carped at the lack of military success and hinted at mismanagement.[94] The latter's offer in May 1434 to lead an expedition himself to France was perfectly consistent with his determination to prevent the subordination of Calais to Normandy's defence. Even though Bedford was unlikely to accept this proposal, Gloucester may have wished to divert attention away from Bedford's own plans and demonstrate that yet another expedition to Normandy could be launched, even if its costs might be as high as £48,000-£50,000. Bedford responded with a final appeal to parliament in June 1434, when he must surely have been contemplating his return to France. The duke's review of Lancastrian fortunes since 1422, and of his own part in shaping them, was doubtless a moving experience for those who witnessed it. Despite his achievements in the 1420s (he said), the French had been revitalized by the Maid; the English were losing mile upon mile of territory and the countryside was devastated. Without further aid from England, those who had already died would be betrayed – which was perhaps the only argument capable of softening an opponent's heart. Bedford's wish to integrate Calais and its march into a Norman defensive design was spelled out in detail to parliament on 9 June and, after threatening to leave England and return to France, he managed to carry the day.[95] On 2 July, Bedford was appointed lieutenant of Calais and captain of all the fortresses in its march for twelve years; the only limitation on his authority was his brother's captaincy of Guisnes, which Gloucester would continue to hold until July 1436, when that too would pass to Bedford.[96]

Bedford's visit to England also enabled him to assemble more men and arms for northern France. Concern was shown early in 1434 for the safety of Crotoy; it was situated not far from the Norman frontier, and St Valéry on the opposite bank of the Somme had just fallen to the French. On 8 February an indenture was concluded with Sir Henry Norbury, an experienced captain, entrusting him with the custody of the town and castle and authorizing him to enlist a retinue of 120 men, in the first instance for three months.[97] Early in March 1434, Lord Talbot took a modest force to France of rather less than 1,000 men at a cost of about £6,500; the siege and capture of Creil-sur-Oise, not far from Senlis, seemed to justify the venture.[98] Later still, in mid-July, Bedford himself led an army to France; it numbered about 1,400 and included retinues which had fought there in 1431 and 1432 – those of Sir Richard Woodville and Lord Clinton, for example. On this occasion, they used the shortest sea route, from Sandwich and Dover to Calais, where Bedford had an opportunity of gauging the garrison's loyalty after the previous year's mutiny.[99]

The argument between Bedford and Gloucester had an inevitable effect on the government's relations with the staplers. Up to 1433, care was generally taken to reassure them, as some of the most reliable of the crown's creditors, by confirming their privileges. They, in turn, responded with a loan of £1,333 6s. 8d. on 19 July 1430, just as the king was about to leave Calais for Rouen. He evidently left the merchants in good humour, for on that same day (and presumably as a condition of the loan) he forbade English subjects from attending the Brabant markets and buying cloth in the Low Countries.[100] The staplers were aware of their importance to the government and did not scruple to project a melancholy picture of customs revenue lost, the Calais mint impoverished, and the trade of Calais's marts undermined if their privileges were not periodically confirmed and the prohibitions on the export of wool, hides, lead, and tin elsewhere than to Calais were not regularly rehearsed.[101] But by 1433 the situation was perceptibly changing, partly as a result of the government's willingness to allow English merchants to bypass Calais, and partly as a result of the failure to pay the garrison's wages on time.[102] The mutiny in February 1433 and Bedford's plans alarmed the staplers further. Hence, when parliament met on 8 July 1433, the merchants required urgent reassurance on a number of points.[103] In the first place, they wanted repayment of unpaid loans totalling more than £2,900, and they were accordingly assigned whatever customs from east coast ports remained after other assignments had been met. They were also concerned about customs evasion at Calais, and parliament introduced new penalties for the guilty. But these assurances fell short of full-hearted backing for Calais, its merchants, and its garrison. This had to wait until after Bedford's return to France in July 1434 and his death in September 1435.[104]

The exchequer's financial provision for Calais, both to repay the staplers' loans and to administer and defend the colony, reflects the argument over strategy that was taking place. The king's visit to France inaugurated three years of substantial expenditure on Calais, with payments in cash or by assignment that ranged from about £7,820 to £11,120 annually. During the first half of 1433, while Gloucester was still chief councillor in England, this same level was maintained (almost £3,500 up to the beginning of July).[105] But when Bedford arrived, the provision fell to an astonishingly meagre level: between July 1433 and July 1434, payment of only £590 was authorized. Even in the year following his departure, the exchequer issued only a modest £4,685. So long as Bedford lived, his conception of how best to protect the Lancastrian territories in France would prevail, with its implications for the subordination of Calais to the defence of Normandy.

The possibility of peace

Negotiations to end the fighting between Lancastrian and Valois were unlikely to make real progress until England's fortunes began to wane with little hope of recovery. After the shock of Orléans, the English were prepared – tentatively and without enthusiasm – to consider proposals for a truce or peace which originated in several quarters, including the pope and the Council of Basle. When it became known in January 1430 that Eugenius IV was about to nominate some cardinals to mediate in France, the English council thought it advisable to insist that known sympathizers with Charles VII should not be among them, though they did not scruple to suggest that Cardinal Beaufort participate in view of his great experience.[106] In parliament a year later, Bedford, Gloucester, Beaufort, and other lords were authorized to take part in the negotiations which papal, Spanish, and Scottish envoys in France were urging; and when additional councillors joined the king in France in May 1431, they were authorized to take part in similar discussions. On this last occasion, it was made clear that nothing more than a truce was possible during the king's minority, whilst – a telling afterthought – if good opportunity should arise for renewing the war, it should be seized.[107] Nor were all influential Englishmen prepared to contemplate a negotiated peace: Beaufort failed to convince Bedford of its desirability,[108] and it is very unlikely that Gloucester was sympathetically inclined.

The situation changed in 1432. Lancastrian fortunes had slumped and Henry VI returned to England with less to show for his two-year stay in France than had been anticipated. Already, on 28 February 1432, negotiations had opened at Cambrai. Towards the end of the year, in November, another group of ambassadors was sent to discuss peace with Charles VII's envoys, though its composition was such that hasty concessions were unlikely to be made: it included the veteran councillor Bishop Langdon of Rochester, Sir John Fastolf, a robust warrior, and Thomas Bekyngton, one of Gloucester's protégés.[109] The talks were leisurely and inconclusive, despite Beaufort's encouragement. Bedford's arrival in England seems to have changed the pace of negotiation, without in any way weakening the Lancastrian resolve to protect Normandy. In 1433 it was suggested that the captive duke of Orléans should be brought into the discussions as a broker and a bargaining-counter for the English, who proposed that a conference he held at Calais at which not only would Orléans be present but also other French aristocrats with whom the English might find it easier to deal: the queen of Sicily, the duke of Alençon, and the duke of Brittany.[110] Yet even this idea was slow to be implemented, and the possibility of taking Orléans to Calais was still being discussed with the duke of Brittany in June and July 1434.[111] The congress of Arras was the eventual outcome.

Cardinal Beaufort led the Lancastrian delegation to this ill-fated conference. He was assisted by the earls of Huntingdon and Suffolk, Archbishop Kemp, the bishops of Norwich and St David's, and the keeper of the privy seal, William Lyndwood. This high-powered embassy journeyed across the channel in sumptuous style, and it conferred with the French from 12 August to 4 September. The actual negotiators representing England and Lancastrian France were Arch-bishop Kemp, Huntingdon, and Suffolk, who were joined by the bishop of Thérouanne and the count of St Pol. Principally, they were authorized to discuss nothing more than a truce during the king's minority, and a possible marriage between Henry and a French princess.[112] The hapless duke of Orléans and his fellow-captive, the count of Eu, were taken as far as Calais to be employed in the negotiations at a later stage.[113] Despite the duke of Burgundy's inclusion in the list of Lancastrian envoys, rumour had already reached England that Philip was planning to desert the English cause and be reconciled with Charles VII. When this was raised with the pope, Eugenius indignantly replied that no French prince had yet asked for, or obtained, a release from any oath he had sworn to Henry V or Henry VI.[114] But the suspicions of the English remained, for the relationship between the two allies had become more and more strained in the years before 1435, despite Beaufort's efforts.[115]

For all the tireless efforts of the principal mediator, Cardinal Albergati, the chief outcome of the congress of Arras was an alliance between Charles VII and Philip of Burgundy, and the latter's conse-quent withdrawal from his allegiance to Henry VI; by the same treaty, several strategic towns on the line of the Somme, including Abbeville and Amiens, were ceded to Philip. This was a calamity for future Lancastrian authority in France and a serious blow to Henry's sovereignty there. Englishmen were angry at what they regarded as the inflexibility of the Valois in demanding Henry's renunciation of the French crown, and they were outraged by the treachery of Duke Philip. In reality, the English envoys were no less inflexible than the French, for they refused to discuss the Lancastrian claim to the French throne, whilst Archbishop Kemp's asperity and bluntness were 'a diplomatic liability to the English side'. It has been said of both French and English envoys that their 'pride was only equalled by their obstinacy'.[116] On the one side, the English dismissed the French offers as 'ridiculous and risible', 'derisions and mockeries', like an apple offered to a child (said Lord Hungerford); for their part, the French stood up laughing when they heard the third English offer.[117] The point was that the French proposals seemed quite fanciful so long as the English had suffered no major military setback. As Beaufort and his colleagues made their way to the French coast, they were insulted and maltreated by the Flemings, and at Poperinge the envoys were forced to carry their horses' dung out of the town.[118] Henry VI burst into tears on opening a letter from Burgundy which addressed him as 'illustrious and powerful prince and dear kinsman', but no longer as sovereign lord. The final insult was the formal promulgation of the Franco-Burgundian treaty on 21 September 1435.[119] The ending of this futile congress, followed swiftly by the defection of Burgundy and the death of Bedford, heralded a significant relaxation of England's stiff-necked attitude to Charles VII, though not without causing further strain between the policy-makers at Westminster.

The defence of Calais and Normandy – and the neglect of Gascony

Gloucester regained the initiative on the king's council after his brother returned to France in July 1434; when Bedford died, he was able to reorder its priorities. Even with the congress of Arras in prospect, the council had resolved to support the English position in France with a substantial new army. Under an able commander, Lord Talbot, and accompanied by the chancellor of France, Louis of Luxembourg, more than 3,300 men made their way to Winchelsea and Barham Down to muster for the journey to Calais; they embarked towards the end of July 1435.[120] The cost of this expedition was high, not only in wages and rewards for the soldiers (totalling £16,500), but also in payments to the captains and sailors of the ships and the dealers from whom arms were purchased.

With Bedford dead and the congress a failure, Lancastrian policy acquired a different emphasis in the second half of 1435. Not only was the strategic importance of Calais reassessed, in the knowledge that Burgundy now dominated the Somme valley, but the reputation of the peace-makers had been tarnished. The years 1435–37, therefore, witnessed a significant change in the respective roles of Gloucester and Beaufort, the place of Calais and Burgundy in Lancastrian strategy, and in England's attitude to the war more generally. In fact, the notions on strategy that held the field in the 1420s experienced a brief revival.

At the parliament which opened on 10 October 1435, Calais, the staplers, and the garrison were reassured: the privileges of the staple were reaffirmed, and powers of search and penalties of forfeiture were authorized against those who persisted in illegal exporting – something which the 1433 parliament had refused to approve.[121] The relationship between the government and Calais was already improving, for in July the staplers had contributed £3,333 6s. 8d. to the chancellor of France for the wages of the soldiers under his command.[122] Moreover, after Bedford's death exchequer expenditure on Calais rose to its former level – to the extent of £9,500 before the siege of Calais in July 1436. Payment of the soldiers' wages was specifically ordered in December 1435 and again in March 1436, so that the garrison would remain loyal and Calais could resist an attack. The government's prudent action was to be fully vindicated within a matter of months.

At the same time, the traditional policy of financing expeditions to northern France was not abandoned. The closing weeks of 1435 witnessed a new alarm as further successes were won by Charles VII's forces and the threat of Burgundy and Charles VII to fortresses like Calais and Crotoy became a reality. Dieppe was lost when its inhabitants rebelled. Arques was burned, and when Harfleur fell at the end of the year, one chronicler wrote: 'And thus Englishmen began to lose a litell and a litell in Normandie'. As a consequence, several detachments were despatched to the Somme and to Normandy during the winter and spring of 1435–36.[123] Crotoy's captain, Walter Cressoner, was authorized to take about 250 men with him at the end of November, and a month later about 1,770 were shipped from Winchelsea and Portsmouth to the Normandy coast, after fast reconnaissance ships from Cherbourg and Honfleur had reported on the embarrassing uprising in the Caux peninsula. The leader of this second expeditionary force was Sir Henry Norbury, the twenty-five-year-old nephew of Sir Ralph Botiller and the son of Henry IV's treasurer. He and his men successfully relieved Rouen.

The largest army of the entire 1430s set sail in 1436, under the command of the duke of York, the count of Mortain, and the earls of Salisbury and Suffolk. It comprised several contingents. The first, under Sir Thomas Beaumont, was modest in size (about 800 men) and was to muster at Winchelsea towards the end of February. Mortain's was far larger (2,000 in all) and followed soon afterwards; whatever its intended destination – probably Lower Normandy and the Angevin border, where losses had recently been alarming – it in fact put in at Calais early in May in response to rumours of a Burgundian advance towards the town.[124] The greatest contingent of all was led by York, Salisbury, and Suffolk, who had assembled more than 5,000 men by the end of May, when they embarked for Normandy. At the age of twenty-five, this was the duke's first command, and arguably his most important.[125] His prime objective was to protect Paris which, after the loss of the Bois de Vincennes and Pontoise, was seriously threatened. But within days of his plans being laid, news arrived of the French capital's fall and the enemy's advance even as far as St Katherine de Mont, outside Rouen. The Norman capital, therefore, became the duke's main objective as final preparations for his expedition went ahead. After years of continuous impressment of merchant ships, extra incentives were now needed to persuade shipowners to surrender their vessels and crews for royal service. Accordingly, licences were given to shippers and their men, allowing them to sail as privateers 'in warfare' for their own profit after the voyage was over, thereby enabling them to recoup their losses in true Elizabethan fashion.[126] This expedient was used at the same time by the channel patrols, a striking consequence of the council's short-sightedness in running down Henry V's fleet.

The armada sailed from Winchelsea with the chancellor of France on board. Weapons continued to stream across the channel after the soldiers had left, many of them gathered from as far afield as Yorkshire, Lincolnshire, and the midland towns. Suffolk was apprehensive about the wisdom of the expedition and may still have preferred to negotiate with the French; at any rate, in the autumn parliament of 1435, when these overseas ventures were still at the planning stage, he secured a statement that absolved him from all responsibility for any misfortune that might arise during the forthcoming campaign and assured him of the king's continued favour after his return.[127] Suffolk's apparent lack of conviction as to the desirability of continuing the war was to recur in other circumstances later on in his career. York's army eventually landed at Harfleur and made its way to Rouen, where the duke stayed for the next three months. Its cost (including Mortain's redirected force) had been prodigious: in wages alone it reportedly amounted to about £50,000, far in excess of the gross annual revenue of England (excluding the customs), and more or less the sum which parliament had estimated Gloucester's proposed expedition would have cost two years earlier – though it is possible that a smaller, less costly force then would have obviated the need for a larger one now.[128]

A series of official appointments at Calais reflect a clear determination to devote a substantial proportion of England's resources to the defence of the town and its fortress, thereby recognizing Calais's supreme commercial and strategic role. Gloucester himself was already captain of Guisnes, and in October 1435 he succeeded his brother as lieutenant of Calais and the marches for nine years. On 10 February 1436, Robert Whittingham, a London draper, replaced the city fishmonger Richard Buckland as treasurer and, eight days later, as master of the Calais mint.[129] Then, by 15 March, Sir John Radcliffe, the long-suffering seneschal of Gascony, was transferred to Calais as Gloucester's deputy, replacing Bedford's servant, Sir Richard Woodville. Finally, the provisioning of the colony, which now stood in the more menacing shadow of the duke of Burgundy's power, was placed on a sounder footing by the appointment of a new victualler on 30 June, William Cantelowe, a merchant and citizen of London; it was his duty to prepare Calais for the expected attack. These measures sprang from Gloucester's resolve to strengthen Calais and leave no one – least of all the Burgundians – in any doubt that whatever Bedford's attitude may have been, it was still the most precious jewel in King Henry's crown.[130]

The council and public opinion were prepared for a Burgundian assault on Calais six months before it actually happened. Duke Philip had been trying to raise an army in the Low Countries since at least February, when he took part personally in discussions at Brussels, and the news soon reached England.[131] The English preparations were lengthy and, in view of the simultaneous crises on the Somme and in Normandy, comprehensive. Parliament responded with its graduated income tax, convocation with a clerical tenth; oaths were demanded in April from Flemings, Brabanters, and Hollanders living in England, and invasion scares led to defensive measures on the south-east coast.[132] The townsmen and garrison of Calais were prepared to stand by a government that had recently begun to show its appreciation of Calais's worth, and the reinforcements under Radcliffe and then Mortain provided a stout defence in anticipation of attack. Philip was believed in England to have assembled a massive army of 60,000 men, who were supported by a considerable quantity of ordnance; his general muster took place at Ghent on 9 June and the march to Calais began immediately afterwards.[133] Within a week his army, swollen by other contingents on the way, was laying siege to Oye castle in the Calais march, and after that fell on 28 June, Marck was invested during 2 – 8 July. Calais itself now lay open and unprotected on its eastern and southern flanks. The main siege began on 9 July and lasted for about three weeks.[133] When, on 29 July, the last Burgundian companies retired ignominiously from their positions, abandoning most of their supplies and artillery, this was not entirely – or even primarily – due to the vigour of the English defence or the news that the arrival of a large relief force under Gloucester was imminent, but rather because deep rifts had opened within the Burgundian ranks.

Philip the Good's ministers had been divided about the wisdom of attacking Calais in the first place, for some of them valued the English commercial connection more highly than any need to demonstrate their duke's Valois allegiance; on the other hand, the Flemish cities had driven a hard bargain before agreeing to provide contingents for the army and were determined to get their hands on the wool at Calais and to destroy its staple organization.[135] During the siege jealousy between the men of Bruges and those of Ghent, coupled with poor tactical planning, sowed dissension among the Flemings, who formed the backbone of the Burgundian army. Philip's fleet failed to blockade Calais at the crucial moment and attempts to obstruct the harbour were foiled by the inhabitants of Calais at low tide;[136] the Bruges contingent was demoralized by a defeat in a skirmish (26 July) and the Gantois when their bulwark overlooking Calais was destroyed soon afterwards (28 July).[137] It was at this juncture that news came of Gloucester's approach. His army was one of the largest to set foot on the continent since Henry V's day and he assumed personal command in response to news of the fall of Oye on 28 June. The most effective way of assembling a substantial army reasonably quickly was for the king to summon all those who were in receipt of his fees and to enlist the retinues of magnates who had recently commanded in France.[138] Thus, Gloucester's own retinue of 5,000 included the duke of Norfolk and the earls of Huntingdon and Ormond, but other retinues under Warwick, Stafford, Devon, and Lords Hungerford, Welles, Beaumont, and Cromwell brought the entire army up to about 7,675. Their aim was the limited one of relieving Calais, and accordingly a short, sharp campaign was envisaged, lasting no more than a month; it is doubtful if the exchequer could have sustained a large land army in France or Burgundian territory for longer.[139]

Having blooded their nose, the Gantois decided to abandon the siege during the night of 28-29 July and the remainder of the duke's army (including the Brugeois) had no alternative but to retreat as well.[140] A few days later, in a letter to his brother-in-law, the duke of Bourbon, Philip tried to minimize the disaster and placed the entire blame for the abortive siege squarely on the shoulders of the Flemings:

> ... we discovered after our arrival certain things which weakened our faith in the determination and loyalty of our Flemish people, and especially of the men of Ghent... So we took up quarters in a camp, and not for a siege, and we neither fired artillery against the town nor did we make the customary preliminary summons to the defenders....
>
> ... these people of Ghent, considering neither our honour nor their own, regardless of the promises which they had that very day [28 July] renewed, and at a time when we were expecting the enemy to arrive on the following Monday or Tuesday, came to tell us that they had decided to decamp that night and to withdraw to a place near the town of Gravelines in Flanders, ... And at once, without listening to our requests or waiting for our advice, they departed that night, together with the men from the castellany of Ghent, and withdrew to the above-mentioned position near Gravelines. Moreover, not content with this, they persuaded the men of Bruges, Ypres, and the Franc of Bruges, who would willingly have stayed to carry out our wishes, to withdraw likewise. Since the contingent of noblemen we had with us was too small to do battle with the enemy... we were forced to depart and withdraw to Gravelines with the Flemings, abandoning what we had begun with the utmost chagrin...[141]

In the event, it was Lord Welles's advance force which put into Calais on or about 28 July; Duke Humphrey with the main force did not arrive until 2 August, only to discover that Philip's men had melted away.[142] To justify his impressive expedition (and perhaps to keep the army occupied and fed for the month of its engagement), it was resolved to conduct a chevauchée along the Flemish coast. After a council of war lasting a few days, Gloucester led his men across the river Gravelines into Flanders on 6 August and spent eleven days burning towns and destroying crops before returning to Calais and thence to England on 24 August.[143] Gloucester's personal achievement was minimal, as one or two contemporaries acutely observed.[144] And although Calais had put up strong resistance, credit for raising the siege must go to the Burgundians! They proved wanting in two of the most elementary aspects of a military operation: they failed to weld their men into one, united force, and the blockade that was vital to deny Calais its supplies and naval aid had been mismanaged. Nevertheless, what was important in England was that Calais had not fallen and that the perfidious duke of Burgundy had been humiliated.[145]

Gloucester's overall strategy seemed vindicated. England's recent record had been dominated by the rebuff at Arras and the defection of Burgundy; now traditional English policy since the days of Edward III had been reasserted, and the commercial and military vulnerability of Flanders had been demonstrated. The government had seemed capable both of sustaining the staple port with vigour and of sending substantial expeditions to Normandy. The parliament of January 1437 praised Gloucester and accommodated the staplers who, later in the year, responded with a 20,000-mark loan for the wages of mounted archers at Guisnes castle.[146] Care was taken to repay the staplers' loans, and Calais was regarded in the first half of 1437 as a major call on the government's resources. Further south, York's army stayed in Normandy beyond its term, and when the duke and the lords with him were thanked on 7 April 1437 for their services, they were requested to remain in France until relieved.[147] Steps were taken to reinforce them with further retinues under Lords Beaumont, Bourgchier, and Willoughby, but eventually, in July, the duke was relieved of his burden and the veteran commander Warwick was appointed king's lieutenant-general in France in his place.[148] A grand army of about 5,320 men was raised and put under his command at Portsmouth in mid-August.

These preoccupations in the north meant that Gascony was left to its own and Sir John Radcliffe's devices – to his considerable financial loss. Even the army bound for Gascony in 1429 was diverted to northern France after Joan of Arc's victory at Orléans. Radcliffe, the seneschal, had been in England since 1427.[149] As an incentive for him to return to his charge, on 6 July 1430 he was assigned £6,620 from the customs of the west-country ports in order to clear the government's debt to him; but this was only on condition that he went to Gascony before the end of September for one year.[150] Radcliffe showed commendable forbearance, especially since the organization of his expedition was a slow business; but eventually, on 16 March 1431, he was retained for one year with 620 men, and his expedition left Plymouth for Bordeaux sometime in mid-June.[151] He took with him £1,000 in cash for distribution to those French lords, captains, and others on whom the security of the duchy partly depended. Such sweeteners had become an important prop of the English régime in the south. But just as the duke of Brittany had slipped gradually away from his English alliance when the Lancastrian armies ran into difficulties, so too did the Gascon allies forget their oaths of loyalty. By 1433, the counts of Foix and Armagnac had declared openly their support for Charles VII, and on 21 March the seneschal was told to warn English subjects that they should no longer enter their service, aid them or ally with them.[152]

This was evidently not the moment to leave the Gascon administration bereft of support and so at the same time the eventual repayment of Radcliffe's enormous debt was guaranteed by the council. On 16 March 1433 he was granted the income from Caernarvonshire, Merionethshire, and the lordship of Chirk for as long as was needed to settle the £7,030 debt; almost a year later, on 10 February 1434, he took over the chamberlainship of north Wales himself and, presumably to hasten the repayment, he was empowered to appropriate the first £728 *per annum* of north Wales income.[153] Even so, at this rate, it would take ten years to eliminate the debt – hardly a satisfactory rate of payment for a loyal Lancastrian servant in a vulnerable post on which the defence of a vital English possession depended. By 1436 Radcliffe's patience was exhausted; at least £800 of the wages due to his 1431 retinue alone had still not been paid. In any case, Gloucester had urgent plans for him at Calais.[154] Radcliffe, therefore, was formally discharged of his Gascon duties on 6 November 1436, though he had been transferred to Calais at least as early as the preceding March. The reorganization of Calais's defence may well have been undertaken at the expense of Gascony's security, for the king's effective authority in the duchy was now seriously weakened. By July 1437 there was no alternative but to empower the resident local officials, the archbishop and the constable of Bordeaux, to negotiate a truce with the count of Armagnac and the seigneur d'Albret, two former allies who had once protected the duchy's frontiers.[155]

The defence of England in the 1430s

The English reverses in northern France after 1428, and the growing estrangement between Henry VI and the dukes of Brittany and Burgundy, made it much more difficult for the government to control the behaviour of the king's own subjects in the narrow seas and protect mainland England from attack. The folly of discarding Henry V's fleet now became apparent. Half-hearted attempts were made to halt the disposal of those royal ships that remained, though the rundown had gone too far; instead, small squadrons of impressed ships were engaged to patrol the seas and deter privateers and enemy vessels. When fear of invasion became real by 1435, the modest efforts of the past to keep the seas and protect the coast were urgently redoubled. The usual method of achieving this was to pay local ships and their crews to put to sea on the king's service for a specified period of sea-keeping duty. On 18 June 1430, for example, the west-country ports assembled a fleet to serve for six weeks; the cost to the crown was £1,400.[156] Later in the month, a belated attempt was made to divert to William Soper, who was still keeper of the king's ships, some of the money raised by the sale of royal ships at Sandwich and in the western ports so that others could be repaired or constructed.[157] The only other, more traditional, resource was the obligation of the Cinque ports; accordingly, on 18 February 1433 their warden, Gloucester, was instructed to ensure that their ships swept the seas and arrested privateers.[158]

The Bretons were causing more trouble than most. Defeats in northern France made the English anxious to improve their relations with Brittany: not only was the duke's recognition of Henry as sovereign of France valuable propaganda, but a *rapprochement* would give security to the Norman frontier and the channel's shipping lanes. By 1432 the two governments had agreed on a mechanism to deal at least with this second matter. On 5 April the council invited all those from southern and coastal counties who had complaints against Bretons to be in London by 22 April to appear before commissioners appointed by King Henry and Duke Jean.[159] On the English side, a veritable bevy of inquiries was subsequently conducted into attacks on Breton ships by westcountrymen from Plymouth, Dartmouth, Teignmouth, and elsewhere in Devon and Cornwall.[160] The normalization of good relations was assisted by the arrival in England in June 1432 of Gilles, the younger son of Jean V; he immediately struck up a close and affectionate friendship with the king, so much so that Henry insisted on keeping him in the realm as a guest, paying his expenses while he stayed.[161] Gilles, for his part, liked England and was eventually to be distrusted in his own land for his Anglophile attitudes. Then, on 2 December 1432, the accord was furthered by the visit of garter king-of-arms to Duke Jean for more discussions.

Despite English goodwill and the government's readiness to perform agreements already made, the Bretons were less than eager to live up to their undertakings. Complaints from Englishmen were not properly examined; in fact, an envoy failed to induce Duke Jean to appoint commissioners to sit at Exeter for this purpose.[162] Nevertheless, the English persisted with the negotiations and parliament, which opened on 8 July 1433, was still not prepared to authorize hostile action against Bretons living in England despite the provocative activities of their fellow countrymen.[163] The eventual arrival of Breton envoys in London in mid-August 1433 does not seem to have accomplished much, and even the minority régime's willingness to restrain English privateers began to wane.[164]

For the first time in years, in April 1435 the English coast was in real danger of attack, presumably from Bretons and Valois French. No longer were Lancastrian arms able to maintain a secure frontier in the fields of northern France; the hostilities were coming nearer home. On 12 April the Isle of Wight prepared for an invasion. In the following weeks almost every county on the south coast, from Sussex to Cornwall, was ordered to be vigilant.[165] The parliament of October 1435 was very worried at the way in which Bretons and others were able to sail unhindered round the coast, thumbing their nose at any English vessel that might put to sea. What was even more alarming was the lack of resolution shown by the merchants, on whom the country relied for ships: the king's right to forfeitures and the rigour of the law against breakers of safe-conducts seem to have discouraged them from taking action against the enemy.[166] The government responded with a temporary suspension of the latter regulation, and positive encouragement was given in the tense months of 1436. From February onwards, ships equipped for sea at their owners' expense were allowed to keep any vessels or booty which they might capture, and these English privateers (for such they were) were further authorized to appoint two of their own admirals. By this means, a fleet could be re-created by private enterprise, enjoying a licence to reap its own rewards.[167] Such an expedient had its dangers, unless official supervision were a reality and treaties with foreign states were respected. But for the moment, all coastal hands were required to repel the enemy, for in 1436–37 hostile vessels frequently sailed the channel. In April 1436 work was carried out on Sandwich's walls and planks were laid across the town gates to make house-to-house movement easier should there be an enemy attack. Soon afterwards, in June, rumours were circulating that Burgundy's army was about to land at Maldon (Essex), and the inhabitants of Essex and Middlesex showed signs of panic. Even after the relief of Calais, another threat from the Flemings alarmed Surrey and Sussex in February 1437.[168]

More energetic measures to defend the shores of England and patrol the narrow seas were being demanded with greater persistence. The *Libelle of Englysche Polycye* voiced this concern, and two of the foremost causes for the summoning of parliament on 21 January 1437 were the defence of the realm and the keeping of the seas.[169] At last, on 17 April, three commanders were nominated for a fleet that was to be assembled by the government itself: Lord Carew, Thomas Neville, and William Wolf. It was a significant step. A month later the entire eastern and southern sectors of the country were alerted to defend themselves against a possible invasion.[170] England's attitude to sea protection and coastal defence was changing and a number of influential men realized that the channel was now England's best – and it might soon be its only – defence towards the south and east.

Notes

1 Above, p. 116. See C. F. Richmond, 'The keeping of the seas during the hundred years' war, 1422–1440', *History*, XLIX (1964), 283-4.
2 The alliance of 1423 was complemented by the marriage of Bedford and Arthur of Brittany to two of Burgundy's sisters and co-heiresses (who, according to one contemporary, were as plain as owls) (G. A. Knowlson, *Jean V, duc de Bretagne, et l'Angleterre* [Rennes, 1964], p. 126; R. Vaughan, *Philip the Good* [1970], p. 9; Armstrong, *Annales de Bourgogne*, XL [1968], 13, 104-5; ibid., XXXVII [1965], 83-5).
3 Knowlson, op. cit., pp. 118-32; *PPC*, III, 181.
4 Vaughan, op. cit., pp. 1-17, 32-48; Vickers, op. cit., ch. IV. This friction also resulted in temporary restrictions on English wool-trading in the Low Countries from the summer of 1428 (J. H. A. Munro, *Wool, Cloth and Gold* [Toronto, 1972], p. 69).
5 Richmond, *History*, XLIX (1964), 285-9; idem, 'English naval power in the fifteenth century', ibid., LII (1967), 7; M. Oppenheim, *A history of the administration of the royal navy and of merchant shipping...* (1896), pp. 16, 22-3.
6 *HBC*, pp. 132-3. Lieutenants seem to have performed his administrative and judicial duties for him (*CPR, 1422–29*, pp. 160-1, 350). Exeter was succeeded by another busy man, the duke of Bedford.
7 ibid., pp. 327, 328, 405, 553.
8 The largest force sent to France appears to have been that accompanying Beaufort in 1429, about 2,750 strong (*PPC*, III, 339-44).
9 *CPR, 1422–29*, p. 404 (1427); *PPC*, III, 349-51 (1429); below, n. 58. For these and other profits of war, see McFarlane, *Nobility*, ch. 2; idem, 'England and the hundred years' war', *PP*, XXII (1962), 3-18.
10 PRO, E28/39/61 (1423, at Dover); *CPR, 1422–29*, pp. 128 (1423), 192 (1424, at Winchelsea), 362 (1426), 404 (1427), 469 (1428, at Sandwich), 552 (1429, at Sandwich), 553 (1429, at Sandwich and Dover); *PPC*, III, 323-4 (1429). For the horses, see PRO, E403/671 m. 9 (1424, 3,400); *CPR, 1422–29*, p. 469 (1428, 5,000). See M. M. Postan, 'The costs of the hundred years' war', *PP*, XXVII (1964), 34-53.
11 Special harbingers were appointed in Kent in 1429 to deal with the retinues of Beaufort and other magnates quartered there and awaiting departure (*CPR, 1422–29*, p. 555); they and other royal officers were plied with gifts by the Cinque ports to win their favour (KentRO, NR/FAc/2 f. 110, 121: New Romney, 1429, 1435). For the lawlessness that often sprang from such concentrations of soldiery, see above, p. 136.
12 Above, p. 108.
13 *PPC*, III, 67-9; PRO E28/40/16; 41/103.
14 *RP*, IV, 191; *CPR, 1422–29*, pp. 390-1.
15 ibid., p. 404; *GEC*, XII, ii, 380.
16 PRO, E28/41/26. William FitzHarry was confirmed as captain of Marck on 17 May 1423.
17 *PPC*, III, 53-4.
18 *Foedera*, IV, iv, 26-7 (corrected in J. L. Kirby, 'The financing of Calais under Henry V', *BIHR*, XXIII [1950], 168); Chrimes and Brown, op. cit., pp. 272-4. These annual figures appear to be representative of the first third of the fifteenth century (Kirby, *BIHR*, XXIII [1950], 166-8).
19 PRO, E403/658-91 passim; *PPC*, III, 19, 40-1. Only the duty on wool exports

from Southampton, which was reserved to Beaufort, was excluded from this grant of 1 February 1423. With minor modifications, this subsidy was periodically renewed throughout the protectorate (PRO, E28/45/30; 47/58; *RP*, IV, 340-1).

20 *PPC*, III, 88-90; PRO, E28/44/1; 45/25; 47/60. In the event, south Wales contributed only £120 to the treasurer of Calais, on 22 March 1425 (PRO, E401/710).

21 PRO, E28/48/38; *CCR, 1422–29*, p. 360.

22 *PPC*, III, 49, 242-3. Expectations that James I would produce his ransom were not high, and in July 1429 the soldiers settled for the duke of Bourbon's ransom instead (ibid., pp. 344-5). Bourbon had been captured at Agincourt, and 40,000 of his 100,000-crown ransom were still unpaid when Henry V died (Wylie and Waugh, op. cit., III, 287-8).

23 Above, p. 157. In July 1424 Calais stood second to Beaufort in successfully realizing its tallies on the wool subsidy (PRO, E28/45/30).

24 A commission was appointed in March 1427 to survey and record all royal lands in Calais and the services (including military) attached to them (*CPR, 1422–29*, pp. 390-1).

25 M. G. A. Vale, *English Gascony, 1399–1453* (Oxford, 1970), pp. 80-1.

26 *PPC*, III, 46-8.

27 ibid., 67-9; PRO, E28/41/2; E403/661 m. 3; *CCR, 1422–29*, pp. 161-2.

28 *PPC*, III, 170.

29 ibid., 303-4.

30 ibid., 204, 339. Some of Radcliffe's assignments were issued on particularly reliable sources (Steel, op. cit., p. 186).

31 Vale, op. cit., p. 235.

32 ibid., pp. 82-98; *PPC*, III, 54-5.

33 Vale, op. cit., pp. 245, 248. He died in office as seneschal of the Landes in 1443.

34 ibid., pp. 245, 247. He appears to have been absent from the duchy only during 1427-31.

35 ibid., p. 247; R. A. Griffiths, 'The rebellion of Owain Glyndŵr in north Wales through the eyes of an Englishman', *BBCS*, XXII (1967), 151-68.

36 Vale, op. cit., p. 247.

37 Newhall, *English conquest*, pp. 290-3, 297-9.

38 PRO, E28/39/82, 61; 41/75; E403/658 m. 13, 14; /661 m. 2, 11, 14; *CPR, 1422–29*, p. 78; *PPC*, III, 59-61, 86-8, 100-1. For Norfolk's retinue, see McFarlane, *Nobility*, p. 25.

39 Newhall, *English conquest*, p. 295. An attempt to take Mont St Michel itself in July 1423 was abandoned (ibid., pp. 300-1).

40 ibid., pp. 297-9, 305 PRO, E403/664 m. 21; 671 m. 9; E28/43/56; 44/65, 3; *PPC*, III, 25; *CPR, 1422–29*, p. 192; *CCR, 1422–29*, p. 141. For New Romney's contribution to the expeditions, see KentRO, NR/FAc/2 f. 100. The capture of Crotoy stirred at least two London chroniclers (*London Chrons.*, p. 283; *Great Chron.*, p. 131).

41 Newhall, *English conquest*, pp. 307-8, 313-15.

42 'Benet's Chron.', pp. 179-80; *Brut*, pp. 441, 497-8, 564-7; *English Chron.*, p. 53; *EHL*, pp. 320-1; Giles, p. 5; *London Chrons.*, pp. 75, 129; Stevenson, II, ii, 759. Sir John Fastolf claimed to have made 20,000 marks out of ransoms, etc. at Verneuil (McFarlane, *Nobility*, p. 33).

43 *CPR, 1422–29*, pp. 299, 302; *CCR, 1422–29*, pp. 176, 205. See R. A.

Newhall, 'Henry V's policy of conciliation in Normandy, 1417–22', in C.
A. Taylor (ed.), *Anniversary essays in medieval history . . . presented to C.
H. Haskins* (Boston, 1929), pp. 205-29.
44 Newhall, *English conquest*, pp. xv, 155, 173-4, 177-84, 246; idem, *Muster
and review* (Cambridge, Mass., 1940), pp. 14-47, 96-7, 101-3.
45 Allmand, *EconHR*, XXI (1968), 463-8; see also Newhall, *English conquest*,
p. 166.
46 Above, pp. 178-9.
47 J. C. Laidlaw, *The poetical works of Alain Chartier* (Cambridge, 1974), pp.
12-13; M. G. A. Vale, *Charles VII* (1974), p. 33; above, p. 158.
48 Newhall, *English conquest*, p. 189.
49 Newhall, *Muster and review*, pp. 45-7.
50 *Brut*, p. 498; *London Chrons.*, pp. 76, 286; *Great Chron.*, pp. 133-5. For
Warwick's title of 'captain- and lieutenant-general of the king and regent
for the wars in Normandy, Anjou, Maine and the Breton marches', see BN,
f. fr. 25767/212.
51 PRO, E403/675 m. 15; *CPR, 1422–29*, p. 362; Ramsay, op. cit., I, 373.
52 *PPC*, III, 229-30.
53 *CPR, 1422–29*, p. 404; PRO, E403/678 m. 12, 19; *PPC*, III, 225-6. Amongst
the others retained were Roger, Lord Camoys, William, Lord Clinton, Sir
Thomas Beaumont, and Henry Bourgchier.
54 Newhall, *Muster and review*, pp. 114-15. It was not an invariable rule after
1427, but increasingly common.
55 PRO, E403/684 m. 18; /688 m. 10; /688 m. 4; *CPR, 1422–29*, pp. 406. 469,
493, 499; *CCR, 1422–29*, p. 408; *Foedera*, IV, iv, 134-6, 138. Siege engineers
were also included in Salisbury's indenture.
56 *Brut*, pp. 434-5, 450-4, 500; 'Gregory's Chron.', pp. 164, 132. Lord Moleyns
and William Glasdale, one of the Normandy captains, also lost their life in
the siege (Giles, p. 10; Newhall, *Muster and review*, pp. 109, 110).
57 *PPC*, III, 322-3. A useful introduction to the mass of writing on Joan is Vale,
Charles VII, ch. 3; two recent accounts in English are J. H. Smith, *Joan
of Arc* (1973), and E. Lucie-Smith, *Joan of Arc* (1976).
58 *PPC*, III, 322-3, 330-8, 339-44; *CPR, 1422–29*, pp. 553, 554, 555. In
mid-April, an attempt was made to intercept French ships that were
believed to be about to convey the Scottish princess to France (*PPC*, III,
323-4; above, p. 158). English landowners in France were ordered to
proceed forthwith to their estates or face forfeiture (*PPC*, III, 349-51). For
Beaufort's concern about the Hussites, see F. M. Bartoš, 'An English
cardinal and the Hussite revolution', *Communio Viatorum*, I (1963), 47-54;
Holmes, *EHR*, LXXXVIII (1973), 721-50.
59 *RP*, IV, 338.
60 Ramsay, op. cit., I, 413-14; Poquet du Haut-Jussé, *Bibl. de l'école des
chartes*, XCV (1934), 312-26.
61 *PPC*, IV, 10-11. Envoys from Normandy pleaded for aid at the parliament
which opened on 22 September 1429 (*Amundesham*, I, 43).
62 e.g., *CFR, 1422–30*, pp. 306-9.
63 *Brut*, pp. 437, 450-1, 454; 'Gregory's Chron.', pp. 165-70; *EHL*, p. 351;
below, p. 220. For the knighting of 33, see Winkler, thesis, pp. 27, 92-5.
64 *Amundesham*, I, 44.
65 PRO, E403/691 m. 22-28 (payments for accompanying the king to France
for one year, 12 April 1430); E404/46 passim. Leo, Lord Welles ordered the

compilation of an inventory of his goods (including books) before he left England (LincsRO, Ancaster 10/A/1; see also McFarlane, *Nobility*, p. 237 and n. 4).

66 PRO, E101/408/9 – and that is an incomplete account! It ignores the personal expenses of individuals: witness Sir John Stourton's attempt to raise cash 'consideryng my nede ate this present hoeure that I have for my goyng ovir see . . .' (SomsRO, DD/L/1/17 [1]).

67 *CPR, 1429–36*, pp. 44, 47, 71, 72, 73; *CCR, 1429–35*, pp. 10-11, 47-8, 71. For the assembly of men and ships in the Cinque ports for the king's voyage, see KentRO, NR/FAc/2 f. 110 (*s. a.* 1428–29, New Romney), 111v (1429–30).

68 PRO, E28/51/68, 47.

69 *Brut*, p. 458; Christie, op. cit., p. 376. Henry had left London for Dover on 17 April (PRO, E364/71 m. Ed). WarwsRO, CR W1618/W19/5 is the household account of the earl of Warwick in France and England for March 1431–32; it records Henry VI at Rouen with the earl during 1431. See H. A. Cronne and R. H. Hilton, 'The Beauchamp household book', *UBHJ*, II (1949–50), 208-18.

70 *DKR*, XLVIII, 281; PRO, E403/696 m. 13-14, 19. FitzWalter was a friend of Gloucester's and his lieutenant in Holland and Zeeland in 1425–26 (Vaughan, op. cit., pp. 39-42).

71 PRO, E403/696 m. 17, 18. Neville had married the heiress of Thomas Montague, who had fallen at Orléans.

72 *CPR, 1429–36*, pp. 133, 112.

73 *PPC*, IV, 81-2.

74 PRO, E403/696 m. 12. Beaufort and Tiptoft had only recently returned to England.

75 *RP*, V, 415-18.

76 For the successful exploitation of Normandy, see R. Doucet, 'Les finances anglaises en France à la fin de la guerre de cent ans, 1413–35'. *Le moyen âge*, 2nd ser., XXVII (1926), 272-303.

77 ibid., pp. 283-4; Allmand, *EconHR*, XXI (1968), 472.

78 C. T. Allmand, 'The collection of Dom Lenoir and the English occupation of Normandy in the fifteenth century', *Archives*, VI (1963–64), 207.

79 *EHL*, p. 351; WarwsRO, CR W1618/W19/5 f. 164ff. Warwick and his wife accompanied Henry VI.

80 'Gregory's Chron.', p. 173; *Brut*, pp. 460-1; WA MS 63504/A-H. Henry was welcomed to Paris by his grandmother, the queen-dowager of France, Isabelle of Bavaria. See Shirley, *Parisian Journal*, pp. 268-73.

81 Ramsay, op. cit., I, 434. For strains between Burgundy and the Lancastrian parlement at Paris, see Armstrong, *Annales de Bourgogne*, XXXVII (1965), 95-6; and for commercial tension, J. H. Munro, 'An economic aspect of the collapse of the Anglo-Burgundian alliance, 1428–1442', *EHR*, LXXXV (1970), 225-44.

82 Ramsay, op. cit., I, 444-6.

83 PRO, E403/704 m. 16, 17; E404/48/315-23; *PPC*, IV, 126; *CPR, 1429–36*, pp. 202, 218. *Brut*, p. 465, puts the force at 1,500 men. For an indenture between Sir William Peyto and a Warws. gentleman to raise a company of archers for this expedition, see ShakesBT, Willoughby MS 469a.

84 Armstrong, *Annales de Bourgogne*, XXXVII (1965), 83-4; Vaughan, op. cit., pp. 20-8.

85 *PPC*, IV, 139 (19 December 1432). The soldiers were promised payment provided Gloucester (perhaps because they trusted him) was assured of their good behaviour. See A. N. E. D. Schofield, 'England and the council of Basel', *AHC*, V, no. 1 (1975), 38ff, including Kemp's and Hungerford's report on the conference (in Emmanuel College, Cambridge, MS 142 f. 148).

86 *RP*, V, 435-8; *PPC*, IV, 222-32.

87 *Brut*, p. 466 (mistaking Chichele for Kemp at Calais); 'Gregory's Chron.', p. 176; PRO, E404/49/156; E403/710 m. 1 (the loan). This army was about the same size as that of 1432.

88 *CPR, 1429-36*, pp. 277, 278; *CCR, 1429-35*, p. 243.

89 J. S. Roskell, 'Sir William Oldhall, speaker in the parliament of 1450-1', *Nott. Med. St.*, V (1961), 87-112; idem, *Speakers*, pp. 242-7, 360-1.

90 *Brut*, pp. 502, 570; *DKR*, XLVIII (1887), 291.

91 *Chron. of London*, p. 119, dates Bedford's entry to 7 April.

92 ibid., pp. 120-1, 135; *London Chrons.*, p. 170; *Brut*, pp. 502, 571.

93 *RP*, IV, 473. A rule forbidding a garrison from being recruited from the residents or businessmen of its town was already in operation in Normandy (Newhall, *Muster and review*, pp. 114-19).

94 *RP*, IV, 420 (13 July 1433), 423 (24 November 1433).

95 *PPC*, IV, 210-13, 22-32; *RP*, V, 435-8.

96 *DKR*, XLVII, 300; PRO, E28/55/8; E101/71/877. Bedford was already captain of Calais, and had been since 1427.

97 PRO, E404/50/60.

98 PRO, E403/713 m. 11, 14; *London Chrons.*, p. 77; *DKR*, XLVIII (1887), 296. He was made lieutenant-general of the Ile de France on 16 May 1434 (Pollard, thesis, p. 152).

99 PRO, E403/716 m. 7, 12-13; /717 m. 1; *CPR, 1429-36*, pp. 356, 358, 359, 424-5. *London Chrons.*, p. 137, puts Bedford's company at only 600. For one of Sir William Peyto's indentures to raise archers in Warws., see ShakesBT, Willoughby MS 472a (14 July).

100 *DKR*, XLVIII (1887), 267, 277; PRO, E403/695 m. 20; *CPR, 1429-36*, p. 26. For the protectionist measures in favour of Calais and its greater merchants, see Munro, *EHR*, LXXXV (1970), 225-44.

101 *RP*, IV, 410 (1432).

102 *DKR*, XLVIII (1887), 289; above, p. 195.

103 *RP*, IV, 452-4, 474-5.

104 On 12 July 1434, a few days after his departure, the treasurer of Calais was granted certain duties imposed on ships entering Calais harbour in order to help meet the town's expenses (*DKR*, XLVIII [1887], 300).

105 PRO, E403/691-719 passim. As far as can be judged, the assignments were eventually honoured. The changes in levels of payment are masked by the figures in Doucet, *Le moyen âge*, 2nd ser., XXVII (1926), 269.

106 *PPC*, IV, 12-15.

107 *RP*, IV, 371; above, pp. 192-3.

108 J. Ferguson, *English diplomacy, 1422-1461* (Oxford, 1972), p. 18. For Beaufort's good relations with Burgundy in 1432-33, see Armstrong, *Annales de Bourgogne*, XXXVII (1965), 107-9.

109 PRO, E404/48/155; E403/707 m. 11; *DKR*, XLVIII (1887), 289. See A. Judd, *The life of Thomas Bekynton* (Chichester, 1961), pp. 10-15, 57.

110 *DKR*, XLVIII (1887), 294; Schofield, *AHC*, V, no. 1 (1975), 39-40.

111 *PPC*, IV, 255-61, 278-80.
112 ibid., 302; PRO, E28/55/19; *RP*, IV, 461-3; *DKR*, XLVIII (1887), 306 (for the envoys' authority). In general, see J. G. Dickinson, *The Congress of Arras, 1435* (Oxford, 1955), ch. I, II, and more briefly, idem, 'The congress of Arras, 1435', *History*, n. s., XL (1955), 31-41.
113 Dickinson, *Arras*, p. 50.
114 ibid., ch. III; *Foedera*, IV, i, 21 (16 July 1435). The bishop of Thérouanne and the count of St Pol were not Burgundy's friends.
115 Armstrong, *Annales de Bourgogne*, XXXVII (1965), 81ff.
116 Dickinson, *Arras*, pp. 41, 126-8, 143-4.
117 ibid., pp. 155-7.
118 *Brut*, pp. 467, 503, 571-2; *RP*, IV, 481.
119 Dickinson, *Arras*, pp. 177-9, 426.
120 PRO, E403/719 m. 6-7, 12, 14; /721 m. 6; E404/51/306-20, 332; *CPR, 1429-36*, pp. 474, 476. One of Talbot's companions, Sir Bertrand Entwhistle, owned the barony of Bricquebec in Normandy from 1429 (Allmand, *EconHR*, XXI [1968], 467). Another, Robert, Lord Willoughby, made his will on 25 July, just before leaving (LincsRO, 2 Ancaster 3/A/21; PRO, E404/51/332).
121 *RP*, IV, 490-2.
122 PRO, E403/719 m. 14. But in June 1435, the mayor of Calais appealed to the mayor and aldermen of London to exert influence on the council for aid to Calais (*Letter book K*, p. 190).
123 PRO, E403/721 m. 6, 8, 12, 16; *CPR, 1429-36*, pp. 525, 526, 607; Monstrelet, *Chroniques*, III, 151-3; *Brut*, p. 504; Stevenson, I, 424-9; *London Chrons.*, pp. 139-40. For Cressoner's indenture, see PRO, E101/71/892; and Bodl, Rawlinson poet. 32, for the quotation.
124 *CPR, 1429-36*, pp. 533-5; *Brut*, p. 468; *Great Chron.*, pp. 172-3; Giles, pp. 15-16; PRO, E403/721 m. 14; /724 m. 14, 16; E404/52/196.
125 ibid., 52/370; E28/56/14, 50; E403/721 m. 14, 17, 18; /724 m. 16, 13-14, 11, 10, 5, 1; *CPR, 1429-36*, pp. 533-5, 536, 607, 608; *CCR, 1429-35*, p. 57. See *Brut*, p. 469; *Great Chron.*, pp. 172-3; 'Benet's Chron.', p. 185; *London Chrons.*, p. 140.
126 PRO, E28/57/66, 85. For ships, men, and stores provided by New Romney and Sandwich, see KentRO, FAc 2 f. 123*v*, 125*v*; Sa/AC 1 f. 30.
127 *CPR, 1429-36*, p. 590.
128 *London Chrons.*, p. 141; above, p. 196. The captain of Rouen was Lord Talbot.
129 *RP*, IV, 483-4; *DKR*, XLVIII (1887), 309, 311. See S. L. Thrupp, *Merchant class*, p. 374 (for Whittingham), and Wylie and Waugh, op. cit., I, 449 n. 4 (for Buckland).
130 PRO, E28/56/41; *DKR*, XLVIII (1887), 313. For the phrase 'a preciouse jewell to this reame', see *PPC*, IV, 352.
131 Vaughan, op. cit., p. 75; for similar discussions at Ghent on 8 March, see *HMC, Var. Coll.*, IV, 197-8 (misdated to 13 January). The fullest reconstruction of the siege is in M.-R. Thielemans, *Bourgogne et Angleterre* (Brussels, 1966), part 1; but see also Vaughan, op. cit., pp. 78-84. The most reliable contemporary chronicles of the siege are *Brut*, pp. 468-70, 504-5, 571-84 (from the English side), and Monstrelet, *Chroniques*, III, 160ff (from the Burgundian).
132 Above, pp. 118, 171.

133 *HMC, Var. Coll.*, IV, 198-200 (26 March), reports the Burgundian strength. See Monstrelet, *Chroniques*, III, 177ff, for its advance up the river Lys, reaching Armentières by 11 June. Some English chroniclers naturally exaggerated the size of the army ('Benet's Chron.', p. 185; *EHL*, pp. 321-2 [100,000]; *English Chron.*, p. 55 [150,000]).

134 This chronology is best established in *Brut*, pp. 577-8. For the opening of the siege, see also ibid., p. 504; *Chron. of London*, p. 121.

135 Monstrelet, *Chroniques*, III, 160-2; Vaughan, op. cit., pp. 75-7. For war fever in Bruges, see *Brut*, p. 572.

136 ibid., pp. 579-80; Monstrelet, *Chroniques*, III, 177ff. There was also jealousy between the Flemings and Picards.

137 *Brut*, p. 580.

138 On 30 June, Henry VI summoned his 'feed men' to join him at Canterbury, but later that day (after hearing the news from Oye) he ordered them to join Gloucester's retinue at Sandwich by 22 July (PRO, SC1/58/47).

139 *Brut*, pp. 574-5; Stevenson, II, i, xlix-lv; PRO, E403/724 (29 August). The soldiers' wages amounted to £6,084 and the transport to £1,196; a few of the indentures are in ibid., E101/71/893-98. For the provision of supplies to the besieged by the victualler of Calais, see ibid., E28/58/47.

140 *Brut*, p. 581; *Chron. of London*, pp. 121-2; Monstrelet, *Chroniques*, III, 186ff. The Burgundian guns were left embedded in the sand (*English Chron.*, p. 55) and foodstuffs were abandoned to the English (*London Chrons.*, p. 142). For the victualler of Calais's account of this booty, see PRO, E101/192/10 m. 6-8.

141 Vaughan, op. cit., pp. 81-2. The letter is published in M.-R. Thielemans, 'Une lettre missive inédite de Philippe le Bon concernant le siège de Calais', *Bull. de la commission royale d'histoire*, CXV (1950), 285-96, though the recipient is wrongly given as the count of Richemont.

142 *Brut*, p. 581; 'Benet's Chron.', p. 158; *Chron. of London*, p. 122. This chronology is preferred to that of *London Chrons.*, p. 142, and *Great Chron.*, pp. 172-3, which places Gloucester's arrival on 27 July. The final muster date at Sandwich had been 26 July (*Letter book K*, p. 206).

143 *Chron. of London*, p. 122; *English Chron.*, p. 55; *EHL*, pp. 321-2; 'Benet's Chron.', p. 185; Waurin, IV, 202-3; Monstrelet, *Chroniques*, IV, 43. *Great Chron.*, pp. 172-3; *London Chrons.*, p. 142, and *Three Chrons.*, p. 62, misdate the sequence of events. Poperinge and Bailleul were badly damaged, and for the English fleet's ravages, see E. Vlietinck, 'Le siège de Calais et les villes de la côte flamande', *Annales de la soc. d'emulation de Bruges*, V. sér., III (1890), 91-101, using the archives of Nieuport and Ostend.

144 Giles, pp. 15-16; *EHL*, pp. 321-2.

145 For the popular scorn of the duke and the Flemings, see below, pp. 223-4.

146 *RP*, IV, 502-3, 508-9.

147 *PPC*, V, 6-7, 8; Newhall, *Muster and review*, pp. 137-8.

148 PRO, E403/727 m. 7, 6, 8; *CPR, 1436-41*, pp. 85, 88; above, p. 455.

149 'Gregory's Chron.', p. 164; *Brut*, pp. 454, 450.

150 *PPC*, IV, 53; *CPR, 1429-36*, p. 69.

151 PRO, E403/696 m. 18, 19; /699 m. 6; *CPR, 1429-36*, p. 152. Most of his men were archers, and 700 horses went with them.

152 *PPC*, IV, 156-7.

153 ibid., 154-5, 198-200; *CPR, 1429–36*, p. 338. In the opinion of an exchequer clerk, Radcliffe had previously been defrauded of £300 (WA MS 12234, for which see above, p. 115).

154 PRO, E403/724 m. 6 (17 July); E28/56/41, 58.

155 *Foedera*, IV, i, 42.

156 *PPC*, IV, 52; *CPR, 1429–36*, p. 74; PRO, E403/695 m. 13.

157 PRO E28/52 (26 June 1430).

158 ibid., 54-61.

159 *CCR, 1429–35*, p. 241.

160 *CPR, 1429–36*, pp. 201-2 (1 June 1432), 219-22, 278, 279-80, 300, 348 (28 October 1433).

161 *Brut*, p. 465; *PPC*, IV, 128, 150-1, 181.

162 ibid., 146-50.

163 *DKR*, XLVIII (1887), 292-3; *RP*, IV, 448, 475.

164 *PPC*, IV, 178-9.

165 *CPR, 1429–36*, pp. 472, 473-4.

166 *RP*, IV, 492-3. This was still felt to be so a year later (ibid., 500-1).

167 *CPR, 1429–36*, pp. 509, 511. For the government's repair of one remaining royal ship and the purchase of another in the winter of 1435–36, see Richmond, *History*, XLIX (1964), 290-1.

168 KentRO, Sa/AC 1 f. 30; *EHL*, p. 352; *CPR, 1436–41*, p. 86.

169 *RP*, IV, 495; Warner, op. cit., passim.

170 *PPC*, V, 19; *CPR, 1436–41*, p. 64; *CCR, 1435–41*, pp. 127-8.

10 Propaganda and the Dual Monarchy

The novelty of the dual monarchy, and the extraordinary emotional and material demands it imposed on Englishmen and northern Frenchmen, prompted Henry VI's advisers to muster every available resource to acclaim the monarchy's inauguration after Charles VI's death in October 1422. They brought the conscious use of the arts of persuasion in a propagandist fashion to a sophisticated pitch, skilfully deploying administrators, designers, illuminators, and writers. Bedford and his companions in France set about convincing northern French opinion – sometimes international opinion – of the legitimacy of Henry VI's claim to the throne of France and the unworthiness of his opponent, whom they termed the dauphin. At the same time, Englishmen needed to be convinced of the justice of their king's French enterprises, reassured that military success would not compromise the independence of their own realm, reminded of the despicable actions of the Valois, and, most immediately, induced to respond sympathetically to requests for money, men, and supplies.

Henry V was quite familiar with the methods of propaganda available to a fifteenth-century king, but after 1422 the offensive was taken up by his brothers Bedford and Gloucester with greater vigour and imagination.[1] Like their brother, these two dukes valued the written word and the striking illumination; they patronized poets and other writers and scholars, were well acquainted with French and Burgundian fashions in the arts, and Gloucester at least sympathized with the ideals of humanism and appreciated their political and social context. Alongside Henry V, they had been more imaginatively educated than the average English magnate and their mother's family, the Bohuns, were noted patrons of culture. Meanwhile, the princely courts of western Europe, from Italy northwards to Berry, Burgundy, and England, were learning the value of officially sponsored propaganda in word and picture.[2] After 1422, Bedford and Gloucester placed their literary and artistic awareness at the disposal of Lancastrian policies. Few of the propaganda methods employed by the house of Lancaster were new, though some reached a higher pitch of development in these decades. The themes they explored – the justice of the king's cause, the soundness of English policy, scorn for the enemy – seem to have roused the population of England and northern France with considerable success and to have produced literary and artistic pieces of lasting quality.

Official appeals to public opinion became more effective in the early fifteenth century as literacy spread more widely through English society. Royal proclamations and open letters to the subject were posted up in Coventry's market-place (for example) and publicized in the so-called 'bull-ring' outside Shrewsbury. Across the channel, the churches of Paris and Normandy were the public posting-places of Lancastrian France, and churches and town gates were used for similar purposes in England – as St Paul's preaching cross certainly was in London.[3] In 1430 copies of statutes passed in the recent parliament were sent to every shire in the land for publication.[4] The lollards were perhaps the supreme propagandists of all – not because their propaganda was ultimately successful, but because they argued a truly revolutionary cause with a repertoire that was rich and up-to-date through its exploitation of the growth of literacy and a vigorous vernacular language. They demonstrated how effectively views could be disseminated through the English countryside, and they accustomed townsmen especially to the reception of the bible, libels, and bills as propaganda. The stream of lollard writings continued unabated during the early years of Henry VI's reign, and it was particularly strong in 1431. In that year, seditious, heretical, and treasonable literature was distributed in London, Salisbury, Frome, and towns further north; libels were passed from hand to hand, and bills affixed to doors, windows, and gateways.[5] Such methods were equally available to the government and their political impact was duly appreciated by the authorities.

Bedford employed all the means at his command to bind Frenchmen's loyalty to their new Lancastrian king, not least by removing the inevitable doubts about the justice of his cause. By refusing the royal style to Charles, 'who calls himself the dauphin', in public ordinances, Bedford was in effect denying the kingly pretensions of the Valois.[6] By his patronage of artists in the workshops of Paris, Rouen, and elsewhere, as well as by means of the cruder, though more popularly effective, media of public picture and distributed verse, the duke stressed directly Henry VI's legitimate descent from both French and English kings and the Burgundian alliance on which he depended. The Book of Hours which he commissioned in 1423 for presentation to his bride, Anne of Burgundy, was peppered with pictorial reminders of the Burgundian tie; its skilful use of political symbolism would be understood by all who saw or used it – including the young Henry VI himself, to whom it was given by the duchess of Bedford when the king was in Rouen in 1430–31.[7] This beautiful book was, of course, a formal and essentially private example of pictorial propaganda, but the legendary genealogies, historical descents, and pictorial demonstrations of Anglo-Burgundian amity which figure in such illuminated volumes were simply accomplished reflections of a propaganda tradition with more common expression on church walls and gates, and in public spectacles.

Lawrence Calot, a notary who served Bedford's council in France, was engaged by the duke in 1423 to produce a large picture and an accompanying poem to be hung in Notre Dame cathedral. They stressed Henry VI's descent in the line of St Louis in a manner compelling to the worshippers of Paris. When a canon of Rheims defaced the genealogy and poem in 1425, his punishment was such – having to make two copies of each – that their dynastic message could be relayed elsewhere in Lancastrian France. After the earl of Warwick had seen this propaganda design in July 1426, he commissioned John Lydgate to produce a translation of the poem ('On the English title to the crown of France'), together with a pictorial genealogy, presumably so that he could take them back to England with him.

> Verily, liche as ye may se,
> The pee-degre doth hit specifie,
> The figure, lo, of the genelagye,
> How that God lost for her purchase
> Thurgh his power and benigne grace,
> An heir of peas by iust successioun,
> This ffigure makith clere demonstracioun,
> Ageins which noman may maligne,
> But that he stondith in the veray ligne,
> As ye may se, as descendid is
> Of the stok and blode of Seint Lowys;
> Of which we aught of equite and right
> In oure hertis to be glad and light,
> That we may se with euery circumstaince
> Direct the lyne of Englond and of Fraunce.[8]

Later still, another English commander in France, the earl of Shrewsbury, had a copy of the genealogy inserted in the presentation volume which he gave to Margaret of Anjou on the occasion of her wedding to Henry VI in 1445.[9]

The unity of the dual monarchy also inspired a new Anglo-French coinage in 1422. Following the example of coins minted in 1387 to mark the union of Burgundy and Flanders, it was produced under the direction of the duke of Bedford, Philip of Burgundy's brother-in-law, and the new coins displayed the shields of England and France juxtaposed beneath King Henry's name, and the leopard and the lily emblazoned side by side.[10] Their message could be expected to reach wide and influential audiences.

Bedford's skill in moulding public opinion was severely tested in 1429, and later, by Joan of Arc's assault on the English position. His propaganda offensive capitalized on the suspicion in some quarters that Joan was a heretic or a witch – or both – and this he encouraged by a well-tried mode of communication, the newsletter. English war leaders of the past had used such letters to educate domestic opinion in the glory of military victories; Bedford adopted them to besmirch the Maid's reputation. On 7 August 1429, some months after her first meeting with the dauphin, he reprimanded Charles for renewing the war and accepting the aid of a disreputable, dissolute, and superstitious girl whose habit of wearing men's clothes was damnable. In May 1431 she was burned by the English at Rouen, and this extreme action by the Lancastrian authorities required swift explanation to avoid condemnation and a possibly serious reaction within France. It was probably Bedford who addressed open letters in Henry VI's name to kings, dukes, and other princes on 8 June 1431, presumably to justify the Maid's burning and to itemize the reasons for her punishment; three weeks later, similar letters were sent to prelates, nobles, and cities within France, and to the duke of Burgundy, with the same purpose in view. English propaganda was being purposefully employed to obscure the achievements and influence of Joan, and to reinforce the doubts of any who were sceptical as to the source of her inspiration.[11]

In fact, the entire sequence of public events between 1429 and 1432 in both Paris and London was, in part at least, a gigantic propaganda exercise. When the duke of Burgundy arrived in Paris in July 1429, Bedford staged a pageant of the assassination of his guest's father at Montereau in 1419; it was a timely reminder to Duke Philip that his best interests lay with Lancaster, not with the treacherous Valois. The coronation of the eight-year-old Henry in Westminster abbey in November 1429 took place at that precise moment because the dauphin had been crowned king as Charles VII at Rheims cathedral the previous July. This ceremonial triumph, made possible by Joan's determination and energy, could only be countered by Henry's crowning at Rheims or, failing that, in Paris, but this could hardly be arranged before the coronation in England. The profound political importance of these solemnities was apparent to the devisers of the pageants that welcomed the young king to London and Paris, and it even influenced the organizers of the accompanying festivities and the chefs who prepared the menus at the two coronation banquets. Those who participated in, or watched, the ceremonies and celebrations were left in no doubt as to their symbolic significance – as, of course, was the intention.

Memories of Henry V and his stirring exploits in France were rekindled in verse and pageant in 1429 so that his son could bask in their reflection as well as benefit from the Valois blood of his mother, Queen Katherine. The life of Henry V was graphically revivified, with exhortations and expectations that his son would shortly prove as virtuous and famous as the father. The imposing figure of the Emperor Sigismund, who had visited England in 1416 and had been captivated by Henry V, was also prominent in 1429, thereby assuring the popular mind that the dual monarchy had imperial approval – even if the practical value of this sanction was negligible.[12] In preparation for the king's return to England in February 1432, John Lydgate, 'who was never one to abandon a tested expedient for eliciting patronage', was commissioned by London (or possibly by the council) to gild Henry's triumphal entry to the city. Poems and ballads lauding Henry's dual descent from monarchs of England and France, and glorifying the achievements of his father, were composed for the occasion by Lydgate and others; the same themes were publicized by trees hung with genealogies reminiscent of the biblical tree of Jesse.[13]

Lancastrian achievements in France during the young king's presence there were likened to David's victory over Goliath, and his London reception to the subsequent rejoicing in Jerusalem.

> The stormy reyne off alle theyre hevynesse
> Were passed away and alle her olde grevaunce,
> For the vi^te Herry, roote off here gladnesse,
> Theyre hertis ioye, theyre worldis suffisaunce,
> By trewe dissent crovnyd kyng off Fraunce,
> The hevene reioysyng the day off his repayre
> Made his komyng the wedir to be so ffayre . . . .
>
> The Kyng roode fforth, with sobre contenauce,
> Towarde a castell bilt off iaspar grene,
> Vpon whos toures the sonne shone shene,
> Ther clerly shewed, by notable remembraunce,
> This kyngis tytle off England and off Fraunce.
>
> Twoo green treen ther grewe vp-ariht,
> Fro Seint Edward and ffro Seint Lowys,
> The roote y-take palpable to the siht,
> Conveyed by lynes be kyngis off grete prys;
> Some bare leopardes, and some bare fflouredelys,
> In nouther armes ffounde was there no lak,
> Which the sixte Herry may now bere on his bak.[14]

A few months earlier, when Henry had formally entered his French capital, Paris, in December 1431, the king had been met by representatives of the citizens, whose approbation of his kingship was publicly represented by a gift of three hearts; a boy balancing two crowns on his head symbolized the dual monarchy of Henry VI of England (and Henry II of France).[15] Tableaux portrayed the duke of Burgundy and his son, the count of Nevers, offering the arms of France to the young king, even though (a blight on the occasion) Duke Philip did not meet his acknowledged sovereign at any time during the latter's French visit.[16] Henry himself may have entered into the propagandist spirit of these festivities, for he addressed the parlement of Paris on 21 December 1431 in English; it is unlikely that a son of Katherine of Valois did so through ignorance of French.[17]

The university of Paris had already been enlisted by Bedford to supplement his efforts at mass persuasion: by issuing proclamations in the Anglo-Burgundian interest, singing masses, and organizing processions to celebrate Anglo-Burgundian victories. In similar vein, the university welcomed Henry to Paris in 1431 and undertook 'through the whole kingdom [to] organise prayers, speeches, processings and sermons exhorting the people to join in our good wishes' to the king. Its Sunday sermons fostered a vehement abomination of Charles VII among Parisians until their city was captured by Charles in 1436, when the university's organizing genius was turned about to serve his interest.[18] Bedford's foundation of a new university at Caen in 1431 provided an alternative propaganda centre for Normandy at least.

The act of consecration during the coronation of 1429 had its own propagandist tale to tell. The sacred oil of St Thomas Becket was used in the ceremony. In England it would demonstrate the divine unction which the king received in the tradition of Plantagenet and Lancastrian monarchs. To Frenchmen, the use of this hallowed oil rivalled the veneration accorded the holy oil of Clovis which French kings had long been wont to use at their coronation.[19]

The glory and justice of Lancastrianism were likely to be ingrained in the mind of most of those who witnessed these ceremonies. Such sentiments were touched in men's minds by familiar symbols, by an appeal to history, tradition, and the bible – even to myth and legend. The popular success of these stage-managed functions is testified by the lengthy accounts of them recorded by contemporary chroniclers and copied in private commonplace books.[20]

The abortive negotiations with Charles VII at Arras in 1435, followed by Burgundy's withdrawal from the English alliance, meant that the royal need for soldiers, mariners, ships, weapons, and money would continue at a high level – and without Burgundian support. In these bleak circumstances, Englishmen's resolve to continue the war might have to be fortified; this could partly be done by publicly emphasizing the justice of the English cause and denigrating the character of the enemy.[21] Accordingly, a robust propaganda offensive was launched by the government in 1436: it stressed the perfidy of Burgundy for his defection, scorned the duke's Flemish subjects who were already disliked in England for commercial reasons, and hinted at the threat to the channel, its shipping, and the safety of England's coastline. This combination was carefully calculated to rouse Englishmen to a swift defence of Calais and a vigorous prosecution of the war in northern France. Gloucester is likely to have played a central role in thus marshalling opinion, now that his elder brother was dead.

Some of Burgundy's advisers were right to fear that the English government would exploit for propaganda purposes the duke's breaking of his oath of allegiance to Henry VI. In England, he was denounced as the 'foundour of new falsehede', and abroad letters in Henry's name publicized Philip's infamy, particularly among his Flemish subjects.[22]

When Gloucester planned his expedition to raise the Burgundian siege of Calais in 1436, sermons were preached from English pulpits extolling the enterprise and deprecating Philip's deceit.[23] Already commissioners had been despatched to the shires, cities, and towns of England with an armoury of persuasive proclamations to induce the well-to-do to disgorge yet another loan, this time for the defence of hard-pressed Calais, 'a preciouse jouell to this reame' (as the commission inspiringly put it). The argument that Calais was vital to England's defence was a familiar one; equally telling was the rumour that failure to protect it or to produce a substantial loan would lead to the invasion of England and 'divers places and shires of this lande joynant to the sea coostes wer putte fronters to the enemys', a vision certain to conjure alarm in the mind of those to whom a frontier meant instability.[24]

English opinion was influenced by a series of carefully composed proclamations that were issued at intervals between March and July 1436. That of 20 March denounced the Flemings for allowing themselves to be seduced from their sworn allegiance to Henry as king of France by the 'perverse and treasonable counsels' of that arch-dissembler 'who calls himself duke of Burgundy and count of Flanders'.[25] Another proclamation on 18 June urged the people of London and the southern coastal shires to provide the earl of Huntingdon, as admiral of England, with free shipping. The explicit justification for this appeal was Burgundy's dastardly change of heart at Arras and the threat it posed to both France and England, whose subjects were now offered the customary justification of defence of the realm for their efforts in the king's service.[26] When Calais was actually threatened by the Burgundian forces a few weeks later, official anger at the craft, malice, and treachery of 'he who calls himself duke of Burgundy, the king's enemy and rebel', was bitterly recorded in a further proclamation to enlist troops for the defence of the fortress-town.[27]

Ballads were sung in the streets and taverns of London especially, sneering at the bravery of the Flemings and, once the siege had been brought to an end by Philip's withdrawal, mocking them and him for their irresolution. At least four different ballads descanted on these themes and attained wide popularity.[28]

> Remembres how ye laide seege with gret pryde and bost
> To Caleis, that littil toun, the noumbre of your host
> Was a hundrid thousand and fifty, to reken by the pollis,
> As it was that same tyme founden by youre rollis.
> And yette for al youre gret host, erly nothir late,
> Caleis was so ferd of you they shitte neuer a gate.
>
> ('Mockery of the Flemings')[29]

> O thou Phelippe, fonder of new falshede,
> Distourber of pees, Capiteine of cowardise

Sower of discorde, Repref of al knyghthode,
Whiche of al burgoigne (that is so grete of pryse)
Thou clepist thiself duc – whan wiltow rise,
And in pleyn felde doo mustre with thy launce?
Se how all knyghthode thy werre dothe despise,
Wite thyn ovne falsnes al thys myschance! . . .

Remembre the, Phelippe, what tyme and how
To kyng henry the fyft by thyn ovne assent,
Withoute his desire, thou madest a solempne vow,
Vsyng goddes body the holy sacrement,
To become trew ligeman with gode entent
To hym and to his heires without variance.
Thou art false to god, by thyn owne assent,
Whiche thou may wite al thy mischange.

('Scorn of the duke of Burgundy')[30]

Some of the ballads bear the hallmark of official sponsorship and John Lydgate once again produced what amounted to syndicated editorials that circulated by bill and word of mouth to literate and illiterate alike in easily remembered verse.[31] Other ballads praised Gloucester for his bravery and his harrying of the Flemish coast; they exaggerated the importance of his intervention, but London merchants (who were among Lydgate's patrons) would find them congenial and inspiriting.[32] The same result was anticipated from the newsletters which were sent from the Calais siege to London, presumably to generate enthusiasm and admiration for the besiegers' efforts.[33] Some of the ballads were even copied into London and other chronicles, and soon afterwards were included in collections and common-place books whose owners found their sentiments heartwarming and still relevant.[34]

Gloucester's interest in this fusillade was many-sided: he yearned to mobilize English sentiment against the Burgundians; he determined to defend Calais, of which he was lieutenant; and he sought to secure his personal position and his preferred policy in the public eye by a successful enterprise that had popular backing. With these aims in mind, he drew upon his international literary connections, and his consciousness of the power of the written word, to complement his belligerent pronouncements and eager campaigning in 1436. He encouraged Titus Livius Frulovisi, the Italian humanist who had recently become his 'poet and orator', to produce a poem ('Humfroidos') celebratory of the duke's deeds: in indifferent Latin verse, it described the passage of events from the congress of Arras to the parade through Flanders. The enthusiasm with which Englishmen responded to this orchestrated campaign culminated in the plaudits of parliament to which the duke returned in January 1437.[35]

The well-known *Libelle of Englysche Polycye* had the same propagandist motive, though its initial audience was quite restricted. Its message was ostensibly intended for the eyes and ears of certain of the councillors, but it was quickly couched in crude and catchy verse that probably reflects the author's hope that it would become familiar to a wider public; moreover, like contemporary ballads of similar theme, the *Libelle* retained its relevance for the times and was frequently copied later on.[36]

> The trewe processe of Englysh polycye
> Of utterwarde to kepe thys regne in rest
> Of oure England, that no man may denye
> Ner say of soth but it is one the best,
> Is thys, as who seith, south, north, est and west
> Cheryshe marchandyse, kepe thamyralte,
> That we bee maysteres of the narowe see. . . .
>
> Therfore I caste me by a lytell wrytinge
> To shewe att eye thys conclusione,
> For concyens and for myne acquytynge
> Ayenst God, and ageyne abusyon
> And cowardyse and to oure enmyes confusione;
> For iiij. thynges oure noble sheueth to me,
> Kyng, shype and swerde and pouer of the see.[37]

Produced soon after the siege of Calais, the *Libelle*, as it survives today, is a political pamphlet with a detailed argument to supplement the broader and simpler appeals of ballad, verse, and proclamation. It advocated certain policies that were both economically profitable and emotionally patriotic – the safety of Calais and the seas, the defence of England, the health of her commerce – and combined them with fiercely anti-alien jibes at the Flemings and Italians. 'Accurate, pithy and vulgar journalism', is G. A. Holmes's verdict on it.[38] For a small but cultured circle, Gloucester further patronized Titus Livius in his writing of a *Life* of Henry V in 1437–38, when the French war was still a burning issue and the glories of the late king could reinforce the enthusiasm of Gloucester and others for continued belligerence. This *Life*, with the hero-king as its centrepiece, was an aristocratic counterpart of the proclamations and ballads that reached wider audiences, and the *Libelle* that was aimed originally at the king's advisers.[39]

Notes

1 C. T. Allmand (ed.), *Society at war* (Edinburgh, 1973), pp. 10, 143-52.
2 McFarlane, *Lancastrian kings*, pp. 115-17; R. Weiss, *Humanism in England during the fifteenth century* (Oxford, 1967), ch. 4; E. C. Williams, *My lord*

of Bedford, 1389–1435 (1963), pp. 3-4, 249-52; E. G. Millar, *La Miniature anglaise aux XIVᵉ et XVᵉ siècles* (Paris, 1928), pp. 30-43; C. C. Willard, 'The manuscripts of Jean Petit's justification: some Burgundian propaganda methods of the early fifteenth century', *Studi Francesi*, XII (1969), 271-80.

3 H. Owen and J. B. Blakeway, *A history of Shrewsbury* (2 vols., 1825), I, 271; G. R. Owst, *Preaching in mediaeval England* (Cambridge, 1926), p. 225.

4 PRO, E403/695 m. 19 (19 July 1430).

5 Thomson, op. cit., passim; Aston, *Past and Present*, XVII (1960), 1-44; PRO, KB9/225/2,3,4,21; 227/2/13, 36; above, p. 139. Compare M. Aston, 'Lollardy and literacy', *History*, LXII (1977), 347-71.

6 B. J. H. Rowe, 'King Henry VI's claim to France in picture and poem', *The Library*, 4th ser., XIII (1932–33), 77. In reply, the French took to referring to Henry VI as *Henry de Lancastre qui se dit Roy d'Engleterre* (Folger Lib. MS 899.1 [3 May 1434]).

7 B. J. H. Rowe, 'Notes on the Clovis miniature and the Bedford portrait in the Bedford Book of Hours', *JBAA*, 3rd ser., XXV (1962), 56-65. See C. A. J. Armstrong 'The golden age of Burgundy', in A. G. Dickens (ed.), *The courts of Europe* (1977), pp. 55ff.

8 Rowe, *Library*, 4th ser., XVIII (1932–33), 77-88; MacCracken, *Minor poems of Lydgate*, pp. 613-22. The number of surviving manuscripts indicates that Lydgate's translation became very popular in England.

9 BL, Royal MS 15 E VI f. 3. This genealogy has been published several times, most recently in C. D. Ross, *The Wars of the Roses* (1976), p. 27.

10 J. W. McKenna, 'Henry VI of England and the dual monarchy: aspects of royal political propaganda, 1422–1432', *JWCI*, XXVIII (1965), 146-51 (with illustrations of the coins facing 145). About 3,000 Anglo-French coins from Henry VI's mints were discovered in Normandy in 1955: R. Monard, 'Le trésor monétaire du prieuré du Plessis-Grimault: monnaies d'Henri VI roi de France et d'Angleterre', *Bull. de la soc. française de numismatique*, IX (1968), 328-30. For contemporary awareness of the political symbolism in coin design, see below, p. 225.

11 W. T. Waugh, 'Joan of Arc in English sources of the fifteenth century', in J. G. Edwards, V. H. Galbraith, and E. F. Jacob (eds.), *Historical essays in honour of James Tait* (Manchester, 1933), pp. 388-91. See above, p. 191.

12 MacCracken, *Minor poems of Lydgate*, pp. 630-48; *London Chrons.*, pp. 97-116; *Great Chron.*, pp. 156-70; R. Withington, *English pageantry: an historical outline* (2 vols., Cambridge, Mass., 1918), I, 141-7; G. Wickham, *Early English stages, 1300–1600* (2 vols., 1959), I, 72-3; and in general, McKenna, *JWCI*, XXVIII (1965), 156-61 (with the quoted phrase on 154).

13 MacCracken, *Minor poems of Lydgate*, pp. 622-30. Sigismund also figured a little later in the *Libelle of Englysche Polycye* (Warner, op. cit., ll. 8-21, 832).

14 McCracken, *Minor poems of Lydgate*, p. 631.

15 ibid., pp. 630, 643-4.

16 Withington, *English pageantry*, I, 138-41, and passim for pageants in general.

17 H. G. Richardson, 'Illustrations of English history in the mediaeval

registers of the parlement of Paris', *TRHS*, 4th ser., X (1927), 58; ct. Armstrong, *Annales de Bourgogne*, XXXVII (1965), 106.

18 J. Verger, 'The University of Paris at the end of the Hundred Years' War', in J. W. Baldwin and R. A. Goldthwaite (eds.), *Universities in Politics* (Baltimore, 1972), pp. 53ff.

19 J. W. McKenna, 'The coronation oil of the Yorkist kings', *EHR*, LXXXII (1967), 102-4; with a more sceptical view by T. A. Sandquist, 'The holy oil of St Thomas of Canterbury', in T. A. Sandquist and M. R. Powicke (eds.), *Essays in mediaeval history presented to Bertie Wilkinson* (Toronto, 1969), pp. 330-44.

20 *Brut*, pp. 458-61, 502, 569; 'Gregory's Chron.' pp. 173-5; *Great Chron.*, pp. 156-70; *London Chrons.*, pp. 97-116, 235-50; A. G. Rigg (ed.), *A Glastonbury miscellany of the fifteenth century* (Oxford, 1968), pp. 48-50; Bodl, Digby MS 102; *Letter book K*, pp. 135-7; English College, Rome, MS 1306 (for which see below n. 29).

21 A. Bossuat, 'La littérature de propagande au XVᵉ siècle: le mémoire de Jean de Rinel, secrétaire du roi d'Angleterre, contre le duc de Bourgogne (1435)', *Cahiers d'histoire*, I (1956), 129-46.

22 Dickinson, *Arras*, pp. 70, 74 n. 2; T. Wright (ed.), *Political songs and poems* (RS, 1861), II, 148; Monstrelet, *Chroniques*, VI, 249-55.

23 Dunstan, *Reg. Lacy*, II, 15-17, for Archbishop Chichele's mandate to his suffragans on 22 July 1436. When Bishop Spofford of Hereford commanded his clergy to observe it, he added the expedition of the duke of York, a local magnate, as also meriting encouragement: A. T. Bannister (ed.), *Registrum Thome Spofford episcopi Herefordensis* (Cant. and York Soc., 1919), pp. 215-16. See in general Owst, *Preaching*, passim.

24 *PPC*, IV, 352 b-e. The *Libelle of Englysche Polycye* represents the Emperor Sigismund describing Calais as a 'jewel moste of alle' (Warner, op. cit., l. 382).

25 *CCR, 1435–42*, p. 58, with the full text in *Foedera*, V, i, 27.

26 PRO, E28/57/83, with the proclamation printed in *Foedera*, V, i, 31. See above, pp. 199-200.

27 *CCR, 1435–42*, pp. 68-9, with the full text in *Foedera*, V, i, 32 (3 July). See above, pp. 202-5.

28 Three are printed in Robbins, *Historical poems*, pp. 78-89 ('The siege of Calais', 'Mockery of the Flemings', 'Scorn of the duke of Burgundy'); the first and part of the third also appear in Wright, op. cit., II, 148-9, 151-6; and the third is printed in full in R. H. Robbins, 'A Middle English diatribe against Philip of Burgundy', *Neophilologus*, XXXIX (1955), 131-46 (from English College, Rome, MS 1306). A fourth ballad is in H. N. MacCracken, 'A new poem by Lydgate', *Anglia*, XXXIII (1910), 283-6, and in *Brut*, pp. 600-1 ('Ballade in despyte of the Flemynges'). See also MacCracken, *Minor poems of Lydgate*, pp. 600-1; *Brut*, pp. 582-4; R. A. Klinefelter, 'The siege of Calais: a new text', *Proc. Modern Language Assoc. of America*, LXVII (1952), 888-95; idem, 'A newly discovered fifteenth-century English manuscript', *Modern Language Quarterly*, XIV (1953), 3-6.

29 Robbins, *Historical poems*, p. 84.

30 ibid., pp. 86, 87.

31 Schirmer, op. cit., pp. 104-8.

32 Holmes, *EHR*, LXXVI (1961), 212-14. For Gloucester and Lydgate, see A.

   S. G. Edwards. 'The influence of Lydgate's *Fall of Princes*, c. 1440–1559: a survey', *MedSt*, XXXIX (1977), 424-8.

33 'Gregory's Chron'., p. 179.

34 ibid., passim; *Brut*, pp. 582-4; Bodl, Digby MS 102; English College, Rome, MS 1306 (for which see n. 29). It is worth noting that some versions of the *Brut* chronicle end triumphantly with a detailed (probably eyewitness) account of the Calais siege (*EHL*, pp. 115, 124-5).

35 T. Hearne (ed.), *Vita Henrici Quinti*... (Oxford, 1716); Weiss, op. cit., pp. 42-3; idem, 'Humphrey, duke of Gloucester and Tito Livio Frulovisi', in *Fritz Saxl, 1890–1948* (1957), pp. 218-27; above, p. 205.

36 Warner, op. cit., ll. 1151–57 and passim; F. Taylor, 'Some manuscripts of the "Libelle of Englyshe Polycye"', *BJRL*, XXIV (1940), 376-418. Lydgate's authorship is now seriously doubted.

37 Warner, op. cit., ll. 1-7, 29-35.

38 Holmes, *EHR*, LXXVI (1961), 215.

39 Hearne, *Vita*; above, p. 224.

2
PERSONAL RULE
1436–1453

11   The King and his Queen

The ending of the king's minority

Those contemporaries who were able to observe Henry VI as a boy were agreed that he grew into a personable, intelligent, even precocious youth. His years as a minor, between the ages of one and fifteen, were naturally of considerable importance to his education as a monarch of two realms. His relatives had already created about him an atmosphere of political bitterness, even of personal hatred, and after Bedford's death both Gloucester and Beaufort strove to be the single most dominant influence on him as he grew older. They would be reluctant to allow him the exercise of his free will as an adult king. The ultimate effect of these intense personal pressures was to accustom Henry to dependence, to being told what to do. Even after Gloucester and Beaufort had receded into the background, he found other pillars on which to lean: the earl of Suffolk, Archbishop Kemp, the duke of Somerset, and, finally, when he was least able to fend for himself, the queen.

At the same time, Henry was developing a distinctive personality of his own. By 1432 he had a youthful awareness of his 'hiegh and royale auctoritee and estate', and two years later his council recognized his unusual powers of perception.[1] Clearly it would not be long before Henry would wish to dispense with the services of a guardian (and Warwick resigned in May 1436) and cast off the tutelage of his council. Moreover, the king assumed his royal prerogatives just when the future of the dual monarchy was threatening to divide English opinion as never before. As a result, Gloucester and Beaufort had not only to fight for the adoption of their respective cherished policies, but also to take account of the inclinations and discernible attitudes of the king.

After the collapse of his mission to Arras in 1435, Beaufort's position was seriously undermined, and the defection of the duke of Burgundy seemed to indicate that England's best policy lay in a determined defence of Calais and a vigorous prosecution of the war in Normandy. But the resourceful Beaufort bided his time. On 28 July 1436, as Gloucester prepared to embark to relieve Calais, Henry VI, who was then at Canterbury, for the first time (according to surviving records) formally exercised his will as king by authorizing a warrant with his own sign manual or signature. This warrant was a grant to Cardinal

Beaufort.[2] The king and several of his councillors (Beaufort among them) had travelled to Canterbury to organize the relief expedition and they had reached the cathedral city by 24 July; there they remained for a couple of days before Gloucester made his way to the coast. No sooner had he departed than Beaufort was able to induce the king to issue his warrant, whereby the cardinal secured the manor of Canford and the town of Poole (Dorset) free of charge and for life. Within a few more days, the royal party (including Beaufort) had returned to London.[3] The king whom Gloucester, for his own purposes, had been encouraging to emancipate himself from both guardian and council was taking the duke at his word, but it was Beaufort who reaped the benefit. With Gloucester absent in Picardy and Flanders, Beaufort swiftly contrived to establish his own influence with the king and pander to Henry's desire to play a more active role.

Gloucester returned to England about 24 August. He realized that once the minority was ended he would have to adapt to a situation in which he would no longer be chief councillor. Nor can he have been unaware that it was a hardening custom in England (if the examples of Henry III and Richard II may be so described) that kings came of age when they were fourteen, and that in Valois France this had been stated as a constitutional custom.[4] Rather than delay or discourage the arrival of Henry VI's majority, the duke, like Beaufort, sought to ensure that Henry would turn to him for counsel, and Gloucester seemed well placed to provide it. His elder brother, Bedford, had died in September 1435 and Humphrey was therefore heir to the throne. Moreover, his mission to Calais had been conspicuously successful and had done much to restore English morale and pride in the achievements of the dual monarchy. His exploits brought him the congratulations of parliament in the following March.[5]

From August 1436 onwards, Henry VI regularly played a recognizable part in government by personally authorizing warrants, using his signet seal and his sign manual; by February 1438 (and possibly earlier) a secretary had been appointed to take custody of the signet – Thomas Bekyngton, who had previously been in Gloucester's household and had kept in touch with the duke.[6] Gloucester was still a powerful figure at court and in the realm, as the king's acts of favour toward him indicate. On 23 November 1436 his 500-mark annuity from Henry V was replaced by a grant of the islands of Jersey and Guernsey, which Bedford had formerly held; this was an appropriate accession of authority for a lieutenant of Calais and lord of Flanders, as well as a better guarantee of his annuity's payment.[7] Furthermore, he and his wife were contemplating converting their Greenwich estate into a large and imposing residence, conveniently close to the capital, and on 6 March 1437 they were authorized in parliament to impark an additional 200 acres and to rebuild the old house with crenellated stone towers.[8] But the signs of political and constitutional change were there. For one thing, Henry expressed his new-found freedom and authority in the most predictable way: he proceeded to reward and patronize those with whom he had grown up and who had protected him in his household.

The winter of 1436–37 saw significant changes of personnel in the government of England and Wales. They were the result less of partisan pressure to further the interests of one faction or another (though that can be detected), than of a wish to strengthen the relationship between the household and the government at a time when Henry VI was beginning to impose his will as king. The consequence was an extension of the influence of the Beaufort faction in which Suffolk, who was steward of the household, was prominent. Household servants were entrusted with a large number of the shrievalties of England, the constableships of royal castles, and with stewardships and receiverships of lordships and estates in both England and Wales. More than half the new sheriffs in November 1436 were household men. The marshal of the hall and keeper of the king's lions, Robert Manfield, became sheriff of Bedfordshire–Buckinghamshire, as well as steward and receiver of the East Anglian estates of the duchy of Lancaster, on 7 February 1437.[9] James Fiennes, who had accompanied Henry to France in 1430 and became Suffolk's closest ally in south-eastern England, was the new sheriff of Kent; John St Lo, one of the king's esquires since at least 1428, secured Somerset.[10] Elsewhere, John Feriby, controller of the household, became sheriff of Surrey–Sussex on 8 November 1436 and steward of the duchy lordship of Knaresborough two months later; in Worcestershire, another king's esquire, John Burghope, was nominated sheriff, to hold the post concurrently with the constableship of Cardigan castle in west Wales.[11] To quote but two further examples, William Ludlowe, a household servant, was appointed sheriff of Shropshire and William Beauchamp, one of Henry's carvers, obtained Wiltshire.[12] Evidence from the duchy of Lancaster is just as striking. The new chief steward of the northern part of the duchy, appointed on 23 April 1437, was Suffolk himself, whereas his colleague in the south from 12 May was Sir William Philip, another long-serving member of the king's entourage and currently his chamberlain.[13] Philip's son-in-law, Lord Cromwell, who had no cause to admire Gloucester after his dismissal in 1432, became steward of Pickering for life on 4 January 1437, and Lord Beaumont was steward of Leicester, Castle Donnington, and Higham Ferrers from 5 January.[14] On the other hand, John Tyrell's son, William, was nominated steward of the duchy estates in the home counties on the same day, presumably because his father was treasurer of the household and one of Gloucester's affinity. The keeper of the king's jewels and wardrobe, John Merston, acquired the constableship of Pleshey castle (Essex) three days later.[15]

These appointments and promotions marked a major, conscious departure in policy from the practice of the past and may be attributed, at least in part, to the king's own role in government by the autumn of 1436. They seem also to reflect an eagerness by the household servants – especially Suffolk – to extend their interests into spheres which they had not previously entered and which had hitherto been subject to conciliar negotiation and a variety of factional influences. These influences had now narrowed to those of Gloucester (to a limited degree) and Beaufort and his kinsman Suffolk. When regarded in the light of the struggle for the king's mind that took place in 1436–37, such official patronage represents a crucial accession of authority for Beaufort, who had shown himself in the past to be far more adept at such manoeuvres than Gloucester.[16] Opportunity arose for the same influences to penetrate the church, for on 20 November 1436 the venerable bishop of Durham died. Within a week, the king had placed before the pope the name of the young bishop of Salisbury, Robert Neville, son of the earl of Westmorland and Joan Beaufort; birth and kin were stressed as his qualifications and there can be little doubt that his Beaufort connection was a powerful commendation. His successor at Salisbury was the king's principal chaplain (and soon to be his confessor), William Aiscough, a cleric whose later association with Suffolk and the Beauforts could not have been closer. Gloucester's opinion, if sought, evidently carried little weight in ecclesiastical circles.[17]

As yet, the king did not use his powers to make life-grants which would have alienated his resources for years ahead. The only exception to this rule benefited Beaufort in July and Gloucester in November 1436. Thus, Henry only gradually, and without formal announcement, began to explore the extent of his prerogatives.[18] However, right at the beginning of the new year (certainly by 8 January), a signet seal was in use to authenticate the king's personal will, but even then no one is certainly known to have been appointed as his secretary. Moreover, his gifts and appointments were still rarely made other than during pleasure, though on 21 March he began to exempt for life several favoured persons (usually from the household) from serving on juries and the like; at least this did not involve the alienation of lands, rents, offices, or cash.[19]

Beaufort's comment on his great-nephew on 13 April 1437 that 'God hath sette ye Kyng in such age yt he [Beaufort] may ye better abbsente him' was manifestly justified, though the cardinal's request for permission to undertake a pilgrimage abroad was probably in anticipation of the king's refusal.[20] Henry's awakening enthusiasm for exercising power was cautiously recognized by the council. When Warwick requested certain assurances prior to undertaking the command in France, on 20 May 1437 the council consulted the king; they did so again on 8 June, when the earl sought to make new arrangements for the lordship of Abergavenny during his absence. On both occasions, the councillors' tact was rewarded, for Henry deferred to their advice.[21] The king's assertiveness was taken an important step further on 17 July, when his signet warrants began regularly to be authorized for life, and once again it was the household servants who were most conspicuously favoured. On that day, the king was at St Albans at the start of a tour of the midlands and west that would symbolize the new era of personal freedom that was beginning for him.[22]

Two major issues arose at this juncture to attract the young king's attention and prompt him to take a greater personal interest in the formulation of policy. And that speeded up Henry's emergence from his minority and eventually determined irrevocably on whom – Beaufort or Gloucester – he would rely for advice. The first issue was the scandalous contest between Pope Eugenius IV and the Council of Basle which in 1436–37 reached the point at which the Council actually suspended the pope on 8 January 1438. To a young king who was admittedly gaining a reputation for piety (carefully nurtured by the coterie of chaplains that had cocooned him since birth) and growing increasingly conscious of his kingly dignity (and therefore of his coronation oath to uphold the faith and protect the church), this was a matter of burning interest. Henry declared himself outraged by this unholy dispute and threw his weight on Eugenius's side.[23] The latter's representative in England, the papal tax-collector Piero da Monte, who had been energetically denouncing the Council of Basle since 1435, was anxious to persuade his master that this happy outcome was the result of his own distinguished efforts in appealing to Henry's council and to the king in person. He was equally anxious to ingratiate himself with Henry VI and his advisers. In November 1437, therefore, in a letter to the archbishop of Florence whose contents may have been intended for publication in England, he testified to the intelligence, wisdom, and kindliness of the king, and to the royal dignity he radiated. His piety and sense of Christian morality had (in da Monte's description) an adolescent quality, the reflection of stern teaching rather than inner conviction or mature experience – as one might expect of a boy yet barely sixteen.

> . . . he avoided the sight and conversation of women, affirming these to be the work of the devil and quoting from the Gospel, 'He who casts his eyes on a woman so as to lust after her has already committed adultery with her in his heart'. Those who knew him intimately said that he had preserved his virginity of mind and body to this present time, and that he was firmly resolved to have intercourse with no woman unless within the bonds of matrimony.

Henry's chaplains had done their work well, and it is hardly surprising that this naive 'priests' king' should appear to a papal envoy in 1437 as a devoted son of the church, more like a monk than a king.[24] If the suspicion is well founded that Gloucester was less than enthusiastic (or interested) in supporting Eugenius in his difficulties, then the duke and his nephew might understandably find themselves drifting apart.[25]

The other issue of current concern was the French war. It soon became apparent that Henry wished to end the bloodshed and resume negotiations. Gloucester's views on these matters (and especially on the defence of Calais) diverged sharply from those of Beaufort and, increasingly, the king. This divergence, exploited by the intrigues of the cardinal, further alienated Henry VI from his uncle. Even by the autumn of 1436, Gloucester was experiencing considerable difficulty in obtaining reinforcements and adequate financial and other support for the garrison at Calais, so much so that some of the soldiers began to desert.[26] By the time parliament met on 21 January, he was sufficiently exasperated to pursue his and Calais's interests publicly. On 25 February he knelt before King Henry and requested that he be discharged of his responsibilities in the fortress because of lack of support from the government. This barely veiled threat seemed to have the desired effect, for not only did parliament make provision for the payment of the garrison's wages by 25 March, but two days later, when parliament was about to disperse, Gloucester and his men were belatedly praised for having saved Calais from the duke of Burgundy the previous summer.[27] There is no doubt that on this important issue, Gloucester had had to fight hard and he had received little sympathy from the council and, in the event, only meagre financial provision. But had it not been for the parliament, he would have gained nothing at all. This assembly proved to be Gloucester's temporary political salvation, for the mercantile lobby in particular was highly critical of the government's neglect of naval defence and the interests of the wool trade, on which the security and prosperity of Calais depended. Gloucester shared their concern.[28] But parliaments did not normally last long and the duke would have a much more difficult task in pleading with, or influencing, the other councillors and the king himself. His lack of success led to his resignation as captain of Calais on 8 January 1438.[29] In the meantime, the groundwork was being laid to prepare for serious negotiations with the Bretons and the Valois, with a crucial role assigned to the duke of Orléans as mediator, despite the misgivings of Gloucester. Eventually, in November 1438 a great conference near Gravelines was authorized by Henry VI, even though 'several of our blood and lineage and of our Great Council' were hostile.[30]

Thus, the year following the siege of Calais witnessed not only an intensification of the rivalry between Gloucester and Beaufort, but also the personal intervention of the king in affairs of state. Both older men needed to take Henry's personality and attitudes into account if either was to emerge as the trusted and all-powerful counsellor of an inexperienced monarch. Gloucester refused to modify his views on how best to preserve the dual monarchy created by his brothers and conduct the war most effectively. Beaufort, on the other hand, was able to attune his political convictions to the youthful passions of his great-nephew. In the immediate future, Gloucester could expect to lose his formal position as chief councillor and the council to surrender much of the authority it had exercised since 1422. The minority of Henry VI was drawing perceptibly to a close.

These were the circumstances in which the *Libelle of Englysche*

Polycye was composed. Its sentiments were approved by Lord Hungerford, who had shown some understanding of the merchants' position in April 1437; John Lydgate, the monk of Bury who had been the favourite propagandist of the dual monarchy and was one of Gloucester's protégés, may have had a hand in its composition; and it was presented to several members of the council with the intention of persuading them to change their French policy, especially their neglectful attitude towards Calais and sea-keeping.[31] Even if the *Libelle* owed more to the mercantile lobby than to Gloucester directly, the duke was a skilled publicist on his own account and was regarded by many (including the commons in 1437) as the best advocate of its interests. It was about this same time that he commissioned Titus Livius Frulovisi to write his *Life* of Henry V and dedicate it to Gloucester as the true successor of the conqueror of northern France, and a companion-piece had as its sole purpose the glorification of Duke Humphrey.[32] If self-glorification and propaganda, supported by the sympathy of parliament, could buttress his position, then Humphrey was secure. But parliament was dissolved on 27 March 1437 and political life was henceforward focussed on the council and, increasingly, the household, where poems and heroic tales had less impact than in the parlours of noblemen and merchants. Moreover, on 2 April, Humphrey lost one of his most valued agents among the household establishment: Sir John Tyrell, treasurer of the household, died and was replaced by Sir John Popham, who at least had the virtue (to Gloucester's way of thinking) of being employed by Bedford, York, and Warwick in France.[33]

During the summer of 1437, Henry VI went on an extended tour through his kingdom. Most of his time hitherto had been spent at the royal residences at Westminster and Windsor, or at manor houses in the Thames valley. The only occasions when he ventured far beyond this customary circuit were towards the end of his minority, when his own curiosity about his kingdom may have been aroused or his advisers felt that more of his subjects should see their king. In the summer of 1434 he travelled as far as the midlands, staying at the duchy of Lancaster castle at Kenilworth, only 5 miles north of his guardian's fortress at Warwick; in the following winter and spring he moved westward to Cirencester and Gloucester, where Christmas was celebrated. It may not have been a coincidence that Gloucester was one of the traditional crown-wearing centres of earlier English kings.[34] In 1435 the king was introduced to the royal pastime of hunting, and the summer months were spent in Rockingham forest, with Henry staying at least part of the time at another duchy castle, Higham Ferrers in Northamptonshire.[35] But the tour of 1437 probably had more than a recreational purpose, for no sooner had he returned to the south-east than plans were laid for major constitutional change. In the middle of July Henry VI set out from London and travelled north; his destinations seem to have been Leicester, Nottingham, and Kenilworth, before once again he wheeled south-westwards into Gloucestershire and returned to Woodstock

(Oxfordshire) at the end of August.[36] Both Leicester and Kenilworth were major centres of the prosperous midlands estates of the duchy of Lancaster and they were currently in the charge of prominent household servants: Lord Beaumont had been steward of the former since 5 January 1437 and three years later would become England's first viscount; the steward of Kenilworth and constable of its castle since 1433 was Sir Ralph Botiller, whose tenure was extended for life just a few months before the king arrived.[37] Who accompanied Henry on this tour is not known, though Archbishop Kemp, one of Beaufort's associates, may have done so.[38] It is certain that no sooner had Henry returned to Berkhamsted and King's Langley than Gloucester paid him several visits prior to the great council that had been summoned to Sheen for 21 October. The duke had every reason to be anxious about what was in the king's mind.[39]

Aside from the fundamental matter of releasing the king from his minority, the two most pressing issues absorbing Henry's mind – the divided church and the war with France – were likely to place Gloucester at loggerheads with Beaufort and probably find him without much support among the rest of the king's advisers. The great council, when it met, was presented by the king himself with further items for discussion, and these probably related to the formal adjustment of the relative roles of king and council that took place on 12 November. The traditional relationship between the king and his advisers was thus re-established at the moment when Beaufort was emerging as the king's most favoured counsellor.[40]

During the ensuing year, Gloucester found himself gradually ignored, whereas Beaufort's authority increased, the peace policy prospered, and good relations with Eugenius IV were consolidated.[41] He experienced a brief revival of influence only in the summer of 1439. Just as his own absence had been crucial in enabling Beaufort to influence Henry VI and encourage him in his desire to act as a king, so in the summer of 1439, when Beaufort went to Calais in pursuit of peace, Gloucester was able to impose his will on Henry. When Archbishop Kemp came back with proposals that would have entailed significant concessions to the French, Gloucester vigorously opposed their acceptance and the king followed his advice.[42] But the eventual return of Beaufort in October, after Kemp's experience had reminded him of the crucial importance of vigilance and a personal presence at court, enabled him to reassert his hold on Henry so quickly that by the end of the year Gloucester had been decisively ousted, never again to return to the king's innermost counsels, even though until his death he remained heir presumptive to Henry's throne. The appeal which he directed to the king against the cardinal in the first weeks of 1440 was a dexterous blend of propaganda, accusation, and smear. It was Gloucester's last attempt to win his nephew's mind and

to estraunge hem [i. e., Beaufort and Kemp] of your councel . . . , that men may be at ther fredom to saye what they thinke of trouthe. For trouthe I dare speke off my trouthe, the power [i. e., the poor] dare not so.

But for all the skill with which he framed his charges so as to appeal to fair-minded men as well as those who, like Archbishop Chichele and a number of magnates other than himself, had suffered from 'the pryde and th'ambusyon that was in his [Beaufort's] persone', Gloucester's protest arose from a deep personal sense of grievance. His own powerlessness is reflected in his denunciation of the presumption of Beaufort and Kemp, who 'had and haue the gouernaunce off you and all your lande'. The patronage which Beaufort had secured, 'to your gret hurt and his avayle', left the duke resentful and jealous. And the peace negotiations, which Gloucester judged to be 'to your grettest charge and hurte to bothe your reames', seemed a betrayal of Lancastrian France and the memory of Henry V.[43] It is inconceivable that English policy on an issue that so closely affected Henry VI's honour as king of France would have been reversed without his agreement; impossible, too, that the advice of his uncle and heir would have been increasingly ignored without the king's connivance.

From this time dates the most finely executed manual of instruction and exhortation for a king that Henry VI probably ever received. This treatise, *On the rule of princes,* is contained in a volume which seems to have been composed and presented to the king soon after the end of his minority (say between 1436 and 1442). It expounded for his young majesty the political qualities most desirable in a ruler and the moral precepts he should ideally follow.[44] Much of its substance lay squarely in a political tradition that was most highly developed in the French 'mirrors' of princes and their age, and best exemplified by the thirteenth-century writing of Egidius Colonna, on which this treatise frequently relied. A more popular and easily digested English tradition of political instruction extended from Chaucer onwards into the mid-fifteenth century.[45] By contrast, most of the moral and religious precepts can be traced to those cardinal virtues which the early church fathers had listed. Henry VI may have been familiar with them from King Alfred's translation of Pope Gregory the Great's *Cura Pastoralis;* they were certainly refined and popularized by St Thomas Aquinas in the thirteenth century and more recently had been briefly rehearsed by Piero da Monte in his description of Henry VI in 1437; when John Blacman wrote his eulogy of the king in the 1480s, they formed the framework of his idealized portrait.[46] But the author of the treatise also showed himself to be well aware of the contemporary situation in France in the late 1430s, and wisely (and without noticeable partisanship) urged the advantages of peace through negotiation, while at the same time vigorously defending the just claims of the dual monarchy, as had recently been done at the sieges of Calais and Roxburgh and in stemming the French advance in Normandy. The author likewise grasped the importance for a king entering manhood of having the advice of well-chosen and experienced lords. In short, he was acquainted with the matters of current debate at court during the late 1430s. Not only that, but his emphasis on the value of a formal education and the foundation of colleges and universities leads one to suppose that he approved of the educational ventures on which Henry VI embarked in 1439-40, and his advice to the king to favour those ecclesiastics who were responsible for his spiritual welfare suggests that one of Henry's own chaplains was the author.[47]

If Henry read this book, he would have encountered much that was familiar to him about the desirable qualities of a ruler, as well as sound practical advice relevant to his own situation: steer a course (he was counselled) between precipitate peace negotiations, which had already failed, and the scornful dismissal of peace (which Gloucester advocated); and choose carefully the best advisers rather than fall victim to flatterers. Whereas Henry seems to have taken to heart much of the familiar moral and religious guidance, he was less attentive to the political cautions. In relations with France, he preferred to press for a peace by means of bold concessions to the French, and his own character and upbringing made it almost impossible for him to show the recommended circumspection in his choice of ministers. Advice of this sort may have come from those observers at court who were uneasy about Henry's early conduct of affairs, for the king seems not to have had the strength of will or the good sense to act otherwise.[48] But whether Henry ever took this particular presentation volume from his shelf (let alone read it) will never be known.

Henry VI, then, emerged from his minority vulnerable to the exhortations and solicitations of those about him. It was acknowledged that he possessed certain distinctive qualities of mind and some laudable traits of character, but they were, as yet, those of a fifteen-year-old boy. To apply these in practice, to decisions, patronage, and actions, required the mature advice and guidance of experienced men. Henry's upbringing was not such as to encourage him to take initiatives of this sort on his own. If anything, he became an effective king too soon not to succumb to the sort of influences to which he had been subjected as a child. Both Beaufort and Gloucester were eager to dominate him, not least in order to preserve their own authority in the land; but the king's personal response to issues that happened to be pressing in 1436-39 made it inevitable that the former, rather than the latter, would become his principal adviser in the immediate future.

Contemporary observations

It is surprising, perhaps, that no detailed contemporary description of the king survives – if, in fact, anyone was ever moved to pen one. But on two occasions when he was a boy he was observed by Frenchmen who recorded their impressions: to one at Rouen in 1430, he was *un très beau fils*; to the French envoys in 1433, he appeared *ung tres bel enfant, et de belle venue*. These comments accord well with the statements of the two Italians who, in 1432 and 1437, observed a dignified and well-mannered boy, every inch a king.[49] One would ordinarily be wary of reporting Polydore Vergil's later description of Henry as 'taule of stature, sclender of body, wherunto all his members were proportionately correspondent', were it not for the fact that when the king's supposed tomb was opened in 1910, a Cambridge professor of anatomy judged the bones inside to be those of 'a fairly strong man' between the ages of forty-five and fifty-five (Henry was fifty when he died in 1471), and 5 feet 9 inches or 5 feet 10 inches in height.[50] Great caution needs to be exercised in extracting historical fact about the king from those oft-quoted statements of approvers in the court of king's bench in the 1440s. 'Woe to thee, O land, when the king is a child', was a well-known text from *Ecclesiastes* which had even been intoned at Henry Bolingbroke's command against his exact contemporary, Richard II, in quite different circumstances in 1399. Nor can one feel much confidence in the powers of discernment of a yeoman who thought that 'the king is a lunatic, as his father was'. Other quips can be relegated to the stock of ill-informed criticisms generated by an unpopular government; as R. L. Storey recognized, they are 'not weighty evidence'.[51] In short, there is nothing to show that as boy and man Henry was anything but normally developed physically and mentally. There is no sign that he suffered ill-health in his youth – indeed, quite the contrary. And he seems to have had no more doctors in his service than Henry V or Edward IV over a comparable period of time.[52]

Henry's spoken words, even in indirect speech, cannot be very usefully examined because too few of them are recorded. We can be reasonably certain of the oath he normally used, 'Forsooth, and Forsooth', which hardly reveals him to be a man of hot or imaginative temper. On other occasions, he was given to exclamations of 'St Jehan, grant mercis', to express his satisfaction or delight. But there was rarely anything intemperate or blasphemous in his utterances.[53] Just as elusive are his written words, as opposed to the official pronouncements of his government: it is known that often, especially in the dozen years after he began to rule in 1436, he put his initials to petitions of which he approved – sometimes even a phrase in French (*nous avouns graunte*). So one may deduce that Henry was a literate man, and, as the French envoys discovered in 1445, he understood and spoke French fluently as well as English. The little Latin prayers he has since been credited with composing need not, however, be dated in their surviving manuscripts earlier than 1485, when his reputation for exceptional piety was under construction.[54]

There is one category of contemporary witness unclouded by the propaganda of civil war: those chroniclers who wrote during Henry VI's reign itself, before 1461. Yet their opinions may be distorted by a reluctance to criticize their monarch during his own reign, and few of them go beyond formal and predictable descriptions of Henry as 'the most illustrious' and the 'most noble and Christian king'.[55] However, one anonymous writer in Latin was courageous enough to hint at the king's habitual dilatoriness. Another contemporary commentator was John Hardyng: he had petitioned the king for a reward and in his chronicle duly acknowledged that the king ruled well enough; but he obliquely criticized him by drawing to the king's attention the need to deal with such pressing matters as civil unrest and local injustice.[56] A further reproof, embedded in eulogy, was penned by John Capgrave about 1446: although dedicated to Henry, his *Liber de illustribus Henricis* regretted that the navy and the keeping of the seas were currently being neglected. A similar attitude was taken by Abbot John Whethamstede of St Albans who, stirred lest the 1456 act of resumption should harm his abbey, tempered his praise of Henry as a simple and upright man with chidings that he could not resist those who led him to unwise decisions and wasteful prodigality.[57] These meagre judgements are slender foundations on which to build an estimate of any king; but they do hint at a monarch who, though possessed of worthy personal qualities, neglected certain aspects of his kingly duty.

Education and foundations

Henry's education had not been neglected. It is unlikely that it would have been in a Lancastrian household, for his grandfather and father were as thoroughly and imaginatively educated as any English magnate. Henry V collected many books, and so did Bedford; but it was Gloucester who was pre-eminent among members of the royal family – indeed, among Englishmen generally – in the patronage of scholars and the breadth of his cultural interests.[58] We have precious little knowledge of the details of Henry VI's own books, although some purchases were made for his household, including the Venerable Bede and certain religious tomes; even more were stored in the exchequer and Henry presented a bundle of more than a hundred of these to All Souls College, Oxford, and King's Hall, Cambridge. The king's habit of reading chronicles and other writings was well known, and from them may have sprung his interest in King Alfred, for whom he tried to secure canonization in 1442. This admiration for a king who was a notable promoter of education and literacy among his subjects reflects Henry's view of himself, for he saw his obligations as a king stronger in this direction than in the more conventional pursuits of a medieval monarch.[59] After all, Henry showed a marked concern for the welfare of Oxford and Cambridge universities, which he may have learned from Duke Humphrey and, to a lesser extent, Archbishop Chichele; whilst some of the clerks of his chapel were notable scholars and were well patronized by the king in later years.[60] When Henry authorized the building of a new library at Salisbury cathedral in March 1445, the purposes he had in mind were 'for ye keping of the bookes to the said Churche belanging and also for thencrece of connyng and of vertu of such as wol loke and studie in the same'.[61]

Henry's devotion to his new foundations of Eton and King's College, Cambridge, was even greater: for both he laid the foundation stone and personally supervised the building details. After the king had been captured by the Yorkist lords at the battle of Northampton in July 1460, the earls of Salisbury and Warwick judged that the surest way to gain the king's goodwill was to promise to continue his patronage of Eton and King's.[62] The two foundations were (or at least quickly became) a single conception: a grammar school at Eton providing recruits for a university college at Cambridge, rather after the manner in which boys passed from William of Wykeham's school at Winchester to his 'new' college at Oxford. Indeed, Henry VI appears to have based the organizational details of his scheme on Wykeham's colleges, and in July 1440 he visited Winchester and attended services in the chapel there. The first provost of Eton was Henry Sever, a distinguished academic who had links with Winchester. His successor round about Michaelmas 1442 was William Waynflete, who had been headmaster of Winchester college since 1429 and was destined to leave the greatest mark on Eton's earliest years; Henry relied heavily on this man, whom he regarded as of 'grete discrecion . . . high trought and feruent zele'.[63]

More is known of the beginnings of Eton because its carefully compiled building accounts survive in considerable number, along with other muniments still kept at the college; it is also true that more of the original fabric designed by Henry VI may be seen at Eton than at King's.[64] Henry regarded the foundation in the shadow of his castle at Windsor as his first major, independent act of initiative as an adult, and Eton certainly expresses most nearly the personality of the young king:

> Wherefore we also, who, by the disposition of the same King of Kings (through whom all kings do reign), have now taken into our hands the government of both our kingdoms, have from the very beginning of our riper age carefully revolved in our mind how, or in what manner, or by what royal gift, according to the measure of our devotion and the example of our ancestors, we could do fitting honour to that our same Mistress and most Holy Mother [i.e., the church], to the pleasure of that her great Spouse [i.e., God]. And at length, while we were thinking over these things with the most profound attention, it has become a fixed purpose in our heart to found a college, in honour and in support of that our Mother, who is so great and so holy, in the parochial church of Eton near Windsor, not far from our birth-place.[65]

His cogitation was far advanced by December 1439, when the rector of

Eton was induced to resign in favour of an obedient incumbent, John Kette, who already held a prebend at Windsor and shortly afterwards agreed to the conversion of his new church into a collegiate foundation. But Henry's intentions were much more ambitious than that, for he envisaged a grammar school for twenty-five poor scholars who would be taught free of charge, and an almshouse for the same number of indigent men; a generous endowment worth 1,000 marks a year was authorized for their support. Within a very few years, the number of indigent men had fallen and the body of young scholars greatly expanded to seventy.[66]

The need for better educational facilities in England had been impressed on the king soon after he came of age. Despite the remarkable advances of the previous century, both in the university towns and elsewhere, there are signs that the vitality in educational patronage was faltering and the quality of teaching declining by the mid-fifteenth century. In July 1439 it was claimed that there was an inadequate number of schoolmasters teaching grammar at Oxford and Cambridge and in the east midlands generally, and William Bingham, a priest at St John Zachary's, London, warned the king that this situation would lead to a disastrous decline in Englishmen's mastery of Latin, which was not only the medium of Christian salvation but had important practical uses too; he knew of more than sixty schools that had recently closed in that region alone.[67] It was soon afterwards that the king embarked on his projects at Eton and King's.

The new college at Eton honoured the Virgin Mary and commemorated the king's parents; but its prime purpose was educational, and that placed the king among a growing number of his wealthy subjects who were founders of English grammar schools. What was remarkable about Eton, however, was its size and the fact that no previous king of England had endowed a public grammar school.[68] On 12 September 1440 Henry nominated a group of clerical commissioners to make the necessary practical arrangements; most of them were, at one time or another, members of his household. Bishop Aiscough of Salisbury was his confessor, Bekyngton his secretary, and Richard Andrew, a king's clerk, had been educated at Winchester and New College, was currently warden of Chichele's college of All Souls, and would soon be Henry VI's secretary. William Alnwick was not only bishop of Lincoln (whose agreement was therefore required for the establishment of a collegiate church in his diocese), but had had a long career as king's secretary and confessor, and keeper of the privy seal; and William Lyndwood, a formidable canonist, was presently head of the privy seal office.[69]

The king took a close personal interest in the organization and building of his college, and he pored over the architectural plans submitted to him at Windsor castle, scratching his initials ('R. H.') on them to signify his approval. His interest never flagged during the 1440s; in fact, it quickened as the buildings began to take shape until, in 1448–49, he decided to transform the appearance of the college in a dramatic fashion. By the beginning of 1448, he had come to the conclusion that the existing plans were inadequate for the purposes he had in mind, and in February modifications were submitted to him that resulted in a much larger chapel and extended college precincts.[70] This new plan, which was eventually finalized in 1449 in the 'kynges owne avyse', envisaged a chapel worthy of a cathedral city in place of the original, but still unfinished, construction. The reason for the king's change of mind is not certainly known, but the suggestion that it was a product of the king's already failing mental powers is the least likely.[71] Buildings of the scope and grandeur that were now proposed are testimony to the inspiration and imagination of the king rather than to any supposed inadequacies. It may be that (as H. M. Colvin supposed) problems relating to the foundations of the first building and the tendency for the low-lying land on the north bank of the Thames to flood easily were threatening to undermine the work of 1441. But that would not explain why the revised scheme was so much more ambitious. May not the modifications have been a response to the expansion of King's College, Cambridge, and to the queen's desire to indulge in educational patronage? The initial plans for King's were considered inadequate as early as August 1443, when a larger site was designated for what was proving to be a popular college, 'considering [the scholars'] own numbers and those of others daily flocking together to the said college'. An expanded institution for seventy scholars was accordingly planned at King's instead of the original complement of twelve.[72] But it was not until 1448 that detailed architectural specifications were approved for the modified scheme. At the same time, the queen was expressing an interest in appropriating the college of St Bernard at Cambridge, even though Henry had recently taken steps to re-endow it himself; the king's patronage was therefore concentrated on King's. An enlarged Eton could appropriately serve this augmented university college, and by August 1446 Eton's own scholar community had been increased to seventy.

This renewed burst of organizational and building activity bespeaks of a continuing sense of urgency on the king's part in pursuit of his educational objectives, and their considerable popularity.[73] When parliament assembled at Bury, not far from Cambridge, in February 1447, it seemed as if the country was no better served educationally than it had been in the previous decade. London, the mecca for the realm's youngsters, made limited provision for the teaching of grammar, so much so that a proposal by a syndicate of four to establish an additional grammar school in the city was approved, despite recent restrictions imposed by Archbishop Stafford on the number of authorized institutions.[74] Henry VI's revised plans for Eton and King's were devised in this context. By 1446 Henry's pride in his new school at Eton was undisguised;

. . . it surpasses all other such schools whatsoever of our kingdom in the affluence of its endowment and the pre-excellence of its foundation, so it may excel all other grammar schools as it ought in the prerogative of its name, and be named henceforth the king's general school, and be called the lady mother and mistress of all other grammar schools.[75]

John Blacman was able to testify from personal knowledge to the king's fatherly interest in the young scholars of Eton, for he was a fellow there himself from about 1443 until appointed warden of King's Hall, Cambridge, in December 1452.

> ...he sought out everywhere the best living stones, that is, boys excellently equipped with virtue and knowledge, and priests to bear rule over the rest as teachers and tutors: and as concerned the getting of priests the king said to him whom he employed in that behalf: 'I would rather have them somewhat weak in music than defective in knowledge of the scriptures'. And with regard to the boys or youths who were brought to him to be put to school, the king's wish was that they should be thoroughly educated and nourished up both in virtue and in the sciences. So it was that whenever he met any of them at times in the castle of Windsor, whither they sometimes repaired to visit servants of the king who were known to them, and when he ascertained that they were of his boys, he would advise them concerning the following of the path of virtue and, with his words, would also give them money to attract them, saying: 'Be you good boys, gentle and teachable, and servants of the Lord'.[76]

As in so many other fields, Henry VI received advice and enthusiastic encouragement from members of his household in promoting his educational ventures. Those whom he commissioned in 1440 to make the preliminary arrangements were mainly his private chaplains, but some of his lay friends also embraced his ideas. Although Waynflete, both as provost of Eton and as bishop of Winchester after 1447, controlled the supply of cash to the workforce on the site, it was Suffolk's role that was paramount, under the king, in making policy decisions. John Hampton, one of the king's most constant companions, acted as purveyor for the enterprise, so that it is not difficult to imagine the *rapport* which existed between those who were frequent residents at the castle on the hill and the royal foundation taking shape below it.[77]

Building work began at Eton in 1441, and although substantial progress had been made by 1453, the alteration in the college's design (which, it was envisaged in 1448-49, would take about twenty years to implement) meant that Henry VI did not witness its completion before his illness and the civil war intervened. Nevertheless, Thomas Bekyngton could be consecrated there in October 1443 and was able to celebrate his first mass on the site of the high altar, even though the new chapel 'was not as yet half finished'; the accompanying banquet was held in some of the other new buildings.[78] Local kilns produced the required bricks and stone was quarried in Kent, Surrey, and at the famous Norman quarries near Caen – until the Valois advance in 1449-50 forced the contractors to lease alternative quarries in Yorkshire and Oxford-shire.[79] Labourers and craftsmen were hired or impressed, often at the sites of other building operations.[80]

Eton was well nigh unique in the extraordinary range of privileges bestowed on it by both king and pope. The confiscated properties of alien priories were assigned to the college as part of the original endowment of 25 March 1441.[81] A further 3,000 marks were obtained in March 1442, as well as other windfalls from the king's prerogative resources.[82] Royal charters, which were periodically confirmed by parliament 'gladly and with good heart', conferred regular grants of land, including the town of Eton in January 1444, and the example set by Henry VI induced others to make donations – Suffolk among them, with a gift of £666 in 1448, and Beaufort's £1,000 to Eton and King's in his will. The duchy of Lancaster was required to find £1,000 annually for at least twenty years when the grandiose plans of 1448–49 were finalized.[83] Eton's privileges were even more notable, for they created an independent jurisdictional enclave, exempt from the authority of the archdeacon of Buckinghamshire, from lay and clerical taxation, and other obligations.[84] Parliament gave it a high degree of protection, particularly when acts of resumption were passed in 1449–51; out of reverence for God, the Virgin, and the devout zeal of the king, Eton's franchises emerged unscathed from the wholesale cancellation of royal grants.[85]

The foundation of King's followed a few months later, and Henry's personal role is no less apparent. Moreover, practically the same group of men played a central part in devising the constitutions of the college as had acted as commissioners at Eton. Once again Bishop Alnwick of Lincoln had a special role as diocesan, and associated with him in drawing up the ordinances on 12 February 1441 were Bishop Aiscough, William Lyndwood, John Somerset, and, appropriately on this occa-sion, the chancellor of Cambridge University, John Langton. It seems to have been Langton's advocacy that persuaded Henry to make Cambridge, rather than Oxford, the site of the new foundation, though the close connection that had existed since the fourteenth century between the chaplains of the royal household and King's Hall, Cambridge, may have been an equally significant factor.[86] In dedicating the new college, Henry initially honoured his birth-saint, Nicholas, but within a short time he had also included the Virgin Mary in the dedication, after the example of Eton. The king's motives were overwhelmingly educational, and at first the college was planned for twelve scholars under the authority of a rector; after it had been decided in 1443 to admit a much greater number, the need for larger college buildings was recognized. As with the revised scheme at Eton, the duchy of Lancaster contributed £1,000 for twenty years to cover the costs of construction.[87]

> We ordain . . . that each and every student to be chosen for our royal college at Cambridge for the years of probation shall be poor and indigent scholar clerks, who have received the first tonsure, adorned with good manners and birth, sufficiently grounded in grammar, honest in conversation, able and apt for study, desiring to proceed further in study, not already graduates, and not bound to any other college, except our royal college of Eton . . .

The privileges of King's, both in grants of land and rights, were comparable with those of Eton, and parliament likewise took this foundation under its wing, confirming its franchises on more than one occasion; it enjoyed the same exemption from taxation and in 1449–51 secured immunity from the acts of resumption.[88] It was a personal tragedy for Henry that by the time of his deposition, the chapel at neither of his colleges was complete.

There is no doubting Henry's unwavering interest in these institutions, especially during the 1440s, or his determination to support and advance those who studied and served in them. The colleges' statutes and constitutions demonstrate that the king's aims were more educational than purely devotional, and it is A. B. Cobban's judgement that 'his projected scheme shows a far deeper concern for true educational values than that evinced by his Yorkist successor'. Here, too, Gloucester's early influence may be discerned, as well as Archbishop Chichele's.[89] Moreover, Henry's foremost teacher and doctor from 1427, John Somerset, was a man of many distinguished parts – grammarian, doctor, author, and administrator – who, after the death of his first patron, Thomas Beaufort, duke of Exeter in 1426, entered the service of Duke Humphrey, whose executor he had become by 1447. One can well imagine the cultured Gloucester recommending the outstanding teacher and doctor after he had emerged victorious from his struggle with Beaufort in 1425–26. Somerset remained in the king's service until his death, probably in 1453, and was intimately concerned with the planning of Eton and King's.[90]

The king's character

In establishing foundations of this sort, educational and religious motives were closely entwined. Henry's encouragement of university reform and the education of clerks, and his promotion of scholars and his own religious advisers and confessors to the episcopate after 1436, reflect a deep concern for the quality of the church and its leaders. It was one of the consequences – perhaps his intention – that he strengthened the theologically trained element in an otherwise political bench of bishops.[91]

The most marked feature of the popular conception of Henry today is his extraordinary piety. As the dedications of his new colleges indicate, he showed a special devotion to the Virgin Mary, and when Richard Wyche was tried for heresy in 1440, he expressed himself publicly and uncompromisingly a firm opponent of idolatry and heretics. However, he did not follow in his father's footsteps and found a monastery, even though he was generous to a number of religious houses, particularly those of the Carthusians. Nor did he expend much energy or cash on chantries, as many of his rich subjects did.[92] The king certainly felt in 1444 that if the University of Oxford abandoned Latin sermons, it would lead to what he described as 'disworship'. But not even the sympathetic abbot of St Albans could discern the saint in him. None of the prayers or the *Sanctus* which Henry is credited with composing can be dated to his lifetime and are more likely the product of Tudor hagiography. Henry, then, was evidently a pious, if orthodox, Englishman, but it is difficult to agree with B. P. Wolffe that the king displayed an 'unique, obsessive and ostentatious piety'. Henry's elevation to the threshold of sanctity owes more to the pathos of his tragic illness and dethronement, his mysterious death in captivity, and to Henry VII's desire to have a saint in the family to buttress his new régime. When John Capgrave produced his eulogy of the king about 1446, he described a man concerned for religion and for priests, and a protector of the church – which was not much more than others had said of Richard II and Henry V.[93]

Less conventional was the compassionate, humane, and sensitive trait in Henry's character. Contemporaries remarked on his penchant throughout adulthood for pardoning even traitors and murderers. The principles of law enforcement in the country cannot have been properly upheld when the number of pardons for serious crime increased markedly during Henry's majority. His reasons for this leniency, where they are known, were humane, merciful, and religious – the hope that a murderer would reform, or the desire, out of 'reverence for the passion of Christ and the Virgin Mary' (a motivation he shared with Henry IV and Henry V), that a traitor should be given another chance. In July 1439 he could not resist the contrition of a thief who 'has now the greatest horror of his ill deeds, intending to avoid all such in the future, and has with tears and sighs besought the king's mercy'.[94] The human consequences of the English defeats in France appalled him at least as much as they shocked his subjects. He was distressed to see the forlorn soldiery limping back to England after the collapse of Normandy in 1450. Some he took into his own household, where they joined the substantial number of poor clerks whom he also supported. All added their wages and gifts to his already inflated expenses bill.[95]

The prudish sensitivity of Henry comes through in a revealing episode that occurred on his visit to Bath in 1449. Taken into the Roman baths, he was deeply shocked and embarrassed to see men and women bathing naked together in the famous waters. Thomas Bekyngton, bishop of Bath and Wells, felt it wise to ban the 'established custom' whereby the citizens of Bath 'barbarously and shamelessly strip them [i. e., the bathers] of their said garments and reveal them to the gaze of the bystanders, and inflict on them not only the loss of their garments but a heavy monetary fine'. It was a form of ransom which Henry VI did not appreciate. In the same vein, Henry was generous in his exhortations to his courtiers to eschew the pleasures of the flesh. His tiresome preaching may have had particular effect on his half-brother, Jasper, whose upbringing was strictly controlled for a time by King Henry, and who did not marry until he was in his mid-fifties – or produce any illegitimate offspring.⁹⁶ The boys of Eton in particular were discouraged from visiting the court at Windsor castle 'lest his young lambs should come to relish the corrupt deeds and habits of his courtiers, or lose partly or altogether their own good characters, . .'⁹⁷

Yet the king was by no means unrelievedly dour or straitlaced. His boyhood experience of the chase in Rockingham forest cannot have been entirely distasteful to him, for after decades of neglect the small, royal hunting lodge not far away at Clipstone, in Sherwood forest, was extensively renovated between 1435 and 1446, presumably in anticipation of occasional royal visits.⁹⁸ Hunting with falcon and hawk evidently gave him considerable 'pleasure and disport' as a young man, whilst indoors he enjoyed the occasional game and diversion, especially with John Hampton, a favoured esquire for the body.⁹⁹ Nor does Henry appear as the dowdy figure whom Blacman later described. He spent freely every year on fine new gowns and hats for himself, and greeted the French envoys in 1445 richly robed in cloth of gold.¹⁰⁰

Henry VI was therefore capable of taking a sustained, positive, sometimes intelligent and constructive, interest in affairs, provided they were to his liking. Military affairs were not. It may be that, as with Richard II, it was a mistake to put the king in the charge of ageing, distinguished soldiers too early in life. His great-uncle Exeter had had a successful military career in the company of Henry V; after he died in 1426, his replacement as the king's guardian, Warwick, was, if anything, a greater paragon of martial virtue – though with wider interests to commend him. If these men were a constant reminder to Henry of the traditional qualities expected of a medieval king, and repetitive in their stories of Henry V's exploits, it is hardly surprising that Henry VI should develop no martial instincts whatever. He was the first English king never to command an army against an external foe. He only once visited France, in 1430–32 to be crowned; the visit projected during 1445–47 to discuss peace with Charles VII never materialized. He never fought in Scotland nor crossed the channel to Ireland, and only once did he set foot in Wales when he visited the duchy of Lancaster town of Monmouth on 4 August 1452 during his tour of the Welsh borderland. The only occasions on which his subjects saw him in battle array before the civil war were unhappy ones: in 1450 and 1452 he clattered through London with his magnates to ride against some of his own subjects.[101] Henry's interest in the order of the garter was sincere enough and he rarely missed the festivities at Windsor on St George's day; but it was during the 1440s that the order began to lose its exclusively military character as the king took to conferring membership on European princes and knights (not always for reasons of diplomacy) and on friends and companions in his household.[102]

Henry proved to be a generous young king – generous to a serious fault. Kindnesses were well repaid (as the prior of Wallingford discovered in 1445), and as soon as he came of age, he began to patronize and reward his friends, courtiers, and servants – in short, the members of his household. This was natural enough in a teenager with new-found powers. It seemed harmless enough at the time and would doubtless bring him popularity. But the extent and permanence of his grants of offices, cash, and land quickly impoverished the crown financially and weakened its control over local administration in several parts of the realm.[103] By the early 1440s the council had become concerned about the way in which the king was dispensing his patronage. In 1444 it tried to modify it by introducing a much-needed element of honesty, efficiency, clarity, and control. Henry's imprudent generosity, his unwillingness to refuse those who petitioned him or pestered him for grants, and his inability to visualize the implications of his actions had led to bitterness and confusion on many occasions during the past seven years. By October 1442 he was being advised to be more circumspect so as to avoid the mistakes of the recent past, though with little success in either England, its dependent territories, or Lancastrian France.[104] Indeed, France, of which Henry had had no direct experience since he was ten, witnessed a number of such blunders in these early years of the king's majority, and they frequently led to disputes among the magnates and lesser men. For example, Edmund Beaufort was given at least three baronies in Normandy to which Sir John Robessart and others had prior claim.[105] It is worth remembering that these were the years that witnessed Henry's energetic promotion of educational foundations and peace with France, and his conscious attempt to promote the interests of the royal family. The king's personality was in large part determining the actions of his government in these most active years of his personal rule.

During the first few years of his majority, Henry VI may have taken advice about negotiations with the French, whether it was Gloucester's to allow no substantial concession at the conference at Oye in the summer of 1439, or Beaufort's to embark on the negotiations in the first place. But Henry soon played his own role, especially when his marriageability became an important factor in the discussions. He wrote and signed letters with his own hand, 'the whiche as ye wote well we be not muche accustomed for to do in other caas', and ordered others 'of our owne mocion' to forward plans for his marriage to a daughter of the count of Armagnac in 1442; he even commissioned portraits of the count's daughters so that he could choose the most attractive of them as his bride. When his negotiators returned from Bordeaux in 1443, they reported first to Henry and only afterwards to a succession of his advisers.[106]

He can have been no less interested in the negotiations preceding his wedding to Margaret of Anjou in 1445, and thereafter his initiative is reasonably clear. In the audience he gave to the French ambassadors in July, he followed the proceedings intently and approvingly; although Suffolk and the chancellor, Archbishop Stafford, appear to have conducted most of the discussion, Henry intervened tellingly and occasionally drew his advisers aside for further consultation. Always willing to grant the requests of his friends, he was just as prepared to listen to the importunings of his young French wife; the sixteen-year-old girl reinforced his own wish to bring the war to an end, as Henry and Margaret both stated in their letters.[107] This royal combination produced the most far-reaching proposal yet from the English side: the surrender of hard-won territory in the shape of Maine. Formally, through the chancellor in parliament, his lords to a man dissociated themselves in April 1446 from the proposed meeting of heads of state that was also planned, and Henry declared formally and in public that it was his responsibility alone. A year later, Suffolk made it clear that his own role in the surrender of Maine was strictly limited: in the midst of the outcry which this proposal had caused it is unlikely that Henry would have assumed practically sole responsibility for what proved to be a blunder if others too were deeply implicated.[108] By 1450 the part which Suffolk had played in England's foreign relations was attracting universal odium. Yet, more than once the king publicly stood by his minister and made it clear that the duke's policy was, in effect, Henry's too; even in the midst of the clamour for Suffolk's condemnation in 1450, Henry was prepared to act alone in suspending proceedings against him and banishing him for five years instead.[109]

Nor can the king be relieved of at least some of the responsibility for the English attack on the Breton fortress of Fougères in 1449, which catapulted England into the final struggle with Charles VII. It may have been prompted in part by Henry's sense of personal outrage at the imprisonment of his boyhood friend, Gilles of Brittany, to whom Henry was devoted, by his brother, the Breton duke. Even without the attack, there was every likelihood that Brittany would join Charles VII in his advance through Normandy. But the English action gave the Bretons their excuse for doing so at this juncture.[110] Judging consequences and implications was not Henry's *forte*.

The king's judgement of other than simple, uncomplicated issues was often seriously at fault. Nor did he have a sound sense of proportion to compensate for it. Henry was a merciful man and generally willing to forgive those who criticized his government. But he was keenly mistrustful of those who attacked him personally and could react with irrational haste to rumours that men were plotting his death. Whatever the political undertones of the trial in 1441 of Eleanor Cobham, duchess of Gloucester, there are several indications that Henry sponsored, and took a close interest in, her prosecution because he believed her to be plotting his death by magical means. When an obscure Kentish woman berated him to his face for condemning the duchess, the king waxed 'wroth, and toke it to hert' – so much so that he immediately and uncharacteristically ordered the woman's arrest and trial, and he did nothing to prevent her subsequent execution.[111] He was no more level-headed when, in 1447, he believed the rumours that Duke Humphrey too was plotting against him. Henry refused to see his uncle and heir, surrounded himself with a large bodyguard that had no idea from whom or from what it was protecting the king, and put on alert hundreds of men in London and Bury St Edmunds, where parliament was assembling to condemn the duke.[112]

Henry's energetic judicial tours in 1450–51 after Cade's rebellion were unprecedentedly severe for this reign, with a 'harvyste of hedys' garnered by the king himself in Kent, and 'great justice' meted out by him elsewhere. The king was truly shocked by the rising, but even more by the mutiny of his own forces and the murder of some of his closest companions. It was these outrages that prompted the king to flee ignominiously and in fear from London to Kenilworth at the height of the revolt, and led him to over-react with alarm when the duke of York suddenly appeared from Ireland later in the year, preceded by seditious bills, threats, and 'moche straunge langage'.[113] Actual or supposed personal affronts like these caused Henry's natural inclination to clemency to be replaced temporarily by irrational fear and suspicion.

The common view of Henry as a king whose sole aim was to practise the virtues of 'charity, long-suffering, gentleness, goodness, faith, meekness and temperance' is a long way from the reality. At another extreme, K. B. McFarlane was disposed to measure the first fifteen years of Henry's adult rule with the yardstick of the last five when he recalled the 'inanity' of Henry VI, by which 'second childhood succeeded first without the usual interval'. B. P. Wolffe has provided an alternative appraisal of the king, but one cannot readily endorse his harsher strictures that Henry was a man 'of perverse wilfulness', in whom 'wilful incompetence and untrustworthiness' were abiding characteristics.[114]

Henry VI was, in reality, a well-intentioned man, with aspirations that were laudable enough, in an age when kings could not rule by good intentions alone. He had an interest in the realities of government with the aim of realizing those aspirations, especially in education, relations with Valois France, and in the reward of friends and servants. Other of his qualities were obstacles to effective kingship. He was extravagant, credulous, over-merciful and compassionate to those at fault, yet fearfully suspicious of those who were rumoured to be doing him personal harm. These were not the qualities of a shrewd and balanced judge of men or policies. Henry also lacked the foresight, prudence, and calculation that make a king's actions responsible ones: he showed little sagacity, subtlety, or discrimination in his administrative acts, and none of the political astuteness necessary to achieve an acceptable balance among his subjects' competing interests – as contemporaries recognized who stressed his simplicity. Not that Henry was uneducated or unintelligent, but he was the least experienced of medieval English kings at his accession and never shook off his youthful dependence on others in the routine and detail of affairs. The Prussian agent in London, Hans Winter, well appreciated the king's situation when he reported to his employers in 1450 that Henry VI 'is very young and inexperienced and watched over as a Carthusian'.[115] And with his naively defective judgement, Henry's advisers were too often unworthy of his confidence.

The new queen

Margaret of Anjou has excited the interest of at least a dozen biographers over the past 200 years, all of whom have been attracted by the personal qualities of the queen as well as by the calamitous events which brought her and her husband to ruin. Seventeenth- and eighteenth-century portraits of her moralized on the implications of her unhappy life, often confusing legend with fact.[116] Early in the nineteenth century, the tragic heroism of her experiences appealed particularly to those parts of western Europe with which she and her family had links: she inspired romantic melodrama in print and on stage in France, Italy, and England, whilst Lorrainer patriotism inspired a study of the 'lost heroine' in 1855.[117] More serious works were written in the second half of the nineteenth century, though the heavy hand of Tudor historians (especially Shakespeare) dictated their assessments of her character and intentions.[118] The first objective account of Margaret was the brief notice of her by T. F. Tout, published in 1893; it was scrupulously based on contemporary chronicles (especially foreign ones) and published documents. Yet this scholarly attention by no means ensured unhindered progress towards authentic historical appreciation, for in the twentieth century it has been the drama of Margaret's downfall in a foreign country and her courage in upholding the rights of an imbecile husband and baby son that have touched the imagination of almost all writers up to the present time.[119] Only the biography by J. J. Bagley has attempted a dispassionate study, though his straightforward chronological account, based upon published materials, was hampered by the inconveniences of wartime. He too viewed the queen as a tragic figure, born somewhat out of her time and thrust to the fore by events; a heroine commended for her bravery and determination.[120] With this tradition of historical study at one's back, it is particularly difficult to assess the character of Margaret of Anjou in the years before the civil war began in England, and to evaluate her role as queen and her new subjects' attitude towards her prior to Henry VI's illness in August 1453.

Margaret's arrival in England in April 1445 had more than usual significance. Not only would she, like all other queens, enjoy the status, influence, and patronage of the king's consort; she had an additional importance. First, she symbolized the truce with France and the hopes of peace which Henry VI cherished; she was therefore fated to have the closest of links with those of his ministers who pursued this policy. Secondly, the marriage of Henry and Margaret took place at a time when the king badly needed an heir to give security to the dynasty, for Gloucester was fifty-five years old, had no legitimate children, and no longer a wife. Although the new queen may bear some responsibility for the fact that she did not conceive for another eight and a half years, during which time the question of the succession became more and more acute and seriously vitiated aristocratic politics in the realm, the souring of the expectations of peace was in no way her fault. Nonetheless, she attracted a certain unpopularity on both counts in the late 1440s, particularly between 1449 and 1453.

Aside from the fact that her very presence in England was a promise of the anticipated accommodation with her uncle, Charles VII, Margaret intervened personally in the diplomacy of peace, though her role was of no more than minor consequence. In December 1445, she exerted girlish pressure (for she was only sixteen) on her husband at the request of Charles and her father, Réné of Anjou, to fortify Henry's resolve to surrender Maine as an aid to peace. And when the cession of this county was soon afterwards conceded, the king confessed that he had responded to the pleas of 'our most dear and well-beloved companion the queen, who has requested us to do this many times'.[121] Thereafter, Margaret's initiative in French affairs seems remote and inconsequential. She was spared the suspicion which a number of her predecessors had earned by their favours to foreign friends and servants, for Margaret brought a very small entourage to England in 1445; indeed, so few were her companions that her lack of state ironically prompted adverse comment.[122] However, as the peace treaty proved elusive, despite the surrender of Maine, one may imagine Margaret becoming gradually more unpopular, especially when, after the outbreak of war in July 1449, her own father joined the Valois armies as they swept through Normandy.[123] Soon after the death of Gloucester, the last great champion of a vigorous military offensive, one of his sorrowful servants, Thomas Hunt, keeper of Gloucester castle, is alleged to have remarked that he would be glad to see the queen drowned because no good had come of her arrival in England.[124] Yet, for the time being the convention that forbade direct criticism of the king appears also to have extended to the queen.

It was otherwise with her apparent failure to do her dynastic duty. It is undeniably strange that Margaret did not conceive a child by Henry VI sooner than she did; there is no sign of a miscarriage at any time during their first eight years of married life. Whatever the reason – and it is likely to have lain in the bedchamber beyond the prying eyes of all but the gossips – the absence of a royal birth led Henry to continue the patronage and advancement of members of his family, especially the Beauforts, at the expense of the duke of York and his line. This created alarm in the duke which bred resentment and fear, and it perhaps encouraged some to contemplate more drastic action against him – even attainder, which would have effectively disposed of his claim to be the king's heir and made it impossible for him or his offspring to sit on Henry's throne.[125] Gossip there certainly was about the queen's continuing childlessness. One rumour had it in 1447 that the impressionable king was deterred by his confessor, Bishop Aiscough, from coming 'nigh her' when he wished to have 'his sport' with Margaret. But this particular malice is more likely to have sprung from the common hatred of Aiscough and others of Suffolk's circle by the late 1440s; Aiscough had married the royal couple at Titchfield abbey and he, more than most, would have longed to see the dynasty secure.[126] Soon afterwards, it was alleged that a Canterbury man had said that

> oure quene was none abyl to be Quene of Inglond, but and he were a pere of, or a lord of this realme he would be on of thaym that schuld helpe to putte her a downe, for because that sche bereth no child, and because that we have no pryns in this land.[127]

Henry may not have been an ardent husband; Blacman, though he was concerned to insert the virtue of chastity in his posthumous eulogy of the king, related that

> with her [Margaret] and toward her he kept his marriage vow wholly and sincerely, even in the absences of the lady, . . . : never dealing unchastely with any other woman. Neither when they lived together did he use his wife unseemly, but with all honesty and gravity.[128]

It was inevitable that Margaret should have developed very close relations with Suffolk, who had done more than most to arrange her marriage and had spent months in France patiently negotiating for her hand and then conducting her in great state to England. These relations were placed on a personal level, for Alice, duchess of Suffolk continued in attendance on the queen even after 1445.[129] Later still, the queen was indebted to the duke of Somerset for his good advice and kindly service, so much so that on 16 November 1451 she decided to award him a 100-mark annuity.[130] Even if her position as queen had not dictated it, her chosen associations were with members of the king's household and court; and when the commons attacked some of these in 1450-51, a few of her companions – including the duchess of Suffolk, the duke of Somerset, and William Booth, her chancellor – were on their list.[131]

By the terms of her endowment, Queen Margaret was a very rich, highly privileged, and, therefore, influential person in her own right, whilst her position at the centre of the court gave her an opportunity, second only to that of the king, to advance her interests and her servants. Margaret – perhaps because she came from France with few attendants of her own – early showed herself to be a conscientious patron, eager to cherish loyalty and determined to extend her 'good ladyship' to those who merited it. A high proportion of those in her household employ were also servants of the king, for not only had the temporary 'household-in-transit' which had accompanied her to England been recruited from Henry's establishment, but a number of its members continued to serve her after 1445. Moreover, after their marriage, Henry and Margaret appear to have been in one another's company for much of the time, and although their households were distinct administrative organizations, they overlapped a good deal in their personnel.[132] Until 1450 Henry and Margaret were together for most of the year, and it was only when the crises of 1450–51 claimed an unusual amount of the king's attention and time (not least when he was on commissions of oyer and terminer) that they parted for more than three or four months in the year. But they were together again in 1452, even on the king's tour of the south-west and Welsh borderland after the duke of York's rising; later the queen's confinement made travel more difficult for her, though her visit to Norwich in April 1453 without Henry, but in the company of one of his half-brothers, may have been *en route* to the shrine at Walsingham, where thanks could be offered for her long-awaited pregnancy.[133] They spent Christmas together – whether it was at Eltham in 1451 or at the queen's own manor of Pleasaunce, near Greenwich, in 1452, when elaborate masques were organized to entertain the royal couple – as well as other major festivals of the year, and they travelled together between Sheen, Westminster, and Greenwich by barge down the Thames.[134] If there is no more sincere form of flattery (or affection) than imitation, then the queen's feelings towards her husband may be reflected in her wish to found a college at Cambridge soon after Henry had re-endowed St Bernard's college in August 1447. One may even detect a proud and assertive young woman in the words of her petition to Henry VI that in Cambridge there was 'no collage founded by eny quene of Englond hidertoward' and that she therefore wished to adopt

the fondacion and determinacion of the seid collage to be called and named the Quenes collage of sainte Margerete and saint Bernard, ... so that beside the mooste noble and glorieus collage roial of our Lady and saint Nicholas founded by your highnesse may be founded and stablisshed the seid so called Quenes collage to conservacion of oure feith and augmentacion of pure clergie ... and to laud and honneure of sexe femenine, ... [135]

She had probably first travelled to Cambridge with the king in July 1446, when he laid the first stone of the chapel of his earlier and larger foundation of King's; they were there again in the spring of 1447. Although Margaret may not have returned for a third visit until June 1448, the foundation stone of her own college was laid on 15 April by her chamberlain, Sir John Wenlock; the college's statutes were formulated with the assistance of William Booth, her chancellor.[136]

Although Margaret had her own household, servants, and administrative departments for the management of her estates, revenue, expenditure, and interests, the relationship between her establishment and that of the king was close and intimate. Even some of those servants who did not continue to serve the king after entering her employ had shown their worth and acquired their experience in Henry's household or administration.[137] Margaret employed, too, a number who made her household service their principal occupation and believed that their careers would be best advanced by her favour. Edward Ellesmere, for example, was clerk of her jewels soon after she arrived in England and by 1452 had risen to the more responsible position of treasurer of her chamber. His devotion to the queen was carried to the battlefield at Towton and was rewarded by attainder in Edward IV's first parliament.[138] Robert Tanfield, a lawyer, was another of her leading officials: her attorney-general by 1453, he became her chamberlain two years later and suffered for his Lancastrian loyalties in 1461.[139]

Margaret rewarded such counsel, service, and devotion from the fund of patronage, influence, and resources which was at her command. The only surviving collection of her letters (eighty-three in all) demonstrates the care she took to offer preferment to those who served her; indeed, as a patron she showed herself to be resourceful and persistent, to the point where she was prepared to compete with others – even the king – for a benefice, an office, or a lucrative marriage.[140] Thus, her 'right welbelovyd clerc and Secretary', Nicholas Caraunt, received her advocacy and protection in 1446–47 when his election to the deanery of Wells cathedral was challenged; so long as he continued to give his secretarial services he received further prebends, but after the accession of Edward IV the stream of patronage dried up.[141] She was equally helpful to John Hals, who had become one of Margaret's chaplains by 1446 and on whose behalf she importuned the duke of Somerset and the earl of Wiltshire in 1453 to secure his promotion to the archdeaconry of Norwich.[142] When the wardship of Anne, the Beauchamp heiress, was granted to her in June 1446, Margaret immediately set about deploying the additional resources temporarily under her control to advance, for instance, the usher of her chamber, John Wenlock (soon to be her chamberlain), to the constableship of Cardiff castle, and the clerk of her signet, the talented George Ashby, to the stewardship of Warwick.[143]

Recently married herself, the queen's interest in other people's marriage plans is well known, and on occasion she intervened to press the suit of a servant. To the widowed (and wealthy) Jane Carew, she strongly recommended her sewer, Thomas Burneby, round about 1447–50:

> for the greet zele, love and affeccion that he hath unto your personne, as for the womanly and vertuouse governance that ye be renowned of, [Burneby] desireth with all his hert to do yow worship by wey of marriage, bifore all creatures lyvyng, as he saith; We desiryng th'encres, furtherance, and preferring of oure said squire, for his manyfold merits and deserts, as for the good service that he hath don unto my lord [the king] and us, and yet therin dayly continueth, praye you right affectuously, that, at reverence of us, ye will have oure said squire towards his said mariage especially recommended, inclynyng you to his honest desire at this tyme; the rather by contemplacion of this oure praier, wherin we trust verreily ye shul mowe pourvcy right well for your self, to your greet worship and hertsease, and cause us to have yow both in suche tendernesse and faver of our good grace, that by reason ye shul holde you right well content and pleased;...[144]

She was not always successful in her advocacy of causes and servants; in these early years, her youth and inexperience imposed limitations on the confidence and authority with which she and her council pursued her interests and cared for her servants.[145] But her qualities of determination, firmness, and concern are evident in more than one letter. Insistence on her rights as a landowner produced a stern reprimand to the city of London, even to a magnate like Lord Ferrers of Groby, for molesting the queen's tenantry; Ferrers was left in no doubt of Margaret's feelings:

> We therefore desire and praye you, and also exhorte and require you, that ye do yeve in commandement unto your said bailiff [of Stebbyng] for to cesse of his said vexacions and oppressing, and put him in suche reule that oure said tenants may leve in rest and peas, so that they have no cause to compleine ayeine unto us for lak of remedie in your defaulte; as ye thinke to stande in the faver of oure good grace, and t'eschewe our displeasir at your peril.[146]

The queen's endowment in March 1446 was substantial and it increased in size as a result of her husband's open-handed generosity. Initially, she received the customary dower of queens of England, worth 10,000 marks *per annum*, and care was taken lest the cold financial winds that blew about the late-Lancastrian monarchy should adversely affect her income.[147] The estates – the sure foundation of wealth and influence – which were granted her were taken from the duchy of Lancaster, £2,000-worth of whose lands were made over to Margaret; they were concentrated on the midlands honours of Tutbury, Leicester, and Kenilworth, a compact stretch of rich property to which Margaret would return again and again during the next fifteen years.[148] For this reason, experienced duchy officials continued to serve the queen while she held these lands, and the receiver-general of the duchy, William Cotton, acted as her receiver-general and treasurer of her household.[149] They would be more likely to ensure that the £1,000 annuity which Margaret also received from the duchy in 1446 would pass regularly into her coffers.[150] In addition, she acquired certain annual sums of cash which her officials would have to collect from specified sources: £1,000 from the customs revenue at Southampton, £1,009 from the duchy of Cornwall, and £1,658 from the exchequer. The queen and her officials did not have direct control over these sources, and hence could not collect them at first hand; she therefore encountered greater problems in realizing this part of her dower income in the difficult financial days of the 1440s and '50s.[151]

In addition to her dower, Margaret gained custody of the richest heiress ever to fall into Henry VI's hands: Anne, the three-year-old daughter of Henry Beauchamp, duke of Warwick. On 15 June 1446 Anne was placed in Margaret's care, and £200 *per annum* was assigned from the estate to maintain the girl in the queen's household. Although Margaret sold this valuable wardship to Suffolk five months later, she spared no time in appointing a number of her servants to significant offices on the Beauchamp estates.[152] The parliament of 1447, which saw the humiliation and death of Gloucester, lavished further lands, annuities, and pensions on Margaret, among them an extra 500-mark annuity from the duchy of Lancaster; moreover, it reaffirmed that her £3,667 in cash should be converted as soon as possible into the greater security of land grants, and to this end Margaret was now given priority in the disposal of any property that might fall to the king in the future. By this means, she was able to acquire the important castle and lordship of Berkhamsted in June 1448.[153] A month later, Margaret received a privilege which many must have envied and the merchant community, particularly the staplers at Calais, bitterly resented: in place of cash tallies worth £1,500, she was licensed to ship wool free of customs from any port in the realm to any destination she chose, thereby breaching the jealously guarded monopoly of the staple.[154] On top of this, in an attempt to improve her ability to realize the dower grant of £1,000 from the Southampton customs, she was accorded the rare privilege of nominating one of the two customs collectors who operated not only in that port, but also at Hull and London, three of the most bustling wool-exporting ports in the kingdom. It was a grant reminiscent of the special position which Cardinal Beaufort had enjoyed in the wool trade for many years – and which had caused so much resentment and suspicion. The intention was that Margaret should also have a more secure means of ensuring that the £1,658 which had been assigned her at the exchequer in 1446 would indeed reach her hands.[155]

Thereafter, great care was taken to give these various grants the protection that few others (apart from those of Suffolk and his friends) enjoyed. Her annuity from the duchy of Lancaster, for example, was given precedence over all subsequent grants from the duchy's resources (apart from a few named exceptions) by the parliament of 1449, and this was reaffirmed when the next assembly made important provisions for the king's household.[156] Her grants were also exempt from the acts of resumption of 1450–51. These very acts made available sources of income which the king, in accordance with his promise of 1447, could now assign to his queen to replace the elusive cash sources that had formed part of her original dower.[157] The co-operative assembly of 1453 went further; it awarded Margaret the grandest grants of all. While it proved extraordinarily generous to Henry VI himself, it was scarcely less indulgent towards his consort. Margaret's earlier grants, including the ability to bypass the Calais staple, were precisely safeguarded. Although preference had been given to the king's needs in the collection of Southampton's customs for two years from Christmas 1450, the queen's special privileges in the port were now confirmed and arrangements made for her to collect whatever arrears were owing to her.[158] The same assembly continued the king's undertaking that escheated lands should be handed over to Margaret in place of her £3,667 cash assignment. Above all, on 21 July 1453 a solemn charter conferred on her for life the right to all moveable possessions forfeited to the king, regardless of their total value; certain other royal prerogatives were surrendered to her so that she had royal rights of justice on her estates and the power to exclude royal officials and impose trading tolls. These privileges created a virtual queenly franchise.[159] They bestowed on Margaret a more extensive patronage, unusually wide powers of lordship, and significant financial resources. 1453 witnessed a handsome second-stage endowment of the queen.

Her good relations with the king and her good accord with this parliament account for these acts of unsurpassed generosity. The initiative in seeking them may have come from Margaret or her advisers, though both crown and parliament were prepared to acquiesce without apparent hesitation or reluctance. After all, complementing her own youthful energy and determination was a body of councillors and officials of devotion and experience who had very close links with the king's household and government. This combination of qualities and talents goes far to explain the scrupulous attention which Margaret paid to the interests of her servants as well as her own, even at the most mundane of levels. It explains, too, the alertness with which her resources were exploited and their successful augmentation, particularly after the acts of resumption in 1450–51. It is not without significance in this regard that several of her household officials, most notably Edward Ellesmere and William Nanseglos, clerk of the queen's receipt, were also assigned financial duties on estates in the south-east that were easy of access from Westminster or Windsor, for such a dual responsibility would the more likely facilitate the collection of revenue and (as A. R. Myers implied) establish an effective link between the queen's local and central administrations. 'A study of Margaret's revenues confirms the impression of her as a woman eager for power and ever watchful to gain and to keep all the income she could, . . .'[160]

By 1453, she was advised by three of the most powerful magnates in the realm: the duke of Somerset, Viscount Beaumont, who was chief steward of her lands and Henry VI's confidant, and Thomas, Lord Scales, a notable soldier who had held the Tower against Cade's rebels in 1450. Her chancellor, Lawrence Booth, had succeeded his half-brother in the office in March 1451; both men were clerks trained in the law and rose high in the English church by their talents and Margaret's patronage. William, the elder, became bishop of Coventry and Lichfield in 1447 (though continuing as the queen's chancellor) and archbishop of York in 1452; Lawrence reached the bishopric of Durham in 1457 and eventually he, too, was translated to York in Edward IV's reign (1476).[161] Her two knights of the body had had distinguished careers in France: Sir Edward Hull, whom she inherited from the king's household, as constable of Bordeaux, and Sir Andrew Ogard as a commander in Normandy under Bedford, York, and Somerset. But both men were dead by the autumn of 1454.[162] Margaret's councillors also included former duchy of Lancaster officials of great experience in the workings of English government, and like most magnates she employed attorneys in the various departments of state; her battery of lawyers – perhaps an unusually large number of these, headed by Robert Tanfield – helped to identify her interests, pursue them vigorously, and bring disputes to a successful conclusion.[163]

One of her most striking interventions in politics in these early years occurred in 1450, when the king faced the gravest challenge to his authority and his ministers since the reign began – certainly since Margaret had arrived in England. The offer of a general pardon to Cade's insurgents on 6 July had her full backing, and she may have urged it in order to reconcile the bulk of the population of the south-east and isolate the committed rebels. After all, her stern treatment of John Payn who, though one of Sir John Fastolf's men, had been forced to join the rebels against his will (so he later claimed), is the reaction to be expected from a spirited young princess of France encountering rebellion against royal authority. Payn

was arestyd by the Quenes commaundment in-to the Marchalsy [prison], and ther was in ryght grete durasse and fere of myn lyf, and was thretenyd to haue ben honged, drawe, and quarteryd; . . .[164]

Notes

1 Above, pp. 59-60. Cf. the report of the bishop of Lodi, Gerardo Landriani, who was received in audience by the king in 1432; he noted Henry's elegance of manner (Schofield, *AHC*, V [1973], 19).
2 PRO, E28/57/92; *CPR, 1429–36*, p. 601.

3 *Foedera*, V, i, 33; PRO, E28/57/97, 106, 115. On 5 August, Beaufort was responsible for ordering in council the implementation of an earlier decision (ibid., 115).

4 It seems to have been regarded as a desirable principle in England, though in practice neither Henry III nor Richard II entered into full possession of their prerogatives when they were 14 (Turner, *TRHS*, new ser., XVIII [1904], 280-1; F. M. Powicke, *King Henry III and the Lord Edward* [Oxford, 1966 ed.], pp. 43-4, 59; Tuck, op. cit., pp. 44-5; Dupuy, op. cit., pp. 6-7, 87-8).

5 *RP*, IV, 502; above, p. 205. Katherine of Valois died on 3 January 1437, though her influence on her son seems to have been slight after her marriage to Owen Tudor (above, p. 60).

6 PRO, E28/58; PSO1/5; Vickers, op. cit., pp. 256-7; Otway-Ruthven, *King's secretary*, pp. 14, 87-8, 96; Storey, *End of Lancaster*, p. 31. He soon acquired a wooden stamp carrying his initials in order to ease the burden on the royal hand; an example of its use with printer's ink is on display in the PRO Museum. Among the king's councillors, Gloucester continued to visit the king frequently between April 1437 and September 1438 (PRO, E101/408/24 f. 4r-40r).

7 PRO, E28/58/19; *PPC*, V, 5. The grant, which was to Gloucester and his male heirs, was not enrolled until 9 April 1437 (*DKR*, XLVIII [1887], 317).

8 *RP*, IV, 498-9; *CPR, 1436–41*, p. 74.

9 Wedgwood, *Biographies*, pp. 569-70; Somerville, op. cit., pp. 594, 596.

10 R. M. Jeffs, 'The later medieval sheriff and the royal household' (Oxford D Phil thesis, 1960), pp. 289-91, 322-3; Wedgwood, *Biographies*, pp. 322-3, 737; below, p. 339. Long before the mid-1440s, St Lo had intimate links with both Gloucester and Beaufort.

11 Somerville, op. cit., pp. 524, 525; Griffiths, *Principality of Wales*, p. 215.

12 Wedgwood, *Biographies*, pp. 516-62; above, p. 57.

13 Somerville, op. cit., pp. 420, 428; above, p. 58.

14 Above, p. 58; Friedrichs, thesis, pp. 27ff.

15 Roskell, *1422*, pp. 226-9; above, p. 58.

16 Above, pp. 94ff.

17 R. G. Davies, thesis, I, 407-11; III, iii-iv, ccx-ccxi; Emden, *Oxford*, I, 15-16; II, 1350; above, p. 103. Aiscough joined the council in June 1437.

18 Below, p. 232.

19 PRO, PSO1/5/230 and passim; *CPR, 1436–41*, p. 76 and passim.

20 PPC, V, 9-13.

21 ibid., 28-31.

22 PRO, PSO1/5/271; E101/408/24 f. 4ff.

23 Schofield, *AHC*, V (1973), 84ff. In November 1436 Eugenius was most accommodating in expediting the episcopal promotions noted above.

24 ibid., 92-8 (esp. pp. 93-4 for the description of Henry, taken from J. Haller, 'Piero da Monte, Ein Gelehrter und papstlicher Beamter des 15 Jahrhunderts, seine Briefsammlung', *Bibliothek des Deutschen Historischen Instituts*, XIX [1941], 43-5).

25 For this suspicion, see Schofield, *AHC*, V (1973), 98.

26 *RP*, IV, 496-7 (February 1437); Holmes, *EHR*, LXXVI (1961), 208-9 (29 October 1436), citing PRO, E28/58/40.

27 *RP*, IV, 499, 502; Holmes, *EHR*, LXXVI (1961), 210; above, p. 205.

28 Holmes, *EHR*, LXXVI (1961), 205-7. For the staplers' hostility to Beaufort, see ibid., 211; and for Londoners' view of Gloucester as 'a gracious and favourable lord to this city', Barron, thesis, pp. 426-7 (1439).

29 For the indenture of Sir Thomas Rempston, his successor, see PRO, E404/55/15.

30 Below, p. 446.

31 Holmes, *EHR*, LXXVI (1961), 214-16; Warner, op. cit., ll. 1150-64. Chichele, Suffolk, and Cromwell seem to have been the initial intended recipients.

32 *EHL*, pp. 52-6; C. L. Kingsford (ed.), *The first English life of King Henry the fifth* (Oxford, 1911), pp. xiv-xv, 6-7; above, p. 224. On 7 March 1437 Frulovisi, as a member of Gloucester's entourage, was made a denizen (*CPR, 1436–41*, p. 50; *Foedera*, V, i, 37).

33 Below, p. 301.

34 PRO, E28/57/96. Henry was still at Gloucester on 15 April 1435 but had returned to Windsor for the St George's day celebrations on the 23rd (PRO, E28/55/48; 57/96).

35 'Benet's Chron.', p. 184.

36 Christie, op. cit., p. 376, supplemented by PRO, E101/408/24 f. 10-14.

37 Somerville, op. cit., pp. 563, 560. Extensive rebuilding was undertaken at Nottingham castle during 1437–41, some of it perhaps as a result of the king's visit (*King's works*, II, 764). The furthest north he reached was Newstead priory, which Henry visited on a day-trip from Nottingham on 8 August.

38 There is a suggestive gap in the known itinerary of the archbishop between 15 July (when he was in London) and 21 October (when he was at Sheen) (Nigota, thesis, p. 553). Henry left Sheen on 15 July and had returned to Bishop's Langley by 14 September (PRO, E101/408/24 f. 10, 14).

39 ibid., f. 15-17*d*. The earls of Huntingdon and Northumberland accompanied Gloucester to see the king on 11 October; the former was named by Duke Humphrey early in 1440 as one of the lords who had been edged out of the king's confidence by Beaufort and Kemp, and both men had been the duke's pledges in 1435 (R. Arnold, *The Customs of London* [1811], p. 280; PRO, E28/55/34). During the king's absence, Gloucester had made the funeral arrangements for Queen Joan (PPC, V, 56; above, p. 62).

40 Below, p. 275.

41 Thus, on 25 November 1437, when the attractions of peace were being sung, the captive brothers, the count of Angoulême and the duke of Orléans, were allowed to meet provided Beaufort approved (*PPC*, V, 80; below, p. 445). See in general, Radford, op. cit., ch. XII.

42 Below, p. 449.

43 Arnold, *Customs of London*, pp. 279-86. Another, early Tudor version is in Hall, *Chronicles*, pp. 197-202, and a late-eighteenth-century copy (Bodl. Ashmole MS 856 f. 392ff) in Stevenson, II, ii, 440-51 (largely printed in modernized English in *EHD*, IV, 254-6). Although Hall's version is not taken from Arnold's printed text, it is probable that both derive from a common original, which ultimately may also be the source of the Ashmole version; no contemporary copy has survived. I am indebted to Miss P. M. Black for a preliminary analysis of the document. For more detailed consideration of Gloucester's charges, see below, p. 451.

44 BL, Cotton MS Cleopatra A XIII, with the treatise on f. 4*r*-135*v*, edited by J.-Ph. Genet in *Four English political tracts of the later middle ages* (Camden Soc., 4th ser., XVIII, 1977), pp. 40-173. The high quality of the MS and the portrait of Henry VI that was formerly on f. 3 suggest that it was a presentation volume for the king. For the date of composition, see ibid., pp. 41, 43-4, 47.

45 ibid., pp. xii-xvi, 170, 172.

46 Above, p. 235. For Henry's interest in Alfred, see below, p. 242.

47 The author's description of himself as *religiosus* (p. 168) may indicate that he was a member of a religious order; as the king's *orator* (p. 53), he may have been a royal chaplain, diplomat, or even feoffee; that he needed the assistance of a bachelor of theology (p. 55) suggests that he may not have been theologically trained himself. He also used the same image of Solomon's throne as Archbishop Stafford in his opening address to parliament on 25 January 1442. These qualifications, together with those of a household chaplain who was concerned with the king's educational foundations and sufficiently prominent to be aware of the political implications of the king's coming of age and of events in France, suggest a relatively small circle: (1) John Somerset was Henry VI's mentor and doctor, a graduate in arts and medicine, from 1418 master of the grammar school at Bury whose library owned a copy of Alfred's homily which the treatise's author read, MP in 1442, and chancellor of the exchequer from 1434 (Emden, *Oxford*, III, 1727-8; Wedgwood, *Biographies*, pp. 780-1). (2) Henry Sever was a king's chaplain by 1437, graduated in arts and law, first provost of Eton, and a great collector of books, including some used by the treatise's author (Emden, *Oxford*, III, 1672-3). (3) Thomas Bekyngton, the king's secretary by 1437, was a graduate in law, frequently an envoy abroad (including to the peace conferences of 1435 and 1439), and the author of a treatise on the English right to the French crown (ibid., I, 57-9; Judd, op. cit.). (4) William Lyndwood, a lawyer and hunter of heretics, was keeper of the privy seal in 1432–43, an envoy to Arras in 1435 and to the Scots in 1438 (Emden, *Oxford*, II, 1191-3). (5) Bishop Lowe of St Asaph, the only religious in this group (an Augustinian), was a theologian, the king's confessor from 1432 and his feoffee in 1441–42, an ambassador in 1441–42, collector of books, and the author of a collection of sermons preached before Henry VI (ibid., II, 1168-9). One can probably get no nearer.

48 Cf. too the advice (p. 120) to keep good records with above, p. 232.

49 Ramsay, op. cit., I, 419 n. 3; Stevenson, II, i, 225; above, p. 235. In March 1428, Henry was said to be 'ser goon and growen in persone, in wit and understandyng', but on this occasion parliament was anxious to find a reason for rejecting Humphrey of Gloucester's claim to be regent (above, p. 53).

50 Ellis, *Polydore Vergil*, p. 156; W. H. St John Hope, 'The discovery of the remains of King Henry VI in St George's Chapel, Windsor castle', *Archaeologia*, 2nd ser., XII (1911), 536-7.

51 B. P. Wolffe, 'The personal rule of Henry VI', in Chrimes, Ross, and Griffiths, op. cit., p. 32; Storey, *End of Lancaster*, pp. 34-5; McKenna, *JWCI*, XXVIII (1965), 145. Cf. the Sussex men in 1450 who misunderstood the significance of the royal sceptre and thought the king 'a naturall Fooll' for playing with 'a staff . . . with a bird on the ende' (R. F. Hunnisett, 'Treason by words', *Sussex notes and queries*, XIV [1954–57], 117-19).

52 C. H. Talbot and E. A. Hammond, *The medical practitioners of mediaeval England* (1965), passim. Apart from John Somerset (above, p. 54), William Godfrey, an apothecary, was paid in July 1448 for attending the king; by 1442–43 two physicians were in the king's employ, John Faceby and one of the Beauchamp doctors, John Arundel; by 1448–49 William Hatclyf, physician, had joined them (PRO, E403/771 m. 9; E404/64/199; E101/409/10; 410/4; Emden, *Oxford*, II, 663; I, 49-50).

53 A. P. Stanley, *Historical memorials of Westminster Abbey* (1868), pp. 509, 512, 513; Blacman, op. cit., pp. 38, 40; Stevenson, I, 111-12.

54 PRO, E28/58/13, 14; E404/61/159; 62/72; 63/104; Storey, *End of Lancaster*, pp. 31, 38; Stevenson, I, 105-6; Blacman, op. cit., p. xiv; Knox and Leslie, op. cit., pp. 7-15; above, p. 6. C. A. J. Armstrong's conclusion that Henry spoke in English at his coronation in Paris in 1431 because he could not understand French may well mistake political propaganda for lack of knowledge (above, p. 221).

55 'Benet's Chron.', pp. 189, 195. Cf. a version of the *Brut*, pp. 477-8, which ends in 1446,

56 Giles, p. 37; Kingsford, *EHR*, XXVII (1912), 462-82, 740-53, where the later Yorkist version of the chronicle is noted as being more directly critical of Henry (Ellis, *Hardyng's chronicle*, pp. 394, 410).

57 F. C. Hingeston (ed.), *John Capgrave, Liber de illustribus Henricis* (RS, 1858), pp. 134-5; *Reg. Whethamstede*, I, xvii, 248-61; II, xvi-xvii.

58 McFarlane, *Lancastrian kings*, pp. 23, 115-17, 233-8; idem, *Nobility*, pp. 243-4; Vickers, op. cit., ch. IX.

59 Ferguson, op. cit., p. 147 n. 2; R. Weiss, 'Henry VI and the library of All Souls College', *EHR*, LVII (1942), 102-5; A. B. Cobban, *The King's Hall within the University of Cambridge in the later middle ages* (Cambridge, 1969), pp. 256-7; PRO, E101/409/2 f. 25r, 29v; Blacman, op. cit., p. 26; *RP*, V, 375-6; *Bekynton Corr.*, I, 55, 118; Ramsay, op. cit., II, 50; Christie, op. cit., p. 129; below, p. 239.

60 *CPR, 1436–41*, pp. 295 (Clare Hall), 558 (New College); ibid., *1441–46*, pp. 141 (All Souls), 25 (Oriel); below, p. 302. For some melancholy verses in English, supposedly written by Henry VI after his capture in 1465 and later to be found in the possession of the Harrington family, one of whom had assisted in his capture, see *The Chronicle of the White Rose of York* (1845), pp. 14 n. 16, 108 n. 1.

61 PRO, E28/75/11-13.

62 The authoritative study of both is still R. Willis and J. W. Clark, *The architectural history of the University of Cambridge and of the colleges of Cambridge and Eton* (4 vols., Cambridge, 1886), I, ch. VII. See also, for Eton, *Royal Commission on Historical Monuments: Buckinghamshire*, I (1912), 142-53; D. Knoop and G. P. Jones, 'The building of Eton college, 1442–1460', *Trans. Quatuor Coronati Lodge*, XLVI (1933), 70-114; H. Maxwell-Lyte, *A history of Eton College, 1440–1875* (1875; revised ed. 1889), ch. I-III; *King's works*, I, 279-92. For King's, see ibid., pp. 269-78; *Hist. Mons. Comm., City of Cambridge* (1959), I, 98-136; *VCH, Cambs. and Isle of Ely*, III, 377-408. The reference to the Nevilles is more satisfactorily attributed to 1460 (when the duke of York, who is not mentioned, was in Ireland) than to May 1455, when York led the victorious lords at the battle of St Albans: ct. Willis and Clark, op. cit., I, 469-70, followed by *King's works*, I, 275.

63 Maxwell-Lyte, *Eton*, p. 5; PRO, E101/409/10; Willis and Clark, op. cit., I, 378-80 (with the quotations from Henry's 'will' in favour of Eton and King's, 1448); Emden, *Oxford*, III, 1672-3, 2001-3. For the influence of New College on the revised design of Eton's chapel, see Maxwell-Lyte, *Eton*, pp. 43-4; *King's works*, I, 284; and for the fraternal links between the four colleges of Henry VI and Wykeham, Maxwell-Lyte, *Eton*, pp. 22-3.

64 For Eton's accounts, see Knoop and Jones, *Trans. Quatuor Coronati Lodge*, XLVI (1933), 71-2, with an additional one noted in *King's works*, I, 280 n. 3. The account roll for 1449–50 is translated in D. Knoop and G. P. Jones, *The mediaeval mason* (3rd ed., Manchester, 1967), pp. 216-19. By contrast, only a fragmentary account (for 4 weeks in 1443) and a few other records survive for King's (*King's works*, I, 269, 274 n. 2).

65 Maxwell-Lyte, *Eton*, pp. 6-7, translated from the foundation charter of 11 October 1440, for which see *Bekynton Corr.*, I, 279-85; *RP*, V, 45-7; *CPR, 1436–41*, p. 556, and an excerpt in *EHD*, IV, 917-18.

66 Maxwell-Lyte, *Eton*, pp. 4, 7; *Bekynton Corr.*, II, 273. For the papal bulls of 28 January 1441 authorizing the college's establishment, see ibid., pp. 270-97 (from the Eton college archives).

67 PRO, E28/62/10; *CPR, 1436–41*, p. 295. In general, see N. Orme, *English schools in the middle ages* (1973), pp. 208ff.

68 ibid., pp. 194-201.

69 *CPR, 1436–41*, p. 455; see *Bekynton Corr.*, II, 274-8, for Alnwick's agreement to the foundation (29 September 1440). The king's agent who acted for the commissioners was William Lynde; perhaps a yeoman of the household in 1429–30, he was steward of the Savoy manor in London from 1439 and became clerk of works at Eton in 1441–43 (PRO, E404/46/302-3; Somerville, op. cit., p. 613; *King's works*, I, 279).

70 ibid., 284-7. For sustained expenditure on building during 1441–53, see Knoop and Jones, *Trans. Quatuor Coronati Lodge*, XLVI (1933), 78. For a plan of the college as proposed in 1448, see *King's works*, I, 286; Maxwell-Lyte, *Eton*, facing p. 45; *Hist. Mons. Comm., Bucks.*, I, facing p. 152.

71 Maxwell-Lyte, *Eton*, p. 44 and n. 1; *King's works*, I, 287. Roger Keys, master of works, was sent to Salisbury and Winchester in January 1449 to measure the cathedrals there. The 'avyse' is printed in Maxwell-Lyte, *Eton*, pp. 500-2; and Willis and Clark, op. cit., I, 366-7. See also A. H. R. Martindale, 'The early history of the choir of Eton College chapel', *Archaeologia*, CIII (1971), 179-98.

72 *King's works*, I, 271-2; *EHD*, IV, 901-3. Henry VI laid the stone of the new chapel at King's on 27 July 1446; for a plan, see *King's works*, I, 270, and for its statutes, *EHD*, IV, 895-901 (1443).

73 During 1446–48 King's Hall was also firmly subjected to the control of Eton and King's, with priority given to the teaching of those Etonians who did not win scholarships to King's College (Cobban, op. cit., pp. 188-93).

74 *RP*, V, 137, reproduced in modernized English in *EHD*, IV, 913-14; *CPR, 1441–47*, p. 432 (6 May 1446).

75 Seventy was the intended complement by June 1446, when Eton secured a monopoly within a radius of 10 miles of Windsor (PRO, C81/1/1439/, with the quotation as printed in *EHD*, IV, 918-19).

76 Blacman, op. cit., p. 34; Emden, *Oxford*, I, 194-5. For other indications of

Blacman's special knowledge of Eton, see Blacman, op. cit., pp. 32-5, 55.

77 *King's works*, I, 279 n. 7, 283. At various times, Chichele, John Stafford, Lowe, Aiscough, Moleyns, John Somerset, Bekyngton, John Carpenter, as well as Henry Sever and William Waynflete (among the clerics), and Hampton, Suffolk, and James Fiennes, laymen of the household, were responsible for overseeing various aspects of Eton's development (*CPR, 1436–41*, pp. 454, 471 [September 1440]; ibid., *1441–46*, p. 50 [March 1442]; *CFR, 1437–45*, p. 207 [January 1442]). Other members of the court interested themselves in the project (*CPR, 1446–52*, p. 21 [Lord and Lady Moleyns]; ibid., *1452–61*, p. 69 [Alice, duchess of Suffolk]).

78 *King's works*, I, 283-4. For Bekyngton's links with Eton, see Maxwell-Lyte, *Eton*, pp. 18-19. Bishop Carpenter (1444) and Bishop Waynflete (1447) were also consecrated there (ibid., pp. 32-3).

79 *King's works*, I, 281-2; Knoop and Jones, *Trans. Quatuor Coronati Lodge*, XLVI (1933), 79-80. For sea-coal brought by sea from Newcastle upon Tyne for making mortar, see *CPR, 1446–52*, p. 330 (June 1450).

80 Knoop and Jones, *Trans. Quatuor Coronati Lodge*, XLVI (1933), 101, 105; E. F. Jacob, 'The building of All Souls College, 1438–1443', in J. G. Edwards, V. H. Galbraith, and E. F. Jacob (eds.), *Historical essays in honour of James Tait* (Manchester, 1933), pp. 129, 133.

81 *RP*, V, 45 (1442); *CPR, 1436–41*, pp. 454, 471, 556. Gloucester was induced to hand over his properties from alien priory confiscations, in return for compensation, in November 1442 (PRO, E28/71/10). For his other endowments, see *CCR, 1441–47*, p. 162.

82 *CPR, 1441–46*, p. 50; *CFR, 1441–47*, p. 207 (wardship); *CPR, 1446–52*, p. 86 (wardship).

83 *RP*, V, 75-87 (1445); Maxwell-Lyte, *Eton*, pp. 30-1, 47; Somerville, op. cit., pp. 221 and n. 6. This perpetuated a shorter-term duchy endowment to Eton and King's in 1444. These duchy endowments may have been the occasion when a copy of Henry V's will was deposited at Eton; the terms of the will had assigned a large segment of the duchy's revenues for the payment of Henry IV's and Henry V's debts and the copy may have been part of the record that this had been done.

84 *RP*, V, 45-52 (1442), 75-87 (1445), 172 (1449-50). For the king's requests for papal indulgences for those visiting Eton on the feast of the Assumption of the Virgin Mary and contributing to its maintenance fund, see *Bekynton Corr.*, I, 217-20, 160-1, 231-2; II, 297-303, 306-9; Maxwell-Lyte, *Eton*, pp. 12-14, 23-5; A. K. McHardy, 'Some late-mediaeval Eton College wills', *JEccH*, XXVIII (1977), 387-95.

85 *RP*, V, 159, 183, 217, 220, 231, 250 (1449-53).

86 *CPR, 1436–41*, p. 521; *RP*, V, 87-102 (March 1446). Langton became the first master of works at King's (*King's works*, I, 272). The decision to found a college had probably been taken by 14 September 1440, when property was made over to the commissioners (*VCH, Cambs. and Ely*, III, 377; Cobban, op. cit., pp. 60-3). See also J. Saltmarsh, 'The founder's statutes of King's College, Cambridge', in J. C. Davies (ed.), *Studies presented to Sir H. Jenkinson* (1957), pp. 337-60.

87 Above, p. 247. For the king's well-known devotion to St Nicholas, see PRO, E28/70/12; *CPR, 1441–47*, p. 51 (1441–42).

88 *King's works*, I, 272-4; Willis and Clark, op. cit., I, 368-70, 378-80; *RP*, V,

132, 161, 172, 183, 217, 220, 231, 250. In March 1444, Henry VI also exempted the college from paying fines for its letters patent (*PPC*, VI, 29). The quotation from the statutes of King's (1443) is taken from *EHD*, IV, 895. Bishop Waynflete, who had general supervision of the construction of King's from 1448, exemplified the links between Henry VI's foundations and those of Wykeham (above, p. 243 ; *King's works*, I, 272).

89 Cobban, op. cit., p. 193; PRO, E159/220, *adhuc communia, recorda*, E, m. 6; E101/409/12 f. 85r.

90 *EHL*, pp. 57-8; Emden, *Oxford*, III, 1727-8; Wedgwood, *Biographies*, pp. 780-1; Talbot and Hammond, op. cit., pp. 62, 182.

91 *Bekynton Corr.*, I, 137; Betcherman, *Speculum*, XLI (1966), 413-18; below, pp. 346-7.

92 *CCR, 1435–41*, pp. 181, 385; PRO, E101/409/9 f. 32r-33r; J. T. Rosenthal, *The purchase of paradise* (1972), ch. III. For Henry V's foundation of Syon, which seems to have been contemplated even by his father, and the Charterhouse at Sheen, see Knowles, op. cit., II, 175-82. For Henry VI's gift of a bible to the London Charterhouse, see Bodl. MS 277; and his relief of the Carthusians from taxes in 1439, PRO, E28/60/53.

93 H. E. Salter (ed.), *Registrum cancellarii Oxon.*, I (Oxford, 1930), 101; Capgrave, op. cit., p. 131; Wolffe, 'Personal rule', p. 38; above, pp. 3ff.

94 Bellamy, *Crime and public order*, pp. 193-7; PRO, SC8/43/184; Blacman, op. cit., p. 39. Many examples of Henry's imprudent pardons could be cited (e.g., *PPC*, V, 88; Storey, *End of Lancaster*, p. 34 and n. 210-16; above, p. 242). For Henry IV's and Henry V's invocation of religious motives in pardoning, see *Foedera*, IV, i, 113; ii, 18; iii, 7-8, 16, 38; for the tearful thief, *CPR, 1436–41*, p. 275.

95 PRO, E404/55/254; 66/215; 'Benet's Chron.', p. 202; A. R. Myers, *The Household of Edward IV* (Manchester, 1959), pp. 5-10, 63-75; below, p. 319. Cf. his compassion to an old sick woman who had supported 13 poor men and women for many years and therefore merited an exemption from taxation and other burdens in 1445 (*CPR, 1441–47*, p. 330).

96 Blacman, op. cit., pp. 29-31; H. C. Maxwell-Lyte (ed.), *Register of Bishop Bekynton* (Soms. Record Soc., XLIX, L, 1934–35), I, 116-17; R. S. Thomas, thesis, pp. 28-9, 37, 251-3.

97 Blacman, op. cit., p. 35.

98 *King's works*, II, 921.

99 PRO, E403/730 m. 7 (December 1437), 12 (February 1438); 786 m. 9 (1449–50). His gaming even cost the king money!

100 PRO, E101/409/9 f. 37r; 11 f. 37r; 16 f. 33r; Stevenson, I, 103, 157. For purchases of jewels from Bruges, see PRO, E403/771 m. 6 (1448).

101 Above, p. 52; *RP*, V, 102, 128; 'Benet's Chron.', p. 203; Giles, p. 43; 'Gregory's Chron.', pp. 191, 196; *Three Chrons.*, p. 69. For the journey to Monmouth, see PRO, E101/410/9.

102 Above, p. 56; J. D. Milner, 'The order of the garter in the reign of Henry VI, 1422–1461' (Manchester MA thesis, 1972), pp. 9-11, 122-38. The ceremony at Windsor seems to have lost some of its formality and regularity after 1445 (ibid., pp. 47-8, 66-7).

103 *CPR, 1441–47*, p. 362 (a grant of £8 *per annum* to the prior in return for past kindnesses); below, pp. 329ff.

104 Below, pp. 282ff, 364ff.

105 Below, p. 193; Vale, *Gascony*, pp. 127-9; E. M. Burney, 'The English rule

of Normandy, 1435–50' (Oxford BLitt thesis, 1958), pp. 233-4; PRO, SC8/57/71; *DKR*, XLVIII (1887), 347.

106 C. T. Allmand, 'The Anglo-French negotiations, 1439', *BIHR*, XL (1967), 3-4, 7, 9, 25-6; N. H. Nicolas, *A Journal by one of the suite of Thomas Beckington*, . . . (1828), pp. 6-7, 10, 95-6; above, p. 236.

107 Below, pp. 490ff.

108 Below, p. 495; *RP*, V, 102, 182-3.

109 Below, p. 682; *Foedera*, V, i, 176-7.

110 Below, pp. 510ff. Gilles first came to England in 1432 and was generously patronized by the king thereafter (above, p. 207; PRO, E404/48/333; 60/105; A. Bourdeaut, 'Gilles de Bretagne entre la France et l'Angleterre', *Mémoires de la société d'histoire et d'archéologie de Bretagne*, I (1920), 57ff).

111 Below, p. 280; R. A. Griffiths, 'The trial of Eleanor Cobham: an episode in the fall of Duke Humphrey of Gloucester', *BJRL*, LI (1968–69), 387, 389, 391-2, 395, 397-8; *Brut*, pp. 483-4.

112 'Benet's Chron.', p. 192; Giles, p. 33; 'Gregory's Chron.', pp. 187-8; below, p. 496.

113 Below, p. 685; 'Benet's Chron.', pp. 204-5; *Brut*, pp. 517-20; Giles, p. 42; R. A. Griffiths, 'Duke Richard of York's intentions in 1450 and the origins of the Wars of the Roses', *JMH*, I (1975), 191-3; 'Gregory's Chron.', p. 197; *Three Chrons.*, p. 68.

114 Christie, op. cit., p. 109; McFarlane, *Nobility*, p. 284; Wolffe, 'Personal rule', p. 44.

115 Quoted by M. M. Postan in *English trade*, pp. 376-7 n. 60. Winter claimed to have influential connections in the English government and may, therefore, have been unusually well informed as an observer (ibid., pp. 129, 377 n. 63).

116 M. Baudier, *An history of the memorable and extraordinary calamities of Margaret of Anjou, queen of England* (1737) translated from a seventeenth-century French MS (BN, Ancien St. Germain Fr. 16940) that was never published; A. F. Prévost d'Exiles, *Histoire de Marguérite d'Anjou, reine d'Angleterre* (Amsterdam, 1740), translated as *The history of Margaret of Anjou, queen of England* (2 vols., 1755).

117 R. C. Guilbert de Pixérécourt, *Marguérite d'Anjou – mélodrame historique en trois actes, en prose* (2nd ed., Paris, 1810), on which was based F. Romani, *Margerita d'Anjou – mélodrame* (first performed in Milan in 1820 and 1826, and in England in 1828); L. Lallement, *Une héroine oubliée des biographes lorrains: Marguérite d'Anjou–Lorraine, reine d'Angleterre* (Nancy, 1855). And in 1857 at Tours, where Margaret was betrothed to Henry VI in 1444, J. T. E. Roy published his *Histoire de Marguérite d'Anjou*. In similar vein is the account in Strickland, op. cit. (1st ed. 1840–48), III.

118 R. Brooke, *On the life and character of Margaret of Anjou* (Liverpool, 1859); M. A. Hookham, *Life and times of Margaret of Anjou* (2 vols., 1872); K. Schmidt, *Margareta von Anjou vor und bei Shakespeare* (Berlin, 1906).

119 T. F. Tout in *DNB*, XXXVI (1893), 138-48; J. Petithuguenin, *La vie tragique de Marguérite d'Anjou* (Paris, 1928); P. Erlanger, *Marguérite d'Anjou et la guerre des deux roses* (Paris, 1961), translated as *Margaret of Anjou,*

queen of England (1970); J. Haswell, *The ardent queen: Margaret of Anjou and the Lancastrian heritage* (1976).

120 J. J. Bagley, *Margaret of Anjou, queen of England* ([1948]).

121 Stevenson, II, ii, 639-40; below, p. 495.

122 Below, p. 487. Margaret's surviving household account for 1452–53 notes very few French servants: A. R. Myers, 'The household of Queen Margaret of Anjou, 1452–3', *BJRL*, XL (1957–58), 404-5.

123 Below, p. 521. Charles VII was still in communication with her as late as 3 June 1449, though his purpose is unknown: G. du Fresne de Beaucourt, *Histoire de Charles VII* (6 vols., Paris, 1881–91), IV, 457.

124 PRO, KB9/256/12; cf. Storey, *End of Lancaster*, p. 46. Indications of her involvement in Gloucester's death are no earlier in origin than the Tudor period: Ellis, *Polydore Vergil*, pp. 71-2.

125 Below, p. 358.

126 Storey, *End of Lancaster*, p. 40, citing PRO, KB9/260/40a (the accusation of an approver); below, p. 488.

127 *HMC*, V (1876), 255, from the dean and chapter of Canterbury Archives, M. 239 (1448).

128 Blacman, op. cit., pp. 7, 29; above, p. 4.

129 PRO, E403/767 m. 11 (July 1447). For Suffolk's supposed poem in Margaret's honour, 'Ryght goodly flour to whom I owe seruyse', see H. N. MacCracken, 'An English friend of Charles of Orléans', *PMLAA*, XXVI (1911), 168-71 (from Bodl. MS 3896 [formerly Fairfax MS 16]). But there is no contemporary warrant for the Tudor suggestion, incorporated in *Henry VI*, Part II, act III, scene 2, that Margaret and Suffolk were lovers: C. L. Kingsford, *Prejudice and promise in fifteenth-century England* (Oxford, 1925), pp. 174-5.

130 Myers, *BJRL*, XL (1957–58), 417.

131 Below, p. 308. See also (below, p. 645) the attacks on Bishop Lyhert of Norwich, who was her confessor from 1445: PRO, E101/409/13,15,18 (1445–48).

132 Above, p. 487; Myers, *BJRL*, XL (1957–58), passim; idem, 'The jewels of Queen Margaret of Anjou', *BJRL*, XLII (1959), 115-31 (with information supplied in the notes to both articles). Compare Crawford, in Griffiths, *Patronage, the crown and the provinces*, ch. 2.

133 These calculations are based on the queen's contributions to the king's household budget in 1446–53: PRO, E101/409/16,20; 410/6,9, and, for 1453, Myers, *BJRL*, XL (1957–58), 429-30. For the Norwich visit, see *PL*, I, 249.

134 'Benet's Chron.', pp. 205, 208; PRO, E101/410/6 (St George's day, 1451, at Windsor castle); 409/16 f. 30; Myers, *BJRL*, XL (1957–58), 422. For Margaret's extensive rebuilding at Greenwich, Gloucester's former residence, including accommodation for the king, see *King's works*, II, 949.

135 The standard history of the college is W. G. Searle, *History of the Queen's College of Saint Margaret and Saint Bernard in the University of Cambridge, 1446–1560* (Cambridge, 1867), with the quotation on pp. 15-16. The charter of 30 March 1448 granting the college to Margaret is noted in *CPR, 1446–52*, p. 143, and printed in Searle, op. cit., pp. 18-26.

136 ibid., pp. 21, 42-3; Christie, op. cit., pp. 382-5; *King's works*, I, 269-77. Among the benefactors of Queen's were Wenlock and Viscount Beaumont, Margaret's chief steward (Searle, op. cit., pp. 37-8, 62; below, p. 262).

137 Myers, *BJRL*, XL (1957–58), 405-11, for lists of her esquires, valets, grooms, and pages.

138 ibid., pp. 426-7. For his accounts as clerk of the jewels, see Myers, *BJRL*, XLII (1959), 113-31, where Margaret's role at court is graphically illustrated by the range of her gifts each New Year's Day.

139 idem, ibid., XL (1957–58), 58; Wedgwood, *Biographies*, pp. 840-1. For her secretary, Nicholas Caraunt, see below.

140 Copies of these letters appear in the late-fifteenth-century commonplace-book which is said to have belonged to John Edwards of Chirk, *temp.* Henry VII, and then passed into the Puleston family of Flints.; it is now BL, Add. MS 46,846. All but seven of the letters are in C. Munro, *Letters of Queen Margaret of Anjou* (Camden soc., LXXXVI, 1863). Most of the 38 or so that have been dated by Mr J. G. Reid (to whom I am indebted for his comments on the letters) can be assigned to the period before 1453. For further comment on the MS, see Otway-Ruthven, *King's secretary*, pp. 119-20, who suggests that it is based on a compilation made by George Ashby, Margaret's clerk of the signet (for whom see below, n. 143).

141 C. Munro, op. cit., pp. 93-4. For a discussion of the dispute, see Maxwell-Lyte, *Reg. Bek.*, II, xliv-xlvii; and for Caraunt, Emden, *Oxford*, I, 353. He was Margaret's secretary by 1445 and still in 1458 (PRO, E101/409/13). The queen to whom John Lydgate's 'Life of Our Lady' (Yale Univ. Lib. MS 281) was presented by a member of the Caraunt family in the fifteenth century may well have been Margaret.

142 Emden, *Oxford*, II, 856-7; Myers, *BJRL*, XLII (1959), 125 n. 7, 129. Hals's patronage, too, came to an end with the fall of Henry VI, though he re-emerged to become keeper of the privy seal at the readeption in 1470. For Margaret's later efforts in his behalf, see *EHD*, IV, 280.

143 *CPR, 1441–46*, pp. 433, 436, 437, 450. For Wenlock, see above; and for Ashby, Otway-Ruthven, *King's secretary*, pp. 135, 139, 142, 158, 185, and Wedgwood, *Biographies*, pp. 21-2. For other examples of the use of the Beauchamp inheritance, see *CPR, 1441–46*, pp. 427, 433.

144 C.Munro, op. cit., pp. 96-8. The suit was unsuccessful. For Burneby, see Myers, *BJRL*, XLII (1959), 127. Her other matrimonial projects are in ibid., XL(1957–58), 426 (a large gift of £200 to one of her ladies, the Burgundian Osan Herman, on the occasion of her marriage in 1454); C. Munro, op. cit., pp. 89-90, 125, 152-4; *PL*, I, 249 (1453).

145 For failures, see above n. 144; C. Munro, op. cit., pp. 125, 138-9, 152-4.

146 ibid., pp. 99, 146-7; see also ibid., pp. 122-3, 126, 127-8, 154. For her efforts to protect her tenants and servants when they went to law, see *CPR, 1446–52*, p. 328; C. Munro, op. cit., pp. 122-3, 154.

147 The best study of Margaret's resources is Myers, *BJRL*, XL (1957–58), 79-99, as an introduction to the account for 1452–53 of William Cotton, Margaret's receiver-general since 1446 (PRO, DL28/5/8). Like many of the queen's estate and financial officials, Cotton was a duchy of Lancaster officer and a member of the king's household, in which he was keeper of the great wardrobe from 1450 to 1453 (below, p. 306; Somerville, op. cit., p. 399). For the assignment of dower in parliament on 19 March 1446, see *RP*, V, 118-20. Annuities already charged on the duchy estates totalled £325 and this sum was made up by cash assignments to the queen.

148 Tutbury alone was worth £928 a year. Other lesser duchy properties were

assigned to her in the southern counties (Somerville, op. cit., p. 340; Myers, *BJRL*, XL [1957–58], 82 and n. 5).

149 Above, n. 147; Somerville, op. cit., pp. 208-9, 340.

150 It was fully paid in 1452–53 (Myers, *BJRL*, XL[1957–58], 110), but ct. Somerville, op. cit., p. 209.

151 Myers, *BJRL*, XL (1957–58), 83-4. During the four years 1446–49, the whole of the exchequer payment was assigned to Margaret, but the tallies on which it was payable were often very unreliable: for example, 87 per cent of £1,525 assigned her in November–December 1446 had to be reassigned in January 1449 (PRO, E403/762-75).

152 *CPR, 1441–46*, pp. 436, 450; above, p. 363.

153 *RP*, V, 133; *CPR, 1446–52*, pp. 56, 260; *CCR, 1441–47*, p. 13. After Gloucester's death she also acquired the reversion of the marcher lordship of Pembroke after a prior grant to Suffolk had expired; but she may not have enjoyed possession after Suffolk's death because Lord Beauchamp was given the lands of the earldom on 31 May 1450, only to have them resumed in July 1451. By the end of 1452 arrangements were being made to transfer Pembroke to Jasper Tudor. Margaret's rights, however, were fully acknowledged and alternative sources of income were promised her. See *RP*, V, 260-1; R. S. Thomas, thesis, pp. 32-3, 49; B. P. Wolffe, *The Royal demesne in English history* (1971), pp. 100, 137, 260. Myers, *BJRL*, XL (1957–58), 83, 104, is not entirely reliable on this matter.

154 *RP*, V, 149; *CPR, 1446–52*, p. 171.

155 ibid., p. 172. For the tallies, see above n. 151. In April 1449, she surrendered £3,658-worth of uncashed tallies at the exchequer and received replacements chargeable on the Southampton customs, which she now had a better chance of collecting (*CPR, 1446–52*, p. 267).

156 *RP*, V, 164, 174.

157 ibid., 183, 217. For receipt of resumed revenues in July 1451, including the earldom of Pembroke and the lordship of Haverford, see *CCR, 1447–54*, p. 222.

158 *RP*, V, 229, 258; Myers, *BJRL*, XL (1957–58), 84. Special licences to allow export from Southampton free of customs were annulled – unless they were held by Genoese merchants.

159 *RP*, V, 260; *CCR, 1447–54*, p. 390.

160 Myers, *BJRL*, XL (1957–58), 85-6, 93 (with the quotation on 86), who stresses the tenacity of the queen and her officials in pursuing her right to 'queen's gold', a proportion (one-tenth) of fines paid voluntarily to the king. For a suit in the exchequer of pleas against the receiver-general of the duchy of Cornwall in 1450, presumably for non-payment of her dower grant, see PRO, Index 9995(i) (a reference I owe to Mr J. G. Reid).

161 Myers, *BJRL*, XL (1957–58), 92-3; Reeves, *Midland Hist.*, III (1974–75), 11-29; Emden, *Cambridge*, pp. 73, 78-9. Lawrence's early career had been advanced by William. For Sir John Wenlock, valet of the queen's chamber by 1445 and her chamberlain by 1448, see PRO, E101/409/13; Myers, *BJRL*, XL (1957–58), 402 n. 5. He had been a diplomat in France in the early 1440s (PRO, E404/57/303; 60/226; below, p. 484).

162 Myers, *BJRL*, XL (1957–58), 402-3; Wedgwood, *Biographies*, pp. 481-2, 644-5. Ogard seems to have left York's service after returning from Normandy in 1450; perhaps he found the criticisms of those who had lost the duchy to Charles VII a severe embarrassment and sought the umbrella

of Margaret's protection (PRO, SC8/14,448; A. E. Marshall 'The role of English war captains in England and Normandy, 1436–1461' [Wales MA thesis, 1975], p. 155; *CPR 1446–52*, p. 537).

163 Myers, *BJRL*, XL (1957–58), 94-5; Somerville, op. cit., passim; above, p. 258.

164 *CPR, 1446–52*, p. 338; *PL*, II, 315; below, p. 640.

12 King Henry and his Council

The king's declaration of 1437

When Henry VI began to take an active part in ruling, his relations with his councillors perceptibly changed and led to a modification of the council's membership and practical powers. For one thing, Henry often attended council meetings himself immediately after 1437.[1] Secondly, a greater flexibility became evident in the way in which he consulted his advisers, not all of whom were assembled in the council chamber, for in the last resort a king could confer with whomsoever he chose.[2] There was, too, a readiness on the part of the young king to arrange larger meetings of councillors and others (i.e., great councils) when it was desirable to consult more widely on important or urgent questions of the day.[3] Thus, after Henry formally announced his intention of playing a central part in government in November 1437, the parameters within which the council had functioned since 1422 lost some of their validity as the councillors tried to adapt themselves to new circumstances.

The return to normalcy under an adult monarch was signalled by Henry himself at a great council which lasted for three days, from 12 to 14 November 1437. At this meeting, the powers of the council were reviewed and its relationship with the king redefined.[4] With these purposes in mind, on 12 November a recent (perhaps the most recent) statement of the usual relationship between an adult king and his council was read; it was dated 1406 and two of the councillors present, Cardinal Beaufort and Lord Tiptoft (who had been speaker of the commons in 1406), would have been able to recall its endorsement by Henry IV.[5] This declaration of the king's need for advice and of the general responsibilities which councillors undertook was suited to the circumstances of 1437; but its more detailed clauses, which had then been publicized in parliament, had placed certain restrictions on Henry IV's freedom of action and these were accordingly omitted in 1437 as inappropriate.[6] On the latter occasion, England was not ruled by a king whose recent activities and methods had alarmed some of his subjects and his parliament, but by a king who, after a long minority, needed to be integrated in the practicalities of government. Although Henry VI had shown a desire to take personal initiatives for about a year before November 1437, these had hardly given cause for concern among his councillors, especially since the king could reasonably be expected to acquire more experience and wisdom as the years passed. Rather than reflect a serious apprehension at the king's approaching manhood and a determination by the council to place him under constraints similar to those of 1406, the declaration of 1437 was simply an announcement that Henry VI would take a prominent part in affairs henceforward, though without jettisoning the councillors who had served him during his youth.

At this point, Henry was barely sixteen years old, and younger than any other king of England since the Norman conquest in bringing his minority formally to an end. It is unlikely, therefore, that the council should itself have proposed such a major constitutional and political change. Regardless of whether Henry or his closest advisers formulated the statement, there can be little doubt that an adjustment was intended in the future role of both Henry and his council. In terms of personnel, the council might be left unchanged for the time being – something that was advisable in the interests of continuity, experience, and the peaceful acceptance of the proposed changes – but its specific, practical powers were decisively readjusted.

Henry, like his grandfather before him, expressed his wish in 1437 for wise counsel to help him shoulder the heavy burden of ruling, and he declared his awareness of his responsibility to maintain the crown's rights and prerogatives, to collect and increase its revenue so that the royal estate could be maintained, and to ensure that the law was enforced and justice offered to all. Such a general justification for the appointment of councillors was not new. In 1437 it was the prelude to the formal nomination of a 'prive Counseill' which was charged with upholding the laws of England, and with discussing and deciding a whole range of state problems. The existing councillors, together with a few additions, were duly sworn and their duties in relation to the king carefully defined. In return, the lay councillors at least were assured of an appropriate fee, which Henry, with characteristic generosity, was prepared to grant for life – and to continue paying even if a councillor were too ill to offer advice.[7] Yet, the council's powers were more circumscribed than they had been during the minority. Pardons were the king's grace to grant, collations to benefices his to bestow, royal offices his to fill, and other areas within the king's own bounty, favour, or goodwill were specifically reserved to him.[8] If he wished to take a decision on them alone, or seek the advice of his friends in the household or of his councillors, that was his prerogative. But the council could not issue such pardons or appointments uninvited – as it made clear in November 1441, when the appointment of the seneschal of the Landes (Gascony) came before it.[9] More significantly, questions 'of grete weght and charge' that were 'moved among' the councillors should be decided in future only with the advice of the king, whereas other, less significant questions 'moved among hem' should be referred to him if the councillors were seriously divided in their opinion or unable to come to a conclusion. Thus, the declaration of 1437 adjusted the spring of decision-making – as the handling of a petition from the duke of York demonstrates. The question of honouring unpaid debts to the duke worth 1,150 marks was too weighty a matter for the council alone to decide on 10 February 1438, especially in view of the government's lack of ready cash; the decision was left to the king who, in consultation with the chancellor and the earl of Suffolk, decided on 23 February to give the duke certain crown jewels as security.[10]

Henry was personally assuming powers which had been delegated to his council during the minority, though the councillors' continued role was assured, especially in routine matters which would normally be referred to (or 'moved among') them. In this respect, it is worth noting that the crucial phrase 'of grete weght and charge' was a vague one: whereas it indicated the king's intention to intervene personally on important matters, English government need not be hamstrung if the king declined or failed to exercise his powers conscientiously. This, then, was no robust return to personal rule, wilfully thrusting aside the ministrations of skilled and experienced counsellors.[11] Even less can it be regarded as an attempt by the council to preserve the authority it had enjoyed since 1422 by encircling the king with restrictions devised thirty years before.[12] Rather did Henry's declaration in 1437 herald the re-establishment, after fifteen years of conciliar government, of traditional royal rule in which the king's councillors had an acknowledged part. Perhaps its only surprising feature was that it was published so soon in the young king's life.

An accurate appreciation of the consequences of the king's assumption of full powers in 1436–37 has been hindered, rather than advanced, by the discussions of historians over the past century or so, and in particular by some misunderstandings about the purport of the royal and conciliar pronouncements made during the years immediately following Henry's coming of age. Perhaps the most serious misconception is the belief that once the king's minority had ended – an eventuality that was, of course, expected and inevitable – a conflict took place between the king and his council over where power in the realm lay; and that this conflict revolved around the authority attributed, on the one hand, to the privy seal, whose keeper was a regular member of the council, and, on the other, to the royal sign manual and signet, which was in the custody of Henry's secretary. This belief was based on a fundamental misunderstanding of the relationship between king and council, and of the authority even of a teenage monarch in the fifteenth century. Henry's declaration marked a return to normality in government under an adult king, rather than a victory of a king over his councillors. The council did not become once again 'a mere instrument in the hands of the king or the court', as William Stubbs would have it; nor did it suffer a 'reverse', as T. F. T. Plucknett maintained.[13] Equally mistaken have been the verdicts of R. L. Storey and B. Wilkinson (lately confirmed by A. L. Brown), whereby constraints were 'forced on the king' by his own councillors.[14] If unmodified, the re-use in 1437 of the conciliar ordinances of 1406 would probably have represented an attempt to 'curb his [i.e., Henry VI's] powers', but these ordinances were, in fact, altered in several crucial respects. Careful comparison has led R. Virgoe and B.P. Wolffe to conclude that in 1437 the council's role 'reverted to the active but necessarily subordinate role that it had played under the first two Lancastrian kings', with the councillors acknowledging that 'the young king was bound to assume responsibility for the government of the realm'.[15] Long ago, in 1913, J. F. Baldwin had seen the events of 1437 as 'the assertion of the complete independence of the Crown'.[16] This was too vigorous and uncompromising a judgement, but it was on right lines from which historians have since diverted us.

The councillors, 1437–45

Most of the councillors who were formally nominated by Henry VI in November 1437 had been his advisers for some time past. Gloucester, Beaufort, and the archbishops of Canterbury and York were stalwarts of Lancastrian rule, as also were the three officers of state appointed in 1432–33: the chancellor, Bishop Stafford, who remained in office until 1450; William Lyndwood, the keeper of the privy seal, and Lord Cromwell, the treasurer, both of whom served until 1443. To this loyal group may be added the only other bishop among the nominated councillors, William Alnwick of Lincoln, who had a similar record of royal service to commend him. Laymen were more numerous: namely, the earls of Stafford, Huntingdon, Northumberland, and Suffolk, Lords Hungerford and Tiptoft, and Sir William Philip, the chamberlain of the king's household who became Lord Bardolf at about this time. All were well versed in conciliar business. The small number of additions in 1437 gave an indication of how important the personality of the king and the influence of his household were likely to be in the future. The newcomers were the bishop of St David's, Thomas Rudbourne, a companion of Henry V and a royal chaplain who had been at Arras in 1435; the earl of Salisbury, a nephew of Cardinal Beaufort newly returned from France; Robert Rolleston, who had been keeper of the king's wardrobe since the beginning of the reign; and another household official, Sir John Stourton.[17] In the months that followed, Henry kept his promise to give life-fees to the lay councillors and on a traditional scale that took account of their status: £40 *per annum* for a knight, 100 marks for a baron, and £100 for an earl.[18] The bishops were to receive no salary at all, and this may partly explain their poor attendance at council meetings. Yet Henry, who could rarely resist a suppliant, was prepared to review an individual's wages in the light of special circumstances and as a result might vary the basic scale.[19]

These were the men who were expected to advise the king at the opening of his personal rule. Compared with the council of the minority, they were a body of advisers that was somewhat unbalanced, and in terms of attendance it became even more so. The ecclesiastical element was noticeably smaller than at any time since 1422. The failure to offer the bishops a salary may have had something to do with this; whatever the reason, the consequences were unfortunate. In the first place, the influence of the best educated and most literate section of the community declined, and lay considerations inevitably came to bulk larger in the council's deliberations. Secondly, the moderating influence of a relatively disinterested group in discussions involving family or dynastic interests and the royal patronage was weakened. On a purely religious and ecclesiastical level, the views of Beaufort and Kemp (Chichele rarely attended by 1439) were likely to go virtually unchallenged. Finally, bishops had generally found in the past that they could attend the council more regularly than lay lords; now they were no longer summoned in such number and consequently the size of council meetings shrank.

Other changes in council membership took place within the next two years. In preparation for the peace conference at Gravelines in the summer of 1439, to which several prominent councillors travelled, some additions were made to the council during May, though none of the new appointees became a particularly regular attender. Lord Fanhope, who had married Henry IV's sister and was therefore the young king's great-uncle by marriage, was an old man; but he had valuable military experience behind him and he knew northern France well. He was joined by John, Lord Beaumont, a man half Fanhope's age who was married to the daughter of another councillor, Lord Bardolf; he had been in France with the king in 1430 and was probably occupied at court thereafter. Prominently linked with the household was the king's confessor, Bishop William Aiscough of Salisbury, who was the only prelate among the new councillors summoned in May 1439.[20] This year also saw Gloucester's influence virtually set at nought. His political eclipse is reflected in his infrequent attendance at council meetings (unless they were large assemblies from which it was impossible to exclude him as heir to the throne), in the direction taken by English policy towards France, and in the pattern of royal patronage. Archbishop Chichele was aged (he was by now in his late seventies) and feeble (he needed the support of a stick to walk), and in any case he shared Gloucester's profound distaste for the Beaufort clique that was gradually encircling and increasingly dominating the king.[21]

This enlargement of the council took place not long before Beaufort journeyed to Calais for the peace conference; with him went other royal councillors, Archbishop Kemp, Bishop Rudbourne, the earl of Stafford, Lord Hungerford, and Sir John Stourton. The new recruits did nothing to redress the balance between ecclesiastic and lay; if anything, they tipped the scales yet further and strengthened the links between the king's household and the council. It is true that Gloucester was able to take advantage of his colleagues' absence (especially Beaufort's) to stiffen momentarily the young king's resolve to resist hasty concessions to the French, and also to insinuate his ally, Lord Scrope, back on to the council (in July 1439). Like Fanhope, Scrope had had a long career as a soldier and his views would command respect, if not agreement, in the peace discussions that were taking place. Yet in the nature of things, Gloucester's opportunity was short-lived, and by the end of the year he was well nigh powerless.[22]

The growing dominance of Cardinal Beaufort during 1439 (with the exception of the few months spent at the peace conference) is echoed in the cryptic comments appended to a number of the bills and petitions which the king and his council dealt with during the second half of the year. Whether he was on his barge, or at his house in Southwark, or merely by slipping a quiet word to the clerk of the council, Adam Moleyns, Beaufort was able to influence the king's decisions and even secure grants in his own favour.[23]

During the next few years, the links between council and household became stronger, though the council meetings themselves, released as they were from the detailed regulations of the minority, were not always well attended.[24] No quorum seems to have been acknowledged, and in any case the council suffered some serious losses in personnel. Although in January 1441 Sir Ralph Botiller began to be summoned (he had been chief butler of the household since 1435, a knight of the garter by April 1440, and would shortly become Henry VI's chamberlain),[25] within a further year two others had died. In June 1441 Lord Bardolf, a stalwart of both household and council, expired, and early in 1442 he was followed by Bishop Rudbourne. Both Gloucester and Chichele were totally ineffective by this stage, and the scandal of the duchess of Gloucester's trial in the summer of 1441, in which several councillors took part, further damaged her husband's reputation.[26] Age, spiritual calls, or a plain reluctance to serve any longer persuaded Bishops Alnwick and Aiscough to withdraw from the council: on 24 April 1442, Alnwick was allowed to absent himself from councils and parliaments for reasons that hint at weariness and a wish to devote his remaining energies to spiritual matters (though he can hardly have been fifty years of age); on 11 July 1443, a similar privilege was conceded to Aiscough, who was a little younger.[27]

Of the lay councillors, Tiptoft died early in 1443 and Hungerford, now an old man of more than seventy, withdrew increasingly from active service after the summer of 1442. At the same time, Huntingdon and Stafford were less in the forefront of politics than they had been, so that the councillors who had a regular part to play formed quite a small coterie. William de la Pole, earl of Suffolk, who attended the council with growing regularity from early in 1441, was fast becoming the most constant and influential of the king's advisers, and he moved in a circle that inherited many of Beaufort's attitudes. Moreover, a significant number of those who were still active councillors could be identified with the royal household, of which Suffolk was steward and Sir Ralph Botiller chamberlain. In 1443 the council and the officers of state were virtually recast to underscore these developments. By such means, control of the government passed decisively into the hands of a group that was equally powerful in council, household, and departments of state, and the group included several kinsmen and protégés of Cardinal Beaufort.

Archbishop Chichele died at last on 12 April 1443 at Lambeth at the grand age of eighty-one; he was succeeded at Canterbury on 25 June by the chancellor, Bishop Stafford, who retained custody of the great seal. Then, on 7 July, Sir Ralph Botiller (Lord Sudeley since 1441) replaced Cromwell as treasurer of England; a fortnight later, the king's secretary, Thomas Bekyngton, became keeper of the privy seal. Although the latter had begun his career in Gloucester's service, he was also a confidant of the young king. The career of another clerk, Adam Moleyns, had been different: clerk of the council since 1436, and a regular observer and recorder of its discussions, he had eventually become a councillor in his own right by February 1443.[28] A few months later, Northumberland and Archbishop Kemp were involved in violent discord in Yorkshire which resulted in Northumberland avoiding council meetings from about May onwards. The ravaging of the archiepiscopal estates and the attacks on Kemp's officials were laid at the door of the earl and other north-country noblemen so that it would doubtless have been an embarrassment for him to have continued as a conscientious attender at the council.[29] This year, therefore, saw a major and speedy reorientation of the council's membership. John Sutton, who was one of the English envoys to the peace conference of 1439 and was recognized as Lord Dudley in February 1440, was appointed to it in November 1443, and in the following January Thomas Brouns, bishop of Norwich, an elderly cleric who, like Dudley, had been on the peace mission, was also summoned. A month later, Beaufort's own nephew, Edmund Beaufort, marquis of Dorset, joined them.[30]

As a result of these events, Beaufort felt able to retire as an active councillor himself, confident that his policies would be pursued by a council controlled by his own satellites; even so, he continued to be consulted informally on important matters and his personal influence could still be exerted in private.[31] Suffolk was usually present at council meetings from 1441, and there is no doubt that he, more than anyone else, enjoyed the greatest authority about the king, both formally through the established institutions of government and more privately in Henry's household. He was supported doggedly by most of the other councillors, but especially by relative newcomers like Adam Moleyns, a knowledgeable and ubiquitous administrator, diplomat, and politician. Indeed, after less than a year in office as keeper of the privy seal, Bekyngton gave way to Moleyns on 11 February 1444, just as a major shift in foreign policy was bringing to an abortive end negotiations (led by Bekyngton) with the count of Armagnac and inaugurating alternative discussions with Charles VII (in which the new keeper was intimately involved). Furthermore, attendance of the councillors at meetings noticeably declined from 1443, thereby leaving Suffolk and his minions securely in charge of affairs. The bishops' enthusiasm had been blunted a few years earlier, but even the lay magnates were now less assiduous in attending, perhaps because of the tightening grip of the household officials on the advisory and executive organs of government and (what was more immediately disturbing from the aristocracy's point of view) their near-monopoly of the king's patronage. No longer guided by the regulations devised during the minority, the procedures of the council allowed this small circle of advisers to dictate the decision-making processes. Not only was there no provision for a quorum at meetings, but the wise practice of excluding from discussion anyone who had a vested interest in its outcome had been abandoned by 1441; Suffolk, for example, seems to have been the only councillor present when, on 13 February 1441, he petitioned for a grant of the marriage of Richard Chamberlain's heir. That the sponsor of petitions was required to record his sponsorship in writing was hardly sufficient to counteract such questionable practices.[32] It is equally striking that among the household recruits to the council were some of those who secured the new peerages which Henry VI created in the early 1440s: Sudeley, Dudley, Fanhope, and Beaumont. Policy-making, administration, and patronage were being gathered into the hands of a small group of like-minded men, led by Suffolk, Archbishop Kemp, and Adam Moleyns; and they could just as easily use their authority in the seclusion of the private apartments at Windsor or Sheen as at the council board itself.

The council's ordinances of 1444

Some time during the course of 1444, this council formulated a series of ordinances recommending improved procedures for dealing with bills and petitions presented to the king. It is a mistake to regard these proposals as a further episode in a continuing struggle between king and councillors that began in 1437. The ordinances were accepted by the king and were followed by Henry's reaffirmation on 7 November 1444 of the validity of grants made by him in the past by procedures other than those now being recommended by the council.[33]

The new proposals involved procedural changes in the exercise of the king's patronage in the interests of efficiency, clarity, and control. The king was prepared to fall in with them and they were couched in respectful language and deferred explicitly to Henry's own wishes ('in the kynges good grace do at all tymes as it shall plese him, and use his power and wille as it perteyneth to his roial estate'). If the proposals were to be implemented, it would only be 'if it plese the kyng, undre his noble coreccion'. In 1444, therefore, it appears that Henry VI was willing to accept proposals that were intended to relieve him of unwelcome burdens and would also ensure more effective government by discouraging petitions that were imprecise in content, suits that were unhelpful or vexatious, and other inconveniences. The king accordingly signified his approval.

It is true that the council in 1444 emphasized its role in dealing with bills and petitions, whereas in 1437 it was perhaps intended that this role should be restricted; and its duty to scrutinize petitions involving matters of law or which were 'of great charge' was affirmed. But this can hardly be regarded as the outcome of a struggle with the king, not even when one considers that more minor, personal grants by the king were henceforward to be recorded fully and should pass through the hands of the keeper of the privy seal – himself a member of the council – on the way to the chancellor. It is vital to appreciate that the council of 1444 was different from that of 1437. The concept of a conflict between Henry and this re-cast council, and of an attempt to shackle the king against his wishes, misconstrues the reality.[34] By 1444 the royal council was a decidedly smaller body, dominated by Suffolk, the steward of Henry's household, by Adam Moleyns, the keeper of the privy seal and already a frequent companion of the king, and by Bishop Stafford, the chancellor.[35] Henry himself may have recognized the need for greater efficiency in his affairs, and it would be true to his character if he were insufficiently interested in the routine of kingship by 1444, when plans for his educational and religious foundations were crowding his mind. To relieve him of certain of his kingly chores and, at the same time, to improve efficiency and clarity in government through his closest associates would be a palatable prospect for him.

One omission from the council's ordinances was any provision to protect those grants which had previously been warranted by the king's signet, or by the king's own hand, or by his chamberlain's signature or that of the clerk of the council (who was Adam Moleyns himself), without passing through the privy seal office as well. Hence, on 7 November 1444 Henry issued a warrant under the privy seal (a procedure recommended by the new ordinances) which declared that such grants since 1432, when the present chancellor had taken office, should have the same force as if they had been authorized by the keeper of the privy seal.[36] This warrant was retrospective in tone and does not represent (as some historians have maintained[37]) an assertion by the king of his right to continue to issue warrants independently of the privy seal and in defiance of the council's recent ordinances. Once again, the misleading suggestion of a struggle between king and council, during which a temporary victory by the latter was soon overthrown in November by the former, has hindered historical understanding. Rather did the November statement supplement the earlier conciliar ordinances, approved by the king, and close an embarrassing loophole in their terms.[38] Either this lacuna was appreciated at the time the ordinances were formulated, and required a formal privy seal warrant to place the earlier grants beyond challenge (in which case the ordinances may date from the beginning of November 1444), or else one or more holders of the original warrants developed doubts about their validity after the conciliar ordinances had been approved and sought formal confirmation of them. As A. J. Otway-Ruthven has concluded, 'the spirit of the whole series of regulations [proposed by the council] is moderate and seems intended rather to secure administrative efficiency than to assert a constitutional position'.[39] She might appropriately have extended her judgement to include Henry's statement of 7 November 1444. A king like Henry VI may well have welcomed the conciliar suggestions, though they also enabled those who controlled the council – Suffolk and Moleyns pre-eminently – to consolidate their influence over both government and king via the privy seal office and, therefore, over the king's patronage.[40] The inherent dangers of the situation were realized in the late 1440s: Henry VI continued to divest himself of much of the routine of ruling, whereas Suffolk and his fellows tightened their hold on the council and, through Moleyns, on the privy seal office.

Suffolk's faction, 1445–49

Henceforward, the king's council gradually ceased to be a coherent body capable of giving considered and dispassionate advice to Henry VI. This was in despite of the recent arrangements that were intended to order its business and its relations with the king. Conciliar decay may be reflected in the disappearance of formal council minutes after 1443, and in indications from the council warrants that it was increasingly absorbed by routine administrative instructions rather than with political decisions.[41] Instead, the nation's affairs were being decided at small meetings of advisers consisting of Beaufort, Suffolk, and their close associates, whilst by the end of 1446 even Beaufort, now an old man, had retired from active politics, leaving the field to Suffolk as the principal royal mentor. Furthermore, the customary payment of a salary to lay councillors partially collapsed; lords tended to turn up less frequently as a result, so that meetings were sometimes reduced to a mere handful of advisers, even to as few as one or two. In J. F. Baldwin's view, the late 1440s were consequently a period of feebleness and inactivity in the council's history.[42] Those who still offered advice from time to time included Suffolk, Kemp, and Cromwell (whose service in each case dated from the minority), along with the officers of state (Stafford as chancellor, Sudeley as treasurer, and Adam Moleyns as keeper of the privy seal and, from 1445, bishop of Chichester), Bishop Brouns (who died in December 1445), and Lord Dudley.[43]

The changes of personnel in the offices of state and the royal household before the crisis of 1449–50 reinforced Suffolk's unmistakable dominance and elevated a group of household servants dependent on him. Several of these changes took place in the winter of 1446–47. On 26 October 1446, one of Suffolk's clients, a king's knight from

Norfolk, Sir Thomas Tuddenham, became keeper of the great wardrobe in the household.[44] Three weeks later, on 15 November, the experienced councillor Sir John Stourton replaced another household servant, Sir Roger Fiennes, as treasurer of the household and was duly raised to the peerage in 1448.[45] After a further month, Bishop Lumley of Carlisle, the energetic client and kinsman of the Beauforts, became treasurer of England on 18 December 1446.[46] By 3 February 1447 Lord Sudeley had replaced his powerful patron as steward of the household, though Suffolk (now a marquess) quickly compensated himself with the honorific title of great chamberlain of England which the duke of Gloucester had enjoyed at his death; somewhat later, in June 1448, he was created duke of Suffolk.[47] Finally, on 1 April 1447 Sir James Fiennes, Roger's younger brother and a long-serving member of the king's household, stepped into Sudeley's shoes as chamberlain of the household, having become Lord Saye and Sele a couple of months before.[48] The most significant feature of these changes is that they considerably enhanced Suffolk's personal position in the realm and made his influence about the young king unassailable – except by violence. Bishop Lumley had already become a councillor in November 1446 and as treasurer he was essential to the conduct of most government business.[49] A few days after that, Walter Lyhert, bishop of Norwich, began to attend the council's meetings; his elevation to the episcopate at the beginning of the year had been the result of Suffolk's personal advocacy and, no doubt, his own position as Queen Margaret's confessor.[50] Suffolk designed these promotions to serve his interests and thereby the king's. To complete them, Lord Saye and Sele and Sir Thomas Stanley, controller of the household since 1442, also joined the council in 1448.[51]

Notwithstanding the intention of 1444 to improve the practical management of the king's affairs, misgivings were soon being expressed by some of Henry's officers. They may have been concerned to preserve efficient and well-considered government in accordance with recently acknowledged principles; though their scruples need not have been shared by all their colleagues, and the remedies they proposed might ultimately serve to buttress the authority of the king's confidants in certain crucial spheres. Probably as a consequence of the king's approval of the council's ordinances of 1444, the chancellor was able to record sometime before 1447 that in important discussions (presumably those 'of grete weght') the king was usually advised by the lords of royal blood and of the council; and as if to reinforce the point, he gave it as his opinion that well-governed realms were those ruled by kings with foresight, acting with the advice of their councillors and abiding by their collective and wise decisions. In a particular matter that had evidently arisen during the summer vacation, when most lords and councillors had retired to their estates, the chancellor strongly urged the king not to take any decision until they had all returned, and he promised to assemble them within a month. Such a forthright exhortation betrays the chancellor's anxiety lest Henry proceed without the advice of his full council, not only on the specific matter in hand – England's reaction to a letter from the emperor about reunion of the Latin and Greek churches – but also (to judge by the principle he expounded) on other important questions.[52]

Similar disquiet was felt by the king's officers in relation to other, less significant issues. Within a month of becoming treasurer in December 1446, Bishop Lumley found it necessary to insist that the king should be more circumspect in his actions. On 1 January 1447, it was formally announced that no port official should henceforward be appointed without the treasurer's consent; and a fortnight later, Lumley succeeded in abridging payments that had been authorized at the ports by the king – unless, once again, the treasurer's agreement had been obtained or they were customary disbursements. These were probably among the proposals concerning 'the profit of the king' which one of the exchequer clerks, Thomas Browne, compiled for presentation to the council at about this time.[53]

The crisis of 1449–50

Suffolk's position may well have 'virtually ended the independent role of the Council', but there probably were still a few discerning councillors who were prepared to speak out when news of disaster upon disaster abroad reached England in 1449.[54] Of the older generation, Kemp and Cromwell had been disenchanted with Suffolk's rule for some time past. Then, in November 1449, a sinister incident occurred at Westminster in which a headstrong Lincolnshire gentleman and esquire of the household, William Tailboys, tried to assassinate Cromwell: Tailboys was known to have been patronized by Suffolk and Viscount Beaumont, and the attack may have been provoked by the strain and apprehension caused by the political and military failures. It is significant that when Suffolk's impeachment was demanded in parliament in 1450, Cromwell gave his encouragement.[55] Kemp, too, may have been disillusioned, let alone Lord Sudeley, the king's steward. Thomas Kemp, the archbishop's nephew and protégé (whose career he had forwarded since 1435), was provided to the see of London in August 1448 after the king had written enthusiastically to the pope in his behalf. He did not secure the bishopric until February 1450 because Suffolk belatedly sponsored a rival candidate in the person of the treasurer, Bishop Lumley. Pope Nicholas V was unimpressed by the English vacillation and counter-claims, and he accordingly refused to withdraw his original provision in favour of Kemp. The whole episode can hardly have failed to displease Archbishop Kemp or undermine his confidence in Suffolk.[56] Meanwhile, attendance at the council was very thin, especially among the lay councillors; it had long since come to be dominated by the three officers and a few ecclesiastics.[57] The earl (later duke) of Somerset was in France in the late 1440s, whilst the duke of York had little sympathy with Suffolk or his régime and in 1449 sailed for Ireland to take up an appointment as royal lieutenant there.[58]

The disastrous record of the government, orchestrated by these internal strains, precipitated a serious, domestic crisis in 1449–50 which 'changed the character and scale of politics for the next decade and more' – though not immediately.[59] Specifically, it raised the question of the character, powers, and personnel of the king's council and household. The complaints launched against the régime in 1449–50 reflect what was believed to be lacking in the king's current advisers: too few of the traditional advisers of the crown, the magnates, were being consulted, especially those of royal blood, and the council was believed to be inexperienced and too restricted in size. From what was said in parliament and outside it, there is no doubt that Suffolk himself was thought to be monopolizing the king and destroying the reality of sound and extensive counsel in the realm.[60] Despite the obvious remedy for these deficiencies, few of the issues raised in 1450 were quickly resolved and when the immediate crisis had passed, the situation remained very much as before. It goes too far to claim that Suffolk's régime 'was destroyed' in 1449–50.[61] The character of the council – even its membership to some extent – remained largely unaltered until after the king's mental collapse in the summer of 1453. But at least a few of the most unpopular individuals – Suffolk, Moleyns, and Lord Saye and Sele – had been disposed of.

The critical months of 1449–50 saw some significant changes in the departments of state and the household, and certain discredited persons were removed. On 16 September 1449 Lord Saye and Sele replaced Lumley as treasurer; even Lumley, who had shown some reformist inclinations at the beginning of his term of office in January 1447, may have deplored the consequences of current policy.[62] A month later, Adam Moleyns, the keeper of the privy seal, sought permission to retire from active politics and to resign his posts, though it seems doubtful that he was allowed to surrender the privy seal just yet.[63] Perhaps he, too, appreciated the dangers that lay ahead and preferred to lay down his responsibilities. Then, when the tide of complaint against Suffolk was at its height, certain measures were either forced on the king and his hated minister, or else were intended as a palliative to the complainants. On 31 January 1450 two significant appointments were made. One was Kemp's replacement of Archbishop Stafford as chancellor; after almost eighteen years in office, Stafford, who was well into his sixties, could be pardoned if he was wearying of his charge in the worsening situation of the late 1440s.[64] The other was the nomination of Kemp's protégé, Andrew Holes, archdeacon of York, as keeper of the privy seal in place of Moleyns, over whom the storm had burst most fiercely, for he was murdered at Portsmouth on 9 January.[65] Holes may also have found favour with Henry VI, for he was the humanist scholar for whom Henry had tried to secure the Norman see of Coutances in 1440, and at Rome in 1441 he had presented the king's case for the canonization of St Osmund.[66]

Under pressure of turbulent events, significant changes were taking place in the régime, but they came late in the day and can hardly be described as far-reaching. At the end of spring, the resolution of the king's household men revived. On 6 May, a few days after Suffolk's murder, the ill-fated duke was replaced as chamberlain of England by Viscount Beaumont, who had protected William Tailboys the year before and was known to be one of Suffolk's allies.[67] Three weeks later, the earl of Northumberland took Beaumont's place as constable of England, though only for a brief period before giving way in September to the duke of Somerset, newly returned from France.[68] Then, on 22 June 1450, just as Cade's rebellion was flaring up, Lord Saye and Sele was removed from the treasurership of England, which he had occupied for barely nine months, and was succeeded by Sir John Beauchamp, a long-serving officer in the king's household.[69] After Saye's execution by the rebels in London on 4 July, Lord Cromwell stepped into his vacated post of chamberlain of Henry's household.[70] Saye had been especially closely identified with the régime against which Cade's rebels were protesting; to remove him from prominence signified a modest concession, but it did not imply a fundamental change in the nature of English government, least of all in its overwhelmingly household hue. To turn to magnates like Beaumont, Cromwell, and Northumberland might meet some of the criticism being voiced, but these men were not brought to the fore on the council.[71]

Continued faction, 1450–53

After the immediate crisis had passed, the king and his ministers may have tried to mollify their critics by broadening the base of the council. When the duke of York in October 1450 offered his services to the king, Henry responded with the announcement that he had decided to engage a 'sad and so substancial consaile yevyng them more ample auctorite and power then evir we did afor this; in the which we have appoynted yow to be oon'. With an apparent change of heart that can only be described as breathtaking, Henry rejected the idea (to which he had been so attached during Suffolk's ascendancy) that he should be advised by one man alone, and professed himself to prefer the 'grettest and the leste, the riche and the power' instead.[72] If this was truly the king's intention, rather than an attempt to arrest the duke's pretensions and draw the sting of the government's opponents, the establishment of such a council proved little more than a cosmetic exercise. Despite his prominence during the parliament of 1450–51, there is no sign that York was consulted as a councillor at this juncture, whereas the return to England of the duke of Somerset in August 1450, and his presence on the council immediately afterwards, were unlikely to promote major reforms.[73] Moreover, although the complete absence of conciliar warrants between November 1450 and May 1451 may mask much, it may equally reflect the council's continued feebleness.[74]

On those rare occasions when criticism was voiced by Henry's own advisers, it was directed towards preserving their powers and curbing his initiative. On 25 January 1451 the treasurer and barons of the exchequer were instructed not to halt any judicial process or judgement on the sole authority of a letter or warrant from the king himself, but only if the communication had been approved by the council and was so noted.[75] The king's readiness to show sympathy to those engaged at law or in search of the royal favour was evidently well understood. The commons in parliament shared this concern in 1450–51, when the act of resumption was under discussion, though for rather different reasons. One of the proposed exemptions concerned pardons which the act would ordinarily have annulled. The commons insisted that such pardons should be exempted by the chancellor, the treasurer, the keeper of the privy seal, and by six lords of the great council, whose names must be subscribed on the relevant letters patent for all to see, and the letters themselves enrolled in the chancery as a permanent record.[76] The king's penchant for unrestrained pardoning demonstrably required urgent curbing if the effectiveness of resumption were not to be undermined.[77] For the commons, the answer to present problems was not to reinforce the supremacy of a small governing group, but to associate as many as six lords from beyond the continual council in the king's decisions.

Controls and restraints of this sort, recommended from several influential quarters in government, were a response to the unwise, even damaging, interventions of the king. His generosity, compassion, and lack of experience lay at their root, not least because responsibility for the undermining of public order, for financial extravagance, and disastrous policies could be laid partly at his door. As to the remedy, however, there was no wide measure of agreement: those who ruled wished to make their position more secure; those who criticized in parliament put their faith in more extensive and substantial counsel. All depended on the individual councillors, be they substantial in number or few.

That there was no fundamental change in the way England was governed is demonstrated by the events of the next two years. As far as the council was concerned, the chancellor and treasurer conducted most of the routine business; even the keeper of the privy seal was frequently absent.[78] It is true that certain experienced councillors continued to be relied on fairly regularly – Archbishop Stafford, Bishop Waynflete, Reginald Boulers (who was elevated to the bishopric of Hereford in August 1450), Lord Cromwell, and the duke of Somerset.[79] More significant, however, were the new councillors consulted in 1451: Sir Thomas Tyrell, a household servant whose father had been treasurer of the household during the minority, and Robert Botill, the prior of the

Order of St John of Jerusalem in England who was engaged as a diplomatic envoy during the late 1440s.[80] Then, in the early summer of 1452 the lay, household element was further strengthened, though at the same time one of the demands of the complainants in 1450 – namely, that more magnates should be consulted – was partially conceded. Yet, each of the magnates now involved had close personal links with Henry VI. The treasurership of the household, for example, passed in March 1452 from Lord Stourton to another of the household circle, Lord Dudley.[81] Within a month, a new treasurer of England had replaced Lord Beauchamp; he was John Tiptoft, the young and intelligent earl of Worcester, who was born in 1427 of a family that had served the Lancastrians for decades. Tiptoft's later sympathy for the duke of York's predicament seems not yet to have compromised his reputation in the king's eyes as a potentially dependable magnate.[82] In June James Butler, earl of Wiltshire, undoubtedly a king's man, also joined the council.[83] He was followed a month later by Bishop William Booth, Queen Margaret's chancellor, whilst on 12 May a new keeper of the privy seal had been appointed in the person of Thomas Liseux, dean of St Paul's and a protégé of Thomas Kemp, bishop of London.[84] Finally, in July 1452 a humbler household official, Robert Whittingham, became a councillor.[85] These official appointments emphasized the role of laymen, including magnates, and they extended the social spectrum from which councillors were drawn in a way reminiscent of Henry IV's day or, quite briefly, the 1420s. The new appointees were hardly 'the grettest and the leste, the riche and the power', but they may possibly represent a modest, conciliatory response to the crisis of 1449–50; they did not significantly modify the nature of royal government or the attitudes of those who directed it. This became clear in mid-July 1453, when further additions were made to the council. On this occasion, Thomas Thorp, a senior exchequer official who was speaker of the commons in the parliament of 1453–54 and a close Beaufort associate, was appointed despite his personal dispute with the treasurer, Worcester. So, too, was Peter Tastar, dean of St Seurin at Bordeaux and now a refugee in England; since his arrival, he had been patronized by John Chedworth, whom Henry VI had recently nominated to the see of Lincoln in February 1451.[86] Tastar's experience, not least as a councillor in Gascony, and Thorp's knowledge of finance and of the temper of the commons were undoubted assets at a time of grave crisis in France. Tyrell, Whittingham, Thorp, and Sir Thomas Browne (who joined the council in July 1453), were firm adherents of the duke of Somerset, and their appearance at the centre of affairs at this juncture confirms the impression that, aside from the non-magnate origins of a few, those who advised the king in the year before his illness differed little in political outlook from the Suffolk clique of the late 1440s.[87]

Notes

1 *PPC*, V, passim.

2 On 28 May 1438 Henry acted with the advice of his chamberlain, Lord Bardolf, two household officials, John Hampton and Robert Felton, and Adam Moleyns (PRO, E28/59/36). At several council meetings in 1443, one or more of the royal justices were present (*PPC*, V, 247, 256, 266, 268). On other occasions, bills were referred to the royal attorney and serjeants-at-law for comment (PRO, E28/60/2-3, 99; 62/36; 63/34; 64/12).

3 A great council was summoned on 7 March 1443 to meet at Windsor, and another was held in the fortnight beginning 11 May in the council chamber of parliament (*PPC*, V, 236, 269-79). Yet another urgent meeting was arranged on 26 February 1439, when the commanders of the Order of St John of Jerusalem were instructed to attend (PRO, E28/59/51).

4 *PPC*, V, 71, 312-15; *RP*, V, 438, reprinted, in Chrimes and Brown, op. cit., pp. 275-6, and, modernized, in *EHD*, IV, 426-7.

5 *RP*, III, 572-3, reprinted in Chrimes and Brown, op. cit., pp. 218-19. For Beaufort and Tiptoft in 1406, see A. L. Brown, 'The commons and the council in the reign of Henry IV', *EHR*, LXXIX (1964), 30.

6 For the most reliable comment on this, see Wolffe, 'Personal rule of Henry VI', p. 45.

7 Cf. J. F. Baldwin, *The King's council in England during the middle ages* (Oxford, 1913),pp. 184-6.

8 Numerous examples of these principles in practice may be found in *PPC*, V, passim, and PRO, E28/59-71 (1437–44).

9 *PPC*, V, 159-61; Baldwin, op. cit., p. 188.

10 PRO, E28/59/12.

11 As in W. Stubbs, *The constitutional history of England* (5th ed., 3 vols., Oxford, 1891–1903), III, 256; Baldwin, op. cit., p. 184; and T. F. T. Plucknett, 'The place of the council in the fifteenth century', *TRHS*, 4th ser., I (1918), 181.

12 As in Storey, *End of Lancaster*, p. 39 (who confused the declaration of May 1406 with the much sterner one of December 1406: Brown *EHR*, LXXIX [1964], 20-7); and A. L. Brown, 'The king's councillors in fifteenth-century England', *TRHS*, 5th ser., XIX (1969), 111.

13 W. Stubbs, op. cit., III, 256; Plucknett, *TRHS*, 4th ser., I (1918), 181.

14 Storey, *End of Lancaster*, p. 39; B. Wilkinson, *Constitutional History of England in the fifteenth century, 1399–1485* (1964), p. 231; Brown, *TRHS*, 5th ser., XIX (1969), 111.

15 R. Virgoe, 'The composition of the king's council, 1437-61', *BIHR*, XLIII (1970), 141; Wolffe, 'Personal rule of Henry VI', pp. 35-6, 45.

16 Baldwin, op. cit., p. 184.

17 Warwick and Scrope, who had recently been councillors but were not renominated, went to France in 1437 (Virgoe, *BIHR*, XLIII [1970], 141).

18 *CPR, 1435–41*, pp. 162, 144, 182. As a baron, Tiptoft was especially fortunate in securing a grant of Bassingbourne manor (Cambridgeshire) for life up to the value of his 100 marks (ibid., p. 193; Baldwin, op. cit., p. 186 n. 2).

19 Stafford received 200 marks and Cromwell's fee was likewise raised to 200 marks a few years later; some of the bishops, too, were recompensed subsequently (Baldwin, op. cit., p. 185), and Archbishop Kemp received £1,492 during 1437–45 (PRO, E403/730-57).

20 Virgoe, *BIHR*, XLIII (1970), 157 n. 2.
21 One of Gloucester's closest allies, Lord Scrope, had not been included among the councillors renominated in 1437 (above, n. 18). Gloucester himself received no payment as a councillor after 16 July 1438 (PRO, E403/730-57).
22 Allmand, *BIHR*, XL (1967), esp. 25-7.
23 PRO, E28/60/36; 61/11; 63/62.
24 Virgoe, *BIHR*, XLIII (1970), 141, 144.
25 *GEC*, XII, i, 419-21.
26 Griffiths, *BJRL*, LI (1968-69), 381-99.
27 *CPR, 1441–46*, pp. 85, 158; Emden, *Cambridge*, 11, 28; *Oxford*, I, 15-16. Alnwick died in December 1449.
28 Moleyns had evidently given advice on many occasions even before he was described as a councillor (Virgoe, *BIHR*, XLIII [1970], 157 n. 4; PRO, E28/59/36 [28 May 1438]; 63/28 [8 May 1440, when he recorded his role in the first person for the first time]).
29 *PPC*, V, 268-9, 273-5ff.
30 Meanwhile, 3 of the lords recruited in 1439, Fanhope, Scrope, and Beaumont, had become more intermittent in their attendance by the autumn of 1443. The only addition to be made to the councillors during the next two years (11 February 1445) was John Lowe, the recently enthroned bishop of Rochester who had once been Henry VI's confessor (Virgoe, *BIHR*, XLIII [1970], 157 n. 5; above, p. 59).
31 Virgoe, *BIHR*, XLIII (1970), 143 n. 2.
32 PRO, E28/61/11; 64/32; 66/58 (Suffolk); 67/2-3 (Huntingdon), 36; 68/5-6 (Aiscough); 69/25 (Beaumont), 35-6 (Suffolk); 70/13-14 (Huntingdon).
33 *PPC*, VI, 316-20, reprinted in Chrimes and Brown, op. cit., pp. 277-9, and, modernized, in *EHD*, IV, 431-3.
34 As in Baldwin, op. cit., p. 189; and Plucknett, *TRHS*, 4th ser., I (1918), 182.
35 Virgoe, *BIHR*, XLIII (1970), 143-4, and above, pp. 278-9.
36 *CPR, 1441–46*, pp. 312-13, reprinted in Chrimes and Brown, op. cit., pp. 279-80, and, modernized, in Wilkinson, *Const. Hist.*, p. 237.
37 See Otway-Ruthven, *King's secretary*, p. 36.
38 B. Wilkinson (*Const. Hist.*, p. 217 and n. 2) seems to appreciate the purport of this order, but does not elaborate on its significance.
39 Otway-Ruthven, *King's secretary*, p. 36; cf. Wilkinson, *Const. Hist.*, pp. 217-18. If the king's reference to 'certain restraintes late made by thadvis of you [the chancellor] and othere of our Counseil' refers to the ordinances, they may date from shortly before 31 October (H. C. Maxwell-Lyte, *Historical notes on the use of the great seal of England* [1926], p. 90 n. 1, quoting PRO, C81/1370/17).
40 Despite B. P. Wolffe's unduly cautious comments ('Personal rule of Henry VI', pp. 36, 46) on the composition of the council in the late 1440s (for which ct. Virgoe, *BIHR*, XLIII [1970], 143-6), and B. Wilkinson's inclination to separate 'court' from 'council' at this time (*Const. Hist.*, p. 218).
41 Virgoe, *BIHR*, XLIII (1970), 143.
42 ibid., 143 and n. 3; Baldwin, op. cit., pp. 190-1.
43 Virgoe, *BIHR*, XLIII (1970), 144, 157.
44 *CPR, 1446–52*, p. 4. A few months later he secured exclusive and

independent authority in the great wardrobe (Wedgwood, *Biographies*, p. 880; below, p. 317).

45 *HBC*, p. 79; *GEC*, XII, i, 301-2.
46 *HBC*, p. 102. In August 1448 it was belatedly proposed that he be translated from Carlisle to London (mistakenly given as Lincoln in Emden, *Cambridge*, p. 377), though Thomas Kemp's name had already been sent to the pope; despite Suffolk's support, Lumley was disappointed, but early in 1450 he secured Lincoln instead (R. G. Davies, thesis, III, clxxviii). See Storey, *TCWAAS*, n. s., IV (1956), 128-30.
47 *GEC*, XII, i, 446.
48 ibid., XI, 480; Jeffs, thesis, pp. 289-91; Wedgwood, *Biographies*, pp. 322-3. Sir Roger Fiennes's loss of the treasurership of the household in 1448 marked his retirement from crown service; he may have done so willingly through ill-health or the like, for he died in 1450.
49 Virgoe, *BIHR*, XLIII (1970), 157 n. 5.
50 ibid., p. 157 n. 5; Emden, *Oxford*, II, 1187-8.
51 Virgoe, *BIHR*, XLIII (1970), 158 n. 4. In the circumstances, it is surprising that whereas Lord Saye and Sele, Stanley, Moleyns, and others shared some of the odium which Suffolk attracted in 1449–50, Sudeley, the latter's successor as head of the household, was not denounced (ibid., p. 145 n. 3; below, pp. 304ff).
52 *PPC*, VI, 337. The document is undated, but it refers to an archbishop who is chancellor, a duke of Gloucester (Humphrey), and a cardinal (Beaufort) who are royal councillors. This places it between 1443 and early in 1447.
53 *CPR, 1446–52*, p. 28; PRO, E404/767 m. 11. Browne was paid for his efforts on 18 July 1447, by which time he had been made under-treasurer of the exchequer by Lumley; the fact that he was referred to simply as a clerk may indicate that the articles were drawn up before his promotion *c*. February (Wedgwood, *Biographies*, pp. 123-4). See below, p. 290.
54 Virgoe, *BIHR*, XLIII (1970), 145.
55 *RP*, V, 200; R. Virgoe, 'William Tailboys and Lord Cromwell: crime and politics in Lancastrian England', *BJRL*, LV (1973), 459-82; below, p. 678. Suffolk had already secured Tailboys a pardon for past crimes.
56 Emden, *Oxford*, II, 1032-4; above, p. 285.
57 Virgoe, *BIHR*, XLIII (1970), 144-5.
58 *CPR, 1446–52*, pp. 185, 238. Suffolk may have planned York's 'exile' to Ireland ('Benet's Chron.', p. 195). See below, p. 420.
59 Virgoe, *BIHR*, XLIII (1970), 146.
60 Below, pp. 634-5.
61 Brown, *TRHS*, 5th ser., XIX (1969), 113.
62 Above, p. 286; *HBC*, p. 102.
63 ibid., p. 92; *CPR, 1446–52*, p. 297. His health and eyesight were said to be failing.
64 *HBC*, p. 85; Jacob, *TRHS*, 5th ser., XII (1962), 1-23, reprinted in idem, *Essays in later medieval history*, pp. 35-57.
65 *HBC*, p. 92; Kingsford, *Prejudice and promise*, p. 166.
66 Emden, *Oxford*, II, 949-50; *Bekynton Corr.*, I, 118.
67 *CPR, 1446–52*, p. 329; Virgoe, *BJRL*, LV (1973), 461ff.
68 *GEC*, IX, 716; XII, i, 52.
69 *HBC*, p. 102; above, p. 613.
70 Below, p. 615; Wedgwood, *Register*, pp. 115, 145.

71 For their non-attendance at council meetings, see Virgoe, *BIHR*, XLIII (1970), 158-9.
72 Griffiths, *JMH*, I (1975), 200-1, 204-6.
73 ibid., 197; Storey, *End of Lancaster*, p. 75.
74 Baldwin, op. cit., p. 195; Virgoe, *BIHR*, XLIII (1970), 147 and n. 1.
75 *PPC*, VI, 104.
76 *RP*, V, 217.
77 For the effect of this restricted exemption, see below, p. 389.
78 Virgoe, *BIHR*, XLIII (1970), 147.
79 ibid., 147, 158-9.
80 ibid., pp. 158-9; Jeffs, thesis, pp. 329-30; Wedgwood, *Biographies*, pp. 891-2. Despite Tyrell's father's association with Gloucester, his own links were with the king's service. For Botill, see Ferguson, op. cit., pp. 179, 188, 199, 206, 214.
81 *HBC*, p. 79.
82 ibid., p. 102; Emden, *Oxford*, III, 1877-9. Some would link him with York in 1452 and regard his appointment as a concession to the duke after the Dartford confrontation. But his family links with the Mortimers were rather tenuous, and his marriage to Cecily Neville in 1449 is unlikely to have taken the young earl to York's side, for the Nevilles themselves had not yet sought his alliance and, in any case, Cecily died a year later (Storey, *End of Lancaster*, pp. 135-6, 239-40; R. J. Mitchell, *John Tiptoft, 1427-1470* [1938], pp. 19-20; below, p. 696).
83 Virgoe, *BIHR*, XLIII (1970), 158 n. 6; *GEC*, X, 126-9.
84 Virgoe, *BIHR*, XLIII (1970), 158 n. 6; Reeves, *MedSt*, III, 11-29; *HBC*, p. 92; Emden, *Oxford*, II, 1197; Booth was provided to the archbishopric of York in succession to John Kemp on 21 July 1452.
85 Virgoe, *BIHR*, XLIII (1970), 158 n. 6; Jeffs, thesis, pp. 338-9; Wedgwood, *Biographies*, pp. 943-4. He was an usher of the chamber, his father had been treasurer of Calais, and his wife was one of Queen Margaret's ladies by 1452-53 (Myers, *BJRL*, XL [1957-58], 405 n. 2).
86 Virgoe, *BIHR*, XLIII (1970), 158 n. 6. For Thorp, see J. S. Roskell, 'Thomas Thorpe, speaker in the Reading parliament of 1453', *Nott. Med. St.*, VII (1963), 79-105; idem, *Speakers*, pp. 248-52; Wedgwood, *Biographies*, pp. 849-51. For Tastar, see Emden, *Oxford*, III, 2220-1; and for Chedworth, ibid., I, 401-2.
87 Virgoe, *BIHR*, XLIII (1970), 158 n. 6; Wedgwood, *Biographies*, pp. 123-4; Jeffs, thesis, pp. 277-8. Browne was a former exchequer official whose family had expanded its landed interests from London into Kent, where Thomas was both sheriff and MP; he was slandered by the populace in 1450. Below, p. 634.

13 The King's Court and Household

The king's coming of age inevitably meant that his household would expand and his friends multiply, and that acquaintances, petitioners, and others would throng to his presence in larger numbers than before. There was thus created a court that was different in size, nature, and function from Henry's entourage during his minority. This posed new problems for the household itself which, if not dealt with effectively, would create difficulties for those who organized the king's daily affairs.

Court and household

It is difficult to do justice to the many-sided character of Henry VI's court by describing those who attended it and their reasons for doing so, the activities that took place within it, and the influence it exerted elsewhere in the realm. G. R. Elton faced similar problems in studying the Tudor court of a century later:

> We all know that there was a Court, and we all use the term with frequent ease, but we seem to have taken it so much for granted that we have done almost nothing to investigate it seriously ... At times it has all the appearance of a fully fledged institution; at others it seems to be no more than a convenient conceptual piece of shorthand, covering certain people, certain behaviour, certain attitudes.·

The late-Lancastrian court has never been studied and what little has been unearthed about the Yorkist and early Tudor courts has led historians to suggest either that no such thing existed in Henry VI's reign in the modern sense of the term, or that it was such a pale reflection of the court of Edward IV, and especially that of Henry VIII and Elizabeth I, that to describe it as a 'court' at all is hardly justifiable.[2]

In their quest for Henry's court, historians are hindered by the nature of the surviving sources. Institutionally speaking, its core was the king's household, whose organization can be examined through the financial accounts of the keeper of the great wardrobe and the treasurer of the household, and the books of the household controller.[3] But beyond this easily identified centre was a world of visitors, hangers-on, and petitioners, of the curious and the great, who had no particular function or special office to perform about the king and yet were temporarily in his company as the court moved round the country or resided at the royal manors, castles, and palaces.[4]

After 1436 Henry VI's household increased in size. Naturally, an adult king who had taken up the reins of government required a larger and more sophisticated organization to manage his household, offer advice, and execute his decisions, and the household servants played a crucial role in each of these spheres. It has been estimated that during the early 1460s, Edward IV's numbered about 550 officials and servants; it is quite evident that Henry VI gathered far more about him during his adult years.[5] By 1445 it was felt necessary to restrict the number to about 420, with the unmistakable implication that of late it had grown far beyond that figure.[6] Writing of Edward's household, D. A. L. Morgan identified a broad structural and organizational division between the household and the chamber, between 'below stairs' and 'above stairs', between the provisioning and consumption departments, between (in short) the commissariat and the ceremonial. In the former, under the supervision of the steward and the financial officers of the household, there were about 250-300 people with designated functions, ministering to the material needs of the entire household and its visitors, and harbouring few pretensions to social advancement or political influence. They were the clerks, valets, grooms, and pages of the kitchen, the buttery, the cellar, the pantry, and the other domestic departments.[7] It should be understood that the working establishment 'below stairs' was the permanent section of the household, occupied in its routine not solely when the king was in residence at Westminster or Windsor castle, or at one of his oft-frequented manor houses (like Eltham, Sheen, or in Windsor park); some of them would accompany the royal entourage as it made its way round the country from manor house to monastery and priory.[8]

'Above stairs' were to be found the chaplains and clerks of the royal chapel under their dean, the officers of the jewel house under the keeper of the king's jewels, and a large body of knights and esquires for the body, ushers, grooms, valets, and pages, all of them acknowledging the king's chamberlain as their head, together with a similar group of knights and esquires of the hall. In sum, they too numbered about 250-300 in Edward IV's early years, and their social standing and place in the household were such that they really could expect rewards and gifts of office and land throughout the realm, in addition to the customary livery and fees.

This entourage 'above stairs' varied in its composition from one occasion to the next, and its members should not be thought of as constantly attending the king or as a daily burden on his household's finances. They were present in what C. D. Ross has described as a 'shift-system', though at important ceremonies and festivals during the year, or when parliament and great councils met, or when foreigners were being entertained, many of them were expected at court and were sustained there.[9] Thus, if daily expenditure on meals, transport, and other necessities during the 1440s was usually about £30, the celebrations at Windsor on St George's day (including at the garter festivities) often ran up a much larger bill, which on 23 April 1447 topped £172. The holiday period from Christmas Eve to Epiphany was another time of unusually heavy expense, while at Windsor at Easter in 1447, £128 was spent on the feast day itself.[10] On these occasions, one may imagine a court complement that was much swollen by scores of household esquires and valets, feed and liveried by the king, and travelling to his court to attend the celebrations; at the same time, they could maintain their friendships and their contacts with influential persons who would doubtless also be there. It was this fluid body of household dependants 'above stairs' which provided the king with a corps of devoted servants, to be employed as needed both at court and in the country, and to be rewarded and patronized accordingly.

During the first two years of the king's majority their number stood at about 360, already well in excess of the total that Edward IV required after his accession.[11] During the early 1440s, the figure probably increased gradually (thereby escalating its cost) so that in the ordinances of 1445 it was proposed to reduce the size of this part of the household drastically to a little over 200. But the reforms were evidently a dead letter, for by 1446–47 the number had risen to about 420 – clerks, chaplains, esquires, valets, grooms, and minstrels (i.e., 117 per cent of the 1437–39 total) – and this excluded those in the queen's employ.[12] By 1451–52 the comparable total stood at 445.[13] The valets and esquires of hall and chamber formed the largest category of those in receipt of livery and fees from the king : respectively 148 and 128 in 1437–39, 171 and 154 in 1446–47, and 183 and 173 in 1451–52.[14] It was inevitable that a king who ruled indeed should attract others who were eager to join his service or, at the very least, were ready to hover in the vicinity of his household in the hope of competing for the crumbs of office and gifts as they fell, catching the king's eye at an advantageous moment, and importuning his companions for favours and rewards. In Henry VI they encountered a sympathetic and generous patron, who was prepared to listen to a sad tale and to content a subject when he could.[15]

The esquires, yeomen, valets, and officers who staffed the household 'above stairs' were recruited through countless contacts which the king and his advisers had made in the past. Some of the younger men, like Alexander Fairford of Southwark, were themselves sons of household officials who could easily commend their offspring to the king or an influential household dignitary. When he became coroner of the Marshalsea court of the household by December 1450, Alexander was entering an office which his father Robert had occupied since 1422. Brotherly ties probably account for the fact that Thomas Stoughton of Guildford (Surrey) became a king's serjeant and a household purveyor by 1444, for his elder brother John had been a yeoman of the catery, with which the purveyors regularly dealt, since at least 1436 (and in the household since 1429-30).[16] Others were more distant relatives whose well-placed kinsmen opened the avenues of advancement when opportunity allowed. A possibility of employment in the household came the way of John Hende (or Hynde) as a result of his mother's remarriage to Lord Sudeley, Henry VI's chamberlain; he was a king's esquire by 1436, became clerk of the household in 1441, and marshal of the hall five years later. His kinsman-by-marriage, Thomas Montgomery, a nephew of Sudeley's, had succeeded him as marshal by July 1447.[17] Yet others were sponsored by magnates or bishops, who were eager to promote the careers of retainers and servants (and thereby their own interests). John Nanfan, for example, was a retainer of the earl of Warwick who, when he was King Henry's guardian, seems to have introduced Nanfan (and others) into the household; by July 1447 Nanfan had become an esquire for the body. Archbishop Kemp was equally solicitous about the interests and careers of his dependants, and not only the clerks among them; thus, it was probably he who, by 1451–52, had introduced his nephew, Robert Strelley, to household service.[18] Nor should the king's own inclinations and affections be ignored. Some of the companions with whom he grew up, and young men of similar age who were at court, became quite friendly with Henry; thus, Gilles of Brittany was an unusually affectionate friend of the king when he came to England, and Henry Beauchamp, Warwick's son and heir, established a close relationship with Henry VI when the earl was the king's guardian and his son the king's ward.[19]

When Henry's queen arrived from France in late spring 1445, she came with a ready-made household; it consisted of very few of her fellow-countrymen, but many of the royal servants who had travelled from England in November 1444 to bring her to her new kingdom stayed in her service.[20] This queenly entourage usually lived close to the king during the following fifteen years, and therefore expanded significantly the size of the royal establishment at Westminster, Windsor, the royal manor houses in the south-east, and elsewhere.[21] In 1453 Prince Edward was born and henceforward he, too, required a domestic establishment, albeit a small and rudimentary household of only several dozen people.[22] Together, these three distinct, yet closely associated, households multiplied the opportunities for service at court, increased the cost of the royal family's establishment, and opened up further corridors that led to the suites of influence and favour that made up the king's court.

Many of those who frequented this court, and especially the servants who had specific duties in the household, bought or leased houses or rooms in Westminster or London; some, like John Noreys, even took quarters close to the castle at Windsor.[23] The wardrobe itself owned a number of shops and houses near the palace at Westminster, and so did St Peter's abbey, which was prepared to let them on long leases to regular residents of the household. For example, two valets of the crown who were entrusted with keeping Eleanor Cobham in protective custody in 1441 were each leased two of the abbey's tenements at Westminster by the abbot and convent: John Beket, who was keeper of the king's private apartments in the palace nearby, concluded a 35-year lease in May 1443 at £2 *per annum*; and John Slyfirst (or Slythurst) agreed in March 1457 to pay £1 6s. 8d. a year for two other tenements over a period of fifty years.[24]

A short distance away lay the narrow, crowded streets of London and Southwark, as well as the household departments within the high walls of the Tower. Several bishops and some of the greater abbots and priors, aside from the bishop of London and the archbishop of Canterbury with his palace at Lambeth, traditionally had their own city inns, while the bishops of Winchester resided at Southwark when visiting the capital or the court. A number of these residences were located beside the Thames, either along the northern shore up-river from the Tower where the bishops of Hereford (including Reginald Boulers, and John Stanbury, the king's confessor, both of whom were constant attenders at Henry VI's court) and the bishops of St David's (among whom William Lyndwood was keeper of the privy seal and John de la Bere the king's almoner) had their houses; or else on the south bank in Southwark. There, the inns of the bishop of Rochester (and John Lowe was a noted court preacher and one of Henry VI's confessors) and the abbot of St Augustine's, Canterbury, could be reached from Bishop of Winchester Stairs, near the imposing residence of Beaufort and Waynflete. Apart from Ely House in Holborn, the other episcopal houses were scattered along the Strand towards Charing Cross and, beyond, to Westminster: between Lincoln's Inn, just outside Temple Bar, where William Alnwick, also a former confessor and councillor, could stay, and the property of the archbishops of York, known as York Place before Henry VIII renamed it White Hall, lay the houses of Bishop Lacy of Exeter (who added a great hall to Exeter Inn), Bishop Bekyngton of Bath and Wells, and the bishops of Llandaff, Coventry and Lichfield, Worcester, Durham, and Norwich – all within walking distance of the royal palace and government offices at Westminster.[25]

A large number of the temporal lords, too, had their own houses in or near London, often on the Thames embankment so that they, like some of the bishops, could be rowed by barge to the Tower or Westminster. Gloucester was occupying Baynard's Castle by 1428 when he rebuilt it after a disastrous fire; in March 1453 the king's brother, Edmund Tudor, moved into it, though two years later the house had reverted to Richard, duke of York, whose Uncle Edward (d. 1415) had once owned it. Opposite in Thames Street was Barklies (or Berkeley's) Inn, which Warwick owned at the time of his death in 1439, while down-river lay the inns of Lord Scrope, Lord Bardolf (which passed to his son-in-law, Viscount Beaumont, in 1441), the earl of Ormond, and, largest of all, Bigod House, belonging to the dukes of

Norfolk; then the residences were reached of William de la Pole, earl of Suffolk, at Pulteney's Inn, which he bought from the duke of Exeter, and Coldharbour which, after Lord Fanhope's death in 1443, became the residence of the Holand dukes of Exeter. Other magnate homes were away from the river smells: the Percies owned Northumberland House not far from the Tower near Aldgate, and the Neville earls of Warwick and Westmorland and Lord Lovel stayed in the vicinity of St Paul's when they were in the city.[26]

These domestic arrangements made easy the comings and goings, to and from the king's court, of all those who, aside from household and government officials, felt it worthwhile – if not vital – to frequent the chambers and corridors of power through which the king and queen passed. The court was the fount of influence, the pre-eminent source of patronage in the realm, an ideal centre at which to pick up news and gossip, and the place where, more than any other – even counting the council and parliament – decisions were taken and things were done.

The critical importance of having an influential ear – and a good pair of lungs – at court is revealed by the attempt during the winter of 1450–51 to bring Sir Thomas Tuddenham and John Heydon, two of Suffolk's former clients, to book for their notorious oppressions in Norfolk. A commission of oyer and terminer was appointed on 1 November 1450 and it was fully expected in the county that the culprits would appear before it at Christmastide. The earl of Oxford, Sir John Fastolf, John Paston, Justice William Yelverton, and others were well pleased; but it was Edmund Blake, a royal serjeant and one of the king's secretary's clerks, who also happened to have a deep interest in East Anglia as steward of the honour of Richmond in Norfolk and bailiff of Swaffham, who ensured that the proceedings would not be abortive. On his arrival in London on 27 December, Blake

> yede streyt to my lord Chauncelere and told my seyd lord that yf the Kynge pardoned Syr Thomas Tudenham and Heydon here issewes that the shire of Suffolk wold paye no taxe; . . . And also he told my seyd lord Chaunceler and many mo lordes that yf the Kynge pardon hym or graunted any supersedeas London shuld with-jnne short tyme have as meche for to do as they hadde for to kepe London Brygge whanne the Capteyn cam thedyr, for he told hym that ther was up in Norffolk redy to rise .v. ml. and moo yf they have not execucion of the oyre and terminer.

Blake was straightway taken to Henry VI to 'telle all this and meche more a-forn the Kynge and all hese lordes, that they blyssed hem whanne they herden yt. And yf he hadde not a seyd thus they shuld an hadde a supersedeas and pardon also, . . .'[27] At the same time, Blake took Fastolf's part against Tuddenham: 'he dede Syr John Fastolf labor to the Kynge and to ye Chaunceler for to lette [i.e., prevent] the supersedeas and the pardon, and the was grette langage atwex Blacke and Tudenham' [as may be imagined!].[28] Fastolf's satisfaction at Blake's efforts at court was undisguised. He instructed two of his servants to persuade the earl of Oxford and Justice Yelverton to write to 'Blake of the Kyngges hous' to thank him for his friendliness towards the county of Norfolk (and, presumably, himself).[29]

Contrariwise, the perils of not having an advocate at court became apparent during the protracted dispute between Lord Moleyns and John Paston over the Norfolk manor of Gresham. Two of Paston's friends, John Damme, MP for Norwich in 1450–51, and James Gresham, his own agent, wrote to John from Westminster to warn him of the consequences of his absence from court:

> ...the Lord Moleyns hadde langage of yow in the Kyngges presence, ... Your presence shuld haue do meche ease here in your own matiers and other, as your weel-willers thynkyn, and your absence do non ease here; ...[30]

Anyone who desired what the king could give (and in England he had the greatest capacity of all) was well advised to visit the royal court as often as favours were sought.

The formation of a household faction

The affairs of the king's household after 1436 were largely ordered by those who had done so earlier. Its formal head was the earl of Suffolk, who had been appointed steward in April 1433, while William Philip, Lord Bardolf was still its chamberlain. Certain aspects of household finance were allowed to remain under the supervision of Robert Rolleston, who had been responsible for handling the income and expenditure of the great wardrobe since the reign began; whilst John Merston, the keeper of Henry's jewels, had just as long and impeccable a record in the more personal department of the royal chamber.[31] But the crucial financial post of treasurer of the household, with its correspondingly decisive control over much of the household's activities (and, if the king were personally involved in warfare, over military expenditure too), did not experience the same degree of continuity from minority to majority. When Gloucester's friend Sir John Tyrell died on 2 April 1437, the duke probably had a hand in ensuring the appointment two weeks later of an experienced soldier and councillor of Richard, duke of York. Yet he, Sir John Popham, held the office for barely two years.[32] Early in April 1439 he resigned to make way for Sir Roger Fiennes, a Sussex landowner in his fifties who had also seen service in France under Henry V and Bedford, but whose political and other links in England were with the Suffolk clique, which eventually included Sir Roger's two sons and his brother James, later Lord Saye and Sele.[33]

301

Indeed, by the spring of 1439 changes were taking place at court which were soon to transform the personal and political complexion of both the king's household and his council. Such developments in turn undermined Gloucester's pervasive influence (which had been strong ever since the king's return from France in 1432) and enabled Beaufort and Suffolk to establish their own predominance. Some decisive changes of personnel – and therefore of political attitude – were required if the current peace negotiations with France were to be sustained, and if Beaufort and other envoys were to feel able to attend a conference abroad without exposing an essential element in their policy, the personal approval of the young king, to contrary persuasions. Thus, not only was Sir Roger Fiennes appointed to a key household post in April 1439, but a new controller replaced the long-serving John Feriby.[34] By then, the new controller was at his post – Sir Thomas Stanley, a rich landowner from Liverpool, with estates in Cheshire, Lancashire, west Derbyshire, and the Isle of Man. Like his grandfather before him, he had been lieutenant of Ireland (1431–37), but had hitherto had no significant connection with either the household or Westminster, though his father, Sir John Stanley, had counted himself a supporter of Beaufort in 1426 in the quarrel with Gloucester. In February 1437 Sir Thomas began to receive valuable grants of land and office in the north-west which would eventually give him and his family the kind of position in Lancashire, Cheshire, and north Wales which the Fiennes kin were coming to enjoy in Kent and Sussex. This may have been no coincidence: a prominent household official who had an unassailable social, economic, and political base in areas of peculiarly exclusive royal jurisdiction (which, by the way, had proved politically valuable in the past, notably in Richard II's reign) would provide a direct link between the household and a strategic source of provincial power. Stanley retained the controllership until 1451 when, significantly, he was replaced by his cousin and ally Sir Richard Harrington, another influential Lancashireman.[35]

When Henry entered the chapel royal, dispensed alms, or sought religious advice, for a while after 1436 he encountered the same group of clerics who had ministered to him since 1432 – men whom Gloucester had approved, patronized, or installed. The dean of the royal chapel since March 1432 was Richard Praty, who had been one of the king's domestic chaplains even before that; in April 1438 he was elevated to the bishopric of Chichester and thenceforward severed his links with the household.[36] His successor was Master John Crouther (or Crowcher), a Cambridge don whose respectable ecclesiastical career had been spent mainly in the diocese of Chichester, to which Praty was now nominated. In 1438 Crouther had been dean of Chichester for twelve years, and there he had been patronized in particular by Bishop Rickinghale (1426–29), Bedford's confessor.[37] Henry's almoner, Robert Felton, had also retired by the autumn of 1438 in favour of John de la Bere, who had served the boy-king briefly in 1431 but had then fallen victim to

Gloucester's assertion of authority in March 1432; by Michaelmas 1438 he had returned to the almonry.[38] These, and other changes of a similar nature among the royal councillors, signalled the end of Duke Humphrey's effective authority in late-Lancastrian England. A dangerous incongruity was thereby unveiled, for henceforward the heir to the throne was starkly and utterly opposed in certain crucial aspects to the personal and political outlook of the young king, his intimate companions, and his principal advisers.

When Lord Bardolf died on 6 June 1441, he was succeeded as chamberlain of the household by Sir Ralph Botiller, soon afterwards created Lord Sudeley; he had been chief butler of the household since 1435 and a knight of the body even earlier.[39] But it was not really until the mid-1440s that the compact little group assembled by Suffolk came to dominate completely life in the household, and patronage and politics beyond it. Robert Rolleston's immediate successors at the great wardrobe were royal servants whose careers were forged in the household, where they attracted the king's attention and patronage and from which they were deployed in several ways and in various parts of the realm to advance the interests of the Lancastrian régime. John Noreys, who was keeper from October 1444 to October 1446, had spent a decade and a half in household service, occupying offices as far afield as Dorset, Anglesey, and Leicester; and yet he consolidated his own landed fortunes elsewhere, especially in Oxfordshire and Berkshire, though his family hailed from the Liverpool area like that of his colleague, Sir Thomas Stanley. Noreys was friendly with the courtier bishops, Adam Moleyns and William Aiscough, and by 1445 he owned a house at Windsor which meant that he could live close to the court even after he ceased to supervise the great wardrobe's finances; in fact, in October 1446 he moved from the great wardrobe to become treasurer of the queen's chamber and keeper of her jewels and personal finances (until June 1452). Noreys was a prototype among Suffolk's household associates, attracting popular odium and denunciation by Cade's followers in 1450.[40] In October 1446 he was succeeded as keeper by Sir Thomas Tuddenham, whose reputation grew even more unsavoury, not least in his native East Anglia, where he was known as a 'common extortioner'. A divorcee, Tuddenham was one of the most notorious of Suffolk's intimates, and towards the end of 1450 his life was threatened and his London property ransacked.[41]

Similar changes were taking place elsewhere in the household. In November 1446 Sir John Stourton stepped into Sir Roger Fiennes's shoes as treasurer; one of the king's councillors in November 1437, Stourton's loyalty earned him one of Henry VI's new peerages (by 1448).[42] Then, on 1 April 1447 Lord Sudeley was succeeded as chamberlain by Lord Saye and Sele; he was rapidly emerging as second only to Suffolk as the most influential (and detested) of the king's lay advisers.[43]

The prominence of Cardinal Kemp on the ecclesiastical side of

Henry's household establishment complemented that of his collaborator, Suffolk. By Michaelmas 1444, John Crouther had given way as dean of the royal chapel to Master Robert Aiscough, the brother of the king's confessor and a cleric who was not only generously patronized by his kinsman and Kemp, but was entrusted by the king in 1448 with the wardenship of the reconstituted King's Hall at Cambridge.[44] Aiscough died about February 1449, and his role in the chapel royal was filled by Master William Say, a product of Winchester and New College in Bishop Beaufort's day. Towards the end of Beaufort's life, Say was actively patronized by Kemp, who made him a canon of York in 1443 and, presumably, favoured his appointment as a chaplain to the king in 1446.[45] Henry's almoner, John de la Bere, may have received the same ecclesiastical encouragement. He had a much murkier personal reputation, but after losing the contest for the deanery of Bath and Wells in 1443, during which he supposedly distributed bribes to right and left, he was advanced by Kemp, who secured for him a canonry at York in February 1444.[46] De la Bere's elevation to the see of St David's in the autumn of 1447 meant that eventually he would lay down his duties in the royal household; they were soon assumed by Master Henry Sever in the spring of 1448. Sever had been one of the king's chaplains since 1437, and had evidently commended himself to Henry VI personally, for the king chose him to be the first provost of Eton in October 1440.[47]

To those who had no *entrée* to this favoured circle in the later 1440s, or who failed by other means to secure access to the king and his patronage, it doubtless seemed that Henry was enveloped by an impenetrable, self-perpetuating oligarchy that (admittedly) protected him, but yet also isolated him from alternative sources of counsel, insulated him from the pleas, petitions, and complaints of his subjects, and detached him from those whom his decisions affected. True power was exercised by this small group of men. If their decisions were shown to be unwise, or their policies failed or proved mistaken, then not only would the reputation of the king's ministers plummet, but the interlocking edifice of court, household, and council would be threatened too.

The household under fire

The crisis of 1449–50 broke with greatest force over the heads of members of the household, and it placed the political organization of which they were a part, both at Westminster and in the country, in serious jeopardy. Suffolk was murdered in May 1450, and Lord Saye and Sele in July. The king's entourage was frightened by Cade's rebels, who condemned a selection of household men; it was alarmed by York's return from Ireland and several courtiers lost their nerve sufficiently to seek his protection as he made his way to London; and it had its confidence badly shaken by physical threats and popular abuse during the winter of 1450–51, especially from the London mob. During this crisis, the king's household felt a severe chill down its collective spine, but it emerged virtually intact, with its personnel largely unchanged and its influence on government fundamentally secure.

In the summer of 1450, there could be no certainty that the household affinity which Suffolk had headed would survive the duke's death unimpaired, or that its coherence could be maintained by someone else. However steadfast Sir Thomas Stanley was in holding part at least of this group together in north Wales at the time of York's arrival in 1450, some of his colleagues elsewhere were more fainthearted – or else quicker to put thoughts of personal security before group loyalty. Either explanation may account for the fact that John Sutton, Lord Dudley and Reginald Boulers, abbot of Gloucester and, from 14 August 1450, bishop of Hereford, rode to meet York at Ludlow; they did so, according to one chronicler, for their own safety.[48] Although neither held any official position in the household, they both had good cause for alarm. They had been intimately involved in the negotiations with France during the 1440s which had recently failed so signally to protect Lancastrian interests there, and both men had joined the council during the course of 1443. They had reaped the anticipated rewards, Dudley by securing a peerage in 1440 and Boulers his bishopric during the summer of 1450 itself.[49]

The same motive is likely to have prompted Thomas Hoo, Lord Hastings, the former chancellor of Normandy whom Cade's rebels had ridiculed, to risk his life and hurry to meet York; near St Albans Sir William Oldhall, one of York's closest councillors, had to intervene to protect Hoo from 'the western men' who were accompanying the duke.[50] And what manoeuvres lay behind the cryptic comment of John Paston's correspondent on 6 October that Oldhall and Lord Scales, who had helped to drive Cade's rebels out of London, 'ar friends become'? For Oldhall, as York's chamberlain, was evidently regarded as the intermediary through whom York's favour might be sought and, perhaps, even as the organizer of strategy for the duke in these turbulent months.[51] Even the Norfolk bullies, Sir Thomas Tuddenham, a former keeper of the great wardrobe, and his partner-in-crime, John Heydon, were prepared to offer £2,000 to be well received, presumably by York.[52] After Suffolk's demise, men like Dudley, Boulers, and Hoo may have concluded that York was destined for greater prominence at court and a more central role in policy-making. The duke of Somerset's emergence as the royal favourite *par excellence* was no foregone conclusion.

The same selfish fears may have been in the mind of William Tresham, who set out from his Northamptonshire home on 23 September 1450 to rendezvous with York. Nothing might have been heard of this journey if Tresham had not been waylaid and hacked to death. He was an experienced lawyer and royal official, MP for

Northamptonshire on many occasions and speaker of the commons on no less than four of them. Apart from a minor connection with York – acting as feoffee in one of his Rutland manors by February 1449 – Tresham's career owed everything to his employment in the royal household and by the duchy of Lancaster.[53] Although speaker for the commons when they launched their charges against Suffolk in the 1449–50 parliament, he must be regarded as their spokesman on that occasion and not as the initiator or formulator of their accusations. After this experience, he continued to benefit from court favour and, like many a household official, was exempt from the 1450 act of resumption. Thus, the most that can be said of his loyalties in September 1450 was that they were in a state of flux and that he himself, like Dudley and Boulers, was in an uncertain frame of mind.[54] It was Tresham's wife Isabella who, in a petition to parliament in 1450–51 for action against her husband's assailants, claimed that he was riding to meet with York in response to a letter from the duke; but this may have been an embroidery of the truth with the object of enlisting the sympathy of an avowedly anti-court assembly which included several of York's servants among its members.[55] The suggestion that the perpetrators of the crime thought that Tresham's intention to meet York would later be a valid excuse for their action argues for a greater degree of forethought than was likely in September 1450.[56] The attack on Tresham, his son Thomas, and their servants was hatched by a Rutland squire, Simon Norwich, as a result of a longstanding quarrel; and those who actually committed the murder had been in violent dispute with the Treshams over property a month or so earlier.[57] As more than one writer claimed, they may have been servants of Lord Grey of Ruthin, a Northampton-shire landowner, but there is no sign that Grey himself was privy to the incident or that it had any other political significance.[58] A number of people were hastening to ingratiate themselves with York at this juncture, and William Tresham may have been one; indeed, he was deceived into informing his attackers of the route he was about to take by a certain William Kyng, who also claimed to be anxious to petition the duke.[59]

The disarray of the royal household after the death of Suffolk and the shock of Cade's revolt was reflected within the household establish-ment itself. At the beginning of December 1450, Tuddenham was induced to resign from the great wardrobe amid a welter of abuse and condemnation that included attacks on his house and personal pos-sessions in the city of London. In these perilous circumstances, a hasty decision was taken to revert to the kind of official who was less of a political favourite and more of an experienced financier. Accordingly, the new keeper, appointed on 3 December 1450, was William Cotton, the forty-year-old scion of one of the London merchant families which had invested in land and acquired influence in the countryside, in the Cottons' case in Cambridgeshire and Suffolk. William had, in truth, been working as a clerk in the great wardrobe since at least 1437, but it was his evident ability that led to his appointment in March 1445 as receiver-general of the duchy of Lancaster and (in July 1446) of Queen Margaret's estates too. There was no question of his loyalty to the king and the queen, but equally there could be no doubting his financial expertise. Cotton remained at the great wardrobe until mid-June 1453.[60] Then, his friend and business associate, Henry Filongley, a lawyer who had married Sir John Fastolf's niece and seems to have had no prior connection with Suffolk or the household, was appointed on 17 June.[61]

In contrast to the long-serving Rolleston, four different keepers were appointed to the great wardrobe between 1444 and 1453, and in the case of the first two of them, Noreys and Tuddenham, they obtained their commission because they were well known in the household already, had shown themselves to be politically reliable, and had the cardinal virtue of belonging to the Suffolk affinity. Both men were denounced in 1450 by the populace as a result. The crisis of 1449–50, therefore, seems to have had the effect of moderating the element of blatant political motive in appointments to this financial office of the household, for neither Cotton nor Filongley was a client of Suffolk or Somerset; rather were they career administrators who had shown their professional worth in decades of service, both financial and legal, and they performed their duties without the selfish ruthlessness and oppression of their predecessors.

Sir Thomas Stanley held the controllership of the household through a wholehearted espousal of Suffolk's régime; but he, like Tuddenham, resigned in the winter of 1450–51 in the face of popular hostility. He survived the Christmas festivities, but was replaced soon afterwards by his cousin and close associate, Sir Richard Harrington, the significance of whose appointment lies in the king's unwillingness to alter drastically the character of the household or, more specifically, to break the vital link between the court and the palatinates of the north-west.[62] Yet if these changes represented a retreat before strongly-expressed popular and parliamentary opinion, they were modest ones and were confined to the removal of the more unpopular of Suffolk's clique and the more glaring of the abuses. Lord Sudeley stayed on as steward of the household, as did Lord Stourton as its treasurer (until March 1453). Lord Cromwell succeeded the late Lord Saye and Sele as chamberlain; although he had detached himself somewhat from Suffolk's friends by 1450, he was nevertheless a longstanding and dependable supporter of the house of Lancaster.[63]

The king's carvers, who had formed an élite among the household knights, esquires, and valets during the minority, retained their positions after 1436 until death removed two of them. Sir John Beauchamp, a kinsman of the earls of Warwick, was dead by 1447, and during the winter of 1448–49 Sir Robert Roos, who had also been brought into the household in February 1430, followed him to the grave.[64] The other two carvers who owed their position to Richard

Beauchamp – Sir William Beauchamp and Sir Edmund Hungerford – continued to give the king their staunch support. They survived virtually unscathed the crisis of 1449–50 and the acts of resumption, though Hungerford was singled out by the commons when an attempt was made to exile certain key household officials from the king's presence. In fact, Beauchamp's role in north Wales complemented that of Sir Thomas Stanley in a wider area, and early in 1449 he was summoned to parliament as Lord St Amand.[65] The only new carver to be recruited to the household was Sir Philip Wentworth, a Yorkshireman whose mother eventually brought him a Suffolk estate with which he was closely identified. Wentworth, a king's serjeant by 1446, had acquired Gloucester's house at Ashingdon in Essex after the duke's death in 1447; he managed to escape the clauses of the acts of resumption and was promoted carver by 1452.[66] Most members of the king's entourage, both significant and minor, held on to their positions of influence and profit, and during 1451 they were able to heave a long sigh of relief.

The most direct and concerted attack by parliament on the king's court occurred late in 1450, probably during the last fortnight or so of the session which ran from 6 November to 18 December.[67] On that occasion, the commons demanded the removal from the king's presence of twenty-nine named individuals, about whom 'universall noyse and claymour of . . . mysbehavyng renneth openly thorough all this youre reame . . .'. This may refer to the public outcry which led to the indictment of three-quarters of the twenty-nine at Rochester soon after Cade's rising had ended.[68] It is indicative of the nexus of influence which the court and household had created that these twenty-nine were regarded as exerting an undesirable dominance over the king from their position in his household or, in a less formal way, at his court; by their 'undue meanes youre possessions have been gretely amenused, youre lawes not executed, and the peas of this youre reame not observed nother kept . . .'. Almost all of them were officers or feed members of Henry's household establishment.

Only three (discounting Alice Chaucer, the widowed duchess of Suffolk) were peers: the duke of Somerset, newly returned from disaster-torn France and, since 11 September 1450, constable of England; Lord Dudley, a royal councillor; and Thomas Hoo, Lord Hastings, the discredited chancellor of Normandy. Dudley had been involved in the recent negotiations with France, Burgundy, and the Hanseatic league, and this diplomatic activity probably earned him the mistrust and dislike of the commons.[69] Only Somerset was a magnate with any claim to venerable lineage, for both Hastings and Dudley were among the new creations of Henry VI.[70] There were only two senior ecclesiastics among the commons' targets: Bishop William Booth, the chancellor of the queen, who was a constant reminder of the French enemy, and Reginald Boulers, a former councillor and envoy, and a colleague of Suffolk's in negotiating French treaties; in 1449 he had been Somerset's emissary to parliament to plead for military aid on the duke's behalf.[71] The only other clerics among the twenty-nine were three who were exceptionally closely associated with the government that had brought England to its current pass. Thomas Kent had been clerk of the council since 1444 and on occasion temporary keeper of the privy seal in place of Adam Moleyns (most recently for ten days after the murder of the bishop on 9 January 1450); he, too, had been involved in French and German negotiations.[72] Master John Somerset had been in the king's household since the minority, and he was well known at court as the king's mentor as well as his physician.[73] Master Gervase le Vulre was himself a Frenchman and had been given responsibility for French affairs as a royal secretary as far back as Henry V's reign.[74]

These apart, the remaining twenty were either knights, esquires, or servants of the household. Although the link with Suffolk doubtless made some of them hated by 1450 – the much-patronized Sir Edmund Hampden and the rough-neck Sir Robert Wingfield, for example – others (such as Bishop Booth and John Hampton) are likely to have been equally distrusted for their relations with the queen. A few had aristocratic connections which seem to have weighed little in 1450 with the commons, who were hostile primarily to the court and the household, and were angry at the collapse of Lancastrian power in France; betrayal by a household régime that appeared to have no attractive side was the sentiment most keenly felt by the MPs.[75] John Newport was employed in the Isle of Wight by the duke of York, though his banditry there may have forfeited the duke's sympathy; John Somerset was formerly in the employ of Exeter and Gloucester, but they were dead; and both John Penycock and Thomas Daniel had once been clients of Suffolk's rival, the duke of Norfolk.[76] But what they all had in common by 1450 was their place at court or in the household, advancement through the king's patronage, a penchant for ignoring the law, and, as far as more than a third of the denounced were concerned, a public involvement in the disastrous events in France. Policies, patronage, and even lawlessness stemmed from the court of a monarch who lacked good judgement and powers of discrimination.

One quality which Henry VI did show in the face of this assault was stubbornness. He responded to the commons' petition by declaring that he 'is not sufficiently lerned of eny cause why they shuld be removed' from his presence, and his attempt at concession was little more than a façade. He agreed that certain of the twenty-nine should be exiled from his court for one year, during which specific charges would be entertained; but his exemption of the lords named in the petition (Somerset, Dudley, and Hastings, let alone the spiritual peers and the duchess of Suffolk), and (an open-ended reservation this)

certein persones which shall be right fewe in nombre, the which have be accustumed contynuelly to waite uppon his persone, and knowen howe and in what wise they shall mowe beste serve hym to his pleasure, ... savyng alwey that if it happen the kyng to take the felde

> ayenst his ennemyes or rebelles, that than it shall be lefull to hym to
> use the service of any of his liege people . . .

enabled Henry to implement as much or as little of the petition as he
chose.[77] Thus, while Sir Thomas Stanley lost the controllership of the
household (perhaps because, as the only one of the twenty-nine to be
returned to this parliament as an MP, he was least able to withstand the
commons' wrath), the others appear to have retained their position in
the household and elsewhere.[78] It is curious that on 17 October 1450
Stanley had also lost the justiciarship of north Wales, ostensibly
because he was occupied with various other matters and therefore had
'no leisure to exercise the office', and in the following April was
succeeded as chamberlain of north Wales by the king's carver, Sir
William Beauchamp. One is bound to wonder whether he had not been
sacrificed by the king, who was faced with criticism from both York (in
September–October) and parliament (in November–December), in an
attempt to satisfy the critics. The choice of Stanley is difficult to
explain, but he was indubitably one of the most prominent household
officials, had been singled out for condemnation by Cade's followers,
and, above all, had been the lynch-pin of the plot to apprehend York
on his arrival in north Wales in September 1450.[79] Stanley's reaction to
his temporary embarrassment is unknown, though it may be wrong to
think of him as victimized. Not only was he quickly restored to his north
Wales posts, but his political influence in the north-west generally was
such that both the Lancastrian régime and York's protectorates felt his
co-operation to be essential. Had his surrender of certain offices in
1450–51, in favour of selected associates of his, been a carefully
contrived response by Stanley and the king to the crowd of critics that
was closing in on them both?[80]

The costs of the household

By the time parliament met in November 1439, the burgeoning cost of
the larger and more active household was apparent. It was sufficiently
disquieting for the commons to propose some action in the session held
at Reading during January–February, though after only two years'
experience of an adult king the matter was not considered very urgent.
Henry was faced with debts to a number of household clerks, some
going back to Henry IV's reign; it was claimed in 1438 that these
neglected servants had not been paid wages or rewards, and some of
them were now quite elderly. Their petition had a pathetic ring which
touched the heart of the sensitive monarch.[81] More serious were the
representations made by the crown's judicial officers, both the justices
of the benches and of assize, and by the king's own serjeants and
attorneys. They, too, claimed not to have been paid for quite some time
(in this case eleven years), while in the meantime some of them had

retired or even died without being recompensed. This state of affairs imperilled justice and good administration in an age when sweeteners and bribes were common, and hence an effort was made in parliament to assure the law officers that regular payment would be made from specified sources.[82] Practical action on this promise took a little time, and it was not until the king had authorized the necessary warrant at Windsor on 16 November that the justices, attorneys, and serjeants could feel secure.[83]

The Reading session of parliament concluded that major steps were necessary to ensure the solvency of the household, but there is no evidence of panic or hysteria. The king was sufficiently roused by the rumours and complaints of unpaid expenses and wages, and by the specific examples brought to his attention, to meet the commons' request. It was accordingly agreed that the revenue from the estates and prerogative rights of the duchies of Cornwall and Lancaster should be assigned to the treasurer of the household for the next five years, though individuals or officers with a prior claim would be protected.[84] The precise details of this provision for the household were not worked out until a council meeting held at the royal manor of Kennington in June 1440. Then, in the presence of Beaufort, Gloucester, and the three officers of state, the treasurer of the household was assigned £10,000 *per annum* for each of the next five years, beginning with 1439–40. The designated sources were a little more diverse than parliament had originally intended: although the two duchies were required to find the bulk of it, 4,000 marks would come from the exchequer itself. In addition, an extra £8,000 was made available immediately as a stand-by credit should the treasurer need it.[85] As far as can be ascertained from the surviving accounts of Sir Roger Fiennes as keeper of the wardrobe (Michaelmas 1441–42 and Michaelmas 1443–44), the receivers-general of both duchies did what was asked of them – and more besides. In 1441–42 they delivered as much as £7,193 to the treasurer and in 1443–44 £8,482. In those same years the exchequer, too, more or less met its target: £2,992 and (a little lower than the expectation of £2,667) £2,601 respectively.[86] Nevertheless, when the treasurer of the household concluded his account at the end of 1441–42, he had overspent by almost £2,200. Evidently, the measures taken at Reading to earmark specific funds could not fully satisfy the needs of the active household of an adult king.

The great wardrobe had a far smaller turnover than the wardrobe, perhaps about one-tenth of it; but its financial fortunes in these years were very similar. In both 1438–39 and 1439–40 the expenditure authorized by the keeper, Robert Rolleston, on clothing and other goods exceeded an income of about £1,400 by £200. As a result of the concern of the Reading parliament to place the household's finances on a more secure basis, more cash was injected into the great wardrobe from the exchequer during 1440–41 – so much in fact (£2,600) that £1,082 was left unspent at the end of the year. But this was a fleeting silver-lining.

During the following two years the deficit reappeared and at double its previous size: in 1442–43 expenditure of £1,534 meant that as much as £514 had been overspent at the conclusion of Rolleston's account.[87]

Despite the capacity of the crown's financial reserves initially to rise to the occasion, the situation was evidently worsening. But the seriousness of the deterioration does not seem to have been appreciated quickly. Sources of finance that had been assigned to the household were later occasionally devoted to other purposes, a practice that undermined the good credit of the household itself. In 1440, for instance, £6,000 was diverted to the army then being assembled for despatch to Normandy, despite the fact that parliament had specifically assigned the cash for household and other purposes. It was small consolation that on 7 July this assignment was replaced by a promise of the first instalment of the duke of Orléans's ransom, which was unlikely to be promptly, immediately, or, it might be anticipated, fully paid.[88]

The lamentable state of repair into which some of the royal palaces and mansions had fallen during the minority was an additional, if less daunting, burden. The manor house at Sheen, a favourite residence with Henry VI, was in a sad state, but the prospect was no more pleasing at Westminster itself, or at the Tower. The king's mentor, John Somerset, was appointed surveyor of these residences in May 1442. But to do anything about their condition would cost money, and in January 1445 another £1,000 was required for Sheen, Eltham, and Westminster – presumably because the expected arrival of a new queen made renovation and redecoration essential.[89]

Resources continued to be diverted from the household and in November 1441 the council took action to stop this financial leak. The treasurer of the household was instructed to bring to the exchequer tallies amounting to more than £7,000 which could not be cashed because they carried the names of specific tax-collectors who may have left office. £4,000-worth of these had been issued to Sir Roger Fiennes on 8 July 1441 as part of the annual subvention to the household; they were replaced by others on 20 November that would enable the customs revenue from Southampton to be directed to the household after Christmas 1441.[90] But the tallies had again to be replaced on 10 February 1442 by further drafts worth £3,933 on the Southampton customs; soon afterwards, parliament had to assign another 15,000 marks from the same source over a three-year period to combat the deteriorating situation.[91] The need for this kind of action made the provision of finance for the household rather unpredictable; the spending of a major department became erratic and thereby bred suspicion among its creditors.

The parliament which opened in January 1442 was admittedly more conscious of the financial difficulties of the household than its predecessor had been. The commons demanded more effective and urgent action by way of remedy. They asked that the assignment of the two royal duchies' revenues as from Michaelmas 1439 be extended beyond the limit of the initial grant (Michaelmas 1444) for a further three years.[92] This at least showed an awareness of the continuing and long-term needs of the king's household and would, it was hoped, facilitate planning. The arrangement would also restore the good credit of the régime so that Henry VI could borrow more freely and be served more willingly. The pressures for better financial organization that were exerted in this parliament were appreciated by the king and his advisers, who doubtless realized the benefits of having more secure credit. Henry himself seems to have been less enthusiastic about the specific proposals of the commons, which were designed to earmark particular revenues. Rather than extend the duchies' assignment, he assured MPs that proper (though unspecified) arrangements would be made for the management of household expenditure, but that they would be made with the advice of those councillors whom he alone chose to consult. There is little sign that this was successful, and the diversion of sorely needed cash from the household continued to take place, as the reassignment of 4,800 marks to the duke of Bavaria on 28 November 1443 testifies.[93] Even though the contributions from Cornwall and Lancaster were maintained, new subventions (as opposed to the replacement of uncashed ones) from the exchequer during 1442–44 were at an unprecedentedly low level for Henry VI's reign.[94] Insufficient resources and some lack of commitment by the government to the support of a household larger in size and more lavish in expenditure than that of the minority are reflected most vividly in Sir Roger Fiennes's inability to honour the household's obligations. Its debts mounted alarmingly during 1439–42, even though many were recorded more than once in the exchequer records as a search was made to find reliable resources.[95] If, during 1442–44, the reduction of the quantity of replaced tallies and the somewhat larger sums made available by the exchequer to the household reflect a more thrifty attitude among the king's ministers, their good intentions were set at naught by the prodigious expense involved in bringing Margaret of Anjou to England in 1445.[96] The arrival of a new queen made a thoroughgoing review of the household's organization, size, efficiency, and solvency desirable, not least because of the costs incurred during her journey and reception in the realm.

The reform of the household's administration was regarded as one, albeit drastic, way out of its difficulties. Proposals were accordingly made to reduce its size, for that in itself would help to solve some of the problems, and would allow an improvement in efficiency and promote more economical management. In raising the matter in 1442, the commons realized that they were treading on sensitive ground connected with the king's person and prerogatives.[97] Nevertheless, Henry VI was persuaded to agree to certain changes, including the nomination of several lords, selected by himself, to reorganize the household and supervise its management. The only important reservation which the king made was that no one with existing interests or position should be prejudiced by any subsequent reorganization – so delicate were the closely allied considerations of influence, patronage, and prerogative. This sensitivity is probably one reason why the proposed changes took a long time to implement – not, in fact, until they were precipitated by the queen's imminent arrival and the assembling of a new parliament on 25 February 1445.

The king's marriage, together with a continuing concern for the state of Henry's household, caused parliament in 1445 to take the initiative and submit certain 'Provisions made for the kynges houshold . . . which be seemene necessarie'. Henry appears to have given his assent to them.[98] These ordinances were designed to grapple with all the major problems posed in recent years by the growth of the king's personal establishment. Henry undertook to prevent unauthorized people from residing at court, including the servants of household officials and others left behind after their masters had withdrawn. Household expenditure was placed under careful and regular scrutiny so that 'it may be seen who is most wastfull'; entertainment would be more strictly controlled, and so would the granting of fees and wages to household officials. It seems as if the very meals prepared in the royal kitchen would be scrupulously weighed:

> . . . .the clerk of the cechyne and the maister cokes taken hede that ther be no waste do by them in there offices ne by noon othir undir hem, and that euery man of the seid office go to the halle at her meles but such as ben ordeyned the contrarie. And that the countrollour or on of his clerkys with the seid clerk of cechynne se that non of the seid officers haue no fees in ther offices but suche as haue bene of old tyme acustumed, and that noon of them take no mete out of the cechynne, neither for hem self ne for noon othir, but by deliueraunce by suche as haue the gouernaunce. Also, that the clerk of cechyne sette the nombir of messes both of the chambre, the halle, and the liueres dayly in the panetrie rolle, and the ussher of the cechynne suffre no mannys man ne other persone to come into the cechynne but such as ben of the office self.[99]

Economy and the abolition of waste and embezzlement were the watchwords. If household expenses additional to those authorized in these ordinances were later incurred, the king would have to find the necessary cash himself; if he did not, even warrants from the keeper of the privy seal might be refused by the financial officials of the household. Other undertakings regulated the household's relations with the king's subjects at large. Efforts to reform and control the behaviour of royal purveyors were long overdue,[100] whilst the realization that a steady income would solve a number of knotty problems explains the declaration that the household should be accorded first access to the revenues of the realm, particularly those from wardships, marriages, and other prerogative sources. In the matter of economy, the chief officers of the household – the steward, treasurer, and controller – were enjoined to set an example by incurring only moderate expenses in future.

As these ordinances make clear, after 1436 the king's 'court' had mushroomed in size. By 1445 it included some who were in residence with the king and had their own entourage, including a duke (presumably the young Henry Beauchamp, duke of Warwick, whose company the king enjoyed), the king's secretary, and his confessor.[101] An attempt was now made to limit this large establishment to about 420 persons, but, as we have seen, it did not have much success.[102] A balance had to be struck between assembling a court suitable for a Lancastrian king of England and France, on the one hand, and containing its cost within tolerable limits, on the other. This balance eluded the king and his advisers during the 1440s.

Suffolk's mission to France to escort Margaret of Anjou to England was the single most expensive enterprise embarked upon by Henry's government after his return from France in 1432. It crippled the royal finances during 1444–45 by extending household costs to unprecedented levels, and its effects were highly relevant to the discussion about resumption four years later. Seldom had a foreign-born queen been brought to England with such pomp, for when Suffolk left England in mid-November 1444, he was accompanied by an entourage fit to escort any queen to her kingdom. The marchioness of Suffolk and her ladies were with him, as were five barons and their baronesses, 17 knights, 65 esquires, and 204 valets. On the return journey, this impressive company was augmented by the queen's own Angevin servants, small in number though these were.[103] It was a royal household-in-transit, all of one-half the size of the king's permanent establishment in England and comparable with the splendid entourage which had accompanied Henry himself across the channel in 1430.

Moreover, the initial estimate of three months for the journey to Nancy to meet Margaret and bring her to England turned out to be very optimistic. When Suffolk arrived, he was faced with a long delay while Margaret was brought to the city and a proxy marriage arranged. This meant that she did not actually set foot on English soil until 9 April 1445; with her was the large entourage that had left England almost five months earlier. At generous daily rates of pay, the queen's companions absorbed large sums of money in the shape of wages and rewards. Moreover, the two royal clerks who were put in charge of the finances of the enterprise, John Brekenok and John Everdon, opened their account on 17 July 1444, for such an enormous undertaking required lengthy and careful preparation once Suffolk had returned from the negotiations in France on 27 June. And their account was not closed until 16 October 1445, thereby allowing provision for the coronation at Westminster abbey on 20 May and the formation of Margaret's own domestic organization in place of the temporary household-in-transit. For fifteen months, therefore, a considerable additional burden was laid upon the nation, and a new – albeit transitory – household department was created for the specific purpose of organizing the queen's journey to England and her establishment in her new realm in queenly state.

The exchequer provided most of the necessary cash: £4,234 of it, though miscellaneous additional contributions were collected, amounting to £895 (£133 being lent at Rouen by a representative of the London merchant, William Cantelowe, formerly victualler of Calais, and £53 from some of the Cinque ports as an expression of their obligation to offer mariners' wages for fifteen days). Expenditure of the whole enterprise exceeded even this large figure by as much as £435, and therefore Brekenok and Everdon closed their account in debt. That the queen's entourage was an extension of the royal household is testified by the fact that the two accountants were household clerks of some experience, and the entire company formed a subsidiary household organization for the specific purpose of providing Margaret with a suitably dignified suite on her journey. Brekenok had been clerk of the controlment in the household since 1436 and recently had been appointed receiver-general of the duchy of Cornwall. Everdon had been a clerk in household service even longer (since 1422) and had performed duties in France as well; perhaps as a reward for a job well done, he was promoted in 1447 to be cofferer of the household in succession to Thomas Gloucester.[104]

The strain of this extraordinary financial burden threw the already parlous state of the household finances into confusion and greater debt. The great wardrobe, with its store of drapery, leather, and general mercery, spent almost twice as much as usual in 1443–44, presumably in preparation for the journey to France. In the following year its expenditure was four times as high, standing at well-nigh £6,200; as a result, Robert Rolleston concluded his account having overspent by £646.[105] As far as can be deduced from the surviving accounts of the treasurer of the household (and those for 1444–46 appear to be missing), expenditure by the household in England was in no way significantly reduced when Suffolk and his train went abroad.[106] The money made available to Brekenok and Everdon was an additional burden at a time when the country could ill afford it. Sir Roger Fiennes received from the exchequer during 1445 sums which in total (about £11,820) exceeded the annual figure for every year of Henry VI's reign but 1430, when the wardrobe had played a central role in organizing the king's visit to France. Not only that, but Henry's personal expenditure in the chamber, under the control of John Merston, keeper of the jewels, also rocketed. Henry's private expenses were bound to grow after 1437; but in 1445 they shot up to such a high level that assignments amounting to £5,700, four times the average for the years 1438–44, were required from the exchequer.[107]

Thus, after the king's return from France early in 1432, there were only two occasions of unusually heavy expenditure by the household departments. The first followed his release from tutelage in 1436–37; the second coincided with the plans for his marriage to Margaret of Anjou. The solvency of the household was intimately and directly connected with both. There was a serious crisis of confidence between 1439 and 1443 which reached its peak in 1441, when unpaid tallies and warrants were returned to the exchequer by creditors in considerable number and with alarming frequency. The economy measures of 1440–42 were the result. Yet whatever might have been achieved, Henry's marriage incurred further crippling expenses and an inflation of the household's debt.

The household's growing financial difficulties, even the expedients that were sometimes used to meet them, eventually precipitated a crisis that had political overtones, and which the commons in parliament tried to combat from 1449 by wholesale resumption of the king's earlier gifts and grants.[108]

Substantial financial windfalls arising from the king's prerogative rights were used to discharge some of the household's debts, and especially to pay the wages of officials and the bills of purveyors, merchants, craftsmen, and victuallers who supplied food, wine, and supplies to the court. On 15 June 1446, for example, income from the estates of Henry Beauchamp, late duke of Warwick, which were still in the king's possession, was assigned to the treasurer of the household so that subjects at large should not be burdened with additional taxes or other imposts.[109] Later that year, John Merston, keeper of the king's jewels and plate, was assigned monies from the customs and subsidies payable at Southampton and London; these included £1,000 from Florentine and Genoese merchants visiting the south-coast port.[110] Even small sums were welcome; for instance, a proportion, amounting to 250 marks, of the value of several forfeited estates was diverted to the household on 1 March 1447.[111] In fact, in July of that year, when Henry's prerogative rights were placed for five years under the general supervision of a small group of royal advisers – the chancellor, the treasurer, the steward, and treasurer of the royal household, and Suffolk – the probable intention was to ensure greater financial security for the household as the very hub of government. This group of men would dispose of the profits with the advice and assent of the council, of which they themselves formed the dominant part, provided that no grant was made without Treasurer Lumley's specific approval. This was a most unusual step, for it put a portion of the king's resources – and therefore of his patronage – into commission.[112]

As far as the household was concerned, the results were swift in coming. Within ten days, on 12 July 1447, Sir Thomas Tuddenham, as keeper of the great wardrobe, was assigned £3,700 from customs and subsidies, and his assignment was given preference over all other grants. The same day, Sir John Stourton, treasurer of the household, received £5,000 under the same exclusive conditions, while John Merston had £4,000 five days later for the expenses of the chamber, with preference over all but the grants to his two colleagues. In addition, William Cleve, the king's clerk of works, secured £2,000 on 29 July for construction work at royal palaces and manor house.[113] But intentions are not necessarily translatable into reality, and it was far easier to grant cash than to ensure that the money was actually paid. Instead of £3,700, Tuddenham received £1,203 during the two years 1446–48; instead of £5,000, Stourton had £1,405 in 1446–47, a mere £230 in 1447–48, and no more than £548 in 1448–49.[114] By November 1447, £12,000 was still needed for household expenses, and accordingly the treasurer of England was authorized to appropriate the £6,000 which the staple merchants had undertaken to lend to the king.[115] Already on 1 October, the council had approved the transfer to the household of £10,000 (in addition to £2,000 from the queen) that was anticipated from customs revenue and from lay and clerical taxation conceded in the parliament of 1445.[116] The queen's contribution, at £6 a day so long as she and her entourage lived in the king's household, only once (in 1448–49) reached the designated £2,000 between 1447 and 1451.[117] Nor could the propensity of the great wardrobe to overspend be curbed and by 1448–49 a debt of £1,055 had been incurred on a meagre income of only £435.[118]

The formal assignment of such large sums proved hardly adequate, therefore, to meet the debts and expenses of the royal establishment, with the result that on 30 January 1448 John Merston was authorized to dispose of some of the king's capital assets, including the crown jewels. In order to meet debts of £4,300 (including £3,150 owed to two London goldsmiths for jewels bought in the past as royal gifts), and to repay loans made to the king's chamber, he was instructed to surrender some of Henry's jewels to the goldsmiths.[119]

The allocations arranged by the commission set up in 1447 were made annual ones in the following year. On 14 July 1448 Tuddenham was assigned a further £3,700 for the great wardrobe, whilst for Henry's personal expenses John Merston secured a somewhat larger sum of £4,150 on 2 August 1449, again from the customs revenue.[120] Despite all, at least one aspect of household finance was a lamentable failure. Many of the household's minor servants – its serjeants, gentlemen, yeomen, priests, and clerks – were well in arrears with their wages by 1449 and those which had accumulated since before 1446 alone amounted to about £3,830. The parliament which met in February 1449 proceeded to make arrangements, presumably through the commissioners nominated in 1447, for a small number of lay and clerical household servants to receive on behalf of their fellows the necessary payments from the crown's prerogative resources.[121] This scheme – and the cash intended to fund it – was not entirely adequate, for repayment of the debt was not begun until 1450, and only by mid-1452 had £3,450 of it been discharged to four household representatives, the esquires Bartholomew Halley, Thomas West, George Heton, and Hugh Kyngeston.[122]

Meanwhile, when parliament met again in November 1449, it was informed that the household's expenses were running at about £24,000 annually – £19,000 above the usual annual revenue from the king's livelihood. The subventions provided each year since 1447, and the periodic expedients, were demonstrably incapable of satisfying this order of debt.[123] Therefore, the main purpose of those who demanded resumption in the parliament of 1449 was to place the household on a financially sound foundation, as well as to meet the essential, routine expenses of government. Henry VI and his advisers faced a cruel dilemma when they considered the commons' petition: they could look forward to increased resources if it were approved, but at the unpalatable price of dishonouring royal gifts and grants, placing constraints on the king's patronage, and running the risk of sullying Henry's reputation as the provider of 'good lordship'. The king accepted the petition, but he also exempted from its terms a long list of household servants and dependents, headed by the treasurer of the household, Lord Stourton.[124] The prospect of resumption meant that far larger sums than hitherto were passed from the exchequer to the treasurer of the household during 1448–52. No longer able to call on the resources of the duchies of Lancaster and Cornwall, he relied on the exchequer as the largest single contributor to household funds. Thus, whereas in 1447–48 £5,340 was paid into the wardrobe by exchequer officials, the annual figure between Michaelmas 1448 and Michaelmas 1452 was in the region of £10,000, and to judge by the total figure for the period between November 1446 and March 1453, given in Stourton's account, the treasurer was at least able to balance his books, though he had little or nothing to spare.[125]

The king's government naturally continued to employ familiar expedients to help meet its financial obligations. On 22 May 1450 the £620 which was owed to merchants from the city of Lucca for expensive silks and gold cloth bought by Sir Thomas Tuddenham for the great wardrobe, was repaid in kind in the form of licences to trade without paying customs duties until the entire debt had been cleared.[126] And later in the year, John Merston was again requested to value some of the crown jewels in anticipation of their sale to yet more royal creditors.[127]

The government's abiding concern with adequate finance, especially for the household, had become more feverish as the months passed. Resources were disposed of, sometimes temporarily, sometimes permanently, to meet short-term situations, and this simply made worse the basic problem of financing an elaborate organization in the long term with inadequate resources. Resumption would cut the Gordian knot provided the exemptions were not allowed seriously to undermine its purpose. On another level, however, the political and personal effects of resumption on the relationship between king and subject might more seriously damage the credibility of the régime and, in some measure, respect for the king.

The unpopularity of the king's purveyors

During the early years of Henry's majoirity, some of the activities of his household servants attracted public criticism, and their high-handed methods brought the institution itself into disrepute. This was especially the case with the ruthless purveyance of food and other materials from the villages and towns of England – especially in the south-east – which an enlarged household required. The king had an undoubted right to buy provisions for his and his dependants' needs at the lowest rate and to compel the owners to sell; but ever since Magna Carta, attempts had been made to regulate the right and prevent its abuse, and in Edward III's reign secular and regular clergy alike had been specifically protected by statute.[128] The problem became more acute after 1436. Complaints were expressed in the parliament of 1439–40 because supplies were being commandeered in large quantities without their owners' consent or without the immediate settlement of bills. Henry undertook early in 1440 to rectify this abuse by insisting that some of the cash recently made available to the household by parliament should go towards alleviating those who were being exploited by the royal purveyors. He was clearly concerned about the problem, but he wisely warned that reforms would take time. The commons were induced to leave the matter to the council to resolve by 24 June 1440.[129] This sensitive question, which touched a number of ordinary subjects where it hurt most, was one reason why the king was anxious to channel more cash into the household – even those duchy of Lancaster revenues that had been assigned to fulfil the provisions of his father's will. Not unnaturally, this particular proposal brought a strong protest from two of the surviving feoffees of the dead king, Beaufort and Lord Hungerford: they stood firmly by their obligation to Henry V, whose will had still not been fully executed. However, even they were persuaded to agree that when the last testamentary instruction had been carried out, these resources should be transferred to Henry VI's household. It was a solution that seems to have been proposed by the king himself.[130]

The best reply to complaints of this sort was an ample supply of cash, for that would reduce the likelihood of oppression and mollify the victims of rapacious purveyors. But the commons were equally perturbed about the behaviour of the purveyors, regardless of whether they had adequate cash in their pockets. Subsequent parliaments were determined to enforce statutes regulating and restricting the activities of the royal agents. Thus, in 1442 they were required to pay on the spot for all but the smallest purchases, and JPs were authorized to protect the exploited tradesman and farmer.[131] Similar grievances were re-hearsed in 1445, when an effort was made to confine purveyance to the personal needs of the king and his bride. The agents of lords, including those of the king's heir, Gloucester, were to be arrested in future if they persisted in their burdensome operations. If unchecked, unscrupulous or high-handed servants might besmirch the reputation of the monarch himself, and hence the regulations devised in this parliament for the reform of the king's household included a new oath which bound purveyors to eschew corruption, force, and favour 'in such wyse that the grete clamour had aforetymes . . . mowe cesse'.[132]

That purveyance continued to be burdensome and to degenerate into enforced seizure – little short of theft in the king's interest – is reflected in the protection which some fortunate individuals secured from the king to present to the royal agents on their rounds. On 16 May 1446, for instance, Henry Somer, the recently retired chancellor of the exchequer, and his tenants were declared immune from the obligation to entertain the king's household and quarter its horses while on its tours; two months later, John Kette, a clerk, was assured that the household officers would not forcibly seize his goods or commandeer lodgings on his property without his consent.[133] Others were not so lucky. The exemption which ecclesiastics had enjoyed for a century and more was repeatedly ignored in the 1440s.[134] Then, in 1449 the commons again remonstrated with the king's ministers, claiming that many a man had had his horses seized without permission or, one suspects, payment by Henry's servants, but an attempt to stop the practice and investigate the more blatant examples of it was rejected by the king, whose household relied heavily on horse flesh acquired in this way.[135] It was reported, too, that even the humbler members of the household – the king's minstrels were mentioned – were in the habit of flaunting their livery and their position as royal employees; some of them demanded exactions as they travelled from place to place, capitalizing on their role as the king's personal entertainers. That it was a profitable and widespread malpractice is indicated by the fact that ordinary husbandmen and artificers, with little skill but plenty of gall, took to posing as royal minstrels. The king was roused by this insult: he determined to stop purveyance by unauthorized men impersonating the king's liveried servants and officials – but not purveyance itself.[136]

The parliament of 1449–50, which wrestled with the desperate problem of household finance and condemned Henry's foremost minister, Suffolk, also examined the heavy material burdens which the household imposed on the king's subjects via purveyance. Complaints on this score were loud and frequent in the commons' chamber. Eventually, it was decided that for seven years, as from 7 May 1450, sums of money should be set aside to meet the annual cost of essential purveyance. In all, £5,630 was assigned, in addition to whatever revenue was left in the duchy of Lancaster after the running costs of duchy administration had been met and the queen's dower paid; and apart from repayment of any future loans obtained by the household, this expenditure was to have priority over all else.[137] This outspoken assembly also took action at long last against the forcible seizure of horses and carriages to transport the king and queen and their entourage on their travels. Hostillers, brewers, and victuallers, on whom the household relied and to whom life-grants were sometimes given as recompense, often exceeded their authority by commandeering horses and carriages even when the court was not on the move; nor were they above holding their owners to ransom as the price of obtaining immunity from their attentions. This blatant abuse was outlawed by parliament, though the king was understandably concerned lest his legitimate needs and his prerogative right to purvey should in any way be prejudiced.[138]

Aside from the odium that clung to a number of the king's ministers, there is no doubt that by 1449 the public reputation of the household and its officials was badly tarnished, and not without reason. It is equally apparent that the commons in 1449–50 were prepared to criticize forthrightly this aspect of Henry's rule and to propose stern measures for its reform that did not rest with the impeachment of an individual. To cleanse the Augean stables would be no quick or easy task, but this parliament was in a mood to act firmly and fearlessly to obtain improvements. Parliaments, however, had an essentially temporary existence and the zeal displayed by its members during a short session would very likely dissipate after dissolution.

Notes

1 G. R. Elton, 'Tudor government: the points of contact, III. The court', *TRHS*, 5th ser., XXVI (1976), 211.
2 ibid., 212, and cf. Dickens, *Courts of Europe* pp. 55-6. For Edward IV's court as a centre of ceremony and political influence, see C. D. Ross, *Edward IV* (1974), pp. 258-62, 313-17.
3 Respectively, PRO, E101/409/2, 4-7, 10, 12-13, 15, 18; 410/4, 7, 10; 408/23; 409/8, 16, 20; 410/1, 9; 408/24-25; 409/9, 11; 410/3, 6. For the use of the word 'court' in an institutional, as well as a locative, sense, see A. R. Myers, 'Some household ordinances of Henry VI', *BJRL*, XXXVI (1954), 456-67, reprinted in idem, *Household of Edward IV*, pp. 69-75.
4 The arrival and departure of distinguished visitors – ambassadors, councillors, magnates and their wives – were frequently noted by the treasurer of the household in his account of daily expenditure on food and drink (e. g., PRO, E101/408/24 [1437–38]).
5 D. A. L. Morgan, 'The king's affinity in the polity of Yorkist England', *TRHS*, 5th ser., XXIII (1973), 2-4.
6 Myers, *BJRL*, XXXVI (1954), 460-7.
7 See the lists (for 1445) in ibid.
8 Hence the implied separation of sections of the household in the daily accounts of food, drink, and transport (e.g., PRO, E101/410/6 [1450–51]).
9 Ross, *Edward IV*, p. 327 and n. 1. This is implied in the 1445 ordinances,

though it is doubtful if the recommendation that those with only few fees or offices from the king should stay in the household was observed under Henry VI (Myers, *BJRL*, XXXVI [1954], 458).

10 PRO, E101/409/16.

11 ibid., 408/25, using, as far as possible, D. A. L. Morgan's mode of calculation in *TRHS*, 5th ser., XXIII (1976), 5.

12 Myers, *BJRL*, XXXVI (1954), 460-7; PRO, E101/409/16.

13 ibid., 410/9.

14 Clerks were also numerous: 68, 76, and 75 in those same years.

15 Below, p. 332.

16 Wedgwood, *Biographies*, pp. 311, 816-17; PRO, E404/46/302-3. Sir Ralph Rocheford, a king's knight from 1428, left instructions in his will (March 1439) that his 3 sons should be taken to court and placed in the charge of his executors, among whom were Lord Cromwell and Bishop Alnwick; but none seems to have found a place in the king's household (above, p. 55; WA MS 14,740).

17 Wedgwood, *Biographies*, pp. 458, 605; Jeffs, thesis, pp. 297-8. Hende's mother, in any case, was a daughter of Sir John Norbury, one of Henry IV's most faithful servants; she had married Sudeley by 1425–26 (PRO, E404/42/266).

18 Wedgwood, *Biographies*, pp. 621-2, 822-3; Jeffs, thesis, pp. 154-5, 327-8. Strelley was the son of Kemp's sister, Isabella.

19 Above, p. 207; PRO, E404/57/273; 62/178. Henry Beauchamp was about 4 years younger than the king and died in 1446 at the age of only 21 (*GEC*, XII, ii, 383-4).

20 Above, p. 258.

21 For payments from the queen to the treasurer of the household while she was in the king's household, at the rate of £6 per day, see e.g., PRO, E101/409/16, and above, p. 257.

22 Below, p. 729.

23 For Noreys, see below, p. 303. Henry Langton, a yeoman of the chamber from 1436, was granted a house in London in 1441 jointly with another royal servant, John Croke (Wedgwood, *Biographies*, pp. 525-6).

24 WA MS 17,759, 17,776; PRO, E404/57/304, 53. Slyfirst was later (by 1450) sent to the Isle of Wight as royal bailiff (ibid., 66/216). The properties owned by the great wardrobe are noted in the treasurer's annual account (e.g., PRO, E101/409/4).

25 C. L. Kingsford, *A Survey of London by John Stow* (2 vols., Oxford, 1908), II, 4, 35, 45, 53-4, 56, 89, 92-3, 99-100, with a city map at the end of the volume. See also idem, 'Historical notes on mediaeval London houses', *London topographical record*, X (1916), 44-144; XI (1917), 28-81.

26 Kingsford, *Stow's survey*, I, 66, 149, 236-7, 247, 343; II, 11, 13, 15, 279-80, 321-2, 344, 350, 358-9. A list of magnate houses in the city, largely (but not entirely) based on Stow's record, is in M. I. Peake, 'London and the Wars of the Roses, 1445–61' (London MA thesis, 1925), pp. 174-83.

27 *CPR, 1446–52*, p. 432; *PL*, II, 60 (3 January 1451).

28 ibid., 61. Cf. also ibid., 523-30, relating to the same matter.

29 Gairdner, *PL*, I, 187 (12 January 1451). For Blake, see Wedgwood, *Biographies*, pp. 80-1.

30 *PL*, II, 56 (11 November 1450).

31 Above, pp. 58ff. Merston was still treasurer of the chamber in 1451–52 (PRO, E404/68/185).

32 *HBC*, p. 79; J. S. Roskell, 'Sir John Popham, knight banneret, of Charford', *Proc. Hants. Archaeological Soc. and Field Club*, XXI (1958), 38-52; idem, *Speakers*, pp. 235-7.

33 Wedgwood, *Biographies*, p. 324; Jeffs, thesis, pp. 289-93; below, p. 339.

34 Feriby had been controller since at least 1429–30 (PRO, E404/46/197).

35 Roskell, *Lancaster knights*, pp. 123-8, 162-72; PRO, E101/410/6; below, p. 343.

36 Emden, *Oxford*, III, 1514: R. G. Davies, thesis, pp. ccxxv-ccxxvi; above, p. 59. For the constitution of Henry's chapel *c.* 1448–49, see W. Ullmann (ed.), *Liber regie capelle* (Henry Bradshaw Soc., XCII, 1961).

37 Emden, *Cambridge*, p. 170; above, p. 72.

38 Emden, *Oxford*, I, 556-7; PRO, E101/408/24, 25; above, p. 58.

39 *GEC*, XII, i, 419-21.

40 Wedgwood, *Biographies*, pp. 637-9; Jeffs, thesis, pp. 311-13. Myers, *BJRL*, XLII (1959), 115-16, 121; above, p. 298.

41 Wedgwood, *Biographies*, pp. 880-1; Roskell, *Speakers*, pp. 244-6; below, pp. 585ff.

42 *HBC*, p. 79; above, p. 278.

43 *HBC*, p. 76; Wedgwood, *Biographies*, p. 65. Suffolk himself surrendered the stewardship of the household to Sudeley by 3 February 1447, though this in no way meant a diminution of his influence over the king (*HBC*, p. 76).

44 Emden, *Cambridge*, pp. 27-8; PRO, E101/409/13; Cobban, op. cit., pp. 188-92, 285.

45 Emden, *Oxford*, III, 1649–50; PRO, E101/410/3. Say remained dean of the royal chapel into Edward IV's reign.

46 Emden, *Oxford*, I, 556-7; Gascoigne, pp. 35-6, 200. De la Bere became bishop of St David's in September 1447.

47 Emden, *Oxford*, III, 1672–3; PRO, E101/410/1; above, p. 243. He seems to have been most consistently patronized by Robert Gilbert, bishop of London and himself the dean of the chapel royal who was dismissed in March 1432 (R. G. Davies, thesis, pp. cxxx-cxxxii).

48 'Benet's Chron.', p. 202. Boulers had recently been attacked by his Glos. tenants for his alleged role in the loss of the French territories (*EHL*, pp. 355-6). It may be significant that, unlike most household officials and courtiers, Dudley was not confirmed in those of his grants cancelled by the 1451 act of resumption (Wolffe, *Royal Demesne*, pp. 282, 285).

49 Ferguson, op. cit., pp. 179, 184, 189, 193; Emden, *Oxford*, I, 228-9; below, pp. 493-4.

50 *PL*, II, 174-5; *GEC*, VI, 562-3. In a cordial meeting with Oldhall, Henry VI himself is reported to have appealed to Oldhall to speak to York about the possibility of his offering assistance to one of the king's esquires for the body, John Penycock, who had earlier been denounced by Cade's rebels (*PL*, II, 174; Roskell, *Speakers*, p. 244).

51 *GEC*, XI, 506; *PL*, II, 176, 179-80 (where men were advised to 'cherse and wirchep well' Sir William Oldhall).

52 ibid.; Roskell, *Speakers*, pp. 244-5. Heydon, like Tuddenham, was one of Suffolk's affinity and he had acted with the duke as a feoffee of Sir Thomas Hoo (Wedgwood, *Biographies*, pp. 452-3).

53 J. S. Roskell, 'William Tresham of Sywell', *Northants. Past and Present*, II (1954–59), 189-203.

54 When Tresham was waylaid, he was wearing a collar of the king's livery (*RP*, V, 211-13). His son Thomas, who was wounded in the ambush, was another household servant who continued in favour after 1450 (J. S. Roskell, 'Sir Thomas Tresham, knight', *Northants. Past and Present*, II [1954–59], 313-23).

55 *RP*, V, 211-13. The pseudo-William Worcester simply records that Tresham was riding towards the duke (Stevenson, II, ii, 769). Tresham was never a member of York's council (as R. L. Storey claimed in *End of Lancaster*, p. 80), and J. S. Roskell has already expressed some unease on the question of his connection with Duke Richard (*Northants. Past and Present*, II [1954–59], 198-99, 201-3, 315).

56 Roskell, *Speakers*, p. 240 n. 2.

57 PRO, KB9/94/1, especially no. 22 (10–12 August).

58 Stevenson, II, ii, 769; *EHL*, p. 372. Thomas Tresham, in fact, became a feoffee of Lord Grey (then earl of Kent) in June 1470 (Roskell, *Northants. Past and Present*, II [1954–59], 320). Among the murderers were 4 Welshmen who may have orginally come from Grey's Welsh estates to live in Northants (R. I. Jack, *The Grey of Ruthin Valor* [Sydney, 1965], p. 74 n.4).

59 *RP*, V, 211-13. For this whole matter, see Griffiths, *JMH*, I (1975), 197-8.

60 PRO, E101/410/7; Wedgwood, *Biographies*, pp. 227-8; Somerville, op. cit., p. 399; *CPR, 1452–61*, p. 77; above, p. 260. Tuddenham was not removed from the keepership in June (as in Wedgwood, *Biographies*, p. 880). Cotton was clerk and porter of the great wardrobe by July 1437 (PRO, E101/409/4, 5). For his account (1452–53) as the queen's receiver-general, see Myers, *BJRL*, XL (1957–58), 79-113, 391-431.

61 Wedgwood, *Biographies*, p. 325. Filongley's brother-in-law, Robert Darcy, another lawyer, seems to have been in Bedford's service; four of his children married into the family of Sir John Tyrell, one of Gloucester's supporters (ibid., p. 258; Roskell, *1422*, pp. 71, 171-2).

62 Roskell, *Lancaster knights*, p. 168; PRO, E101/410/6; above, p. 302.

63 *HBC*, pp. 76, 79; Wedgwood, *Biographies*, p. 115; PRO, E101/409/20.

64 PRO, E101/409/16, 18; Roskell, *1422*, p. 213.

65 Wedgwood, *Biographies*, p. 55; Chrimes and Brown, op. cit., p. 293; below, p. 343.

66 PRO, E101/410/9; Wedgwood, *Biographies*, pp. 934-5.

67 *RP*, V, 216-17, reprinted in Chrimes and Brown, op. cit., pp. 292-4. The dating is suggested by the fact that the commons' petition spoke of those whom it attacked forfeiting their offices and profits as from 1 December, and because Sir Thomas Tuddenham, who had resigned the keepership of the great wardrobe by 3 December, was not among the discredited royal servants: above, p. 306.

68 Below, p. 641. The fact that their trial had produced few punishments goes some way to explaining the renewed attack in the following winter – a suggestion made by R. E. Archer, 'The court party during the ascendancy of the duke of Suffolk, 1444–50' (Bristol BA dissertation, 1977), p. 53.

69 Ferguson, op. cit., pp. 184, 193, 207. There is a useful analysis of these courtiers in Archer, dissertation, pp. 26ff.

70 Below, p. 355.

71 Emden, *Oxford*, I, 228-9; below, p. 350.
72 Emden, *Oxford*, II, 1037–8; Ferguson, op. cit., pp. 181, 190, 207. Kent stayed in office despite the petition.
73 Above, p. 54.
74 Otway-Ruthven, *King's secretary*, pp. 95-102, 156. He served in England from 1436.
75 Wedgwood, *Biographies*, pp. 413-14 (Hampden), 415-16 (Hampton); Storey, *End of Lancaster*, pp. 226-7 (Wingfield).
76 Wedgwood, *Biographies*, pp. 630-1 (Newport), 676-7 (Penycock), 253-5 (Daniel).
77 *RP*, V, 216-17. R. L. Storey (*End of Lancaster*, p. 81) mistakenly notes that 20 persons were attacked in the petition.
78 Above, pp. 288ff. In addition, John Somerset was still the king's doctor in 1450–51, and John Penycock, Thomas Daniel, John Say, John Stanley, Thomas Pulford, Bartholomew Halley, and Ralph Babthorp were among the squires of the household in 1451–52 (PRO, E101/410/7, 9).
79 *CPR, 1446–52*, pp. 403, 419; Roskell, *Lancaster knights*, pp. 168-9; Archer, dissertation, p. 46; below, p. 361. It is also relevant to note that in the second act of resumption of 1451, Stanley did not receive an exemption for his grant of Mold castle, manor, and town (*CPR, 1446–52*, p. 539).
80 Sir William Beauchamp was not only one of Stanley's colleagues in the household, but was associated with him in north Wales as constable of Caernarvon and Beaumaris castles (since 1446); at Beaumaris, moreover, he had custody of Eleanor Cobham (PRO, E28/76/33; E. Breese, *Kalendars of Gwynedd* [1873], p. 122; below, p. 343).
81 *PPC*, V, 16.
82 *RP*, V, 13.
83 PRO, E28/65/4-5. Bishop Aiscough seems to have been the only royal adviser present.
84 *RP*, V, 7.
85 PRO, E28/63/29. The 4,000 marks from the exchequer was first paid on 16 July 1440 (PRO, E403/739 m. 13). The duchy of Lancaster had been transferring cash to the wardrobe since the end of 1436 at a modest rate (i.e., £5,779 during Michaelmas 1436–38 [PRO, E101/408/23 m. 1]). It was able to do so because the duchy's portion of Queen Katherine's dower (worth about £2,400 *per annum*) returned to the crown on her death in January 1437 (*RP*, IV, 183-9; above, p. 61).
86 PRO, E101/409/8, 9, 11.
87 ibid., 2, 4, 5, 7, 10.
88 *PPC*, V, 122.
89 *CPR, 1441–46*, p. 82; *PPC*, V, 31.
90 PRO, E28/69/40; E403/742 m. 7; 744 m. 5. ibid., E28/69/42 is a list of some of these tallies (worth £4,133).
91 PRO, E403/744 m. 10; *RP*, V, 62. The £10,000 would have covered the rest of the outstanding £7,167-worth of tallies.
92 *RP*, V, 62.
93 PRO, E28/71/28 (undated but assigned to 1443).
94 PRO, E403/737-56 passim.
95 ibid., 733-47 passim.
96 It may be noted that in 1442 the great wardrobe received far less cash from the exchequer than at any time since 1434 (ibid., 713-44 passim).

97 *RP*, V, 63.
98 Myers, *BJRL*, XXXVI (1954), 456-66. Questions about the date of these ordinances and the king's assent to them are satisfactorily dealt with here and in idem, *Household of Edward IV*, pp. 63-75.
99 Myers, *BJRL*, XXXVI (1954), 457.
100 For purveyors, see below, pp. 320-2.
101 It is not known at what precise point in the parliament of 1445 these ordinances were presented or approved; Warwick was created duke on 5 April 1445, and the parliament did not end until 9 April 1446. It is just possible, though unlikely, that Gloucester was the duke referred to.
102 Above, p. 297.
103 Kingsford, *Prejudice and promise*, pp. 157-8; 'Benet's Chron.', p. 190; below, p. 486. The account of John Brekenok and John Everdon is printed in Stevenson, I, 443-60; it is enrolled in PRO, E364/82 F 26 Henry VI E.
104 Wedgwood, *Biographies*, pp. 106-7; Somerville, op. cit., p. 642; PRO, E404/39/330; 42/278, 279; 46/236; E101/409/16.
105 PRO, E101/409/12, 13.
106 ibid., 11 (1443-44), 16 (1446-47).
107 PRO, E403/756-7, 760.
108 The fundamental studies of the petitions for resumption are by B. P. Wolffe, 'Acts of resumption in the Lancastrian parliaments, 1399-1456', *EHR*, LXXIII (1958), 583-613, and *Royal demesne*, ch. IV, V, appendix C.
109 *CPR.*, *1437-46*, p. 437.
110 ibid., *1446-52*, pp. 13 (12 September 1446), 31.
111 ibid., p. 46.
112 ibid., p. 61; above, p. 286.
113 ibid., pp. 67, 68, 75. After the king's marriage, considerable repairs were undertaken at Westminster, Windsor, and Clarendon manor (ibid., pp. 375, 394, 412).
114 PRO, E101/409/18, 20.
115 *CPR, 1446-52*, p. 114.
116 ibid., p. 123; below, p. 380. £5,000 of this was specifically earmarked for the king's personal alms-giving.
117 It more usually stood at between £1,364 and £1,726 (PRO, E101/409/16, 20). The rate of payment was increased from £6 to £7 per day in the spring of 1453, perhaps as a result of her pregnancy (ibid., 409/20; Myers, *BJRL*, XL [1957-58], 429-30).
118 PRO, E101/410/4. For overspending in 1446-48, see ibid., 409/18.
119 *CPR, 1446-52*, p. 156.
120 ibid., pp. 183, 233, 261; *CCR, 1452-61*, p. 90.
121 *RP*, V, 157, 158.
122 Their account is PRO, E101/410/5.
123 *RP*, V, 183. In 1451-52 the treasurer of the household received only £963 from customs and subsidies, the ports of Lynne, Hull, and Yarmouth producing nothing at all (PRO, E101/410/9). If 'livelihood' meant the crown's ancient revenues from shire, town, and feudal sources, £5,000 may have been a slight underestimate; Cromwell had estimated a total of about £7,000 in 1433, though the king's generosity is likely to have reduced this (see above, p. 108).
124 *RP*, V, 186ff.

125 PRO, E101/409/20; 410/4, 9. See also PRO, E403/774-5, 778-9, 783, 785-6, 788. Similar increases in exchequer payments were received by the treasurer of the great wardrobe during 1450–53, and from 1451 he was able to keep his account in balance (ibid., E101/410/7, 10; Longleat MS misc. 1).
126 *CPR, 1446–52*, p. 375.
127 ibid., p. 401.
128 F. W. Maitland, *The constitutional history of England* (Cambridge, 1909), p. 183. It was also customary for the purveyors to pay when they liked.
129 *RP*, V, 7.
130 ibid., p. 8; above, p. 111.
131 *RP*, V, 55.
132 ibid., pp. 103, 115; Myers, *Household of Edward IV*, pp. 67-8.
133 *CPR, 1446–52*, pp. 427, 441. Kette had had to supply food for Louis of Luxembourg, the former chancellor of Lancastrian France, on one occasion (PRO, E404/62/112).
134 WA MS 12,734, 1,540 (for Westminster abbey's Surrey manors in 1443 and 1448); BristRO, Museum deed 5,139 (463)(confirming Tewkesbury abbey's privilege, January 1453).
135 *RP*, V, 154. For horses bought by the treasurer of the household in 1437–39, costing more than £11, see PRO, E101/408/25.
136 *CPR, 1446–52*, p. 262. Seven of his own minstrels were appointed to inquire and punish the guilty.
137 *RP*, V, 174. The duchy officers paid £400 into the great wardrobe in 1451–52, while the exchequer supplied £1,832 (PRO, E101/410/10).
138 *RP*, V, 202. For the widespread suspicion of purveyors in Kent by 1450, see below, p. 631.

14   The King's Patronage and the Royal Household

The favoured servants

Membership of Henry VI's enlarged household afforded sure access to his patronage. Household servants and court friends – and there were many more of them after 1436 than at any time since Henry V's reign (and perhaps earlier, in view of that monarch's frequent absences abroad) – were foremost among its recipients. The way in which the king rewarded, patronized, excused, and encouraged this veritable regiment of men (and women) can scarcely be paralleled in medieval England for its indulgence, generosity, and liberality – often to excessive lengths. The extent to which Henry allocated his resources in this way, and deployed his patronage in response to petitions from his household and his court, is a large and complex subject that merits detailed investigation. An impressionable monarch who was indulgent by nature, inexperienced in his craft, and as a result possessed of an imprecise appreciation of his available resources, was likely to respond readily to the advice of friends and companions, and to the importunings of associates, servants, and acquaintances. By so doing, he submitted gradually to their influence. He not only dangerously impoverished himself and alienated others who were denied his favour, but gave opportunity to the unprincipled to abuse an entrenched position; and, by a regrettable lack of supervision, Henry seriously weakened central control over his agents at large.

Henry VI's household servants were foremost among those who received lands, cash, offices, and favours from the king after 1436. Such men had a unique opportunity to attract the king's favour, and they were usually able to take advantage of it successfully and, in some cases, handsomely. They received custody of lands temporarily in the king's hands: Thomas Daniel, one of Henry's more notorious esquires, secured for life in February 1446 two-thirds of the manor of Troutbeck in Westmorland for £17 8s. 6d. per annum.[1] Others were installed in important and, presumably, profitable offices on the crown estates; this was the good fortune of Edmund Blake, a king's serjeant who was described as clerk 'for the king's secrets' (i.e., in the signet office) in July 1450 when he became steward of the honour of Richmond in Norfolk and Suffolk for life.[2] Some were rewarded within the household for services that may have extended far beyond its comfortable world:

John Bury, a yeoman-usher of the king's hall who had spent more than twenty-four years in Henry's employ, both in the household and in France, and had been imprisoned on one occasion during the war, was appointed a royal serjeant-at-arms for life on 26 May 1447.[3] A number availed themselves of the wardships and marriages that were part of the king's prerogative resources and from which a custodian could expect to reap temporary benefits by vigorous exploitation and, as far as the marriage went, a careful deployment of the widow or maiden. This was precisely the prospect before Master Richard Andrew, the king's secretary from 1442, when he paid 50 marks on 23 October 1449 for a wardship.[4]

Several of these grants did not even guarantee the king the customary modest fine or payment in return.[5] At the same time, a substantial number of grants which had formerly been issued during pleasure were now (after 1436) converted into life-grants. This was a common enough practice, but under Henry VI there was little or no justification for its extension to offices of considerable political or financial importance. Thus, the customer of the wool subsidy at Calais, John Stoughton, who had held office during pleasure, was made a life-appointee on 13 December 1437; Stoughton was clerk of the great catery (or purchasing department) of the household at the time.[6] Other patents granted for life in the early years of the king's majority were new ones but they favoured similar people: James Fiennes, an esquire of the body, secured the constableship of Rochester castle in March 1442.[7] Some of these appointments, such as that of John Fenwyk, a royal serjeant, of the receiver-generalship of Bamburgh castle (Northumberland) on 6 June 1444 for life, ran the risk of weakening the recipients' obligation to account at Westminster.[8] Certain household employees were especially favoured to enable them to advance their family's dynastic interests. James Fiennes, one of the most generously endowed and universally detested of Henry's companions in these years, received lands in fee simple on 11 February 1440, and two and a half years later he and his heirs secured £40 *per annum* in place of an earlier life-grant to James alone.[9] The depletion of the crown's resources for an indeterminate period in the future was the inevitable consequence, and the accountability to which officials would normally have been subject was shadowy indeed when they became hereditary appointees.

There was a complementary willingness in Henry to countenance the accumulation of valuable properties and worthwhile offices in a single, much favoured hand, with consequences that smacked of absenteeism and encouraged inefficiency and a near-monopoly of royal patronage by a restricted group of king's friends and servants. Reliance on absentee officials in all quarters of the realm was a significant outcome of this imprudent course. John Everdon, for example, was not only clerk of accounts in the household (which, to judge by its financial problems, should have been a full-time occupation) but also receiver of the lordship of Guisnes (a taxing undertaking at a time of military alarm) from 2 November 1440.[10] One may reasonably doubt whether Everdon was able to devote himself properly to both tasks simultaneously. The same may be said of Sir Robert Roos's position as chamberlain and customer of Berwick-on-Tweed, an office to which he was appointed for life on 30 March 1443, even though he was a knight-carver in the royal household and a regular attendant on the king.[11] Berwick could hardly afford an absentee official: its defensive role on the Scottish border required careful and regular financing, and any profit from the town might be frittered or salted away without constant vigilance.

The security of the realm, too, might be imperilled by the appointment of household servants to the constableships of royal castles, for it is ironic that this should have been a frequent practice just when invasion scares were alarming the southern coasts of England. Salisbury castle was placed in the charge of two household officials in survivorship on 1 July 1442, and the same had happened at Odiham castle (Hampshire) on 30 September 1441.[12] Even fortresses far from Westminster and Windsor received household custodians, with all the implications for neglect which that involved. At Beaumaris (so a patent of August 1442 ran) Sir William Beauchamp, a royal carver, was to be installed whenever the sitting constable, Richard Walkestede, should die, whereas on 28 January 1445 a royal serjeant-at-law and clerk of the counting-house, who could hardly perform his legal and financial duties if he were not within easy call, was installed at Winchester castle for life.[13]

The influence of these men on the formulation of public policy was probably not very significant, unless they happened to be senior members of the household who were also royal councillors or, when the council itself lacked vigour and coherence, had a personal attachment to the king. Otherwise, a household man was influential only in so far as his position gave him opportunity to seek a favour for a friend, obstruct the advancement of a rival, or create a minor 'connection' of his own at court. Thus, John Penycock, a prominent household servant who benefited much from the king's favour, was able to secure a royal pardon for an acquaintance on 18 February 1449; Henry himself signed the pardon to excuse a monk's violation of the fourteenth-century statute of *praemunire* in accepting bulls from the pope without royal permission.[14]

The spate of ill-conceived appointments extended even beyond the store of offices, lands, and resources which at any moment were currently at the king's disposal. Henry began to anticipate his resources, making grants that would take effect at an unspecified date in the future; his ability to reward and act in response to particular circumstances as they arose was thereby curtailed. Sir William Beauchamp's appointment at Beaumaris is a case in point; but equally on 2 January 1443 two royal esquires, Geoffrey Pole and Thomas West, were nominated in survivorship to the constableship of Leeds castle (Kent) after the death of the present constable, Sir John Steward.[15]

Among those household servants who benefited most handsomely from the king's generosity after 1436, a small number stand head and shoulders above the rest. James Fiennes, the younger brother of Sir Roger Fiennes, treasurer of the household, enriched himself in Kent and Sussex, where his family was already prominent.[16] John St Lo's standing further west was based no less securely on his household connection.[17] Although a royal esquire and annuitant as early as 1428, his greatest gifts were received after the king came of age. Of Somerset stock, he acquired the constableship of Bristol castle in fee tail in 1443, and extended his landed interests in Wiltshire by marriage and royal grants. He, Fiennes, and a number of other household friends were nominated as feoffees in Henry VI's will of 1443–44. It may be that St Lo's career had been set fair by Cardinal Beaufort, but there can be little doubt that his later closeness to Henry VI himself was of the utmost value to his advancement in the western shires. An older man who had been at the king's side since the 1420s, was John Somerset, his tutor and physician.[18] Immensely learned and a polymath of his day, Somerset was a teacher and doctor of distinction. Ecclesiastical pensions were lavished on him, especially when the king grew to manhood. He became chancellor of the exchequer and warden of the king's exchange and mint (in 1439), and surveyor of works at the royal residences (1442). The extent of Somerset's learning and his influence on the king were relatively unusual and he reaped very substantial rewards in consequence.

Such patronage had its attractive side, for it showed the king to be a sympathetic and generous man who was loyal to friends and servants alike. He rarely neglected the nurses who had cared for him in his childhood, and later on he guaranteed their pensions for life.[19] Yet in a king, this unstinting liberality was foolhardy and, if continued, financially disastrous and politically dangerous. The crown's material resources were being depleted in an improvident fashion. The degree of accountability to which officers, both central and provincial, were subjected was weakened in an increasing number of cases. Inefficiency, pluralism, and absenteeism were able to flourish, and even the country's security might be compromised in certain circumstances. After a year or so of personal rule, his council began to appreciate the significance of what was happening. On 3 February 1438 it expressed concern on two grounds: the threat to sound financial administration posed by appointments for life, and the implications of grants that allowed a deputy to act for a receiver.[20] The cautionary advice was disregarded. More constructive criticism was formulated during 1444, when the council returned to the whole question of patronage and suggested a number of practical rules to modify its application.[21] Almost seven years of royal prodigality were having damaging effects. But they hardly seem to have been appreciated by the king. A lack of awareness of the need for solvency in the household and for efficient administration among his servants dictated the pardon to his esquire, John Thorley, on 4 February 1446. Thorley was excused from paying all the arrears and current income for which he had responsibility as clerk of the market and clerk in the avenar's office.[22] His role as a purchaser for the household meant that sums of money constantly passed through his hands; in a sound organization, he would have accounted for them regularly, but the obligation to do so was now lifted from his shoulders at a stroke. Equally ill-considered, though in a different way, was Henry's readiness to forgive his household servants the offences and misdemeanours which ordinarily would have brought them to court. Thus, on 5 February 1446, John St Lo was pardoned a series of offences which included the illegal giving of livery, and this favour was coupled with a general pardon.[23]

Patronage and the provinces

The king's patronage of household servants had important implications for government and the kingdom at large, and its provincial dimension requires major study. Henry's characteristic attitude to administrative appointments had predictable results on the quality of local government, order and security in the realm, and the effectiveness of the central government's control over the provinces. The king's disposal of his prerogative rights and profits had similar consequences: his attitude towards wardships and marriages, the estates of royal wards, and the forfeited properties of criminals and traitors rested on principles that were frequently devised by an entourage that fully expected to be generously patronized. These principles reveal much about Henry's conception of the duties of a king and the business of ruling.

The English shires

The king's promotion to office of loyal and valued servants knew few bounds. Little account was taken of the nature of the office involved – whether it was the constableship of a castle that needed defending or a fortress that was in ruins, a receivership that required expert financial knowledge and at least a periodic presence, a stewardship that involved supervising an estate and placating tenantry, a distant royal franchise like the principality of Wales or the duchy of Cornwall where lawlessness might have to be overcome and corruption eliminated, or more central offices in or near London which, like the three principal offices of state, were crucial to good government or, like offices in the Tower, vital to the realm's security. To employ loyal men from among the country gentry or less in offices in their own localities would facilitate the co-ordination of the realm's administration, ensure an effective and resident officialdom, and encourage obedience to instructions – considerations that were important to the central government and took account of the needs of the locality itself. This presupposed, however, a sophisticated, integrated, and well-regulated national administration, and such notions did not receive a high priority from Henry VI or his advisers. Rather was the quality of England's governors allowed to evolve in response to the private desires of those closest to the king or working in his household as they sought advancement and employment for their dependants, friends, servants, and 'connection' by every available means. Within a decade of Henry's coming of age, a labyrinth of household officials and royal servants, with their relatives, was to be found throughout England and Wales, with perhaps greatest concentration in the most politically and socially advantageous places, especially the home counties and the south, or where local circumstances posed no significant challenge to royal authority, as in the principality of Wales and Cheshire.[24]. Its growth was gradual and unplanned, the consequence of considerations and decisions focussed on the king and his court; and this 'king's affinity' proved of uncommon value when it was enlisted for purposes that were only tenuously linked with royal office or the locality to which an individual was appointed. Despite the protests of Cade's rebels, the duke of York, and, as far as the king's personal companions are concerned, the commons in 1450, there is no sign that the golden age of the household official was brought to an end before the king became ill in the summer of 1453.

The motives behind grants of office, land, and fees to royal dependants are not difficult to fathom. There were no statutory constraints on the king's prerogative to patronize, except in relation to the shrievalties of the English counties. Sheriffs were required to be resident in the county they served and they should stay in office only for one year and not be chosen again for a further three.[25] The first constraint was rarely challenged after 1436, though in view of the large body of available household esquires, valets, and other servants, drawn from all parts of the realm (and, in some cases, beyond it), this was hardly an irksome limitation.[26]

Naturally, with the court normally resident near London or in the Thames valley, making infrequent excursions elsewhere, to secure office and property in the south of England or in the home counties was the most desirable goal of an ambitious royal servant. For this reason, more household officials were appointed to the sheriff's office in this region than anywhere else, and household men acquired a disproportionate amount of property here compared with the realm beyond. During the sixteen years between 1437 and 1453, as many as 12 men with household associations were appointed to the Surrey–Sussex shrievalty, and 8 in Bedfordshire–Buckinghamshire, with an extension west to Wiltshire (where there were 8 between 1437 and 1453) and, rather less commonly, to Somerset and Dorset (5 in 1437–53), which had reasonably good communications with the capital.[27] By contrast, it is striking that household officials rarely became sheriff in the counties on the Welsh border, in the north of England, or in the far south-west, where, in most cases, powerful magnates dominated local society and the local officialdom. Where a Percy or a Neville, a Beauchamp or a

Stafford stalked there was little room for a coterie of royal officials who depended primarily on the king and his court for their advancement and protection. An exception which goes far towards proving this rule is the de la Pole presence in East Anglia, for it coincided with a household dominance masterminded by Suffolk: during 1437–53 as many as seven of the sheriffs of Norfolk–Suffolk were king's men, among them clients of Suffolk like William Calthorpe and John Say.[28]

Appointments during Henry's majority reflect the importance that still attached to the sheriff's office – a financial, administrative, and military importance, apart from the sheriff's role as returning officer for shire and borough elections to parliament. Thus, although a sheriff risked leaving office poorer than when he entered it and with new enemies at his back, the office temporarily conferred considerable influence on its occupant, not least because the king relied pre-eminently on him to enforce central authority in the provinces. The financial liability of the office was fully appreciated; and when prospective sheriffs overcame their natural reluctance to serve, they all too often resorted to abuse and extortion in order to make the sacrifice worthwhile.[29] The hostility which a sheriff could attract was exemplified in most extreme fashion during Cade's rebellion, when those who had recently held the office in Kent went in fear of their life – and, as William Crowmer's execution demonstrated, with good reason.[30] Yet, in October 1450 John Heydon was reportedly prepared to spend £1,000 in order to secure a shrievalty that could be exploited to protect his territorial interests in East Anglia.[31] Moreover, a sheriff's favour was curried by all sections of the local community which could muster the gifts and sweeteners he required. When the city of Exeter found itself involved in a dispute with the prior of Holy Trinity, London, the sheriff of Devon in 1438–39 was suitably entertained in an Exeter citizen's house to discuss the matter; a dozen years later, Edward Hull was similarly fêted in order to induce him to intercede with the king on the citizens' behalf.[32] It is not surprising, therefore, that after 1436 a significant number of household servants became sheriffs, though local susceptibilities would be offended and statutory regulations breached if a complete stranger were pricked to serve in any particular locality.[33] A degree of pressure may have been required on occasion to persuade a household servant to undertake this onerous task, but ready service would guarantee further patronage in the future.

Although by no means a novel phenomenon in medieval England, this reliance on court-connected sheriffs was most evident at the annual nominations made in November 1438; but it was maintained over the next four years, so that in November 1441 (to take an example) as many as 10 of the 23 new appointees were linked with the household, and almost all of them had local interests worth protecting in the shires over which they presided.[34] There is a strong suspicion, therefore, that special effort was made to nominate household men who might not otherwise have attained the office of sheriff quite so quickly in their careers. At least one-third of all sheriffs pricked during 1437–44 are known to have had household affiliations. They formed a close-knit affinity dedicated to the service of the king. They and their families married within their own circle, disposed of their property and possessions with one another's aid, and, if occasion demanded it, supported the crown with their loyalty and influence.[35] Their rewards came overwhelmingly from the king and his household, though others – magnates, cities, and ecclesiastics – recognized their worth as men who had access to the court. John Basket, who lived at Bagshot (Surrey) and was sheriff of Surrey–Sussex in 1443–44 and of Wiltshire a year later, had probably been in Queen Joan's service towards the end of her life; he was regarded as sufficiently influential in the south-east for him to be taken into Archbishop Stafford's household and be made steward of the liberties of his see.[36] William Calthorpe of Norfolk, on the other hand, was courted by the duke of Norfolk, who thought so highly of his capabilities (as displayed, *inter alia*, while sheriff of Norfolk–Suffolk in 1441–42) that he tried to entice him from Suffolk's service into his own. The duke of York valued his support too, for in October 1450 he asked Calthorpe 'to awayte on hym at his comyng in-to Norffolk to be oon of his men'; some thought that 'it is to th'entent that he shuld be outhir shiref or kynght of the shire, to the fortheryng of othir folkes', and although neither eventuality occurred, Calthorpe can be regarded as a dependable client of the duke by 1452.[37] Norfolk had more success with John Penycock, who had been in the king's employ since 1424–25; he later became an official on one of Norfolk's estates, as well as sheriff of Oxfordshire–Berkshire in 1448–49 and Surrey–Sussex the following year.[38] In the shires where these courtier-sheriffs were most numerous, they were able to use their office for their own purposes, as well as those of their sovereign; Thomas Daniel, for example, may have sought the shrievalty of Norfolk–Suffolk in 1446 in order to strengthen his hold on the Norfolk manor of Rydon, which he seems to have acquired by fraud.[39] Around London, in particular, was a belt of territory in which the king could feel secure, where he travelled with greatest regularity, and where his courtiers waxed rich and powerful by fair means and foul.

Cardinal Beaufort cultivated his own interests both before and after the king came of age. Between 1437 and 1441 as many as eleven of his associates (who were also in his nephew's household) were promoted to shrievalties in England. Thereafter, it was Suffolk who grasped the available opportunities most resolutely. He was foremost among the king's ministers in the later 1440s in influencing the disposition of offices and, by so doing, strengthening his personal position. With only modest inherited estates of his own, where a tradition of service and bonds of loyalty could develop, he capitalized on his role as the king's most intimate adviser to advance his dependants to positions of influence in the south and east of England especially. His political affinity owed much to his Beaufort connections and to his marriage with

Alice Chaucer, for by these means his influence in Oxfordshire–Berkshire was assured (via men like John Noreys, Sir Edmund Hampden, and Edmund Rede); it owed something to his own landed position in Norfolk and Suffolk (via Sir Thomas Tuddenham, John Heydon, and others), despite the suspicion of the duke of Norfolk; but above all it was his place in the larger affinity of the king (as steward of the royal household until 1447, and then as Henry's confidant) that enabled him to regard the Fiennes 'connection' in Kent and Sussex as his own. During the late 1440s Henry VI's affinity became very largely Suffolk's too.[40]

In other respects, Suffolk was not unique. Beaufort had been just as adept during the minority, and other magnates – like the Staffords, the Percies, and the Beauchamps – showed themselves to be hardly less so, though the scale of their operations was more restricted and less ambitious.[41] It was to the lasting reproach of the duke of Gloucester that he did not properly appreciate that his position as heir to Henry VI's throne needed to be buttressed by 'good lordship' in carefully calculated directions. The motives of the cardinal and Suffolk in so disposing of Henry's patronage of office did not seem sinister to the contemporary mind. As 'good lords', they were anxious to reward loyal servants and attract men with ability or other qualities, thereby extending their own influence and gratifying their self-esteem. But the propensity for abuse which had long characterized the office of sheriff came to alienate a number of men who stood outside the favoured circle: the monopolizing of patronage roused their jealousy and resentment; and the knowledge that protection would be forthcoming from Westminster or Windsor for any household servant who rode rough-shod over others created bitter resentment. It was a foregone conclusion that this animosity should ultimately be focussed on the king's household and his court.

The appointment of constables and custodians of the royal castles or of seignorial castles which, like those of the duke of Warwick, came into the king's hands during the late 1440s and early 1450s was governed by similar considerations. At least two-thirds – and probably nearer three-quarters – of them went to men who were connected in some way with the king, even if they did not frequent his household except on periodic visits. King's serjeants, esquires, and (to a lesser extent, because there were fewer of them) king's knights dominated these posts: at least a third of the appointees are known to have occupied a specific position in the household; a much smaller number can be identified with the queen's establishment or government service at Westminster.[42] On 20 June 1446, the constableship of Gloucester castle, which was currently held for life by Duke Humphrey, was granted to the king's knight Sir John Beauchamp of Powick and his heirs whenever the duke should die.[43] Life was set fair for Beauchamp, for Gloucester died in the following February and Sir John was himself raised to the peerage just about a year after he had been promised the castle. A colleague in the household, Thomas Daniel, proved to be less fortunate

in the event, for although he too was promised a castle-constableship
on 8 September 1448 – that of Castle Rising in Norfolk, along with the
stewardship of the lordship – the present occupant was Lord Cromwell,
who was nothing like as obliging and lived on until 1456. Long before
that Daniel had been denounced by the commons in 1450 as one of the
king's more notorious companions, and as such he had plenty of
opportunity meanwhile to pull the household's strings.[44] Lower in the
social scale was Thomas Yerde, the king's harbinger and esquire, who
became constable of Winchester castle for life on 21 February 1451,
thereby succeeding in the post his father John, himself a king's serjeant
and household harbinger.[45] From the queen's household came Edward
Ellesmere, treasurer of her chamber and clerk of her jewels; he
acquired, also for life, custody of Launceston castle (Cornwall) in June
1451.[46] Even John Nayler, a chancery clerk, commanded sufficient
influence to secure the reversion of the constableship of Salisbury castle
on 30 November 1446.[47] The few peers who became castle-constables
at this time often had a personal relationship with the king and
frequented his court. Among them was James Fiennes who, when he
was created Lord Saye in February 1448, was granted the constableship
of Dover castle and the wardenship of the Cinque ports, together with
a handsome annuity of £200, to maintain his new dignity.[48] This pattern
of household appointments was a striking feature of the military
establishments on the south coast and in the lower Thames valley; there
foreign and domestic uncertainty may have fortified the king's
inclination to rely on known men to fill key defensible positions and
maintain public order. If so, it was a consideration that marched well
with his desire to bestow marks of favour and profit on his friends,
companions, and servants. But the east coast and the west country
exhibit these tendencies in some measure, too, and the conclusion
inevitably suggests itself that, regardless of region, personal loyalty and
reliability, and a record of service, had become the exclusive criteria for
appointment to the custody of English and Welsh castles.

Stewards, receivers, and other administrative and financial officials
were recruited from the same stable. Philip Wentworth, formerly a
king's serjeant and esquire for the body, was steward of the Worcestershire manor and forest of Feckenham from 6 June 1449; he had become
constable of Llanstephan castle (Carmarthenshire) within a year, by
which time he was one of that small circle of leading household servants,
the knights carver.[49] Another king's serjeant, Robert Berd from Kent,
received a life-grant much nearer home in August 1447, when he became
steward of the royal manor of Eltham.[50]

At least a third of these appointees had designated posts within the
household; at least two-thirds of them were linked with the king as his
esquires, servants, serjeants, or knights, with a preponderance among
the serjeants, a category of household servant which Henry VI
considerably enlarged by way of reward – often to old soldiers, defeated
or wounded or simply scurrying back from France and seeking a living

at home in England. One old soldier, who had lost all and had been forced to sell much of his property in England to pay his ransom, found it desperately difficult to support himself and his wife after his return – until, that is, the king gave him the constableship of Bridgnorth castle and town (Shropshire) on 30 May 1451.[51] Another who had fought long and hard in France beside Thomas Montague, earl of Salisbury was made a serjeant-at-arms for life by the king on 10 August 1451, taking the usual daily allowance of 1s. for his livelihood.[52] Even the strictly military commands in London were disposed of in this way. The Tower, which lay in the nominal charge of the duke of Exeter as hereditary constable, passed into the effective control of a group of household officials and personal servants of King Henry: they supervised the mint, the ordnance, and the fabric of what was the principal armoury of the realm. After the death of John Holand, duke of Exeter in 1447, and while his son and heir was under age, the king's chamberlain, Lord Saye, took charge of the Tower. He was joined by Thomas Montgomery, Lord Sudeley's nephew and a king's esquire and marshal of the hall, who was appointed warden of the mint on 25 October 1449.[53] A yeoman of the crown, Bartholomew Halley, had already been made porter of the Tower for life in January 1446 and therefore controlled access to the fortress when his superiors were absent; he was appropriately involved in the initial stages of Eleanor Cobham's imprisonment in 1441 and the arrest of her husband in February 1447.[54] An observer travelling round the country in 1450 might be pardoned for concluding that household men monopolized every significant or profitable position and had laid hands on almost all the attractive items of patronage. They might not be physically present in Launceston or Leeds, in Bamburgh or Bassingbourne, for more than a few weeks now and then, but their authority was real enough, if only serving to channel a fee into their pockets.[55]

Disquiet at the nature of the king's patronage was being voiced in a number of quarters by 1450. Cade's rebels were the most vehement of critics. The south and east of England had probably experienced the effect of the king's will more consistently than areas further afield; what the Chaucer 'connection' was to Oxfordshire and the Beauforts earlier in the reign, the Fiennes and their associates were to the south-east and the household in the 1440s.[56] The family, it is true, hailed from Herstmonceux (Sussex). Sir Roger was one of Henry V's knights and fought in France both before and after 1422; he became treasurer of Henry VI's household in 1439 and was a prominent Sussex gentleman and county official. His younger brother, James, had an equally distinguished military career in Normandy, but he excelled as a royal servant at court, both in the king's household (of which he was chamberlian from 1447) and as a councillor. He was richly rewarded in the 1440s, accumulating pensions and other sources of income that were estimated to be worth £302 annually by 1450. His social, political, and economic predominance in Kent (where he bought Knole manor) complemented that of his brother in Sussex (where Herstmonceux was rebuilt); whilst his close relations with Suffolk and Henry himself procured him the barony of Saye and Sele (1447). When the tide of criticism washed high in 1450, his name was linked with that of Suffolk, Moleyns, and Aiscough, and he was accordingly executed by Cade on 4 July.[57] Sir Roger's two sons, Richard (later Lord Dacre of the South) and Robert, who had joined the king's household in about 1446, helped to perpetuate their father's and uncle's influence in the south-east.[58] Although only twenty, William, Lord Saye's son and heir, had become a knight of the body by 1448 and two years before that joint constable of Pevensey castle (Sussex) with his father. From this family nexus sprang relationships, formed in the south-east and at court, which gave the Fiennes 'connection' a well-nigh unique position in the realm by 1450. James's daughter, Elizabeth, married two husbands who were successively sheriffs of Kent: William Crowmer, whose lack of scruple and ready oppression brought him to the block with his father-in-law in July 1450; and Alexander Iden, the very man who captured Cade soon afterwards.[59]

Social and business ties extended the Fiennes' tentacles beyond their immediate family. Nicholas Carew was a Surrey gentleman who represented the shire in parliament in 1439–40 and became sheriff of Surrey–Sussex on three occasions during the 1440s. As early as 1435 James and Roger Fiennes were acting as his feoffees, and when Carew came to draw up his will in 1456, Robert Fiennes witnessed it.[60] William Isle, a Kentish lawyer, MP, and sheriff, and Stephen Slegge, another local official from the same county (where he was sheriff in 1448 and MP for Hythe and Dover), were close friends of James and incurred some of the odium which engulfed him in 1450.[61] More fortunate were two others in the same circle. Gervase Clifton, a midlander from Nottinghamshire, deputized for James Fiennes as constable of Dover castle and warden of the Cinque Ports; he also joined Stephen Slegge as one of James's feoffees, and in 1440 and 1450 he was sheriff of Kent and its MP in 1439–40. The other was Robert Radmyld, sheriff of Surrey –Sussex in 1447, MP for Sussex in 1449, and a recipient of James's favours. No other region of the kingdom was dominated so completely by such a close-knit body of gentry who had the highest sponsorship and the most influential patronage that the king's household and court could provide. A number of them not only took full advantage of their opportunities, but even resorted to oppressive methods to assert their rights, flay their opponents, and, of course, promote the royal interest. In 1450 Cade's rebels rose in their midst. Yet, despite the execution of James Fiennes and William Crowmer early in July and the death in more sedate circumstances of Sir Roger Fiennes during the same year, the family's local influence and 'connection' persisted.[62]

The group of king's servants and county administrators of which John Noreys was a central figure was hardly less coherent in its personal attachments centred on royal patronage and an *entrée* to the household.

Noreys, who was a sheriff on no less than six occasions between 1437 and 1448, and in shires as far afield as Wiltshire and Worcestershire, Somerset–Dorset and Oxfordshire–Berkshire, had entered the household as an usher of the chamber by 1429 and rose to become keeper of the great wardrobe in 1444–46. His father's home was in Berkshire, where John was MP on no less than seven occasions between 1439 and 1453. A friend of courtiers like Adam Moleyns, Bishop Aiscough, and William Catesby (whose wardship he purchased in 1438) Noreys acted as feoffee for Catesby (and he for Noreys) and they were evidently friends; Catesby became sheriff of Northamptonshire in 1442 and 1451, and represented the shire in parliament in 1449 and 1453–54 – as well as Warwickshire, his other county of residence, in 1449–50.[63] The interests and social connections of these two attracted others, who strengthened the household 'connection' in the east midlands, helping at the same time to construct an officialdom – even, sometimes, a parliamentary lobby – in which the king's interests were coherently represented. Among Catesby's feoffees were William and Thomas Tresham, father and son, who were wearing the king's livery when they were attacked in Northamptonshire in 1450. William had been retained by Henry VI with a £20 fee in 1443; his son Thomas was brought up in the household and served as sheriff of Cambridgeshire–Huntingdonshire in 1451–52.[64] Catesby married the daughter of a Herefordshire gentleman, Thomas Barre, and thereby became the brother-in-law of Sir John Barre, MP for Herefordshire in 1445–46 and 1447 and of Gloucestershire in 1450–51, as well as sheriff of his home shire in 1450–51 (which may explain why he was returned to parliament by a neighouring county on this occasion). Sir John acted as feoffee for Catesby, whose links with the midlands esquire for the body Thomas Everingham are equally significant. Possibly a kinsman of Viscount Beaumont, Everingham's war service in France may have brought him to the notice of John Beaufort, earl of Somerset, and the earl of Shrewsbury, with whom his contacts continued. Aside from being MP for Leicestershire in 1449 and 1453–54, Everingham was sheriff of Warwickshire–Leicestershire in 1446–47.[65] Thus, across a considerable stretch of midland England in the 1440s the crown had at its command a society of gentlemen who knew one another well, engaged each other's service for their private purposes, and maintained direct links with the household which could be of benefit to them and to the king.

The duchy of Lancaster

A similar pattern is observable on the duchy of Lancaster's estates, whose senior central offices were especially attractive to courtiers like William Tresham and John Say, who obtained successively the reversion of the duchy's chancellorship.[66] Similarly, the financial and legal offices of receiver-general and attorney-general were reserved for two conscientious financiers who were employed elsewhere. Richard Alred, appointed on 26 December 1437, was well known at court. A citizen of London and a landowner in Essex, he was a feoffee for Henry VI's will and tried, not always successfully, to combine his duchy duties with the clerkship of the king's works. Alred was also a feoffee for the will of Lord Cromwell in 1444, and when he drew up his own testament three years later, three esquires for the king's body, as well as the duke of Buckingham and two of the Bourgchiers, guaranteed its implementation.[67] Alred's successor on 31 March 1445 was William Cotton, a notable king's esquire who became an usher of the royal chamber and a faithful employee in the great wardrobe.[68]

More striking still were the chief stewards of the duchy, officers whose routine duties were less precise or personally demanding. In April 1437, Suffolk himself acquired the northern stewardship and a month later the Lancastrian veteran Sir William Philip was appointed for Wales and the south. After Philip died in June 1441, he was succeeded by Sir Roger Fiennes and then by Suffolk and his friend Sir Thomas Stanley jointly and also for life. Meanwhile, about Michaelmas 1443 the earl associated his East Anglian henchman, Sir Thomas Tuddenham, in the stewardship of the north. Thus, soon after Henry VI came of age, the link between duchy administration and the royal household was snapped shut. The assault on the régime in 1450 led to Suffolk's murder; Tuddenham was forced to surrender his life patent early in 1451, and for a few months at least Stanley lost control of the southern stewardship, which underpinned his growing dominance of Lancashire. Into their place stepped Lord Cromwell in March–April 1451, though after the protests had abated, Stanley retrieved his position so that by 15 June he was back in office, occupying the chief stewardship of Wales and the south jointly with Cromwell for life.[69]

Of the more localized offices in the duchy organization, those in the south and east were eagerly sought by household servants. That unruly pair who were the bane of many a gentleman's life in East Anglia, Tuddenham and Heydon, added the stewardship of the duchy lands in eastern England to their list of offices in November 1443.[70] Earlier still, William Tyrell had been steward of the duchy estates in the home counties since the beginning of 1437; in November 1440 he was joined by his brother Thomas. They were the sons of Sir John Tyrell, formerly treasurer of the royal household and a partisan of Gloucester; their father's distinction and accumulated wealth, especially in Essex, provided them with a ready-made provincial base and an *entrée* to the king's service. Thomas was *persona grata* with Bishop William Booth, who was one of the queen's intimates; he helped to suppress Cade's revolt and subdue the Essex rebels, and by 1452 was a king's knight. Brother William was in the household when Gilles of Brittany arrived in 1444, for he attended the young Breton while he was in England; moreover, his father-in-law was Robert Darcy, an official of the court of common pleas. However devoted Sir John Tyrell and his sons had been to Gloucester in earlier days, by the 1440s Thomas and William were part of the king's affinity.[71] At Pleshy (Essex) stood the duchy castle of which John Merston secured the constableship in January 1437, and he successfully petitioned in November 1438 that his patent be converted into a life-grant; some months later he was allowed to associate his brother Richard in the office. John had been keeper of the king's jewels since the 1420s, and Richard was found a clerkship in the same office as well as the joint controllership of the king's works.[72]

By contrast, the more outlandish (at least in the eyes of aspiring courtiers) of the duchy offices were not half so attractive, partly because they frequently lay in areas ruled by powerful magnates. Thus, Richard Neville, earl of Salisbury, had been installed as steward of the Yorkshire lordship of Pontefract since 1425 (and that meant control of its castle too); several years later he became steward of the lordship of Tickhill.[73] Further south in Staffordshire, the honour of Tutbury was under the control of the earl of Stafford, after 1435; when he surrendered it in May 1443 to Fulk Vernon, he was handing it over to the son of one of his own councillors, Sir Richard Vernon.[74]

Wales and Cheshire

If the prime concern of the king and his advisers was to use office as a means of reward, the regular use of a deputy would enable household servants and courtiers to be appointed in royal franchises much further afield, where no residence qualification existed. Thus, the principality of Wales acquired in the late 1430s and 1440s a significantly high proportion of officials with household links, and a number of them had no prior connection with the region. From the beginning of the reign, the council had looked after its own in Wales. In the early 1430s, it also granted profitable offices to household servants, probably at the prompting of Suffolk. Single-faction government was already in the making.[75] By June 1438, Suffolk himself was justiciar of south Wales, and soon afterwards he transferred to the north, where opportunities for patronage were greater and many of his household subordinates were already installed. To make way for him, Gloucester moved to Carmarthen as justiciar in February 1440, ostensibly to 'ease the great debates' there. But the change was probably the earl's idea; it was unlikely to be Gloucester's, for at that moment he was lambasting Beaufort and confessing by the way that he no longer had the king's confidence. The two chamberlainships of the principality had already been recast. Within the space of a month, Sir Ralph Botiller was appointed to south Wales and Sir William Beauchamp, the king's carver, to the north. When the latter was replaced in 1439 by the controller of the household, Sir Thomas Stanley, Suffolk's influence increased, and in 1443 he went so far as to associate Stanley with him as joint justiciar of north Wales and Chester in survivorship – a unique step in fifteenth-century Wales.

The change of gear after 1436 was more marked and rapid in north Wales than in the south, and signalled a veritable household invasion. The occasional life-grant began to be issued in April 1437, and it soon turned into a flood. Minor offices, perquisites, and estates, as well as influential positions, were disposed of: 23 of the 37 northern grants recorded on the patent roll between 1436 and 1461 were made during 1437–40; in the south, the figure was 17 out of 32. Half of this total of 40 patents were for life. Henry VI in his household was indubitably affixing the seal – in many cases his signet – and within months of assuming his prerogative he had given away (often for life) a third of the Welsh offices, in north Wales more than half. Most of the appointments were of household servants; and in the north every single minor official was a household man, except John Fray, and he was baron of the exchequer.

Suffolk's acquisition of the northern justiciarship is, therefore, readily explicable: it enabled him after 1440 to extend protection to his household subordinates there, and in this he was assisted by the Lancashire knight Sir Thomas Stanley. There was less patronage available in south Wales, where there were a number of Herefordshire men already installed, some of them retainers of Richard, duke of York. Moreover, since 1433 Edmund Beaufort had held the two most important castles there (Carmarthen and Aberystwyth) and there was no need to challenge his influence.[76] When Gloucester died in 1447, the coping-stone was placed on this household edifice by the nomination as his successor of Sir John Beauchamp of Powick, the king's carver. A battery of similar appointments to the castle-constableships and shrievalties ensured that by 1450 the northern principality especially was a household preserve – and with a distinctly Cheshire and Lancashire flavour about it. Notable were Sir Ralph Botiller, constable of Conway castle until 1461 and Suffolk's successor as steward of the household, and John Stanley, usher of the chamber and Sir Thomas's kinsman. John's earlier appointments as constable of Caernarvon castle and sheriff of Anglesey were extended for life in 1437, and he had other positions there besides. Equally blatant was the intrusion of household men into offices rarely occupied by absentee non-specialists in the past. The most unlikely individuals now took charge of the king's works and artillery in Wales: grooms of the cellar and pages of the kitchen were transformed into armourers, master carpenters, and masons. Scarcely an influential or profitable office was not reserved for a household servant at some time during Suffolk's régime as steward, and a few that had long been forgotten were revived to furnish financial rewards for favoured servants. The distinction between effective and archaic offices was gradually blurred – with fatal consequences for the king's authority: '. . . yf hit were that the kyng hade .ii. gode shirreffs a bidyng opon thair offys in Caern'shir and Anglesey...', lamented one contemporary clerk.[77]

Resumption was the only means of challenging this household ascendancy, in Wales as elsewhere, but most household servants with patronage in the principality successfully petitioned for exemption in 1449–51, and the parliament of 1453 confirmed this. The one instrument capable of restoring the balance between patronage and the needs of government, between those inside and those outside the household, between court and country, was thereby seriously blunted. However salutary the effect of resumption on the crown's finances, it did not fundamentally alter crown patronage in Wales. Rather was the whole structure jeopardized by Suffolk's fall, for far fewer appointments of this sort were made thereafter. But when Richard of York landed in north Wales in September 1450, the household servants among the officers of north Wales were still there to bar his path.[78]

Several generations of a family were consistently partronized in some regions, as the fortunes of the Troutbecks of Frodsham (Cheshire) and the story of their hold on the chamberlainship of Chester and other offices in the county illustrates.[79] Military or defensive considerations were secondary, though it was undeniable that castles in Wales and the north of England, as well as those along the English coast, might be more secure in the hands of constables bound specifically to the royal service when a crisis arose or the central government wished to assert its authority. Similarly, although the local population would ordinarily live undisturbed under the nominal authority of an absentee household official (with effective power shipping inevitably into local hands), at moments of political alarm or necessity the king's influence could be directly exerted in the shires and lordships of the provinces. It is likely that family dominance and absenteeism were equal threats to efficiency, equitable administration, and central control. If effective authority were allowed to fall into the hands of local deputies, it would offer them the temptation to abuse their authority, and that would ultimately arouse hostility and unrest within their own community. Such was the case in west Wales, where Gruffydd ap Nicholas, the Welsh gentleman recently made denizen, created bitter resentment by his unscrupulous pursuit of power, wealth, and office on the coat-tails of magnate and household officials who rarely visited their posts.[80] On the other hand, in those areas close to the centre of government, the monopoly of office by a relatively small cadre of influential men with access to the court, sometimes insinuated into office and property where they previously held little or none before, could create resentment in those who were ignored or elbowed aside; if these same household men were inclined to be oppressive or abused their good fortune, such resentment would almost certainly escalate into disorder or worse. For the local knight, esquire, or gentleman to be excluded from royal patronage could involve more than the loss of rent or an annual fee; it could mean the denial of power, influence, and prestige in his own community. In those circumstances, the court circle would be faced with as much hostility in Kent or Essex or Hertfordshire as unsupervised deputies might encounter in Carmarthenshire, Caernarvonshire, or Lancashire. The political and governmental flaws in Henry VI's patronage outweighed the financial benefits enjoyed by a household servant or the glow of pleasure experienced by a prodigal king.

Bishops, lords, and king

Appointments at the highest levels of all in church and state reveal similar motives at work, and here the personal role of the king was often crucial. Between 1437 and 1445 a dozen bishoprics fell vacant through either death or translation. There can be no question but that the court, and especially the household, lay behind several of the new nominations recommended to their respective cathedral chapters. Four of the nominees were prominent clerks in the royal chapel and had ministered to Henry's spiritual needs for some years past. Richard Praty was a household chaplain by February 1430, when he joined the king on his journey to France; on his return in March 1432 he became dean of the chapel royal, and it was Henry's own advocacy that secured him the see of Chichester on 21 April 1438 after Bishop Sydenham's demise. Although he subsequently withdrew from court and proved an energetic and decisive bishop, Praty's links with former colleagues were maintained, for among his proctors at the 1442 parliament were Lords Beaumont and Sudeley, and the king's secretary Thomas Bekyngton.[81] Another king's chaplain to attain a bishopric soon after Henry came of age was William Aiscough, who may have been the king's confessor by the time he was provided to Salisbury in February 1438; he was certainly keeper of the king's conscience thereafter until his murder in 1450. Both John Carpenter (bishop of Worcester from December 1443) and John Lowe, the learned Augustinian friar who was translated from St Asaph to Rochester in April 1444, had done service in the household, Lowe as Henry's confessor from February 1432. These personal links with the king, let alone the ecclesiastical experience and spiritual inclinations of each aspirant, made them eminently suitable for an English bishopric now that the king ruled. They seem to have been Henry's own choice, and Carpenter at least was consecrated at Eton's newly founded chapel on 22 March 1444.

Three others merited election on grounds that would have been universally approved in the fifteenth century; indeed, they would have attained promotion at almost any time in the middle ages. John Stafford, bishop of Bath and Wells, had been chancellor of England since 1426; in May 1443 he was chosen archbishop of Canterbury in succession to Chichele, who had strongly recommended him. The king's secretary since 1437 had been Thomas Bekyngton, a product of Winchester and

New College who was a generous benefactor of his *alma mater* later on in life when his humanistic leanings had heightened his awareness of the importance of education and study. For all his earlier service with Gloucester, Bekyngton's career advanced most rapidly under the patronage of Archbishop Chichele, Beaufort, and the king himself. In July 1443, he was provided to the see of Bath and Wells.[82] The other outstanding candidate was William Lyndwood, a noted theologian who, as a scholar, stood head and shoulders above the rest of the fifteenth-century English and Welsh bishops. The wonder is that, at the age of sixty-one, he had been denied a bishopric for so long. As keeper of the privy seal since 1432, he was now (ten years later) presented to the distant and hardly enticing see of St David's.[83]

The influence of the wider court is reflected in the careers of the remaining new bishops, all of whom were servants of a councillor or royal favourite.[84] Few could rival the aristocratic connections of Thomas Bourgchier, who was successfully translated from Worcester to Ely on 20 December 1443, after being baulked six years before when the archbishop of Rouen and chancellor of Lancastrian France, Louis of Luxembourg, was allowed to hold Ely *in commendam*. Bourgchier was a young man of thirty-two, but his brothers were Henry, count of Eu, William, later Lord FitzWarin, and John, later Lord Berners; a sister had married the duke of Norfolk and his family's relations with the Staffords were very close. From comparable stock came Robert Neville, a nephew of Cardinal Beaufort and the younger brother of the earl of Salisbury; on 27 January 1438 he was translated, at the king's special request, from Salisbury to the premier see of Durham, with its extraordinary franchises in Neville country. Yet, all things considered, it cannot be said that Henry's appointments in these years were inappropriate for the episcopal bench. Most of the men elected were demonstrably capable and, as far as Praty, Lyndwood, Bekyngton, and Lowe are concerned, had more than a passing interest in spiritual matters. Above all, they either had a record of proven competence in the personal service of the king or the state, or else they had inspired sufficient confidence that they would perform such service in the future.

In the later 1440s, it was Suffolk who increasingly interpreted these considerations to the king and therefore placed his stamp as well as the king's on the character of the episcopate – and more firmly than even Beaufort had been able to do. A connection with the king or his household or with some of his courtiers was still of decisive value to an aspiring cleric. After the crisis of 1450, there is even a sign that Henry, bereft of his all-powerful minister, preferred to promote those who had been raised to the bench earlier, translating known loyal servants to richer sees rather than introducing new, untried clerks. Whether this was in response to the chorus of complaint is doubtful; it rather reflects a continuing desire to reward the faithful and the congenial, coupled

347

with a greater sense of insecurity which led the king to rely more, rather than less, heavily on those about him.

Adam Moleyns's nomination as bishop of Chichester in September 1445 was a reward for a former clerk of the council, then a councillor himself, a close protégé of Suffolk, and, above all, the current keeper of the privy seal. Walter Lyhert's promotion to Norwich on 24 January 1446 also owed much to Suffolk, and he may even have been promoted in preference to Henry's personal choice, his confessor, John Stanbury. However, the king was likely to fall in with Suffolk's wishes, especially since Lyhert had become Queen Margaret's confessor; one need not seek for private tensions between king and queen in this matter.[85] A similar comment can be made in relation to William Booth, the sole common lawyer among the fifteenth-century bishops; he secured the see of Coventry and Lichfield in April 1446 with the support of both king and queen (whose chancellor he had recently become) and with the advocacy of Suffolk. In the late 1440s there can be little doubt about the latter's irresisitible influence, but the fact that his clients and the queen's servants were elevated need not mean that the king had been overruled or ignored, or that Henry was unwilling to recognize the merit in their proposals, as his espousal of Booth's candidacy indicates. Rather did the situation reflect the decisive importance in matters of public policy of the close-knit circle in which Henry moved and the restricted range of the advice he received.

The king's personal inclinations were in any case crucial in the advancement of William Waynflete, whom he provided to the richest see of all, in succession to his uncle, on or about 17 April 1447. Patronized also by the king's former secretary and mentor, Thomas Bekyngton, Waynflete was a man after Henry's own heart: the head of Winchester college for many years (1429–42), he seems to have been chosen by the king as the first head of Eton in 1441; certainly, he was provost of the king's new college from 1442. Waynflete was actually consecrated within the half-finished walls of Eton, and Henry did him the honour of attending his enthronement at Winchester cathedral. The new bishop's training, personality, interests, and service to the king strongly reccommended him for Beaufort's great see.

Henry's thoughts were now moving unmistakably in the direction of a vigorous promotion of education and the faith; his own role in bishop-making became correspondingly more positive. This is evident in the case of John Langton, who had already been provided to St David's on 28 January 1447; a former chaplain of the king and a learned man who bequeathed books to Cambridge in his will, he was one of those household servants patronized handsomely by the generous king. When Langton died not many months later, a new bishop of St David's was sought among clerics of similar character. John de la Bere, a household servant of long standing whom Henry had tried to inflict on the chapter of Wells as dean in May 1443 but then deserted in favour of Queen Margaret's secretary, was not (it is true) a man of learned reputation; but he had been almoner to the king since 1431 and as a result received the king's support. The new bishop of Bangor, appointed by 23 June 1448, came from the same circle. John Stanbury, a member of the Carmelite order which Henry particularly favoured, was a royal chaplain and, later, the king's confessor; he was a theologian and writer on canon law, and although he may have been disappointed at Norwich in 1446, he now at least secured a see in north Wales.[86] Another king's chaplain was Thomas Kemp, promoted to the see of London on 21 August 1448. He had additional support at court in the person of his uncle, Cardinal Kemp, but Thomas's presence in the household and, to judge by his benefactions to Oxford later on, his scholarly inclinations doubtless swayed the king just as much, though Henry showed characteristic vacillation in contemplating moving Marmaduke Lumley from Carlisle to London even after he had signified to the pope that Kemp was his choice. Indecision was a facet of Henry's character and one of his weaknesses as a king. Since bishoprics fell vacant infrequently and yet a substantial number of clerks and chaplains were in the royal service or brought to the king's attention by eager patrons – a far greater number than could ever attain a see – careful thought may have crumbled into vacillation in the mind of an inexperienced monarch like Henry VI. His willingness to accommodate and his readiness to be persuaded – in the case of Lyhert and Booth, for example – probably reflect the same trait; it need not represent a struggle between the king and more insistent patrons.[87]

One suspects strong household influence in the nomination of Richard Beauchamp as bishop of Hereford in December 1448. One of the Beauchamp brood which had supplied knights for the king's protection (one of whom, Sir John Beauchamp, had recently been created Baron Beauchamp of Powick), Richard was of noble stock. There is every likelihood that he was suggested to the king as a possible bishop by influential relatives and friends at court.[88] Even at the height of the movement against Suffolk and his clique, the same considerations prevailed. Indeed, during the 1449–50 parliament Suffolk continued to exert influence on ecclesiastical promotions. Marmaduke Lumley was translated on 28 January 1450 from one of the poorest sees, Carlisle, to one of the richest, Lincoln. Now about sixty years of age and having recently resigned the treasurership of England, he had over the years cultivated a long line of Beaufort associates, beginning with Queen Katherine and the cardinal himself. His work as envoy, treasurer, and councillor, and as a one-time critic of Gloucester, made him an admirable choice for this large diocese.

There were as many as fourteen appointments to English and Welsh sees in the three years before the king's illness; nine of them were by translation, whereby former household clerks exchanged one see for a better and hence came to occupy the most senior dioceses in the realm. In Archbishop Kemp's case, his move from York to Canterbury on 21 July 1452 was his fifth translation in a third of a century. Six of the exchanges took place between January and August 1450, when the household and court were under strongest attack and were most apprehensive. It may have been too risky to introduce untried clerks to the bench of bishops and thereby provoke louder howls of protest against favourites (though the ambition of some deserving clerics may have lost its edge after the murder of Moleyns and Aiscough); there was also much to be said for relying on known, loyal men at such a critical moment. The majority of the translated bishops were, therefore, former household officials or servants of the queen, and almost all of them had been provided to their first see since Henry had attained his majority; they were his choice and not that of the council or his lords.

Several of these men are likely to have shared Henry's own abiding interest in education and religion. Nicholas Close, for example, who replaced Lumley at Carlisle on 23 January 1450, was doubtless chosen because he was a fellow of King's College, Cambridge; he had become master of works there in 1447 and warden of King's Hall in 1446.[89] He was highly regarded for his efficient supervision of the building operations at King's and had become one of Henry's chaplains by 1448. Such dedication to one of the king's own foundations was as sure an avenue to a bishopric as one could imagine. Suffolk may still have been able to support the translation of Reginald Pecock from St Asaph to Chichester on 23 March 1450. A friend of Lyhert, Suffolk's client who was now bishop of Norwich, Pecock was a popular literary figure and theological writer who had perhaps found favour with the king, especially if it were known that his intellectual activities were complemented by staunchly orthodox views on heresy. It is unfortunate that his over-zealous preaching proved so tiresome and embarrassing to his fellow bishops that his episcopal career – which might ordinarily have been expected to advance him beyond Chichester – came to a sudden halt. His replacement at St Asaph, Thomas Bird, a Dominican friar, had a passing connection with Suffolk and the queen, whom he had accompanied on her journey to England in 1445. Bird proved an energetic heresy-hunter and a steady adherent of the king in 1460–61; he may have been attached to the household as early as 1450.[90] When Richard Beauchamp was translated to Salisbury from Hereford on 14 August 1450, the vacant see was allocated to Reginald Boulers, long a friend of the king, who had tried to persuade him to take the obscure see of Llandaff in 1440; Boulers had then declined, preferring to remain abbot of the wealthier monastery of St Peter at Gloucester. Since that date he had thrown himself into the royal service with considerable verve: as councillor and envoy to France, and the duke of Somerset's emissary to the 1449 parliament. By 1450 he was commonly identified with Suffolk, and his role at court led the commons to demand his banishment from the king's presence. Henry would have supported his candidacy at Hereford with enthusiasm.

Despite the complaints and protests of 1450, the translation of former household clerks continued, and the small number of new bishops came from the same mould. Thus, John Chedworth, who was promoted to Lincoln on or about 11 February 1451, had been a fellow of King's since 1443 and its second provost in 1446. He had evidently already attracted Henry's attention and shown his worth; receiving this wealthy see was confirmation of that. Stafford's death on 25 May 1452 caused a minor upheaval among the bishops, for four changes ensued, only one of which involved a new recruit to the bench. Predictably, the chancellor at last surrendered York, over which he had presided since 1425, to become primate of all England, though he was destined to remain so for only two more years. In Kemp's place was installed William Booth; his consecration in the archdiocese marked the most rapid rise of a clerk to York since Alexander Neville in 1373; Booth's service as Queen Margaret's chancellor was doubtless a powerful recommendation. From Carlisle to Coventry and Lichfield went Nicholas Close, whilst up to Carlisle, the poorest see in this particular sequence, went William Percy, the son of the earl of Northumberland. By 30 August 1452, when Percy was elected, the rearrangement of the bench was complete. Only Percy, in the least attractive of the four sees, was new to a bishop's throne; noble lineage and lack of court experience were somewhat exceptional qualifications for the times, but Northumberland's predominance in the area is explanation enough.

The last five appointments of all before the king fell ill in August 1453 were translations of experienced and loyal bishops who were close associates of the king, the queen, or the court. They took place on 7 February 1453 and were precipitated by Boulers's promotion to Coventry and Lichfield: John Stanbury moved from Bangor to take his place at Hereford, and John Blakedon crossed St George's channel from Achonry in Ireland (which he rarely, if ever, visited) to Bangor. This latter appointment may be regarded as promotion, but there is little sign of any prior connection between the Dominican friar and the king's service. Nevertheless, Blakedon was something of a theologian and scholar, and as such would have fulfilled King Henry's idea of what a bishop should be. In any case, in the past he had been patronized by Cardinal Beaufort, whose chaplain he had once been.

There were few practical constraints on the king's ability to advance favoured clerks. That prospective bishops had already to be ordained priests was taken for granted, and no hasty adjustment, such as was made when Henry II insisted on Thomas Becket as archbishop of Canterbury in 1162, was required during Henry VI's reign. Likewise, the decree that bishops must have reached the canonical age of twenty-five was generally observed, though the plan to make the twenty-two-year-old Thomas Bourgchier bishop of Worcester in 1433 was eventually successful despite the pope's misgivings. Diocesan waywardness in the election of bishops was rare, and papal provisions were hardly ever pursued against the king's wishes. The English and Welsh episcopacy was, therefore, generally reserved for clerics who had earned their monarch's gratitude or regard, or of whom good service could confidently be expected in the future.

The lay aristocracy was the most effective buttress of the crown. This was especially true of a usurping dynasty with formidable military commitments to which the greater nobility still had an essential contribution to make in the mid-fifteenth century. The incentive for Henry VI to regard his baronage creatively, as an incomparable support of his dynasty and a major avenue of patronage, was a strong one; and it led to notable developments in the character and role of the peerage during Henry's mature years. By the mid-fifteenth century, the titled nobility was well on the way to becoming a clearly identifiable and strictly defined and hereditary social caste, with a formally acknowledged status that was closely bound up with summons to parliament and great councils. The titled nobility had become almost synonymous with England's parliamentary peerage.[91] This sense of corporate identity had been hardening since the late fourteenth century, and juridically it was expressed in the privilege that had become a right of trial in parliament by fellow peers for treason and felony – something which, in the aftermath of Eleanor Cobham's trial, was extended in 1442 to a peer's wife as well.[92] Still, at the time Henry VI came of age, the relationship between parliament and peerage was not yet immutable, and there was some room for manoeuvre by the king. He could still accord (or withhold) parliamentary status to (or from) an individual baron, and his initiative was immense in the creation of new barons and the elevation of existing ones. Here lay an opportunity for patronage that was of the utmost significance because of its political, social, economic, and, above all, constitutional implications.

The importance of 'the lords' in both council and parliament had been graphically illustrated during Henry's minority, when the king's powers and prerogatives had resided in them as a body. And their importance had been cultivated during a century of virtually annual parliaments, constitutional crises of unprecedented complexity, and noble leadership of conquering armies in France. After 1436, the lords were only a whit less crucial, even though their collective responsibility for political decisions was now reduced. Their service in peace, war, and defence, at home and abroad, was stressed time and again in the 1440s when barons were created or titles bestowed, as also occasionally was their role as a buttress to the crown or a stabilizing influence in the realm.[93] The English monarchy functioned best with a substantial nobility about it, as the king acknowledged in his patents of creation and his critics insisted when they put their faith in the greater nobility to improve the condition of the realm.[94] This emphasis on the practical value of a well-stocked baronage, coupled with a realization that a usurping dynasty needed as extended a royal family as was available, were considerations in the forefront of Henry's mind when he approached the matter of creating and elevating barons. And these considerations so modified the conventions surrounding a hereditary baronage that Henry's majority may be considered one of the most creative periods in the evolution of the English peerage, comparable perhaps with Charles II's extravagant creations in the seventeenth century or the explosion in life peerages in the twentieth.[95]

Henry adopted several means by which to replenish the English peerage; they may have been modestly prefigured during Richard II's reign or his own minority, but now they were used more frequently and self-consciously, and with greater sophistication.[96] Ultimately, on questions of title, precedence, and heredity, it was the king's own initiative that was decisive, and Henry VI, suborned by petitioners or advised by favourites though he may have been, showed a constructive will in the way in which he augmented the baronage, altered its character, and did much to establish conventions for its future development. In so doing, he had a golden opportunity to act the part of the royal patron.

So close an identity had come to exist between the English baronage and a parliamentary peerage that a number of Henry's new barons were acknowledged as such by receipt of an individual writ of summons to parliament, where they joined the titled nobility in a separate upper house.[97] About half of these new creations between 1439 and 1452 are datable to writs of parliamentary summons. Thus, Sir John Beauchamp, a former soldier and one of the king's carvers, was summoned to the 1447 parliament by a writ issued on 3 March; he was thereby held to have become Lord Beauchamp of Powick, his family estate in Worcestershire.[98] Sir William Bonville of Chewton (Devon) received his title by a similar writ dated 10 March 1449, one month after parliament had assembled.[99]

The first grant of a barony by letters patent or by charter took place in 1387. Henry VI followed Richard II's sole example and created a number of barons in this way. The first of them, it is true, was elevated in his name by the lords in parliament in 1432: Sir John Cornwall, an elderly and rich widower who had distinguished himself in arms under Henry V and his son, and who had married the king's great-aunt, Elizabeth, sister of Henry IV and dowager countess of Huntingdon, was created Lord Fanhope, taking his title from a Herefordshire manor which he had recently purchased. The lords declared themselves 'willing therefore to reward the said John with some, if inadequate, prerogative of honour'.[100] Henry VI's own first creation by letters patent was that of his chamberlain, Ralph Botiller, who took the title of Lord Sudeley on 10 September 1441. This derived from a barony in Gloucestershire which Botiller had inherited and whose lord had last been summoned to parliament in 1321. But above this, it was the king's own deliberate act in 1441 which determined that the personal qualities of his chamberlain – his knowledge, loyalty, and industry – were those of 'a noble of our realm' and a peer of parliament.[101] This act of creation – and it is a feature of almost all subsequent creations of new barons

– was also an act of patronage; the title was designed to lend dignity to its recipient and a sense of historical precedent to his barony.

In the revival of extinct or dormant baronies, the timing of the creation usually expressed the king's wish to favour and to patronize. However, it was recognized practice that a noble title should descend through an heiress, whose husband might be allowed to adopt her title when he came of age or secured the hereditary estates of her family. Thus, Edward Neville, who married the grand-daughter and heiress of William Beauchamp, Lord Abergavenny, received a writ of summons to parliament only in September 1450, after he had acquired the Abergavenny estates following the duke of Warwick's death in 1446, though he had actually used the title twenty years before.[102] Thus, the traditional link between an hereditary estate and a baronial title could still lead to the creation of a parliamentary peer, though Edward Neville's earlier use of the title demonstrates that marriage to an heiress was itself regarded by contemporaries as a sound qualification of baronial status. In Neville's case, the scope for the exercise of royal patronage through the creation of a barony was limited, but had he so wished, Henry VI could have withheld the writ of summons until a later date.

Henry, Lord Bourgchier acquired his barony in a similar, indirect way, after the death in 1433 of his distant cousin, Elizabeth, daughter and heiress of Bartholomew, Lord Bourgchier. After he had entered Elizabeth's estates in August, Henry was summoned to the parliament that was already in session.[103] The lords during the minority had evidently called him to join them as soon as it was appropriate to do so. Contrast the treatment of Sir John Radcliffe. He had married Elizabeth, daughter and heiress of Walter, Lord FitzWalter, by 1444 and secured her lands a year later. Although contemporaries referred to him as Lord FitzWalter, he never received a writ of summons from Henry VI to cap his marital success. His father had undertaken a long sojourn as seneschal of Gascony (until November 1436), but had then proved tiresomely insistent that arrangements should be made to repay the government's massive debt to him. His son was hardly, therefore, in the same category as Fanhope: here the patron-king declined to observe current convention for comprehensible reasons.[104]

On other occasions, a writ of summons to the husband of a baronial heiress could be unaccountably delayed – unaccountably, that is, unless the king's own predilections are taken into account. Henry Bourgchier's younger brother, William, had secured the estates of his wife, the heiress of the barony of FitzWarin, as early as 1437, but his writ was not issued until 22 May 1449 – though admittedly the lord of this particular barony had not previously been summoned to parliament since 1336.[105] In such cases, an inherited estate or marriage to an heiress was treated as justification for the title rather than for the conferment of the barony itself, which is better explained by other, often political, motives. When Sir Richard Woodville was created Lord Rivers by letters patent on 9 May 1448, he took his title from a Norman barony which his father had once held; but this had never been the basis for a noble dignity in England and Sir Richard's elevation in 1448 surely stemmed (as the king himself declared) from his outstanding personal and military gifts which had recently been tested in war and diplomacy, and which (it was conceded) might be valuable in an uncertain future.[106] Lord Saye's elevation was manifestly an outright act of royal patronage. James Fiennes, one of the king's intimates, received his patent on 24 February 1447. As a title, by no stretch of the imagination could it be grounded in a plausible hereditary claim, for James had an elder brother, Roger, as grandson of the co-heiress of the Saye barony, which had been extinct in the male line since 1382. In any case, there was a more senior representative of the Saye line, Sir John Clinton, who also had a claim. On 1 November 1448, sometime after James's creation, the impecunious Clinton was induced to sell the title of Lord Saye to the new baron, thereby removing at the same time any possibility that Roger Fiennes could claim it in the future.[107] It was an extraordinary and unique insurance taken out by a newly created English baron whose title had not even the pretence of being inherited or associated with an hereditary baronial estate.

With so much latitude available to the monarch in dispensing what, in some respects, was the most prized part of his prerogative, Henry VI's creation of new barons and his elevation of others reveal some cherished principles of patronage which helped to mould his relations with his greatest subjects and determine his priorities as king. As in the case of Lord Abergavenny, the writ of summons to parliament was sometimes an acknowledgement of a rank already popularly recognized by contemporaries, though the point at which this formal acknowledgement was conceded might depend on who the baron was and the king's attitude towards him. John Sutton, who at a council meeting in April 1434 was referred to as Lord Dudley, did not receive his writ of summons until February 1440, though the delay may be explained by his absence in France for a good deal of the interval.[108] The hereditary claim which he had to his barony and title was tenuous indeed: rather did the king confirm it when Dudley returned to England.[109]

Ennoblement was also looked upon as a means of providing compensation for those who, after the congress of Arras, found that their French estates were gradually reduced in value and size by the resurgent French. Sometime in 1445–46, Lord Bourgchier was granted the title of viscount, a French style which he received just when his Norman county of Eu was slipping from his grasp; it had only once been conferred in England and then in not dissimilar circumstances.[110] Others in the same unfortunate plight were James Fiennes, whose county of Court-le-Comte can hardly have been of much value to him by the time of his ennoblement in 1449; Sir Thomas Hoo, whose crumbling authority as chancellor of Normandy may partly explain his creation as Baron Hoo and Hastings on 2 June 1448; and Lord Beaumont who, when he was created the first viscount in English history on 12 February 1440, may have given up all hope of controlling the Burgundian county of Boulogne which he had been granted in July 1436.[111] Yet even in this connection, when overseas losses in the service of Lancaster were at their worst, Henry VI did not feel obliged to compensate all who suffered. His patronage did not extend, for example, to Sir John Fastolf, whose wealth and military distinction placed him on a par with others who were ennobled by the king and who had lost valuable French provinces when the tide of war began to ebb. Fastolf's strong hostility to Suffolk's attempts at peacemaking, and his record of devoted service to Bedford and York, may well have ensured that no baronial dignity came his way in the 1440s. Thereafter, he was an embittered septuagenarian reduced 'to a state of querulous and unmanageable senility.'[112]

Outstanding personal qualities and loyal service to the crown were probably among the fundamental reasons for Henry's ennoblements. Sir John Cornwall had set a pattern for himself (and for others during this reign) when he was created Lord Fanhope (1432). His further acquisition of the barony of Milbroke in parliament in January 1442 should be regarded as added recognition of his considerable contribution to, and close kinship with, the house of Lancaster.[113] An impressive record in the French war also accounts for both the elevation of Lord Talbot to the earldom of Shrewsbury on 20 May 1442, and the writ of summons to Sir William Bonville on 10 March 1449 during a turbulent period as seneschal of Gascony (since 1442).[114]

The personal favour of the king may be observed most clearly in the creation and elevation of his friends and household servants, rather than of notable military leaders. Henry Beauchamp, earl of Warwick was one of the king's companions at court – indeed, he was only a few years the king's junior. On 2 April 1444 the king accorded him precedence as England's premier earl, thereby ranking him next after the dukes and marquesses (of whom there would be only two); then, on 5 April 1445 he was elevated to the rank of duke in recognition (as his patent put it) of meritorious personal qualities (which, at the age of twenty, can hardly have been displayed in any practical service) and the remarkable reputation of his father, the king's former guardian and the realm's most accomplished knight.[115] Prominent courtiers and household men received ennoblement less because they were close friends of the king than because they were indispensable servants and royal confidants, whose attainment of baronies (or more) was yet another aspect of the rich patronage which they monopolized in the 1440s. James Fiennes's elevation in 1447 springs immediately to mind, especially in view of the attempt to remove all possibility of a counter-claim to his barony. But William de la Pole presents the crowning example among the king's favourites: on 27 February 1443 he secured the reversion of the earldom of Pembroke in the event of Gloucester's death; then, in 1444, a marquessate (only the second conferred in England since Richard II's day) and finally, in June 1448, a dukedom.[116] Alongside them was Sir John Stourton, a Wiltshire landowner who had strong links with Suffolk and the household, where he had been treasurer since 1446; he received a patent as Lord Stourton on 13 May 1448.[117] Two Beauchamp cousins, both of whom were carvers in the household, received their baronies in the late 1440s too. John, Lord Beauchamp of Powick was sent a writ of summons on 3 March 1447 to attend the parliament which had just witnessed Gloucester's arrest and death; William Beauchamp, Lord St Amand by virtue of the king's writ of 22 May 1449, had, it is true, married the heiress of the St Amand barony some years before, but that he was elevated now rather than immediately after his marriage indicates that the title was a reward for one of Suffolk's entourage.[118]

Some of the greatest of the new dignities had important dynastic implications. They represented the king's eagerness to strengthen the royal family and its central place in the baronage of England, for Henry had a keen sense of dynasty in an environment that was politically perilous for his line.[119] By 1435 the dynastic prospects of the house of Lancaster had deteriorated alarmingly: Bedford was dead and had left no legitimate heirs; Henry VI at the age of fourteen was unmarried and childless; and even Gloucester, by then aged forty-four, had little chance of fathering the legitimate heir that had hitherto eluded him and his two wives – something which contemporaries realized when, from 1440 onwards, steps were taken formally to dispose of his property in the event of his death.[120]

The personality and political attitudes of Duke Humphrey and his second wife, Eleanor Cobham, intensified contemporaries' concern for the succession even while he lived. It was apparent after 1435 that should anything happen to Henry VI, Gloucester would succeed to the throne and Eleanor would become queen (for no previous English king had not made his wife queen). But beyond the Gloucesters there was no further Lancastrian heir in existence and no likelihood of one in the direct line until Henry VI married. Then, too, Duke Humphrey had acquired a long list of enemies over the past twenty years. For these reasons, the possibility of his succeeding King Henry probably played a part in the scandal that enveloped his wife in 1441.[121] Her trial highlighted the fragile dynastic hold which the Lancastrians had on the English (let alone the French) throne, even aside from whether Gloucester himself was personally acceptable or not in some influential quarters.

In these circumstances it was imperative that the Lancastrian house should be fortified dynastically. Accordingly, discussions were soon being held to arrange a marriage for the king[122]; but even with Henry married or about to be married, it was almost as urgent to fortify the dynasty less directly, though up to the point where a next heir could be indicated. This was a sensitive and delicate business in view of the claims of the duke of York, and the imprecision of the rules then governing inheritance of the crown – certainly there was no unequivocal law of succession to guide the thoughts of contemporaries beyond Henry VI and Duke Humphrey.[123] Urgency was made more urgent by the enviable fertility of Richard of York and his wife, Cecily Neville. Starting with a daughter, Anne, in 1439 and a son, Henry, in 1441, in the thirteen years between 1439 and 1452 they produced eight sons and three daughters.[124] Comparison with this prolific progeny was bound to underline the extreme poverty of the Lancastrian family and increase the dynastic threat from the most senior line of Edward III, now represented by York.

It was natural that Henry VI and his advisers should turn cautiously, yet unmistakably, to the extended Lancastrian family in the search for dynastic support, and noble creations were one of the two principal means (the other was marriage) employed to realize the king's design.[125] In preparation for John Beaufort, earl of Somerset's expedition to France, on 30 March 1443 the king resolved to create his cousin, who was a grandson of John of Gaunt, duke of Somerset; he was given a handsome endowment of 600 marks a year and accorded precedence over the duke of Norfolk, in acknowledgement of his blood relationship with Henry VI.[126] Less than a year later, in January 1444, John Holand, earl of Huntingdon, was created duke of Exeter specifically (as the patent has it) because of his proximity in blood to the king, for the Holands were descended from Henry IV's full sister, Elizabeth. At the same time, he was given precedence over all other dukes save York.[127] In September 1444 Humphrey Stafford was created duke, only a few months after Somerset had died, leaving a one-year-old heiress. In May 1447 the new duke of Buckingham, who descended from Edward III's youngest son, Thomas of Woodstock, was given precedence over all who might in the future be created duke, unless they were of the king's own blood; and this happened only three months after the death of the king's sole heir, Gloucester.[128] Stafford, then, was created duke and given this special precedence specifically because he was close in blood to the king, and these steps were taken immediately after the impoverishment of the Lancastrian house by sudden death.

In March 1448 Edmund Beaufort was created duke of Somerset; he was the younger brother of the late Duke John, and had already (1442–43) been raised rapidly to the successive dignities of earl and marquess of Dorset.[129] It is not without significance that Edmund's own daughter, Margaret, had married none other than Buckingham's son and heir in 1444. Edmund's niece, Margaret, the senior Beaufort heiress, was married soon after March 1453 to the king's eldest half-brother, Edmund Tudor, who had been raised in the previous November to the earldom of Richmond which the late duke of Bedford had enjoyed; at the same time, his younger brother, Jasper Tudor, became earl of Pembroke, one of the dignities held by the king's other dead uncle, Gloucester.[130] Though Edmund himself could not conceivably have a claim to the throne, his marriage would undoubtedly strengthen the royal family and give it greater cohesion.

Some of the lesser creations of baronies, particularly during the later 1440s, may reflect the same preoccupation of the king, though admittedly rather less clearly. Both Edward Grey, who was promptly issued a writ on 14 December 1446 as the husband of Elizabeth, grand-daughter and heiress of William, Lord Ferrers of Groby (d. 1445), and his brother Thomas, created Lord Richemont-Grey by royal charter on 25 June 1450, were fairly young men at the time of their respective creations and did not occupy a prominent position at court or in the household. But they were closely related to the Holands, the former being a stepson and the latter a grandson of Constance, daughter of John Holand, duke of Exeter, and the wife of Reginald, Lord Grey of Ruthin. Edward and his brother Robert were in any case members of the affinity of the Staffords, whose head had recently been created duke of Buckingham.[131]

Sir Richard Woodville, Lord Rivers also had a relationship with the royal family that may partially explain his elevation at this juncture. His wife was none other than Bedford's widow, Jacquetta of Luxembourg, though they had been married for some years (in fact, since about 1437); however, his sister was now the wife of Charles of Anjou, uncle of Henry VI's queen, and it may have been this relationship, at a time when the credibility of Henry VI as king of France was being seriously challenged, that prompted Woodville's creation and his resort to a title derived from a Norman barony which his father had once held.[132]

Those who received the highest dignities the king could bestow were not necessarily those to whom his patronage of office, lands, and fees was most frequently channelled. The Staffords, Beauforts, and Tudors were elevated primarily to provide the king with a wider family from which, if need be, an heir might ultimately be designated. By contrast, the most worthwhile gifts, grants, and appointments went to some of the newly-created barons of the 1440s: to Dudley, Sudeley, Stourton, and the Beauchamps, as well as to Suffolk at their head. This was predictable, but in the essentially kingly matters of title, precedence, and marriage Henry's own sense of dynasty was an equally potent factor, particularly before the birth of his son and heir in 1453.

The king's special agents

The dependable complement of paid household servants, and others linked with them, was large enough to provide the king with a body of agents for special, temporary tasks up and down the country. On a minor level, it was Richard George, a serjeant-at-arms, who in March 1446 transmitted from the council to the town officials at Coventry the renunciation of errors which a local friar had agreed to proclaim from the pulpit in Coventry's parish church. If heresy or treason were to be refuted, then a household envoy could be relied on by the king to convey the news and make the necessary arrangements.[133] Of greater significance, but very delicate in nature, were the commissions given to household agents to keep important prisoners of state in custody. The most diplomatically valuable – not to say culturally cultivated – of the Agincourt captives still in prison in England when Henry VI came of age was Charles, duke of Orléans. Towards the end of the minority, he was put in the care of high-ranking courtiers: Suffolk, as steward of the household, from 1433; Sir Reginald Cobham, the duchess of Gloucester's father (who was certain to keep him safe, if only for his son-in-law's sake), from May 1436 to July 1438; Sir John Stourton, who kept him in Somerset and was responsible for escorting him to Calais in 1439 for the peace negotations; and Lord Fanhope, the last of the duke's gaolers before his release in the summer of 1440.[134]

The sensitive political issues raised by the duchess of Gloucester's dabblings in witchcraft and sorcery were handled in 1441 by the king's councillors, and her subsequent imprisonment was supervised by household servants.[135] During the investigation of her activities, she was kept under guard in Leeds castle (Kent), whose constable, Sir John Steward, had recently been the king's master of horse; he was helped by several of the chamber officials, including John Stanley. After sentence, Eleanor was assigned to Sir Thomas Stanley, controller of the household, and in January 1442 he conveyed her to Chester, where he was constable of the castle. Perhaps in relaxation of the rigours of imprisonment, in October 1443 she was moved to Kenilworth, where Lord Sudeley, chamberlain of the household and the newly-appointed treasurer of England, was constable of the fortress. But rumours of rescue bids resulted in her return to Stanley's care, and this time, in July 1446, the isolation of the Isle of Man (of which Stanley was lord) was preferred. Her last move was also organized by the household: in March 1449 Eleanor was taken to Beaumaris castle (Anglesey), where the constable was Sir William Beauchamp, long a household figure and soon to be recognized as Lord St Amand.[136] North Wales and north-west England had, after all, become a provincial retreat for the king's household under the leadership of Suffolk who, jointly with Sir Thomas Stanley, was justiciar of north Wales and Chester.[137] It was at Beaumaris that the hounded lady died on 7 July 1452, still in the custody of Henry's personal servants.

The household provided a section of the large company that journeyed to France with Suffolk in 1444 and returned to England with the new queen as a temporary household-in-transit. Thus, John Hampton, who travelled home with her in 1445 as her master of horse, had evidently been seconded from Henry's household, where he had been an usher of the chamber since 1427–28 and master of the ordnance by 1429; his organizational talents, which the king valued sufficiently highly to employ them in the building of Eton, could be put to good use during Margaret's journey.[138] Another example is afforded by Gilbert Parr, whose experience as an usher of the king's chamber since 1427–28 and keeper of the privy wardrobe in the Tower of London by 1436–37 fitted him extremely well to act as usher of the queen's chamber in 1445.[139] There is ample evidence that even after her marriage, Margaret's household was staffed by a number of people who had earlier served the king (and in some cases continued to do so) or had been engaged on Suffolk's mission to France. Sir John Wenlock, a substantial Bedfordshire landowner, had become her chamberlain by 1448.[140] Originally one of the affinity of the king's great-uncle, Lord Fanhope, he had joined Henry's household by 1441 and gathered experience as a frequent envoy to France. Having accompanied Suffolk's cavalcade across the channel, he secured appointment as usher of Margaret's chamber by the time the coronation took place on 30 May 1445. This brotherhood of household service was very much Suffolk's achievement. Accordingly, when his career and life were threatened in 1450, Henry put him in congenial protective custody. He was assigned to three servants whose careers he had assisted in the 1440s: William Mynors, John Stanley, and Thomas Staunton were all king's esquires, whilst Stanley and Staunton were ushers of the chamber in 1450 and had special responsibility for the armoury at the Tower. Suffolk's importance and the king's determination to keep him safely made them eminently suitable custodians.[141]

It was again the household which was given the task of barring York's path to Westminster from Beaumaris early in September 1450, when he arrived unexpectedly from Ireland. His arrest, perhaps even his death, was made the responsibility in particular of those household officials who had virtually monopolized the government of north Wales and Cheshire for a decade and more. In a bill which the duke placed before Henry VI at about the end of September, he complained that.

> ...at suche tyme as I proposid for to arreyved at your haven of Beammereys..., my landyng was stoppid and forbarred be Herry Norys, Thomas Norys, William Buklay, William Gruffe and Bartilmew Bolde, your officers of Northwalys, that I schulde not land there, nor have vitaile, nor refreschyng for me and my fellischip, ... So ferforth that Herry Norys, depute to the chambirlayn of Northwalys, sayde unto me that he had in comaundement that I schulde in no wyse have landyng there, nor refreschyng nor lodging for man, hors, nor othir thyng that myght torne to my worschip or ease, puttyng the blame unto William Say, usscher of your chambir, ... And more ovir certain lettres was wretyn, made and delivered unto Chestir, Schrowsbery and to othir places for to lette myn entre into the same...[142]

William Say, a prominent member of the household, had evidently had a great deal to do with conveying the king's instructions to north Wales. York further remonstrated about the elaborate steps taken by a squad of household men to apprehend him and his more prominent companions:

...certayne persones have layn in wayte to herkyn upon me as Sir John Talbot knyght at the castell of Holte, Sir Thomas Stanlay knyght in Chesschire, [Thomas] Pulforthe at Chestir, [William] Elton at Worcestre, [William] Broke at Glowcestre and Richard [Belth] Grome of your Chambir at Beammerreys, whilke had in charge as I was enformed for to take me and put me in the castell of Convay, and to strike of the hede of Sir William Oldhalle knyght, and to have put in prison Sir [Walter] Devoreux and Sir Edmond Mulso knyght...

The vital and possibly secret nature of the commission with which these servants were entrusted is indicated by the unedifying rush of certain courtiers to make their peace with York once it became known that he had slipped past the king's agents and successfully reached his own estates around Ludlow.[143]

The grounds of criticism

Increasing unease about the character of the king's political, administrative, and military appointments was matched by a growing dissatisfaction with other aspects of his patronage. Wardships and marriages were more often granted away than kept by the king, and their disposal was frequently dictated by political or personal motives rather than financial ones. Suffolk used his position as steward of the king's household to secure the wardship and marriage of Lord Morley's daughter and heiress on 11 October 1442, and also the most desirable marriage, dynastically speaking, that became available after 1436, that of Somerset's heiress, Margaret Beaufort, on 8 June 1444.[144] Smaller prizes were no less coveted, and Suffolk was one of the most regular recipients – and on generous terms. The wardship and marriage of the godson and heir of William FitzRauf, for instance, became his on 20 December 1444, apparently in return for no payment at all.[145] Others, less influential and therefore less favoured, had to pay up – even Sir Thomas Stanley.[146]n Suffolk's personal aggrandisement merely served to flaunt more widely and irritatingly his growing influence in the household and at court.

The estates of royal wards and the properties that came to the crown in other ways were rarely retained by the king for other than short periods. Soon after Lord Fanhope died in 1443, his lands were handed over to two of his executors who were close to the king, Archbishop Kemp and Lord Cromwell. Yet they were soon carved into smaller portions for distribution to several household servants: the Cornish lands went to John Trevilian and his partner in piracy, Thomas Bodulgate, on 1 February 1444 for seven years.[147] When Lord Tiptoft died on 22 January 1443, his estates were at first retained by the crown, administered by royal agents, and used to satisfy a chorus of royal creditors. But within a year, their fragmentation had begun: John St Lo received the Somerset properties for seven years on 16 October 1443, and eventually all the Somerset and Dorset estates went to Edmund Beaufort, earl of Dorset, and his male heirs on 4 October 1444.[148]

It was rare for such estates to be granted away without any guaranteed financial return to the crown, unless the recipient were exceptionally fortunate or extraordinarily favoured. Lord Hungerford and his eldest son, Robert, secured the wardship of the dower estates of Margaret, late Lady Moleyns, on 30 March 1439 at a price of £180 which was eventually fixed more than a year later.[149] In November 1439, Lord Dacre paid 50 marks more than the extent for William Legh's Cumberland, Westmorland, and Norfolk estates, and he further increased the payment within ten days.[150] Such transactions were often negotiated at the exchequer by the hopeful recipient, and hence they might be expected to give satisfaction to both sides. Warwick managed to keep his estates out of the king's hands after his death and thereby saved them from disposal during his heir's minority. He had already taken the precaution of enfeoffing them to himself and his wife jointly, and the countess was allowed to maintain the enfeoffment after her husband's death and to make one of her own that covered 600 marks-worth of the properties for the performance of her will. The remainder eventually went to Gloucester on 2 July 1440 during the minority of Henry Beauchamp, the Warwick heir.[151] Henry died in June 1446 at the age of twenty-one, and his sole daughter and heiress, Anne Beauchamp, survived him by less than three years to die at the age of six.[152] As a result, in the week beginning 12 June 1446 scores of appointments on the Warwick estates were confirmed by the crown and the late duke's properties were farmed or given to temporary custodians. Almost without exception, the recipients were either king's knights (like William Beauchamp), king's esquires (like Thomas Vaughan and Edmund Mountford, a former Warwick servant), king's serjeants (like Edward Ellesmere and, in Glamorgan, Ralph Gamage), or other royal servants; some like Thomas Montgomery, marshal of the hall, and Thomas Daniel, usher of the chamber, were household officials. Yet others were associated with the queen's establishment (witness John Wenlock, usher of her chamber), and Margaret herself secured the custody and marriage of the young heiress. The only peer to benefit from this windfall was Lord Sudeley, who was chamberlain of the household.

To control an heir or an heiress meant having the opportunity to manage his or her estates and determine his or her marriage – and all to the profit and advancement (if only temporarily) of the guardian's interests. Some wardships were small in value and inconsequential in prospects, with no local influence at stake and only a small property to be exploited. Others were larger. Not long before his death, the duke of Warwick was granted the marriage of John Arundel, son and heir of Thomas Arundel, on 24 September 1445; and a king's serjeant and esquire of the household, Lewis ap Maredudd, was fortunate enough to obtain custody of the lands of William Clement in Herefordshire and

Cardiganshire, and the custody and marriage of his daughter and heiress.[153] The custody of legally-declared idiots and their property was another source of profit and, in the nature of things, often enjoyed for longer, as Sir Edmund Hampden, a king's carver, and John Hampton, an esquire for the body, realized when they petitioned for John Crandon and his property in February 1446.[154] Throughout the 1440s, men with access to the court or an official position in the household made up the vast majority of grantees, and peers (other than favourites like Cromwell, Sudeley, Saye, or Somerset) were low on the list of beneficiaries from the king's prerogative rights. Some were expected to pay for their grant; others – a greater number – were not. If the acts of resumption threatened their grants for a moment in 1449–51, the danger was swiftly removed either by the specific exemption of a large number of household servants, or else by a reissue of the original grant soon afterwards.[155]

Henry VI was equally willing to confer privileges. He was prepared to lift the obligation to give public service from some men's shoulders, and the number of such exemptions in the late 1440s was truly astonishing, though the crisis of 1450 seems to have ended this particular irresponsibility. He was, too, indulgent towards royal officials who found it difficult to honour even their financial obligations, and on one occasion in 1439 the crown surrendered 2,000 marks of much-needed income.[156] The spate of pardons to such officials was especially striking in 1447–50, and after a brief lull in 1450–51, they reappeared in the years that followed. The well-to-do were excused from distraint of knighthood; others were pardoned for marrying without the king's licence, while certain fortunate institutions and individuals were even exempt from parliamentary taxes.[157] Nor did pardons for a whole variety of offences stop when protests were made in 1450, though once again they seem to have fallen sharply in number in that particular year; thereafter, they climbed to a yet higher level. So little did the government and the king heed the warnings and threats of parliament, peers, and popular opinion. King Henry was evidently easily swayed by an eloquent request or a pathetic plea, whether it came from a worthy old woman in difficulties late in life, or an old soldier suffering in body or possessions; and simple, hard-luck stories elicited a sympathetic response from the credulous monarch.[158] Traits which in a subject might be considered laudable, in a king ran the risk of increasing waste and feeding resentment.

Disquiet was frequently expressed at the improvident, even reckless, disposal of the king's resources. For one thing, the ready way in which the king responded to petitions occasionally led to confusion. His lack of foresight enabled numerous conflicting grants to be issued, one gift being superseded later by another; bitter arguments resulted in several parts of the country. The warning signs were flashing as early as 1438. At times Henry seemed uncertain whether a grant was capable of implementation, and a significant number of them carried the proviso that they should take effect only if an identical patent had not already been issued.[159] John Ardern, the king's clerk of works, received a life-grant of the priory of Romney and the parsonage of Upchurch (Kent) on 30 July 1438, but it was overtaken by an identical grant to Gloucester, and Upchurch was later appropriated by Archbishop Chichele for All Souls' College, Oxford. It was only after Ardern had protested to the king that his original grant was affirmed on 22 May 1439 – and a £40 annuity added.[160] Some grants proved, through carelessness, to be more ample than had been intended, as Thomas Daniel discovered to his delight in 1441; but his position in the household did not prevent the treasurer of England from cancelling his acquisition of the manor of Frodsham (Cheshire) on 14 May and duly pruning the initial grant.[161] One blatant example of maladministration involved the alien priory of St James, near Exeter, which was conferred in two separate instruments on two different individuals on consecutive days in February 1438.[162] Bungling of this kind – for it can be regarded as no less – sometimes led to violence, as one party was ejected from land or office by a rival. The well-known feud between the Bonvilles and the Courtenays in the west country was intensified by a particularly serious blunder whereby the stewardship of the duchy of Cornwall estates in Devon was bestowed on both families simultaneously.[163]

The council could not fail to be concerned at these developments, not least because of the imprudent granting of pardons to financial officials. Early in the king's personal rule, it urged him to change his habits, but there was a fundamental conflict betwen Henry's personal inclinations and his advisers' political and administrative judgement. It is true that by 1440 the number of life-grants of offices seems to have declined, but by 1443 it was at its previous level once more. If an attempt had been made to introduce restraint and greater prudence, perhaps in the wake of the Reading parliament, it was only temporary. An effort was also made to ensure that the terms of such grants were made more specific, so that the conditions under which wardships, marriages, and properties were leased were not left to the recipient to negotiate directly with the exchequer or allowed to be determined by competition. This latter practice seems to have been suspended in 1440, though it, too, reappeared after 1443.[164]

The problem was approached from another direction. Inquiries were periodically instituted into those resources of the crown that were slipping away almost unnoticed; but without an efficient and regular system of investigation, their identification and retention would be difficult. The period of greatest activity by commissions of inquiry was 1439–41, and some of them may have been intended to inform the king of what was actually at his disposal. Equally, they may have been partly responsible for the tighter control which seems to have been exerted immediately afterwards. The commissions examined wardships, marriages, and escheats that had been lost without authorization; waste and the destruction of royal property; concealments, escapes, and the evasion of responsibilities; and those eligible for knighthood.[165] This activity coincides with the concern felt by the commons in parliament in 1439–40, when they correctly focussed attention on the role of the king's household. Such concern seems to have revived in 1443 when, on 9 March, all those with fees or grants from the duchy of Lancaster were summoned before the council 'for the good of the realm'; in the following July, a number of grants made in Ireland were subjected to review by the Irish parliament.[166] It may have been a blow to the prospects of better management that on 7 July 1443 Lord Cromwell, who had insisted on the household's financial solvency in the past, was replaced as treasurer by Lord Sudeley, one of the most prominent courtiers; during 1443 some of the more wayward features of royal patronage revived.[167] Major procedural improvements for the implementation of the king's will were proposed by the council and accepted by the king in 1444, but they did not grasp the fundamental problem, namely, the quality of the decision rather than the efficiency of its execution.[168] There is no real sign that sounder judgement prevailed in the later 1440s, and indeed the entrenched power of Suffolk's household clique made it most unlikely that a reorientation of the king's patronage could be achieved without upheaval.

Specific warnings were voiced in parliament. In 1450–51, for instance, the city of York remonstrated at the granting of exemptions to citizens so that they could avoid office, and its petition was adopted by the commons as a whole perhaps because the frustration was felt in other parts of the realm.[169] The king felt it wise to concede their point at that unsettled juncture, and in general exemptions ceased over the next couple of years; but by 1453 bad habits had returned and the situation was fast becoming as unsatisfactory as before. Another aspect of the king's lack of circumspection and prodigality was raised in parliament in 1453–54. Not for the first time the statutes which protected the monopoly of the Calais staplers in the export of wool to northern Europe had been breached by royal licences which allowed direct shipment to Normandy, Flanders, and elsewhere in the Low Countries. Such licences were issued with increasing frequency after 1436, and eight years later the staplers had demanded assurances that their privileges would be respected. But the government's promises proved worthless, and the matter was raised again in 1449. Early in 1454, the commons insisted that such preferential licences should be withdrawn and abandoned, and that merchants who procured them should spend two years in prison. They even proposed a network of informers, who would report illicit trading and receive a proportion of any merchandise recovered.[170] The government's response to these demands is not recorded; they may have been rejected, for although the staplers felt most strongly about this matter, it would have been humiliating for the government to withdraw licences already issued or forego a valued means of patronage. In any case, important persons, including the queen, were recipients of these licences.[171]

In the English ports, the long-established expedient of surrendering to government creditors authority to appoint one or more customs officers seems to have resulted in inefficiency and abuse. Presumably as a result of representations to the exchequer, on 1 January 1447 it was agreed that no port official or customs collector whose appointment was the treasurer's responsibility should receive his commission in any way other than with the treasurer's assent. Bishop Lumley had been treasurer a mere fortnight before this regulation was introduced.[172] The kind of situation that could arise was illustrated at Great Yarmouth, where the bailiff had defrauded the crown of £1,000 by allowing uncustomed wool to be exported and hindering the customs officers in the exercise of their duty. Other customs officials were said to be of little 'haveour and valeur', and in London wool packers, gaugers, and wiredrawers took advantage of their position to impose illegal imposts, presumably for their own profit.[173] The parliament of 1453 decided to deal with these problems on a national level, but its lack of success reflects the fundamental cause. A statute of Richard II's day, whereby port officials should serve for one year only, was ignored by those who secured letters patent from the king authorizing them to hold office for life or for a term of years.[174] Parliament requested the annulment of such letters and strict control by the treasurer over future appointments. The petition was granted, but the exemptions that were attached to it rendered it quite ineffective: two household officials were exempt by name – John Penycock and Giles St Lo – as well as all menial or domestic servants of the household and the queen's employees.

Notes

1 *CPR, 1441–46*, p. 399. For Daniel, see below, p. 336.
2 *CPR, 1446–52*, p. 334; Wedgwood, *Biographies*, pp. 80-1; above, p. 300.
3 *CPR, 1446–52*, p. 68.
4 ibid., p. 305. For Andrew, see Otway-Ruthven, *King's secretary*, pp. 172-3.
5 e.g., *CPR, 1436–41*, pp. 92, 99, 124.
6 ibid., p. 123; Wedgwood, *Biographies*, pp. 816-17.
7 *CPR, 1441–46*, p. 83.
8 ibid., p. 266.
9 ibid., *1436–41*, p. 383; ibid., *1441–46*, p. 133. Cf. John St Lo in *CCR, 1435–42*, p. 103, and below, p. 332.
10 *CPR, 1436–41*, p. 488. For Everdon's other tasks, see above, p. 315.
11 *CPR, 1441–46*, p. 158. Roos was also a frequent envoy to France in the 1440s (Ferguson, op. cit., pp. 183, 192, 197).
12 ibid., pp. 81, 98.
13 ibid., pp. 89, 323.
14 *PPC*, VI, 66; Wedgwood, *Biographies*, pp. 676-7; Jeffs, thesis, pp. 314–16; above, p. 309. For another example of household advocacy, this time on behalf of a Bristol merchant in 1449, see *CPR, 1446–52*, p. 215.

15 *CPR, 1441–46*, p. 137; above, p. 331. For West, see Wedgwood, *Biographies*, p. 937; and Pole, R. S. Thomas, 'Geoffrey Pole: a Lancastrian servant in Wales,' *NLWJ*, XVII (1972), 277-86. They did not actually enter the office until 1449.

16 Wedgwood, *Biographies*, pp. 322-3; *GEC*, XI, 479-81; Jeffs, thesis, pp. 289-91; below, p. 339.

17 Jeffs, thesis, pp. 322-3; Wedgwood, *Biographies*, p. 737.

18 Emden, *Oxford*, III, 1727–8; above, pp. 54-5.

19 *CPR, 1436–41*, pp. 126 (Maud Fosbroke), 127 (Joan Asteley), 367 (Alice Botiller); ibid., *1441–46*, pp. 180 (Fosbroke), 319 (Asteley); above, p. 51. When Fosbroke died early in 1448, her executors included the queen's secretary, Nicholas Caraunt, and her attorney, Robert Tanfield (North-antsRO, Δ 1102; above, p. 258).

20 *PPC*, V, 87.

21 Above, pp. 282ff.

22 *CPR, 1441–46*, p. 399. Thorley had been a clerk in the office of the household controller as long ago as 1430, when Henry went to France (PRO, E404/46/263).

23 *CPR, 1441–46*, p. 408; above, p. 332.

24 Griffiths, 'Patronage, politics and the principality of Wales', passim.

25 E. C. Lodge and G. A. Thornton (eds.), *English constitutional documents, 1307–1485* (Cambridge, 1935), p. 343.

26 Jeffs, thesis, pp. 14-17.

27 ibid., appendix VI, pp. 341-3. The main road from London to the west country and Cornwall ran through Basingstoke and Andover (Hants.) to Salisbury (Wilts.), Shaftesbury and Sherborne (Dorset), and on to Taunton (Soms.) or Exeter (Devon), as the inhabitants of Andover stressed in 1435 (PRO, SC8/90/4477). This was the very route taken to and from the capital by the mayor of Exeter in 1459 (DevonRO, Exeter receivers' accounts, 37-38 Henry VI).

28 Jeffs, thesis, pp. 278-9; below, pp. 584ff.

29 PRO, C49/26/11 (1445); *RP*, V, 323-4 (1455). The worst financial difficulties of sheriffs were sometimes alleviated after 1444 by replacing their obligation to pay the county's fee-farm into the exchequer by the obligation to declare what their actual receipts had been. The sheriffs of Lincoln (from 1444) and Warws.–Leics. (from 1450) in particular were accorded this privilege, though it was rare elsewhere before 1461. Jeffs, thesis, appendix IV, pp. 269-73, and, more generally, pp. 38-128.

30 Below, p. 615.

31 *PL*, II, 51.

32 DevonRO, Exeter receivers' accounts, 17-18, 24-25, and 30-31 Henry VI.

33 The Herefs. esquire Walter Sculle was appointed sheriff of Oxon.–Berks. in 1439–40, though his royal service hitherto had been confined to Wales and the border shires; he later became a member of the king's household, but his appointment in a 'foreign' shire in 1439 may be explained by his recent marriage to a daughter of Sir John Beauchamp of Holt. Griffiths, *Principality of Wales*, p. 153; Wedgwood, *Biographies*, pp. 773-4; Somerville, op. cit., pp. 641-2; Jeffs, thesis, pp. 323-4.

34 The number would only be as large again in 1448–49; these figures are based on Jeffs, thesis, appendix V, VI.

35 Cf. the Kentish group, below, p. 633.

36 Jeffs, thesis, pp. 275-6; Wedgwood, *Biographies*, pp. 48-9; F. R. H. DuBoulay, *The lordship of Canterbury* (1966), p. 396.
37 Wedgwood, *Biographies*, pp. 149-50; Jeffs, thesis, pp. 278-9; *PL*, II, 51, 77-8.
38 Jeffs, thesis, pp. 314-16; Wedgwood, *Biographies*, pp. 676-9; PRO, E404/41/143; above, p. 331. Cf. the importance which the archbishop of Canterbury attached to securing the services of James Fiennes in Kent (below, p. 630), and the city of Exeter's wooing of the sheriffs of Devon (above, p. 335).
39 Jeffs, thesis, p. 286. Cf. the charges levelled in 1450 at former Kent sheriffs (below, p. 632).
40 Above, p. 280; Jeffs, thesis, passim. Sir Edmund Hampden's brother, Sir John, was one of Suffolk's servants slain in 1450 (below, p. 643).
41 The Beauchamps, for instance, were hereditary sheriffs of Worcs.
42 *CPR, 1441–46*, passim; ibid., *1446–52*, passim.
43 ibid., *1441–46*, p. 460; *GEC*, II, 47.
44 *CPR, 1446–52*, p. 203; Wedgwood, *Biographies*, pp. 253-5; Jeffs, thesis, pp. 286-7; above, p. 336. Daniel came from Cheshire, but he married a sister of the Norfolk knight Sir John Howard.
45 *CPR, 1446–52*, p. 416; Jeffs, thesis, pp. 339-40; PRO, E404/56/162; the Yerde home was at Cheam in Surrey (below, p. 659). For another example, William Stone, see Wedgwood, *Biographies*, pp. 813-14; *CPR, 1446–52*, p. 109.
46 ibid., pp. 456, 563; see Myers, *BJRL*, XLII (1959), 113-31.
47 *CPR, 1446–52*, p. 24.
48 ibid., p. 87; *GEC*, XI, 479-81.
49 *CPR, 1446–52*, pp. 283, 329; Wedgwood, *Biographies*, pp. 934-5; Jeffs, thesis, pp. 335-7. Wentworth was a Yorkshireman.
50 *CPR, 1446–52*, p. 77; *CCR, 1445–52*, p. 81. For his household connections, see Wedgwood, *Biographies*, p. 78.
51 *CPR, 1446–52*, pp. 426-7.
52 ibid., p. 468.
53 ibid, pp. 84, 305; Wedgwood, *Biographies*, pp. 605-6; Jeffs, thesis, pp. 306-7. The king's indulgent attitude towards such men is revealed in 1450 when Henry described Montgomery as 'a young son [who] hath nothing to live on, saving only of our gift' (*RP*, V, 193).
54 *CPR, 1441–46*, p. 398; Wedgwood, *Biographies*, pp. 409-10; below, p. 497.
55 *CPR, 1441–46*, pp. 456 (Launceston), 511 (Leeds); ibid, *1446–52*, pp. 246 (Bamburgh), 329 (Bassingbourne).
56 The following paragraphs are based largely on Wedgwood, *Biographies*, s. n.; Jeffs, thesis, appendix V, s. n.; *GEC*, XI, 479-81. For a fuller exposition, see below, pp. 633-4.
57 Below, p. 615.
58 Richard was sheriff of Surrey–Sussex in 1452–53; Robert was MP for Hampshire in 1447, sheriff there in 1448–49, and secured the reversion of some of his father's grants.
59 Below, pp. 633-4.
60 Below, pp. 633-4.
61 Below, p. 633.
62 According to Wedgwood, *Biographies*, p. 324, Sir Roger's death occurred

sometime between 11 February and October 1450. He was not mentioned in the attacks on household servants, so it may have been earlier rather than later (above, p. 304). Richard Fiennes was sheriff of Surrey–Sussex in 1452–53, and after the Lancastrian triumph in 1459 his brother Robert was appointed; Iden was sheriff of Kent in 1456.

63 Jeffs, thesis, passim, *s. n.*; Wedgwood, *Biographies*, passim, *s. n.* For Catesby, see also J. S. Roskell, 'William Catesby, counsellor to Richard III'; *BJRL*, XLII (1959–60), 149-52.

64 idem, 'William Tresham of Bywell', *Northants. Past and Present*, II (1954–59), 189-203; idem, 'Sir Thomas Tresham, knight', ibid., 313-23; above, p. 305.

65 Henry Everingham, who may have been Thomas's brother, was also an esquire for the body.

66 Somerville, op. cit., p. 390. For Tresham, see above, p. 305; and for Say, J. S. Roskell, 'Sir John Say of Broxbourne', *East Herts. Arch. Soc. Trans.*, XIV, pt. 1 (1959), 20-41, and idem, *Speakers*, pp. 231-2. Both men were chancellor of the county palatine of Lancaster as well (Somerville, op. cit., p. 476).

67 Jeffs, thesis, pp. 274a-b; Somerville, op. cit., pp. 398-9.

68 ibid., p. 399; above, p. 306.

69 Somerville, op. cit., pp. 420-1, 428-9. Among the lawyers who acted as deputy-steward for these influential courtiers were John Heydon, Suffolk's client, deputy-steward in the south in 1437–41 and the north in 1444–45, and Thomas Yonge, deputy-steward in the south in 1442–47 (Somerville, op. cit., pp. 424-5, 430-1). The chief stewardship of Lancashire was held jointly with the northern stewardship (ibid., p. 492).

70 ibid., p. 594.

71 ibid., p. 605; Roskell, *1422*, pp. 226-9; Jeffs, thesis, pp. 329-30; Wedgwood, *Biographies*, pp. 891-3; PRO, E404/67/20; 39/215; 64/162; 60/143.

72 Somerville, op. cit., pp. 611, 607; *King's works*, II, 1046; above, p. 65.

73 Somerville, op. cit., pp. 513-15, 528.

74 ibid., pp. 539-40; C. Rawcliffe, *The Staffords, earls of Stafford and dukes of Buckingham, 1394–1521* (Cambridge, 1978), pp. 81, 224-5. Sir Richard had been treasurer of Calais and his son captain of Hammes castle while Stafford was captain of Calais in the 1440s.

75 The following paragraphs are largely based on Griffiths, 'Patronage, politics, and the principality of Wales', pp. 83-5, where full references are given.

76 Beaufort was also steward of the duchy of Lancaster lordships of Kidwelly (Carmarthenshire), Monmouth, and the Three Castles (Grosmont, Skenfrith, and White Castle in Gwent), and constable of Monmouth castle from 1433 (Somerville, op. cit., pp. 640, 647, 649). His patents in both principality and duchy were converted to life in April and July 1438.

77 PRO, E28/76/19.

78 Below, p. 361.

79 William Troutbeck and his son John between them held the chamberlainship for 45 years from 1412. William was chancellor of the county palatine of Lancaster during 1423–39, and both father and son were steward and receiver of Hawarden and Mold; John became sheriff of Cheshire in 1438–39. His father had been an official of Queen Katherine, while John was a king's esquire and had lands in Herts., which he represented in

parliament in 1442 and 1447; his son, William II, married a daughter of Sir Thomas Stanley. See Wedgwood, *Biographies*, p. 897; Somerville, op. cit., pp. 476, 486; *DKR*, XXXVI (1875), 477; J. T. Driver, *Cheshire in the later middle ages* (Chester, 1971), pp. 76, 118, 121-3.

80 R. A. Griffiths, 'Gruffydd ap Nicholas and the rise of the house of Dinefwr', *NLWJ*, XIII (1964), 256-68; idem, 'Gruffydd ap Nicholas and the fall of the house of Lancaster', *WHR*, II (1965), 213-31.

81 These paragraphs are based on Emden, *Oxford*; idem, *Cambridge*; and R. G. Davies, thesis, III, *s.n..* For Praty, see C. Deeds, 'Extracts from the episcopal register of Richard Praty', *Sussex Record Soc.*, IV (1905), 89, 91; and ChichRO, Ep.1/1/2 (Reg. Praty), f. 50v.

82 Judd, op. cit., passim.

83 It is possible that his promotion had been delayed by a fear that he would feel bound to devote himself to his diocese; this consideration may have dictated the choice of the uninviting St David's, though Lyndwood continued as keeper of the privy seal only for a further year (above, p. 278).

84 Nicholas Ashby presumably owed his nomination to Llandaff late in December 1440, at the suggestion of Henry VI himself, to his being a Benedictine monk at Westminster who had made a name for himself as a capable administrator of the abbey.

85 Note, in any case, the degree of overlap in the personnel of their households (above, p. 257). J. M. George, 'The English episcopate and the crown, 1437–50' (Columbia PhD thesis, 1976), pp. 76-89, plausibly proposes a Tudor origin for the story of Stanbury's candidature.

86 For Stanbury, see A. Rhydderch, 'Robert Mascall and John Stanbury: king's confessors and bishops of Hereford' (Wales MA dissertation, 1974).

87 ct. R. J. Knecht, 'The episcopate and the Wars of the Roses,' *UBHJ*, VI (1957–58), 110-11.

88 His father was Sir Walter Beauchamp (above, p. 55).

89 Cobban, op. cit., pp. 285-6. Close left books to King's in his will.

90 A Thomas Bird was engaged in the building of Eton in 1449–50 (PRO, E404/66/123). Bird, Close, and John Blakedon were the only friars promoted in these years.

91 This difficult subject is best approached via McFarlane, *Nobility*, ch. I and appendix A; and T. B. Pugh, 'Magnates, knights and gentry', in Chrimes, Ross, and Griffiths, op. cit., pp. 86-128.

92 *RP*, IV, 56, reprinted in Chrimes and Brown, op. cit., pp. 276-7, and Lodge and Thornton, op. cit., p. 170, and translated in *EHD*, IV, 466. See Griffiths, *BJRL*, LI (1969), 399, for the duchess's trial, and Lodge and Thornton, op. cit., pp. 137-8, 158, for the privileges of peers in the fourteenth century.

93 *RDP*, V, 233ff.; for their stabilizing role, see ibid., 241-3.

94 Below, p. 356. Cf. Gloucester's complaint in 1440 that lords, especially of the royal blood, were being ignored (above, p. 238).

95 Though Lord Fanhope's peerage in 1432, the second ever to be created by letters patent, appears in effect to have been a grant for life (*RDP*, V, 213). He was then an elderly widower with no surviving legitimate heirs.

96 Powell and Wallis, op. cit., ch. 23-27. There is a useful analysis of most of

Henry's creations in M. K. Jones, 'The new nobility, 1437–50' (Bristol BA dissertation, 1977),

97 Powell and Wallis, op. cit., pp. 436-7; S. B. Chrimes, *English constitutional ideas in the fifteenth century* (Cambridge, 1936), pp. 126-30, 145-56; idem, '"House of Lords" and "House of Commons" in the fifteenth century', *EHR*, XLIX (1934), 494-7.

98 Beauchamp received a patent of creation two months later on 2 May (Powell and Wallis, op. cit., p. 484). See *GEC*, II, 46-7; and Griffiths, *Principality of Wales*, pp. 152-3.

99 Powell and Wallis, op. cit., p. 487. A patent, now unrecorded, may also have followed this writ to ensure the normal heritable character of the Bonville barony in the male line.

100 ibid., pp. 461-2; *RP*, IV, 400-1; *RDP*, V, 213; *GEC*, V, 253-4. Fanhope was held in Edward III's reign by Roger Chandos, who had been summoned to parliament, but none of his successors were. The link between title and estate was therefore tenuous but still of some force.

101 *RDP*, V, 239; Powell and Wallis, op. cit., pp. 470-1. For Botiller's personal service to the king, and his mother's role as Henry's nanny, see above, p. 52.

102 Powell and Wallis, op. cit., pp. 480-1; *RDP*, IV, 928; *GEC*, I, 27-30. Although the Abergavenny estates had been entailed on Warwick and his male heirs, Neville had great difficulty in securing them against the claims of Richard Neville, the husband of the duke of Warwick's sister.

103 Powell and Wallis, op. cit., pp. 467-8; *RDP*, IV, 889; L. S. Woodger, 'Henry Bourgchier, earl of Essex, and his family' (Oxford DPhil thesis, 1974), p. 53. Henry was not summoned with other lords on 8 July 1433, and he is first recorded in the upper house on 3 November (*RP*, IV, 422).

104 M. K. Jones, dissertation, p. 5; *GEC*, V, 484-5; above, p. 205. Radcliffe died fighting for York in 1461.

105 Powell and Wallis, op. cit., p. 486; Woodger, thesis, pp. 51, 56-7. Though his wife was only 14 in 1437, Bourgchier was probably of age, for the couple had seisin of the FitzWarin lands on 15 August (*GEC*, V, 507-8).

106 Powell and Wallis, op. cit., pp. 484-5; *RDP*, V, 263. He had married Bedford's widow, Jacquetta of Luxembourg, as long ago as 1437. Rivers also chose to emphasize his supposed connection with the Norman earls of Devon (1141–1262), the Reviers.

107 ibid., IV, 917; Powell and Wallis, op. cit., pp. 481-4.

108 ibid., pp. 466-7; *RDP*, IV, 902; the Dudley barony was held by Sutton's forebear, John de Somery, who was summoned to parliament until his death in 1322. Similarly, Sir Henry Bromflete was known as Lord Vesci as early as 13 May 1438, even though his writ was not issued until 24 January 1449 (*RDP*, IV, 919; Powell and Wallis, op. cit., pp. 486-7). The title derived from distant ancestors in Edward II's reign who had been summoned to parliament until 1314; Bromflete's stronger claim to the barony of Alton was ignored.

109 Bromflete's title may have been in recognition of his diplomatic and other services to the house of Lancaster since Henry IV's day (*GEC*, XII, ii, 285-8).

110 He is first referred to as viscount in the writ of summons of 14 December 1446. Woodger, thesis, pp. 55-6, noted that military service was the declared reason for the creation, but the French count of Eu, Charles

d'Artois, a prisoner in England since Agincourt, had returned to France in 1438 and played a significant part in the French recovery of Normandy (*Dict. Biog. Franc.*, VIII, 561-2).

111 Powell and Wallis, op. cit., pp. 485, 468-9; *RDP*, V, 235, 266. Beaumont's belated grant of the vicomté of Beaumont in January 1441 followed his viscountcy, though his ancestors had originated in Beaumont (Maine). Hoo had been granted the lordship of Hastings 3 years before his creation, on 19 July 1445 (*CPR, 1441–46*, p. 350). For other examples, see below, n. 116.

112 K. B. McFarlane, 'The investment of Sir John Fastolf's profits of war', *TRHS*, 5th ser., VII (1957), 91-116 (with the quotation on p. 93); Allmand, *EconHR*, 2nd ser., XXI (1968), 273-6. Another of York's councillors, Sir Andrew Ogard, is a further example (Wedgwood, *Biographies*, pp. 644-5); for his extensive French and English acquisitions, see J. H. Harvey (ed.), *Itineraries of William Worcester* (Oxford, 1969), pp. 47-9.

113 *RP*, V, 40; Powell and Wallis, op. cit., p. 471: 'The change in, or addition to, Cornwall's title seems to have been no more than a piece of vanity', for he continued to be known as Fanhope.

114 *RDP*, V, 237-8; IV, 922; Powell and Wallis, op. cit., p. 487; Vale, *English Gascony*, p. 245. Talbot may also have merited his earldom, with its £20 in annual rent from Shropshire, by his territorial losses in France; he had been granted extensive lands in Normandy and the Ile de France, including the county of Clermont, north of Paris, See Pollard, thesis, pp. 328-32.

115 Powell and Wallis, op. cit., pp. 473-4; *GEC*, XII, ii, 383-4; above, p. 52; *RDP*, V, 242-3, 244. As a duke, Warwick was to have precedence after Norfolk, but before Buckingham.

116 *RDP*, V, 240, 249-50, 259-60; Powell and Wallis, op. cit., p. 486. His marquessate emulated the extraordinary grant to Richard II's favourite, Robert de Vere, marquess of Dublin.

117 ibid., pp. 484-5; *RDP*, V, 264-5; above, p. 303. Stourton's commendations were listed as personal probity, impeccable origins, and service to both Henry V and Henry VI.

118 Powell and Wallis, op. cit., pp. 484, 486; Wedgwood, *Biographies*, p. 55. For John Beauchamp's subsequent patent of creation, see above, p. 353.

119 R. A. Griffiths, 'The sense of dynasty in the reign of Henry VI', in C. D. Ross (ed.), *Patronage, pedigree and power in later mediaeval England* (Gloucester, 1979) pp. 13-36.

120 *CPR, 1436–41*, pp. 401, 444; ibid., *1441–46*, pp. 63, 74.

121 Griffiths, *BJRL*, LI (1969), 381-99.

122 Above, p. 251.

123 Chrimes, *Const. Ideas*, pp. 22ff.

124 Ross, *Edward IV*, pp. 5-7.

125 Griffiths, 'The sense of dynasty', pp. 19-23.

126 *PPC*, V, 252-3; *EHL*, p. 341; *GEC*, XII, i, 47. At the same time, or soon afterwards, he was given Bedford's former earldom of Kendal (*PPC*, V, 285-8 [the charter being formally enrolled on 28 August: *RDP*, V, 241]).

127 ibid., 248; the patent also noted John's affection for the king and his services. Somerset had meanwhile returned to England in disgrace and soon died (May 1444).

128 ibid., 243, 257-8. Once again, it was kinship with the king that was specially emphasized in these patents.

129 ibid., 238, 240-1, 258-9. The initial creation on 28 August 1442 laid great stress on his royal lineage.

130 ibid., 293-4; Thomas, thesis, pp. 32-7. PRO, E159/231, *adhuc communia, recorda*, Michaelmas, m. 22d., establishes that Jasper's ennoblement took place at the same time as Edmund's.

131 *GEC*, V, 358-9; X, 777-8; *RDP*, V, 275; Rawcliffe, op. cit., pp. 74, 232-3.

132 *RDP*, V, 263; M. K. Jones, dissertation, pp. 16, 20 n. 37; above, p. 354; no mention, however, was made of the relationship in the patent of creation. The ennoblement of Northumberland's sons – Henry as Lord Poynings in December 1446 (a title acquired through his wife) and Thomas as Lord Egremont in November 1449 – probably stemmed from the Percies' influence in the north and their Beaufort connections (*GEC*, X, 665; V, 33; *RDP*, V, 272-3; above, p. 36).

133 *PPC*, VI, 41.

134 PRO, E404/50/130; 52/358 (Suffolk, 1433–36); 55/128, 297 (Stourton, 1438–39); 56/259 (Fanhope, 1440); E403/735 m. 9 (Cobham); 737 m. 7 (Stourton); 739 m. 8 (Fanhope, from 29 January 1440); Stevenson, I, 432-4 (Stourton); II, i, 231 (Suffolk).

135 Griffiths, *BJRL*, LI (1968–69), 387-99.

136 idem, *WHR*, VIII (1976), 23-4.

137 Above, pp. 343-4.

138 Stevenson, I, 448; PRO, E404/44/334; 46/307; 58/126; Wedgwood, *Biographies*, pp. 415-17. For other aspects of this journey, see below, pp. 486-8.

139 PRO, E404/44/234; 53/164; Stevenson, I, 445. Parr's wife, Agnes, accompanied him as one of the queen's ladies (ibid., 454-5).

140 Roskell, *Speakers*, pp. 258-62; idem, 'John, Lord Wenlock of Someries', *Beds. Hist. Record Soc.*, XXXVIII (1958), 12-48; Wedgwood, *Biographies*, pp. 931-2. For other instances of the overlap of service, see above, p. 257.

141 *PPC*, VI, 311; Wedgwood, *Biographies*, pp. 797-9, 803; Jeffs, thesis, pp. 326-7. They were discharged of their responsibility on 19 March 1450 (*CPR, 1446–52*, p. 311).

142 This and the next quotation are from Griffiths, *JMH*, I (1975), 203 (Beverley Corporation archives, Town 'Chartulary', f. 36-37, supplemented by J. Stow, *The chronicles of England* [1580], pp. 666-8). For the relationship of these north Wales officers to one another and to the king's household, see Griffiths, *WHR*, VIII (1976), 16-22.

143 Above, p. 305.

144 *CPR, 1441–46*, pp. 133, 283.

145 *CFR, 1437–45*, p. 313.

146 ibid., p. 75. Salisbury had to pay 2,500 marks in August 1438 for the earl of Arundel's marriage (*CPR, 1436–41*, p. 194).

147 *CPR, 1441–46*, p. 240; *CCR, 1441–47*, pp. 222-3; *CFR, 1437–45*, p. 287; Kingsford, *Prejudice and promise*, pp. 101-4, 200-2. For popular hostility to Trevilian and Bodulgate, see below, p. 641.

148 *CPR, 1441–46*, pp. 145, 176, 228, 324; *CFR, 1437–45*, pp. 271, 278, 295-6, 298. For St Lo, see above, p. 332.

149 *CFR, 1437–45*, p. 159. Robert soon afterwards (by November 1440) married Margaret's granddaughter, the Moleyns co-heiress, and as a consequence

was summoned to parliament as Lord Moleyns in January 1445 (*GEC*, IX, 41-3).

150 *CFR, 1437–45*, pp. 113, 115.
151 ibid., pp. 77, 122; *CPR, 1436–41*, pp. 279, 360, 435, 359-60.
152 *GEC*, XII, ii, 384-6; *CPR, 1441–46*, 391, 419, 432-7, 443, 446, 448-9; Anne's heiress was her aunt, also called Anne. The conclusions of the following paragraphs are largely based on a detailed study of *CPR, CCR, CFR*.
153 *CPR, 1441–46*, p. 372; ibid., *1446–52*, pp. 2, 6; Griffiths, *Principality of Wales*, pp. 222, 426.
154 *CPR, 1441–46*, p. 452.
155 Wolffe, *Royal demesne*, ch. V.
156 *PPC*, V, 88.
157 *CCR, 1435–41*, p. 255; *CPR, 1436–41*, pp. 160, 469; ibid., *1441–46*, p. 330.
158 ibid., pp. 330, 348.
159 *CFR, 1437–45*, p. 34.
160 PRO, E28/60/57-58. Other grants had to be annulled (*CPR, 1436–41*, p. 186).
161 *PPC*, V, 144.
162 *CPR, 1436–41*, p. 255.
163 Storey, *End of Lancaster*, pp. 85ff; below, pp. 574-7.
164 Haggling with exchequer officials was also less frequent by 1441 and did not really return until 1443, and then only for a brief period.
165 *CPR, 1436–41*, pp. 314-15. But Henry's willingness to pardon undermined these inquiries (*CCR, 1435–41*, p. 255).
166 *PPC*, V, 238-9, 296.
167 Above, p. 281.
168 Above, pp. 282-4.
169 *RP*, V, 225.
170 ibid., p. 275; Lloyd, op. cit., pp. 270, 272.
171 Haward, in *English trade*, pp. 294-5 and n. 4. The queen, Suffolk, and 3 household officials had been specifically exempt from the 1449 statute banning licences.
172 *CPR, 1446–52*, p. 28.
173 *PPC*, VI, 50, 328.
174 *RP*, V, 268.

15   In Search of Money

The financial problem

If there was an 'habitual disparity between the crown's revenue and its obligations' in the middle ages, the financial health of Henry VI's government was particularly gravely compromised. This was by no means entirely the king's fault. During the minority his income had barely sufficed for his normal needs; after 1436 the costs of government, an expanded household, and an inherited war, in which the English were thrown increasingly on to the defensive, imposed demands that far outweighed the country's normal resources and severely tested the goodwill of Englishmen to support their monarch's ventures with direct taxation.[1] Henry's imprudence in allowing his resources to be reduced by carelessness and unwonted generosity made matters worse.

In the first place, the royal household after 1436 was a costly affair, and both council and parliament were conscious of the inadequate funds available to run it efficiently. In 1450 it was reported that its expenses amounted to £24,000 a year; although this was an exaggeration as far as normal current expenditure goes (closer to £17,000), the increased costs associated with the queen's arrival and the accumulation of unpaid debts may well have brought the figure within reach of that larger sum on a few occasions.[2] Secondly, the record of the council in meeting crown debts during the minority was not impressive. By 1437 a number of officials were unpaid and in some cases had been neglected for years.[3] Some of these debts were large: Sir John Radcliffe was dead, but his executors were still owed £7,015 from his term as seneschal of Gascony (1423–36) and a further £68 for his journey to Arras (1435); Sir John had reportedly mortgaged or disposed of much of his personal wealth and was indebted to many friends as a result of the crown's defaulting.[4] More seriously, Lord Fauconberg and the earl of Salisbury on the Scottish border and Buckingham at Calais held strategic commands which might be gravely weakened if lack of finance were to lead to mutiny or desertion.[5] The war with France was an increasingly heavy burden too, for it was going badly for the English by the late 1430s and substantial financial support from Normandy and elsewhere was no longer forthcoming.[6] The cost of sending expeditions to Normandy, Gascony, and Calais, as well as frequent embassies to and from various parts of France, not to speak of the formal conference at Oye (1439), fell almost entirely upon English shoulders. In October 1437 Lord Cromwell warned that there was no cash available to pay envoys who were being despatched to Cherbourg and that every foreseeable item of future revenue had been assigned; in February 1441 the council recognized that there was insufficient money available to send a new army to Normandy.[7] Henry VI's government was living a hand-to-mouth existence in a fundamental state of bankruptcy.

Nor were his resources under prudent management, at least to judge by the complaints of royal creditors.[8] Those who had lent money to the king in good faith, sometimes many, many years before, found themselves neglected and with little prospect of repayment; merchants among them were allowed to ply their trade free of customs, but that was a short-term expedient that ultimately further compromised the crown's income.[9] Even the king's own servants and courtiers and those who worked in the government offices at Westminster were issued with questionable assignments that led to unseemly squabbles as certain sources were over-assigned by a desperate government. This practice simply transferred the burden from one foot to the other and in the process alienated creditors and exasperated the revenue-collectors.[10] Indeed, more and more of the income normally available to the government seems to have been assigned well in advance of its collection; on some occasions, the temptation to anticipate revenue that had not even been authorized was too strong to resist.[11] By the time parliament was dissolved in July 1449, the king's current charges and debts had reportedly risen to the 'grete and grevouse' level of £372,000 (compared with £225,315 in 1433). The need for immediate relief was stark; according to the commons, the only course open to Henry was a wholesale resumption or cancellation of grants of lands and rents issued since 1422.[12]

Lord Cromwell struggled manfully with the gigantic task before him, and he did not shrink from telling the council that it could not undertake all it wanted to do.[13] By 1443, by which time he had again tried to convince his colleagues of the financial realities, he was brought to the point of resignation. The ostensible reason for his departure from office was ill health and it may be that the strain imposed on a treasurer in Henry VI's reign is comparable with that borne by a chancellor of the exchequer in the twentieth century; moreover, by a fair margin, Cromwell had been the longest serving treasurer for almost a century. Yet he lived on for another thirteen active years, and reading between the lines of his act of resignation one may detect a final exasperation at the lack of understanding shown by the king and his advisers of the parlous state of England's finances.[14] His retirement removed from the exchequer a man who had the rare combination of clear-sightedness, realism, and determination to manage the king's financial affairs in a particularly difficult era. His four successors between 1443 and 1452 were all household figures closely identified with Suffolk's clique; with the possible exception of Bishop Lumley, they showed little of

377

Cromwell's skill or interest in managing the realm's finances. Each of them may have authorized, at least nominally, a review of the king's income and expenditure for the benefit of parliament (though there is no unequivocal evidence that Lord Sudeley and Lord Beauchamp did so), but it was Lumley (1446–49) who tried with greatest determination to correct some of the more obvious deficiencies arising from the king's intervention in financial affairs, and to raise more cash.[15] Yet his measures lacked sensitivity and evenhandedness: he showed a partiality for the hard-pressed wardens of the Scottish marches, whose problems he fully understood, and twice in six months (at Christmas 1446 and in June–July 1447) he dismissed some of the customs collectors so that assignments on their revenues could be cancelled and money thereby saved.[16] All this aroused an hostility that found an outlet in the Bury parliament of 1447, which incidentally made no grant of direct taxation to the king. Lumley's resignation in September 1449, when the financial situation was grave and talk of resumption free, removed a strong-minded treasurer and substituted the hated Lord Saye; his preoccupation – and that of Lord Beauchamp who followed him in June 1450 – was probably to extricate the household and its clients from the several acts of resumption with as much as possible of their patronage intact.

Parliamentary taxation

Parliament's contribution to the king's resources after 1436, by way of direct taxation and customs on trade, was far from generous. Despite the presence of courtiers and household servants among the lords and commons in every parliament, MPs from shire and borough had responsibilities other than those to the king. As taxpayers they were naturally averse to direct taxation that grew steadily heavier; burgesses and merchants were sensitive to the conditions under which the wool subsidy and tunnage and poundage on wine and general merchandise were imposed; shipowners had an interest in fitting out expeditions to France; and they all had to keep in mind the views of their constituents, who were ready to plead poverty at every opportunity. Such considerations tempered any awareness which MPs might have had of the government's financial difficulties and dictated their reaction to its requests.

The 1437 parliament made a grant of one tenth and fifteenth on moveable possessions which, if fully realized, would have raised about £33,000; it was scheduled for payment in two equal instalments in November 1437 and November 1438. This was the pattern of the next dozen years: the equivalent of about half a subsidy each year, or rather less than 50 per cent of the annual rate before 1436.[17] The poll tax imposed on aliens for the first time in 1440 raised only a small additional sum during 1440–44 (£350 *per annum*).[18] Both these taxes were less valuable to the king than they at first appeared. For one thing, so many towns and communities asked for exemption on grounds of poverty that the total remission of £4,000 authorized in 1432 was increased to £6,000 in April 1446.[19] As a result, a half-tenth and -fifteenth was likely to produce an annual maximum of only £15,500. This concession was agreed at the end of an unprecedented fourth session of parliament; the government had signally failed to impress three earlier sessions with its request for money, and a remission of this magnitude may have been the price of the commons' reluctant co-operation in this fourth meeting.[20] One suspects, too, that Henry VI's impulsive generosity and his readiness to accommodate an acquaintance or a servant contributed to a notable increase in the number of individual exemptions from lay as well as clerical taxation. Perhaps Selby abbey (Yorkshire) was successful in its petition because noblemen and others flocked there 'well-nigh daily' for entertainment and hospitality, rather than because of the floods which it also claimed to have suffered.[21] These exemptions were most numerous in 1446 itself, though there was an unusually large number of them during 1445–48. The majority (perhaps two-thirds) were in favour of religious houses alleging poverty and hard times; but a significant number gave relief from lay taxation – again frequently on grounds of poverty.[22] Whether or not they were all justified is now impossible to gauge, but their extraordinary incidence in a very short period of time is suspicious; after all, natural and other calamities rarely occur with such striking coincidence.[23] The later acts of resumption were intended, of course, to annul most of these grants, though opportunity to circumvent the acts' provisions damaged their impact as a financial restorative. Nevertheless, after 1448 the king resorted to exemptions of this kind far less often; plain speaking by the commons in 1449–50 ensured that.

The cheeseparing grants of the commons were hedged about with other restrictions. The rate of poundage charged on imports and exports of general merchandise, which had been raised by parliament from the traditional 1s. in the £ to 1s.8d. early in 1440, was reduced to its former level in 1442, and the customary exemptions were made to this subsidy in order to facilitate the importation of much-needed food in years of dearth and the victualling of Calais.[24] Indeed, the customs revenue as a whole was generally at a lower level during the 1440s than in the previous two decades; according to figures assembled by J. H. Ramsay, between 1441 and 1452 the customs revenue *per annum* was only 83 per cent of the figure for 1422–32.[25] The worsening military situation in France and the desertion of England's allies, coupled with the readiness of Henry VI to grant licences to government creditors to export without paying customs duties, go some way towards explaining this decline.

The king's plight was particularly desperate in the late 1440s. The insistent demands of Henry's ministers for more cash were presented to a sceptical and unhelpful series of parliaments, even though individual MPs and speakers might be beholden to the king or were members of his household.[26] This hardening attitude was partly due (so the MPs claimed) to the fact that subjects could not afford to pay recurrent taxes; one may also speculate that the depth of the crisis in France was not yet widely appreciated and therefore did not weigh as heavily with the commons as did the repeated demands for taxation by an unpopular régime.[27] Accordingly, the 1445 parliament granted a mere half-tenth and -fifteenth in its first session, and nothing at all in its second and third when Suffolk sought extra cash to finance the king's marriage; indeed, only in its unique fourth session were tunnage and poundage and the wool subsidy at last renewed – and the tax on aliens was allowed to lapse.[28] The assembly at Bury St Edmund's in February 1447 offered no financial grant at all, and by 1449 the commons were so critical of the régime that they were in no mood to be generous.

The first session of the parliament held at Westminster in February 1449 was decidedly niggardly (granting a mere half-tenth and -fifteenth), and to allay at least some of the criticism the king had been forced to concede that grants by letters patent or under the privy seal which had already anticipated the subsidy should be annulled.[29] This small, preliminary measure of resumption might save something, but only at the risk of alienating the royal creditors. After this experience, and the refusal of the second session to increase its grant, Henry decided to adjourn parliament a second time and reconvene it in the calmer and (it was doubtless hoped) more amenable atmosphere of Winchester, well out of reach of the Londoners and their powerful merchant lobby. Even there, however, a further half-tenth and -fifteenth was all that could be extracted, with difficulty, by 16 July 1449.[30] As to the wool subsidy which was renewed, most of its proceeds were earmarked for the defence of Calais and the repair of its fortifications; and officials were authorized to conduct searches to ensure that the money was spent in accordance with parliament's directions.[31]

This parliament also shifted perceptibly the burden of taxation from the king's subjects to the foreigner, for a new subsidy was imposed in the Winchester session on all aliens living either permanently or temporarily in the kingdom. The rate was generally the same as it had been in the early 1440s (1s.4d. for householders and 6d. for others), but alien merchants (particularly the Italians and Hansards) were required to pay 6s. 8d. and their clerks and factors 1s. 8d. These harsh poll taxes were to last for three years.[32] At the same time, efforts were made in parliament to tap those ecclesiastical sources which were not comprehended within the tenths granted by the two convocations. In July 1449, a subsidy of 6s. 8d. on each unbeneficed priest was proposed as from Michaelmas 1449; in return, an amnesty was offered to all clergy convicted of rape or of receiving excessive fees. The king realized that it was a delicate matter for parliament to encroach on what was patently the prerogative of convocation, and he accordingly referred the proposal to the bishops. At St Paul's some days later, the southern convocation duly adopted it, though the price it exacted was a more general pardon of all transgressions, felonies, and outlawries.[33] The commons had responded grudgingly to the crown's request for more money. In terms of direct taxation, they showed reluctance and parsimony; they preferred to transfer the burden to foreigners and obscure clergymen of slender means.

Once war broke out in July 1449, and the catalogue of disasters to English arms began to lengthen, these modest grants were shown to be woefully inadequate. A new parliament quickly followed in November (the interval since the previous assembly was the shortest between two parliaments for a very long time) and was presented with more requests for cash. Further direct taxation was ruled out by the commons, if only because the terms of payment of the 1449 grant still had two years to run. Instead, they agreed to examine some supplementary expedients. Even so, not until 6 May 1450, four days after the murder of Suffolk and after the king had agreed to an act of resumption, did they authorize a graduated tax on freehold estates which were worth more than £1 in net annual value. Life interests in annuities and jointures would be taxed at the same rate; lands in Wales and the marches were included as they had not been in 1436; and not even the estates of minors escaped, for their guardians were required to pay up like the rest. Offices and fees held for a term of years were mulcted too, though the level at which the tax would operate was here raised to £2 *per annum*. Four special treasurers and receivers were appointed, on the precedent of 1404, to supervise the collection of what was stated to be an extraordinary grant that should not serve as a precedent.[34] This, in fact, was the only new financial provision made since July 1449; yet when the next parliament met in November 1450, it had still not been properly apportioned, largely because of resistance or inefficiency on the part of the local commissioners. On 18 December 1450, therefore, the grant had to be reaffirmed.[35] Acknowledging the hostility which this tax had aroused, the level at which it was to begin to operate was now raised so that a number of smaller freeholders would be exempt: those with possessions worth less than £2 net *per annum* and with offices less than £3.

By this stage, Normandy had been utterly lost, and without massive financial aid there was poor prospect of recovering it. The danger to Calais seemed serious, and so was the threat to Gascony and the English coast. But in view of the chastening experience of 1449–50, it was unlikely that the commons would concede any additional grants and hence no parliament met between May 1451 and March 1453. By the latter date, however, the climate of opinion in England had changed markedly. The assembly of March 1453 proved as royalist and complaint as any during King Henry's reign. The shock of the loss of Normandy, and the realization that Gascony too might fall to Charles VII, induced it to make swift and generous financial provision for the kingdom's defence and the keeping of the seas. On 28 March the commons announced themselves ready to grant a full tenth and fifteenth, with half of it payable on 11 November 1453 and the remainder one year later. Tunnage and poundage were extended at the customary rate of 1s. in the £ on all imported and exported merchandise, with the exception of tin (whose duty was so arranged that aliens paid 2s.) and all supplies shipped to Calais (which were exempt); and for the first time in the reign, these duties were granted to the king for life. The only reservation inserted carefully by the commons stressed that this was an unusually generous act on their part which should never be quoted as a precedent. The wool subsidy was likewise extended for the king's life, with none of the exemptions or reservations that had so emasculated the 1449 grant; denizens were required to pay 43s. 4s. per sack, and aliens (even those made denizen) a hefty £5 per sack.[36] As in 1449, foreigners were treated harshly in 1453.[37] The poll tax was renewed at the customary rate on alien residents born outside England, Ireland, Wales, Gascony, and Normandy. But that imposed on alien merchants from Spain, Italy, and the Hanse was massively increased – from 6s. 8d. to £1 for foreign brokers and from 1s. 8d. to £1 for their factors – and was designed to last throughout the king's life. Those who had been made denizen, presumably in an effort to avoid the burdens which the government might impose on foreign communities, were no longer allowed to escape, for they were required to pay at the rate of 6s. 8d.

The generosity of this parliament was still running strong during its second session; on the last day (2 July), a further half-tenth and -fifteenth was granted and declared payable within a relatively short period of time (compared with recent practice): half on 2 February 1454 and the remainder on 12 February 1455.[38] The king himself went down to the commons' chamber to thank the assembled MPs personally – as well he might.[39] But it all came too late. While the crises were breaking, parliament's provision was miserly and reluctantly made. Lack of provision in 1449–51 ensured the Lancastrian collapse in France and posed a real threat to England's security. The commons failed to appreciate the dangers or, if they did identify them, they refused to act in concert with a mistrusted government. When, in 1453, an assembly meeting outside London in Reading abbey was prepared at last to make liberal grants to the king – to the extent of conferring on him a considerable measure of financial independence for the rest of his reign – the news from Gascony was truly desperate; as for the rest of Lancastrian France, it came too late.

Clerical taxation

It was customary for the archbishop of Canterbury to summon, at the request of the king, the southern convocation to coincide as far as possible with meetings of parliament. The reason was primarily financial.[40] On only two occasions after 1436 did convocation meet when there was no parliament in the offing, and on only one of these (in 1444) did convocation make a grant that was not matched by direct lay taxation.[41] Correspondingly, there were only two occasions when no Canterbury convocation was held to coincide with a parliament (in 1447 and 1450–51), but the government secured a grant from the commons on neither occasion and presumably did not feel it appropriate to request one from the clergy either.

The return from clerical tenths was much smaller than that from lay taxation. The Canterbury convocation rarely authorized more than a half-tenth of clerical wealth, based on its antiquated assessment, for collection in any one year; only in the more understanding atmosphere of 1453 was a whole tenth offered.[42] In the smaller and poorer northern province, the grants were worth even less (averaging no more than £360 *per annum* during 1436–53), partly as a result of the large number of exemptions that operated.[43] Furthermore, the terms under which clerical tenths were granted in the 1440s were more tightly circumscribed than before. In 1438 some clergy were reported to be refusing to pay their share of the Canterbury tenth; later in the year convocation rejected on grounds of poverty and dearth a further request from the king.[44] In York exemptions for reasons of poverty and desolation mounted, and in any case the northern grant was usually earmarked for border defence.[45]

When war began in July 1449, the king persuaded Archbishop Stafford and his suffragans to use extraordinary methods to obtain an additional sum of money from their clergy. At St Paul's in July convocation voted an extra quarter-tenth from those clergy who were normally exempt from clerical taxation, most commonly because they were poor; at the same meeting, the 6s. 8d. poll tax on unbeneficed clergy was accepted at the suggestion of the commons.[46] Just as a second parliament quickly followed the first in 1449, so a further meeting of Canterbury's convocation opened on 14 November (and lasted until July 1450, an extraordinarily long session). The political and military crisis provides the explanation.[47] The usual tenth was granted, and in addition (and for collection forthwith) the quarter-tenth on exempt clergy was repeated and a new poll tax of 2s. in the £ was required of beneficed clergy. These unusually heavy clerical taxes were needed to despatch armies to France in an effort to halt the Valois conquests. One may imagine the disquiet felt by the poorer unbeneficed clergy, by those who had believed themselves exempt from clerical taxation, and by those whose benefices were doubly assailed by the royal demands. If the expedients devised by parliament in 1449–50 were disappointing in their return, one may equally doubt whether the new imposts on clergymen fared any better. What is so remarkable, therefore, is that the Canterbury convocation of February 1453 (meeting only days before the opening of parliament on 6 March) agreed not only to the usual annual half-tenth, but also authorized its collection for an unprecedented period of four years; parliament was about to go further and grant indirect taxes to the king for life.[48] After a period during Henry's personal rule when clerical taxation stood at a level considerably below that of the 1430s, it required the crushing disasters of 1449–51 to bring the laity and clergy to realize that without substantial aid Henry VI could not adequately discharge his responsibility to protect the realm and the church. It was the misfortune of the dynasty that this realization came too late.

Direct taxation, 1436–53

Tax	Total	1436–45 p.a.	1445–53 p.a.
Lay subsidies:			
10th and 15th at £33,000 to 1446, £31,000 from 1446	239,500	12,833	15,500
Clerical subsidies:			
10th Canterbury at £12,000	114,000	5,333	8,250*
10th York at £ 1,400	6,300	467	263
Other taxes:			
alien poll tax in 1440–44, 1449–53	2,800+	c. 156	c. 175+
income tax 1450–51	?		?
Total		18,789	24,188+
Authorized borrowing level		44,444	25,000

* An extra half-tenth has been added to accommodate the expedients of 1449–50; this is probably a generous addition.

Desperate expedients

The government resorted to several temporary, extra-parliamentary expedients in order to buttress its financial position. Their value was very likely small (though it cannot be precisely calculated), but their incidence reflects the desperate plight in which the late-Lancastrian régime found itself. Several of the expedients were grounded in the king's prerogative rights, though their implementation might be oppressive; some were a flagrant abuse of royal authority; and yet others, though ingenious in conception, were frankly bizarre. The government was most fertile in devising such schemes after 1449, but it was inevitable that they should encounter a certain amount of resistance and obstruction.

Distraint of knighthood, which was applied to all who were believed to be worth at least £40 annually in land or rent over a three-year period, evoked a storm of protest in parliament in 1439. To the well-off who deemed the accolade of knighthood less valuable than their rentals, this device seemed like an attempt to soak the modestly rich by resurrecting an antique custom.[49] Nevertheless, the practice continued, and another protest, apparently originating with the gentry of the East Riding, was made early in 1450, when the new graduated income tax was under discussion. Many evidently resented being subjected to both, and the objections were sufficiently weighty to ensure that no one who paid the tax should be distrained for knighthood for at least two years.[50]

The customary right enjoyed by lords to demand *dona* or subsidies or aids on entering their Welsh lordships or shires for the first time was exploited in the crown's interest in 1437–38, after Henry had recovered lands in Anglesey, Flint, and Chirk from the estate of Queen Katherine; unfortunately, the king quickly frittered away part of this windfall by granting Chirk to Cardinal Beaufort in fee simple.[51] By the mid-1440s other opportunities were being seized to exploit the king's position as lord of the principality in order to negotiate extraordinary contributions from the communities of north Wales; in 1446 a *donum* was discussed with Anglesey and not long afterwards with Caernarvonshire and Merioneth as well as Flintshire.[52] Then, on 12 August 1453 the decision was taken to extract another contribution from north Wales, and especially Merioneth which was perpetually in arrears with its normal payments to the crown and was now induced to offer a subsidy in return for a pardon of its accumulated and intractable debt.[53]

The gold and silver mines of Devon and Cornwall had long been a valuable asset to the crown, not least because the metals they produced were vital in the manufacture of coin. In the later 1440s attempts were made to intensify their exploitation as if they were outposts of El Dorado. On 14 July 1446 the mines were farmed for eight years to a group of men headed by Suffolk and two London merchants for £100. Like many of Henry's grants at this period, the lease involved the disposal of an important crown asset for a fixed annual farm; it was open to the farmers to exploit it in their own, rather than the crown's, interest. This attitude to the Cornish mines changed dramatically with Suffolk's death. On 29 July 1451, a German clerk, Adrian Sprynker, was appointed governor of the king's mines in Devon and Cornwall for seven years, with a further option beyond that. He undertook to extend the work-face over the next three years and reorganize metal production; for this he would receive an annual salary of 100 marks. In order to ensure that the anticipated growth in profit materialized, the government offered Sprynker 2 per cent of the mines' profit over and above an initial £1,000. Such an arrangement reveals how generous had been the earlier concession to the farmers and the extent to which the government's hopes now reposed in Sprynker.[54]

He set to his task without delay and issued relatively modest leases, sometimes to fellow-countrymen whom he may have known already or had been attracted by his plans for mining development.[55] The government kept a close watch on these undertakings, presumably because much was expected of them. On 23 September 1452 a commission was ordered to seize all metals produced in the west country mines after 25 March 1453; the reason was that rumours were reaching the government that they (and other merchandise) were being exported from the western ports in contravention of the bullion laws.[56] These investigations need not mean that enlisting German expertise in the development of the crown's mineral resources was ineffectual or corrupt, but it does indicate the government's determination to reap every penny of profit that rightly belonged to it. Sprynker continued his work until, on 20 June 1453, Master John Botright, a king's clerk, was appointed governor of the mines in his place for an indeterminate period. In other respects, his contract was similar to Sprynker's: he was required to develop the mine-workings at his own cost and was authorized to conclude twelve-year leases with sub-contractors, reserving a 10 per cent profit to the crown. But – and this may provide a clue to Sprynker's disappearance – new shafts beneath private homes or castles were forbidden; this concern for the violation of private property above ground by operations below it may have emerged out of Sprynker's operations and caused his contract to be prematurely terminated.[57]

Not unconnected with this eagerness to lay hands on more gold and silver was the curious interest which Henry VI began to show in 1452 in alchemy. On 30 April, John Mistelden was licensed for life to experiment with the transmutation of base metals. Always presenting a great temptation to the hopeful and the greedy, within a few months others too were claiming mastery of this supposedly profitable art and were defrauding the gullible of money and jewels in order to finance their dubious operations. On 18 August the government was forced to appoint a commission in London and Middlesex to investigate the activities of such charlatans.[58] They were the inevitable outcome of official encouragement of a foolish art by a bankrupt king.

Seizure of cargoes of Genoese alum at Southampton in 1450 was yet another scheme to which the government resorted; the aim was to force the Genoese merchants to give £8,000 to the king in return for an authorization allowing four of their number to ship wool and other merchandise to the Mediterranean and to import their commodities without paying the usual customs duties. The Genoese were also allowed to appoint one of the English customs collectors at Southampton to ensure the security of their investment. It was plain blackmail, but whatever was gained from the gift and the alum sales was eroded by the reduction in the customs, on which the king already had first call. The Genoese may have benefited most, for they obtained a monopoly of the sale of alum in the kingdom during the next two years, and at an additional 2*s*. per cwt.[59]

Finally, the government was increasingly prepared to take advantage of the loyalty or personal difficulties of a highly paid servant who was owed a large sum of money and was anxious for repayment. In these circumstances, the servant might be persuaded to take a reduced sum rather than maintain his right to the entire debt and run the risk of receiving little or none of it in the long run. Such an arrangement profited the crown, removed a major debt from its records, and, in part at least, satisfied a creditor with cash-flow problems. This was precisely Lord Fauconberg's experience in 1453. He was a substantial creditor of the crown through his custody of Roxburgh castle; whilst as a result of imprisonment in France, he found himself alarmingly short of cash. His personal resources were practically exhausted after paying his ransom and footing the bills at Roxburgh. Hence in July 1453 the government proposed to settle its £1,000 debt to him by means of a 1,000-mark grant from the customs imposed at Newcastle-upon-Tyne. To his credit, Archbishop Kemp, as chancellor, was reluctant to authorize the transaction until he had heard from Fauconberg that the arrangement was acceptable to him. After all, it was a rather arbitrary way of dealing with a long-suffering official who had grown poor in the royal service and of whom an impecunious government was now taking advantage. On the other hand, Fauconberg may have felt that in the circumstances of 1453 if he could recover 1,000 marks of his debt, he would be a lucky man.[60]

Resumption

Resumption was the most drastic expedient of all. Writing from experience in the early 1470s, Sir John Fortescue, in *The Governance of England*, championed it as a means of achieving solvency and predisposing the king's subjects to provide any extra cash that might be needed:

> ... yff suche gyftis, and namely tho wich haue be made inconsideratle, or aboff the merytes off hem that haue thaim, were refourmed; and thai rewarded with money, or offices, and some with livelode terme off lyff, wich aftir thair dethis wolde than retorne to the Crowne, the kyng shulde haue suche livelod as we now seke ffor, sufficiante ffor the mayntennance off his estate. And yff it wolde not than be so gret, I holde it for vndoubted, that the people off his lande woll be well wyllunge to graunte hym a subsidie, ... as shall accomplishe that wich shall lakke hym off such livelod; so that is highnes woll establyshe the same livelod than remaynynge, to abide perpetuelly to his crowne, withowt translatynge theroff to any other use.[61]

Resumption was first proposed as a formal measure in parliament in 1449, but it was not until the second assembly of that year that a commons' petition on the subject was accepted by the king early in May 1450. A foretaste of what was in the commons' mind was contained in several of the petitions presented to the king and lords in the earlier assembly. For instance, a successful attempt was made to annul all grants and assignments that had been issued prematurely from the taxation and subsidies approved on 3 April 1449.[62] A similar step was taken on 16 July, following the grant of a further half-tenth and -fifteenth. These provisos amounted to a modest resumption of grants which had anticipated not only the collection of revenue but even its authorization; it was a prelude to the long petition for resumption which the commons later presented in the new parliament.[63] The king's reluctance to acquiesce in the withdrawal of patronage already bestowed on friends, servants, and others is understandable, and he was determined to maintain his freedom of action by insisting that the treasurer should continue to deploy his resources and that no one with a prior grant from the king should be victimized. Apart from associating the treasurer with the making of such grants in the future, the king's response was rejection of the principles underlying the commons' demands, principles which, if accepted, would seriously damage the king's credibility and his pride. According to one chronicler, it was this parliament's insistence on a measure of resumption, and the king's refusal to go further than he had, which led to its dissolution at Winchester on 16 July 1449.[64]

When the parliament of 1449–50 met for its third session at Leicester on 29 April 1450, the commons were as resolute as ever in their determination to carry through proposals for resumption: now their bold aim was the wholesale cancellation of grants made since the reign began so that substantial resources could be made available without unduly burdening the king's subjects as a whole.[65] The proposed bill comprehended grants both at home and overseas, and from the duchy of Lancaster too; hereditary grants (the commons believed) ought to be converted into life grants so that they might eventually revert to the crown, and all grants that had been issued during the present parliament should be annulled forthwith. The commons appreciated the implications of what they proposed and the difficulties likely to be encountered; they recognized, too, that well judged patronage was an intrinsic quality of good kingship. A number of exceptions were therefore inserted right at the beginning. Queen Margaret and Cardinal Beaufort's executors (who might be importuned for loans) were among the first to be excused from the bill's provisions; so too were the educational foundations close to the king's heart. As to the magnates, it was acknowledged that grants to newly-ennobled peers to enable them to maintain an appropriate state ought to remain in force. Others sporting letters of confirmation from the king (rather than grants of first instance) or receiving compensation for earlier losses or exchanges should continue to enjoy their grants, provided these did not involve a gratuitous augmentation of the original award. Grants which produced for the crown an annual return were sufficiently profit-making to remain in force as well. It was further conceded that the privileges of towns and cities, and murage grants for civic building projects, did not deplete the royal treasury and hence deserved to be exempt from the bill. And certain key royal officials, including the three principal officers of state and legal officers who, in order to preserve their independence, required adequate financial reward, were also exempt.[66] These carefully worded exemptions had justice on their side or else made no substantial inroads on the king's resources.

The commons' purpose in proposing such a radical measure was plainly stated and was related to the increasing demands which the régime had presented to parliament in recent months: the expenses of government and household required it, even though Calais and Guisnes might be able to survive on their own revenue provided it was not in any way depleted. The MPs were encouraged to be forthright by the confusion and doubt that gripped the ruling clique in the immediate aftermath of Suffolk's downfall. The resumption bill was accepted by the king on 6 May, though within a month 186 clauses of exemption were attached to it by royal warrant. Grants made to persons in Calais and Ireland were allowed to stand, presumably because the successful defence of these two outposts required the goodwill of their residents. But some of the exemptions challenged the very purpose of the act itself: individuals had been invited to submit petitions for special treatment, many of which were approved and attached to the bill as it made its way through parliament. As B. P. Wolffe has revealed, the most significant group comprised servants of the state and household who had conspired beforehand to secure their own position; they agreed amongst themselves to surrender almost exactly one-third of the value of their grants as the price of retaining the rest.[67] The result caused one of John Paston's correspondents to write rather guardedly of this act: 'the Kyng hath *sumwhat* graunted to haue the resumpsion agayne, in *summe but nat in alle*'.[68]

The weakening of the first act of resumption led to agitation for a second in the parliament of 1450–51. A bill may have been introduced in the first session, but it probably did not complete its passage until the end of the second on 29 March. On this occasion, the number of exemptions included in the bill itself was much smaller and some of the earlier ones were modified.[69] For example, although the king's favourite foundations were again mentioned, some of the grants to Eton and King's were no longer protected because they were regarded as unusually burdensome; they and all other grants since 1422 were to be resumed as from the first day of the previous parliament, 6 November 1449. The queen was again fully protected and so were the three officers of state and the crown's legal officers. The duke of Buckingham, who as captain of Calais was seriously out of pocket, was added to the list; towns and cities which had received privileges and murage grants were likewise included. This second act attempted to control Henry VI's patronage by a far-reaching (and humiliating) device: it was proposed to submit his grants to scrutiny by the three principal officers and at least six councillors, who would record their names on each grant they authorized.[70] The principal justification for this act, with its more restrictive provisions, was the need to relieve the king's overtaxed subjects, especially since the first attempt at resumption had not been very successful. The king was induced to give his assent to this bill, but he rejected the provisions limiting his personal initiative, particularly the establishment of a supervisory committee; this device accordingly fell by the wayside, and so did the clauses affecting his two foundations and exchanges that he had personally arranged.[71] If the original bill had been introduced during the autumn session of 1450, when the duke of York enjoyed unusually powerful backing among the commons, its passage during the spring of 1451 was in a stabler atmosphere which enabled Henry VI to stand firm against some of its radical demands.[72] Moreover, additional exemptions were attached to the bill before it received the king's assent, though these were authorized with the advice and assent of the lords (rather than by the king alone) and probably for that reason were more restricted in number and scope (43 in all). Grants from the duchy of Lancaster and those to support newly ennobled peers were once more exempt, and so were those made in exchange for, or instead of, earlier grants; fees and wages to royal officials were confirmed.[73] Both parliament and government were more scrupulous in their handling of this petition: those who had received appropriate grants from the king were treated equitably, and an effort was made to identify the unwise grant, which was the product of Henry's ill-considered patronage. Sheriffs were not ordered to implement the new act until 2 August 1451, more than two months after parliament was dissolved (which gave ample time for petitions for exemptions to be considered); their reports on what had been resumed were expected at the exchequer within a further six months.[74] 'The prayer of the commons that the resumption might "take good and effectuell conclusion" had thus at last been answered'. Henry VI's reward came in the parliament of 1453: the supplementary grants and taxes then voted by an assembly dominated by a group of household servants and courtiers were unusually generous.[75]

Loans

Only if loans were forthcoming in sufficient quantity and without undue difficulty could the king and his advisers implement their domestic and foreign policies with reasonable freedom and flexibility. But the willingness to lend depended squarely on the ability to repay. The level of borrowing authorized by parliament on guaranteed security had risen dramatically in the 1430s and continued to do so until the mid-1440s, when a truce was concluded with Charles VII. In so doing, it fell wildly out of step with the level of direct taxation, which, after all, provided much of the necessary security: during 1428–36 authorized borrowing and direct taxation on an average annual basis had more or less coincided, but during 1436–45 the taxation level was halved and yet the borrowing level was allowed to rise by a third.[76] Parliament's approval of borrowing, therefore, was not matched by any willingness to find the necessary resources. A most dangerous situation developed. Parliament in 1445 declined to authorize any further loans for the time being; the French war had come to a halt, but more significant was the fact that it was increasingly difficult to secure repayment, even when parliament offered formal guarantees.[77] The futility of this financial procedure was appreciated by 1449, for no further loans were formally authorized by parliament for the rest of the reign; instead, the commons put their faith in the recovery of resources by resumption and life grants of indirect taxes to the king in 1453. The nature of Henry's patronage and the uncertain health of English trade detracted from the effectiveness of both as a means of restoring the government's credit.

Henry VI's subjects had a traditional obligation to respond to appeals for loans justified by necessity or a threat to the king or kingdom. There is no doubt that a convincing case could be made that the peril in which English France found itself in the 1440s was a direct menace to England itself. Several general, corporate loans were therefore demanded of the subject in these terms. In 1442–43 a countrywide effort was made to induce towns, communities, and individuals to offer a substantial loan which, if one excludes Cardinal Beaufort's and the staplers' contributions, amounted to more than £17,600 (including £2,000 from London); it was needed primarily to finance Somerset's expedition to Gascony.[78] This loan could be repaid from the proceeds of the taxation recently granted by both parliament and convocation, and large numbers of lords, townsmen, merchants, and clergy were approached with appropriate security for any loans they might give.[79]

The other large corporate loans were sought when the crisis in France was at its height, in September 1449 and January 1453. Requests of a similar nature (quoting the subject's traditional obligation) in 1444 to finance the reception and coronation of Queen Margaret, and in 1446 to enable the king to visit Charles VII in France, elicited decidedly smaller sums; perhaps the relevance of these requests to England's security seemed remote, and in any case no army was being assembled or planned to give point to a plea of necessity.[80] But in September 1449, when the survival of Lancastrian Normandy was at stake, and Calais and the seas appeared suddenly exposed, an urgent request for a corporate loan elicited promises of at least £12,250, including £2,000 from London.[81] This was no great windfall, and no further loans of this kind were sought until early in 1453, when the imperative need to aid the earl of Shrewsbury in Gascony produced the most generous response yet, more than £22,450 (though only £333 was contributed this time by London).[82] Whether or not such corporate loans were fully realized by the government's collectors, the abandoment from 1449 of the formal procedure of guaranteeing repayment may have discouraged lenders at a most critical point in Henry's reign: a request to London in September 1450 to provide cash for Gascony was refused, and there is considerable doubt whether another six months later was any more successful.[83] The return to corporate borrowing in 1453, and at a relatively high level, may well have spurred on the life-grants of taxation in the ensuing parliament.[84]

Among individual lenders, Cardinal Beaufort remained the government's pre-eminent creditor until shortly before his death on 11 April 1447. He had been prepared to lend prodigious sums to three Lancastrian kings, and he continued to do so until his retirement from active politics by 1444; £21,667 was lent in the early summer of 1443 alone, when the expedition of his nephew, John Beaufort, absorbed considerable amounts of cash.[85] As security, he acquired not only a substantial haul of crown jewels, which he could keep if repayment of the loans were delayed, but also a firm grip on the customs administration throughout the realm.[86] Moreover, financial aid of this dimension consolidated his political power, as a result of which he was able to dictate the kind of security he wanted for his loans. As Gloucester reflected in May 1443, there was little point in the council discussing at length the conditions for honouring Beaufort's loans since the cardinal would insist on precisely what he wanted – or refuse to lend any more.[87] Henceforward, preference over every other individual was usually accorded the cardinal in the repayment of his loans – sometimes even over the government and the household.[88]

After the enormous loans of 1443, Beaufort appears to have offered relatively little further financial aid to the crown.[89] But once he was dead and buried, the government, with the emergency of 1449 upon it, turned to his executors for help; between July and December 1449 they lent £9,333, with a further £2,000 in August 1452.[90] Thus, over practically half a century, Cardinal Beaufort, whether dead or alive, supported the Lancastrian dynasty to the tune of a quarter of a million pounds, about half of it during the critical years 1428–45. No other single individual came remotely close to establishing himself as such a prominent banker of the English state.[91]

The interest of the staple merchants in the defence of Calais, in the repair of the port's facilities, and in ensuring that the garrison was regularly and adequately paid coincided with the government's own responsibilities.[92] It was inevitable, therefore, that the Lancastrian régime should turn to the staplers more frequently for financial help as the situation in northern France deteriorated. Their loans in the 1440s were accordingly twice as large as they had been before the siege of Calais in 1436. During 1449–51, £16,667 was lent to the government, but when it was seen that Calais was able to weather the storm and the government's attention was drawn to Gascony, the staplers declined to lend any more; nothing at all was offered for Shrewsbury's expeditions in 1451–53, for Gascony doubtless seemed a distant province to merchants at Calais.[93] The government paid a price for these larger loans as the staplers seized their opportunity to buttress their privileges and demand redress of their grievances. In February 1449 an undertaking was given in parliament that licences to bypass the Calais staple would be restricted and the government confirmed that it would devote part of the wool subsidy to Calais's needs. When parliament reassembled in November, the staplers continued their campaign against the hated licences, and Henry reluctantly agreed to annul all but those granted to the queen, Suffolk, and four others, three of whom were members of the household.[94] This successful lobbying was directly linked to the loans which the staplers offered. They acted largely out of self-interest, inducing a hard-pressed régime to make concessions at a time when many feared that Burgundy and Valois would launch an attack on Calais.

Some prominent lenders, 1436–53*

Loans	1436–45		1445–53
London	25,514 —	2,835 *p.a.*	21,807 — 2,726 *p.a.*
Calais merchants	34,551 —	3,839 *p.a.*	25,601 — 3,200 *p.a.*
Cardinal Beaufort (or executors)	*c.* 72,000 — *c.* 8,022 *p.a.*		12,666 — 1,583 *p.a.*
	c. 14,696 *p.a.*		7,509 *p.a.*

* These figures are based on Barron, thesis, pp. 611-12; Harriss, *TRHS*, 5th ser., XX (1970), 134 n.1.; Steel, op. cit., passim.

The other wealthy commercial sector that was likely to respond to royal pleas for loans was London, but setting aside its contribution to the staplers' loans, it appears that the city's enthusiasm for acting as a government creditor waned during the 1440s.[95] The Italian merchants – from Genoa, Venice, Florence, and in smaller numbers, Lucca – were far less wealthy as a group, though much more at the mercy of the government. They lent cash regularly to Henry VI but not a great deal; the Genoese, for instance, advanced about £465 *per annum* during 1438–46 and the others rather less.[96] But by the mid-1440s they were encountering serious difficulty in recovering their loans, whilst the intensification of anti-alien feeling made them much less willing to lend.[97] The only others who might be prepared to support the government financially were the richer members of the court and household. Suffolk himself invested £2,773 in his own policies in the second half of 1449 – almost double the total loans he had contributed since 1437.[98] And the treasurers of England could not easily escape the unwritten obligation on them to contribute some of their personal wealth to the exchequer when they were seeking to persuade others to lend: between December 1449 and March 1450, Lord Saye provided £1,400, and at the height of the Gascon crisis in 1453, the earl of Worcester found £2,300.[99]

By 1449 – and probably earlier – the Lancastrian régime was well and truly bankrupt. Beaufort was dead; recent treatment of the Italian merchants made them reluctant to lend; the staplers had little alternative but to underwrite the defence of Calais, but at a price; parliamentary and clerical taxes were becoming difficult to raise; whilst the government's policies were on the brink of disaster.[100] The reaction of the commons was to demand resumption, but the king's stubborn determination to protect his friends and confidants damaged this strategy. The crown's response was to seek alternative sources of money, but most of these were temporary expedients or 'dangerous drugs', which failed to realize the sums expected of them. The government's good credit had evaporated, as parliament recognized when it discontinued formal guarantees of loan repayments in 1449.[101] This was the background to the unusual grants made to Henry VI by the Reading parliament in 1453. On the continent, only Calais and parts of Gascony remained in Lancastrian hands and the commons, presided over by Thomas Thorp, an official of great experience at the exchequer and the mint, authorized the enlistment and payment for six months of 20,000 archers.[102] In the longer term, it was hoped that resumption and life-grants of indirect taxes would so underpin the king's normal revenue that it would suffice for most purposes, including the provision of security for creditors. The financial acts of the 1453 parliament were not in the nature of a spontaneous gift to a popular monarch (how could they be in view of events since 1449?); rather were they an attempt to streamline the financial administration by removing the need to borrow hugely and spend prodigiously. Whether these arrangements were a sufficient basis for solvent royal government was never put to the test, for within four months Henry VI had lapsed into a state of such incapacity that for a season the country was virtually kingless.

Notes

1 G. L. Harriss, 'Preference at the mediaeval exchequer', *BIHR*, XXX (1957), 17-40 (with the quotation on p. 39); above, p. 108.
2 *RP*, V, 183. The estimate of £17,000 is the average annual expenditure of wardrobe and great wardrobe during 1437–53 (above, p. 311). The available livelihood of the king was put at only £5,000.
3 *RP*, V, 13.
4 *CPR, 1436–41*, p. 542; *CCR, 1435–42*, p. 416.
5 *RP*, V, 205, 206 (1449–50); *CPR, 1441–46*, p. 440 (1446).
6 Doucet, *Moyen Age*, XXVII (1926), 302-3, 316-17.
7 *PPC*, VI, 7, 132.

8 Above, pp. 312-13. Cf. the £10,426 debt owed to the earl of Shrewsbury by 3 December 1443, when arrangements were made to discharge it at the rate of £1,667 *per annum*, provided Beaufort was satisfied of his £21,000 first (*CPR, 1441–46*, p. 227; PRO, E28/71/47-48).

9 *CPR, 1446–52*, p. 206; *CCR, 1447–54*, p. 82 (William Beaufitz, 1449).

10 *RP*, V, 157, 158, 167 (1449).

11 *PPC*, V, 264; *CPR, 1446–52*, p. 573.

12 *RP*, V, 183. K. B. McFarlane, *CHJ*, IX (1947–49), 64, regards the £372,000 as representing debts alone, and compares this with £168,000 of debt in 1433. The picture may not be quite as black as this, since the current year's charges are included in the first sum. For a comment, see Wolffe, *Royal demesne*, p. 114.

13 Above, p. 115. For a further declaration of the state of the realm's finances (presumably similar to the well-known statement prepared in 1433) which was prepared for the king and his council by the exchequer staff about Christmas 1438, see PRO, E403/733 m. 9.

14 *PPC*, V, 298. That there were reasons other than Cromwell's health may be indicated by the undertaking given on 6 July 1443, the day of the resignation, that he would be allowed to reply to any attacks on his conduct as treasurer; the suddenness of the resignation is reflected in the six months' grace allowed him to put his books in order. The decision to send a large expedition to France under Somerset may have been the last straw for Cromwell (below, p. 466).

15 *PPC*, V, 220-33, suggests that treasurers' declarations of the state of the realm were made in parliament by Sudeley, Lumley, Saye, and Beauchamp between 1443 and 1452, but the issue rolls contain none of the usual indications that clerks were employed on this task by either Sudeley or Beauchamp. For investigations especially by Lumley but also by Saye, see PRO, E403/765 m. 16; 771 m. 11 (for parliament, 1447); 767 m. 11; 769 m. 9 (for the council, 1447); 778 m. 9 (for the council, 1448); 778 m. 15 (for the council, 1450); Wolffe, *Royal demesne*, p. 114 n. 47 (for parliament, 1450).

16 Below, p. 405; Harriss, *EconHR*, 2nd ser., VIII (1955–56), 195-6. For Lumley, see Storey, *TCWAS*, new ser., LV (1955), 128-30.

17 *RP*, V, 502-3 and passim; above, p. 110.

18 *RP*, V, 4-6, 37-9. S. L. Thrupp estimates that 'not much more than half its potential maximum' of £700 could be realized in a year (*Society and history* [Ann Arbor, 1977], p. 134). The alien subsidy was renewed for 2 years in 1442, but was allowed to expire in November 1444.

19 *RP*, V, 142, 144; *CPR, 1446–52*, p. 80 (for Lincoln's persistent petitions). See also Great Yarmouth, Carlisle, Oxford, Cambridge, Bedford, and Gloucester, among the more important towns pleading poverty (ibid., *1441–46*, p. 458; ibid., *1446–52*, pp. 36, 70; *RP*, V, 142, 144, 205).

20 ibid., 69-70. Wedgwood, *Register*, p. 89, erroneously says that the increased exemption was conceded in 1449. Commissioners were regularly appointed to apportion the deductions in each county (e.g., *CFR, 1435–42*, p. 137).

21 *CPR, 1441–46*, p. 398 (December 1445). Selby had been exempt since 1431–32 (R. B. Dobson, *Durham priory, 1400–1450* [Cambridge, 1973], pp. 177-8). Most exemptions are recorded in *CPR, 1441–52*, passim, and *RP*, V, passim.

22 More than three-quarters of the exemptions recorded during 1445–53 were issued in 1445–48.

23 Durham priory's plea for exemption in 1444 was based on claims of poverty, expense, and past services, though the mother house's average annual payment was only £18 compared with total annual receipts of over £2,000; the petition was successful in 1448, at the time of Henry VI's personal visit to Durham (Dobson, *Durham priory*, pp. 178-82).

24 *RP*, V, 4-6, 37-9.

25 Ramsay, op. cit., p. 266. The annual average in 1441–52 was £30,509, though it was more often than not well below that.

26 e.g., John Say, speaker in 1449, and William Tresham in 1439, 1442, and 1447 (Roskell, *Speakers*, pp. 218-22, 229-33).

27 *RP*, V, 173 (1450).

28 In fact, the commercial grants had expired and had to be backdated in April 1446, tunnage and poundage to 1 April 1445 and the wool subsidy to November 1445. For this parliament, see Roskell, *Speakers*, pp. 225-8; Wedgwood, *Register*, pp. 45-7. For Suffolk's request for 1½ fifteenths to cover the expenses of Margaret's journey, see *Fabyan's Chron.*, p. 618.

29 *RP*, V, 142. For the apportionment on 4 April 1449 of £6,667 of the first half (*c*. £7,750) of the half-tenth and -fifteenth for defence of the seas, Calais, and the Scottish border, see A. R. Myers, 'A parliamentary debate of 1449', *BIHR*, LI (1978), 81-2, from College of Arms MS 2 H. 13 f. 390.

30 *RP*, V, 144; R. A. Griffiths, 'The Winchester session of the 1449 parliament: a further comment', *HLQ*, XLII (1979), 181-91. The same annulment proviso was inserted and the terms of payment were longer than usual: not until November 1451 would this tax be fully realized.

31 *RP*, V, 144-7. An annulment proviso was attached to this grant also, but it excluded grants to Lord Fauconberg as captain of Roxburgh castle, and the supervisor of repairs at Berwick and Roxburgh (Wedgwood, *Register*, p. 90).

32 It is difficult to estimate what difference the increased rate for merchants made to the actual return.

33 *RP*, V, 152; Wedgwood, *Register*, p. 91; *Reg. Lacy*, III, 55. J. S. Roskell, *Speakers*, p. 234, appears to be mistaken in believing that the bishops, to whom this proposal was referred, eventually turned it down. The York convocation does not seem to have assembled to discuss the matter (*HBC*, p. 562).

34 *RP*, V, 172, 183; Roskell, *Speakers*, p. 240. For a protest from Cheshire at being included in the tax, see H. D. Harrod, 'A defence of the liberties of Chester, 1450', *Archaeologia*, LVII (1900), 71-86.

35 *RP*, V, 211. The receivers and treasurers were Sir William Lucy, Sir Thomas Tyrell, Sir James Strangways, and Richard Waller (ibid., 173). A second act of resumption was also passed by this assembly (below, p. 389).

36 *RP*, V, 228-30. Not since Henry V's reign had the rate on denizens been charged at 43s. 4d; the alien rate was almost doubled. Only Richard II (in 1398) and Henry V (in 1415) had been accorded similarly generous treatment by an English parliament, though on both occasions the circumstances had been quite different (Roskell, *Speakers*, pp. 135, 161-2).

37 *RP*, V, 230; above, p. 380.

38 It was intended to finance the war in Gascony and was in return for a reduction in the number of archers which the parliament had earlier granted to the king for six months' service (*RP*, V, 233).

39 ibid., 236. For the purpose of these grants from the commons' point of view, see below, p. 394.

40 *EHD*, IV, 599-600. The less important York convocation, which normally assembled in York minster, coincided less frequently with meetings of parliament, and no meeting at all seems to have taken place between 1445 and 1452 (D. Wilkins, *Concilia Magnae Britanniae et Hiberniae, A. D. 466–1718* [4 vols., 1737], III, passim).

41 *Reg. Chichele*, III, 526, 260; *Reg. Lacy*, II, 325; *HBC*, pp. 561-2.

42 Ramsay, op. cit., II, 259-60. For the Canterbury grants, worth about £12,000 per whole tenth, during 1437–53, see *Reg. Chichele*, III, 526; *Reg. Lacy*, II, 272-6, 325, 386; III, 55, 77, 177-8. They are tabulated above, p. 384.

43 In all, the equivalent of four tenths was granted between 1437 and 1453, with nothing between 1446 and 1453 (Wilkins, op. cit., III, 525, 533, 544, 563). J. H. Ramsay, op. cit., II, 259-60, estimates the yield as £1,400 per whole tenth. Archbishop Kemp had personally to exhort the clergy assembled at York on more than one occasion, stressing the expense of defending the Scottish border, before they would make a grant (e.g., *CFR, 1437–45*, pp. 8, 257). Yet the burden on Durham priory and its dependencies was not great: about £77 every time a tenth was granted (Dobson, *Durham priory*, p. 177). For exemptions, see above, p. 117.

44 *CPR, 1436–41*, p. 154; *CCR, 1435–42*, p. 174; *Reg. Chichele*, III, 526, 260.

45 *CFR, 1437–45*, p. 8; Harriss, *BIHR*, XXX (1957), 25 n. 3. For the question of exemptions, which were said in 1461 to halve the return from clerical taxes, see M. Oldfield, 'Parliament and convocation, with special reference to the pontificate of Henry Chichele, 1413–1443' (Manchester MA thesis, 1938), pp. 146-7, 168-69.

46 *Reg. Lacy*, III, 55; above, p. 380. The recent spate of exemptions may have made some realize that too many individuals and institutions were escaping taxation unjustifiably.

47 *Reg. Lacy*, III, 77; *CPR, 1446–52*, p. 313. By contrast, no York convocation seems to have been held until June 1452 (Wilkins, op. cit., III, 563; *HBC*, p. 562).

48 *Reg. Lacy*, III, 177-8; above, p. 380. The York convocation, too, granted a half-tenth on 29 January 1453, more than a month before parliament began (Wilkins, op. cit., III, 563). The meeting had first begun on 12 June 1452, but it took a very long time before it made a grant.

49 *CCR, 1435–42*, p. 255; *RP*, V, 26. One of the main complaints was that some had been fined already in 1430, when this custom was last revived; the complaint was parried by the king. For resistance to distraint in Derbs. and Notts, see Belvoir, grants royal 560 (April 1441). Cf. the government's attempt to induce 8 lawyers to become serjeants-at-law, under threat of a £1,000 fine, in February 1453 (*CCR, 1447–54*, p. 381).

50 *RP*, V, 172. On 21 March 1450 a special commission was sent to Yorkshire to investigate the complaints (*CPR, 1446–52*, p. 379).

51 *CPR, 1436–41*, pp. 147, 148; McFarlane, 'At the death-bed of Beaufort', p. 423. Gloucester appreciated the folly of disposing of Chirk in this way, as

his attack on Beaufort in 1440 makes clear (Arnold, *Chronicle*, pp. 284-5). Anglesey and Flint alone were expected to find £1,122 for the king (PRO, E403/735 m. 14).

52 PRO, E403/762 m. 13 (21 July 1446); 771 m. 9 (12 July 1448). On each occasion, the exchequer clerk, John Brown, travelled to north Wales to lead the government's negotiators (Wedgwood, *Biographies*, p. 120). The government seems to have concentrated on the north, rather than the south, because its influence was greater there (above, p. 344). Compare an extraordinary *mise* demanded of Cheshire in 1442–44 (PRO, Chester 2/100 m.4, a reference I owe to the work of Miss D. J. Clayton).

53 *CPR, 1452–61*, p. 124. About £2,876 were sought in gifts from London between October 1449 and January 1453 to cope with the threats to Normandy, Calais, and Gascony; the most recent before that (£1,333 in August 1444) was intended to finance London's own welcome to Queen Margaret. See Barron, thesis, pp. 630-3.

54 *CCR, 1441–47*, p. 397; *CPR, 1446–52*, pp. 467, 494, 501. Suffolk's predecessor as lessee of the mines had been none other than Beaufort (PRO, E403/765 m. 11). Suffolk had granted free leases to work the mines, including one to Sprynker himself (Bodl, MS ch. Suffolk a. 12 [February 1448]).

55 *CPR, 1446–52*, pp. 561, 571, 569.

56 ibid., p. 532.

57 ibid., *1452–61*, pp. 47, 110. For the commons' concern that silver-mining in the south-west should be under closer royal control, rather than farmed wholesale to a small number of individuals, see *RP*, V, 212 (1453).

58 *CPR, 1446–52*, pp. 547, 583. See W. H. L. Ogrine, 'Western society and alchemy from 1200 to 1500', *JMH*, V (1980), 103-32 (esp. 119-20).

59 *RP*, V, 214, 216. The alum was sold to London merchants, who were authorized to resell it for £8,800, provided they lent the extra £800 to the crown to help equip an army for Gascony: those who refused would be dealt with by the council. This was double blackmail. *PPC*, VI, 152 (7 August 1453).

60 *RP*, V, 146. For similar treatment of the duke of York in 1446, involving far larger sums, see below, p. 674, and Griffiths, *JMH*, I (1975), 195; and in general, Harriss, *BIHR*, XXX (1957), 21.

61 C. Plummer (ed.), *The Governance of England* (1885), ch. XI. See *EHD*, IV, 526, reaffirming the date of composition, though Wolffe, *Royal demesne*, p. 113 n. 44, appears to believe that the treatise was written before 1450.

62 *RP*, V, 142. Grants or assignments issued before 1 April were annulled.

63 ibid., 144; cf. ibid., 157.

64 Flenley, pp. 125, 126; Wolffe, *Royal demesne*, p. 116 and n. 60.

65 *RP*, V, 183–200. This matter is expertly analysed by Wolffe, *EHR*, LXXIII (1958), 583-613, and more recently and fully in *Royal demesne*, ch. V, sect. 1.

66 The offspring of foreign mothers who had married English since 1413 were assured of their rights, something on which the soldiers returning from France needed assurance.

67 ibid., pp. 127-8, citing PRO, E163/8/14, which lists the exemptions and resumed grants affecting 101 household men.

68 *PL*, II, 37 (my italics).

69 *RP*, V, 217-40; Wolffe, *Royal demesne*, ch. V, sect.2. Even franchises like Ireland and Lancashire were included within this act's scope.

70 Those grants which were simply exchanges and letters patent initiated by the treasurer that incorporated a clause enabling the highest bidder to claim a particular grant also escaped annulment. But exchanges to which the king had been a party were resumed – a reflection of men's lack of trust in Henry VI.

71 Moreover, the king would only authorize the act's operation as from 25 March 1451, rather than from 6 November 1449 (*RP*, V, 217).

72 Wolffe, *Royal demesne*, p. 132; below, p. 692.

73 A major problem of interpretation had arisen by the time parliament met again in March 1453: were the fees and wages of officers appointed by previous kings included among the exemptions or not? The commons then declared that they should be (*RP*, V, 267).

74 *CFR, 1447–54*, p. 229. Writs to the sheriffs ordering them to implement the first act were not sent out until about March 1451 (Wolffe, *Royal demesne*, p. 128 n. 1). For the effect of these two acts on the surrender of grants and their reissue, see ibid., pp. 133-4 and appendix C.

75 ibid., pp. 135 (for the quotation), 136; Roskell, *1422*, p. 136 and n. 3. At least 17 per cent of the commons had household connections in 1453, the highest proportion known.

76 *RP*, V, 6, 39, 136, 143; see tables, pp. 110, 384.

77 Thus, of London's corporate loans, that of March 1439 was still being repaid in July 1447, and that of August 1442 in March 1450. The city reacted by insisting on new tallies for uncashed old ones as the price of further loans in February 1441, March 1442, and March and July 1444 (Barron, thesis, pp. 625-9).

78 Guisnes was also in need of funds (*PPC*, V, 198, 201, 203, 215, 218, 219, 231, 414, 238, 272, 276, 284; *CPR, 1441–46*, pp. 61, 68, 92; PRO, E28/70/72). For instructions to the commissioners on how to levy the loans locally, see *PPC*, V, 418, and Harriss, *HJ*, VI (1963), 13-15; and for London's contribution, Barron, thesis, p. 628. The overall calculation is based on PRO, E403/745-50, where repayment is recorded.

79 For the use of household confidants like John Langton, Adam Moleyns, and Geoffrey Pole to stimulate lending, see Harriss, *HJ*, VI (1963), 14; PRO, E404/59/153 (Yorks, 1442–43); 60/247 (1443–44); 62/101 (1446).

80 PRO, E403/754-56 (August 1444–February 1445, *c.* £6,200, including £1,766 from London), 762-65 (July–December 1446, *c.* £2,750, including at least £1,333 from London); for London, see Barron, thesis, pp. 629-30. See also *CPR, 1441–46*, pp. 311, 430-1; *PPC*, VI, 52. For the commissioners' instructions, see ibid., 46; resistance was especially strong in 1446 (Harriss, *HJ*, VI [1963], 15-16).

81 PRO, E403/775-79 (September 1449–August 1450); Barron, thesis, pp. 631-62; *PPC*, VI, 86; *CPR, 1446–52*, pp. 267, 297, 307. The figures given in relation to these loans may only be approximate, but at least they have a comparative value. For difficulties experienced in collecting money in Suffolk, see the abbot of Bury's report on 3 May 1450 (Bodl, Tanner cccxlii f. 195).

82 PRO, E403/791-93 (February–July 1453); Barron, thesis, p. 634; *CPR, 1452–61*, p. 52.

83 For these proposed London corporate loans, see Barron, thesis, p. 632.

84 The bulk of the large loan was recorded after the taxation grant on 28 March. See *RP*, V, 228.

85 PRO, E403/751-57; Harriss, *TRHS*, 5th ser., XX (1970), 134 n. 1; table, p. 393.

86 *PPC*, V, 115; VI, 28, 277, 76, 194, 240. He first secured the right to appoint one customer at Southampton in 1417 and began nominating one in every other port in November 1422; these privileges were confirmed in 1436 and 1443 (McFarlane, 'At the death-bed of Beaufort', pp. 412ff; *PPC*, VI, 160, 182).

87 ibid., 279; McFarlane, 'At the death-bed of Beaufort', pp. 416-17; *PPC*, VI, 279. See Harriss, *EconHR*, 2nd. ser., VIII (1955–56), 197-8.

88 *PPC*, VI, 182.

89 PRO, E403/757 m. 3; 762 m. 13. Beaufort received more crown jewels as security for £1,333 in February 1444 (ibid., E28/72/86). K. B. McFarlane ('At the death-bed of Beaufort,' pp. 425-6) finds it strange that neither Suffolk nor his wife (Beaufort's cousin) is mentioned in the cardinal's will and he suggests that a certain coolness had arisen between them by 1447; the decline in his lending may indicate this too.

90 PRO, E403/776 m. 13; 778 m. 1, 2, 3, 7, 8; 791 m. 5; 793 m. 8. On 22 August 1449, the executors also restored to the treasurer crown jewels which Beaufort had retained in place of unpaid loans since 1424; they were given assignments worth £2,403 instead (McFarlane, 'At the death-bed of Beaufort', pp. 427-8; PRO, E403/775 m. 11).

91 Harriss, *TRHS*, 5th ser., XX (1970), 133; Steel, op. cit., p. 252. This overall figure includes the executors' loans. The question of whether Beaufort accumulated his fortune partly by charging heavy interest on these loans to the government has been argued by McFarlane, 'At the death-bed of Beaufort', pp. 405-28, and Steel, op. cit., pp. 251-2 (who believe he did), and Harriss, *TRHS*, 5th ser., XX (1970), 129-48 (who is more sceptical). The matter has not been finally resolved.

92 *English trade*, pp. 73-4, 293-4. The staple company was dominated by about 50 or 60 wealthy merchants, most of whom were based in London.

93 Barron, thesis, pp. 611-12; Haward, in *English trade*, p. 296; tables, pp. 119, 393. In October 1449, too, the staplers were given a guarantee of repayment of £10,700 for unpaid loans which had accumulated since the mid-1440s.

94 Haward, in *English trade*, pp. 294-6. The abolition of licences was incorporated in a statute to last for 5 years; the four additional exemptions were in favour of Thomas Walsingham, Thomas Browne, John Pennington, and the prior of Bridlington (*RP*, V, 183; Wedgwood, *Biographies*, pp. 123-4, 676-7; Jeffs, thesis, pp. 277-8, 314-16; above, p. 290). In the November parliament the staplers were also assured of an annual income of £2,667 (Steel, op. cit., p. 236); for the usefulness of staplers as MPs., see Roskell, *1422*, pp. 51-2, 120. Earmarking half the wool duty for Calais's expenses began in the 1437 parliament (Steel, op. cit., p. 210).

95 Above, p. 119.

96 PRO, E403/732-65. The merchants of Lucca lent only £167, in August 1446 (ibid., 762 m. 13).

97 ibid., 765 m. 13; 767 m. 10, 11; 769 m. 11; 774 m. 16; 778 m. 9 (the difficulties); 779 m. 10; below, p. 555; Steel, op. cit., pp. 269-70. The Venetians alone seem to have been able to recover their loans without appreciable delay. There were no alien loans at all during 1446–50.

98 PRO, E403/775 m. 11; 778 m. 5. For loans during 1442–52 from the courtier bishops, Kemp, Aiscough, and Moleyns, see Steel, op. cit., p. 253.

99 PRO, E403/778 m. 5, 6, 14; 793 m. 15. Bishop Lumley as treasurer (1446–49) also contributed substantial sums, even though his bishopric (Carlisle) was one of the poorest (ibid., 765 m. 14 [£1,333]; 771 m. 10 [£100]; 775 m. 9 [£100]).

100 For the sense of financial doom in 1450–51, see Steel, op. cit., pp. 233, 236-7, 268-9.

101 ibid., p. 271 (for the quotation). Several lenders in the summer of 1451 insisted on crown jewels or silverware as security, rather than tallies of assignment (ibid., p. 238).

102 *RP*, V, 228-31; above, p. 290. For Thorp, see Roskell, *Nott. Med. St.*, VII (1963), 79-105; idem, *Speakers*, pp. 248-52, 366-7.

16 Scotland, Ireland, and the Defence of the Realm

Anglo-Scottish relations

Official relations between England and Scotland were relatively peaceful after 1436. This was not because of any new accord reached between Henry VI and James II. Indeed, the disorder of the borderland and the periodic raids and acts of reprisal that disturbed its peace continued to demand attention and had a relentless and debilitating effect on frontier folk. Rather was it because the Scottish government was distracted by a series of internal problems and crises, for it is a fact of Anglo-Scottish relations between 1437 and 1453 that England played an apprehensive, yet largely passive, role while the Scots were the more likely to initiate diplomatic and military offensives in partnership with their allies on the continent.

For the moment, however, a sensational murder riveted the attention of Scotsmen and English observers alike.[1] The assassination of James I in February 1437 caused domestic upheaval and noble dissensions, and it left Scotland to be ruled by a boy of six mothered by a queen who was Cardinal Beaufort's niece. These circumstances made the formulation of an aggressive policy towards England a remote possibility in the immediate future.[2] Accordingly, on 31 March 1438 a nine-year truce between the two kingdoms was negotiated, with a panel of conservators nominated by each side to supervise its functioning and to deal with complaints and other irritations.[3] On this formal level at least, relations between England and Scotland during the remainder of Henry VI's reign were governed by a series of truces, that of May 1444 being designed to last until 1454. Notwithstanding, the Franco-Scottish alliance, cemented by the Dauphin Louis's marriage to James I's daughter Margaret in 1436, might still spell diplomatic and military danger for England and Lancastrian France.[4] This willingness to regularize relations for as much as ten years ahead reflected the desire of both sides in the early 1440s to establish more peaceful conditions on the border. Each was preoccupied elsewhere, the English in France and the Scots at home. Attempts were made to keep open the trade routes between the two countries, and Scotsmen were invited as guests to Queen Margaret's coronation in May 1445.[5]

Yet, these truces left unresolved a number of long standing issues, aside from the implications of the Franco-Scottish alliance; and these were bound to lead to tension and bloodshed between the inhabitants of the two kingdoms. For example, the English negotiators at Durham in September 1449 made it plain that they could not contemplate abandoning Henry VI's claims – so vigorously prosecuted by Edward I – to the homage and fealty of the Scottish king and to sovereignty over his kingdom.[6] There were, too, bitter disputes over the 'debateable land' in the western marches; and these defied settlement at the further conference held at Durham in November 1449.[7] The envoys were prepared to come to temporary agreements and conclude truces in order to gain a respite from widespread warfare, but their frequent parleys failed to remove any of the rooted and tendentious issues that divided the two realms. If circumstances were to prove favourable to one side or the other (and in these years they were more likely to favour Scotland than England), then an excuse for a reopening of major hostilities could easily be found.

The financial burden of guarding and administering the Scottish marches was as heavy as any of the various theatres of English administration. This fact explains the anxiety of Henry VI's ministers to reduce wherever possible the cost of border defence, partly by the negative (and perilous) decision to keep the Berwick garrison short of funds and delaying the honouring of tallies for the payment of wages and loans, and partly (and more constructively) by endeavouring to attract wardens who would assume responsibility in the marches at lower rates of pay. Both the west and east marches were without a warden during the second half of 1436, the former since 12 September and the latter from 25 July.[8] The increasing difficulty experienced in financing these posts was doubtless one important reason for the hiatus, but in the summer and autumn of 1436 the government at Westminster was also engrossed in repelling the Burgundian threat to Calais and in coping with the political consequences of Gloucester's successful raising of the siege.[9]

In the event, it proved easier to find a suitable warden for the west march, and on 24 November, Bishop Lumley of Carlisle agreed to take the commission. Though it was rare for an ecclesiastic to be appointed to either wardenship (and Lumley was associated with several laymen, including some of his relatives, who might more properly perform certain of the warden's duties), Lumley had the cardinal merits of belonging to a north-country family with direct interest in the borderland and presiding over a diocese which had suffered much from frontier feuds and lawlessness. The bishop began his term on 12 December 1436 at a salary which, at £1,050 *per annum* in peacetime and in war, was significantly lower than that enjoyed by previous wardens.[10] Even so, he received an average annual assignment that was about £150 below the sum promised. Yet Lumley suffered less than others from the crown's inability to meet its obligations, for on 18 December 1446 he was appointed treasurer of England. This placed him in an ideal position from which to scrutinize the uncashed tallies he had been given years

403

before. As a result, on 22 April 1447 he authorized for himself an exchange of thirty-five tallies, originally issued between May 1438 and November 1446 and worth £1,018, so that he could secure more prompt payment.[11]

When Lumley's kinsman, Richard Neville, earl of Salisbury returned from France in 1437, he showed himself eager to relieve the bishop of his charge – or at the very least to succeed him when his term ended in 1443. The Neville family's vested interest in the region was as great as Lumley's, and the earl even offered to accept a rate of payment that was £50 less than the bishop's modest remuneration. Eventually, on 18 December 1439 the king granted Salisbury's petition, taking advantage of his enthusiasm to reduce the annual salary still further to £983. But he had to wait until Lumley's term had run its course before beginning his ten-year tenure of the western wardenship on 12 December 1443.[12]

By contrast, it was not until near the end of March 1437 that a new warden for the more onerous east march was found. That a young, twenty-two-year-old magnate with no territorial interests in the north was appointed – and for one year only – may well reflect the extraordinary difficulty encountered by the government in finding a suitable candidate. John Mowbray, duke of Norfolk was inexperienced (not least of conditions in the north) and he may have owed his appointment to his association with Gloucester, most recently at the siege of Calais.[13] In mid-November an effort was made to find someone else who would assume the wardenship and the custody of Berwick for less than the £2,000 *per annum* which was currently the peacetime rate. Expectations of finding such a person were not high, and the council was reconciled to maintaining Sir Ralph Grey, a local landowner, in office at the old rate until at least midsummer 1438 if no alternative came forward. At one stage in the discussions, Salisbury was mentioned as a possible warden of both marches.[14] Eventually, Norfolk was replaced by two north-country knights, Sir Ralph Grey and Sir Robert Ogle, who were intimately acquainted with the problems of the north; but theirs, like Norfolk's, was a short-term contract and after two years it was allowed to lapse at the end of March 1440.[15]

The one man who could most appropriately occupy the eastern wardenship, Henry Percy, earl of Northumberland, was evidently reluctant to do so: he had been in office for seventeen years before resigning in 1434 and by that stage his frustration at the government's inability to pay him his due had reached the point of exasperation.[16] Yet, the attraction of these wardenships to those whose estates and interests were concentrated in the north was compelling: the patronage associated with them was valued by local magnates; the opportunity they offered to advance private interests alongside those of the crown was fully appreciated; and a stable frontier was essential to any magnate with property within reach of Scottish raiders or English plunderers. Accordingly, on 1 April 1440 Northumberland's nineteen-year-old eldest son, Henry Percy, was prevailed upon to act as warden of the east march, initially for four years; but the indenture was renewed for a further ten years on 1 April 1444, and on 15 December 1445 for seven years after that.[17] Percy's annual payment was fixed at £2,500 during peacetime and double that if war should break out; he had an additional allowance of 100 marks (or £200 in wartime) for the upkeep of Berwick castle. When his contract was confirmed on 7 March 1452, the government's grave financial position was revealed, for on that occasion Percy's payment was fixed at £2,567 in both peacetime and war; eleven months of wartime payments during 1448–49 had presumably proved crippling.[18]

On the west march, Salisbury was joined as warden by his eldest son, Richard, soon to be earl of Warwick; the arrangement was made on 4 April 1446, but it did not take effect until 12 December 1453 when the father's original indenture expired.[19] Meanwhile, financial problems were being experienced there too, though Salisbury's influential position in the realm ameliorated their impact to some degree. Thus, assignments to the earl from the customs revenue appear to have been honoured fairly promptly, and by August 1450 his arrears amounted to only £1,239 on nine uncashed tallies. Indeed, between 1443 and 1449 he was assigned three-fifths of his due and, to judge by the rate of his reassignment, much of this was eventually realized in cash.[20]

It was Salisbury's brother William who, as keeper of Roxburgh castle, had the worst financial fright of all. Known as Lord Fauconberg after his marriage to a wealthy north-country heiress, he took custody of the fortress on 27 March 1443 for a five-year term. It was agreed that he should be paid at the rate of £1,000 *per annum* so long as England and Scotland were at peace, but that this rate would be doubled if war broke out.[21] The fortresses of the north, including Roxburgh, needed to be kept permanently in a state of good repair, not only to deter a Scottish attack but also to impose order on a volatile populace. For all these good intentions, and the occasional effort to provide the constables with supplies and arms, mainly from the northern and eastern counties of England, Lord Fauconberg's wages slipped seriously into arrears.[22] For the first five years or so of his term, he received assignments from the exchequer which were well up to peacetime expectations, and any tallies that could not be cashed easily were replaced by his obliging kinsman, Bishop Lumley, on 17 July 1447. The bishop's sympathy for the sentinels of the Scottish marches was extended to Fauconberg as well as to Salisbury and Northumberland.[23] Ordinarily, the government was prepared to respond stonily to pleas for payment from important castellans like Fauconberg, hoping that in the last resort and in their own interests they would discharge their responsibilities rather than desert their post. There was, too, always the possibility that payment might eventually materialize if one waited long enough, and in the meantime private sources could be tapped as a form of loan to the king.

Lord Fauconberg's unforeseen capture at Pont de l'Arche on 16 May 1449, whilst on a diplomatic mission in Normandy, jeopardized this kind of arrangement as far as Roxburgh was concerned.[24] Before leaving England, he had instructed his servants to use his personal resources in Roxburgh's defence if payments were not forthcoming from the crown. By the time parliament met on 6 November 1449, the unpaid wages of his men amounted to more than £3,500 and he had already spent over two years' worth of his own income and had realized in cash some of his plate, not to speak of loans he had personally incurred for the same purpose. Fauconberg's misfortune, with a consequent demand for a ransom, came on top of these weighty financial commitments. Faced with the prospect of imprisonment and inadequate resources to purchase his freedom, he appealed to the lords for aid: he calculated that he required £100 in hand for Roxburgh castle and £300 for the wages of his soldiers. If these requests were not met, then he was prepared to abandon unilaterally his responsibilities as custodian. The lords in parliament agreed that Fauconberg's plight merited sympathy, and £400 was duly assigned to buy supplies for the castle and pay the wages of the garrison. This seems to have been a sufficient indication of good will to induce Fauconberg to remain as keeper of Roxburgh after he had secured his release from France.[25]

The situation deteriorated very quickly. By 25 September 1451, the government's debt to Fauconberg amounted to £4,109. Lest he again threaten to abandon his post, assignments were issued in his favour on the customs revenue.[26] Some felt twinges of conscience at his predicament, especially in view of his long and largely unpaid service at Roxburgh. Yet even this measure of understanding failed to produce many tangible results: Fauconberg was eventually forced to forego part of what was owed him in order to secure the rest.[27] What is so remarkable about this tale is that the Lancastrian crown could command the loyalty of such long-suffering servants as Fauconberg, who found himself heavily in debt through his official commitments in the north, and the recipient of promises the government could not fulfil. When they also had to dig deep into their already mortgaged pockets to meet personal crises, bankruptcy stared them in the face and serious doubts arose as to the wisdom – or even the practicality – of continuing to serve this regime much longer.

The Percies and Nevilles had long dominated the borderland, but the restoration of their personal control over the wardenships in the early 1440s set the scene for a rivalry that threw Yorkshire into turbulence a decade later and threatened the effectiveness of the defence of northern England against James II and his undisciplined borderers. Northumberland and Salisbury took to retaining prominent members of the local gentry in the northern shires in increasing numbers, and if Percy spent rather more of his income on this (as much as one-third in 1445), it may have been because of the greater favour lavished on his rival by the Beaufort-dominated court of Henry VI, and because Salisbury managed to secure his warden's salary and expenses with greater regularity. Moreover, from 1438 the palatinate of Durham was ruled (until 1457) by Salisbury's brother, Bishop Robert Neville, who retained several of the northern gentry in his service, whilst Roxburgh castle was kept (from 1443) by another brother, Fauconberg – and he was granted an annual fee of £20 for life by the earl in May 1444.[28]

Life itself in the borderland continued uncertain and violent, to judge from the messages received periodically at Westminster. It was reported that the lands of Carlisle cathedral priory were badly wasted by the incessant warfare, and Bishop Lumley was forced to support twenty of the canons out of his own pocket; the alternative would have been to disband them.[29] It was small compensation that in June 1443 Lumley was authorized to appropriate two churches, one in strife-torn Cumberland and the other in the no less stricken county of Northumberland, to augment the ravaged estates of the bishopric and repair some of the damage caused by Scottish raiders.[30] The town of Appleby in Westmorland was no better off, for in May 1440 it was described as utterly laid waste.[31] In the eastern march, the church at Bamburgh had declined in value catastrophically; by the summer of 1438 it was worth merely one-fifth of its original 500 marks *per annum*. Its sad state was the consequence of burning and devastation in the vicinity of one of the most notable of English bastions, though the famines and exceptional frosts of 1438–40 increased the hardship; few of the town's inhabitants were prepared to remain living there by March 1439.[32] Seven years later, Bamburgh still lay largely burnt, wasted, or destroyed and it was claimed that only thirteen burgesses were left where (according to an inquiry in April 1439) there had once been 120.[33] Durham's cathedral priory had cause to complain bitterly, for many of its estates lay close to the border or, as in the case of its cell at Coldingham, on the Scottish side of it. Cattle was rustled from its pastures in Redesdale, and the few monks with the stamina to remain at Coldingham suffered severe and frequent attacks from both sides, from English raiders and from the Scots who looked on the monastery as 'a serpent nourished in the bosom of the kingdom'.[34] Not only did the anomalous geographical position of Coldingham, 9 miles north of the Tweed, place the English monastery in the front-line of border devilry ('By the fifteenth century there was no ready parallel to the position at Coldingham where a small colony of English monks lived among their traditional enemies'), but up until 1442 the abbey at Dunfermline was striving to displace Durham as its mother-house. Accused of spying and smuggling, and of succouring their fellow-countrymen to the south in the 1440s, the Coldingham monks also had to bear the hostility of the formidable bishop of St Andrews, James Kennedy, their diocesan.[35]

On the border itself, Berwick was so poverty-stricken that on 18 January 1440 the council authorized a relaxation of the ordinances that restricted the commercial activities of its inhabitants; for three years they were enabled to enjoy a greater measure of latitude in buying wool and hides between the rivers Cocket and Tweed for shipment abroad. Otherwise, it was feared, the populace would continue to fade gradually away before Scottish onslaughts and urban decay.[36] Despite the occasional commission to undertake repairs at all the border fortresses, by the end of 1451 Berwick was in a dilapidated state.[37] A considerable portion of its perimeter walls had fallen down, while the remainder – even the castle itself – was said to be ruinous.[38] £400 spread over four years and raised from the customs of Newcastle-upon-Tyne, and a further 100 marks from Berwick's own customs, were earmarked for the repairs. Nor were the English borderers a whit better behaved than their Scots counterparts. 'Opyn wer of Inglischmen' was a hazard with which the Scots had to cope, and the men of Tynedale and Hexhamshire 'and of other partes nigh unto Scotland' had such a ferocious reputation that Archbishop Kemp's tenants were ready to engage their services in 1441 against the men of Ripon; 'the marchmen were ashamed to come so farr, and not to be noysed with none affray, or they went out of the Country'.[39]

So long as the Anglo-Scottish truce provided at least a framework for stability, society in the borderland was spared the worst barbarities of rapine and warfare. But at one stage in the late 1440s, relations between the two kingdoms came within an ace of open strife. Developments within the Scottish realm were partly responsible. James II (or 'Fiery Face', as he was known from the distinctive birthmark that disfigured his face) began to show the independent will of a teenager by 1444, and as the decade drew to a close he resolved to take the reins of government firmly into his hands. His mother, Joan Beaufort, died in July 1445, and England thereby lost a powerful advocate at the Scottish court. Meanwhile, the factions which had rent the Scottish aristocracy since the 1430s appear to have composed their differences to some extent so that James was not faced with an irreconcilable group of noblemen determined to resist his assertion of kingly power.[40] Moreover, by 1448 the slow pavane of negotiations between England and France had demonstrated little more than mutual distrust and the inability of Henry VI to translate his peace-loving inclinations into practical guarantees. Hence, whereas Charles VII had previously attempted to restrain James lest he commit some provocative and hostile act against the English, the French monarch now no longer felt any compunction about reviving his links with the northern kingdom to encircle the Lancastrians.

These ancient links had been sustained not only by Scottish diplomats and soldiers of fortune employed by the French king, but also by the marriage of the dauphin to Margaret Stewart in 1436; although she was to die in misery in France in 1445, other alliances were contemplated – and some concluded – between the clutch of daughters of James I and continental princes in the Valois orbit. In 1437 Breton envoys, with Charles's blessing, visited Scotland to discuss a marriage between Gilles of Brittany and one of the princesses. This particular proposal came to nothing, but in July 1441 Gilles's elder brother, the widowed heir to the Breton dukedom, agreed to marry Isabelle of Scotland. The Scoto-

Breton alliance which this match symbolized reflected the gradual, yet decisive, shift in Breton opinion to the French side in the closing decades of the Hundred Years War.[41] Then, in 1445, the French court suggested that another of James's daughters, Eleanor, should marry Frederick III, king of the Romans, and accordingly towards the end of the summer she and her deaf-mute sister, Joan, were conveyed to the city of Tours, where they were honourably treated. Frederick's prospects quickly faded, and a proposal that Eleanor should instead marry her recently widowed brother-in-law, the dauphin, was also abandoned; rather did Charles VII content himself with promoting a plan to marry her to one of his allies, Sigismund, duke of Austria; a series of alliances could thereby be concluded between France, Scotland, and Austria. The marriage eventually took place on 8 September 1448 near Chinon, in the presence of the king and queen of France; the treaties of alliance had been sealed the previous day.[42] The coping-stone of this matrimonial edifice was laid in July 1449, when James II himself was wedded in Edinburgh to Mary of Guelders, a great-niece of the duke of Burgundy. This was an event looked upon with satisfaction by both Duke Philip the Good and King Charles VII, and it was preceded by Scottish treaties of alliance with Brittany (22 October 1448), France (31 December), and Burgundy herself.[43]

Well aware of the diplomatic implications of these negotiations and marriages, and having to admit that the project of a meeting with his uncle of France was abortive, Henry VI undertook his first major journey to the north-east parts of his kingdom in the autumn of 1448. The disturbances in Yorkshire between the tenantry of Archbishop Kemp and the earl of Northumberland, as well as the prevailing instability of the border, were probably additional reasons for the king's journey. According to the Auchinleck chronicle, English bands had inaugurated this summer's campaign of raids, in which Dunbar and Dumfries were burned, but the Scots responded by putting Alnwick and Warkworth to the flames.[44] Repairs were authorized to the fortifications at Carlisle, Berwick, and Roxburgh on 27 July, and Henry himself set off from Westminster on 4 September. He reached Durham, the most northerly stage of his itinerary, three weeks later and spent about three days there, during which large numbers of the curious flocked to see him; he returned to Westminster by 3 November.[45]

The Scottish king seems to have led a raid into Northumberland on the very eve of Henry's arrival in the north, but the Scots withdrew as the king approached Durham, where a council meeting favoured stern retaliation.[46] With a cunning born of centuries of guerrilla warfare, the Scots waited until the king was on his way south before resuming their devastation over the border. Insurgents advanced as far as Carlisle, where they burned the suburbs of the city. The king again ordered retaliation, and according to one contemporary an army of 5,000 men was sent into Scotland, only to return with some 500 cattle. At the river Sark the Scots broke the habit of generations and gave battle on 23

October: some of the English leaders, including Sir Henry Percy, Sir John Pennington, and Sir Thomas Harrington, were trapped in a 'mire ground' and captured.[47] A further punitive expedition was assembled in Yorkshire, Cumberland, and Westmorland, this time under the command of the warden of the west march, Salisbury; beacons were built to serve as signals in case of more enemy attacks. But his success was negligible: advancing towards the border on or about 11 November, he managed to lose 2,000 horses and after three days his dejected force returned with little achievement to its credit.[48] It may have been this ignominious engagement which attracted to the government, and especially Suffolk, a measure of odium for its Scottish policy in 1448.[49]

The events of the autumn persuaded Henry VI and his council that it was wiser to repair relations with Scotland and confirm the truces between the two countries.[50] Moreover, the deteriorating situation in northern France, with the invasion scares which it revived along the English coast, alarmed Henry's ministers. Accordingly, the northern nobility, headed by the bishop of Durham, the earl of Westmorland, and Lords Clifford, Greystoke, Dacre, Poynings, FitzHugh, and Scrope, as well as the Nevilles, Percies, and Lumleys, were excused attendance at parliament on 3 February 1449 so that they could remain in the marches.[51] Salisbury was instructed to co-ordinate their defence and to enlist the co-operation of all border landowners.[52] The negotiations which took place at Durham and elsewhere not many months later, with the keeper of the privy seal, Adam Moleyns, himself leading the English delegation, eventually succeeded in removing the immediate danger, but they did not – nor could they be expected to – resolve those intractable problems which in a century and a half had hardened into principles. The state of truce was finally restored when James II ratified the Durham agreements on 8 June 1450.[53]

There is no mistaking the powerlessness of the English and their consequent concern to maintain the truce. After the resignation of Bishop Lumley as treasurer in September 1449, meagre provision indeed was made to support the wardens of the marches and Fauconberg at Roxburgh. Priorities had changed with the outbreak of war in France, the appointment of Lord Saye as the new treasurer, the dislocation caused by Cade's revolt, and the losses incurred in Gascony. Almost nothing was assigned to either Salisbury or his brother after 1449, and Percy's funds slumped badly in 1451–53.[54] All the English diplomats could do was to engage in yet another round of negotiations to confirm and extend the threadbare truce which had been in operation since 1438.[55]

If respite came, it did not result from any political or military initiative conceived at Westminster, but rather, as in 1437, from events within Scotland itself. The financial problems of James II were just as inhibiting as those of Henry VI, so that although he and his court were delighted to hear news of the Valois victories in Normandy in 1450,

James confined himself to confirming his adherence to the Franco-Scottish alliance of 1448 and did not offer the more tangible aid which Charles VII appears to have sought.[56] Then, on 22 February 1452, James plunged a dagger into his greatest rival, the earl of Douglas, with whom relations had been particularly strained after the king had encroached on the Douglas estates while the earl went on pilgrimage to Rome in October 1450.[57] The king's direct complicity in his death led to a full-scale revolt, during which (in June 1452) Henry VI entered into communication with the earl's heir, who promptly sought refuge in England.[58] This threat to James's authority relieved some of the pressure on the wardens of the march and removed, at least for a time, the possibility of open war between the kingdoms.

The English government's capability in the north had allowed it to undertake no more than a holding operation, from which the inhabitants of the borderland could expect little in the way of material recovery, social stability, or lasting peace. It hoped to buy time (and this limited aim was aided by events in Scotland), but to what ultimate purpose it had no clear conception, as the foolish neglect of the financial requirements of the wardens indicates.

Lordship in Ireland

The deep-seated Celtic prejudices that were nurtured by the ruthless imperialism of the medieval English state still flourished in a number of quarters in the mid-fifteenth century, even though (or perhaps because) the Lancastrian monarchy of Henry VI was relatively powerless in its external relations, or else beleaguered on several sides. In January 1442, during the struggle to sever the parental tie between Durham cathedral priory and Coldingham, the abbey at Dunfermline reported to Bishop Kennedy of St Andrews that the 'tyranny and cruelty of the English are notorious throughout the world, as manifestly appears in their usurpations against the French, Scots, Welsh, Irish, and neighbouring lands'.[59] By this period, there was no question of the English embarking on a robust, offensive campaign against their neighbours within the British Isles or on the continent. On the contrary, English arms and English settlers were experiencing a sobering reversal of fortune in France, Scotland, and, not least, in Ireland.

The isolated administration entrenched in Dublin and its 'pale' was more often than not subject to the rough dictates of Anglo-Irish magnates like Desmond and Ormond, and for some time past it had been assailed by a Celtic resurgence among the native Irish themselves that was cultural and social as well as military in character.[60]

> That wylde Yrishe so muche of grounde have gotyne
> There upon us, as lykelynesse may be,
> Lyke as England to shires two or thre

> Of thys oure londe is made comparable;
> So wylde Yrishe have wonne on us unable
> It to defenden and of none powere,
> That oure grounde there is a lytell cornere,
> To alle Yrelonde in treue comparisone.[61]

Even the Anglo-Irish lords were subjected to this Gaelic pressure and it made them all the more anxious to fortify their liberties and assert their independence of any outside authority, whether it be English at Dublin and Westminster or Irish from the west and north. Political morcellation and seignorial separatism grew apace in the mid-fifteenth century, and whilst such developments need not have promoted instability and disorder in the Anglo-Irish and Gaelic lordships, they bade fair to immobilize yet further the authority of the king's representative in Dublin castle.[62] Notwithstanding this possibility, Ireland, like the Scottish marches, offered an appealing prospect to the great magnate families if they could secure their own grip on the delicate royal administration: from its patronage and the use of its modest revenue might flow political power, franchises, and privileges, as well as the opportunity to outwit competitors. But in contrast to the northern borderland, the substantial obstacles in Ireland to practical control from Westminster and the king's court threatened to convert such magnate dominance into something worse than lawlessness – tyranny. The danger which this state of affairs posed to the realm of England was clearly perceived by the author of *The Libelle of Englysche Polycye* in 1437. This persuasive, versified tract lamented the decay and poverty of royal government, and voiced an obsessive concern (based on information supplied by the earl of Ormond) with the threat to England's security if her French, Spanish, Scottish, and Irish enemies should forge an alliance.[63]

After 1436 it was as much as the English government could do – or afford – to hold on to the shrunken territory of direct exploitation and administration in order to give some semblance of reality to the king's title of lord of Ireland. Though perhaps prosperous, the land no longer contributed sufficient wealth to the king's resources to enable him to support his official establishment. During the 1430s no more than £1,000 a year was available in Ireland to pay the fees and wages of the officials, not to speak of their expenses and the upkeep of Dublin castle and other buildings. Senior officers like Archbishop Talbot found it very difficult to extract their due remuneration (and the archbishop was still owed £87 in October 1438 after a decade of waiting). In 1441 it was reported that 'the charges of the justiciar of Ireland and his officials this year exceed the revenues by £1,456', and that this was no great exaggeration is indicated by a further estimate in 1444 that the king's Irish revenues were quite inadequate to meet the costs of government, not least because of the dishonesty and embezzlement of the earl of Ormond.[64] Rivalries, oppressions, corruption, and war were frequent, and the long-standing feud between Archbishop Talbot and his kin, on the one hand, and Ormond, with the support of the earl of Desmond, on the other, vitiated most seriously attempts to govern peaceably and profitably. The fourth ('White') earl of Ormond was a self-willed magnate of violent disposition who discharged his delegated responsibilities from the king with a very heavy hand; few were able to establish a relationship with him that was other than servile.[65]

Ireland was without a royal lieutenant after Sir Thomas Stanley's commission expired in April 1437. During the ensuing vacancy, Archbishop Talbot enjoyed supreme power in the pale as justiciar of Ireland, and in the winter of 1437–38 Thomas Chace, the chancellor, nominated some new members to the king's Irish council. In mid-February 1438 the council at Westminster discussed the implications of these nominations. In the event, the senior officers were confirmed in their posts for life, thereby perpetuating the character and quality of the administrative hierarchy formed in the 1430s.[66] At the same time, the archbishop was instructed to pursue every conceivable policy that would bring peace to the troubled island in expectation of the arrival of a new lieutenant. After Stanley's departure, some difficulty was experienced in persuading anyone to take his place, for Lionel, Lord Welles, who was eventually retained in December 1437, seems to have been far from eager to shoulder such an unattractive responsibility.[67] At the age of thirty-one, his career to date had been that of a courtier-councillor, though recently he had joined Gloucester at the siege of Calais. The chancellor of Ireland, who had been in office since 1432 and was reappointed on 8 March 1438, was Thomas Chace, a learned cleric who, when he was proposed as bishop of Meath in 1434, was one of Gloucester's chaplains.[68] The early months of Henry VI's majority may have witnessed, therefore, an attempt to limit the worst consequences of partisan rule; Chace was cautioned not to leave his post as chancellor except for genuine reasons, and then to hurry back to it as soon as possible.

Welles's appointment was for seven years, and a force of 300 archers was scheduled to accompany him to Ireland with the specific purpose of restoring order and resisting those who disturbed it.[69] Like his predecessor, Welles was denied the ultimate authority to appoint to the highest positions of all in the Dublin government (that is, the offices of chancellor, treasurer, and chief justice of the king's bench); though Chace, as one of Gloucester's protégés, may have been an acceptable colleague. The Northumberland esquire Giles Thorndon was already *in situ* as treasurer, and he also had custody of Dublin castle (since 1434); in March 1439 he became constable of Wicklow castle and from April 1438 enjoyed joint custody of Cardigan castle, with its direct sea communication with south-east Ireland. After decades spent in the household of Henry V, Queen Katherine, and Henry VI, Thorndon appears to have joined the circle about Thomas Chaucer and the earl of Suffolk by the 1430s. The presence in the small English establishment at Dublin of officers who were linked with bitterly opposed factions at Westminster may not have made for smooth or co-operative government in an environment already fissured by local rivalries and feuds.[70] Yet, when preparations were underway at Chester in April 1438 for the journey of the new lieutenant to Ireland, they included arrangements for his deputy, who was none other than the factious earl of Ormond.[71] Steps were taken in the following year to repatriate all Irishmen without kinsfolk or a recognized occupation in England, ostensibly for the defence of Ireland, though one suspects that the prospect of removing footloose Irishmen from the lanes and streets of England was at least as powerful a consideration.[72]

It is hardly surprising that in the thraldom of Ormond and the archbishop the condition of English authority in Ireland continued to deteriorate. By the end of 1441 there were serious rifts within the Dublin establishment which imperilled English rule and the peace of the pale; they even promoted bickering and disorder in Dublin itself. The complaints which flooded across the channel to the king and his council at Westminster were admittedly sponsored by Ormond's enemies, but there is nevertheless a strong suspicion that the earl's actions were indeed selfish ones, careless of the king's interests and almost entirely designed for his own aggrandisement.[73] To achieve his ends decisively, he proceeded to discredit the chief officers of the administration and subject the Irish council and courts to his will. In the absence of Lord Welles in 1441, Ormond posed as the champion of the independent jurisdiction of the Irish courts and administration, and its underpinning by adequate financial provision.[74] If such principles have a modern air about them, representing an attempt to loosen the bonds by which Westminster dictated the most senior appointments in the Irish government and kept it exasperatingly short of funds, they should not be mistaken for a yearning for national independence. Rather was Ormond bent on strengthening his own powers as deputy lieutenant (and shortly as lieutenant) in order to tighten his grip on Irish affairs by easing the king and his English council further into the background and pandering to the self-esteem of Irish institutions and most of those who staffed them (who in any case were gradually falling under Ormond's brazen authoritarianism). To the Irish officers of state – the chancelor, treasurer, and chief justice of the king's bench especially – such moves were welcome and to the Talbots they were positively dangerous.

According to Archbishop Talbot, the Irish parliament, meeting at Dublin early in November 1441, responded with charges that Ormond showed an intolerable high-handedness as deputy lieutenant and a shameless unscrupulousness in insinuating his servants in key offices and into parliament itself, that he ousted duly appointed officials, and embezzled the king's revenue. Parliament had begun to disintegrate under Ormond's régime, for he evidently allowed the members to absent themselves frequently, himself pocketing the fines paid in return for this privilege. True justice was on the verge of collapse, according to the archbishop and other petitioners, largely because of the prevailing fear of reprisals from Ormond's men; if independent proof were needed of his unsuitability for public responsibility, it lay in his advancing years (he was about fifty-one) and in his alleged inability to prevent the native Irish from encroaching on his own estates. The king was accordingly urged to authorize a full-scale inquiry into the earl's activities, taking evidence from those who had served as lieutenant of Ireland during the past twenty years.

This forthright protest was inspired by the news that Ormond was likely to be appointed lieutenant of Ireland in succession to Lord Welles, who had concluded that he would be better off resigning than serving his full term of seven years.[75] Yet despite the efforts of the archbishop, on 27 February 1442 Ormond's appointment was formally ratified, to take effect from the following Easter and to last for seven years; his eagerness to acquire supreme authority is displayed in his willingness to accept a salary which, at 3,000 marks for the first year, was 1,000 marks less than that received by Stanley and Welles.[76] Ormond's appointment at this stage reflects a lack of resolve on the part of the king's ministers to act on the information supplied by the Irish parliament. Choosing his ground carefully – in council meetings at Trim and Naas outside Dublin – the earl reacted sharply, inducing (some would say intimidating) the Irish councillors to reject the charges against him as utterly false and declaring the chancellorship vacant after Richard Wogan's flight from the country (July 1442).[77] At Westminster, the king's ministers were justifiably alarmed at the intemperate recriminations on both sides, but they could not bring themselves to abandon either Ormond or Talbot, or to establish a less partisan régime at Dublin. The archbishop still had his sympathizers, but his reappointment as chancellor on 7 August 1442 merely served to guarantee a continuation of the rivalries of recent years.[78]

Yet Talbot's appointment sprang from a decision by the English government, after nine months' hesitation, to open a full-scale inquiry into the condition of Ireland's government, summoning not only Ormond but also the archbishop and the treasurer, Giles Thorndon, who had just as much reason to denounce the lieutenant, to give evidence.[79] According to Thorndon's testimony, based (as he himself stressed) on experience in the royal service going back thirty-eight years, the enmity between Ormond and the Talbots had undermined impartial justice and perverted the workings of the Irish exchequer. The latter at least might be remedied, in Thorndon's opinion, if the chief baron of the exchequer were a trained lawyer and freed from dependence on one or other of the Anglo-Irish lords, and if the independent powers of the treasurer were strengthened; moreover, the habit of employing deputies undermined the effectiveness of all government departments and should be discontinued.[80] Inadequate financial resources were at the heart of the problem, not least because they led to the neglect of the English-held castles and towns of the south and east. These beleaguered bastions of

415

royal authority – Drogheda, Dublin, Waterford, Wicklow, and, in the west, Limerick – were in a desperate and destitute state, with defences that were ruinous, inhabitants who had fled, and merchants who were deterred from their normal trading operations.[81] Not only were the native Irish a constant threat, but Anglo-Irish rebels were feared no less, whilst sea attacks by Scots, Spaniards, and Bretons seemed to be increasing. Some effort was made to support those English administrators who, like Thorndon, Richard Wogan, and Christopher Bernevale, were in the van of the struggle with Ormond, but it may be doubted whether formal protections and pardons granted at Westminster were at all respected in Dublin and beyond.[82] In October 1442 the tenacious lieutenant summoned another council meeting, this time to Drogheda where he secured a declaration endorsing his recent actions; this seems to have fortified his determination actually to remove Archbishop Talbot from the office of chancellor (albeit illegally since he was the king's appointee).[83] For the government in England to grasp the nettle more resolutely would ultimately mean dismissing the all-mighty Ormond from office, and that it was disinclined – or unable – to do.

As a result, the tenuous hold which the English administration had on affairs in Ireland slackened yet further: income from customs duties collectable at the ports and from fee farms payable by the loyalist towns seeped inexorably away. It was a disastrous misfortune that at this very juncture Henry VI adopted the habit of making generous, yet ill-conceived, grants to practically all who requested them, whether for life or during pleasure or for a term of years; these had the effect of worsening the financial situation and depriving Dublin of badly needed cash. Soldiers in the lieutenant's retinue went unpaid and his establishment as the king's principal representative could not be properly supported; officers were likely to desert and Irish merchants in English ports ran the risk of arrest for debts owed by their home town. Accordingly, on 4 July 1443 Ormond was instructed to summon the Irish parliament and conduct an urgent financial review, especially of unwise grants and patents; the intention was that they should be resumed, a device that would soon commend itself to an English commons faced with a similar problem.[84]

The harvest of years of failure on the part of the king to tackle the fundamental problem of Anglo-Irish magnate dominance over the Dublin administration was now being garnered. Ormond, the lieutenant who was instructed to implement these reforms, was himself a root cause of the ills which they were designed to remedy. He preferred his personal and private interests before those of the crown, and yet his and the Talbots' influence in England ensured that Henry VI's divided counsels would not undertake a radical reformation of the Irish political scene.[85] Although Ormond visited Limerick during 1443 to investigate the town's failure to pay its fee-farm, he confined himself to issuing a pardon, apparently in return for a £100 gift to himself. The treasurer,

Thorndon, found himself in an impossible position. If he returned to England to submit his usual account (and, very likely, to remonstrate) without the lieutenant's permission, he risked Archbishop Talbot's fate of being deprived of office in his absence; when he received Ormond's permission to leave in 1441, it was at the price of nominating one of the earl's retainers, William Chevirs, as deputy treasurer, a man who abetted Ormond in his embezzlement and oppression. When Thorndon refused to nominate Chevirs a second time in 1443, Ormond seized the treasurer's lands and offices and proceeded to appropriate the crown's resources by flagrantly browbeating the craven Irish council; Thorndon's attempts to resist him in the great council and parliament were easily thwarted. For his pains, Thorndon was disdainfully ignored as treasurer and deprived of his constableship of Wicklow castle; Henry VI's instruction that he be restored went unheeded. These events were the burden of Thorndon's complaints in the winter of 1443–44.[86] Henry VI's council might summon the earl to England to discuss 'certain grete and chargeable matteres the weill of our Reaume, Lordshipes and subgittes concerninge' on 23 March, but Ormond's complete mastery of the supine Irish council enabled him not only to secure a total exoneration of himself at Drogheda (June 1444), but to take the offensive and declare Thorndon relieved of his office because of desertion and certain misdeeds (30 March). The reputation of Chief Justice Bernevale was similarly besmirched by a series of accusations of law-breaking and sharp practice.[87]

The crown's paralysis in Ireland is well illustrated by the experience of Michael Gryffen, whose loyal service to the king was rewarded on 31 October 1441 with an appointment for life as chief baron of the Irish exchequer. With the connivance of Ormond as Lord Welles's deputy, Gryffen was speedily ejected from the post by John Cornwalsh and it was not until July 1443, when Westminster was momentarily making a closer scrutiny of Irish affairs, that his reinstatement was commanded by the king. Yet letters from Henry VI might condemn the meddling of the lieutenant (as Ormond had become) and the Irish council, but it was only in June 1445 that Gryffen obtained justice.[88] By this time, a new royal lieutenant had at last been appointed. On 12 March 1445, John Talbot, earl of Shrewsbury accepted the post; his indenture ran from 20 April for seven years, and it was evidently envisaged that he would remedy some of the ills fathered on the land by decades of neglect.[89] The appointment of the sixty-one-year-old earl, who had spent much of the past twenty years fighting in France, admittedly represented a victory for the Talbot faction, but it at least had the merit of decisively altering the political climate at Dublin and neutralizing the selfish influence of the White earl. On 7 May, Ormond was licensed to leave Ireland for a period of three years, though he could receive his landed income during his absence.[90] This withdrawal inaugurated a more peaceful relationship between his family and the Talbots, though it also had the effect of rekindling the hostility between the Butlers and the FitzGeralds so that in 1444 and again in 1446 Tipperary, which was under Ormond's control, was ravaged and burned. The FitzGerald earl of Desmond had decided to take advantage of his former ally's relative weakness to advance by violence his own interests.[91] Ireland was exchanging one master for another, though perhaps a less perfidious one; but the condition of the country and the vigour of English rule were hardly affected.

During 1446 Ormond lived in or near London under some form of restraint, for he was forbidden to travel more than 40 miles from the capital unless it were to Canterbury as a pilgrim. He was required to hold himself in readiness to appear before king and council to answer the accumulated charges against him.[92] As winter approached, he was brought to trial in the king's prerogative court of the constable and marshal of England, where he was accused of treason and *lèse-majesté*. His accuser was Thomas FitzGerald, the prior of the hospital at Kilmainham of the Order of St John of Jerusalem, who had been in England since October 1444 insisting on the earl's treasonable conduct. This exceptional procedure was available for crimes committed outside the realm, and resort might even be made to the duel if, as seemed likely in Ormond's case, there was some difficulty in assembling witnesses.[93] The Ormond–Talbot feud was moving to a climax in which at one stroke Ormond might be swiftly removed from the scene.

FitzGerald, who was a member of the Anglo-Irish family of the earls of Desmond, had recently added his appeal of treason to that of Giles Thorndon and others.[94] It was now to be resolved by an age-old procedure that may have been considered by some as the only possible way of dealing with Ormond. Even so, it was an extraordinary episode and one which attracted a good deal of attention at the time, especially in London.[95] Elaborate preparations were made at Smithfield for the forthcoming spectacle of a prominent Anglo-Irish magnate defending himself in the lists.[96] The commons of the city showed their partisanship (and perhaps their anti-clericalism) by rallying to Ormond's side, and a bevy of Irish ecclesiastics arrived at Chester to cheer him on (though the prior and Giles Thorndon persuaded the king to forbid the visitors from speaking with the earl or his men).[97] Although the prior engaged a knight to fight for him (since it would have violated his order to have done so himself), at the last moment the king cancelled the arrangements and reserved judgement to himself. Henry VI had responded to an appeal from a group of prominent preachers and clerics in London, led by Master Gilbert Worthington, who was himself a distinguished canonist.[98] Both Ormond and the prior subsequently accepted a pardon from the king.[99]

Meanwhile, Shrewsbury and his family held sway at Dublin and in the English pale. Even though the earl did not visit Ireland until the autumn of 1446, Talbot ascendancy was assured and Sir John Talbot, his son and heir, was associated with the ageing archbishop in the most important positions of responsibility; when other officials and castle-constables were chosen, loyal Talbot sympathizers were preferred.[100]

Shrewsbury's own authority was significantly extended in July 1446, when he was granted the title of steward of Ireland with powers comparable to those of the steward of England; no matter how ceremonial these may actually have been compared with those of the lieutenancy, the emphasis accorded to Shrewsbury's status was unmistakable. His proven and 'strenuous probity', shown during decades of service to Henry V and Henry VI, seemed to be just what was needed in a war-torn Ireland whose government lay paralysed. His mighty defence of the Anglicized areas was duly rewarded (doubtless in the hope that it would continue) on 17 July by his creation as earl of Waterford in tail male, and by a grant of the fee-farm of the county and city of Waterford to complement the stewardship.[101] His eldest son became chancellor of Ireland on 12 August. But already (on 16 May 1446) two household servants of the king and queen had been offered the treasurership of Ireland and the constableships of Wicklow and Dublin castles whenever Giles Thorndon should die. The fact that these men would almost certainly be absentee officials did not prevent their appointment by Henry VI. In fact, this particular promotion of personal companions of the king seems to have been one of those thoughtless decisions to which Henry was prone, for not only did it offend Thorndon but it also seems to have upset Shrewsbury, who confirmed the treasurer in office on 22 July by his own letters patent.[102] Safe in the knowledge that his opponent, Ormond, was in disgrace in England, and that his own family's grip on the Irish administration was reasonably secure, Shrewsbury was in no hurry to visit Ireland personally; he even secured a licence on 7 August 1446 to absent himself for ten years and yet continue to receive the income from his estates.[103] Nevertheless, he eventually did spend some months in Ireland between the autumn of 1446 and the summer of 1447.[104]

On 30 July 1447 Shrewsbury was replaced as lieutenant by Richard, duke of York, with effect from 9 December. His salary was fixed at the usual level of 4,000 marks in the first year of his ten-year term, and £2,000 in each of the remaining years. The situation in Lancastrian France has some bearing on what was a premature change, for in 1447 Shrewsbury's indenture still had several years to run. During the previous year York found himself increasingly at odds with Suffolk's government and resentful of its witch-hunt of those in the Norman administration suspected of corruption. Then, on 24 December 1446, York was deprived of his authority in France by the appointment of the duke of Somerset as lieutenant-general and governor of France, Normandy, and Aquitaine. The change of scene may not, therefore, have been entirely unwelcome, and Ireland offered new channels into which his energies could be diverted.[105] One needs to remember, too, that contemporaries were by no means certain that the Ormond–Talbot feud would not burst into life again once the treasonable accusations against Ormond had been disposed of. Some may have regarded York as the only person of stature and with an interest in Ireland who was capable of preventing such an outbreak: not only was he the greatest landowner in Ulster, Meath, and Connacht, but both Shrewsbury and Ormond were obligated to him. Indeed, the two deputies he successively appointed during 1447–49 were, first, Archbishop Talbot (who died in 1449) and then Richard Nugent, Baron Devlin, who had been Ormond's representative in 1444.[106] The view of late-fifteenth-century chroniclers that York was exiled to Ireland against his will should probably be relegated to the list of exaggerated criticisms levelled against Suffolk.[107]

The task of extending English authority through the island was barely tackled in these years. Shrewsbury's rule might have accomplished something in this direction had it been allowed to continue; for the first time in Henry VI's reign one of the two warring factions in Ireland had established a virtually unchallengeable control over the English administration. In addition, a serious effort seems to have been made to provide him with adequate finance; during a term of less than three years Shrewsbury received assignments worth more than two-thirds of his agreed salary.[108] But his régime was all too brief and his own stay in Ireland a short one. York therefore faced lawlessness and dangers every whit as daunting as those with which earlier lieutenants had had to contend.

In 1448, parts of Kilkenny, Tipperary, Wexford, and Waterford were in rebellion and had united with certain Gaelic elements and foreigners to raid, slaughter, and burn in the city of Waterford itself.[109] Soon afterwards, co. Louth within marching distance of Drogheda was invaded by Irish lords, whilst Cork and nearby ports in the south-west found themselves surrounded by hostile Irishmen. By June 1450 parts of co. Meath were being subjected to raiding, arson, and murder.[110] Among the Franciscan friars were many Gaels, regarded as an insidious fifth column, insinuating themselves in the more loyalist areas, winning promotion in their order and threatening, like a Trojan horse, a régime that was all too precariously sustained from England. Even their former minister provincial in Ireland, William Crailly, was in communication with the Irish rebels and some of his brothers occasionally gave refuge to the enemy. At the request of the order, stern action was enjoined on the duke of York and the Irish council on 28 July 1451 so that the admission of new friars would be more carefully scrutinized.[111] It was an act of overt racial discrimination. A little later still, when Normandy had been lost, Calais lay under threat, and Bordeaux had fallen, hasty efforts were made to victual Wicklow castle.[112] Enfeebled by the rifts in Irish society, paralysed by feuds that had only recently abated, deserted financially by a government headed by a king whose conception of patronage sometimes offended those on whom he had to rely, the lordship of Ireland now felt itself threatened from abroad.

Plans for York's journey to Ireland were in hand by October 1448, though it was not until the summer of the following year that he set sail from Beaumaris in ships brought speedily from the west-country and

Cheshire ports – and he did so then only at the king's exhortation. Those who see in the duke's initial acceptance of the lieutenancy an eagerness to attract allies and construct a power-base in Ireland, preparatory to making political demands in England, are trusting too readily in their powers of hindsight.[113] Meanwhile, another ill-conceived act of generosity on the king's part had annoyed Sir John Talbot and poisoned relations within the Talbot circle. On 5 April 1448 Thomas FitzGerald, the prior of Kilmainham who had recently been harrying Ormond, was granted the reversion of the office of chancellor. Only when parliament met at Westminster in February 1449 was Sir John able to have his position clarified and confirmed in the face of efforts by FitzGerald to take the great seal from him.[114]

As a result of the efforts of Baron Devlin and, to a lesser extent, of Ormond (who had accompanied York from England), the Irish lords of Ulster were brought to submit to the new lieutenant soon after his arrival on 6 July 1449. As the Irish chronicler quaintly put it, he was

> received with great honour, and the earls of Ireland went into his house, as did also the Irish adjacent to Meath, and gave him as many beeves for the use of his kitchen as it pleased him to demand.

It was perhaps natural that the duke should turn his attention first to his own earldom of Ulster, where the Irish lords owed him fealty. The indentures which he concluded with Irishmen at Drogheda in August were a promising start to his tour of duty and opened up tentatively a prospect of stability in the north-east at least; a few other lords from the centre, as well as the earl of Desmond, came in a month later. A swift campaign followed to the south of Dublin in the Wicklow mountains which induced the O'Byrnes and the MacMurroughs to submit, though one may question the sincerity and practicality of their undertaking to wear English clothes and speak the English tongue.[115] A great council summoned to Dublin on 17 October set about ensuring that hard-pressed castles and towns were properly protected and fortified, and that the more flagrant oppressions and abuses of government were removed. An impression of fairer and firmer government marked York's first months in Ireland and the lieutenant himself appears to have acted with vigour and speed, though with a weather-eye on safeguarding his own interests.

It was at this juncture that the duke was seriously affronted by Henry's ministers and deeply humiliated after his unsuccessful attempts to gain the king's ear and dislodge his rival, Somerset, from the king's inner counsels.[116] One consequence of this rupture with the government was that the exchequer ignored its obligation to pay his annual salary. Even in his first two years of office, York received only slightly more than half of what he had been promised (tallies worth £2,533 instead of £4,667); after December 1449 he obtained none at all.[117] This neglect merely served to try the duke's patience, not least because it threatened him with bankruptcy. After he had been in Ireland barely two months, he was contemplating selling or mortgaging some of his English manors 'to helpe hym to the charges and costes that he hath and shall at this tyme bore to do your highnesse service' in Ireland.[118] Sometime in the first half of 1450 he could claim with justice that as lieutenant he was so far owed £3,133, let alone £6,000 that had failed to materialize from other sources. Although Henry VI ordered the exchequer to settle its account with him on 17 May, little had been done before the duke suddenly arrived in north Wales a few months later.[119] Meanwhile, he had informed his brother-in-law Salisbury, who was also one of the king's councillors, that unless his army in Ireland were paid soon, he might have to abandon Ireland and his campaign to restore law and order, and return to England to live. Yet not even this threat stirred a government that was admittedly confronted by urgent financial problems in Normandy, Calais, and Gascony, and would shortly be engaged in suppressing Cade's revolt. Nothing of significance was done to meet York's demands arising from his service in either France or Ireland: 'for paiement wherof, mony promises have been to me made, not parfourmed'.[120]

York tried to raise what money he could within Ireland itself. At a council at Drogheda in April 1450 the expedient of resumption of royal grants, which was currently being recommended in England, was adopted to provide cash with which to pay the king's Irish officers; the council also imposed a scutage levy on those owing military service to the crown in Ireland – something which had been suspended for ten years as recently as 1445. York justified this particular action by claiming that he 'has no payment of the king for the protection of this his said land'. The energy and unusual dedication shown by the duke may partly be explained by his determination to buttress his personal position as an Anglo-Irish magnate, but this should in no way detract from the integrity and resolution exhibited in his letter to Salisbury in June 1450: 'I had liever be dead than any convenience shall fall thereunto [i. e., Ireland] by my default: for it shall never be chronicled nor remain in scripture, by the grace of God, that Ireland was lost by my negligence'.[121]

The souring of relations between York and the king's court from 1450 put at risk whatever the duke may have achieved in restoring respect for Henry VI and his government during his brief sojourn in Ireland; his unheralded return in September 1450 also demonstrated how vulnerable were the western approaches to the realm. Ireland could be identified as the same serious threat to England as it had appeared to be to the author of the *Libelle* a dozen years before. With the earl of Shrewsbury preoccupied in France (and shortly to be slain in Gascony), Ormond dead by 23 August 1452, and York of uncertain loyalty, by 1453 the appointment of a new lieutenant seemed overdue – at least from the point of view of the government in England. James Butler, who had succeeded his unruly father in the earldom of Ormond, was admittedly in his youth one of York's companions and retainers, but his nomination for a ten-year term as lieutenant on 5 March 1453 signalled a return to faction rule and a setback for the Talbots. It also alienated York, who had not been consulted and whose own term still had more than four years to run.[122]

Butler was thirty-three years old and, despite his own and his father's connection with York, he was well regarded at court: as a boy (he was only one year younger than the king) he had accompanied Henry VI to France in 1430; and on 8 July 1449 he was raised to the peerage as earl of Wiltshire, three years before he inherited the Ormond title.[123] York's break with the court in 1450–52 seems to have reinforced Butler's loyalty to the king and henceforward he walked boldly with the circle that provided staunch support for Henry and his ministers; he even became treasurer of England in March 1455, after York had been discharged as protector and defender of the realm.[124] His appointment to the Irish lieutenancy, therefore, was strongly influenced by political considerations at court, and it is doubtful if he ever intended travelling to Dublin in person. Within two months Wiltshire had enlisted John May, archbishop of Armagh and primate of Ireland, as his deputy whenever he himself was absent from Ireland, and in July the exchequer assigned him his entire first year's salary of 4,000 marks.

Though openly favoured by the Lancastrian régime, Wiltshire's was an inauspicious appointment: with little apparent interest in Ireland's peculiar, vexatious problems, he was at odds with the most senior Anglo-Irish landowner, whose service he had deserted and whom he had brusquely displaced as lieutenant. The involvement of senior magnates like Wiltshire and York in the politics of Irish government was bound to influence their attitudes to one another on other, non-Irish matters, including the power struggle that was developing about the person of the last Lancastrian king. In those circumstances, Ireland's security in a Lancastrian world that seemed to be crumbling on several sides rested on the promise of an English army, which was being assembled at Chester, Liverpool, and Beaumaris during the summer months of 1453; it is not known whether it ever reached Ireland, and if it did, it accomplished nothing that contemporaries considered noteworthy.[125]

The Coasts and Seas

Henry VI's advisers showed greater concern for the safety of English shipping and for the protection of the seas and shores of the realm when French armies began to penetrate to the Normandy coast, especially after the abortive peace negotiations of 1439. On occasion in these years, the government gave more serious attention to the defence of the south coast than at any time since Henry IV's reign. But it had no clear-sighted policy and responded to particular crises as they arose and then usually at the insistence of the mercantile community or coastal population.[126] Furthermore, piracy round England's shores was a serious problem from the mid-1430s, to judge by the number of cases that were brought to the government's attention by way of complaint and demands for restitution or compensation. Not all of these suits arose out of the maritime activities of foreigners, for freelance Englishmen, particularly from the west country, were organizing themselves in freebooting enterprises, laying the foundations of that distinctive way of life associated with many a seaman from Cornwall and Devon in the following century.[127] How the dispersal of Henry V's fleet after 1422 must have been regretted twenty years on!

The channel had become a front line of defence for the realm. This, in turn, meant expenditure of money on ships, fortifications, and harbours, and also increased vigilance by the local populace. Yet the most effective way of protecting the realm and its commerce was, as the *Libelle* argued, by preserving English dominion over the seas around it. Advice of this nature was in ample supply, for in the years that followed Henry's coming of age, when Cardinal Beaufort was steering the king towards a peace treaty with Charles VII, those who were knowledgeable about naval defence and free passage across the seas considered that the Lancastrian régime was doing insufficient to ensure either. In the mind of Sir John Fastolf, who surveyed the scene from the standpoint of a military strategist, effective sea-keeping had a triple merit: it shielded the Norman and English shores, protected English commerce, and would provide naval support for the armies sent to northern France. As the French turned the tide of war, by 1440 this last consideration, which he urged on behalf of the duke of York's council in France, was felt by him to be the weightiest consideration of all.[128] The author of the *Libelle of Englysche Polycye*, writing sometime in 1436–38, also stressed the naval, commercial, and military importance of English control of the channel, with its 'tweyne eyne' of Dover and Calais.

> For if this see be kepte in tyme of werre,
> Who cane here passe withought daunger and woo?
> Who may eschape, who may myschef dyfferre?
> What marchaundy may forby be agoo?
> For nedes hem muste take truse every foo,
> Flaundres and Spayne and othere, trust to me,
> Or ellis hyndered alle for thys narowe see.

His commercial assessment buttressed an argument that was designed to persuade the council to adopt an aggressive policy in defence of England and her French possessions. Then would the honour of the king and his reputation abroad be upheld, for that was the haughty purpose of this propaganda.

> So shulde he [the king of England] be lorde of the see aboute,
> To kepe enmyes fro wythine and wythoute,

And to be holde thorowgh Christianyte
Master and lorde environ of the see,
For all lyvinge men suche a prince to drede,
Of such a regne to be aferde indede . . .

Kepe than the see abought in speciall,
Whiche of England is the rounde wall,
As thoughe England were lykened to a cite
And the wall environ were the see.
Kepe than the see, that is the wall of Englond,
And then is Englond kepte by Goddes sonde;
That, as for ony thinge that is wythoute,
Englande were than at ease wythouten doute, . . .[129]

Within a decade of these exhortations, John Capgrave, the Franciscan chronicler, was still moved to regret that so little had been done along these lines. It was no longer appropriate, during an interval of peace, for him to stress the aggressive potentiality of command of the seas, but he stressed its defensive and commercial implications:

. . . . if the sea were kept by our navy many good results would follow – it would give a safe conduct to merchants, secure access to fishers, the quiet of peace to the inhabitants of the kingdom, to our king himself a large measure of glory.[130]

The needs of defence and safe trading produced some appropriate measures, and occasionally the government financed a fleet to discourage intruders and to remain at sea for a limited period. But it was slow to respond to circumstances and advice, once the threat posed by the siege of Calais had passed. Royal naval organization was allowed to decay during the king's majority, and down with it sank the king's remaining ships.[131] In the two years following 31 August 1437, only £8 9s. 7d. was spent by the exchequer on ships, while during the night of 6-7 January 1439 the great ship *Grace Dieu* caught fire as it stood rotting in the river Hamble, near Southampton.[132] But in 1440, with the situation at several points on the Norman coast deteriorating, more purposeful measures were taken. The government looked to the seafaring community for assistance and lighted on a west-country knight, John Speke from Devon. His public service hitherto had been confined to membership of the commons in 1427, but when he appeared in parliament in November 1439, he attracted the government's attention (not least because of the violence which accompanied his election) and soon afterwards was enlisted on sea-keeping duties.[133] The plan was a modest and short-term one, for Speke was engaged for three short periods, each lasting no more than two months: first, on 2 May 1440 with 400 men, though he enthusiastically assembled an extra 300; then, on 22 July with 600; and finally, on 7 September, he agreed to provide an even larger force of 800 men.[134] He sailed on two voyages, the second of which was mainly concerned with the siege of Harfleur.[135] All things considered, this was an *ad hoc* arrangement of a very temporary kind, relying on a particular individual whose reputation in Devon had commended him to the king for a brief period of official service at sea. Speke died, probably on board ship, on 5 October 1441.

To judge by the complaints voiced in parliament early in 1442, the restraints imposed on English traders themselves by truces and treaties were a discouragement to the merchant community and a disincentive for them to supply ships for the royal service. The practice of granting safe-conducts to foreigners and foreign vessels was widely believed to encourage piracy and attacks on English merchantmen and coastal dwellers by Breton captains and the like.[136] Many who owned or mastered ships were quite demoralized, and the government had to concede that the law should be eased at least in the case of ships sailing without a safe-conduct and seized by Englishmen.

Ten days after parliament ended, the king embarked on a modest reorganization of his few remaining seaworthy ships. On 7 April 1442 the keeper of Henry V's ships, William Soper, who was now well into his fifties, finally resigned; he may not have been sorry to relinquish a post that had lost much of its importance since the heady days of shipbuilding and fleet manoeuvres, and he had developed his own commercial interests in Southampton in the meanwhile. He was replaced by Richard Clevedon, a member of the king's household, whose appointment emphasized the direct control which the household would now have over the king's ships; but in practice his duties were performed by deputy. Soper's vigorous administration was at an end. If Clevedon's appointment signalized anything, it was the importance that was being attached, at a time of renewed military effort in Normandy, to raising a fleet that would be under a household chain of command.[137]

Some were now heeding the proffered advice that what was needed was a more sustained and coherent policy of sea-keeping, preferably with a fleet financed by the crown which would be constantly at sea between February and November; it should have a proper chain of command ultimately linked with the king himself so that the indiscipline and violence on board impressed ships (for which merchants and shipowners declined to take responsibility) could be reduced. If implemented, these proposals would have amounted to a considerable reform, and presumably they emanated from the merchants' spokesmen in parliament.[138]

At the commons' urging, therefore, Henry commissioned three of the recent MPs who had a close interest in coastal defence: Sir William Eure, a Yorkshireman who had recently been sheriff of Northumberland and was experienced in negotiations with the Scots; Sir Miles Stapleton from Norfolk, a younger man with family links with the earl of Suffolk; and Sir John Heron, the youngest of all, who lived in

Northumberland and was constable of Bamburgh castle. They were joined by a household knight well versed in the needs of Lancastrian France: Sir John Popham from Hampshire had been treasurer of the household in 1437–39, had fought with Henry V and Bedford in Normandy, and was currently a councillor of the king's lieutenant-general in France, York.[139] It was a well-designed command which showed a broad appreciation of naval defence on the entire eastern and southern seaboard of the realm. The four knights were engaged on 26 June 1442 'for the seure and saufkeping of the see for the seuretee of us oure Reaumes, lordships and subgettz and in especiall of oure marchauntes with theire marchandises resorting on the sea', and in their eight capital ships and twenty smaller ones they were to have 2,260 armed men.[140] As was often the case with late medieval military and naval plans, execution was less impressive than intention. The rendezvous at The Camber near Winchelsea did not take place according to schedule, and eventually on 23 August the government designated the roads off the Isle of Wight as the assembly point: Popham would bring his contingent of 565 men from the west country to meet the other three commanders with their 1,695 drawn from ports and counties further east and north.[141] They were contracted and paid by the king for three months' service, rather than the six months requested by parliament.[142]

The commons had envisaged a repeat of this exercise in the spring of 1443, when the fleet would be financed for eight months from 1 March. But this plan was completely abortive, for by May the traditional arrangement had been substituted, whereby merchants and shipowners contributed a number of ships for sea-keeping purposes for half a year. Moreover, the undertaking that they would be financed by the king, who would institute a hierarchy of command, was abandoned; rather were owners allowed to recoup their outlay by retaining prizes and captured enemy ships. This represented a return to the improvisation of the past, with maritime lawlessness harnessed in the king's service rather than superseded by the measures of 1442.[143]

Ashore, Dover, the first port of entry from France and the Low Countries, was widely acknowledged to be of critical importance. The condition of its defences was under consideration by the government in May 1438, and two years later steps were taken to renovate the harbour installations and strengthen the town walls.[144] Further west, Plymouth was encouraged in 1439 to reconstruct its walls and towers in stone, by which time raids by pirates and enemy vessels had increased.[145] And although these two major ports were treated in isolation, the fear of invasion was common in the south as news arrived of the French successes in Normandy.[146] The vulnerability of the English coast was most graphically revealed in 1443, one of the gloomiest of years for Lancastrian fortunes at sea. Remedial measures were taken, and communities within reach of the coast were required to pay for their own defence on the basis of the traditional general obligation of all subjects to protect their king and his kingdom. More would be heard of this obligation later as the situation in France deteriorated further.[147] The Isle of Wight felt particularly threatened, not only because it was geographically exposed to marauding Frenchmen and their allies, but also because the islanders' capacity to defend themselves was severely handicapped. In July 1443 some of the weapons which the king had bought for Sir John Popham's ships the previous year were transferred to the island instead.[148]

The Lancastrian conception of sea power and coastal defence did not easily attune itself to the dramatic changes of military fortune on mainland Europe. Even if the government appreciated the need for greater continuity and royal control, the financial implications were too daunting. Despite the measures taken in 1442, therefore, the temptation to resort to piecemeal arrangements and, during the period of truce from 1444 to 1449, to ignore both the idea of a fleet and the reality of strong fortifications was irresistible. Faced with the disasters of 1449–50, the preparations of Henry's government were quite inadequate, as the strictures of Cade's rebels underlined.[149]

The seizure of Fougères (Brittany) in March 1449 and the surreptitiously planned offensive of which it may have formed a part were accompanied by a more vigorous attempt to patrol the seas and keep them safe for English commerce and for the transport of armies to the French mainland. The tone and tempo of the government's measures altered dramatically during 1449; indeed, its sea-keeping activities became progressively more urgent as the months passed. Shortly before 1 April, an ungenerous half-subsidy was granted by the commons in parliament for the defence of the realm, and just before parliament adjourned on 4 April it was announced that the first part of it (collectable in November 1449) would be allocated to the defence of the Scottish border (£2,333), Calais and Crotoy (£2,433), and the seas (£2,000).[150] Three servants of the crown, Gervase Clifton, Alexander Iden, and Robert Winnington, were retained that same day to undertake the naval commission; they were authorized to commandeer ships and to equip and victual them with the money that was promised. To co-ordinate the effort, a novel expedient was employed: Thomas Daniel, one of the most influential of all the household servants, was ordered a few months later to take a posse to sea and assume full command over the ship-masters and mariners so that discipline could be imposed and the naval attack on the enemy be co-ordinated in the king's interest.[151] But this promising initiative encountered the inevitable reef on which most of Henry's attempts at sea-keeping foundered: lack of money. It was realized in April that the proposed fleet could not wait until November for at least part of the allocation of £2,000, and accordingly, on 26 April, Clifton and Iden were authorized to borrow 1,000 marks on the security of the forthcoming half-subsidy in order to augment the 200 marks which the exchequer had advanced them on 7 April. Yet even by March 1450, when a further 400 marks were issued for naval operations, the provision fell far short of the intended £2,000.[152]

On 22 March 1452 a similar attempt was made to assemble a coherent fleet, this time with Lord Clifford at its head. Ships were impressed at ports as far afield as Hull and Hampshire, Newcastle and the west country, and the squadron was intended in the first instance to convey the king himself to Calais to forestall Charles VII's rumoured siege of the sole remaining Lancastrian bastion in northern France.[153] Overall naval command, however, was vested in the earl of Shrewsbury, and a considerable army of 3,000 men was placed at his disposal. Even when he was instructed to take this force to Gascony, sea-keeping duties still figured among his orders, which included a vigorous offensive against the ships of Castile and Leon, Brittany and France.[154] At the same time, Gervase Clifton, one of the commanders of 1449, and Sir Edward Hull were commissioned to serve at sea for three months with a force of 1,000 men each; this they did to the letter, with Clifton even extending his patrol for an extra two months at his own cost – though he might have known that some difficulty would be encountered in recovering the £400 he over-spent.[155]

This very real concern for the safety of the seas was to be one of the foremost preoccupations of the English government henceforward. The realm itself would now bear the brunt of foreign hostilities at sea, for nothing more than Calais and the Channel Islands stood between her and the enemy. As to the islands, the king's governor there, John Nanfan, an esquire for the body, kept in periodic touch with the mainland and on 18 September 1452 arrangements were finally made to place a force, 130-strong, under his command.[156]

Closer in, the Isle of Wight's security was bound to give grounds for renewed concern. The parliament of 1449–50 was informed, with some sense of drama, that pestilence, war, and officers' extortions had seriously reduced its able-bodied population during the past five years; what was worse, there were no prominent islanders left, with the possible exception of Henry Bruyn, an esquire of the king's household, to organize its defence. Carisbrooke castle had been sadly neglected and its garrison was depleted. Thus, when soldiers retreating from Normandy brought news of French preparations for an invasion, the inhabitants were well-nigh panic-stricken. Henry VI responded by appointing one of his intimates, Lord Beauchamp of Powick, to take charge of the island as a virtual royal lieutenant. Among Beauchamp's more immediate problems was that of re-establishing internal order. The Isle was terrorized by the duke of York's steward, John Newport, who had recently been discharged from office for misgoverning the island in the duke's name; during the summer of 1449 he had taken to piracy with some aptitude and operated with such effect that many fled to the mainland for safety while he rejoiced in the sobriquets of 'Newport the Galaunt' and 'Newport the Riche'. Nevertheless, the islanders' plea in parliament that Henry Bruyn be retained as lieutenant and steward of the island was rejected by the king, partly perhaps because Newport was an influential courtier.[157] The danger increased after the fall of France, and from the autumn of 1450 the government's attention was focussed intently on the Isle of Wight, where a small company was mustered to defend Carisbrooke castle; it was placed on a five-day footing under one of the king's serjeants-at-arms, John Baker.[158]

On the mainland of the realm, the government had formerly contented itself with the periodic repair of castles like Bristol and Gloucester, and with the gathering of arms and artillery that might be used for expeditions as well as for home defence.[159] But with the prospect of total defeat opening before it during 1449, more major and urgent steps were taken from September onwards. During the ensuing two years and more, commissions of array were issued with some regularity and in various parts of the country, so that sufficient armed, able-bodied men could be made available in the localities to repel the invader. These commissions were naturally most frequent in the southern counties: in Hampshire, where Southampton and Portsmouth, as well as the Isle of Wight, provided an *entrée* to the realm; in Somerset, at the head of the Bristol channel where an enemy fleet might penetrate to the Somerset ports and perhaps even to Bristol; in Norfolk, which was open to attack from the Burgundian Low Countries; in the Thames estuary and the approaches to London; and in Kent, gateway to Calais.[160] On 7 October 1450, immediately after the arrival of the duke of York in the north of the principality, south Wales was similarly alerted.[161] The Cornish peninsula, with its notorious propensity for piracy and maritime self-indulgence, presented an additional problem; on 16 August 1451, therefore, the sale of arms there to any enemy was forbidden.[162] All in all, an elaborate scheme of defence and communication was devised, with men keeping watch and ward in each of these coastal counties, presumably in touch with one another and with the king's officers, partly by means of the beacons that were ordered to be erected.

These efforts may have deterred attackers, but they could not remove the fears. That these were well justified is illustrated by the French attack on Queenborough (Isle of Sheppey) in April 1450, and by the sack by French and Norman night-raiders of the Essex port of Harwich, which regretted that it did not enjoy the protection of stone walls. On 24 March 1452, the construction of better defences for Harwich was belatedly authorized, to be financed by the free export of cloth from Ipswich by four of Harwich's merchants; the building operations were placed under the supervision of the earl of Oxford, himself an Essex landowner, and Sir Thomas Tyrell, a noted soldier who was also from Essex.[163] Further precautions of a similar nature were taken in the summer, when repairs were made at Rochester and Leeds castles and at the royal manor of Havering (Essex).[164]

Englishmen's apprehension was heightened by the insecurity at sea caused by pirates. Apart from those of foreign provenance, it seems likely that a number of commissioned English captains were prepared to take advantage of a royal licence or a tour of duty in the king's service to feather their own nests by capturing or plundering merchant vessels on the high seas. Hence, some of the raids by Frenchmen and others on the English coast may have been in the nature of reprisals, for Queenborough seems to have harboured a veritable nest of English pirates, rivalling the narrow creeks of Devon and Cornwall.[165] One of the most famous exploits, which stimulated the pride and fired the imagination of contemporaries, was conducted by Robert Winnington, who had been retained with Clifton and Iden in April 1449 on sea-keeping duties. He appears to have left the main force and, while lying in wait for a Breton fleet, fell in with

a flotte of a c. grete schyppys of Pruse, Lubycke, Campe, Rastocke, Holond, Selond, and Flandres, betwyte Garnyse and Portland; and then I cam abord the Admirall, and bade them stryke in the Kyngys name of Englond, and they bade me skyte in the Kyngs name of Englond; and then I and my feleschyp sayd, but he wyll streke don the sayle, that I wyld over sayle ham by the grace of God, and God wyll send me wynd and wether; and dey bade me do my wurst, by cause I had so fewe schyppys and so smale, that they scornyd with me. And as God wuld, on Fryday last was, we had a gode wynd, and then we armyd to the number of ij. m^1. men in my felyschyp, and made us redy for to over sayle them; and then they lonchyd a bote, and sette up a stondert of truesse, and com and spake with me. And ther they were yolded all the hundret schyppys to go with me in what port that me lust and my felawys; but they faothe with me the day before, and schotte atte us a j. m^1. gonnys, and quarell owte of number, and have slayn meny of my felyschyp, and meymyd all soo. Wherfor me thyngkyt that they haye forfett bothe schypps and godys at our Soverayn Lord the Kyngys wyll . . .

Such actions were not in the interest of the king or of the commercial community, for some of the ships seized by Winnington belonged to the powerful Hanseatic league, whose good will was highly valued by English governments of every hue. Yet Winnington, after he had reported his exploit to the English squadron's organizer, Thomas Daniel, and to the chancellor and other councillors, received considerable sympathy from some of the council and from certain members of the king's household, whereas the merchant community had to bear the brunt of the reprisals which the Hanse predictably took.[166]

What was lacking in the ability of the Lancastrian government to protect the realm in these difficult years was not the will, nor even the imagination, to do so, but rather adequate resources. Defence of the realm was an acknowledged obligation imposed on the king's subjects and extraordinary parliamentary taxation was accordingly granted for this purpose in many crises. In the past, when England's protection was best achieved by offensives on the continent, this customary justification had been interpreted generously; now, in the parliament meeting at Leicester in 1450, the commons could give sharper point to their monetary grants. They nominated a commission of four – Sir William Lucy, Sir Thomas Tyrell, Sir James Strangways, and Richard Waller, who between them could boast an impressive record of military and royal service – to act as receivers and treasurers of the new graduated estate tax so that the proceeds could be handed directly to the captains and soldiers engaged in the realm's defence.[167] A renewed subsidy on householders and non-householders of foreign origin in 1453 was likewise intended for the 'tuition' and defence of the realm.[168] Thus, inadequate though the king's customary resources might be, and difficult the collection of new taxes, the commons at least attempted to make their contribution to combating the threat.

Their most novel expedient of all was devised in 1453. When parliament met in March, the gravity of the crisis at sea and in Gascony resulted in a grant to the king of a force of 20,000 archers for half a year, to be deployed as he thought fit at four months' notice. It was to be raised from the cities, boroughs, towns, and villages of the kingdom, including franchises like Cheshire and Wales that were famed for their archers' skill. It amounted to a concerted and co-ordinated commission of array throughout the realm, replacing the localized measures of previous years; and it would rely not on the traditional obligation of unpaid service in defence of king and kingdom, but on a series of wage-contracts supervised by officers appointed by Henry VI. Although the size of the projected army proved a useful bargaining weapon in financial negotiations with the commons, its conception proves that the threat to the realm was clearly appreciated in 1453.[169] One month after the original grant on 28 March, it was reduced by 7,000, though each of the remaining 13,000 archers would, when called on, be paid 6*d*. a day from contributions raised by local officials; their captains would be appointed by Henry himself. Soon afterwards, even the arraying of this reduced complement was deferred as fear of invasion was overshadowed by concern for the fate of Gascony. As a result, the commons agreed instead to finance a new expedition to the duchy to take precedence over the needs of domestic defence which the archers had originally been designed to meet. Henry VI, in return, agreed to delay for two years any summons of the 13,000 men and then would lead them in person – unless a sufficiently grave crisis in the meantime demanded their earlier assembly at three months' notice. Within a few short months, the king himself was seriously ill.

Not since the late fourteenth century had England's coastal communities experienced the ravages of raids, the fright of surprise attack, and the alarm of invasion. Most of the measures taken by the government were traditional ones, though by 1449 something more was required in default of the royal fleet which no longer existed. Powers of command, punishment, and general discipline were formulated and conferred on commanders who were virtual royal lieutenants at sea, and, as in so many other spheres of administration in these years, the king looked to his own companions and household servants for the men he needed. Henry's own initiative in these matters, though difficult to detect, may not therefore have been as inconsequential as has been supposed; but it must be admitted that no successor was appointed in 1452 to succeed the household official Richard Clevedon as keeper of the king's ships.[170]

Notes

1 Above, p. 162.
2 Nicholson, op. cit., pp. 325ff; W. C. Dickinson, *Scotland from the earliest times to 1603*, ed. A. A. M. Duncan (Oxford, 1977), pp. 226-8.
3 Bain, IV, 228; *Foedera*, V, i, 47-50.
4 ibid., 132; *CCR, 1441–47*, p. 221; Bain, IV, 238. For the truces of July, September, and November 1449, August 1451, and May 1453, see ibid., 245-8, 251-2, 255-6; *Foedera*, V, ii, 10-11, 14-19, 47-52.
5 Bain, IV, 228ff, 239. But care was taken to prohibit the export of weapons and armour to Scotland (ibid., p. 235 [14 May 1441]).
6 ibid., IV, 246; Nicholson, op. cit., pp. 329-30. Cf. also at Newcastle upon Tyne in August 1451 (Bain, IV, 251; *Foedera*, V, i, 16-19). These claims had been brought to Henry VI's attention by the secret agent and chronicler John Hardyng (*CPR, 1436–42*, p. 431).
7 *Foedera*, V, i, 15, 51-2; Bain, IV, 247. Cf. in May 1453 (ibid., p. 256). For the extent and origin of the 'debateable land' between the rivers Sark and Esk, see W. M. MacKenzie, 'The Debateable Land', *ScotHR*, XXX (1951), 109-25 with a map on p. 112.
8 Storey, *EHR*, LXXII (1957), 605, 613-14.
9 Above, pp. 203-5.
10 Storey, *EHR*, LXXII (1957), 605, 614; idem, *TCWAS*, new ser., LV (1955), 125-7; R. G. Davies, thesis, III, clxxvi-clxxix.
11 PRO, E403/732-50 passim; 767 m.l. In all, tallies worth £1,507 were issued in the bishop's favour while he was treasurer; very few of them had proved uncashable by the end of 1453 (ibid., 765-75).
12 Storey, *EHR*, LXXII (1957), 605; PRO, E28/63/40. This petition was sponsored before the council by Bishop Aiscough. Salisbury had already been warden of the west march from 1420 to 1435.
13 Storey, *EHR*, LXXII (1957), 605, 614. The Mowbray estates were in Gloucester's care during John's minority (*DNB*, XXXIX, 223).
14 *PPC*, V, 75, 90, 100; above, p. 173. Grey may have acted as Norfolk's lieutenant in 1437-38; he was certainly appointed chamberlain and customer at Berwick on 16 February 1437 (PRO, E28/74/6).
15 Storey, *EHR*, LXXII (1957), 614. Ogle was sheriff of his home shire of Northumberland in 1437-38 (*List of sheriffs*, p. 98).
16 Storey, *EHR*, LXXII (1957), 604-5; Bain, IV, 230; above, p. 161. He was still drawing assignments two decades later for his unpaid wages (e.g., PRO, E 403/793 m. 13 [20 July 1453]). It may have been one of the benefits of having Bishop Lumley as treasurer that on 18 July 1447 a payment of £3,709 was authorized to Northumberland (PRO, E 403/767 m. 11).

Moreover, the amount of uncashed tallies in the hands of wardens of the east march that were exchanged at the exchequer for other (presumably more reliable) ones was far greater during Lumley's treasurership than at any comparable period in Henry VI's reign. Cf. above, p. 378.

17 Storey, *EHR*, LXXII (1957), 614 and n. 4. The first commission was settled on 14 July 1439.

18 ibid., 614 n. 4; *CPR, 1446–52*, p. 374. Between Michaelmas 1448 and Michaelmas 1450, £5,232 had been forthcoming from the exchequer instead of £7,500, and this aside from the fact that a substantial proportion of it proved difficult to collect (PRO, E 403/774, 775, 778, 779). The clerk of works at Berwick, Roxburgh, and Carlisle similarly received only £100 of the £400 allocated to him during 1442–49 (*King's works*, II, 570).

19 Storey, *EHR*, LXXII (1957), 605-6, 614.

20 *CPR, 1446–52*, pp. 184, 335; *CCR, 1447–54*, p. 149; PRO, E403/751-75 passim. For the unusual nature of the assurances of payment given to Salisbury in 1450, see *RP*, V, 347. Cf. his grant of £333 in March 1452 to cover various additional expenses as warden (*CPR, 1446–52*, p. 520).

21 PRO, E403/750 m. 3; *RP*, V, 205. On 14 September 1444 his indenture was extended to sixteen years.

22 *CPR, 1441–46*, p. 390 (19 November 1445); ibid., *1446–52*, p. 138 (1 February 1448); Bain, IV, 241 (22 November 1445).

23 PRO, E403/750-74. Lumley exchanged for Fauconberg 31 tallies issued between 19 February 1444 and 19 July 1446 (ibid., 767 m. 10). Cf. above, p. 378.

24 *GEC*, V, 281-5; d'Escouchy, I, 166. He was captured (and almost killed) when Pont de l'Arche fell to Charles VII's forces.

25 *RP*, V, 205.

26 *CPR, 1446–52*, p. 496; *CCR, 1447–54*, p. 291.

27 *PPC*, VI, 146; above, p. 387.

28 Storey, *End of Lancaster*, ch. VII, VIII. For the Percy and Neville retainers, see Bean, *Percies*, pp. 91-4, 106-7; A. J. Pollard, 'The northern retainers of Richard Neville, earl of Salisbury', *Northern Hist.*, XI (1976), 52-69. For the Nevilles' earlier close connection with Durham priory, see Dobson, *Durham priory*, pp. 184-91. For 2 additional indentures between Salisbury and Sir James Strangways (1446) and Sir Ralph Greystoke (1447), see NorthantsRO, FitzWilliam MS 2051-2.

29 *CPR, 1436–41*, p. 185 (13 July 1438).

30 ibid., *1441–46*, p. 183.

31 *CFR, 1435–41*, p. 157. Cf. PRO, E28/70/45 (May 1442).

32 *CPR, 1436–41*, pp. 190, 270; *Brut*, pp. 472-3. For complaints from Northumberland about Scottish depredations in about 1437, 1440, and 1445, see PRO, SC8/128/6373; E28/63/22; SC8/198/9861.

33 *CPR, 1441–46*, p. 403. The nearby coastal settlement of Newton was also desolate, probably for the same reason (ibid., *1446–52*, p. 239 [6 April 1449]).

34 A. A. Cardew, 'A study of society in the Anglo-Scottish borders, 1455–1502' (St Andrews PhD thesis, 1974), pp. 40, 47, 42-4; Bain, IV, 227; Dobson, *Durham priory*, pp. 146-8, 316-27 (with the quotation from John de Fordun's *Scotichronicon* on pp. 319-20).

35 R. B. Dobson, 'The last English monks on Scottish soil' *ScotHR*, XLVI

(1967), esp. pp. 3-6 (with the quotation on p. 5); idem, *Durham priory*, pp. 316-27.

36 *CPR, 1436–41*, p. 379. Nevertheless, the government continued to insist on the payment of customs dues at Berwick (ibid., *1441–46*, p. 368 [30 May 1445]).

37 *CPR, 1446–52*, p. 183 (commissions to repair Berwick, Roxburgh, and Carlisle castles and towns, 27 July 1448).

38 ibid., p. 508.

39 Duke of Roxburghe MSS in *HMC*, XIV, appendix, pt. 3, p. 10 (December 1454); T. Stapleton (ed.), *The Plumpton correspondence* (Camden Soc., 1839), pp. liv-lv.

40 Nicholson, op. cit., pp. 340-5; Duncan, op. cit., p. 228. The queen-mother's second husband, Sir James Stewart, the 'Black Knight of Lorne', fled to England in the autumn of 1445 (Bain, IV, 240).

41 De Beaucourt, op. cit., III, 320 and n. 4. By the time the marriage took place on 30 October 1442, the bridegroom was duke of Brittany. For Scotsmen in France, see A. I. Dunlop, *Scots abroad in the fifteenth century* (1942), pp. 4-9 (including the striking example of Sir William Monypenny), and for the select Scottish corps among the king's life guards, created in 1445, P. Contamine, *Guerre, état et société à la fin du moyen âge* (Paris, 1972), pp. 294, 400, 457-8.

42 De Beaucourt, op. cit., IV, 180-1, 365-6, 369-70; Stevenson, I, 194-6. For Frederick III, whose suit was strongly supported by the duchess of Burgundy, see Register house, Edinburgh, treaties with the Empire, Burgundy, etc., no. 2, calendared in C. Macrae, 'Scotland and the wars of the roses' (Oxford DPhil thesis, 1939), pp. 566-7 (20 April 1445).

43 James had been pressing Charles VII on the matter of a suitable bride since the beginning of 1448. De Beaucourt, op. cit., IV, 367, 370-1; Stevenson, I, 197-8, 221-3, 239-40; Vaughan, op. cit., pp. 111-12; Bodl, Carte MS vol. 90, f. 4v-6, calendared in Macrae, thesis, pp. 567-8 (6 May 1448). The Breton treaty is in Register house, Edinburgh, treaties with France, no. 13, noticed in Macrae, thesis, pp. 119-21.

44 Quoted in ibid., pp. 124-5.

45 *CPR, 1446–52*, p. 183; Christie, op. cit., p. 384; 'Benet's Chron.', p. 195 n. 99; Giles, p. 35. As he came south, 'the voice of people blessed him' (Bodl. MS 857 f. 1v).

46 Giles, p. 35; Flenley, pp. 123-4.

47 ibid.; Macrae, thesis, pp. 127-30, 454-60. The Auchinleck chronicle (as in ibid., pp. 127, 130) estimates the English army at 6,000, those taken prisoner at 500, and the dead at 1,500; it also claims that the Scots lost only 26. Cf. 'Benet's Chron.', p. 194, and Giles, p. 35. This may have been the occasion when the estates of Carlisle cathedral priory were ravaged, houses burned, servants kidnapped, and produce stolen (*CPR, 1446–52*, p. 228). For the efforts of the border gentry in resisting the Scots, see Stevenson, I, 491 (3 April 1449).

48 *CPR, 1446–52*, p. 238; 'Benet's Chron.', p. 194 (which puts the size of his force at 30,000). Flenley, pp. 123-4, adopts a more enthusiastic attitude to Salisbury's engagement.

49 ibid., p. 125.

50 Giles, p. 35.

51 *PPC*, VI, 65-6.

52 Stevenson, I, 491; *Foedera*, V, ii, 9 (3 April 1449), reproduced in Macrae, thesis, pp. 493-4. See also *HMC, Beverley MSS*, pp. 163-4, for the expenses of soldiers sent to Scotland in the first half of 1449.

53 For the negotiations of July, September, and November 1449, see Bain, IV, 245-8; *Foedera*, V, ii, 10-11, 12-19. For further extensions, for three years from 15 August 1451 and for four years from 21 May 1453, see ibid., 32-8, 47-52; Bain, IV, 250-2, 254-6. There is some evidence that the English negotiators in November 1449 tried unsuccessfully to secure a more permanent peace with Scotland (*PPC*, VI, 89: Macrae, thesis, pp. 145-7).

54 PRO, E403/778-93. Hence the attempt by letters patent in 1452–53 to assure Percy of his arrears (*CCR, 1447–54*, pp. 374, 392, 393).

55 Above, n. 53. The capture off Whitby on 5 November 1451 of a French delegation to the Scottish court – it included the Scottish émigré Sir William Monypenny (but not Pierre de Brézé and the Bastard of Orléans, as in *EHL*, p. 367, and *Chron. of London*, p. 137) – is a curious episode of no major significance (Flenley, p. 139; Bodl. Roll 5).

56 Stevenson, I, 299-306. For James's mounting debts by 1449–50, see A. L. Murray, 'The comptroller, 1425–1488', *ScotHR*, LII (1973), 5-6. The marked increase in the crown's landed wealth, by annexation and the vigorous exploitation of feudal rights, seems to have begun under James I; it partly explains the crown's turbulent relations with the Scottish nobility (C. Madden, 'Royal treatment of feudal casualties in late-mediaeval Scotland', ibid., LV [1976], 172-94 [especially 172, 192-3].

57 Henry VI had received Douglas with some state when he arrived in England on his return from Rome in February 1451 (Bain, IV, 249).

58 Nicholson, op. cit., pp. 361-2; Duncan, op. cit., pp. 230-1.

59 J. Raine (ed.), *The correspondence, etc., of Coldingham priory* (Surtees Soc., XII, 1841), p. 247, quoted in Dobson, *ScotHR*, XLVI (1967), 5.

60 Nicholls, op. cit., pp. 17-20, 44-8. The concern of many at the advance of Irish law may have been behind the plea to the king in August 1439 that any Irish who wanted to study English common law at the inns of court should be allowed to come to England (PRO, E28/62/91; 63/19). See also C. A. Empey and K. Simms, 'The ordinances of the White Earl and the problem of coign in the later middle ages', *PRIA*, LXXV, section C, no. 8 (1975), 163-4, for the place of Irish and Anglo-Norman practices in seignorial legislation.

61 Warner, op. cit., p. 37.

62 See, in general, Lydon, *Later middle ages*, ch. 5; idem, *The Lordship of Ireland in the middle ages* (Dublin, 1972), ch. IX.

63 Warner, op. cit., pp. 34-40; for the reference to Ormond, see ibid., p. 39. The brief comment on the *Libelle* by Lydon, *Later middle ages*, pp. 141-2, is marred by his belief that the tract was composed by Bishop Moleyns.

64 Lydon, *Later middle ages*, p. 130; idem, *Lordship of Ireland*, p. 259; PRO, E28/63/59; 62/28.

65 Griffith, *IHS*, II (1940–41), 376-97; above, p. 164. For other feuds and disorders, even involving senior ecclesiastics, see Nicholls, op. cit., pp. 100-1, 171, 174.

66 PRO, E28/62/28; *PPC*, V, 89-90; *CPR, 1436–41*, pp. 132, 184. For the archbishop, see Bernard, *PRIA*, XXV, section C (1919–20), 218-19.

67 *PPC*, V, 88; Otway-Ruthven, *Medieval Ireland*, p. 369. Welles is first noticed as lieutenant on 10 December 1437 (PRO, E403/730 m. 11).

68 *GEC*, XII, ii, 443-4; *DNB*, LX, 168; *CPR, 1436–41*, p. 151; Emden, *Oxford*, I, 379-80.
69 His indenture was formally sealed on 12 February 1438 (*CPR, 1436–41*, p. 140; PRO, E101/71/901; E404/54/161).
70 Griffiths, *Principality of Wales*, pp. 216-18; above, p. 65; *CPR, 1436–41*, pp. 197, 240. Thorndon's appointment as treasurer was confirmed on 6 January 1440 (ibid., p. 361).
71 *CCR, 1435–41*, p. 177; *CPR, 1436–41*, pp. 154, 198, 200. Chace travelled to Ireland at the same time (ibid., p. 153).
72 *CCR, 1435–41*, p. 255. Several licences were issued on 8 May 1439, allowing Irishmen, particularly clerics, to remain in England despite the recent measure (*CPR, 1436–41*, p. 281).
73 *PPC*, V, 317. For further complaints against him, see ibid., 327; below, p. 415. This phase in the Talbot – Ormond quarrel is dealt with by Griffith, *IHS*, II (1940–41), 385-91; Otway-Ruthven, *Medieval Ireland*, pp. 370-4.
74 ibid., pp. 370, 374.
75 Exasperation at the failure of the English exchequer to pay his salary is probably the reason for his premature resignation. Between 1437 and 1441, £4,168 was assigned to him instead of £6,667 – and that included a mere £113 in 1440–41 (PRO, E403/730-40 passim). He left office with £1,000 in March 1442; but he was still owed more than £2,000 and special arrangements were made in April for his future payment (ibid., 744 m. 14; *CPR, 1441–46*, p. 100). Some of his tallies were being reassigned in June 1448 (PRO, E403/771 m. 7).
76 ibid., 744 m. 14; *CPR, 1441–46*, p. 45; PRO, E404/58/121. Between 1442 and 1445, Ormond also tolerated a low rate of payment: he received £2,007 instead of £6,000, and some of this was in the form of uncashable tallies (PRO, E403/ 744-57 passim). He was assigned the usual lieutenant's retinue of 300 archers but was denied the authority to create peers of parliament (*PPC*, V, 184, March 1442).
77 J. Graves (ed.), *A roll of the proceedings of the king's council in Ireland* (RS, 1877), pp. 276-94; Griffith, *IHS*, II (1940-41), 386. There was undoubtedly some exaggeration in the charges against Ormond (Otway-Ruthven, *Medieval Ireland*, pp. 371-2).
78 *CPR, 1441–46*, p. 91. For a substantial grant in his favour on 3 June 1442, see ibid., p. 92.
79 *PPC*, V, 201, 203. The inquiry was to be held at Westminster in February 1443.
80 ibid., 321-4. For other accusations of Ormond's perversion of justice, see the petition of Richard Wogan, chancellor of Ireland in 1441–42 (*CPR, 1436–41*, p. 514; ibid., *1441–46*, p. 91).
81 ibid., pp. 58 (March 1442), 97 (April), 102 (June), 132 (November); *CCR, 1441–47*, p. 22 (March 1442). See also *CPR, 1441–46*, p. 358 (August 1445).
82 *CPR, 1436–41*, p. 548 (June 1441); ibid., *1441–46*, pp. 73 (June 1442), 91 (July 1442). Bernevale had been chief justice of the king's bench in Ireland since February 1435 (J. L. J. Hughes [ed.], *Patentee officers in Ireland, 1173–1826* [Dublin, 1960], p. 11).
83 Graves, op. cit., pp. 295-303; Griffith, *IHS*, II (1940–41), 386.
84 *PPC*, V, 325, 296. One may also assign to the early 1440s a 'lost' treatise by Archbishop Talbot 'on the abuse of rule of James, earl of Ormond while

he was lieutenant of Ireland' (Bernard, *PRIA*, XXXV, section C [1918–20], 222 n. 6).

85 *GEC*, X, 123-6; XI, 698-704.

86 *PPC*, V, 327. For Chevirs, see Hughes, op. cit., p. 26. It was unfortunate that the government licensed several great Anglo-Irish magnates to absent themselves from their lordships, while at the same time they continued to received their Irish revenues; Ormond, as a result, had few to oppose him (*CPR, 1441–46*, pp. 167 [Shrewsbury, March 1443], 273, 312 [York, November 1444]).

87 Otway-Ruthven, *Medieval Ireland*, p. 374; Griffith, *IHS*, II (1940-41), 388-9, 395-7 (where the accusations against Bernevale are taken from BL, Cotton, Titus B XI f. 1-41). It was recognized at Westminster in May 1444 that Thorndon had decided to leave Ireland for good, though he was allowed to retain Dublin and Wicklow castles (*CCR, 1441–47*, p. 92).

88 ibid., p. 104; *CPR, 1441–46*, pp. 7, 352.

89 ibid., p. 345; PRO, E403/762 m. 4; E404/61/138 (a copy of the indenture).

90 *CPR, 1441–46*, p. 351. He was evidently summoned to England to hear charges against him (PRO, C49/34/31/3).

91 Empey and Simms, *PRIA*, LXXV, section C, no. 8 (1975), 164, quoting PRO, E101/248/15. Shrewsbury's son John had married Elizabeth, Ormond's daughter, by March 1445 (Pollard, thesis, pp. 34, 134); the dowry included £300-worth of uncashed tallies issued to Ormond as lieutenant (Lydon, *Later middle ages*, p. 128). One wonders who had the last laugh!

92 *CPR, 1441–46*, p. 404; *PPC*, VI, 52; PRO, C49/34/31/4. The earl was increasingly concerned at the delay in hearing the charges (ibid., 34/31/1).

93 *PPC*, VI, 57; Bodl, Carte 30 f. 10. In his absence, the prior was expelled from his priory (*CPR, 1446–52*, pp. 46-7). The prior was indulgently supported by the exchequer during his stay (PRO, E403/760 m. 1, 12; 762 m. 2, 7; 765 m. 10 [£200 in all]); a further £100 was paid to him long after, in July 1448 (ibid., 771 m. 8). See also PRO, E28/74/19. For the court of the constable and marshal, see Lodge and Thornton, op. cit., pp. 254ff.

94 For Thorndon's connection with the prior before March 1444, see Otway-Ruthven, *Medieval Ireland*, p. 374. Other charges were levelled by Edmund Brian (PRO, C49/34/31/3; E403/771 m. 6).

95 'Benet's Chron.', p. 192; *Great Chron.*, p. 178; Flenley, pp. 118-19; *Brut*, pp. 487, 510-11.

96 The prior's representative had to be taught the passage of arms appropriate to such a trial by a London fishmonger (PRO, E403/767 m. 10). The trial itself seems to have been placed in the jurisdiction of the steward of the household (PRO, E403/774 m. 6), and in December 1446 the prior was in the custody of the duke of Norfolk, presumably as earl marshal of England (ibid., 765 m. 10).

97 Flenley, pp. 118-19; PRO, C49/34/31/2. The clerics were led by the heads of the Dublin monasteries and the dean of Dublin.

98 Emden, *Cambridge*, p. 652. *Brut*, p. 487, wrongly states that the prior failed to turn up and was therefore convicted. Lydon, *Later middle ages*, p. 137, is probably equally mistaken in believing that Ormond failed to appear and that, therefore, the prior won his case.

99 'Benet's Chron.', p. 192; Flenley, p. 122; *CPR, 1446–52*, p. 255. The reversionary grant to the prior in June 1447 of Archbishop Talbot's lands

smacks of a reward for services rendered (ibid., p. 38). He also received the king's protection in March 1447 (ibid., pp. 46-7).

100 *CPR, 1441–46*, pp. 410, 455; ibid., *1446–52*, pp. 4, 6. For John Talbot's association with his uncle, the archbishop, in one of the latter's grants, see ibid., p. 56 (13 June 1447).

101 ibid., *1441–46*, p. 448.

102 ibid., pp. 424, 457. This John Wenlock (of Someries, Beds.) must be distinguished from his namesake (of Blackmere, Salop) who, coincidentally, was a servant of Shrewsbury, his heir, and his wife (Roskell, *Beds. Hist. Record Soc.*, XXXVIII [1958], 12 n. 19, 23-4). Later in the year, Nicholas Arthur, who had been made constable of Limerick castle with Archbishop Talbot's blessing in September 1445, was confirmed in office (*CPR, 1446–52*, p. 4).

103 ibid., *1441–46*, p. 455.

104 Otway-Ruthven, *Medieval Ireland*, p. 375. He was at Trim on 17 May 1447 (*CPR, 1446–52*, p. 217).

105 *PPC*, VI, 89; *CPR, 1446–52*, p. 185, though *PPC*, VI, 92, implies that his term began at Michaelmas 1449. In a letter, dated 3 April, to his 'cousin' ordering him to go to Ireland, Henry VI stated that it was the recipient's own desire to go (PRO, E28/59/59). Though the year 1439 has been assigned to this document, it may more suitably be placed in 1449, with the recipient as the duke of York, Henry's blood cousin.

106 Otway-Ruthven, *Medieval Ireland*, pp. 375, 378-9. York's plan to send Ormond independently to Ireland as his deputy was not well received by the king in April 1449 because it might rekindle the disorder associated with the Ormond – Talbot feud (PRO, E28/59/59 [for which see above, n. 105]). For York's close links with Ormond's son and Shrewsbury, see below, pp. 670, 672; Rosenthal, 'Estates and finances of York', pp. 180, 190.

107 Below, p. 508; Otway-Ruthven, *Medieval Ireland*, p. 379.

108 PRO, E403/762 m. 4, 11, 13; 767 m. 7; 769 m. 6. Shrewsbury's value as a military commander to Henry VI's government is reflected in its efforts to pay the debts arising from his tour of duty in Ireland: £1,300 in 1448 and a further £1,900 between February 1450 and August 1451, apart from some reassigned tallies (ibid., 769-85 passim).

109 *CPR, 1446–52*, p. 132.

110 Otway-Ruthven, *Medieval Ireland*, pp. 379, 381-2.

111 *CPR, 1446–52*, p. 467.

112 ibid., p. 494 (25 September 1451).

113 PRO, E28/59/59; *CPR, 1446–52*, pp. 227, 238; Lydon, *Lordship of Ireland*, pp. 267-8. York was still at Denbigh on 6 June 1449 (BirmPL, Hagley Hall 25/407/351404).

114 *CPR, 1446–52*, p. 167; *RP*, V, 166. A further confirmation of 10 November 1451 allowed him to depute his kinsman, Thomas Talbot, the new prior of Kilmainham, to act as chancellor for him (*CPR, 1446–52*, p. 560).

115 Otway-Ruthven, *Medieval Ireland*, pp. 379-81. See, for details, E. Curtis, 'Richard, duke of York, as viceroy of Ireland, 1447–1460', *JRSAI*, LXII (1932), 165-73. See briefly J. L. Gillespie, 'Richard, duke of York as king's lieutenant in Ireland', *The Ricardian*, V, no. 69 (1980), 194-201.

116 Below, pp. 674-6.

117 PRO, E403/774 m. 7; 778 m. 6; *PPC*, VI, 89. But during the embarrassment of the attack on the court in the winter of 1450–51, York's original

appointment as lieutenant was confirmed (11 February 1451) (Otway-Ruthven, *Medieval Ireland*, p. 385).

118 PRO, E28/79/3. On the other hand, for his building activities at Trim, which seems to have been a favourite residence, see Curtis, *JRSAI*, LXII (1932), 173.

119 Griffiths, *JMH*, I (1975), 195-6.

120 ibid.; *RP*, V, 255 (1454).

121 Otway-Ruthven, *Medieval Ireland*, p. 382. Ormond was retained by York for life in July 1450, and was left by him as deputy in Ireland, a responsibility he discharged with some vigour in the west and centre of Ireland (*Cal. Ormond deeds*, III, 167-8; Flenley, p. 135). His indenture as York's deputy and as 'captain and governor of the king's wars' in Ireland, 22 August 1450, is Bodl, Eng. hist. c. 34.

122 *CPR, 1452–61*, pp. 75, 102. He was married to the sister of the duke of Somerset, and his appointment was evidently against York's wishes (below, p. 672).

123 Rosenthal, 'Estates and finances of York', pp. 180, 190; R. Virgoe, 'The Cambridgeshire election of 1439', *BIHR*, XLVI (1973), 97, 99-100.

124 Rawcliffe, op. cit., pp. 79-80; *GEC*, X, 123-6.

125 *CPR, 1452–61*, pp. 82, 102, 120; PRO, E403/793 m. 9. Wiltshire, in fact, never visited Ireland as lieutenant (Otway-Ruthven, *Medieval Ireland*, pp. 385-6).

126 Richmond, *History*, LII (1967), 1.

127 C. F. Richmond, 'Royal administration and the keeping of the seas, 1422–1485' (Oxford DPhil thesis, 1962), pp. 94ff; M. E. Meehan, 'English piracy, 1450–1500' (Bristol MA thesis, 1971), pp. 118, 143ff, 176-7.

128 Stevenson, II, ii, 582-3 (1435), 588 (1440).

129 Warner, op. cit., ll. 21, 22-8, 858-63, 1092-9.

130 Capgrave, op. cit., p. 134, translated in Richmond, *History*, LII (1967), 1-2. This work was composed in 1446–47: P. J. Lucas, 'John Capgrave, O. S. A. (1393–1464), scribe and "publisher"', *Trans. Cambridge Bibliog. Soc.*, V (1969–71), 2 n. 4.

131 *CPR, 1436–41*, p. 369 (October 1439); Richmond, thesis, pp. 74ff.

132 Turner, op. cit., p. 44; Oppenheim, op. cit., p. 23; Richmond, *History*, XLIX (1964), 291.

133 Wedgwood, *Biographies*, p. 785.

134 PRO, E28/66/25; E404/57/323; E403/739 m. 17; Richmond, *History*, XLIX (1964), 296-7, with Speke's indenture of 26 May and associated documents noted from PRO, E101/53/30.

135 PRO, E403/744 m. 6.

136 *RP*, V, 52. For the unusual number of safe-conducts issued between 1435 and 1440, see Meehan, thesis, p. 12.

137 Wedgwood, *Biograhies*, pp. 782-3; Richmond, thesis, pp. 76-82.

138 *RP*, V, 55, 59; *CPR, 1441–47*, p. 108.

139 Wedgwood, *Biographies*, pp. 306, 804-5, 446-7, 692-3; PRO, E28/70/62; *PPC*, V, 190-1; *CCR, 1441–47*, p. 113.

140 PRO, E28/70/63, 66; *RP*, V, 59.

141 *PPC*, V, 191, 198; *CPR, 1441–46*, p. 105; PRO, E28/70/75; E403/745 m. 5, 6; E404/58/170-71; E101/71/911 (Popham's indenture of service). Even so, the fleet did not in fact muster until 13 September (Richmond, *History*, LII [1967], 6 n. 25).

142 *London Chrons.*, pp. 149-50. On the issue roll under May–June (*sic*) 1442, £2,548 was assigned them (PRO, E403/745 m. 5, 6), but even in February 1446 Popham, who had since died, had still not been fully paid. *CPR, 1441–46*, p. 407.

143 *PPC*, V, 236 (March 1443); PRO, E28/73/7 (May 1443).

144 *PPC*, V, 98; *CPR, 1436–41*, pp. 392, 399.

145 *RP*, V, 18.

146 *CPR, 1436–41*, p. 409; *CCR, 1435–41*, p. 324.

147 *PPC*, V, 418 (n. d.). This request may be linked with the commission of array issued to coastal and southern shires early in March 1443 (ibid., 235; *CPR, 1441–46*, p. 199). For French attacks on Sussex before 16 June 1443, see PRO, E28/73/51.

148 ibid., 71/18.

149 *HMC*, VIII (1881), part 1, p. 267. It is true that the *Grace Dieu* was being rebuilt in June 1446 (*CPR, 1441–46*, p. 432; above, p. 425). The obligation of the Cinque ports to supply 59 ships for 15 days' service was hardly suitable for patrolling the seas, and Rye at least was no longer capable of making its contribution (*CPR, 1446–52*, p. 276). The 26 vessels provided in the winter of 1444–45 was almost the last instance of the obligation at work (Oppenheim, op. cit., p. 26).

150 *RP*, V, 142; Myers, *BIHR*, LI (1978), 81-2; Griffiths, *HLQ*, XLII (1979), 181-91.

151 *CPR, 1446–52*, pp. 270, 265, 271. Daniel was given £250 on 29 July for a large quantity of weapons (PRO, E403/775 m. 9). For these men, see Wedgwood, *Biographies*, pp. 194-5 (Clifton, who was deputy-warden of the Cinque ports in 1449), 353-5 (Daniel); Jeffs, thesis, pp. 283-4 (Clifton), 304 (Iden), 285-7 (Daniel).

152 PRO, E403/774 m. 18; 775 m. 1; 778 m. 16; E404/65/130, 145; Stevenson, I, 516-17. Sandwich agreed to provide a ship for Clifton's fleet in May for 4 months (KentRO, Sa AC 1 f. 75*v*).

153 *CPR, 1446–52*, pp. 540, 579; *PPC*, V, 119, 122-3. Henry never, of course, went to Calais.

154 *CPR, 1446–52*, p. 562; *CCR, 1447–54*, p. 360; PRO, E404/68/149 (Shrewsbury's indenture of service). £2,000 was assigned to the earl and his men on 18 July 1452 (PRO, E403/788 m. 5).

155 *CPR, 1446–52*, p. 583; ibid., *1452–61*, p. 78; PRO, E404/68/144-45; E403/788 m. 4. For Sir Edward Hull, a knight of the body and constable of Bordeaux until his death at Castillon, see Wedgwood, *Biographies*, pp. 481-2; Jeffs, thesis, pp. 299-301. Lord Roos agreed to raise at his own cost a small fleet in the East Anglian ports for the protection of the sea-lanes nearby (*CPR, 1452–61*, p. 55; PRO, E404/69/212).

156 *CPR, 1452–61*, p. 55; ibid., *1446–52*, p. 585; PRO, E404/68/160. The muster of Nanfan's force should have taken place on 9 August, for which he was paid £296 on 18 July for the first 3 months of his half-yearly contract (PRO, E403/788 m. 5). See Wedgwood, *Biographies*, pp, 621-2; Jeffs, thesis, pp. 309-11.

157 *RP*, V, 204. For Bruyn, see Wedgwood, *Biographies*, p. 127; and for Newport, ibid., pp. 630-1.

158 *CPR, 1446–52*, p. 445. John Baker's indenture for 20 men ran from 18 October 1450 to at least Michaelmas 1452; the master of the king's ordnance, Thomas Vaughan, provided weapons early in October 1450

(PRO, E403/783 m. 1; 785 m. 14; 786 m. 6; 791 m. 7; 793 m. 15; Stevenson, II, ii, 474-5).

159 *CPR, 1446–52*, pp. 42, 172, 228.

160 ibid., pp. 316, 319, 379, 381, 383, 389, 442, 477. See also ibid, pp. 480. (Cornwall), 540 (Sussex), 582 (Isle of Wight).

161 ibid., p. 432.

162 ibid., p. 480. For a French landing near Teignmouth in 1451, see DevonRO, Exeter receivers' account 13 (1450–51).

163 *CPR, 1446–52*, p. 528; Flenley, p. 129. For Tyrell, see Wedgwood, *Biographies*, pp. 891-2; Jeffs, thesis, pp. 329-30.

164 *CPR, 1446–52*, p. 570.

165 Richmond, *History*, XLIX (1964), 295.

166 ibid., 295-6; Gairdner, *PL*, II, 104-5 (for the quotation). See also Postan in *English trade*, pp. 127-9. Winnington may have been licensed to capture whatever ships he could, for the most prominent landowners of Devon were instructed on 3 April to aid him in 'the clensing of the [sea] and rebukyng of the robbeurs and pirates therof', and he was not paid any money by the exchequer; but the attack on the Bay fleet can hardly have been the precise objective, as Winnington's lengthy explanation to Daniel and the council indicates (Stevenson, I, 489). Cf. the report of the Prussian agent, Hans Winter, for the implication of Daniel and Trevilian in another attack on Prussian ships in 1450 (G. von der Ropp [ed.], *Hanserecesse, 1431–76* [7 vols., Leipzig, 1876–92], II, iii, nos. 647, 669-70).

167 *RP*, V, 172. The wealthy were felt to be the only remaining section of the community capable of being burdened with further demands for cash. For these 4 men, see Wedgwood, *Biographies*, pp. 559-60, 891-2, 820, 915-16; *DNB*, LIX, 130-1 (Waller); Jeffs, thesis, 305-6 (Lucy), 329-30 (Tyrell).

168 *RP*, V, 230. For the concern for defence in the parliaments between 1449 and 1451, see ibid., 142, 144, 172, 210, 214, 216.

169 ibid., pp. 231-3.

170 Richmond, *History*, LII (1967), 7-8.

17 The Fall of Lancastrian France – I

The duke of Orléans and the search for peace, 1437–40

The death of the duke of Bedford on 15 September 1435 and the calamities that followed it – notably, the invasion of the Ile de France and the fall of Paris to Charles VII on 13 April 1436, and the alarming disorders in Normandy itself – did much to convince an influential section of opinion in England that to continue offensive operations in northern France, with the ultimate aim of conquering the kingdom, was out of the question. This view was shared by the young king who, moreover, harboured a sincere, Christian revulsion at the further shedding of blood in his name in a 'werre that longe hath contynued and endured, that is to saye, an hundreth yeares and more'.[1] The clearest revelation of the king's feelings came at the beginning of 1440, when the decision to release Charles, duke of Orléans was finally taken in an effort to promote peace.[2] A declaration was then formally issued by the council on the orders of King Henry himself, and it stated explicitly that what the king 'hath doen in the saide mater he hath doen of hymself and of his owen advis and courrage . . . moeved and stured by God and of raison . . .' Among the factors which he listed to justify his quest for peace by means of the duke's release was 'the first, bigynnyng at God and that toucheth Goddes worship, whose ministre he [i.e., the king] is, and by whom he regneth kyng', for Henry was outraged at the scandal of a divided church which the Anglo-French conflict merely served to perpetuate.

The killing and destruction, and the consequent impoverishment of France, deeply distressed Henry, while the more practical problems of war, particularly the relentless financial strain on the resources of England and northern France, strengthened his conviction that some kind of arrangement with Charles VII, either temporary or (preferably) permanent, was essential in order to bring the fighting to an end.[3] In his statement of 1440, Henry enlisted what was said to have been the eventual opinion of both Edward III and Henry V (and no stouter support could be envisaged for the king's views) that the material, financial, and human burden of the war pointed unmistakably in the direction of peace, 'what for the unlyklyhode of the conqueryng of the royaume of Fraunce by the werre, whiche is so ample, so greet and so mighty' in the number and strength of its defences. During the minority, everything possible had been done to stabilize Lancastrian rule in France,

> as wele in sending over of personnes, suche as for the tyme of thoo that might and wolde be entreated were thought moost bihovefull for the saide gouvernance with as gode and notable instruccions and advis putte in writing and yeven, as couth to thayme be thought for the tyme or conceyved, as in sending thider from tyme to tyme notable puissance of men and not oonly men, but also grete and notable sommes of money and goode.

It was all to no avail, and the king was bitterly aware

> that the kynges cuntre there, namely the duchie of Normandie that longe hath souffred such wrongs and borne them with suche charges as some royaumes might nat have borne and endured, is nowe broughte to that myschief and extreme miserye that unneth thoo that ben left therinne may pourly lyve.[4]

An accommodation between the two kings would, strictly speaking, imply that both would rule in France in the future. This fundamental concession was ultimately unavoidable in the absence of a decisive English victory or a comprehensive English surrender. But even Henry VI found it difficult to contemplate that, for it would involve conceding rights and territory which were regarded as his undoubted inheritance and had been hard won by his revered father.

The failure of the congress of Arras in 1435 was a serious blow to those who had hoped to negotiate a lasting peace to England's advantage; yet, even with Bedford dead, the triumphantly successful defence of Calais against the treacherous Burgundians reinforced the belief that it was perfectly feasible to hold on to substantial parts of France. Accordingly, the years immediately following the abortive congress witnessed, on the one hand, a renewed effort to agree terms with Charles that would also embrace Brittany, England's uncertain ally, and Burgundy, now reconciled with the Valois; and, on the other, a determination to sustain the Lancastrian armies and governors in France.[5] As far as negotiations were concerned, the government believed that it had a cardinal asset at its disposal in the person of Orléans, who had been a prisoner in England since 1415. The captive duke became, therefore, the focus for discussions between English, French, and other envoys in the late 1430s. Henry and his council hoped that he might personally ease the way towards agreement if he were released, though the extent of his influence with a Valois king he can scarcely have known and who distrusted him, and with a French nobility that had learned to live without him for more than twenty years, may be doubted.[6] Be that as it may, proposals of peace emanated from all sides during 1437–39, and they included the suggestion that Orléans be taken to Cherbourg in the Cotentin peninsula as a contribution to the reopening of negotiations. The duke of Brittany, who was always reluctant to choose between his allegiance to France and his alliance with England, eagerly encouraged them; he did so in large part for his own purposes, for a duke of Orléans restored to his rightful position in French politics would be likely to discomfort other French nobles and provide King Charles with an additional distraction.[7]

Philip of Burgundy's advocacy of a general peace, in which Orléans would be freed, was also motivated by self-interest, for he had recently been humiliated by the failure of his assault on Calais and, as his councillor, Hue de Lannoy, pointed out in September 1436 in a remarkable analysis of Burgundy's position,

> I do not see any way, considering past events and your relation to these two kings and kingdoms, in which you can maintain the lands, peoples and merchants along the seaboard, who are inclined towards rebellion and disturbance, in peace, justice and obedience towards yourself (as they ought to be), while the war continues between the two above-mentioned kings.[8]

At first some of Henry VI's ministers were less than enthusiastic about the duke of Brittany's specific invitation to Orléans to play a part in a conference, and they insisted on financial guarantees before he went. Towards the end of October, the council was still spending more time discussing how the visit to Cherbourg could be financed (with the treasurer, the economy-minded Lord Cromwell, digging in his heels and insisting that the duke should pay his own expenses since the 12,000 saluts required could not be found by the exchequer) than in planning how best to deploy the duke's efforts.[9] It may have been the formal assertion of the king's will in matters of government in the weeks that followed that eventually enabled a decision to be made. That Beaufort was a leading proponent of the peace negotiations cannot be doubted, and this is perhaps indicated by the concession made on 25 November 1437 to Jean, count of Angoulême, who was also a prisoner in England, allowing him to go and talk with his brother Orléans, provided the cardinal approved.[10] Then, probably in January 1438, the king removed the financial obstacle by authorizing the expenditure of money to pay for Orléans's journey to Normandy on the security of the anticipated ransom which the duke would have to find.[11] Evidently, by the beginning of 1438 the decision had been taken, with Henry's full approval, to embark on peace negotiations at Cherbourg, with Orléans as a central figure in them. Opposition and scepticism had been overcome, even though Orléans's captor was Sir Reginald Cobham, Gloucester's father-in-law.[12] An English envoy had already been despatched to Brittany on 20 December 1437, presumably to convey to Duke Jean the English government's attitude; just before he returned on 29 March 1438, a more significant ambassador left London to cross the channel 'pour conclure un certain traité' – Sir John Popham, treasurer of the king's household.[13] Preparations for Orléans's journey went on apace during the spring: a retinue of westcountrymen was raised to accompany him in some state, and on 9 May a bishop, an earl, a baron, and a clerk were appointed to conduct the actual negotiations from the English side. Meanwhile, the duke himself was brought to London on 17 May in preparation for his departure.[14]

A conference opened at Vannes, in Brittany, shortly before 30 May under the presidency of the duke of Brittany and, in anticipation, the duke of Orléans.[15] But the latter failed to turn up, presumably because the prospect of guaranteeing the cost of his own journey proved beyond his available personal resources. This signalled the failure of the duke of Brittany's efforts in the cause of peace. On 17 July, Henry VI reaffirmed his own willingness to allow Orléans to travel to France in February 1439, but only if the required finance could be found by the duke, the first instalment by 1 October.[16] It is likely, too, that in the divided counsels of the English king, the sceptics had reasserted themselves. Meanwhile, Sir John Popham was recommissioned on 28 July to renew discussions with the French; but he arrived in Normandy to discover the prospect of negotiations receding, for Charles VII was much more cautious than his greatest princes and preferred to send his own envoys to interview Orléans in England and await their return.[17] Presumably the machinations of the dukes of Brittany and Burgundy were well known at the French court and some assurances were sought by the king on the subject of Orléans's political intentions if he were released; more practically, the divisions among the English councillors and the understandable niggardliness of the English government in insisting on financial guarantees had postponed yet again fruitful discussions to achieve a cessation of hostilities.

Serious negotiations between representatives of the adversaries eventually took place in the summer of 1439, though not at Cherbourg; the conference was held at Oye on the plain between Calais and Gravelines.[18] After the failure of the duke of Brittany's efforts to arrange a peace conference and negotiate the release of Orléans, the initiative was taken up by Philip of Burgundy, whose strained relations with Henry VI had hitherto precluded such a step. Nevertheless, during 1438 contact was resumed between the English and Burgundian governments, and Philip's envoys visited England in March and May. Eventually the English responded, and on 23 November 1438 a delegation headed by Cardinal Beaufort and Archbishop Kemp was empowered to open discussions with the Burgundian representatives.[19] The Duchess Isabelle played a central role at the meeting held near Calais towards the end of January; she did so in preference to her husband, with whom Henry VI still found it difficult to communicate directly.[20] They discussed not only commercial matters but also the more general question of peace between England and France, and the part which Orléans might play in achieving it. These preliminary discussions went well, for the duchess seems to have been regarded as a trustworthy envoy; on 8 February she was able to announce that a peace convention would be held in the near future. Henry VI confirmed this on 4 March and declared his preference for Calais as a suitable meeting-place (though he was prepared to consider Cherbourg if the French wished), and his willingness to allow Orléans to attend.[21] Breton envoys travelled to England later in March to make sure that their duke was not excluded, but Charles VII once more displayed caution before he too agreed to the meeting.[22]

At a council held at the royal manor of Kennington on 8 May, in the presence of both Gloucester and Beaufort, the choice of the English envoys was made.[23] Diplomatically speaking, it was a highly experienced delegation: its collective knowledge of the fighting was extensive; it was evenly balanced between laymen and clerics; and it reflected the differing political views within the council. The bishops of Norwich (Thomas Brouns) and St David's (Thomas Rudbourne), along with Archbishop Kemp and the three lesser clerics, Nicholas Bildeston, Stephen Wilton, and William Sprever, may be regarded as sharing Beaufort's belief that peace was essential; indeed, Bildeston, Wilton, and Sprever were protégés of Kemp and the first two had served as Beaufort's chancellor in the past.[24] On the other hand, most of the laymen probably sympathized with Gloucester's hostile attitude towards any concessions to the French, for Stafford, Lord Bourgchier, and Sir John Popham were landowners in northern France; Lord Hungerford was a veteran campaigner, and the earl of Oxford and Robert Whittingham, treasurer of Calais, had recently co-operated in raising Burgundy's siege of Calais.[25] Sir John Stourton had none of this diplomatic and military experience, and it would be rash to attempt to divine his attitude to the forthcoming conference, but he had recently (in July 1438) assumed custody of the duke of Orléans from Gloucester's father-in-law.[26] Thomas Bekyngton may have found it difficult to choose between Gloucester's and Beaufort's views, for he owed much to the duke, in whose service his early career had been spent, whereas since 1437 he had been the king's secretary; his role at the conference was evidently that of an official recorder, for he produced a most informative journal of the entire embassy.[27] Technical expertise in diplomatic exchanges undoubtedly reposed in Kemp and his fellow ecclesiastics, but the material implications of the negotiations – particularly the defence of Calais and Crotoy, and the protection of Englishmen's rights in France – were most clearly understood by the noblemen in the delegation.[28] For this reason, perhaps, the formal authorization of their mission gave these English representatives very little scope for negotiation and almost none for concessions.

An advance party left England in May to make the necessary arrangements and to discuss with the French and Burgundians details of the site, the buildings, and the facilities that a large conference required.[29] Meanwhile, the commissioning and formal appointment of the envoys proceeded. Their procuration issued on 21 May was hardly a suitable basis for negotiation, for Charles VII was bluntly referred to as 'Charles of Valois, our adversary', and great emphasis was laid on extracting from the French those territories which the English king regarded as rightfully his. The possibility of a marriage between Henry and one of Charles's daughters would not be raised until after peace was concluded – which effectively put it beyond discussion, as Gloucester doubtless intended. Two days later, the English delegates were formally appointed; a few additions were made to the earlier list, especially the young duke of Norfolk, who would share leadership of the mission with Archbishop Kemp, and four delegates from Lancastrian France.[30] Rather than appear responsible for the early collapse of the convention, the English envoys were authorized, as a second stage, to allow the French to occupy large stretches of territory south of the Loire, provided they were held of Henry VI as king of France. This was hardly more accommodating and no more likely to promote fruitful discussion. On 25 May, however, a less rigid procuration was allowed to Cardinal Beaufort, who was given sole responsibility for discussing anything relating to Henry's title to the crown and kingdom of France. In relation to such a delicate question, Beaufort was the envoy 'to whom the King hath opened and declared al his intent in this matter'.[31] If neither of the envoys' demands proved to be a basis for negotiation, then Beaufort should make a direct appeal for peace to the French on grounds that encompassed the general good of all involved in the war. 'Both sides would only give up what they did not hold, and by making this concession hoped to win what the other held'.[32]

It was intended that the role of Beaufort and the duchess of Burgundy should be different from that of the other ambassadors. Although nominated to represent their respective sides, whose efforts they would fortify, they also performed the function of interested mediators expected to aid the negotiators when necessary; as the English said of Beaufort, he was to be the 'Mediatour and Sterer to the Peas'.[33] The two were well fitted to work together, for Beaufort was the duchess's uncle, and they quickly established a *rapport* with one another and won the respect of both sides. Orléans's role was similar, though his mediation was sought less regularly and consistently at critical junctures.[34]

Most of the English envoys had arrived at Calais by 26 June.[35] The French ambassadors were already in the vicinity. They were led by the duchess of Burgundy, acting on behalf of her husband, and Regnault de Chartres, archbishop of Rheims and chancellor of France. They and their colleagues were equally experienced in diplomacy and very knowledgeable of Anglo-French relations.[36] But for a month both sides proved unbending in their demands and the conference at times degenerated into a mere forum for wrangling. Despite the efforts of the mediators, the original commission of the English envoys could not be set aside; moreover, the suspicion and distrust with which each side viewed the other – in which Bekyngton was able to dismiss French proposals as 'full of wormwood and snares', and the French believed that for military reasons the English were playing for time – made the negotiators even more stubborn.

It became evident that a breakthrough was required if the talks were not to founder, for the French were now on the point of abandoning the convention and returning to Paris. Beaufort decided, therefore, to send some of the English envoys back to England for further instructions, while he and Orléans remained at Calais. By 8 August, Kemp, Stafford, Hungerford, and three others had reached London, and at Windsor castle they presented the case for relaxing their original instructions. In the absence of Beaufort and the main clerical negotiators, Gloucester had no difficulty in persuading the king and his council to reject this suggestion, particularly when news arrived that the French had seized the important town of Meaux, north-east of Paris. Early in 1440, Gloucester recalled to the king how the returning envoys had been received in the council:

> ...the saide archebisshop of York, sent with other into youre royaume of France from the saide cardinal, after communicacon had with youre adverse partie at your towne of Calais, made in youre presence at his commyng hoom, at youre castel of Windesore, alle the suasions and colourable mocions in the moost apparent wise that he couth for to enduce youre highnesse to yeve youre aggrement to the desires of youre saide capital adversarie, as I sawe by his owen writing shewed there in youre high presence. At whiche tyme, to my understanding, hit was his single opinion and labour, that is to saye, that ye shulde leve youre right, title and youre honneur of youre coroune of Fraunce, of you being kyng of Fraunce, during certain yeeres ye shulde utterly absteyne you, and be content oonly in writing, 'Rex Angliae', etc., to the grete note of infame that ever felle to you, my doubted lord, or to any of youre noble progenitours sith the taking on hem first the saide title and right of youre saide royaume and coroune of France, To the whiche mater in youre saide presence, thereafter that it liked you to aske myn advis thereupon, with other lords of youre bloode and counsaille, I answered and saide that I wolde never agre me therto, to dye therfore;...[37]

The chastened envoys left London at the end of August and arrived at Calais on 9 September, bearing the discouraging news to Beaufort and Orléans. The only concession which could be pursued was the possibility that Orléans might be encouraged to work for peace, though under strict financial guarantees. There can be no doubt that any other proposals that could have been put to the French would have been rejected. As it was, the English were spared this, for the French had not even bothered to return to the conference table; they were in no hurry to resume negotiating when their armies were doing so well in the field.[38]

The only constructive outcome was a commercial truce with Burgundy which was concluded on 29 September before the English envoys returned to London by 10 October.[39] Yet, because the French had not formally terminated the negotiations, the door was still open for future discussions; accordingly, before the English departed, the duchess arranged for a further meeting during the next year, and this Henry accepted on 12 October.[40] The expectation was that Orléans would play a part in it and eventually be allowed to ransom himself.[41]

The deep divisions among the English statesmen were embarrassingly revealed during the Oye negotiations, and so long as Gloucester and Beaufort were able to command influential support for their diametrically opposed opinions, peace would prove elusive and any conference would collapse. The duke, as heir to the Lancastrian throne, expressed with considerable force the classic view of the war, the justice of English claims to sovereignty in France, and the crown's duty in the tradition of Henry V and the treaty of Troyes. Current military and financial difficulties need only be transitory and should not dictate concessions of principle that would permanently affect the king's title, the rights of Englishmen, or the duty of Frenchmen to acknowledge their Lancastrian monarch. The middle-aged duke found it impossible to adopt any other attitude and in this he was doubtless supported by others, especially among the Lancastrian nobility; to regard him as 'blind to events' shows too little sympathy for his position.[42] Beaufort, on the other hand, is dubbed 'a realist' for having astutely analysed the significance of events since Joan of Arc's appearance, and he may indeed have foreseen further territorial losses and financial strain (though the attractions of hindsight are all too seductive). May he not also have acted from ecclesiastical motives, for the pope and the Council of Basle were generous in their exhortations to the English to reach an agreement with the French and a delegation from Basle attended on the cardinal at Calais during the convention?[43] It is equally possible that the deep hatred between Beaufort and Gloucester had now made it impossible for the two men to adopt other than utterly opposed views on the war, and Beaufort may have realized that the king's own inclinations were toward peace; it would be more profitable politically for him to encourage these sentiments in Henry rather than allow him to succumb to the vigorous advocacy of Gloucester. Nor ought one to forget that in recent years it had been Beaufort's wealth that had substantially sustained the English war effort and not necessarily to the cardinal's profit.[44] After Beaufort returned to England, Gloucester's influence seriously waned. When parliament opened at Westminster on 12 November, the chancellor, Bishop Stafford, expounded the official policy of the king's ministers, and it is clear from his remarks that Beaufort and his friends had reasserted themselves in the month following their return from Calais: a more constructive attitude would be adopted henceforward to the question of peace with France.[45]

The failure of the conference at Oye brought into yet sharper focus the role of the duke of Orléans, and perhaps exaggerated his significance in the eyes of those in England who were determined to achieve a peaceful settlement with Charles VII (and, incidentally, of those who were opposed to his release). During 1440 Orléans's role in securing an arrangement with Charles (in return for a substantial ransom) was the subject of constant argument, though the recent collapse of the conferences at Vannes and Oye encouraged those influential Englishmen like Gloucester to continue to express forcefully their hostility to such a move[46]

When the king asked his councillors to weigh the advantages and disadvantages of the proposed release, Gloucester made his views abundantly clear. Nevertheless, the arguments put forward by Beaufort and Archbishop Kemp won the day, and early in 1440 Gloucester heard that 'the deliveraunce of the sayd Duke of Orlyaunce is utterly appoynted by the mediacion, councel, and steryng' of these two clerics.[47] Humphrey maintained that his views had not been given sufficient weight and he genuinely seems to have feared for the consequences in years to come. Therefore, some time afterwards he requested from the king a formal assurance, authorized by the great seal, that he would not be held responsible for the decision and could not be blamed for its results. This the king granted on 2 June, in the process reciting Gloucester's 'Advys and Oppinion unto my said Lord and his Counseill', as the duke requested. It was a persuasive and skilful document which showed an enviable knowledge of current politics and the military situation in France, as well as of recent history.[48] The burden of his advice was, firstly, that Orléans could not be trusted to honour his undertaking to work for peace once he was released, and that, on the contrary, he was more likely to strengthen the French position; secondly, that his release would demoralize Normandy (whose lengthy sufferings would hardly seem worthwhile), Gascony (which would be faced with an alliance of Orléans, Armagnac, Foix, and d'Albret), and potential allies (who would regard the release and the losses in Normandy as a sign of weakness). The conclusion was inescapable:

what may all this Roialme crie, and sey, and sorrowfully grucche, when they remember of the pitous and inestimable Losse that ever Land lost, that was my Lord my Brother of most Noble Memory (whom God assoille) [i.e., Henry V], my Brother of Clarance, my Brother of Bedford, and many other Dukes, Erles, and Lordes, and many tristy a Knight and Squier, all for the keeping and defense of thoo Landes: And also what good this Roialme hath spent for the kepyng and defense of thoo Landes; And also what good this Roialme hath spent for the keeping of the said Roialme and Duche, and it were thus mischieffully Lost, which God defend: Forsoth I trowe it grucched never so sore nor had so grete cause sorowefully to bewaille to see the Worship, that God soe long hath eured him with, to here

451

grete Labour and Charge, shuld so voluntarily be put in likelyhod of total Perdition be Meen of the Deliverance or Eslargissement of the said Duke.

This was a strong, emotive plea which mobilized the glorious memory of the royal and aristocratic dead to considerable effect. Gloucester insisted that he be publicly dissociated from such a shameful decision.

> ... consideryng a gret part of this Roialme paraventure wold ymagyn or thynk that the Deliverance or Eslargissement of the said Duc, which that toucheth soe nygh my Lord and his Roialmes, wold not be woon, assentid, nor concluded withoutyn myn advis, conseill, or consent, for the which, if any of the said Inconvenienz fill, Men wold arrette upon me to my grete Charge; I Protest, for my Excuse and my Discharge, that I never was, am, nor never shal be Consentyng, Conseiling, nor Aggreyng to his Deliverance or Eslargissement, nor be noon other manere of Meen, which shuld take effect, otherwise then is expressed in my seid Lord my Brother's Last Wille (whom God asseille) or else Suerte of so grete Good whereby my Lorde's both Realmes and Subjettis shuld be encreced and easid; ...

Humphrey's 'Advys and Oppinion' was signed by his own fair hand.

It appears to have been the king's personal views which eventually tipped the scales against Gloucester. Henry's justification for Orléans's release amounted to a moving exposition of his deeply felt convictions in the search for peace, and nothing less would serve to counteract the blast from the heir to the throne and companion-in-arms of Henry V than an equally formal and public statement from the great monarch's son. Henry's own conclusion, as well as that of all those who had served as envoys to France in recent years, was that Charles VII, though prepared to discuss peace terms, was 'not disposed effectuelly to entend to eny traite of the saide peas withoute the saide duc [of Orléans] be appointed therinne and part therof'.[49] Moreover, peace was more likely to result from present negotiations if Orléans were free to exert his influence on Charles than if he continued to stand on the side-lines. Aside from the basic conviction that peace was essential and that the military burden on England and Normandy could no longer be tolerated, the arguments in favour of Orléans's release lacked substance: namely, that to keep a man in prison indefinitely was contrary to the law of arms and a discouragement to other soldiers (though this does not seem to have worried the English government over the past twenty-five years); that the possibility of securing a ransom was receding annually (which was a conclusion tardily come to); and that Orléans had acquired no more sensitive knowledge of English affairs than any other prisoner (though he would be uniquely placed to use whatever he had learned later on).

The flurry of diplomatic activity required to finalize arrangements for a peace conference and Orléans's release was intense during the spring and early summer of 1440. Envoys were despatched across the channel by both England and France from April onwards; the duke of Brittany, who was anxious not to be left out of any convention, had sent his secretary to England at the end of 1439, and eventually Jean V elicited a promise from Henry VI on 25 June 1440 that he would be included in any treaty that might be concluded. Calais was chosen as the venue of the negotiations.[50] The arrangements for the duke's release, after twenty-five years and with so many misgivings expressed as to its wisdom, took some months to finalize and many sheaves of parchment to record. Eventually, on 2 July 1440 the terms were formally agreed by all concerned and Orléans undertook to abide by them: he was required to find a ransom of 40,000 nobles on the occasion of his release and a further 80,000 within six months; if he succeeded in arranging peace within that time, the entire ransom would be cancelled, but alternatively, if he failed to do so and to produce the required sum on time, he was bound on his honour to return to captivity.[51] It was a customary arrangement according to the law of arms and the dictates of a chivalrous society. In order to dispose finally of Gloucester's taunt that Henry V on his death-bed had counselled that Orléans should not be released lightly, the king added that his father's intention had been to keep the duke in custody until just such a time, when the achievement of a final peace between the two kingdoms seemed imminent.[52] By a remarkable countrywide collection among the French princes, the duchess of Burgundy managed to raise the required initial payment, and Charles VII, though conspicuous by his omission from the list of contributors, ratified the release agreement on 16 August.[53] Everything bade fair for the freeing of the duke by the beginning of November.

When Orléans gave his solemn undertakings to Henry in Westminster abbey on 28 October, Gloucester stalked out. The scene evidently created something of a stir, as Robert Repps reported to John Paston a few days later:

> ... the Duk of Orlyawnce hath made his ooth vpon thesacrement, and vsyd it, neuer for to bere armes ayenst Englond, in the presence of the Kyng and all the lordes except my lord of Gloucester; and in prevyng my seyde lord of Gloucester agreyd neuer to hys delyueraunce, qwan the masse be-gan he toke hys barge, etc.

A feeling that a risk was being taken was not confined to Humphrey alone, for Repps added: 'God yef grace the seide lord of Orlyaunce be trewe, for this same weke shall he toward Fraunce'.[54] But his angry last-ditch stand during the first half of 1440, and his complete dissociation from the policies of the king's ministers, was eventually to seal his fate as a power in the land. This year saw Humphrey's influence set at nought as the French duke prepared to journey to France and to freedom.

On 3 November the formal instrument authorizing the release was at last sealed by Henry VI.[55] That very day, Lord Fanhope was discharged as Orléans's custodian, a letter of protection was issued enabling him to leave the realm, and a group of prominent Englishmen were commissioned to receive his oath anew after he had set foot in France and to open negotiations at Calais. These included Fanhope himself, Bishop Wells of Rochester, and Sir Thomas Kyriell, lieutenant of Calais town; they set sail immediately and reached Calais on 5 November.[56] Orléans dutifully swore his oath at Gravelines one week later and then embarked on a grand tour of the duke of Burgundy's Flemish dominions.[57] With a gallantry he had been able to display only in his poetry during the past quarter-century, he greeted the Duchess Isabelle with the words: 'In view of all you have done for my deliverance, I surrender myself your prisoner'.[58] In the city of Orléans and other of the duke's towns, celebrations which had been held prematurely and expensively on more than one occasion during the past year to herald their lord's freedom could now be staged in the certain knowledge that Charles would shortly appear at their gates.[59] His impeccable behaviour so far, and the tone of his reception by Duke Philip and his duchess – he was admitted to the order of the golden fleece and married to Philip's niece, Marie of Cleves – augured well for the realization of the promise which many attached to his release and for his re-entry to the forefront of French politics.[60]

Keeping up the guard, 1437–40

During these three years of diplomatic exchanges and occasional conferences, sometimes abortive and rarely constructive, it was common prudence for the council to sustain the Lancastrian military and governmental position in France; opinion at home would have had it no other way. The death of Bedford had left a yawning gap in the ranks of the English commanders and impoverished their military thinking; it had also removed the young king's next heir and his supreme representative in his second realm. Gloucester, who was now the sole surviving brother of Henry V, was the king's new heir and he was required at the council in England; therefore, the need to provide France with a royal lieutenant became suddenly acute.

At first, this role was filled by Richard, duke of York, a young man of twenty-five who had no military experience to his credit and was quite unprepared for the administrative duties assigned to Henry VI's representative in France. He owed his appointment on 1 May 1436 to his position as England's premier duke after Gloucester.[61] Misgivings about his youth and inexperience, about the treason committed by his father, the earl of Cambridge, in 1415, and his own provocative lineage were doubtless overcome by the realization that able and dependable councillors would control the young lieutenant-general and uphold the aims of the dead Bedford.[62] Richard's agreement to undertake the awesome commission had been secured some months earlier, on 22 February, when he undertook to serve in France for one year with 500 men-at-arms and 2,200 archers.[63] His was evidently intended to be a temporary appointment, and may have had the support of both Gloucester and Beaufort. Duke Humphrey may have felt that he could hardly travel to France himself at this juncture and leave the council open to the aggressive influence of his rival. York may also have been acceptable to the cardinal, for he had been brought up in a Beaufort household – that of Joan Beaufort, countess of Westmorland – and he had married Cecily Neville, one of Joan's daughters.[64] In these circumstances, his formal commission as lieutenant-general withheld certain powers from York which Bedford had enjoyed: he was not allowed to appoint to the major military and financial offices in Lancastrian France, and whereas Bedford had been 'governor and regent' of France, York and his successors had to rest content with the lesser title of 'lieutenant-general and governor'.[65]

During York's term, the counter-offensive which was launched against the French in the Ile de France was conducted by the brilliant Lord Talbot who, early in 1437, succeeded in recovering a number of towns and fortresses near Paris (especially Pontoise to the north-west) and even threatened the capital itself.[66] The duke seems to have played little part in these military operations and stayed comfortably at Rouen, the Norman capital. In any case, his councillors were wary of engaging in any ambitious manoeuvres if only because York's authority would lapse after one year.[67] His indenture in fact expired at the beginning of May 1437, and he may not have been entirely sorry, for in 1439 £18,000 was still owing to him and he had not at first been allowed to receive the proceeds of Norman taxation.[68] As it was, he remained in Normandy until his replacement, the veteran campaigner Warwick, arrived in November after a hair-raising sea crossing.[69]

Richard Beauchamp, earl of Warwick was hardly eager for the commission. Not only was he feeling his age at fifty-five, but he had no intention of incurring further financial loss in the service of the crown when £12,606 was due to him for the custody of Calais ten years before.[70] Moreover, he was adamant that he must be assisted by several other noblemen, and he actually named Viscount Beaumont, Lord Willoughby, and Lord Bourgchier as his preference; in the event, only Willoughby was prepared to join him.[71] After negotiating with the council on these and other points, Warwick agreed to sail for France, but he cautioned the council that if the agreed terms of service were not fulfilled, he would feel free to return home after informing the king. Even though he was not a nobleman of royal blood, it is difficult to think of anyone who was Beauchamp's equal in military experience and reputation; he had, moreover, until recently been the king's guardian.

As the new lieutenant-general, therefore, he is likely to have been one of the very few magnates to be acceptable to all shades of opinion among the king's councillors.[72]

The earl received his formal commission as lieutenant-general on 16 July 1437 and the powers it contained were identical with those of York.[73] He tried to embark at once and with some optimism included his wife, Isabelle, and his fifteen-year-old son and heir, Henry, among his entourage. But that summer was a particularly stormy one, and seven times in eleven weeks the Warwick company put to sea only to be driven back, on one occasion almost drowning the lieutenant and his family; after a frustrating and distinctly harrowing experience, they were able to pull away from the shore (though without the countess, who had wisely concluded that she had best remain behind) and head for Honfleur, which they reached at the beginning of November.[74] After his unpleasant trip, the earl made for Rouen and there he seems to have stayed for much of his sojourn as the king's lieutenant.[75]

He was charged with the defence of Lancastrian territory against further French encroachments, even to the extent of assembling a large field army as well as maintaining castle garrisons. For this purpose, £24,000 was sent over to him in November 1437.[76] He was also instructed to conduct a thorough review of the state of the English dominion, and in particular the garrisons of Normandy were to be inspected; perhaps as a result of this, on 6 May 1438 large quantities of saltpetre were bought at Southampton for the count of Mortain to take to the fortresses.[77] Lord Talbot was the principal commander in the field, but the record of this lieutenancy was largely confined to winning a success here, suffering a reverse there: thus, after a four-month siege, Tancarville in the Caux peninsula fell to Talbot, whilst for his part the Dauphin Louis spent three months besieging Montereau-sur-Yonne before its castellan, Thomas Gerard, was induced to capitulate in default of relief. A more significant reverse involved Harfleur, which was lost by a ruse towards the end of December 1438, when a fleet of forty-two French ships flying the standard of St George sailed into the harbour and surprised the town.[78]

Calais presented special problems of defence, partly because of its extraodinary commercial and military importance to England, and partly because on land it was isolated from the rest of Lancastrian France by Burgundian territory. Moreover, for all practical purposes, it lay beyond the reach of the king's lieutenant-general and instead was the effective responsibility of its own captain. Despite the security won for the colony by the raising of the siege of 1436, the turning of the tide of war meant that the strategic needs of Calais, including adequate finance for its garrison, and proper protection for the supporting fortresses of Guisnes, Marck, Hammes, and Oye, would appear regularly on the council's agenda.[79] Steps were taken to ensure the security of these bastions, to survey the state of Calais and its march, and, as far as resources allowed, meet their requirements.[80]

Barely eighteen months after Philip the Good's attack, the precariousness of the situation was brought home to Englishmen. In November 1437 intelligence reached the government that Philip was about to besiege Guisnes, whose relationship to Calais was regarded as akin to that of Calais to England itself, namely, as a vital element in its defence. Accordingly, plans were laid to provision the fortress in anticipation of the attack and to muster a force in England for its rescue, should that be necessary.[81] A new lieutenant for Calais's castle was hastily nominated, and on 25 November Lord Dudley, a former royal lieutenant of Ireland and, to judge by his later career, a man in whom Beaufort had great confidence, was ordered to Calais without further ado.[82] Yet, the war-weary English were no longer easily mobilized for such enterprises, and difficulty was encountered in rousing the knights and esquires of the shires who would be needed to serve as captains and commanders of any relieving force.[83] Eventually, in the spring an expedition was fitted out under the king's cousin, the earl of Huntingdon, and the duke of Norfolk; it sailed from Sandwich at the end of March.[84] Sir Thomas Rempston probably seemed an inauspicious choice to some for, although an active soldier, he had managed to fall into the enemy's hands not too long before.[85] Fortunately, the threat passed, and during the next two years Calais and its march enjoyed a temporary respite as diplomatic and commercial contacts with Burgundy were resumed, the benefits of peace were stressed by influential men in both countries, and the 'pale' of Calais was chosen as a suitable venue for the Anglo-French negotiations.[86]

Warwick died at Rouen on 30 April 1439. His demise left the Lancastrian council in France, headed by the chancellor, Louis of Luxembourg, archbishop of Rouen, in charge not only of the government but also of the direction of the war. A delegation was accordingly sent to England to urge a more satisfactory arrangement, and as a result measures were taken to assist the chancellor by associating with him three Norman clerics, Pierre Cauchon, bishop of Lisieux and the man who, as bishop of Beauvais, had led the prosecution of Joan of Arc, and the abbots of Fécamp and Mont St Michel; five English lay councillors were designated at the same time. The latter included, significantly, two nephews of Cardinal Beaufort, John, earl of Somerset and Edmund, count of Mortain, as well as the field commanders, Lords Talbot, Scales, and Fauconberg. Together, they were to rule Normandy until Warwick's successor had been announced. To judge by their likely attitudes to the war, this council was the military and administrative counterpart of the elaborate embassy to Oye that was being given its instructions just at that moment: experienced war commanders were associated with others closely attached to Beaufort, the pursuer of peace.[87] Somerset appears to have been singled out as supreme military commander with the title of 'lieutenant- and governor-general of the war'; civil authority does not seem to have been entrusted to him, and in fact no formal commission akin to that of York or Warwick is known. Somerset had spent seventeen of the last eighteen years in prison in France and can hardly have acquired much knowledge of the war since his capture at Baugé in 1421. It is difficult to imagine a less qualified successor to the great Warwick, and his incompetence was proved during the next few years; the suicide which is said to have been responsible for his death in 1444 perhaps indicates that he too became aware of his shortcomings.[88]

Somerset's temporary appointment may have been devised to forestall the despatch of an expedition to France under Gloucester, who had offered to lead an army across the channel. It is not impossible, in mid-1439, that Duke Humphrey offered himself as Warwick's successor now that his opinion on the peace negotiations and on the release of Orléans was unacceptable to the king and council. Compared with 1435–37, supreme authority in France may have looked more enticing than the prospect of vanishing influence in England. As he indignantly remarked some months later,

> how oft tymes that I have offerd my service unto you [i.e., the king] for the defence of youre Royaume of Fraunce and lordeshippes there, where I have be put there fro by the labour of the said cardinal, in preferring othre of his singular affection [i.e., presumably, his nephew].[89]

Meanwhile, following Warwick's death, a modest force was hastily assembled at Winchelsea to support the leaderless Lancastrians. It was placed under the command of Sir Richard Woodville (who provided the largest retinue), Sir William Peyto, and Sir William Chamberlain, each of whom had had recent experience of the fighting under Bedford.[90] Woodville, the son of the regent's old councillor, may have been entrusted with the leadership of this army, which totalled about 900 men and cost only a whit less than £6,000. It eventually sailed for Honfleur towards the end of July.[91]

Somerset himself showed no sense of urgency in crossing to Normandy, though the fact that preparations for his expedition were being made in the depths of winter may partly explain the delay.[92] He did not leave with his 2,100 men until some time in February 1440. Before his departure, he agreed his conditions of service with the council, and extracted certain financial concessions in the process.[93] Thus, as far as the availability of men, money, and royal lieutenants allowed, England's guard was kept raised and this policy ran parallel with the quest for a peaceful settlement; indeed, as the attitude of the French showed occasionally at Oye in 1439, greater progress was likely to be made in negotiations if the English could restrain the advances of Charles VII and his Burgundian ally. Accordingly, in the north, Calais and Guisnes were likewise reinforced in the spring of 1438 and Mortain's expedition, which landed at Cherbourg later in the year, was intended to succour Gascony.[94]

Defeats and disasters, 1440–44

Orléans's mission had none of the results anticipated by those who had championed it; it certainly produced no new peace initiatives.[95] Continued vigilance was therefore required in the English-held provinces, and on the very day when terms for the release of Orléans were finally agreed by Henry VI (2 July), a new lieutenant-general was at last appointed to take Warwick's place. The choice fell for the second time on the king's cousin, Richard, duke of York, who was now thirty years old.[96] His lineage and his loyalty were the qualities which secured for the duke the approval of Gloucester and Beaufort, as well as other members of the great council. This time the appointment was scheduled to run for more than five years, until Michaelmas 1445. York was granted the extensive civil and military authority which Bedford had enjoyed, and specific provision was made for an annual payment of £20,000. Such comprehensive powers were probably necessary in order to persuade the duke to take up the post again, and in any case considerable confidence could be placed in his 'chieff councelle' who closely advised him in governing English France; it was they who had counselled him to extract from the king the carefully defined and yet wide-ranging articles of appointment. These councillors – Sir John Fastolf, Sir William ap Thomas, and Sir William Oldhall (who was singled out by one chronicler as the chief adviser at Rouen) – were experienced and dedicated soldiers who had been bequeathed by Bedford and would remain staunchly loyal to their new master through all adversity.[97]

The French siege of Creil-sur-Oise, south-east of Beauvais, made the despatch of a new commander with ample reinforcements and supplies overdue.[98] Yet, an unconscionable time was spent in making the arrangements for York's journey. The mustering of his troops and the necessary ships was delayed from month to month during the spring of 1441, and accumulating the necessary stores and ordnance seems to have been a leisurely business too.[99] By 23 May the council was sufficiently alarmed by the French advance to urge York to cross as soon as possible. At Rouen the embattled council felt deserted and deceived, for over the past two years they had been led to expect first Gloucester and then York, 'since promised by you [i.e., the king], and for long expected by us' but in vain.[100] It was only on or about 25 June, almost exactly one year after his appointment, that the duke at last entered Rouen with 5,000 men to take up the reins of government and to supervise the direction of the war.[101] He was accompanied by a goodly retinue which included the earl of Oxford, Lord Bourgchier (who was also count of Eu and recently appointed captain of Crotoy), Sir Richard Woodville, Sir James Ormond, as well as several wives, including the duchesses of York and Bedford, and the countesses of Oxford and Eu. A lengthy stay, with as many of the comforts of home as was possible, was evidently envisaged for the high-ranking commanders.[102]

Despite all, the following autumn saw a vigorous resurgence of French arms on practically all fronts, but most notably in the advance on Crotoy at the mouth of the Somme in October, and against the strategic towns of Harfleur, Honfleur, and Caen soon afterwards.[103] The government in England was deeply disturbed by the news it received and undertook an urgent review of how best York's annual subvention of £20,000, together with the proceeds of Norman taxation, should be spent. It was concluded on 27 November that a mainly mounted army in excess of 3,000 men was still perfectly feasible within the financial limits imposed.[104] Such an army could confront invading French forces wherever they might appear and its mobility should enable the threatened towns and castles to be relieved. Provided the cash was readily available from Westminster and Rouen, much could be achieved. This was the crucial point: at the beginning of his second term as lieutenant, it had proved impossible to find York the £20,000 that was his due, and so in November 1441 a mere £5,000 was authorized as the first quarter's contribution.[105]

Of the two detached Lancastrian establishments, Crotoy had always been in the more exposed position. Now, in the early 1440s, its survival became distinctly problematical, as the French began to edge closer along the northern march of Normandy and to the east the Burgundians were decidedly hostile. By the spring of 1439, the long-serving custodian of the fortress, Walter Cressoner, evidently felt the world to be closing in on him. Even ostensibly friendly English garrisons nearby were slipping away from the discipline imposed from Rouen by the lieutenant-general. Soldiers from the garrison at Neufchâtel, some distance to the south, indulged in skirmishes with the Crotoy men, holding to ransom those whom they captured, demanded *appatis* from the French countryside adjacent to Crotoy and St Valéry on the opposite shore, and committed other depredations which not only breached good order and undermined English justice, but also weakened Crotoy.[106] The failure of the peace negotiations during 1439–40, and the release of the French count of Eu in 1438 in exchange for Somerset, together with the recent run of French successes, brought the war even closer to the walls of the outpost. One consequence of this was the decision of the council to place a noble commander in charge of the fortress, if only to give the impression that serious attention was to be paid to it in the future.[107]

Henry, Lord Bourgchier was well suited to the assignment; as the English count of Eu, he had a vested interest in halting the French advance in the environs of Crotoy in order to protect his own estates in northern Normandy. On 22 May 1441, therefore, as he prepared to join the new lieutenant-general on his journey to France, Bourgchier was given the captaincy of Crotoy for seven years, from the following 19 October, with an annual grant of £1,000 in wartime and £867 during a peace.[108] By that stage, York had also appointed him (on 26 September) to the captaincy of Neufchâtel, whose garrison had caused Cressoner so much concern two years before.[109] As an encouragement to vigorous effort, it was further agreed that should Dieppe, Eu, and Caux be recovered from the Valois, he would receive an extra 1,300 marks a year, presumably because they would be added to his dominion in the northern frontier zone of Normandy. Bourgchier, for his part, was under no illusions as to the difficulty of his task, and he extracted from the king a promise that if Crotoy were besieged, a rescue bid would be launched within one month or else Bourgchier could disclaim all responsibility for any disaster that might follow. With some success, Bourgchier held on to Crotoy during the next seven years and more, but although stores and equipment continued to arrive from London, Winchelsea, and Chichester, the promised payments from England rarely fulfilled the undertakings of the government in May 1441.[110] Bourgchier's official posts and his personal estates were the foundation for a position as 'governor-general' of the Normandy–Picardy borderland by March 1442, though most likely under the overall command of York as lieutenant-general.[111] The appointment of York and Bourgchier seemed to herald a more energetic phase of the English war effort and a commendable determination to stem the oncoming tide of Frenchmen.

At the same time (and most inappropriately), the English showed a renewed interest in seeking a peaceful settlement – or at the very least a truce – with the French king. In April and May 1441 Henry VI had attempted in good faith to establish contact with French envoys, but at first none came to discuss the preliminaries.[112] Orléans's oath was very much in mind, and in some desperation on 28 November 1441 the king agreed to enact it formally to give it greater publicity and, if possible, to stress its binding power. As Gloucester had perceived, with the French duke set at liberty, what more could be done?[113]

The deteriorating situation in northern and south-western France, combined with the absence of any constructive response from the French to proposals for negotiation, persuaded the council to take a more belligerent attitude towards Charles VII in 1441–42. The vigorous defence of Normandy, prefigured by the appointment of York and Bourgchier, was accompanied on the diplomatic front by a major initiative at the highest level. Moreover, the threat to Bordeaux and Bayonne was very much in the king's mind, especially in view of the defection of several of the Gascon nobility from their English allegiance. Henry hardly needed reminding that Gascony 'is oon th'oldest lordship longing to your coroune of Englande'.[114] The initiative took the form of a proposal of marriage between Henry VI and one of the daughters of the greatest of the southern French nobility, the count

461

of Armagnac. Such a match might give to English Gascony the kind of security which direct military aid from England could not provide easily or swiftly. It was certain, on the other hand, to anger King Charles, but by the spring of 1442 so little had been forthcoming from that monarch by way of concession – or even negotiation – that this particular risk held no terrors for most of the English council. As a result, the count's envoys were welcomed in England in the first weeks of May 1442 and by the end of the month royal ambassadors had been nominated to arrange the marriage; they included Sir Robert Roos, one of the king's senior household servants, Thomas Bekyngton, his secretary, and Edward Hull, an esquire for the body, who had recently returned from Bordeaux.[115] It was felt necessary to justify this somewhat unexpected turn of events, and of the reasons advanced the prosperity of Gascony (through its wine trade) and the political advantages likely to accrue to both sides in their relations with Charles VII must surely rank above the religious and dynastic motives that were also mentioned.[116] That the proposal came to nothing is no reflection on the diligence with which the envoys went about their task (as the surviving diary of the mission from 5 June 1442 to 26 February 1443 demonstrates), but is attributable rather to Charles VII's presence in force on the frontier of Armagnac just when the discussions should have begun, his sweeping victories within Gascony itself, and (some contemporaries hinted) the machinations of those councillors at home, especially Suffolk, who preferred an accommodation with Charles VII.[117]

As the duke of York tried to hold the line in Normandy during 1442 (with the aid of a new army under Talbot, who had earlier returned to England), at the same time as reinforcements were packed into Calais and the citadel of Crotoy, the search for peace became more and more intensive on the English side. Contacts were made even while the Gascon initiative was being pursued, though before the end of August the mission to Armagnac was on the brink of withdrawing.[118] The king's chamberlain, Lord Sudeley, had been sent to the Breton march in the summer of 1442 to reopen communication with Orléans.[119] It was something of a humiliation for York himself to be ordered by the council in October to inaugurate negotiations, assisted by Louis of Luxembourg and the king's chamberlain. No previous lieutenant had been required to sue for peace under such circumstances.[120]

England's position at any negotiating table was weakened at this juncture not only by the universally acknowledged difficulty of providing sufficient men and money for the defence of northern France, and the unprecedented success of the French in gnawing away at Lancastrian-held territory, but also by a disastrous paucity of capable commanders.[121] With the single exception of Talbot, who was created earl of Shrewsbury on 21 July 1441 in recognition of his personal qualities and military successes, the English magnates could produce no one of the stature of Bedford, Salisbury, or Warwick.[122] Somerset and

York were short on soldierly talent and commonsense, and the government's ill-considered association of the former with York in the rule of English France caused profound misunderstandings and fostered deep resentment in the lieutenant-general and an irreconcilable bitterness between the two men.[123]

Moreover, disagreements in England about future military strategy reached a turning-point as the available resources were declared to be inadequate. Discussions about sending yet another army to France to aid the duke of York were held as early as August 1442, soon after Talbot's expedition set sail.[124] But the logistical problems involved, and the attempt to initiate peace negotiations in the autumn, postponed any decision. Nor did the plan (formulated by 21 September 1442) to despatch the earl of Somerset and 'a right noble puissance of war' to defend Gascony fare any better.[125] When Cherbourg came under threat from the French by January 1443, all the council could say to John Burgh, Lord Scales's lieutenant as captain of the town and castle, was that 200 longbows, 40 crossbows, some gunpowder, and 40 labourers were on their way and that he would have to make do with that.[126] When these measures proved barren of result, the wranglings resumed. No longer was it simply a question of when an expedition could be sent, or how large it should be, or who should lead it; now, more fundamental questions had to be considered. A council meeting held on 6 February 1443 was faced for the first time with the painful dilemma of choosing between the defence of Gascony and the defence of Normandy. Some councillors still clung to the belief that both could be assisted by an army, but others were more doubtful; only the treasurer, Lord Cromwell, who had the clearest conception of what was financially practicable, was emphatic that only one duchy could be aided at any one time, but as to which, he was prepared to give preference where the need was considered greater.[127] The arguments raged for at least another week, and it was no help that Somerset, who had been designated the commander of any expedition that might eventually be organized, was away from London ill. Moreover, the return of the king's emissaries from Bordeaux led to a frantic round of discussions as Bekyngton reported, doubtless in vivid terms, to several of the councillors (including Gloucester, Beaufort, the chancellor, the treasurer, and the bishop of Norwich), and to the king himself during 21–26 February.[128] At one stage, it seemed as if the decision about the expedition's destination would be left to Somerset alone until, on 2 March, with the treasurer insisting that to recruit two armies was inconceivable, it was concluded that the decision must be taken by the king, his lords, and his captains.[129] At this critical juncture, indecision and incompetence were the hallmarks of the council. A decisive, if bullish, intervention by someone of Gloucester's stature was sorely needed in its counsels – though he had been politically neutralized some time ago. One thing all were agreed on: both Gascony and Normandy were in urgent need of relief. It is astonishing, therefore, that several months were allowed to slip by before Somerset's expedition was ready to sail.

Although the Gascon problem was less immediate that that of Normandy, the vital wine trade and the fundamental fact of a 300-year-old lordship meant that Gascony's defence was a residual preoccupation of Henry VI's council. Like the English territories in the north, it was subject to serious attack and enemy inroads.[130] Somerset's ill-starred expedition in 1443 was originally intended to provide a bold initiative in defence of the duchy. To begin with, however, it seemed more expeditious, and certainly cheaper, to encourage the merchants who controlled the trade with Bordeaux and Bayonne to arm themselves in convoy rather than await the inevitably laborious gathering of a fleet to protect their shipping.[131] But by the spring of 1439, ships were being commandeered in the west, east, and south of the country, to assemble at Plymouth, for an expedition to Gascony. The king's lieutenant, the earl of Huntingdon, would sail with them.[132]

In the face of revived French power and the defection of some of the southern nobility (including the Sieur d'Albret, and the son of the count of Longueville) from their English allegiance, military reinforcements and other aid were required fairly constantly throughout the 1440s.[133] As Thomas Bekyngton and his fellow envoys discovered in July 1442, the inhabitants of Bayonne and the Bordelais were feeling increasingly isolated and demoralized by the seeming lack of interest shown in their plight in England.[134] Of Bordeaux, they commented on 24 July that it was

> As sorowful a town and as gretly dismayed and discoraged as any might be in th'erth, as poeuple desolat and cast out of al comfort of any socour to be had from your said mageste ayeinst your ennemies that ben in this country in grete puiseaunce; . . .

A fortnight later the Dauphin's army had moved closer to the city,

> wher, as God knoweth, is division and never was so litel help nor store of Englissh pouple, the lak of whom is cause of losse of al this cuntry; as we doubt not on lesse that succour be had withoute any delaie all is goon.

The insecurity of the English administration was exemplified by the nervousness which the council felt about leaving important Gascon offices in Gascon hands any longer. In November 1441, for example, the council rescinded a recent appointment by the lieutenant of Ame de Canpenne to the seneschalcy of the Landes, and a number of lords expressed the view that an Englishman ought to fill the post.[135] But there were other grounds for their reaction, for it had become the king's policy of late to dispense his patronage of offices, lands, and revenues in

Gascony in much the same way as he had done nearer home. From about 1439 he had been persuaded to 'passe upon suche graunts of your demaynnes or of other lands, rents, or revenues here, as peraventure shall be axed of your said Highnesse', frequently by members of the royal household. This aroused resentment among the councillors at Bordeaux and precipitated rivalries that were sometimes violent. Circumspect patronage was likely to inspire confidence and encourage the loyal in Gascony, as elsewhere, but protests in October 1442 went unheeded.[136]

Then, in the summer of 1442, supplies and men, partly recruited in Bristol, one of the main centres of the wine trade, were despatched to Bayonne, the more vulnerable of the two great Gascon cities, on a short-term contract of three months; they were placed under the command of a west-country knight, Sir Philip Chetwynd, who had been appointed mayor of Bayonne on 26 November 1441 and was now ordered to prepare the city for the expected French invasion.[137] Even councillors who, like Suffolk, were anxious to arrange peace with Charles VII, baulked at deserting the king's Gascon subjects; the earl had been party to the decision to send this force 'to goo thider for the helpe, succour and defense of our said cite [of Bordeaux] and of all our cuntreyes there'.[138]

Overtaking Chetwynd's orders a month later, presumably in response to the arrival of worse news from Bekyngton and the other envoys in Gascony, were instructions to prepare a larger expedition and to despatch considerable quantities of grain and other supplies to the population. Widespread and compulsory aids were authorized on 24 August among the great and the small, the thrifty and the townsmen, with security offered in the form of assignments on future taxation, the crown jewels, and other sources of revenue.[139] A new seneschal, Sir William Bonville, from Chewton in Devon, was engaged to accompany this army, which was placed under the command of Sir John Popham, a reliable and experienced Lancastrian servant.[140]

With the usual delays, it does not seem likely that this expedition left Plymouth much before mid-February 1443.[141] Meanwhile, to support the flagging political initiative of negotiations with the count of Armagnac, as well as to aid the demoralized duchy, an even grander design was envisaged for the relief of Gascony. Already by late September 1442 discussions were under way with the earl of Somerset, not only for his own journey to the province, but also for his appointment to a special position comparable with that of York in Normandy, with widespread authority extending far beyond the Gascon frontier.[142] While he haggled and delayed, and the king's council weighed inconclusively the relative demands of Normandy and Gascony, realizing that both could not be succoured, the situation deteriorated in both. Up until Christmas 1442, King Charles's progress in the Landes had been virtually unchecked and already by October, Bekyngton was reporting to the king that Bordeaux itself had little means with which to defend itself,

> The which causeth grete hevynesse, desolacion, and sorowe amongis al your pouple here, seing that after promisse of succours declared unto theym by your commaundement is passed so longe a tyme and no comfort commeth . . .

The time was past when a modest-sized army like Bonville's would do, and the envoy doubted if £20,000 could now achieve very much.[143] In January Bekyngton and Sir Robert Roos decided to return home, their mission to the count of Armagnac a failure. Soon afterwards, the French king's forces prepared to renew their assault on the vulnerable towns of Gascony. Furthermore, the Castilians were reported to be preparing to blockade both Bordeaux and Bayonne by sea and on land.[144] For the second time within a year, loans, ships, and supplies were urgently sought in England, and royal agents were sent hot-foot to Bristol – even to Ireland – to secure aid.[145] In this increasingly desperate situation, Somerset's expedition was of no assistance whatever.

Preparations were under way by 7 March 1443 to assemble troop-ships at The Camber near Winchelsea, and evidently the decision had been taken by then to concentrate the war effort on Somerset's forthcoming expedition to Gascony.[146] At the end of the month, his conditions of service as lieutenant and captain-general of Aquitaine and France were agreed with the king, and they represent an extraordinary accession of authority, wealth, and status. He was assigned the duchy of Anjou and the county of Maine for seven years once the grant which his younger brother, Edmund, enjoyed had run out; he was created duke of Somerset with precedence over all other English magnates save Gloucester and York; and an annual income of 600 marks was conceded (after the lords had resisted 1,000 marks). He was allowed to inspect the exchequer's financial records in order to choose the most reliable source for his annuity, and he was created Bedford's successor as earl of Kendal on the very same day (28 August) that his formal patent as duke was sealed.[147] These unique marks of favour were intended to emphasize Somerset's position as a senior magnate of the royal blood and to provide him with an authority appropriate to his new commission.

His powers in France were equally extraordinary and their practical relation to those of the duke of York is not easy to visualize.[148] His authority was to be effective in those lands at present beyond the king's obedience and 'in the whiche my said Lorde of York cometh not'. It was scrupulously stated that it was not intended to prejudice Duke Richard's position as lieutenant-general of France and Normandy, and initially at any rate it was envisaged that Somerset would confront the forces of Charles VII in Gascony.[149] Nevertheless, the grant of Anjou and Maine meant that Somerset's interests would extend northwards well beyond the river Loire, and the terms of his appointment allowed him to campaign wherever the French were to be found.[150] The details of these powers which garter king-of-arms was charged on 5 April with conveying to York in Rouen demonstrate that an even more decisive shift in policy had occurred since Somerset's original commission on 30 March; it was prompted perhaps by news that Charles VII had transferred his field of operations (or was about to do so) from Gascony to Normandy.[151]

The revised brief makes it clear that Somerset was to lead a large field army in an offensive war against Charles personally, since 'it is semed ful behoveful and necessarie that the maner and the conduit of the werre be chaunged...' This military role of seeking out and destroying Charles's army would serve as 'a shield' for York in Normandy. At the beginning of April it still seemed likely that after landing in Normandy, Somerset would 'passe over the water of Leyre [i.e., Loire]', but it was also acknowledged that if King Charles moved north from Gascony, the new English army should pursue him wherever he went. Thus, although Somerset's lieutenancy of Gascony in no way encroached on York's position, his military authority, expressed in the title 'lieutenant and captain-general of France and Gascony', was much more likely to do so. As an imaginative, strategic decision, the appointment was not without merit, for Charles VII's marches through the length of France were a striking proof of his claim to be truly king of all France, whereas York's reputation could not but raise doubts as to the ability of Henry VI's lieutenant to halt this run of successes. Yet in executing its decision, the council blundered badly; it showed insufficient sensitivity towards York's feelings; it failed to realize that in sustaining Lancastrian Normandy it was no longer possible to separate governmental considerations from military ones; and at his request it committed supreme authority in the field to a magnate of royal blood who owed his elevation more to political and dynastic qualifications than to proven ability or lengthy experience.

York, when he received news of Somerset's appointment, may be pardoned for suspecting that he (and his commanders) were being superseded in their military duties, and that his own authority was being confined to the defence of little more than Normandy. Somerset would succeed to the bulk of the powers previously exercised by Bedford and his immediate successors. The council went to considerable lengths to persuade York of the merits of Somerset's appointment. Moreover, he was informed that the French intended to launch a major assault on Rouen itself, in the repelling of which Somerset's 'shield' would be vital. But although Duke Richard was promised support – perhaps a force of 1,600, depending on the cash available, and saltpetre for his gunners – his request for the £20,000 which he had been promised in 1440 was met by the scarcely digestible plea that he be patient because Somerset's expedition was very expensive and would leave little to spare for other enterprises![152] Almost the whole of the English establishment in Normandy protested at the new departure. Their protest waited until Somerset's patent of appointment was formally issued on 4 June, and then a formidable delegation was despatched from Rouen to demand that the king and council reconsider the matter.[153] It was led by England's greatest living soldier, the earl of Shrewsbury, and it included one of York's most capable councillors, Sir Andrew Ogard, as well as two representatives of the Norman administration, John Stanlow, treasurer of Normandy, and Henry's French secretary, Jean Rinel. It is evident that not one segment of the English régime in northern France approved of the reorganization. The particular grounds for their complaints are not entirely clear, but the core of their concern was the implied threat to York's supreme authority in Lancastrian France. The council was unrepentant when it replied to the duke on 21 June, even though Somerset was already displaying exasperating dilatoriness in embarking on his expedition.[154] It reiterated its publicly stated view that Somerset's task would in no way prejudice York's authority where that was effective, and Somerset himself assured the envoys of this and ventured the hope (somewhat naively in the circumstances) that the two dukes would be able to co-operate in a friendly way.

If military factors alone had been considered, the choice of Somerset was a poor one; and if, as one contemporary believed, he had been chosen for his courage and ability (though these qualities had had little enough opportunity to show themselves so far), it was a monumental miscalculation.[155] Somerset displayed little urgency in preparing for the journey, and even the king and his council came to suspect that his enthusiasm for the mission left something to be desired. He was retained to serve in France for one year, and on 6 April more than £13,500 had been placed at his disposal.[156] The preparations extended throughout April, but on 3 May he sent his servant, Thomas Gerard, to the council to ask that muster day, fixed for 17 June, should be brought forward a fortnight.[157] The council may have been more sanguine than Somerset, for it doubted the wisdom of this suggestion and on 21 May affirmed the original date.[158] Meanwhile, substantial quantities of saltpetre and sulphur were made available by the master of the king's ordnance, John Stanley, for Somerset's military stores, under the control of his own master, John Dawnson; whilst haggling went on about the precise composition of his army of over 4,000 men.[159] Ships were brought in from all but the northern ports – even from Calais which could ill afford to provide them.[160]

When the day came and the musterers, including the earl of Salisbury, turned up for three days, Somerset did not; the same thing happened at least once more so that the king and his advisers grew annoyed and expressed their astonishment; after all, the delay was costing the government £500 daily. Somerset's excuses and requests for more money were rejected, whilst his organization for assembling and retaining the men was believed to be riddled with corruption and inefficiency.[161] The duke was reminded that he had been given the signal honour of a dukedom and that a greater proportion of the king's meagre resources had been invested in his enterprise than in any other since the reign began. Round about 9 July, he was ordered peremptorily to leave for Normandy, for the potential consequences of his failing to do so were alarming: not only would the situation in France deteriorate yet further, but in England the counties in which the assembled army was quartered would become rebellious, and the ships, sailors, and soldiers would contrive to desert (as they had evidently begun to do for some weeks past).[162] Even though Cardinal Beaufort sent another £1,000 to bring Somerset's fleet up to adequate strength, it was not until late in July that eventually the expedition arrived at the Cotentin peninsula, somewhere near Cherbourg.[163]

To compound the foolishness of the government and the laziness of Somerset might be considered treasonable, but that was precisely what followed. The duke committed a blunder of the first water by crossing the Breton frontier, devastating part of the countryside, and sacking one of Brittany's border towns. The new duke of Brittany, Francis I, was outraged and the incident threatened his alliance with England at a time when, for his own reasons, he was prepared to mediate a truce between England and France in which he would be included. According to Francis, Somerset entered Brittany 'like a conqueror', for although the Bretons treated him in a friendly fashion, he responded by pillaging and destruction, especially at La Guerche. Somerset exacted an enforced payment of 20,000 saluts, half of which had been handed over by Francis I before Breton envoys arrived in England late in the autumn.[164] But Francis was understandably incensed and demanded reparations; the English were decidedly embarrassed. Henry's council placed the blame squarely where it belonged, on Somerset's shoulders, and it redirected to him all complaints and demands relating to the sorry venture.[165] He was commanded to avoid similar action in the future. Had it not been for the usefulness of Brittany's mediation, and the friendship which had blossomed between Henry VI and Gilles, the younger brother of Francis I, it is likely that Anglo-Breton relations would have been seriously ruptured by the end of 1443. As it was, Gilles was taken into the king's service and given a handsome annuity of 1,000 marks, and his close affection for Henry VI lasted until his murder in 1449 by fellow-countrymen who mistrusted his Anglophile attitudes.[166] More-over, the mediation of Duke Francis was gratefully accepted by the English and the reciprocal promise to include the duke in any treaty that might be signed with Charles VII was highly valued in Nantes. Nevertheless, the events of 1443 had boosted Charles's confidence, demonstrated England's inability to finance properly its commitments across the channel, and revealed all too clearly the alarming poverty of talent and the divisions in the English high command.

The protection of Calais and the maintenance of its prosperity depended on the government's ability to keep the Burgundians at bay and to provide the necessary conditions for the wool staple to function profitably. In the early 1440s its record on both counts was adequate, but in the longer term it was hardly impressive. The failure of the duke of Orléans to explore avenues of peace would in time renew the threat of attack by Philip the Good.[167] The siege mentality is well conveyed by the concern felt by the Calais authorities in October 1441 for the physical wellbeing of the soldiers, merchants, and other civilians who were huddled within the town walls; the inveterate medieval habit of casting refuse and other 'offensive stuff' into the streets had become a health hazard and a dumping-ground was therefore designated beyond the town limits.[168] The English council had also become very apprehensive about the large number of French fishermen from Dieppe, now in French hands, who were allowed to put into Calais while fishing for herring; the fear that such a large number of visitors might establish a fifth-column in the town and thereby undermine its safety led to the suspension of this facility in October 1441.[169]

Meeting the needs of Calais and its supporting castles, in terms of feeding their population, renovating their walls and bastions, and securing the wages of the garrisons, was a recurring problem for the authorities at Westminster and in the Calais pale.[170] The staplers, who bore most of the expenditure, were induced to lend £10,000 to the crown in the autumn of 1441 and in return they were enabled on 22 November to appropriate a portion of the subsidy which they normally paid when importing wool into the port.[171] Loans continued to be sought from the staplers and from the lords in England, but they were only secured in return for promises of repayment from mercantile and taxation revenue which had not yet been collected by the exchequer. Moreover, shortly before the earl of Stafford, the new captain of Calais, left England to assume his responsibilities at the beginning of September 1442, news arrived that once again the exasperated and unpaid soldiers of the Calais garrison had seized the wool stacked in the mart in lieu of their overdue wages.[172] It was scarcely adequate for the government to express its thanks to the soldiers at Calais and Guisnes as Sir Thomas Kyriell's term of office came to an end on 29 August 1442.[173] If the soldiers went unpaid and seized their wool, the merchants would in turn be unable to provide the loans which were the only source of ready income available in Calais for the payment of wages. When the assurance given by the council that the staplers could take one mark from the subsidy which they paid for importing wool turned out to be vain (for, as Cardinal Beaufort pointed out in October 1442, others had prior claim to these subsidies), even the staplers reacted sharply.[174] The government was becoming the butt of numerous complaints that were mutually irreconcilable.

The appointment as captain of Calais of the king's kinsman, Humphrey, earl of Stafford was an earnest of the government's determination to resolve the dilemma. Stafford's appointment on 10 February 1441, along with that of the earl of Suffolk as captain of Guisnes on the same day, was made by the council hastily and in secret.[175] Whatever the reason for the speed and secrecy, little was done to give effect to the authority now vested in Stafford and, to a lesser extent, Suffolk for the coming decade. Lord Dudley stayed on as the lieutenant of Calais castle into the summer of 1442, even though his indenture had long expired; and Kyriell did not relinquish his post as captain until about the same time. Indeed, it was inconceivable that Suffolk would ever be able to give much thought to Guisnes, much less visit it during his term of office; William Pirton accordingly soldiered on as its lieutenant, though the earl provided funds for him by way of a large loan.[176] One is driven to the conclusion that the appointment of these great magnates was a cosmetic operation designed to inspire confidence in the staplers and in the garrisons, who desperately needed powerful advocates at the exchequer. They joined a Calais establishment which, like all other facets of Henry's government, had a prominent element of absentee household officials in it.[177]

Stafford himself was not without some knowledge of the situation in Calais, and when he at last prepared to visit the colony late in August 1442, 1,000 marks were to be paid to him annually, and he secured an undertaking from the council that if the soldiers revolted again before he arrived, he should not be regarded as responsible.[178] His task was a formidable one. Nevertheless, under Stafford at least some steps were taken to repair the defences of both Calais and Guisnes, and to provide sufficient ordnance for the garrisons. In response to rumours that the Castilian navy in French pay was about to invest Calais in March 1443, a series of harbour works and repair projects was undertaken in the town and castle.[179] All this, of course, required further expenditure, and once more the customs duties collectable at Calais were preyed upon to the extent of £1,000 before the winter of 1443 set in.[180] More ominously, the council felt able to contribute only £3,400 (again from the customs) to the wages of the new lieutenant and his men, though £5,000 was owing to them by 5 June 1443. A further £200 was promised from the same source on 28 June to pay for repairs to Guisnes, and further works were authorized by a commission appointed on 10 July.[181] The unsatisfactory nature of assigning these revenues for collection by creditors at source was revealed by the case of the long-serving (and evidently long-suffering) William Pirton, the lieutenant at Guisnes. In accordance with his indenture, dated 10 February 1441, his wages were to be taken from Guisnes's own revenue and his initial commission was extended on 10 February 1444 until 1449. It was a naively optimistic award, but the council at least had the grace to add that if war should occur, then alternative (though unspecified) sources would be found. Pirton had been able to survive until 1444, running up a wages bill of £2,378 since February 1441, by incurring a loan from Suffolk as captain of the fortress.[182]

It was apparent that all that was considered desirable in the defence of Calais could not be afforded. The unpaid wages of the garrisons and imperfect protection of the trading lanes could eventually prove as damaging to the colony and the reputation of the Lancastrians as any threat from Burgundy. And the Calais problem was likely to get worse rather than better, unless an international peace treaty were sealed soon. Moreover the protection of the wool trade was as vital to the prosperity of England's mercantile community, particularly in London, as it was to the survival of English dominion in Calais. The merchants, in turn, looked to the government to preserve their trading monopoly and to provide the conditions under which their interests – which were the interests of Calais – enjoyed adequate security. For this reason, in November 1437 measures were confirmed to regulate the bullion traffic by the establishment of two exchanges, one at Calais and one in England, and also to reaffirm the basic staple principle that wool exported from England should go to Calais before being released to the European markets, unless the bales were destined for the Mediterranean.[183] Peace with the Burgundian Low Countries was essential if the commercial link were to function efficiently and profitably; hence, on 29 September 1439, just as the peace conference at Oye was dispersing, a commercial treaty for three years was concluded with the Low Countries.[184] At last wool exports from England could be safely resumed and the bales and fells which had stockpiled in Calais as a result of the Burgundian ban on their sale in the duke's territories could be released.[185]

It was unfortunate that the English government's actions ran clean contrary to the declared principles of its policy and the normal practice of decades. These were characterized, in trading as in other spheres, by misplaced generosity in the granting and distributing of favours and privileges. John Stevens, a London merchant who had admittedly done good service at sea in 1436, was allowed in March 1440 to export 20,000 wool fells to Holland and Zeeland directly, without passing through the Calais staple.[186] In the 1439–40 parliament the regulation was relaxed that required exports of cheese and butter, which were cheap and perishable commodities, to be taken to Calais before being disposed of elsewhere.[187] As yet, it is true, there was a reluctance to extend his privilege to other goods like hides, which were less perishable. But Henry VI's lack of circumspection may be detected in the growing habit of licensing merchants and shippers to export wool elsewhere than to Calais; it brought a protest from the staplers and in parliament an assurance was given that such licensing would cease.[188]

Moreover, in response to a demand from the staplers, who feared for the health of their commerce in the face of Burgundian enmity, the government conceded in October 1442 that the restrictive bullion laws should be relaxed to encourage trade. This was sufficient for wool exports to Calais to revive dramatically in the winter and spring of 1442–43.[189] But the government was not prepared to confine the privilege of electing the mayor of the staple to those wool merchants who actually traded at Calais and were members of the staple company. It is evident that, as with parliamentary elections in England, the existing regulations were so elastic as to result in informality and even disorder; and the staplers were anxious to tighten their own control over Calais's trade and to protect their position in uncertain times. The government did not oblige.[190] Without the good will and continued prosperity of the staplers, the defence of Calais and its commercial wealth would be endangered. If this were to be avoided, then the government had no option but to accede to most of the merchants' requests; any persistence in the licensing of wool exports elsewhere would risk forfeiting the support of these powerful men.

Notes

1 Stevenson, II, ii, 452 (1440); *PPC*, VI, 20 (December 1443). In the latter letter, issued from Sheen manor under Henry's own signet, the king declared himself a true Christian prince who sought peace through his reverence for God, a desire to avoid bloodshed, and a concern for the souls of Christian people involved in the war.

2 Stevenson, II, ii, 451-60 (with the quotations on 452-3).

3 See *PPC*, V, 132 (February 1441), for the financial burden.

4 Stevenson, II, ii, 454-6.

5 The French army continued to suffer from inherent weakness, particularly the 'la carence de la noblesse française' (Contamine, op. cit., pp. 253-62, 271-2).

6 There is some evidence that the English hoped Orléans would aid them in operations against Burgundy, if he were released (P. Champion, *Vie de Charles d'Orléans* [2nd ed., Paris, 1969], pp. 277, 279, citing 'Exposé de Louvet', président de Provence, in the Archivio di stato, Negoz. colla Francia, in Turin). For Charles's sojourn in England, see Champion, op. cit., ch. VIII, XI (and an itinerary on pp. 668-72); and, in English, E. McLeod, *Charles of Orleans* (1969), ch. 11-12.

7 *PPC*, V, 64, 67, 85; Knowlson, op. cit., pp. 163-4.

8 Translated in Vaughan, op. cit., pp. 102-7; see also Champion, op. cit., pp. 276-7.

9 *Foedera*, V, i, 38 (29 April 1437); *PPC*, V, 64, 67 (24-31 October 1437). See also Champion, op. cit., p. 282, quoting AN, K 67 no. 37 (11 July 1437).

10 *PPC*, V, 80 (25 November).

11 ibid., 85.

12 Above, p. 360.

13 Knowlson, op. cit., pp. 164-6, based on PRO, E101/323/4-6. Popham had been appointed to lead the English envoys on 17 March 1438 (*Foedera*, V, i, 45); for him, see above, p. 301.

14 *PPC*, V, 90 (c. February), 95, 101. On 27 April there was a public procession in Rouen 'pour la paix' (Allmand, *BIHR*, XL [1967], 2 n. 1, citing Archives de la Seine-Maritime, Rouen, G. 39).

15 Champion, op. cit., p. 283; *Foedera*, V, i, 54.

16 ibid.; Champion, op. cit., p. 284.

17 *Foedera*, V, i, 55; Knowlson, op. cit., pp. 165-6.

18 A full account appears in Allmand, *BIHR*, XL (1967), 1-33, with accompanying documents printed in *Camden Miscellany*, XXIV (Camden

Soc., 4th ser., IX, 1972), 79-149. The following paragraphs are largely based on these works.

19 *Foedera*, V, i, 56, 57. Commercial negotiations with Holland, Zeeland, and Friesland were authorized the same day.

20 *Brut*, p. 506.

21 *Foedera*, V, i, 59.

22 ibid.; *DKR*, XLVIII (1887), 326; Allmand, *Camden Misc.*, XXIV (1972), 85-8 (BN, n. a. q. 6215 f. 93*v* – 95*v*).

23 PRO, E28/60/66.

24 Emden, *Oxford*, I-III, *s.n.*; above, pp. 46, 278.

25 *GEC*, II, 388-9; V, 137-8; VI, 613-16; X, 236-9; Roskell, *Speakers*, pp. 235-7.

26 *GEC*, XII, i, 301-2; above, p. 303.

27 Judd, op. cit., ch. I, III; *PPC*, V, 334-407. Bekyngton's account extends from 26 June, when the main delegation reached Calais, to 10 October, when it reported to the king at Kennington. A comparable French account, probably by one of the French envoys, lasts from 4 June to 29 July (Archivio General de Simancas, Spain, K. 1711 f. 489*r*-198*v*, printed in Allmand, *Camden Misc.*, XXIV [1972], 108-25). See also Allmand, *BIHR*, XL (1967), 4-5.

28 Thus, when envoys were commissioned to discuss a commercial truce with Burgundy, the magnates' names were omitted (*Foedera*, V, i, 63).

29 Allmand, *Camden Misc.*, XXIV (1972), 96-8 (BN, n. a. q. 6215 f. 100*v*-101*r*), 99-104 (ibid., f. 102*r*-104*v*). A safe-conduct for 500 to attend the convention was issued by Henry VI on 8 May (*Foedera*, V, i, 59).

30 ibid., 61, 64; *DKR*, XLVIII (1887), 328. Norfolk was authorized on 2 June to take 2,000 marks-worth of goods with him (*CPR, 1436–41*, p. 285).

31 C. T. Allmand (*BIHR*, XL [1967], 9 n. 4) suggests that Gloucester may have been absent from the council that day; but it is highly unlikely that such latitude would have been given to Beaufort without the duke's knowledge.

32 ibid., 11 n. 1.

33 *Foedera*, V, i, 61.

34 On 26 May, his departure with his custodian, Stourton, was duly authorized (PRO, E28/60/76), and the city of Orléans began celebrating his return to France (Champion, op. cit., 288-9).

35 Three days before, Beaufort had been granted £1,000 to cover his expenses on the embassy since 29 May (PRO, E403/735 m. 9).

36 The French and Burgundians had spent much of June concerting a common attitude, and Burgundy's son and heir, Charles, was married to Katherine, daughter of Charles VII, during these weeks (Allmand, *BIHR*, XL [1967], 6).

37 Arnold, *Customs* p. 283 (with other versions in Hall, *Chronicle*, pp. 197-202, and, from an eighteenth-century copy, in Stevenson, II, ii, 440-51, partially reprinted in *EHD*, IV, 254-6, and Wilkinson, *Const. Hist.*, pp. 52-6). There was no purpose in Gloucester distorting his recollection, since the king himself had been present at the envoys' interview.

38 The English took a self-righteous view of the French withdrawal, blaming the dauphin for the fruitlessness of the entire conference (*Great Chron.*, p. 174).

39 Such negotiations had been authorized on 23 May (above, p. 446).

40 *DKR*, XLVIII (1887), 331.
41 The duke had left Calais on 13 October with his captor, who took him to Stourton in Wilts.; from there he announced on 25 October that he would be freed to pursue peace and raise his ransom (Champion, op. cit., pp. 294, 297).
42 Ct. Allmand, *BIHR*, XL (1967), 30.
43 Allmand, *Camden Misc.*, XXIV (1972), 105-8 (Bibliothèque Publique et Universitaire, Geneva, Latin MS 27 no. 59, 57; Archivio Segreto Vaticano, Reg. Vat. 359 f. 98r-v).
44 Above, p. 235; Harriss, *TRHS*, 5th ser., XX (1970), 129-48.
45 *RP*, V, 3.
46 Arnold, *Customs*, p. 283; *Foedera*, V, i, 76-7, partially reprinted in modernized English in Wilkinson, *Const. Hist.*, pp. 51-2.
47 Arnold, *Customs*, p. 283.
48 *Foedera*, V, i, 76-7. In character, it may be compared with Hue de Lannoy's memorandum to Philip the Good in September 1436 (Vaughan, op. cit., pp. 102-7; above, p. 445). For Henry V's cautionary words in his will of 1421 about the release of Orléans and the count of Eu without a guarantee that they would keep the peace between England and France, see Eton Coll. MS.
49 Stevenson, II, ii, 457.
50 *DKR*, XLVIII (1887), 332, 333, 334, 336, 337, 338; *Foedera*, V, i, 73, 75, 77, 78, 79.
51 ibid., 81; *DKR*, XLVIII (1887), 337.
52 Above, p. 452. This was a reasonable interpretation of the will of 1421 (above, n. 48), though at that time Charles VI was king and at peace with Henry V; the deathbed codicils made no mention of the captives. According to Monstrelet, what Henry V had advised was the custody of Orléans until Henry VI came of age (Wylie and Waugh, III, 417).
53 *Foedera*, V, i, 85, 87, 88, 89, 97; Champion, op. cit., p. 300. Since the previous autumn Orléans had been alerting his friends and servants and his fellow princes about his need to raise a large ransom (ibid., pp. 297-9).
54 *PL*, II, 21-2.
55 *Foedera*, V, i, 96; *DKR*, XLVIII (1887), 341.
56 *Foedera*, V, i, 93, 99, 100; Champion, op. cit., pp. 311-12.
57 *Foedera*, V, i, 101; Vaughan, op. cit., pp. 124-5. Orléans left his younger brother, Jean, in England as security for the fulfilment of his promises.
58 Champion, op. cit., p. 313 (citing the lost Registre de l'hôtel de ville de Saint-Omer).
59 Champion, op. cit., pp. 288-9, 299, 328 (citing Archives communales d'Orléans, CC 655).
60 For the Burgundian reception, see Champion, op. cit., pp. 313-25; Vaughan, op. cit., pp. 124-5.
61 BN, f. fr. 5330 f. 137; and see Marshall, thesis, p. 13, citing BN, MS fr. 23,189 f. 137.
62 He was still regarded as inexperienced and under the control of subordinates at the beginning of his second term as lieutenant-general in 1440 (below, p. 459).
63 PRO, E404/52/208.
64 *GEC*, XII, ii, 905-91. Both Gloucester and Beaufort were present on 8 May when the appointment was resolved (BN, f. fr. 5330 f. 137).

65 Bedford was designated 'regent' between Charles VI's death (October 1422) and Henry's coronation (December 1431); thereafter he was 'governor and regent', perhaps to emphasize his practical powers of government (Stevenson, II, i, 43, 44-5, 141, 207, 266, 268; II, ii, [534], [554]; BN, n.a. fr. 1482 f. 116, 117).

66 Contamine, op. cit., p. 262.

67 *London Chrons.*, p. 143; Marshall, thesis, pp. 14-15.

68 E. F. Jacob, *The fifteenth century, 1399–1485* (Oxford, 1961), pp. 465-6.

69 York evidently returned only after Warwick had arrived (*Brut*, pp. 471-2).

70 Stevenson, II, i, lxvi-lxxi (11 May).

71 *Brut*, p. 471. Willoughby was made captain of the town and castle of Bayeux by 28 November 1437 (*CPR, 1436–41*, p. 117) and of Lisieux by 26 September (Marshall, thesis, p. 257).

72 His appointment was noted as being 'with the advice' of both Gloucester and Beaufort (ibid., p. 17, from *Foedera*, V, i, 42).

73 *Foedera*, V, i, 42. The appointment had been resolved on 23 May in the presence of Beaufort and Gloucester (BN, f. fr. 5330 f. 137).

74 *CPR, 1436–41*, p. 144; *PPC*, V, 69, 72; *London Chrons.*, p. 143; *Brut*, p. 472; 'Benet's Chron.', pp. 185-6. A delay of 11 weeks would make early November, rather than 8 September (the preference of 'Benet's Chron.'), more likely as the time of landing. The long wait in port explains why some masters and sailors on the ships assembled in Devon and Cornwall deserted before sailing – even though they had received their wages (*CPR, 1436–41*, p, 200).

75 According to Giles, pp. 16-17, he could accomplish little because of French strength. He was also ill for a considerable time before he died on 30 April 1439 (NorthantsRO, Westmorland MS Box 1, XI no. 4 [L]).

76 *PPC*, V, 70.

77 ibid., 73, 88, 94. Envoys were despatched on 11 February 1438 to aid in the survey.

78 *London Chrons.*, pp. 143, 145.

79 *PPC*, V, 64, 69, 70, 73-4 (October–November 1437).

80 ibid., 69, 94; *CPR, 1436–41*, p. 340.

81 *PPC*, V, 73-4, 79. Crotoy was under siege at the same time, and Lords Fauconberg and Talbot were commissioned to relieve it; they did so by 11 January 1438 (BL, Add. Ch. 3830, 561).

82 *PPC*, V, 80.

83 ibid., 90.

84 *CPR, 1436–41*, p. 149; *Foedera*, V, i, 46; *DKR*, XLVIII (1887), 321, 322. Huntingdon, who evidently had the principal command, was assigned certain revenues to finance Guisnes's defence (*Foedera*, V, i, 46).

85 *CPR, 1436–41*, p. 139; PRO, E404/52/411; 55/15.

86 For the phrase 'sur le pale', see Allmand, *Camden Misc.*, XXIV (1972), 101, 103.

87 Above, p. 447.

88 Marshall, thesis, p. 18 (from BL, Add. MS 11,542 f. 78, 81); *Foedera*, V, i, 85; *GEC*, XII, i, 46-7. He was certainly captain of Cherbourg by 8 November 1439 (*DKR*, XLVIII [1887], 330). *Brut*, p. 475, says rather vaguely that he went to govern France and Normandy. Somerset was

exchanged for the French count of Eu round about April 1438 (*Foedera*, V, i, 50).

89 Arnold, *Customs*, p. 285.

90 *CPR, 1436–41*, pp. 312, 314. For their earlier military experience in the 1430s, see PRO, E404/50/305, 298; 51/130; 48/320.

91 *London Chrons.*, pp. 145-6; PRO, E403/735 m. 6, 12.

92 *CPR, 1436–41*, pp. 372, 408; *DKR*, XLVIII (1887), 331; PRO, E403/737 m. 11. See M. Jones, 'John Beaufort, duke of Somerset and the French expedition of 1443', in Griffiths, *Patronage, the crown and the provinces*, ch. 4.

93 *PPC*, V, 112-13; *CPR, 1436–41*, p. 370. He was at Bernay by 17 February, withdrawing men from the Norman garrisons to join his troops (J. F. Reed Lib., Penn., MS 33). Somerset at least seems to have concluded a truce with Brittany which Henry VI ratified on 2 July 1440 (BN, f. fr. 5330 f. 138).

94 Below, p. 469.

95 Champion, op. cit., pp. 329ff. Duke Charles became immersed in the princely intrigues against Charles VII.

96 Stevenson, II, ii, 585-91; *Foedera*, V, i, 85.

97 *EHL*, pp. 339, 341.

98 *PPC*, V, 146.

99 ibid., 132, 142, 145, 146; *CPR, 1436–41*, pp. 534, 536, 538, 539, 571; PRO, E28/66/56 (February–May 1441).

100 PRO, E28/68/30; Stevenson, II, ii, 603-7 (June 1441).

101 'Benet's Chron.', p. 187.

102 *Brut*, p. 477; *London Chrons.*, pp. 147-8. The duchess of Bedford was Woodville's wife. The company left London on 16 May but did not cross the channel until June (Flenley, p. 115).

103 *PPC*, V, 154, 159, 163.

104 ibid., 171. For all purposes, 440,000 *livres tournois* (evidently misprinted as 340,000) were expected from the Normans and 68,000 *l.t.* would be provided by England; both estimates were wildly optimistic on the threshold of the 1440s. See Doucet, *Moyen Age*, 2nd ser., XXVII (1926), 272-303.

105 PRO, E28/69/41, 64 (13, 28 November).

106 PRO, E28/60/75 (25 May 1439). For Cressoner, see above, p. 201.

107 Cressoner died in 1441, and John Sherwyn's appointment as captain in his place on 20 April only lasted a month (*DKR*, XLVIII [1887], 346).

108 PRO, E28/68/31-33; E101/53/35.

109 Woodger, thesis, pp. 18-19 (from Longleat MS 215). During his year-long appointment, Bourgchier was required to employ a garrison that was predominantly non-Norman, and he was instructed to wipe out brigands and enforce discipline.

110 *DKR*, XLVIII (1887), 330, 331 (October 1439); PRO, E403/743-78. See Woodger, thesis, pp. 18-44, for a full account of Bourgchier's term as captain.

111 ibid., 21.

112 *PPC*, V, 139; *Foedera*, V, i, 107, 108; *DKR*, XLVIII (1887), 347.

113 *PPC*, V, 173. Orléans was in touch with Brittany, Burgundy, and other French princes in 1441–42, but the purpose is unknown (BN, n.a.fr. 5848 no. 21).

114 *Bekynton Corr.*, II, 189 (a reminder from Thomas Bekyngton in July 1442). For the situation in Gascony, see below, p. 464.
115 *Foedera*, V, i, 112; *DKR*, XLVIII (1887), 354. On 29 May the envoys were described as being sent to Gascony on business that lay very close to the king's heart (PRO, E28/79/56).
116 *Bekynton Corr.*, II, 177-248 (from Bodl, Ashmole MS 789 f. 174ff), with a summary in ibid., I, xxxvi-xlii, and translated in Nicolas, *Journal*. Charles VII made for Tartas in southern Gascony, in the sieur d'Albret's territory, after Easter 1442 (Champion, op. cit., p. 338). In general, see S. E. Dicks, 'Henry VI and the daughters of Armagnac: a problem in mediaeval diplomacy', *Emporia State research studies*, 1967, pp. 5-12.
117 *Bekynton Corr.*, II, 201, 210-12, 220-2, 225-7. For Suffolk's opposition, see *Great Chron.*, p. 176; *Brut*, pp. 509, 511; *London Chrons.*, p. 155. But ibid. puts the failure of the abortive negotiations down to the military situation.
118 *PPC*, V, 210 (7-8 October 1442); *Bekynton Corr.*, II, 201. For the reinforcement of Crotoy, see *CPR, 1441-46*, p. 80 (16 June 1442); and for Talbot's expedition, 2,500 strong (May), ibid., pp. 79, 106; *PPC*, V, 186; PRO, E28/70/51. 'Benet's Chron.', p. 189, dates his crossing with 3,000 men after 27 May, but *Brut*, p. 483, suggests 25 May; *London Chrons.*, p. 150, puts the size of the army at 4,000.
119 PRO, E403/745 m. 10 (16 July). For Orléans's renewed activity in the cause of peace in the second half of 1442, following the agreement between Charles VII and his princes, see Champion, op. cit., pp. 339-40.
120 *PPC*, V, 212, 214. The negotiations were to take place within a fortnight. York had been instructed on 9 September to choose a site for such a convention (*Foedera*, V, i, 115; *DKR*, XLVIII [1887], 355).
121 The English difficulties were well appreciated by the Burgundian Hue de Lannoy as early as September 1436 (above, p. 445), whilst reluctance to serve in France had been growing of late (*PPC*, V, 90-1 [February 1438]).
122 *RDP*, V, 237-8; above, p. 356.
123 For a sober judgement on York and Somerset as military commanders in the early 1440s, see Giles, p. 31.
124 *PPC*, V, 198, 203.
125 *Bekynton Corr.*, II, 216; below, p. 465.
126 PRO, E28/70/89 (25 January, probably in 1443). Talbot's attempted siege of Dieppe in November 1442 had to be abandoned when his men threatened to desert (*London Chrons.*, p. 150; *Chron. of London*, p. 131; 'Benet's Chron.', p. 189).
127 *PPC*, V, 223. For 'la petitesce de nos finances' in Normandy, see BN. n. a. fr. 1482 no. 167 (29 June 1443).
128 *Bekynton Corr.*, II, 244.
129 *PPC*, V, 226, 229.
130 *CCR, 1435-41*, p. 194.
131 ibid. (September 1438).
132 *CPR, 1436-41*, pp. 247, 273, 312. Huntingdon arrived in Gascony on 2 August 1439 and served for only a year and a half before he was recalled in December 1440 for reasons that are obscure (Vale, *English Gascony*, pp. 115-16).
133 For d'Albret's defection, see *PPC*, V, 121 (July 1440); and Longueville's, ibid., 291 (June 1443).

134 See the letters to King Henry dated, respectively, 24 July and 9 August 1442 (*Bekynton Corr.*, II, 186-90, 196-7).

135 *PPC*, V, 247.

136 *Bekynton Corr.*, II, 214-15; Vale, *English Gascony*, pp. 116-19, 243. Huntingdon's servants, as well as household men like John St Lo and Edward Hull, benefited nicely.

137 *PPC*, V, 192 (29 July); PRO, E404/58/182; Vale, *English Gascony*, p. 120.

138 *Bekynton Corr.*, II, 180 (23 June 1442).

139 *PPC*, V, 201, 198, 203, 207, 217; Bodl, Tanner cccxlii f. 187v (abbot of Bury). The archbishop of Bordeaux, Pey Berland, was in England between August and November 1442 and doubtless added his plea from first-hand knowledge for more aid (*Bekynton Corr.*, I, xl n. 2; Vale, *English Gascony*, p. 123). See R. Corbin, *Histoire de Pey Berland et du pays bordelais au XVᵉ siècle d'après les documents de l'époque* (Bordeaux, 1888).

140 *PPC*, V, 203; Vale, *English Gascony*, p. 124. Bonville's indenture was for one year only.

141 *CPR, 1441–46*, pp. 107, 114, 154. Bonville was reported on 5 February to be at Plymouth; he was still waiting to leave on 15 February, but seems to have departed by 2 March (*Bekynton Corr.*, II, 439-40; Vale, *English Gascony*, pp. 125-6). One ship and more than a third of his men were lost at sea.

142 *PPC*, V, 218; below, p. 466.

143 *Bekynton Corr.*, II, 214.

144 *PPC*, V, 414; *Bekynton Corr.*, I, xl-xli. For a list of the towns that fell to Charles VII even before 18 October, see ibid., II, 215-16.

145 *PPC*, V, 242, 247. Those taking badly needed wheat to Bordeaux or Bayonne were exempt from customs duties on 27 March 1443 (ibid., 249).

146 *PPC*, V, 236; *Foedera*, V, i, 118. For his title see S. Luce (ed.), *Chronique du Mont St Michel, 1343–1468* (2 vols., Paris, 1879–83), II, 157; PRO, E403/747 m. 15 (2 April 1443). For a full treatment of the expedition, see Jones, in Griffiths, *Patronage, the crown and the provinces*, ch. 4.

147 *RDP*, V, 241; *PPC*, V, 280; above, p. 358. Although Maine was still in English hands, Anjou was not; Maine was confirmed to Edmund Beaufort on 19 July 1442 (BN, n. a. fr. 3642 no. 800A).

148 For somewhat differing views, neither of which is quite that expressed below, see Jacob, *Fifteenth Century*, pp. 471-2; Vale, *English Gascony*, pp. 128-9.

149 *PPC*, V, 258ff.

150 *PPC*, V, 251-6. At the same time, his family received some security when it was agreed that should anything happen to the duke, his widow would have custody of the Somerset heiress, Margaret, rather than that she should become a ward of someone else.

151 ibid., 259-63.

152 ibid., 258.

153 ibid., 288; *DKR*, XLVIII (1887), 359.

154 Below, p. 469. For Rinel, see Otway-Ruthven, *King's secretary*, pp. 91-3; Ogard had been captain of Caen since 26 January 1440 (BN, f. fr. 22468 no. 50).

155 Giles, p. 31.

156 PRO, E403/747 m. 15. Between 5 June and 26 July a second instalment of almost £14,200 was paid to him (ibid., 750 m. 6-19).

157 *PPC*, V, 256, 266, 409; *CPR, 1441–46*, pp. 199, 201.

158 *PPC*, V, 275, 276, 409.

159 ibid., 280 (28 May), 409.

160 ibid., 236, 276, 278, 282; *CPR, 1441–46*, p. 201.

161 *PPC*, V, 409 (*c.* 9 July).

162 By 27 June, ten days after the date on which the army should have set sail, many of those who had taken the king's wages had disappeared (ibid., 291, 301). At the same time, it was reported that insufficient ships were now available to transport the army and two journeys might be necessary (ibid., 293 [28 June]). For reluctance to join the expedition, see *Brut*, p. 484. See PRO, E403/750 m. 12-16, for the provision (under 6 July) for payment of the fleet. The whole sorry tale of Somerset's proposed expedition may have been the last straw as far as the treasurer was concerned; Cromwell resigned on 6 July 1443 (*Foedera*, V, i, 123; above, p. 377).

163 *PPC*, V, 306 (13 July); *CPR, 1441–46*, p. 202. *Brut*, p. 484, says that he set sail on 21 July. See also 'Benet's Chron.', p. 189; *Three Chrons.*, p. 64; *London Chrons.*, p. 151; *Chron. of London*, p. 132.

164 *PPC*, VI, 11. Bonds were concluded for payment of the other half by Christmas.

165 ibid., 16-18, 19, 22-3 (12-17 December).

166 ibid., 3, 7, 9, 16, 19, 20; *CPR, 1441–46*, p. 229; below, p. 511. Henry VI agreed to examine the revived Breton claim to the earldom of Richmond, but it was in effect rejected. For Gilles's friendship with Henry, formed as long ago as 1432, see D. S. Cottam, 'Anglo-Breton relations, 1435–91' (Wales MA dissertation, 1972), pp. 17-18; and above, p. 207.

167 *PPC*, V, 73-4 (November 1437), 187 (May 1442); PRO, E28/66/31-32 (Guisnes, February 1441).

168 *DKR*, XLVIII (1887), 349.

169 *PPC*, V, 153.

170 ibid., 64, 69, 70, 79, 94, 185; *CPR, 1441–46*, p. 33; *DKR*, XLVIII (1887), 336, 338, 343; PRO, E28/60/78-79. A report from the surveyor of works on 16 April 1441 showed that much more needed to be done (ibid., 67/51). In 1442 proceedings were initiated against the treasurer of Calais for failure to undertake repairs (ibid., E101/193/5).

171 *PPC*, V, 163.

172 ibid., 163, 187, 198, 203. The privilege of leave of absence, which was authorized on 16 June 1440, was hardly sufficient to mollify the soldiers (*DKR*, XLVIII [1887], 336).

173 *PPC*, V, 198, 207.

174 ibid., 215. A similar obstacle had been encountered in repaying the staplers 3,000 marks from the wool subsidy in April 1441 (PRO, E28/67/56).

175 PRO, E28/66/68; *DKR*, XLVIII (1887), 347. His indentures are PRO, E101/71/908-10. He also succeeded Sir Maurice Bruyn as captain of Rysbank tower.

176 PRO, E28/68/40; 70/65; above, p. 470. Stafford took no steps to garrison Calais with his own relatives (Rawcliffe, op. cit., p. 75).

177 e.g., Giles St Lo, an esquire of the household by 1429–30, was appointed controller of Calais on 19 November 1437; and William Port, one of Beaufort's servants, became customer there on 8 January 1438. Both

offices were crucial to the commercial and financial health of Calais. *DKR*, XLVIII (1887), 322; Jeffs, thesis, p. 312; PRO, E404/55/294-95. See also *DKR*, XLVIII (1887), 329 (William Ludlowe), 330 (George Ashby); below, pp. 472-3.

178 *PPC*, V, 203 (August 1442). His renewed indentures are PRO, E101/71/912-13.

179 *PPC*, V, 207; *DKR*, XLVIII (1887), 354-5.

180 *PPC*, V, 283.

181 ibid., 285, 293; *CPR, 1441–46*, p. 203.

182 PRO, E28/66/31-32, 34; 67/17; *CPR, 1441–46*, pp. 242, 243; *CCR, 1441–47*, pp. 173, 181; *DKR*, XLVIII (1887), 344.

183 *CPR, 1436–41*, pp. 139, 146.

184 Above, p. 450; *CCR, 1435–41*, p. 357; *Foedera*, V, i, 65.

185 T. H. Lloyd, *The English wool trade in the middle ages* (Cambridge, 1977), p. 263, with table on p. 264. For further details, see Thielemans, op. cit., pp. 116-45.

186 For this and other examples, see *CPR, 1436–41*, pp. 384, 441; *DKR*, XLVIII (1887), 331, 341, 343, 347, 352-60.

187 *RP*, V, 24. It presumably occurred towards the end of the session in mid-February 1440, after the granting of a licence on 28 January to export cheese to Flanders (*DKR*, XLVIII [1887], 332).

188 At first, unlicensed exports to other ports were the main target of parliament in 1440 and 1441–42, but the increasing number of licences accentuated the problem by 1441–43 (*RP*, V, 30, 54; *PPC*, V, 316; *CPR, 1441–46*, p. 49).

189 *RP*, V, 64; *PPC*, V, 215, 219, 221; Lloyd, op. cit., pp. 268-9 (and table on p. 264). This was done despite Cardinal Beaufort's misgivings.

190 *RP*, V, 105 (1444).

18 The Fall of Lancastrian France – II

The king's marriage, 1444–45

One cannot be certain of the origin of the proposal that Henry VI should marry Margaret, the second daughter of René, duke of Anjou, Lorraine, and Bar, and titular king of Naples, Sicily, and Jerusalem. On the other hand, there can be no doubt that the king's marriage would be a momentous event, and that a bride who was closely related to the king's adversary (for her aunt was Charles VII's queen) would arouse apprehension in many quarters and hostility in some. After all, Henry V's marriage to Katherine of Valois in 1420 had had outstanding advantages to commend it; not least among them was the fact that she was Charles VI's eldest daughter and the marriage was indissolubly linked with a treaty that disinherited her brother, the dauphin, and opened the way for the accession of Henry and Katherine as king and queen of France. In 1444 circumstances were entirely different. England was now the suppliant in negotiations and the king's marriage to a French princess might do no more than stop the fighting and yet leave the large questions of sovereignty and occupation of territory unanswered. When it became clear that the prospective bride was Margaret of Anjou and that no final treaty was forthcoming, but merely a short-term truce that was just as likely to give the French opportunity to strengthen themselves as it would give the English a much-needed breathing-space, hostility to the match would probably increase even among those who had previously been prepared to tolerate it.

The marriage proposal may have been transmitted to Henry by the duke of Brittany's envoys, from whom the king had sought information about any French proposals as early as August 1443; at the same time, the king was preparing to send his own ambassador to France to investigate the possibility of concluding peace. Reports were forthcoming from the Bretons in the autumn, despite Somerset's foolish provocation at La Guerche. They informed the council that Suffolk was expected shortly in France to discuss a treaty, though there is no sign that the earl had yet been assigned this task.[1] Francis I's envoys were engaged in delicate diplomatic footwork between the two adversaries in order to maintain their duchy's independence and ensure its inclusion in any Anglo-French peace treaty. But still, on 17 December, when the Bretons were again told that Henry welcomed Francis's mediation, no

English embassy had been despatched to France.[2] Whether Margaret's name figured in these exchanges is unknown. There is no indication that the duke of Orléans played any significant part in forwarding the cause of peace at this juncture, and the duke and duchess of Burgundy are unlikely to have done so because their relations with Charles VII had deteriorated markedly in recent years.[3]

A truce in the war may have been welcomed by Charles VII for his own domestic purposes, for during 1444 he decided to move against Burgundy in conjunction with his brother-in-law, Duke René. After years of inconclusive negotiating, a royal marriage was most likely to achieve this end, though Charles understandably baulked at offering one of his two unmarried daughters, Jeanne and Madeleine, to Henry VI.[4] As Thomas Basin observed, the French king had no intention of buttressing the English claim to his own throne by forging another family link between Lancaster and Valois.[5] One of René's daughters would avoid this risk and in view of the Angevins' prominence at the French court, the choice was an appropriate one. Charles's queen was Marie of Anjou, Duke René's sister, and their younger brother, Charles of Anjou, had long been one of the king's intimate advisers. By the beginning of 1444, René was himself an honoured member of the Valois court and when Charles VII moved against Burgundy later in the year, he did so ostensibly in René's interest in Lorraine.[6] One may presume, therefore, that the proposal for Margaret's marriage to Henry VI originated at the French court, where a strong Angevin lobby favoured it. It suited Charles's purpose diplomatically in isolating Burgundy, militarily in providing a respite during which army reforms could be contemplated and tested against Philip the Bold, and dynastically in avoiding a potentially dangerous liaison between the French royal house and the Lancastrians.[7]

From the English point of view, the choice of Margaret was far from auspicious: she was not René's heiress (for she had brothers living and an elder sister). René himself, for all the influence of his family at court, was hardly an imposing figure diplomatically, militarily, or politically, for he had been a captive of the duke of Burgundy from 1431 to 1437 and was still pledged to pay an enormous ransom for his release; his claims to the kingdoms of Naples, Sicily, and Jerusalem were nothing more than extravagant illusions, and those to the islands of Majorca and Minorca little better; even his position as duke of Anjou was threatened by the English in Normandy and Gascony.[8] To involve Henry in marriage for military reasons was hazardous enough; if the results proved not to be substantial – and strikingly so – then the entire venture would be seen to be hardly worthwhile.

By the end of January 1444, the English council had taken the weighty decision to pursue the possibility of a marriage alliance with a French princess, and probably by that stage Margaret's name was being considered. By 1 February it was resolved to send Suffolk to France (as the French had anticipated) at the head of an embassy to negotiate with

Charles VII's representatives a termination of the war and the conclusion of a marriage. The significance of this step and the risks that were involved were fully appreciated by the earl, and he expressed serious misgivings about the wisdom of his own participation in the mission.[9] He seems to have felt that the dual approach of the last three years to relations with Charles VII, combining a willingness to discuss peace with a readiness to defend territorial positions, should still be the guiding principles of English policy. In the circumstances, therefore, he doubted whether he was at all appropriate as a negotiator, partly because the French had requested him and partly because he had close personal relations with certain French noblemen.[10] This latter factor especialy worried him, for he feared that his contacts in France would be misinterpreted in England (and hostile rumours were already circulating in London) and therefore prejudice the success of a mission led by himself. As he pointed out to the council, others who had been engaged in peace-seeking embassies had returned home to popular denigration by those who disagreed with, or misunderstood, their best intentions (and Gloucester's reaction to the conference at Oye and to the release of Orléans was fresh in the mind).[11] Despite these warnings, the king insisted on nominating Suffolk as his envoy, and the earl, as the loyal Lancastrian he was, undertook to do his best; it was a fateful decision as far as Suffolk's future reputation was concerned and (as he himself feared) it probably increased popular scepticism of the whole enterprise. Nevertheless, he had his conditions to make. He requested experienced colleagues to accompany him, and the king accordingly commissioned Adam Moleyns, the dean of Salisbury who had just been made keeper of the privy seal and had long been an advocate of peace in the shadow of Cardinal Beaufort; Sir Robert Roos, one of the king's most senior and trusted household servants; Master Richard Andrew, Henry's secretary, and John Wenlock, another household servant whose diplomatic knowledge was already extensive.[12] Suffolk also requested a public declaration that no blame should attach to him and his companions should their mission fail, and this the king provided by letters patent under his great seal.[13] In short, this was to be an embassy intimately connected with the inner circle of the king's household (as was appropriate for discussions about Henry's marriage) and sympathetic to past efforts to achieve peace.

Suffolk's reluctance to go to France was a medley of self-interest, political apprehension, and a genuine unease about his own suitability for the task. In agreeing to discuss an Angevin marriage, the English were making a major conciliatory offer to the French, and that would probably have been enough to elicit a positive response from Charles VII. An envoy who was less committed to the cause of peace than Suffolk might well have been able to bargain for better terms than a two-year truce and the negligible dowry which was all Duke René could provide.[14] Moreover, a tougher negotiator would have scotched decisively any French demands for further concessions – and with greater conviction in the eyes of those at home.

Meanwhile, the French envoys had already been nominated, for on 22 January the English government in Normandy issued a safe-conduct to Dunois, bastard of Orléans, the count of Vendôme, Louis de Bourbon, the archbishop of Vienne, and others, to enable them to attend a meeting in France in safety in order to discuss a peace treaty.[15] It had evidently been arranged that the meeting of envoys should take place near Compiègne, north-east of Paris, and the English envoys were accordingly expected to land at Calais.[16] But at short notice Suffolk and his companions decided to proceed by a different route, to the apparent mystification and inconvenience of the French and Burgundians; it is possible that the change was caused by news that the king's prospective bride was to be an Angevin. At any rate, the envoys landed at Harfleur on 15 March 1444 and made their way, via Rouen and Le Mans, to René's duchy.[17] This diversion had the effect of postponing the meeting with the French, partly because Charles VII himself was unwell, but also because it took much longer to bring the Burgundian envoys to Anjou rather than to Compiègne. (It is not impossible, of course, that the move from Compiègne was welcomed by René and Charles simply because it would inconvenience the Burgundians and delay their arrival at the peace conference.) Be that as it may, a preliminary meeting was eventually held at Vendôme on 8 April.[18] Suffolk then passed on to Blois, where he was a guest of the duke of Orléans, and thence down the Loire to Tours, which was reached on 16 April. There the English met Duke René, as well as the dukes of Brittany and Alençon and many other French noblemen. Next day, they visited Charles VII nearby at Montils-les-Tours; the Burgundians did not arrive until 3 May. With all the participants now assembled, the girl at the centre of the discussions, the fifteen-year-old Margaret of Anjou, was brought from Angers to Beaumont-les-Tours next day to meet the English ambassadors.

Negotiations began in earnest almost two months after Suffolk had crossed the channel. It quickly became apparent that there was no likelihood of the French making any significant concessions to the English, who appear to have requested acknowledgement of their possession, without homage, of Gascony and Normandy, setting aside for the moment the intractable question of the crown of France. Charles VII was not in such a precarious military position that he felt it necessary to discuss the dismemberment of his kingdom or the alienation of his rights. By 20 May, therefore, it was recognized that a general truce was all that could be achieved.[19] The arrangements for the marriage between Henry VI and Margaret were made two days later. Two days after that the formal ceremony of betrothal took place in St Martin's cathedral, in the presence of two kings (Charles VII and René), two queens (of France, and Naples–Sicily), the dukes of Brittany and Alençon, the dauphin and his wife, Margaret of Scotland, and a large concourse of French nobility. The papal legate, Piero da Monte, bishop of Brescia, presided, and at the altar stood Suffolk, taking the place of his king.[20] In substance, the truce was a minor achievement: formally sealed on 28 May, it was scheduled to last for only twenty-three months until 1 April 1446.[21] But it was the first general truce to be concluded in the war since 1420; the popular expectations to which it gave rise were expressed in celebrations at Tours itself, and at Rouen and London as the English envoys made their way home.[22] They left for England next day (29 May). King Henry's gratitude was expressed extravagantly to the returning Suffolk. Already, during his absence and probably as a result of receiving advance news of the agreements of 20-22 May, the king had granted him the wardship of the most dynastically significant heiress in England, Somerset's one-year-old daughter, Margaret Beaufort, who in due time was wedded to Suffolk's only son John in 1450.[23] A few months after his arrival, he was raised to the rank of marquess, a rare distinction.[24]

Suffolk's second mission to France in 1444 was charged with bringing the new queen to her kingdom and with continuing the peace negotiations begun at Tours. The new embassy was much larger and more dignified than its predecessor – as befitted its purpose. Apart from Suffolk, it included the earl of Shrewsbury, Lords Greystoke and Clifford and Sir James Ormond (who could provide youthful company for the teenage queen)[25]; two prominent members of Shrewsbury's household, his sister-in-law, the Portuguese-born Beatrice, Lady Talbot, who had been in Katherine of Valois's service, and Sir Hugh Cokesay, his kinsman from Herefordshire; as well as Walter Lyhert, bishop of Norwich and a loyal associate of Suffolk's.[26] Among the noble wives forming an appropiate entourage for a queen were the duchess of Bedford (Jacquetta of Luxembourg), the marchioness of Suffolk, the countesses of Shrewsbury and Salisbury, and Lady Scales and Lady Grey; several of them remained in Margaret's household after she reached England.[27] A large fleet of ships was assembled from the south-east ports and a major appeal was launched throughout the realm to raise loans by Lady Day (25 March 1445) at the latest.[28] Meanwhile, on 21 August a delighted Henry VI had urged Charles VII to send envoys to England so that a final concord could be reached before the truce of Tours expired. Charles responded in co-operative terms.[29]

Suffolk's final instructions before leaving were issued on 28 October,[30] and a week later he rode through London with an imposing retinue the like of which had not been seen since Henry VI returned to his kingdom in 1432.[31] The cost of the entire enterprise (put at a little less than £3,000) and the length of time it was expected to take (three months) were serious underestimates, a miscalculation whose financial and diplomatic implications had unforeseen effects on the Lancastrian régime.[32]

On this occasion, the English train had to travel to Nancy in René's duchy of Lorraine, for the duke and King Charles had installed their courts there while they laid siege to Metz, about 50 miles to the north, as part of a new campaign to keep the duke of Burgundy in his place. Queen Margaret, however, was still in Anjou and she was not brought to Nancy until early in February 1445, two months after Suffolk and the English had arrived. The new destination, and especially the delay in producing Margaret (which meant lengthening the stay and cost of the embassy), were almost bound to fuel rumours that the French were trying to blackmail Suffolk into making further concessions, and they would certainly encourage those who were sceptical of the marriage's value to voice their misgivings once more.[33] Yet Suffolk, on more than one occasion after his return to England, asserted that he had not exceeded his instructions and certainly had not promised on behalf of Henry VI that the English claims to Anjou and Maine would be ceded to Duke René.[34] In view of his own sensitivity to the domestic perils involved in the negotiations with the French, his denial can be accepted, though it need not follow that Charles did not put some such suggestion to him at Nancy.[35] In England, the arch-rumour-monger of late-Lancastrian England, Dr Thomas Gascoigne, was the only contemporary to give outspoken and written credence to these tales; he claimed that the French had threatened to withhold Margaret's safe-conduct if Suffolk did not promise to cede the territories to her father. But the continuing friendly correspondence between the French and English kings belies this suggestion, and no other member of the English delegation at Nancy sprang forward to lend it any authority.[36]

The wedding, with Suffolk again standing in for Henry VI, was celebrated at Nancy soon after Margaret's arrival in the city, and on 2 March the English embassy began its journey home, with Queen Margaret in tears at the prospect of leaving her family and friends.[37] René accompanied her as far as Bar-le-Duc and her brother, John of Calabria, was with her until St Denis was reached; there the duke of Orléans met the cavalcade and conducted it through Paris to Pontoise (18 March), the last Valois-held town on the road west.[38] Here the queen was met by Richard, duke of York, the king's lieutenant and governor-general of France and Normandy, and, aside from the modest number who would travel with her to England, the Frenchmen said goodbye to Margaret and returned to Lorraine. From Mantes the party took to barges and sailed down the Seine to Rouen, which was reached by 22 March. The grand ceremonial entry to the capital of English France was marred by the seclusion of the queen herself, who was probably unwell; the countess of Shrewsbury took her place in the processions, presumably lest the crowds be disappointed and the propagandist value of the occasion be lost.[39]

Margaret was again ill before she embarked at Harfleur on 9 April, and the sea journey did her no good either, as Henry VI discovered when he met her for the first time on 14 April, still sea-sick and suffering from some indeterminate 'pokkes'.[40] If a story related to the Milanese envoy by an Englishman in 1458 has any truth in it, the surreptitious

487

inspection which Henry contrived to make of his wife is therefore unlikely to have gladdened his heart:

> When the queen landed in England the king dressed himself as a squire, the Duke of Suffolk doing the same, and took her a letter which he said the King of England had written. When the queen read the letter the king took stock of her, saying that a woman may be seen over well when she reads a letter, and the queen never found out that it was the king because she was so engrossed in reading the letter, and she never looked at the king in his squire's dress, who remained on his knees all the time. After the king had gone, the Duke of Suffolk said: Most serene queen, what do you think of the squire who brought the letter? The queen replied: I did not notice him, as I was occupied in reading the letter he brought. The duke remarked: Most serene queen, the person dressed as a squire was the most serene King of England, and the queen was vexed at not having known it, because she had kept him on his knees.[41]

Preparations for the wedding and coronation proceeded with some urgency, for the entire timetable of events had been upset by the delay at Nancy as well as by the queen's indisposition. A dispensation had already been secured from the pope to enable the union of Henry and Margaret to be solemnized during Lent; and the ceremony took place at Titchfield abbey in the New Forest on 22 April, with William Aiscough, bishop of Salisbury, Henry's confessor and one of his councillors, officiating.[42] Then, while Henry returned to Westminster, Margaret was placed in the care of Cardinal Beaufort, who had striven so hard for the truce with France of which she was the symbol. She stayed at one of his manors, probably Bishop's Waltham, and then made her way through Sussex and Surrey, being entertained as she went, to Archbishop Stafford's house at Croydon before proceeding to Eltham, where the royal palace had been newly decorated to receive her.[43] Margaret's entry into London had been arranged for 28 May and her coronation at Westminster abbey two days later.

Aside from the dignified deference that was customarily extended to a new queen, the London reception of Margaret of Anjou by the mayor and the massed commonalty of city officials and guildsmen was sponsored by the king himself as a gigantic display of propaganda to stir the citizenry. Margaret was first greeted by many of the lords, each richly dressed and accompanied by a retinue, and heading them all was Gloucester, the king's uncle and heir.[44] The pageants that were then staged as the queen made her way into the city from Southwark, the emblems that were displayed, the themes stressed and the addresses delivered, all descanted on the theme of peace and the hope that the Anglo-French conflict would soon end. Queen Margaret was identified as the dove of concord.[45] Each guild was instructed to play its part, and John Lydgate, the English propagandist on whom the government had relied for twenty years past for literary accompaniments to such visual demonstrations, was enlisted to produce celebratory verses for the occasion.[46]

> Oo declared Pryncesse vn to youre noble grace
> How god hath made this conducte and conueye
> Thus throgh youre Cite from place to place
> More hertly welcome then youre folk can seie
> Enioieng entierly youre highe nobleye
> Tis pagent wold mene youre excellence
> That ther is ioie in verrey existence[47]

It was a well-orchestrated and imposing scene and, as far as one can judge, the Londoners joyfully entered into its spirit.

Others, too, expressed their relief at the marriage and the news of peace. John Capgrave, who completed his eulogy of the Lancastrian kings toward the end of 1446, included similarly enthusiastic sentiments about the wedding and the fruits that were confidently expected of it.[48] Parliament had committed itself to supporting Suffolk's mission after it heard the chancellor report on 24 February 1445 (at the opening of the session) on the progress of the negotiations.[49] But these formal and public demonstrations of loyalty and good will towards the queen could not obliterate the more cautious and sanguine – even sceptical – attitude of many of the politically aware in the kingdom. Even Suffolk, when he reported to the commons on 2 June, and next day to the lords, acknowledged the possibility that the forthcoming peace negotiations, which the truce of Tours and the king's marriage had inaugurated, might collapse. Should this happen, he counselled, Lancastrian France should be vigorously defended. He was also aware of the suspicions of some that a secret undertaking had been made at Nancy, and he accordingly assured parliament that he

> nethir uttered ne communed of the specialite of the matiers concernyng in any wyse the saie Tretie of peas, nor of what maner of thyng the same Tretie shuld be, but only referred it to oure said Soveraigne Lorde, and to all tho the whiche he will calle to hym in this matier, atte the comyng of the said Ambassiatours into his Roialme; . . .

For his own future security, he asked that his report be formally recorded on the official roll of parliament. This was duly done, and on 4 July the speaker, William Burley, commended the marquess to the king for his efforts and Gloucester led the lords in his support.[50] It was a wise precaution of Suffolk's, but it did not prevent the rumours from gathering strength or Suffolk's reputation from plummeting disastrously.

As the demands of the French during the ensuing negotiations became more widely known, so the hostility to the idea of peace and to the queen herself became more pronounced. Even Lydgate, who of course numbered Gloucester among his patrons, allowed a stanza sounding a cautious plea to intrude on his lengthy (and somewhat obscure) encomium of the truce of Tours:

> Undir fals pees ther may be covert ffraude;
> Good cheer outward, with face of innocence;
> Ffeyned fllaterye, with language of greet laude;
> But what is wers than shynyng apparence,
> Whan it is prevyd ffals in existence?[51]

Such sentiments, ostensibly substantiated by the claim that Suffolk had secretly promised at Nancy that Henry VI would cede Anjou and Maine to René, were articulated more offensively and directly by Thomas Gascoigne in the 1450s and by several chroniclers later on.[52] René's pretensions as king of Naples and Sicily and Jerusalem, and lord of Majorca and Minorca, came to attract considerable scorn when it was realized that he was unable to provide a dowry suitable for a queen of England; this embarrassing feature of the royal marriage attracted criticism and adverse comment after 1445. Probably as early as 1446, when the French envoys' brief was all too apparent, a bitter satirical proclamation, which seems to have been aimed at René, the 'Constable of Jerusalem', was publicized in England.[53] Its theme was taken up by a number of chroniclers not long afterwards, stressing as they did with some exaggeration the poverty of the queen's Angevin entourage (as compared with the prodigious company of English men and women who disembarked with her at Southampton).[54] It was a perverse criticism, for when larger numbers of foreigners had accompanied new queens to England in the past, they had usually aroused even greater odium.

The elusive peace, 1445–49

The truce of Tours was due to expire on 1 April 1446, and almost as soon as it was sealed, the government, with some sense of desperation, tried to extend it and sought, better still, to conclude a final and lasting peace with the French. This course of action had the fervent support of the peace-loving Henry VI. Envoys crossed the channel in both directions in the period following the royal wedding, but a series of truce extensions was ultimately their only tangible result.

The to-ing and fro-ing began with the arrival of the French embassy that had been promised when Suffolk was in France. A powerful delegation reached London on 14 July; it was led by Louis de Bourbon, count of Vendôme, and Jacques Juvenal des Ursins, archbishop of Rheims, and it included several other councillors of Charles VII as well as representatives of the dukes of Brittany and Alençon, René of Anjou, and the king of Castile.[55] They spent about three weeks in England and one of their entourage compiled a journal of extraordinary interest from which our knowledge of the proceedings of this embassy is largely derived.[56] This lengthy, careful, and dispassionate record begins with the arrival of the first of the French envoys at Calais on 2 July and it records the unusual courtesies which each side showed to the other throughout. On their entry to London on 14 July, they were greeted in state by Suffolk, Dorset, Salisbury, Shrewsbury, Exeter, Warwick, and several bishops (including Adam Moleyns as keeper of the privy seal), whilst the mayor and city authorities conducted them through streets lined with curious and good-humoured citizens.[57] The ensuing discussions were conducted in an atmosphere of conscious informality that cut through the wearisome formalism customary in international negotiations; both sides were eager for plain speaking, an open exchange of views, and a speedy conclusion. There can be no doubt that Suffolk, whose credit with Charles VII and his envoys was very high, dominated the English side of the discussions, though he was ably assisted by Cardinal Kemp and Lord Sudeley, the king's chamberlain and, since 1443, treasurer of England.[58] The king's role was nevertheless a crucial one, for not only did he set the tone of the talks by his friendliness towards the Frenchmen and by his declarations of affection for Charles VII and of devotion to the cause of peace, but when the talks reached a crucial stage, his advice had to be sought by Suffolk and the others.

The French envoys' first meeting with Henry VI at Westminster on 15 July was a formal one:

> And they found the king upon a high stool, with a bed stretched over it, of blue tapestry, diapered, of the livery of the late king [Henry V], that is to say, pods, and his motto 'Jamais', of gold, and a back-piece of tapestry representing some ladies who present to a lord the arms of France; and the whole was of gold, very rich, and a high chair under the said back-piece; and he himself was clothed in a rich robe down to the ground, of red cloth of gold.[59]

If the symbolism took the French envoys somewhat aback, the king's behaviour was a warm encouragement:

> And as soon as the count of Vendôme and the archbishop of Rheims, who were the first, had entered into the said hall, and the king perceived them, he came down and stood exactly in front of his chair, and there waited for the said ambassadors, and took by the hand all those of the king's [of France's] party right humbly, taking off his hat a little to the said count and archbishop.

Later in the interview,

> ... the said king of England made a very good appearance of being well pleased and very joyful; and especially when the king, his uncle,

was mentioned, and the love which he bore towards him, it appeared that he rejoiced at the heart ... ... his chancellor commenced speaking, thanking God and the king [of France] for the good love, and also for the inclination of the king [of France] for a good peace, and that the king [of England] would let them know the hour at which he could hear them. And the king, while the said chancellor was speaking, advanced and addressed him in English, and we were told afterwards that he was not pleased that he had not spoken words of greater friendship. And in fact he came to the said ambassadors, and putting his hand to his hat and raising it from his head, he said two or three times, 'Saint Jehan, grant mercis'; Saint Jehan, grant mercis'; and patted each one on the back, and gave very many indications of joy, and caused them to be informed by the said earl of Suffolk that he did not consider them as strangers, . . .[60]

The detailed and substantive discussions with the three English representatives began in earnest on 19 July. And at that point it became clear that, for all the friendliness and declarations of intent, the negotiating positions of the two sides were a considerable distance apart. The English echoed a major concession which Beaufort and Kemp had been prepared to offer at Oye in 1439 (but which Gloucester had then successfully prevented) and which Suffolk had put to Charles VII at Tours the previous year, namely, that the Lancastrians should be allowed to occupy Normandy and an enlarged Gascony (including Poitou) as the price for implicitly abandoning the claim to the French throne.[61] The French envoys held to their brief and were conscious that militarily speaking their king was in a stronger position than Henry VI (a point which they had already made obliquely to the king himself)[62]; they thereupon conceded to the English a greater Gascony as well as Ponthieu, but on the question of Normandy they would not be moved. Not even the presence of Buckingham to assist the English on 21 July, and subsequent emotional appeals for peace from both sides later in the day could break the deadlock over the occupied territory.[63] It was Bertrand de Beauvau, seigneur de Précigny, who then interjected with a novel proposal to make progress: he suggested a personal meeting between the two kings of England and France, and it was at this point that the meeting had to be adjourned so that this significant suggestion could be placed before Henry VI himself.[64] This was done at the bishop of London's Fulham palace on 27 July, and after a brief discussion, Henry instructed Kemp to inform the waiting envoys that although he regretted the inability to come to an agreement there and then, he would be happy to travel to France to meet Charles; but he cautioned that such a meeting needed careful preparation and that in the meantime a truce was required.

This, then, was the only outcome of what had admittedly been a most amicable series of discussions. At the end of the day, all that could be recorded was an extension of the truce by the French envoys, in accordance with their instructions, until 11 November 1446.[65] Neverthe-less, the high-ranking French embassy testifies to the seriousness with which Charles VII approached the peace negotiations, and the English were no less sincere in their intentions. The archbishop of Rheims suggested that Henry allow some English emissaries to accompany him back to France so that a further extension of the truce could be negotiated and, presumably, the question of a royal meeting pursued with Charles VII in person.[66] This may have been done: certainly, a second group of French envoys, smaller than the first, had arrived in England by November. They were led by Guillaume Cousinot, Charles's councillor and chamberlain, assisted by Jean Havart, for this was a work-a-day delegation of officials rather than an imposing embassy. On 12 November, Henry VI commissioned Suffolk, Moleyns, Sudeley, and Viscount Beaumont, who had been intimately involved with the peace discussions to date, to negotiate with them.[67] As the archbishop of Rheims had foretold during the summer, another extension of the truce proved easy to arrange, this time until 1 April 1447, which would afford ample opportunity to make arrangements for the proposed meeting of kings which both had formally approved.[68] Moreover, the terms of the truce were to apply more widely than the original arrangement at Tours had provided: they would apply in Ireland and Gascony and include the allies of both monarchs.

The proposal for a conference of kings was actively canvassed in France and England fairly continuously throughout 1446 and 1447, but it eventually ran into the sand and Henry never set foot in France. After the idea had received a welcome from both Henry and Charles in the second half of 1445, its details were examined further in the months that followed. In London on 19 December it had been agreed that the historic meeting should take place in November 1446.[69] By the summer, it had become Henry's firm intention to travel to France in October and to take Queen Margaret with him; the site of the conference would lie somewhere near Le Mans on the river.[70] Its declared purpose was to seal a final peace between England and France which, from the English point of view, would bring to an end the bloodshed that Henry so loathed, relieve the burden on his subjects, and end the crippling losses which his armies had lately been suffering. It was a laudable intention, and after 1445 the opportunity for its fulfilment was the most auspicious that had arisen for years – perhaps even since 1420. It failed. In the first place, the expense of such a meeting was far from negligible, even though a stable peace would ultimately have removed the financial and human strain of war. On 1 June 1446 Henry appointed commissioners to negotiate a suitable loan to enable him to make the journey to France in appropriate state, and the duke of York, as lieutenant-general and governor, was assured that additional English soldiers would be provided and that the special measures to raise money would meet the increased cost.[71] Accordingly, Bishop Moleyns and Lord Dudley were sent to France on 20 July to complete the arrangements.[72]

October came and went, and the king remained in his realm. Nevertheless, when parliament assembled at Bury St Edmunds on 10 February 1447, the chancellor, preaching on a text from Proverbs, 12:20, 'In praise of the peacemakers', announced that it was still the king's intention to talk personally with his Uncle Charles.[73] Indeed, new French envoys arrived in England soon afterwards, led by Dunois, the bastard of Orléans, whose presence alone indicates that the French were eager to arrange the meeting; and on 25 February, Charles VII made it known at Tours that he would travel to Paris or Chartres at any time before 1 November to meet his nephew.[74] With the Bury parliament thankfully at an end, on 26 April Henry formally confirmed that the personal interview would take place.[75] But events in Maine served to thwart the best-laid plans of Charles VII and Henry VI and to undermine the agreements into which Henry had entered. One important casualty was the meeting of kings. More diplomatic activity, and a further public commitment by Henry VI, could not prevent postponement of the meeting until November 1448.[76]

The impossibility of ever bringing Charles and Henry together, despite their own conviction that a personal meeting was highly desirable, was evidently realized by the English embassy that crossed to France in February 1448. The discussion which Bishop Moleyns, the abbot of Gloucester, and Sir Robert Roos (three men who had been closely involved in the Anglo-French *rapprochement*) had with Dunois and the archbishop of Rheims, themselves much experienced by now in exploring the possibilities of peace, produced merely a proposal that further ambassadorial meetings should be held in September to discuss the question of the royal interview.[77] Meanwhile, on 12 June, Charles VII signified his willingness to accept Pont de l'Arche and Louviers as possible meeting-places, but this was the last that was to be heard about a meeting of kings.[78] It was overtaken by other events, particularly in England and Lancastrian France. One may guess that the doubts expressed by some about the wisdom of any such meeting had caused the earlier delays. Then, the shock with which parliament – nay, England – heard in late February 1447 that the greatest critic of Henry's policy towards France, his uncle and heir, Gloucester, had died in suspicious circumstances in the custody of those who had played a prominent part in implementing that policy, doubtless counselled further caution.[79] And finally, the even more controversial proposal for the achievement of peace – the cession of Maine to Duke René – threatened to precipitate violence in the county itself and a humiliating rejection of Henry's entire policy by his own subjects.

The Lancastrian government's eagerness for peace was regarded with increasing suspicion and even hostility in a number of quarters, most notably by Gloucester and some of the Lancastrian soldiery holding the line in France. A second proposal which, like that for a meeting of kings, was intended to break the deadlock of July 1445 over territorial questions, thoroughly alarmed them. In November 1445, Charles VII's envoys, Cousinot and Havart, presented Henry VI with a demand that the county of Maine, including the castle and city of Le Mans, should be ceded to Duke René; this demand, which was René's idea, had not hitherto figured in the discussions. Shortly before the envoys were given their final instructions in mid-October, René put it to Charles VII, along with a reciprocal proposal that he should offer Henry VI an alliance to last for René's lifetime and a truce for twenty years. Charles agreed to this bold stratagem and the accompanying carrot, and he allowed René to commission his envoys accordingly.[80] Indeed, Charles seems to have regarded a favourable response to the demand for Maine as proof of the sincerity of the English and as the price to be paid by Henry VI for French agreement to a royal conference.[81] Charles had also enlisted the youthful wiles of Queen Margaret in his campaign to influence Henry's attitudes. Margaret, indeed, writing to her uncle on 17 December 1445, declared herself ready to 'stretch forth the hand', and in the cause of peace to 'employ ourselves herein effectually to our power in such wise that reason would that you, and all others, ought herein to be gratified'. She wisely (and no doubt with good advice) allowed her husband to respond specifically about Maine.[82] But from Henry's own testimony, she persistently exerted what influence she could to persuade him to agree to the cession. Charles had judged his nephew shrewdly. '. . . wishing effectually to prove the great desire and affection which we have to attain the said blessing of peace, and to seek all fitting means to arrive thereat, ... and because we hope that on this account the matter of the principal peace will proceed better, and will come to a more speedy and satisfactory conclusion', on 22 December Henry agreed to the fateful step and to implement it by 30 April 1446. His only conditions were virtually those offered by René himself, namely, an alliance to last during the lifetime of René and his brother, Charles of Anjou, and a truce for twenty years; this (Henry hoped) would stabilize the Norman frontier with Anjou and Maine after the county had been surrendered.[83] The king's letter amounted to an implicit renunciation of sovereignty over Maine and a peaceful withdrawal from English-held territory beyond the frontiers of Normandy. 'For the greater security of the matters abovesaid, and for your [Charles VII's] satisfaction, and that you may give greater faith thereto, we have been pleased to sign these presents [i.e., the agreement] with our hand, . . .' The king's personal responsibility is clear and the extent of the concession undoubted. It was this momentous undertaking, the very first of its kind since 1420, which enabled the subsequent truces to be concluded and the plans for a royal meeting to go ahead; at the same time, it pushed many of the opponents of peace towards outright obstruction of the government's intentions and thereby, paradoxically, towards a renewal of war.

As Henry VI discovered elsewhere in his relations with France, it was easier to seal agreements than to ensure their implementation. The first day of May 1446 arrived and Maine was still in English hands. Charles

VII was relatively understanding about the matter, presumably believing that such a *coup* was worth waiting for and should be pursued with firmness rather than violence. He may also have appreciated the strength of the resistance with which Henry VI had to contend from those who steadfastly opposed the cession. Furthermore, on 24 December 1446, Cardinal Beaufort's nephew, Edmund, marquess of Dorset, replaced York as lieutenant-general and governor of France; it was the culmination of a campaign against the duke which had been resisted by the Lancastrian establishment in Normandy.[84] Leading the opposition in England to the régime's policy was Gloucester. It seems likely that by the end of 1446 Henry and his advisers had resolved to confront Duke Humphrey and his friends in parliament. The session which had been summoned on 14 December to open at Cambridge was rearranged at relatively short notice (on 20 January) to meet instead at Bury St Edmunds, a quiet abbey-town far from the source of Humphrey's mercantile support in London, bereft of disruptive elements such as the University of Cambridge could provide, and, most important of all, situated in Suffolk where de la Pole influence was strong.[85] The parliament was planned to begin with the duke's arrest. Although later chroniclers spoke somewhat loosely of treason as the justification for this step – and the deposition of the king and the release of Eleanor Cobham were alleged when some of his companions were seized – the real reason must surely have been the urgent need to remove him from harm's way (which meant placing him in protective custody) so that opposition to the king's French policy could be overcome without an embarrassing intervention by the king's heir.[86]

The ground was well prepared. Humphrey, who when he received the summons to parliament was probably in Wales, where he had extensive marcher lordships in Pembrokeshire and reserves of authority in the principality shires of Carmarthenshire and Cardiganshire, was instructed to attend with only a small company.[87] By contrast, the king and his friends stocked the countryside around Bury with their own men to ensure against violence and any attempt by the government's opponents to overawe parliament.[88] As the duke approached Bury on 18 February, eight days after the parliament had opened on a note lauding the king's efforts to make peace, he was met by a group of officials from the king's household. Half a mile outside the town, the treasurer of the household, Sir John Stourton, and its controller, Sir Thomas Stanley, handed the duke a message from the king which (if Gloucester's attendants are to be believed) displayed the duplicity of Henry's circle; it urged Gloucester to go straight to his lodgings in Bury because of the cold weather. Accordingly, he entered the town just before noon on the 18th and, with about eighty men in his retinue, made his way to St Saviour's hospital in north Bury where he was to stay. There, probably later that same day, several magnates – Buckingham, Dorset, Salisbury, Viscount Beaumont, and Lord Sudeley – called on him on the king's business. Beaumont, who as steward of England would preside over any tribunal

The Anglo-French
lineage of Henry VI
supported by (left)
Richard, duke of York
and (right) Humphrey,
duke of Gloucester,
from a book presented
by John, earl of
Shrewsbury to Queen
Margaret, c. 1445

Queen Joan of Navarre (d. 1437), second wife and widow of Henry IV,
from her tomb effigy in Canterbury cathedral

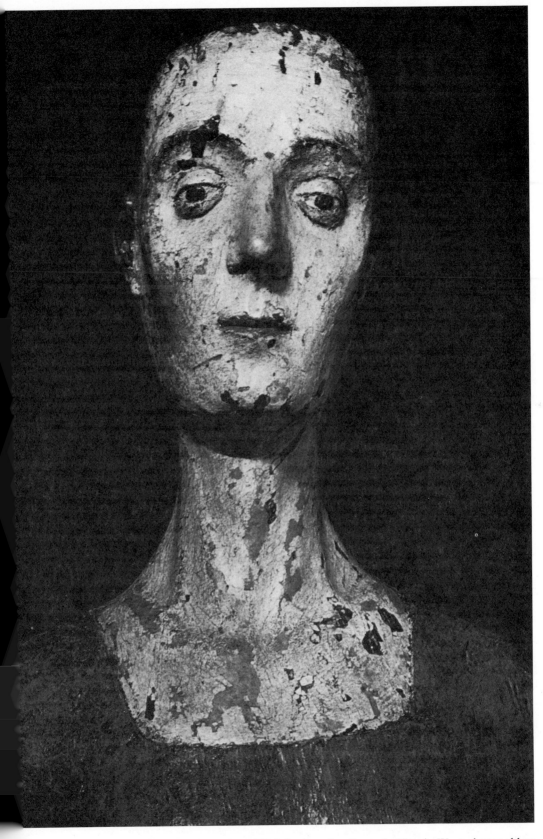

Queen Katherine of Valois, from her funeral effigy in Westminster abbey

Margaret of Anjou, a portrait from the medal
struck by Pietro da Milano, c. 1464

Medal portraying René, duke of Anjou (d. 1480),
father of Queen Margaret

Portrait of Charles VII, king of France (d. 1461), attributed
to Jean Fouquet; the frame commemorates his recovery
of Lancastrian France with the inscription *Le tresvictorieux
roi de France Charles septiesme de ce nom*

Portrait of Philip the Good, duke of Burgundy (d. 1467), after van der Weyden

Charles, duke of Orléans and Marie of Cleves, from a tapestry *c.* 1460

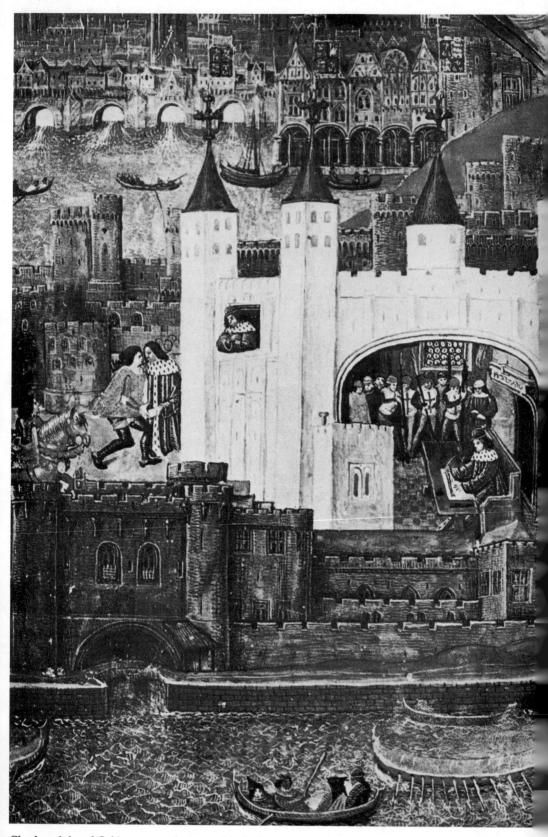

Charles, duke of Orléans as a prisoner at his desk
in the Tower of London after 1415

Henry VI on the arm of his guardian, Richard Beauchamp, earl of Warwick,
who holds his chantry chapel at Warwick in his right hand, c. 1483

Henry VI, from Ricart's *Mayor's Kalendar of Bristol, c.* 1480

Drawing of Richard Neville, earl of Warwick (the 'Kingmaker'), from the English version of the Rous Roll, *temp.* Richard III

Henry VI, by an unknown artist, *c*. 1518–23, though
probably based on an original *ad vivum* likeness which
may have been painted in the mid-fifteenth century

Henry VI, by an unknown artist, *temp.* Henry VIII

Henry VI, by an unknown artist, late sixteenth or early seventeenth century

Henry VI, from the king's bench plea roll. Trinity term 1460

Henry VI, and two king's bench justices, from the plea roll. Michaelmas term
1460–61

Thomas Montague, earl of Salisbury (d. 1428) being presented by
John Lydgate with a copy of Lydgate's *The Pilgrim*

John, earl of Shrewsbury presenting a book of romances to Queen Margaret in the presence of Henry VI, c. 1445

A pilgrim badge depicting Henry VI and commemorating a visit to his tomb, late fifteenth century

A London noble of Henry VI, annulet issue 1422–27, from the

Queen Margaret at prayer, from her prayer roll, mid-fifteenth century

John, duke of Bedford kneeling before St George, from the Bedford
book of hours commissioned by the duke, c. 1423–30

Sir William Oldhall (d. 1460) and his wife, Margaret Willoughby,
kneeling before St George, from his book of hours

Ralph Neville, earl of Westmorland (d. 1425), with his twelve
children by Joan Beaufort, daughter of John of Gaunt

John Talbot, earl of Shrewsbury (d. 1453), by an unknown artist;
the painting is now at Compton Wynyates

Drawing of Humphrey, duke of Gloucester by the herald Jacques le Boucq
(d. 1573) and possibly based on an earlier work c. 1424–25

Peter Christus's portrait (1446) of Edward Grimston, one of Henry VI's servants (hence the SS chain in his hand) and envoy to the Low Countries

Portrait of Edward IV (d. 1483), by an unknown artist apparently
of the Netherlands school, *c.* 1534–40

James III of Scotland by Hugo van der Groes, *c.* 1480; with St Andrew
and the later James IV (b. 1473)

Richard Beauchamp, earl of Warwick (d. 1439), from his tomb-effigy
in St Mary's church, Warwick, c. 1449–56

Marble bust of Pope Pius II (d. 1464), by Paolo Romano, 1463;
it is now in the Vatican

Archbishop Chichele (d. 1443), from his tomb-effigy
in Canterbury cathedral

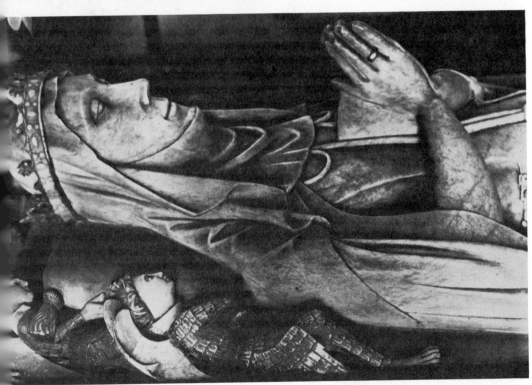

John Tiptoft, earl of Worcester (d. 1470), from his
tomb-effigy in Ely cathedral

Alice, wife of William de la Pole, duke of Suffolk (d. 1450),
from her tomb-effigy in St Mary's church,
Ewelme, Oxfordshire

Sir Robert Waterton (d. 1424), guardian of Richard, duke of York, from his tomb-effigy in St Oswald's church, Methley, Yorkshire; the Lancastrian SS collar is about his neck

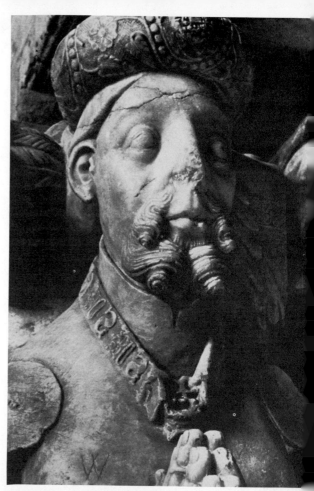

Francis II, duke of Brittany (d. 1488), from his tomb-effigy at Nantes

Henry VI as a saint, with (*left*) St Edmund, from the
screen of Ludham church, Norfolk, *c.* 1500

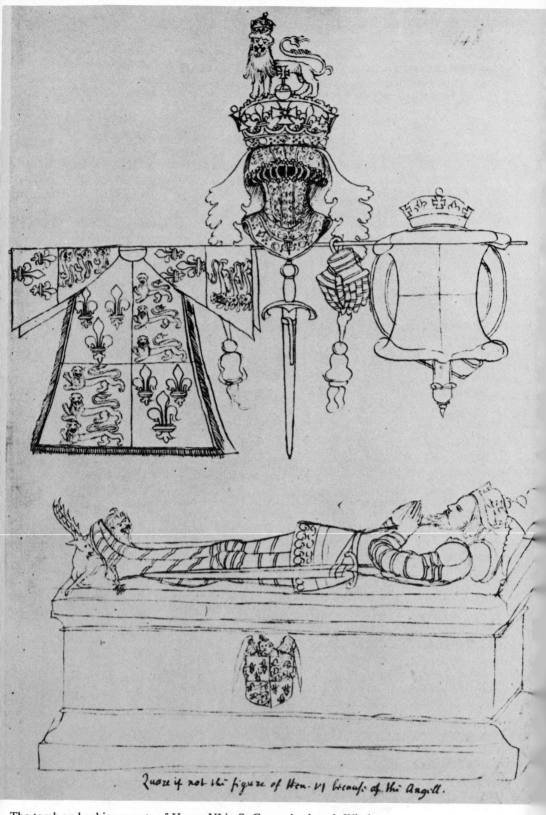

Quære if not the figure of Hen. VI because of the Angell.

The tomb and achievements of Henry VI in St George's chapel, Windsor castle, as they were in the late sixteenth century (but since vanished)

held at the royal court, arrested him; two prominent household servants, Bartholomew Halley and Thomas Pulford (who, incidentally, had had custody of his disgraced wife some years before), and a serjeant, Thomas Calbrose, were instructed to keep the duke in his quarters in strict custody.[89]

Gloucester had been appealed of treason before Henry VI, his nephew. By whom he was appealed and on what grounds are crucial, yet obscure, questions. According to a Yorkist writer in the 1460s, he fell victim to a long-maturing conspiracy headed by Suffolk and Lord Saye who, realizing that the duke's behaviour stopped short of providing a basis for any judicial charge against him, resorted to malicious slander.[90] What indications there are suggest that Suffolk, Saye, and Bishop Aiscough were at the centre of this conspiracy, and when the commons formulated their petition against Suffolk in 1450, they declared him to be the 'cause and laborer of the arrest, emprisonyng and fynal destruction of the most noble, valiant, true Prince youre right obeissant uncle the duke of Gloucestre'.[91] Realizing that he was a frequent visitor to Wales, and exploiting the knowledge that he had an influential position there, these courtiers were believed to have persuaded Henry VI that his uncle was preparing to raise the Welsh in rebellion against him.[92] If true, it would indeed have amounted to treason, and this may have been the charge, spurious though it was, to be preferred against the duke in the parliament at Bury. The real reason was undoubtedly the severe embarrassment caused by Humphrey's implacable hostility to Suffolk's French policy.[93]

Later on 18 February (or soon afterwards), royal officers arrived to arrest some of Gloucester's more important companions, among them Sir Roger Chamberlain, whom Gloucester had made constable of Queenborough castle (Kent), Sir Henry Wogan and five other members of his family, and others who are likely to have accompanied the duke from west Wales.[94] Two days later, the more personal servants of his household, including Sir Robert Vere, Sir John Cheyne, William Buckland (his controller), and his bastard son Arthur, were also seized. They were separated and spirited away to safe prisons, some to castles in the Thames Valley, others as far afield as Winchester and Nottingham.[95] Their master, Duke Humphrey, was denied access to Henry VI, who therefore had little opportunity to judge objectively the accusations made by his advisers or to test them against Gloucester's own explanation. Overcome by the shock of his arrest, crushed by the fabricated charges against him, and frustrated by his inability to plead his case before the king, Gloucester seems to have lapsed into a state of acute depression. For three days, he refused to move or to communicate, and then, on Thursday afternoon, 23 February, he was found dead in his lodgings.[96]

Apprehension lest the duke's death be attributed directly to the machinations of members of the king's circle led to the public display of the body next day in the abbey church so that the lords and commons assembled in parliament, and anyone else who so wished, could view it and conclude (it was hoped) that Gloucester had not met his end violently. His close attachment during life to the abbey of St Albans was maintained in death, for his body was taken inconspicuously and escorted only by his household servants (apart from the three king's men charged with his custody on 18 February) to the abbey for burial. The solemn journey began on 25 February and took six days; on 2 March the body of the heir to the throne and England's premier duke was laid to rest near the tomb of the protomartyr of England, St Alban, in the vault which had been prepared for him during his lifetime.[97]

Of his servants who had been arrested, eight were singled out for trial and condemnation some months later, when the public shock of the duke's death had abated a trifle. Indictments were heard against Sir Roger Chamberlain, Richard Middleton, Thomas Herbert, Arthur de Cursy (Gloucester's son), Richard Nedeham, Thomas Wylde, Robert Cappes, and William Buckland at Deptford (Kent) on 8 July and the trials took place in the court of king's bench during the following week. This was just when the king and Suffolk were renewing their diplomatic offensive to secure a meeting between Henry and Charles VII and to set a new deadline for the surrender of Maine. Moreover, on 18 June the king's commendation of Suffolk's role in the agreement to cede Maine had been published and it may have been felt wise to try and undermine the opposition by discrediting Gloucester's associates. Accordingly, on 8 July these eight members of his household were indicted of plotting to make their master king and release Eleanor Cobham from prison, and of marching to Bury in force to overawe parliament. Those who heard the indictment and referred it to king's bench were none other than Suffolk himself and several influential household officials, Sir John Stourton, Sir Thomas Stanley, and Sir William Tresham.[98] However, with Gloucester dead, the need to execute his servants was less compelling. After their condemnation to death and the assignment of their bodily quarters to strategic centres in the realm (including the marches of Wales), and even while the drawing, hanging, and quartering were in progress, the king reprieved them. By one of those extraordinary displays of compassion for which he was noted – and perhaps in this case tinged with a feeling of remorse – Henry VI ordered them pardoned; Suffolk himself took charters to the scene of execution and the men were cut down and released. The others who had been arrested in February were ultimately freed and had their possessions restored to them before the end of October; those from west Wales returned to their estates and resumed their influential careers.[99] This action hints at the falsity of the charges against Gloucester and reveals the fundamentally political reason for his arrest.

Duke Humphrey's death certainly removed a principal obstacle to a final peace with France, as well as to the cession of Maine and the arrangement for a meeting with Charles VII. That being so, the suspicion is bound to arise, and it certainly arose amongst contemporaries, that the duke's death was not fortuitous. On the other hand, Suffolk and his associates had long been conscious of the delicacy of their French negotiations and of their impact upon English opinion. On several occasions in the recent past, it had been felt necessary to affirm publicly their own good faith and their determination not to surrender essential English interests. They could hardly have failed to realize that to murder Gloucester would simply outrage more Englishmen and deepen the distrust and suspicion with which the king's French policy was regarded. On balance, therefore, it may be concluded that the duke's death was not actively contrived by Suffolk and his friends. His arrest, while a grave matter in itself, would have seemed a more practical alternative. The success with which the duchess of Gloucester had been proceeded against in 1441, and then consigned to discrete captivity without provoking serious or widespread protest, may have encouraged the king's ministers early in 1447 to attempt something similar against her husband. Moreover, the king was now married and (it was fervently to be hoped) would produce an heir before long, while in the meantime steps had been taken to strengthen the position of the immediate royal family by extending unwonted patronage to the Staffords and the Beauforts; indeed, Buckingham and Dorset were among those who confronted Gloucester in Bury on 18 February. The possibility that Gloucester himself might produce an heir had long been regarded as exceedingly remote.[100] No one in 1447 is known to have intimated that murder had taken place, though it would have been more than life was worth for anyone to have done so publicly; but later on propaganda hostile to the court and the Lancastrians placed responsibility for his death squarely on Suffolk's shoulders.[101] Already by 1450 the myth of 'The Good Duke Humphrey' had been born and as it matured, the belief spread that his sudden demise in suspicious circumstances had been planned by the king's servants. This proved to be a damaging charge against the régime of Henry VI from the 1450s onwards.[102]

It soon became clear that the duke's death did not stifle opposition to the cession of Maine; indeed, it became more insistent even to the point of obstructing the king's intentions. With Gloucester dead on 23 February and the Bury parliament dissolved on 3 March, Henry was soon able (on 24 May) to affirm his trust in Suffolk and pay tribute to the marquess's dedication in implementing the king's policy.[103] Peace was evidently to be pursued with vigour once more; if possible, the meeting with Charles VII was to be arranged and the cession of Maine concluded. On 27 July 1447 Henry promised that the surrender of the county would be completed by the following 1 November.[104] But this proved to be a wildly optimistic timetable, because it failed to take fully into account the unwillingness of the English officials and commanders in France to do as they were bidden. Next day two captains, Matthew Gough and Fulk Eyton, were appointed the king's commissioners to receive the towns and fortresses of Maine from the marquess of Dorset, who had been granted lordship over Anjou and Maine in 1442, and to deliver them to Charles VII's representatives. By now the king was aware of the hostility with which his order would be received in Maine, and he duly authorized Gough and Eyton to use force if necessary to carry out their instructions.[105]

It is not easy to comprehend the reasons behind the choice of Gough and Eyton as the king's commissioners. Both men were brought up in the Welsh borderland and had served their military apprenticeship in France under two outstanding commanders, the earl of Arundel and Lord Talbot. They are unlikely to have relished their commission or discharged it with enthusiasm. It is not surprising that the government at home soon began to suspect that they were wilfully dragging their feet. If their choice had the approval of the new lieutenant-general of France, Dorset, then the latter's resistance to the final surrender also can be understood. Yet no other kind of commissioner may have been feasible. It was doubtless recognized that it would require all the force of a royal command and the diplomacy of the royal agents to persuade the captains in Maine to hand over their authority to the Valois French; commissioners from England would be less likely to command respect and obedience than Gough and Eyton.

Aside from a feeling of revulsion at the prospect of surrendering Lancastrian territory over which much English blood had been shed during the past generation, the commanders well appreciated that they were being required to sacrifice their own interests in the lands, rents, and offices which had been granted them over the years. The government was rather slow to admit that at the very least they would have to offer compensation to those who, from Dorset down, would be dispossessed. It was not until 9 September 1447 that the government nominated three commissioners, carefully drawn from the English-born in France, to negotiate some suitable provision with Charles VII's representatives.[106] The three men chosen were experienced in the government of English France and could identify the needs of the dispossessed: Nicholas Molyneux was a master of the *chambre des comptes* at Rouen; Osbert Mundford, an English esquire, was *bailli* of Maine and Alençon; and Thomas Direhille was *vicomte* of Alençon. After some delay, the commissioners of both sides were able to meet at Le Mans by 1 November, the very day on which the county was to have been surrendered to Charles VII. It was now apparent to the French – though they must have suspected it for some time already – that those charged with arranging the transfer of territory and negotiating compensation were bent on obstructing the implementation of their orders. While continuing the discussions with a whole series of French envoys, the English skilfully exploited the fine script of the relevant warrants, authorizations, agreements, and treaties in order to raise objections, spring delays, and, when the surrender could no longer be averted, to challenge the very nature of the transaction.

The three Lancastrian commissioners evinced righteous indignation when they discovered at Le Mans on 1 November that their French counterparts had left much of their documentation behind at Sablé, some distance to the south-west; they also contrived to make heavy weather of the relationship between any award of compensation and the timing of the county's surrender. Henry VI, they asserted, had never intended the transaction to appear like a sale![107] After the French retorted that Dorset had already received compensation, a number of agents for other Lancastrian landowners in Maine, probably with the commissioners' encouragement, presented detailed claims for advance compensation, insisting that it should be calculated on the same basis as his.[108] These were unashamed delaying tactics that exploited resourcefully all the problems to which a cession of territory can give rise. To ensure themselves against possible prosecution for disobedience later on, the Lancastrian commissioners carefully recorded their meeting with the French emissaries and had the record authenticated by the archbishop of Rouen and the cathedral chapter on All Saints Day (1 November) 1447.[109]

Meanwhile, Gough and Eyton, were engaged in a series of similarly tortuous discussions which had the effect (perhaps even the intention) of delaying the county's surrender; in fact, the likelihood of collusion among both groups of Lancastrian commissioners must be kept in mind. When Gough and Eyton demanded that the fortresses of Maine be handed over to them by their custodians, acting on behalf of the marquess of Dorset, Osbert Mundford, captain of Le Mans, Fresnay-le-Vicomte, and Beaumont-le-Vicomte, and Sir Richard Frogenhall, captain of Essay and Harcourt (and probably other captains too), raised objections by a rigid adherence to correct procedures: as Mundford pointed out, the king's instruction, signed by Henry VI personally in the presence of Suffolk, was not accompanied by a warrant from Dorset, with whom the captains had originally indented. They assured the king of their loyalty but without proper authorization what more (they asked) could they do? Like Molyneux and his colleagues, Gough and Eyton took the precaution on 23 September 1447 of compiling a record of their exchanges with Mundford.[110] The king hastily closed this loophole through which Dorset's captains were endeavouring to slip; on 23 October the marquess was unequivocally commanded to deliver Maine to the king's commissioners. Henry expressed his 'bitter displeasure' at the obstruction they had encountered and reiterated his own determination: 'after the great and ripe deliberation of many of our blood and the members of our council [including Dorset himself, as the king pointedly reminded the marquess], we order, command, and as strictly as may be we charge you by these presents, in as much as you dread our displeasure', to obey the royal command.[111]

It was none too soon. At Bourges on 16 and 17 October, Charles VII had appointed his own commissioners, Guillaume Cousinot and Jean Havart, to make the compensation arrangements and to receive Maine;

these two councillors 'already have many times by our appointment and commandment visited our said nephew [Henry VI] upon the said business, and on this account, are better acquainted with his wishes herein, and better instructed in the merits of the same'.[112] King Henry's strongly-worded letter to Dorset suggests that the government in England suspected that its own envoys were in collusion with the custodians in Maine, perhaps even with Dorset himself. The marquess's participation in the decision of 28 July 1447, affirming the king's intention to cede Maine to Charles VII, was underlined and the implication was barely disguised that Dorset was very reluctant to honour his own undertaking. The 'pretences, excuses, or delays' must cease. But by this stage, it was no longer practicable to conclude the entire transaction by 1 November 1447.

Showing remarkable forbearance in the circumstances, Charles VII resolved to negotiate with the English once more. He despatched a high-ranking delegation led by the bastard of Orléans, Pierre de Brézé, seneschal of Poitou and the king's chamberlain, and Cousinot de Précigny, and at Rouen on 30 December they came to certain agreements with Matthew Gough which dealt with all the outstanding issues. In return for a twenty-year truce with Duke René and Charles of Anjou, and compensation for the dispossessed English, Maine's delivery to the French would be completed by 15 January 1448, and the prospect of a general truce for one year between England and France was offered as well. The stubborn resistance of some – particularly of the garrisons at Sillé, Fresnay-le-Vicomte and Beaumont-le-Vicomte – to any form of cession was recognized, but Charles agreed that they should not prejudice the agreement and could be dealt with later.[113] Yet even now, there was too little will on the part of the Lancastrians – even those like Gough who had negotiated the recent terms – to carry out their undertakings. 15 January arrived and still nothing had been done. This third delay finally exhausted Charles VII's patience, for now Henry VI was shown to be incapable of honouring his promises. Charles's protest was sharp and threatening. In his view, 'Subterfuges, pretences and dissimulations' marked the English tactics. Charles's exasperation was communicated to Henry personally by the French king's cup-bearer, Raoulin Regnault, who took with him to England a French version of recent events so that the sincerity and the restraint of the Valois could be fully demonstrated.[114] Charles VII can hardly have failed to realize that, faced with outright disobedience by the English officials in Maine, there was no alternative left but war if the county were to be recovered.

Within days of the expiry of the most recent deadline (15 January 1448), Charles's troops were massing on the borders of Maine. To begin with, this may simply have been a last attempt to exert pressure on Henry VI and his subordinates. But at Rouen, the Lancastrian council was thoroughly alarmed. Sir Thomas Hoo, the chancellor, wrote hastily to Pierre de Brézé to assure him (and the king) that Henry VI had every intention of handing Maine over at the earliest opportunity.[115] Hoo's alarm was all the greater because he had no illusions about the nature of late medieval warfare: 'if the fighting men were once assembled over the country, either upon the one side or the other, it would be no easy matter to cause them to withdraw and depart'. The inevitability of war stared him in the face. Despite his assurances and appeals, Charles's military preparations continued and by mid-February the siege of Le Mans itself was in prospect. When Hoo wrote to Brézé again on 18 February, he knew that Charles had a large army in the field intent on besieging the capital of Maine.[116] Hoo desperately tried to avert war by reporting the arrival of yet another – this time a 'notable' – English embassy; Bishop Moleyns and Sir Robert Roos were already at Honfleur *en route* to the French court.[117] This flurry of activity at Rouen was of no avail; Charles VII had concluded that the English in Maine would respect only force of arms. Soon after the beginning of March, the siege of Le Mans began 'and sharpe werre dayly [is] made to oure subgettes being therin'.[118] The guns of the French engineer, Jean Bureau, were ranged against the city's walls and the bastard of Orléans led the assault force of 6-7,000 men; King Charles installed himself in the château of Lavardin not far away so that he could witness the entire operation.[119] Charles's assessment of the situation was correct. The reopening of hostilities brought the English quickly to the conference table; on 11 March 1448 Moleyns and Roos reaffirmed the agreement reached at Rouen the previous 30 December for the surrender of Le Mans and the other fortresses of Maine. The only unresolved problems concerned Fresnay-le-Vicomte, which had to be exempt from the agreement, and Maine-la-Juhez; though on 15 March the English agreed to surrender the latter castle within twelve days.[120] The Lancastrian garrison thereupon withdrew without a shot being fired or the truce broken – at least in a technical sense.

The obstinacy which Matthew Gough and Fulk Eyton showed in their negotiations for the cession of Maine sprang from a fundamental distaste for their mission and a conviction that their instructions were a shameful error that might rebound on them (and their king) in the future. Like others involved in hazardous and controversial enterprises during the closing years of the Hundred Years War, they insisted on security for themselves through a formal and public registration, staged at the gate of the city of Le Mans on 15 March 1448, of their dealings with the French.[121] As far as they were concerned, they were ceding the county solely in the interests of peace; Henry's sovereignty was not in question, and should the agreement founder, the English might legitimately re-enter Maine. With these conditions attached and Fresnay excepted, English captains, *baillis*, and castellans like Osbert Mundford and William Herbert were prepared to witness this declaration. Several months later, on 12 June, Henry VI issued a declaration of his own, probably at the request of Gough and Eyton, to the effect that they had done nothing beyond their duty in handing Maine over to Charles VII.[122]

The end of the Lancastrian occupation of Maine had been unseemly and hasty. Although Charles VII seems never to have doubted his nephew's sincerity in agreeing to cede the county, Henry VI's nerveless control over his own subjects in the county had been amply demonstrated and so had his inability to overcome their obstructions and deceptions. The consequence was far from Henry's intention. Diplomatic relations between the two courts deteriorated badly in the autumn of 1447, and far from advancing the cause of peace the squalid negotiations over Maine made the renewal of war more likely.

The collapse of peace

The optimism generated by the events of 1444–45 extended beyond the marriage contract between Henry VI and René of Anjou, the plans for a personal meeting between Henry and his uncle, and the Anglo-French truce. By the time that Margaret arrived at Nancy in February 1445, the French court was considering a second proposal of marriage which could only strengthen the accord between England and France. With the arrangements finalized for Henry's wedding to Margaret, Charles VII was no longer averse to an English marriage for one of his own daughters, and by mid-February he was considering sympathetically a suggestion that his youngest girl, Madeleine, should be betrothed to Edward, the eldest son of the lieutenant-general of France and Normandy, Richard, duke of York. Who first made this proposal is unclear, though Suffolk (it appears) forwarded it in his discussions with the French early in 1445. By 19 February, Charles was able to write from Nancy to York at Rouen that he was prepared to entertain the idea; this was the news that Suffolk conveyed to Duke Richard when the new queen of England arrived in Normandy in March.[123] The prospect of a supportive marriage alliance was welcomed on all sides: by the French king, by Henry VI and his ministers, and most of all by York, who was well nigh obsequious in his communications with Charles VII during the succeeding months. 'I am well aware [he told Charles in June], that my said eldest son could not be placed in, and appointed to, a more lofty position and connexion'.[124]

The subsequent delay in finalizing the arrangements reflects no lack of enthusiasm on York's part, but rather his public preoccupations as lieutenant-general: first, his reception of Queen Margaret in Normandy in March–April 1445 and the organization of her journey to England; then, in September, his summons to London for a new session of parliament on 20 October.[125] Moreover, Richard was himself responsible for one hitch in the discussions, for on 10 June he expressed reservations about his three-year-old son marrying the king's youngest daughter (who was all of one and a half); he thought her older sister,

Jeanne, more suitable. When Charles dashed this hope, York hastened to resume negotiations for Madeleine's hand.[126] The last envoys known to have been sent by him to Charles's court arrived there on 4 February 1446; thereafter, nothing more is heard of the project and the young Edward was to remain unmarried until he had been on the throne of England for three years (1464).[127]

There can be no doubting York's undiminished enthusiasm for a royal French marriage. Nor is it likely that Henry VI or Suffolk insisted that the negotiations should be broken off, for not only had Suffolk participated in their initial stages, but York continued his respectful correspondence with the French king after he had returned to England in the autumn of 1445 and spoken with Henry VI; and his last envoy to Charles VII was none other than Lord Dudley, a man who was close to Suffolk.[128] The decision to suspend these matrimonial discussions seems rather to have been Charles's, presumably as a result of a change in his attitude to York and his family. The French king's desire for peace with England was still strong during 1446, as the negotiations for a royal meeting and the surrender of Maine proceeded. On the other hand, Charles may have become aware of dynastic developments in England which were emphasizing the importance of the Beauforts, the Staffords, and the Holands among the blood royal at the expense of York and his line.[129] Soon afterwards he submitted his own proposal for a marriage between the recently widowed Dauphin Louis (whose wife, Margaret of Scotland, died in August 1445) and one of the daughters of Humphrey Stafford, the newly created duke of Buckingham.[130] In fact, the year 1446 witnessed the frustration of several of York's designs as lieutenant-general and the souring of his relations with Henry VI's advisers. The duke does not seem to have disapproved of his king's policy in France (as his eagerness to secure a French princess for his son demonstrates), but personal slights against him and his family gradually made him an opponent of the Suffolk régime and ultimately presented him to the public as a victim of discredited ministers. It was a short step for the disillusioned and disgruntled to look to him as a potential protector and leader and for him eventually to adopt this role himself.

Richard's indenture as lieutenant-general was due to expire on 29 September 1445 and he and his councillors travelled to England for the third session of parliament, where they could support with first-hand detail the government's request for a grant to defend Lancastrian France, and (as the Tudor chronicler Edward Hall put it) 'to visit their wifes, children, and frendes, and also to consulte, what should be doen, if the truce [of Tours] ended'.[131] York remained in England for this parliament's fourth session (lasting until April 1446), which was found to be necessary in view of the commons' reluctance to make a grant to the king. During his stay, his commission as the king's lieutenant-general was extended, for evidently there was still no reason to question his support of the current negotiations with the French. Indeed, on 20

July 1446 he was promised an additional force of 200 men to accompany Henry VI to France for the projected interview with Charles VII.[132] At the same time, not only were new stocks of weapons sent to those who were protecting Normandy in the duke's absence, but in mid-July a genuine attempt was made to pay most of the £20,000 that was owed to York as lieutenant-general for the period up to Michaelmas 1445.[133]

In the months that followed, relations between the king's government and the duke of York steadily deteriorated. The reason is unclear. Perhaps the full enormity of the surrender of Maine became apparent to the lieutenant-general, particularly its implications for many of his captains in France; it would certainly strip the southern borderland of Normandy of its protective march. More immediately, a financial scandal in Normandy in the second half of 1446 enmeshed the duke. Well before 1446, Sir Thomas Kyriell, the English captain of Gisors, was accused by his men of appropriating their wages. Kyriell's reputation was already tarnished: although he had fought in France periodically since 1421, he had been a harsh conqueror and on at least one previous occasion (in 1442) complaints about his conduct had been forwarded to the king.[134] Now, in 1446, an inquiry by the marshal of Lancastrian France, John Talbot, and the constable of England, Viscount Beaumont, the most senior officials of martial justice, evidently found against Kyriell; but he challenged its findings, and on 13 November a second commission was appointed under two highly respected persons in England – Bishop Bekyngton, the king's former secretary, and Lord Cromwell, a distinguished councillor. These inquiries may have been part of a wider-ranging investigation of alleged corruption and peculation, during which York himself was criticized by the keeper of the privy seal, Bishop Moleyns. The duke was accused of financial maladministration and of seeking to favour his own councillors at the expense of the garrisons protecting Normandy; more generally, Moleyns's criticisms were directed at the effectiveness of his defence of the duchy from French attack. The particular charges were indignantly refuted by York's councillors and representatives from the Norman administration, and once more John Stanlow, treasurer of Normandy, and Sir Andrew Ogard, one of the duke's senior councillors, along with Sir William Oldhall, his right-hand man, travelled to England to rebut the charges.[135] They may have been successful in their mission, for no further action was taken against the duke; and a confrontation between York and Moleyns at a council meeting seems to have papered over the cracks temporarily. But it would be readily comprehensible if the incident seriously alienated Duke Richard. Furthermore, Suffolk's determination in the winter of 1446–47 to move against Gloucester, and the fact that York was manifestly cold-shouldered as the king's next heir presumptive, may have been decisive factors in Richard's disillusionment with current Lancastrian policies and those who devised them. Before the end of 1446 his removal as lieutenant-general had been decided upon.

Edmund Beaufort, marquess of Dorset was appointed lieutenant-general and governor of France, Normandy, and Aquitaine (an accession of authority akin to Bedford's regency before 1435) on 24 December 1446; his commission was to run for three years as from 1 March 1447.[136] Aside from the favour shown in England to the Beauforts, the situation in France justified this change. York's reputation as ruler of Normandy had been besmirched by the rumours of embezzlement and malfeasance, and if Bishop Moleyns is to be believed, 'such noyses as bene pretended come not by the sayd bysshope at any tyme of his beinge in Normandye nor sythe, for it is well confessed that they were here [in England] longe before'. Furthermore, York's competence as a commander had been suspect from the very beginning and Moleyns's was only the most recent aspersion to be cast on his military abilities. Whatever fate was planned for Maine, the continued defence of Normandy was still a priority of the Suffolk régime. As Moleyns declared to the king's councillors, with every confidence that they could corroborate what he had to say,

> he hathe alway semed, and yet dothe, that Normandye is not lost nor shuld be lost of reason but welle kept and the kyngys obeysaunce there encreased with good provision lyke as often tymes in this same place he hathe declared his mynd there in. Where of some of my lords the kyngs counseylars now present he supposethe can well remembar, without that that evar he spake any worde of discoraginge the kepinge of the sayde countrie but that he evar semed it right profytable.[137]

And Bishop Moleyns was keeper of the privy seal.

Dorset was also lord of Maine; if anyone could facilitate its transfer to the French and overcome resistance from the local Lancastrian captains, it would be he. Accordingly, arrangements were made on 1 February 1447 to send him to France with an army of 1,200 men.[138] The Bury parliament and its aftermath intervened to delay his departure, and it was only after the failure to hand Maine over to Charles VII in the autumn of 1447 that preparations were resumed to despatch Dorset on his expedition.[139] The advice offered by that old campaigner with landed interests in Maine and elsewhere in northern France, Sir John Fastolf, reflects the formidable task before a royal lieutenant-general in 1447–48 and the particular expectations pinned on Dorset. Fastolf let slip no hint that the marquess was regarded as anything other than a promising new broom. But the veteran knight's cautionary words were well directed. Recent experience had shown that Dorset would do well to ensure that he had loyal friends in England to cope with any charges that might be made against him while he was engaged on his hazardous mission, and also that before he embarked he should make sure that he was paid his due and provided with adequate arms and supplies. Once across the channel, Dorset was advised that he should appoint to the Norman administration and to the military captaincies able men who would be honest and just so that the sorry scandals of York's later years might be avoided. At this stage, Fastolf was prepared to put his faith in Dorset's ability to wage a defensive war in Normandy by sustaining the Lancastrian fortresses and deploying their garrisons as a field army when required; the ports (he sensibly commented) should be supported by a naval force. As for Gascony, it was recognized that this was a separate theatre of operations, and Dorset was counselled to nominate a reliable lieutenant to organize its defence. This was wise, if unsolicited, advice; regardless of whether it ever reached the new lieutenant-general, it betrays scarcely a doubt about Dorset's determination to defend Normandy, whilst its implied criticism of York's lieutenancy reflected the belief of at least some Lancastrian landowners in France that his replacement could be expected to do better.[140]

Furthermore, the French army had been reformed of late, and incidents along the Norman frontier had been a source of increasing irritation to the English.[141] Dorset's principal commission, therefore, was the overall protection and supervision of Lancastrian France and, in particular, 'the sure and save garde' of Normandy.[142] It was planned that he should lead a substantial new army which would defend a duchy now bereft of the protection that Maine had hitherto afforded.

The duke of York had meanwhile been shunted to the sidelines. On 9 December 1447 he was appointed the king's lieutenant of Ireland. His new commission need not be regarded as an 'exile' imposed by Suffolk; indeed, York was in no hurry to cross St George's channel and did not do so until 1449.[143] But the manner and timing of his removal from the French scene rankled with the duke and fortified his growing dislike of the king's advisers. After all, Dorset's elder brother had superseded York's military powers in France in 1443, and Edmund's own creation as duke of Somerset on 31 March 1448, preparatory to his embarkation for Normandy, was an unmistakable sign of the favour which Henry VI was lavishing on the royal family, with the notable exception of Lionel of Clarence's progeny.[144] If his elder brother's term had been ignominious in its results, Edmund's was to prove disastrous: the irony would not be lost on Richard of York.

Contrary to the roseate expectations of Henry VI, the eventual surrender of Maine did not significantly promote a final peace. Discussions between Lancastrian and Valois envoys continued during 1448–49, but they encountered mounting obstacles. The French placed most of the blame on their adversaries for the deterioration in relations to the point of war, and in particular on Somerset and his captains in France. In the first place, the English soldiers had retired from Maine to certain fortresses on the Breton–Norman frontier which were in disputed territory; they proceeded to fortify them in contravention (so the French insisted) of the truce in order to deter Duke Francis I from openly siding with Charles VII. Thus, St James de Beuvron, Mortain, and Pontorson, which had previously been deserted by the military, became Lancastrian bastions and as such were regarded by Francis and Charles as a provocation.[145] Protests on this and other matters (among them the descent by English garrisons on the traffic along Norman roads) produced no satisfaction; indeed, Osbert Mundford, who was now treasurer of Normandy, was accused of disrupting the smooth relations between the English and the French by his unwillingness to promote further negotiations. Moreover, Somerset showed a lack of sensitivity in his personal dealings with Charles VII, who regarded the discourteous tone of the lieutenant-general's letters as insulting.[146]

Somerset was swift to respond with his own accusations of bad faith and incitement to violence. The French were denounced for encouraging attacks upon Lancastrian positions around Louviers on the south bank of the Seine, and in particular for assaulting Vanuray and other places, where

> some of your party had by force taken a great quantity of wines, without reasonable cause, which they have not, and will not, restore to those persons to whom they belong . . . . [but rather] had distributed in the bulk at their pleasure, amounting in value to more than eight hundred pounds, without taking into calculation the damage and loss of the sailors and other people by the hindrance of trade, . . .

The degree to which national antipathy had developed during the long Anglo-French conflict was graphically demonstrated at a small village near Pont de l'Arche, also on the Seine; there the *bonnes gens* gave an unenthusiastic welcome to French soldiers from the Louviers garrison, who promptly 'beat them and gave them much foul language, calling them false traitors and English dogs, and did much damage to their property'. As far as the Lancastrians were concerned, the existing arrangements for restitution and for the appointment of commissioners and conservators of the truce were inadequate and unworkable.[147]

Yet neither side was quite ready to precipitate renewed fighting on a wide scale or unilaterally to abrogate the truce. In fact, in the spring of 1449 both France and England withdrew from the brink and reopened negotiations in March in a spirit of relative conciliation. Despite the air of injured innocence which the Valois affected as the hapless victims of deceitful English aggression, Charles VII agreed that commissioners should meet between Avranches and Mont St Michel to iron out the differences between the parties on the Breton–Norman frontier and to attend to individuals' complaints.[148] This atmosphere of cautious co-operation was roughly dispelled by news of the seizure of Fougères, a Breton *bastide* which stood near the Norman frontier, by an Arragonese knight in Henry VI's service. The attack decisively alienated the duke of Brittany and provided Charles VII with apparent justification for claiming that Henry's representatives had broken the truce and committed further depredations immediately afterwards.[149]

After the truce of Tours and the marriage between Henry VI and Margaret of Anjou, Anglo-Breton relations were far from satisfactory: they fluctuated between an uneasy peace fraught with incidents and outright hostility. Although the English clung to the hope that a final rupture could be avoided (for if it were to occur, it would range the Bretons on the side of Charles VII), it was only a question of time before this lingering hope was dashed. Earlier truces, which had established procedures for the periodic examination and amelioration of friction between English and Breton subjects, were still respected, at least in the letter. On 4 November 1445 sheriffs in England were instructed to announce that any Englishman nursing a complaint against a Breton should present his case in London during the following March when, it was expected, commissioners from Brittany would hold hearings with their English counterparts in accordance with the existing machinery.[150] This proved to be hardly more than an empty gesture, for during the next year and more the government had to acknowledge that there was faint hope of securing redress of grievances from the Bretons, even though Gloucester and Henry VI himself intervened on one occasion on behalf of an Englishman captured during an official mission to Ireland.[151] Francis I had declared his own preference for an alliance with Charles VII by travelling to Chinon to swear homage to the king in March 1446, and the duke's younger brother, Gilles, a well-known advocate of the English connection, was put in prison in the following June. The parliamentary commons at Bury St Edmunds responded belligerently early in 1447 and supported a petition from two other Englishmen for letters of marque against a Breton ship.[152]

Despite a distinct lack of interest on the part of the Breton government in discharging their truce obligations conscientiously and maintaining their English alliance, Henry VI's ministers viewed the prospect of a breach with less and less enthusiasm as the Lancastrian position in France became more precarious after the surrender of Maine. The instructions issued to Henry's envoys to France in October 1448 were clear in their references to Brittany. The duchy was to be regarded as England's ally, bound by allegiance, treaties, and truces, and its duke a subject of Henry as monarch of all France. Even if the Bretons were to insist on flaunting their preference for French suzerainty, the king's ambassadors were not to allow this to impede their pursuit of peace; they were rather to content themselves with a protest and do everything in their power to avoid a rift.[153] By 1449, therefore, it would merely require a provocative incident to precipitate a rupture, for Francis had already resolved to sever his ties with England.

The attack on Fougères in 1449 is a celebrated episode in the history of the Hundred Years War, and its significance has been much discussed. Its role in hastening the collapse of Lancastrian fortunes in northern France and in assisting Charles VII's successful recovery of almost the whole of his kingdom by 1450 is crucial, and yet until recently certain significant features of the incident have not been clearly understood.[154] The assault itself, and the subsequent sack of the town, seems on the surface to have been a major miscalculation by the English because as a result England and France were catapulted into a war which the English had been trying to avoid and in which the duke of Brittany openly supported Charles VII. But neither the motives of the attacking commander, François de Surienne, whose Spanish origins earned him the nickname 'L' Arragonais', nor the degree of collusion of the council at Westminster were satisfactorily explained. Recent reassessments of the entire affair and of de Surienne's English loyalties provide a more convincing explanation of the strategy behind the sack of Fougères and document the close relationship between the Arragonese knight and Henry VI's advisers in England and France.[155]

On 24 March 1449 Fougères fell to de Surienne by an assault launched in Henry's name. It was a wealthy town, and after pillaging it and robbing its rich merchants, the attacking force, some 6-7,000 strong, occupied the citadel for more than seven months until, on 5 November, Francis I procured its surrender.[156] De Surienne had been a man honoured in England for at least ten years before this critical phase of his life. He himself claimed that he had served Henry VI in France since 1424; certainly by 1437, when he was employed as the Lancastrian captain of Montargis, not far from Orléans, he was in personal contact with Suffolk, who was then steward of the king's household.[157] On 10 June 1441 Henry VI granted him a 100-mark annual pension after hearing his petition that he and his wife had lost an inheritance worth £100,000 through holding to the English cause. In gratitude, de Surienne offered a personal gift to Henry VI in 1442–43.[158] So far his career in Lancastrian service had been similar to that of other foreigners – like the Dane Sir Andrew Ogard – who were involved in military operations in France. But in the later 1440s de Surienne was drawn into the tortuous world of Anglo-Breton relations, becoming an instrument of the English government in its endeavours to protect Gilles, the younger brother of the duke of Brittany and a close friend of Henry VI, from the consequences of his robustly Anglophile attitudes. As a result of the enemies Gilles had made by his outspoken opinions and his ambition, and the exasperation felt by his brother, the duke, at certain independent activities that often ran counter to Francis's own policy, Gilles found himself in prison by June 1446.[159] Henry VI's ministers were anxious to free such a committed ally and restore him to a position of influence in Brittany so that (it was hoped) he might restrain the duke's strong inclinations for an open alliance with Charles VII. In these circumstances the reinforcement of the Breton–Norman frontier in the wake of the cession of Maine must be regarded in large part as an attempt to separate Francis from Charles VII prior to some military manoeuvre on Gilles's behalf.[160]

De Surienne became the English government's agent in the plan to set

Gilles free. Towards the end of 1447, his son, John l'Arragonais, crossed from England to France in the company of a pursuivant of Lord Dudley, one of the royal councillors, and two of Gilles's servants, and it is possible that plans were already being laid for a demonstration of English power along the Breton–Norman border in Gilles's interest that would influence Breton attitudes and discourage the duke's *rapprochement* with Charles VII.[161] Moreover, de Surienne's important role in this new phase of Anglo-Breton diplomacy was marked on 27 November 1447, during a visit which he paid to England, by his election to the order of the garter and by his receipt of other patronage from Henry VI. Furthermore, Suffolk seems to have persuaded Sir John Fastolf to transfer one of his castles, that of Condé-sur-Noireau, situated within striking distance of Fougères, to de Surienne in 1448; it could be a useful base from which to harry the Bretons.[162] The seizure of Fougères was the dramatic outcome of this plan. There can now be little doubt about the complicity not only of Suffolk, but also of the king's lieutenant-general in France, Somerset, and de Surienne himself later stated that they were both centrally involved in the adventure.[163] At the meeting of parliament at Winchester in mid-June 1449, the lords offered their congratulations to de Surienne on a job well done and by implication they may be considered to have thoroughly approved the town's sacking.[164]

Much of this plotting and intrigue came to light after Fougères was captured, when de Surienne grew disillusioned with the reluctance of the English to support his beleaguered force inside the fortress. Although the earl of Shrewsbury's army was placed on alert and supplies were ferried across the channel from England, a relieving force under Sir Robert Vere never ventured far from Caen and certainly did not bring the aid that de Surienne desperately needed. Eventually, after five weeks, l'Arragonais and his men could withstand the Breton siege no longer; although he claimed to have refused an initial offer of 50,000 crowns if he would surrender the fortress to Duke Francis, he finally capitulated when no aid arrived. Dispirited and bitterly disillusioned, he and his men were allowed to withdraw.

If the sack of Fougères led to recriminations by the French and Bretons against the perfidious English for breaking the truce in such a blatant fashion, the surrender of the fortress on 5 November 1449 poisoned the diplomatic atmosphere yet further and prompted other accusations: by Henry VI and his council, who claimed that de Surienne had submitted to French bribes;[165] and by de Surienne himself, who denounced the English for deserting him and announcing that the entire operation had been conducted without the knowledge or approval of the English government.[166]

Much of our information about the incident and its aftermath comes from a lengthy justification which de Surienne published after his surrender of Fougères in order to clear his name and dispel the accusations that were levelled against him as a truce-breaking mercenary who had acted on his own account for personal gain.[167] After November 1449 de Surienne, with his wife and children, made his way to Naples and the dominions of the king of Aragon. By 24 January 1450 he was on his way north again and at Pisy (in the Yonne valley) he wrote to Charles VII, whose favour he hoped to win, stating that he had returned the order of the garter to Henry VI, whose ministers had disowned and dishonoured him by their refusal to shoulder their share of responsibility for the seizure of Fougères. He had also renounced his English allegiance and accepted the sovereignty of the king of Aragon. A full explanation of the events of 1449 was sent to the kings of Aragon, France, and England as well as to Rome, and de Surienne appealed to Charles for understanding and indulgence so that he could return to France and recover the property he had been forced to leave behind. This he was allowed to do in the following November.[168]

The sack of Fougères was an inglorious episode. Its covert aim of influencing Brittany's diplomatic attitudes is comprehensible, though Gilles was unlikely to be able to rally his countrymen against Duke Francis and King Charles. The risk that the former might rather turn decisively towards the latter was much more real, and in fact Francis appealed to Charles for aid soon after the attack was launched. Fougères's seizure and the subsequent English desertion of de Surienne reflect little credit on the Lancastrian régime. It is difficult to argue, in any other than a strict, legal sense, that the assault did not breach the Anglo-French truce, for Francis's sworn homage to Charles VII in 1446 had more fundamental and practical significance than the surreptitious inclusion of Brittany among the allies and lieges of Henry VI when the truce of Tours was last renewed in 1448 (when the texts were exchanged 'without so much as a candle, and without looking at the contents').[169] To disown de Surienne, a garter knight and royal pensioner, was little short of despicable. To a well-executed operation in March 1449, the English responded with unfulfilled promises, inadequate aid, and ultimately broken faith. The events at Fougères hastened the collapse of English morale and, therefore, of English Normandy. The duke of Somerset compounded the régime's blunders by steadfastly refusing to return the fortress to Francis I or alternatively to provide reparations for this and other outrages against both Frenchmen and Bretons.[170]

A belated attempt by Somerset to halt the hostilities was scorned by Charles VII. Although Osbert Mundford led a delegation to Louviers to hold discussions with the French, they came to nothing. Not unreasonably, the French maintained that the attack on Fougères had absolved them from their obligation to observe the truce, and in their view the Bretons were well justified in seeking revenge against castles in Normandy (like Pont de l'Arche, which was captured by Frenchmen and Bretons by a ruse on 9 May).[171] Moreover, by one of those unfortunately timed ventures of which the English were capable in these years (perhaps as a result of the disintegrating political and military command in Normandy), Lancastrian forces attacked Neubourg without warning while the discussions at Louviers were taking place. In any case, Somerset's demands were inordinate, for he insisted that English sovereignty over Brittany should be acknowledged (in accordance with the truce of 1448), despite the fact that Francis I had sworn homage to Charles VII in 1446. To make this 'an open question [commented the French] would be to occasion far greater harm to the king than the restitution of Fougères could be to his profit'. Equally unacceptable was the demand that even if Fougères were surrendered to Brittany, it must be acknowledged that Henry VI had the right to demand its return at any time. Somerset was regarded as haughty and disingenuous when he asserted that he had powers to negotiate on no other bases than these for, as Charles VII later recalled, the duke had been given full powers to act in Henry VI's name.[172]

By mid-1449, Charles's complete lack of trust in Somerset was a major obstacle to the avoidance of war. He found it difficult to believe that the duke was serious in his professed desire for peace, and the French thought the worst of him as a Lancastrian negotiator. The recent disasters in northern France were turning English opinion against him, too. Some at home believed that he had promoted the Fougères enterprise for his own profit, to the point of obstructing every chance of an agreement with Charles VII. He was accused of neglecting to repair town walls and castles and of failing to pay officers and soldiers their wages. Then, too, the compensation owed to English landowners who had recently been ejected from Maine was believed to have passed into his pockets and remained there. These and other reproaches against Somerset in 1449 contrast sharply with the hopes reposed in him only two years before, after his appointment as lieutenant-general.[173] For Sir John Fastolf, the disillusion had set in with the surrender of Maine, and a bitter taste of sour grapes doubtless lingered in the mouth of other erstwhile property-owners in English France.

The military expression of these accusations and reprisals was the preparations of Charles VII and Francis I on their frontier with Lancastrian-held territories for a major assault on upper and lower Normandy. At this very moment, the English garrisons faced serious problems of morale and supply as they awaited the anticipated onslaught. Westminster was aware of the situation, for by the middle of May the master of the king's ordnance in Normandy, William Gloucester, was preparing to travel to Normandy with Suffolk himself, in response to urgent pleas from the earl of Shrewsbury and the English council in France.[174] Efforts were made to support the custodians of Rouen, and Sir John Fastolf was as prodigal as ever with unsolicited advice.[175] The scale of his recommendations demonstrates how near-hopeless the situation had become by August 1449.[176] If Fastolf's proposals were at all close to the mark, any English hope of retaining a substantial territorial position in northern France was vain. He urged the government to assemble a large new army for Normandy and Aquitaine which would be 40,000 strong, and this, he calculated, would require a total expenditure on wages of about £140,000 spread over six months. Harking back to the strategic perceptions of the minority, whereby England's defence was best assured in Normandy, he regarded 'fortress England' as dangerously isolating Calais and inviting invasion by the French and their allies. He used, too, the seductive, emotive argument that those Frenchmen and Englishmen who had fought long in France in the Lancastrian cause ought not to be deserted in dire poverty; Fastolf himself claimed to have lost an annual livelihood of 4,000 marks, and he raised the further spectre of footloose, rootless bands arriving in England and behaving in lawless fashion, perhaps even kindling insurrection. These recommendations represented the opinion of those in England for whom recent events in France were a shameful betrayal; they advocated greater efforts, rather than humiliating negotiations, in order to maintain the Lancastrian dominion in Normandy and Aquitaine. Fastolf's analysis was generally sound, not least in its prediction of the impact on England of migrants fleeing from defeat in France and of the threat of invasion after a military collapse on the continent. Grounded in the vested interest of many soldiers and settlers in the continuance of English rule in Normandy, Sir John's conclusions appreciated the burden on England of the obligation felt by Henry VI to compensate former Norman residents for their losses after 1449.[177] But the massive army which he saw as the principal means of averting these disasters was well beyond the capacity of the Lancastrian régime to raise.

The failure during April 1449 of the attempts to repair some at least of the damage to Anglo-French relations caused by the sack of Fougères led within a matter of weeks to a Valois descent on key Lancastrian positions in central Normandy.[178] On 9 May the town and castle of Pont de l'Arche fell as a result of a Franco-Breton ruse, and this notable success was taken as a signal by the residents of several fortified towns in English hands to rise against their English commanders and deliver themselves like overripe apples into Charles VII's hands.[179] Quite unexpectedly, the men of Conches betrayed their town to the French soon afterwards, and the castle's captain, Robert Prynstrop, had no alternative but to negotiate the surrender of the fortress too. There were similar scenes in the lower Seine valley, at Gerberoy and Verneuil, where the French defeat of 1424 was at last avenged. These events, and the attacks that were launched against other fortresses in that area, led the frightened Lancastrians to abandon Pont l'Evêque without a blow by August.[180] What had been originally intended as an act of reprisal for the seizure of Fougères became the cue for a co-ordinated campaign of far greater significance. The deteriorating military power of the English, the diplomatic impasse in which Somerset refused to exchange Fougères for the recently captured Lancastrian strongholds, and the state of Anglo-Breton relations encouraged Charles VII to declare formal war on the English, and this he did on 31 July 1449; the truce was finally at an end.[181]

Two crucial successes were achieved at Pont Audemer and Lisieux. At the former two French armies, under the bastard of Orléans and the count of Eu, converged on 12 August, cutting the town off from Rouen up river and from the port of Harfleur at the mouth of the Seine.[182] At Lisieux on 16 August, the bishop, who was none other than Thomas Basin, the chronicler, and the town representatives sealed their formal surrender to the bastard, Dunois, after only a token resistance, and this document also included in its terms a series of subsidiary fortresses and protective strongholds round the city.[183]

These were severe blows to the Lancastrian presence in upper Normandy, and they triggered off a number of capitulations during the following two months which brought Charles's armies to the very gates of Rouen. The king himself advanced north from Amboise in the Loire valley to play an active role in the campaign, and by 26 August he had joined Dunois and the counts of Eu and St Pol outside the walls of Mantes.[184] Between mid-August and mid-October a score of surrenders was negotiated without so much as an assault or a siege or, apparently, a shot fired in anger; Lancastrian morale had been shattered and the garrison commanders' expectation of aid from England or Rouen seemed forlorn. Furthermore, the daunting array of siege artillery and cannon, under the supervision of the Bureau brothers, Jean and Gaspard, respectively treasurer of France and *maître d'artillerie*, was enough to persuade many English captains that capitulation was advisable.[185] Only two places held out for more than a day: the castle at Harcourt was defended by John Worcester for eight days and the rocky fortress at Touques on the coast, south-west of Harfleur, for only three under Edward Bromfield. Several others were betrayed by their own inhabitants; at Roche Guyon, for example, the captain, a Welshman named John Edward, who had married a French lady, preferred to join the Valois cause after his surrender rather than face the English music.[186] A few strongholds were deserted by their commanders, who had concluded that withdrawal was the better part of valour in a swiftly deteriorating situation. Meanwhile, the emboldened armies of Brittany under the duke himself and his brother Arthur, count of Richemont and constable of France, were advancing from the west into lower Normandy, securing the countryside as they went but skirting the English strongholds of Fougères and Avranches. A considerable prize was secured in mid-September with the surrender of the city of Coutances, whose captain took one look at Duke Francis's large army of 7,000 men and decided to capitulate.[187]

This catalogue of successes soon brought Charles's forces to the suburbs of Rouen. The fall of the capital of Lancastrian France on 29 October, after a siege directed by Charles himself from Pont de l'Arche but hampered by heavy rain, was a catastrophe for the English. To begin with, there was a hard-fought and bitter struggle, which contrasts with the relatively easy pickings which the French had elsewhere in Normandy; but under pressure from the archbishop of Rouen, Raoul Roussel, and the citizens (who feared the destruction of their city and the slaughter that would accompany it) the duke of Somerset was soon induced to open negotiations with the French king. Rouen's surrender was the culmination of a series of rapid capitulations of towns and fortresses with what twentieth-century strategists would call a domino-effect, and it accelerated a collapse of morale throughout the duchy that was irreversible. The city's loss was a shock to Henry VI's government and to the nation at home, where every contemporary chronicler was moved to record the melancholy details. Not the least distasteful aspect of this sorry affair was the terms of surrender which Somerset concluded with Charles VII.[188]

Somerset secured for himself, his wife and children, and for his entourage (which included the earl of Shrewsbury, Lord Abergavenny, and Lord Roos) a safe-conduct to enable them to leave the palace at Rouen and return to England unharmed and with their possessions intact. But in addition to surrendering Rouen and its fortifications, and other fortresses like Caudebec, Tancarville, Montivilliers, and Harfleur, the duke agreed to find a large ransom of 50,000 *écus* within one year and to leave some high-ranking hostages behind to guarantee the fulfilment of the negotiated terms.[189] It seemed to many in England a heavy price to pay for the freedom of a lieutenant-general whose period in office had seen the entire Lancastrian kingdom of France virtually swept away. On 10 November 1449, Charles entered Rouen with much pomp to take possession of the Norman capital.

> The king of France rode...into his said city, on the side of the Carthusians, by the Porte-Beauvoisine. ...To meet the king there came on horseback into the fields the archbishop of the said city, accompanied by many bishops, abbots, and other churchmen, arranged according to their rank, who made their reverence to him very humbly, and then returned.
>
> Afterwards came the said lord of Dunois, the lieutenant-general, mounted upon a great horse, entirely covered with red velvet, with a great White Cross, clothed with a jacket likewise furred with sable martins, upon his head a cap of black velvet, and a sword at his side, garnished with gold and precious stones, valued at 20,000 crowns; and the seneschal of Poitou [Pierre de Brézé] and Jacques Coeur, banker, mounted upon war-horses, and dressed and covered like the said lord of Dunois.
>
> Then came the burgesses of the said town and city of Rouen in great number and multitude, clothed in blue with red hats, with the keys of the said city, who made reverence to the king of France, and talked much with him in fair and pleasant language, and presented to him the said keys of his city. He received them graciously, and gave them to

the said seneschal of Poitou, who was made captain of the said city; . . . .

Then came the churchmen dressed in their copes, in great numbers, as well seculars as regulars, carrying the relics and other precious things with the cross, saying *Te Deum laudamus*.

And thus as the king entered into his city, four of the chief men of the said city conducted him to the cathedral, a canopy being over his head. The boulevard of the said Porte-Beauvoisine, and the gate and the towers of the same were hung with cloth of the king's livery, having his arms in the middle. And wherever he passed, the streets were hung and covered with a canopy very richly, all full of people crying 'Noel'.

And where the streets met were devices; and among the others there was a fountain with the arms of the said city, which, under the figure of an *Agnus Dei*, ran drink by its horns, and in another place there was a tiger and its whelps, who looked at themselves in mirrors. And near Notre-Dame, there was a winged stag [Charles VII's personal emblem], exceedingly well made, having a crown on his neck, which knelt, by machinery, when the king passed by to go to the said church. And near this place to see these things was the Lord Talbot and the other English, who were with the wife of the said count of Dunois.

The king dismounted at the cathedral, where he was received by the said archbishop and the members of the church, nobly robed, and there he made his prayer; . . . .[190]

After the surrender of Rouen, the Lancastrians attempted to withdraw through the Caux peninsula to the Cotentin, with the intention of concentrating their retreating forces on the defence of Caen and the major port of Cherbourg. Somerset stood by all his earlier undertakings, with the single exception of his promise to surrender Harfleur. That port was retained in English hands until New Year's Day 1450, when, after a hard siege by land and sea in driving rain and snow and freezing cold, the keys of the town were handed over to Dunois, Charles's lieutenant-general.[191] Faint hopes were raised that a relieving army might be despatched from England during the winter, and large sums of money were required to pay the soldiers' and sailors' wages and to buy the necessary supplies and weapons. They were not forthcoming in sufficient quantity. The storerooms at the Tower of London were cleared of longbows, arrows, and gunpowder for the reinforcement of Caen, while further purchases were made in London for the captain of Cherbourg, Thomas Gower.[192]

Indeed, in each of the four years 1448–51 a major expedition had to be launched across the channel, and as the strain of war increased in the summer of 1449, the problems presented by this assemblage of men, equipment, and ships re-emerged in all their gravity. In the spring of 1448, it had been the expedition sailing from Portsmouth under the new lieutenant-general, Somerset, which encountered delays in mustering its men and eliciting wages from the exchequer.[193] Just over a year later, Portsmouth and the nearby haven of Poole were the assembly points for another expedition, and later that same year, when the military situation in Normandy was plainly critical, yet another fleet of transports was fitted out and at the least auspicious time of the year, late autumn. Ships were gathered at Portsmouth from the east coast ports (the southern ones having provided the necessary transports during the summer) and soldiers were also mustered there.[194] This autumn army was placed under the command of Lord Powis and Sir Thomas Kyriell; its formation was laboured – as usual, commented one Englishman writing ruefully with hindsight in the mid-1450s – but eventually about 4,500 men had been retained for the initial period of three months and in November–December the payment of their wages was authorized up to the sum of £9,000. Even with the £13,277 assigned to the duke of Somerset for his men already in Normandy, this was a fraction of the £140,000 which Sir John Fastolf had recently recommended for a major new army to defend Normandy and Aquitaine.[195]

During the latter days of December, when the English positions in the Caux were collapsing one by one, urgent efforts were made to raise loans, and the treasurer of England, Lord Saye, called in as many of the crown jewels as he could to use as security.[196] Dogged by financial problems, the government experienced difficulty in assembling a fleet of transports for the waiting retinues and, in a spirit of desperation, it appealed to the major landowners of Devon (and perhaps elsewhere along the south coast) to aid directly the hard-pressed Lancastrians in lower Normandy.[197] Not only was Somerset experiencing serious difficulty in paying his men, some of whom either were sent home (as one critical commentator believed) or deserted their post in Normandy, but the second instalment of wages payable to the waiting army was delayed until March 1450.[198] During the frustrating weeks at Southampton the mood of the expectant soldiers and sailors grew dangerously volatile, and when the keeper of the privy seal, Adam Moleyns, arrived in Portsmouth with their back-pay, he was hacked to death on 9 January – and by one of the force's own captains, Cuthbert Colville, who had been in the king's service for some years.[199] The exasperation felt by Colville and his men at their treatment by the harried and indigent government drove them to violence.

The problems attending these frantic military and naval manoeuvres were as great as ever they had been. The soldiers and their commanders were as much a nuisance in the countryside near the ports as in the past, and by September 1448 the abbey at Dover was close to despair after 'entertaining' an army on its property for weeks without proper recompense; the abbey lands had begun to suffer badly.[200] Another problem was finance, for the soldiers needed wages and so did captains and sailors in the transport ships. Loans were sought for both purposes.[201] As we have seen, the payment of these wages was not always prompt and sometimes not forthcoming at all, and in June 1449 stern measures were resorted to in order to compel sailors and masters to serve at the king's cost. As a result, desertion among the soldiery was not uncommon.[202] Moreover, the camp-followers of fifteenth-century armies were equally unwelcome to the civilian population on whom they were quartered. Along with the English soldiers and loyalist French who began to retreat across the channel in considerable numbers towards the end of 1449, their behaviour resulted in restrictions being imposed in the vicinity of Dover and other ports: strangers to the area and men with no honest occupation were ordered to return home until they found legitimate employment.[203]

The crumbling English position also meant that desperate measures were required if the Norman garrisons that were holding out against Charles VII's armies were to be supported. This involved further demands on southern England for foodstuffs and weapons. In December 1449, after the fall of Rouen had become widely known, food was hastily conveyed across the channel to the ports of Honfleur and Harfleur, while in July 1450 sheaves of arrows were drawn from the stores at the Tower and despatched, along with contingents of fletchers and workmen, to the Normandy coast, where a few outposts still remained untaken.[204]

Eventually, the French braced themselves for battle. It would be the first time they had seriously challenged the English in the field since the 1420s. The contest took place on 15 April 1450 at the village of Formigny, near the Norman coast north-west of Bayeux. The resounding Valois-Breton victory (for the constable of France had brought badly needed Breton reinforcements from St Lô) destroyed the lingering myth of English invincibility on the battlefield and sealed the fate of the remaining English-held towns in Normandy. The Lancastrian commander at Formigny, Kyriell, who had recently arrived from England with his relief force, was captured, along with a number of captains whose careers had been made in France – Sir Thomas Dring, Sir Henry Norbury, William Herbert, and Elis Longworth. One dejected English estimate put the total of captured English at 900 and their dead at much more (2,300).[205] So rarely were the French able to win battle honours from the English in the Hundred Years War, and so notable was their success at Formigny, that a heated argument broke out immediately after the fighting as to whether the count of Clermont, who had first confronted the English forces, or the constable of France, Arthur de Richemont, who had brought the required assistance, should be credited with the victory.[206]

The final extinction of all English garrisons in northern France (with the exception of Calais) followed by 12 August 1450. These last positions – because they were the very last – were the most hotly contested. The castle and city of Bayeux had to be subjected to a shattering assault by cannon for fifteen or sixteen days, under the direction of Dunois, before its surrender was agreed on 16 May by Matthew Gough (or 'Mathago', as he was known with respect in France), whom an English contemporary described as 'surpassing all the other esquires in war at that time in bravery, hardihood, loyalty and liberality' – in other words, all the chivalric virtues of the best of the war's commanders.[207] The sight of hundreds of wives retiring from the town to Cherbourg with their children and their despondent husbands moved even the hardened besiegers to pity:

> Some were carrying the smaller infants in cradles on their head or around their neck, others had them hanging round their body or by strips of linen, and yet others were holding and leading the bigger children by the hand as best they could.[208]

Not far away, the siege of Caen, the understudy of Rouen as the administrative headquarters of Lancastrian Normandy, was, if anything, even more strenuously conducted from every side by four assault divisions of French troops accompanied by Dunois, the duke of Alençon, King Réné, and Charles VII himself; altogether, they numbered well over 20,000, the largest force yet to be gathered for an assault on a Lancastrian position. Inside Caen lay Somerset and his family, as well as 3-4,000 English. A further stream of advice from Sir John Fastolf, if it was ever heeded by Henry VI and his council, could hardly be acted on in time.[209] With the signing of Caen's instrument of surrender on 24 June, after a battering lasting seventeen days, the end was in sight.[210] Apart from the capitulation of a few outposts in the heart of Normandy, the fall of Cherbourg on 12 August, the only significant foothold remaining to the English in northern France west of Calais, marked the complete triumph of Charles VII and the Bretons, though Francis I had recently died on 28 July, a little too soon to savour the ultimate Lancastrian humiliation. Desperate attempts to hire ships for Cherbourg's protection and furnish arms for its defence availed it nothing.[211] The confidence of the French under de Richemont was such that they were even ready to defy the tides in deploying their artillery:

> ... there were various bombards on the beach, despite the fact that the sea came up twice a day. And these were loaded with stones and powder, though they were completely covered with water when the tide rose. Nevertheless, by means of hides and tallow with which they were coated and covered, the sea did no damage to the powder. But as soon as the sea retreated, the gunners lifted the coverings, and fired and shot as before against the town. At this the English were quite dumbfounded; for they had never encountered such mysteries before.[212]

The English had been brought to such a pitch by their inadequate resources, the lack of immediate aid from England, the collapse of morale, desertion by the Norman population, and the failings of their own commanders. It was the inner decay of Lancastrian power in France, rather than simply the overwhelming strength and superior equipment, organization, and leadership of the French, that ultimately destroyed the achievement of Henry V and the duke of Bedford.[213] To the French the conquest of Normandy 'within the space only of a year and six days' seemed 'a great miracle and an extraordinary marvel'. Jean Chartier expressed their pride in this almost unbelievable accomplishment in heroic phraseology of Churchillian splendour:

> ... never had so great a country been conquered in so short a space of time, with such small loss to the populace and soldiery, and with so little killing of people or destruction and damage to the countryside.[214]

The French were triumphant. On 31 August 1450, as he looked back at the speed of his victorious advance during the past year, Charles VII felt the presence of God close at hand:

> Which recovery and reduction, when due consideration is given, as well to the shortness of time which has been employed therein, as also to the manner in which it has been effected, in which no one can reasonably blame any cruelty or inhumanity, nor have those detestable evils which frequently occur in time of war been perpetrated, make it the rather to be regarded as a divine and miraculous work than aught else.

Charles ordered public celebrations of thanksgiving to be held throughout his realm on 14 October 1450, and henceforward the events of 12 August would be commemorated annually in all cathedral churches.[215]

Holding Calais, losing Gascony

The withering of the English dominion in Normandy isolated Calais and posed a real threat to the fortresses of its march. By March 1449 rumours were current in England that Burgundian forces were massing at St Omer and the English government was concerned about this ominous development for several months.[216] The attitude of the duke of Burgundy and his Low Countries subjects was a critical factor in the continuing prosperity of Calais and its wool staple and, indeed, in the ultimate survival of this toehold in northern France. If Philip the Bold were to hamper the staplers' commerce, then their prosperity would be severely damaged; if his armies advanced against the fortresses of the march, then the last English bridgehead on the mainland would be endangered. During 1449, when the French were overrunning Normandy, Philip's attitude to Calais and its merchants hardened into a real threat to its trade and to Henry's dominion there.

The Anglo-Burgundian agreement sealed at Bruges on 9 April 1445 had provided a mechanism whereby complaints and counter-charges by the subjects of both rulers could be investigated, and guiding principles for the award of reparations in order to avoid reprisals had been devised.[217] Subsequent treaties and truces with the French, in which Burgundy was included, had likewise assured freedom of commerce to the merchants of both states. But by 1449 these undertakings were no longer being observed. In March relations between England and Burgundy were so strained that a Burgundian attack on Calais was expected daily.[218] In parliament the commons spoke out strongly against the recent ban which the Burgundian authorities had imposed on English cloth merchants trading in the Low Countries; they claimed that it was producing unemployment in England, that in time it would reduce the king's revenue from Calais and was likely to harm the merchants and their trade. The commons resorted to a well-directed threat, announcing that if no satisfaction were forthcoming by Michaelmas 1449, then the English would impose their own ban (to last until the next parliament) on all imports from the Low Countries to Calais.[219] At the same time, the government despatched an embassy to convey the strong feelings expressed at Westminster and, by means of this sabre-rattling, to try and open negotiations. Accordingly, William Pirton, the lieutenant of Guisnes castle, and Edward Grimston, a reliable household official who had been employed as a diplomat before, were instructed to convey Henry's personal regret for the present state of Anglo-Burgundian relations and to stress that he was fully prepared to act reasonably, provided the Burgundians made a similar response that would benefit the merchants of both sides.[220]

Their mission was seemingly abortive, though the envoys undertook to return to their respective masters and to meet again before the end of the summer of 1449. To judge by the instructions given to its envoys, the English government appears to have been conciliatory and prepared to offer concessions, even to examine Burgundian complaints against English merchants in the latter's absence. Faced with a rapidly deteriorating situation further south, the English were most anxious to avoid a complete rupture with Burgundy, for that could only damage trade, threaten Calais, and cost much money. To this end, the new envoys appointed on 30 July were more senior officials: Lord Dudley and Master Thomas Kent, clerk of the council and Bishop Moleyns's deputy as keeper of the privy seal, were given wide discretion in negotiating an agreement to avoid a breach.[221] They appear to have been no more successful than their predecessors, for when parliament again met in the autumn of 1449, the commons had lost none of their sense of outrage or determination to pay the Burgundians in their own coin. At first they wanted to erect a permanent trading barrier against Calais's imports from the Low Countries, but in the event this stern proposal was modified to the extent that unless a satisfactory agreement were reached by Michaelmas 1450, a seven-year ban would be imposed.[222]

Nevertheless, efforts continued to be made by the government to repair the tattered truces and agreements with Burgundy for the benefit of both countries. Thomas Kent again travelled to Calais to meet the Burgundian envoys in May 1450 and reopen the discussions on complaints and reparations so that the possibility of armed reprisals and commercial disruption could be avoided.[223] Henry VI and his council were undoubtedly anxious to maintain the truces they had earlier concluded, and relations had sufficiently improved by February 1452 for the duchess of Burgundy to ask Henry to receive her young nephew (and therefore the king's relative), John of Coimbra, into the royal service.[224]

Yet the situation was no better by the time parliament assembled in March 1453. The Burgundians were now imposing tolls at Gravening on wool bought at Calais for the Burgundian Low Countries. It was not such a hindrance to trade as the recent cloth ban, but associated with it were Burgundian restrictions on the amount of bullion passing into Calais for minting into English coin there or in England. During the parliamentary session, the government responded with a ban as from 3 April 1453 on all wool exported to the Burgundian industrial centres, and this would remain in force until the duke's unfriendly acts ceased.[225] Soon afterwards, the hearing of complaints against the inhabitants of both countries was resumed.[226] Thus, some of the tension that had vitiated Anglo-Burgundian relations at the time of the French successes of 1449–50 subsided when it became clear that the capture of Calais was no easy task. Amicable relations were not fully restored, but the essential features of past undertakings were salvaged. The commons in parliament, fortified by the mercantile members and their sympathizers, were vigilant in insisting on unhindered access to the markets of the Low Countries.

As for Calais itself, the main preoccupations of the Lancastrians in these years were its defence and proper garrisoning, the regular payment of its defenders, the repair of its walls and other fortifications, and the supply of its inhabitants and soldiers with arms and supplies. Parliament sympathized with these aims, and the commons gave priority to Calais's need except when the requirements of the king's household, the queen, or the crown's creditors – but no other – demanded precedence. The simplest and most direct way to provide Calais with funds for wages, repairs, and supplies was by assigning to the treasurer and victualler of the town the customs duties payable at Calais on wool exported through the staple; hence, the parliament of 1449 earmarked 20s. per sack to Calais's needs and instilled some longer-term confidence by guaranteeing this arrangement for four and a half years.[227] To prevent this resource being significantly reduced even before collection, at the same time those licensees who were enabled to export free of custom duties would now forfeit half their wool.[228] To improve the morale of the inhabitants and soldiers at Calais, the resumption act of 1449–50 contained a specific clause whereby those who had received grants of one sort or another in Calais or its marches were exempt from the act's provisions, while it was requested of the king that all revenue from Calais and Guisnes should be handed over to the local treasurer to meet the soldiers' wages and necessary repairs.[229] The other major source of cash for Calais came in the form of loans, overwhelmingly provided by the staple merchants themselves, who had a vital interest in the proper defence of the port. They therefore contributed out of self-interest and in return for commercial concessions that frequently allowed them to avoid paying customs duties until they had recouped their loans.[230]

Without a flourishing and profitable commerce organized by the staple, and generous financial support from its merchants, the Lancastrian position in Calais would have crumbled from within at the slightest pressure from Burgundy or Valois France. And yet, Henry VI's government was in danger of falling between two stools as a result of its relations with the staple and its attitude to the staplers' privileges. The patronage offered to those favoured by the government took the form sometimes of licences to export wool free of customs duty at Calais and, what was worse, sometimes of permission to export wool to north European ports other than Calais. Both, but especially the latter, incensed the staple merchants because their monopoly of the wool trade was thereby eroded and the speed with which they could recover their loans to the crown from customs duties collected at Calais consequently reduced. The staplers' reactions could not, therefore, be ignored, and when it seemed likely that a moratorium might be placed on further loans, the king's ministers would have to give way on the question of licences.

The staplers' views, as communicated to the government by the commons in parliament, were expressed clearly in 1449. Licences had once again become a lively issue, for it was felt, probably with some exaggeration, that wool exporters who avoided the staple were defrauding the king of his customs income; corrupt customs officials were also condemned, for their activities further reduced the total income from the customs. According to the commons in 1449, the income from Calais amounted to only £12,000 *per annum*, whereas in Edward III's reign, when the staple had first been established, it had stood at about £68,000. The staplers and their allies refrained from making the obvious and fundamental point that the nature of England's overseas trade had altered significantly since those early days, when the amount of wool exported was much greater than in 1449. Nevertheless, they were justified in painting a gloomy picture of the effects of inadequate revenue on the prosperity and security of the mercantile community at Calais, on the regular payment of the garrison's wages, and on the repair of the fortress, town, and harbour. For its part, the embattled government was fully prepared to confirm the century-old privileges of the staple, even the extensive judicial powers of its mayor and officials; but the demand for an end to the vexatious granting of licences was a more delicate matter, for the queen and Suffolk were among those who were currently benefiting from them. It was eventually agreed that such licences should no longer be granted (with certain minor exceptions in favour of royal servants) and that the ban on them should last for five years. This concession was reluctantly made, and indeed proved difficult for the hard-pressed government to honour.[231]

Henry's ministers found it well-nigh impossible to allay the staplers' misgivings about the reduction of customs revenue as a result of concessions to export wool to Calais freely. Furthermore, so long as the borrowing requirements of Henry's régime were high and its resources hopelessly inadequate to satisfy them, similar grants to the merchant-lenders themselves could not be avoided. Thus, by October 1449, when a total of £10,700 which had been lent by staple merchants had not yet been fully repaid, they had to be allowed to export from London as many sacks of wool as would ordinarily produce a subsidy of £9,875 over four years, beyond the 20s. per sack which had already been assigned earlier in the year for Calais's needs. This meant that from this source of income, there was available for other purposes at Calais no revenue at all during 1449–53.[232]

The government's undertakings on the subject of licences soon proved a dead letter, for when the commons had another opportunity to echo the complaints of the staplers in the parliament of March 1453, they did so with greater force, proposing stern remedies which the government found it impossible to endorse. Licences for export were still being granted and not always in return for loans; the commons therefore advocated the use of informers, who would be rewarded for bringing to light breaches of the earlier act. Existing licences (they further demanded) should be annulled, the staple should be enabled to take to law anyone who used a licence, and the king's subjects should be encouraged to seize the illegal shipments by a kind of 'citizen's arrest'. If implemented, these proposals would have meant the withdrawal of privileges and favours granted to king's servants, friends, and others, thereby forfeiting their good will and abandoning a prerogative right by which the king could meet his obligations. Needless to say, the commons' petition was rejected.[233] Moreover, aspersions had recently been cast on the ability of the mayor of the staple and his aldermen to deal impartially with disputes brought before them and this may have intensified the staplers' annoyance by the time this parliament met.[234] Meanwhile, the impoverished crown had no alternative but to honour some of its debts by allowing the free export of wool to Calais, provided the basic 20s. subsidy for Calais's needs was paid first.[235] Trapped in its own financial dilemma, the most the government could offer was an inquiry on 8 April 1453 in the south coast ports into wool that was exported illegally to Brittany, Normandy, and elsewhere.[236]

Neither the state of the crown's finances nor the constant agility required to soothe the staplers would allow the government to escape the consequences of its position for very much longer. It was surely evident to all interested parties that the revenue from the wool trade was inadequate for the purposes to which it was now being put. The consequent strains had serious political repercussions, not least because the patience of the staplers wore thinner and thinner as inroads on their cherished privileges continued to be made. Whatever its public posturings, in the final analysis Henry VI's régime was in no position to guarantee the terms of the franchise of Calais which it had reaffirmed. A rupture in relations between government and staple was likely in the long run if this unsatisfactory situation deteriorated further and the bonds of interest between the two parties began to break.

The wages and other payments owed to the captain of Calais and the garrisons under his command in the marches were not matched by income from Calais itself or by the loans from the staplers, whose own repayment from the customs at Calais in turn reduced the available revenue. In February 1449 £220 was still outstanding of expenses incurred at Calais twenty years earlier.[237] The monies currently owed to the captain, his lieutenants, and their men were enormous in comparison. When parliament met in November 1449, it was reported that the duke of Buckingham, who had been captain at Calais since 1442, was a creditor of the government to the tune of £19,395 for the wages and rewards of himself and his men up to Michaelmas 1449. It is true that arrangements were immediately made by parliamentary authority to recompense him, and he was granted the customs and subsidies levied at Sandwich from 2 February 1450, together with 6s. 8d. a sack from the subsidy on wool exported from every other port in the realm, not to speak of the privilege of naming one of the customs collectors at Sandwich so that he could keep a personal eye on his new investment in the port.[238]

The government attempted to give high priority to the revenue assignments for Calais's defence, and in particular to Buckingham's debts.[239] But the next captain, Somerset, quickly accumulated another list of unpaid debts. When parliament met in 1453, it learned that he was owed £21,649 up to 6 June. All that could be done was to grant him the Sandwich customs after Buckingham's claims had been met, with the right to appoint the collector formerly nominated by Buckingham, and, in due course, to give him an identical subvention from the subsidies collected in every other English port.[240] Yet not even the king's principal confidant could work a financial miracle, and one may doubt whether he received more than a small proportion of his due before he was killed at St Albans in May 1455.

The physical protection of Calais depended on an adequate provision of arms, foodstuffs, and other supplies, and the channel link with Kent, especially Dover. To ensure that sufficient foodstuffs were available at this and other moments of crisis, in May 1449 the king's purveyors were instructed not to scour the area between Canterbury and the sea and from Sandwich to Appledore in order to purchase or confiscate supplies for domestic consumption, but rather to reserve this rich area for the needs of the victualler of Calais and of Dover castle.[241] In order that cross-channel transport could be organized safely, it was desirable that the town of Dover should be properous and its defences kept in a state of good repair – something that was only a whit less important than the defence of Calais itself. Hence, in June 1451 the 'common passage' between Calais and Dover was placed under the government's special protection, and efforts were made to funnel the commerce of Kentishmen through this, the most important port in the county.[242]

After weathering for the moment the Burgundian danger, in 1451 it was the victorious French who posed the gravest threat to England's outpost. An English army was assembled during the summer to sail from Dover to Calais under Gervase Clifton, an experienced soldier who had been Lord Saye's lieutenant as warden of Dover (1447–50), had served at sea during the darkening days of 1449, and was currently treasurer of Calais.[243] Two of Henry VI's closest companions, Lords Beauchamp and Sudeley, also crossed over, while the mayor of the staple, Robert White, the controller of Calais, Giles St Lo, and Robert Manfield, a squire for the body and victualler of the town, mustered at Sandwich a further contingent provided by the merchant community of London.[244] Reinforcements were despatched in the middle of winter, so serious was the situation felt to be.[245] This intense activity was in response to the news that Charles VII was advancing to lay siege to Calais and – who knows? – to invade England itself after it had fallen.[246] A substantial English expedition was eventually placed under the command of two other of Henry's favourites, Lords Rivers and Saye, while the king himself planned to visit Calais before spring in order to sustain the morale of those bracing themselves for the fight in his name. Whether or not this was a serious intention on the king's part or simply a propagandist announcement to deter the French and revive Lancastrian spirits cannot now be ascertained. In any case, the proposed royal visit, like the similar (though more pacific) project in the 1440s, never materialized. Despite extensive preparations and the gathering of a fleet at Sandwich, as well as the appointment in March 1451 of Shrewsbury to command the sea, and the raising of an army to accompany the king, Henry did not set foot outside his realm; events in the west of his kingdom, culminating in the confrontation with York at Dartford (Kent), diverted his attention and thwarted his plans.[247]

When parliament met on 6 March 1453, the needs of Calais were as great as ever, and there is reason to believe that the arrangements made in 1449 to assign revenues to Calais from the customs duties imposed at the port were not being implemented satisfactorily. Nevertheless, the government insisted that prompt payment would be made to creditors, and a further £9,300 was promised on 16 May for repairs to the gates of Calais and to Rysbank tower after parliament had heard a report on their dilapidated condition.[248] The new victualler, Sir John Cheyne, and his agents were encouraged in their duties by being offered on 6 July the king's special protection for as long as Cheyne remained in office.[249] Rather remarkably, Calais weathered the alarums of these years, for by the end of 1453 it had become the sole English possession on the continental mainland. It survived by the skin of Lancastrian teeth and with a good deal of luck as a result of major preoccupations elsewhere.

The record of defeat in Normandy in 1449–50 was matched by events in Gascony. Indeed, Charles VII's successes in the north encouraged him to believe that victory would come as easily – if not more quickly – in the south.[250] Gascony had been in the charge of Sir William Bonville as seneschal since 1442, when it had been hoped that he would divert his ample energies from the west country (where his expanding wealth and authority had led him into rivalry with the earl of Devon) to resist the Valois threat.[251] Likewise, John Strangways had been captain of Fronsac's impregnable castle at the entrance to the Dordogne since 1438.[252] On their shoulders pre-eminently rested responsibility for the military defence of Gascony after war with King Charles was renewed in July 1449.[253]

Alarm spread to the south when Normandy fell. Charles's agent in the south-west was the count of Foix, his lieutenant-general between the Garonne and the Pyrenees. His first offensive was directed against Mauléon-Soule, a fortified town near the Pyrenean foothills and not too far from the second city of Gascony, Bayonne. This fell at the end of September, despite an intervention by the king of Navarre, whose constable was Mauléon's custodian for the English. By the spring of 1450, the country around Bayonne in the Landes had been subdued by the count of Foix and his large army.[254] In September, Charles ordered his own forces southwards, with Jean Bureau's artillery in its train. Their first success in the Dordogne was at Bergerac, a fortified town about 50 miles east of Bordeaux; its capture in October 1450 opened the way for the advance on the capital itself.[255]

The authorities at Westminster soon recognized that reinforcements from England were needed urgently. Henry's government found its hands securely tied so that a rapid response was out of the question. Financial difficulties and problems of logistics in raising a suitable navy dogged its efforts to despatch a substantial expedition under the command of Lord Rivers, who was accorded supreme authority in the duchy on 18 October as seneschal; the embarkation of his army was postponed time and again from the summer of 1450 onwards, just when the French inroads were digging deeper into the Gascon countryside.[256] While these laborious, and largely ineffective, military and naval preparations were in progress far away in England, Bordeaux succumbed to a French attack on 29 June 1451. And Rivers had not even set sail.[257] One year after the preparations had begun, his men were still in the west country, frustrated by the delays and annoyed at the failure to produce any wages; they had attracted, too, camp-followers who were such a burden to the local populace that they had to be sent home. Eventually, in July – August 1451 the huge sum of £29,500 was assigned for the expedition – but by then it was too late.[58] By contrast, Charles VII, flushed with his Norman successes, was ready to transfer his energies and his armies to the Gascon campaign, confident that support would be forthcoming from the southern nobility, despite the tradition of English loyalty felt by some of them.[259] Dunois, the victor of the Norman conquest and the king's lieutenant and captain-general of the war, was instructed to march south by May 1451 with an army of at least 7,000 men; the carefully conceived strategy also envisaged a force from Maine and a joint French, Spanish, and Breton fleet in the Gironde estuary to support the French besiegers of Blaye and Bourg, a few miles down river from Bordeaux.[260] It was a faultless plan that successfully severed the capital's communications with the open sea and surrounded it by substantial land forces. As the latter made their way irresistibly towards Bordeaux, even the great protective fortress of Fronsac, 'the key of Guienne and the Bordelais country', whose vital importance was signified by a garrison of native Englishmen, was induced to negotiate a surrender on 5 June, after a brief but vigorous siege. Superior French forces, heavy bombardment from the Bureau cannons, and swollen rivers prevented relief from reaching the town.[261]

After a triumphal entry into Bordeaux which lacked nothing in magnificence and dignity save the person of Charles VII himself (though a lone white horse bearing the royal seals symbolized the monarch's presence), the king contemplated a siege of the southern city of Bayonne.[262] It began on 6 August, and the count of Foix was assisted by Gaspard Bureau and his guns. They were soon joined by Dunois himself, and on 22 August, after a siege lasting about a fortnight, the French took possession of the city and its citadel.[263]

The recovery of Bordeaux by the Lancastrians in October 1452, and the possibility that the earl of Shrewsbury might regain at least some of the lost territory, eventually stirred the government to purposeful action.[264] The earl appears at first to have been ordered to secure the sea approaches and trading lanes to England, now that most of the French coastline was in enemy hands; in this he was aided from July 1452 by the dispossessed constable of Bordeaux, Sir Edward Hull (who was also retained for service on the island of Jersey), and by Gervase Clifton, treasurer of Calais. But the indentured force of Hull and Clifton, which alone totalled 2,000 men, may equally have been intended from the beginning for a more ambitious venture than mere sea-keeping; certainly the French feared a major descent on Normandy. Moreover, not only was there an influential Gascon lobby in England, led by Peter

Tastar, dean of St Seurin at Bordeaux, but from 1 July numerous grants of land, office, revenues, and benefices in Gascony were made to several Gascons living in England; these would be a powerful incentive to the recovery of the duchy and they indicated the government's hope that it might be soon achieved.[265] Thus, in the autumn of 1452 Shrewsbury and his companions made for the Gironde, and if French spies had done their work well, they would have discovered that the earl had been named lieutenant-general in Gascony on 25 September.[266] With an army 5,000-strong, and assisted by a group of Anglophile Gascons, whom Jean Chartier reproachfully compared to Judas, he was able to capture King Charles's men in the city of Bordeaux on 23 October.[267]

The sense of shock which the fall of Bordeaux caused at the French court is well conveyed by a report written on 7 November by the Milanese envoy who was with the king.[268] It gave way to an angry determination on the part of Charles VII to punish those responsible for the city's betrayal. He resolved to recover it, and those who had broken their oath of allegiance, so recently sworn, would be severely dealt with as 'an example to others and a perpetual memory'. The king's willingness in 1451 to conciliate the Gascons, for whom the English link represented a strongly felt sentiment as well as an economic lifeline, had disappeared a year later.[269] Before the walls of Bordeaux, he personally berated envoys from the city thus:

> It is our intention, with the help of Our Creator, to have the town, and all those in it and their goods, placed at our disposal, in order to punish their bodies according to their deserts for having broken their oaths and expressions of loyalty to us, so that it would be an example to others and a reminder in the future.[270]

The Milanese observer at Tours in late March 1453 appreciated the priority which Charles now attached to the recovery of the Gascon lands:

> The king and all his officers are making great provision for this war, and all are so intent on it that they pay heed to few other things; and audiences are more unsatisfactory and difficult than they used to be. The king is confident that he will regain Bordeaux – nor is it known that the English are arraying powerful forces – and, indeed, the king's preparations are mighty.[271]

In England, the need to support Shrewsbury's enterprise and stem a renewed French attack produced urgent appeals for loans from spiritual and temporal persons alike; any who failed to respond with a contribution would be stigmatized as 'a hinderer of the army'. It also prompted the hasty assembly of a force of 2,400 men, mostly of infantry, under Viscount Lisle, Shrewsbury's son and heir, and Lords

Camoys and Moleyns, in January–March 1453.[272] The commercial interests of the wine merchants were temporarily subordinated to the military and naval emergency, and Shrewsbury ruthlessly condemned deserters and reluctant helpers, and commandeered a number of merchant ships for his own use.[273] In the Bordelais and coastal regions, the English troops were ill-disciplined and spent much of their time pillaging and defiling churches; moreover, Shrewsbury's efforts to raise taxes and appropriate merchant ships displeased the Gascons. These expedients had attendant risks, and in any case the English commanders were so short of cash for their men that they had to dig deep into their own private purses for the required wages. By contrast, the French army was strictly policed and adequately recompensed, and Charles VII's banker extraordinary, Jacques Coeur, gave a substantial contribution to the war in 1451 and his confiscated wealth supported the French campaign of 1453. 'Foresight and strategic planning had become an integral part of Charles VII's political armoury by his later years'.[274]

While a second army of 2,200 men was being raised in England in July–August 1453 to aid Shrewsbury, news arrived that the English had been defeated at Castillon on 17 July, with great loss of life (over 4,000, it was claimed) and Shrewsbury himself unhorsed and slain – and his eldest son too.[275]

> And thus died this famous and renowned English leader [commented one admiring French contemporary], who for so long had been reputed to be one of the most formidable scourges of the French, and one of their most sworn enemies, and had seemed to be the dread and terror of France.[276]

The French, Spanish, and Breton ships blockading the Gironde estuary prevented wheat and other supplies from England from reaching Bordeaux, which accordingly was in danger of being starved into submission.[277] Difficulties were even experienced in England in ensuring that these provisions were in fact sent to Gascony, and at the same time further appeals for loans were made to London merchants, royal household servants (who could hardly ignore such a request), and certain London churchmen. A combination of carrot and stick was employed to assemble more ships from the south coast ports:

> ...exerte, stire, moeve and enduce.... alle the oweners and maistres of shippes belonging to oure port of Plymmouthe [and Dartmouth, Fowey, and Bristol] and there being, that this yere dispose thayme towardes oure citee of Bourdeaux, that thai be redie by the last day of this monthe to accompany oure saide armee towardes our said duchie. And over this, that ye do openly to be proclaimed, in suche places as ye thinke most expedient, that alle persones that wol dispose thaim to be redy in maner abovesaide with thair shippes to accompaigny oure said armee, shalle frely passe

withoute paying of any custume for any vitaile that thai shalle carie withe thayme, what ever it be, And that that wol differe thaire going unto the tyme our said armee be passed, shalle in noo wyse enjoye that benefice, but duely pay alle manere custumes according to oure lawes and statutes, . . .[278]

Whilst Henry VI's government realized the extreme precariousness of Shrewsbury's position, and appears to have had the will to take urgent steps to aid him in the summer of 1453, its demands on the king's subjects had outrun their ability (or perhaps their willingness, after the catalogue of disasters) to meet them.[279] Towards the end of July, Charles VII had arrived in the Bordelais, and eventually his forces were able to re-enter Bordeaux in October. Plans to send Sir William Bonville once more to Gascony were abandoned soon afterwards.[280] Gascony, like Normandy before it, had become a lost province of the Lancastrian crown, almost 300 years to the year since Henry II had first united it with England in 1154.

English fortunes in France during the eight years following Henry VI's marriage are a record of frustration in the search for peace, commercial disruption, military defeat, and the loss of every English possession on the European mainland apart from Calais. A special medal struck by order of Charles VII carried the triumphant legend:

When I was made, everyone in France, without dispute, obeyed the prudent king, loved by God; – except at Calais which is a strong place.[281]

Public celebrations were held in many parts of France, with morality and other plays expressing Frenchmen's gratitude to God and their king; at Compiègne one performance relived what in the popular mind was one of the key episodes in the recovery of Gascony; the *Desconfiture de Talbot*.[282]

The effect of the calamities on Henry VI, his government, and his subjects may be imagined in terms of personal distress and dejection, and national shame and despair; as far as contemporaries were concerned, the alleviation of the material and human burden on the realm weighed lightly by comparison. Cauterization by defeat and expulsion was unwelcome treatment for the problems afflicting Henry's French inheritance. The impact of its loss on the Lancastrian commanders and soldiers, and on public opinion at home, was severe and bred deep dissatisfaction with, and disdain for, the ministers associated with it. The effect on the king himself, who had striven for an honourable and negotiated peace, and yet had suffered crushing defeats and the loss of his second realm, was bound to be shattering.

Notes

1 The Bretons may have been conveying the French hope that Suffolk would be nominated, as Suffolk himself later inferred (below, p. 484).
2 *PPC*, VI, 3, 11.
3 Champion, op. cit., pp. 340-1; Vaughan, op. cit., pp. 114-16.
4 Catherine, the eldest, was already married (1439) to Charles of Charolais, Philip the Bold's heir, and Yolande had been married to Louis of Savoy, prince of Piedmont, in 1436 (Vale, *Charles VII*, pp. 84, 73).
5 Basin, II, 292-3. A French proverb current at the time scorned the 'tristes noces et des hyménées malheureux' experienced by French wives in England in the past.
6 Vale, *Charles VII*, pp. 86-7.
7 For the military reforms, see Contamine, op. cit., pp. 278ff.
8 Lecoy de la Marche, *Le roi René* (2 vols., Paris, 1875); Vaughan, op. cit., p. 118. Several of the earlier proposals for Margaret's hand had come from French noblemen in the Burgundian circle (*DNB*, XXXVI, 138-9).
9 *PPC*, VI, 32-5, reprinted in modernized English in Wilkinson, *Const. Hist.*, pp. 59-61.
10 For his correspondence with Orléans, his former prisoner in England, in the weeks before he arrived in France, see Stevenson, I, 67-76. Suffolk also struck up a friendship with Orléans's bastard brother, Dunois, who had been his captor when Suffolk was a prisoner in France in 1429-30 (Kingsford, *Prejudice and promise*, p. 148).
11 Above, pp. 450ff.
12 *Foedera*, V, i, 130, 133 (11 February 1444). For Moleyns, see Emden, *Oxford*, II, 1289-91; for Roos, above, p. 57; for Andrew, Otway-Ruthven, *King's secretary*, pp. 154, 172-3; and Wenlock, Roskell, *Beds. Hist. Record Soc. Publ.*, XXXVIII (1958), 16-22. 'Benet's Chron.', p. 190, says that Reginald Boulers, abbot of Gloucester and one of Suffolk's clients, also went, though there is no other indication of this (Ferguson, op. cit., p. 179); and John Say, an esquire of the king's chamber, seems to have accompanied them too (ibid., p. 184).
13 *Foedera*, V, i, 130 (20 February); *DKR*, XLVIII (1887), 361.
14 De Beaucourt, op. cit., III, 277, puts the dowry at 20,000 francs. René also conveyed his claim to Majorca and Minorca to Margaret.
15 *Foedera*, V, i, 129; *DKR*, XLVIII (1887), 363. They were mostly Charles VII's councillors (Vale, *Charles VII*, p. 87). For Dunois, see *Dict. Biog. Franc.*, XII, 279-83; and Bourbon, ibid., VI, 1404–5.
16 Stevenson, I, 67-76.
17 ibid., 69; Ramsay, op. cit., II, 59.
18 Despite A. Vallet de Viriville, *Histoire de Charles VII et son époque* (3 vols., Paris, 1862–65), II, 452, it is evident that Burgundy did not travel himself to Tours (de Beaucourt, op. cit., III, 275). For the dauphin's bitter hostility to Suffolk's arrival, see Stevenson, I, 77-8 (1 April, though the year is not given).
19 ibid., I, 131-5 (as recalled in July 1445). The French appear to have offered Gascony and Calais only.
20 Bodl, Digby MS 196 f. 155-56 (an account written by one of the English delegation), is analysed in Vallet de Viriville, op. cit., II, 451; *English Chron.*, p. 61.
21 *Foedera*, V, i, 133 (its English confirmation on 27 June 1444); *DKR*, XLVIII

(1887), 362. The release of the count of Angoulême, Orléans's younger brother, was also arranged at Tours (de Beaucourt, op. cit., IV, 19-20).

22 C. M. de Robillard de Beaurepaire, *Les états de Normandie sous la domination anglaise* (Evreux, 1859), p. 83, transcribing Reg. capit. de la cathédrale de Rouen, 4 and 8 June.

23 This grant was authorized by the king at Berkhamsted on 31 May 1444, four days after Somerset's death; the letters patent were issued on 8 June (S. Bentley [ed.], *Excerpta Historica* [1831], p. 4; *CPR, 1441–46*, p. 283).

24 *RDP*, V, 251; above, p. 356. Although the patent was not issued until 14 September 1444, Suffolk was being referred to as marquess on or about 17 August (PRO, E403/754 *s. d.*)

25 All three lords were under 30 years of age and may have been considered congenial company for a young queen (*GEC*, III, 293; VI, 197; X, 126-7).

26 BL, Add. MS 23,938. For Lady Talbot, see *CPR, 1416–22*, pp. 415-16; *GEC*, XII, i, 619; for Cokesay, Pollard, thesis, pp. 225-8; and Lyhert, above, p. 136. 'Benet's Chron.', p. 190, says that Suffolk's entourage numbered about 1,000 on horseback.

27 Stevenson, I, 447; BL, Add. MS 23,938 f. 13-14; 'Gregory's Chron.', p. 185; d'Escouchy, I, 87; Myers, *BJRL*, XL (1957-58), 48-50. For the place of household servants of the king in the company, see above, p. 360.

28 Stevenson, I, 445-59. For the preparations, see *CPR, 1441–46*, p. 292; *Foedera*, V, i, 137. The enrolled account of Peter Bowman, who was charged with assembling the fleet, is PRO, E364/87 m. 48; he was not paid the £17 which he had overspent until 16 October 1454.

29 Stevenson, II, i, 356-60; J. B. Sheppard (ed.), *Literae Cantuariensis*, III (RS, 1889), 176-82 (29 October, though the year is not given), preserved in a register of Canterbury cathedral priory. For other letters concerning peace, forwarded at about the same time by the duke of York from Rouen to the queen of France, Margaret of Anjou, the duke of Orléans, and the bastard of Orléans, see Stevenson, II, ii, 468-9.

30 *Foedera*, V, i, 128; PRO, E403/760 m. 1; *DKR*, XLVIII (1887), 366.

31 Flenley, p. 118, for the impression it made.

32 PRO, E364/79, printed in Stevenson, I, 443-60; the detailed particulars on which this account was based are BL, Add. MS 23,938. See also Stevenson, I, 462-4.

33 De Beaucourt, op. cit., IV, 91. But in his letter to Henry VI on 29 October which may not have arrived in England before Suffolk left London on 5 November, Charles had pointed out that he and René needed adequate notice of the arrival of the English so that proper preparations could be made to bring Margaret in suitable state to meet them (Sheppard, op. cit., III, 176-82).

34 *RP*, V, 67, 176-83.

35 Anjou was not, of course, in English hands, though most of Maine was and had been granted in reversion to the duke of Somerset in 1443; even though Suffolk was now the guardian of Somerset's heiress, it is doubtful if he had the power to dispose of the county, in which the marquess of Dorset, Edmund Beaufort, also had an interest (above, p. 466).

36 Gascoigne, pp. 190, 204-5, 219-21. Elsewhere (ibid., pp. 219-21) he says that the cession was agreed at Margaret's request. These passages are partially translated in Wilkinson, *Const. Hist.*, p. 68. The story was, of course, taken

up by later (often hostile Yorkist) writers (*Great Chron.* pp. 176-7; *London Chrons.* p. 155; *Brut*, pp. 509-10, 511-12).

37 Stevenson, I, 448, 80; BL, Add. MS. 23,938 f. 10*v.*; de Beaucourt, op. cit., IV, 93-4.

38 King Charles had previously agreed that the queen should be brought to Pontoise, where she would become the responsibility of the English (Sheppard, op. cit., III, 176-82).

39 AN, K. 68 no. 1³; Stevenson, I, 449; BL, Add. MS 23,938; d'Escouchy, I, 86-90. For the queen's need of doctors on the journey, see Stevenson, I, 452; BL, Add. MS 23,938 f. 10*v*. For York's preparations to greet her with a suitable retinue, see d'Escouchy, I, 86-7 (where the editor, de Beaucourt, also cites AN, K. 68 no. 1³); and Luce, *Chron. Mont-St.-Michel*, II, 176-8, printing BN, quittances, t. 82/5107, which indicates that the preparations to receive her were in hand as early as 24 November 1444. Rouen's gifts to the queen cost more than £2,000 (BL, Add. MS 26,805-7).

40 Stevenson, I, 447-8, 453; *PPC*, VI, xvi n. 1; *Brut*, p. 488. On reaching the English coast on 9 April, her ship, the *Cog John*, put in at Portsmouth and there she spent the night before re-embarking for Southampton next day; see also *English Chron.*, pp. 61-2 (mentioning Porchester instead of Portsmouth); *EHL*, p. 347; Flenley, p. 119; BL, Add. MS 23,938 f. 9.

41 *CMilP, 1385–1618*, pp. 18-19. The envoy's informant may have been one of the queen's servants, for he referred to her as 'his mistress.'

42 *CChR*, VI, 81; PRO, E403/760 m. 1; 'Benet's Chron.', pp. 190-1; *English Chron.*, pp. 61-2.

43 Flenley, pp. 119-20; J. Nichols (ed.), *Collection of the wills of kings and queens of England* (1780), pp. 339-40. The king had returned to Westminster by 16 May ('Benet's Chron.', p. 191).

44 *Great Chron.*, pp. 177-8; *Brut*, p. 510; *London Chrons.*, p. 156.

45 *Great Chron.*, pp. 177-8; Flenley, pp. 103, 119-20; *Chron. of London*, p. 134; 'Gregory's Chron.', p. 186.

46 Above, pp. 219ff.

47 BL, Harleian MS 3,869 f. 2-4, printed in C. Brown, 'Lydgate's verses on Queen Margaret's entry into London', *MLR*, VII(1912), 225-34 (with the quotation on p. 230). This is an imperfect version of the entire work and for an even less complete version (BL, Harleian MS 542 f. 101-2), see R. Withington, 'Queen Margaret's entry into London, 1445', *Mod. Philol.*, XIII (1915), 53-7.

48 Capgrave, op. cit., pp. 135-7.

49 *RP*, V, 66. The session was prorogued on 15 March partly because these negotiations were as yet incomplete (ibid., 67).

50 ibid., 73-4.

51 BL, Harleian MS 2,255 f. 131, printed in Wright, op. cit., II, 215-20 (with the quotation on 216), and in MacCracken, *Minor poems*, II, 813-18.

52 Above, p. 487. Cf. perhaps *PL*, I, 28: writing from Norfolk to her son Edmund in London on 4 February 1445, Agnes Paston asked him 'to sende me tydynggis from be-yond see, for here thei arn aferde to telle soche as be reportid'.

53 BL, Cotton, Vespasian, B XVI f. 5, printed in F. J. Furnivall (ed.), *Political, religious and love poems* (EETS, old ser., XV, 1866), pp. 12-13. The contemporary date 'mccccxvj' is probably a mistranscription of

'mccccxlvj'. This is the most satisfactory explanation of the poem's extravagant allusions.

54 'Benet's Chron.', p. 190 (which restricts her companions to 3 or 4 French maids). Admittedly, a number of Angevins came to England in April 1445 to witness the coronation and then report to René (PRO, E403/757 m. 2, 6). For a comment on her lack of dowry as late as 1458, see *CMilP*, I, 18-19.

55 Etienne Chevalier was Charles VII's secretary and one of the dauphin's councillors; Bertrand de Beauvau, seigneur de Précigny, was one of his councillors as well as René's confidant; Guillaume Cousinot, seigneur de Montreuil, was Charles's chamberlain, a member of the dauphin's household, and a former servant of the duke of Orléans; the archbishop was a lawyer and one of that remarkable group of brothers who served Charles and Louis XI; and Guy, count of Laval, was the king's kinsman. See Stevenson, I, 105; Vale, *Charles VII*, pp. 99-100, 33, 99; P. S. Lewis, *Later mediaeval France* (1968), pp. 177-9, 297; Lecoy de la Marche, op. cit., I, 133, 135, 496-7.

56 BN, MS Baluze 8448/2 f. 171ff, printed in Stevenson, I, 87-148. Other versions of this journal are in BN, MS Baluze 9037/7ff. 45-57 (of which part is printed in Stevenson, I, 149-59), and Bodl, Carte MS 94/124.

57 Several chroniclers noted their arrival ('Benet's Chron.', p. 191; Flenley, p. 120; *Brut*, p. 490; *London Chrons.*, p. 134).

58 The envoys told Henry VI that Charles regarded Suffolk as a 'familiar and confidential friend' (Stevenson, I, 117).

59 ibid., I, 103-4.

60 ibid., 110-11. Although the envoys were encouraged to speak in French to Henry VI, who understood it well enough, the king appears to have used English whenever he interjected (ibid., 105-6).

61 ibid., I, 129ff; above, p. 449.

62 Stevenson, I, 117.

63 ibid., 137-40. Kemp, Suffolk, Sudeley, and Buckingham had been authorized on the previous day to treat with the French envoys (*Foedera*, V, i. 146).

64 Stevenson, I, 142. The English representatives were forewarned that this suggestion might be made, for their commission of 20 July had mentioned it (*Foedera*, V, i, 146).

65 ibid., 147, 149 (13 August, confirmed by Charles VII on 18 September); Stevenson, I, 143-4.

66 ibid.

67 *Foedera*, V, i, 149, 150. For their procuration from René, as well as Charles VII, see Lecoy de la Marche, op. cit., II, 257-60 (17 October); below, p. 495.

68 *Foedera*, V, i, 151, 153, 155-6, 157. The agreements about the meeting and the truce were reached in London on 19 December and confirmed by the two kings shortly afterwards, by Henry on 3 January and by Charles on 20 February 1446.

69 ibid.; Stevenson, II, i, 368-71.

70 *PPC*, VI, 46, 50; *CPR, 1441–46*, pp. 430-1; Stevenson, I, 183-6. An attempt was made to extract money from the estates of Normandy and the *pays de conquête* to pay for the visit (BN, n. a. fr. 7692 f. 176: 16 February 1446).

71 *CPR, 1441–46*, pp. 430-1; *PPC*, VI, 52. It was hoped to receive the loan by 1 July 1446, but it was disappointing (above, p. 391).

72 *Foedera*, V, i, 163.

73 *RP*, V, 128.

74 *Foedera*, V, i, 157, 170.

75 ibid., 174. A further French embassy, again headed by Dunois and the count of St Pol, but also including the seigneur de Précigny, who had originally proposed the royal meeting, arrived in England in mid-June (ibid., 172). They seem to have stayed until about 2 August ('Benet's Chron.', p. 193; Flenley, pp. 121, 122).

76 *Foedera*, V, i, 178, 180, 183.

77 ibid., 186, 191. The envoys' meeting concluded at Lavardin on 11 March 1448.

78 ibid., V, ii, 4.

79 The commoners and the newly-arrived French ambassadors who witnessed the punishment of Gloucester's retinue were said to have been very distressed (Flenley, p. 122). For Gloucester's arrest by Buckingham, Dorset, Salisbury, Beaumont, and Sudeley, see *English Chron.*, pp. 116-18; below, p. 496.

80 Lecoy de la Marche, op. cit., II, 258-9 (17 October). That Charles VII had only recently approved the demand is indicated by René's reference to his receipt of the king's letters patent authorizing it.

81 Stevenson, II, i, [639]. Shortly afterwards, on 2 January 1446, Henry VI wrote to Charles VII affirming his intention to travel to France for the meeting; garter king-of-arms was sent to discuss the arrangements (ibid., II, ii, 368-71; above, p. 493). This being so, Charles was content to renew the truce on 31 March 1446 (Stevenson, I, 175-6).

82 ibid., I, 164-7; II, ii [639]. For another letter from Charles to Margaret on 24 March 1446, urging her to work in the cause of peace, see ibid., I, 183-4. To this she replied on 20 May, inviting Charles 'to signify to us all matters agreeable to you, with a view to their accomplishment, by us to the best of our ability, joyfully and with a right good heart, ...'.

83 ibid., [639] – [642]. Charles of Anjou had not been mentioned in René's original plan, but it was a minor inclusion.

84 PRO, E403/765 m. 14; below, p. 506.

85 *HBC*, p. 531. It is possible that the government believed that Gloucester was preparing to come to parliament with a substantial body of men to challenge English policy, and perhaps even to remove Suffolk and his followers.

86 'Benet's Chron.', pp. 192-3; *EHR*, XXIX (1914), 513; *Chron. of London*, p. 135; Flenley, pp. 104, 121; *English Chron.*, pp. 62-3; *Brut*, pp. 512-13 (whose speculations drew on rumours relating to other royal deaths, namely, by smothering between two feather-beds, which was associated with the earl of Gloucester's murder in 1397, or by a spit in his 'foundement', which was commonly believed to be Edward II's fate; see also *Great Chron.*, pp. 179-80, which adds drowning in wine, a fate reserved also for Clarence in 1478). One Yorkist writer (*English Chron.*, p. 62) even went so far as to claim that the purpose of the parliament was to slay Gloucester. For the charges against his followers, see PRO KB9/255/2; KB27/745 rex m. 22.

87 Giles, pp. 33-4. On his way to Cambridge, Gloucester spent Christmas at

his Wiltshire castle of Devizes ('Benet's Chron.', p. 192). He passed through Colchester and Lavenham (PRO, KB9/255/2/22), and he may have travelled via Greenwich where, according to the indictment of his servants, a plot was hatched on 7 and 11 February to depose the king (ibid., 21; KB27/745 *rex* m. 22-22*d*).

88 Despite the severe cold weather, armed men from the adjacent counties were summoned to Bury in order to attend the king; some chroniclers were so impressed by this extraordinary mobilization that they put the number at an impossible 60,000 and claimed that most of those who came had no idea why they were there (*Three Chrons.*, p. 65; 'Benet's Chron.', pp. 192-3; *English Chron.*, pp. 62, 116-18 [40,000]; Flenley, pp. 104, 121).

89 The fullest fifteenth-century account written by Richard Fox, a monk of St Albans, in 1447–48, is in *English Chron.*, pp. 116-18; but see also *Three Chrons.*, p. 65; 'Benet's Chron.', pp. 192-3; *Great Chron.*, pp. 179-80; *English Chron.*, pp. 62-3; Giles, pp. 33-4. For the steward's wide judicial powers, see Lodge and Thornton, op. cit., pp. 253-4, 283-4; for Halley and Pulford, above, pp. 319, 361.

90 *English Chron.*, pp. 62-3.

91 Giles, pp. 33-4; *RP*, V, 226. A popular verse satire current around 1460 maintained that a bishop, a 'bryber' (or thief), had spun damning yarns about Gloucester, gleaned from the confessional, to the king (*EHL*, p. 397). According to *English Chron.*, pp. 62-3, it was Suffolk who ordered the mass mobilization in the vicinity of Bury.

92 *English Chron.*, pp. 62-3. For the Welshmen in his retinue, see below, n. 94, and for the supposed plotting at Greenwich on the way to Bury, above, n. 87.

93 'Benet's Chron.', p. 192, comments that the treason charges were mostly obscure.

94 *English Chron.*, pp. 116-18; *EHL*, p. 363 (with another copy of the list of companions in H. Ellis [ed.], *Original letters illustrative of English history* [2nd ser., 4 vols., 1827], I, 108-9); *CPR, 1446–52*, p. 569. They also included Thomas Herbert, Owain Dwnn, Thomas Wyriot, Gruffydd ap Nicholas, Hywel ap Dafydd, and a number of Welshmen with family ties that bound them together and to Gloucester. For the association of two-thirds of them with Gloucester in Pembrokeshire and Carmarthenshire, see Griffiths, thesis, pp. 507-16. The timing of the arrests is a little uncertain, but they took place between 18 and 23 February (*English Chron.*, pp. 62-3; 'Benet's Chron.', pp. 192-3 [which specifically notices the arrest of his Welsh affinity]).

95 *English Chron.*, pp. 116-18 (Buckland's name was evidently William, not John as given here [PRO, E404/63/126; below, p. 498]); Ellis, *Original letters*, II, i, 108-9. Among the others were Thomas Wylde, Richard Nedeham, Richard Middleton, and John Swafylde; in all they numbered 28. The total arrests on both days was variously put at 54 (*EHR*, XXIX [1914], 513) and 32 (*Three Chrons.*, p. 65; *London Chrons.*, p. 157; *Great Chron.*, pp. 179-80). For two Welshmen taken by a serjeant-at-arms from Bury to the Tower, see PRO, E403/767 m. 5.

96 *English Chron.*, pp. 116-18; Giles, pp. 33-4. One writer said he died 'for hevynes' (Flenley, p. 121), another of sorrow (*English Chron.,*, pp. 62-3). But *EHR*, XXIX (1914), 513, says that he died in bed, and Bodl, Digby 201 that it occurred at midnight.

97 *English Chron.*, pp. 116-18; *Great Chron.*, pp. 179-80. For Gloucester's arrangements for his own funeral at St Albans, see *English Chron.*, pp. 194-5. The possibility that Eleanor Cobham might claim dower or jointure from the dead duke's estate was eliminated on the last day of parliament (3 March); this was to make unequivocal what was implicit in the earlier annulment of their marriage (*RP*, V, 135; above, p. 280).

98 *CPR, 1446–52*, pp. 74, 104, 110, 112. The official record in PRO, KB27/745 *rex* m. 22, and KB9/255/2/21, mentions only the first five. *EHR*, XXIX (1914), 513, says that nine were indicted, but no trace of the ninth has been found.

99 Griffiths, thesis, pp. 515-16; *English Chron.*, pp. 116-18; Flenley, pp. 104, 121-2; *EHR*, XXIX (1914), 513; *Three Chrons.*, p. 65; *London Chrons.*, p. 157; 'Benet's Chron.', p. 193; *Great Chron.*, pp. 179-80; *Brut*, p. 513; *Grey Friars' Chron.*, p. 18. Six of the pardons were enrolled on 14 July (Thomas Herbert), 14 September (Wylde, Cappes, and Buckland), 11 October (Nedham), and 26 October (Middleton) (*CPR, 1446–52*, pp. 74, 104, 110, 112).

100 Above, pp. 357-8.

101 *Great Chron.*, pp. 179-80; *English Chron.*, pp. 62-3; *Brut*, p. 513. Neither 'Benet's Chron.' (*c*. 1462), nor *English Chron.*, pp. 116-18 (written at Bury *c*. 1448), nor Giles (*c*. 1457), nor the register of Abbot Whethamstede of St Albans (*Reg. Whethamstede*, I, 178-83, *s. a.* 1455), mentioned the possibility of murder.

102 See the charges in 1450, below, p. 638, and popular ballads current then (Wright, op. cit., II, 224, 268).

103 *Foedera*, V, i, 176-7. This was at Suffolk's request in response to charges levelled against him. The king's affirmation took place in Henry's chamber in the palace of Westminster, in the presence of the queen, York, the king's principal officers of state and household, and others of his *familia*. It was formally published under the great seal on 17 June.

104 Stevenson, II, ii, [638] – [643].

105 ibid., II, ii, [696] – [702]; above, p. 466. For Gough, see Y. Probert, 'Mathew Gough, 1390–1450', *Trans. Cymmrodorion Soc.*, 1961, pp. 34-44; for Eyton, Marshall, thesis, pp. 287-90.

106 Stevenson, II, ii, [666] – [669]. Charles VII's envoys, nominated on 16 October, were Cousinot and Havart, 'who have always been present at all the agreements, treaties, and arrangements made and discussed . . . .' (ibid., [654] – [658].

107 ibid., [670] – [685].

108 ibid., [687] – [689].

109 ibid., [690] – [692].

110 ibid., [704] – [710]. For Frogenhall's role, see ibid., [702] – [703]. For Mundford's and Frogenhall's captaincies, see Marshall, thesis pp. 234, 246, 251, 254-5, 257.

111 Stevenson, II, ii, [702] – [703], [692] – [696].

112 ibid., [645] – [650]; above p. 495. For Cousinot's ability, see Vallet de Viriville, op. cit., III, 136-7. The two groups of commissioners met again at Le Mans on 31 October (Stevenson, II, ii, [634] – [637]).

113 ibid., II, ii, [710] – [718]. Dorset would be allowed to collect his income from Maine until 15 January, and Englishmen who wished to stay in the county under Valois lordship could do so. Sillé-le-Guillaume had been in Sir John

Fastolf's possession in 1433–35 and was presumably held by one of his men in 1447–48 (ibid., pp. 434, [549], [575]). Fresnay-le-Vicomte was another of Fastolf's former fortresses which may have been in Mundford's hands by 1447; he was certainly its captain by June 1449 (ibid., I, 494; II, ii, [544]; Marshall, thesis, pp. 250-1). Beaumont-le-Vicomte was in Mundford's custody by 1447 (Stevenson, II, ii, [704], [707]).

114 ibid., II, i, 361-8 (n. d., but evidently soon after 1 November 1447).

115 ibid., I, 198-201 (20 January). De Brézé was warned to ignore anything that Fulk Eyton, the reluctant commissioner, may have told him about the king's will to hand Maine over. It is likely that the mobilization of the French had begun before 15 January in anticipation of yet another English failure to honour commitments.

116 ibid., 202-6.

117 Along with Reginald Boulers, abbot of Gloucester, they had been empowered on 30 January to treat with the French, and an advance payment had been authorized for Roos the previous day; he and Moleyns had evidently travelled to France in some haste, though there is no sign that Boulers actually went with them (*DKR*, XLVIII [1887], 377; Ferguson, op. cit., pp. 179, 183).

118 Stevenson, I, 482-3 (6 March).

119 Vallet de Viriville, op. cit., III, 138.

120 Stevenson, II, ii, [710] – [718]; *Foedera*, V, i, 189. Charles VII undertook to pay 24,000 *livres tournois* in return for the delivery of Maine; the recompense to those holding grants in Maine from Henry VI was calculated at 10 years' value (*Foedera*, V, i, 188-9).

121 ibid., 189.

122 ibid., V, ii, 4; *DKR*, XLVIII (1887), 378. Mundford was *bailli* of Maine as well as captain of Fresnay-le-Vicomte and other castles in the county (above, p. 500). Fresnay-le-Vicomte was finally surrendered on 22 March 1450 (Marshall, thesis, p. 251 n. 2).

123 Stevenson, I, 79-82.

124 ibid., I, 83-6.

125 ibid., I, 79-82, 160-3. He had left Rouen by the time a great council was held there on 30 September (BN, n. a. Latin 2320 no. 270).

126 Stevenson, I, 160-3 (21 September), 168-70 (21 December).

127 *Sotheby Catalogue of . . . W. W. Manning, Esq.*, 24-25 January 1945, p. 45 (with a facsimile). See also *HMC*, IX, pt. 2, p. 410, where the document is misdated to 1456.

128 ibid.; Stevenson, I, 160-3. For Dudley, see above, p. 305. York's earlier ambassadors had been members of the Anglo-Norman establishment in France.

129 Above, p. 358.

130 Griffiths, 'Sense of dynasty', 23-4.

131 Roskell, *Speakers*, p. 227; Hall, *Chronicle*, p. 205.

132 *PPC*, VI, 52. York was still lieutenant-general on 6 November 1446 (BN, n. a. fr. 7692 f. 297). He seems to have returned to France sometime during 1446–47 (Stevenson, I, 189-93 [21 July 1447]), despite what J. T. Rosenthal says ('The estates and finances of Richard, duke of York', in W. M. Bowsky [ed.], *Studies in medieval and renaissance history*, II [1965], pp. 197-8); but during his absence 'messieurs les commis' ruled France and Normandy (BN, n. a. fr. 1482 no. 179: 5 July 1446). He was in England 28

July 1446 (at Hunsdon) and 6 January 1447 (Fotheringhay) (Pierpoint Morgan Lib., autographs, RE).

133 PRO, E403/760 m. 15 (7 March 1446); 762 m. 8 (12 July), 12, 13 (16, 21 July, 19 August).

134 *CPR, 1446–52*, p. 6; Wedgwood, *Biographies*, pp. 521-2; Marshall, thesis, pp. 290-4. The earlier complaint may have been responsible for his premature resignation as lieutenant of Calais town in August 1442.

135 BL, Harleian MS 543 f. 161-63; see McFarlane in *CMH*, VIII, 404-5, and Wolffe, 'Personal rule', pp. 41-2. This document is a copy of York's counter-charge against Bishop Moleyns. The original was drawn up after York had returned from France in the autumn of 1445 to attend the Westminster parliament but before he was replaced as lieutenant-general (24 December 1446); it refers to a recent visit by Moleyns to Normandy (probably that of July 1446). See PRO, E403/765 m. 14; Ferguson, op. cit., pp. 182, 29. Both K. B. McFarlane and B. P. Wolffe were mistaken in dating the document to 1447 or 1448.

136 PRO, E403/765 m. 14.

137 BL, Harleian MS 543 f. 161-63.

138 PRO, E403/765 m. 14. Dorset was allocated £1,883 for the men for six weeks.

139 Above, pp. 499ff. On 5 December £2,667 were assigned him (PRO, E403/769 m. 7; Stevenson, I, 477-8; II, ii, 575 n. 1.). Some weeks later, on 31 January 1448, when the French were known to be gathering, he was assigned 1,000 yeomen for six months and £20,000 as lieutenant-general (though he received only £2,275 at this juncture) (ibid., I, 479-80).

140 Stevenson, II, ii, [592] – [594]. The advice is still to be found among the papers of Fastolf's secretary, William Worcester.

141 For the French army, see Contamine, op. cit., part 4. The plot to seize Argentan in the summer of 1447 was revealed to the captain, Sir Richard Harrington, by the duke of Alençon; he, Orléans, and a number of other French noblemen were said to be anxious to avoid war (Stevenson, I, 187-93; Marshall, thesis, p. 230).

142 Stevenson, I, 477-8; II, ii, 575. Representatives from the baillages of Caen, Cotentin, and Alençon were in England by 20 December 1447, presumably to stress the dangers to Normandy (ibid., I, 476-7). For 'injustice', 'vices', and 'sins' committed by the English in Normandy, with attacks on the merchants and others who travelled the roads to Paris, Orléans, Abbeville, and Amiens, see Stevenson, I, 192-3 (July 1447); Chartier, II, 78-80.

143 Above p. 419. For the idea that Suffolk 'exiled' York to Ireland, see Giles, p. 35; 'Benet's Chron.', p. 195.

144 *RDP*, V, 258-9; Stevenson, I, 477-8; II, ii, [575]; above, p. 466. Further sums of cash were authorized for Dorset on 20 February and 30 May 1448 (PRO, E403/769 m. 14 [£2,500]; 771 m. 4 [£2,275]).

145 D'Escouchy, I, 132-3. Osbert Mundford was one of the leading commanders occupying these fortresses.

146 ibid., 133 n. 2; Stevenson, I, 209-20 (22 August 1448). Henry VI's envoys, Bishop Moleyns and Sir Robert Roos, who were then in Brittany presumably to soothe the ruffled Francis, were regarded by Charles VII as more amenable than the English administration at Rouen. For Henry's attempts to calm Charles's anger, see BN, f. fr. 4054 f. 93 (October).

147 Stevenson, I, 223-32 (28 February 1449). The French at Dieppe had even

killed two Lancastrian officials and captured a third, Sir Simon Morhier, a day or two earlier.

148 ibid., 233-8, 241-64.
149 The impact of the attack on Fougères is well illustrated from the French side by Charles's instruction to two Lancastrians who were returning to Somerset in April 1449 (ibid., 243-64).
150 *CCR, 1441–47*, p. 354.
151 *CPR, 1441–46*, p. 418 (28 May 1446). The unfortunate captive, who had been seized in August 1437, was Walter Dolman, receiver of Pevensey.
152 D'Escouchy, I, 97 n. 1; *RP*, V, 135. The letters were to take effect immediately the current truce expired. See also *CPR, 1446–52*, p. 104 (26 September 1447). For Gilles, see below, p. 511.
153 *PPC*, VI, 62 (30 October 1448).
154 See M. H. Keen and M. J. Daniel, 'English diplomacy and the sack of Fougères in 1449', *History*, LIX (1974), 375-91, on which the following account is largely based.
155 Cottam, dissertation, pp. 25-37, had already hinted at these factors, and valuable material appears in A. Bossuat, *Perrinet Gressart et François de Surienne, agents d'Angleterre* (Paris, 1936), esp. chs. X-XIII.
156 D'Escouchy, I, 154; Chartier, II, 60-1, 172-4. For the various estimates of the value of the booty seized at Fougéres, see ibid., pp. 63, 72.
157 *CPR, 1436–41*, p. 543; PRO, E404/53/319, 334. When Henry was in Paris in December 1431, he authorized a payment of £67 to de Surienne (Bodl, MS ch. England 24). In 1439 he sent his servant, Thomassin du Quesne, to England on business relating to his duties in English France (PRO, E404/55/303). For du Quesne as de Surienne's servant and escalade-master, whom he sent to England again in 1443, see Stevenson, I, 281, 438.
158 *CPR, 1436–41*, p. 543; PRO, E404/59/258. The size of the lost inheritance must surely be exaggerated.
159 Keen and Daniel, *History*, LXI (1974), 377, 378-9, 383-6. See also Bourdeaut, *Mémoires de la société d'histoire et d'archéologie de Bretagne*, I (1920), 53-145.
160 Keen and Daniel, *History*, LIX (1974), 388. The subtle alteration of the terms of the truce renewed at Le Mans on 30 March 1448, so that the duke of Brittany could be shown to be a vassal of Henry VI and not of Charles VII, had a similar purpose (below, p. 513).
161 Keen and Daniel, *History*, LIX (1974), 379; PRO, E404/64/99.
162 Stevenson, I, 278-98; Keen and Daniel, *History*, LIX (1974), 377-8. De Surienne's membership of the garter and Henry VI's great council were regarded by Charles VII as of damning significance (Stevenson, I, 243-64).
163 ibid., I, 278-98 (15 March 1450), a letter from de Surienne to Henry VI. For the belief in England in the autumn of 1449 that Somerset was involved in the attack, see ibid., II, ii, [718] – [722].
164 The best version of the record of this parliamentary session is Huntington MS 202 f. 30*v*-31*r* (printed by Griffiths, *HLQ*, XLII [1979], 189-91),though a 17th-century copy appears in Myers, *BIHR*, LI (1978), 81-2. An inferior version of the record (BL, Harleian MS 6849 f. 77) is discussed by Myers, 'A parliamentary debate of the mid-fifteenth century', *BJRL*, XXII (1938), 402-4 (reprinted in *EHD*, IV, 468-9), and W. H. Dunham Jnr, 'Notes from the parliament at Winchester, 1449', *Speculum*, XVII (1942), 402-4.

165 For this rumour in England in the autumn of 1449, see Stevenson, II, ii, [718] – [722].

166 See Chartier, II, 62-3, for Somerset's denials of involvement as they were conveyed to Charles VII after the seizure.

167 Stevenson, I, 275-7. See also the inquiry instituted by Charles VII at Rouen in October 1449; its findings corroborate de Surienne's statements, though they may be open to charges of bias in Charles's favour (J. E. J. Quicherat (ed.), *Histoire des règnes de Charles VII et de Louis XI par T. Basin* [Paris, 1855], IV, 290-347); for comment, see Keen and Daniel, *History*, LIX (1974), 379-82.

168 Stevenson, I, 278-98, 310-11. For his subsequent career in the pay of Burgundy and Louis XI, see Bossuat, op. cit., ch. XIV.

169 For this example of English sleight-of-hand, see Keen and Daniel, *History*, LIX (1974), 387-8, quoting from R. Anstruther, *Prétensions des Anglois à la couronne de France* (Roxburghe Club, 1847), p. 91.

170 Stevenson, I, 243-64. The returning English envoys had to endure a diatribe from Charles VII, during which it was claimed that the English had committed 'sacrileges, murders, thefts, fire-raisings, women have been violated, prisoners have been made and held to ransom, and all other evils which could be committed in time of war, . . .'.

171 Chartier, II, 69-74.

172 Stevenson, I, 243-64.

173 ibid., II, ii [718] – [722]. These questions that were asked rhetorically of the duke were posed about August–October 1449, probably by Sir John Fastolf, for they survive among the archives of his secretary, William Worcester. Ct. above, p. 507.

174 Stevenson, I, 496-9 (12-13 May).

175 For the messages passing between Sir Richard Curson, lieutenant of Rouen, and Westminster, see ibid.; PRO, E404/66/77. And envoys from Normandy, including the bishop of Avranches, were in England in July (PRO, 403/775 m. 9).

176 Stevenson, II, ii, [723] – [730].

177 Above, p. 178. See Allmand, *EconHR*, 2nd ser., XXI (1968), 478-9.

178 The following paragraphs are based largely on a list of places lost to the French between May 1449 and August 1450 (Stevenson, II, ii, [619]–[634]), and on the several French chronicles that resulted in Charles VII's victories: Chartier II, 69-239; d'Escouchy, I, 159-319; Robert Blondell's *De Reductione Normanniae*, in J. Stevenson (ed.), *Narratives of the expulsion of the English from Normandy* (RS, 1863), pp. 23-238; Gilles le Bouvier, Berry herald of the king of France, in his *Recouvrement de Normandie*, in ibid., pp. 245-376; and Basin, II, 79-157.

179 Chartier, II, 69-74. Lord Fauconberg was taken and ransomed for 8,000 écus.

180 ibid., II, 74, 81ff.

181 Keen and Daniel, *History*, LIX (1974), 388-9. On 17 June 1449 Charles had agreed with Duke Francis the aid which he would provide to his vassal (Chartier, II, 73, 75-7).

182 ibid., II, 85-7. Osbert Mundford and Fulk Eyton surrendered at Pont Audemer.

183 ibid., 93-4.

184 ibid., 84, 87, 94, 101, 110-11. This chronicle (ibid., 97-101) gives the terms

of Mantes's surrender; they are model of those negotiated at most of the Norman towns that surrendered without a fight. By the time the king reached Louviers, he had a court with him of great size, not to speak of the four armies of the duke of Brittany, the counts of Eu and St Pol, Dunois, and the duke of Alençon.

185 ibid., II, 237-8 (translated in *EHD*, IV, 262-3); M. G. A. Vale, 'New techniques and old ideals: the impact of artillery on war and chivalry at the end of the Hundred Years War', in C. T. Allmand (ed.), *War, Literature, and Politics in the Late Middle Ages* (Liverpool, 1976), pp. 66-72. For the innovations in gun-transports by Louis Giribault, a Genoese engineer, in this campaign, see ibid., p. 66.

186 Chartier, II, 115-16, and Le Bouvier, op. cit., pp. 273-5, claim that the Harcourt siege lasted 15 days. On the other hand, Loigny in Perche was handed over to the French by its captain, Richard aux Espaules, seigneur de Ste Marie, who had married a daughter of François de Surienne; he may have shared his father-in-law's disgust at being deserted at Fougères by the English government (Stevenson, II, ii, [624]; Chartier, II, 102-3; Blondell, p. 82). For Roche Guyon, see Chartier, II, 116-19; Blondell, op. cit., pp. 88-9.

187 Chartier, II, 91-2, 122-4.

188 Stevenson, II, ii, [607]-[618]; Chartier, II, 137-72; d'Escouchy, I, 211-44; Blondell, pp. 120-50; Le Bouvier, pp. 290-320. See the English reports in Flenley, pp. 125-6; 'Benet's Chron.', p. 196; *English Chron.*, p. 63; Giles, pp., 36-7; *Brut*, pp. 515-16 (misdating the capital's fall to December).

189 The hostages included Shrewsbury, Roos, Abergavenny's son, Ormond's son, and Richard Gower (Chartier, II, 158 [though the French chroniclers are mistaken that Roos's son, rather than Roos himself, was held captive: *GEC*, XI, 105-6]). See Stevenson, II, ii, [611]. Gower was released in mid-August 1450 as one of the conditions whereby his father, Thomas Gower, agreed to surrender Cherbourg (Chartier, II, 233; Le Bouvier, p. 367).

190 Le Bouvier, pp. 316-19. For the ritual significance of this (and other) royal entries as dramatizations of the French monarchy, see Vale, *Charles VII*, pp. 198ff.

191 Le Bouvier, pp. 323-4; Chartier, II, 159, 176-80. Charles VII took part in this siege from his headquarters at Montivilliers.

192 Stevenson, I, 501-2 (21-22 November 1449), 513 (4 February 1450); PRO, E403/778 m. 8 (22 December).

193 Above, p. 508.

194 *CPR, 1446–52*, pp. 270, 317; PRO, E403/775 m. 10; /778 m. 2, 5.

195 ibid., 775 m. 9, 12; /778 m. 4, 5, 6, 15; above, p. 515. The reference to Lord Powis leading this expedition is otherwise unknown; presumably John Tiptoft is the nobleman involved, though he had been created earl of Worcester in July 1449.

196 Stevenson, I, 503-8 (20,22 December); above, p. 391.

197 ibid., pp. 508-12. For the payment of ships assembled between 11 October and 24 December, see PRO, E403/779 m. 5-7.

198 *English Chron.*, p. 68; PRO, E403/778 m. 15. See also d'Escouchy, I, 314, and William Worcestre, *The Boke of Noblesse*, ed. J. G. Nichols (1857), pp. 71-2 (reprinted in Allmand, *Society at War*, pp. 95-6), on the consequences of non-payment.

199 'Benet's Chron.', p. 196; Giles, pp. 37-8; *English Chron.*, p. 64; Griffiths, *JMH*, I (1975), 191.

200 *CPR, 1446–52*, p. 203. Cf. Giles, pp. 37-8.

201 CPR, 1446–52, p. 267.

202 ibid., pp. 270, 384.

203 ibid., pp. 478, 577 (1451–52).

204 ibid., pp. 301, 335; PRO, E403/778 m. 6.

205 Stevenson, II, ii, [630]; Le Bouvier, pp. 330-8; A. le Vavasseur (ed.), *Guillaume Gruel, Chronique d'Arthur de Richemont* (Paris, 1890), pp. 205-8; d'Escouchy, pp. 276-86; Chartier, II, 191, 192-200, who put the English dead at 3,764 (a figure corroborated by d'Escouchy, I, 285, and Le Bouvier, p. 336), and the captives at between 1,200 and 1,400, according to the testimony of heralds and others present. The total English army seems to have been about 5-6,000 strong and the French considerably less at about 3,000. For the various estimates of the strength of the army under Kyriell, and the date of their arrival at Cherbourg (just before 16 March), see d'Escouchy, I, 277 and n. 1.

206 Chartier, II, 199-200; *Chron. Arthur de Richemont*, p. 208 and n. 1. Charles VII contrived a wise compromise that apportioned credit to both men.

207 Stevenson, II, ii, [630]-[631]; Le Bouvier, pp. 340-3; Blondell, pp. 209-12; Chartier, II, 204-11 (including the terms of Bayeux's surrender).

208 Chartier, II, 206-7. The English were forbidden to retreat to Caen, and in general these terms of surrender were more severe than those negotiated at other towns. The scent of complete victory may have been in French nostrils and Charles's men were now determined to give as little succour as possible to those of the enemy they temporarily had in their grasp.

209 Stevenson, II, ii, [596]-[597]. Once again, Fastolf's was a realistic appraisal: he pinpointed the danger arising from quarrelsome subordinates, the vital importance of holding the ports, and the fatal weakness of divided command between a lieutenant-general and a field commander.

210 The terms of surrender, taken from AN, K 69 no. 45, are printed in *Chron. Arthur de Richemont*, pp. 275-9. It is worth noting that the recently captured city of Rouen sent 200 men to help the assault on Caen and Falaise (ibid., p. 211 n. 3).

211 Stevenson, I, 517-18, 520-1; Chartier, II, 214-35; Le Bouvier, pp. 345-67; Blondell, pp. 213-36; *Chron. Arthur de Richemont*, pp. 208-15. Two days after Cherbourg's fall, efforts were being made to assemble a fleet at Southampton to relieve it and Calais.

212 Chartier, II, 232. See also *Chron. Arthur de Richemont*, pp. 213-15.

213 Chartier, II, 235-8 (translated in *EHD*, IV, 262-3). See also Le Bouvier, pp. 369-76; d'Escouchy, I, 305-6. The French chroniclers describe the recovery of Normandy as a truly national and co-operative effort, with military leadership from the nobility complemented by good counsel and financial support from such as Jacques Coeur (Chartier, II, 239; Le Bouvier, p. 375).

214 Chartier, II, 234.

215 Stevenson, I, 307-9 (a letter to the cathedral chapter at Chartres). See Chartier, II, 234-5, who evidently knew of this order, and d'Escouchy, I, 317 n. 3, where the letters sent to several bishops are cited.

216 *PPC*, VI, 69, 74 (11 June).

217 ibid., 76.

218 Above, p. 523.
219 *RP*, V, 150.
220 *PPC*, VI, 69; Ferguson, op. cit., 183, 191, 180, 189. Grimston's portrait, painted by the Flemish master Petrus Christus, is in the National Gallery, London. It was presumably done on one of Grimston's missions to the Low Countries.
221 *PPC*, VI, 76. Like the earlier envoys, Dudley and Kent were accredited to the duchess of Burgundy, who in the past had shown herself more amenable in discussions than the husband who had deserted England in 1435.
222 *RP*, V, 201.
223 *PPC*, VI, 92.
224 *CPR, 1446–52*, pp. 520, 521. John was 15 years old; he was now promised an annual pension of 2,000 *saluts*. Cf. *PPC*, VI, 110.
225 *RP*, V, 275.
226 *CCR, 1447–54*, pp. 443, 451; *CPR, 1452–61*, p. 158.
227 *RP*, V, 146, 147. Soldiers' wages were the largest single expense.
228 ibid., 146. The queen was among a very small group of exceptions.
229 ibid., p. 183, 186.
230 e.g., ibid., p. 207 (1449-50): a £2,000 loan for the expedition of Viscount Beaumont and Lord Sudeley to Calais and Rysbank. See above, pp. 392-3.
231 *RP*, V, 149; *PPC*, VI, 117. On 17 February 1449, five days after parliament opened, the way the wind was blowing was indicated by a pardon for exporting elsewhere than to Calais (*CPR, 1446–52*, p. 213). Cf. a similar reservation in favour of the city of Lincoln on 24 July, eight days after the dissolution of parliament (ibid., p. 28).
232 ibid., p. 314. A further loan of £2,000 in March 1450 for the expedition of Sudeley and Beaumont to Calais elicited a similar grant to 16 staplers (ibid., p. 323).
233 *RP*, V, 275. For the relaxation of the prohibition on licences before 1453, see *PPC*, VI, 117.
234 *CPR, 1446–52*, p. 42.
235 e.g., ibid., pp. 103 (in favour of a much-patronized esquire for the body, John Penycock, for whom see above, p. 324), 114 (the earl of Shrewsbury).
236 ibid., p. 117.
237 ibid., p. 229.
238 *RP*, V, 206; *CPR, 1446–52*, p. 376. For Buckingham's financial problems at Calais, see Rawcliffe, op. cit., pp. 117-19 (where the above arrangements are misdated to 1451).
239 *RP*, V, 217, 233.
240 ibid., 233. Somerset was appointed captain in September 1451.
241 *CPR, 1446–52*, p. 244.
242 ibid., p. 427.
243 ibid., p. 479; Wedgwood, *Biographies*, pp. 194-5.
244 *CPR, 1446–52*, p. 480; *PPC*, VI, 112. Manfield had been victualler since 6 March 1442, having been appointed the previous 1 January (PRO, E403/760 m. 7).
245 *CPR, 1446–52*, p. 536 (early January 1452).
246 ibid., p. 512; *PPC*, VI, 119, 122.
247 *CPR, 1446–52*, pp. 515, 537; above, pp. 492ff.

248 *RP*, V, 229, 234, 235. See also *CCR, 1447–54*, p. 372, on the condition of Calais in September 1452.

249 *CPR, 1452–61*, p. 90.

250 D'Escouchy, I, 324. By March 1450 it was believed in England that Charles planned to invade Gascony with Spanish help (Bodl, Tanner cccxlii f. 194).

251 Vale, *English Gascony*, p. 245; below, p. 575.

252 His appointment had been renewed in November 1441, March 1445, and May 1447 (PRO, E404/54/148; *CPR, 1446–52*, p. 67). £1,042 was assigned to him on 20 February 1450 (PRO, E403/778 m. 11) and £1,092 on 27 May 1451 (ibid., 785 m. 2).

253 Though Cognac and St Maigrin, situated not far from Angoulême on Gascony's northern border, had been seized already by the duke of Brittany in reprisal for the English capture of Fougères (Le Bouvier, pp. 251-3; Blondel, pp. 31-32; Chartier, II, 74; d'Escouchy, I, 168).

254 Chartier, II, 127-30, 186-7; Le Bouvier, pp. 280-5, 325-6; Blondel, pp. 115-17, 152-3.

255 Chartier, II, 241-2. For subsequent victories in the Dordogne and in the estuary below Bordeaux, see ibid., pp. 242-3, 254-77.

256 *CPR, 1446–52*, pp. 389, 437-9, 444, 462, 476-8 (August 1450–June 1451); *PPC* VI, 105; *CCR, 1447–54*, pp. 219, 221. At least 86 ships were to be assembled at Portsmouth to take Rivers's men to Bordeaux (*CPR, 1446–52*, pp. 447-50).

257 Chartier, II, 277-313; d'Escouchy, I, 337-9, 356-60; 'Benet's Chron.', p. 205. For this attack, and the struggle for control of Gascony in 1451-53, see especially, in English, Vale, *English Gascony*, pp. 131-53, and M. G. A. Vale, 'The last years of English Gascony, 1451–1453', *TRHS*, 5th ser., XIX (1969), 119-38.

258 *CPR, 1446–52*, p. 478; Vale, *English Gascony*, p. 234. The duke of Somerset, to whom the men had appealed for cash, sent them a statue of St George wrought in silver and gold, and an alms-dish that had once belonged to Gloucester (*London Chrons.*, pp. 162-3).

259 Vale, *TRHS*, 5th ser., XIX (1969), 120-33.

260 ibid., 122 and n. 4; Chartier, II, 254. For the surrender of Blaye on 24 May, and of Bourg on 29 May 1451, see ibid., pp. 256-9, 261-4; d'Escouchy, I, 329-36.

261 ibid., 335-6; Chartier, II, 266-75. Fronsac opened its gates a couple of weeks later.

262 ibid., 277-313; d'Escouchy, I, 358. For an eyewitness account of the entry, written by a pursuivant of arms on 1 July, see BN, MS fr. 5028 f. 182, printed by A. du Chesne, *Les oeuvres de M. Alain Chartier,...* (Paris, 1617), p. 846.

263 D'Escouchy, I, 361-7; Chartier, II, 313-23; P. Champion (ed.), *Chronique Martiniane* (Paris, 1907), pp. 62-3. The £80 assigned on 13 July 1451 to the mayor of Bayonne, Sir John Asteley, for the garrison of 100 men was probably irrelevant to the situation (PRO, E403/785 m. 6; Vale, *English Gascony*, p. 232).

264 Vale, *TRHS*, 5th ser., XIX (1969), 124ff. Shrewsbury's achievement was noted by 'Benet's Chron.', p. 208, which records that he captured 33 ships and 32 towns and castles.

265 *CCR, 1447–54*, p. 360; *CPR, 1452–61*, pp. 108,78; PRO, E404/68/143-44,

149, 157; E403/788 m. 4, 6; Chartier, II, 330-3; d'Escouchy, I, 413-16; II, 28-30. For Hull and Clifton, see Wedgwood, *Biographies*, pp. 481-2, 194-5; Jeffs, thesis, pp. 299-301. See also Vale, *TRHS*, 5th ser., XIX (1969), 124-31, 136-8. For fears of an English attack on Normandy, see Vallet de Viriville, op. cit., III, 230.

266 Vale, *TRHS*, 5th ser., XIX (1969), 246.

267 Chartier, II, 331.

268 P. M. Kendall and V. Ilardi (eds.), *Dispatches, with related documents, of Milanese ambassadors in France and Burgundy, 1450–1483*, vol. 1 (1450–1460) (Athens, Ohio, 1970), pp. 78-80. The envoy was Angelo Acciaioli.

269 D'Escouchy, III, 30-1. Great stress was laid on the seriousness of oath-breaking (ibid., 70). For the beheading of Gascons at Chalais, north-east of Bordeaux, see ibid., 31; and stiffer terms imposed, especially on native Gascons, at the towns of Cadillac, Rions, and Benauges in the Garonne valley, ibid., pp. 66-7. See D. Brissaud, *Les anglais en Guyenne* (Paris, 1875), pp. 235-8.

270 D'Escouchy, III, 90.

271 Kendall and Ilardi, op. cit., I, 114-16. See also, for the king's preoccupation, ibid., 118 (10 April).

272 *CPR, 1452-61*, pp. 104, 33, 52, 59, 61; *PPC*, VI, 143, 330; PRO, E404/69/87, 91; Chartier, II, 333. Sir John Lisle and the bastard of Somerset were also commanders in this expedition (PRO, E404/69/90, 92), though 'Benet's Chron.', p. 209, claims that only 1,000 men left for Gascony in March. For the numerous loans, see PRO, E403/791 m. 9ff; 793 m. 1ff; and the assignments to the retinues, ibid., 791 m. 14, 15, and Stevenson, II, ii, 479-81. A very sharp letter had to be sent to Lord Vesci on 13 July 1453, reminding him of his earlier promise to lend 200 marks, which, needless to say, had not been received (Stevenson, II, ii, 481-2), and for even later defaulters, ibid., 485-7, 491-2.

273 *PPC*, VI, 152, 156; *CPR, 1452-61*, p. 76. For ships arrested in the ports between London and Fowey for the March expedition, see PRO, E403/791 m. 14, 15. See, in general, E. M. Carus-Wilson, *Medieval merchant venturers* (3rd ed., 1967), pp. 272-5, and M. K. James, *Studies in the medieval wine trade* (Oxford, 1971), pp. 42-3.

274 Vale, *TRHS*, 5th ser., XIX (1969), 131-2, 135-6; *CPR, 1452-61*, pp. 78, 108. For Charles's ordinances for the proper behaviour of his soldiers, especially when quartered on the Gascon population, see d'Escouchy, I, 325-9. The confiscation of Jacques Coeur's possessions was ordered on 29 May 1453, though he had been arrested in July 1451 (M. Mollat [ed.], *Les affaires de Jacques Coeur*, I [Paris, 1952]).

275 *PPC*, VI, 151, 155; *CPR, 1452-61*, pp. 123-5; Chartier, III, 1-9; d'Escouchy, II, 33-43; *Chronique Martiniane*, pp. 64-6. This second army, under William, Lord Saye, included a number of captains who had recently retired from Normandy (e.g., Sir Richard Frogenall and Elis Longworth) (PRO, E404/69/198-206; Stevenson, II, ii, 483-4; PRO, E403/793 m. 15, 18; Vale, *TRHS*, 5th ser., XIX [1969], 132-3). On this occasion, the indentures provided that the first instalment of wages should be handed over to the captains 2 months before the muster. For efforts from mid-July onwards to assemble ships, see Stevenson, II, ii, 482-3; PRO, E403/793 m. 13, 14.

276 Chartier, II, 7, translated in *EHD*, IV, 271. For the crippling ransom of the captured Lord Moleyns, see McFarlane, *Nobility*, pp. 29, 126-8.

277 Stevenson, II, ii, 485-6. For Bristol's role in victualling the besieged Bordeaux, see *English trade*, p. 208.

278 Stevenson, II, ii, 487-90 (with the quotations on p. 490). See above, pp. 393-4.

279 One London chronicler also attributed it to corruption in raising loans (Flenley, pp. 136-7).

280 Chartier, III, 12-19; d'Escouchy, I, 64-79. The appointment as seneschal of Lord Camoys on 4 July 1453 (he attempted to defend Bordeaux after Castillon and was captured for his pains) and of Bonville on 12 September (he never had the opportunity to act) availed the English nothing (Vale, *English Gascony*, p. 246; Stevenson, II, ii, 492).

281 Vale, *TRHS*, 5th ser., XIX (1969), 119.

282 Valet de Viriville, op. cit., III, 238, citing Archives de Compiègne, C. 19.

19   The Aliens in the Realm

The treatment of aliens in England depended partly on the reputation which they acquired as a result of their activities within the realm, and partly on external factors, notably the state of diplomatic and commercial relations between England and foreign states. In the wake of the English reverses in France after the congress of Arras, and the siege of Calais, a wave of anti-alien feeling swept across parts of England. The commercial truce with Burgundy in September 1439, still less the abortive conference at Oye a little earlier in the year, did little to contain it, so that a crescendo was reached in the parliament which opened on 12 November 1439. Acts of piracy and anti-foreign demonstrations in London and elsewhere were closely related to the progress of the French war, as well as to jealousy of what was thought to be the unwarranted wealth of foreign merchants. And when English fortunes in Normandy slumped badly in 1449–50, the hostility towards foreigners was sharpened yet further.

It might be thought that in this troublous decade and a half the size of England's alien community would have been reduced, for alien merchants were increasingly distrusted and military defeats led to tighter controls on foreign residents. However, many who had lived in the realm for years preferred to secure protection for themselves and their families by purchasing letters of denizenship or other privileges that would allow them to own and dispose of property, sue at common law, and live unmolested by the authorities. Those who belonged to royal or noble households found this easy enough; others may have encountered greater difficulties or obtained privileges that were more limited in scope.[1] There was inevitably a rash of such letters, licences, and pardons, during and after the coercive parliament of 1439–40. Frenchmen and natives of the Low Countries were the most common recipients, but Italians too were anxious to obtain protection, for in the current witch-hunt they incurred considerable odium for their wealth (and perhaps the strangeness of their language?).[2] The Lancastrian collapse in 1449–50 led to a further spate, many of the grants being issued to former French subjects of the king who preferred to settle in England rather than run the risk of persecution by Charles VII.[3] Indeed, the dual monarchy had a social dimension that embraced travel, employment, and settlement to an extent not experienced in England since the disintegration of the Angevin 'empire' – and perhaps not experienced since. Paradoxically, it was the beginning of the English withdrawal in northern France in the 1430s, after a decade and a half of Lancastrian rule, which persuaded many Frenchmen that their future was more secure in England than on their native heath.

The king's assumption of practical powers in 1436–37 affected the administration of the French realm as well as of England, especially since Bedford had died in 1435. Westminster and the king's court were henceforward more intimately involved in matters which previously the Lancastrian council in France had handled. Not only did several French laymen provide a constant messenger service between England and Rouen, but Henry VI engaged for his French business a number of French secretaries, who lived in England for considerable periods and probably brought with them families and households that swelled the immigrant population of London and its suburbs. Several of these secretaries chose to stay permanently in England and, like Gervase le Vulre in 1441, obtained letters of denizenship. They were encouraged to do so not only because of the nature of their work, but also because they fell victim to the Valois advance after 1436; some, like Michael de Paris and Jean Rinel (whose possessions in Paris, Champagne, and Brie had been seized by 1439) lost lands and goods in France and sought recompense in England.[4]

The king's marriage to a French princess in 1445 might ordinarily be expected to have led to the arrival of a coterie of French servants and attendants, after the manner of foreign-born consorts since William the conqueror's bride, Matilda of Flanders. But among the various accusations cast at Margaret of Anjou in after years, that of insinuating and patronizing foreign companions and servants was conspicuously absent. The small group of Angevin esquires who came with her were emissaries of her father to attend the coronation and then return to France to report. Indeed, so modest was her entourage at her landing at Southampton that one English chronicler could record, doubtless with a degree of misrepresentation, that she was accompanied merely by three or four maids.[5] Some of the Frenchwomen who applied (and received) letters of denizenship in 1449 were probably connected with Margaret's household; they had waited four years partly because the truce with Charles VII had made it unnecessary and partly because the foreign queen's unpopularity may not have been particularly pronounced immediately after her arrival.[6]

On the other hand, the loss of Normandy in 1449–50 produced a stream of Norman and other immigrants, most of them with families but few with possessions; they abandoned lands that were confiscated by the adherents of Charles VII. Many of these Frenchmen quickly decided to seek letters of denizenship and not a few elicted pensions or other grants from a king who was well known for his generosity and compassion. Simon de la Chapelle, for example, a Norman by birth, suffered such losses in Lancastrian service that he was granted £16 13s.

4*d*. a year by Henry VI when he retired to England in the spring of 1450. Of the Normans who secured letters of denizenship between 1445 and 1453 half did so during 1449–50.[7] Frenchmen and women who had been born outside the former English territories were even more anxious to obtain such letters in 1449, when the fighting resumed and Charles advanced steadily towards Rouen and the channel coast; without their protection, those of Charles's subjects who lived in England would find their position most vulnerable.[8]

Scotsmen were in a similar position. They were settled the length of England, though mostly on the eastern side of the kingdom, from the northernmost counties to London and Canterbury. Of all those Scots who felt it wise to purchase denizenship between 1445 and 1453, half did so in the single year 1449, when James II renewed hostilities in the north in alliance with the French.[9]

For the rest of the alien community, commercial considerations were the most potent factor determining their relationship with Englishmen. The profit motive, as appreciated by English freebooters and merchants with royal letters of marque in their hose, was linked with a deep suspicion of the wealth which Spanish, Italian, German, and Low Countries traders had accumulated through their trade with England, and these sentiments served to reinforce the age-old mistrust of the foreigner to provide a plausible veneer of justification for acts of hostility and even lawlessness towards them. Spanish vessels carrying the cargoes of Genoese and Portuguese were preyed on by pirates from the west country, and a Bristol merchant was authorized in February 1449 to seize a Castilian ship in retaliation for assaults on him in the past.[10] The publication of a truce with Spain in November 1448, whilst it forced the government to investigate these incidents, seemingly had little restraining effect in reducing their incidence.[11]

The merchants of Holland and Zeeland were threatened no less frequently by English pirates. An official letter of marque enabled a Boston merchant in February 1447 to proceed against them for the loss of £1,234 some time before. Then, when English fortunes collapsed at the end of the 1440s and Calais was threatened by a Burgundian army, there was a serious outburst of resentment against the Dutch-speaking Flemings in London and its suburbs; they were attacked by some of the soldiers assembled to relieve Calais who evidently shared the *Libelle*'s opinion of

> . . . . oure cruell enmyes,
> That is to saye Flemmynges wyth here gyle,
> For chaungeable they are in lytel whyle.[12]

For ten years repeated exchanges of emissaries between Henry VI and the duke and duchess of Burgundy had preserved the commercial treaty of 1439, but the dire situation of 1449–50 undermined its provisions for a time.[13]

Hostility towards the Italians reached the most dangerous pitch of all. Their goods were stolen by Englishmen, and in Southampton the Genoese were occasionally subjected to personal assaults despite the possession of a safe conduct.[14] The salvation of these Italian visitors was their role as bankers to the crown, particularly in the desperate years after the renewal of war. The Florentines, Venetians, Genoese, and Luccese contributed valued, though not large, sums to the exchequer and in return received protection from the king; whether or not this was respected depended on the temper of the king's subjects and, of course, on the efficiency of his officers. The preferential terms of trade which were conceded them in repayment of their loans were likely to increase the resentment of English merchants rather than reduce it.[15]

Merchants of the highly privileged (and therefore much envied) Hanseatic league were also badly treated, particularly in East Anglian ports like Grimsby and Bishop's Lynn which handled much of their trade.[16] The source of this ill-treatment was the refusal of the Hanse towns of north Germany to accord visiting English merchants the same privileges which Germans enjoyed in England. Despite much negotiating and a number of protests on this score, Henry's government was able to extract few concessions from the giant trading community; indeed, the treatment of Englishmen in its towns was ungenerous at best, many of them being arrested, imprisoned, or plundered.[17] The fortuitous interception of the huge Bay fleet, consisting of a large number of Hanse ships, in July 1449 by an English captain (Robert Winnington) who was on the king's service prompted retaliation from the Hanse, and for a while English merchants in German towns found themselves arrested and those of the Hanse who visited England did so at their peril. Not until a special diet was held at Utrecht from May 1451 was some of the damage repaired.[18]

The king and his government were never so consumed with xenophobia as to refuse a welcome to foreigners with special skills, and small groups were encouraged to come to England and made a distinctive contribution to its life. Francis Panizonus, for example, an Arab from Alexandria who excelled in the medical arts for which his race was renowned, had become personal physician to Henry and Margaret by 1 March 1446, when he was awarded £100 *per annum* from the customs of Southampton.[19] Also from the eastern Mediterranean were two Greeks who came to England from Constantinople with four servants and in January 1445 were allowed to practise their rare skill in damask work.[20] Others were welcomed as industrial developers: John de Schiedamme, for instance, successfully reclaimed hitherto worthless land near Winchelsea in 1440 and developed salt-beds with the aid of as many as sixty men.[21] And the Fleming John Utynam was retained for life in April 1449 as a glass manufacturer; he was employed initially on the king's foundations of Eton and King's College, Cambridge, but his skills eventually led to his retention for twenty years as a teacher of glass-making and associated crafts that had been unknown in the realm hitherto.[22] Adrian Sprynker, the Dutchman who had been engaged to develop the king's mines in Devon and Cornwall, was so conspicuously successful that his lease was renewed in July 1451 and he was encouraged to expand his mining activities; as an incentive, not only would he receive a salary, but he was allowed to keep a proportion of the profits.[23] But whatever the services offered by Melchior Richenbeck, a servant of the duke of Silesia, they were never explained to Henry VI for the simple reason that no one could be found who could understand the Silesian's language; Henry explained to the duke in July 1452, not, one suspects, without some embarrassment, that Melchior's services would have to be declined[24]

The merchant class of fifteenth-century England had a unique forum in which to make their demands. No other single group represented in the commons, except perhaps the king's servants, had such a golden opportunity to influence the deliberations and resolutions of parliament.[25] Not only were the burgesses likely to respond to a lead from the citizen-MPs of London, Bristol, and Southampton, but the shire knights, too, were intimately involved in the wool trade, whilst the king's advisers fully appreciated the value of merchants and townsmen as a source of loans. Parliament, therefore, was a sounding-board for the attitudes and prejudices of the merchant class, most of whose demands were conceded by Henry VI. In particular, the assembly of 1439-40 was, as we have observed, the scene of some forthright criticisms of the alien merchants in England. Here the commons sponsored several anti-alien petitions which were designed to control the movements and the activities of foreigners in the realm.[26] Already, a number who had neglected to observe existing legislation governing the purchase and sale of land sensed that it would be a wise precaution to secure a pardon and swear fealty to Henry VI in order to avoid being deprived of their possessions.[27] Interference in the lives and careers of aliens led some of the more prosperous – even the occasional Welshman who was worried about Henry IV's statutes – to take steps to secure their position.[28]

Aliens had every reason to be alarmed by what they heard of the proceedings of this parliament. Although the subsidies it imposed on foreign merchants followed precedent, one of its measures, taken at the commons' instigation, was novel and more extreme. An annual tax of 1s. 4d. was assessed on each alien householder (with the exception of Welshmen and denizens) and 6d. on every foreigner who was not a householder but rather a servant or clerk. It was a foreigners' levy in aid of naval defence, with the Welsh (but not for the moment the Irish) properly classed as the king's subjects. Its records have been designated by S. L. Thrupp as 'the only nation-wide surveys of immigrants that any European nation possesses from so early a period'. The measure was to remain in force for three years, and only those foreigners who were married to Englishmen or Welshmen, or who were under twelve years of age, or were members of a religious order were exempt.[29] Hostility to the foreign community probably ranked higher than the financial needs of sea-keeping in the collective mind of the commons, for even if every penny of the tax had been collected – and hardly more than half was in fact realized – it would have amounted to only £700.

The most mistrusted of all foreigners, the alien merchants, were treated with yet greater severity. Although foreign merchants were able to strike up a friendly – or at least a tolerable – relationship with the townsfolk of Southampton, most historians are agreed that these foreign merchants were an object of mistrust, suspicion, and at times hatred more generally in late medieval England. Certainly, the government's attitude towards them was powerfully influenced by propaganda of the sort purveyed by the author of the *Libelle of Englysche Polycye* and by those strident complaints of the parliamentary commons which in the late 1430s coincided with the *Libelle*'s sentiments. It is not, therefore, just to allow the tranquillity of individual relationships in south-coast ports to obscure the significance of anti-alien strictures and demands in Henry VI's reign.[30] But the propaganda and complaints relied more on emotion and prejudice than on the actual terms of trade. J. L. Bolton's recent researches suggest that 'the anti-alien movement was based on feelings rather than facts and that it was inspired as much by the belief that English trade should be in English hands as by theories about the balance of trade, by jealousy of the aliens and above all of the Italians'.[31] Herein may lie an explanation of the paradox: outside the council chamber and parliament, and beyond the environs of London, where anti-alien feeling could be exaggerated and stoked by merchants and others for their own purposes, relations between Englishmen and visitors from overseas were perhaps calmer and mutually profitable. It was to England's lasting misfortune that Henry VI and his advisers did not resist this pressure more resolutely.

Accusations that had been heard earlier in the century were revived in 1439–40. It was well known – so the commons maintained, partly no doubt to enlist popular support for proposals which probably sprang from the commercial lobby – that foreign merchants manipulated commodity prices for their own profit and enriched themselves at the expense of English traders. Their commercial and other activities drained wealth from the realm and consequently undermined the mercantile marine on which effective sea-keeping depended. Existing hosting regulations were no longer regarded as adequate to control their movements, and accordingly the commons proposed that no alien should henceforward be allowed to buy or sell to other aliens inside the realm, that they should be hosted as soon as they arrived, and that the hosting system should be carefully supervised by surveyors appointed in each town. The hosts, it was said, should be Englishmen who had some commercial knowledge and a particular acquaintance with the trade of foreigners so that the restrictions on them would be effective.

> What reason is it [argued the *Libelle* a few years earlier] that we go
> to oste.
> In there cuntrees and in this Englisshe coste
> They schulde not so, but have more liberte
> Than wee oure self? . . .
>
> Therefore lett hem unto ooste go wyth us here,
> Or be wee free wyth hem in like manere
> In there cuntres; and if it woll not bee,
> Compelle them unto ooste and ye shall see
> Moche avauntage and muche profite arise,
> Moche more than I write can in any wyse.

In an effort to prevent the suspected seepage of wealth from the realm, all alien merchants were required to sell their wares within eight months of arrival, and with their earnings to buy within the same time-limit goods that were available in England. It was a crude attempt, and one that had not been particularly successful in the past, to ensure a favourable balance of trade in cash terms. The king agreed that these proposals should be put into effect for seven years (though they seem not to have lasted more than five), and elaborate records of aliens, hosts, and the business transacted were kept by the exchequer. The Hanseatic merchants, with their guaranteed privileges, were given immunity; the Genoese persistently claimed it.[32]

The commons expressed special irritation at the Italians and their prominent role in English commerce. A barefaced attempt was made to capture the trade in non-Italian goods between England and those ports that lay along the sea-route from the Mediterranean. Such cargoes had often been brought to England in Italian bottoms, with Italians reaping the benefits as a result and (so the xenophobic commons claimed) seizing the opportunity to fix their own profiteering prices.[33] To wrest this trade from the Venetians, Genoese, and Florentines might have important political implications, for the countries situated *en route*, particularly the Spanish kingdoms, might henceforward feel beholden to England instead of to the north Italian city-states. But there were delicate naval and political questions at stake here, as well as commercial ones, and the government therefore moved cautiously; the king declined to give his assent to this petition, though it reflected unmistakably prevailing attitudes in England.

Such feelings had hardly abated by the time parliament met again in January 1442. The new tax on alien residents was extended for a further two years, though certain anomalies which had appeared since 1440 were corrected to give exemption to the king's Irish subjects and the Channel Islanders, as well as to the already exempt Welsh.[34] The commons also turned their attention to the banking operations of foreign brokers, presumably because the scope for profit-making at English expense was resented. An earlier statute of Edward III's reign which had imposed restrictions on such activities, particularly in London, the centre of the brokerage business, was reaffirmed by the king.[35] It was directed mainly against the Italians, who stood in the forefront of the European banking community; but the vindictive commons cast their net more widely. The Hansards were causing considerable resentment, and they were accordingly threatened with a reduction in status which would place them on a par with the Italians, unless English merchants were accorded worthwhile privileges in the Baltic ports.[36] As for the Genoese, news had recently reached England of the alliance concluded between Genoa and the Saracens during the latter's attack on Rhodes; this provided an excuse for an outburst of Christian indignation that fuelled the anti-alienism of the commons. But before he was prepared to brand the Genoese as enemies of Christ, Henry VI requested further information about their role at Rhodes.[37]

This hostility and the general conviction that foreigners enjoyed inordinate wealth were behind the increase in the taxation burden on alien communities, as the government cast about for additional sources of revenue in the late 1440s. Special subsidies on alien residents, heavier customs and other dues on their commerce – these were the peaceful consequences of anti-alien feeling. After a five-year respite, the parliament of 1449 reimposed for three years the earlier tax on alien residents, and at the same time it created two new categories of the taxable: the alien merchant, who had largely escaped hitherto but was now required to pay 63s. 8d., and his foreign clerk (1s. 8d.). [38] The Reading parliament of 1453 went even further: merchants were now assessed at 40s. and travellers visiting the realm for less than six weeks at 20s.; and these and the earlier residents' taxes were to last during the king's life.[39]

This escalation of the mulcting of aliens forced the government to reassure them that although the financial pressures could not be alleviated, at least all aliens would be equitably treated by the tax assessors. Even those who had circumspectly purchased letters of denizenship could no longer escape the arm of the tax-collector. A more precise definition of those who were exempt from the alien subsidies – namely, those actually born in the realm, or in Ireland, Wales, or the former Lancastrian duchies of Normandy and Aquitaine – contributed to the imperceptible tendency to distinguish legally those who were denizens from those who were aliens. A conception of nationality hardened as a consequence. Although newly-made denizens were no longer exempt from the government's imposts, their privileged status was acknowledged by a considerably lower rate of subsidy. Perhaps the marked rise from 1449 in the number seeking denizenship had made the more restricted definition of 1453 necessary.

The vulnerability of aliens without letters of denizenship was a powerful stimulus to securing them – especially those who wished to remain in England and own property. When, on several occasions, it was discovered that aliens had unwisely purchased land without securing a special licence or letters of denizenship – even an Irishman at Oxford – they were deprived of their land.[40] The law of naturalization could even be maliciously exploited to destroy the reputation of an English-born whose possessions were coveted by others who claimed he was an alien.[41] The Italians, though squeezed hard by taxation and demands for loans, could not be pressed too far because of their commercial and financial value to the government as bankers and paymasters, as well as traders. Thus, care was taken to authorize the prompt repayment of their loans by allowing them to keep the customs chargeable on their imports and exports; and they were given precedence even over the king's and queen's assignments on the Southampton customs.[42] The dilemma of a foreigner doing business in the hostile environment of England, especially London, was matched by the dilemma of a government that distrusted the foreigner and yet needed his wealth.

Notes

1 *CPR, 1436–41*, passim; ibid., *1441–46*, passim.
2 Similarly, in 1443, following the parliament of 1442, an unusually large number of denizenships was conferred (ibid.).
3 Below, p. 552.
4 Otway-Ruthven, *King's secretary*, pp. 89-105, with a list of the French secretaries on p. 156. Le Vulre may have sought denizenship to avoid the aliens tax of 1440 and later (Thrupp in *Studies in London history*, p. 254). S. L. Thrupp (ibid., p. 259) perhaps underestimates the number of Frenchmen coming to England in the 1440s.
5 PRO, E403/757 m. 5, 6; E404/61/228, 230, 243; 'Benet's Chron.', p. 190; above, p. 490.
6 *CPR, 1446–52*, pp. 212, 240, 261 (22-23 March). They included Marie, the bastard daughter of Charles of Anjou, Duke Réné's brother.
7 ibid., pp. 276, 305, 324, 416; PRO, E403/779 m. 1 (Chapelle), 9; 785 m. 5, 8, 13; 786 m. 4, 5, 8. Breton merchants, whose duke was also at war with England after 1449, withdrew from the ports of south-west England (H. Touchard, *Le Commerce maritime breton à la fin du moyen âge* [Paris 1967], pp. 185-6).
8 *CPR, 1446–52*, pp. 249 (from Blois), 260 (Picardy), 407 (Paris).
9 ibid., *1441–46*, passim; ibid., *1446–52*, passim; above p. 409.
10 *CPR, 1446–52*, pp. 238, 215 (1449); *CCR, 1442–47*, p. 367 (1445); PRO, E28/64/17-18 (1440). For the fear of attack which Spanish merchants in England felt, see *CPR, 1446–52*, p. 40 (1446).
11 *Foedera*, V, ii, 5; *CCR, 1447–54*, p. 103.
12 *CPR, 1446–52*, pp. 42, 317; *PPC*, VI, 74; Warner, op. cit., ll. 137-9. For Englishmen's difficulty in distinguishing Hollanders and Zeelanders from

Flemings in the fifteenth century, see N. J. Kerling, *Commercial relations of Holland and Zeeland with England* . . . (Leiden, 1954), p. 186.

13 *Foedera*, V, i, 56-7, 63-6, 71, 78, 85, 92, 108, 111, 117, 136, 158-9, 161, 163-6; ii, 11 (1439–49); PRO, E28/73/63 (1444). For earlier incidents between Englishmen and Flemings at sea, see PRO, E28/71/51 (1443–44). See Kerling, op. cit., pp. 185-9.

14 PRO, E28/71/29 (1444); *CPR, 1446–52*, pp. 381, 404, 405 (1450), 441 (1451). These attacks on the Genoese may have been launched by outsiders at this time (1450–51) (below, n. 30). For Cade's demands on the Italians and other aliens in London, see below, p. 625.

15 Above, p. 393; *CPR, 1446–52*, pp. 375 (1450), 554 (1452); ibid., *1452–61*, p. 109.

16 ibid., *1446–52*, pp. 384, 430 (1450); ibid., *1452–61*, p. 119; *Foedera*, V, ii, 12.

17 ibid., i, 35, 39 (1436), 79 (1440); ii, 4 (1448), 14 (1449), 26 (1450).

18 Above, p. 431; *CPR, 1446–52*, p. 445; *Foedera*, V, ii, 29. Even so, men from Lubeck, which had refused to take part in the diet and closed the Sound to English shipping in 1451, continued to run risks in England (*CPR, 1452–61*, p. 123 (1453); *Foedera*, V, ii, 38, 41).

19 *CCR, 1442–47*, p. 336; *CPR, 1441–46*, p. 406; *Foedera*, V, i, 158; PRO, E403/762 m. 7. He especially attended on the queen.

20 PRO, E28/74/11; *Foedera*, V, i, 139.

21 *CPR, 1436–41*, p. 485; *Foedera*, V, i, 75.

22 *CPR, 1446–52*, p. 255.

23 ibid., p. 467.

24 *Foedera*, V, ii, 42.

25 Roskell, *1422*, pp. 51-5, 125-9. Though perhaps less than in Edward III's time, the influence of the merchants in the commons of Henry VI's reign was still great.

26 *RP*, V, 24, 27, 31, 32. See Giuseppi, *TRHS*, n. s., IX (1895), 78-84; Flenley, *EHR*, XXV (1910), 645-7.

27 e. g., *CPR, 1436–41*, pp. 94, 95.

28 ibid., p. 416 (William ap Gwilym ap Gruffydd, whose mother was Joan, daughter of Sir William Stanley); *PPC*, V, 251 (Thomas Vaughan, who was sponsored by the duke of Somerset and Adam Moleyns); above, p. 551.

29 *RP*, V, 5, 6. A census of aliens was accordingly commissioned on 28 February and 3 June 1440 (*CPR, 1436–41*, pp. 409-10); the number of alien householders and other residents was established again in July 1441 (below, n. 34). For discussion of the surviving taxation returns for 1440 and subsequent years (PRO, E179), see Giuseppi, *TRHS*, n. s., IX (1895), 90-8; N. J. M. Kerling, 'Aliens in the county of Norfolk, 1436–1485', *Norfolk Archaeology*, XXXIII (1965), 200-12; Thrupp, *Speculum*, XXXII (1957), 262-73, and *Studies in London history*, pp. 251-72 (with the quotation on pp. 251-2). A hitherto unknown record of aliens taxed in Soms. and Dorset for several years in the 1440s and 1450s, is DorsetRO, D 10/X 1, X 2. For the different attitude to Welshmen and Irishmen in the mid-fifteenth century, see above, p. 168.

30 See Ruddock, *EHR*, LXI (1946), 1-17, and idem, *Italian merchants in Southampton*, ch. VI, for Southampton; and Flenley, *EHR*, XXV (1910), 647-54, and Holmes, *EconHR*, 2nd ser., XIII (1960–61), 198, for the hostility. For the mayor of Southampton's defence of the Italians in the port

from attack by the men of Romsey in 1450, the year of popular disturbances throughout southern England, see Ruddock, *EHR*, LXI (1946), 3.

31 J. L. Bolton, 'Alien merchants in England in the reign of Henry VI, 1422–61' (Oxford BLitt thesis, 1971), p. 157.

32 *RP*, V, 24; Flenley, p. 114; Giuseppi, *TRHS*, n.s., IX (1895), 86-91; Warner, op. cit., ll. 496-9, 506-11. Proclamations to give effect to the statute were issued on 1 March 1440 (*CCR, 1435–42*, p. 310). For analysis of the hosting records (PRO, E101/128; E179) relating to Southampton, see A. A. Ruddock, 'Alien hosting in Southampton in the fifteenth century', *EconHR*, XVI (1946), 30-7; and in general, Giuseppi, *TRHS*, n.s., IX (1895), 85-91. For tacit disregard of the hosting regulations on occasion by host and hosted, see Touchard, op. cit., p. 138, and Ruddock, *EconHR*, XVI (1946), 35-6.

33 *RP*, V, 31. See M. E. Mallett, *The Florentine galleys in the fifteenth century* (Oxford, 1967), pp. 82-92, 132-43.

34 *RP*, V, 38-9; the necessary survey was not instituted until 1 December 1442 (LeicsRO, DE 221/10/3/4). In the meanwhile, a further investigation had been made on 27 July 1441 into the aliens resident in the realm (*CPR, 1436–51*, p. 576).

35 *RP*, V, 56; cf. Warner, op. cit., ll. 396-433.

36 *RP*, V, 64.

37 ibid., 61.

38 ibid., 144-7; *CPR, 1446–52*, pp. 272, 390, 479.

39 *RP*, V, 228, 230. The respite may have been accidental, since only the politically-charged parliament of 1447 met between the tax's lapse in 1445 and its renewal in 1449 (Thrupp in *Studies in London history*, p. 252).

40 *CFR, 1445–52*, pp. 25, 59 (1446).

41 *CCR, 1442–47*, p. 365 (1446).

42 *RP*, V, 214, 216, 258 (1453).

20 Lawlessness and Aristocratic Violence

Country and Town

The king's coming of age had no immediate perceptible effect on the frequency or seriousness of violent crime in England, or, initially at any rate, on the ability of the machinery of law enforcement to deal effectively with it. These conclusions have perforce to stand as provisional and impressionistic: not only have few found the courage to quantify the amount of violent crime that occurred in mid-fifteenth-century England, but in a world of charge and counter-charge, official favour and disfavour, accusations of corruption and threats, one may doubt whether the changing nature of crime can ever be assessed from surviving judicial records alone or with the precision that would satisfy the statistically-minded. Nevertheless, it has proved feasible and instructive to analyse county by county the way in which the king's courts, including their local commissions, dealt with violent crime in the Lancastrian period, and, in a contrasting approach, to examine the effectiveness of the central courts in dealing with such crime throughout the kingdom in a single year (or two).[1] Such studies need to be pursued for more counties and other years before a clearer picture can be painted, based on the admittedly defective materials available.

It might reasonably have been anticipated that a young and vigorous monarch who was alive to the obligation expressed in his coronation oath to offer impartial justice and peace to all in his kingdom would bring a firm and salutary influence to bear on this matter. We may assume that a man like Henry VI was fully conscious of oaths solemnly sworn and by temperament was likely to be stirred by the sufferings of his subjects. And yet, some of the king's own actions and decisions, particularly his passion for pardoning and his incautious and short-sighted indulgence of courtiers, servants, and friends, had the effect of stimulating, rather than pacifying, quarrels and rivalries. As a consequence, a number of the nobility especially were emboldened to resort to criminal activity and to thumb their nose at the common law and the king's council; it was a greater threat to the upholding of the law and the preservation of stability when they, rather than any other section of the community, did so. Moreover, Henry VI was rare among medieval English kings in his disinclination to travel extensively throughout his realm, and thereby to impress the reality of kingly power on a broad spectrum of his people. Before his illness in 1453, he never travelled to the north-west; he traversed Yorkshire only once, when he journeyed to Durham in 1448; he likewise visited Wales on only one occasion, in 1452 when he broke his journey through the border shires to cross into the lordship of Monmouth; and yet neither was he particularly fond of the city of London or Westminster.[2] It was not that he failed to appreciate the value of a royal tour as a unique demonstration of his sovereignty and as a means of impressing his authority on communities that rarely, if ever, saw him – hence his plan to undertake an extensive journey through the realm in the summer of 1453 and the projected visit to Calais in 1451.[3] But personal inclination, the onset of serious illness, and other circumstances combined to frustrate both these designs.

Those parts of the realm that were furthest from the centre of government and the king's presence, and large conurbations like London, were still the most turbulent regions and posed special problems for those responsible for executing the law and maintaining peace. In the north, the counties adjacent to the Scottish border contained unusually volatile communities that were perpetually disturbed, even though for much of Henry's majority formal relations with Scotland were peaceful.[4] The sprawling county of York, with its proud and powerful magnate houses, experienced a level of violent crime that was probably more dangerous than that of any comparable stretch of English countryside, and after 1450 aristocratic rivalries there became so intense that the shire was on the verge of civil war. At the other corner of the realm, Somerset, Devon, and the Cornish peninsula were almost as turbulent, with the king himself contributing to this state of affairs by his imprudent treatment of the earl of Devon and Sir William Bonville.[5] Cheshire and Lancashire, whose great franchises complicated their jurisdictional relationship with neighbouring shires, were Henry's private domain; there was no earl of Chester after 1413 and no duke of Lancaster after Henry IV's accession, and neither county could look to any other peer of the realm to provide a focus of political power. Distance, privilege, and a society of self-important knights and esquires, who were often 'so grete kynred and alyed', made for ill-co-ordinated and precarious peacekeeping.[6] Likewise, Derbyshire, with its remote peaks and dales, had lost its greatest aristocratic landowner when the duke of Lancaster had seized the crown in 1399.[7] After all, the English magnate was central to social stability in those localities where his major interests lay; though, as the situation in East Anglia and Yorkshire indicates, the presence of too many of them, with their estates in close proximity to one another, was likely to promote rivalries, disorder, and violence.[8]

Kent and the home counties exhibit different social forces at work. This was a region defined by the presence of the largest administrative and commercial centre in the kingdom, with a suburban extension into Kent, Essex, Surrey, Middlesex, and Hertfordshire; here the upper reaches of society were infiltrated by government employees, household servants, courtiers, and others in search of property, wealth, and influence, and Henry VI's patronage facilitated the formation of a household nexus in the south-east by the middle decades of the fifteenth century. Such migration and resettlement would have been resented by the traditional social and administrative hierarchy of any county, but in Kent especially it coincided with the passage of ill-disciplined armies to and from the ports and, in the late 1440s, of bands of refugees.[9] Moreover, problems of sea-keeping undermined the flourishing trade of the south-coast ports and in the 1440s even the English coastline was threatened when the Lancastrians began to lose control of the opposite shore. Hampshire, with its major ports of Southampton and Portsmouth, situated opposite a particularly vulnerable Isle of Wight, in this respect had greater cause for concern than most English counties.[10]

London stood in a class apart. Trade and craft rivalries were deep-seated and of long-standing; the struggle between the drapers and victuallers in Richard II's reign was echoed later by an animosity between the drapers and tailors that marred the mayoral elections of 1441 and 1448.[11] The foreign merchants and their households in the city were also a focus of disturbance; not only was the well-protected Steelyard of the Hanseatic merchants, situated on Thames-side, a monument to foreign privilege, but the inns occupied by Italians, Flemings, and others were often at the centre of anti-alien agitation, though not, as yet, on the scale of the late 1450s.[12] Some of the Flemings had concentrated in Southwark, which in any case had an unsavoury reputation for its disreputable inns (many of them owned or run by foreigners) and its stews and brothels; despite the regulations imposed by successive bishops of Winchester, whose London house fronted the Thames in Southwark, brawls were frequent in this quarter and the quality of suburban life produced periodic demonstrations of moral indignation by other Londoners.[13]

On the westerly edge of the city, the inns of court, those universities for lawyers that were attracting young men to London from all parts of the kingdom, were growing in number and expanding in size. Their *curiales* forged very poor relations with the citizenry of London, especially those living in nearby streets; during the night of 31 August 1441, a particularly violent skirmish took place between the apprentice lawyers and the residents of Fleet Street, and several chroniclers seem to have observed at first-hand the bows and arrows that were used and the casualties that afterwards lay in the streets.[14] The presence in or near the capital of the departments of government and of the king's household meant a significant influx of major and minor officials, together with their servants, families, and friends, who sometimes had uneasy relations with the citizens and the city authorities. Two household servants from the king's stable, for example, were said to have been responsible for riots in Southwark in the spring of 1443.[15] Moreover, a score of magnate and episcopal houses were situated in the city or along the road to Westminster, each of them capable of accommodating a household staff and retainers. They, too, posed serious problems for the city's officials, who not only had to find additional housing for their visitors, but also tried to ensure that the retinues of rival lords were kept well apart. The difficulties are well illustrated by the events at the opening of parliament in November 1450; York, Warwick, Norfolk, and Devon were among those magnates who arrived in London at the head of large followings which contributed to the violence accompanying the debates in the parliament chamber. The impossibility ultimately of controlling lordly retainers was apparent during Cade's revolt, when many of them refused to obey their lords and resist the approaching rebels.[16]

Not only was mid-fifteenth-century London an exceptionally violent place for these special reasons, but as the largest city in the land it acted as a veritable magnet for the petty criminal.[17] Furthermore, its scriveners' shops came as close to providing a factory of seditious propaganda as the pre-printing age could muster. The contemporary publishing business was largely concentrated in the city, particularly in the vicinity of St Paul's churchyard, where John Shirley, amongst others, set up his copying and distributing shops; not only did such entrepreneurs supply the well-to-do with chronicles, but they also provided the bills and seditious literature that littered the city in disturbed times.[18] Fairly constant vigilance was required to man the barricades of an orderly society and this was the permanent preoccupation of the mayor and his colleagues.[19] After 1436 their task seems to have been particularly difficult. The Burgundian volte-face of 1435 and the siege of Calais that followed placed the Flemings of London in a delicate position: they were regarded with intense suspicion, so much so that many of them affirmed on oath their loyalty to Henry VI as king of England and France. Nevertheless, it proved irresistible to attribute the lawlessness of Southwark to them.[20] The disruption of smooth trading relations with the Hanseatic League in 1449, together with the unrivalled privileges which German and Baltic merchants had long enjoyed in England, inevitably fed English resentment.[21] The political crisis of 1450 drew unusually large numbers of retainers to London, especially in time of parliament, and these presented a danger to public order that was worse than anything hitherto experienced in Henry's reign. Furthermore, the unpopularity of the government was frequently visited on its representatives who happened to be in the city. Into this increasingly charged atmosphere in 1449–50 entered substantial numbers of defeated, disgruntled, and unemployed soldiers from France who were all too ready to display their exasperation openly and violently against the duke of Somerset and Lord Hoo.[22]

The other urban centres of the realm were neither as large nor their social relationships as complex as those of London. But many of them experienced at least some of the causes of tension and violence that afflicted the capital. Conflicting jurisdictions embroiled city and university at Oxford and Cambridge, whilst at the former the traditional student feuds between northerners and southerners were responsible for a particularly savage incident at the end of August 1441.[23] More commonly, ecclesiastical corporations found themselves at odds with adjacent urban authorities. At Norwich, the city and the cathedral priory were at each other's throat during 1442–43, and so were the abbot of St Mary's and the city of York, though their disputes may not have been quite so violent.[24] Similar factors explain some of the violence accompanying the murder of Bishop Aiscough in 1450, for assaults were then made on Salisbury cathedral and the property of its dean and chapter; at Gloucester, Abbot Boulers was detested by the populace, who made their feelings plain in 1449–50 by raiding his manors, quaffing his wine, and appropriating his property and stock.[25] Such incidents were more serious during Henry VI's majority because several of those who headed these great clerical corporations were closely associated with the discredited Lancastrian régime.

Provincial towns were not infrequently riven by faction as occupational groups of tradesmen, merchants, and craftsmen sought exclusive privileges or even a stranglehold on town government. At their most complex in London, such rivalries and struggles were present in smaller centres like Hereford and Norwich. By the fifteenth century, these quarrels were often second nature to the participants, for they might date from the granting of charters of privileges or the conferment of administrative and commercial self-government. They also provided raw material for manipulation by other interests, as fourteenth-century Flemish and Italian cities exemplify. In England in the following century, noble factions sought support from, and influence in, towns up and down the realm by enlisting one faction against another for purposes which had little to do with the town itself. The duke of York and his councillors embarked on such a campaign in a number of towns situated in or near York's personal estates, and perhaps the best-documented example involved the duke's retainer and councillor, Sir Walter Devereux, who enlisted the 'Welsh faction' at Hereford during 1451–52 in order to assist his lord's political manoeuvres in the realm at large.[26] Similar, though perhaps less provocative, exploits at the instigation of outsiders can be observed elsewhere: livery was being distributed at Hull in 1443; Lord Grey of Ruthin, who owned substantial Northamptonshire estates, tried to overawe Northampton at about the same time, and during the early 1450s the city of York was drawn into the county's magnate disputes.[27]

Such divisions were most likely to erupt in violence at election time, whether at the annual election of a mayor or other town official, or at the rare elections of borough and county MPs. The mayoral elections in London were such violent affairs that in October 1443 steps were taken to prevent interference in the election procedure and obviate the disorders of recent times; but nevertheless Mayor Podesly had to consign several disappointed tailors to Newgate gaol for their behaviour.[28] At Cambridge in 1439 the followers of Sir James Ormond and Lord Tiptoft, both Cambridgeshire landowners, came to blows at the parliamentary election, an incident that gave rise to dangerous uproar among the citizens and students. Ormond, 'with men, harnessit in jakkys and salates to the numbre of .1. persones, comen to Cambrigge on the evyn that the shire [court] shuld be holdyn on the morne, takyng up all the innes in the stretes goyng to the castell ther as the shire shuld be holdyn for his men shuche as shuld come to hem'. Tiptoft 'came to the said towne of Cambrigge wythe power sufficiaunt to se the pees kepte, and was logid atte the Freres Austyns and ther abode all the tyme he was in the towne'. The sheriff, wishing to avoid an ugly incident, decided to abandon the election temporarily; but Ormond 'a gayne the will and intent of the shirrefe, takyng upon hem the said shirrefs office, atte vj of the belle atte nyght whan the most partye of the commones war departid', insisted on conducting the election with a packed and illicit electorate.[29]

Relations between the larger towns and the surrounding countryside were somewhat ambivalent for much of the middle ages for, despite the privileged status of towns and their inhabitants, the two communities were interdependent and for much of their daily life could hardly be distinguished. In the Welsh borderland, however, what urban-rural tension existed was heightened by the proximity of the peculiar marcher lordships, the existence on the statute book of Henry IV's punitive legislation against Welshmen, and by a racial antipathy that was still keenly felt in border towns. Both Hereford and Tewkesbury had their 'Welsh factions', and rough-neck Welshmen were frequently responsible for disrupting elections and were able to escape to a neighbouring lordship in an attempt to thwart the peace-keeping agents of an English county. The situation seems to have deteriorated in the 1440s, perhaps because of renewed emphasis on Henry IV's statutes and the attempts made from Richard of York's extensive marcher estates to gather support in important border towns like Shrewsbury, Ludlow, and Hereford.[30]

Thus, circumstances during Henry VI's majority made the vital questions of lawlessness and disorder of more urgent concern than for some time past. This was partly the result of the unpopularity of the régime itself and its lack of success in many of its policies; but it also sprang from the king's disinclination to contain – let alone resolve – magnate quarrels; indeed, he and his ministers promoted them! The communities of country and town were too frequently caught up in the consequences of an ineffective and partial régime headed by an inexperienced and short-sighted monarch.

Property, the source and symbol of influence, lay at the heart of most quarrels and violent disputes. Breaking and entering the parks, houses, and estates of the affluent, with violence offered to their tenantry and servants, even to the landowners themselves, were commonplace in an overwhelmingly rural society. Most of the commissions of oyer and terminer that were regularly nominated in these years were intended to investigate such occurrences throughout the length and breadth of the land.[31] There were arguments over the ownership and possession of property and inheritances, over offices and positions of power in the community, and these disagreements were more likely than not to degenerate into violence and implicate magnates and gentry alike.[32] Maud Clifford, countess of Cambridge indignantly informed the council in October 1439 how her manor at Danby in Eskdale (Yorkshire) had been attacked by Salisbury's son Thomas, Sir Thomas Lumley, and their 'grete parentelle and alianus'; how they had hunted in it and shot deer at a daily rate of sixteen, some of the pregnant beasts included.[33] Nor were the estates of laymen the only – or even prime – focus of disorder, for several of the king's properties were attacked by criminal elements, and so were those (it goes without saying) of the clergy, both secular and religious.[34]

Indeed, the religious were fair game in an age which, however much respect it might show for individual piety, was still critical of the more obviously temporal aspects of the institutionalized church. In town and country, its franchises, buildings, and parks, not forgetting the servants who staffed them, were attacked by the envious, the poor, and the disaffected. At York the citizens clashed head on with the abbot of St Mary's in 1443; the abbeys at Bury (Suffolk) and at Fountains (Yorkshire), along with Archbishop Kemp's manors at Southwell, Ripon, and Bishopthorpe, were subjected to vicious attack in the 1440s by veritable armies of men.[35] Among less important houses, Hartland (Devon), Basingwerk (Flintshire), and Rowney priory (Hampshire) suffered no less severely.[36] The anticlerical temper of the times occasioned personal outrages: the Augustinian canons fled from Hartland for their lives, whilst a parson had to appeal to the king for protection against a malicious indictment of multiple rape.[37] It also emboldened sanctuary-violators at St Martin-le-Grand in London.[38]

Yet by this time, there was little sign of widespread heresy, with its occasional blasts against the very foundations of the social and religious order; perhaps the collapse of the 1431 rebellion had cowed its spokesmen. One or two burnings were arranged *pour décourager les autres*, and at the merest suspicion of heresy the lay and ecclesiastical authorities closed ranks to snuff it out, confident in their knowledge that the king was staunchly orthodox in matters of faith. On the occasion of a burning in London in 1438, it was recorded that

> The king is zealous for justice and the catholic faith, willing to uphold the church and defend the rights and liberties thereof, and so far as in him lies to extirpate heresies from the realm and award condign punishment to convicted heretics, and is aware that by the law of God and men and by the canons and institutes such heretics ought to be burned with fire.[39]

The government's vigilance grew keener when it was discovered that Richard Wyche, an old heretic of Henry IV's time who was burnt in June 1440, attracted more devoted followers in death than he had done in life, for among the superstitious it was said that miracles were being worked at the site of his execution; the authorities, which were ever ready to associate heresy with treason, stepped in to prevent the spot from becoming a place of pilgrimage and idolatry.[40] But this incident was no more than a nine days' wonder, and even less of a threat to public order was the preaching of a Franciscan friar at Coventry early in 1446; he was simply removed to a more distant house, though the thoroughness with which his opinions on ecclesiastical authority and wealth were refuted by order of the council may reflect Henry VI's personal horror at religious deviation.[41]

The government and its agents were sometimes the victims of the criminal, and unpopular officials who discharged their duty with zeal found themselves subjected to assault or worse.[42] One of the customers at Exeter and Dartmouth complained of dispossession by an armed band that was maintained by Sir Nicholas Carew. Carew and 'sum of his consell' had not only overawed the assizes in Devon by bribery and maintenance, but could also count on JPs who were their kinsmen; he was therefore able to ignore an arbitration award and the unfortunate customer 'dar not abide in tho parties to sue as lawe woll'.[43] Even those armed with sealed writs were treated with scant respect, and it seems to have been a particularly unpalatable snub to force a royal servant to eat the writ, wax and all.[44] Suspicion of the powerful and the privileged is not an exclusively medieval trait, but in the fifteenth century the officials and servants of the king's counsellors ran a real risk of violence: those in the service of Cardinal Beaufort, Gloucester, and Suffolk were vulnerable, despite the fact that the political views of their masters were poles apart.[45] Even an MP, travelling to the commons from Cumberland for the parliamentary session in March 1446, could be set upon in the city of London: Sir Thomas Parr immediately demanded in the commons that the culprits be tried in king's bench, though the affront to parliamentary privilege was not so serious as to prevent an out-of-court settlement that led to the act being rescinded in the next assembly (1449).[46] Such incidents seem to have been relatively few in number, and the government may be relied upon to have recorded them with more than usual care; but by 1450 they had increased to a disturbing level.[47]

Noble lawlessness

Apart from the petty criminal, the heretic, and the obscure rioter, the most serious crimes, those with the most dangerous implications for the peace of the realm, were perpetrated by well-to-do members of the magnate, knightly, and gentle classes. They had most to gain from success in quarrels over local office and coveted properties, whilst the reality of their 'good lordship' needed to be demonstrated in order to be maintained. As a group, they all but monopolized regional influence; as individuals they felt it to be worth breaching the law in order to retain their share of this influence. And where the magnates marched, the gentry followed, not least because the latter could hardly ignore the causes of their patrons. A number of the fracas in which they were involved make fascinating and instructive reading: these incidents expose the dearly-held concerns of the gentry and the aristocracy, the attitude of the crown towards their waywardness, and the capacity of England's law enforcement machinery to control it. One is left with the distinct impression that there were more of such incidents, and ones of great seriousness, during Henry VI's adulthood, and that the government proved less and less capable of dealing with them.

The riots which took place in Bedfordshire in the late 1430s were of a sort not uncommon in aristocratic England. A well-established magnate, the elderly Reginald, Lord Grey of Ruthin, had his principal residence at Wrest Park, near Silsoe; although not a landowner of the front rank, his estates in Bedfordshire, Northamptonshire, and north-east Wales (the lordship of Ruthin) were the foundation of a position which he and his forebears had carefully maintained since the fourteenth century.[48] One can easily imagine the suspicion and apprehension with which he received the news that a prominent veteran of Henry V's campaigns, Sir John Cornwall, had decided to invest the proceeds of his soldiering in France in a brand new castle at Ampthill, barely 4 miles from Silsoe. Cornwall, moreover, was well placed at the Lancastrian court, for he had married the widowed sister of Henry IV, Elizabeth of Lancaster, and was accordingly, if somewhat belatedly, raised to the peerage as Lord Fanhope in 1432.[49]

The first serious disagreement between the two men occurred shortly before May 1437, when a commission of oyer and terminer was sent to Bedfordshire to investigate a series of felonies. Most of the commissioners appear to have been well disposed towards Fanhope, and they included at least one of his retainers, John Wenlock (who was later his executor in 1443).[50] Moreover, the commission decided to open its sessions at Grey's manor of Silsoe, much to the distaste of the old man; indeed, he so much resented the insult that, it was soon alleged, a number of his men, led by his attorney John Enderby and his retainer Sir Thomas Waweton, accused the commissioners of maliciously seeking to indict Grey's tenants and servants.[51] This allegation, which, to judge by the personnel and procedure of the commission, had some substance to it, was laid before the council when it met in June and July 1437 to examine the news of discord from Bedfordshire. Grey's representative asserted that a new commission of the peace should meet at which Enderby and Grey could be present in order to refute the charges of their enemies, and the danger of serious fighting arose, for Grey was accompanied at Silsoe by several hundred men, including a number brought from his Northamptonshire estates. Fanhope promptly retired to his seat at Ampthill to gather reinforcements. The commission seemed on the point of dissolving in chaos. For the moment, however, the quarrel was settled by arbitration, with each side offering security for its future good behaviour towards the other. The sessions of the peace were adjourned to avoid further provocation, and on 15 February 1438 a general pardon was issued to a number of Northamptonshire men (presumably in Grey's employ) for any murders, treasons, or other offences they may have committed before the previous 10 December.[52]

Unfortunately for the future peace of the Bedfordshire countryside, the fundamental cause of the discord was not easily removed – certainly not by what amounted to promises of future good behaviour secured by monetary sanctions alone. The intrusion into Bedfordshire society and politics of a wealthy, well-connected soldier-magnate presented a challenge to a long-established magnate house, headed by an elderly peer. Apart from Fanhope's decision to take up residence in the vicinity of Silsoe, he posed a real threat to Grey's political prominence in the shire: after decades in which Grey's clients (including Roger Hunt, Waweton, and Enderby) had been among the most active justices of the peace, in 1437 Fanhope seemed determined to change the complexion of local politics and all that entailed in terms of 'good lordship'.[53] In mid-January 1439, therefore, fresh disturbances occurred, and this time at the county town of Bedford.[54] The sympathizers of both magnates collided on the commission of the peace in the house where the sessions were being held. At least eighteen men were thrown down the stairs of the shire hall; some were badly hurt and jurors and others were suffocated.[55] Each side accused the other of precipitating the violence. John Enderby later claimed that Fanhope had attended with about 140 armed men and proceeded to insult Grey's entourage and interrupt the sessions, mainly because four of the justices were beholden to Lord Grey. To add to the observer's confusion, Fanhope's followers claimed that as many as 800 of Grey's men were there, armed to the teeth and drawn not only from Bedfordshire, but also from Grey's Northamptonshire estates; they, it was said, insulted the justices.[56]

It is more than likely that neither side was blameless, though the favour which Fanhope could command at court was sufficient to secure for him more lenient treatment than that meted out to Grey, who had admittedly raised the larger force to overawe the commissioners. Fanhope and his adherents were the first to secure a pardon on 7 March 1439, after the entire episode had come before the council on 10 February; and it was the king himself who decided to extend his grace to his kinsman-by-marriage, after payment of a fine. The councillors present that day included Gloucester, the chancellor (Bishop Stafford), Salisbury, Northumberland, and Cromwell, the treasurer.[57] Moreover, the new commission of the peace, nominated on 12 March, excluded Enderby, Waweton, and other servants of Lord Grey, and yet it still

571

included Fanhope and a number of his retainers. Indeed, Enderby had to wait several more months for his pardon, towards the end of May 1439. Such treatment was hardly calculated to assuage the deep-seated feelings of personal malice and local rivalry.[58] Death did so more effectively: Lord Grey died in 1440 and Fanhope in 1443, and whereas the former was succeeded by his twenty-four-year-old grandson Edmund, Fanhope's only child, a son, had been slain at Baugé in 1421.

The tangled history of the Berkeley inheritance exemplifies most clearly the skein of claim and counter-claim, argument and negotiation, stubbornness and violence which the complex provisions of English land law could weave by the fifteenth century. The Lisle barony which Thomas, Lord Berkeley had enjoyed in right of his wife passed after his death in 1417 to his daughter and heiress, Elizabeth; she in turn took its estates in Wiltshire, Berkshire, Northamptonshire, and the south-west as a handsome windfall to her husband, Richard Beauchamp, the much-admired earl of Warwick. Earl Richard continued to enjoy them for seventeen years 'by courtesy of England' after Elizabeth's death in 1422.[59] Elizabeth also had a claim of sorts to the Berkeley estates, centred on the fortress at Berkeley itself, but neither she nor her powerful husband was able to sustain it against her cousin, James Berkeley. The dispute between these two was under way by 1420, but even after Elizabeth's death two years later it proved difficult to reach a compromise; eventually, in 1426 it was agreed that Warwick should enjoy for life seven of the Berkeley manors in Gloucestershire and Somerset (with a few other properties besides) but that the remainder of the estate should be acknowledged as James's rightful inheritance.[60] It was an intractable problem, and it seems likely that James, though brought to a compromise by the earl, cherished the hope that he would recover not only the Berkeley manors after Warwick's death but perhaps also the barony of Lisle. To accomplish this, he would have to contend with the three daughters and heiresses of Elizabeth Berkeley and Richard Beauchamp, one of whom, Margaret, 'a dangerous woman' (to quote T. B. Pugh), was particularly tenacious and indomitable – witness the chilling inscription on her tomb, 'Her reson was *Til deth departe'.*[61]

In July 1439, soon after Warwick died, his wife's Lisle inheritance was partitioned between the three daughters: Margaret, the wife of John, Lord Talbot; Eleanor, the wife of Edmund Beaufort, count of Mortain; and Elizabeth, the wife of George Neville, Lord Latimer. Their half-brother, the new earl of Warwick, was only fourteen years old and James Berkeley seized the opportunity to lay claim to both the Beauchamp and the Lisle properties.[62] His boldness was rewarded with confinement in the Tower and a requirement that he enter into a recognisance of £1,000 that he would cease such unilateral action. Once again, lengthy negotiations took place which culminated in an arbitration award between the three sisters and James Berkeley, delivered by three of the king's justices who were acceptable to them all. In February 1441, and again a year later, the four disputants undertook to abide by the award.[63] Whatever its details, it was Margaret Berkeley, spurred on perhaps by her husband's creation as earl of Shrewsbury on 20 May 1442, who forcibly seized some of the Berkeley estates during 1442. Intermittent agreements, appearances before the council, and another arbitration in April 1448 solved nothing.[64]

An especially bitter phase of the dispute opened in 1450, by which time the settlement of such labyrinthine problems had frequently become a matter of bows and staves and swords. Doubtless taking advantage of the upheaval in the realm at large, in the summer of 1450 James Berkeley sacked the manor at Wotton-under-Edge which Countess Margaret held by a life-tenancy (by virtue of the arbitrations). This trespass sparked off months of private feuding in the west of England. Both Shrewsbury, who was no mean soldier for all the ignominy of his return from Normandy, and his younger son, Lord Lisle, intervened on behalf of the countess; their efforts culminated early in September 1451 in the capture of Berkeley castle; inside was one of James Berkeley's sons who (it was claimed in 1466) was held prisoner for eleven weeks.[65] Berkeley was arraigned before commissioners of oyer and terminer, sitting at Chipping Campden in October 1451, to answer for his seizure of Wotton-under-Edge. He was condemned, ordered to pay 700 marks in damages to Lisle and to hand Berkeley castle over to the Talbots for two years as security for a compensatory payment of £1,000, and required to let his eldest son William enter Lisle's household, where a careful watch could be kept on him as a hostage for his father's future good behaviour. That done, on 20 November a general pardon was issued to Berkeley and his sons for all offences committed by them before Michaelmas 1451.[66]

It was a highly satisfactory settlement from the Talbots' point of view; that it was so owed much to the regard in which Shrewsbury was held at court as England's greatest living war captain. On the other hand, such a punitive settlement was scarcely likely to keep James Berkeley at bay for long. Yet, as with the Grey–Fanhope quarrel in Bedfordshire some ten years earlier, the fortuitous death of several of the participants during 1452–53 had the effect of improving relations between the feuding families. James Berkeley's wife, Isabel Mowbray, who had wholeheartedly supported her husband in his struggle, died at Gloucester on 27 September 1452 after being apprehended by the Talbots. Then, at Castillon in Gascony on 17 July 1453 not only Shrewsbury and Lisle, but also one of James Berkeley's sons died on the battlefield; another Berkeley was captured by the French. The second earl of Shrewsbury was less inclined to pursue the vendetta and saw some merit in Berkeley's case; indeed, the discord was temporarily calmed by a marriage in 1457 between James Berkeley (who was now all of sixty-three) and Shrewsbury's sister Joan.[67] Private dissension had escalated into dangerous feuding largely through the personal inclinations of certain individuals; yet, it was also the quality of royal government and waning respect for its legal process that enabled the dispute to erupt in violence and civil strife.

Henry VI was directly and more centrally involved in the ugly clashes between the earl of Devon and Sir William Bonville in the west country. The Courtenay earls were not only the largest landowners in Devon, with considerable properties in Cornwall and, to a lesser extent, in Somerset, Hampshire, and Dorset, but they could justifiably claim to occupy the highest social and administrative niches among the king's subjects in the south-west. It so happened, however, that Earl Thomas, who was born in 1414, was only eight years old when his father died; and for years he was in financial straits because his widowed mother clung to substantial dower and jointure lands until 1441. Moreover, in the recent past, the earls of Devon had seen their influence in the region challenged on more than one occasion by the advancement, through royal patronage, of lesser gentry and noble families.[68] The Bonvilles represented a renewed threat to Courtenay influence and prestige. Sir William, who had inherited properties at Shute in Devon and Chewton in Somerset, his principal residences, was born in 1392 and had married successively a daughter of Lord Grey of Ruthin and one of the Courtenay girls, the latter none other than Earl Thomas's aunt. A capable, energetic, and well-connected man, he had, like many of his contemporaries, won his spurs in France beside Henry V, Clarence, and Bedford; when he returned home, he passed naturally into the Lancastrian administration of Devon, Cornwall, and Somerset. Sir William's Courtenay connections were intimate ones, and he seems to have formed a friendship with Sir Philip Courtenay of Powderham, a kinsman of the earl but by no means an obedient relative. For his service as seneschal of Gascony in the mid-1440s, Sir William was raised to the peerage in March 1449. An able and prominent west-country knight could be a valuable adjunct to Courtenay power in the south-west; but a peer favoured by the Suffolk group at court signalled jealousy and trouble.[69]

The fundamental cause of the violent clashes between Earl Thomas and Sir William lies, then, in the readjustment of the relative positions and wealth of the two men in Devon, although Bonville's marriage into the comital family, with the control which that gave him over certain Courtenay properties, may have made relations yet more delicate. Matters came to a head following an ill-judged act of Henry VI's government in 1437 which angered the suspicious and sensitive earl. On 8 March, Bonville was appointed royal steward in Cornwall for life, in place of Sir John Courtenay of Powderham; it was a post which, however imprecise its title, must surely have implied the stewardship of the duchy of Cornwall estates in Cornwall.[70] The grant of a life-annuity of £100 to Devon in November 1438 may have done something to ease the earl's financial plight, but it could hardly compensate for the encroachment on his west-country influence which Bonville's stewardship implied.[71] Serious criminal attacks on Bonville's Devonshire estates were taking place by the summer of 1439, though these may have resulted from a private dispute with Thomas Carminow, a Cornish esquire with a Devon estate.[72] By 1440, however, relations between the new steward and Earl Thomas had reached breaking-point; armed demonstrations were organized by each side and they eventually led to both men being summoned to appear before the council in October.[73] It was symptomatic of the deeper issues at stake and the political implications of the quarrel that Sir William, who had been favoured immediately Henry VI came of age, travelled to London to receive his medicine whereas the earl disdainfully made his excuses.[74]

It did not take Devon long to realize that he might be as successful as his rival in eliciting patronage from the open-handed Henry VI – hence the earl's petition in May 1441 that he be given the stewardship of the duchy of Cornwall. If the king was initially persuaded that this office was sufficiently distinct from that already given to Bonville for life, he was speedily disabused.[75] The duchy's main estates were in Cornwall itself, where Bonville's commission was operative; to confer virtually identical powers on the earl of Devon was certain to result in friction.[76] In reality, the king had precipitated a brawl between the parties. The blunder – for such it was – was realized within a week; optimistically, Devon, who had secured precisely what he wanted, was urged not to implement his warrant, but predictably this appeal was ignored.[77] Disorder was inevitable. One of Bonville's old friends, Sir Philip Chetwynd, was attacked on the road between Bristol and London, near Hungerford, by men who were said to be wearing Devon's livery; and although on this occasion both Devon and Bonville attended the council to be examined (November 1441) and were induced to surrender their stewardships, the arbitration that was arranged by 1 March 1442 either found in Devon's favour or, more likely, was ineffective.[78] Certain it is that the earl continued to regard himself as rightfully steward of the duchy of Cornwall.

Peaceful relations were temporarily restored only when Bonville set sail for Gascony as the duchy's new seneschal. Though his earlier military reputation was impeccable, in December 1442 (when he was appointed to the post) he was fifty years of age and had not seen France in almost twenty years; nor was he the government's only choice.[79] One may wonder, however, whether his appointment overseas was not part of the arbitration agreed in 1442 in order to bring stability to the west country.[89] Having been granted a general pardon on 7 December for all past offences, he left Plymouth for Bordeaux at the beginning of March 1443 and spent about four years in the duchy before returning to England.[81] With Bonville safely abroad, on 4 November 1443 the king could extend his favour to Earl Thomas and release him from all debts and suits which had arisen before the previous 1 January. The slate seemed to have been swept clean.[82] Nevertheless, Sir William's creation as Lord Bonville of Chewton in March 1449 was doubtless not only in recognition of his efforts in Gascony, but also as a decisive expression of the favour in which he was held by Suffolk's régime; indeed, de la Pole's henchman, William Tailboys, was Bonville's son-in-law. Moreover, the new west-country magnate had recently attached himself to another lately ennobled knight, James Ormond, son of the earl of Ormond; he was a west-country landowner by marriage and, to judge by his role in the Cambridge elections of 1439, none too law-abiding by nature.[83] Bonville and the earl of Wiltshire (as Ormond had become), fortified by the patronage of the court, together represented the most formidable challenge yet to Earl Thomas's sway in the south-west.

The fall of Suffolk and the discredit into which the king's government had fallen by 1450 persuaded the earl of Devon that these alarming inroads into his domain could at last be countered by resolute action. In any case, he had formed his own associations by this stage, notably with Edward Brook, Lord Cobham, who, as a landowner in Dorset and Somerset, was no friend to his neighbour, Wiltshire; by the autumn of 1450 he had also made contact with the duke of York, whom he joined at the November parliament with a substantial retinue. It was York and Devon who briefly controlled the situation in London and demonstrated their mastery of the city by extending their protection even to the duke of Somerset when he and his property were assailed by an enraged mob of citizens and soldiers.[84]

Cade's rebellion and York's return from Ireland prompted Devon to risk another armed confrontation with his enemies in the west. With aid from Cobham and Lord Moleyns, in August 1451 he gathered a veritable army of 5-6,000 men to overawe Bonville and the earl of Wiltshire. Marching north-eastwards from Taunton, he forced Wiltshire to flee from his house at Lackham, which was plundered along with other of his estates in Somerset and Wiltshire. Earl Thomas then retraced his steps to Taunton in order to deal with Bonville, who had installed himself in the castle there. Its siege lasted for three days at the end of September and was only raised when York arrived unauthorized and unannounced, accompanied by Sir William Herbert, the most prominent tenant from his lordship of Usk. Devon was persuaded to withdraw and Bonville surrendered the castle into York's hands.[85] The duke had successfully saved Earl Thomas, one of his few sympathizers among the English nobility, from the consequences of his own rashness in raising local war against the royal clients, Wiltshire and Bonville. For the moment, Henry VI seems to have been angry with all parties in the affray and the leaders were briefly placed in custody in two royal castles in the home counties: Wiltshire and Bonville in Berkhamsted and their adversaries, Moleyns and Cobham, in Wallingford. York showed his partisanship by omitting to bring the earl of Devon to book and repeated summonses failed to elicit any response from either of them, though in November the earl was removed from the commission of the peace in

Devon and Cornwall.[86] No judicial proceedings were taken against Devon until 11 January 1452, by which time the wider political situation had become seriously polarized with Devon actively popularizing York's cause in the west country preparatory to the march to Dartford. Wiltshire and Bonville, by contrast, were released from confinement and received a pardon on 19 February 1452 for contravening the legislation against the giving of livery; no charges at all were laid against them.[87] Bonville, after all, was now being employed by the government to crush the risings in the west country which might have provided York with crucial support.[88]

Through King Henry's thoughtless liberality and the government's carelessness, personal jealousies in the west country had been exacerbated; in 1452 the régime compounded its foolishness by treating with partiality those who had been involved. The earl of Devon's resentment had been increased rather than diminished, whilst Bonville was confirmed in undisputed possession of the stewardship of Cornwall (or rather of the duchy of Cornwall, in order, it was said, to remove the ambiguity of 1441) for life on 8 March 1452; a year later (7 April) he became constable of Exeter castle for life.[89]

The collision between Henry Percy, earl of Northumberland and John Kemp, archbishop of York was the result, in its essentials, of a tussle between two powerful Yorkshire landowners, although the prevalent anticlericalism may have been an encouragement to the earl and his affinity, whilst Henry VI's local patronage of Kemp as a lifelong Lancastrian servant and influential councillor may have further offended Northumberland.[90] Kemp proved to be a cardinal-archbishop who was unusually sensitive of his rights and prerogatives and determined to exercise them as vigorously as he could; his régime in the north, therefore, caused unease and some resentment. He had no personal ties or prior association with his archdiocese, and the political controversy surrounding his translation from London in 1425–26 may have alienated some elements.[91] Moreover, he introduced to the spiritual and temporal administration of his see a considerable number of outsiders who either were members of his household, or had served him earlier at Rochester, Chichester, or London, or had entered his service from the king's chancery when he himself was chancellor; several of them stayed with him when he eventually moved to Canterbury in 1452. Such a record may account for the strictures of that disillusioned and sour intellectual Dr Thomas Gascoigne, who condemned Kemp for appointing evil-doers, foreigners, and papal courtiers at York.[92] He was proud of his position as a cardinal of the church since 1439 (and after the death of Beaufort in 1447 he had no rival in that capacity in England), and round about 1445 he issued a proclamation declaring his prerogatives and franchises, and threatening excommunication against any who would challenge them. That can hardly have endeared him to the lay magnates of Yorkshire and the north.[93]

Kemp was a major landowner in Yorkshire and Nottinghamshire, where influence and repute were jealously guarded by a number of lay magnates, most notably by the Nevilles and the Percies. The archbishop seems to have been on cordial terms with the Nevilles, not least because his political and ecclesiastical associations were with Cardinal Beaufort, Adam Moleyns, Marmaduke Lumley, and the household circle. He cemented good relations with Robert Neville, bishop of Durham and he helped launch the career of Robert's young nephew, George Neville.[94] But with the Percies his contacts were much less friendly, even though Northumberland's youngest son, William, received early patronage from the archbishop in 1436 and later. The Percies, along with Lord Dacre and perhaps others, resented the independent jurisdiction enjoyed by Kemp at Beverley, Bishopthorpe, Ripon, Southwell, and even in the city of York, whilst the authority of the archbishop was brought home to most of the shire by a series of visitations conducted between 1439 (at Ripon) and 1442 (in the archdeaconry of Richmond).[95] There had been cases of assault and robbery against some of Kemp's servants and tenants from the very beginning of his episcopate, but by 1440, soon after the red hat was conferred on him and the visitations had begun, the hostility reached a new and violent pitch. The king may have inflamed the situation by confirming and extending Kemp's secular franchise in Yorkshire in July 1442; the fact that he was also a royal councillor close to Beaufort and Suffolk, and a prominent instrument of their policies, readily explains why Northumberland in particular could contain his exasperation no longer.[96]

During 1440–44 the confrontation focussed on the archbishop's fairs at Otley and Ripon, where tolls were demanded of the tenants of the duchy of Lancaster lordship of Knaresborough, whose steward, Sir William Plumpton, had once been Northumberland's ward in the early 1420s and in February 1442 became steward for life of his Yorkshire manors.[97] Kemp took the precaution of fortifying Ripon 'like a towne of warr' and in 1441 he enlisted contingents of rugged men – 200 in all – from Tynedale, Hexhamshire, and the Scottish border, as well as 100 more from elsewhere in Yorkshire, to help protect his interests and defend his rights. The Knaresborough men congregated in the lordship's forests and plotted an assault on the fairs, 'be the covyne and assent of' Plumpton and others of Northumberland's affinity. Lives were lost during a skirmish at Thornton bridge on 5 May 1441, on the road between Ripon and Boroughbridge. What could happen to mere servants and tenants who were impressed or inveigled into those armed detachments is exemplified by the painful fate of Christopher Bee, who (reported Kemp) was

> smitten in the mouth and so through the mouth into the throat, by the which he hath lost his cheeke bone and three of his fore teeth, and his speech blemished and hurt, that it is not easy to understand what

he speaks or saies, and may not use therefore the remnant of his teeth and jawes to th'use of eating, as he might before.

And John Creven, another of the cardinal's men and a tailor by trade,

> was greivously beaten and wounded on divers parts of his body by the said misdoers, in especiall in his right legg, the which was neerhand hewen in two, with many other wounds, so that the said John Creven was left as for dead; and so left, lay there after tyme that all other folkes was departed, till was about iiij after noone the same day, at the which tyme happened of the dwellers of the said town of Helperby to come to the place where as he lay; the which finding not fully dead, of compassion and pittie brought him to the said towne of Helperby, and there refreshed him and releived him in such wise that he was turned to life. How it be, that he is perpetually letted of occupying of his crafte of Tayler that he used before, in so much that he may not indure to lay his legg under him in such wise as his crafte would aske.[98]

The earl himself seems to have embraced his men's cause by the beginning of 1442, to the extent of initiating a propaganda campaign against the archbishop and his officials in Yorkshire.[99] The archbishop's powerful position is reflected in the arbitration terms recommended to both sides in July 1443: Kemp received assurances from the council that the damage inflicted on his property and tenantry would be made good, whereas the earl surrendered himself at the Tower to face the council's wrath.[100] A commission of oyer and terminer under Edmund Beaufort, earl of Dorset and Lord Willoughby had been despatched to the troubled shire on 18 May. Meanwhile, the sheriff of Yorkshire was instructed to deploy the county posse to arrest those who had attacked Kemp and his servants.[101] In these circumstances, it is probable that the king's confirmation of Kemp's franchises in February 1444 served only to rekindle the hostility rather than pacify the shire, so much so that in July 1447 even more violent scenes occurred, with Northumberland's boisterous sons, Thomas and Richard, engaging in a skirmish with some of Kemp's Beverley tenants at Stamford Bridge.[102] By influencing officials and bribing jurors, Kemp secured the conviction of the Percy brothers and their imprisonment.

Henry VI's intervention on behalf of his councillor, far from bringing peace and justice to the north, had merely incensed one of his greatest magnates and prejudiced the re-establishment of order. It may have been this renewal of violence which determined the king to undertake his first and only journey to the far north of his realm in 1448.[103] But the translation of the tenacious prelate to Canterbury in 1452, and the dramatic change in the fortunes of the Nevilles in Yorkshire at about the same time, made the Percies review their attitude to the king and his peace in northern England.[104]

To ensure social stability and public order, a circumspect government needed to avoid antagonizing prominent magnates by failing to respect their local predominance or by patronizing some at the expense of others. Wise and, as far as politics allowed, impartial patronage was the key to regional control. This is precisely what Suffolk's régime did not appreciate, and not least in Lincolnshire, where several powerful noblemen were deeply offended by blatant interference in the judicial process and by a thinly concealed encouragement of criminals for political reasons. The former treasurer of England, Lord Cromwell, was a rich, self-made man whose abilities in government had long been recognized; by the 1440s he was one of the most senior and respected of Lancastrian magnates.[105] But in the later 1440s he was bitterly estranged from the duke of Suffolk and his life was placed in jeopardy on more than one occasion by some of Suffolk's henchmen, particularly William Tailboys.[106] The Tailboys home at Kyme was situated not many miles from Cromwell's new brick castle at Tattershall, and indeed the Tailboys family had in the recent past been on good terms with Cromwell.[107] But young William had a violent temper; although he had entered the king's household by 1441, he was implicated soon afterwards in a catalogue of murders, maintenances, and other offences. Doubtless his patrons at court obtained for him the general pardon that was issued in November 1446, and in that same year he married the daughter of another household client, Sir William Bonville, whose Lincolnshire properties had been acquired by marriage.[108] Tailboys's principal protectors at Westminster seem to have been Suffolk himself and Viscount Beaumont, Henry's chamberlain. In Lincolnshire, he was careless of the traditional loyalties of his family, for his lawlessness was all too often directed against Robert, Lord Willoughby and Willoughby's uncle-by-marriage, Cromwell.[109] On 5 May 1448 a commission of oyer and terminer, headed by the earl of Salisbury and Cromwell himself, was nominated to investigate Tailboys's behaviour. But once again, influence was exerted to protect him: the commission was superseded within a month and on 14 July another was nominated which excluded the two magnates and had a more modest purpose, namely, the investigation of assaults and threats against another Lincolnshire gentleman, John Dymocke. Dymocke was a servant of Lord Willoughby. The flagrant attempt by Suffolk to protect the wayward Lincolnshire lout alienated both Willoughby and Cromwell and probably other landowners like Lionel, Lord Welles, just as similar happenings in East Anglia were alienating many of the gentry there.[110]

During the course of 1448 and 1449, aristocratic resentment in the shire was polarized so sharply that Tailboys could rely only on the sympathy of Suffolk and Beaumont among the Lincolnshire magnates. Cromwell, Willoughby, and Welles were determined to bring him to justice, and they sought out his servants wherever they could be found;

as yet, however, the knave-in-chief sheltered beneath the umbrella provided by his patrons, who enabled him to secure a pardon on 8 November 1448 and a place on the bench of justices for Lindsey.[111] Matters came to a head on 28 November 1449, when Tailboys made an attempt on Cromwell's life outside the star chamber in the palace of Westminster. He was quite capable of plotting such a daring throw himself, but there is a strong suspicion that he had been prompted to it by his master, Suffolk. Cromwell certainly believed that the king's chief minister was behind the outrage and it is likely, therefore, that he encouraged the commons in parliament to impeach the duke, lending his expert advice to those who compiled the bills of impeachment against him. By this means, the scandal of Suffolk's involvement with Tailboys provided concrete evidence on which to base a general condemnation of Suffolk's flagrant abuse of position and power.[112] About the same time, Cromwell sponsored a bill in the same parliament to bring Tailboys to justice, while he, Willoughby, and John Dymocke prosecuted suits in king's bench. They eventually secured substantial damages and Tailboys had a spell in prison after further attacks on Cromwell during 1450. But this obdurate ruffian had still not learnt his lesson or appreciated the greater danger in which he stood after the removal of Suffolk; for in 1451–52 he continued to plot shamelessly against Cromwell for all he was worth.

In large measure, this entire sequence of episodes has the air of a local quarrel in several acts, played out between minor esquires who, as a result of aristocratic connections, succeeded in embroiling several magnates. When a man of the wild audacity of Tailboys turned on these magnates themselves, with encouragement from influential quarters at Westminster, the banditry in Lincolnshire was subsumed in lawlessness and corruption on a grander scale, practised by the king's own intimates, though not by Henry himself. The impact on the shire is not easily assessed, but one is bound to wonder whether Richard of York, himself a Lincolnshire landowner, when he heard of these events and of Cromwell's role in bringing Suffolk down, may not have directed his appeals in the autumn of 1450 to Grantham and Stamford in the high expectation of a favourable response – and not simply because these towns lay close to his own estates. If this was so, the gamble did not come off, for Cromwell declined to take the duke's part in 1450–52 and remained loyal to the Lancastrian king he had served since 1422. Cromwell's objective had been Tailboys and, through him, Suffolk and Beaumont; with the collapse of Suffolk's power in 1450, one of his main anxieties was removed.[113]

Another remained. It was this second concern, grounded in the two passions of his life – his Lancastrian loyalty and his carefully accumulated inheritance – which led Cromwell, as he approached his sixtieth birthday, to seek a closer connection with the Neville family. He already had a strong affinity with the earl of Salisbury and his sons through their Beaufort blood: Bishop Beaufort seems to have been

Cromwell's most consistent patron in the first two decades of the reign, and enduring relationships were forged with several other Beaufort protégés (John Kemp among them) from Henry V's reign onwards.[114] If Cromwell had thoughts in the 1440s about the succession to Henry VI's throne, one may assume that he regarded a Beaufort as the king's most appropriate heir. These associations of his probably made him reluctant to embrace York's cause in 1450–52, and the Nevilles showed no sign of doing so either. As with so many of the political alignments and commitments of these years, the personal, private, and landed interests of Lord Cromwell, combined with the loyalties of a lifetime, dictated his attitude to wider questions, including the Suffolk régime, the posturings of the duke of Exeter in 1454, and the claims of the duke of York. Cromwell believed that his interests, both political and personal, would be best served by the destruction of Suffolk and an alliance with the Neville kinsfolk of the Beauforts.

Cromwell's heirs were his two nieces, Maud and Joan Stanhope. Towards the end of his life, he made plans for the marriage of both.[115] Maud, the eldest, had been a widow since the death of Lord Willoughby in July 1452, and Cromwell spared no time in making arrangements for her remarriage rather than run the risk of leaving her and her inheritance without adequate protection in the event of his own demise. By 1 May 1453 he had made the necessary arrangements to marry her to Thomas Neville, a younger son of the earl of Salisbury. The king's permission for the match was obtained that day, and the wedding took place at Tattershall in mid-August. His second niece, Joan Stanhope, was married at about the same time in 1453 to Humphrey Bourgchier, Richard of York's nephew.[116]

The Neville match was by far the more significant of the two: to acquire control of part of the extensive Cromwell estate would augment the Nevilles' already vast northern possessions and 'connection'; it would extend the family's interests southward from their Yorkshire and Durham properties; and it would enhance the influence of a prolific brood that had already absorbed the ancient earldoms of Salisbury and Warwick. On these grounds alone, the other great northern house, that of the Percies, who had been jealous rivals of the Nevilles for generations and nervous spectators of their rise, would view this marriage with alarm. But there were other, more particular, reasons why the disposal of part of the Cromwell inheritance to the Nevilles should have exasperated the earl of Northumberland, not to speak of the duke of Exeter.

Northumberland had been attempting for some years to reassemble the Percy inheritance after its forfeiture and partial dismemberment in Henry IV's reign. Two important manors – Wressle in Yorkshire and Burwell in Lincolnshire, which Lord Cromwell had secured for life in February 1438 and in fee simple two years later – were still unrecovered. This bestowal of patronage by Henry VI on the treasurer of England was an affront to Northumberland, who saw his two manors likely to disappear for ever into the Cromwell family. It was treatment of a similar nature which doubtless dictated the earl's attitude to the pretensions of Archbishop Kemp in Yorkshire at exactly the same time.[117] The possibility that Wressle and Burwell might pass into the hands of a Neville hardly bore contemplating. As the Nevilles' wedding party made its way back to Yorkshire from Tattershall in August 1453, it was set upon at Heworth, near York, on the 24th by a Percy force under the command of two of the earl's sons, Thomas and Richard.[118]

The Holands' interest in the disposal of the Cromwell estate was revived when Henry Holand, duke of Exeter entered into his father's inheritance in 1450 at the age of twenty (Duke John had died in 1447) and dusted off a somewhat tenuous claim to the manor of Ampthill and other Bedfordshire properties. These lands had been acquired by Lord Fanhope in October 1440 from the co-heiress of the St Amand estate; but before his death without heirs in December 1443, Fanhope had transferred them to a group of feoffees on the understanding that Cromwell, one of his executors, should have first option on their sale for £1,000.[119] Although this arrangement was made without the king's licence, in January 1444 it was regularized and eventually Cromwell secured the manors, with Edmund, Lord Grey of Ruthin witnessing the transaction. Enlisting the support of Grey was a shrewd move on Cromwell's part, for both Grey and Exeter had a claim to Ampthill through Elizabeth of Lancaster, widow of the duke of Exeter who died in 1400 and subsequently Fanhope's wife.[120] When Henry Holand reasserted his family's claim in 1452, it was based on this relationship; but Lord Grey decided, for reasons of his own, to support Cromwell in defending his right to the manors, both at law (where Exeter appears to have lost) and by force (when Cromwell was ejected from Ampthill by Exeter's men).[121] This resort to violence was condemned by the king, who ordered the arrest of all three magnates and their confinement for a short period: Exeter in Windsor castle, Cromwell in Wallingford, and Grey in Pevensey on the Sussex coast.[122]

The crown's role in precipitating the outbreak was minimal, though it had perhaps unwisely allowed Fanhope to make the preferential arrangement in Cromwell's favour in 1443 without taking into account Exeter's claim.[123] There is no evidence of judicial partiality; rather should due account be taken of the rumbustious character of the youthful and shallow-minded Exeter. Yet, coming as it did when Cromwell was pondering the disposal of his property after his death, the incident confirmed his inclination to seek a closer connection with the powerful Nevilles as a protection against the onslaught of Exeter and the animosity of the Percies.[124] When Salisbury and Warwick decided to throw in their lot with the duke of York at the end of 1453, and Exeter raised his banner against York in 1454, Cromwell found his hitherto unshakeable loyalty to the Lancastrian crown severely tested by his alienation from the court in the last years of his life. Cromwell had, in fact, outlived his usefulness and he felt himself to be increasingly out of tune with political developments in the mid-1450s. He showed no inclination to join York and his Neville allies, and yet he could hardly bring himself to make friends with Exeter or the Percies. He died in 1456 before his devotion to the dynasty could be put to the ultimate test.

What makes our view of East Anglia in the mid-fifteenth century so exceptionally translucent is, in three words, the *Paston Letters*. The uniqueness of their revelations lies less in the nature of the society which they uncover – for the preoccupations of land, office, influence, and repute were as compelling in the rest of the kingdom – nor even in the intense and intricate rivalries among magnates, country gentry, and city folk observable in their pages (for Yorkshire at least provides as rich and tangled a tapestry). Rather does it lie in the microscopic detail of the picture which is painted by the letters to and from relatives, friends and acquaintances, servants and patrons, even from the king. One may conclude, therefore, that the society they reveal was in no fundamental sense peculiar in fifteenth-century England – if it were, then the chroniclers of London and elsewhere would surely have reported some of the events in Norfolk and Suffolk more prominently – and indeed it may not have been so explosively violent as Devon or Yorkshire in the 1440s and 1450s, or even Bedfordshire a little earlier.[125] It is the very fabric of society which the letters allow one to examine in extraordinary detail; they do not in themselves frame a society that was more violent, more materialistic, or more corrupt than that to be observed elsewhere in contemporary England.

In the decade or so before the crisis year of 1450, the counties of Norfolk and Suffolk, like Kent, were dominated socially, politically, and governmentally by William de la Pole, successively earl (1415, when he was nineteen years old), marquess (1444), and duke (1448) of Suffolk, along with his councillors, servants, and protégés. According to the *Paston Letters* (and their laments are substantially confirmed by other evidence), his affinity maintained itself in the two counties by means of extortion, high-handed demands, seizures of property, denials of justice, and even by perverting due legal process; his representatives manipulated the courts and abused their own position and offices, perpetuating their local sway often by unashamed fear.[127] In Margaret Paston's opinion, by April 1448

> ther xal no man ben so hardy to don nother seyn ayens my lord of Sowthfolk nere non that longyth to hym; and all that han don and seyd ayens hym, they xul sore repent them.[127]

To be able to count the duke as one's 'good lord' was fervently to be desired by anyone who aspired to influence or office, or who simply wished to gain security for himself and his property. Margaret Paston earnestly advised her husband, John, on these lines probably in May 1449:

> Sondery folkys haue seyd to me that they thynk veryly but if ye haue my lord of Suffolkys godelorchyp qhyll the werd is as itt is ye kan neuer leven jn pese wyth-owth ye haue his godelordschep. Therfor I pray you wyth all myn herth that ye wyll don yowre part to haue hys godelordschep and his love jn ese of all the materis that ye haue to don, and jn esyng of myn hert also.[128]

To have him as one's 'heavy lord' meant that he was one's rival, one's enemy. Although to some extent it may be a distortion of the Pastons' correspondence, Suffolk's ascendancy appears to have been at its height in the second half of the 1440s, immediately before his impeachment in 1450. An apprehensive juror was advised by Edmund Paston, perhaps in 1447, that Thomas Daniel and Suffolk were at that time rivals for authority in Norfolk:

> He enqueryd me of the rewle of myn master Danyell and myn lord of Suffulke, and askyd wheche I thowte schuld rewle in this schere, and I seyd bothe, as I trowh, and he that suruyuyth to hold be the vertue of the suruyuyr, and he to thanke his frendes and to aquite his enmyys. So I fele by him he wold forsake his master and gette him a newh yf he wyste he schuld rewle. And so wene I meche of all the contre is so disposyd.[129]

The king's role in sustaining his chief minister was crucial. Henry, perhaps partly (and to begin with) out of ignorance of the nature of Suffolk's hold on East Anglia, but partly also from a willing indulgence of his chief councillor's ambition and greed, enhanced his control of the shires to such an extent that by 1450 his power was greater than that of other magnates with landed interests in the region.[130]

The means by which Suffolk achieved this position were not novel. His agents were frequently local men whom he retained as his councillors or servants and who repaid his offer of good lordship by acting in his (and, incidentally, their own) interest in shire matters. Foremost among them was Sir Thomas Tuddenham of Oxburgh, near Norwich, who alone among the duke's East Anglian affinity was advanced to high office in the king's household, where Suffolk was steward until 1446. Tuddenham became keeper of the great wardrobe in 1446, preserving thereby the command of the Suffolk circle when the duke himself resigned in favour of another of his associates, Sir Thomas Stanley.[131] A close friend and colleague of Tuddenham, and if anything even less scrupulous, was John Heydon, a lawyer from Baconsthorpe (Norfolk). He championed the duke's interests and advanced his own by threats and naked force, and his harsh treatment of his first wife and their young child seemed to confirm to members of the Paston family

585

that here was a particularly unmannered and vicious gentleman who represented Suffolk's regional dominance. As Margaret Paston reported to her husband John in July 1444,

> Heydonnis wyffe had chyld on Sent Petyr Day. I herde seyne that herre husbond wille nowt of here, nerre of here chyld that sche had last nowdyre. I herd seyn that he seyd zyf sche come in hesse precence to make here exkewce that he xuld kyt of here nose to makyn here to be know wat sche is, and yf here chyld come in hesse presence he seyd he wyld kyllyn. He wolle nowt be inretit to haue here ayen in no wysse, os I herde seyn.[132]

Of more lowly standing and importance in Suffolk's affinity were three men who nevertheless served him loyally by fair means and foul: John Wymondham, who resorted to threats and violence in 1448–49 as easily as Heydon; William Prentis, who usefully manipulated juries and was one of Tuddenham's rougher henchmen; and John Ulveston.[133]

The means which the duke and his following employed to further their designs were not unusual ones in fifteenth-century England, nor, one may hazard, any more violent than those practised elsewhere. Their forcible expulsion of Sir John Fastolf from one of his manors for three years is well known because the old campaigner was capable of making a louder noise in his own defence than almost everyone else among his contemporaries.[134] But their attempts to use their influence to secure pliant sheriffs can be paralleled elsewhere.[135] Their championship of one of the factions in the city of Norwich, usually that associated with the prior of the cathedral priory, can be mirrored in other towns and cities, though their intervention here was all the more decisive because John Heydon had been recorder of Norwich in 1431–33.[136] The protection which they extended to their clients and servants, even to those who were outlawed, and the way in which they contrived legal suits in order to secure their ends by fraudulent methods, and, finally, their resort to arms – these are all features of political society more generally in this period. What made the Suffolk clique so brash and effective was the protection and implicit encouragement it received from the king's government, simply because Suffolk and some of his more prominent cronies stood at its head and King Henry showed them every favour in the late 1440s.[137]

In an East Anglia dominated by de la Pole, the duke of Norfolk, John Mowbray, had no alternative but to play second fiddle. He was not a member of the king's council and seems to have had little influence at court, as Cade's rebels recognized in 1450 when they demanded the recall of Norfolk and other magnates to the council board as a remedy for the kingdom's ills. In any case, Mowbray was barely seventeen when his father died in 1432, and in the 1440s he was not as wordly-wise or well connected as his rival.[138] In the disputes with Suffolk's associates in which he and his men engaged, Norfolk was the more likely, therefore, to emerge the loser. Indeed, on two occasions he found himself detained briefly in the Tower of London. In 1440 he and his retainer Sir Robert Wingfield of Letheringham (Suffolk), who had served the duke's father, were involved in a quarrel with Heydon, and when Norfolk and Wingfield took high-handed action against a certain John Lyston in Nottinghamshire and Suffolk, de la Pole disapproved and seems to have played a part in securing Norfolk's and Wingfield's arrest.

> ...an esquyer of Suffolk callyd John Lyston recoueryd in assisa noue disseisine vij c. marc. in damno ayenst Ser Robert Wyngfeld etc. In avoydyng of the payement of the seid vij c. marc. the seide Ser Robert Wyngfeld sotylly hath outlawed the seide John Lyston in Notyngham-shire be the vertue of qwych outlagaré all maner of chatell to the seide John Lyston apparteynyng arn acruyd on-to the Kyng, etc. And anon as the seide vtlagaré was certyfyed my lord Tresorer grauntyd the seide vij c. marc. to my lord of Norffolk for the arrerage of hys sowde [i.e., soldiers] qwyl he was in Scotland, and accordyng to this assignement forseide taylles delyuered, etc. And my lord of Norffolk hath relesyd the same vij c. marc. to Ser Robert Wyngfeld. And here is greet hevyng and shovyng be my lord of Suffolk and all his counsell for to aspye hough this mater kam aboute, etc.[139]

A few years later, perhaps by 1443, Norfolk and Wingfield had fallen out, and Suffolk took full advantage of the breach. Their quarrel, which seems to have arisen when Norfolk tried to recover property assigned to Wingfield by the duke's father, was temporarily composed in 1444 by an arbitration award which probably declared in Wingfield's favour; but when the dispute flared up again in 1447–48, Suffolk offered Wingfield his protection, and by this stage the Suffolk knight had made friends at court after his inclusion in the entourage accompanying Queen Margaret to England in 1445. It was consequently Norfolk who found himself in prison once more in August 1448.[140] Thus, relations between the dukes of Suffolk and Norfolk in East Anglia were generally tense in the 1440s, and the latter was powerless in the face of Suffolk's supreme authority at court.

John Heydon had a secondary protector and patron in the shape of Robert Hungerford, Lord Moleyns in right of his wife and grandson of Walter, Lord Hungerford, Henry V's household treasurer and a true pillar of the minority régime.[141] By 1448 Robert was abetting Heydon in his activities in East Anglia and proffering him protection.[142] Moleyns's best-known exploit in the region, and one which identified him as a member of the Suffolk clique bent on personal aggrandisement, was his seizure of the Paston manor of Gresham in February 1448 and his subsequent tenacious attempts to keep it, even during the critical years 1450–51. Heydon seems to have played a significant part in planning this piece of crude lawlessness, whilst Moleyns was encouraged to fight the Paston counter-claims by the support which he, as a member of the court circle, received from the king.[143] Negotiations between the parties proved barren even when John Paston travelled to Wiltshire, in Hungerford country, to press his case in person on Lord Moleyns. Paston was forced to move to another house at Gresham until, on 28 January 1449,

> the seid lord [Moleyns] sent to the seid mansion a riotous peple to the nombre of a thowsand persones, with blanket bendes of a sute [i.e., in livery] as riseres a-geyn your [the king's] pees, arrayd in maner of werre with curesse, brigaunderes, jakkes, salettes, gleyfes, bowes, arows, pavyse, gonnes, pannys with fier and teynes brennyng there-in, long cromes to draw doun howsis, ladderes, pikoys with which thei myned down the walles, and long trees with which thei broke vp yates and dores and so came in-to the seid mansion, the wiff of your seid besechere [John Paston] was, and bare here oute at the yates and cutte a-sondre the postes of the howses and let them falle, and broke vp all the chambres and coferes with-in the seid mansion, and rifelyd and in maner of robery bare a-wey all the stuffe, aray, and mony that your seyd besechere and his seruauntes had there, on-to the valew of cc li., and part there-of sold and part there-of yaffe, and the remenaunt thei departed among them to the grete and outrageous hurt of your seid besechere; sayng opynly that if thei myght haue found there your seid besechere, and on John Damme which is of councelle with hym, and diuers oder of the seruauntes of your seid besechere, thei shuld haue died.

Moleyns hounded Paston's tenants at Gresham by menace, force, and vexatious court summonses, whilst Paston found himself 'not abille to sue the commune lawe in redressyng of this heynos wrong for the gret myght and alyaunce of the seid lord'.[144]

The crisis of 1450–51 delivered a serious blow to the position of the Suffolk covin in East Anglia; it certainly disposed of the duke himself, leaving a young boy of eight as his heir. It was a time, too, of uncertainty for Moleyns, whose hold on Gresham was now more easily challenged. Within two months of Suffolk's murder, both John Paston and Moleyns were resorting to law over their conflicting claims to Gresham, but the latter's greatest patron of all, the king, made an undisguised attempt to delay the proceedings so that Moleyns could remain in possession of the manor.[145] Tuddenham, Heydon, and others of Suffolk's faction also found themselves in danger and faced with the likelihood that the political complexion of the community would change dramatically, most probably in favour of the duke of Norfolk. Just as the situation in the provinces of the realm had had much to do with the fall of Suffolk, so his murder had profound implications for the local influence of those who had aided, served, or supported him in the past. In East Anglia, de la Pole's death was followed by the appointment of two commissions of oyer and terminer, with the specific purpose of inquiring into complaints of misdoing and judicial corruption, especially by former Suffolk men. These commissions of 2 August and 9 October 1450 were staffed by, amongst others, the duke of Norfolk, the bishop of Ely (Thomas Bourgchier), the earl of Oxford, Lord Scales, and Sir John Fastolf.[146] At the same time, in October–November, Tuddenham and Heydon were excluded for the first time in years from the local bench of JPs; and care was taken that the new sheriff should be an impartial individual rather than one of the mainly household servants who had filled the office in recent years.[147] Men who, like John Paston and Sir John Fastolf, had not been members of the charmed court circle recognized how crucial it was to secure a sheriff of repute and fairness. It was their hope that

> we may haue a good shereve and a good vndershereve that neythir for good fauore no fere wol returne for the Kyng ne betwix partie and partie non othir men but such as are good and trewe and in no wyse will be forsworne, for the pepil here is loth to compleyne til thei here tidynges of a good shereve.[148]

It was hardly a coincidence that at this very juncture, in October 1450, the duke of York arrived in East Anglia, where he was a considerable landowner, both to gauge the feelings of the country after the fall of Suffolk before returning to London to see the king and attend parliament, and to gather support in a region that had a goodly proportion of disgruntled gentry resentful of their victimization by the Suffolk affinity.[149] On his arrival, York showed a marked coldness toward Moleyns and 'louyth hym nought', whilst the oppressed who looked on his coming with hope of reform set about organizing demonstrations and appeals to the duke to enlist his goodwill in destroying the pernicious rule of Suffolk's former henchmen. Tuddenham and Heydon, for their part, made desperate efforts to ingratiate themselves with the duke and to cultivate his councillors, notably Sir William Oldhall. All three wished to preserve as much of their local influence as possible.[150]

They were not unsuccessful in their intrigues. When the jurors presented their indictment on 2 December, it included a tally of charges of illegality and violence in Norfolk, Suffolk, and the city of Norwich that went back to 1435. Tuddenham's guilt was self-evident and earned him the enormous fine of £1,396.[151] Yet, during the first days of 1451 it was being rumoured that the commission of oyer and terminer might not be able to proceed as had at first been intended or some of its members, particularly Oxford, had hoped.[152] Others feared that Tuddenham and Heydon would be pardoned by the accommodating king and thereby escape retribution; indeed, the hefty fines imposed on Tuddenham were substantially reduced in the following July. Some observers seem to have been poised to take matters into their own hands if the 'ryche extorssioners and oppressours' escaped.

> ...yf the Kynge pardon hym [Tuddenham] or graunted any super-sedeas London shuld with-jnne short tyme have as meche for to do as they hadde for to kepe London Brygge whanne the Capteyn [Cade] came thedyr, ... ther was vp in Norffolk redy to rys v m¹ and moo yf they have not execucion of the oyre and terminer.[153]

Tuddenham and Heydon also managed to arrange their reappointment to the bench of JPs in March 1451, and thereafter, if with some caution, they resumed their machinations to influence the nomination of sheriffs and to move against some of their enemies. Margaret Paston wrote to her husband from Norwich on 15 March 1451, doubtless in some despair:

> It is seyd here that the Kyng shuld com in-to this contré, and Ser Thomas Todenham and Heydon arn well cheryshid wyth hym; and also it is seyd they shall have as grett rewill in this contré as evyre they hadde, and many more folkys arn sory therfore than mery. Ser Thomas Todenhamys men and Heydonys sowyn this sedde all abowte the contré, that here maysteris shull com in hast in here prosperité and be als well att ese as euer they were.[154]

They received support from an unexpected quarter. Thomas, Lord Scales, the respected warrior who had recently manned the Tower when Cade's rebels burst into London, was one of those appointed to the commissions of oyer and terminer in the autumn of 1450. He was also married to Lord Moleyns's aunt.[155] Indeed, although he showed himself eager to come to an accommodation with the duke of York when the latter arrived from Ireland, grave doubts were expressed about his impartiality on the commissions. These misgivings were justified.[156] Scales seems to have offered his protection to Tuddenham, Heydon, and Prentis, and he proved decidedly hostile to those who moved in Paston and Norfolk company.[157] According to the duke of Norfolk's information,

> serteyne servaunts of the Lord Scales schulde in his name manasse and put men in feer and drede to compleyne to us at this tyme of the seide hurts and greves, seynge that we wolde abyde but a schort tyme her, and aftir our departynge he wolde have the rewle and governaunce as he hath had affore tyme ... her hath ben the grettest riotts, orryble wrongs and offences done in thise partyes by the seide Lord Scales, Thomas Tudenham, Mylis Stapilton, John Heydon, and suche as ben confedred on to theym that evir was seen in our dayes; ...[158]

His own household was accused of harbouring thieves, though widespread disappointment and disillusion with the commissions of 1450 may have contributed to these onslaughts.[159] Scales made some effort to be impartial and to foster links with gentry on both sides, but his basic loyalties led him, in the final analysis, to be lenient to the Suffolk men and to provide them with that shelter which enabled them to recover something of their former power during 1451.[160]

The remaining magnate with major interests in this region was John de Vere, earl of Oxford, who had residences at Wivenhoe (Essex) and Winche (Norfolk).[161] There can be no mistaking his attitude in 1451 (when the earl was forty-two); he was a good friend of the duke of Norfolk, to whom he declared in August 1450 that for 'sad rule and governaunce to be had I wold full fayn a ben with your good Lordship'.[162] He regarded York's visit to East Anglia in October as an opportunity to break the hold of the Suffolk faction. Oxford served on the commissions of oyer and terminer, and it was he, along with Norfolk, who tried to rally gentlemen like Paston to ensure the nomination of an impartial sheriff and the election in October 1450 of MPs who would not be former supporters of the dead Suffolk.[163] His actions against Tuddenham and Heydon carried greater conviction than those of Lord Scales.

Out of the feverish activity of 1450–51 – with the frightened seeking refuge and protection, and the ill-used bent on revenge – the duke of Norfolk emerged as the dominant figure in East Anglia; he inherited Suffolk's mantle and employed, it must be admitted, some of his methods. From his castle at Framlingham (Suffolk), he extended his influence throughout East Anglia, in alliance with Oxford and York. As a commissioner in 1450, his role in bringing Suffolk's affinity to justice was widely approved.[164] He, Oxford, and York did their best to manage the Norfolk elections to parliament in October 1450, and his determination to 'have the princypall rewle and governance throw all this schir, of whishe we ber our name whyls that we be lyvynge, as ferre as reson and lawe requyrith, hoso ever will grutche or sey the contrary', was openly announced.[165] His dominance in the region was acknowledged at court by the king's new chief adviser, the duke of Somerset.[166] The desirability of country gentry winning Norfolk's good lordship was apparent to John Paston, though the duke's means of exerting his authority fell little short of de la Pole's in its use of violence and its unscrupulous quality – except that Norfolk did not enjoy anything like Suffolk's unchallenged position at Westminster before 1450.

> .... the stedfast godlordship and ladiship of my lord [Norfolk] and my lady ... geuith cause to all her seruantis to trost verily in them and to do hem trew seruise.[167]

By 1452 Norfolk was claiming Sir John Fastolf's new castle at Caister and showed grim determination in securing it.[168] He also allowed some of his retainers and servants, led by Charles Nowell, a notorious outlaw, to terrorize parts of East Anglia in the early 1450s. Nowell had had his uses during the disturbed months of 1450–51, and in March 1450 he had struck up a friendship with York's councillor, Sir William Oldhall; together, they may have plotted a demonstration against the king and the duke of Suffolk, perhaps even supported John Cade. Thereafter, Norfolk employed him in a series of ventures which flouted the law and brought fear to many a household in East Anglia, including those of Norfolk retainers like John Paston.[169] To John's surprise and puzzlement,

> Charlis Nowell, with odir, hath in this cuntré mad many riots and savtis, and among othir he and v of his felachip set vp-on me and to of my seruantis at the Chathedrall chirch of Norwich, he smyting at me whilis on of his felaws held myn armis at my bak . . . whech was to me strawnge cas, thinking in my conseyth that I was my lordis man and his homagere or Charlis knew hys lordschipe and that my lord was my god lord, that I had be with my lord at London within viij days be-for Lent, at which tyme he grantyd me his godlordship so largely that it must cause me euer to be his trew seruant to myn power.[170]

Suffolk had been justifiably condemned for his abuse of power and his disregard of justice and the law; but had Norfolk enjoyed the same support from the king, it seems likely that he too would have misused it without hesitation to strengthen his position in East Anglia. If York were to pose as the restorer of public order and lawfulness, then his alliance with Norfolk might soon prove an embarrassment and Mowbray's assistance would remain invaluable only so long as it advanced, rather than prejudiced, their local interests.

The law's effectiveness

Such magnate brawls and 'battles' betokened danger beyond the immediate world of those involved, for on the aristocracy, more than on any other section of the community, depended the peace of the realm and the implementation of the law. The genuine effectiveness of inquiries and commissions of oyer and terminer and of the peace relied on their involvement and impartiality. They were the men who were most frequently the king's councillors, and as such they were the last resort of those who could not find justice elsewhere; if councillors were to be among the most blatant of the lawless, then confidence in the king's ability to provide peace and justice would ebb away.

Despite statutes passed and republished over the previous half-century, the casual giving of livery by magnates and lesser men was a provocation and incitement to others and a significant accompaniment of violent wrangling. The government's desire to confine the practice to the king and his household and to lords and their domestic servants was not entirely successful, both because such restrictions ran counter to social and political need and also because their enforcement depended on the very men who gained most from their breach, either as employers or retainers.[171] Moreover, Henry VI was willing to license the granting of livery by pardoning those who, like John Hampton, a household official, or Sir Walter Devereux of Herefordshire, offended against the legislation.[172] Ineffectual resolutions and half-hearted enforcement would have little effect on a phenomenon which, though it could cement social and other relationships, might also lead, if unsupervised or unchecked, to oppression, injustice, and corruption. 'Mighty persons' with the cash, the inclination, and the following were able to maintain their own and their friends' quarrels, extend the means of pursuing them by calling on a wider body of sympathizers, and ultimately overawe sheriffs and other royal officials. When news reached Westminster in 1439 of the presence of retainers in the small Dorset town of Bridport, giving and receiving livery, badges, and cognisances in contravention of the statutes, Henry VI and his ministers had no doubt that divisions would be deepened and dissensions encouraged as a consequence.[173]

The general response of Henry's government to threats to public order lacked conviction, however. It is true that many commissions of inquiry and of oyer and terminer were issued regularly soon after the king came of age, and especially during 1438–41; but thereafter until 1450, their number declined whereas serious crime did not.[174] Moreover, commissions of oyer and terminer were issued to deal with offences in the northern counties with far less frequency after 1440 than before. Indeed, it became a rarity for the Cumbrian counties to figure at all in the records of the king's central courts or their regional commissions. Distance, aristocratic autonomy, and a preference for out-of-court settlements to the slower procedures implemented by royal justices and others who were often strangers to the region, provide part of the explanation.[175]

A number – perhaps a growing number – of cases were referred to the king's council, frequently because the normal machinery of law enforcement was paralysed or perverted by local forces. One Lancashire landowner was pestered by an esquire who was 'so grete kynred and alyed' in Lancashire that the law could provide no remedy; two other gentlemen had such an affinity and alliance in Yorkshire that their misdeeds could not be brought before the common law courts; and a Leicestershire man proved too poor and friendless to seek justice against his attackers and could only appeal directly to Henry and his council.[176] By 1443, the council was being asked to grapple with the Devon–Bonville dispute in the south-west, the archbishop of York's complaints from Yorkshire, and the disturbances at Hull.[177] Not surprisingly, in view of the prominent persons involved, it did so hesitantly and without noticeable success.

Others might prefer to appeal to the chancellor, who was the most dignified and authoritative of the officers of state. His speedier and more flexible procedures were grounded in a combination of common law and his own reason and sense of equity; but by mid-century much of his time was mortgaged to the unravelling of enfeoffment disputes – though admittedly they were the cause of a high proportion of violent crime among the nobility.[178] By the autumn of 1443, the city of Hereford was so disturbed that it was well nigh impossible to implement common law procedures in a case arising from the disruption of an inquisition *post mortem* after the death of the prominent gentleman John Abrahall; the culprits were summoned instead to wait on the chancellor, though they were required to answer for their behaviour before the council.[179]

Parliament, when it met, was an articulate forum of complaint, and by the end of 1449 the commons showed that they understood the wider implications of increasing violence. They pleaded with the king to consider

> howe that the honour, welthe and prosperite, of every Prynce reynyng uppon his people, stondith moost principally upon conservation of his peas, kepyng of Justice, and due execution of his lawes, withouten which no Roialme may long endure in quyete nor prosperite; and for lak herof, many Murdres, Manslaughters, Rapes, Roberies, Riottys, Affrayes and othur inconvenientes, gretter than afore, nowe late have growen within this your Roialme; . . .[180]

But Henry's parliaments rarely provided new or vigorous remedies and preferred to put their faith in existing legislation.[181] Edward I's statutes of Westminster and Winchester were, in truth, adequate enough if executed energetically, and loopholes which had appeared – as, for instance, when some of the legislation of Henry V's last parliament had lapsed on his death because it could not be renewed in his next parliament as had been intended – were carefully closed.[182] The only brand-new legislation relating to order and justice that passed through parliament between 1437 and 1446 dealt with false accusations by approvers (1444) and the perversion of legal procedure by delays or vexatious tactics. Approvers had long ago lost much of their credibility, and as a means of securing the conviction of actual lawbreakers they were fatally discredited; yet in discouraging the transfer of pleas from one shire court to another in the hope of securing a sympathetic hearing, the government was only prepared to concede a short trial period.[183] No action at all was taken in 1449 on a commons' petition which would have redefined the clerical class that could legitimately claim 'benefit of clergy'. The growth in education and the spread of literacy was extending this facility to an ever-widening class in late fourteenth- and early fifteenth-century England, and in 1449 the commons tried to restrict the number of people who might seek to avoid the full rigour of the law by claiming more lenient treatment in the ecclesiastical courts.

This proposal would merely have tackled the fringes of the problem of lawlessness, and yet the wary government contented itself with referring the proposal to the bishops.[184]

More concern was shown about the continuing tendency for local officials to be less than honest and conscientious in the performance of their duties, and the well-rehearsed problem of the sheriff was as serious as ever. Unpaid though he was, the English sheriff often encountered difficulty in recovering the costs incurred during his term of office; the temptation to resort to extortion and financial exploitation was, therefore, irresistible in some cases.[185] Moreover, many sheriffs were retainers or neighbours of magnates, and sometimes breakers of the law and the perpetrators of violence themselves.[186] The abbot and convent of Fountains complained bitterly of vexatious suits and distraints contrived by the sheriffs of Yorkshire, Westmorland, and Cumberland, and their officials; although there was room for argument about the justice of these actions, the oppressions and extortions of which the abbey also complained in August 1451 suggest that the king's officers were (to put it mildly) heavy-handed.[187] To judge by the cases of uncustomed exports and imports that came to light, customs officers were frequently ineffective and lacked diligence.[188]

The king's use of his prerogative of pardoning with characteristic abandon harmed, rather than promoted, respect for the law and helped to dislocate an already creaking judicial machine. It required perseverence, patience, and plain good luck to secure a judgement (let alone a conviction) in the courts of king's bench and common pleas, for by the mid-fifteenth century their machinery was hampered by long delays and the difficulty of enforcing summonses, as well as by the periodic abuses of maintenance, bribery, and threats.[189] 'A mountain of process and . . . a molehill of justice' is M. Blatcher's verdict on the workings of king's bench in the fifteenth century.[190] On top of this, Henry VI proved especially prone to forgive those of his servants and household officials who flouted the law relating to livery, but even treason was pardonable in his compassionate eyes, particularly in the years before 1450.[191] As R. L. Storey has concluded, 'some of the crimes which Henry pardoned were atrocious, and by admitting their perpetrators to his grace he not only appeared to condone them but openly admitted the powerlessness of his government'.[192] The near-revolutionary state of southern England in that year was in part a protest at the current level and nature of crime and especially at the inability of the régime to control it. Yet Cade's revolt was regarded by the government less as a symptom of the country's ills than as a treasonable uprising. Corrupt and oppressive officials were, it is true, proceeded against in the wake of the rising, but only reluctantly and as a cosmetic exercise to quell the rebels' anger; when it was safe to do so, Henry VI and his ministers resorted to repression.[193]

Recourse to arbitrators and referees or umpires ('Noumpers', as contemporaries quaintly called them) to resolve quarrels was not novel in the fifteenth century; indeed, as an extra-curial arrangement it had certain affinities in some cases with the blood-feud compensation-system popular in early medieval England and Wales. Although *wergild* had all but disappeared from the vocabulary of English common lawyers by Edward I's day, in Wales the comparable *galanas*-system survived in some corners of the land as an attenuated, antiquated phenomenon even beyond the middle ages. And the comparison with the tariff for wounds and slayings in a fifteenth-century 'warde, ordinance and dome' is striking.[194] The custom of resorting to arbitration in private, out-of-court settlements or awards, regulated by financial penalties, was kept alive and remained familiar to many disputants in the fifteenth century. During Henry VI's majority there appears to have been an increasing number of truly violent disputes submitted to agents of self-help rather than to tardy common law procedures or to the council or the chancellor; and they were not confined to frontier regions or areas of peculiar jurisdictions.[195] Many of these arbitrations, with recourse to an umpire if a solution acceptable to all parties did not emerge, were doubtless arranged at the informal 'love-days' which abounded in medieval England for the discussion and peaceful resolution of quarrels and disputes. Men with their counsellors or attorneys, and the agents of neighbouring jurisdictions, often met with the minimum of formalism to examine their differences. Thus, Lord and Lady Rivers attended a *dies amoris* between the earl of Devon and Lord Bonville at Colcomb (Devon) in 1451, though that particular feud was not so easily ended; and in the Welsh marches, a whole series of exclusive jurisdictions made 'love-days', usually held near the common border of adjacent lordships, a regular occurence.[196] If such meetings proved fruitless, then the matters in dispute might be submitted to an agreed arbitrator or panel of arbitrators.

This is a subject of legal, social, and political import that merits much closer study than it has so far received, particularly since a number of arbitration awards survive in private and local archives.[197] The popularity of the device in Henry VI's reign was symptomatic of the crumbling domestic order; it testifies also to the growing feebleness, unreliability, and delays of the normal judicial machinery of the state and to an awareness by some that they could better secure a fair and respected verdict by seeking the intervention of acceptable arbitrators who would deliver a judgement to which each side was bound by financial penalties or recognisances.[198] It was a somewhat primitive mechanism that had no sanction for its enforcement at law save that of financial loss for non-performance and none socially except the risk of renewed violence. Arbitrations were rarely buttressed by the common law in any but their monetary clauses, and hence such agreements were hardly successful in removing the root cause of a dispute.[199] Without engaging the cumbrous and slow-moving machinery of the law, there was little possibility of a permanent settlement of intractable problems. When strong doubts arose as to the impartiality of the king's courts themselves

– as happened in the 1440s – their most appealing virtue vanished.[200] The acceptance of arbitration as an acknowledged facility among the peace-keeping agencies of the realm was signalled by the seal of approval given to its procedure not only by the chancellor and the council, but also by parliament.[201] A decision of the 1439 assembly is significant in this respect: Bishop Alnwick's arbitration in a dispute between the dean and the chapter of Lincoln had earlier been accepted by both parties; now, Alnwick successfully petitioned that his award be authorized in perpetuity by parliament.[202]

The activities of the duke of York in 1450–52 were inspired by the same motives that moved his fellow magnates – personal resentment, ambition, jealousy – but they also capitalized on the popular recognition that Henry VI and his government fell far short of their obligation to ensure peace and justice throughout the realm. The treatment of the duke and his supporters was often partisan and vindictive, for the Lancastrian régime under the leadership of Edmund Beaufort was just as ready to bend judicial processes to its own purpose and to seek revenge more often than justice as it had been during Suffolk's rule.[203] The king himself may have been well-meaning, but he was also ineffectual and a blunderer by turns. The only indication that Henry recognized the dangers threatening his kingdom came in July 1453, when he announced plans to tour various parts of his realm in order to combat extortion, maintenance, riots, and other disorders, and to punish those responsible. He requested MPs to publicize his intentions when they returned to their constituencies.[204] Within a matter of weeks, however, he had been struck down by incapacitating illness.

Notes

1 Notably Herbert, thesis (Herefs., 1413–61); idem, in Griffiths, *Patronage, the crown and the provinces*, ch. 5; Blatcher, op. cit., (king's bench, 1488–89). The material from the king's bench indictments in Storey, *End of Lancaster*, is a rich *apéritif*. For a recent critique of approaches to this problem, see M. R. Weisser, *Crime and punishment in early modern Europe* (Hassocks, Sussex, 1979).

2 Above, pp. 250, 409; below, pp. 790ff.

3 *RP*, V, 236; above, p. 528.

4 Above, p. 402.

5 Griffiths, *Speculum*, XLIII (1968), 589–632; Storey, *End of Lancaster*, ch. V; above, p. 132. Lesser men were also involved: witness the forcible dispossession by two Yorkshire gentlemen and their affinity in November 1438 (PRO, E28/61/15).

6 Bennett, thesis, passim. Dr Bennett also allowed me to see his unpublished paper, 'Power, patronage and political crime in late mediaeval England: the rise of the Stanleys in the north-west'. For the quotation, see the complaint to the king's council of Sir John Holand against Harry Kyghley, esquire,

in Lancashire in 1438 (PRO, E28/59/19). For a similar armed disseisin in Cheshire, see ibid. 60/55 (1439).

7 Storey, *End of Lancaster*, pp. 150-1.

8 Below pp. 577ff.

9 Above p. 339. For soldiers returning from Normandy 'in great necessity as starving beggars', see McFarlane, *Nobility*, p. 27, citing PRO, PCC Stokton f. 13-14.

10 Above, pp. 423ff.

11 *London Chrons.*, pp. 154-5; *Brut*, p. 509.

12 Postan in *English trade*, pp. 114-18, 124, 127-9; below, p. 790.

13 Post, *JSA*, V (1977), 418-28. John Cade established his headquarters in one of the Southwark inns (below, p. 614).

14 'Benet's Chron.', p. 188; *London Chrons.*, p. 154; Flenley, p. 102; *Brut*, p. 509.

15 *PPC*, V, 278.

16 Below, pp. 624, 690.

17 e.g., *CPR, 1436–41*, p. 412.

18 ibid., p. 278; H. S. Bennett, *Chaucer and the fifteenth century* (Oxford, 1947), pp. 116-18.

19 Barron, thesis, passim; Peake, thesis, pp. 19-20.

20 Above, p. 169.

21 Above, p. 554.

22 Below, pp. 690-1.

23 'Benet's Chron.', pp. 187-8. To judge by the detail given, this unknown chronicler was probably at Oxford at the time. For Cambridge's students, see below, n. 29. Cf. B. A. Hanawalt, 'Violent death in fourteenth- and early fifteenth-century England', *Compar. Studies in Soc. and Hist.*, XVIII (1976), 304.

24 Storey, *End of Lancaster*, pp. 220-4; *PPC*, V, 225, 231. Nor ought the dearth and disease suffered widely in 1438–39 be forgotten (*Brut*, pp. 472-73 [York and the north], 507; *Great Chron.*, p. 174; *Chron. of London*, p. 173; Flenley, p. 114). For details of the York dispute, see R. B. Dobson (ed.), *York city chamberlains' account rolls, 1396–1500* (Surtees soc., CXCII, 1980), pp. 37-58.

25 Below, p. 644; *EHL*, pp. 355-6.

26 Storey, *End of Lancaster*, pp. 228-30, and more fully in Herbert, thesis, pp. 107ff; below, p. 695.

27 *CPR, 1436–41*, p. 505; ibid., *1441–46*, pp. 180, 305; *PPC*, V, 191; Griffiths, *Speculum*, XLIII (1968), 597ff. For the Grey lands in Northants., including the county town, see Jack, *Grey valor*, pp. 66-78.

28 Flenley, p. 123. Cf. the Norwich mayoral elections of 1433 and 1437 (Storey, *End of Lancaster*, pp. 219-20; W. J. Blake, 'Thomas Wetherby', *Norf. Arch.*, XXXII [1961], 63-4).

29 Virgoe, *BIHR*, XLVI (1973), 95-101, with the quotations on pp. 100-1 (from BL, Eg. Roll 8792). A not dissimilar situation arose at the election at Huntingdon in October 1450, though no magnates intervened (J. G. Edwards, 'The Huntingdonshire parliamentary election of 1450', in *Essays to Wilkinson*, pp. 383-95; Wedgwood, *Register*, pp. cii-civ).

30 Herbert, thesis, ch. IV, VIII; idem, in Griffiths, *Patronage, the crown and the provinces*, ch. 5; above, p. 566. For Welshman involved in riots at

Tewkesbury in 1437, see *CPR, 1436–41*, p. 226. See, in general, Griffiths, 'Wales and the marches', pp. 154-8.

31 e.g., *CPR, 1441–46*, p. 290 (Suffolk, 1444), 466 (Herefs., 1446); ibid., *1436–41*, pp. 201 (Yorks., 1438), 268 (Salop, 1439); ibid., *1446–52*, p. 531 (Cornwall, 1451).

32 e.g., below, p. 574 (Devon); *CPR, 1436–41*, p. 475 (Suffolk); ibid., *1441–46*, p. 246 (Derbs.).

33 PRO, E28/63/31. The countess wanted the council to intervene because she felt that she had no hope of redress in a county where Nevilles and Lumleys were powerful figures.

34 e.g., *CPR, 1436–41*, p. 147 (Rutland, 1438).

35 *PPC*, V, 124 (Bury, 1440), 241-2; *CPR, 1441–46*, p. 133 (Fountains, 1443); below, p. 578 (Yorks.). See also *CPR, 1441–46*, pp. 287 (Dunstable priory, 1444), 340 (Northampton priory, 1445); *RP*, V, 130 (Pontefract church, 1447); *CPR, 1446–52*, pp. 285 (Burton abbey, 1449), 320 (Barking abbey, 1450), 378 (Ramsey abbey, 1450), 476 (Axholme priory, 1451), 581 (Bristol abbey, 1452); ibid., *1452–61*, p. 48 (Abbey Dore, 1451); PRO, E28/71/23 (Buckfast abbey, *c.* 1437–43).

36 *CPR, 1441–46*, p. 292; PRO, E28/73/2 (Hartland, 1444); *CPR, 1441–46*, p. 42 (Basingwerk, 1442), 209 (Rowney, 1444).

37 ibid., p. 292; ibid., *1436–41*, p. 118 (1437). The latter charge had become something of an epidemic by 1449 (*CPR, 1446–52*, p. 302; *RP*, V, 152).

38 *CPR, 1436–41*, p. 569 (1440); below, p. 699. And at Westminster abbey (WA MS 13175).

39 *CCR, 1435–41*, p. 118; see also ibid., p. 197 (Kent, 1438).

40 ibid., p. 385; 'Benet's Chron.', p. 187; *English Chron.*, pp. 56-7; *EHL*, p. 339; *Brut*, pp. 476, 508; *London Chrons.*, pp. 147, 153-4; *Chron. of London*, p. 173; Flenley, pp. 101, 114; *Three Chrons.*, p. 63; *CPR, 1436–41*, p. 426; W. W. Shirley (ed.), *Fasciculi Zizaniorum* (RS, 1858), pp. 370-82, 501-5 (for his views). Wyche's reputation soared when his prediction that the postern gate of the Tower of London would collapse came true (*Great Chron.*, pp. 174-5). See Thomson, *Later lollards*, pp. 148-50.

41 *PPC*, V, 40-3. For a few other incidents in London and its environs in 1451–52, see *CPR, 1446–52*, pp. 440, 584; ibid., *1452–61*, p. 55.

42 *CFR, 1436–42*, p. 212 (Kent, 1441).

43 PRO, E28/60/66 (11 May 1439).

44 *CPR, 1441–46*, p. 370 (Suffolk, 1445).

45 ibid; *CPR, 1436–41*, p. 101; below, p. 643.

46 *RP*, V, 168; Wedgwood, *Biographies*, p. 662. The assault may have been an incident in a northern feud, because Parr's attackers were Bellinghams, a Cumberland and Northumberland family.

47 For attacks on household officials, see below, pp. 639ff; *CPR, 1452–61*, p. 58 (1452).

48 See, in general, Jack, thesis, pp. 23, 333-41; Roskell, *1422*, pp. 176-7; *GEC*, VI, 155-8. Grey was born in about 1362.

49 Jack, *Grey valor*, p. 34 and n. 92; *GEC*, V, 253-4, 199-200. The marriage took place before December 1400. The peerage preserved the name of Cornwall's recently-acquired manor in Herefs. It is ironic that in 1413 Lord Grey's son John married Fanhope's stepdaughter, Constance, the daughter of Elizabeth of Lancaster and her second husband, John Holand, duke of Exeter. Constance died in 1437, though after the rupture between her

husband's father and her own stepfather; but some bitterness over property may have played a part in the subsequent discord (*GEC*, VI, 159; V, 199-200).

50 He had been MP for Beds. in 1433 and 1437 (Wedgwood, *Biographies*, pp. 931-2; Roskell, *Speakers*, p. 259; Roskell, *Beds. Hist. Record Soc.*, XXXVIII [1958], 18-19). Fanhope owned estates in Shropshire, the Wenlocks' home county; Sir Thomas Wenlock had served with Fanhope in France (ibid., p. 16).

51 Roskell, *Speakers*, p. 370; idem, *1422*, pp. 234-5 (for Waweton).

52 *CPR, 1436–41*, pp. 142, 246; *CCR, 1435–41*, p. 186.

53 Jack, *Grey valor*, pp. 24-5. See Roskell, *Speakers*, pp. 422, 207-8; idem, *1422*, p. 193, for Hunt. The two Beds. MPs in 1439–40, John Wenlock and William Peck, were both Fanhope's associates (Roskell, *Beds. Hist. Record Soc.*, XXXVIII [1958], 18-19).

54 The renewal of violence between the two magnates may have been caused by property disputes concerning Elizabeth of Lancaster's inheritance; Sir John Grey died in August 1439 and his and Constance's son, Edmund, took livery of his inheritance in October 1440; Fanhope had his own claims as the widower of Elizabeth of Lancaster. See above, n. 49.

55 *Great Chron.*, p. 174; *Brut*, p. 507; Giles, pp. 17-18; PRO, E28/59/49-50. The chroniclers differ in their estimates of the dead and wounded.

56 ibid.; *CPR, 1436–41*, p. 246; PRO, E175/4/5 m. 3d; Roskell, *1422*, pp. 176-7.

57 *CPR, 1436–41*, pp. 246, 282; PRO, E28/59/52.

58 *CPR, 1436–41*, p. 282. In 1442 Fanhope was created Baron Milbroke, after another manor he had recently acquired (*GEC*, V, 200).

59 *GEC*, II, 131-3; Ross, *Estates and finances of Beauchamp*, pp. 4-5. For Elizabeth's household account (preserved at Longleat), see C. D. Ross, 'The household accounts of Elizabeth Berkeley, countess of Warwick, 1420–1', *TBGAS*, LXX (1951), 81-105. The Lisle estate retained its administrative identity until Countess Elizabeth's death in 1422 (Ross, *Estates and finances of Beauchamp*, pp. 6-7). A valor of the barony, compiled while it was in Warwick's possession and indicating that it was worth about £550–£600 *per annum*, is PRO, SC11/18/42, for which see McFarlane, *Nobility*, pp. 197-8.

60 Ross, *TBGAS*, LXX (1951), 82-3; *GEC*, II, 132-3; WarwsRO, Warwick castle MS 373. Warwick had actually seized Berkeley castle by 1420, and after his wife's death tried to get more of the Berkeley manors (Ross, *TBGAS*, LXX [1951], 83, 86; McFarlane, *Nobility*, p. 119). James Berkeley was knighted in May 1426. The dispute is traced in J. Smyth, *Lives of the Berkeleys*, ed. J. Maclean (2 vols., Gloucester, 1883), II, 41ff., on which is based J. H. Cooke, 'On the great Berkeley law-suit of the 15th and 16th centuries', *TBGAS*, III (1878–79), 305-24 (with a pedigree facing 305).

61 *GCH*, III, 193-4. For the inscription, see *GEC*, VIII, 55 n. (f).

62 Ross, *Estates and finances of Beauchamp*, p. 19 and n. 1. The most recent full commentary on the Shrewsbury involvement in the dispute is Pollard, thesis, pp. 38-49.

63 *CCR, 1435–41*, pp. 224, 325, 464; ibid., *1441–47*, p. 60.

64 PRO, E28/74/10; Pollard, thesis, pp. 38-49.

65 Storey, *End of Lancaster*, p. 91 n. ; Smyth, op. cit., II, 65-8. For Berkeley's arrest in the autumn of 1451, see Flenley, p. 139.

66 *CPR, 1446–52*, p. 511; *CCR, 1447–54*, p. 325.

67 Cooke, *TBGAS*, III (1878–79), 310-12; *GEC*, VIII, 55.

68 See, in general, Storey, *End of Lancaster*, pp. 84-92; Lander, *BJRL*, XLIII (1960), 59ff; M. Cherry, 'The Courtenay earls of Devon: the formation and disintegration of a late mediaeval aristocratic affinity', *Southern Hist.*, I, (1979), 71-97.

69 Storey, *End of Lancaster*, p. 165; *CPR, 1446–52*, p. 526; ibid., *1452–61*, p. 91. For further life grants in Devon, see ibid., p. 18 (7 September 1452). For the Devon–Bonville dispute, see now M. Cherry, 'The struggle for power in mid-fifteenth-century Devonshire', in Griffiths, *Patronage, the crown and the provinces*, ch. 6.

70 *CPR, 1436–41*, p. 133. Bonville also received 40 marks *per annum* (*CCR, 1435–42*, p. 195). For the stewardship in Cornwall, see J. Hatcher, *Rural economy and society in the duchy of Cornwall, 1300–1500* (Cambridge, 1970), pp. 42-6.

71 *CPR, 1436–41*, p. 222.

72 ibid., pp. 314, 448; Wedgwood, *Biographies*, p. 158. Carminow had abducted one of Bonville's wards in 1438.

73 Several commissions of oyer and terminer were despatched to the south-west between October 1439 and September 1440 (*CPR, 1436–41*, pp. 370, 450, 500).

74 A councillor, Sir John Stourton, was accordingly sent to Devon to receive a promise from the earl that he would behave himself in future (*CCR, 1435–42*, p. 396; PRO, E28/65/54; Storey, *End of Lancaster*, p. 87).

75 The stewardship was given to Devon for as long as it remained in the king's hands (*CPR, 1436–41*, p. 532).

76 Cf. the ostensibly subtle differences in constitutional detail between the appointments of York and Somerset as lieutenant-general of France in 1443 (above, p. 467).

77 PRO, E28/68/22 (14 May).

78 *PPC*, V, 157, 159, 163, 173, 408. Some suspected that Chetwynd jumped too readily to the conclusion that the attackers were Devon's men. Others thought they belonged to John Beaufort, earl of Somerset, who was Devon's father-in-law (*GEC*, IV, 326-7). The arbitration was to be publicly announced by 1 April 1442 (not 1 March, as in Storey, *End of Lancaster*, p. 188).

79 PRO, E404/59/119; E101/71/914; Vale, *Gascony*, p. 245. Bonville's retainer, Sir Philip Chetwynd, had already been made mayor of Bayonne for 7 years in November 1441, though he did not embark for Gascony until the end of August 1442 (ibid., pp. 120, 127). Other of Bonville's men were set at bail by the council on 18 October 1442 (*PPC*, V, 219).

80 Vale, *Gascony*, p. 120; Storey, *End of Lancaster*, p. 188.

81 *CPR, 1441–46*, p. 136. Storey, *End of Lancaster*, p. 188, is mistaken in saying that he left in the early summer of 1444.

82 *CPR, 1441–46*, p. 218. The debts presumably covered the recognisances for good behaviour that had been extracted from Devon at various times in the past (e.g., *PPC*, V, 408; *CCR, 1435–41*, p. 396). Devon's Beaufort connections (above, n. 78) doubtless assisted his rehabilitation.

83 See above, p. 567.

84 Below, pp. 691-2.

85 PRO, KB9/105; 'Benet's Chron.', p. 205. York had a force of 2,000 with

him; for Robert Hungerford, Lord Moleyns, another local landowner, see below, pp. 587-90.

86 'Benet's Chron.', p. 205; Storey, *End of Lancaster*, p. 92. This episode helped to poison relations between Wiltshire and York (above, p. 423).

87 *CPR, 1446–52*, p. 525. This pardon was not extended to Devon or Cobham (Storey, *End of Lancaster*, p. 101 and n. 20). For the rumour that Cobham prompted the casting of a spell over Henry VI which led to his illness in August 1453, see ibid., p. 136 (based on PRO, KB9/273/7).

88 Storey, *End of Lancaster*, pp. 98-9.

89 *CPR, 1446–52*, p. 526; Roskell, *1422*, pp. 153-5.

90 Witchell, thesis, pp. 242-53; Nigota, thesis, pp. 509-17.

91 Above, p. 70. For Kemp's Kentish origins, see Witchell, thesis, ch. I; Nigota, thesis, ch. I.

92 ibid., ch. VI; Witchell, thesis, pp. 198ff.; Gascoigne, pp. 38, 194-5. Gascoigne based part of his critique on Kemp's provision of 3 Italians to 4 prebends during 1427–37; Gascoigne's own provision to the chancellor-ship of York a week after Kemp's translation to Canterbury was disdainfully refused, but coming as it did at that juncture, it may have had some bearing on his hostility to the archbishop (Le Neve, VI, 9, 34, 55, 61, 65).

93 Witchell, thesis, p. 252 (from Borthwick Institute, York, Reg. Kemp, f. 97). See W. Ullmann, 'Eugenius IV, Cardinal Kemp, and Archbishop Chichele', in J. A. Watt, J. B. Morrall, F. X. Martin (eds.), *Mediaeval studies presented to A. Gwynn* (Dublin, 1961), pp. 359-83.

94 Witchell, thesis, pp. 211-13; Nigota, thesis, p. 392; Emden, *Oxford*, II, 1347–49. For his employment of Neville retainers in his temporal administration, see Nigota, thesis, pp. 502-7.

95 Emden, *Cambridge*, p. 450; Witchell, thesis, p. 251. When Kemp's commissioners visited the deanery of Coupland (Westmor.) in Percy country in 1442, they were attacked (Nigota, thesis, pp. 491-3).

96 Witchell, thesis, pp. 250-1; Nigota, thesis, pp. 502-7; above, p. 446. The documents relevant to this significant grant are PRO, C66/454 m. 11-14; C47/21/11/3-4; E28/72, 80 (1 February 1444).

97 Somerville, op. cit., pp. 524-5; *Plumpton corr*, pp. 1, lxvi. Plumpton, whose father died in 1421, was born in 1404; he had been joint-steward, constable, and master-forester for life in survivorship since January 1439. The incidents are described in Witchell, thesis, pp. 244-53; and Nigota, thesis, pp. 509-17.

98 Stapleton, op. cit., pp. lx-lxi. The clashes are described, from diametrically opposed points of view, in reports to the council by Kemp and Plumpton. See in full ibid., pp. liv-lxii, as extracted from Sir Edward Plumpton's Coucher-book (now in Leeds RO), pp. 108ff, which was copied in the early seventeenth century from earlier materials. For a comment, see J. Taylor, 'The Plumpton letters, 1416–1552', *Northern Hist.*, X (1975), 72-87.

99 *CPR, 1441–46*, p. 77 (12 February), 203 (July 1443).

100 *PPC*, V, 268, 273, 309; *CCR, 1441–47*, p. 98. Percy tenants like Sir William Normanville, Sir John Salvin, Sir Alexander Neville and his son William, Christopher Spencer, and John Hothom were summoned, along with Plumpton, to the council on 11 May; Sir John Pennington had already been interrogated before the chancellor. ibid.; *PPC*, V, 269; *CCR, 1441–47*, pp. 145-6. See Bean, *Percies*, pp. 92 n. 1, 96-7, for these Percy annuitants.

101 *PPC*, V, 273, 275; *CCR, 1441–47*, pp. 143-4, 145. Dorset and Willoughby were paid their expenses on 20 May (PRO, E404/59/223).

102 For their subsequent activities, see below, p. 583. For an incident in Beverley in the summer of 1444, see *CPR, 1441–46*, p. 291; and for Percy outrages in Northumberland, Cumberland, and Westmorland in 1444, *CCR, 1447–54*, p. 217.

103 Above, p. 349.

104 Cf. R. L. Storey's estimate of Kemp's character in *End of Lancaster*, p. 82. See also Witchell, thesis, pp. 252-3.

105 *GEC*, III, 552-3; Friedrichs, thesis, passim; Price, thesis, passim. For his term as treasurer (1433–43), see above, p. 377. His income had more than doubled between 1429 and 1447 (to £2,263 *per annum*): Friedrichs, thesis, p. 192.

106 These incidents are fully described in Virgoe, *BJRL*, LV (1973), 459-82. See also the comments in R. L. Storey, 'Lincolnshire and the wars of the roses', *Nott. Med. St.*, XIV (1970), 76-8; Friedrichs, thesis, pp. 242-6, 262-5.

107 Virgoe, *BJRL*, LV (1973), 460; Friedrichs, thesis, pp. 34, 241. A John Tailboys was in Cromwell's employ as late as 1444–46 (Price, thesis, p. 239).

108 Virgoe, *BJRL*, LV (1973), 462, 464; above, p. 576.

109 Willoughby (d. 1452) had married Maud Stanhope, one of Cromwell's nieces and co-heiresses; both men had been in the service of Thomas, duke of Clarence, and Willoughby's nephew, William Willoughby, was one of Cromwell's annuitants (Friedrichs, thesis, p. 23; Virgoe, *BJRL*, LV [1973], 464 n. 3).

110 Tailboys's attacks on Dymocke took place in March 1448 (ibid., p. 464). Storey, *Nott. Med. St.*, XIV (1970), 68, perhaps exaggerates Welles's connection with the court in the 1440s: his contribution to Lancastrian government was primarily as lieutenant of Ireland in 1438–42 and deputy-captain of Calais after 1451. His son also married Lord Willoughby's daughter and heiress. Virgoe, *BJRL*, LV (1973), 465 n. 2; above, p. 413. For East Anglia, see below, pp. 584ff.

111 Virgoe, *BJRL*, LV (1973), 465. Some of the evidence for the polarization of opinion (Gairdner, *PL*, I, 96-8; *PPC*, VI, 336-7) is imprecisely dated, but all commentators agree that it belongs to 1448 or 1449: Storey, *Nott. Med. St.*, XIV (1970), 76-8; Virgoe, *BJRL*, LV (1973), 463, 465 n. 2; Friedrichs, thesis, pp. 242-5.

112 Above, p. 678. Storey, *Nott. Med. St.*, XIV (1970), 78, misdates the assault on Cromwell to 1450.

113 Above, p. 689. With Suffolk removed, Cromwell became chamberlain of the king's household in March 1451. For his links with York, see below, p. 673; Friedrichs, thesis, pp. 252-6.

114 This point is well made in ibid., pp. 27-8, 32-7, 54, 62-4, 67-8, 72-4, 81, 145-8. Cromwell's wife's grandmother was a sister of Ralph Neville, earl of Westmorland, who married Joan Beaufort and fathered Richard Neville, earl of Salisbury (ibid., p. 26).

115 Griffiths, *Speculum*, XLIII (1968), 589-632 (with the implications of the marriage on 593-4, 606-8); Storey, *End of Lancaster*, pp. 130, 143.

116 Storey, *Nott. Med. St.*, XIV (1970), 69.

117 Above, p. 578. Perhaps because of his presence on the council in the early

1440s, Northumberland's siege mentality in the north of England may have been insufficiently recognized by historians.

118 This 'battle' is fully described in Griffiths, *Speculum*, XLIII (1968), 597-602. Thomas and Richard were also the Percy 'trouble-shooters' in the dispute with Archbishop Kemp (above, p. 579). For the impact of the Percy–Neville struggle on the city of York, see Dobson, *York chamberlains' account rolls*, pp. 89-98.

119 Fanhope, like Cromwell and Welles, had served the duke of Clarence and he was an old friend of Cromwell's (Friedrichs, thesis, pp. 151-2).

120 Both Grey and Exeter were descended from Elizabeth; a delay in Cromwell securing Ampthill in 1444 may have been due to a counter-claim by John, duke of Exeter (Friedrichs, thesis, pp. 266-9). For Grey, see Jack, *Grey valor*, pp. 34-5, 105 n. 4; above, pp. 570-2.

121 The violence, in which £2,000-worth of furnishings were taken by Exeter's men, occurred after Exeter and Cromwell had agreed on 15 July 1452 to submit to arbitration by 11 November: *CCR, 1447–54*, pp. 360, 398; Griffiths, *Speculum*, XLIII (1968), 607-8; Friedrichs, thesis, pp. 177, 266-9, quoting PRO, E13/145B/78. Grey's reasons for supporting Cromwell are unclear: he may have had a personal preference for the elderly magnate, or he may have felt his own and Exeter's claims to be slight. It is possible that his support was bought by Cromwell with a promise that Grey would be allowed to buy Ampthill before Cromwell's death; the reversion was granted to him in November 1454 for 6,500 marks, which was eventually fully paid in 1473 (Jack, *Grey valor*, pp. 34-5; Friedrichs, thesis, pp. 214-15). For the earlier enmity between Grey's grandfather and Fanhope, see above, p. 570.

122 'Benet's Chron.', p. 210, which says that the arrests took place on 4 July. Cromwell and Grey had also resorted to violence in an attempt to force a decision in their favour in a plea of novel disseisin at Westminster in 1453.

123 It should be noted that Exeter's assault on Ampthill in 1453 was led by Richard Caudray, dean of St Martin-le-Grand, London, since 1435. One of Archbishop Kemp's servants, he was an executor of John, duke of Exeter in 1447 and a chaplain who had been closely connected with the royal household since Henry V's day; between 1431 and 1448 he was warden of King's Hall, Cambridge (PRO, E13/145B/78; Emden, *Cambridge*, pp. 126-7; Cobban, op. cit., p. 285). For his role as clerk of the council during 1421–35, see A. L. Brown, *The early history of the clerkship of the council* (Glasgow, 1969), pp. 20-9.

124 For loans, totalling £1,800, which Cromwell made in 1453 to Salisbury, his two sons (Warwick and Thomas Neville), and their clients, perhaps as the price of the marriage between Thomas and Maud Stanhope, see Friedrichs, thesis p. 209 (from Magdalen College, Oxford, Misc. MS 303).

125 The disturbances in the city of Norwich are the only episodes to receive much attention from contemporary chroniclers (Storey, *End of Lancaster*, pp. 217-25).

126 See, in general, ibid., pp. 54-7. For the kind of offences perpetrated, see *PL*, II, 525-8.

127 ibid., I, 222. Cf. ibid., II, 518 (before 1444).

128 ibid., I, 236. In 1440 the abbot of Bury likewise regarded Suffolk as his 'grete lord' (*PPC*, V, 124).

129 *PL*, I, 147-8. For the phrase 'heavy lord', see *CCR, 1454–61*, p. 77 (referring to Suffolk's activities in 1431); and 'hard, unfavourable and unloving lord', in Storey, *End of Lancaster*, p. 218 (from PRO, KB9/267/23 [referring to 1441]).

130 *GEC*, XII, i, 443-8; Kingsford, *Prejudice and promise*, ch. VI; Somerville, op. cit., I, 420.

131 Above, p. 303. For Tuddenham, see Wedgwood, *Biographies*, pp. 880-1; Somerville, op. cit., I, 420-1, 492, 594. He was joint-steward (with Suffolk) of the northern parts of the duchy of Lancaster and of Lancashire for life from September 1443; he had been steward of the duchy estates in Norfolk, Suffolk, and Cambridgeshire since 1425.

132 *PL*, I, 220. For Heydon, see Wedgwood, *Biographies*, pp. 452-3. He was in the duchy of Lancaster's service by 1437 (as deputy-steward of the southern parts) and deputized for Suffolk and Tuddenham as chief steward of the northern parts in 1444–45; he and Tuddenham were joint-steward of the duchy estates in East Anglia for life from November 1443 (Somerville, op. cit., I, 425, 430, 453, 594). It says something of Suffolk's circle that Tuddenham deserted his wife too (Jacob, *Essays to Feiling*, p. 76).

133 For Wymondham (or Wyndham), see Wedgwood, *Biographies*, pp. 976-7; *PL*, I, 224-5, 235, 232 (in association with Heydon); for Prentis, *PL*, II, 33; I, 239; and for Ulveston, Wedgwood, *Biographies*, p. 895.

134 Storey, *End of Lancaster*, p. 54; for Fastolf, see above, p. 515.

135 *PL*, II, 83 (by Tuddenham and Heydon), 524.

136 Wedgwood, *Biographies*, p. 452; Storey, *End of Lancaster*, pp. 217-25; Blake, *Norf. Arch.*, XXXII (1961), 63, 66-71; above, p. 147.

137 See *PL*, II, 528-30, 50-1, for a sample of the alleged behaviour of Tuddenham and Heydon.

138 *GEC*, IX, 607-8. He spent much of his early manhood soldiering and on diplomatic missions; and for his connection with Gloucester, see above, p. 204.

139 *PL*, II, 22 (1 November 1440); *CPR, 1436–41*, pp. 413, 381; Storey, *End of Lancaster*, pp. 78-9, 226. Wingfield had been patronized by the late duke of Norfolk and become chief steward for life for the son. For the Lyston episode, see also PRO, E403/751 m. 5; E28/65/26; *CPR, 1436–41*, pp. 475, 395; *CCR, 1435–41*, p. 420. Wingfield secured a pardon on 11 November 1440.

140 Storey, *End of Lancaster*, pp. 226-7; *CPR, 1441–46*, pp. 337, 290; *CCR, 1441–47*, pp. 196, 213. Norfolk had been the first to resort to force by attacking Wingfield's house at Letheringham in 1443 and purloining goods worth £5,000. For commissions of oyer and terminer in Suffolk in February 1448 and in Norfolk the following July, see *CPR, 1446–52*, pp. 186, 188.

141 *GEC*, VI, 618-20; IX, 42-3; Kirby, thesis, pp. 91-2; above, p. 34. Through his wife, Elizabeth Moleyns, whom he married before 1440, Robert acquired lands in Oxon., Bucks., and Berks.

142 *PL*, II, 29-30, 53; I, 55-6, 233-4.

143 This celebrated dispute is fully reported in the *Paston Letters*. See the commentary in H. S. Bennett, *The Pastons and their England* (Cambridge, 1951), pp. 5-8; Kirby, thesis, pp. 57-8.

144 *PL*, I, 51-3 (Paston's petition to the king and lords in parliament before 16 July 1449). Cf. ibid., pp. 55-6 (a similar petition to the chancellor in 1450), 225, 227-32; II, 38-9, 519-20, 521.

145 ibid., II, 38-9, 41, 45.
146 Storey, *End of Lancaster*, p. 56; Gairdner, *PL*, II, 171; *PL*, I, 57.
147 *CPR, 1446–52*, pp. 592, 595. Men like Thomas Daniel (sheriff in 1446–47), Philip Wentworth (1447–48), Giles St Lo (1448–49), John Say (1449–50) (Wedgwood, *Biographies*, pp. 253-5, 934-5, 744-6; PRO, E404/46/211; 63/4 [St Lo]).
148 *PL*, II, 524 (the opinion of Justice William Yelverton, one of Norfolk's councillors), 51, 523.
149 Below, p. 689.
150 *PL*, II, 47-51, 53, 525-7; it was rumoured that Tuddenham and Heydon were prepared to offer more than £1,000 to secure York's good lordship. Lord Moleyns's support for Devon in the west country in 1451 is explained by local circumstances and cannot be regarded as a *rapprochement* with York (above, p. 576).
151 Storey, *End of Lancaster*, pp. 56-7 (quoting PRO, KB9/267/1-42), 246 n. 5.
152 *PL*, II, 525, 529.
153 ibid., pp. 60-2; 63; Storey, *End of Lancaster*, p. 78.
154 *PL*, I, 238-41; II, 68, 83. A case in which Fastolf was involved could be described by June 1451 as 'ruled by' Tuddenham and Heydon (HL, Newhall MS IX). For efforts to stiffen the resolve of the commission and parliament in 1451 to act against Suffolk's former friends, see *PL*, II, 525-30.
155 *PL*, I, 57; *GEC*, XI, 504-7. Scales was born in 1399.
156 *PL*, I, 48, 62-3; for Scales and York, see above, p. 305.
157 *PL*, I, 60-3, 75. Scales and Sir Miles Stapleton received custody of Suffolk's lands in 1451 (*GEC*, XI, 504-7). Stapleton married in 1438 Catherine, daughter of Suffolk's brother, Sir Thomas de la Pole (Wedgwood, *Biographies*, pp. 804-5).
158 Gairdner, *PL*, II, 258-9 (redated by Storey, *End of Lancaster*, p. 79, to February 1451).
159 *PL*, I, 69 (4 March 1451).
160 For Scales's links with John Paston and his wish to compose differences, see ibid., pp. 60-1, 77, 81, 524-5, 34-5.
161 *GEC*, X, 236-9. Several of Oxford's letters in the Paston collection were written at one or other of these two manors.
162 Gairdner, *PL*, II, 165-6.
163 *PL*, I, 57; II, 525, 529, 42-4, 54-5, 56-7, 48, 53. For Oxford's friendly relations with Paston, see ibid., II, 70, 84, 29. He had also accompanied York on his expedition to France in 1441 and he was related, through his wife, Elizabeth Howard, to the Mowbrays (*GEC*, X, 236-9).
164 *PL*, I, 57; II, 50-1.
165 *PL*, II, 54-5; Gairdner, *PL*, II, 258-60 (*recte* February 1451). For his influence on the nomination of sheriffs, see *PL*, II, 83 (1450–53); and his servants' supposed intimidation of the Suffolk parliamentary election in 1453 (which the duke denied), *PPC*, VI, 183 (with a comment in Virgoe, thesis, pp. 309-11).
166 *PL*, II, 76-7. Norfolk was elected to the order of the garter on 28 May 1451 (*GEC*, IX, 607-8).
167 *PL*, I, 69.
168 ibid., 39. On 6 September 1452, Fastolf entered into a £1,000 recognisance

to appear before the council, which he did on 6 November 1453 and secured a release (*CCR, 1447–54*, p. 398).

169 *PL*, I, 64-6; II, 80-1; *RP*, V, 269; Storey, *End of Lancaster*, p. 79; above, p. 591. Norfolk himself received on 20 March 1452 a pardon for all trespasses (*CPR, 1446–52*, p. 530). The treason charges against Nowell were laid by a hostile jury in February 1453.

170 *PL*, I, 66-7. For Paston's service to the duke of Norfolk, see ibid., II, 23, 54-5, 83.

171 McFarlane, *Nobility*, pp. 106-7, 122-3. For the effect on public order of the granting of livery, see *CPR, 1441–46*, p. 180. A subsidiary aim of the legislation was to restrict the wearing of livery except in domestic and military contexts (ibid., *1436–41*, p. 480).

172 ibid., p. 490 (Hampton, 1440); Herbert, thesis, pp. 237, 240-1. See also *CPR, 1441–46*, pp. 396 (1446, Thomas Wesenham, a king's esquire and household servant), 408 (1446, John St Lo, an esquire for the body); ibid., *1446–52*, p. 147 (1448, John Somerset, the king's doctor and mentor).

173 *HMC*, VI (1877), 496-7. The king ordered that such activities should cease; if they did not, the names of those responsible were to be sent to Westminster. See also *RP*, V, 16 (Derbs., 1439). For the phrase 'mighti lordship', see *CCR, 1447–54*, p. 325 (1449).

174 *CPR, 1436–52*, passim. For the various commissions, especially of oyer and terminer, whose frequency was often a sign of a breakdown in government or the institutions of justice, see Avrutick, thesis, pp. 13-18.

175 ibid., pp. 210-17.

176 PRO, E28/59/19 (February 1438); 61/15 (1438-39); 68/47 (1441). Cf. ibid., 62/47 (1439); 70/45 (1442); ShakesBT, DR 98/477 (in which the duke of Warwick is said to have been 'so mighti and of so muche strength that by the mean of your comon lawe ayene him thay [Richard Verney and his wife] may have no remedie').

177 Above, pp. 566, 575, 578.

178 Avery, *BIHR*, XLII (1969), 130-45; and more fully in idem, thesis, passim. Increasing recourse to the chancellor in the fifteenth century helped to formalize the use of the supreme court of exchequer chamber in dealing with cases of exceptional difficulty, doubt, or delay. Henry VI's reign saw its most significant development. M. Hemmant, 'The exchequer chamber, being the assembly of all the judges of England for matters of law' (London PhD thesis, 1929), pp. 39-44, 55-6.

179 PRO, E28/71/54 (January 1444).

180 *RP*, V, 200.

181 Cf. in the Welsh context, Griffiths, 'Wales and the marches', p. 157.

182 *RP*, V, 28 (1439), 106 (1444); *PPC*, V, 83 (1437), 212 (1442); *CCR, 1441–47*, p. 224 (1444).

183 *RP*, V, 106, 112. The innate caution of the government led it to warn specifically that a successful petition in an individual case need not automatically apply in other similar cases. Cf. ibid., 111, 109.

184 ibid., 151; J. W. Adamson, 'The extent of literacy in England in the fifteenth and sixteenth centuries: notes and conjectures', *Library*, 4th ser., X (1929–30), 167-71. M. Gollancz ('The system of gaol delivery as illustrated in the extant gaol delivery rolls of the fifteenth century' [London MA thesis, 1936], pp. 234-5) has established that in Yorkshire and Devon in the Lancastrian period many convicted laymen demonstrated their ability to

read in order to qualify for benefit of clergy and thereby to save their life.

185 Jeffs, thesis, pp. 41-3, quoting PRO, C49/26/11, a bill prepared for the 1445 parliament and almost identical with that actually passed in 1455 (*RP*, V, 323-4). It attempted to control extortions by local officials as well as by those at the exchequer itself. For further details, see Jeffs, thesis, pp. 80-119, 146.

186 *RP*, V, 110 (1444), directed against bribery and extortion by sheriffs and their subordinates.

187 *CCR, 1447-54*, p. 220.

188 *CPR, 1436-41*, pp. 147, 372, 411, 413; ibid., *1441-46*, pp. 108, 369; *RP*, V, 200; *PPC*, VI, 50, 328; *CPR, 1446-52*, pp. 191, 536; ibid., *1452-61*, p. 123.

189 Herbert thesis, ch. V; Blatcher, op. cit., ch. IV-V; M. Hastings, *The court of common pleas in fifteenth-century England* (Ithaca, New York, 1947), ch. XV; Williams, *BIHR*, I (1923-24), 69-72.

190 Blatcher, thesis, p. 26.

191 Above, p. 249. For murder, see *CPR, 1436-41*, pp. 123, 125, 142, 171, 300, 406; ibid., *1441-46*, p. 438; ibid., *1446-52*, pp. 62, 121; for treason, ibid., *1436-41*, pp. 142, 548; ibid., *1441-46*, p. 278; ibid., *1446-52*, pp. 68, 255, 330, 420, 470, 507; ibid., *1452-61*, p. 17. For a detailed reconstruction of one such case, see C. A. F. Meekings, 'Thomas Kerver's case, 1444', *EHR*, XC(1975), 331-46. The pardon, dated 4 August 1444, was to be kept secret; its unfortunate effects on the judicial system may have been appreciated by the king's advisers.

192 See Storey, *End of Lancaster*, pp. 210-16, for the massive increase in royal pardoning after 1437, particularly by means of general pardons in 1437, 1446, and 1452 (with the quotation on p. 215). Complaints about the misuse of the royal right to pardon in criminal cases had been voiced in the fourteenth century, but nevertheless the reign of Henry VI appears exceptional (Blatcher, thesis, pp. 311-14; idem, *Kings bench*, p. 87).

193 Below, pp. 641ff.

194 DerbsRO, Vernon papers, Box 1/432. See R. R. Davies, 'The survival of the blood feud in mediaeval Wales', *History*, LIV (1969), 338-57 (esp. 354-7); its appropriateness in cases of violence between entire families, whereby kinship ties had a significant role in determining the course and length of a dispute, is well brought out.

195 Stapleton, op. cit., pp. li-lii (23 July 1435), from the Plumpton Cowcher Book, p. 102; also ibid., p. 100, for an earlier award (March 1432). Both refer to land disputes without apparent violence. See, in general, W. S. Holdsworth, *A history of English law*, vol. XIV (1964), 187-96.

196 DevonRO, Exeter receivers' accounts 13; Davies, *March of Wales*, pp. 245-8 (days of the march); Griffiths, 'Wales and the marches', pp. 154-5. See also SomsRO, DD/CC/110739/15 (*dies concordie* between Thomas Cheddar and the chapter of Wells), 14; DD/L/Box 1/17 [3] m. 2.

197 From Derbs., see DerbsRO, 410M/Box 14/488 (arbitration by Sir Thomas Stanley, controller of the king's household, between the Venables and Bulkeley families, September 1446); Vernon papers, Box 1/432 (by the duke of Buckingham between the Vernon and Gresley families, September 1455); *HMC, Rutland*, IV, 29 (by Lord Ferrers between Gresley and Vernons, 1447). From Warws. and Staffs., see ShakesBT, DR98/497A (by John Vampage and John Brown between the Verneys and the earl of

Warwick's executors, 1446). For Chesh., see JRL Ch. 1618 (by Sir Thomas Stanley between the abbot of Vale Royal and Randulf Wenere, 1446). For Beds.–Bucks., see NorthantsRO, Brudenell A. x. 3 (by Sir John Cheyne and others between Thomas Reynes and John Ansty, 1439). Many are referred to in peaceful circumstances, usually in the context of property and jurisdictional disputes (e.g., *CCR, 1435–42*, pp. 178, 235, 358; ibid., *1441–47*, pp. 138, 268; *PPC*, V, 225); others were concluded amidst more violent clashes (above, p. 569; *CCR, 1435–42*, p. 276; ibid., *1447–54*, pp. 66, 276, 355, 358).

198 Above, p. 595. For recognisances for future good behaviour in such circumstances, see *CCR, 1447–54*, pp. 398, 400, 411, 426, 442.

199 Holdsworth, op. cit., XIV, 187-96. If consequential deeds, etc., were concluded, they were enforceable at law, but not the original award in its entirety. See ShakesBT, DR98/497A.

200 Above, p. 595.

201 The chancellor sometimes helped by making the arrangements for an arbitration (*CCR, 1441–47*, p. 444). On other occasions, it was agreed that if an arbitration award was not made on time, then a dispute would be referred to the chancellor; at other times, the council authorized an arbitration. These arrangements (together with the official standing of some arbitrators), demonstrate men's preference for this swifter, less formal means of solving a dispute and the government's endorsement of its use (*CCR, 1447–54*, p. 66; ibid., *1441–47*, p. 138; *PPC*, V, 225; above n. 196). For an example of one party preferring the common law procedures to an arbitration authorized by the king, see S. A. Moore (ed.), *Letters and papers of John Shillingford, mayor of Exeter, 1447–50* (Camden Soc., 1871), pp. 133-5.

202 *RP*, V, 10.

203 Below, pp. 687ff.

204 *RP*, V, 236.

21   Cade's Rebellion, 1450

The rebellion led by John Cade occupies a prominent place in accounts of fifteenth-century English history, not least because contemporaries were shocked by it and chroniclers correspondingly dwelt on it at considerable length. Paradoxically, few historians have examined its course or estimated its significance in the light of advances in our understanding of late-Lancastrian England. Only one major study of the rising has ever been undertaken, and that by a German scholar almost a century ago; that apart, one has to rest content with a pamphlet published in 1950, and some minor revelations since then.[1] The principal events of the rising are well chronicled in these writings, and the statements of the rebels as to their aims are clearly rehearsed. But over the years, a number of other sources have come to light and our appreciation of the nature of English society in the south-east has been considerably enhanced. As a result, several questions need to be reopened and others, which were hardly identified by earlier writers, can now be tackled more satisfactorily.

A chronology

As a mass, popular movement, the rebellion appears to have begun in the woods and vales of south-west Kent towards the end of May 1450.[2] Before advancing to London in the second week of June, Kentishmen were reported to be assembling in the vicinity of Ashford and Appledore, and on Calehill heath, which lay a short distance north-west of Ashford and was the traditional meeting-place of the hundred of Calehill.[3] It was presumably while the rebels were in this area that John Cade was chosen as their leader, or 'captain', assuming the evocative name of John Mortimer. He tried energetically to extend their appeal elsewhere in Kent, but he was denied entry to Canterbury on 7 June, and his messages were treated cautiously in ports like Lydd, Rye, and Romney, which despatched scouts to inspect the rebel force as it moved towards the south coast.[4] The king and his ministers, who were then attending parliament at Leicester, had certainly been alerted by 6 June, for on that day a number of senior noblemen – the duke of Buckingham and the earls of Oxford, Devon, and Arundel – were commissioned to move against the Kentishmen and to arrest and punish them.[5] At the same time, parliament was adjourned, probably in a state of some alarm after receiving the news from Kent, and Henry VI quickly arranged to return to his capital.[6] A second commission was issued on the way, on 10 June at Newport Pagnell (Buckinghamshire), to Viscount Beaumont and Lords Scales, Rivers, Dudley, and Lovel, in order to reinforce the government's earlier response to the rising. These were older men, who either were closely associated with the governing group about the king or had spent long years in France fighting with Bedford and his successors.[7] But before these lords could raise the anticipated force of men, the Kentishmen had reached Blackheath, from which they could gaze northwards across the Thames to London itself. They had encamped there by 11 June; fortifying their position with stakes and ditches, they stayed at least a week, contemplating their next move, popularizing their cause, and making contact with persons of authority at Westminster.[8]

Meanwhile, by 12 June an advance party from Leicester had arrived in London, headed by some of those who had been instructed to suppress the rising a few days before, namely, Buckingham and Rivers. Henry was close behind, with a large company that included the archbishops of Canterbury and York, the dukes of Exeter and Norfolk, and several earls and barons; on the thirteenth the king lodged at St John's priory, Clerkenwell.[9] Two days later, messengers were despatched to the rebels to order them to disperse, and later the same day a delegation, consisting of the earl of Northumberland and Lords Scales and Lisle, rode to Blackheath to discover the precise strength of the insurgents. Henry VI planned to go himself next day (16 June) to confront the rebels, taking with him Buckingham, Exeter, and other magnates. The government's reaction to the rising so far was to suppress it with the king's and the magnates' retinues which had arrived from Leicester. It may have been the assessment of the rebels' strength brought back from Blackheath by Northumberland and the others which induced a change of attitude, for Henry's councillors now advised against the king himself crossing the Thames and persuaded him to send emissaries in his place.[10]

This delegation was charged, it seems, with the task of persuading the rebels to seek the king's pardon. It was led by Archbishop Stafford, who was the largest single landowner in Kent; Cardinal Kemp, a Kentishman by birth and a former bishop of Rochester; Buckingham, who also had valuable property in the county; the bishop of Winchester, William Waynflete, whose diocese was perilously close to the infected region; and Viscount Beaumont, constable of England.[11] Next to the king himself, these envoys stood highest in the social and political hierarchy of the realm and had an immediate interest in the happenings in Kent. Yet they reached no substantive agreement with the rebels, who disdained a proffered pardon; but at least they seem to have clarified their own minds as to the rebels' intentions.[12]

These discussions took place on or about 16 June. Thereafter, Henry decided to make the short journey himself from Clerkenwell through London to Blackheath, accompanied by a large and heavily armed company; he took with him a train of guns and 'the most party of temporalle lordys of thys londe of Engelond in there a beste raye', headed by Northumberland, Rivers, Scales, and Lord Grey. They arrived at Blackheath on the morning of 18 June only to discover that the rebels had retired under cover of darkness, perhaps reluctant to confront their anointed king.[13]

Some of the king's men pressed on into Kent in pursuit of the retreating rebels. A small contingent (said to have been about 400-strong) followed them into an ambush. This incautious pursuit had been recommended by some on the grounds that a modest company was all that was required to harry a poorly armed and ill-disciplined rabble. Thus, two kinsmen, Sir Humphrey and William Stafford (the latter described by one contemporary as 'one the mannylste man of alle thys realme of Engelonde'), led their men into a skirmish at Tonbridge, Buckingham's estate near Sevenoaks, and there the first blood of the revolt was drawn. The Staffords were killed; a number of their men were slain by the very rebels they were hunting, and the rest turned tail and fled. Sir Humphrey's expensive accoutrements – his brigandise of velvet decorated with gilded nails, his salet, and his spurs – were donned by Cade himself 'to advance his pride and display his victory'.[14] Had it not been for this disaster, the rebels might well have dispersed relatively peacefully to their homes, but the Staffords' defeat polarized men's attitudes. It showed the rebels that they were capable of success, no matter how modest this might so far be, and they accordingly regrouped in the Kentish countryside, perhaps even seeking aid on a wider front from both north and south of the Thames. It indicated, too, that the authorities were prepared to hunt down insurgents; indeed, in the days following the withdrawal from Blackheath several prominent loyalists went on the rampage in north Kent.[15] To the ordinary retainer of the king and his magnates, the Sevenoaks incident demonstrated what rustics from the south-east could accomplish, and as a result the loyalty of a number of these retainers began to waver. Finally, the king and his ministers were jolted into a realization that stern and swift repression was required if a more serious rising were to be averted.

About the time of the Staffords' death, therefore, some members of the king's entourage – and especially Lords Dudley and Rivers, Sir Thomas Stanley, and Thomas Daniel – devoted several days (18-20 June) to a ruthless harassment in Kent while they pursued the retreating rebels with 2,000 men.[16] Such harsh and (if later charges are to be believed) indiscriminate repression simply served to stiffen the resolve of the rebels. Meanwhile, in the vicinity of Blackheath the restive retainers of the king and his magnates took to decrying their masters and, in some cases, deserted them. Moreover, a number of soldiers who had returned defeated from Normandy were now being temporarily taken into the king's household, where they seem to have formed something of a fifth column of discontent; before the end of June, therefore, responsibility for them was transferred to Lord Scales, a former war captain who was installed in the Tower.[17]

On 19 June many of the discontented retainers threatened to join the rebels unless several royal servants whom they regarded as traitors (and Lords Saye and Dudley, Bishop Aiscough, Abbot Boulers of Gloucester, John Trevilian, John Say, John Noreys, and the infamous Thomas Daniel were specifically named) were arrested; many ran amuck in London, robbing the houses of Dudley and Sir Thomas Stanley. When Buckingham returned from Blackheath to Greenwich to report all this to Henry VI, the king capitulated to the extent of authorizing Saye's arrest; he was taken from the king's presence and lodged in the Tower (where in any case he would be relatively safe).[18] At this point, the mettle of the king was cruelly tested: instead of taking resolute action, he seems to have vacillated, then panicked.

After Saye's arrest, Henry VI publicly encouraged the seizure of others who were popularly regarded as traitors; and on 20 June, he withdrew to London from the Kentish border. Until that point, the king had taken up lodgings at Greenwich, in the queen's manor house; now he hurried back to Westminster, riding through London arrayed for war against his own subjects.[19] That night he secretly summoned Saye from the Tower, presumably to accord him the same protection that he had extended to Suffolk less than two months before, but the constable, the duke of Exeter, refused to give him up. Dislike of the king's household servants and closest advisers had evidently spread well beyond the ranks of the Kentish rebels.[20] An attempt to use the county posse of Kent, Surrey, and Sussex to arrest some soldiers, who had presumably just returned from France and were engaged in robbery and lawless acts at Edenbridge, a little to the south-west of Sevenoaks, came to nothing; the commission was headed by Robert Poynings, an esquire from Twineham and Sutton (Sussex), but either on this occasion (22 June) or soon afterwards he defected to Cade and became his carver and sword-bearer.[21]

In view of these ominous developments, urgent discussions began about the advisability of the king withdrawing from London altogether. The decision to do so seems to have been taken by 23 June, when all business in the law courts was suspended until the autumn term because it was envisaged that the king would need the justices to attend on him personally to give him their advice for quite some time.[22] Probably most of the justices accompanied the king when he left London on the morning of 25 June, consigning the defence of the city to the mayor and common council; Henry made his way, first, to Berkhamsted castle and then on to Kenilworth. For the journey, a barge full of horses was brought into London from Gravesend and Rochester by river, thereby avoiding the rebels congregating on the shore.[23] It is difficult to ascertain who, apart from the justices, went with Henry to the midlands. Although the chancellor (Cardinal Kemp), Archbishop Stafford, and Bishop Waynflete appear to have stayed in or near London, Buckingham is known to have travelled to Kenilworth and other lords and courtiers probably did so too; sufficient numbers of government personnel withdrew to warrant a reward (though it was belatedly paid on 8 April 1451) to two exchequer officials, who bravely stayed at their post.[24] Appeals by the mayor to dissuade Henry from abandoning his capital, even to the extent of offering to underwrite the expenses of his household for six months, were unavailing in circumstances that posed a direct danger to the person of the king and his companions.[25]

When news of these events reached the rebels, it is readily comprehensible why they reassembled and returned to Blackheath at the end of the month, arriving probably on 29 June.[26] Their aims were now more clearly formulated, and they had decided to march on London as a preliminary to securing remedy of their grievances and the implementation of their demands. On 1 or 2 July, Cade took his men down into Southwark, immediately south of London bridge; there they installed themselves in the local inns and hostelries, Cade himself lodging at the White Hart. For the moment, the rebels were denied access to London itself by the mayor.[27] But their entry was soon assured by two other developments. In the first place, an independent (though possibly co-ordinated) rising in Essex brought large numbers of men streaming along the road to London from the east, and by 1 July (or soon afterwards) they were at the city walls.[28] Secondly, the king's desertion of his capital dealt a blow to the morale of those in the city.[29] He had probably reached Kenilworth by 1 July, when the nearby counties of Cheshire and Lancashire were requested to supply a force of men for the king's service, under Sir Thomas Stanley, who accompanied the king from London, and Sir Thomas Harrington.[30] The abandonment of London by the frightened king was a fateful step. On the one hand, it made the immediate task of withstanding the rebels almost impossible, while on the other it hindered and delayed any negotiations designed to bring the rebellion to a speedy end. To that extent, the situation had become more intractable than that of 1381, when the king and his ministers were close at hand in the Tower of London.

On 3 July, Cade finally crossed London bridge into the city, though not without some difficulty.[31] He came determined to demonstrate how orderly his large company of common folk could be, but such commendable intentions could not in practice prevent the rebellion from degenerating into a series of lootings, burnings, and murders. Even at the time of his arrival at Blackheath on 29 June, Cade had beheaded one of his own captains (a man called Parys) in order to show that he could dispense justice, and his proclamations to uphold the peace were issued in Henry VI's name.[32] On 3 and 4 July a commission of oyer and terminer which the king had nominated in an act of conciliation on 1 July, when he was presumably unaware of the imminent entry of the rebels into London, held sessions at the guildhall under Cade's scrutiny; it proceeded to try some of the hated ministers and royal servants under a cloak of legal forms.[33] Several of these were arraigned before the mayor, the chief baron of the exchequer, and Nicholas Assheton, justice of common pleas; in the absence of most of the other justices, they constituted the commission's quorum.[34]

The increasing turbulence of the rebels hardened the hearts of the more prominent and prosperous citizens, perhaps even of some who had hitherto sympathized with Cade. At 5 p.m. on 3 July, Cade entered the city in bombastic fashion, cutting the ropes of the bridge to prevent it from being raised against him later. And for all his proclamations at St Magnus church and Leadenhall that anyone who committed acts of robbery would be put to death, the captain himself perpetrated a number of criminal acts. Lord Saye was brought from the Tower to the guildhall sessions, where about twenty others were indicted and condemned; Saye's request that he be tried by his peers was scornfully rejected. Rather did it require all the powers of persuasion of one of Cade's captains to prevent him from being hacked to death before the very justices themselves; eventually, he was allowed to confess before being taken to the standard in Cheapside for execution. The hated sheriff of Kent, William Crowmer, who was the son of an unpopular alderman of London as well as Saye's son-in-law, was dragged from the Fleet prison, where he had been confined at the time of Saye's arrest; he was paraded through the streets to Tower Hill and on to Mile End, where he too was beheaded, along with a number of others.[35] The heads were stuck on pikes and the gruesome procession made its way to Cheapside. Saye's head was placed on another pike and made to kiss the lifeless head of his son-in-law at prominent places in the city for the entertainment of the mob. Saye's body, tied to Cade's saddle, was dragged through the city streets and across the bridge into Southwark. Others, including Alderman Robert Horne, managed to escape either by bribery or with the aid of friends – or both. Outrages like these continued into the evening, when the victims included a thief snatched from sanctuary in St Martin-le-Grand.[36]

By 5 July some Londoners had resolved to try and prevent Cade and his men from entering the city from Southwark ever again. A battle ensued on London bridge that night from about 10 p.m. until 8 or 9 a.m. the following morning; after a hard fight the rebels found themselves unable to force their way across the bridge, and Cade accordingly set its drawbridge alight. Sheriff Hulyn was eventually able to shut and bolt the gateway at the bridge's entrance.[37] The loyalists were led by Lord Scales, who had been holding out in the Tower, Matthew Gough, the veteran soldier, and several London aldermen. When the dust cleared and the flames died down, Gough, Alderman John Sutton, a goldsmith, and Roger Heysant, a draper, lay dead along with several hundred others, some of whom had fallen from the burning bridge and were drowned in the Thames.[38] During the mêlée, or immediately afterwards, Cade threw open the Marshalsea prison on the south bank, and the inmates were set free to swell the rebel ranks.[39]

Meanwhile, a few hours' truce had been arranged between the exhausted combatants, with each side agreeing not to cross to the other's side of the bridge. This allowed the available members of the government an opportunity to initiate negotiations with the rebels in order to induce them to disperse.[40] At the instance of the queen, a general pardon was offered to Cade (in the name of John Mortimer) and his men on 6 and 7 July. A delegation of churchmen, consisting of the two archbishops and Waynflete, finally brought about a cessation of the fighting at a meeting with Cade in St Margaret's church, Southwark. They received the petitions of the rebels and offered charters of pardon in return. Large numbers of insurgents availed themselves of the offer. Cade, however, seems to have disdained the pardon and, clutching his booty, planned to hold out in north Kent. He and a small group made for Dartford and Rochester on 9 July, and then for Queenborough castle. He was prevented from entering the latter by Sir Roger Chamberlain, and he therefore turned aside into Sussex. His booty had meanwhile been put on a barge in the river and sent by water to Rochester, where it was hoped to transfer it to a ship. A predictable quarrel over the booty broke out among some of Cade's own men, and on 10 July it was all seized at Rochester while Cade sped away.[41] The exchequer was authorized to take custody of the goods of all the rebels on 12 July and to deploy it to crush the rising once and for all.[42] Two men were sent to Rochester by the new treasurer of England, Sir John Beauchamp, to collect Cade's personal belongings, and they spent four days doing so. These goods were then sold to raise cash and several London merchants were among the purchasers, including Philip Malpas (who may have been buying back property stolen from his own house during the revolt), and Richard Joynour, as well as Thomas Rothewell who, as clerk to the treasurer of England, had organized the sale.[43]

On 10 July, Cade was proclaimed a traitor in his own name (rather than as John Mortimer), and a price of 1,000 marks was placed on his head; 500 marks were said to have been offered for the capture of any of his lieutenants, and 5 marks were posted for any of his adherents still in revolt who could be apprehended.[44] This had the desired effect. Cade was captured two days later by Alexander Iden, the new sheriff of Kent, with some assistance from John Seyncler (or Sinclair) of Faversham, and John Davy. The capture took place at Heathfield in Sussex, not far from those haunts in south-west Kent where the rebellion seems first to have begun. On the way back to London, Cade died of wounds sustained at the time of his capture. His naked body was brought to Southwark next day for proper identification by the wife of the innkeeper of the White Hart, and three days later it was solemnly beheaded at Newgate lest the captain of Kent escape a traitor's fate. The head was placed on London bridge, and the body dragged through the city, from Southwark to Newgate, before being quartered.[45] The Kentish revolt was over.

The rebel leader

One of the more vexatious problems connected with the revolt is posed by the identity of its leader. Contemporaries were unanimous that a man called John Cade headed the main rebel host as the 'captain of Kent', but precious little information has been recorded about him, and contemporaries appear to have been just as mystified as modern commentators as to his origins and early career. Some thought him an Irish immigrant, though this opinion may have been based solely on his adoption of the emotive name of Mortimer, for the Mortimer forebears of the duke of York had been substantial Irish landowners since the thirteenth century.[46] One writer identified him with John Aylmere, a physician who had married the daughter of a Surrey squire; although these circumstantial details invite belief, there is no corroboration of the statement.[47] The royal proclamation issued on 10 June for the arrest of Cade announced that he had once served Charles VII and that he had been residing in Sussex in the household of Sir Thomas Dacre – until, that is, he killed a pregnant woman and had to flee.[48] Yet these revelations smack of a determination on the part of the government to blacken the rebel's reputation by every available means. All one can conclude with any degree of confidence is that Cade had a prior connection with south-eastern England before he appeared as 'captain of Kent'.

Whatever military experience and gentlemanly connections he did or did not have, there is a measure of agreement among contemporaries that Cade came from the lower ranks of society rather than from the county squirearchy or the urban patriciate: to one chronicler he was a 'ribaud' and a 'knave', to another a 'sympylle' man.[49] His assumed name of Mortimer masked his true identity, and for a time many believed (as was the intention) that he was a kinsman of the duke of York. Eventually most people in the fifteenth century, including the chancery clerks, had no doubt that he took this name for propaganda purposes, 'forto haue the more fauour of the peple'.[50] A name with political implications and suggesting aristocratic connections would help to support his pretensions, attract sympathizers, and give weight to the rebels' demands.[51] York's name was certainly worth conjuring with by anyone critical of the king's government in the late 1440s. There is no strictly independent or unbiased evidence that Cade's revolt was actually incited by York or his agents. The rebel demands afforded the duke no clear precedence among the magnates in whom the rebels put their faith – indeed, his name figures only once in their written manifestos and in one context only.[52] Moreover, the duke returned to England at least two months after the revolt had ended, and although rapid communication across St

George's channel faced formidable physical obstacles, a direct connection between the two events may be discounted.[53] Again, later accusations that the duke and councillors of his like Sir William Oldhall were actively engaged in rousing the rebels stem from formal indictments presented to a hostile Lancastrian jury that was determined to besmirch York's reputation and secure the condemnation of his supporters.[54] Tudor writers rehearsed and elaborated these charges, giving them a definition that seemed to convert them into historical fact.[55] Nevertheless, after all these qualifications have been sounded, it remains a plausible suggestion that Oldhall and others associated with York appreciated the political capital that could be made out of Cade's large-scale protest and established cautious communication with his rebel throng.[56] In doing so, they may have been *plus ducale que le duc*.

In the fearful circumstances in which they found themselves in 1450, Henry VI and his ministers may have accepted all too readily Cade's feigned aristocratic pretensions, and when a pardon was offered him on 6 July, it was couched in the name of John Mortimer.[57] Four days later, this pardon was superseded by a proclamation for the arrest of John Cade for crimes other than those connected with the rising; it made no mention of the name of Mortimer.[58] Accordingly, the parliament which met in the winter of 1450–51 proceeded to attaint him as the self-styled John Mortimer, to corrupt his blood and declare his possessions forfeit, possibly as a final precaution lest he prove later to have had, after all, at least a drop of aristocratic blood in his veins; by that stage Cade had been dead for half a year, no heirs had been identified, and his possessions had been seized and sold immediately after the revolt collapsed. The justification for this attainder lay not in the rising itself, even though the revelation that Mortimer was not Cade's real name would have invalidated his pardon; it lay in his continued rebellious activities after 7 July in the vicinity of Dartford and Rochester. Not until 1453, in a parliament that was exceptionally loyal to Henry VI, was this first act of attainder extended to encompass all of Cade's rebellious and treasonable activities in 1450. On this occasion, his assumption (or accroachment) of the king's authority during the revolt itself was particularized, and especially his attempt to condemn certain lords, royal servants, and subjects by manipulating due legal process. The parliament thereby ensured that none of those indicted before the guildhall sessions of 3–4 July would suffer embarrassment in the future.[59]

One other morsel of information, contributed by a contemporary writer, has an incidental bearing on the leadership of the revolt. Cade apparently liked to refer to himself as John Amende-alle, an expressive nickname that indicated his intentions in a clear and simple way that might serve as an effective rallying-cry.[60] Less helpful to the historian is the statement in 'Gregory's Chronicle' that the leader whom the rebels chose on their return to Blackheath on 29 June was different from the original captain of Kent, though the Kentishmen themselves claimed that this was not so.[61] It is a unique claim and perhaps Cade's adoption of the name of Mortimer had confused this writer, too.

Contemporary evaluations of Cade's character and abilities are few and brief. The proclamation of 10 July painted a predictable picture of a base criminal who displayed all the worst qualities of a contemporary rogue: a dabbler in magic, a consorter with the devil, a murderer of pregnant women, a traitor and 'tale-teller' who had aspirations beyond his station.[62] Apart from what may be revealed indirectly by his actions and proposals (if they were his), the chroniclers offer no more than a rudimentary assessment of the man with whom the king's ministers had to deal. He was evidently chosen by the Kentishmen as their leader at a very early stage in the rising, before they reached Blackheath, though one writer implies that it was the imminent prospect of negotiation with the king's envoys that prompted the rebels to make him their spokesman.[63] He is reported to have been a brave individual who stood out easily from his fellows.[64] His discussions with the two archbishops and Buckingham left them with the distinct impression of a courageous man, well spoken, and of transparent intelligence.[65] If the formulation of the rebel programme owed anything to him, this latter quality is amply corroborated.[66]

The rebel host

Every description of the company which Cade led to Blackheath suffers from the imprecise – and often wild – estimates of its size offered by fundamentally innumerate contemporaries. The result is bewildering. All that can reasonably be hazarded is that the throng which converged on Blackheath on 29 June was considerably smaller than that which had assembled there earlier in the month. According to the most conservative estimate of all, 20,000 Kentishmen congregated on the heath on the second occasion, with 6,000 more from Essex converging on Mile End by the beginning of July.[67] Even these figures may be notional ones. The reports of the dead on or beneath London bridge after the fracas of 5–6 July are likely to be more precise because the numbers involved were more easily computed: about 40 Londoners and 200 Kentishmen, according to one writer.[68]

The composition of the rebel host has been analysed by historians, without exception, in terms of those who accepted the pardon offered on 6 and 7 July.[69] The long list of the pardoned needs to be reviewed with great caution. A general pardon was made available to Cade and his followers, and to anyone who wished to avail himself of it, without paying the customary fine or fee.[70] It is likely, therefore, that other than active rebels sought pardon for their own future security in the event of either recriminations after the revolt or a possible campaign of punishment or, conceivably, an attempt to remedy some of the rebels' grievances by instituting legal proceedings against those whom they criticized. And in the first weeks of July it was by no means certain which course the government would follow. The foresight of those from the south-east who availed themselves of the pardon was well justified, for initially the king ordered an inquiry into the rebels' complaints and began to punish those who were guilty.[71] Later on, when the extreme danger had passed, the government's attitude hardened and many were harshly treated for taking part in this and other disturbances.[72] Thus, common prudence dictated that those who had participated in the revolt, others who had stood on the sidelines, and those who had, by their oppressions, helped to precipitate the violence, should seek pardon on 6 or 7 July.

Some specific examples from among the two thousand and more who were pardoned will demonstrate their diverse motives and, as a result, should counsel caution in relying on this pardon-list to deduce the nature of the rebel force. It is true that two of Cade's supporters in London early in July, Simon Shipton and John Frenssh, were among those who secured a pardon, along with Cade himself.[73] Yet so did John Seyncler, mayor of Faversham, who less than a week later played a crucial part in the capture of Cade. Or take Stephen Norton, a Kentishman who by 1459 was one of the executors of Alexander Iden, the newly appointed sheriff of Kent who actually apprehended Cade in the Sussex countryside.[74] More striking still are the dozen or so men who were among the more notorious oppressors of whom the rebels complained and yet who received a pardon, presumably to fend off investigations. Robert Est, a Maidstone gentleman, was denounced by Cade and his men as one of the principal extortioners in Kent – and with good reason for, as a commission of oyer and terminer would soon establish, throughout the 1440s he had abused his authority by committing fraud, extortion, forcible disseisin, and maintenance, especially as the keeper of Maidstone gaol. His pardon was granted on 7 July.[75] John Watte of Sandhurst was no less adept at abusing his position as a bailiff in the service of William Crowmer, the sheriff of Kent, and he sometimes (as in 1449–50) committed his illegalities in association with Stephen Slegge, another of Cade's targets. Yet, Watte, too, successfully sought the king's pardon on 7 July.[76] So did John Ram, the lieutenant of Richard Bruyn, an esquire from Islington and a notorious extortioner as Lord Cromwell's steward in his lordship of Hoo (Kent). Ram's thieving and lawbreaking during the 1440s were brought to the commissioners' attention in the autumn of 1450, though he had already acquired a pardon; he is quite unlikely to have been out with Cade at the very time when he was oppressing his fellow Kentishmen.[77]

There were some among the pardoned who were unlikely rebels, to say the least. John Thornbury, esquire, had been sheriff of Kent in 1445–46 and was a highly experienced local government official during Henry VI's reign; and far from being a disgruntled Kentishman suffering from the malevolence of an unpopular régime, he was one of that band of enterprising property purchasers who were resented by the native Kentishman, for Thornbury was a newcomer to the county where he had acquired an estate as recently as the 1430s.[78] Equally unlikely as a follower of Cade was Roger Appleton of Dartford; he, together with his wife and son Roger, probably took the royal pardon in order to protect his family and his interests, which were connected with the royal exchequer, where Roger served regularly as an auditor during Henry's reign.[79] Sir John Cheyne, of Eastchurch on the Isle of Sheppey, was the only knight to receive a pardon on 6–7 July. He had been MP for Kent in 1449, when his colleague was none other than William Crowmer; he was a royal serjeant-at-arms by 1445, and after the revolt he became sheriff of Kent (in 1454–55) and victualler of Calais (in February 1452). Cheyne's concern to obtain a pardon in July 1450 may well have sprang from apprehension lest accusations like those directed against Crowmer would also be thrown at him.[80] Finally, three former officials of the archbishop of Canterbury are only a whit less likely to have been among the rebels on Blackheath, and yet each sought a pardon for himself in July 1450: James Hope had been clerk to the archbishop's auditor in 1436–37; Simon Morley was the archbishop's receiver in 1437–39; and William Green would be his receiver-general in Kent in 1453–59.[81]

To regard those who received a pardon as active rebels to a man, deducing therefrom conclusions about their occupations and geographical origins, is thus quite unwarranted. The most that can be said of the pardon-list is that it undoubtedly contains the names of many rebels – but also of many loyalists and others who took no part at all in the incidents of 1450. It represents, in brief, a cross-section of society in the south-east of England, but little more.[82] Indeed, several towns, districts, and institutions appear to have bought a collective pardon through the officials of their bailiwick, and by this means townsmen, villagers, household servants, and tenantry could be protected in the event of a commission of oyer and terminer arriving to make its investigations.[83] William Ederiche and his wife Alice, whose family was well established in East Greenwich by 1450 and owned property in London, were pardoned on 7 July along with 'all others of that town', not because East Greenwich had risen *en masse* with Cade, but rather because the Ederiches were leaders of their community and probably negotiated the collective pardon on behalf of their fellows as well as themselves.[84] Little different was the pardon granted to Richard Dartmouth, abbot (1437–63) of the Sussex abbey of St Martin at Battle, for it included the abbey convent and its men and servants.[85] In the same category stands John Danyel, prior of St Pancras priory in Lewes, whose pardon was obtained for the convent as a whole and its employees, and Katherine de la Pole, abbess of Barking (Sussex) and the sister of the late duke of Suffolk; Katherine's 'men, tenants and servants' were thereby protected by the pardon which she duly received.[86] The possibility that she had joined a popular movement which had as its purpose the denunciation of her brother's friends and colleagues is singularly remote. For different reasons, Bartholomew Bolney of West Firle and Bolney (Sussex), who was pardoned on 7 July with 'all his men and servants', was no insurgent; he continued to take his place on local commissions, including one that investigated treasons committed by other rebels in Sussex in May 1451. Furthermore, his sound reputation in the county of Sussex, where he was a prominent yeoman-farmer and steward for both the abbot of Battle and the archbishop of Canterbury, gave him a strong vested interest in an orderly society.[87] Were such men likely to chance all in Cade's company?

To regard the scores of constables who negotiated pardons on behalf of their respective hundreds as thereby admitting their involvement in the rebellion as recruiting agents (a view commonly held by historians) profoundly misunderstands the role they played on 6–7 July; each constable was certainly acting as an agent for his hundred community, but merely to secure protection for neighbours and fellow subjects.[88] That this was so is perhaps indicated by the record of a chance conversation in an alehouse in Brightling (Sussex) three weeks later. On 26 July, two yeomen of Brightling, John and William Mirfield, denounced the constable of Netherfield hundred, William Burford, who had secured a pardon probably on behalf of the men of Brightling, because the pardon 'made of the First insurrection was fals and he also'. Burford's representation of their interests was evidently not appreciated.[89]

Rather than make a virtue of extreme scepticism, the pardons may be regarded as indicating where Cade's rebellion was most serious. Of the thousands of pardons issued, about 65 per cent went to Kentishmen either singly or collectively, 14 per cent to Sussex men, 12 per cent to the inhabitants of Surrey, and 8 per cent to those of Essex. These figures confirm what is well known, namely, that Cade's revolt was overwhelmingly a Kentish movement, with significant support from Sussex, Surrey, and Essex. With less confidence, its rank and file may be said to have come from the lower orders; from the 'ribaudmen' and 'rustics', as one chronicler called them; 'a fulle rude peple', according to another.[90] It is possible that Cade forced a few gentlemen to join him, as one London chronicler related, but the most significant accession of strength came from the populace of London and the mutinous retinues of the magnates; even a few royal household servants were thought to be involved.[91] If some urban communities expressed cautious sympathy with the rebels at first, they seem to have repented of it quite soon. The gift of a porpoise to Cade from the town of Lydd was a precautionary move, intended 'to have his friendship' rather than as a sign of adherence. It followed a mission to Ashford by the constable, John Fermour, to gain news of 'the Capitaine of the oste'; a little later, a letter from the town to the captain of Kent was 'in excuse of this town'.[92] After Cade and his rebels had moved further south to the outskirts of Appledore, a soldier was despatched from Rye to find out if the rebel army had entered the town or not.[93] Cautious reconnaissance was the order of the day as far as these Kentish ports were concerned.

The collective behaviour of the rebels was the behaviour of commoners, ill-organized, poorly armed, and badly disciplined, acting beyond the limits of their normal political ken.[94] Throughout they stressed their abiding sense of loyalty to Henry VI, and their proclamations of protest castigated in traditional vein the evil advisers of the king rather than the king himself.[95] By 18 June, they had melted away rather than face their sovereign in person. Admittedly, one contemporary thought that they were then too weak to engage in a fight, but this is an unlikely reason for their initial withdrawal, for when they returned to Blackheath, they were fewer in number and more belligerent, but by then the king had retired to Kenilworth.[96]

Cade attempted to organize this vast array of Englishmen into a disciplined force, with a small cadre of lesser captains acknowledging his leadership, apparently by a sworn oath.[97] He issued proclamations to control their behaviour as soon as they appeared on Blackheath; he even beheaded one of his lesser captains on 29 June to demonstrate his authority.[98] After London had been penetrated on 3 July, two further proclamations against plunder were publicized.[99] But it was a forlorn hope that peace could be preserved when such vast numbers were careering through the city's streets. Order quickly collapsed, with the result that robbery, destruction, and murder followed. It was this that turned the tide of sympathy away from the rebels and made possible the successful attempt to keep them out of the city during the night of 5-6 July.[100]

The king's men

The royal forces pitted against the rebels were considerable and testify to the alarm which caused Henry VI to adjourn parliament at Leicester and hasten back to London. He was accompanied by a goodly number of his magnates, including the three dukes who were then in the realm (Exeter, Buckingham, and Norfolk), and the earls of Devon, Arundel, Oxford, and Northumberland, Viscount Beaumont, and Lords Scales, Rivers, Dudley, Lovel, and Grey among the barons.[101] At St John's priory, Clerkenwell, a large force assembled, each lord with his retinue well armed and preparing to confront the rebels.[102] Estimates of its size only serve to confuse, for whereas 'Benet's Chronicle' and the 'pseudo-Worcester Annals' record that 20,000 armed men made their way towards Blackheath, 'Gregory's Chronicle' puts the figure at 10,000, and the *English Chronicle* at 15,000.[103] Even if these computations indicate that the royal army may have been decidedly smaller than the rebel host, it was probably better organized and better equipped for a fight.[104] Yet this superiority was more apparent than real.

In the first place, the ambush of the Staffords gave heart to Cade's men and precipitated a crisis of morale and discipline among the royal and magnate retainers.[105] Their mutiny was one of the most critical events of the entire rising. The captains and men of both the king and his magnates faltered, and then threatened to go over to the rebels unless certain ultimata were conceded.[106] The most important of these was identical with the Kentishmen's principal demands, namely, that certain of the king's advisers should be dismissed; the retainers were therefore aligning themselves with the commons of the recent parliament and the rebels. Several captains promptly fled through fear of their own men, while the king and his lords, faced with this desperate turn of events, had little alternative but to retreat to London and, eventually, to Kenilworth.[107] Meanwhile, the mutineers had ransacked parts of the city, especially the houses of hated favourites like Lords Dudley and Rivers, Sir Thomas Stanley, and Thomas Daniel, who were away harassing the Kent countryside. It was in response to the clamour of the retainers that Saye was arrested and put in the Tower.[108] In coping with Cade's rebellion, the king and his companions suffered from a fatal weakness: the loyalty of their own men was too fragile to permit of stern and decisive repression at the beginning of the revolt. It was this, more than anything else, that prompted the initial concessions to the rebels and the short-lived undertaking that their complaints would be considered.[109]

The Londoners' attitude

The transitory success of Cade's rebels owed much to their entry into London, where they were welcomed by the mass of inhabitants and tolerated by a majority of the ruling patriciate. The former seem to have sympathized with the aims and actions of the Kentishmen, whereas the latter were probably influenced partly by fear and partly by their own internal rivalries, which had a long history of dividing the gildsmen and embittering relations within the city's governing circles.[110] Early in the year, when parliament had met at Westminster, there had been rioting in the city: for example, in Dowgate ward on 12 January a mob had gathered, chanting ominously.

> By this town, By this town,
> For this array the king shall lose his crown.

Now, in the summer of 1450, the preservation of order in London and the avoidance of destruction and wholesale robbery were the main concerns of the common council.[111]

When the magnitude of the Kentish rising came to be appreciated, the common council took precautions to protect the city and maintain order within its walls. On 8 June a permanent guard was placed day and night on the gates and on the wharves and in the lanes leading down to the river: ballistic machines were stationed on the wharves and ground nearby was cleared to allow of easier manoeuvre. Lordly retinues, which normally accompanied their masters on visits to the capital, had their movements restricted: they were only to be allowed into the city for specific purposes and were forbidden to take up quarters there. Meanwhile, as a security measure, the armourers of London were warned not to sell their wares outside the walls for the time being.[112] Next day, the two masters in control of London bridge were provided with four hand-guns with which to defend the bridge – a pretty inadequate step when one considers the speed and accuracy of contemporary firearms and the number of Kentishmen that would soon swarm into London from Southwark.[113] Overall responsibility for guarding the city's gates rested with the aldermen of London; Robert Horne, the alderman of Bridge ward, had charge of the strategic gateway leading from London bridge.

Once Cade and his men had encamped on Blackheath by 11 or 12 June, urgent problems faced the city fathers, especially if the rebels proved hostile or intransigent. On 13 June, therefore, two barges were used to keep open the supply-line to the city.[114] Relations between the common council and the king at this point were cordial, and on about 19 June the city authorities undertook to provide beer and white wine for the royal entourage and their retainers.[115] But when these very retainers threatened to mutiny after the Staffords' death, Henry took the decision to leave London and make for the midlands, consigning the defence of the city to the mayor and common council alone.[116] The mayor, Thomas Charlton, a mercer, had desperately tried to dissuade the king from leaving, assuring him that the citizens would stand by him, but his pleas were unavailing.[117] Accordingly, on 26 June further precautions were hurriedly taken and spies were sent to discover the purpose of the rebels' reappearance on Blackheath. The bridge was kept raised from 28 June onwards, and next day discussions were held with the constable of the Tower, the duke of Exeter, presumably to co-ordinate the defence of the city's wards more effectively.[118]

As soon as Cade returned to Blackheath on 29 June, the common council steeled itself to negotiate with him. Alderman Thomas Cooke, a draper and the son-in-law of Alderman Philip Malpas, was nominated on behalf of the city to go to the rebel camp; Cade issued him with a safe-conduct to enable him to pass through the lines. Cooke took back to London certain demands which Cade made of the citizens: he wanted weapons, horses, and 1,000 marks in cash which, the rebel leader opined, might be collected not only from Londoners but also from the unpopular alien merchants in the city.[119] It was probably the flight of the king which decided the city council to treat cautiously with the rebels at their door. At first, the mayor bravely denied Cade entry into the city itself. But with the king gone and the rebels massing on Blackheath, resistance withered.[120] The care taken by the common council to avoid offending the rebel leader unnecessarily led to the imprisonment of Alderman Robert Horne, who had vigorously opposed the negotiations with the rebels and a proposal to allow them into the city; he was, in any case, associated in the popular mind with the late duke of Suffolk. On 26 June Alderman Malpas, an unpopular draper, former sheriff and MP for the city, whose nomination as alderman for Lime Street ward had been forced through on 1 April 1448 by royal command after its initial rejection on 26 February by the court of aldermen, was now stripped of his authority by demand of the citizens.[121] There were evidently already some sympathizers in London who were gathering to aid Cade.[122]

Despite these conciliatory gestures on the part of the citizens, the prospect of the mob running wild through the streets of London remained a fearful one, and Cade was only able to gain entry on 3 July by a subterfuge. By threatening to set fire to the bridge, with all the danger which that spelled for the houses and shops nearby, the keys of the city's gate were handed over by a spurrier, Thomas Godfrey. As he crossed London bridge, Cade cut the ropes to prevent the drawbridge from being raised against him again.[123] Cade affected some semblance of regal state to begin with, having his sword carried before him by Robert Poynings, his carver and sword-bearer.[124] He then proceeded to appoint his own aldermen – among them Lawrence Stokewode, a salter and therefore from one of the minor gilds, who fed information about the other aldermen to Cade and in return was allowed to hold some of the citizens to ransom.[125] Yet, for all his good intentions to limit disorder and destruction, it was beyond Cade's power to prevent the plundering – and even murder – that now took place. Initially, it was confined to the houses and property of that section of the city community that had earlier opposed the rebels. Alderman Malpas's house was despoiled of goods worth £20,000 (including gold and silver, merchandise and luxuries such as jewels and tapestries, some of which belonged to the duke of York).[126] Another man called John Gest, who lived near Tower Street, had his house ransacked after Cade had dined there.[127] Alderman Horne, who had been put in Newgate goal, managed to escape death through the pleadings of his wife, his friends, and the mayor, and by providing a large bribe of 500 marks; his experience was shared by a number of others, including Malpas and Gest.[128] One eyewitness, perhaps William Gregory, denounced the rebels as half-demented when he penned his account of the revolt not long afterwards, and he blamed them squarely for numerous acts of spoliation, though it seems that many of the Londoners were also responsible.[129]

Some of the citizenry, including Mayor Charlton, participated in the guildhall sessions which, with a veneer of legality, dealt with some of those whom the rebels had denounced. On 3 or 4 July, the sessions opened before the mayor, the chief baron of the exchequer, Justice Assheton of common pleas, and Robert Danvers, a merchant who had been recorder of London since 1442.[130] This commission of oyer and terminer was overawed by Cade and his men, and most of the justices (including the chief justices) had already beat a hasty retreat from the city to avoid being involved as victims or judges. In all, twenty persons were formally indicted of treason and extortion before this court, among them the infamous Lord Saye, the duke and duchess of Suffolk, Thomas Daniel, Bishop Aiscough, and John Say.[131]

Even this flimsy veil of legality was torn away when the rebels proceeded to punish not only the indicted but others too. The plea by Lord Saye, who had been brought from the Tower where the king had reluctantly confined him, that he be tried by his peers was ignored; he was beheaded by some of the lesser captains, and his body abused by Cade himself.[132] That same day, Cade rode through London with his sword drawn and held high. Crowmer, the unpopular sheriff of Kent, was dragged from the Fleet prison and also beheaded.[133] Other killings followed, which do not seem to have had even a formal justification in law. Richard Hayward (or Hawerdyn), a thief and murderer who had taken sanctuary in St Martin-le-Grand, was executed at the Tabard inn in Southwark.[134] A clerk and a London goldsmith suffered the same fate, as did Thomas Est and a man called Wodhouse, two yeomen of the crown whom the rebels had castigated bitterly; a Colchester squire named Thomas Maine was executed on 5 July at the request of the Essex rebels, and to his death went a necromancer called Bayley who is said to have known Cade in the old days and was done away with lest he should tell what he knew about him (whatever that may have been).[135] These killings on 4–5 July convinced some of the Londoners that Cade and his rebels should be ejected from the city as soon as possible. The violence of the past few days had hardened opinion against him, certainly among the more prosperous and prominent citizens, though the common folk may still have regarded him as a saviour.[136] Thus, a businessman, John Mabyowe, who with his associates happened to be in London at the time of the rebel incursion, was asked by his friends on 5 July to join them in arming themselves and forcing the rebels out; he refused because he feared that his enemies in the city would slay him if he did so.[137]

During the religious services that day, a Sunday, the common council discussed ways of shutting Cade out of the city.[138] Some sought the advice and aid of Lord Scales, who was still in command of the impregnable Tower, and the Welsh captain who was with him, Matthew Gough. Scales had under his command a number of soldiers who had recently returned from France, and although their loyalty may have been in doubt, at least the experience of Scales and Gough would be invaluable in what was, after all, a military situation.[139] It was decided that the Londoners should seize London bridge during the night of 5–6 July in order to prevent Cade's re-entry to the city the following morning.[140] 'Gregory's Chronicle', whose writer had understandably by this stage lost all sympathy with the rebels, implied that the whole of London rose against Cade, but it seems likely that it was the mayor, the aldermen, and the most prominent of the citizenry who took the lead – in other words, the men who had most to lose from the continued orgy of robbery and destruction.[141] They made their way across the bridge to the stulps at the Southwark end, and there the fighting began. Sheriff Hulyn, a fishmonger, managed to close the gate into Southwark and this so roused the rebels that a veritable battle ensued and lasted all night.[142]

At the moment of crisis in 1450, London had proved equivocal in its loyalty to Henry VI. Many of the inhabitants were ready to join the rebels and shared their common grievances. It was obvious to the king that they could not be trusted and hence he withdrew to the midlands; this simply had the effect of quickly handing the city over to the rebels and their sympathizers – but only for a few days, until mob rule showed itself for the destructive force it usually was in the later middle ages.

The rebel grievances and proposals

Cade's rising was the first popular rebellion in English history to produce a coherent programme of grievances, requests, and remedies in the form of written, publicized manifestos. From the extant versions – some contemporary and others dating from the sixteenth century – it is possible to analyse the rebels' aims and their motives. These manifestos survive today probably because they were well publicized in 1450, both within the rebel ranks and during the negotiations with the authorities.

Three days after the king arrived in London from Leicester on 13 June, the two archbishops led a delegation to Blackheath to establish the precise cause of the rising. They tried to persuade the captain and his men to seek the king's pardon and disperse, whilst Cade, for his part, presented them with a bill of petitions relating to the state of the realm and the king. The demands contained therein became well known to contemporaries: to reform the wrongs and abuses of England's government, and remove and punish the king's advisers and personal companions. At the same time, and as an earnest of their good intentions and sincerity, the rebels affirmed their loyalty to Henry VI, and Cade issued a proclamation forbidding any destruction of property or other lawless behaviour. The Kentishmen wanted the king and his council to receive their petitions for, as one chronicler recorded, they considered themselves to be petitioners, not rebels.[143] Henry's emissaries seem to have responded by promising that the grievances would be examined and an answer given by the king within a designated time-limit.[144] Henry evidently refused to concede any changes.[145]

It is not easy to establish with any certainty what these petitions contained. Indeed, in the pre-printing age, there may have been no single text, duly authorized by the rebels or their leader, that was superior to all other lists of complaints and requests. Moreover, the rapid passage of events during June 1450 is likely to have prompted the compilation of different manifestos to suit different audiences in different situations: perhaps one for the men of Kent who had to be roused in the first instance; another for a wider public to whom appeals were made at a later stage; and yet a further document for presentation to the king and his councillors, who alone could grant the rebels' petitions. It is not surprising, therefore, that the surviving documents that purport to have originated with Cade's men differ from one another in their character, their details, and, one suspects, in their overall purpose.

To galvanize large numbers of Kentishmen required carefully designed and widespread propaganda. Accordingly, the captain sent messages to several towns to elicit aid. Moreover, the simultaneous rising in Essex may have been co-ordinated with the Kentish movement, for communication across the Thames was easy, as is indicated by the accusation that Sir William Oldhall and others incited the rising from Bury St Edmunds (Suffolk). Political ballads and poems served not only to popularize a cause, but also to inspire a movement and give a common identity and a rallying-cry to its enthusiasts.[146]

In an increasingly literate society, a more precise exposition of complaints, in the form of a well-publicized, written manifesto, would be the most effective way of stimulating support in the community at large. John Stow included in his *Chronicles of England*, published in 1580, a document which (he claimed) the rebels had entitled 'The complaint of the commons of Kent, and causes of the assembly on the Blackheath'. No contemporary version of these complaints now survives, but Stow is known to have been a voracious collector of manuscripts, while his father and grandfather, as London citizens, could well have obtained materials relating to Cade's rebellion.[147] This manifesto pinpointed a number of political calamities and administrative abuses which were attributed to the king's advisers and household servants, and to certain corrupt shire officials. One-third of the fifteen clauses of complaint refer specifically to oppressions in Kent, and the remainder embody problems which that county in particular experienced, as the inquiries in the autumn of 1450 demonstrated. In only two instances did the rebels succumb to rumour 'openly noysed... by common voyces': the fear that Kent would be harried 'and made a wilde forest' in retribution for Suffolk's recent murder was surely unfounded; while the belief that the king's territories in France had been alienated and his subjects there betrayed may have arisen from news of the surrender of Rouen by the duke of Somerset under humiliating conditions. Generally speaking, then, this manifesto was an outpouring of currently-felt and easily identified oppressions, especially in Kent. It is a Kentish document, drawn up by Kentishmen and directed at fellow Kentishmen – especially the landholding peasantry – most likely before the rebels reached Blackheath on 11 or 12 June. It was a manifesto to launch a campaign, rather than a programme for reform and remedy, for its proposals for change were few.

There was, indeed, something unmistakably Kentish about Cade's revolt. It was unlike the rising of 1381 in the same region, for that was primarily a rural movement spearheaded by a peasantry in economic and social difficulties. By contrast, the rebel complaints of 1450 reflect the frustrations and resentments of practically all sections of Kentish society, including the substantial and well-to-do, the townsmen and the traders as well as the peasantry and yeomen.[148] By the middle of the fifteenth century, Kent was a shire in which few labour services were still being demanded from an unfree peasantry; rather was it a shire supporting prosperous and independent – if small – peasant proprietors, though it must be admitted that of late the less successful of these had been migrating in increasing numbers to the towns and villages where they became labourers.[149] The occasional insistence on residual labour dues on the archbishop of Canterbury's estates by such agents as John Alpheigh, one of the extortioners denounced in 1450, would seem all the more irritating.[150] Frustrations of this sort also appear to have roused resentment on the estates of Battle abbey, where the reviving land market was awakening in the abbot a consciousness of his seignorial rights.[151] Thus, there is evidence that in 1450 tenants living within the abbot's franchise (including prosperous burgesses of Battle itself) were eager to sweep away surviving customary dues that were the vestiges of traditional seignorial authority; they refused payment for a while, taking advantage perhaps of the current restlessness of the region.[152] Furthermore, service in the archbishop's employ provided a close link with the royal household, for the archbishop recognized that it was to his advantage to have a steward of his lands who was of 'standing about the king'; it was this awareness that involved Lord Saye ever more closely in the exercise of lordship, both royal and ecclesiastical, in Kent in the 1440s.[153] On secular estates, too, the obligations of tenants could place them at the mercy of unscrupulous officials wielding the seignorial powers of their master: at Hoo in Kent, the agents of Lord Cromwell abused their authority at a court baron in May 1449 by forcing twelve men to act as jurors and then unjustly fining them for eating and drinking before their verdict was delivered.[154]

The more enterprising tenantry of Kent, themselves acquiring properties where and when they could, were naturally suspicious of royal servants and those who came from the environs of London; by foul means as well as fair, they bought up estates or forcibly seized them or procured them by chicanery.[155] Since the mid-fourteenth century, prosperous Londoners had been investing their commercial wealth in the fertile acres of Kent, and Gloucester's lavish expenditure on his manor at Greenwich is only the most striking and best-documented example in a movement that took rich merchants and government and city officials to the Kent countryside in search of country residences.[156] A number of household servants had recently been buying estates in Kent and the home counties that were within easy reach of Westminster, and had been extending their properties by means that were not always peaceful or lawful.[157] William Crowmer's family were parvenus in the county, for his father hailed from Cromer in Norfolk; but as a

London alderman he acquired some property in Kent.[158] William Wangford, a royal serjeant-at-law, acquired his lands at Northfleet legally, so far as is known; but Robert Est of Maidstone, who was described as one of the 'grete extorcioners beyng in Kente', expelled a fellow townsman from his property in 1441 and still held on to it in 1450.[159] Fraud and deception to the extent of £100 were the means employed by Lord Saye and his wife in 1448 to obtain an extensive stretch of countryside in the Kent parish of Seal from a man who thought he was exchanging it for other property.[160] Household servants were also accused of wrongfully securing the indictment and imprisonment of otherwise innocent men for the simple, though deceitful, purpose of appropriating their lands and possessions. As inquiries after the revolt discovered, instances of such activities abounded in Kent; support and maintenance by influential gentlemen like Richard Bruyn, steward of Cromwell's lordship of Hoo and a local JP, often had the same outrageous end in view.[161]

The area around Cranbrook in Kent supported a profitable cloth-weaving industry, while the fishing and trade of the ports in the Thames estuary and on the south coast were flourishing at this time.[162] Yet the impact of an inept government and its dishonest officialdom on the occupations and livelihood of Kentishmen here, as in the countryside, may have drawn many of them into the rising. The strain of the French war was felt directly by a county through which English armies marched to embarkation points like Dover and other Kentish ports; soldiers and camp-followers were quartered on the countryside to the profound distaste of the local population, which was rarely paid promptly for the food, clothing, and shelter it provided.[163] These ports were also badly hit by the commercial disruption that followed the loss of a friendly French coastline when Lancastrian power in Normandy collapsed in 1449–50; and the inconvenience (to say the least) that stemmed from the commandeering of merchant ships to transport troops to France, most recently in the autumn of 1449.[164] Moreover, there was an increase in piracy and in the number and seriousness of French attacks on the poorly-guarded English coast; in 1448 Rye and Winchelsea were burned by Frenchmen.[165] Most recently of all, the movement of troops had increased in the reverse direction, with disappointed soldiers and embittered settlers crossing the channel from Normandy after the fall of Rouen in October 1449; they 'cam into this land in greet mysery and poverte be many companyes and felawships and yede into severall places of the land to be enherite and to lyve upon the almes of the peple. But many of them drewe to theft and misrule and noyed sore the cominalte of this land . . .' Well might rumours of treason germinate in English soil, fed by the resentment of the defeated and expelled.[166]

The decay of the Cinque ports had long reduced their effectiveness in defence of the channel against enemies and pirates alike, and of late an attempt had been made to extend their customary naval obligation to certain inland communities: when Rye and Winchelsea defaulted, aid was demanded of Tenterden.[167] The cloth trade of the Kentish ports was severely curtailed by the deteriorating situation at sea and in France; to take an example, Sandwich's exports of wool and cloth slumped disastrously in 1449 compared with previous years, and wine imports fell to a quarter of their recent level. The decline of this Kent port was far greater and more damaging than that of ports across the country as a whole. Furthermore, the mismanagement of the kingdom's trading relations with the Low Countries and the Hanseatic league could not but cause further exasperation, for it brought instability to the channel and increased the possibility of piracy.[168] Already by 1448 the trading community of the small north Kent port of Faversham had become agitated by violent arguments between, on the one hand, the merchants, brewers, and victuallers of the town and, on the other, the common porters whose livelihood from dues charged at the quayside seemed in danger. New regulations had to be promulgated on 10 July by the mayor, John Seyncler. It is noteworthy that the continued violence in Kent later in 1450 was centred on this port.[169]

One cannot ignore the reputation of Kent in explaining why the rising began in this county: it was a reputation founded in part on the memory of 1381, and it was justified by the ease with which its lanes, roads, and waterways, linking London and the coast with the villages and towns of the Weald, enabled 'rumour, news, alarm and hope . . . . [to] spread as rapidly as they did'.[170] Its receptivity to 'new chaung and new fangelnes' was noted by the Croyland chronicler later in the century and by Edward Hall and others early in the next; this quality doubtless owed something to its cross-channel links with the Low Countries and north-western France, and to the consequent ease with which new ideas or unsettling news spread through the Kent countryside.[171] The duke of York, when he challenged the king's government a second time in 1452, made for Kent because, among all the shires of England, it was the most likely to respond to his call. In such an environment, the political songs and popular ballads that were current in 1450 may have helped forge an *esprit de corps* among the commons of the south-east. The confident verse which was incorporated in one of the rebel manifestos served the purpose well:

> God be oure gyde,
> and then schull we spede.
> Who-so-euur say nay,
> ffalse for ther money reuleth!
> Trewth for his tales spolleth!
> God seend vs a ffayre day!
> A-wey traytours, a-wey![172]

At the root of men's frustrations was the knowledge that remedy for the oppressions of Kentishmen (and others) was baulked by a corrupt officialdom, headed by the sheriff, whose office had become notorious, and his under-sheriff. They and the bailiffs to whom they often farmed their offices were determined to reap the best profit they could by methods that sometimes strayed across the frontier of legality into extortion, fraud, and false indictment. One of the bailiffs of William Crowmer, himself an extremely unpopular sheriff of Kent, was accused of abusing his position to extort cash from a hapless Chatham man in May 1442 without any warrant or other authorization. John Alpheigh, who attracted odium for other reasons as one of the 'common extortioners and oppressors of the lord king's people', acted unscrupulously for his own gain when he was under-sheriff of Kent in 1442.[173] Officials of private landowners like Cromwell and the archbishop were no better, while the franchisal courts of Dover had taken to extending their jurisdiction beyond its customary limits by 'divers subtile and untrue meanes and actions falsely fained . . . in great hurt of the people in all the Shire of Kent'.[174]

Symptomatic of the alleged venality of shire government was the interference in free parliamentary elections in Kent by 'letters . . . . sent from divers estates to the great rulers of all the country, the which enforceth their tenants and other people by force to choose other persons then the common will is'.[175] The complainants believed that such surreptitious influence was being exerted by members of the king's household. Although there is no surviving evidence of contested elections in Kent during the 1440s, or accusations at Westminster of corrupt practices at election time, the record of shire representation lends weight to the charges.[176] The household circle of Lord Saye, with its powerful Kentish dimension, was able to dominate the election of county members in the 1440s, not least because the sheriff, the county's returning officer, was one of this circle of 'great men' denounced by Cade and his followers. Stephen Slegge, sheriff in 1448–49, made the returns of the county members, as well as those of Canterbury and Rochester, for the parliaments of 1449 and 1449–50; he was closely associated with Lord Saye, had served the archbishiop in the past, and was bitterly attacked for his oppression and corruption in 1450. He had been under-sheriff in 1441–42 for John Warner, who was related to William Isle, another of Cade's *bêtes noires* and himself the sheriff who made the Kent returns for the Bury parliament of 1447; Warner and Isle together represented Kent in 1449–50. The notorious William Crowmer was sheriff in 1444–45 and conducted the election for the 1445–46 parliament, while he was himself MP for Kent in 1447 and 1449. Thus, all four sheriffs who had responsibility for making the returns for the five parliaments immediately preceding Cade's rebellion came from Saye's charmed, but unpopular, circle. For the ten county seats available in these parliaments, six persons were elected: both William Isle (1442 and 1449–50) and William Crowmer (1447 and 1449) were MPs twice, while James Fiennes, before his elevation to the peerage as Lord Saye, was Kent's MP on three occasions (1442, 1445–46, and 1447). Warner was Isle's colleague in 1442. The remaining two members,

Thomas Browne (1445–46) and Sir John Cheyne (1449), were connected with the régime at Westminster, for the former was a prominent exchequer official and the latter a royal serjeant-at-arms; both, therefore, would have been known to the Saye circle and, one may presume, favoured by it.[177] After the murder of Saye and Crowmer in London, and the fierce attacks on Isle, Slegge, and the rest, Cheyne's haste to secure a general pardon on 7 July 1450 can be well understood.

The grounds for rebel misgivings about the elections in the urban constituencies of Canterbury and Rochester were fewer, though by no means negligible. Seven men represented Rochester in these same five parliaments between 1442 and 1450; of these, two (1442 and 1449–50) were minor officials in the household organization that Saye headed, whilst one other was among the group whose lawless activities in Kent were investigated by the commission of 1 August 1450.[178] In Canterbury, there were likewise seven different MPs during these years; only William Say (1442 and 1447) appears to have been a household official, but another (1449) turned out to be an active pursuer of rebels in 1450, and five felt it desirable to avail themselves of the royal pardon on 7 July.[179] It is significant, too, that the elections in the Cinque ports were arranged by the lieutenant of the warden, Lord Saye (since 1447); accordingly, Gervase Clifton made the returns for him and sent to the chancery more new names for the two parliaments of 1449 than had been usual in the recent past.[180] There are strong indications, therefore, that the influence of Saye and the régime at Westminster controlled Kentish elections to parliament in the 1440s. As a comment on the grip which these 'great men' had over the county's representation, the rebels' accusation was soundly based; their presence in parliament was simply a further facet of their dominance of local society and national politics. When the crisis broke in 1450, many of them attracted the rebels' condemnation or hurried to secure a general pardon before worse befell them. This near-monopoly of representation of the county and its major towns by a small group of men closely connected with Saye, the household circle, or government service provides circumstantial proof of the rebels' charges; it is unfortunate that none of the 'letters' mentioned by them has yet come to light.

Once elected, it seems, the knights of the shire bought and sold the post of tax-collector 'for gifts and bribes...extortionously at the Knights lust'.[181] Any expectation of reform was ultimately baulked by the dispiriting realization that the traditional, or 'natural', counsellors of the king – especially the lords of the blood royal – were prevented from influencing Henry VI by others of less exalted lineage who dominated his council, shielded him from complainants, and feathered their own nests by accepting 'bribes and gifts' as 'messengers to the hands of the said counsell'.[182] The rebels showed a touching, conservative faith in traditional, aristocratic government, and in the cleansing of an inefficient and corrupt régime rather than in its complete substitution by something better.

The only radical proposal for widespread reform was adopted from the programme of the commons in the parliament of 1449: that alienation of the king's resources should cease and with it the heavy taxation that was required instead.[183] Indeed, the authors of this manifesto confined themselves to proposing implicitly the end of abuse, illegality, and oppression, and a return to sound, time-honoured principles of good government. The single specific and practical exception was, significantly, a Kentish one: in order to remove the inconveniences whereby men from the far west of the shire were summoned to sessions in the far east and spent as much as five days on the road, the rebels advocated the establishment of two sessions for the eastern and western parts of the county.[184] All in all, this was a politically cautious programme in view of the revolutionary events of 1450: Suffolk was not maligned and the Kentishmen hastily denied that they had had anything to do with his murder. None of the king's advisers was mentioned by name, even though responsibility for most of the oppressions and disasters was set firmly at the door of 'the king's meniall servants of housbold'. It stopped short of making truly treasonable utterances.

After the rebels had encamped on Blackheath, the tone of their complaints changed because the audience to which they now had to appeal had also changed. The rebels realized that the success of their enterprise depended on enlisting the support of a wider public beyond Kent: the Londoners, the retainers whom the king was certain to be marshalling against them, loyal and patriotic Englishmen and, if possible, even men in high places who might espouse the rebel cause and sponsor the rebel petitions to the king. Many people in and around London, Sir John Fastolf among them, were bound to be curious as to the precise intentions of the rebels, especially when their leader claimed kinship with the duke of York, a magnate whose reputation as a war commander and an opponent of the Suffolk régime, stood him high in popular esteem. A contemporary copy of a manifesto of complaint, appeal, and exhortation survives in Fastolf's archives, and it rehearses certain rebel attitudes in great detail and in a way calculated to impress several interests apart from those in the south-east.[185] According to the recollection fifteen years later of John Payn, one of Fastolf's servants, he had been ordered by the aged knight 'to take a man and .ii. of the beste orsse that were in his stabyll with hym to ryde to the commens of Kent' then assembled on Blackheath, in order 'to gete the articles that they come for'. After a hair-raising experience that brought Payn almost to the block, 'I gete th'articles and brought hem to my maister'.[186] They presumably comprise the document now deposited in the library of Magdalen College, Oxford.

This second document is in no sense a peculiarly Kentish document; rather does it express universally felt grievances in a mood more of sorrow than of anger: 'These ben the poyntes, mischeves, and causes of the gederynge and assemblynge of us, youre trew lege menne of Kent, the weche we triste to God for to remedye, with helpe of hym oure Kynge, our Soveraigne lorde, and alle the comyns of Inglond, and to dye therefore'. Its main purport is a detailed indictment of 'the false traytours abowte his hyghnesse' for their greed, deceit, and maliciousness, and for their mismanagement of the king's affairs. This was no narrow, sectionalist complaint, but a skilful plea for the restoration of sound and equitable government, 'wherfore we exorte all the Kynges trew lege mene to helpe us'. Several of the charges against Henry VI's advisers had been heralded by the catalogue of Kentish ills – isolating the king from his subjects, monopolizing his patronge, securing judicial decisions for selfish ends, advocating heavy financial demands on his subjects – but the tally was now considerably extended. Thus, the king's companions were denounced for encouraging the king to believe that he could make and unmake law at his pleasure, thereby breaking his coronation oath (rather after the manner of the ill-fated Richard II, the memory of whose deposition may have occurred to some as a salutary lesson to be applied in 1450). In particular, they were said to be stressing the king's traditional, but little used, prerogative of pronouncing a traitor by his own declaration or 'record' for their selfish purposes.[187] The law, in short, was felt to be seriously defective, and not even the court of chancery seemed able to provide a remedy.[188] Yet the appeal went far beyond issues of personal security and access to the courts, for this manifesto also pressed the accusation that the king's advisers opposed resumption of royal grants, a proposal which had been presented to the Leicester parliament by the commons.[189] The self-seeking of the king's companions was matched only be their maliciousness in poisoning Henry's mind against his subjects by implying that they wished to replace him by the duke of York. The depths to which they were prepared to sink in order to preserve their own position and destroy their opponents was (the manifesto claimed) demonstrated by the unwarranted appeal of treason of the duke of Gloucester just before his death in February 1447; a contrast was tellingly drawn with the reprieve of Suffolk before his murder in May 1450. Moreover, Suffolk's affinity had seemingly recommended the use of force against loyal subjects, presumably in response to the rebels' advance to Blackheath. The indictment of the royal ministers was, in sum, a damning one. In one pithy sentence, the rebel advocates reviewed their principal accusations: the king

hath hadde ffalse counsayle, ffor his londez ern lost, his marchundize is lost, his comyns destroyed, the see is lost, ffraunse his lost, hymself so pore that he may not for his mete nor drynk; he oweth more than evur dyd kynge in Inglond, and yit dayly his traytours that beene abowte hyme waytethe whereevur thynge schudde coome to hyme by his law, and they aske hit from hyme.

It was an adroit and resourceful piece of propaganda and exhortation, which enlisted the untainted name of the duke of York and the growing posthumous reputation of 'the good Duke of Gloucester'. Shrewd minds had devised its appeal to a threatened landowning community, obstructed in its litigiousness, disappointed in its expectations, and affronted by the power of selfish household men.

The sole specifically Kentish grievance in this manifesto was overtly propagandist in nature and directed at the same kind of audience; it was calculated to rouse the gentlemen of Kent, who were told that the king's advisers coveted their possessions and were bent on convicting them as traitors and rebels.[190] Yet Cade's men were prudent enough to avoid any impression that they were social revolutionaries of the calibre of John Ball or the lollards. The manifesto refrained from naming the guilty men (in case they immediately fled, one contemporary suggested),[191] but the skilled author assured the influential and the propertied that the rebels did not blame all lords, all gentlemen, all lawyers, all bishops, all priests, nor even 'alle that biene aboute the Kynges persone'. This was no egalitarian or anti-clerical movement; only the guilty were blameworthy.[192] Above all, the manifesto affirmed the rebels' loyalty to the king and their determination to act in a restrained manner: '.... but these fawtes amendid we schall go hoom'. Until their entry into London on 3 July, the rebels strove to honour their guarantee that they would commit no acts of lawlessness.[193]

The practical remedies proposed were few in number and traditional in character, but at least they elevated the document above a mere list of complaints and grievances. The rebels placed their faith in the king and the restoration of customary legal process. Accordingly, they requested that an inquiry be established in Kent 'with serteyne trew lordez and knyztes', so that 'justyse may be done upon hem [the traitors and bribers] whoso evur they be'.[194] If the king had acted promptly on this request, it is possible that the subsequent course of the revolt would have been different. But he either equivocated or else rejected the rebel demand. At any rate, it was only after the rebels had rampaged through London that on 1 August a commission of oyer and terminer was nominated for Kent.[195] The king was also recommended to retain in his own hands the lands and possessions of any found guilty by the commission, so that they could augment the king's resources or else be used to finance the French war and service his debts – two obligations that were universally acknowledged to be pressing. Finally, access to the king should no longer be governed by the offering of bribes or the proffering of *douceurs* to those who stood about him. Honest, open, and successful government was what the rebels wanted, and they felt confident that such aims would be widely applauded in the country at large. If the king and his ministers conceded some of the demands, they did so with great reluctance, and the commission of oyer and terminer appears to have had a minimal result as far as the punishment of the guilty is concerned.[196]

The third extant manifesto survives today in a contemporary body of miscellaneous political material which C. L. Kingsford designated 'Collections of a Yorkist partisan'. It seems to have been compiled shortly after May 1452 by a citizen of London with a highly developed and analytical political sense.[197] 'These ben the desires of the trewe comyns of your soueraign lord the Kyng', and they come closest to representing the bill of petitions presented to the king and his ministers during the rebellion.[198] Each clause is a clear, simple, and brief demand for action, and together they may very well have been the document given to the archbishops on Blackheath on 16 June. The grievances for which remedy was sought had been rehearsed already in the other rebel manifestos, but, as befitted an address to the king himself, who alone had the power to remove them, names were now named of the 'opynly knowyn traitours'. The rebels advocated resumption of the king's demesnes to enable him to 'raign lyke a Kyng Riall'; and the punishment of Suffolk's traitorous and 'false progeny and afynyte', who were considered to be responsible for the disgrace and death not only of Gloucester (1447), but also of the dukes of Exeter (1447), Somerset (1444), and Warwick (1446), and of Cardinal Beaufort (1447), as well as for the loss of Lancastrian France and the betrayal of the men who served there.[199] In relation to Kent, the rebels requested an end to all extortions, particularly the collection of debts by false warrants, and the use of the court of king's bench presumably to secure wrongful indictment, imprisonment, and conviction.[200] The statute of labourers, first promulgated in 1351 and most recently in 1445, was resented for its attempt to fix maximum wages and to restrict the movement of (in Kent) a highly mobile labouring community, unburdened by antiquated customary dues.[201] Accusations of unauthorized purveyance of grain, meat, and other foodstuffs were levelled at the 'grete extorcioners beyng in Kente', Stephen Slegge, William Crowmer, William Isle, and Robert Est; their punishment was demanded by a predominantly Kentish rebel host.

The rebels looked for reform to the magnates of the realm who, it was felt, had been displaced by the Suffolk clique: to the four dukes of York, Exeter (who was just twenty years old), Buckingham, and Norfolk, but significantly not to the duke of Somerset, who had just surrendered Rouen; and to the earls and barons of England, the king's natural counsellors.[202] The particular emphasis laid on York as 'the hye and myghty prince' and 'the trewe blode of the Reame' can hardly have failed to alarm King Henry and his court, now that they were faced by a rebel leader who, to all appearances, was a kinsman of the duke. Once again, the reputation of both Gloucester and York was being skilfully exploited with only moderate respect for the truth, to attract sympathy to the rebel cause. It was to this bill of petitions that the king apparently returned a clear, negative answer, once again showing that unwillingness to desert his friends and companions which had briefly protected Suffolk earlier in the year.

If Cade's followers professed themselves anxious to behave with restraint – and their petition denounced only a handful of individuals – these statements were merely the formal expression of a much larger and more scathing body of complaint that was current in the tense atmosphere of May–June 1450. To gauge popular sentiments in fifteenth-century England is extraordinarily difficult; nevertheless, the verses and ballads that were on men's lips or were chanted in meetings and conventicles convey something of commonly held political attitudes, even though they were couched in narrowly personalized terms. Several poems, still surviving, harshly ridiculed Suffolk and his cronies, but one in particular, which even today exists in several manuscripts and three different versions, surpasses them all for the cruel irony of its indictment of fifty councillors, household and government servants, and assorted ecclesiastics, apart from Suffolk, Adam Moleyns, and Sir Robert Roos who were already dead.[203] They were each assigned a role in a parody of the Office of the Dead sung for Suffolk's soul:

> Who shall execute his exequies with a solempnite?
> Bisschopes and lordes, as grete reson is,
> Monkes, chanons, prestes, and other clergie
> Pray for this dukes soule that it might come to blis,
> And let never suych another come after this!
> His interfectours blessed might thei be,
> And graunte them for ther dede to regne with angelis,
> And for Iac Napes soule, Placebo and dirige.[204]

The poem was current after the death of the hated duke on 2 May, but probably before the murder of Bishop Aiscough on 29 June, and certainly before that of Lord Saye in London on 4 July. To judge by the absence of the names of purely Kentish extortioners like Crowmer, Isle, and Est, it did not originate with the Kentishmen. It is more likely to have been popular among the Londoners and the magnate retainers in the last two weeks of June as they surged restlessly inside and outside London prior to Cade's return to Blackheath. Thus, among those portrayed as offering their prayers were a number of royal servants involved in the last dismal phase of the French war (among them, Lord Hoo, lately chancellor of France, and negotiators like Abbot Boulers, Master Thomas Kent, and Master Gervase le Vulre),[205] certain London merchants connected with the government (including Aldermen Horne and Malpas, who urged resistance to the rebels and consequently fell foul of them, John Judde, and William Cantelowe, formerly victualler of Calais[206]), and Lords Dudley and Rivers, Thomas Daniel, and Sir Thomas Stanley, who had borne down upon north Kent in the wake of the retiring rebels after 18 June.[207]

Others singled out by name were the heads of certain religious houses situated in or near London: for example, John Stoke, abbot of St Albans, a notorious Benedictine, 'lax in administration, malicious and indiscreet in his personal dealings'; the abbot of St Mary Graces on Tower Hill, 'with his fate face'; Katherine de la Pole, abbess of Barking and Suffolk's eldest sister; and Edmund Kyrton, the disreputable abbot of Westminster who had been charged in 1446 with being 'a fornicator, dilapidator, perjurer, simoniac', and much else besides.[208] The king's council, with its heavy leaven of bishops like Kemp of York, Aiscough of Salisbury, Lowe of Rochester, and Lyhert of Norwich, attracted some of the satire, and so did recently created barons like Saye, Dudley, Sudeley, Stourton, and Rivers, who were courtiers; they were linked with other household servants – Thomas Daniel, John Trevilian, Sir Edmund Hungerford, John Say, John Penycock, Sir Thomas Tuddenham, and others of that ilk.[209] Bartholomew Halley and Thomas Pulford had been given charge of Eleanor Cobham in 1441 and Gloucester in 1447, and this may still have rankled in 1450, when the rebels accused them of having 'drownyd the duke of Glocestar'.[210] William Mynors was one of Suffolk's keepers for a short period in March 1450 when King Henry was attempting to protect him.[211]

Just as the insurgents laid great stress on their fundamental loyalty to the king, so they showed no obvious hostility to the queen; indeed, Margaret may have played a modest role in the offer of a general pardon to the rebels and others on 6–7 July.[212] It is true that her chancellor, Bishop Booth of Coventry and Lichfield, and her confessor, Bishop Lyhert of Norwich, were subjected to insults and threats in 1450, while Bishop Aiscough, who had performed the royal marriage ceremony in 1445, was slain at Edington. But these men are more likely to have been regarded by the rebels as part of the group of eleven bishops, most of whom had been royal chaplains, some of whom were councillors, and three of whom were former confessors to the king, than as prominent members of a queenly circle whose unpopularity was second only to that of the king's own entourage. All but Aiscough and Kemp had been provided to their present sees since 1443, during Suffolk's ascendancy.[213]

To hear these and other names bandied about by desperate men was unnerving enough; in a parody of the funeral mass, following upon the murder of Suffolk and Moleyns, it was a fearful experience and doubtless played its part in persuading the king to leave London before the end of June. His alarm was well justified. After all, Saye and Aiscough would shortly be murdered by rebels; Horne and Malpas imprisoned by popular demand; Booth, Lyhert, and Boulers assaulted; and Daniel, Slegge, Dudley, Trevilian, and John Say threatened by mutinous retainers on Blackheath. The dire notions in such broadcast poems catch, as do the tales of destruction and killing, the morphology of Cade's rebellion.

Conciliation, turmoil, and retribution

Royal caution or uncertainty dictated conciliation when the rebels first appeared on Blackheath. Henry VI accordingly instituted an inquiry into their complaints, and Lord Saye and his son-in-law, Crowmer, were placed in custody. After the rebels entered London, however, they were brought out to face a tribunal, set up on 1 July but overawed and manipulated by Cade and his men once its sessions began in the guildhall. Both men were executed.[214] Even so, after Cade had been repulsed on London bridge during 5–6 July, the government still felt it wisest to offer a general pardon to the leader and any of his men who cared to take it. Sending the two archbishops and William Waynflete as mediators was in itself a conciliatory move, though admittedly most of the lay lords were probably with the king at Kenilworth and therefore not available to take an initiative.[215]

Henry returned to his capital before the end of the month: he was at St Albans by 24 July, holding a council meeting, and on the 28th he was received in London, where a service of thanksgiving was held at St Paul's cathedral.[216] Yet pacification continued even after the mass of the pardoned rebels had retired to their homes. Despite Cade's capture and death, disturbances were still common in London and the south-east, so that on 1 August a commission of oyer and terminer was appointed to investigate the oppressions of which the rebels had complained.[217] The commissioners were the two archbishops and the bishop of Winchester, who may have won the rebels' confidence by their earlier efforts at reconciliation, and also Buckingham and Sudeley, neither of whom had been closely connected with Suffolk, and a panel of eleven justices, of whom eight were to form the judicial quorum of the commission.[218] They held their sessions at Rochester, Maidstone, Canterbury, and Dartford from 20 August to 22 October; as one chronicler noted, their intention was to placate the Kentishmen.[219] This commission may have been the price paid to induce the rebels to accept the pardons of 6–7 July, for among the extortions, frauds, forcible disseisins, and other malpractices and oppressions investigated were those committed by several royal officials and their aides: by Lord Saye, who was already dead; the most recent sheriffs of Kent, Stephen Slegge and William Crowmer (the latter of whom had been executed), and several of their subordinates[220]; by John Trevilian and Thomas Bodulgate, who were household servants of west-country origin but guilty of forcible disseisins in Kent; some local officials of the archbishop of Canterbury; and a few other Kentish landowners who were especially obnoxious to the Kentishmen, mainly because of their activities in the 1440s.[221] Also indicted were Lords Dudley and Rivers; William, Ralph, and Sir Thomas Stanley from Cheshire; Thomas Daniel, Richard, Edmund, and William Vernon from Staffordshire; Sir John and Roger Griffith, also from Staffordshire; and Robert Legh from Cheshire, who were all accused of thefts, assaults, and forcible entries while they were pursuing the retreating rebels from

Blackheath.[222] To hear their names called in court must have gladdened the heart of many an erstwhile rebel! Even Alexander Iden was accused of unlawfully seizing cash from Henry Wilkhous, one of Cade's closest companions, while Iden was tracking down the rebel leader on 11 July.[223] Whether prompted by weakness or calculation, these proceedings constituted an astonishing act of reconciliation. But in the event, little true punishment was meted out to the accused: some were declared not guilty, as they had pleaded; others paid a fine; while the fate of many, though unknown, is unlikely to have been harsh.

It was equally necessary in the long term for the king and his ministers to demonstrate that rebellion and treason could not be tolerated as a means of political or personal protest, for England remained in a turbulent state long after Cade's death. Further commissions of oyer and terminer pursued those who continued in rebellion after 7 July, or who had not petitioned for a pardon at that time; and new disturbances in the south-east and elsewhere required sterner measures before the year was out. Several strands can be discerned in these later waves of unrest.

York's arrival from Ireland in September 1450, and his adoption of a number of the demands made by parliament and Cade's rebels, introduced a new element of instability into an already explosive situation. Moreover, some of the rioters perpetuated the belief that Cade's blood was Mortimer blood and that the captain was not only still alive but should be king – an opinion which obliquely emphasized York's dynastic position.[224] A number of Cade's Kentish adherents had refused to disperse after the death of their leader. In the vicinity of Sevenoaks, Cranbrook (the main cloth-weaving area), and elsewhere, rebels were active between September 1450 and January 1451, though bands of criminals bent on sheer robbery and murder soon began to set the pace. At Faversham, Canterbury, and other places in August–September 1450 William Parmynter, a Kentish smithy, declared himself to be the second captain of Kent, with a force of about 400 at his command; by his very title he implied that Cade's cause was not yet dead and ought to be fought again.[225] In January 1451 Stephen Christmas attempted to raise Kent once more, warning that the king was proposing to assemble soldiers in Lancashire and Cheshire in order to devastate the rebellious county; it was a rumour which would strike a chord with those who had read or heard Cade's manifesto or who knew about the force which the king had raised early in July 1450 in the north-west.[226] The more credulous were led to believe that Henry VI was about to seek aid from the French king, a charge calculated to rouse the ire of many a patriotic, if gullible, Englishman, just as a similar belief had heightened the distrust against Richard II.[227] Such plots, fuelled by rumour, invention, and historical allusion, continued well into May 1451.[228] An attempt was made to coerce the king himself when he arrived at Canterbury in February, in the hope of inducing him to grant wholesale pardons; in March the myth was being elaborated that Cade still lived.[229] In April a rising led by Henry Hasildene in Sussex and Kent directed its hostility towards the duke of Somerset and ventilated a common frustration at the disappointing results (from the protesters' point of view) of the parliament of 1450–51. Hasildene's most extreme proposal was to create twelve peers from the ranks of his own men who would henceforth rule the land.[230] To label such men as lollards and heretics who were anxious to turn all things to common ownership, was nothing more than a device whereby the common stock of contemporary charges could be assembled to ensure conviction for treason.[231] Then, in July a rising began in Kent which was led by Cade's notary and secretary, Henry Wilkhous (or Wilcotes), a lawyer who had once been procurator for the bishop of Rochester.[232] Others, concealing their identity with long beards and charcoal-blackened faces, and calling themselves servants of the queen of the fairies in a manner reminiscent of the rural Rebecca-rioters of nineteenth-century Wales, broke into Buckingham's park at Penshurst sometime in 1450 or 1451.[233] There can be no doubt that Kent, the home of revolt and the scene of the most chronic and widespread rioting in recent years, was in a state of seething unrest during 1450 and 1451; the conciliatory treatment of the autumn of 1450 would have to be succeeded by sterner punishment.

Popular devotion to Cade's memory, even belief in his personal survival, spread beyond Kent and was still alarming the authorities in 1452.[234] During the second week of September 1450 dissidents at Colchester, led by a local fuller, used his name as a rallying-cry; perhaps some of the Essex rebels of June–July had not yet dispersed to their homes.[235] The discord may have been less severe outside the south-east, but it nevertheless seriously alarmed the authorities. It was by no means confined to the south of England, but the concentration of chronicle-writing in London and the home counties may have obscured the outrages that took place in Flintshire, East Anglia, and elsewhere.[236] In some degree, these disorders were provoked by news of events in Kent – perhaps even were incited by the Kentishmen. In some areas, criminals used Cade's revolt as an excuse or as a shield for the prosecution of personal enmities and private greeds.[237] In others, the populace voiced similar sentiments to those of the Kentishmen, denouncing the mismanagement and oppression of the government and especially the household men. The contagion of rebellion spread quickly and effectively, but it was rarely co-ordinated, except possibly across the Thames estuary to bring Essex men to the gates of London just as Cade was arriving in Southwark.

Suffolk's steward, Sir John Hampden, was slain in Flint castle in 1450; the duke's chaplain, a Suffolk parson, was murdered and his secretary was arrested – all three unfortunates reaping the whirlwind that dragged their master down.[238] At Tewkesbury the sheriff of Worcestershire had an arm cut off and his clerk a hand – outrages that probably reflected detestation of a royal official at a time when sheriffs were particularly mistrusted by the populace.[239] In Northamptonshire,

William Tresham and his son Thomas, both of whom were household servants and Thomas a notorious extortioner, were assaulted on the king's highway by men in the service of Lord Grey of Ruthin, who was engaged in a personal feud with the Treshams. The impression given by William's widow that her husband was attacked and murdered because he was on his way to welcome the duke of York in September 1450, is likely to have been a ploy to secure revenge (and perhaps compensation) from a sympathetic parliament in 1450–51.[240]

In Wiltshire, yet another of the king's advisers, William Aiscough, bishop of Salisbury, who had actually married Henry VI and Margaret of Anjou in 1445, was hacked to death by his own flock at the monastery of the Bonhommes at Edington on 29 June 1450 while he was on his way to Sherborne castle (Dorset). This outrage was thought at the time to have been precipitated by news of the Kentish rising further east. The monastery at Edington was stripped of its possessions, especially its jewels, and the houses and other buildings were seriously damaged.[241] Hostility in the diocese towards the bishop was deep-seated, and the rebels of Wiltshire may have taken advantage of the unruly state of England in 1450 to settle old scores as well as to strike a blow at 'these [spiritual] lords and all other temporal lords around the king and of his council, traitors to the king'. Aiscough was relieved of £1,000-worth of personal possessions, and £3,000 in cash, that is, double the annual value of his bishopric. R. L. Storey may be right in suggesting that Aiscough, among Suffolk's associates, had enriched himself by means which the Kentishmen had recently condemned.[242]

Wiltshire society had some features in common with that of Kent, and the disturbances in the county were the most serious to occur in 1450 outside the south-east. Ecclesiastical landowners dominated the shire, and although there were indications of prosperity in agriculture and industry (especially the cloth industry), there was also by mid-century a certain resistance to the payment of rents and dues, and an increase in the mobility of labour.[243] The interruptions in cloth exports on the eve of Cade's revolt had an adverse effect – albeit temporarily – on many areas of Wiltshire, and it is significant that Salisbury, west Wiltshire, and Sherborne, where the most serious depredations occurred, were notable centres of cloth-making. It appears, therefore, that the Wiltshire rebels in 1450 were mainly craftsmen and labourers, whilst some of their specific targets exemplified deeply felt grievances against unpopular local figures and the representatives of an incapable government.[244]

In the ten days prior to Aiscough's murder, there had been several attacks on his property.[245] Hearing of the bishop's death, his tenantry proceeded to plunder the episcopal manors and lands near Salisbury and Sherborne, preying especially on their valuable sheep flocks.[246] In the city of Salisbury, the dean and chapter of the cathedral were attacked on the very day of the bishop's death, suggesting that rebel activities in the county were co-ordinated. A few days later, Aiscough's palace at Salisbury was ransacked and the episcopal archives largely destroyed.[247] With the heinous deeds done, remorse and fear for the consequences caused the bishop's tenants at Sherborne to club together to make restitution for their descent on the episcopal manors there, and in fact they obtained a general pardon from the king. But another, apparently unrelated, issue caused further rioting at Sherborne soon afterwards. A local grievance against a clerical landowner led to the renewal of an old quarrel between the abbot of Sherborne and his tenants in September 1450. Although on this occasion the cause of the unrest was relatively minor, relating to the position of a communal font in the abbey church, it produced several ugly incidents and even the desecration of the abbey itself. The abbot eventually gave way, fearing especially for his sheep flocks and his own fate in the aftermath of Aiscough's murder. The new bishop of Salisbury, Richard Beauchamp, agreed to consecrate a new font in the parish church instead.[248]

In the neighbouring diocese of Winchester, the palace of Bishop Waynflete, who had actually negotiated with the Kentish rebels, was sacked. More comprehensible was the siege of Bishop William Booth, a member of the queen's household, in his palace; the threats against Bishop Lyhert of Norwich in his diocese; and the plundering of the manor of Wyreyard, which belonged to Abbot Boulers, by the men of the city of Gloucester.[249] Both Lyhert and Boulers, like Aiscough and perhaps Waynflete, were bitterly disliked by their neighbours and tenants for reasons that may have sprung from a century-old anticlericalism associated with resentment of a conservative ecclesiastical landowner. But these common sentiments were given particular point in 1450 by the connection of these men with the discredited régime of the duke of Suffolk, the wilful illegalities of royal officials and household servants, and the humiliating shame of French territorial losses. Lyhert, a Cornishman who was provided to the see of Norwich in January 1446 at Suffolk's express request, had turbulent relations with the city of Norwich, had engaged in peace negotiations with France in 1447, and at some stage became the confessor of Queen Margaret. Boulers had been abbot of Gloucester since 1437, though at the time of the attacks upon him he was in process of being elevated to the bishopric of Hereford; a councillor since 1443, he too had been on missions to France. His experiences in 1450 probably led him to seek the protection of the duke of York, who put him briefly in Ludlow castle.[250]

In London, the populace who had sympathized with Cade early in July continued volatile well into 1451, and frequently vented their spleen against the same royal and household servants who had been attacked at the height of the rising. The soldiery limping home from Normandy, the sensational arrival of York in the city, and the prospect of a new parliamentary session at Westminster on 6 November 1450, made the atmosphere electric and the city and government authorities very apprehensive. Defeated soldiers were still arriving in London during the first week of August 1450; men, women, and children were to be seen passing through the streets in carts, with all their belongings hastily salvaged from Normandy. They added an explosive element to a highly disturbed city.[251] The soldiers themselves were placed temporarily under the supervision of Lord Scales, but such an arrangement proved impractical not least because the means available to Scales to marshal them properly were probably inadequate.[252] On 21 July, a number of them made their way to the house of the Grey Friars, where Saye's body had recently been buried; his coat of arms, which was displayed to mark his tomb, was torn down and reversed. More soldiers returned from France with Somerset round about 1 August, and they too sought out the arms of Saye and Suffolk and insulted them wherever they could be found.[253] A number burst into the precinct of the Tower and stole arms and weapons from the stores; an inquiry was instituted on 5 August into this potentially dangerous occurrence.[254] The soldiers even prevented Henry VI from leaving the city for his beloved Eton, where he hoped to attend celebrations on 15 August.[255]

St Bartholomew's fair, which was traditionally held on 23 August, was likely to spark off further disturbances, and the deputy-mayor, sheriffs, and aldermen, with 300 men to help them, tried energetically to keep the peace while the fair lasted, keeping an eye particularly on the dejected soldiers lest they run amuck and attack traders and residents alike.[256] These soldiers remained a problem throughout the autumn, not least because they had kept their weapons and acquired more from the Tower armoury. Hence, the formal procession marking the installation of a new mayor on 29 October became the focus of trouble. The new mayor, Nicholas Wyfold, a grocer, was constantly harassed as he made his way through the London streets. After this incident, during which Wyfold and his men had to disarm forty of the soldiers who were rampaging through the city, the mayor issued a proclamation that banned, on pain of imprisonment, the bearing of arms by soldiers or lordly retainers in the city, for should a fight occur, a bloodbath might ensue. Mayor Wyfold rode tirelessly about his city desperately trying to keep the peace.[257] Meanwhile, the keeper of Newgate gaol, who had heard that he was to be replaced at Michaelmas 1450, set all the prisoners free; they took over the prison, burned some of the buildings, and threw stones at anyone within reach before the city authorities regained control.[258] An attempt to divert the unemployed soldiery to Bordeaux for its defence backfired, for the money raised to finance the expedition fell into the pockets of the corrupt.[259]

York's arrival in London in the first week of October heightened the uncertainty and promoted further unrest, particularly since it was known that efforts had been made by some household servants to impede his journey, perhaps even to arrest him. York was fast becoming the symbol for all the disaffected elements in the city, the south-east, and the realm at large. On 30 October his arms and badges were replaced by those of the king in London and the suburbs, but his supporters quickly restored them.[260]

Early in November, lords and their retinues began arriving in the capital in preparation for the opening of parliament on 6 November. York, Norfolk, and Warwick arrived two weeks late, with men from East Anglia whither York had gone to seek allies and supporters. Their heavily armed and liveried retinues were sizeable.[261] Despite the chains that were thrown across the London streets to hinder the gathering of a mob and impede riots, and in the face of an order on 6 November that no one should interfere with the lords who were present or the parliament that was about to begin, the concentration of armed men in the city proved disastrous.[262] Bills and seditious posters appeared on the doors of St Paul's cathedral, Westminster hall (where parliament was meeting), even on the door of the king's own chamber in the palace of Westminster.[263] When there was no indication from this parliament that the king and his lords were disposed to act, especially against Somerset for the losses in France, on 30 November a mob that included many of the seignorial retainers broke into Westminster hall and three times denounced the allegedly guilty men and demanded justice.[264] Next day, these same retainers engineered a veritable uprising against Somerset, with more than 1,000 of them attacking him in the city.[265] He was hurriedly escorted by barge from Blackfriars to the Tower on the king's order and for his own safety, rather as Lord Saye had been protected earlier in the year. This was achieved as a result of the steadfastness of the mayor, the duke of York, and the earl of Devon, who was responsible for conducting him secretly from the house of the Friars Preacher beside the Thames to the fortress downriver.[266] In the event, the duke faired better than Saye, for his life was spared even though his possessions at the Friars Preacher were ransacked on 2 December by the aristocratic retinues.[267] Responsibility for maintaining order in the city rested primarily with the mayor, assisted on this occasion by the dukes of York and Norfolk and the earl of Devon, who were almost the only magnates not identified with the king and his discredited régime and yet capable of attracting respect from the insurgents. On 2 December they issued a proclamation which, on pain of death, was directed against robbers and despoilers in London; to serve as an example, York took one thief and handed him over to the king, who ordered the earl of Salisbury to behead him publicly at the standard in Cheapside.[268]

These commotions impelled a number of the magnates closely associated with the government to withdraw from the city, for they were understandably embarrassed by, and fearful of, the activities of some of their own men.[269] The king, by contrast, made a personal effort to assert his authority and overawe the malcontents; he was supported by a powerful group of his magnates. A commission headed by the earls of Warwick, Salisbury, and Wiltshire, Lords Audley and Scales, the mayor of London, and a bench of eight justices, was nominated on 3 December to investigate the disturbances which had occurred in the city since parliament opened on 6 November. It met in the guildhall two days later, apparently in Henry VI's presence; its proceedings are unknown, but among other things it may have confirmed Somerset's temporary confinement in the Tower.[270] On the 3rd, too, the king and his magnates rode noisily through the city armed to the teeth and at the head of a force that has been put at 10,000. Norfolk and Devon were in front with 3,000; York, Salisbury, Arundel, Oxford, Wiltshire, and Worcester followed with the king and 4,000; while Buckingham and Warwick brought up the rear with a further 3,000 men. They made their way from the city to Westminster, with the citizens and populace gazing at them with some awe and apprehension as they passed through the streets. '. . . . a gay and gloryus syght if hit hadde ben in Fraunce, but not in Ingelonde, for hyt boldyd sum mennys hertys that hyt causyd aftyr many mannys dethe.'[271] It was intended as a demonstration of official power that would quell the unrest and discourage troublemakers. Nevertheless, many hurriedly packed their bags and left the city, including Sir Thomas Tuddenham, who was chamberlain of the royal household, and Lord Hoo, lately chancellor of Normandy. Their property in the city was looted by the enraged rioters, among whom were some of their own retainers.[278]

The widespread nature of the disorder in England is gruesomely reflected in the destinations of the heads and quarters of rebels executed during 1450–51: the limbs of Cade, and a score of others were distributed to Rochester, Canterbury, Blackheath, and the Cinque ports in Kent, to London, to Chichester (Sussex), Colchester (Essex), and other towns in the midlands (Coventry), Norfolk (Norwich), Lincolnshire (Stamford), Berkshire (Newbury), Hampshire (Winchester and Portsmouth), Wiltshire (Salisbury), and as far west as Gloucester.[273] York's arrival in September had, if anything, heightened the expectations of many rebels, and therefore severe repressive measures were required in place of the commissions of conciliation issued on 1 August. In September new commissions had been issued for Kent, but this time their intention was to suppress rioters and lawbreakers and bring them to justice.[274] The hated duke of Somerset himself went to Kent at this time and seized John Smyth, who had announced himself to be a captain of Kent; the duke tried with a will to re-establish peace and punish rebels.[275] September also witnessed a series of commissions covering Gloucester, Essex (under the earl of Oxford), and Wiltshire; in October, Gloucestershire and Wiltshire; and in November, Norwich.[276] In December, York himself was assigned to hold sessions in Kent and Sussex.[277] Then, in the new year Henry VI embarked on a personal tour of the most disaffected areas in the realm. First, he travelled to Kent, following the appointment of yet another commission in that troubled shire on 27 January.[278] The intention was to investigate offences committed since 8 July 1450 other than those which had been dealt with by the commission of 1 August. From 28 January onwards, the king spent about a month in the shire with a substantial number of his magnates, including the dukes of Exeter and Somerset, four earls, and six other lords, not to speak of three judges who provided the necessary legal expertise. He had, too, a large number of men with him, and the commission held sessions at Canterbury (on 2 February), Rochester, and Faversham.[279] Some rebels were pardoned after they had submitted to the king at Blackheath (significantly), naked to the waist and with ropes about their neck.[280] Others were captured: for instance, Robert Spencer, a soap-maker from Faversham who had been a sworn companion-in-arms of the arch-villain, Cade, was taken by none other than Alexander Iden, Cade's own captor; and Sir Roger Chamberlain, who had held Queenborough castle against Cade, apprehended Geoffrey Kechen and 'Captain Butcher'. William Parmynter, the self-styled second captain of Kent, with others of his company fell into the hands of Thomas Waryn, an esquire of the duke of Somerset who headed this investigation.[281]

A further commission on 20 May 1451 to more or less the same men accompanied the king once again into Kent, and this time they made their way westwards to hold sessions in Sussex (at Lewes on 29 June), Surrey, Hampshire, Wiltshire (at Salisbury from 20 July), and in the west country beyond.[282] Numbers of guilty men were brought humiliatingly before Henry VI to seek his pardon, and many were hanged.[283] Meanwhile, similar commissions, headed by the duke of Norfolk and the earl of Oxford, had been nominated on 18 February 1451 to investigate treasons in Suffolk.[284] All in all, this was a far less conciliatory campaign than that of August 1450. It was said that on one occasion eight rebels were adjudged to death in one day, and that when it was all over, twenty-three heads were carried back to London bridge for display.[285] It is striking testimony to the seriousness of the near-revolutionary situation facing the Lancastrian monarchy in 1450 that King Henry himself took such an active part in the eventual suppression of his rebellious subjects. This was noted by all contemporary chroniclers, as was the unprecedented severity of the punishments: 'Men calle hyt in Kente the harvyste of hedys', said one.[286]

The events of 1450–51 amounted to the most serious crisis encountered by the house of Lancaster since Henry IV's early days. Not since 1381 had the government and the realm been subjected to such a dangerous popular assault; the disastrous conduct of affairs at home and overseas by the king's ministers had not been condemned so harshly by the king's subjects since then. On both occasions the protests were made in the aftermath of military humiliation and scandalous revelations of official corruption and malpractice. Whatever social attitudes or economic grievances may have predisposed Englishmen to assail their masters and rulers in 1450, the king's ministers, servants, and companions must bear a heavy responsibility for creating the situation in which the realm found itself.

Notes

1 G. Kriehn, *The English rising in 1450* (Strassburg, 1892); H. M. Lyle, *The rebellion of Jack Cade, 1450* (Historical Assoc., 1950). As a result of editing *The Paston Letters* and several of the fifteenth-century chronicles, J. Gairdner constructed an account of the rebellion in *Fortnightly Rev.*, old ser., XIV (1870), 442-55; *PL*, I, 68-78 (rev. ed., 1904; original ed., 1872-75); and *DNB*, VIII (1886), 171-4. Interesting details uncovered more recently are noted below.

2 *English Chron.*, p. 64. This dating is supported by Stevenson, II, ii, 767, which states that the rising originated in Kent during the week beginning 24 May. Sir William Oldhall, York's councillor, was accused in February 1453 of proclaiming Cade as the rebel leader and of sending letters to Kent on 26 May to stimulate a rising (Storey, *End of Lancaster*, p. 79).

3 *HMC*, IX, pt.i (1883), 140 (Canterbury city archives); V (1876), 520 (Lydd corporation archives); *CChR, 1427-1516*, pp. 122-3 (with the original of the city charter of 4 May 1453 noticed in *HMC*, IX, pt. i [1883], 167-8). For Calehill heath, see J. K. Wallenberg, *The place-names of Kent* (Uppsala, 1934), pp. 387, 392. According to the Prussian agent, Hans Winter, writing in Bruges on 3 July, the rebels had gathered on 2 June (von der Ropp, op. cit., II, iii, no. 338).

4 *CChR, 1427-1516*, pp. 122-3; *HMC*, V (1876), 490 (Rye corporation archives), 520 (Lydd), 543 (New Romney corporation archives).

5 *CPR, 1446-52*, p. 385. A messenger sent to Faversham 'on the king's business' may have been on a mission of reconnaissance; the fact that he is recorded on the issue roll as having been paid 6s. 8d. on 18 May need not mean that he went on his errand quite as early as that (PRO, E403/779 m. 3). More than 70 yeomen of the duke of Buckingham made their way from Stafford to London to be with the duke at this time (K. B. McFarlane, 'The wars of the roses', *PBA*, L [1964], 91; Rawcliffe, op. cit., pp. 47, 77).

6 Giles, p. 39. The session ended on 6 June ('Benet's Chron.', p. 198). Parliamentary business was apparently left unfinished.

7 *CPR, 1446-52*, p. 385.

8 'Benet's Chron.', p. 198; Flenley, pp. 129, 153; 'Gregory's Chron.', p. 190. *Grey Friars' Chron,*, p. 173, says that they stayed 7 days, which would put their arrival on 11 June. One minor writer, however, maintains that the rebels reached Blackheath on 4 June (Flenley, p. 105), and B. Wilkinson adopts this faulty chronology (*Const. Hist.*, p. 36 n. 2).

9 'Benet's Chron.', p. 198; Stevenson, II, ii, [767]; Flenley, p. 129; *Great Chron.*, p. 181 (which puts the king at the Tower); *EHL*, pp. 371-2.

10 'Gregory's Chron.', p. 190; *English Chron.*, p. 65; Flenley, pp. 129-30; 'Benet's Chron.', pp. 198-9.

11 The most reliable chronicles on balance place the delegation's visit to the rebels at this point (Giles, pp. 39-40; *English Chron.*, p. 65; 'Benet's Chron.', pp. 198-9; Flenley, p. 130). But *Great Chron.*, pp. 182-3; *London Chrons.*, p. 160; and *Brut*, p. 518, place it after the return of the rebels to Blackheath at the end of June. See below, p. 614.

12 Below, p. 628.

13 *Three Chrons.*, p. 67; Flenley, p. 131; *Brut*, p. 517; 'Gregory's Chron.', p. 191 (with the quotation); *PPC*, VI, 94. William Stanley of Hooton (Cheshire) was one of those accompanying the king (*CPR, 1452-61*, p. 570).

It was believed in Bruges that they were reluctant to confront the king because they thought that he shared their devotion to the common good (von der Ropp, op. cit., no. 338).

14 *Three Chrons.*, p. 67; *EHL*, pp. 360, 366 (140 slain), 371-2 (27 slain); 'Benet's Chron.', p. 199 (40 slain); Stevenson, II, ii, [767] (26 slain); *Brut*, p. 517; *English Chron.*, p. 66; Flenley, p. 154; Giles, pp. 39-40 (where the skirmish is placed in a narrow lane at Bromley); *Great Chron.*, pp. 181-2; *London Chrons.*, p. 159 (which associates another esquire with the Staffords, who are reported to be brothers). William Stafford apparently fought valiantly, if recklessly (*EHL*, pp. 371-2; 'Gregory's Chron.', p. 191, for the quotation). The news in Bruges was exaggerated: 350 killed, Northumberland wounded, and Scales captured (von der Ropp, op. cit., no. 338).

15 Below.

16 R. Virgoe (ed.), 'Some ancient indictments in the king's bench referring to Kent, 1450–1452', in F. R. H. Du Boulay (ed.), *Kent records: documents illustrative of medieval Kentish society* (Kent Record Soc., 1964), pp. 223, 224, 225, 232, 241, 242, 243. Others involved included Cheshire and Staffs. gentry whom the king and magnates like Buckingham had probably brought from Leicester. See above, n. 5, 13. Thomas Daniel's activities were especially notorious: contemporaries claimed rather extravagantly that he plundered churches and murdered men and boys in Kent ('Benet's Chron.', p. 199; Flenley, p. 131).

17 PRO, E403/779 m. 8, 9.

18 *Three Chrons.*, p. 67; 'Benet's Chron.', p. 199; Flenley, pp. 131-2, 154; *Brut*, pp. 517-18; *Great Chron.*, p. 182; *English Chron.*, p. 65; Giles, p. 40. It was also the intention to arrest Thomas Daniel, but he went into hiding (Flenley, p. 132). Hans Winter in Bruges had heard (probably incorrectly) that Daniel, Dudley, Trevilian, and others had been seized by the royal forces and that Bishop Aiscough was being sought (von der Ropp, op. cit., no. 338).

19 Flenley, p. 132; 'Benet's Chron.', p. 199; *Great Chron.*, p. 182; *English Chron.*, p. 65; Giles, p. 40; *Brut*, p. 518; *EHL*, pp. 371-2. See above, p. 251.

20 'Benet's Chron.', p. 199.

21 *CPR, 1446–52*, p. 386; below, p. 656. Poynings had personal reasons for joining in a rising against the household regime (R. M. Jeffs, 'The Poynings – Percy dispute', *BIHR*, XXXIV [1961], 148-64).

22 Flenley, p. 154; *CCR, 1447–54*, p. 149; below, p. 624. The king sent spies to keep an eye on Cade's movements, among them John Hillesdon, a yeoman of the crown and a household servant; he was not recompensed for his £100 expenses until 20 September 1457, when he received a 7-year grant in Calais of £9 *per annum* (PRO, E404/67/170; *CPR, 1452–61*, p. 385).

23 'Benet's Chron.', p. 199; *English Chron.*, p. 66; Stevenson, II, ii, [768]; *Great Chron.*, p. 183; *Chron. of London*, p. 136; PRO, E403/779 m. 8. For the absence of the justices from London, see below, p. 615. The king had evidently left London by 29 June, when a messenger was paid for travelling to him at Kenilworth (PRO, E403/779 m. 8).

24 Rawcliffe, op. cit., pp. 77-8; PRO, E404/783 m. 12 (John Iwardby and John Poutrell). Serious disruption of the government offices at this juncture may

be reflected in the unusually short issue roll for the Easter term of 1450, and the virtual suspension of business between 4 July and 29 August (ibid., 779).

25 *Three Chrons.*, p. 67. The flight to Kenilworth is explained by one writer by the attacks on the household servants by the king's own retainers (Giles, p. 40).

26 'Benet's Chron.', p. 199; *Great Chron.*, p. 182. 'Gregory's Chron.', p. 191, places the return on 1 July; Flenley, p. 154, on 30 June. On 23 June a man called Stanlow (perhaps John Stanlow, a former treasurer-general of Normandy) was drawn and hanged at Maidstone, possibly by the rebels, or else by the vengeful royal agents who were in pursuit of the Kentishmen and any disorderly soldiers from Normandy (*EHL*, p. 371; *Grey Friars' Chron.*, p. 173). For Stanlow, see above, p. 468

27 'Benet's Chron.', p. 200; Flenley, p. 132; *English Chron.*, p. 66; *Great Chron.*, p. 183; 'Gregory's Chron.', p. 191.

28 'Benet's Chron.', p. 200; *Great Chron.*, p. 183. Flenley, p. 132, says that the Essex men had reached Mile End by 3 July.

29 'Benet's Chron.', p. 199; *Great Chron.*, p. 183; and Stevenson, II, ii, [768], link the rebels' return with the prior departure of the king.

30 *PPC*, VI, 95. For Harrington, see above, p. 410.

31 'Benet's Chron.', p. 200; 'Gregory's Chron.', p. 191.

32 *Great Chron.*, pp. 182-3; *London Chrons.*, p. 160; Flenley, pp. 133, 155. A John Parys was living at Rye on the eve of the revolt (*HMC*, V [1876], 515).

33 *Great Chron.*, p. 183; 'Gregory's Chron.', p. 192. Flenley, p. 155, indicates that the sessions lasted two days. The commission of 1 July amounted to a renewal of the proclamation of 19 June for the arrest of those of whom the rebels were complaining (*CPR, 1446–52*, p. 388; above, p. 613).

34 'Benet's Chron.', p. 200. The indictments of a household servant, Edward Grimston, and a government clerk, Thomas Kent, both of whom had acted recently as envoys (sometimes together) to Charles VII and the duke of Burgundy, and were associated with Suffolk, survive as PRO, KB9/265/120-21, 144-45. See Ferguson, op. cit., pp. 180, 189, 181, 190, 198, 204, 207. Kent may in fact have been abroad at the time of his trial.

35 *English Chron.*, p. 67; Stevenson, II, ii, [768]. For Crowmer's father, see Thrupp, *Medieval London*, p. 336.

36 'Benet's Chron.', p. 201; *Brut*, pp. 518-19; *Great Chron.*, pp. 183-5; below, p. 625.

37 'Benet's Chron.', p. 201; *London Chrons.*, p. 160; Flenley, p. 156; *Brut*, p. 519; 'Gregory's Chron.', p. 193; *Three Chrons.*, p. 68 (which says the fight lasted from 9 p.m. to 6 a.m.); *English Chron.*, p. 67 (where the fighting is said to have continued until 10 a.m.); Flenley, p. 134 (till 4 a.m.). Giles, p. 41, comments that the Londoners' resistance was made at night because most of the commoners still supported Cade.

38 'Benet's Chron.', p. 201; Stevenson, II, ii, [768]; Flenley, p. 156; *English Chron.*, pp. 67-8; *Great Chron.*, pp. 183-5. Scales and Gough had been invited to lead the citizen force.

39 'Gregory's Chron.', p. 193. For a prisoners' mutiny at Newgate at the time of the revolt, see M. Bassett, 'Newgate prison in the middle ages', *Speculum*, XVIII (1943), 241.

40 *Fabyan's Chron.*, p. 625; Hall, *Chronicle*, p. 222.

41 'Benet's Chron.', p. 201; Stevenson, II, ii, [768]; Flenley, p. 156; *Brut*, p. 519; *Great Chron.*, pp. 183-5; *CPR, 1446–52*, pp. 328, 338-74; 'Gregory's Chron.', p. 193; R. Holinshed, *Chronicles of England, Scotland, and Ireland*, ed. H. Ellis (6 vols., 1807–08), III, 226-7. Hall, *Chronicle*, p. 222, who has an unusually detailed account of the fighting, says that Archbishop Stafford came from the Tower and Bishop Waynflete from Holy Well (now Sadler's Wells) outside the city; he does not mention Cardinal Kemp.

42 *RP*, V, 224; *English Chron.*, p. 67; Flenley, p. 156; Stevenson, II, ii, [769]; Giles, p. 41; *PPC*, VI, 96-8; *CPR, 1446–52*, p. 387. Sir Roger Chamberlain was given a 40-mark reward (Barron, thesis, p. 526). Six of Cade's horses were handed over to the keeper of the privy seal for official use, and £40-worth of goods were later assigned to the bailiff of Rochester to rebuild the east gate of the town on the Canterbury road (*PPC*, VI, 98 [18 July], 101 [25 August]). A list of Cade's confiscated possessions is reproduced in F. Palgrave, *The ancient kalenders and inventories of the treasurer of His Majesty's exchequer* (3 vols., RC, 1836), II, 217, and in W. D. Cooper, 'Participation of Sussex in Cade's rising, 1450', *Sussex arch. coll.*, XVIII (1866), 32-3; there was £106 in cash and the goods were sold on 29 August for £274.

43 PRO, E403/779 m. 8; *CPR, 1446–52*, pp. 332, 334. The sale included some of the duke of York's jewels which were taken from Malpas's house (and originally deposited there perhaps as security for a loan); the duke was recompensed by a grant of £86 on 6 October 1450, which was the sale price of the jewels (PRO, E403/783 m. 2).

44 The proclamation appears in Stow, *Chronicles*, pp. 661-62, whence it was copied by Abraham Fleming into the 1580 edition of Holinshed, op. cit., III, 226-7. For the relationship between Stow, Fleming, and Holinshed, see Griffiths, *JMH*, I (1975), 190, 206. A damaged contemporary copy of it is among the muniments of the dean and chapter of Canterbury (M. 295) (*HMC*, V [1876], 445).

45 PRO, E403/783 m. 2; Flenley, p. 134; *Brut*, p. 519; 'Benet's Chron,', pp. 201-2 (which notes that Cade did not have a proper trial); 'Gregory's Chron.', p. 194 (where he is said to have been killed in the Sussex Weald); *EHL*, p. 297, and Flenley, p. 156 (where his death is placed near Maidstone in Kent); *Great Chron.*, pp. 183-5 (in a Sussex garden); *English Chron.*, pp. 67-8 (near Lewes, Sussex); *Chron. of London*, p. 136 (in Sussex); *Three Chrons.*, p. 68 (dating his capture to 13 July); *London Chrons.*, p. 62 (in a Sussex garden). Iden was paid 400 marks for his reward very quickly, and the king's gratitude extended beyond the grave, for on 6 August 1459 Henry VI pardoned Iden's two executors all of his debts (PRO, E403/779 m. 9; *CPR, 1452–61*, p. 506). For Seyncler's and Davy's role in the capture, see PRO, E404/67/24, 31; E403/783 m. 2. For the tradition that Cade was apprehended near Westwell, in the Kent parish of Hothfield, where a 'Jack Cade's Field' existed centuries later, see G. Hasted, *The historical and topographical survey of the county of Kent* (new ed., 12 vols., Wakefield, 1972; original ed., 12 vols., Canterbury, 1797–1801), VII, 417, 516; but this may refer to one of the early assembly-points of the rebels, for Calehill heath is only 2 or 3 miles away (above, p. 610). The likely Heathfield in Sussex is a little to the north-east of Lewes in the Weald.

46 *Brut*, p. 517; *English Chron.*, p. 64; Giles, p. 39. The government also

appears to have accepted his Irish origins (PRO, E403/779 m. 9; Stow, *Chronicles*, pp. 661-2).

47 *EHL*, p. 365. The squire supposedly lived at Tandridge (Surrey).

48 *HMC*, V (1876), 455; Stow, *Chronicles*. pp. 661-2.

49 *English Chron.*, pp. 64, 66; 'Gregory's Chron.', p. 192.

50 *English Chron.*, p. 64 (including the quotation); *Chron. of London*, p. 136; *Brut*, p. 517; Flenley, p. 154; 'Benet's Chron.', p. 198. It is just possible that Cade was also an assumed name (*Great Chron.*, p. 181).

51 *English Chron.*, pp. 64-5.

52 Below, p. 638.

53 Griffiths, *JMH*, I (1975), 196-7.

54 Storey, *End of Lancaster*, pp. 63, 79; *RP*, V, 265, 329. Cf. York's attainder in 1459 which implied for the first time that some of Cade's adherents, at the point of death, had confessed that they were acting on York's behalf in 1450 (ibid., 346).

55 Hall, *Chronicle*, p. 220; Polydore Vergil, op. cit., p. 84.

56 Above, p. 650. Several retainers of the duke of Norfolk were said to be involved with Oldhall (Storey, *End of Lancaster*, p. 79).

57 *CPR, 1446–52*, p. 328. By the end of the revolt, it was commonly known that his real name was not Mortimer, and that the charter of pardon was therefore void (*Three Chrons.*, p. 68).

58 *HMC*, V (1876), 455; Stow, *Chronicles*, pp. 661-2.

59 J. G. Bellamy, *The law of treason in England in the late middle ages* (Cambridge, 1970), pp. 97, 124-5, 186-7; *RP*, V, 224, 265; *PPC*, VI, 96-7. Accroaching the royal power was a rare justification for a treason charge in the fifteenth century.

60 *English Chron.*, p. 64.

61 'Gregory's Chron.', p. 191. J. Gairdner was inclined to accept the existence of two leaders (*DNB*, VIII, 172). But 'Benet's Chron.', p. 199, clearly implies that the captain who brought the rebels to Blackheath on 29 June was the same man who had led them two weeks earlier.

62 *HMC*, V (1876), 455; Stow, *Chronicles*, pp. 661-2.

63 'Gregory's Chron.', p. 190.

64 'Benet's Chron.', p. 198.

65 *English Chron.*, p. 65 ('a sotill man'); *Fabyan's Chron.*, p. 623 ('right discrete in his answerys'); *Brut*, p. 518 ('witty in his talkynge and request').

66 Below, pp. 635ff.

67 'Benet's Chron.', pp. 198-200 (50,000 Kentishmen *c.* 6 June, and 20,000 on 29 June, apart from the 6,000 from Essex); 'Gregory's Chron.', p. 190 (40,000 early in June); Flenley, p. 130 (over 60,000 in early June); von der Ropp, op. cit., no. 338 (60,000 with more coming every day). But *Great Chron.*, p. 182, states that the victory over the Staffords caused the rebel ranks to swell rather than diminish.

68 'Benet's Chron.', p. 201.

69 *CPR, 1446–52*, pp. 338-74. All modern interpretations are based on W. D. Cooper, 'John Cade's followers in Kent', *Arch. Cant.*, VII (1868), 233-71 (reproducing the list of Kentish rebels); idem, 'Participation of Sussex in Cade's rising, 1450', *Sussex arch. coll.*, XVIII (1866), 19-36 (the Sussex list). Both W. D. Cooper's articles are reprinted in B. B. Orridge, *Illustrations of Jack Cade's rebellion* (1869), pp. 24-82. For commentary,

see Storey, *End of Lancaster*, p. 63; Wilkinson, *Const. Hist.*, p. 36; McFarlane, *CMH*, VIII, 408; Lyle, op. cit., pp. 18-21; Gairdner, *Fortnightly Rev.*, old ser., XIV (1870), 442-55.

70 'Benet's Chron.', p. 201. *Brut,* p. 519; Giles, p. 41; and *Great Chron.*, pp. 183-5, record that the pardon was offered to the Kentishmen and others. A copy of it still exists in the dean and chapter of Canterbury muniments (M. 309) (*HMC*, V [1876], 455).

71 'Benet's Chron.', p. 202; *London Chrons.*, p. 160; below, p. 641.

72 Virgoe, 'Some ancient indictments', pp. 243-65.

73 Barron, thesis, pp. 520-1; Kingsford, *Prejudice and promise*, p. 50; *CPR, 1446–52*, pp. 341, 342.

74 PRO, E404/67/31; Barron, thesis, p. 526; *CPR, 1446–52*, pp. 366, 339; ibid., *1452–61*, p. 506. John Davy, who also helped to capture Cade, had a pardon (PRO, E403/783 m. 2; *CPR, 1446–52*, pp. 342, 368).

75 Virgoe, 'Some ancient indictments', pp. 221, 224, 227, 231, 233, 234, 235, 236, 240; *CPR, 1446–52*, p. 356. For Cade's denunciation of Est, see *Three Chrons.*, p. 99.

76 Virgoe, 'Some ancient indictments', pp. 224, 239; *CPR, 1446–52*, p. 341 (where he is said to hail from nearby Hawkhurst). For Slegge, see below, p. 633.

77 Virgoe, 'Some ancient indictments', pp. 226, 227, 229, 230; *CPR, 1446–52*, pp. 352, 370. Bruyn was also the archbishop of Canterbury's heavy-handed steward in his manor of Wingham by 1443 (Virgoe, 'Some ancient indictments', p. 240). When the Dartford inquiries were launched in May 1452, Bruyn was one of the commissioners nominated to investigate treasons committed since 7 July 1450 (ibid., p. 259; *CPR, 1446–52*, p. 577). Cf. Richard Snelgrove, Hamo Bele, Thomas Henry, Thomas Remee, Roger Twysden, William Carter, Walter Langley, and perhaps John Carter; others pardoned reappear as jurors co-operating in the indictment of subsequent rebels in 1451–52 (ibid., pp. 338-74 passim; Virgoe, 'Some ancient indictments', passim).

78 *CPR, 1446–52*, p. 364; Wedgwood, *Biographies*, pp. 547-8.

79 ibid., pp. 15-16; *CPR, 1446–52*, p. 363. For the son, see Wedgwood, *Biographies*, pp. 15-16.

80 *CPR, 1446–52*, p. 339; Lyle, op. cit ., p. 19; Wedgwood, *Biographies*, p. 181. Cf. John Septvans, a gentleman whose effigy with its SS collar in the Mollan chancel of Ash church (Kent) indicates that he was a faithful Lancastrian servant before his death in 1458 (R. Tower, 'The family of Septvans', *Arch. Cant.*, XL [1928], 115; *CPR, 1446–52*, p. 373 [his pardon]).

81 *CPR, 1446–52*, pp. 347, 338, 365, 370; Du Boulay, *Lordship of Canterbury*, pp. 399-400.

82 An analysis of surviving Kentish wills reveals an almost identical range of occupations as does the pardon-list, and in similar proportions, with the single exception of labourers, who were unlikely to leave wills anyhow (A. J. F. Dulley, 'Four Kent towns at the end of the middle ages', *Arch. Cant.*, LXXXI [1966], 96, 101).

83 *CPR, 1446–52*, pp. 338-74 passim.

84 ibid., p. 356; A Brown, 'London and north-west Kent in the later middle ages: the development of a land market', *Arch. Cant.*, XCII (1976), 152-3. Cf. John Seyncler as mayor of Faversham (above, p. 620; *CPR, 1446–52*, p. 366); this pardon is still lodged in KentRO, Faversham corporation

archives (*HMC*, VI [1877], 509). The pardon now in the archives of New Romney may have a similar origin (ibid., IV [1874], 442).

85 *CPR, 1446–52*, p. 372.

86 ibid., pp. 350, 355.

87 *CPR, 1446–52*, pp. 355, 478-9; Wedgwood, *Biographies*, p. 91; E. Searle, *Lordship and community* (Toronto, 1974), pp. 397, 422-3. Many of his 'men and servants' are among the tenantry listed in his surviving estate-book, which records the accumulation of Bolney's properties, mainly before 1450 (M. Clough [ed.], *The Book of Bartholomew Bolney* [Sussex Record Ser., LXIII, 1964]). Cf. Thomas Fynhow and Richard Beche, both of whom came from prosperous Wealden families (Searle, op. cit., pp. 334-6; *CPR, 1446–52*, p. 346, 362, 345, 360).

88 Ct. Lyle, op. cit., p. 19.

89 Hunnisett, *Sussex notes and queries*, XIV (1954–57), 119-20 (citing PRO, KB9/122 m. 28); *CPR, 1446–52*, p. 353. The Mirfields were echoing Cade's own alleged dismissal of the pardon as a royal snare (*HMC*, V [1876], 455; Stow, *Chronicles*, pp. 661-2). To judge by their subsequent behaviour, it is likely that the Mirfield brothers were rebels in 1450, for on 11 October they declared that they would rise again.

90 *EHL*, pp. 347-9; Flenley, p. 132. 'Gregory's Chron., p. 190, put it quaintly: 'als goode was Jacke Robyn as John at the Noke, for alle were as hyghe as pygys fete'. *Great Chron.*, p. 181, notes that there were no 'nobles' among them.

91 Gregory's Chron.', p. 190; below, p. 624.

92 *HMC*, V (1876), 520 (Lydd corporation archives).

93 ibid., p. 490 (Rye corporation archives). A similar inquiry was made on behalf of Romney (ibid., p. 543). For a possible rebel from Rye, see above, p. 652.

94 Yet as early as 10 June, the court of aldermen in London was told that men had been seen travelling down river to Gravesend with bundles of arms in their barges, possibly on their way to join the rebels (Barron, thesis, p. 485).

95 'Benet's Chron.', p. 199; *Great Chron.*, pp. 181, 182-3.

96 'Benet's Chron.', p. 199 (which says that the rebels withdrew, even though they were strong enough to resist; another writer states that they were certainly not afraid of the king (*EHL*, pp. 347-9).

97 'Benet's Chron.', p. 200. One chronicle (*EHL*, pp. 347-9) maintains that captains were nominated in several places, though he may be referring to the leadership of subsidiary risings in other parts of the country. For some of the lesser (or petty) captains, see *RP*, V, 396 (Thomas Bigg, a yeoman of Lambeth); Barron, thesis, p. 403 (William Caym of Sittingbourne, Kent); and for Cade's carver and swordbearer, Robert Poynings, see above, p. 613. For a reference to 'sworn brothers', see PRO, E403/785 m. 2 (Robert Spencer).

98 *Great Chron.*, pp. 182-3.

99 ibid., pp. 183-5; *Brut*, p. 518; above, p. 614.

100 *Brut*, p. 518; *Great Chron.*', pp. 183-5; 'Benet's Chron., p. 201; *London Chrons.*, pp. 160-1; below, p. 615.

101 Giles, p. 39; *EHI*, pp. 371-2.

102 'Benet's Chron.', p. 198. For details of Buckingham's retinue, see above, n. 5; and for Warwick's summons to Lord Ferrers for men on 9 June, M.

C. Carpenter, 'Political society in Warwickshire, 1401–72' (Cambridge PhD thesis, 1976), p. 195, citing *Notes and queries*, XIV ser., V (1919), 120.

103 'Benet's Chron.', pp. 198-9; Stevenson, II, ii, [767-8]; 'Gregory's Chron.', p. 191; *English Chron.*, p. 66.

104 It required considerable finance, some of which was provided by Cardinal Beaufort's executors, one of whom, William Port, had not been entirely repaid by November 1456 (*CPR, 1452–61*, p. 329; *CCR, 1454–61*, p. 154).

105 Above, p. 612.

106 *Three Chrons.*, p. 67; *Brut*, pp. 517-18; *Great Chron.*, p. 182; Giles, p. 40.

107 'Benet's Chron.', p. 199.

108 ibid.; *Three Chrons.*, p. 67; above, p. 613. According to *Brut*, pp. 517-18, the king initially rejected the demands of the mutinous soldiers.

109 'Benet's Chron.', p. 199.

110 'Benet's Chron.', p. 200; *English Chron.*, pp. 65-6; *Great Chron.*, p. 183. For London's attitude to Cade, see Peake, thesis, and Barron, thesis.

111 Storey, *End of Lancaster*, p. 62.

112 Sharpe, op. cit., I, 283, citing GuildhallRO, Commons Journal V f. 36b.

113 Barron, thesis, pp. 484-5.

114 ibid., pp. 485-6; Kingsford, *Prejudice and promise*, p. 50. The two Londoners who supervised this expedition were later arrested when Cade entered the city. Meanwhile, shops and taverns were closed (von der Ropp, op. cit., no. 338).

115 Barron, thesis, p. 491.

116 Flenley, p. 154.

117 *Three Chrons.*, p. 67; above, p. 614.

118 Sharpe, op. cit., III, 283-4, citing GuildhallRO, Commons Journal V f. 39, 38b. Four citizens 'of dignity and discretion' were nominated in each ward on 30 June to assist the aldermen in supervising defence (Barron, thesis, pp. 500-1). Supplies were also conveyed to the Tower (*PPC*, VI, 95).

119 Stow, *Chronicles*, p. 653, reprinted in Holinshed, op. cit., III, 221. For Cooke's friendly links with alderman Philip Malpas, see Barron, thesis, pp. 503-4.

120 *Great Chron.*, p. 183.

121 Orridge, op. cit., pp. 2-5, citing GuildhallRO, Commons Journal IV f. 208b, 213b; V, f. 38b; *London Chrons.*, p. 160; *Great Chron.*, p. 183 (like Flenley, p. 155, placing the humiliation of Horne and Malpas on 3 July at the guildhall sessions); Gairdner, *Fortnightly Rev.*, old ser., XIV (1870), 450-1; Furnivall, *Political, religious and love poems*, p. 11 (for Horne in an anti-Suffolk ballad). Barron, thesis, pp. 495-9, suggests that Malpas's removal was amicably arranged, but this is not entirely convincing.

122 A chapman or yeoman, Lawrence Broke, assembled a number on 20 June in the parish of St Mary Matfelon outside Aldgate (ibid., p. 506).

123 Sharpe, op. cit., III, 284 n. 2; *English Chron.*, p. 66; *London Chrons.*, p. 160; *Great Chron.*, pp. 183-5; Barron, thesis, pp. 510-11; 'Gregory's Chron.', p. 191. See Wilkinson, *Const. Hist.*, p. 38 n. 4.

124 *RP*, V, 265; above, p. 613.

125 Lyle, op. cit., p. 12; Kingsford, *Prejudice and promise*, p. 50.

126 'Benet's Chron.', p. 200; *Great Chron.*, pp. 183-5; *Brut*, p. 518; Stevenson, II, ii, [768]; Flenley, p. 133. 'Gregory's Chron.', pp. 191-2, says that the rebels were 'halfe be-syde hyr wytte', though as a London chronicle its

opinion may not be entirely objective. York later recovered the value of his jewels stolen from Malpas's house (PRO, E403/783 m. 2 [6 October 1450]; above, p. 625).

127 *Great Chron.*, pp. 183-5; *Brut*, p. 518; *London Chrons.*, pp. 160-1.
128 *English Chron.*, p. 66; *Fabyan's Chron.*, p. 624; *Great Chron.*, pp. 183-5; Flenley, pp. 132, 155 (which suggests that Cade himself authorized Horne's ransom). A London skinner, Ralph Harris, and 40 of Cade's men seized Richard Delwold, one of Lord Saye's servants, in Southwark and held him for a £20 ransom (Barron, thesis, p. 501 – and also ibid., pp. 520-1).
129 'Gregory's Chron.', pp. 191-3; *Brut*, p. 518; *London Chrons.*, p. 160.
130 'Benet's Chron.', p. 200; Stevenson, II, ii, [768]. The summons to the sessions was issued on 2 July (*London Chrons.*, p. 160). *Great Chron.*, p. 183, maintains that it opened on 3 July. For Danvers, see Cooper, *Sussex arch. coll.*, XVIII (1866), 20; and *CPR, 1446–52*, pp. 58, 316, 333.
131 'Benet's Chron.', p. 200; *London Chrons.*, p. 160; 'Gregory's Chron.', p. 192; Flenley, p. 155.
132 'Benet's Chron.', pp. 200-1; Stevenson, II, ii, [768]; Flenley, pp. 106, 133, 156; *English Chron.*, p. 67; *Three Chrons.*, p. 67. According to 'Gregory's Chron.', p. 193, before he died Saye admitted involvement in the death of Gloucester in 1447.
133 'Benet's Chron.', pp. 200-1; Stevenson, II, ii, [768]; *Great Chron.*, pp. 183-5; 'Gregory's Chron.', p. 192; *English Chron.*, p. 67.
134 'Benet's Chron.', p. 201; Flenley, p. 106; 'Gregory's Chron.', p. 193; *Chron. of London*, p. 136; Stevenson, II, ii, [768].
135 For a list of the killings, see *EHL*, p. 366. See also Flenley, pp. 106, 133, 155-6; *Brut*, p. 519; *Fabyan's Chron.*, p. 624; *Great Chron.*, pp. 183-5; 'Gregory's Chron.', pp. 192-3 (which says that Maine came from Southampton); Stevenson, II, ii, [768]; *Grey Friars' Chron.*, p. 173. It is possible that Bayley was the John Baylly, formerly one of the duke of Gloucester's esquires, who had been involved in a divination scandal in 1436–37 (A. Vallance, 'A curious case at Cranbrook in 1437', *Arch. Cant.*, XLIII [1931], 173-86, using PRO, C1/12/210). Flenley, p. 133, gives his name as William, but there were 'Bayles' (including a John) living in the town of Rye immediately before the revolt (*HMC*, V [1876], 515). For Cade's own alleged dabblings with magic which, if true, may have been the cause of his nervousness on meeting Bayley in 1450, see *HMC*, V (1876), 455, and above, p. 619.
136 Above, p. 615; *Great Chron.*, pp. 183-5; Giles, p. 41; Stevenson, II, ii, [768].
137 Mabyowe was pardoned for treason on 6 April 1453 (*CPR, 1452–61*, p. 63).
138 Flenley, p. 133.
139 PRO, E403/779 m. 8, 9; above, pp. 500, 590.
140 *Brut*, p. 519; *English Chron.*, p. 67.
141 'Gregory's Chron.', p. 193; *Grey Friars' Chron.*, p. 173.
142 *Chron. of London*, p. 136; *London Chrons.*, p. 160; Flenley, p. 106; above, p. 615.
143 'Benet's Chron.', pp. 198-9; Giles, pp. 39-40; *Brut*, p. 517; 'Gregory's Chron.', p. 190; Flenley, pp. 105, 130, 154. Other chronicles place the mission of the archbishops and Buckingham at the time of the second advance to Blackheath (above, n. 11), and *English Chron.*, pp. 65-6,

mistakenly suggests that the petitions were forwarded to a parliament at Westminster which was dissolved after the Staffords' death.

144 Flenley, p. 130 (the most precise contemporary account of these negotiations). See also ibid., pp. 105, 154.

145 'Benet's Chron.', p. 199.

146 Above, p. 650.

147 Stow, *Chronicles*, pp. 654-7; Holinshed, op. cit., III, 222-3.

148 A point made by Du Boulay, *Lordship of Canterbury*, pp. 190-1.

149 Lyle, op. cit., pp. 6-7; Dulley, *Arch. Cant.*, LXXXI (1966), 97-8, reprinted in M. Roake and J. Whyman (eds.), *Essays in Kentish history* (1973); Du Boulay, *Lordship of Canterbury*, pp. 140-1, and his 'The Pagham estates of the archbishops of Canterbury during the fifteenth century', *History*, new ser., XXXVIII (1953), 208; 'A rentier economy in the later middle ages: the archbishopric of Canterbury', *EconHR*, 2nd ser., XVI (1963-64), 433, and 'Who was farming the English demesnes at the end of the middle ages?', ibid., 2nd ser., XVII (1964–65), 449. See also B. Harvey, 'The leasing of the abbot of Westminster's demesnes in the later middle ages', ibid., 2nd ser., XXII (1969), 19-20 (some of the most important Westminster estates lay in Middlesex and Surrey). The almost total leasing of the demesnes of the archbishop of Canterbury and the abbot of Battle by the beginning of the fifteenth century provided excellent opportunities for the advancement of local families (Du Boulay, *Lordship of Canterbury*, pp. 218ff; Searle, op. cit., pp. 324ff, 362-4).

150 Du Boulay, *Lordship of Canterbury*, p. 175 n.; Virgoe, 'Some ancient indictments', pp. 223, 224, 225, 227-8, 242. For extortion by one of the archbishop's officials, John Ingham, who was a well-known oppressor, see ibid., p. 233; below, p. 633.

151 Searle, op. cit., pp. 371-2, 374, 380-2, 397.

152 ibid., pp. 398-9.

153 Du Boulay, *Lordship of Canterbury*, p. 270; above, p. 339.

154 Virgoe, 'Some ancient indictments', p. 227.

155 Du Boulay, *Lordship of Canterbury*, pp. 148-9; Brown, *Arch. Cant.*, XCII (1976), 145-55.

156 Brown, *Arch. Cant.*, XCII (1976), 150-5. Alderman Malpas, against whom the commons of the city clamoured in 1450, had acquired lands in Essex (Thrupp, *Merchant class*, p. 354; see above, n. 121).

157 It has been calculated that of 358 Londoners noted in the lay subsidy roll for 1436 (tabulated in Thrupp, *Merchant class*, pp. 378-88) as having an assessment of £5 or more, 237 had property in nearby shires, especially in those east of the city: 37 in Kent, 33 in Essex, 35 in Middlesex, but only 17 in Surrey and 15 in Hertfordshire (Brown, *Arch. Cant.*, XCII [1976], 145).

158 Thrupp, *Merchant class*, p. 336.

159 Du Boulay, *Lordship of Canterbury*, p. 149 n. 1; Virgoe, 'Some ancient indictments,' p. 234.

160 ibid., p. 234.

161 ibid., pp. 220-43 passim (for example, pp. 222-3). For Bruyn, see ibid., pp. 226-7, 229.

162 Lyle, op. cit., p. 6.

163 Above p. 320. In 1449–50 Lydd offered a sweetener to John Yerde, the king's harbinger, to secure his good will in refraining from quartering large

numbers of soldiers on the town (*HMC*, V [1876], 519-20; PRO, E404/59/183). For unpaid debts of the royal household to constables of certain hundreds, possibly for quartering, see PRO, E403/760-79 passim (1445–50).

164 PRO, E403/779 m. 5-7. Ships were commandeered in the Thames estuary on this occasion.

165 Lyle, op. cit., p. 7; above, p. 430.

166 Flenley, p. 128; above, p. 520.

167 Lyle, op. cit., p. 7.

168 ibid., p. 8; E. M. Carus-Wilson and O. Coleman (eds.), *England's export trade, 1275–1547* (Oxford, 1963), pp. 61-2, 96-7.

169 F. F. Giraud, 'Faversham: regulations for the town porters', *Arch. Cant.*, XX (1893), 219-21; below, p. 642. For Seyncler, who secured a pardon in July 1450, see above, p. 620.

170 Du Boulay, *Lordship of Canterbury*, pp. 115-16.

171 Lyle, op. cit., p. 8; *Croyland Chron.*, pp. 466-7; Hall, *Chronicle*, p. 219. Cf. Polydore Vergil, op. cit., p. 84 ('They are desirous of novelties'). For the impact of continental links on the freedom and mobility of Kentish society, see Du Boulay, *Lordship of Canterbury*, p. 143.

172 *HMC*, VIII, appendix I, section 2, p. 267; Robbins, op. cit., p. 12. For similar poems current in 1450, see ibid., pp. 186-9, 203-5; below, p. 639.

173 Virgoe, 'Some ancient indictments', pp. 222, 223-5, 230, 237, 239, 241-2 (with the quotation on p. 224). The use of writs sealed with green wax to collect debts, both real and contrived, seems to have been a special irritation (ibid., p. 233; Stow, *Chronicles*, p. 389; below, p. 638).

174 Stow, *Chronicles*, p. 389; Virgoe, 'Some ancient indictments', passim. For an instance of an encroachment in Faversham, see KentRO, Fa/LC 1 f. 50v-51r (1446–47).

175 Stow, *Chronicles*, p. 389.

176 The following paragraphs are largely based on Wedgwood, *Register*, and *Biographies*; there is additional information on the sheriffs in Jeffs, thesis, passim.

177 For Browne, see also below, p. 286. One of his feoffees, William Benet, was accused of extortion in Kent in August 1450 (Virgoe, 'Some ancient indictments', pp. 235-6).

178 Respectively, John Bere, perhaps a royal servitor by 1445–46; John Chester (or Wryxworth), a chamber messenger in 1438–41; and John Nicholl (PRO, E404/62/143; 55/122; 56/270; 57/322; Virgoe, 'Some ancient indictments', pp. 222, 228, 231-2.

179 For the 1449 MP, Thomas Walter, see PRO, E404/67/94.

180 Rye sent a Southwark lawyer and a king's serjeant to the first parliament of 1449, and a London fishmonger and household purveyor to the second; Stephen Slegge himself represented Dover in 1449 and a chancery clerk from Middlesex the Romney constituency.

181 Stow, *Chronicles*, p. 389.

182 ibid.; below, p. 638.

183 Stow, *Chronicles*, p. 389; below, p. 638.

184 Stow, *Chronicles*, p. 389.

185 Magdalen College, Oxford, Misc. Doc. 306, printed in *HMC*, VIII, appendix 1, section 2, pp. 266-7.

186 *PL*, II, 313-15. Fastolf was certainly in London on 24 June (Folger Lib. MS 1007.1).

187 Bellamy, *Law of treason*, pp. 26-57, 154-5, 201.

188 More particularly, the chancery was well used in the mid-fifteenth century to protect the interests of landowners who employed feoffments to use in order to gain greater control over the future disposition of their properties, and this practice was frequently followed in Kent by men like John Alpheigh, one of the local extortioners in the 1440s (Du Boulay, *Lordship of Canterbury*, pp. 113, 157 and n. 2; above, p. 633).

189 Flenley, p. 130, states that on 16 June, Cade explained that he wanted 'to have the desires of the comones in the parliament fulfilled'.

190 Cf. above, p. 633.

191 *Great Chron.*, pp. 182-3.

192 But it was claimed by H. E. Drake (ed.), *Hasted's History of Kent*, part 1 (1886), p. 84 n. 6, that while they were in London, the rebels burned the office of arms and destroyed rolls, registers, and books of arms in a naive attempt to set everyone on an equal footing by obliterating such documentation. The evidence for this statement is elusive, and the incident is reminiscent rather of the rebels' behaviour in 1381 (C. Oman, *The great revolt of 1381* [2nd ed., Oxford, 1969], p. 59).

193 Above, p. 623.

194 A 16th-century copy of this manifesto adds that the rebels regarded the chief justices as unacceptable on this inquiry, presumably because they presided over a corrupt judicial system. Hence the flight of the two chief justices when the rebels approached London for the second time towards the end of June (*Three Chrons.*, p. 98; above, p. 613).

195 *CPR, 1446–52*, p. 388.

196 Virgoe, 'Some ancient indictments', p. 216.

197 *EHL*, pp. 165-6, 360-2. See Stow, *Chronicles*, pp. 654-7, for a 16th-century version with two minor amendments (below n. 199, 200).

198 Above, p. 628.

199 The charges involving the death of these lords were exaggerated for effect; apart from Gloucester, only Somerset died in strange circumstances and in disgrace (for his military failures in France), though Warwick's death at the early age of 21 was surprising (*GEC*, XII, i, 48 n. [b]; ii, 383-4). For Exeter, Beaufort, and Gloucester, see ibid., V, 205-11; McFarlane, 'At the death-bed of Beaufort', pp. 405ff; above, p. 497. Somerset's name was omitted from Stow's version. This entire document is reflected in Hans Winter's report from Bruges on the rebel demands at this juncture, though he added the loss of 2 castles on the Scottish border as a grievance (von der Ropp, op. cit., no. 338).

200 The clause about king's bench was omitted from the contemporary copy of the requests.

201 *RP*, V, 112.

202 It may not be entirely coincidental that Henry, duke of Exeter was granted special livery of his father's estates on 23 July 1450, without having to show proof of age and despite the fact that he was not yet 21 (*GEC*, V, 212-15).

203 (i) The 16th-century Lambeth MS 306 f. 51a, in Stow's handwriting, printed in Furnivall, *Political, religious and love poems*, pp. 6-11; and *Three Chrons.*, pp. 99-103. This is the fullest version (116 verses). Stow copied

the poem 'owt of david norcyn his booke'; Norcyn seems to have been another Elizabethan antiquary (A. G. Watson, *The Library of Sir Simonds D'Ewes* [BM, 1966], p. 199). (ii) BL, Cotton MS, Vespasian B XVI f. 1b, in a 15th-century collection, printed in Robbins, op. cit., pp. 187-9; J. P. Collier (ed.), *Trevilian papers* (Camden Soc., 1857), pp. 72-4; and Wright, *Political songs*, II, 232-4. This has some modifications in its 72 verses. (iii) Trinity College, Dublin, MS 516 f. 116, a 15th-century version extending to 65 verses and so far unprinted. For commentary, see Robbins, op. cit., pp. 351-5.

204 ibid., p. 187.
205 *GEC*, VI, 561-4 (Hoo); Emden, *Oxford*, I, 228-9; II, 1037-8; and Ferguson, op. cit., passim; Otway-Ruthven, *King's secretary*, pp. 89, 95-103, 138 (le Vulre, the king's French secretary, and envoy to France in 1442-44).
206 Above, p. 625. Malpas and Horne had also been negotiating with Burgundy in 1449 (Ferguson, op. cit., p. 190). See *CPR, 1446–52*, pp. 265, 389, for Judde as a commissioner arresting ships and sailors, soldiers and victuals for service at sea in 1449–50; and PRO, E404/64/73 for Cantelowe, who was still victualler in 1447–48.
207 Above, p. 612.
208 Emden, *Oxford*, III, 1780 (Stoke); II, 1080 (Kyrton). The abbess of 'seynt Alborghe' is surely the abbess of St Ethelburgha's, Barking; small wonder that she took a general pardon on 7 July (above, p. 621). Other local religious were Abbots John Thorne of Reading and John Bromley of Bermondsey ('full of lechery'), and John Thurston, master of the College of St Laurence Pountney.
209 Also Sir Thomas Stanley, Master John Somerset, Master William Say, and John Blakeney.
210 Above, p. 497; Furnivall, *Political, religious, and love poems*, p. 11.
211 *CPR, 1446–52*, p. 311. He was a king's serjeant and usher of the chamber (ibid., p. 130).
212 Above, p. 616.
213 Lowe of Rochester was also on embassy in 1442 with Abbot Boulers, Bishop Moleyns, and the abbot of Westminster (R. G. Davies, thesis, III, *s. n.*; Ferguson, op. cit., pp. 118, 211). Bird of St Asaph had frequently been a diplomat in the 1440s and had joined Suffolk and a number of household men in bringing Margaret to England (ibid., pp. 115, 117, 178; Emden, *Oxford*, I, 191).
214 Above, pp. 614-15.
215 *CPR, 1446–52*, p. 338. Since the pardons were issued at the instance of Queen Margaret, it is possible that she remained in London.
216 'Benet's Chron.', p. 202. For a similar celebration in Westminster abbey on 15 August, the feast of the Assumption of the Virgin, see WA MS 33289 f. 70. Somerset, his son Dorset, Scales, Sudeley, Lisle, and St Amand were the magnates present.
217 *CPR, 1446–52*, p. 388. Other commissions were nominated for Norfolk and Suffolk, where presumably there had also been unrest.
218 It is significant that the chief justice of king's bench, John Fortescue, to whom the rebels had been particularly hostile, was not included among the justices (Furnivall, *Political, religious, and love poems*, p. 10). The indictments taken by the Kent commission survive as PRO, KB9/46, calendared by Virgoe, 'Some ancient indictments', pp. 220-43. It was said

that a newly created justice was one of the commissioners because other justices (which may mean the chief justices) were regarded by the Kentishmen as themselves extortioners ('Benet's Chron.', p. 202). It is true that Robert Danvers, who had been at the guildhall session on 4 July and therefore might have been acceptable to the rebels, was appointed a justice of common pleas on 14 August 1450 and joined the Kent commission (*CPR, 1446–52*, p. 333). Cardinal Kemp did not receive his expenses (£253) as one of the commissioners until 19 July 1451 (PRO, E403/785 m. 8).

219 'Benet's Chron.', p. 202. Some historians have mistakenly regarded this commission as being intended to apprehend those who were still in revolt after 7 July (Cooper, *Sussex arch. coll.*, XVIII [1866], 34; *VCH, Kent*, III, 291)

220 e.g., Richard Snelgare, one of Crowmer's bailiffs as sheriff; John Alpheigh, undersheriff for both Slegge and Crowmer in Kent and, later, an official of Archbishop Bourgchier there; and John Watte, a bailiff for both sheriffs. For Alpheigh, see Du Boulay, *Lordship of Canterbury*, pp. 113, 396.

221 e.g., John Basket, steward of the archbishop's liberty by 1449 (ibid., pp. 291, 396; Virgoe, 'Some ancient indictments', pp. 233-5); Thomas Est, whose notoriety was doubtless partly earned when he was the archbishop's receiver from about 1444 (Du Boulay, *Lordship of Canterbury*, pp. 272-3). For the jurisdiction of the archbishop's courts exercised by such as Basket, see ibid., pp. 304-12. A list of the indictments at Rochester appears in a contemporary collection of material critical of the government (*EHL*, pp. 364-5).

222 Virgoe, 'Some ancient indictments', p. 241; Flenley, p. 131; above, p. 612.

223 Virgoe, 'Some ancient indictments', p. 236; above, p. 616.

224 Virgoe, 'Some ancient indictments', p. 245.

225 ibid., p. 253; *CPR, 1446–52*, pp. 423, 453. On 2 August the quarter of Cade's body sent to Deptford strand was stolen, presumably by those who still believed in his cause (Flenley, p. 134). There were also plots in Sussex to kill the king and his lords (*CPR, 1446–52*, p. 472).

226 Above, p. 614; PRO, KB9/257/93, referred to in Virgoe, 'Some ancient indictments', p. 246.

227 ibid..

228 ibid., p. 248.

229 *CPR, 1446–52*, p. 505. The last occasion when Cade's name was invoked in a rising appears to have been in 1456 (Storey, *End of Lancaster*, p. 68).

230 Virgoe, 'Some ancient indictments', pp. 217, 244-5.

231 Above, p. 131; *CPR, 1446–52*, pp. 469, 472.

232 Virgoe, 'Some ancient indictments', pp. 255-6; above, p. 642.

233 ibid., p. 254. Buckingham seems to have alerted all his local officials in case of trouble in 1450 (Rawcliffe, op. cit., pp. 77-8).

234 Virgoe, 'Some ancient indictments', pp. 218, 258.

235 The leader was pardoned on 23 February 1451 at the instance of Viscount Bourgchier (*CPR, 1446–52*, pp. 415, 503). For continuing unrest in Suffolk and Essex in summer 1450, see PRO, KB9/118, 26.

236 See *English Chron.*, p. 68; Giles, p. 41; *EHL*, p. 344, for the widespread nature of disturbances. For precautions taken in Yorks., Oxon., and Northants., see Jeffs, thesis, pp. 20-1.

237 *EHL*, pp. 347-9. See, for example, the forcible entry of lands at Brampton in Suffolk under cover of the prevailing disorder (Kingsford, *Prejudice and promise*, p. 49).

238 ibid., p. 49; *EHL*, p. 366.

239 ibid.; above, p. 632.

240 Flenley, pp. 134-5; 'Gregory's Chron.', p. 195; Stevenson, II, ii, [769]; Griffiths, *JMH*, I (1975), 198.

241 *EHL*, pp. 347-9; *CPR, 1446–52*, p. 560. 'Gregory's Chron.', p. 194, dates it to 14 June, and Stevenson, II, ii, [768], to 30 June. The city of Exeter was sufficiently alarmed to send a messenger to Salisbury to inquire about the murder (DevonRO, Exeter receivers' account 13).

242 Storey, *End of Lancaster*, p. 66. For the quotation (from PRO, KB9/134 m. 14), see J. N. Hare, 'Lords and tenants in Wiltshire, c. 1380 – c. 1520' (London PhD thesis, 1975), p. 318. For Aiscough's role in the fall of Gloucester in 1447 and his appointment as a sequestrator of his goods, see above, p. 497; George, thesis, pp. 197-8.

243 Hare, thesis, pp. 27-33, 159-60, 170, 191-2. The author's contrast with the Kentish revolt rests on his reliance on the pardons of 6–7 July to reflect the Kentish personnel (ibid., p. 324).

244 ibid., p. 327.

245 ibid., pp. 297-300. He had been robbed of goods, valued in all at £172.

246 ibid., pp. 301-3, 321-4; 'Gregory's Chron.'; pp. 194-5; 'Benet's Chron.', p. 199.

247 Hare, thesis, pp. 301-2. For his occupational analysis of the rioters, based on PRO, KB9/133, see ibid., pp. 306-8.

248 *EHL*, pp. 347-9.

249 Lyle, op. cit., p. 15; Storey, *End of Lancaster*, p. 66.

250 Emden, *Oxford*, II, 1187–8; I, 228-9; above, p. 305.

251 Flenley, pp. 106, 128, 134; *Fabyan's Chron.*, p. 626.

252 Scales was paid only 100 marks for the purpose (PRO, E403/779 m. 8, 29 June 1450, probably misdated).

253 Flenley, p. 134.

254 *CPR, 1446–52*, p. 388.

255 'Benet's Chron.', p. 202.

256 Flenley, pp. 134-5.

257 ibid., p. 136.

258 ibid., p. 135; 'Benet's Chron.', pp. 202-3; above, n. 39.

259 Flenley, pp. 136-7.

260 ibid., p. 136.

261 ibid., pp. 106, 134 (York was said to have 3,000 with him); 'Gregory's Chron.', p. 195; Giles, p. 42; 'Benet's Chron.', p. 202 (5,000).

262 Flenley, p. 136.

263 'Gregory's Chron.', p. 195.

264 'Benet's Chron.', p. 203; Flenley, p. 137.

265 'Benet's Chron.', p. 203.

266 Flenley, pp. 137, 157; Stevenson, II, ii, [769].

267 Flenley, pp. 106, 134-5; *London Chrons.*, p. 162; *Great Chron.*, p. 185; *Chron. of London*, p. 137; 'Gregory's Chron.', pp. 195-6; 'Benet's Chron.', p. 203.

268 ibid., p. 203; *Great Chron.*, p. 185; *London Chrons.*, p. 162; 'Gregory's

Chron.', p. 196; *EHL*, p. 297 (misdated to the previous day); Flenley, p. 157.
269 Giles, p. 42.
270 *CPR, 1446–52*, p. 438. On 5 December a similar commission covered Middlesex.
271 'Benet's Chron.', p. 203; *Great Chron.*, p. 185; Flenley, p. 157; 'Gregory's Chron.', p. 196 (with the quotation); *London Chrons.*, p. 162.
272 'Gregory's Chron.', pp. 195-6.
273 *PPC*, VI, 107.
274 *CPR, 1446–52*, p. 431 (headed by Somerset).
275 *PPC*, VI, 101. He was paid £40 expenses on 3 October 1450 and (PRO, E403/783 m. 3) £200 on 29 October.
276 *CPR, 1446–52*, p. 431. The household played a direct part in the investigations in Kent and Essex, through Thomas Scargill, an usher of the chamber (PRO, E403/783 m. 2; E404/67/27).
277 *CPR, 1446–52*, p. 435. Four days later (18 December), a commission was sent to Kent to search for and arrest further rebels (ibid., p. 436).
278 ibid., p. 442. For other investigations earlier in the month into the activities of particular Kentish rebels, see ibid., p. 437.
279 ibid., p. 442. Shrewsbury, Arundel, Wiltshire, and Worcester were the earls; Bourgchier, Cromwell, Roos, Sudeley, Lisle, and St Amand were the lords. The justices spent 25 days with the king on this commission (PRO, E403/783 m. 8; 785 m. 1, 2). While at Canterbury, on 9 February a rising tried to coerce the king into granting wholesale pardons (*CPR, 1446–52*, p. 505).
280 ibid., pp. 423-4, 426, 453-5, 497. For at least one execution, that of Geoffrey Kechyn, one of Cade's men, see ibid., p. 417. The king returned to London on 23 February (*EHL*, p. 372).
281 PRO, E403/785 m. 2 (27 May 1451), 13 (4-5 August). For the commission of 13 January 1451 to arrest them, see *CPR, 1446–52*, p. 437.
282 ibid., pp. 477, 478; 'Benet's Chron.', pp. 203-4. Only Exeter and Bourgchier were missing on this occasion. The indictments delivered at Tonbridge (Kent) between 26 June and 1 July 1451 survive as PRO, KB9/47, calendared in Virgoe, 'Some ancient indictments', pp. 243-56. For the Salisbury sessions, see Hare, thesis, pp. 295ff (quoting PRO, KB9/133); and the Sussex, Hunnisett, *Sussex notes and queries*, XIV (1954-57), 119-20 (quoting PRO, KB9/122).
283 *CPR, 1446–52*, p. 508 (pardons at Chichester on 12 July 1451).
284 ibid., p. 440.
285 'Gregory's Chron.', p. 196; *Great Chron.*, p. 185; *Brut*, pp. 19-20; *Three Chrons.*, pp. 68-9; Flenley, pp. 138, 157; *London Chrons.*, pp. 162-3.
286 'Gregory's Chron.', p. 197.

22   The Political Education of Richard, Duke of York

Upbringing and early experience

Apart from their common Plantagenet lineage, Henry of Lancaster and Richard of York had little in common. Henry was the great-grandson of Edward III's fourth son, John of Gaunt; Richard was the grandson of Edward's fifth son, Edmund of Langley, but, on his mother's side, a great-great-grandson of Lionel of Antwerp, third son of the great Edward. Yet they were almost of different generations, for Richard was ten years older than Henry and seems never to have developed a close relationship with him or, indeed, to have lived at court for any length of time during the formative years of either prince.[1] This has something to do with the fact that Richard's father, the earl of Cambridge, had rebelled against Henry V and was attainted and executed for his treason in August 1415. This rebellion reminded contemporaries that the usurpation of the throne by Gaunt's eldest son in 1399 had thrust aside Lionel's descendant, the young Edmund Mortimer, earl of March, who was the brother of Anne, Richard of York's mother. But March himself took no part in the events of 1415 and his four-year-old nephew Richard, though perhaps regarded with suspicion by the Lancastrians, could hardly be blamed for the indiscretion of his father in a cause that was not actively supported – in fact was betrayed – by the best claimant to the English crown. Nevertheless, Henry V soon afterwards consigned the young Richard to the care of one of his most trusted companions and an old Lancastrian retainer, Sir Robert Waterton. He was not without experience of high-ranking 'guests', for he had received the deposed Richard II at Pontefract castle in 1399 and the duke of Orleáns after Agincourt.[2] York remained with Waterton for the next seven and a half years, out of the public gaze, to be brought up in a small household dedicated to the service of Henry V.

Richard was a distinguished magnate in the making. Although his father's title and most of his modest estates were declared forfeit in 1415, when his father's brother, Edward of York, died childless two months later at Agincourt, Richard inherited the great dukedom of York; and so long as his mother's brother, Edmund of March, also remained childless, he was heir to the equally extensive earldom of March. Such a potentially wealthy and powerful prince did not remain in Waterton's custody long after Henry V's death, for in December 1423 he was transferred to the guardianship of the earl of Westmorland, one of the new king's councillors, and his second wife, Joan, Bishop Beaufort's niece.[3] For the next nine years, he was brought up at the Neville hearth, for even after the earl's death in 1425 he continued in the countess's charge. A wife was found for Richard when he was about thirteen: Westmorland's own daughter Cecily, number twenty-two in the list of his prolific brood.[4] In the circumstances, it was a natural match, and doubtless Westmorland and his wife appreciated the value of a close link with such a man. In January 1425, Richard's uncle of March died suddenly in Ireland, and he thereby became earl of March and Ulster, and heir to the extensive Clare properties in England as well as the lordships of Trim and Connaght in Ireland. Little more than a year later, in May 1426, he was knighted, along with the young king, by Bedford at the Leicester parliament. Richard was gradually being brought into English aristocratic society.[5] His personal ties at this time, so far as they can be identified, were strongest with the Beauforts and the Nevilles. Though an only son himself, his marriage introduced him to a kindred of unusual size which eventually penetrated practically every major magnate household in England; but the quarrel which his guardian, Countess Joan, had with the children of her husband's first marriage may have inclined York to associate more readily with his own wife's full brothers and sisters (and especially with Richard Neville, earl of Salisbury from 1429), rather than with his wife's half-brothers and half-sisters, headed by Ralph Neville, second earl of Westmorland.[6]

His first known contact with Henry VI was made when the king was eight. On 6 November 1429 Richard attended Henry's coronation in Westminster abbey and was decked in clothing provided by the royal household.[7] Then, in April 1430 he joined the vast entourage that accompanied Henry to France. Richard travelled with a personal retinue appropriate to a magnate of nineteen: he had twelve lances and thirty-six archers with him, and on 3 August 1431 £400 was authorized for the payment of his expenses while he was abroad. Richard was with Henry on his visit to Paris for his crowning in December 1431 and he probably returned to England with him a few months later.[8] It was probably this personal service that explains Richard's entry to his estates in May 1432 without undergoing the usual formality of an inquiry to verify his age; he would, in fact, reach his twenty-first birthday in the following September.[9] Two months after that, he was able to secure control of the dower estates of Anne, widow of the earl of March, who died in September. Richard admittedly encountered some difficulty in securing all his due from the March inheritance, but his friends and advisers were able to establish the justice of his claims in the parliament of 1433, provided he honoured the outstanding obligations of his two dead uncles, March and York, and of those (the king and Gloucester among them) who had enjoyed Richard's lands during his minority.[10] In 1433, too, he was admitted to the order of the garter, and evidently much was expected of him militarily in the future. At the age of twenty-two,

667

then, Richard, duke of York, earl of March and Ulster, lord of Wigmore and Clare, stood on the threshold of an auspicious career, sustained by the king's favour and by a multiplicity of family connections.[11]

Aside from the fact that Richard was never engaged by Henry VI as a regular councillor (and this may reflect a basic suspicion of his lineage), there is no sign in these early years that he was treated other than as a leading prince of royal blood.[12] On one occasion in January 1430, he took Bedford's place as constable of England, and it may have been similar considerations of dignity and seniority which determined the direction of his career thereafter.[13] After Bedford's death, Richard was appointed to succeed him as the king's lieutenant-general and governor in France.[14] It is true that he did not enjoy the title or powers of a regent, but a royal representative of more distinguished blood could hardly have been found. Admittedly, his formal appointment on 1 May 1436 was for one year only, and his inexperience led to his replacement by Warwick in July 1437; but when Warwick himself died two years later, it was to York, then in his late twenties, that the Lancastrian government again turned. This French interlude of 1436–37 extended several of the duke's earlier associations, for the expedition which left Winchelsea late in May included his kinsman, Edmund Beaufort, count of Mortain and his wife's brothers, Salisbury and Sir William Neville; his comrade Sir John Beaumont led the reinforcements across the channel in the summer of 1437.[15] Much of the actual campaigning was conducted by Lord Talbot, whom York had inherited as an annuitant from the late earl of March.[16]

This wartime experience had one result which, when repeated on several other occasions, introduced a note of bitterness and disillusion to his relations with the government: Richard found himself out of pocket. The crown failed to meet its financial obligations to the lieutenant-general and by 1439 he was owed £18,000. This doubtless blunted York's enthusiasm for further Lancastrian employment in France, but it was nevertheless to him, the realm's senior duke after Gloucester, that the king again turned in 1440 after Warwick's death. The conditions of York's appointment as lieutenant-general and governor of France and Normandy on 2 July 1440 differed significantly from those of 1436.[17] Sufficient confidence was felt in him (and especially in his councillors) to persuade the government to issue a five-year commission and he was given the full civil and military authority previously enjoyed by Bedford, though without the latter's title of regent. Moreover, he was assured of an annual subvention of £20,000 to meet his expenses. Arriving at Rouen in June 1441, York spent more than four years in Normandy, along with his family; at Rouen, his second son, Edward (the so-called 'Rose of Rouen'), was born in April 1442.[18] For a time, he had Talbot's invaluable assistance, and he was able to continue an association with Henry Bourgchier, to whom he delegated considerable authority on the Norman–Picard border, based on Crotoy. The Bourgchiers were half-brothers of

Richard's aunt, the countess of March, and Henry had married York's only sister, Isabel, in October 1426. Moreover, Henry and John Bourgchier were not too far removed in age from the duke and all three were knights of the garter.[19] This Bourgchier connection would prove of crucial importance to the duke later on.

The duke's counsellors

Aside from his relatives, York had a group of capable and experienced confidants, several of whom were known to him before he went to France. But his residence at Rouen gave him opportunity to enlarge this group from among the Lancastrian establishment of soldiers and administrators in northern France.[20] It was a rare magnate who had interests as far-flung as those of Duke Richard after 1432. His inherited estates were scattered in practically every county of England, as well as in the march of Wales and northern and central Ireland, and he spent half of the decade after 1436 in Normandy. The supervision of such diverse interests was beyond the capacity of Richard himself, even had he not been a young man of little military or political experience, and a close-knit handful of councillors would have found the task scarcely less daunting. It was inevitable, therefore, that during his absences a council should manage his affairs in England, Wales, and Ireland with a certain latitude and autonomy.[21] Moreover, the various administrative traditions of his estates meant that he could draw servants and officials from several quarters, whereas his role as Bedford's successor enabled him to attract professional commanders and strategists to be his French councillors.

Richard's first thirteen years or so as a wealthy magnate were years when he formed and shaped his administrative and advisory organization. At the same time, and even when he was in France, he did not neglect his contacts with the government and the departments of state, or with the king and his court at a time when Henry and his household were becoming increasingly influential. It was natural that the duke should have inherited servants and officials, as well as estates, from his father and his uncles of York and March. Cambridge's circle had been modest enough; that of his brother, Edward of York, was larger. John Russell, a Herefordshire lawyer, had been employed by Edward both as a feoffee and as overseer of his will; he retained responsibility for the ducal estates right up to the point when Richard of York received seisin of them; he may, indeed, have been in the new duke's employ until his own death in 1437.[22] Sir John Popham's early career followed a similar track: first as an annuitant, retainer, and treasurer of Duke Edward; then in the service of Bedford, not least as his chamberlain and as chancellor of Anjou and Maine; and then in the pay of Duke Richard, from whom Popham received confirmation (1433) of Edward of York's

669

annuity and a further payment when Popham was assigned to Richard's French council in 1436. His spell as treasurer of the king's household in 1437–39 afforded Richard valuable access to Henry VI and his ministers at a time when cash problems were seriously afflicting the régime. Popham, then, commended himself to Richard for a range of reasons (not the least of which was his connection with Hampshire, where some of the York estates lay), but by 1449 the political pressures seem to have become too much for a man who was then about sixty years of age and in poor health; he declined election as speaker of the commons in November and probably retired from public life (though he had another fourteen years to live and continued to receive an annuity from Richard).[23] On the military side of the Mortimer connection, Talbot was at least as welcome a recruit to Richard's circle. The latter's introduction to the French war in 1436 was much to Talbot's taste and he gave matchless support to the new lieutenant-general throughout his term in France; Richard reciprocated by creating him marshal of France in August 1436, leaving the military operations entirely to Talbot's judgement. But he, too, withdrew from Richard's side in the later 1440s, less because of the possibility of political embarrassment, but rather because he preferred to remain in France – with ultimately fatal consequences for himself.[24]

It was his two terms as lieutenant-general that enabled York to entice into his service a number of resourceful, experienced, and determined men who had made their fortunes in France in Bedford's company; when their revered leader died in September 1435, they saw their future advancement in the service of the new lieutenant-general, and to a man they remained faithful to York until 1446.[25] Popham and Talbot were prominent amongst them, but others were almost their equal in repute. The Norfolk knight Sir John Fastolf had an extraordinarily successful war, during which he rose to be steward (or master) of Bedford's household, as well as a rich landowner in Normandy, Maine, eastern England, and around London. At the age of about fifty-six, he joined York in France in 1436 as one of the royal councillors and in May 1441, after he had returned to England, he became one of York's life-annuitants; thenceforward, in petulant retirement, he counselled the duke sagely and (to judge by some of his surviving memoranda) persistently.[26] A Dane, Andres Pedersen, whose devotion to Bedford (and, it must be confessed, his reasonable hope of reward in England that was realized by the acquisition of property in Hertfordshire and Norfolk) led him to seek denizenship in 1433 as Sir Andrew Ogard, was another captain who joined York's personal service as a councillor.[27] Closely associated with both these men was Sir William ap Thomas, a knight from Raglan, in the Mortimer lordship of Usk, who invested his war profits in estate- and castle-building. The 'Blue Knight of Gwent', he was already one of York's councillors when he joined the duke's expedition to France in 1441; by 1442–43 he was chief steward of his Welsh estates. By the time he died in 1445, Sir William was one of the leading Welsh gentry of his day.[28]

Sir William Oldhall was from the same stable. A war captain under Henry V and Bedford, he was nominated by the regent as an executor of his will; thereafter, his knowledge of Normandy made him a worthwhile member of York's and Warwick's entourage as successive lieutenants-general. Oldhall soon passed permanently into the service of York, whose chamberlain he had become by 1441; he was to prove one of the duke's most ubiquitous and forceful lieutenants throughout the tribulations of the early 1450s. Like a number of York's councillors, Oldhall was able to add to his patrimony (in Norfolk and Cambridgeshire) substantial estates in both France and England, including Hertfordshire, where his building at Hunsdon excited the admiration of William Worcester.[29] It was Oldhall, along with Fastolf and Sir William ap Thomas, whom the king and other contemporaries identified as the most prominent of York's councillors at Rouen.[30] Henry VI spoke thus of him in about 1444: 'he that of reason shulde have moost perfite knowlege in [France], considering his longe abode with you there, and of your counseil'.[31]

Almost all of these warrior-councillors were a good deal older than the lieutenant-general they were pledged to serve, and one may imagine them taking him under their collective wing and lavishing on him the fruits of an experience gained in Henry V's reign and the glorious campaigns of conquest. One may imagine further that in such a position of trust they exhibited an unusually tenacious devotion to his service, comparable with that inspired by Bedford. It was they who conveyed to the council in England in 1443 their deep displeasure at the authority proposed for John Beaufort; when Bishop Moleyns delivered his accusations against York late in 1446, Scales, Oldhall, and Ogard were condemned with him, and Oldhall, Ogard, and John Stanlow replied vehemently with a protest.[32]

No less vital to the duke were those younger men who were linked with these intimates by marriage, interest, or neighbourliness, rather than by long war service: men like Sir Edmund Mulso, who came from a Suffolk and Northamptonshire family that was patronized by Edward of York and the Bourgchiers and which sprang to prominence during Henry V's and Bedford's campaigns.[33] He was only slightly older than the duke himself and whatever the Mulsos' past links with Richard's family, Sir Edmund seems to have joined him for the first time on the expedition to France in 1441. He was one of a number who entered York's service in the 1440s. Others were Thomas Young, the Bristol lawyer who had become York's attorney by March 1449 and risked his own safety when he pressed the duke's dynastic claim in parliament in 1451; and William Burley, another lawyer, who hailed from a part of Shropshire not many miles from Ludlow, was steward of York's lordship of Montgomery by 1442 and had been in Talbot's service before that.[34] Sir Walter Devereux held his Herefordshire estate at Weobley directly of the duke and married the daughter of John Merbury, a Herefordshire neighbour who had been York's feoffee in 1436; Devereux joined York's council during the 1440s, having sailed with him to Normandy in 1441 and assumed important captaincies in the duchy.[35] Finally, Sir James Ormond was a prominent member of the 1441 expedition and he was appointed steward for life of York's Somerset and Dorset estates on 24 March 1446; but their close relationship fell victim to the political crises after 1450.[36]

These men stepped gradually into the shoes of the councillors inherited from March, Edward of York, and Bedford.[37] Among the younger generation were men whose association with Richard was frequently forged at home, especially on the York estates, or by intermarriage, or in that political society domiciled between East Anglia, the midlands, and the Welsh march.[38] Led by Oldhall, they provided the duke with counsel and encouragement in the late 1440s and early 1450s. Their sense of obligation, underpinned by service in France, led many of them to stand by him during the perils to come. After all, some had benefited handsomely from grants of land, rents, and houses in the towns and countryside of Normandy and Maine, so that peace negotiations that involved the surrender of territory were viewed by them with growing hostility; the outbreak of war in July 1449 and the rapid collapse of Lancastrian France were an unrelieved disaster for them all.[39] As the disgraced lieutenant-general, York seemed their best source of sympathy and succour; yet it is K. B. McFarlane's remorseless judgement that 'we may sympathise with their aspirations while remembering that for a quarter of a century at least they had helped each other to suck France dry'![40] Those councillors shared the disgust with which news of the capture of Rouen and other strongholds in Normandy was greeted in England, and the duke probably understood their feelings. When his successor as lieutenant-general, Somerset, demonstrated his incompetence in defending English France, York's personal resentment of his supplanter coincided with the attitudes of magnates, councillors, and commons. He may have welcomed the opportunity to withdraw to Ireland in June 1449 in order to reassess the situation undisturbed.

Every magnate felt the need to employ agents at Westminster, in the government departments, at the council board, and in the king's household. York was no exception; in fact, his need was all the greater the longer he stayed in France. The councillors he left in England were able to protect his interests through agents whom he regularly retained. Nicholas Dixon, for example, was York's receiver-general in 1437, and as a long-serving baron of the exchequer he could be useful if the aid of the crown's financial officials were sought in the duke's interest.[41] Robert Darcy, who was York's feoffee in March 1441 and still in his service in 1443–44, was equally well placed as keeper of writs and rolls at the court of common pleas.[42]

Even more valuable were York's contacts among the king's councillors, foremost among them Lord Cromwell; he was a feoffee for the duke in March 1441 and his annuitant by 1442, and he continued the association with York almost until his own death in 1456. It may have been Cromwell's serious misgivings about Somerset's expedition of 1443 which eventually dictated his resignation as treasurer.[43] Walter, Lord Hungerford was a venerable Lancastrian councillor; by 1436 he too was sufficiently well disposed towards the duke to be one of his feoffees, and the connection continued for some years yet.[44] On the episcopal side, William Alnwick, successively bishop of Norwich and Lincoln, was a cherished acquaintance in the 1430s and 1440s, perhaps because he was the king's confessor at the time the association began.[45] These three men could look after York's interests at the highest level, especially during his absences abroad. Unfortunately for the duke, they were also a fading asset: both Hungerford and Alnwick died in 1449, and for some years had gradually retired from public affairs (Hungerford, indeed, was seventy-one at his death), whilst under the Suffolk régime Cromwell's influence was far less than it had been when York first established contact with him. By 1450, therefore, the duke had few influential advocates in government. Those on whom he had chosen (or been advised) to rely were rarely men of his own age, with influential careers ahead of them; few were able to preserve their influence in the face of faction rule, exclusivist royal patronage, and precious years spent by some of them in France. The political world of the late 1440s, after Duke Richard had returned from France, saw them curiously powerless.

Richard had also had his placemen in the king's household, a fact which perhaps emphasizes that so long as Gloucester or Beaufort ruled he was not cold-shouldered by the king, for his lineage commanded respect from both statesmen. Thus, among his annuitants of 1443–44 (indeed, among the most highly paid of them at £100 *per annum*) were the king's confessor, Bishop Aiscough, and Sir John Beauchamp, who in 1443 became steward of Henry's household. Receiving an annual retainer of £40 was James Fiennes, a key household official who would soon embody all the qualities of ruthlessness and corruption which York would declare himself anxious to eradicate.[46] With such men on his payroll in the early 1440s, the duke had influence at court and a means of access to the king even though he himself might be in France. But later, when issues of dynasty, faction, and peace strained relations between Richard and the king's ministers, the household officials closed ranks and the duke lost his advocates where they mattered most. By 1450, none of these three courtiers was likely to press the duke's views in household or council.

When Richard returned to England in October 1445, a number of the warrior-councillors returned with him, joining his domestic councillors and perhaps bringing a rough determination to their deliberations. Although Talbot, Scales, and Hoo stayed in France to assist Somerset – Talbot as the military genius, Scales as seneschal of Normandy, and

Hoo as the duchy's chancellor – Fastolf, Ogard, and especially Oldhall chose to settle in England alongside William Burley, Thomas Young, and John Wigmore, supporting and serving Richard during the chilly years of Suffolk's ascendancy.[47]

For much of his time as lieutenant-general, York was courteously treated by Henry VI and his advisers. His interests and property in England were protected in his absence, and in March 1445 the king, acting on the advice of the chancellor, Gloucester, and Cromwell, a triumvirate likely to be favourable to the duke, restored to him the Mortimer lordship of Crickhowell which the Pauncefot family had occupied with royal approval.[48] The king was delighted to have news in 1441 that York's first-born son was to be named Henry, and he facilitated the negotiations for marriage alliances between York's family and the Holands and Valois in 1444–45.[49] But by the time Richard returned to England in the autumn of 1445, his financial position had deteriorated badly, largely due to the government's inability to honour its debts. Symptomatic of this had been the transfer of certain crown jewels to York as security in February 1438, and the resort to letters patent in February 1444 to guarantee payment of £11,667.[50] He now found himself in a serious financial plight. Not only was his modest inherited pension of £83 paid irregularly, but as a result of his French service he was owed the enormous sum of £38,667. In desperation, he agreed to forego about one-third of it as the price of the government's promise in July 1446 to find the remaining £26,000; but some of the tallies proved difficult to cash and even in 1451 were being replaced by the exchequer.[51] The charges of peculation levelled against York by Bishop Moleyns a little later in 1446 may not have been unconnected with the government's gross indebtedness to him as his term as lieutenant-general drew to a close. Nor does it seem likely that the income from his lands enabled York to tolerate such treatment by the 1440s. His Welsh lordships which, at about £2,900, were annually worth more than half his entire estate (about £4,500), seem to have been declining in value during Henry VI's reign, whilst at the same time these very properties were expected to sustain annuities and wages that in 1442–43 alone amounted to £965.[52] York's spell in Ireland in 1449–50 made his financial situation worse, for he experienced insurmountable difficulties in obtaining subventions from the exchequer for himself and his men. The duke was forced to borrow from, and sell property to, his friends in order to make ends meet, but these expedients merely impoverished him further.[53]

In other ways, Richard's treatment by the government was a provocation. In March 1443 the government of Gascony was consigned to John Beaufort, earl of Somerset, together with command of a field army that was authorized to pursue Charles VII wherever he might be found; this commission was regarded by York as a derogation from his own position as lieutenant-general. Moreover, the patronage and honours bestowed on Beaufort at this juncture might well have seemed ominous to the duke: Somerset received Bedford's dignity of earl of Kendal in August 1443 and he was formally raised to the dukedom of Somerset on the same day; the promise of Anjou and Maine after his brother's term had ended seemed to presage an authority in France that would encroach seriously on that of York himself. At the same time, preference was given to Somerset in the provision of exchequer funds, whereas forbearance and patience were enjoined on York. When Beaufort proved a sluggish organizer and a blundering commander, York could be forgiven feelings of bitterness and exasperation towards the government at home.[54]

York's position within the royal family as a possible heir presumptive to Henry VI changed significantly while he was in France. The disgrace of Eleanor Cobham in July 1441 and the annulment of her marriage to Gloucester raised the question of the succession to the throne. The elevation, in turn, of John Beaufort to the dukedom of Somerset (1443), John Holand to the dukedom of Exeter (1444), and Humphrey Stafford to the dukedom of Buckingham (1444), each with precedence over every other duke save Gloucester and York, had considerable dynastic significance, for they were closely related to Henry VI. York may well have suspected that his own line was being ignored, with all the implications which that might have for the succession to the throne. The king's marriage in 1445, therefore, is likely to have come as something of a relief to Richard, for it at last offered the prospect of an heir being born to Henry VI himself; that would make the dynastic issue a little less sensitive. Margaret of Anjou was accordingly nobly received by York when she passed through Normandy on her way to England, and the duke seems to have been genuinely honoured by the proposal of a match between his son Edward and one of Charles VII's daughters.[55] But as the months passed and Margaret did not become pregnant, dynastic uncertainty and suspicions revived. Edmund Beaufort's appointment as lieutenant-general in place of York in December 1446 was followed two months later by the sudden demise of Gloucester – and still the king and queen were childless. Although Richard managed to secure custody of his young son-in-law, Henry Holand, duke of Exeter in August 1447, he nevertheless had reason to believe that his legitimate claims were being submerged by the patronage shown to other members of the royal family: Buckingham's special precedence as a duke was formally acknowledged in May 1447 (soon after Gloucester's death), and ten months later Edmund Beaufort was created duke of Somerset. The implications were clear to some at least, for when the Beaufort heiress, Margaret, was married to Suffolk's son John at the beginning of 1450, it was regarded as a manoeuvre by the hated minister to place a de la Pole on the throne.[56] By this stage, York was bereft of powerful friends at court who could counter these moves. Nor was the patronage he received between 1446 and 1450 at all generous.[57] Even the marriage in 1445 of his daughter, Anne, to Henry Holand was no unmixed blessing, for York had to pay substantially for the privilege – 6,500 marks, the largest marriage portion known to have been paid by a nobleman in late medieval England.[58] These were hardly the pickings of an heir presumptive, which is what York must surely have regarded himself after Gloucester's death.[59]

York's withdrawal to Ireland in June 1449 was badly timed. He appears to have borne the slights on his position with resignation; certainly, his former well-wishers were unlikely to champion his cause now, and his councillors were politically powerless. Even in the parliament of February 1449 scarcely more than three of his servants secured election to the commons.[60] Yet not long after Richard arrived in Ireland, Suffolk's régime began to crumble as it was assaulted on several sides by interests that had much in common with York. But the initiative owed little to the absent duke.

Had he been in the realm and attended the second parliament of 1449, in which the commons strenuously attacked Suffolk, it is more than probable that he would have emerged as leader of the régime's critics. His presence might have fortified the resolve of his old companion, Sir John Popham, to stay on as speaker. And more of his councillors, in addition to the half-dozen or so elected to this parliament, might have been able to play a part in the commons' deliberations rather than spend their time negotiating with Irish chieftains.[61] Instead, York was many miles away; perhaps, too, he was by no means certain that the condemnation of the government for its moribund policy in France would not rebound on him as the only living lieutenant-general apart from Somerset (he had, after all, welcomed the prospect of peace which the king's marriage had offered). He therefore held back, presumably with the counsel of those advisers who, like Sir William Oldhall, accompanied him to Ireland, and he did not return to the mainland until September 1450.[62] Neither news of the resignation of the treasurer of England, Bishop Lumley, on 16 September, nor intelligence of the French advances in Normandy was sufficient to bring him back. Moreover, the murder of Bishop Moleyns at Portsmouth on 9 January 1450, and the rising clamour against Suffolk personally emphasized their responsibility for the military débâcle. Events were moving rapidly and in Ireland they may have sounded exceedingly confused. At about this time, Sir William Oldhall travelled to England, probably to assess the situation; he returned to Ireland at the beginning of the summer of 1450 with much to report.

The indictment of the duke of Suffolk

The parliament which met on 6 November 1449 was arguably the most difficult assembly with which an English king had had to deal since 1399. Faced with a military and financial emergency in northern France and a need to take measures for the defence of the kingdom itself, the writs of summons were issued on 23 September, barely two months after the dissolution of the old parliament. The temper of the commons was indicated at the outset. Having just heard about the capitulation of Rouen (29 October), the capture of Shrewsbury, and the flight of Somerset (4 November), on the customary second day of parliament an experienced diplomat, soldier, administrator, and servant of the duke of York was elected speaker: Sir John Popham's service in France was unrivalled among the commons for its length, and the loss of his Norman estates qualified him to represent the interests of the dispossessed.[63] It was a choice which Suffolk and his fellow ministers could not accept: pleading advanced years and troublesome war wounds, Popham submitted to pressure and declined the doubtful honour of representing the angry and determined commons. This was unprecedented, but it indicates that, uncertain though Henry's control over this new parliament may have been, his residual authority to direct its course was unquestioned; Popham was replaced immediately by a more amenable speaker, the king's servant and duchy of Lancaster official William Tresham – though he, too, had some connection with York.[64] The choice of Popham reflected a widespread movement of opinion against the government, and against Suffolk in particular, for the humiliating losses in France; as the duke shortly afterwards admitted, the rumours and accusations that flew about London and Westminster were alarming.[65] Matters came to a head in the second session, which opened on 22 January 1450 in Westminster hall.

On the very first day, Suffolk, unnerved by the death of Moleyns a fortnight before and stories of deathbed utterances, requested Henry VI that he be allowed to make a formal statement before the lords and have it enrolled, so that innuendo could be checked before it engulfed both himself and the government. The duke resolutely declared himself ready to answer any accusations that might be made against him; he evidently felt that it would be easier to counter charges that were publicly made rather than 'odious and horrible langage that renneth thorough your lande, almost in every Commons mouth', which might acquire a reality of its own if not quickly scotched.

The commons took full advantage of the duke's invitation. Skilfully – and capable, experienced men, including several lawyers, were present in parliament – they concluded that there was a *prima facie* case to answer, based on the rumours and accusations to which Suffolk referred, and that therefore the duke should be committed to custody so that the law could take its course. This recommendation, delivered to the chancellor by a commons delegation on 26 January, was rejected by the lords next day on the not unreasonable grounds that rumour and generalized criticism were no basis for an arrest; in truth, the commons can hardly have expected otherwise. Nothing daunted, and presumably prepared for this eventuality, the commons next day made a specific accusation to the chancellor and a delegation of lords: Suffolk was planning to assist an enemy invasion by surrendering to Charles VII

Wallingford castle, of which he was constable and to which the king had just given him permission to retire for his own safety. This was treason within the meaning of the statute of 1352.[66] In the tense atmosphere of defeat, it was the French war that was uppermost in the commons' mind. Fantastic though it may seem to us today, this specific, concrete charge merited investigation in January 1450; Harfleur had fallen on 31 December 1449 and the threat of invasion seemed real. The king accordingly agreed to Suffolk's arrest, though his intention of allowing him to withdraw to Wallingford was vigorously opposed by the commons, who insisted on the Tower. And to the Tower Suffolk went on 29 January. His arrest was followed two days later by the resignation of the chancellor, Archbishop Stafford, an elderly Lancastrian servant who had been in office for eighteen years; he represented the discredited government and it was inevitable that, with Suffolk under arrest, he should go too. Thus, by the end of January 1450, the three chief officers of state of the late 1440s had been removed.[67]

The tension of these days in London and its suburbs is vividly conveyed by the chroniclers of the city. What was feared most was that the lords and their retainers would counter-attack and use force to overawe parliament.[68] But too many of the lords were privately relieved to see Suffolk pilloried: he was the man who had channelled the king's patronage into an exclusive circle and had alienated a number of them, in addition to York. In particular, Lord Cromwell, a strong-minded individual who had been disenchanted with the régime since 1443 and was well disposed towards York, had his own reasons for seeking revenge on Suffolk. In November 1449 he had been assaulted at Westminster by one of Suffolk's henchmen, William Tailboys. A wealthy Lincolnshire gentleman with household connections and an ungovernable temper, Tailboys had personal grudges against several Lincolnshire magnates; his attack on Cromwell may have been his own idea, but when Suffolk attempted to protect the ruffian, Cromwell threw his influence behind the commons' campaign against the king's minister.[69] Hence, a bill impeaching Suffolk of treason and misprision of treason was presented by Speaker Tresham on 7 February to the new chancellor, Archbishop Kemp, who had his own reason for welcoming Suffolk's downfall, and to a large delegation of lords. Kemp was asked to present it to the king for approval in parliament, after the manner of the state trial devised during 1376–86.[70] Five days later, the bill was read before the lords, who recommended that it should be referred to the judges for their advice. But Henry had no intention of allowing the matter to proceed so far. He stepped in at that point and suspended proceedings in an attempt to protect his favourite. It was not the lords who snatched Suffolk from the hands of his enemies, but Henry VI himself.

The contents of what amounted to a bill of impeachment reveal closely the issues that crowded the commons' mind at the beginning of 1450. Every one of its eight charges related to Anglo-French relations and their alleged mismanagement – to the point of treason – by Suffolk, who

> falsely and traiterously hath ymagined, compassed, purposed, forethought, doon, and committed dyvers high, grete, heynous, and horrible treasons ayenst your moost roiall persone, youre corones of youre reames of Englond and Fraunce, youre duchies of Guyan and Normandie, and youre olde enheritaince of your countees of Anjoye and Mayne, the estate and dignite of the same, and the universall wele and prosperite of all your true subgettes of your seid reames, duchies, and countee, ...[71]

His personal involvement in discussions with Charles VII, his envoys and councillors led the commons to imply that he had placed his own advantage before all else in the negotiations for peace, and had traitorously betrayed the security of the dual monarchy: whether by secretly promising the surrender of Maine in return for a bribe, revealing state secrets to King Charles, or alienating England's allies of Aragon and Brittany. These, like most of the charges, were based on undoubted fact – Maine was eventually surrendered and Brittany did join the Valois campaign – but the implications which the commons now deduced from these facts were at best doubtful, at worst purposely distorted to blacken the duke's reputation and secure his condemnation.[72] Yet, as Suffolk had feared, these imputations of treason gained widespread currency in 1450.[73]

The first of the charges also concerned Suffolk's supposed dynastic ambitions, which (it was alleged) would be forwarded by a French invasion. The prominence accorded the Beaufort family by Henry VI enabled the commons to claim that Suffolk plotted to make his son king by marrying him to the Beaufort heiress, Margaret, who had been Suffolk's ward since 1444: 'presumyng and pretendyng her to be next enheritable to the Corone of this youre Reame, for lakke of issue of your Soverayne Lord'. A marriage was indeed arranged between the two children (both of whom were about seven years old) at the beginning of 1450; but for the moment it simply meant allying with the family of a wealthy heiress with close dynastic links with the royal house.[74] The bill, then, was a skilfully compiled series of treasonable accusations, generally based on well-authenticated incidents whose real significance was purposely misrepresented by the commons' managers in a way that ignored the sincere hopes of the peace negotiators. This concentration on the alleged folly and deceit of the peace policy can hardly have set York's mind at ease, and although the dynastic issue was close to his heart and lineage, he had good reason to be dismayed to hear that what was condemned in the Beaufort marriage was Suffolk's effrontery, not the suggestion that a Beaufort might be a suitable heir of Henry VI. Neither the commons nor, it seems, anyone else mentioned the claim of the duke of York.

Suffolk spent about six weeks in the Tower. Even though the king had suspended the impeachment proceedings, some felt that the matter could not be left in cold storage indefinitely; to do that would not dispel the uncertainty surrounding the duke's future. Eventually, on 7 March, by which time both lords and commons were ready to return to the attack, 'the moost parte of the lordes in the parlement then beyng present' announced that Suffolk should answer the charges laid against him, and the commons were ready with a second bill. This time they wanted it enacted as a parliamentary statute. The intervening month had evidently been put to good purpose in taking legal advice on how best to obviate the king's hostility to all proceedings against his favourite, and a majority of the lords had concluded (how reluctantly is not known) that the commons were not to be deflected. Enactment was a relatively new departure, foreshadowing the process of attainder that was frequently used against political enemies during the ensuing civil wars.[75] In 1450 it would have the crucial merit of making it difficult for the king to suspend a procedure whereby both lords and commons had given considered judgement. Suffolk appeared in the parliament chamber before king and lords on 9 March to hear the new charges of the commons. Not unreasonably, he asked for a copy of them and was allowed time to prepare his answer. Perhaps at the instance of his friends, certainly with the sympathetic agreement of the king, the hapless duke was not returned to the Tower but was installed in the Jewel Tower of the palace of Westminster, close at hand for the parliamentary session and probably in greater comfort.[76]

Four days later, he reappeared before the king and the lords and on his knees proceeded to reply to the first set of charges in an intelligent fashion. He dismissed them in such a way as to embarrass not a few of the lords present: he denied that anything remotely akin to treason had been implied by his actions; the official record would vindicate him, and in any case (he reminded the assembly) others had been involved in the peace negotiations apart from himself. Too many of those who heard this answer would have felt uneasy about proceeding further, and if York had been present, he would surely have felt his own face redden. It perhaps did Suffolk less credit to add that Moleyns, as keeper of the privy seal, had technically authorized the surrender of Le Mans, and any deathbed accusations by the bishop were 'full falls and untrue'. The murdered bishop could neither deny nor corroborate these assertions. Hence, when the lords were asked how they wished to proceed, they hesitated and on 16 March conceded that 'noo thyng [be] doon in that matier'. Suffolk had meanwhile withdrawn to prepare his reply to the second set of charges. There were eighteen of them, altogether more specific though individually more minor. Although some of the emphasis was now shifted to a more vulnerable side of Suffolk's activities – his personal aggrandisement through the king's favour, administrative mismanagement, and the perversion of justice – above all it was his relations with the French king, French envoys and prominent Frenchmen which formed the substance of the bill. The precision which characterized these latter charges suggests that the information about lands, castles, and lordships in Normandy and Gascony which had been transferred to Frenchmen was provided by those (like York's councillors) who had lost practically all their French possessions. Henry VI's unwise patronage in France and England was said to have originated with Suffolk, with the result that the king's resources were depleted, the duke enriched, and allies and servants of the enemy favoured. Suffolk's protection of William Tailboys was singled out as a blatant example of his disregard of justice and due legal process. Corruption, including the nomination of pliable sheriffs (and therefore of MPs), maintenance, extortion, and bribery were listed as features of his rule.

Once again, the factual element in the charges was often undeniable – Tailboys did escape justice by the intervention of the duke, and Suffolk was well known for his 'greet hevyng an shovyng' locally – but the duke's intentions were frequently misinterpreted, and some of the commons' conclusions were a matter of judgement or opinion (particularly in relation to the peace negotiations).[77] In a few cases, the commons exaggerated in their eagerness to bring the minister down: in the west country, for example, there is no sign that he nominated only subservient sheriffs, though the situation may have been different in East Anglia, where his own territorial interests were concentrated, and in Kent and the home counties, where household servants all but monopolized the shrievalty and parliamentary representation. But, of course, other magnates – the Beauchamps in Worcestershire, the Staffords in Staffordshire and Warwickshire, the Courtenays in Devon – attempted to do exactly the same. Perhaps the difference lay in Suffolk's use of the full resources of the king's household to dominate political society in the most populous and prosperous areas nearest the capital.[78] Even so, these were flimsy grounds indeed for charges of treason; if proven, they would have amounted to little more than an indictment of bad character and misgovernment. The substantive treasonable matter arose from his relations with the king's enemies. The bill 'of attainder' was a document produced by the duke's critics, distorting, exaggerating, even inventing where it could be done plausibly to destroy the power of a royal minister.

The king and Suffolk's associates were sufficiently alarmed by the carefully constructed and widely supported attack on the duke to realize that little mercy could be expected from either house in parliament. For this reason, on 17 March, Henry VI summoned all forty-five of the lords who were still in London to a further meeting held, not in the parliament chamber, but in 'his innest chambre with a gabill wyndowe over a cloyster within his paleys of Westmynster'. Suffolk knelt before them. The duke reiterated his response to the first bill and, through the chancellor, the king formally dismissed its charges. As to the second, Henry removed Suffolk from the jurisdiction of parliament and placed him under his own 'rule and governaunce', but not 'by wey of jugement, for he is not in place of jugement'. Henry may have been soundly advised in this by his justices and serjeants-at-law, but he can hardly have expected the support of the commons or of many of the lords for this course of action. Indeed, the king went out of his way to make it clear that he was acting 'by his owne advis, and not reportyng hym to thadvis of his lordes'. They publicly dissociated themselves from the chancellor's statement. Thus, the king had both dismissed the bill of impeachment and offered his protection against the proposed act of attainder. The parliamentary proceedings were aborted. Henry VI had acted decisively to save his friend, and he was able to do so probably because the charges and Suffolk's own defence had divided opinion among the lords. The sense of embarrassment among them and their lack of will to rally to Suffolk's defence in significant numbers appear all the more marked when it is realized that of the forty-five lords who witnessed the dénouement of these proceedings, more than half had been closely associated with the duke's régime during the 1440s. Several of the bishops had been elected to their sees under his scrutiny, and especially among the barons was there a substantial group who owed their creation to his patronage. In March 1450 they hesitated to rush to his side, and when York arrived from Ireland in the autumn, some actually threw themselves on his mercy.[79]

The proceedings against Suffolk had taken place either in the parliament chamber or in the palace. But it must not be forgotten that opinion outside was in a more volatile and potentially violent state, for the rumours current during the winter had not abated while parliamentary discussions were taking place. When, on 13–14 March, Suffolk answered the accusations against him and the lords decided to proceed no further with the commons' bill, certain elements either inside or, more probably, outside parliament expressed their exasperation and tried to rally opinion against him. A lengthy indictment of the duke, less formal, more emotive and propagandist in tone, not directed specifically to the king or the lords, was composed to re-emphasize Suffolk's responsibility for the French disasters and also his personal aggrandisement at the crown's expense.[80] Some of its assertions were wholly malicious; speaking of his capture in France in 1415, for instance:

> The nighte before that he was yolde he laye in bede with a Nonne whom he toke oute of holy profession and defouled . . . by whom he gate a daughter.

Others attributed every calamitous consequence of the French defeat to his evil machinations, thus:

> ther by the kynge's obeisaunce was and ys lost, the more partie God amende it, therby the kynge's adversaries . . . werre releved and sore encressed, therby the kynge's people and soudeours were put from

their Garisons exiled, poverysshed, and distroied; therby were robbers, pillages, murders, ydelnesse, and cursedenesse brought amonge us, therby our frendes of the kynge's amite and of his linage were departed from the leige of oure sovereigne ... therby the Frenshemen alied them selfe and enlarge their amite oure soveriegne lorde; therby were alle the Garrisons in Fraunce and Normandie of the kynge's obeysiaunce; therby were alle soudeours clane piked oute of the countree ...

It has the air of a compilation hastily thrown together and colloquially expressed, probably for popular consumption, by a group of those who had suffered particularly severely from the losses in France in the late 1440s. Its immediate purpose is likely to have been to prevent just the kind of lenient treatment of the duke which the king announced on 17 March. It failed initially in its purpose, but six weeks later it was all too successful for on 2 May, Suffolk was murdered by an apparently obscure company of sailors.

That same night, 17 March, the duke was secretly spirited from the Tower and allowed to go to his manor of Eastthorp (Suffolk). He was pursued part of the way by a large crowd of Londoners, and some of his servants were manhandled.[91] On 30 March the troublesome parliament was adjourned and the king felt able to announce the mild punishment which he had decided to impose on Suffolk, more for his own safety than to accommodate his critics: as from 1 May he would be exiled from the realm for five years, and was forbidden to go to France or any other of the king's territories.[82] By the time that parliament had reassembled on 29 April at Leicester, one of the queen's towns that was certain to be less turbulent than London, Suffolk would be on his way abroad. The commons nevertheless renewed their demand for his condemnation – and indeed for the punishment of Lord Saye, Bishop Aiscough, and Thomas Daniel as well – but the bird had flown.[83]

After protesting his innocence before a farewell gathering of Suffolk gentry, he wrote a moving letter to his young son and heir before setting sail from Ipswich on 30 April. Exhorting John de la Pole to honour God, the king, and his mother, he concluded his advice with cool irony:

... flee the company and councel of proude men, of coveitowse men, and of flateryng men, ... And to drawe to you and to your company good and vertuowse men, and such as ben of good conversacion, and of trouthe, ...[84]

With a small flotilla of three or four ships, he was bound for the duke of Burgundy's lands in the Low Countries. He had a safe-conduct from Philip the Good and sent a reconnaissance craft ahead to Calais to verify that, in response to letters which he had from the king, he would be welcome there. This ship betrayed Suffolk's whereabouts to another vessel, the *Nicholas of the Tower*, which seems to have been privateering in the channel. Off Dover the *Nicholas* encountered Suffolk's ships and stopped them; the duke was taken on board and subjected to a form of trial, though in reality it was nothing more than a kangaroo court. On 2 May he was put into a small boat and beheaded on the gunwale with a rusty sword by a sailor from Bosham (Sussex). The body was thrown up on the beach near Dover and later buried on the king's order at Wingfield college, Suffolk.[85] His companions were released.

Suffolk had at last suffered the fate of his confrère Moleyns, and others – Aiscough and Lord Saye among them – would soon follow. Popular indignation had claimed its victim, regardless of the formally prepared charges of the commons and in despite of the king's determination to protect him. The lords as a body were disinclined to shield him, though they were equally unprepared to confront the king and prevent Suffolk's exile. The duke himself so distrusted his fellow peers that he refrained from appealing to them for judgement, as was his right, in accordance with Magna Carta.[86]

Popular agitation

The commons' charges against Suffolk offered no direct or specific encouragement to the duke of York to hasten back to England and no expectation that his personal grievances would be championed by the politically influential. On the contrary, he had reason to be aware of his own vulnerability when it came to assigning responsibility for the failures in France, though, as one chronicler astutely observed (taking his cue, perhaps, from York's later denunciation of the duke of Somerset in 1452), it was not the ideal of peace, as pursued to a conclusion in the king's marriage in 1445, that was blameworthy so much as the blunders which brought war in 1449; the country had thereby been deceived by some of the peacemakers.[87] Unfortunately for the duke, there is no sign that this distinction was being drawn early in 1450. Then again, the commons had carefully avoided blaming the king or commenting on the delicate matter of his heir. Parliament as a whole observed the constitutional proprieties and stopped short of encroaching on the king's undoubted prerogative.

Yet what may have been absent from formal pronouncements in parliament – even from the more extreme castigation of Suffolk publicized in March 1450 – may nevertheless have exercised several minds. Moreover, the populace at large, in expressing its views, would feel none of the constraints imposed on lords and commons. From the autumn of 1449, there was a groundswell of popular agitation and violence in several parts of southern England (or, rather, that is where the chroniclers noticed it) which had political overtones connected with the parliamentary attack that was in progress. The weight of chronicle and other evidence is too great to be dismissed, even though the experience of Cade's revolt and knowledge of its manifestos may have sharpened chroniclers' and jurors' recollections. Bills were posted up in London, seditious talk passed from mouth to ear, and suspicious assemblies were held here and there.[88] One of the main grievances was the defeat in France, but these popular agitators, unlike the commons, were prepared to go further: they blamed King Henry for not governing properly; they spread rumours about Gloucester's death in 1447, accusing Suffolk and other ministers and royal servants of murdering him; and they raised the spectre of deposition and the recall of York ('another person then outside the kingdom') to remove the traitors and ascend the throne.[89] It was a time of rumour and innuendo worthy of Renaissance Italy, and such stories and accusations were likely to spread quickly in such an atmosphere. The tales of Gloucester's death may have originated with a servant of one of his former esquires; the servant was executed at Tyburn on 31 January 1450.[90] The suggestion that York might be the realm's saviour may have been put about by his wellwishers, led by Sir William Oldhall and working assiduously (as later indictments claimed) during March and April 1450 in the vicinity of Ipswich, Norwich, and Bury St Edmund's, where York and some of his affinity were landowners.[91] When, towards the end of April, the king reached Stony Stratford on his way to the Leicester session of parliament, he was confronted by a shipman from Yorkshire, John Harries by name, who wielded a flail in front of Henry and declared darkly that York would do the same to the traitors when he returned from Ireland.[92]

In the autumn of 1450 King Henry himself admitted

> that a lang tyme the pepill hath yeven upon yow [i. e., the duke of York] moche straunge langage and in special anon eftir the disordinate and unlafull sleyng of the Bischop of Chichestre, divers and many of the untrue schypmen and othir sayden in their maner wordys ayenst oure astate, makyng manasse unto oure persone be your sayeng, that you schuld be fechid home with many thousandis, and that ye schulde take upon you that that ye nothir aught nor as we doutenat ye wole not attempte . . . And also ther were divers of suche fals pepill that wentyn and had suche langage in divers of your townes in oure londe, which be oure true subiectes were takyn and deuly executid . . . .[93]

Such manifestations of popular opinion and unrest could have been communicated to York in Ireland, if only by Sir William Oldhall, who evidently returned there in the summer of 1450.[94] The duke could have deduced that there was some tentative sympathy for him in southern England, even if this was not openly expressed by anyone of political or social consequence; but the indications were few and their source unimpressive – in part perhaps his own affinity.

685

Cade's rebellion in June and July changed the situation significantly. This was a serious expression of popular revulsion at the dishonour inflicted by Charles VII's forces, but especially at the perfidious Suffolk and his friends; it also offered a further sign to York that his popular reputation was comparatively unblemished by what was happening in France.[95] Whether or not Oldhall continued his agitation in May 1450 and fanned the prevailing discontent in Kent (as an indictment of 1453 maintained), the most telling sign of York's growing popularity was the rebel leader's provocative use of the emotive surname of Mortimer. Not only would this prompt men to recall that in 1399 Richard II's most obvious heir had been a member of the family whose senior representative in 1450 was Duke Richard (and which might therefore attract support for Cade's enterprise), but it would also indicate to the duke that he was widely regarded as Henry VI's heir presumptive – though not, to judge by the rebels' own professions of loyalty, his supplanter.[96] Cade was no revolutionary bent on deposing Henry VI and elevating York (or anyone else) to the throne in his place. If more extreme elements existed, they hovered on the fringes of the movement; they were not the authors of its manifestos or directors of its actions. That York was regarded by the rebels rather as the embodiment of the ideal of good government is reflected in their hostility to his old councillor, Sir John Fastolf, and by the seizure of the duke's jewels in Philip Malpas's house in London.[97] Some sympathy for his claim to be Henry VI's rightful heir underlay the rebels' reference to him as 'the trewe blode of the Reame, that is to say the hye and myghty prince the Duke of Yorke', but they looked to him as one of several magnates whose counsel would improve the king's government rather than as an alternative monarch. Cade's rebellion was no attempted Yorkist *putsch*, but it marked an important stage in the blooming of York's reputation among the masses. Nevertheless, the duke would need to act cautiously, for the motives behind Cade's uprising were unlikely to commend themselves to the nobility, gentry, or commercial community, and in any case by the end of the first week in July the rebels had mostly been defeated or dispersed. The government and the city of London continued suspicious of the context in which the duke's name had been mentioned and the king more vigilant in monitoring his movements.[98]

The return to England

Early in September 1450, York landed in north Wales, at Beaumaris, in whose castle the divorced widow of the last acknowledged heir presumptive of Henry VI, Humphrey of Gloucester, was immured.[99] His arrival alarmed the government greatly. '... your sodyn comyng withouten certayn warnyng' was responsible for the extravagant reaction of the king's household and its frantic attempt to prevent the duke's landing and impede his journey to England.[100] Whatever the true contribution of York to the agitation of the past six months, the king's closest companions were convinced of the danger which his return posed.

The timing of York's arrival is not easy to explain. If he wanted to take advantage of the expressions of sympathy towards his predicament in the months since Moleyns's murder, then he was singularly slow to grasp the opportunity.[101] If he was stirred by news that Somerset had returned to England on 1 August, accompanied by a disconsolate army, and within a fortnight had joined the council, then it is strange that he did not denounce Edmund Beaufort for presiding over the loss of Normandy.[102] He prepared two bills of complaint during the weeks following his arrival and these were received by the king at the end of September. The first demonstrates that York's concern at this stage was a personal one. He had travelled to London to declare his loyalty:

> I have bin informed that diverse language, hath bene sayde of me to your moste excellente estate whiche shoulde sounde to my dishonour and reproch, and charge of my person: howe be it that, I aye have bene, and ever will be, your true liegeman and servaunt: . . .

Henry accepted his assurances in a friendly fashion. Claims that it was otherwise are no more than Lancastrian propaganda dating from 1459, when relations between king and duke had seriously deteriorated.[103] York was certainly not coming to rally sympathizers to dethrone Henry VI. This first bill repeated complaints which York had already made to the king, namely, that household servants had tried to intercept him and arrest his councillors; but his principal purpose concerned himself and his lineage. He protested at attempts made to attaint him of treason and defame his family, for if successful, such moves would have destroyed all prospect of his securing peaceable acknowledgment as Henry VI's heir presumptive:

> . . . certayne commyssions ware made and directed unto divers persones which for the execucion of the same sette in certayne placis and the iniures [sic] enpaneld and charged, the which jures certeyn persones laboured instantly for to have endited me of treson, to thentent to have undo me, myn issue and corrupt my blode, . . .

In his reply, Henry denied that any such indictment was contemplated, though the events of the 1440s, culminating in the marriage of John de la Pole and Margaret Beaufort early in 1450, and the rumours that attended it, may have led York to conclude that a direct attack on himself was the next step. News and opinion reaching Ireland may have been distorted or exaggerated during the journey.[104] Yet there can be little doubt that York would have achieved more in this direction if he had returned while the parliament of 1449–50 was still in session; his intelligence service or his nerve had failed him.

The opportunism of the duke and his advisers is reflected in the changed tone of the second bill, written probably after they had been able to gauge at closer quarters the state of opinion in England in the wake of Cade's revolt.[105] The duke could judge for himself the fearful disarray into which the court had been thrown by Suffolk's murder, Cade's executions, and the indictment of household officials during and immediately after the rising. Several prominent members of the régime hurried to meet York when they heard that he had avoided the household ambush: some, like Lord Hoo, Lord Scales, and William Tresham, may have been eager to renew a previous acquaintance with York in order to secure his favour; others, like Lord Dudley, Bishop Boulers of Hereford (who could appeal to the duke as a fellow magnate of the Welsh border), John Penycock, Sir Thomas Tuddenham, and John Heydon, were scared for their own safety and were prepared to pay the duke to guarantee it.[106] Oldhall, York's chamberlain, seems to have been the impresario who organized York's strategy and whom suppliants were advised to 'cherse and wirchep well'.[107] One or two had a rather rough reception – Lord Hoo seems to have been menaced by York's 'western men' – and others, to judge by the duke's subsequent statement, did not receive the sympathetic hearing for which they had hoped. Indeed, York proceeded to take up some of the complaints which had been heard parliament and during Cade's rebellion; he adopted those which harmonized with his own grievances. Thus, he drew the king's attention to the failure to bring to justice those who had been indicted by the commissions of oyer and terminer in August:

> ...to considere the grett grutchyng and romore that is unnuversaly in this your reame of that justice is nouthe dewly ministrid to suche as trespas and offende a yens your lawes and in special of them that ben endited of tresone and other beyng openly noysed of the same...

The duke presented himself as the champion of justice and the smiter of the corrupt in the tradition of the parliamentary commons and Cade's rebels:

> Wherefor I your humble sugett and lyge man...councel and advertyse your excellent [i.e., excellency] for the conservacion of good tranquillite and pesable rewle among alle trew sogetts for to ordeyn and provyde that dew justice be had a yenst alle suche that ben so endited or openly so noysed, where inne I offre and wol put me in devoure for to execute your commaundements in thes premises of suche offenders and redresse of the seid mysrewlers to my myth and powere...

It was a modest enough proposal in anticipation of the new parliament which had been summoned on 5 September to meet at Westminster on

6 November. Education had come slowly to the duke of York, but this at least represented a first step towards appealing to that body of influential opinion which had attacked the king's ministers and companions for a year past and towards converting his own grievances into a more general bid for sympathy.[108] Yet not even now did he so much as mention Normandy or Gascony, or the misdeeds of Somerset. His confidence to do so was undermined by his own involvement in France, but more especially was his vision restricted by more personal, selfish concerns: the problem of Henry VI's heir and his own future political role in England.

York spent the weeks prior to the opening of parliament in Northamptonshire and East Anglia, where he had the support of his niece, the duchess of Norfolk, and her husband, as well as of his own tenantry.[109] The city of Norwich and East Anglia more generally were fiercely hostile to the henchmen of the late duke of Suffolk, and that is why Tuddenham and Heydon sought to come to terms with York.[110] The reason for the latter's tour became apparent after parliament had begun: not only were York and Norfolk enabled to bring to London a substantial following, but Duke Richard managed to ensure that a caucus of wellwishers was present in the commons. At least a dozen known associates of the duke arrived at Westminster – about twice as many as in November 1449 – and five of them came from this eastern area, including Oldhall (MP for Hertfordshire), who had never sat in parliament before and yet was presented as the commons' speaker.[111] Furthermore, York and Norfolk had met on 16 October at Bury St Edmund's; Norfolk reported that they 'haue fully appoynted and agreed of such ij. persones for to be knightes of shire of Norffolk as oure said vnkill and we thinke conuenient and necessarie for the welfare of the said shire'. John Paston was urged to 'make no laboure contrarie to oure desire', and the earl of Oxford declared cautiously that 'me thynkith wel do to parforme my lordes entent'. Only one of the two sponsored candidates, Henry Grey, was in fact elected at the county court three days later, but their other nominee, Sir Roger Chamberlain, was returned for Suffolk. One may assume that Oxford's retainer, Sir Miles Stapleton, the second MP for Norfolk, was probably of like mind.[112] In the shires of Northampton and Oxford, York tried to secure the election of other sympathetic men; he did so by writing to the sheriff and to local magnates like Lords Zouche and Lovel. A modest degree of success was achieved, since Thomas Mulso, Sir Edmund's brother, was elected for Northamptonshire.[113]

York's second purpose in making his tour was to gather a large affinity to accompany him to London. Some were summoned by letter, but there was no substitute for a personal appearance and appeal in his own estates and in those parts of East Anglia which resented most bitterly the régime of the duke of Suffolk and 'stonde right wildely ... by-cause the peple is so wylde'.[114] Norwich and the county were ready to receive him. Their attitude is well reflected in a letter to John Paston from a clerk in the employ of Justice Yelverton of the king's bench, an East Anglian with no love for the Suffolk clique. York was evidently regarded less as a wronged heir presumptive or a magnate deprived of his rightful place at court and council, than as someone powerful enough to turn the tables on Tuddenham, Heydon, and their friends. York's appearence offered them an opportunity to strike at their oppressors. Yelverton's clerk recommended an organized demonstration at the town of Swaffham when York visited his estates in north-west Norfolk:

> late Swhafham men be warned to mete with my seyd lord [York] on Friday nest comyng atte Pykenham on horssebak in the most goodly wyse, and putte sum bylle un-to my lord of Sir Thomas Tudenham, Heydon, and Prentys, and crye owte on hem, and that all the women of the same towne be ther also, and crye owte on hem also and calle hem extorcionners, and pray my lord that he wyll do sharp execucyon vp-on hem. And my mayster counceyll yow that ze shuld meve the meyer and al the aldernmen [of Norwich] with all here comoners to ryde ayens my lord, and that ther ben madde byllez and putte them vp to my lord, and late all the towne cry owte on Heydon, Todenham, Wyndham, and Prentys, and of all here fals mayntenours, and telle my lord how meche hurte thei have don to the cetye, and late yt be don in the most lamentabyl wyse; for, syr, but yf my lord here sum fowle tales of hem and sum hyddows noys and crye, be my feyth thei arne ellys lyke to come to grace.[115]

York might have his purposes in East Anglia, but the people there had their own uses for the duke.

York's mission had been quite successful, and Norfolk, too, assembled his men early in November; John Paston, for example, was instructed to make his way to Ipswich by 8 November 'with as many clenly people as ye may gete for oure worship at this tyme'. Such recruiting probably provided the foundation for later accusations of treasonable meetings at which (so hostile juries claimed) the deposition of the king was discussed.[116]

When the two dukes arrived in London about 23 November, they found the city tense and seething with unrest.[117] This was partly due to the fact that others, including the king and Warwick, had also come to the parliament with large retinues; but it was especially due to the presence in the city of angry and bewildered soldiers, recently thrown out of France and facing an uncertain future in England. Even before the session began, they committed acts of vandalism and not even York's coat of arms escaped unscathed when it was spotted. But it was on their erstwhile commander, Somerset, that the full weight of their wrath descended, for if one person were to be identified as responsible for their frustration, it was he. Although the magnates and the city fathers would not countenance a repetition of the violence and looting of the summer months, York could be pardoned for looking upon the extreme unpopularity of Edmund Beaufort with wry satisfaction. It was potentially useful capital if the situation were handled with care. Together with the mayor, Norfolk, and the earl of Devon, who seems to have formed a close relationship with Duke Richard at this time, he posed as the champion of justice and the bulwark of order in London, setting a grim example by executing a rioter on 1 December. At the same time, he, Devon, and the mayor managed to save Somerset from his tormentors and despatch him to the Tower for his own safety. No one can say whether York's principal motive was to save a fellow magnate from an ill-disciplined mob and prevent an ugly incident, or to seize the opportunity to incarcerate a dynastic and political opponent. But the depth of feeling and its source, the soldiery, could not be mistaken and these violent days in London may have begun an important change in the thinking of the duke and the formulation of his political strategy. By blending the various burning issues of the day – the loss of France, the succession to the throne, public order, and a reformed council – York could appeal to a larger number of discontented and at the same time pursue his own objectives.[118] His posturing as the upholder of order did not last long, however, for on 3 December the king asserted himself and, in company with other magnates, took steps to overawe the city. York was soon (14 December) despatched to Kent and Sussex, where he was commissioned to try and punish the rebels of 1450; and Somerset was appointed captain of Calais in April 1451.[119]

Meanwhile, parliament itself proved almost as difficult for the government to direct as its predecessor, though for different reasons. York and his advisers had an unusually receptive forum in which to publicize his grievances, and with the aid of Oldhall as speaker, he could personally guide the discussions. If the chancellor, Cardinal Kemp, expected the commons to settle down quickly to deal with the two main causes of summons – to provide funds for the defence of the realm, the keeping of the seas, and the defence of Gascony, and to punish those who had earlier caused disturbances 'so as grievously to shake the kingdom itself and to be like to overturn it' – he was wildly optimistic.[120] It is true that the commons showed a sense of responsibility in introducing a bill of attainder against Cade for his treasonable activities. But a good deal of their discussion was far less to the government's taste. In addition to resistance to the granting of the required subsidies, the first session saw the introduction of a bill demanding the dismissal for life of a number of the king's entourage, headed by the dowager duchess of Suffolk and the duke of Somerset, as from 1 December. This and other affronts to the king spilled over into the second and third sessions in 1451. The king himself, 'of his own mere moving, and by none other authority', eventually granted the commons' petition, but skilfully inserted so many exceptions that its purpose was defeated.[121] They proposed to attaint the dead duke of Suffolk, on whom the commons explicitly fathered certain crimes which had not figured among the charges against him a year earlier, but had materialized from the events of 1450: he was now regarded as responsible for the death of Gloucester and the estrangement of 'full grete Lordes to you right nygh' (and York was surely in the commons' mind).[122] This proposed attainder held great interest for Duke Richard, for if passed, it would effectively put an end to any possibility that Suffolk's son and daughter-in-law might mount the throne as Henry VI's successors. But the king refused his assent. The final sessions in May witnessed the greatest insult of all to the king and the clearest reflection of York's mind. Thomas Young, York's lawyer-councillor, moved that the duke should be formally acknowledged as Henry's heir presumptive.[123] This issue had dogged English politics since the mid-1440s at least, and for almost as long York had felt uneasy about his own line's claims; it was now brought into the open with expectation (for the duke cannot have been oblivious of Young's intention) of a decision at last. Circumstances were more favourable to the duke than they had ever been, for the commons gave their full support: York was far preferable to a Beaufort or a de la Pole, and he seemed to embody their desire for a radical change in government and household. The commons refused to proceed to any other business until the lords undertook to designate York. And therein lay the rub: the duke's gravest and decisive weakness was his failure to gain the confidence of the king or a majority of the lords. Whereas several senior magnates – Norfolk, Exeter, Salisbury, Warwick, Northumberland, and Arundel among them – may have been inclined to join York in humbling the duke of Somerset when parliament first began, not one of them was prepared to support his cause a year later. Their and the king's sensitivity on this dynastic issue is reflected in Henry's swift and stern reaction to Young's request: the Bristol MP was arrested and sent to the Tower, while parliament was instantly dissolved at the end of May.[124]

This rebuff on a matter which had moved York most deeply for several years, followed by the dissolution of a parliament in which he had considerable influence, left him with little alternative but to withdraw from Westminster.[125] The king had shown unwonted powers of decision and determination, and York had no means of challenging them. An effort was made to remain in contact with both York and Norfolk, and in mid-September the former was sent to the west country to calm the renewed violence between his friend Devon and Lords Moleyns and Cobham, on the one side, and Wiltshire and Lord Bonville on the other. All except Devon were arrested and placed in captivity for a month, but York seems to have treated Devon more leniently, and despite repeated summons, neither York nor the earl appeared at council meetings held before Christmas.[126] Having retired to Fotheringhay early in November, Richard went to Ludlow for the Christmas festivities.

The Dartford incident

By the beginning of 1452, York had resolved on another political campaign. It was a more daring venture than his return from Ireland and the parliamentary strategy of 1450–51, for on this occasion he not only declared publicly his loyalty to the king, but also announced his intention, for personal and political reasons, of destroying the influence of the duke of Somerset. His determination to remove Edmund Beaufort for, on the one hand, contriving the attainder of himself and his family, and, on the other, neglecting the defence of Normandy and consequently endangering Gascony and Calais, sprang from a coincidence of motives which had not been achieved earlier.

Since the prorogation of parliament at the end of May 1451, criticism of the household and other royal servants had waned for lack of a suitable forum and a number had been able to regain lost influence. On 4 July, Sir Thomas Tuddenham was pardoned all but £200 of the substantial fine of £1,396 imposed on him for his misdeeds in East Anglia, and several household officials were able to recover some at least of their resumed grants. Nor had the king's promise to provide a 'sad and so substancial consaile, yevyng them more ample auctorite and power then evir we did afor this', been fulfilled.[127] York later claimed that Somerset's pernicious influence was responsible for this resistance to the broadening of counsel; his own recommendations for 'dew justice' had, he commented, been completely ignored 'through the envy, malice, and untruth of the said Duke of Somerset'.[128]

On the other hand, York's personal position had improved since May 1451. For one thing, the king, after nearly seven years of marriage, had still not fathered an heir and the passage of time steadily increased men's anxiety about the succession. Then, too, full realization came that the recovery of Normandy was out of the question for the moment and might not be financially possible for a very long time; moreover, on 10 June, Bordeaux capitulated to French armies so that all seemed lost in Gascony as well. Not only that, but Calais was threatened by the duke of Burgundy in the winter of 1451–52.[129] Furthermore, the essential need which York had felt in 1450 for magnate support for his causes was satisfied to some degree by the earl of Devon's renewal of his link with York after a bloody struggle had taken place in the west country with Bonville and Wiltshire during September 1451. Devon and Lord Cobham, a Dorset and Somerset landowner, were evidently ready to give the duke armed support.[130]

York had appreciated the value of popular opinion and mass support in the autumn of 1450, when his correspondence with the king had been widely publicized and he had appeared in person in the eastern counties to drum up assistance; to the extent that in the ensuing parliament the commons were prepared to take his part on several issues, this propaganda campaign was a success. Accordingly, at the beginning of 1452, he issued a personal statement from Ludlow castle on 9 January

693

that declared unequivocally his allegiance to Henry VI. There is no reason to doubt its sincerity; York's dynastic aim was to secure acceptance as Henry's heir, not as his replacement. But it was a matter of great regret to the duke that the king was 'my heavy lord, greatly displeased with me and hath in me a distrust by sinister information of mine enemies, adversaries, and evil-willers'. He was anxious to disabuse Henry and solemnly to give the lie to the accusations of his traducers by inviting to Ludlow the highly respected earl of Shrewsbury and Bishop Boulers of Hereford, another border landowner whose links with the court went back a long way; they heard York's profession and with authority could report the duke's willingness to swear on the sacrament that he was a true and faithful subject.[131]

That obligation discharged, York was ready to unfurl his political colours and make his attempt to induce the king to remove Somerset, by force if necessary, from his side (and therefore as a prospective Lancastrian heir) and to restore himself to the king's favour and his counsels (and, it was doubtless hoped, to secure his own nomination as the king's heir). A second letter sent from Ludlow to Shrewsbury on 3 February contained the elements of York's appeal, which now set great store by Englishmen's pride and patriotism, virtues which Somerset had betrayed by his disastrous record in France. The prospect of commercial loss and the spectre of invasion would prove equally irresistible to an urban community in York country.

> ... what laud, what worship, honour, and manhood was ascribed of all Nations unto the people of this Realm, whilst the Kingdom's Sovereign Lord stood possessed of his Lordship in the realm of France, and Duchy of Normandy; and what derogation, loss of merchandise, lesion of honour, and villany, is said and reported generally unto the English nation, for loss of the same; namely unto the Duke of Somerset, when he had the commandance and charge thereof: the which loss hath caused and encouraged the King's enemies for to conquer and get Gascony and Gyanne, and now daily they make their advance for to lay siege unto Calais, and to other places in the Marches there, for to apply them to their obeisance, and so for to come into the land with great puissance; to the final destruction thereof, if they might prevail, and to put the land in their subjection, which God defend.[132]

York skilfully introduced his own grievances by implying that his proposals of 1450 would have remedied the realm's condition and that Somerset had ensured their rejection. This enabled him to conclude with an indictment of Somerset himself for plotting 'my undoing, and to corrupt my blood, and to disinherit me and my heirs'. The declared intention to proceed against the wicked duke, with the help of kin and friend alike, seemed eminently reasonable; what Richard required of the townsmen was a force that would put itself under his command.

Forewarned by Shrewsbury and Boulers, Henry VI moved to pre-empt any drastic action which York may have been contemplating. On 27 January it was decided to send Thomas Kent, clerk of the council and a senior official in the privy seal office, to Ludlow; he returned a fortnight later with the news that York was in no mood to be conciliatory or to be deflected from his purpose.[133] As a precaution, Henry decided to hold a council at Coventry and within days of receiving Kent's report, he and the bulk of the lords, led by Somerset and Buckingham, left London (16 February) to confront Richard. Contemporary chroniclers make it plain that this was a show of strength on the king's part, with the royal livery of white and blue, 'written like rope on bawdrikewyse', being distributed to his men.[134] Despite letters from the king, York refused to travel to Coventry and instead proceeded to raise a substantial force with which to march on London. His intention, other than to avoid the king in the midlands, is unclear; but the prospect of a hostile duke entering the capital caused the king to retrace his steps and hastily return to London.[135] Meanwhile, men were being raised for York not only in the Welsh borderland and the west country, but also, most likely under Oldhall's direction, at Stamford, Fotheringhay, and elsewhere in the eastern shires, where the duke had been greeted in 1450; later indictments record that talk was free about the forthcoming deposition of the king.[136]

Henry, by contrast, despatched a delegation on or about 23 February to find the duke and dissuade him from any precipitate or armed action. Bishop Waynflete, Lord Stourton, and York's own kinsman, Henry Bourgchier, were entrusted with this delicate and unsuccessful mission. As a further precaution, he wrote to the mayor, aldermen, and commons of London on 24 February, instructing them to bar York's entry into the city, and indeed when the duke arrived at the gates, the city fathers, true to their allegiance, refused to allow him in. York thereupon moved south, crossing the Thames at Kingston and making for his own property near Dartford in Kent, a county which had shown itself ready to challenge governments in the past.[137]

The king's force arrived in the capital soon afterwards, early in the morning of 27 February. Henry took quarters at the bishop of Winchester's Southwark house, ready for the advance next day into Kent. York had meanwhile reached Dartford and was awaiting the approach of the royal army.[138] The king's tactic seems to have been to coerce the duke into negotiation, for on 1 March the king made his way up to Blackheath with such a large force augmented by county levies drawn from the nearby shires that one chronicler estimated its size at 24,000. York's army, drawn up on Brent heath, between Crayford and Dartford, was a trifle smaller (20,000-strong according to the same chronicler); but in the Thames estuary he had seven ships loaded with supplies and 3,000 guns. Yet the only magnates who were prepared to join this daring throw were Devon and Cobham, each of whom commanded 6,000 of York's force. Some at least of the king's men moved forward along Watling street from Blackheath and over Shooter's hill as far as Welling, well within sight of York's defensive position, which was strongly appointed with bulwarks and bastilles. In the event, not even a skirmish took place and the duke was drawn from his position to meet the king on Blackheath.[139]

York submitted to the persuasions of emissaries despatched to Kent by the king on 28 February. Waynflete and Bishop Bourgchier of Ely were likely to have some influence with Richard; Salisbury and Warwick were, respectively, his brother-in-law and nephew; only the household magnates, Beauchamp and Sudeley, would lack sympathy for him. They rode back and forth between king and duke until an agreement was reached, whereby Henry undertook to receive York's petition against Somerset, who would be placed in the Tower pending an inquiry. Richard may have been persuaded to come to this agreement rather quickly by the conciliatory words of the negotiators, but he must also have realized that the Kentishmen, after their experience in 1450 and their taste of royal justice at York's own hand, were far from eager to turn out in his behalf.[140]

What is so striking about York's letter to Shrewsbury and his petition to the king in 1452 is their emphasis on the fate of the dual monarchy as the single most calamitous consequence of Somerset's career.[141] His earlier coyness on this subject had disappeared, though the careful phrasing of his charges reflects an uneasy awareness of his own role as lieutenant-general in making peace with France and maintaining the Norman defences. With all Normandy lost by the summer of 1450, Gascony apparently overrun in June 1451, and Calais seriously threatened, it was perfectly possible to distinguish between, on the one hand, the virtues of the peace policy of the mid-1440s and York's capacity to hold the frontier, and, on the other hand, the bungling of Somerset which had led to the renewal of war in 1449 and his inability to stem the Valois tide; moreover, under York's rule, both Gascony and Calais seemed reasonably secure. The 'articles and pointes' were designed:

> to bryng to knawlege and understondng the meanes and causes of the grete myscheves and inconvenientz which late befel unto this youre said noble roiame, as in losse of your lyvelode by yonde thee see and otherwyse in ponisshment of deservitours and excuse of innocencie, and also in puttyng aside and eschuyng of the grete and importable hurte and prejudice which ben like, withouten that purviaunce be had of remedie, to succede in shorte tyme.

Compared with York's régime, Somerset had replaced good officers by bad, alienated the Normans by his oppressions, neglected the duchy's defences, embezzled the wages of English soldiers, and dispossessed landowners in Normandy and Maine. When faced with a deteriorating military situation, he panicked and capitulated at too great a cost, and as the new captain of Calais he was undermining morale by his pusillanimity. As for Gascony, the collapse in the north allowed Charles VII to switch his effort to the south – with disastrous consequences for the Lancastrians. To these charges, York himself was prepared to testify, and undoubtedly a strong case could be built upon the events of 1449–52.

York had every expectation that this case would indeed be heard when he concluded the agreement with Henry VI on Blackheath on 2 March. Along with Devon and Cobham, he knelt before his sovereign and presented the petition to him. When they entered the king's tent, one may imagine their astonishment, turning to consternation, at discovering that Somerset was there too, apparently under no restraint at all. They had been deceived.[142] York was disarmed and, flanked by two bishops, escorted to London by the royal army in an entourage that included his hated rival. He was conducted to his own house at Baynard's Castle, where he spent about two weeks in protective custody. On 10 March, a week after his arrest, he was taken to St Paul's cathedral, where he solemnly swore never again to rebel against the king but always to refer his grievances to the law.

All these things above said I promise truly to observe and keep, by the Holy Evangelists contained in this book that I lay my hand upon, and by the Holy Cross that I here touch, and by the blessed Sacrament of our Lord's body that I shall now with His mercy receive. And over this I agree me and will that if I any time hereafter, as with the grace of our Lord I never shall, anything attempt by way of fear or otherwise against your royal majesty and obeisance that I owe thereto, or anything I take upon me otherwise than is above expressed, I from that time forth be unabled, held and taken as an untrue and openly forsworn man, and unable to all manner of worship, estate and degree, be it such as I now occupy, or any other that might grow unto me in any wise.

And this that I here have promised and sworn proceedeth of mine own desire and free voluntee and by no constraining or coercion.[143]

On 13 March he and Somerset concluded formal recognisances with one another in the sum of £20,000 that they would observe an arbitration award that embodied York's promises. Only when rumours started circulating that some of his men were preparing to rescue him was the duke allowed to retire to Ludlow to join his wife.[144]

The crisis was passed and the only immediate retribution exacted by the government was as a result of a commission led by Shrewsbury to Kent in mid-March to quell any incipient rising on York's behalf. His treatment of a number of the convicted at Deptford, including a former Cade adherent, John Wilkins, was harsh and a score or more of heads were placed on London bridge, much to the disgust of the city authorities. What York's presence had not achieved, this stern action did: on 9 April there was a minor demonstration of resentment in the county. Otherwise the king offered a general pardon on 7 April, and only those involved in the murder of Bishops Moleyns and Aiscough were excluded from its terms.[145] It was not until the summer and autumn of 1452 that the king and his advisers set about demonstrating to York, his tenantry, and his allies the consequences of their actions. Henry VI had kept in touch with the duke, but on 1 July he embarked on a series of judicial tours in the west country, the Welsh borderland, and those eastern counties where York's estates were concentrated; these tours were intended to bring the weight of the king's power home to the duke's sympathizers and supporters. Henry himself joined the commissioners of oyer and terminer as they made their way during July and August to Winchester, Exeter, Bristol, Gloucester, Hereford, and Ludlow, returning to London via the midlands.[146] In the autumn the king set off again with a panel of justices that included the earl of Wiltshire, whose feud with Devon gave him a special interest in the commission. Between 15 October and 3 November they visited Hitchin, Huntingdon, Stamford (skirting York's Fotheringhay estates nearby), Grantham, and Cambridge. Many petitioned for, and were received into, the king's grace, but on Somerset's recommendation others were forced to submit in humiliating circumstances, and a few were ordered to be hanged.[147] At Kenilworth, for example, Robert Ardern, who had been returned to parliament in 1449–50, and John Mattys were clapped in irons and put in the charge of two household servants, Thomas Est (whom Cade's rebels had denounced) and John Beaufitz.[148] The earl of Devon had been escorted to Wallingford castle by Christmastide.[149]

The king and the court recovered their nerve in other directions. On 23 November, Henry resolved to ennoble his two half-brothers, Edmund and Jasper Tudor, who had recently come of age. Neither, of course, had the slightest claim to the English throne, for if their lineage was at all royal, it was Valois, not Lancastrian. But their ennoblement buttressed a dynastically enfeebled royal house when it was most needed; the two young men were raised, respectively, to the earldoms of Richmond and Pembroke, which had previously been held by the king's uncles of Bedford and Gloucester, and they were accorded precedence of all other magnates save the dukes.[150] The wedding followed later of Earl Edmund and Margaret Beaufort, whose marriage to John de la Pole was annulled (probably for this precise purpose) in February or March 1453. Even at this stage, it may not have been appreciated that Queen Margaret was pregnant at last (the baby being born on 13 October 1453), and, as S. B. Chrimes has shrewdly commented, Henry VI is unlikely to have made these arrangements 'without some expectation that the collateral lines [of the house of Lancaster] would become entwined' – as, of course, they did in Edmund's and Margaret's son, King Henry VII.[151]

Edmund and Jasper were also knighted, at a ceremony in the Tower on 5 January. Sharing the limelight with them on that occasion were

Thomas and John Neville, the sons of the earl of Salisbury; William Herbert, son and heir of York's former councillor, Sir William ap Thomas; and two loyal Lancastrian gentlemen, Roger Lewknor and William Catesby, both of whom were returned to the submissive parliament of 1453.[152] In the case of Herbert and the Nevilles, the knighting may have been an attempt to retain a loyalty that had been recently strained, for Herbert was York's marcher tenant and Salisbury had just been deprived of his stake in the Yorkshire estates of the earldom of Richmond by Edmund Tudor.[153] As for York's principal lieutenant, Sir William Oldhall, he was hounded from pillar to post soon after the Dartford débâcle. Having failed in his attempts to organize a successful *coup* – and they seem to have continued after he ceased to be speaker in May 1451 – he sought sanctuary in St Martin-le-Grand, London, on 23 November 1451. Attempts to winkle him out were resisted by the dean; indeed, he was accused of helping to raise men in support of York's Dartford venture and may even have had a hand in urging the duke's Welsh tenantry to rescue York from his subsequent confinement. Indicted of treason on several occasions during 1452, he was gradually stripped of his possessions, including his favourite house at Hunsdon (Hertfordshire), which was granted to Somerset and his heirs on 24 May 1453; one month later, a bill for his attainder passed the commons.[154]

This Reading parliament marked the zenith of the king's political recovery after the crises of 1450–52. It proved to be one of the most royalist and accommodating parliaments with which Henry VI ever had to deal.[155] Scarcely one or two of the dozen or more of York's supporters who had sat in the 1450–51 assembly were elected to the new one, whereas an unusually large proportion of household men were in the commons (17 per cent of the MPs compared with 6 per cent in 1450).[156] The new speaker, Thomas Thorp, was an experienced exchequer official who had invested in property in Northamptonshire and Essex – and attracted the hostility of Cade's rebels as a result.[157] The parliament in which he presided marked the rejection of the criticisms of 1450–51: the petition then presented against the court was now consigned 'in oblivion' as being contrary to God, king, and reason, and all grants in favour of anyone who had been with York at Dartford were resumed. These acts, together with the attainder of Oldhall and the ennoblement of the Tudors, gave sufficient indication to York that his personal ambitions were frustrated and the public demands to which they had been linked rejected. York was even deprived of his most effective weapon against the régime, for on 20 October 1452 the earl of Shrewsbury, his old councillor who put service to the crown before his association with Duke Richard, managed to recover the wine city of Bordeaux. Hopes were high that the catalogue of disasters in France was closed.

York's resort to force in 1452 had been a failure. He had pondered long, perhaps too long, before resorting to direct action against

Somerset – for that could be construed as treason against the king – and he had eventually done so without the support of a parliamentary movement such as had been available in 1449–51. Accompanied only by Devon and Cobham among the lords, his rising was resisted by the bulk of the magnates, no matter how much sympathy some of them may have had with him in the autumn of 1450.[158] His naivety is revealed in his belief that Somerset could be dislodged by an agreement reached with a delegation which, because it included several who were personally well disposed towards York, may not have represented the court as a whole. He lacked sufficient political astuteness in 1452 to realize that little could be achieved without magnate or parliamentary backing, and the failure to persuade London to open its gates and his inability to stimulate a rising in Kent were signal indications of this weakness. York's bid had failed. It would require a major change of circumstance before he could attempt another; yet in the summer of 1453 circumstances did suddenly alter in a way that was least expected and owed nothing to the duke at all.

Notes

1 There is no authoritative study of Richard, duke of York, but see *GEC*, XII, ii, 905-9; *DNB*, XLVIII, 176-85 (by J. Gairdner); Scofield, op. cit., I, ch. 1; and F. M. Wright, 'The house of York, 1415–1450' (Johns Hopkins PhD thesis, 1959). Rosenthal, 'Estates and finances of York', is an important study that does not, however, claim to be a rounded appreciation of the duke. See also his 'Fifteenth-century baronial incomes and Richard, duke of York', *BIHR*, XXXVII (1964), 233-40.

2 Somerville, op. cit., pp. 185, 418-19. Richard was placed in Waterton's charge on 9 March 1416, and 200 marks were allocated for his expenses at Methley manor (Yorks.) (*CPR, 1429-36*, p. 35; Wylie and Waugh, op. cit., I, 534-5). See PRO, E404/39/309, 320.

3 Though Waterton did not die until January 1425 (Somerville, op. cit., p. 419).

4 The marriage to Cicely, aged 9, took place between December 1423 and October 1424 (*GEC*, XII, ii, 906 n. [a], 908 and n. [g]). Richard was in Joan's custody, at least legally, probably until 1432, though they may have spent time at court (PRO, E404/47/314; above, p. 54).

5 For the moment, a mere 100 marks were added to the original 200 marks to cater annually for his upbringing (above n. 2; *CPR, 1422-29*, p. 343; ibid., *1429-36*, p. 35; *Foedera*, IV, iv, 121).

6 For this quarrel, see Storey, *End of Lancaster*, p. 113.

7 PRO, E101/408/10 m. 7. But according to *DNB*, XLVIII, 176, he was summoned to attend the household in the spring of 1428.

8 *GEC*, XII, ii, 906; *PPC*, IV, 27. In November 1429, when he was 18, Richard received a further 200 marks *per annum*, bringing the annual allocation for his expenses to 500 marks (*CPR, 1429-36*, p. 35).

9 *CCR, 1429-35*, pp. 150-1; *CPR, 1429-36*, pp. 207-8. He paid 1,000 marks to the king for this privilege (*CFR, 1430-37*, p. 122).

10 *RP*, IV, 465-6, 470-1; *CCR, 1429–35*, pp. 242, 260; *CFR, 1430–37*, p. 122. He was allowed to receive his Irish revenues *in absentia* (*CPR, 1429–36*, pp. 225, 241).

11 This recitation of his titles is taken from his letters patent, dated 20 December 1448 and reproduced in facsimile in *Catalogue of the Lyttelton papers* (Sotheby, 12 December 1978), pp. 28-9.

12 For two rare appearances at the council before 1450, see PRO, E28/65/51, 39 (25 November 1440); 66/18-19 (25 January 1441); for five in all, see Virgoe, *BIHR*, XLIII (1970), 157-8.

13 *CPR, 1429–36*, p. 38.

14 Above, pp. 454-5.

15 PRO, E28/57/19 (Neville). Beaumont was one of York's feoffees on 4 May 1436, before the departure for France, and as Viscount Beaumont he performed the same service in March 1441 (PRO, E28/57/23; 67/13-14, 18-19; *PPC*, V, 136).

16 Pugh, 'Magnates, knights and gentry', p. 123 n. 84; for his later connection with Richard, see above, p. 455.

17 Above, pp. 455, 459.

18 Rosenthal, 'Estates and finances', p. 197. His third son, Edmund, was born there too, in May 1443.

19 Woodger, thesis, pp. 2, 4, 10-11, 16-17, 36, 50. Henry Bourgchier was knighted with Henry VI and York in 1426 and was in their company on the visit to France in 1430–32.

20 *EHL*, p. 341; above, p. 459. See the list of his feoffees on 4 May 1436 and 16 March 1441 (PRO, E28/57/23; 67/13-16, 18-19; *PPC*, V, 136, 288). Biographical notes on most of them are in Wedgwood, *Biographies*, *s. n.* This whole subject is illuminated by Marshall, thesis, chs. III, IV.

21 e.g., BL, Eg. Ch. 8782 m. 2.

22 Roskell, *1422*, pp. 214-15. It may have been a help to York that Russell was speaker of the parliament of 1432 in which York was granted seisin of his lands. I was unable to consult T. B. Pugh, 'The lands and servants of the duke of York in 1415' (Oxford BLitt thesis, 1950), but see *CCR, 1429–35*, p. 260, for some of Duke Edward's annuitants who were still alive in 1433 and taken over as a charge on Richard's estate: they included John Russell, John Popham, and Richard Dixon, who was one of Richard's feoffees in 1436 (PRO, E28/57/23).

23 Wedgwood, *Biographies*, pp. 692-3; Roskell, *Proc. Hants. Arch. Soc. and Field Club*, XXI (1957), 38-52; idem, *Speakers*, pp. 235-7; Marshall, thesis, p. 50. Popham was York's treasurer in February 1438 (Rosenthal, 'Estates and finances', p. 179).

24 Marshall, thesis, pp. 50-1; Pollard, thesis, pp. 144-92; above, p. 455.

25 Stevenson, II, ii, 434-7, an incomplete translation of Lambeth MS 506 f. 8*r*-11*r* (Bedford's retinue in 1435).

26 Marshall, thesis, pp. 51, 53; McFarlane, *TRHS*, 5th ser., VII (1957), 91-116; P. S. Lewis, 'Sir John Fastolf's lawsuit over Titchwell, 1448–1455', *HJ*, I (1958), 1-20. For his role as York's councillor in England, see BL, Eg. Ch. 8782 m. 2 (1443–44); Friedrichs, thesis, p. 253 (quoting PRO, CP25 [i] /224/118) (1449). J. Crosland, *Sir John Fastolfe* (1970), is a slight study.

27 BL, Eg. Ch. 8782 m. 2; Marshall, thesis, p. 51; Wedgwood, *Biographies*, pp. 644-5. He had been Bedford's second chamberlain (Stevenson, II, ii, 434).

28 *PPC*, V, 136; BL, Eg. Ch. 8782 m. 2; Marshall, thesis, p. 51; D. Thomas, 'The Herberts of Raglan as supporters of the house of York in the second half of the fifteenth century' (Wales MA thesis, 1967), ch. 1; G. H. R. Kent, 'The estates of the Herbert family in the mid-fifteenth century' (Keele PhD thesis, 1973), pp. 1-10; Griffiths, *Principality of Wales*, I, 147-8. For the most recent account of the building of Raglan castle, though with less emphasis on Sir William's contribution, see A. Emery, 'The development of Raglan castle and keeps in late mediaeval England', *AJ*, CXXXII (1975), 151-86.

29 *PPC*, V, 136; VI, 52; Marshall, thesis, pp. 51, 56-61 (especially quoting PRO, C1/26/475); C. E. Johnston, 'Sir William Oldhall', *EHR*, XXV (1910), 715-22; J. S. Roskell, *Nott. Med. St.*, V (1961), 87-112; idem,*Speakers*, pp. 242-7, 360-1; Wedgwood, *Bigraphies*, pp. 647-8. He acquired Hunsdon and other properties from York himself in the 1440s.

30 *EHL*, p. 341; above, p. 459.

31 Munro, op. cit., pp. 69-70. Consider also John Clay, who served in France from 1421 and was treasurer of York's household in France by 1443; William Mynors, captain of Harfleur in 1426 and controller of York's household by 1442; Thomas Hoo, a captain in France in the 1430s and master of York's household by 1442 (Roskell, *Speakers*, pp. 179, 180; Wedgwood *Biographies*, p. 187; Marshall, thesis, pp. 54 and n. 2, 69). Others who had been in France before 1436 include Lord Scales, Sir John Montgomery, a councillor of York's by 1448-49, and Sir John Salvin, a councillor by 1443 (ibid., pp. 54-5, 66, 69; Rosenthal, 'Estates and finances', pp. 179-81; Wedgwood, *Biographies*, p. 187; *GEC*, XI, 504-7).

32 Above, pp. 468, 506. For Stanlow, one of York's councillors by 1448–49, see PRO, SC6/1113/9 m. 2.

33 BL, Eg. Ch. 8783 m. 3; Marshall, thesis, pp. 61-6; Wedgwood, *Biographies*, p. 618. See also Roskell, *1422*, pp. 206-7 (for Henry Mulso), and BL, Eg. Ch. 8783 m. 4 (for the award of a 100-mark annuity to his brother William by York on 25 June 1450).

34 For Young, see Wedgwood, *Biographies*, pp. 981-2; Rosenthal, 'Estates and finances', p. 179; for Burley, Roskell, *1422*, pp. 159-60; idem, *Speakers*, pp. 216-17, 225-7; idem, 'William Burley of Broncroft, speaker for the commons in 1437 and 1445–6', *Trans. Salop Arch. Soc.*, LVI (1960), 263-72. In 1449 Burley, like Oldhall, bought lands from York; he was steward of the duke's lordship of Denbigh by 1446 (ibid., pp. 264, 270).

35 *GEC*, V, 321-5; BL, Eg. Ch. 8782 m. 2; Marshall, thesis, pp. 52-4, 79. For Merbury (d. 1438), see Griffiths, *Principality of Wales*, pp. 132-4.

36 Above, p. 422; BL, Eg. Ch. 8783 m. 1-3; Rosenthal, 'Estates and finances', p. 180.

37 For another, see Simon Reynham, receiver of Pont à Mer in 1441–43, cofferer of the duke's household from 1448, and possibly the brother-in-law of Edmund Mulso (Rosenthal, 'Estates and finances', p. 179; BL, Eg. Ch. 8785 m. 1; Marshall, thesis, p. 71).

38 e.g., Margaret Mulso married John Langley, one of York's annuitants (Wedgwood, *Biographies*, p. 618 n. 6; Marshall, thesis, pp. 70-1); Simon Reynham may have married Mulso's sister (ibid., p. 71); Oldhall's daughter married Walter, son of Sir Theobald Gorges, one of York's companions (ibid., pp. 72-3); and Sir William ap Thomas's son, William Herbert,

married a daughter of Sir Walter Devereux (Griffiths, *Principality of Wales*, p. 155).

39 McFarlane, *TRHS*, 5th ser., VII (1957), 105-7 (Fastolf); Roskell, *Nott. Med. St.*, V (1961), 99; idem, *Speakers*, p. 243 (Oldhall); and more generally, Allmand, *EconHR*, 2nd ser., XXI (1968), 461-79.

40 McFarlane, *TRHS*, 5th ser., VII (1957), 107.

41 PRO, E404/40/72; 51/37; BL, Eg. Ch. 8781 m. 1. He was York's feoffee in March 1441 (*PPC*, V, 136). John Gloucester, an exchequer clerk, was also his attorney at the exchequer in 1443–44 (BL, Eg. Ch. 8782 m. 1; Wedgwood, *Biographies*, pp. 379-80).

42 *PPC*, V, 136; Roskell, *1422*, pp. 171-2; BL, Eg. Ch. 8782 m. 2; Wedgwood, *Biographies*, p. 258. For his son's service with York by April 1448, see *CPR, 1446–52*, p. 231. John Thrusby and Richard Pytte represented York's interests in king's bench and common pleas in 1443–44 (BL, Eg. Ch. 8782 m. 1; Wedgwood, *Biographies*, p. 687 [Pytte]).

43 *PPC*, V, 136; BL, Eg. Ch. 8782 m. 1, 2; Friedrichs, thesis, passim; above, p. 377. Cromwell was York's agent in arranging the marriage of York's daughter with Exeter's son and heir in 1444–45 (PRO, DL41/2/8, cited by Friedrichs, thesis, pp. 155, 212). For his connection with York throughout the 1440s, see ibid., pp. 252-6.

44 PRO, E28/57/23 (1436); 67/15-16 (1441); *GEC*, VI, 613-16; Kirby, thesis, ch. V; above, p. 34.

45 PRO, E28/57/23; *PPC*, V, 136; Emden, *Cambridge*, p. 11; above, p. 33. He was Henry's confessor still in 1436 and in any case his two bishoprics were in York country (R. G. Davies, thesis, III, v-viii).

46 BL, Eg. Ch. 8782 m. 2; above, p. 340.

47 Wigmore was in York's service by July 1433 and may have been inherited from the earl of March (PRO, E403/710 m. 12; see also *CPR 1446–52*, pp. 244, 394; Rosenthal, 'Estates and finances', p. 179). For Scales and Hoo, see below, p. 688.

48 *CPR 1436–41*, p. 473 (1440); PRO, E28/73/90 (c. 1444); *PPC*, VI, 36; *CPR, 1441–46*, p. 334.

49 PRO, E404/57/172; DL41/2/8; above, p. 504. York's sons Edward (b. 1442) and Edmund (b. 1443) had been given, presumably by the king, the titles of earls of March and Rutland respectively by September 1445 (BN, n. a. fr. 5848 no. 389; BirmPL, Hampton MS 504039; see *HBC*, p. 447).

50 *DNB*, XLVIII, 177 (hence, perhaps, Richard's presence with the king at Windsor on 14 February 1438: PRO, E101/408/24 f. 25d); *CPR, 1441–46*, p. 242. For some minor relief of charges on his inherited estates, see ibid., *1436–41*, pp. 167, 168 (April 1448).

51 In October 1447 an order was issued to pay him the arrears of his pension, but it was only paid intermittently thereafter (in 1447–48, 1450–51, and 1457–58) (*CPR, 1441–46*, p. 117; PRO, E404/64/82; 67/113; 71/2/70). For the debt, see PRO, E403/762 m. 12-13.

52 The reasons for this unsatisfactory situation include the declining value of the seignorial (especially judicial) rights of marcher lords after the Glyndŵr revolt, Richard's own minority, a lingering and substantial burden of uncollected arrears, and perhaps the need to engage, at high cost, councillors and servants during York's long absences in France (Shrewsbury received £200 *per annum*). See C. D. Ross, 'The estates and finances

of Richard, duke of York', *WHR*, III (1966–67), 299-302; Rawcliffe, op. cit., p. 114, citing PRO, SC11/818.

53 *PPC*, VI, 92; above, p. 421. Very few new payments (as opposed to the reissue of uncashed tallies) were made to him in the late 1440s, and none in 1451 or 1452 (PRO, E403/760-93 passim). The transfers of land to Burley, Fastolf, Oldhall, and other of York's annuitants and councillors, may have been in return for cash advances; a number were arranged in 1448–49, when the duke was preparing to leave for Ireland (above, n. 34; ChichRO, Winterton MS catalogue, 1/17; 28/77; BirmPL, Hagley Hall, 25/351402-6; LeicsRO, DE221/10/5/11).

54 Above, pp. 358, 466-7. It was soon after this episode that Claudian's early fifth-century Life of the soldier-consul Stilicho was 'translate et wrete at Clare' and completed in 1445 probably by Osbern Bokenham, a monk of Clare priory (Suffolk) which had long been patronized by the Mortimers. Its unmistakable comparison of York with the 'gode prince' Stilicho, and its likely identification of Stilicho's enemy, the overmighty Ruffinus, with Suffolk (rather than with Henry VI, as in A. Cameron, *Claudian. Poetry and propaganda at the court of Honorius* [Oxford, 1970], pp. 429-31) was small consolation for the slighted duke. The manuscript, BL, Add. MS 11814, with its Yorkist badges, is printed by E. Flügel, 'Eine Mittelenglische Claudian-Ubersetzung (1445)', *Anglia*, XXVIII (1905), 255-99, 421-38; several of the illuminated pages have been reproduced, most recently f. 10 in A. G. Watson, *Catalogue of dated and datable manuscripts, c. 700–1600, in the department of manuscripts, British Library*, II (1979), plate 470. For Bokenham, see Emden, *Oxford*, I, 210; *DNB, s. n.*

55 Above, pp. 358, 504.

56 Griffiths, *JMH*, I (1975), 193-4. For this dynastic question, see idem, 'Sense of dynasty', pp. 19-25.

57 e.g., *DNB*, XLVIII, 178; *CPR, 1446–52*, pp. 43, 66, 83, 334.

58 Pugh, 'Magnates, knights and gentry', p. 118 n. 11 (August 1445); *CPR, 1446–52*, p. 86.

59 His own benefits from Gloucester's death were meagre (e.g., *DNB*, XLVIII, 178 [Great Wratting manor, Suffolk]; *CPR, 1446–52*, p. 83 [justice and warden of the forests south of the Trent]).

60 Thomas Young (Bristol), possibly Everard Digby (Rutland, for whose connection with York in 1449, see *CPR, 1446–52*, p. 218), and John Gloucester (Southwark and Melcombe Regis). Even Gloucester is more likely to have been elected because of his exchequer post than because of his service as York's agent five years earlier (Wedgwood, *Biographies*, pp. 981-2, 273, 379-80).

61 Roskell, *Speakers*, pp. 235-7. At least six of York's servants were returned to the 1449–50 parliament, excluding two royal officials (John Gloucester and Richard Pytte) who had once been his agents at Westminster: Young, Digby, Burley, Popham, John Skelton, and Sir Robert Conyers (Wedgwood, *Biographies, s. n.*; Marshall, thesis, p. 96 [Conyers witnessing the duke's charter in 1447]).

62 Roskell, *Nott. Med. St.*, V (1961), 98-100. John Malpas, John Flegge, and John Langley were also with him in Ireland (Marshall, thesis, pp. 69-74; Rosenthal, 'Estates and finances', p. 190.

63 Roskell, *Proc. Hants. Arch. Soc. and Field Club*, XXI (1957), 38-51; idem, *Speakers*, pp. 235-7; above, p. 516. Popham's connection with York is

unlikely to have been the main reason for his choice. A full study of the parliament is in Virgoe, thesis.

64 *RP*, V, 171-2; Wedgwood, *Biographies*, pp. 871-2; Roskell, *Northants. Past and Present*, II (1954–59), 189-203; idem, *Speakers*, pp. 229-30, 238-9. Tresham had been speaker of the Bury parliament of 1447. He had been one of York's feoffees in February 1449, though that is the extent of his known connection with the duke (*CPR, 1446–52*, p. 218; Griffiths, *JMH*, I [1975], 198).

65 *RP*, V, 176. The parliamentary record of Suffolk's impeachment (ibid., pp. 176-83), on which the following paragraphs are largely based, is partly reproduced and partly summarized in Chrimes and Brown, op. cit., pp. 285-90.

66 'Benet's Chron.', pp. 196-7; Flenley, p. 127. See Bellamy, *Law of treason*, p. 124 and n. 3.

67 Above, p. 518. For Stafford's forced resignation, see Kingsford, *EHR*, XXIX (1914), 514.

68 *Great Chron.*, pp. 180-1; *EHL*, pp. 344, 370; Flenley, pp. 127-8.

69 Stevenson, II, ii, 766; above, p. 580; Virgoe, *BJRL*, LV (1973), 459-82. Tailboys was described as 'a Common Murderer, Mansleer, Riotour and contynuell Breker of your [i.e., the king's] peas' in 1449 (ibid., p. 463). For Suffolk's lack of confidence in magnate support, see below, p. 684.

70 Above, p. 286. For the evolution of impeachment, see T. F. T. Plucknett, 'The impeachments of 1376', *TRHS*, 5th ser., I (1951), 159-64; idem, 'State trials under Richard II', ibid., II (1952), 159-71; idem, 'Impeachment and attainder', ibid., III (1953), 145-58; and the useful comments in Bellamy, *Law of treason*, pp. 96, 98, 124, 163, 170, 187.

71 *RP*, V, 177-9 (with the quotation on 177), summarized in Chrimes and Brown, op. cit., p. 287.

72 For Maine and Brittany, see above, pp. 495-504, 510-13.

73 e.g., the story of the secret surrender of Maine in 1445 as the price of Queen Margaret's hand (Gascoigne, pp. 190, 204-5, 219; above, p. 487).

74 *RP*, V, 177. The marriage seems to have taken place between 28 January and 7 February 1450 (Griffiths, *JMH*, I [1975], 193-4). The same accusation was voiced again on 4 July 1450 in London's guildhall at the height of Cade's rebellion (above, p. 614). Suffolk's dismissal of such implications in the marriage ('it is ayenst lawe and reason to make the seid Margarete soo nygh the Corone') does not carry great conviction (*RP*, V, 182 [13 March]).

75 e.g., below, p. 824. For the procedure of attainder, see Plucknett, *TRHS*, 5th ser., III (1953), 155-7; Bellamy, *Law of treason*, ch. 7 and pp. 124, 170, 211.

76 Kingsford, *EHR*, XXIX (1914), 515. Suffolk was placed in the care of three household servants who probably owed their offices to him: William Mynors, Thomas Staunton, and John Stanley (*RP*, V, 182; above, p. 361). Margaret Paston had heard by 12 March that Suffolk 'is pardonyd and hath his men azen waytyng up-on hym, and is rytz wel at ese and mery, and is in the Kyngys godegrase, and in the gode conseyt of all the lordys, as well as ever he was' (*PL*, I, 237).

77 Virgoe, *BJRL*, LV (1973), 463-7; *PL*, II, 22; cf. ibid., I, 222.

78 Above, pp. 334ff. The council had attempted to curb such practices in 1427 (*RP*, V, 409).

79 For the 45 lords, see ibid., p. 182, which may be compared with the peerage

creations above, pp. 353-9. Attendance of 45 (out of 92 summoned) was not unusual in Henry VI's reign (Roskell, *BIHR*, XXIX [1956], 182-9). The lords' declaration (*RP*, V, 183) may have been issued to convince the commons that they nevertheless sympathized with the moves against Suffolk.

80 *HMC*, III (1872), 279-80, a mutilated paper roll now Bodl, Eng. hist. b. 119. Note, too, that bills appeared in London predicting the death of Suffolk (and the bishop of Salisbury and Lord Saye) by May (*EHL*, p. 370).

81 Flenley, pp. 128-9; 'Benet's Chron.', p. 198; *EHL*, p. 344; Kingsford, *EHR*, XXIX (1914), 515. For the circumstances of Suffolk's death, see R. Virgoe, 'The death of William de la Pole, duke of Suffolk', *BJRL*, XLVII (1964-65), 489-502. The details of Suffolk's execution came to light in June 1451, when two of those responsible were tried (PRO, KB9/47/13, printed by Virgoe, *BJRL*, XLVII [1964-65], 501-2).

82 'Benet's Chron.', p. 198. An order for the assembling of ships from the East Anglian ports was issued on 6 April and four days later one of the queen's servants was instructed to accompany Suffolk (Virgoe, *BJRL*, XLVII [1964-65], 492).

83 *Three Chrons.*, p. 66; *Brut*, p. 516 (which is mistaken in saying that Henry VI brought Suffolk to the Leicester session). For the sullen hostility of this session, see Roskell, *Speakers*, p. 240.

84 Gairdner, *PL*, II, 142-3.

85 Giles, pp. 38-9. It is impossible to prove that any influential person (such as the duke of Exeter, admiral of England) lay behind the interception of Suffolk (Virgoe, *BJRL*, XLVII [1964-65], 494-7). The body lay in a church for one month; perhaps no one dared claim it ('Benet's Chron.', p. 198); this chronicle also maintains that Suffolk was initially making for Brittany, which seems unlikely.

86 *RP*, V, 183.

87 Giles, pp. 38-9. For the attack on Somerset, see below, p. 694.

88 *EHL*, p. 370; Kingsford, *EHR*, XXIX (1914), 514, 515; Flenley, pp. 128, 129; Virgoe, *BJRL*, XLVII (1964-65), 497; 'Benet's Chron.', p. 197; *Great Chron.*, p. 181.

89 Flenley, p. 129; *EHL*, p. 371; *English Chron.*, p. 64; Giles, p. 41; *Three Chrons.*, p. 66; *Great Chron.*, pp. 180, 181; Virgoe, *BJRL*, XLVII (1964-65), 497, 499, 500.

90 Kingsford, *EHR*, XXIX (1914), 514; 'Benet's Chron.', p. 197. See Griffiths, *JMH*, I (1975), 193, for Gloucester's appearance in Cade's manifesto.

91 Virgoe, *BJRL*, XLVII (1964-65), 497, 500, quoting PRO, KB9/118/30; 47/13 (printed on pp. 501-2); Griffiths, *JMH*, I (1975), 191, 192. Indeed, one wonders whether the anonymous condemnation of Suffolk in mid-March (above, n. 80) did not originate with Oldhall and his friends: notice its emphasis on the loss of territory in Normandy and the impoverishment of those who returned ('the trewe subjects lost her londe, her goods, her catall, ther wyfes, ther childrenne, and over that exiled and fleed the countree'), as well as on the alienation of members of the royal family (which must surely have meant York above others). Bury might also have been a useful source of rumour about Gloucester's death there in 1447 (above, p. 497).

92 *EHL*, p. 371; Griffiths, *JMH*, I (1975), 191 and n. 9. He was promptly arrested and eventually executed at the insistence of members of the royal household, led by Thomas Daniel.

93 Griffiths, *JMH*, I (1975), 204 (from Beverley corporation archives, Town 'Chartulary', f. 37-38). For the reputation of shipmen, see ibid., 191.
94 ibid., 197.
95 Above, pp. 636-8.
96 At York's attainder in 1459, some of Cade's adherents were said to have confessed that they rebelled on York's behalf (*RP*, V, 346; Griffiths, *JMH*, I [1975], 192). The suggestion that York might be invited by the rebels to displace Henry VI was sufficiently plausible for the rebels to deny that this was their intention (above, p. 636).
97 Above, p. 635. The former commanders, Lord Scales and Mathew Gough, led the Londoners' resistance to Cade on 5-6 July.
98 Even after Cade's death, there were some who claimed that he was still alive, was a Mortimer, and should be king (above, p. 642). Hence, perhaps, the government's precaution of introducing an act of attainder against John Mortimer *eo nomine* in the following parliament of 1450-51 (*RP*, V, 224; above, p. 618).
99 Griffiths, *WHR*, VIII (1976), 22-4. But this coincidence had no perceptible impact on the course of events.
100 ibid., 15-22; idem, *JMH*, I (1975), 204.
101 Further alleged plots against the king were hatched in July–September 1450 (ibid., 206 n. 9).
102 ibid., 197.
103 ibid., 189, 203-4 (with the quotation on 203). The Prussian envoy's report confirms that Henry VI was friendly towards York (von der Ropp, op. cit., no.669).
104 Griffiths, *JMH*, I (1975), 193-4. On 18 August 1450 a papal dispensation allowed John and Margaret to remain married despite their relationship in the fourth and fifth degrees (*CPapReg, 1447–55*, pp. 472-3). A few of York's grants had been resumed in May–June 1450, in accordance with the act of resumption, though apart from the Isle of Wight, they did not involve significant estates (Wolffe, *Royal demesne*, pp. 256, 258).
105 Griffiths, *JMH*, I (1975), 204-5, from which the two quotations below are taken.
106 ibid., 197-8 and n. 27, 28; Roskell, *Speakers*, pp. 244-45. For the earlier links between York and Hoo, Scales, and Tresham, see above, pp. 305-6.
107 Even Henry VI appealed to Oldhall for York's protection for John Penycock (*PL*, II, 47; above, p. 324). Oldhall was later said to have plotted the king's death, or else to bring discord to the realm, on 27 September 1450; this may have been a distorted reference to Oldhall's role in presenting York's bills to Henry VI, for a week later he was in Henry's presence at Westminster (Roskell, *Speakers*, p. 244; *PL*, II, 47).
108 Griffiths, *JMH*, I (1975), 201. One man who had seen this second bill said it was 'meche after the Comouns desyre' (*PL*, II, 47). A German envoy in London at this time reported that several lords might be prepared to support York – Exeter, Salisbury, Warwick, Arundel, and Northumberland – and that Scales and Rivers accompanied the duke to present his bills to the king (Friedrichs, thesis, p. 259, quoting Göttingen, Staatliches Archivlager, O. B. A. Reg. No. 10422); and before November 1451 Warwick employed York's councillor, Oldhall, as his steward of Saham (Norfolk) (P. B. Chatwin, 'Documents of Warwick the Kingmaker in the possession of St.

Mary's Church, Warwick', *Trans. and Proc. Birmingham Arch. Soc.*, LIX [1935], 2).

109 Above, pp. 588ff. For his extensive Clare properties in Essex, Norfolk, and Suffolk, and the estates in Northants (especially Fotheringhay castle), see Rosenthal, 'Estates and finances', pp. 194, 174-5 (their relative value).

110 Griffiths, *JMH*, I (1975), 200; above, p. 589.

111 *RP*, V, 210; McFarlane, *PBA*, L (1964), 89-91; idem, 'Parliament and "Bastard Feudalism" ',*TRHS*, 4th ser., XXVI (1944), 56-8. Of these associates, the four who had never been in parliament before – Sir Edmund Mulso, John Leynton, Sir Robert Darcy, and Oldhall – were all returned from this area (Wedgwood, *Biographies, s. n.*). Unlike Popham, the initial choice as speaker in November 1449, Oldhall was an exclusive York servant (above, pp. 669-71).

112 *PL*, II, 54-5, reprinted in Chrimes and Brown, op. cit., pp. 291-2; although Sir William Chamberlain is mentioned as York's and Norfolk's candidate, this is probably an error for Sir Roger. For York's link with Zouche and, through Ogard, with Lovel, see T, B. Dilkes (ed.), *Bridgwater borough archives, 1445–68* (Soms. Rec. Soc., LX, 1945), p. 113; A. Clark (ed.), *Lincoln diocese documents, 1450-1544* (EETS, CXLIX, 1914), p. 74.

113 McFarlane, *PBA*, L (1964), 89-90, quoting BL, Eg. Ch. 8783 m. 3. Thomas Mulso had served in France in the 1430s (Marshall, thesis, pp. 61-2).

114 *PL*, II, 51.

115 ibid., 48 (6 October); cf. ibid., pp. 49, 53. William Prentis was an associate of Tuddenham, and John Wyndham (or Wymondham) was connected with Heydon (ibid., I, 239, 224, 232; II, 75, 526; above, p. 586). For York's estates at Bircham and Walsingham (Norfolk), see Rosenthal, 'Estates and finances', p. 194; and for the duke of Suffolk's interest in Swaffham, Wolffe, *Royal demesne*, p. 272.

116 *PL*, II, 55. Meetings of York's and Norfolk's men were organized by Thomas Mulso, Oldhall, John Wykes, and others at Fotheringhay (Northants.), Royston (Cambs.), Grantham and Stamford (Lincs.), and Chelmsford (Essex) between 3 and 12 November (Griffiths, *JMH*, I [1975], 200; *CPR, 1452–61*, p. 23). It seems unnecessary to follow Storey, *End of Lancaster*, p. 249, in redating these events to 1451 in defiance of the indictments (PRO, KB9/7/1, 26/1, 65a, 94/1, 278; KB27/777, *rex* m. 7; as cited by Marshall, thesis, pp. 165-8).

117 Flenley, p. 123; above, p. 647. The king had 'wretyn to alle his men that be in the chekroll [of the treasurer of the household] to awayte on hym atte parlement in their best aray' (*PL*, II, 50.).

118 Cf. the judgement on York in Storey, *End of Lancaster*, pp. 73-4. Somerset had been released by Christmas, which he spent at the Friars Preacher ('Benet's Chron.', p. 204). For York's changed attitudes, see below, p. 693. According to Hans Winter, York had the support not only of Norfolk and Devon, but also of Exeter, Salisbury, Warwick, Northumberland, and Arundel at this juncture (von der Ropp, op. cit., no. 669).

119 Above, p. 648.

120 *RP*, V, 210. For a summary of this parliament, see Wedgwood, *Register*, pp. 146-51; Roskell, *Speakers*, pp. 245-7.

121 Above, pp. 308-10.

122 *RP*, V, 226. The 'murder' of Gloucester had been raised by the commons

soon after parliament opened (von der Ropp, op. cit., no. 670 [15 November]).
123 *RP*, V, 337; Wedgwood, *Register*, p. 147.
124 *Chron. of London*, p. 137; Stevenson, II, ii, [770]; von der Ropp, op. cit., no. 669, 670.
125 For the reassertion of household authority, see above, p. 309. Marshall, thesis, p. 169, suggests that York may have forfeited some goodwill in parliament itself, for Oldhall, the speaker, may have been involved on 30 November or 1 December in the assaults on the lords meeting in Westminster hall; the implication later was that the retinues brought to London were mobilized by Oldhall to attack the king's courtiers. See above, pp. 645-8, and PRO, KB27/777, *rex* m. 7.
126 PRO, E403/785 m. 7, 12; 786 m. 2, 4; 'Benet's Chron.', p. 205; Rosenthal, 'Estates and finances', p. 198. For Wiltshire's alienation from York thereafter, see above, p. 423.
127 Griffiths, *JMH*, I (1975), 205; above, p. 589.
128 Below, n. 132.
129 Above, pp. 528-30.
130 Storey, *End of Lancaster*, pp. 89-92 (with a map of the campaign between 22 and 30 September on p. 90; above, p. 576). Other magnates were much more cautious (below, p. 700).
131 J. Stow, *Annales, or A General Chronicle of England* (1631), p. 393, reprinted in Gairdner, *PL*, I, 96. For Shrewsbury and Boulers, see above, pp. 506, 688. For York's letters allegedly sent to towns and individuals in Norfolk during the previous September, see PRO, KB9/85/10.
132 Ellis, *Original letters*, 1st ser., I, 11-13, reprinted in modernized English in *EHD*, IV, 269-70; Flenley, p. 107, mentions plans by Somerset to destroy York. Sir Henry Ellis printed (1825) York's letter from the original which had been in the possession of Godolphin Edwards, a Salop gentleman who was mayor of Shrewsbury in 1729; he was an antiquarian of sorts and may have appropriated the letter before his death in 1772. Its present whereabouts are unknown. But an independent, though inaccurate, copy is in R. Gough's edition (1789) of W. Camden's *Britannia*, and another, made by James Bowen from the original, which was still in Shrewsbury's archives in 1769, was deposited in Bodl. and is printed in Owen and Blakeway, op. cit., I, 222-3. I am grateful to Mrs M. Halford, Salop county archivist, for help with this note.
133 PRO, E403/786 m. 9; Flenley, p. 139. Kent set out from Westminster on 1 February (Storey, *End of Lancaster*, p. 98n, citing PRO, E404/68/79). On 28 January an attempt was made by Shrewsbury, Wiltshire, Moleyns, and Lisle to drag Oldhall from the sanctuary he had sought in St Martin-le-Grand the previous November (Marshall, thesis, p. 173; below, p. 699).
134 Flenley, p. 129; *Great Chron.*, pp. 185-6. *London Chrons.*, p. 163; *EHL*, pp. 297-8. Exeter, Salisbury, Shrewsbury, Worcester, Wiltshire, even Norfolk, were with the king, as well as Beaumont, Lisle, Grey of Ruthin, Clifford, Egremont, Moleyns, Stourton, Camoys, and Beauchamp (ibid., pp. 372-3). As a conciliatory gesture and to remove some of the grounds of York's complaint, on 15 February Henry ordered inquiries into alleged embezzlement by recent officers in Normandy, including Hoo and Sir Andrew Ogard (*CPR, 1447–52*, p. 537).
135 Giles, p. 43. Warwick seems to have returned with the king, bringing some

of his midlands tenantry with him (WarwsRO, CR 895/7B, 1451–52). One may note that in 1451–52 Warwick appropriated £59 from the revenue of Warwick town (valued at £100 *per annum*) for annuities; his predecessor in 1422–23 had spent only £9 on this purpose at a time when the town was valued at £114 (WarwsRO, Warwick castle, 485, 491).

136 *RP*, V, 265; *CPR, 1452–61*, pp. 23, 31; Marshall, thesis, pp. 172-9. Aside from Oldhall's possible involvement, Sir Edmund Mulso (at Ludlow and Fotheringhay), Fulk Eyton (Ludlow), Sir Walter Devereux (Hereford), Thomas Mulso and Sir Theobald Gorges (Fotheringhay), and John Wykes (Cambridge) were indicted for their activities in York's interest. Devereux's efforts to rouse the 'Welsh faction' in the city of Hereford are fully examined by Storey, *End of Lancaster*, pp. 119-20, and Herbert, thesis, pp. 119-20, 233-45. For Devon's contribution, see Storey, *End of Lancaster*, p. 98. A letter from York was read in Bristol's common council on 14 February (E. M. W. Veale [ed.], *The great red book of Bristol* [5 vols., Bristol record soc., 1931–53], IV, 136).

137 'Benet's Chron.', p. 206; *EHL*, pp. 297-8; *English Chron.*, pp. 69-70; *London Chrons.*, p. 163.

138 'Benet's Chron.', p. 206; *EHL*, pp. 297-8.

139 'Benet's Chron.', p. 207. See also *Brut*, p. 520; *EHL*, pp. 297-8, 372-3; *Grey Friars Chron.*, p. 19; *London Chrons.*, p. 163; *Great Chron.*, pp. 185-6. The sheriff of Surrey – Sussex had raised his levies initially at his own cost (PRO, E403/793 m. 4).

140 *Great Chron.*, pp. 185-6; *EHL*, pp. 298, 372-3; 'Benet's Chron.', p. 207; *London Chrons.*, p. 163; Flenley, p. 107; *Brut*, p. 520; *Three Chrons.*, p. 69; *Chron. of London*, pp. 137-8; *English Chron.*, pp. 69-70. York seems to have delivered an earlier ultimatum that he would die fighting if Somerset were not handed over (*EHL*, p. 298).

141 Gairdner, *PL*, I, 103-8, printed from BL, Cotton MS, Vespasian C. XIV f. 40. The beginning is also in Stow, *General Chron.*, p. 397, but is there mistakenly ascribed to 1453–54. Cf. the similar estimate of his purpose in 1452 in 'Benet's Chron.', p. 206 (which associates Cardinal Kemp with Somerset). For the charges of embezzlement, see above, n. 134.

142 *Three Chrons.*, p. 69; *Chron. of London*, pp. 137-8; *Great Chron.*, p. 185-6; *London Chrons*, p. 163. Messengers from the king and the duke of Exeter, constable of the Tower, brought news of the agreement to the mayor and aldermen of London at about 4 p.m. (Guildhall, Journal V f. 71, reproduced in Peake, thesis, p. 214). *EHL*, p. 298, erroneously gives the date as 3 March.

143 Giles, p. 43; 'Benet's Chron.', p. 207; *Three Chrons.*, p. 69; *Chron. of London*, pp. 137-8. The oath is here taken from the record of the 1459 parliament, which was reminded of it (*RP*, V, 346). Holinshed, *Chronicles*, III, 234-5, includes a version (taken from Stow, *Chronicles*, pp. 671-2), that is only slightly different.

144 The arbitrators were Waynflete, Bishop Bourgchier, Bishop Boulers, Buckingham, Salisbury, Shrewsbury, Lord Beauchamp, Lord Bourgchier, and the prior of the Hospital of St John of Jerusalem (*CCR, 1447–54*, p. 32). Rumour had it that the 10-year-old earl of March was leading 10,000 men to free his father (*Great Chron.*, pp. 185-6; *London Chrons.*, p. 163; *Brut*, p. 520). J. S. Roskell has suggested that the appointment of John Tiptoft

to replace Lord Beauchamp as treasurer of England on 15 April may have been a concession to York (*Speakers*, p. 248).

145 'Benet's Chron.', p. 207; PRO, C67/40 (special pardon roll); Storey, *End of Lancaster*, p. 101. Shrewsbury was paid his expenses on 23 March (PRO, E403/786 m. 13).

146 *CPR, 1446–52*, p. 580; 'Benet's Chron.', p. 208; Storey, *End of Lancaster*, pp. 96-7 (a map of the journey); PRO, E403/788 m.1; 791 m.1, 8, 15. The intinerary of the household is detailed in PRO, E101/410/9, and the commissioners were headed by Somerset. For the king's and Bonville's reception at Exeter, see DevonRO, Exeter receivers' account 13. For the fine imposed at Wells on Sir Theobald Gorges, York's retainer, see PRO, E403/791 m. 1 (£115 of it was given to the earl of Wiltshire and Lord Moleyns, two of the warring magnates in the west country), and for the commission's treatment of Sir Walter Devereux and his companions at Hereford, Herbert, thesis, pp. 233-45. Earlier in the summer, Somerset had led a commission in the south-east counties (PRO, E403/788 m. 3 [15 June 1452]).

147 PRO, E403/791 m. 4, 8; 'Benet's Chron.', p. 208; *CPR, 1452–61*, p. 54; Storey, *End of Lancaster*, pp. 96-7 (for an itinerary).

148 PRO, E403/791 m. 12; E404/69/89; Wedgwood, *Biographies*, pp. 18-19. For Ardern's alleged misdeeds in 1450 and 1452, see Marshall, thesis, pp. 161-2; the alleged involvement of Ardern and others in the murder on 20 April 1452 of a royal messenger sent to Ludlow with letters for the duke probably accounts for the severe treatment of York's tenants there (*EHL*, p. 368; PRO, KB9/103/1 m. 15). Unless the weather was extraordinarily inclement in 1452, Flenley, p. 107, is probably exaggerating Somerset's iniquities when it records that he required some of York's tenants to come stripped, with cords about their neck, in severe frost and snow, to beg the king's pardon. See also *CPR, 1452–61*, pp. 23, 31.

149 'Benet's Chron.', p. 208; above, p. 577.

150 The creations are fully discussed in R. S. Thomas, thesis, pp. 30-7, relying on *CChR, 1427–1514*, p. 122; *RDP*, V, 293-4 (for Edmund); PRO, E 159/231, *adhuc communia, recorda*, M, m. 22d (for Jasper). No marquesses were in existence in 1452. The ceremony of ennoblement was held at the opening of the Reading parliament on 6 March 1453, when both earls were formally recognized as the king's uterine brothers (*RP*, V, 250-3; 'Benet's Chron.', p. 208).

151 ibid., p. 209; Chrimes, *Henry VII*, p. 13. The Tudor brothers jointly received Margaret's wardship on 24 March (*CPR, 1452–61*, pp. 78-9).

152 Stevenson, II, ii, [770] (misdated to 1449); 'Benet's Chron.', p. 208; R. S. Thomas, thesis, p. 34; Winkler, thesis, pp. 348-53. Catesby was a household esquire whose family estates were in Northants. and Warws. (Wedgwood, *Biographies*, pp. 163-4; J. S. Roskell, *BJRL*, XLII [1959–60], 148-50).

153 Griffiths, *Principality of Wales*, pp. 155-6; Kent, thesis, pp. 18-19; R. S. Thomas, thesis, p. 40. Cf. the lenient treatment of Sir Walter Devereux, who received a general pardon on 8 August 1452 and some valuable grants later on (Wedgwood, *Biographies*, pp. 271-2; Herbert, thesis, pp. 240-1; *CPR, 1452–61*, pp. 49, 71).

154 Roskell, *Nott. Med. St.*, V (1961), 104-6; *CPR, 1452–61*, pp. 31, 103; *RP*, V, 252. His other estates had passed to Jasper Tudor on 25 March (*CPR, 1452–61*, pp. 111-12).

155 Wedgwood, *Register*, pp. 175-86; above, p. 390.
156 Roskell, *Speakers*, pp. 248-53. Richard Blyke (MP for Bridgnorth, Salop) and John Gresley (for Staffs.) were returned in 1450 and 1453; both were connected with York (Wedgwood, *Biographies*, pp. 83, 395-6.
157 Above, p. 290; Roskell, *Nott. Med. St.*, VI (1962), 79-105. Did the court in 1452–53 try to establish in Yorkist areas a hierarchy of gentry more loyal to Henry VI? Cf. William Catesby, another Northants. man (above, p. 341), and the grant of the Isle of Wight, York's former property, to Somerset in September 1452 (Wolffe, *Royal demesne*, pp. 258-9).
158 A malicious attempt by Suffolk's old crony, William Tailboys, and others to implicate Lord Cromwell in York's rising was eventually shown to be false in February 1453 (*CPR, 1452–61*, pp. 93-102; above, p. 581; Virgoe, *BJRL*, LV [1973], 470-1).

3

THE APPROACH OF CIVIL WAR

1453–1461

23 York's Opportunity, 1453–1456

The king's illness

Henry VI suffered a severe mental collapse, accompanied by a crippling physical disablement, while he was at the royal manor of Clarendon, near Salisbury, about the beginning of August 1453.[1] He remained more or less prostrate for the next seventeen months, which he spent in seclusion mainly at Windsor castle. The cause of his illness is unclear and speculation as to its nature is perhaps fruitless after a lapse of four and a half centuries; what is important is its effect on the king and his capacity to rule. No other English monarch since the Norman conquest had been in such an impotent state, and no other English dynasty had found itself so cruelly vulnerable as did that of Lancaster in the summer of 1453. Edward III in the last few years of his reign had deteriorated both physically and mentally, but the change was a gradual one and the old king had lucid moments; moreover, the Black Prince, though diseased himself, lived on until 1376 and had younger brothers living who could care for the kingdom, as well as a son (later Richard II). Henry IV was dogged by ill health during his short reign, but he never seems to have been completely incapacitated, and in any case he too had sired a brood of sons to foster his fledgling dynasty. By contrast, in 1453 Henry VI's collapse was sudden, unexpected, and absolute. All his uncles were dead; he himself had no children; and although Queen Margaret was pregnant, there was time for many an accident before she would be brought to child-bed. The Lancastrian hold on the throne was never so precarious as it was in 1453, for to the succession problem was now added the more immediate question of who should rule the realm.[2]

Henry appears to have emerged from the first two sessions of the 1453 parliament in good spirits, grateful for the commons' financial and other aid, and intent on making a tour of his kingdom to restore peace and order.[3] Within days of the adjournment, he began his journey westward, probably to pacify the west country.[4] But by the end of July news reached England of the crushing defeat at Castillon (Gascony) on the 17th, and of the death of the great Talbot and his son, Lord Lisle, on the battlefield. One can well understand it if the king were cast into the depths of despond as he saw his French realm disintegrate further and almost reach the point of disappearing altogether.[5]

There is no evidence that the sick king manifested the more violent and eccentric symptoms of his maternal grandfather, Charles VI of France, who became a lunatic long before his death in 1422, although the onset of Henry's condition was accompanied by what contemporaries described as a 'ffransy' or 'a rash and sudden terror'.[6] It may have been katatonic schizophrenia, as R. L. Storey concluded; certainly it left the king utterly helpless so that he had to be fed and supported by two men when he moved from room to room.[7] Mentally he was totally unresponsive; and to observers it seemed as if 'his wit and his reson [were] withdrawen', and that henceforth he had 'no natural sense nor reasoning power'. There was no doctor and no known medicine that could cure him.[8] During this time, Henry recognized nobody, understood nothing, and, when it was all over, remembered nothing. His mental and physical state is revealed to us on two occasions in the early months of 1454. Soon after New Year's day, a newsletter, written by one of the duke of Norfolk's servants, reported Henry's reaction when he was presented at Windsor with his three-month-old son, Edward:

> ... at the Princes comyng to Wyndesore, the Duc of Buk' toke hym in his armes and presented hym to the Kyng in godely wise, besechyng the Kyng to blisse hym; and the Kyng yave no maner answere. Natheless the Duk abode stille with the Prince by the Kyng; and whan he coude no maner answere have, the Queene come in, and toke the Prince in hir armes and presented hym in like forme as the Duke had done, desiryng that he shuld blisse it; but alle their labour was in veyne, for they departed thens without any answere or countenaunce savyng only that ones he loked on the Prince and caste doune his eyene ayen, without any more.[9]

Two months later he was no better. When a delegation of lords waited on him at Windsor on 24 March to discuss the implications of the death of the chancellor, Archbishop Kemp, two days before, they found conversation with him completely useless:

> they cowede gate noo answere ne signe, for no prayer ne desire, lamentable chere ne exhortation, ne eny thyng that they or eny of theim cowede do or sey, to theire grete sorowe and discomfort.

After two further attempts to communicate with him, 'they cowede have no aunswere, worde ne signe'; and therfore 'with sorowefull hartes come theire way'.[10]

Meanwhile, the king had been committed to the care of a committee of doctors and surgeons, under the scrutiny of the councillors. The fact that on 15 March the council instructed the chancellor formally to enlist their services reflects the delicacy of the doctors' situation and their nervousness about treating a royal patient whose affliction mystified everybody. Three of the doctors – John Arundel (who had once attended the king's friend, Henry Beauchamp, the late duke of Warwick), William Hatclyf, and John Faceby – were already in Henry VI's service; they were now joined by two surgeons, Master Robert Wareyn and John Marchall. They were authorized to recommend a diet for the helpless monarch, prescribe a regimen of medicines for him, and administer a range of treatments which, for lack of any better guidance, were culled from the writings of learned physicians past and present. In the circumstances, it was a wise precaution for these five doctors to receive formal authority, under the signatures of twenty-eight lords, for their experiments.[11]

The universal joy that doubtless the entire realm felt when the king recovered at Christmas 1454 is reflected in Edmund Clere's letter to John Paston, written from Greenwich on 9 January following:

Blessid be God, the Kyng is wel amendid, and hath ben syn Cristemesday; and on Seint Jones Day [27 December] commaunded his awmener to ride to Caunterbury with his offryng, and commaunded the secretarie [Richard Andrew] to offre at Seint Edward. And in the Mondeday after noon the Queen come to hym and brought my lord Prynce with here; and then he askid what the princes name was, and the Queen told him Edward; and than he hild vp his handes and thankid God therof. And he seid he neuer knew him til that tyme, nor wist not what was seid to him, nor wist not where he had be whils he hath be seke til now. And he askid who was godfaderes, and the Queen told him; and he was wel apaid.

And she told him that the Cardinal [Kemp] was ded, and he seid he knew neuer therof til that tyme; and he seid oon of the wisist lordes in this land was dede. And my lord of Wynchestre and my lord of Seint Jones were with him on the morow after Tweltheday, and he spake to hem as well as euer he did; and when thei come out, thei wepte for ioye.

And he seith he is in charitee with all the world, and so he wold al the lordes were. And now he seith matyns of Oure Lady and euesong, and herith his masse deuoutly; . . .[12]

Yet after such a long and serious illness, one is bound to wonder whether Henry's recovery at the end of 1454 was as complete as some contemporaries thought and hoped. Had his illness perhaps fatally weakened at least his mental powers? Was he fully capable of acting as king thereafter? There are several pointers which together indicate that perhaps he was not. In the first place, it is surprising that Henry, if a fit man in full possession of his faculties, should have been kept so much in the dark during the exchanges between his ministers and the Yorkist lords on the eve of the battle of St Albans in May 1455. There are signs that the duke of York himself doubted whether the king was fully aware of what was being done in his name immediately before the fighting began.[13] Moreover, Henry reacted to the skirmishing in the streets of the town on 22 May in a confused and apprehensive fashion, deserted by his followers, wounded in the neck as he stood beneath his own banner, and fleeing to the tanners' house to hide.[14] It was a relief to some that 'thanked be God he hathe no grete harme'.[15]

Nor can Henry's supposed second bout of illness in 1455–56 be dismissed as entirely spurious. J. R. Lander has convincingly demonstrated that there is no indisputable or specific evidence for a sudden or complete relapse. Nevertheless, it is remarkable that the lords in parliament should have agreed to a second protectorate and the virtual suspension of personal rule unless the king were incapacitated, especially since the terms of York's appointment in October 1455 were identical with those of the first protectorate (1454–55), when Henry was undoubtedly in a state of impenetrable collapse.[16] No clear explanation was given at the time, though it is suggestive that the king was said to be unable to involve himself in parliament or in the protection of the realm 'for certain just and reasonable causes'. Moreover, it was felt that a protector would prevent the king from being 'vexed and troubled' with the petitions and complaints which were 'overe grevous and tedious' to the king. A king was hardly normal who was so perturbed by the routine conduct of government, which, it was said, he found 'ful tedious and grete to suffre and bere'.[17] In attempting to gauge the state of the king's health and his ability to rule effectively, James Gresham's tantalizingly fragmentary letter, sent from London to John Paston on 28 October 1455, provides some, albeit equivocal, corroboration:

> . . . .at Hertford, and summe men ar a-ferd that he is seek ageyn. I prey God . . . my lordes of York, Warwyk, Salesbury, and other arn in purpos to conveye hym . . . etc. . . . [18]

One is bound to wonder whether Henry VI, after his serious incapacity in 1453–54, thenceforward lacked the intellectual or mental toughness to cope with the job of being king. Was he able thereafter to apply his mind to his kingly responsibilities other than intermittently?[19]

The birth of a prince

It was a considerable consolation to the queen and the court that on the feast of the translation of Edward the Confessor, 13 October, Margaret was delivered of a baby boy. The birth of a son, who was appropriately named Edward, might ordinarily be expected to have taken the heat out of the dynastic question and to have provided badly needed support to the house of Lancaster during the king's illness. But, coinciding as it did with Henry's collapse, it simply thrust to the fore the problem of who should govern the realm during the king's incapacity and while his heir was a minor – or, if the king should die, during the inevitable long minority. Moreover, whatever provisions were made now for the kingdom's governance, they were almost bound to have implications for the succession in a situation in which it was far from clear who the next heir to the throne should be, after Prince Edward.[20]

Edward's birth was greeted with the ringing of bells and the singing of the *Te Deum*.[21] Henry may have been oblivious of this happy event and in no condition to show fatherly interest in the babe, but there can be little doubt that he was delighted when the queen became pregnant earlier in the year. Richard Tunstall could testify to that from personal experience, for when, as an esquire for the body and usher of the king's chamber, he 'made unto us the first comfortable relation and notice, that oure most entierly beloved wyf the Quene was with child, to oure most singuler consolation, and to all oure true liege people grete joy and comfort', he was awarded a life annuity of £40 by the overjoyed monarch.[22] And when Henry emerged once more into rationality at Christmas 1454, his elation at news of the birth and the naming of the child was genuine and unrestrained.[23] The slanderous stories that were current rather later in the 1450s to the effect that Edward was not Henry's son owe more to the machinations of the régime's opponents than to the surprise which many may have felt that after eight years of marriage the royal pair had at last been able to conceive.[24] Nor is there any justification for the speculation that the king's sudden collapse in August 1453 was caused by his learning of the queen's pregnancy by someone other than himself; if Margaret's condition was widely known by the summer, it would have been apparent to the king long before.[25]

Prince Edward was baptized in Westminster abbey by the bishop of Winchester, William Waynflete, Henry's confessor. His godparents were high-ranking courtiers: Cardinal-archbishop Kemp, the venerable chancellor, the duke of Somerset, and Anne, duchess of Buckingham. In January 1454, Henry expressed himself well pleased with the choice.[26]

The struggle for power

It was wise to refrain from taking any precipitate action involving the king and the government during the first weeks of Henry's illness, for his recovery might be as sudden as his breakdown. Moreover, the final stages of pregnancy, and the queen's convalescence after Edward's birth, inhibited Margaret of Anjou from taking any initiative. In these unique circumstances, it doubtless seemed best to await the baby's birth and hope for an improvement in the king's condition. As a result, no public announcement of Henry's incapacity was made. Even when parliament reassembled at Reading on 12 November after the summer adjournment, there was no official admission that the king was ill; at the last moment (6 November) it was decided to prorogue the session as soon as it met on the grounds that Reading was riddled with plague and 'for other causes'.[27] Yet, there were matters that required attention, and if the king continued insensible, the question of how the realm should be governed in the immediate future would have to be resolved. England had coped with minorities in the past and in 1422 by a novel and successful constitutional device; but the mental and physical collapse of an adult monarch suggested no obvious precedent to guide the chancellor, Cardinal Kemp, the treasurer, the earl of Worcester, the keeper of the privy seal, Thomas Liseux, and the lords and councillors. Furthermore, the situation in Gascony was grave: the Gironde was blockaded after Castillon and eventually, on 19 October, Bordeaux surrendered to Charles VII.[28] The king himself had recently admitted that the realm needed pacification, and in the summer and early autumn the disorders in Yorkshire and the west country (to look no further afield) required urgent attention to prevent disputes from being fought out in the dales and villages rather than at the council table or in the courts.[29]

In the course of planning for the forthcoming parliamentary session on 12 November, a great council was summoned to which a substantial number of magnates and others were called. It was at this stage that the most bitter and disruptive quarrel of all came to the surface: that between the discontented and discomforted duke of York and his powerful rival, Somerset. So long as the king retained his senses, Somerset was secure as his principal adviser, whereas the Dartford incident had discredited York and led to his withdrawal from national politics.[30] Bereft of the king's protection, and with a reputation blackened by recent disasters in France, Somerset became vulnerable to those who resented his ascendancy and sought to clip his wings. The great council in late October was the scene of the first trial of strength between the two men. An attempt was made to exclude York from the meeting, though it would have been astonishing if the king's cousin and the realm's premier duke were to be ignored at such a time of crisis for the dynasty. York protested at the failure to send him an invitation, and his wife appealed direct to the queen. It is unlikely that Cicely Neville's gossip about her own ill-health or even her motherly expressions of comfort to Margaret in the last stages of pregnancy had much effect, but on 24 October a belated letter was taken to York by Sir Thomas Tyrell, one of the king's household officials who had fought in France.[31] Even so, the duke was cautioned to come 'peasiblie and mesurablie accompanied' so that his and other magnates' grievances could be settled in a calm atmosphere.[32]

Members of the court and the household, under the direction of Lord Sudeley as steward and Lord Dudley as treasurer, still exercised significant influence, and along with the chancellor they seem to have favoured an even and cautious tenor to the government in these uncertain weeks.[33] At the annual nomination of sheriffs, which this year took place on 5 November, several gentlemen in the king's employ – Thomas Whalesburgh in Cornwall and Robert Fenne in Rutland, for instance – were pricked, along with William Vaux in Northamptonshire, who had links with the queen, and Thomas Stonor in Oxfordshire–Berkshire, a man formerly patronized by the late duke of Suffolk.[34] But the fluidity of conciliar politics may be reflected in the failure to find a suitable sheriff in a few counties and the nomination of known adherents of the duke of York in Gloucestershire, Yorkshire, and Warwickshire–Leicestershire.[35] Next day, it was decided to delay the meeting of parliament until 11 February 1454, by which time the health of the king might have improved or, failing that, an accommodation reached among the queen, York, and the lords.

Duke Richard was not without his advocates among the councillors, and commonsense and justice demanded his presence at Westminister in the extraordinary circumstances of 1453. Apart from Norfolk, he could probably count on the sympathy of the Neville earls of Salisbury and Warwick, who had their own reasons for resenting Somerset's dominance, and his kinsmen, Viscount Bourgchier, Bishop Bourgchier of Ely, and Lord Berners; even the bulk of the remaining spiritual and temporal lords who were regular members of Henry's council were capable of being persuaded of (or cajoled into accepting) the justice of York's complaints against Edmund Beaufort. Moreover, Exeter and Northumberland, who were at odds with the Nevilles and Lord Cromwell, were conveniently absent from a council meeting on 12 November, most probably because they were conspiring to protect their interests in Yorkshire.[36]

All this became fully apparent as the great council assembled in the star chamber at Westminster on 21 November 1453.[37] Twenty-five lords attended, including the two archbishops and eight bishops, two dukes (York and Buckingham), and six earls; Somerset and Norfolk were also present and the meeting was largely taken up with hearing the latter's accusation against the former and the demands for Somerset's arrest. Norfolk appealed Somerset of treason by means of articles that mainly related to the defeats in France.[38] These dwelt primarily on the 'over greete dishonneurs and losses' suffered by the realm at the hands of Somerset in particular, whilst the latter's defence of his actions was stigmatized as 'but falsenesse and lesynges'. Norfolk urged the lords to cast aside their caution and do justice on the duke.[39] Two days later, Somerset was arrested and conveyed to the Tower, where he languished for more than a year; the fact that he was never brought to trial or presented with formal charges demonstrates the essentially political and personal nature of the campaign against him.[40] At about the same time, York's noble companion at Dartford, the earl of Devon, was released from Wallingford castle. The council listened to his refutation of the charges laid against him and soon afterwards he was invited to join the council in its deliberations on the future government of England.[41] By the end of 1453, therefore, York had been able to recover his political fortunes and, with the aid of several other magnates, had temporarily neutralized his chief rival. His next step would be to establish his ascendancy and ensure his dominance over the government so long as the king remained impotent.

The opportunity came during the winter, when Henry's health was known not to be improving and yet the date of reassembly of parliament (11 February) crept closer. Queen Margaret and the court appreciated the implications of these facts just as clearly as York and the council. About the beginning of the new year, perhaps as a result of witnessing the king's reaction to seeing his baby son, Margaret staked her claim to the regency of England during the incapacity of her husband and for as long as the prince was incapable of taking his father's place. It is a major misfortune that her role at this juncture is almost completely shrouded from our view. One may imagine her concern at the utter hopelessness of the king's condition and the threat which this posed not only to Somerset, but also to herself as a French-born consort and, even more important, to her son, on whom alone rested the future of the dynasty. Steeled in the matriarchal society of the Angevin court, where her mother and grandmother had at times assumed power in default of the males of the family, and familiar perhaps with the French habit of appointing queens as regent, Margaret resolved to lay claim herself to the regency of England.[42]

She is likely to have been aware that Henry V's wish to make his brother Gloucester regent in 1422 had been ignored by the council, but this did not deter her from presenting a bill of five articles which proposed the transfer of kingly authority and patronage to herself. The only surviving indication that this was her intention is imbedded in a newsletter written at Westminster on 19 January 1454:

> . . . the Queene hathe made a bille of five articles, desiryng those articles to be grauntid; wherof the first is that she desireth to have the hole reule of this land; the second is that she may make the Chaunceller, the Tresorere, the Prive Seelle, and alle other officers of this land, with shireves and alle other officers that the Kyng shuld make; the third is, that she may yeve alle the bisshopriches of this land, and alle other benefices longyng to the Kynges yift; the iiij is that she may have suffisant lyvelode assigned hir for the Kyng and the Prince and hir self.[43]

John Stodeley, the author of this letter, had only an imperfect knowledge of the queen's demands, for he was forced to admit that 'as for the vth article, I kan nat yit knowe what it is'; and it must be confessed that we are no better informed of it today.

Revolutionary though her proposals were in an English context, Margaret may not have been without her supporters. These months were therefore an extremely tense period both at Westminster and in the country, with rumour and accusations abroad and many of the magnates taking armed precautions: '. . . every man that is of th'opynion of the Duke of Somerset makethe hym redy to be as stronge as he kan make hym'. Among the councillors, Cardinal Kemp, the duke of Buckingham, and the earl of Wiltshire took care to enlist and arm bands of retainers, whilst Lords Bonville, Beaumont, Poynings, Clifford, and Egremont 'maken all the puissance they kan and may to come hider [to Westminster] with theym'. Members of the household understandably feared for the safety of the king and the prince, and they assembled a garrison at Windsor for their protection. In London Somerset's officials were rumoured to be acquiring lodgings near the Tower, presumably for the duke's retainers who may have been planning to release their master from confinement. Moreover, his spies were said to be 'goyng in every Lordes hous of this land; some gone as freres, som as shipmen taken on the sea, and som in other wise; whiche reporte unto hym all that thei kun see or here touchyng the seid Duke'. On the other side, York was bringing together 'his houshold meynee, clenly beseen and likly men'. With his son March (who was not yet twelve), Norfolk, who rightly feared for his safety if Somerset were released, Warwick, and the king's half-brothers Richmond and Pembroke (who evidently had no love for Somerset and preferred York's company), he was expected in London towards the end of January.⁴⁴ If a *coup* were to be contemplated against the king's ministers and his household, it would have had a greater prospect of success at the beginning of 1454 than even in 1450: Henry VI was helpless, his ministers frightened and confused, the magnates deeply divided, and the queen bent on a course of breathtaking novelty.

Many lords had returned to the capital by the beginning of February in preparation for the opening of parliament on the 11th.⁴⁵ But the diametrically opposed intentions of York and Margaret, which could hardly be reconciled, indicated a lengthy and determined political struggle. As a result, on 6 February it was decided to prorogue parliament yet again, though York may have won this second round, for the session was only postponed for three days and its meeting-place transferred from Reading to Westminster.⁴⁶ It was further decided to nominate York as the king's lieutenant to open parliament on 14 February, though as a political counterweight Buckingham was simultaneously appointed to the largely honorific position of steward of England.⁴⁷

The opening of parliament was not reassuring, for during the recess York, by one of those disconcerting and abrasive acts of which he was occasionally capable, had secured the imprisonment on a charge of trespass of the speaker of the commons, Thomas Thorp, a long-time exchequer official. As soon as they had assembled, therefore, the commons sought confirmation of their cherished customary liberties and privileges and demanded the release not only of Thorp but also of Walter Raleigh, MP for Devon, who had been arrested too (though possibly on a different charge).⁴⁸ It is indicative of York's position by this stage that the arrest of Thorp was reaffirmed by the lords at the request of the duke's counsel, and that his cousin, Bishop Bourgchier of Ely, led the delegation of lords to convey this unpalatable decision to the commons and invite them to elect a new speaker.⁴⁹ We may

723

assume that the queen's unprecedented demand for regency powers had failed to rally significant support, though her son's position at least was secured, for on 15 March, Edward was created prince of Wales and earl of Chester.[50] Events might have proceeded indefinitely in this makeshift fashion had it not been for the death of the chancellor on 22 March.

If the current power struggle were to reach a significant conclusion about the future government of the kingdom and the relative claims of the queen and York, then as full an attendance as possible of lords was desirable, for since 1422 it had been openly recognized that in the absence of a capable monarch (though then a minor had been in mind) the royal authority reposed in the lords as a body. It had been rare in the past for more than half of the spiritual and temporal peers summoned to actually turn up at a parliament, but the situation in 1454 was so grave and fraught with constitutional as well as political and personal problems that as large an attendance as possible was desired. Therefore, on 28 February, for the first and only time in medieval England, parliament imposed fines on those peers who failed to attend without a specific licence to stay away.[51] The sponsors of this petition are unknown, but York is likely to have been prominent among them.[52]

The commons too had a vital part to play in the discussions about the government of the kingdom. As at times of crisis in the past, they put their faith in a publicly nominated council, something which Henry himself had promised to provide in the aftermath of 1450 and 1452 but which does not seem to have been conceded in practice before he fell ill. When they met York and the lords on 19 March, the commons recalled the occasion at Reading in March 1453 when Henry had undertaken to establish 'a sadde and a wyse Counsaill of the right discrete and wise lordes and othir of this land, to whom all people myght have recours for mynistryng of justice, equite, and rightwesness'. [53] Their concern, it may be thought, was the restoration of peace and order in the realm, and less with who might wield power at the centre, York or the queen. But consideration of all these matters was pre-empted by the death of Cardinal Kemp three days later. A man of wisdom, experience, and moderation, who had attempted to restrain the anti-Somerset campaign during the past few months, he seems to have been worn out by the buffeting and threats to which he had been subjected, notably by Norfolk.[54] It was Kemp's death and the consequent need to appoint a new archbishop of Canterbury and a new chancellor that precipitated a decision about the long-term exercise of the royal authority during Henry's continuing illness.

Not even York was prepared to force through decisions on these weighty questions before verifying that the king was still utterly incapable of playing his customary part in the appointment of a new archbishop and chancellor, as well as a reconstituted council. On Saturday, 23 March the lords in parliament nominated several of their number to wait on the king next day at Windsor. The delegation was not a partisan one, though in seeking the king's opinions it went armed with certain names to present to him, if not for the vacant positions at Canterbury and the chancery, at least for the 'discrete and a sadde Counsaill the whiche was to the seid Communnes a grete rejoysing and comfort'. Although the emissaries were headed by Bishop Waynflete, Henry's confessor, much of the talking was done by another courtier-bishop, Reginald Boulers of Coventry and Lichfield. Moreover, Lords Beaumont, Dudley, and Stourton were loyal councillors of some years' standing; but they were complemented by several others who represented more nearly the views and interests of the duke of York – Bishop Bourgchier and his brother, Viscount Bourgchier, the earls of Warwick and Oxford, and Warwick's uncle, Fauconberg. Their visit was a melancholy one and largely unproductive. All that could be reported to the lords on the following Monday was that the monarch showed no sign of recognition or understanding.[55] Having set aside the possibility of a regency, there was no alternative to the appointment of a protector and defender of the realm during the king's pleasure.

The first protectorate

In 1454 the precedent of 1422 was followed in circumstances the like of which had never arisen before, yet the powers conferred on Bedford and Gloucester more than thirty years earlier were appropriate to the new situation. York was aware of the delicacy of his position, the pitfalls that lay ahead, and the likelihood of opposition from influential quarters. He was especially vulnerable because he was not the king's acknowledged heir, not even after Prince Edward, whereas Bedford and Gloucester had in turn been Henry VI's presumptive heirs in 1422. To make him protector in the constitutional uncertainty of 1454 might be deemed by some a dynastic challenge on York's part, and the duke may have regarded it in precisely the same light.[56] For this reason, he was careful to safeguard himself by elaborate conditions presented on 28 March to the lords as the temporary repository of royal power. York posed as the reluctant protector dragged unwillingly and with modesty to the king's seat, and he insisted that the lords take full responsibility for his appointment and give him their support:

> hit be enacted that of your selfe, and of your free and mere disposicion, ye desire, name, and calle me to the seid name and charge [of protector], and that of eny presumcion of my self I take thaym not uppon me, but onely of the due and humble obeissaunce that I owe to doo unto the kyng, our most dradde and souveraine lord, and to you the perage of this lande, in whom, by thoccasion of thenfirmite of our said souveraine lord, restethe thexcercice of his auctoritee, . . .[57]

The strictly limited powers enjoyed by the royal brothers after 1422 were now conferred on York: no more and no less. The formal act, dated 3 April, constituting him protector and defender and chief councillor was to remain in operation during the king's pleasure or until Prince Edward reached years of discretion. This latter clause safeguarded the prince's position as Henry's heir and may have been inserted at the insistence of the queen, who had been overridden on practically every other front.[58] Henry VI thereupon entered the second protectorate of his reign without even realizing it. The circumstances were unprecedented and York's elevation was unlikely to achieve the same consensus of opinion as the settlement of 1422. Aside from the captive Somerset, whose Lancastrian blood gave him a plausible claim to be placed high in the line of succession to the throne, and the frustrated queen, whose recent defeat permanently poisoned her relations with York, the duke of Exeter could hardly be expected to welcome the new régime. Henry Holand, duke of Exeter was the king's closest relative by blood then in England, a kinship which Henry VI had recognized on several occasions in the recent past. If the conferment of the protectorate on York implied any dynastic precedence, then this belligerent young man would not accept Richard's appointment with good grace. On the contrary, it strengthened Exeter's alliance with the Percy family and led to his campaign of violence and rebellion in the north of England.[59] In short, anyone with a grudge against York or the Nevilles, and anyone who was prepared to take advantage of the unsettled times had available prominent figures to whom they could rally. York's task as protector of the realm was a daunting one.

The councillors who were associated with the new protector came close to providing that 'sad and substantial' counsel which Henry VI had been induced to promise. During the tense autumn and winter of 1453–54, there were few among the greater magnates who were not prepared to offer their services at one or other of the council meetings: Cardinal Kemp strove to prevent a stark polarization of view, despite the arrest of Somerset, and a reasonably wide spectrum of opinion among the lords appears to have been sought. Perhaps the only conspicuous and consistent absentees were Exeter and Northumberland.[60] York's appointment towards the end of March was no triumphant victory for the duke and his friends, for the councillors nominated to assist him (and their names had been shown to the king a few days earlier) formed no narrow clique.[61] Although Somerset's closest adherent, Wiltshire, was not among them, a fair balance of interests was maintained. After all, York was in no position to remove the officers of state or of the household; only the chancery was actually vacant. Worcester, the treasurer, and Liseux, keeper of the privy seal, stayed in office, but at the chancery York had a golden opportunity to exert his new authority. On 2 April 1454, less than a fortnight after Kemp's death, he secured the nomination of his own brother-in-law, the fifty-four-year-old earl of Salisbury, Richard Neville, as chancellor of

England; that Salisbury was the first layman to occupy the office for upwards of fifty years underscores the enormous political significance of the appointment.[62] Salisbury, whose sons were currently engaged in a violent feud in Yorkshire with Exeter and the Percies, proved eager to lend his weight in support of the new protector.

Prominent among the councillors were York's brother-in-law, Henry, Viscount Bourgchier and Henry's younger brother, Bishop Bourgchier of Ely. They were two of the most frequent attenders at council meetings in the late spring and summer of 1454, and on 23 April the bishop was elected to the see of Canterbury. The young cleric whose appointment to Worcester in 1433 had caused the pope such misgivings, had reached the pinnacle of the English ecclesiastical hierarchy at the age of forty-two.[63] His qualities were not necessarily those of a partisan of the new protector; rather was he a man skilled in delicate missions, for it was he who had communicated to the commons the unwelcome news that their speaker would remain in prison, who had visited the prostrate king at Windsor on 24 March with other lords, and who, at Dartford in 1452, had undertaken to negotiate with York. The Bourgchiers, moreover, were half-brothers of the duke of Buckingham.[64] Indeed, the cleric whom the council recommended should succeed Bourgchier at Ely was William Grey, the son of Buckingham's north-country nephew and an exceptional figure in the English church as a gifted humanist who had been educated in Italy and Germany. Like the Bourgchiers, the Staffords may have played a crucial and constructive – rather than a partisan – role in the penumbra of politics in these months.[65]

The rest of the regular councillors counterbalanced any 'Yorkist' group that may have been emerging. Several had been councillors well before the king fell ill, among them Robert Botill, prior of the Hospital of St John of Jerusalem, the king's confessor, Bishop Waynflete, and the duke of Buckingham. Archbishop William Booth of York was the queen's chancellor and could be relied on to tend her interests.[66] Lord Dudley was treasurer of the household and the dean of St Seurin had joined the council in 1452, bringing expert knowledge of Gascony's difficulties to conciliar discussions.[67] Furthermore, among those who had not previously been members of the council but now began to attend quite often, Bishop Lyhert of Norwich was the queen's man and Chedworth of Lincoln had been closely associated with the king and his educational foundations.[68] Lord Beaumont was a courtier, Sir Thomas Stanley was controller of the household, and John Say had a long career as a household servant behind him (though he later found favour with Edward IV).[69] Salisbury's eldest son, the earl of Warwick, was the only one of York's intimate circle to be formally appointed to the council (along with Chedworth, Say, and Beaumont) on 15 April 1454, but he did not attend very often.[70]

In all, two dozen councillors were available for consultation by the new protector, though rarely more than half this number attended at any one time. They represented a broad cross-section of political opinion, particularly among the lay magnates: there were strong links with the household (for Henry might recover at relatively short notice) and the queen's entourage, while at the same time a few were openly friendly to York. This was no narrow faction led by a duke with unfettered authority. That this was so is perhaps indicated by the fact that Somerset was never brought formally to trial and in mid-July a meeting of the great council discussed a suggestion that he be released. York parried this proposal, not by a stern refusal, but by seeking a postponement of the matter until the judges had been consulted and a fuller attendance of lords achieved.[71]

Practical as well as political constraints made it difficult for Duke Richard to mould the government of the kingdom to his taste. On 28 March all the major offices at Westminster and in the shires were occupied, with the exception of the chancery. As a result, no major changes in the administration of the duchy of Lancaster took place during the protectorate, and the English sheriffs were not due to retire until November 1454. But when the time came, the protector seized his opportunity to recast the shrievalties, and at least a quarter of the new sheriffs were in some way connected with the duke, particularly in areas where his main estates lay. Sir John Barre, for instance, became sheriff of Herefordshire and others from his affinity were Sir Henry Radford (Lincolnshire), John Wingfield (Norfolk–Suffolk), Sir Thomas Green (Northamptonshire), and Richard Quartermain (Oxfordshire–Berkshire); Sir John Saville (in Yorkshire) was one of Salisbury's retainers.[72] In contrast with the sheriffs appointed in 1453, there were few household servants or adherents of courtier-magnates among those pricked a year later, with the exception perhaps of Sir John Cheyne in Kent, a county which had long been the preserve of court appointees.[73] The complexion of English government was changing slowly and perceptibly, but the result was by no means decisive. If the protector had had a longer term in office, who can say to what lengths he might eventually have gone?[74]

The household was virtually impregnable. It was not the case in 1454 (as it had been in 1422) of a king who did not need a large and influential household with a part to play in government; Henry VI, though sick, might recover his senses and his will to rule at any time. His large household organization, with its nexus of patronage and influence throughout the realm, remained in suspended animation; its principal officials clung to their posts and bided their time. The queen's household was even more vigilant after the birth of the prince. Neither organization could be penetrated by York's sympathizers and neither was easily controlled during the short time available to the protector. Suffolk's protégé Sir Thomas Stanley was still controller of the king's household and had a place on the council; so did Lords Sudeley and Dudley, who stayed on as the household's steward and treasurer.[75] Lord Cromwell, the elderly chamberlain, probably showed more understanding of York's point of view, but Henry's secretary, Master Richard Andrew, kept control of the signet seal, even though it was little used during the months of illness.[76]

Not until the summer of 1454 did York and the council decide to curb the size and cost of the king's establishment. The first step in this direction was a modest one: in late July the king's stable was inspected and the decision taken to sell some of its neglected horses and equipment.[77] The protector was on safe ground in practising economy in such a relatively uncontroversial manner, and in any case Henry VI at Reading in 1453 seems to have undertaken to find ways of reducing the expense of his establishment; with the onset of his illness and the birth of a prince who would soon require his own household, the implementation of this promise was overdue.[78] Accordingly, on 13 November far-reaching ordinances were issued by the council to limit the size not only of Henry's household but also of the queen's and the prince's. Interviews were arranged with household employees to achieve a reduced complement for the royal family of 599 persons, more than half of them in the king's household.[79] This was soon followed, perhaps as a protest, by the resignation on 3 December of the treasurer of the household, Lord Dudley. One might assume that this eventuality gave York an opportunity to gain an entrée to the king's inner court circle. However, the new treasurer, William Fallan, archdeacon of London and until recently a baron of the exchequer (1436–52), had no political weight and no apparent connection with the protector; his extensive financial experience demonstrates that the object of household reform was retrenchment and Fallan's record of service to three Lancastrian kings made him acceptable to the household itself.[80]

Much broader issues of finance constituted one of the major problems with which the protector had to grapple, and the duke's record reflects the narrow parameters within which he had to rule. The taxation grants of 1453 were available to the government despite the king's illness, but their relative generosity inevitably inhibited the protectorate from tapping additional resources, including loans. Prior to York's appointment in March, familiar expedients continued to be exploited: mines in the Cornish peninsula were being leased for a percentage return to the crown; Genoese alum cargoes were once again seized for sale on the open market; and licences enabled favoured merchants to avoid the staple and its customs duties.[81] York and the protectorate council found themselves in a weaker position than the king in seeking loans and the accent was therefore on realism and economy. An effort was made to preserve the good will of some of the larger lenders of the past, notably William Beaufitz, a prominent London merchant-banker, and the Calais staplers.[82] In November 1454, the government examined realistically the obligations of some sheriffs, who were finding it impossible to levy outdated farms; the personal losses they thereby sustained were leading them all too easily toward extortion and illegality.[83]

The protector made the most of two more minor sources of potential income. On 19 July 1454 he decided to assume custody of the Devon and Cornwall mines himself, rather than allow them to be leased for exploitation; the suspicion arises as to whether this action amounted to personal aggrandisement.[84] The aliens, however, were regarded as fair game, and a commission was instructed to ensure that the subsidy authorized in 1453 was duly imposed on all foreigners throughout the realm.[85] But the true bedrock of solvent government, substantial loans, was denied to a régime that had influential enemies and whose future was uncertain. York was able to extract loans only from a small group of wealthy men, most of whom were members of the council. Even so, it required a grave threat to Calais in May 1454 to produce a sizeable sum, most of which came from the Calais merchants for the defence of their own interests. The bulk of the remainder was contributed either by the treasurer and victualler of Calais, or by the chancellor, the treasurer, Viscount Bourgchier, and York himself.[86] Once again, the strict limitations on the protector's power are revealed.

York's prime obligation was to defend the realm. With Normandy and Gascony lost, practically the entire French coastline was in enemy hands. This perilously isolated Calais, gave the French and their allies a greater advantage in the narrow seas than they had enjoyed since before Agincourt, exposed channel commerce and English coastal traffic to attack, and increased the likelihood of enemy raids on the communities of the south and east. The defence of Calais, seaborne commerce, and the English coast were therefore important responsibilities of the government, including the protectorate.

The protection of Calais during York's two periods in power, with the eventual installation of Warwick as captain, have been judged to be the duke's one enduring achievement in a campaign to reform the lethargic Lancastrian régime and to secure his own political ascendancy.[87] This conclusion, in so far as it relates to the first protectorate of 1454–55, imputes to York a greater degree of foresight, planning, and mastery of events than actual circumstances allowed. By the terms of his commission as protector, he could not fail to be fully sensible of the need to defend English territorial and commercial interests, though there were special reasons why he should strive to secure effective command of one of the few fortresses that housed a permanent garrison of any size. Somerset had been captain of Calais since September 1451, and the soldiers there were under the direct command of two of his affinity, Lord Rivers and Lord Welles, the latter of whom had married Somerset's sister-in-law, his brother John's widow.[88] The resignation of all three was bound to be an urgent priority of the new protector, if only to remove the possibility of a counter-attack to free the captain of Calais from the Tower of London. This and the relief of Calais from the anticipated French siege are sufficient explanations for York's deep concern to bring Calais, 'a jewell ... to this oure reame' (as Henry VI was made to describe it), under his control during 1454.[89]

Within a month of his appointment as protector, he had refined his conditions for Calais's future government. All castles in the march were to be surrendered into his hands, and the patents of appointment of all those officers who had been serving under Somerset were to be placed at his disposal; that was an essential preliminary to erasing Somerset's authority from the colony. To keep the garrison loyal would be difficult and he recognized the importance of speedily providing reinforcements in the event of an attack, as well as a regular supply of cash for the soldiers. Equally sensitive were the staple merchants, on whom the government depended for financial aid just as much as the staplers relied on support from England and a loyal garrison at Calais; accordingly, their unpaid loans, amounting to 12,000 marks by April 1454, were guaranteed by York in parliament and several of the irksome regulations controlling their trade (among them price-fixing, the bullion laws, and high levels of customs duty) were temporarily abandoned. These were major concessions from the government, for they incidentally prejudiced some of its precious financial resources. But they were necessary if the staplers were to agree to a further loan of 10,000 marks to meet the wages of the garrison.[90] With these arrangements and conditions agreed by the time that parliament was dissolved in mid-April, a council was summoned for 6 May to discuss the practical details of Calais's defence.[91]

Before these discussions could be concluded, one of the government's greatest fears materialized: the situation at Calais exploded, largely as a result of delays in paying the garrison, but partly, one may suggest, as a result of the rumoured siege and the impending changes in command. Sometime early in May, the exasperated soldiers resorted to a tactic which they had employed more than once in the past: they mutinied and seized the bales of wool in the Calais warehouses and the food supplies stored there; the latter were promptly sold.[92] This mutiny had dangerous implications for the protector, for Somerset's lieutenants, Rivers and Welles, were still in the fortress and in at least nominal command of the garrison. Viscount Bourgchier was hastily sent to negotiate with the soldiers, offer them a pardon, and distribute 6,000 marks in cash. The staplers, for whom the rising was just as dangerous, quickly found the promised 10,000 marks, most of which was transmitted to Bourgchier.[93] By early July he had succeeded in calming the soldiers and bringing them under his command; the news in London on 5 July was that 'the Lord Bourcher hath a gode ronomee of hys wyse demenyng at Calix, but he ys no yhyt comen. The soudeours be more temperat then they were'.[94] On the 17th York could at last assume the captaincy of Calais for seven years, with a generous financial provision of £1,000 in hand and £1,500 a year in assignments, and with £3,000 issued to the treasurer of Calais for the garrison; repairs were ordered to be made to Rysbank tower at the same time.[95] Eventually, in October, elaborate arrangements were made to fulfil the promise made to the staplers in April to repay the government's outstanding 12,000-mark debt, but delays in paying the garrison's wages caused York to be refused entry to the port. He never in fact gained access before the protectorate came to an end and he was relieved of the captaincy early in March 1455. Somerset's lieutenants still held their commissions in the fortress and York's strenuous efforts to subject Calais to his control had failed for the time being.[96]

The protection of Calais from foreign attack was central to the measures taken by the government to keep the seas safe. On 1 September 1453, Henry VI's ministers ordered the impressment of English and foreign ships in the west-country ports in order to assemble a fleet for sea-keeping purposes.[97] But such piecemeal efforts were inadequate in the circumstances. On 13 March 1454 Kemp spelled out the seriousness of the threat to Calais and the sea approaches to the kingdom in a speech to the commons in parliament, but his conclusion that a suitable remedy would cost more than £40,000 prompted the reminder on 19 March that the king had already been granted the customs and subsidies for life. The commons believed that they were sufficient for both purposes and refused to concede any more for the time being; so strongly did they feel on the matter that they insisted that their refusal and their reasoning should be entered formally on the official parliament roll.[98] It was left to York to devise as best he could a means of channel and coastal defence that would also succour Calais, if required, and be funded from available resources. His answer was a specially assembled fleet that would remain in being for three years,

> ...to the entent that all your Navire bee redye togedirs, and of power for to assemble in such place as is most convenable for th' assemblyng of thaim, for to breke the puissance of the Navire of the seid Adversarie, before thaeire assemblyng...[99]

On 3 April 1454, therefore, an indenture was concluded with several noblemen, including the new chancellor and the treasurer, as well as two reliable (from York's point of view) magnates, William Bourgchier, Lord FitzWarin and the earl of Oxford; politically it was a finely-balanced group, for household magnates like Wiltshire, the young Shrewsbury, and Lord Stourton were also engaged.[100] Their commission was to command 'a grete Naviey' at sea for three years, funded by the customs and subsidies. To ensure that the necessary cash was forthcoming, not only were the chancellor and treasurer retained but the commissioners received authority to appoint one customs collector in each of the realm's major ports.

In order to send the fleet to sea as soon as was practicable, loans were sought on parliamentary authority, to be repaid from the customs and subsidies; an initial £990 was anticipated from certain towns and cities by 20 April. This loan-raising operation was a signal failure; rather less than £200 seems to have been forthcoming and most of that came from members of the government.[101] Had it not been for the mutiny at Calais and the consequent massive loans from the staplers (£7,333), together with £467 from the officials at Calais, little cash would have been available to fit out the ships.[102] Even so, of £2,500 issued to the naval commissioners between 25 May and 6 June 1454, half was in the form of assignments that had to be changed at least once over the next twenty-one months before payment was realized.[103]

It was part of the protectorate's strategy to establish its control of commerce in the channel. In April 1454 it insisted that no English ship should sail to an enemy port without the council's express permission, warning that few safe-conducts would be issued henceforward.[104] Then, in late May and June, when the situation at Calais had worsened, the south and east coasts were alerted to the possibility of an invasion: men were mustered, watches kept, and beacons prepared on the cliffs between Yorkshire and Cornwall.[105] The provisioning of the fleet went ahead simultaneously: ships of over 50 tons were assembled at Sandwich, the *Grace Dieu* was refitted, and during June further vessels were commandeered in the south-west and the Bristol channel.[106] A great council was summoned to meet at Westminster on 25 June to co-ordinate the entire strategy of defending the realm, resisting the enemy at sea, and protecting Calais.[107]

Salisbury and the other lords do not seem to have put to sea until the summer; it was their first and only campaign season. The most that their expedition could achieve was to deter the enemy at sea and relieve Calais, for the unpredictability of naval warfare in the fifteenth century made it highly unlikely that a decisive engagement could be fought afloat.[108] Whatever benefits the fleet brought must be offset by the lawlessness to which its captains were prone; some of them were tempted to prey on friendly ships, even on English merchantmen, perhaps because the enemy had been successfully deterred from venturing to sea. Among the most flagrant of the freebooters was Andrew Trollope, whose carvel took to seizing and robbing the ships of allies and subjects alike. Before the end of August 1454, demands for an investigation proved irresistible.[109]

It is difficult to assess the degree of success achieved by the protectorate in reverting to a mode of sea-keeping that had not been employed for a decade. Calais stood fast, though that owed just as much to the staplers' financial rescue-operation. The English coast was for the moment spared enemy raids, and English trade any interruption. The cost was not high, but difficulties were encountered in finding the money for the first year's operations, let alone others in 1455 and 1456. By then, however, the political rifts in England itself inhibited renewed efforts to equip 'a grete Naviey'.

York was equally determined to assert his authority in Ireland, though for somewhat different reasons; there it was not a case of removing a real threat to his power in England, but of reasserting an authority that had once been his. He had resented Wiltshire's appointment as lieutenant in 1453, not least because his own commission still had several years to run. Moreover, some years before, in 1448, the appointment of the prior of Kilmainham as chancellor had annoyed Sir John Talbot on similar grounds.[110] York, therefore, seized his opportunity as protector to retrieve the lieutenancy and restore Talbot (who had become earl of Shrewsbury in July 1453 and sat on the protectorate council) to the Irish chancery; these two magnates would thereby enhance their authority in England. On 6 February 1454, all payments to the Irish government were suspended until the question of the lieutenancy was settled; an agreement had been reached by 15 April between the two claimants and York re-emerged as lieutenant and raised the embargo on Irish expenditure. The related dispute was ended late in August, when Shrewsbury's appointment (of 1446) was reaffirmed.[111] Thus, during the protectorate, York's position in eastern Ireland at least was strengthened, while his estates and personal record consolidated his reputation among the Anglo-Irish more generally. He was better able to stand above the rivalries and violent disputes in which Wiltshire had become embroiled, and a petition to York in June 1454 from the distraught inhabitants of Kildare seems to have prompted energetic measures from his successive deputies, Sir Edmund FitzEustace (until his death in October 1454) and Thomas FitzMaurice, earl of Kildare and Wiltshire's bitter foe.[112] If, then, the duke of York had an enduring achievement to his credit during his first protectorate, it was in Ireland rather than in Calais.

By contrast, the protector largely abstained from intervening in affairs on the Scottish border. After all, James II was pretty well entangled in a difficult struggle with some of his magnates, among whom the earl of Douglas had appealed to Henry VI for aid in 1452.[113] This eased the pressure on the border country by removing the threat of invasion or serious organized raiding. In any case, Lord Poynings, Northumberland's eldest son, was firmly entrenched at Berwick as warden of the east march and he could hardly be challenged even at the height of the Percy–Neville feud.[114] At Roxburgh and Carlisle, York's Neville cousins were well ensconced. Fauconberg's wages as constable of Roxburgh were still hopelessly in arrears, but he nevertheless was an obedient, loyal, and conscientious custodian.[115] Warwick joined his father, Salisbury, in the wardenship of the west march in December 1453, and on 6 August 1454 the chancellor was granted special authority for twenty years in the city of Carlisle to collect the fee farm in return for £80 *per annum*. Though this grant might confer added influence in a city whose bishop was a Percy, it was no financial bargain; later in the year, therefore, the city's merchants were empowered to export 25 sacks of wool annually from Hull to Calais without paying the usual subsidy, a concession that would bring modest wealth to Carlisle and make Salisbury's hold on the fee farm more worthwhile.[116] York's reliance on the Nevilles in the far north was fundamental to his position in England, but he never felt able to challenge the Percy presence there at any time during the protectorate, not even when Northumberland's unruly sons were arrested for their rising in Yorkshire.

With lordships stretching from the valley of the Dee to the Usk, York was well placed to regard the march of Wales as a rich preserve of men and money, and as protector he was careful to maintain his authority there and suppress disorder. The extensive Neville estates in Glamorgan and elsewhere in the south were a valuable adjunct to his own. Probably during the late summer of 1454, he paid a visit to the march, and at Montgomery castle he dealt with a disruptive boundary dispute between his own tenants of Chirbury and those of Buckingham's lordship of Caus; the presence of the protector may also have done something to calm unrest in the vicinity, for since 1453 the men of Caus had been sniping at the tenantry of the lord of Powis, Richard Grey.[117] More serious, if more distant, was the violent and disorderly conduct of the Carmarthenshire esquire Gruffydd ap Nicholas. His indifference to lawful authority in the west of Wales had frequently led him to abuse the powers entrusted to him as a local official and to obstruct those who carried ultimate responsibility for good government in Cardiganshire and Carmarthenshire.[118] On 25 May 1454, the protectorate council resolved to remove him and his relatives from the offices which they occupied in the crown's principality lands and in those marcher lordships adjacent, basing their action on the largely dormant statute passed in Henry IV's parliament:

> . . . we woll ye call to remebraunce it is youre duete to confourme you to oure [i. e., the king's] lawes and not be taking upon you the contrarie therof to wronge oure liege men as it is surmised ye doo, . .[119]

Perhaps the most worrying matter was the apparent freedom with which Gruffydd pursued his criminal activities in lordships much closer to the English border. During 1454 he was in Buckingham's lordship of Brecon and he 'did receave, maintaine and comfort' wrongdoers in York's own Maelienydd. Though found guilty at Shrewsbury and soon afterwards, on 16 August, apprehended at Hereford, he was rescued from the clutches of the law by one of the most prominent Herefordshire gentlemen of his day, Sir John Scudamore, who had married Gruffydd's daughter.[120] More than any other single incident, it may have been Gruffydd's trail of lawlessness in York's own territory that brought the duke to the marchland about the end of August 1454.

It is difficult to escape the conclusion that York's régime as protector in 1454–55 showed him to be less of the reformer or the restorer of good government, and more the proud magnate of royal blood, determined to capitalize on his opportunity to consolidate his own political and territorial power (particularly in Ireland, Calais, and the Welsh march), to advance the interests of his Neville friends, and, as far as was possible in a brief period, to secure his position for the future. His success was limited.

That these were the considerations uppermost in York's mind is indicated by his handling of much the most serious threat to the continuance of the protectorate and to his own position as chief councillor and prospective heir to the throne. This was the rising of the Percies and the duke of Exeter during the spring of 1454.[121] The rival houses of Percy and Neville came into most bitter conflict in the vale of York, where their manors were situated not many miles apart and the city of York, with its magnate residences and other interests, provided a focus for a power struggle. In the later years of Henry's reign, each side enlisted substantial support from its friends, dependants, tenants, and sympathizers, offering livery to many in contravention of statutes that restricted the practice. The Percies, in particular, seem to have strutted the northern shires like kings, not only on their own estates but also more generally. Their sense of grievance rose with the marriage of one of Lord Cromwell's heiresses to Sir John Neville, Salisbury's younger son, for Northumberland now faced the prospect of his ancestors' properties falling into the hands of an implacable enemy.[122] This, then, provided the occasion for an outbreak of violence whose consequences rocked the very foundations of the protectorate.

Over the span of a year or so, a number of vicious and interconnected incidents took place in Yorkshire; the Percies, who felt themselves worse threatened, were especially responsible. The city of York was invaded on more than one occasion; two serious confrontations occurred and were regarded by contemporaries as veritable battles; the government's measures were largely ineffective or else were ignored; and practically the entire magnate community of Yorkshire was implicated in the imbroglio. The Percies were led by Northumberland's younger sons, Thomas (created Lord Egremont in 1449), Ralph, and Richard, but they were supported at various times by their elder brother, Lord Poynings, warden of the east march, by Lords Clifford, Roos, FitzHugh, and Scrope, and by their greatest ally of all, Henry Holand, duke of Exeter. The Nevilles attracted, numerically speaking, less sympathy from the Yorkshire nobility; but although Salisbury's younger sons, Thomas and John, bore the brunt of Percy violence, they were aided by their elder brother, the powerful earl of Warwick, and by the protector himself who, after the announcement of Exeter's involvement at the beginning of 1454, had compelling reasons, apart from the protection of his own Yorkshire estates, for intervening decisively. Furthermore, Salisbury and Warwick enjoyed a major advantage, for they were prominent members of the council in 1453–54.[123]

Relations between the two warring families deteriorated sharply in the summer of 1453 with the attempted ambush of the Neville wedding party on its way back to Yorkshire from Cromwell's Lincolnshire castle of Tattershall. The 'battle' of Heworth on 24 August was a major encounter, not far from the east wall of York, but its outcome is uncertain. Both sides were apparently able to disengage and prepare for further clashes during the following year. The enfeebled government of the indisposed king made half-hearted attempts to cope with the violence, but the two earls of Salisbury and Northumberland, who do not seem to have been personally or directly involved at this stage, were either powerless or disinclined to restrain their boisterous sons. Moreover, during the autumn and winter, relations worsened as Warwick took his father's part, having just emerged from a dispute in Glamorgan with the discredited and imprisoned Somerset; at the same time, the Nevilles were forging that alliance with York which culminated in the latter's nomination as protector, Salisbury's appointment as chancellor, and the despatch of commissions to Yorkshire that were likely to be sympathetic to the Nevilles' cause. On the other side, events in those same winter months persuaded Exeter, who had his own reasons for resenting Cromwell's familial ties with the Nevilles, that he should try to arrest the growing power of York and assert his own claims, as the king's nearest male relative in England, to leadership of Henry VI's government. Before 19 January 1454

> ... the Duk of Excestre in his owne persone hathe ben at Tuxforthe beside Dancastre, in the north contree, and there the Lord Egremond mette hym, and thei ij. ben sworne togider, ...[124]

Neither Exeter nor Northumberland had played a part in the conciliar régime of 1453–54, and it was likely that when parliament resumed on 14 February, and especially after a protector had been appointed on 28 March, firmer action would be taken against disturbers of the peace. Exeter, Northumberland, Poynings, Ralph Percy, and Lord Roos were summoned to attend the council, and Exeter at least travelled to London to listen to York's appeal that he disband his men. But neither Exeter nor his northern allies heeded the protector's pleas and by 8 May the 'politique and restfull rule of this noble Realme' was once more in jeopardy. The situation was sufficiently serious to require York's presence in Yorkshire and by 16 May he was on his way north. Exeter was meanwhile planning a major rising based on the Percy manor of Spofforth and with the city of York as its initial objective; Lancashire- and Cheshire-men were summoned as well as the Holand tenantry from Bedfordshire. The duke's political intentions are not entirely clear, but his reported actions – raising his own standard, distributing the duchy of Lancaster livery, appealing to the Scots, claiming the rule of England – seem to reflect a deep resentment that York, rather than he, had been made protector of England.[125] Exeter and his allies laid plans for the murder of York (and perhaps Cromwell too) when they arrived in Yorkshire; but the plot was foiled and sessions held at York and Newcastle between 15 and 26 June heard detailed indictments of the Holand–Percy forces. The commissioners were headed by York and

Warwick; already Exeter had fled secretly to London, where he was eventually captured on 23 July, after York had returned to the capital. His rebellious following could now be treated with leniency and an attempt was even made to reconcile several of the disaffected magnates. After all, as far as the protector was concerned, the most important threat had been removed when Exeter was despatched under guard to Pontefract castle, where the constable was none other than the earl of Salisbury. As for the Percies still at large, after a further 'battle' at Stamford Bridge on 1 or 2 November, Egremont and Richard Percy were captured and transferred to Newgate gaol.

The protector's success in the north had been primarily the success of force. There had been a serious assault on his constitutional position as well as on the territorial power of the Nevilles. The Percy–Exeter rising was arguably the most serious challenge the protectorate had to face, partly because it was led by a rival for the special powers conferred on York during the king's incapacity; it was of little initial significance that Exeter's dynastic qualities were matched by neither ability nor experience. The Yorkshire problem absorbed a good deal of the protector's time and energy during the spring and summer of 1454, just when the situation in Calais was at its most desperate and events in the Welsh march demanded attention; at least twice he made the journey to Yorkshire, followed by a visit to Montgomery and probably elsewhere in eastern Wales.[126] But as the chroniclers realized, it was the Yorkshire rising that was the most pressing concern. It prevented York from devoting any time to the simmering Devon–Bonville dispute, which produced further violence in Exeter in April.[127] And York's only intervention in the acrimonious squabbles among the Derbyshire gentry was on 1 July when, after months of official exhortations, warnings, and commissions, he paused at Derby on the way south to hold sessions to deal with the Longford–Blount feud that had embroiled other local gentlemen in raids, assaults, and killings.[128] During his brief ascendancy, York found himself reacting to, rather than dictating, events, responding to the actions – usually hostile actions – of others. There is some sense in which he attempted to fulfil the commission entrusted to him to protect and defend the realm, but events inextricably linked with his personal concerns and political survival crowded in on him.

Recovery and reaction

Henry VI's apparent recovery from his long illness on or soon after Christmas 1454 could not fail to have a profound effect on the protectorate and on the political and personal enmity between York and Somerset.[129] The constitutional justification for a protector disappeared, and Henry VI, Queen Margaret, and many courtiers and magnates are likely to have desired Somerset's release from the Tower at the earliest opportunity; some had evidently been unhappy for some months about his continuing captivity without trial.[130] The earl of Wiltshire had no love for York for personal reasons; Buckingham and his kinsman, Archbishop Bourgchier, in welcoming the return of Henry VI to personal rule, could see no grounds for imprisoning any longer a man who, for all his faults, was a close blood-relative of the king – and therefore of the Staffords – and who had not been formally indicted or convicted of any offence. Yet they can have had few illusions that his release would be strongly opposed by York and the Nevilles. For that reason when, on 26 January, Somerset was brought from the Tower, he was said to have been 'straungeley conveied'. The release was made official on 5 February at a well-attended great council at which York, Salisbury, and Warwick were present; but there were strings attached.[131] Several prominent magnates – Buckingham, Wiltshire, Lord Roos (who had recently sided with Exeter and the Percies in Yorkshire), and Lord FitzWarin – stood surety for Somerset pending his reply to the accusations that had been laid against him, and it appears that he solemnly undertook not to involve himself in politics or approach within 20 miles of the king. Such conditions were of some small consolation to York and his friends.[132]

Hard upon these arrangements (though the exact date is unknown), York tendered his resignation as protector to Henry at Greenwich. This may have been settled at the council meeting which had authorized Somerset's release, and was not unexpected.[133] What was probably not foreseen by York was the sequence of political adjustments that followed. From about 21 February certain significant changes in the council emphasized the role of courtiers like Wiltshire and Lords Dudley and Beauchamp (the latter of whom joined the council that day) and cold-shouldered Salisbury, the chancellor, and Worcester, the treasurer.[134] Even more telling was the decision on 4 March to discharge Somerset's sureties, repudiate the charges against him, and abandon the conditions under which he had been freed. The king himself presided over the council, again at Greenwich, which authorized the removal of these remaining constraints on Somerset and encouraged him to resume his former place as the king's principal minister.[135] Buckingham and Archbishop Bourgchier appear to have been willing parties to this decision. York was induced to agree to submit all outstanding disputes between himself and Somerset to a panel of arbitrators. Accordingly, the two dukes entered into a recognisance of 20,000 marks towards each other that they would abide by the arbitration, which would be announced by 20 June.[136] Though the panel of arbitrators included the earl of Worcester and Lord Cromwell, who would probably have looked sympathetically at York's case, the earl of Wiltshire and Lords Beaumont and Stourton were closely identified with the court; and after recent events, Archbishop Bourgchier, Bishop William Grey, and the duke of Buckingham could hardly be considered strictly impartial.

No award is known to have been made by these arbitrators, and in any case events were overtaken by Somerset's death at St Albans on

22 May; but this tacit rejection of York's accusations against Somerset, which can be dated at least to 1452, was decisive as far as Duke Richard and the Nevilles were concerned. The former was relieved of the captaincy of Calais, perhaps at his own request, and on 6 March, Somerset was reinstated.[137] Next day, Salisbury, who is said to have strenuously opposed this rehabilitation of the duke of Somerset, resigned the great seal to Henry VI, who was still at Greenwich, and Archbishop Bourgchier was appointed chancellor in his place.[138] A week later, on 15 March, Worcester was replaced as treasurer, on this occasion by an out-and-out partisan of the court who had his own grievances against York – the earl of Wiltshire.[139] By mid-March, therefore, major constitutional and political changes had occured at the queen's manor house of Greenwich, though the role of Queen Margaret in precipitating them remains obscure. York and the Nevilles had been stripped of all office and authority, whereas Somerset, with the concurrence of a weighty section of the aristocracy that included the Bourgchiers and the Staffords, had been restored to his former position at Henry's side, and his associate Wiltshire had been appointed to a crucial office of state.

The *bouleversement* was concluded by the return of a dynastically important member of the royal family to the king's presence and favour. Exeter was freed from confinement in Pontefract castle and on 19 March no less a person than his cousin, Humphrey Stafford, son and heir of the duke of Buckingham, was sent to Yorkshire to bring him back to court.[140] The Lancastrian royal family, on which Henry VI had purposefully lavished extraordinary honours and patronage in the 1440s, was reassembled in the spring of 1455 to buttress his throne. Once again, York had reason to feel that his person and his line were being threatened, but this time he would have the aid of the powerful Nevilles in any defence he might mount.

The events of February–March 1455 represented an humiliation for the duke and his allies, who could be pardoned for suspecting that acts of sheer revenge would follow. Already on 5 March, York had been deprived of the only item of personal patronage which he had pocketed during his year in power: though allowed to retain custody of the Devon and Cornish mines, he was now required to pay £95 a year for the privilege and had to match any higher offer that might be made for them. Even this arrangement was overturned by 23 March, when two household yeomen were installed as receiver-general and controller of the mines on behalf of the king.[141] Likewise, on 16 March, Salisbury was relieved of the custody of the ancient castle and town of Portchester (Hampshire) which he had been granted during pleasure only three months before.[142] Thus, unmistakable signs of victimization could be read in the air; it was, indeed, the view of several chroniclers that Somerset was busily poisoning the king's mind against York, Salisbury, and Warwick, implying that they were traitors.[143] When, in mid-April, it was resolved to summon a special great council to Leicester on 21

May, well out of reach of the excitable Londoners who had once before shown their hatred of Somerset, the Yorkist lords seem to have concluded that even more punitive measures were being contemplated against them. According to one plausible observer, they thereupon abruptly withdrew from the court without even seeking the king's permission.[144]

St Albans

C. A. J. Armstrong's masterly exposition of the available materials relating to the battle of St Albans on 22 May 1455 has produced a careful and detailed reconstruction of events immediately before and after the fighting, and of the intentions of the participants. Though uncertainties remain, certain conclusions emerge with reasonable clarity.[145] After their withdrawal from the court, York and the Nevilles appear to have retired to Salisbury's Yorkshire estates, perhaps to Sandal castle, where they could consider how best to react to the restoration of personal rule by the king and the return of Somerset as his principal minister.[146] To judge by their own statements on the eve of the battle, they were resentful of the fact that they had not been invited to the council meeting at Westminster in mid-April which had decided to summon the extraordinary great council to Leicester, and they were indignant that the question of their own loyalty should be on the agenda of the Leicester meeting. To the chancellor on 20 May they protested that

we understond the callyng and stablishyng of the Kynges Counsail at his Towne of Leycestre, toke the grounde by such as we conceyve caused th'appointement therof there, for suertee of his moost noble persone, which of commun presumption implieth a mistrust to somme persones: . . . We also, understond what colerable and subtile meanes be made by oure Enemies, holdyng thaim colorably aboute the seid moost noble persone of oure said Soveraine Lord, of might of men and habilementes of werre have the more surely accompaigned us, to th'entent that at oure commyng to his most high presence, we mowe be of power to kepe oureself oute of the daungier whereunto oure said Enemies have not ceessed to studie, labour and compasse to bryng us, such as in allewise we will eschewe with Goddes grace . . . . we understonde that other Lordes of this lande have be late sent fore by the Kynges commaundement under his Letters, to comen unto his Counsail privately late called at Westmynstre, whereunto we have not been among the said Lordes called, we conceyve a jelosy had ayenst us, wherof we purpose with Goddes grace to declare us, and to shewe us such as we bee in oure trouthe, duetee and ligeaunce, to oure said Soveraine Lord, entendyng in alle wyse to remove the said Jelosy, which we woll eschewe to have liyng dormant upon us . . . .

741

To Henry next day, they declared that

> we here and understond to oure grettest sorowe erthly, that oure
> Enemies of approved experience, such as abide and kepe theimself
> undre the wynge of our Mageste Roiall, have thrawen unto the same
> right cediciously and right fraudelently, many ambiguitees and of the
> feith, liegeaunce and duetee, that God knoweth we bere unto youre
> Highnesse, and have put thaim in as greet devoir as they coude to
> estraunge us from youre moost noble presence, and from the faveur
> of youre good grace;...[147]

In requesting a full discussion of the matter with all lords who were loyal
to the king they were barely masking what they could not yet express
in writing, namely, that Somerset and their enemies at court should be
removed. In sum, the three 'Yorkist' lords were adopting the same
strategy as had been adopted at Dartford in March 1452: to demand the
dismissal of Somerset and the end of personal victimization, and to
support these demands with force.[148]

The intentions of the court are less clear and must be inferred from
events. The purpose of the council scheduled to meet at Leicester seems
to have been to review publicly the loyalty of the Yorkist lords and force
them to conclude an agreement with Somerset – perhaps, indeed, to
announce the arbitration award which both sides had commissioned on
4 March.[149] Even as the date of the council approached, there is no sign
that the court intended any military demonstration at Leicester, though
its decision to summon two knights from each shire as well as the lords
indicates a determination to hold as substantial, authoritative, and
representative an assembly as possible. By such means, the confrontation on dynastic, political, and personal grounds between two of the
most senior magnates in the realm would be resolved rather as the
quarrel between Beaufort and Gloucester had been composed in the
self-same town in 1426 – but this time presumably to Somerset's
advantage.[150]

The speed of the Yorkists' advance towards London, and the size of
their retinue – one contemporary put it at 7,000 – took the court by
surprise. It may be that the initiative to react so belligerently came from
the Nevilles; their Yorkshire estates (as well as those of York himself)
could certainly have provided sufficient men. When news of the rising
reached the king, a delegation of three was sent to mediate with the
presumed intention of persuading the lords to come to Leicester more
peacefully. The choice of emissaries was no affront to either York or
the Nevilles, for although Bishop Boulers was a courtier-politician and
diplomat of Suffolk's acquaintance, the earl of Worcester had been
treasurer during the protectorate, and the prior of the Hospital of St
John of Jerusalem was a councillor then and a skilled negotiator. Their
mission was futile, and according to one chronicler the Yorkists

detained them while they continued their march south, probably in order to preserve the element of surprise.[151]

This tactic resulted in confusion and panic in the royal ranks by about 18 May, when the court seems to have finally realized what exactly it was up against. The plan to travel to Leicester by 21 May may have been abandoned in favour of a more cautious strategy whereby the king would make his way to St Albans to meet reinforcements so that he could advance towards Leicester in greater safety, though not by the 21st. The mediators' mission having misfired, on the 19th York, Salisbury, Warwick, and the duke of Norfolk (who was regarded as being in their confidence by this time) were commanded to disband all but their personal retinue.[152] After all, several of the magnates with the king were not without sympathy for York's plight, and it is doubtful if any of them (apart perhaps from Somerset, Wiltshire, and Northumberland) saw a battle as any kind of solution.[153] Accordingly, when he reached St Albans on the 22nd, Henry appointed the duke of Buckingham as constable of England, and therefore commander of the royal forces, in place of Somerset. Buckingham believed that actual fighting could and should be avoided and that the Yorkist lords would prefer to negotiate – but not, naturally enough, with Somerset. The letters which York and his companions sent to the chancellor (on 20 May) and the king (the following day) gave substantial hope that negotiations were in fact possible on the basis of reassuring the insurgents that they would not be ruthlessly victimized.[154] Apart from York himself and in the absence of Exeter, Buckingham was the realm's senior duke and the king's closest blood relative; for all his willingness to see Somerset released from prison in January 1455, he was far from anxious to see York, Norfolk, and the Nevilles alienated to the point of rebellion. What the king did not fully comprehend was that York and the Nevilles had reached the end of their patience and were no longer prepared to risk the kind of deceitful treatment to which York had been subjected at Dartford or a compromise that might later enable the king to restore Somerset to favour. Experience during 1452–55 is likely to have made York sceptical of negotiations on terms that did not include the final and irrevocable removal of Somerset. The Nevilles would have fortified his resolve and when skirmishing started in advance of the battle, it was Warwick and his men who were responsible.

The pre-battle exchanges conducted by heralds and at personal interviews with the leaders of both sides show the Yorkist lords to be adamant that Somerset should be handed over to them, presumably so that the formal trial which had never been held during the protectorate could adjudicate on the accusations York had repeatedly levelled against him.[155] Though he had fewer magnates with him (and no bishops), the duke was a determined man. He had relied heavily on his councillors throughout his public career – perhaps unusually so in view of the frequency with which contemporaries noticed it – and in May 1455 he had the Nevilles and their northern retainers at his elbow.[156] He had, too, superiority of numbers; although contemporary estimates show their usual variations, C. A. J. Armstrong avers that York commanded perhaps 3,000 men against about 2,000 who had so far assembled to protect the king. It was to Duke Richard's advantage, therefore, to bring matters to a speedy conclusion before reinforcements, which the court had already summoned, could arrive in Hertfordshire.[157]

In the negotiations, the attitude of the king's ministers was at first robust, for both Somerset and Buckingham threatened the insurgents with forfeiture if they did not disperse. When that was ignored, Buckingham, who conducted the negotiations on the king's side, adopted more skilful tactics, hoping to wean Norfolk from the Yorkist side by stressing their kinship, and to delay a decision until some of the bishops could arrive from London and bring the persuasive sanction of the church to bear on York and his allies. The role of the king was a passive one. He took no direct part in the discussions and interviewed none of the heralds; when Mowbray herald gained audience, he was immediately referred to Buckingham who, he was told, had full authority to negotiate on Henry's behalf. There was even a suspicion in the Yorkist camp, which was hardened into fact in the official account presented to the subsequent parliament, that York's pre-battle letters to the king had not in fact been shown to him. Henry VI was not a cipher, but the extent of his participation in the exchanges immediately prior to the fighting was strictly limited. This is undeniably strange for a man whose keen interest in peace and reconciliation had led him to take personal initiatives in relations with France in the 1440s and who had been much involved in the crisis of Cade's rebellion and at Dartford. One cannot but wonder whether, after his debilitating illness not many months before, he was still in a somewhat precarious physical or mental state.[158] On 22 May the king relied totally on Buckingham and clung to Somerset. Although the defiant words attributed to Henry later by Yorkist propaganda were calculated to justify the resort to arms that was about to occur (and C. A. J. Armstrong has said of his speech that there is 'a high degree of probability that it is a forgery'), it is doubtful if any constable of England in Buckingham's position would have contemplated surrendering a royal duke like Somerset to his enemies against the will of the monarch, or considered it at all a wise precedent to do so.[159] Buckingham's own declaration to Mowbray herald at their last meeting before the skirmish rings true of the duke's attitude:

> We wish the whole world to know that we have not come here to support any one person or for any other cause but only to be in company with the king our said lord, as by right we are bound to do.[160]

The battle of St Albans began in earnest at about 10 a. m. and lasted for only a few hours until early in the afternoon.[161] The fiercest fighting took place in the centre of the town, especially in the market-place, for there the king stood with his banner unfurled. The barricades which defended the wall-less town, under the command of Lord Clifford, had held the insurgents back for perhaps an hour, but then Warwick's northerners broke through some of the houses and by a flanking movement from the east entered one of the main streets. The Yorkist forces quickly gained the upper hand. Henry VI was deserted beneath his banner and wounded in the neck; Buckingham was struck several times in the face and then retired to the abbey. Somerset was killed after retreating to a house.

> ... to save himself by hiding, but he was seen by the men of the Duke of York, who at once surrounded the house.... And at once York's men began to fight Somerset and his men who were in the house, which they defended valiantly. And at last after the doors were broken, Somerset saw that there was nothing for it but to come out with his men; this he did and immediately they were surrounded by York's men. And after... the duke of Somerset had killed four men with his own hand, he was, it is said, felled with an axe, and was at once wounded in so many places that he died.[162]

The king had meanwhile taken refuge in the tanners' house where York took charge of him and escorted him to the abbey as soon as it was possible to do so. The leading dead included Somerset, Northumberland, and Clifford, and it may well be that they had been particularly sought out by York's and the Nevilles' men; certainly the slaughter of these magnates at the battle perpetuated a feud between the respective families at least until March 1458, when Henry arranged an arbitration settlement.[163] For the moment, however, their death brought the battle of St Albans to an end. A spate of looting followed as the defeated were stripped of their possessions, the town ransacked with some verve by the northerners, and fear spread that the abbey itself would be desecrated. The earl of Wiltshire managed to flee dressed as a monk, but Bishop Percy of Carlisle was robbed before being allowed to make off on foot; other fugitives had to rely on charity to keep body and soul together.[164]

Having achieved his victory, York made his way to the abbey, where he solemnly submitted to the king, who accepted the duke, along with Salisbury and Warwick, as his liege man:

> and on here knees be soughte hym of grace and foryevenesse of that they hadde doon yn his presence, and be sought hym of his Heynesse to take hem as hys true legemen, seyng that they never attendyde hurt to his owne persone, and therfore [the] Kyng oure sovereyn Lord toke hem to grace, and so desyred hem to cesse there peple, and that there shulde no more harme be doon.[165]

In the king's name, York thereupon proclaimed an end to the fighting, and the bodies of the dead magnates were carried to the abbey for burial.[166] The losses on the king's side were naturaly the heavier, though the total is unlikely to have exceeded sixty (which is C. A. J. Armstrong's estimate after a careful review of conflicting contemporary statements). Most of the dead were members of the king's household or servants of the duchy of Lancaster.[167]

The second protectorate

The duke of York's problems after the battle of St Albans were different from those he had faced before, but hardly less intractable. The task now was to resume political life, reconcile the combatants and their sympathizers, and secure acceptance from lords and commons of himself as the king's dominant adviser. This had been the purport of the letters he had written to Archbishop Bourgchier and the king on the eve of the fighting. The duke made his first approach in person to Henry VI in the abbey of St Albans itself and he was able to make his peace with him.[168] Next day, the company made its way to London, where the citizens could witness Henry's apparent reconciliation with the Yorkist lords; all honour was shown to the monarch as he was led by York, Salisbury, and Warwick (who had carried the king's sword from St Albans) to the bishop of London's palace, and a ceremonial public procession was arranged later in the day. During a solemn crown-wearing that was staged at St Paul's cathedral on 25 May, Henry received his crown from York's own hands.[169]

Wider reconciliation was best achieved by erasing from the public mind as soon as possible the memory of the deaths and divisions at St Albans. This was not easy, for the battle had been the first occasion since Henry IV's reign when a king had been personally involved in a major passage of arms within the realm, and Henry VI had been wounded beneath his own unfurled banner, which had been assaulted by subjects who were demonstrably rebels in all but name. The politically dispossessed and the relatives of the fallen were certain to be deeply resentful and outraged; the opponents of York and the Nevilles would not readily submit, whilst the Lancastrian court about the queen and the young prince would be hostile. Nevertheless, the day after the ceremony at St Paul's (i.e., 26 May) parliament was summoned and, with the exception of Somerset's son who was barely twenty, even the heirs of the dead Lancastrian lords were sent writs in the usual way; to do otherwise would have defeated York's purpose and given rise to the same kind of charge that York himself had levelled when he and the Nevilles were excluded from the April council at Westminster.

One of the declared objects of this parliament, as announced by Archbishop Bourgchier on 9 July, was to heal magnate divisions, and to this end the lords were warned not to come to Westminster with forces larger that their household retinues.[170] Few can have been under any illusion as to the difficult problems ahead. Buckingham, who had been placed in custody after the battle, seems to have submitted, though substantial bonds to ensure his good behaviour indicate that he did so grudgingly. Worcester, on the other hand, played a prominent role in the St Paul's ceremony. The earl of Wiltshire's absurd demands – reinstatement at court or permission to go to Ireland – were too extreme to be acceptable; Lord Dudley, a senior household official, continued to make embarrassing accusations and was put in the Tower; and on 26 June the duke of Exeter, one of York's most dangerous rivals, was ordered to be kept under strict guard at Wallingford.[171] Even after parliament opened, Warwick and Lord Cromwell fell to an angry exchange during which the former accused the latter of having caused the recent battle – not without some justice if one considers the consequences of the marriage between Sir John Neville and Cromwell's niece and Cromwell's private property dispute with the duke of Exeter, though it was less than fair to blame the elderly Cromwell for not having had the foresight to realize that his personal arrangements would snowball into something larger. Shrewsbury intervened to offer him his protection. Furthermore,

> ... all my Lord of Warrewikke men, my Lord of York men, and also my Lord of Salesbury men goo with harnes, and in harnes with strang wepons, and have stuffed their Lordes barges full of wepon dayly unto Westminster. And they day of makyng of this letter [19 July], ther was a proclamacion made in the Chauncerie, on the Kyngs behalf, that noman shuld nether bere wepon, ner were harnes defensible, etc....[172]

Thus, the path of reconciliation was a perilous one.[173]

The centrepiece of the first session of parliament (9-31 July) was an extraordinary pardon, introduced on 18 July and granted by the king on parliamentary authority. Its terms offered an indemnity to all who had fought beside York and immunity from future prosecution for their acts that day, 'and nothing doon there never after this tyme to be spoken of'.[174] Three persons were excluded from its provisions, Somerset, Thomas Thorp, and William Joseph, ostensibly because they had withheld York's letters from the king. Somerset was safely dead, and the more obscure Thorp and Joseph were relatively uncontroversial scapegoats: York had a personal grudge against the former and the latter represented the royal household. At the same time, the loyalty of York, the Nevilles, and their supporters was formally recorded.[175] Their authorized version of events prior to the battle included York's two letters to Archbishop Bourgchier and Henry VI, and the preamble of the parliamentary pardon has therefore the air of a propaganda exercise in political expediency intended to halt recriminations and promote unity. The commons, led by their speaker, Sir John Wenlock, acquiesced in the wide-ranging indemnity, 'though mony a man groged full sore nowe [the bill] is passed'.[176] As a public example of the reconciliation for which York hoped, on 24 July sixty of the lords, meeting as a great council during parliament, swore an oath of loyalty to the king and solemnly undertook to protect him, the spiritual peers with hand on breast, the lay lords taking Henry by the hand. On the last day of the session, the king issued his own general pardon.[177]

Reconciliation was an essential foundation for stable rule, but much more immediate was the Yorkists' need to take a firm grip of the king's government. The new régime was no mere partisan faction, though only those likely to sympathize with the Yorkist position were given office. By 25 May the important changes had been decided. Archbishop Bourgchier was allowed to retain the great seal and Thomas Liseux the privy seal, but Viscount Bourgchier, who may have been with York at St Albans, was appointed treasurer in place of Wiltshire, who had fled the field. York himself assumed the constableship of England which Somerset and Buckingham had successively occupied; he also appropriated Somerset's two constableships of Carmarthen and Aberystwyth castles in order to buttress his authority in Wales and defend his marcher interests against such attacks from the west as Gruffydd ap Nicholas had perpetrated in 1454.[178] At Calais the earl of Warwick was installed as captain, though he was not able to give reality to his authority for some time to come.[179] At Windsor, whence the king, the queen, and the prince withdrew towards the end of May, the constableship of the castle was entrusted jointly to Salisbury's brother, Lord Fauconberg, and to Bourgchier's brother, Lord Berners; both these men had been with the king at St Albans and their appointment may therefore have been a small concession to the royal family.[180] It was to be expected that the councillors who had served during the first protectorate would be summoned again to provide broad support in the government of the realm. Though significantly weighted in favour of the victorious Yorkists, the council during the six months following the battle included others who had connections with the court (but not necessarily with Somerset).[181]

Nor did York forget those who had been his friends in adversity. Two of his councillors who were among the new MPs, Sir Walter Devereux and Thomas Young, presented petitions, most likely in the first session, for the removal of any stain upon their character. Indeed, the act of 1453 which had resumed all royal grants to those who had sided with York at Dartford, or had failed to turn out for the king except for good reason, was repealed on the ostensible grounds that it perpetuated divisions, especially among the lords.[182]

York also gave some thought to his personal position. After eight years of fruitless campaigning, this parliament rehabilitated the reputation of Humphrey, duke of Gloucester: it declared him to be a true liege man of the king to the day of his death.[183] For York to associate himself with the memory of a man who had struggled against the policies which Somerset embraced, with disastrous consequences, was inspired. It linked him in the popular mind with Henry VI's last undoubted heir presumptive, whose isolation after 1437 had certain affinities with that of York after 1447. York's rivals for the succession were by now either dead or in disgrace, and there was no telling if the young prince would survive to manhood or a protector of the realm be required long before then. The rehabilitation of Gloucester could only emphasize York's dynastic significance.

More detailed study of individual MPs is required before one can be certain of the tone of the new parliament. Not for the first time, York and his friends tried to ensure that constituencies where their largest estates lay returned congenial representatives. The duchess of Norfolk, on behalf of her husband, wrote to enlist the support of John Paston on 8 June, well before the election took place at Norwich a fortnight later:

> ... for as muche as it is thought right necessarie for divers causes that my lord have at this tyme in the Parlement suche persones as longe unto him, and be of his menyall servaunts, wherin we conceyve your good will and diligence shal be right expedient, we hertili desire and pray you that ... ye wil geve and applie your voice unto our right welbelovid cosin and servaunts, John Howard and Syr Roger Chambirlayn, to be Knyghtes of the shire, ...

And sure enough, despite 'moch to do' in the shire during which Paston himself was canvassed, Howard, who was Norfolk's kinsman and was described by one hostile elector 'as wode as a wilde bullok', and Chamberlain, Gloucester's former servant, were elected.[184] The *Paston Letters* highlight these manoeuvres in Norfolk, but one may assume that similar campaigning took place elsewhere. It certainly did in Kent, and if the council's order on 5 July to the sheriff to follow proper procedures was intended to discourage the return of the usual household servants, it was partially successful, for Kent's new MPs were two soldiers, Sir Thomas Kyriell and Sir Gervase Clifton.[185] The parliament which assembled on 9 July included a solid block of Yorkist supporters, especially from shires in eastern England between Yorkshire and Essex, the Neville-dominated counties of Warwick and Worcester, and the Welsh border, where York's own influence was strong.[186] A well-chosen phalanx of councillors, servants, and sympathizers, modest though their total number might be, could have a decisive voice in the chamber.

To judge by the temper of the electors in Norfolk, this parliament would have an independent spirit. John Jenny, a supporter of John Paston's candidature, declared that:

> It is a evill precedent for the shire that a straunge man shulde be chosyn [and he had in mind Howard, who was said to have no lands in the county], and no wurshipp to my lord off Yorke, nor to my lord

of Norffolk to write for hym; for yf the jentilmen of the shire will suffre sech inconvenyens, in good feithe, the shire shall not be called of seche wurshipp as it hathe be.[187]

In fact, the assembly showed a belligerence reminiscent of 1449–50. Sir John Wenlock, therefore, might seem a surprising choice as speaker; yet when they first assembled, many members may have been uncertain and apprehensive in the unique circumstances created by the battle of St Albans, and on 11 July they chose as speaker one who was acceptable to the court but had associations beyond it. Although Wenlock had been Queen Margaret's chamberlain until at least January 1454 and had been wounded on the king's side at St Albans, he may already have forged those links with John Bourgchier, Lord Berners (who was also with the king on 22 May), which led them to found a gild together at Staines in March 1456, with a chantry where masses could be sung for the king and queen.[188]

Many of the petitions which the commons sponsored during this parliament attacked forthrightly abuses and deficiencies in the realm's administration; as in 1450, they responded to a critical situation by pressing for desirable changes. Even though an unprecedented number of their requests for administrative reform were rejected – the government was reluctant to alienate the bishops by restricting benefit of clergy, and proposals to curb the powers of sheriffs ran into the sand – their collective initiative is noteworthy.[189] One need not assume that this outspokenness was necessarily directed at members of the court or that it coincided precisely with York's attitudes, though he may have shared some of the commons' views and adopted others to his advantage in appropriate circumstances. Wenlock himself is not known to have been disowned by the commons at any stage in the proceedings: indeed, in the first session, they specifically recommended his exemption from the bill of resumption, and in the third they again assured him of repayment of his crown loans.[190]

Relations between the commons and the lords were not easy. Not only did the latter consider most of the commons' administrative proposals too extreme – and they therefore rejected them – but the agitation for the appointment of a protector found them hesitant and suspicious. Whatever leverage York was able to command in the commons, he was less successful in securing co-operation from the lords. The discussion of a new bill of resumption revealed some of the tensions present in this parliament.

The need for financial solvency and a determination to establish firm control over the royal household, which had provided the backbone of the royal forces at St Albans, probably led York to support the bill recommended by the commons in the first session.[191] The household and its expenditure were on the parliamentary agenda announced by the chancellor in his opening speech, and a special committee was set up on 9 July to examine the matter.[192] But it was the commons who introduced the bill. It referred to the household's 'outragious' debts and the harm done to its reputation by unpaid and oppressive purveyance. The commons looked back nostalgically to the 'worshipfull, noble and honorable' household supposedly kept by Henry V. By 1455 Henry VI's reputation was evidently being contrasted with the honour and success brought to the realm by his illustrious father, whose reign was taking on the aspect of a golden age in the mind of those who remembered the warrior king or had been nurtured on tales of his exploits.

The new bill's clauses were partly intended to regulate the royal family's private use of the crown's resources so that the household could be adequately funded: Queen Margaret's dower should not exceed 10,000 marks; the king's half-brothers were not exempt from its provisions; and the duchy of Lancaster's resources should no longer be used to fulfil the terms of Henry V's and Henry VI's wills. The lords' committee is the most likely body to have examined the details. Not surprisingly, the bill was considered too draconian and too restrictive of the king's prerogative. As a result, the more extreme clauses were removed before it was approved by the lords and received the king's assent: the queen was given complete exemption and so were the Tudors, and Henry VI was enabled to make further exemptions at his pleasure, with the advice of the lords but without having to seek the approval of the commons (as the original bill had requested).[193] This act of resumption was therefore a compromise, and it had a lengthy and probably stormy passage. Although introduced in the first session, when it was intended that it should take effect from the following Michaelmas, it was not accepted in its amended form until the second session.[194]

Even so, the anxiety of many to gain exemption is likely to have raised doubts that it would ever be effective. It was still a matter of lively debate when the third session opened on 14 January, and the opportunity was taken a few weeks later to reinforce its demands, on the grounds that unless many grants were resumed, the county farms would be too low to encourage qualified men to take on the office of sheriff in case they found themselves out of pocket when their term came to an end. The resistance of the lords to resumption is clear: they dissented from this further demand and to some observers this confrontation precipitated the resignation of York as protector on 25 February 1456:

> ... the duke of York and the house of commons of parliament worked hard for the resumption of royal rents, and almost all the lords resisted them, so that they went to see the king and came with him to Westminster in order that he should reject the resumption, and there in the king's presence the duke of York resigned his office and withdrew from parliament before the session ended.[195]

To accompany the act of resumption, parliament had assigned £3,935 for the household's use during 1455–56, of which £2,325 would come from the prince's inheritance while it was in the king's hands.[196]

The gulf between the speaker and presumably other MPs, on the one hand, and, on the other, York and his affinity in the commons widened in mid-November 1455. The circumstances surrounding York's appointment as protector and defender of the realm on 19 November present a series of puzzles. It has long been recognized as strange that when, on the second day of the resumed parliament (13 November), a delegation from the commons waited on the lords to discuss the protection of the realm, it was led not by the speaker, but by William Burley. Representing Shropshire, Burley was one of the most experienced MPs and a councillor of the duke of York. So far as is known, Speaker Wenlock was in no way indisposed during this parliament and so the choice of Burley to lead the delegation must have been deliberate. Its purpose confirms it. The delegation wanted York to be appointed protector and defender for the second time and on three occasions in the space of four days it urged the lords to agree.[197]

The reason which the delegation advanced for their petition was the likelihood that Henry VI would not be able to discharge his responsibilities personally. It is true that there is no incontrovertible evidence that the king suffered a major relapse in the autumn of 1455, but there are sufficient indications to suggest that he was far from well and may have been subject to periods of feebleness, either mental or physical.[198] Just before parliament was due to resume on 12 November, a great council had concluded that Henry was unable to preside at the opening; in view of the lords' later reluctance to establish a protectorate, one may assume that they would not have agreed on 11 November to nominate York as the king's lieutenant unless Henry was genuinely indisposed.[199] The commons' delegation on the 13th appreciated that there was a strong possibility that Henry might not be able to attend to his more strenuous duties in person and hence someone ought to be ordained at once to take his place. With Burley leading the delegation, there can be no doubt that York was the protector it had in mind. In any case, the duke's position after St Albans and his term as protector in 1454 allowed of no alternative: the lords were forced to agree, though their decision was couched in dignified language: 'considered the grete noblenesse, sadnesse, and wysdome of the duc of York, [and] the sad governaunce and polletique rule had in this lande the tyme that he was last protectour and defensour of the land'.

According to J. R. Lander, the speed with which the delegation met the lords, on the second day of parliament, and the insistence with which it put its demands three times in four days, indicate careful planning.[200] Moreover, within two days York was able to produce a list of the conditions under which he would accept the appointment. Thus, when the delegation returned for the third meeting with the lords on 17 November, the chancellor was able to accompany them back to their house to make the necessary announcement. York's patent of appointment was sealed two days after that, with all his conditions satisfied. The king's precarious state of health and the presence of a persistent body of opinion in the commons, led by his councillors, were the two factors that enabled York to emerge as protector once again. If the commons were less than united in advocating this step, then the replacement of Wenlock by Burley as leader of the delegation – but for no other purpose – is explained.

Why York should have wanted the powers of a protector is another puzzle. Burley and the common's delegation made much of the disorders in the realm, particularly in the west country, where Devon and Bonville were again at one another's throat. The reason for this particular outburst may have been Courtenay resentment at the way in which Bonville was ingratiating himself with the new Yorkist régime. In October the earl's sons stormed into Exeter and disrupted the sessions of the peace; on the 23rd Sir Thomas Courtenay's men burst into the house of the respected lawyer and councillor of Lord Bonville, Nicholas Radford, and hacked him to death outside; the subsequent coroner's inquest was a mockery. Radford's murder has been pronounced by R. L. Storey as 'the most notorious private crime of the century, an outrage which is distinguished from most other violent deeds of the time by the fact that it was so obviously premeditated'.[201] A week later, Devon himself joined his sons and a much larger force and occupied the city of Exeter; they advanced, too, on Powderham castle, which belonged to Sir Philip Courtenay, an ally of Lord Bonville, whose daughter had married Sir Philip's son. The outrages – threats, robberies, extortion, and assaults, even on priests and Exeter cathedral – continued during the first three weeks of November, until, on the 22nd, Bonville threatened the duke with open war.[202] It may be, as J. R. Lander suggests, that the commons' delegation exaggerated the extent of these disturbances in order to strengthen their demand that York be nominated protector; their claim that the king's subjects needed someone to whom they could 'have recours to sue for remedie and injuries and wronges done to theym' was not very persuasive in view of the existence of the council, parliament, and the chancellor, not to speak of the (admittedly cumbersome) courts of common law. Other, less publicized, motives may have been in the mind of York and his friends.

Despite his victory at St Albans, York's dominance over the government and the court was far from complete; the status and powers of a protector would considerably enhance his position and enable him to advance causes that were of immediate concern to him. Ireland was not one of them: the country seems to have been relatively tranquil at this juncture, and in any case York's authority there was not challenged by that of any other magnate. The Scottish threat had revived earlier in the summer, when James II was getting the better of the rebellious Douglases; the king and his forces then laid siege to Berwick. The government at Westminster left the relief of the fortress early in July to the northern magnates, including the new earl of Northumberland, who was warden of the east march and custodian of Berwick.[203] The emergency was long over by November. Skirmishes along the border may have continued, for King James took defensive measures in October and endeavoured unsuccessfully to galvanize the French into launching a co-ordinated attack on Calais and Berwick soon afterwards. But if these intrigues were known in England, they were not considered serious enough to be quoted by the commons' delegation in mid-November.[204] Less satisfactory was the progress through parliament of the bill of resumption. As we have seen, the commons' bill was in danger of being emasculated by the time the second session opened, and York may have felt that as protector and chief councillor he might be more able to influence the extent of the exemptions.[205] Even closer to his heart was the state of his personal finances. York's debts had increased alarmingly of late, not least because his salary and expenses as protector in 1454 had not been paid. Paradoxically enough, he may have regarded his reappointment as the only sure way of recovering some at least of what was owed him. Accordingly, in November 1455 he secured a guarantee of his due, together with an annuity of 3,000 marks that was half as much again as that granted in 1454.[206]

On a more political level, one of the most vital tests of York's authority in the autumn of 1455 was his ability to bring Calais to obedience, an achievement that had eluded him in 1454. Warwick had been nominated captain of Calais immediately after the battle of St Albans, but to gain practical control of the fortress and the garrison was exceptionally difficult. It depended on being able to convince, firstly, the garrison that the new régime had the authority to pay the soldiers' wages and, secondly, the staple merchants that it could repay their large loans.[207] Somerset had been on the point of negotiating a nationwide loan for the defence of Calais when he fell at St Albans; nothing further was heard of it, for York's position was too delicate for him to risk pursuing Somerset's appeal to the king's more prosperous subjects.[208] When parliament met on 9 July, the resumption of trade with Calais and the payment of the garrison were important priorities, not least because of the fear of a French attack to coincide with Scottish incursions in the north. A committee was set up to discuss both Calais and Berwick, and it included the treasurer and victualler of Calais (Sir Gervase Clifton and Sir John Cheyne), the new captain, Warwick, the duke of Buckingham, one of his predecessors, and Lord Fauconberg, who had negotiated with the garrison during York's first protectorate.[209] Fauconberg, in company with York's councillor, Sir Edmund Mulso, was again sent to meet the leaders of the garrison, including Lord Rivers, Somerset's former lieutenant, in mid-June and at the same time the staplers were asked for a loan. The discussions took over four months to complete, until at the end of October the merchants were sufficiently reassured to advance the government 20,000 marks – with more to come – but only at the expense of the soldiers' wages and victuals.[210] This prompted resistance from the victualler of Calais and once again the garrison responded by seizing the merchants' wool and selling it. It was by no means certain, therefore, that York would be able to fulfil his side of the bargain with the staplers unless he strengthened his own position. The desire to become protector in November may have had a good deal to do with the determination to install Warwick effectively as captain of Calais.

Not one of the foregoing reasons could safely be used to justify York's claim to the protectorship: resumption was hotly contested by many lords; the question of unpaid salary and expenses was a personal matter; and Warwick's installation at Calais and the consequent removal of Lords Rivers and Welles may not have been to every lord's liking.[211] But dangerous disturbances close at hand in the west country, in despite of the oath sworn by most lords on 24 July, might elicit a broader spectrum of agreement for such a step. That the Devon–Bonville dispute was more in the nature of a pretext for demanding York's appointment is demonstrated by the leisurely way in which action was taken against the two peers after 17 November. Parliament was not adjourned, as the commons had urged; Devon's occupation of Exeter lasted until 21 December; and skirmishes between the two sides continued in the neighbourhood of Exeter and Powderham. Bonville was able to plan retaliation in alliance with Sir Philip Courtenay, though on 15 December at a 'battle' at Clyst, just south-east of Exeter, they were worsted by the earl's men. So far all that had been done had been to remove Devon from the commission of the peace (3 December) and, rather belatedly and in response to the commons' agitation, to nominate a group of noblemen, led by Wiltshire, Arundel, FitzWarin, and St Amand, and including Bonville and Sir Philip Courtenay, to assist York (5 December). It may be that the duke was embarrassed by the lawlessness of his former ally and none to eager to take up the cause of Lord Bonville. The fighting at Clyst at last persuaded him to ride westwards. He had reached Shaftesbury when Devon came to meet him, submitted and, after Christmas, was placed in the Tower.[212]

York's hold on power was uncertain throughout the second half of 1455. His appointment as protector did not assure him unchallengeable authority, for although his commission differed in one significant respect from that of 1454, namely, that it could be terminated at the king's pleasure only with the advice of the lords, the duke's relations with several noblemen were sufficiently strained for this reservation to afford him little protection. With Henry VI less than utterly prostrate, Richard's position was even more precarious, for on 22 November Henry required his councillors 'that in all such matiers as touchen the honour, wurship and suertee of his moost noble persone, they shall late his highnes have knowelech what direccion they take in theym;...'.[213] Moreover, the lords' caution and suspicion led them in November to emphasize anew the prince's right to assume the protectorship when he reached years of discretion, and both his and his mother's interests were scrupulously safeguarded against prejudice or financial loss on several occasions during the parliament.[214] The personality and determination of Queen Margaret are factors of cardinal importance in any analysis of political realities in these years, though her activities are largely shielded from view. According to one of Sir John Fastolf's correspondents, writing from Westminster on 9 February, Henry was reconciled to having York as his chief councillor, though with somewhat reduced authority: 'and hise patent to be made in that forme [as chief councillor and lieutenant], and not soo large as it is by Parlement'. As for the dark and handsome queen, she was 'a grete and strong labourid woman, for she spareth noo peyne to sue hire thinges to an intent and conclusion to hir power'.[215] The implication is unmistakable: by February 1456 the court was restless under the constraints imposed by York's nomination as protector of the realm.

On York's handling of the thorniest problems of government during the winter of 1455–56 depended the survival of his régime. The question of Calais dogged him throughout both protectorates: at last, in December 1455, major concessions were offered to the staple merchants, guaranteeing repayment of their loans, whilst the garrison was faithfully promised 20,000 marks, along with a guarantee of future wages, within twenty days of Warwick or his deputy being admitted to the fortress. Even so, the prospects were not encouraging, and Warwick was moved in parliament to request that he be relieved of any further responsibility for Calais's defence. Still further concessions to the wool merchants were therefore needed before they would provide sufficient sums to satisfy the soldiers; these had been made by the time that parliament reassembled on 14 January 1456. The way was now open to negotiate Warwick's entry to Calais as its captain, though not until July was he actually able to sail into the port and not be resisted by the garrison. The staplers had meantime acquired a large investment in the continuance of the present régime at Westminster, with which it had made the recent agreements based on control of the customs revenue (up to £49,580), and the soldiers' loyalty was bought by payment of arrears of wages for the period up to 31 March 1455 (£24,020). As G. L. Harriss has concluded, these agreements and Warwick's eventual entry were an important achievement: slow and costly it may have been, but Warwick was to hold the captaincy for the rest of the reign, and without Calais the Yorkist lords would have been denied a refuge in 1459 and would have been hard put to return to England in force in 1460.[216]

In the west country, the Devon–Bonville dispute was still unsettled at the end of 1455, though the earl was taken into custody after Christmas. The violence continued and Devon does not seem to have been badly treated, partly perhaps because his criminal activities were considered by York to be a serious embarrassment but little more. It was an indication of the protector's weak position that he felt unable to proceed more decisively against a magnate who had once been his only prominent ally. 'This day [9 February] was my Lord Devenshire at Westminstre, and shuld have apperid, but he was countermaundid'.[217]

The protector was doubtless pleased to witness the election of Warwick's younger brother, George, to the see of Exeter in February, though the appointment is likely to have been hard-fought. Soon after the death of Bishop Lacy, Henry V's friend, on 18 September 1455, the queen's chaplain, John Hals, was chosen to succeed him. But Neville's champions were able to remind the council that on 1 April 1454 its predecessor had promised that the next episcopal vacancy should go to the young aristocrat-cleric (he was then twenty-two). Hals was accordingly induced to withdraw, and on 4 February, George Neville was provided to Exeter.[218] Ten days later, his father, Salisbury, was appointed for life chief steward of the northern part of the duchy of Lancaster, a post which considerably enhanced his dominance in the north.[219]

What caused the protectorate to founder and enabled the king, the queen, and the court to strip York of his special powers was the question of resumption. On 25 February the duke at last resigned in the face of a refusal by the king and most of the lords to contemplate further resumption of grants since 1422.[220] Richard was not cast immediately into the wilderness – for Henry VI at least was prepared to accord him the position of lieutenant for such purposes as the opening and closing of parliament, and chief councillor – but the succeeding months saw his influence dwindle and the familiar prospect opened before him of a resurgence of courtly power and his own enforced withdrawal.

Henry VI's health, the birth of Prince Edward, and the queen's strength of will created an impossible situation for a man with York's personal grievances, political objectives, and dynastic significance. So long as Henry VI could be persuaded that the duke was his enemy, there would be no security for him or his friends. Protectorships could not survive the king's recovery, for the monarch's undoubted powers were easily withdrawn; and there were always some lords who resented York's claims and his temporary ascendancy. Yet, apart from the clash at St Albans, political life during 1453–56 did not degenerate into frequent or widespread violence. These years demonstrate with unusual clarity the fundamental weaknesses of a personal monarchy: divisions deepened and mistrust grew under the uncertain rule of the listless Henry VI, whilst the embarrassing claims of a man of York's lineage and ambition could not be accommodated by (in its origin) a usurping dynasty. The more attempts were made to do so, the more incidents of conflict arose and the less likely that eventually domestic peace would be preserved. The years that followed, 1456–59, mark a decisive step toward a realization that domestic peace could not be preserved without a major alteration of direction.

Notes

1 'Benet's Chron.', p. 210, with its precise chronology, says about 1 August. BL, Royal MS. 13 C I (cited in Gairdner, *PL*, I, 130 n. 3) puts the attack as late as 10 August, though T. B. Pugh, *GCH*, III, 612 n. 214, believes this to be rather late. According to Giles, p. 44, Henry arrived at Clarendon on 7 July, rather than fell ill there on that day, as in Lander, 'Henry VI and the duke of York's second protectorate, 1455 to 1456', *BJRL*, XLIII (1960), 46 (which misdates the event to 3 July), and Pugh, *GCH*, III, 612 n. 214. *Great Chron.*, p. 186, and Stevenson, II, ii, [771], simply record the onset of illness at Clarendon. According to J. H. Ramsay, op. cit., II, 166 n. 2 (using privy seal warrants), Henry was still at Westminster or Greenwich on 7 July but had reached Clarendon by 7 August.

2 Griffiths, 'Sense of dynasty', pp. 25-8; above, p. 357.

3 Above, p. 597. The second session ended at Westminster on 2 July with a personal appearance by the king in the parliament chamber.

4 Above, p. 698.

5 Above, pp. 532-3. Inevitably stories spread that the king's collapse was brought about by sorcery (Storey, *End of Lancaster*, p. 136).

6 Flenley, p. 140; Giles, p. 44 (*subita et temeraria formidine*). Stevenson, II, ii, 771, notes that the attack was sudden and that it affected the king's head and seemed to affect his mind (*subito cecidit in gravem infirmitatem capitis ita quod extractus a mente videbatur*). For Charles VI's illness, see Lewis, *Later mediaeval France*, p. 113. For a recent opinion by a medical historian, who rejects heredity as an important factor and favours a '"schizoid personality" not unlikely to lapse into psychoses', see B. Clarke, *Mental disorder in earlier Britain* (Cardiff, 1975), ch. 7; but this diagnosis is disputed by a medical colleague in *WHR*, VIII (1977), 356. Another informed diagnosis is that of 'depressive stupor' (J. Saltmarsh, *King Henry VI and the royal foundations* [Cambridge, 1972], p. 11).

7 Storey, *End of Lancaster*, pp. 136, 252 n. 13; *RP*, V, 241; *Reg. Whethamstede*, I, 163. Several of Henry's pages and grooms stayed with him day and night during the 17 months (PRO, E403/800 m. 7 [a reward of £150]).

8 Flenley, p. 140; Giles, p. 44 (*nec sensus naturalis nec virtualis ratio regiminis*).

9 Gairdner, *PL*, II, 295-6 (19 January), reproduced in modernized English in *EHD*, IV, 272. If the new barge that was made for the king for use on the Thames was intended to afford him rest and relaxation, it failed (PRO, E403/796 m. 2, 6 [5 November, 7 December 1453]).

10 *RP*, V, 241-2; below, p. 724.

11 Their commission was enrolled on 6 April (*PPC*, VI, 166; *CPR, 1452–61*, p. 147). See Emden, *Oxford*, I, 49-50; II, 663; Talbot and Hammond, op. cit., pp. 115-16, 143, 398-9, 305, 168. For attendance by his two principal doctors, Master John Faceby, a physician, and especially Master William Hatclyf, see PRO, E403/796 m. 14; 798 m. 4; 800 m. 4; 801 m. 1, 5 (1453–55); and for Faceby's reward of £100 *per annum* for life from 20 May 1454, *RP*, V, 313. See also G. E. Burtt, 'The activities of household officials in the fifteenth century as illustrated by the Hatteclyff family' (London MA thesis, 1955).

12 *PL*, II, 108. The recovery is less reliably placed by others on 31 December or 1 January ('Benet's Chron.', p. 212; Flenley, pp. 108, 158; Gairdner, *PL*,

I, 130 n. 3). For possible signs of partial recovery in September 1454, see Clarke, *Mental disorder*, p. 179, but the evidence is very unclear.

13 C. A. J. Armstrong, 'Politics and the battle of St. Albans, 1455', *BIHR*, XXXIII (1960), 22-3, 30, 33-9; *RP*, V, 280-2, 284-5, 290; below, p. 744.

14 'Benet's Chronicle', pp. 213-14?; Armstrong, *BIHR*, XXXIII (1960), 39-44; Ramsay, op. cit., II, 229, 244-6, 303. For the surgeons attending the king after St Albans, see PRO, E403/801 m. 7 (15 July 1455); and Gilbert Kymer, dean of Salisbury and a distinguished physician who had accompanied Henry V to France as a doctor, was summoned to Windsor on 5 June (PRO, E404/33/19; *Foedera*, XI, 366.)

15 *PL*, II, 116 (or so it was thought at Lambeth on 25 May 1455).

16 Lander, *BJRL*, XLIII (1960–61), 50-67.

17 *RP*, V, 284-90, reprinted in Chrimes and Brown, op. cit., pp. 305-9.

18 *PL*, II, 127. J. R. Lander does not dispute that Gresham is here referring to King Henry (*BJRL*, XLIII [1960–61], 52).

19 For later signs of feebleness, see below, p. 775; and Clarke, *Mental disorder*, pp. 183-5, 200-2.

20 See Griffiths, 'Sense of dynasty', p. 28, for a comparison with events in 1422 and 1483. Contemporaries were agreed on the date of birth and the naming of the prince clinches it (e. g., 'Benet's Chron., p. 210; *CPR*, *1452–61*, p. 57).

21 Flenley, pp. 140-1.

22 *RP*, V, 318.

23 Above, p. 717.

24 For these stories, the first of which dates from early in 1456, see 'Benet's Chron.', p. 216; *English Chron.*, p. 79; Flenley, pp. 140-1.

25 For a reference to the queen's pregnancy on 19 August, see *HMC, Various*, I, 223.

26 *English Chron.*, p. 70; Flenley, p. 140; above, p. 717.

27 *RP*, V, 238. Cardinal Kemp took the message to parliament.

28 Vale, *Gascony*, pp. 152-3. News of the fall of Bordeaux would have reached England within days.

29 e. g., *PPC*, VI, 159 (8 October), a warning to the earls of Salisbury and Northumberland. See Griffiths, *Speculum*, XLIII (1968), 593ff.

30 Above, p. 699. It is worth recalling, too, that Somerset was Queen Margaret's councillor by 1452–53 (above, p. 262).

31 *PPC*, VI, 163. The duchess's second appeal (HL, Battle abbey 32 no. 937/4) is undated but can be placed very shortly before 13 October; Cicely could speak of childbearing with true feeling (above, p. 357). The choice of Tyrell may have been intended to calm York's indignation: he had served under Bedford and later, and his father had been one of Gloucester's affinity (Wedgwood, *Biographies*, pp. 891-2; Roskell, *1422*, pp. 236-9).

32 York may have arrived at the council on 12 November with a small entourage as instructed ('Benet's Chron.', p. 210).

33 Two other courtiers, Lord Beauchamp of Powick and his first cousin, William, Lord St Amand, had less formal supervision of the sick king (*RP*, V, 248; below, p. 761).

34 Jeffs, thesis, pp. 337-8; Wedgwood, *Biographies*, pp. 904, 814-15. A handful of other examples could be cited.

35 Respectively, Giles Brugge, Sir John Melton, and Sir Leonard Hastings (ibid., pp. 110, 583-4, 433; Rosenthal, 'Estates and finances of York', p.

190). The financial burden may also have discouraged some from becoming sheriffs (below, p. 335).

36 Griffiths, *Speculum*, XLIII (1968), 606ff; Pugh, *GCH*, III, 193-6; Storey, *End of Lancaster*, pp. 135, 231-41; above, p. 582. 'Benet's Chron.', p. 210, hints at magnate sympathy for York.

37 *CPR, 1452–61*, p. 143.

38 'Benet's Chron.', p. 210; *English Chron.*, p. 78; Giles, pp. 44-5. Because of their position as appealer and accused, the two dukes were not noted among the councillors present (*CPR, 1452–61*, p. 143).

39 Gairdner, *PL*, II, 290-2. Somerset's deeds in France should be judged (Norfolk said) by those skilled in French law, and he wanted his charges exemplified under the great seal for his own protection. This document is not a copy of Norfolk's original articles but a response to Somerset's reply to them.

40 *Great Chron.*, p. 186; 'Benet's Chron.', pp. 210-11; below, p. 739. Sometime before April 1454, a Scottish envoy, Sir James Stewart, was informed that Somerset was held on suspicion of treason (*PPC*, VI, lxiii – lxv; Dunlop, op. cit., p. 154 n. l).

41 'Benet's Chron.', p. 211; above, p. 698. Devon became a JP again on 15 December (*CPR, 1452–61*, pp. 662, 664). For his indictment in parliament on 14 March and his complete exoneration after York had declared him unblemished, see *RP*, V, 249-50; L. W. Vernon Harcourt, 'The baga de secretis', *EHR*, XXIII (1908), 508-29.

42 Bagley, op. cit., pp. 24-9; above, p. 19.

43 Gairdner, *PL*, II, 297, reprinted in modernized English in *EHD*, IV, 272.

44 ibid. Jasper Tudor was at council meetings on 21 November and 6 December 1453 (*CPR, 1452–61*, pp. 143-4; *PPC*, VI, 104-5). See R. S. Thomas, thesis, pp. 151-2.

45 According to 'Benet's Chron.', p. 211, York, Salisbury, Warwick, and Devon arrived in London on 2 February, though they had been expected for a week or more (Gairdner, *PL*, II, 297-8). For the precautions taken in London to prevent disturbances, see Peake, thesis, pp. 113-14.

46 The court would have had pleasant memories of the session at Reading in the spring of 1453 (above, p. 699). News of this prorogation was not conveyed to the assembled parliament on 11 February by the chancellor, but by the treasurer. Kemp's disapproval of the treatment of Somerset and the claims of York may have led him to refuse the commission, or else he was suffering from the exhaustion that caused his death six weeks later (*RP*, V, 238). Nor did he invite the commons on 15 February to elect a new speaker; Bishop Bourgchier did that (below).

47 'Benet's Chron.', p. 211. Note also that two leading courtiers, Wiltshire and Dudley, could still secure profitable patronage on 5 and 11 February respectively, though Dudley was required later (in July 1454) to pay £1,018 for his (*CFR, 1452–61*, pp. 73, 82, 85).

48 *RP*, V, 239. For Thorp, see Roskell, *Nott. Med. St.*, VII (1963), 79-105, and idem, *Speakers*, pp. 253-4; and for Raleigh, Wedgwood, *Biographies*, pp. 707-8.

49 *RP*, V, 240. Cf. also York's successful defence of Devon in parliament on 14 March (ibid, 249-50; above, n. 41). Lord Cromwell's petition for a large sum as security of the peace from the duke of Exeter was at first resisted in parliament between 9 and 20 March, but eventually it succeeded and

York despatched the bill for approval by the commons on 22 March; York's advocacy as lieutenant may have been crucial in a case directed against one of his and the Nevilles' rivals, Exeter (*RP*, V, 264). The new speaker, Sir Thomas Charlton, seems to have had links with both the royal household and the Nevilles, and his election on 16 February may therefore reflect the caution of the commons (Roskell, *Speakers*, pp. 255-6, 352-3).

50 *RP*, V, 249. He did not receive his patrimony, however, until November 1455 (below, p. 755).

51 Roskell, *BIHR*, XXIX (1956), 153-204, with this parliament discussed on pp. 189-92. Sickness or feebleness was regarded as a sufficient excuse; Somerset and Cobham were in prison; Lords Rivers, Welles, and Moleyns were abroad; and Lords Beauchamp and St Amand were attending the invalid king. Such fines were well known in the Irish parliament.

52 ibid., 189-90, 192. The act's effect was negligible; 45 attended out of 105 summoned. For the list of fines imposed, see PRO, E159/230, *communia, recorda*, E, m. 36.

53 *RP*, V, 240.

54 Giles, pp. 44-5; 'Benet's Chron.', p. 211 (though the date of death is mistakenly given as 13 February); *English Chron.*, p. 70. For Kemp's wisdom and the trust placed in him to bring order to the realm in November 1450, see von der Ropp, op. cit., no. 669. See Storey, *End of Lancaster*, p. 82, for an interesting assessment of Kemp.

55 *RP*, V, 240-2; Giles, pp. 44-5. The prior of St John of Jerusalem, another ecclesiastic drawn from the court circle, was also present.

56 Griffiths, 'Sense of dynasty', pp. 26-8.

57 *RP*, V, 242-4, reprinted in Chrimes and Brown, op. cit., pp. 299-302. The actual appointment had been made the previous day, 27 March; York's conditions were presented the next day, and the formal patent was issued on 3 April. The lords were just as reluctant to appear as eager despoilers of the king's authority and accordingly stressed (after the manner of 1422) the extreme necessity of this step. See, in general, Roskell, *EHR*, LXVIII (1953), 226-7.

58 It was arranged that Edward should assume the position of protector when he came of age, if he so wished. A salary of 2,000 marks *per annum* was agreed with York, as well as reasonable expenses, and minor rights of patronage were conferred on him.

59 Griffiths, 'Sense of dynasty', p. 27; idem, *Speculum*, XLIII (1968), 612-18. Moreover, there were riots in London in March–April against the men of York and Salisbury (Peake, thesis, p. 117).

60 Above, p. 288; Virgoe, *BIHR*, XLIII (1970), 148-9, professes to see a significant change on 6 December 1453 when a small meeting of York's supposed friends was held, but in view of events early in 1454 this may be premature (*PPC*, VI, 164-5).

61 Above, p. 725.

62 *HBC*, p. 85; R. L. Storey, *End of Lancaster*, p. 140, suggests, not altogether convincingly, that there were no suitably experienced ecclesiastics available.

63 R. G. Davies, thesis cited, III, xxxvi-xxxix; Emden, *Oxford*, I, 230-2; above, p. 100. For his prominence during February and March 1454, see above, p. 725.

64 Woodger, thesis cited, pp. 70-6. Bourgchier was named as archbishop by

the council at the request of the commons on 30 March, only two days after York's appointment, in view of 'his great merit, virtues and great blood'. Salisbury's nomination as chancellor came three days after that; and the licence to Canterbury to elect a new archbishop was issued a week later on 9 April (*PPC*, VI, 168). Although it would be hasty to regard the Bourgchiers as York's political adherents at this stage, their exact affiliation is not easily defined. Viscount Bourgchier had, of course, been closely associated with York in France and was his councillor by 1449–50, yet his brother William had been made Lord FitzWarin in 1449 and his other brother, John, Lord Berners sometime in 1453 (before 21 November). Their ties with Buckingham were very strong (Woodger, thesis, pp. 56-69).

65 *PPC*, VI, 168; Emden, *Oxford*, II, 1347–8. He was provided on 21 June. By contrast, the council at the same time (1 April) recommended Warwick's younger brother, George Neville, for the next vacant see.

66 Above, pp. 289-90.

67 Above, pp. 290, 307.

68 Above, pp. 348, 350; Emden, *Oxford*, II, 1187–8; idem, *Cambridge*, p.133.

69 Beaumont had been constable of England in 1445, and served as an envoy to France in 1445 and to the Scots in 1450 (*GEC*, II, 62; Ferguson, op cit., p. 178; PRO, E404/66/126). For Say, see Roskell, *Speakers*, pp. 231-3, 276-80; idem, 'Sir John Say of Broxbourne', *E. Herts. Arch. Soc. Trans.*, XIV, part 1, 25-41. Say's stepdaughter and ward married a nephew of Viscount Bourgchier and Bishop Bourgchier, and he may have owed his appointment as a councillor to them. His brother William was dean of the royal chapel (Emden, *Oxford*, III, 1649–50). For Stanley, see above, p. 302.

70 The formal nomination of Chedworth, Say, Beaumont, and Warwick on 15 April demonstrates the care taken to preserve a balance of interests among the councillors (PRO, E403/807 m. 9; 814 m. 2, 3; 817 m. 4). See also Virgoe, *BIHR*, XLIII (1970), 150 n.3, for payments to other councillors as from 15 April. A good indication of attendance is provided by *PPC*, VI, passim; a more thorough investigation is in Virgoe, *BIHR*, XLIII (1970), 148-51, 156. As after 1422, the councillors took to recording their names on warrants authorized during the king's illness (ibid., pp. 148-51; above, p. 30).

71 *PPC*, VI, 206. Nor was he in any hurry, since the matter was deferred until the next great council, scheduled for 31 October (ibid., pp. 214, 216).

72 Wedgwood, *Biographies*, pp. 44, 955-6, 703-5, 743; Rosenthal, 'Estates and finances of York', pp. 180, 181-2, 190-1.

73 Wedgwood, *Biographies*, p. 181.

74 The chronicler ('Benet's Chron.', p. 212) who noted that Somerset was expelled from all his royal offices was too sweeping: e.g., he continued as constable of Carmarthen and Cardigan castles (Griffiths, *Principality of Wales*, pp. 202, 237). The reference is probably to his replacement as captain of Calais (below, p. 731).

75 Above, p. 307.

76 As the Percy–Neville feud grew more bitter in 1454, so Cromwell was probably drawn closer to the Neville family (above, p. 583). For Andrew, see Otway-Ruthven, *King's secretary*, ppp. 154, 172-3; Emden, *Oxford*, I, 34-5.

77 *PPC*, VI, 209. The number of horses was reduced from 70 to 24.

78 ibid., 220-33. He had intended reducing it to the size of Henry V's household.

79 That this represents a contraction is indicated by the fact that in 1452–53 the queen paid wages to 151 servants (Myers, *Edward IV's household*, p. 9 n. 3, citing PRO, DL28/5/8 f. 12a-14b, printed by Myers, *BJRL*, XL [1957–58], 99-113, 391-431).

80 *HBC*, p. 79; Emden, *Cambridge*, pp. 219-20. For the much-reduced level of new exchequer payments (as opposed to reassignments) to the wardrobe during 1454 (about £6,000) compared with 1453 (in excess of £9,700) and 1455 (about £8,400), see PRO, E403/791-805 passim.

81 *CPR, 1452–61*, p. 142 (5 September 1453, confirming a mine lease concluded on the previous 20 March), 155; PRO, E403/796 m. 5 (alum seized and sold in late summer 1453); *PPC*, VI, 164 (6 December 1453).

82 *CPR, 1452–61*, p. 64 (12 December 1453), 165 (12 April 1454); *CCR, 1447–54*, p. 464 (13 April); ibid., *1454–61*, p. 12 (24 February 1455). For the staplers' debts, see below, p. 731.

83 Jeffs, thesis, pp. 79-119. See *CPR, 1452–61*, p. 203.

84 *CFR, 1452–61*, p. 86 (as from Easter for 10 years).

85 ibid., p. 222; above, p. 558. For the resulting inquiry at Dover, see KentRO, Sa/Fa. t. 2 (Sandwich treasurer's rolls, 1454–55).

86 PRO, E403/796-800 passim; below, p. 731. Aside from the staplers, the treasurer contributed £1,500 by 18 November. For London's resistance to granting loans, see Barron, thesis, p. 634. See also Steel, op. cit., pp. 274-76; *CPR, 1452–61*, p. 204.

87 Harriss, *EHR*, LXXV (1960), 30-53.

88 ibid., 31-32.

89 For talk of the siege, perhaps exaggerated for the government's purpose, see *CPR, 1452–61*, pp. 147, 171 (April 1454); for the quotation, *PPC*, VI, 175. The nervous authorities at Sandwich put the town on alert on 18 February 1454 (KentRO, Sa ACl f. 94*v*).

90 *RP*, V, 254, 256, 263, with comment in Harriss, *EHR*, LXXV (1960), 34-5, and Haward in *English trade*, pp. 299, 301-2 (though she mistakenly dates these arrangements to July). The new loan was to be repaid in two instalments: in November 1455 and November 1456.

91 *PPC*, VI, 174 (17 April).

92 Harriss, *EHR*, LXXV (1960), 36; Haward in *English trade*, pp. 304-5; *CPR, 1452–61*, p. 154.

93 According to PRO, E403/798 m. 2, 3, the decision to send Bourgchier to negotiate with the soldiers had been made by 21 May.

94 *PL*, II, 95. On 15 June, Bourgchier had been authorized to muster Lords Rivers and Welles and the men under their command (*CPR, 1452–61*, p. 176).

95 Harriss, *EHR*, LXXV (1960), 37; PRO, E403/798 m. 11. York's indenture as captain (17 July) is in *PPC*, VI, 199. On 24 July, York was granted £1,000 in cash, £1,500 by assignment, as well as £200 for Guisnes and Hammes castles and a reward of £200, the entire assignment to be a charge on the clerical tenth payable in 1455 and 1456 (Stevenson, II, ii, 501-2). Apart from the ready cash, this was no swift provision.

96 Harriss, *EHR*, LXXV (1960), 37-9. For the arrangements to repay the loans, see *CPR, 1452–61*, pp. 209, 210, 212, 226, 253; *CCR, 1454–61*, pp. 1, 5, 13, 17, 21, 22.

97 *CPR, 1452–61*, p. 166.
98 *RP*, V, 240.
99 ibid., 254-5. For the lack of a naval organization by the 1450s, see Richmond, *History*, LII (1967), 9.
100 *RP*, V, 244. Though not mentioned on the parliament roll, Shrewsbury and Sir Robert Vere were included in the commission (PRO, E403/798 m. 3; E404/70/1/68-69; E101/71/935 [the indenture]).
101 *RP*, V, 244-5; *CPR, 1452–61*, p. 156 (Bristol's anticipated £150); PRO, E403/798 m. 4. London eventually decided on 7 June 1454 to offer £300 for sea-keeping (Barron, thesis, p. 634).
102 Above, p. 731; PRO, E403/798 m. 5, 8.
103 ibid., m. 3, 4, 6; /800-6 passim. In 1457–58 the Devon and Cornwall customs were producing £748 for them (WiltsRO, 192/55 m. 2).
104 *RP*, V, 244.
105 *CPR, 1452–61*, pp. 170, 177.
106 ibid., pp. 172, 173, 175. For the *Grace Dieu*, see Richmond, *History*, LII (1967), 7; R. C. Anderson, 'The Grace Dieu of 1446–86', *EHR*, XXXIV (1919), 584-6.
107 *PPC*, VI, 184.
108 *CPR, 1452–61*, p. 178; Richmond, *History*, LII (1967), 3-5.
109 *CPR, 1452–61*, p. 179 (22-29 August). For Trollope's capture of a friendly Portuguese ship contrary to the truce, see ibid., p. 281.
110 Above, pp. 421, 423.
111 *PPC*, VI, 172; *CPR, 1452–61*, pp. 163, 202. Sir William Wells, who had been Talbot's deputy since 1446, had his position regularized at the same time (ibid., pp. 163, 179).
112 Otway-Ruthven, *Medieval Ireland*, pp. 385-6. No new payments were made by the exchequer to the Irish lieutenant in 1454 (PRO, E403/796, 798, 800 passim).
113 Above, p. 411; Nicholson, op. cit., pp. 354ff (p. 362 for the appeal to Henry VI). James II's envoy to the captive duke of Somerset received short shrift from the council sometime before April 1454 (*PPC*, VI, lxiii-lxv).
114 Above, p. 405; Storey, *EHR*, LXXII (1957), 614 and n. 4. Who else could be induced to undertake a commission that was badly funded by Westminster? No new payments were made to Poynings by the exchequer during 1454 (PRO, E403/796-800 passim).
115 ibid.; above, p. 406.
116 Storey, *EHR*, LXXII (1957), 614 and n. 6; *CFR, 1452–61*, p. 98; RP, V, 217. The Nevilles' commission was extended on 9 August 1454 for 20 years. Although Salisbury had been granted £1,000 in November 1453, he received nothing further as warden of the west march during York's ascendancy (PRO, E403/796 m. 3 and 796-800 passim).
117 Longleat MS 3988 m. 6. See *Great Chron.*, p. 187, and *London Chrons.*, p. 164, for a vague reference to York's suppression of 'great trouble' in Wales. He may not have had an opportunity to visit Wales before the end of August (Griffiths, *Speculum*, XLIII [1968], 618-21).
118 Griffiths, *NLWJ*, XIII (1964), 256-68; idem, *WHR*, II (1964–65), 213-31.
119 PRO, E28/83/63, 64, 37 (wrongly dated to 1453 in the file). Apart from officers of the principality, the council wrote to the lords of Cemaes, Llandovery, Gower, and Laugharne, and to the bishop of St David's.
120 Cardiff CL, Brecs. MS 16 m. 7. These events, as recorded in the

17th-century history of Gruffydd's family, printed in *Cambrian Reg.*, I (1795), 61-2, are substantiated in significant particulars by contemporary sources (Griffiths, *WHR*, II [1964–65], 220 and n. 28, citing especially PRO, E364/44 m. 69*d*; KB27/771, *rex*, m. 23*d*).

121 A detailed account of what follows, with full references, is in Griffiths, *Speculum*, XLIII (1968), 589-632; see also Storey, *End of Lancaster*, ch. X. There are a few extra details in P. Kelly, 'Henry Holand, duke of Exeter, 1430–75' (Keele BA dissertation, 1980), ch. 3.

122 Above, p. 582. For Neville retainers, see Pollard, *Northern Hist.*, XI (1976), 52-69.

123 Above, pp. 582-4.

124 Gairdner, *PL*, II, 296.

125 This is argued fully in Griffiths, *Speculum*, XLIII (1968), 612-15. For York's appeals, reminding Exeter of their close blood relationship, see HL, Battle abbey, 32 no. 937/3 (8 May, with the quotation).

126 Griffiths, *Speculum*, XLIII (1968), 612, 618-21; above, p. 735. The itinerary in Rosenthal, 'Estates and finances of York', p. 199, is a sketchy one.

127 Devon's two sons, Thomas and Henry, invaded the city by night with more than 400 men, thereby disrupting a meeting, at which Bonville was present, that was negotiating a royal loan (Lander, *BJRL*, XLIII [1960], 60).

128 Storey, *End of Lancaster*, ch. XI, for a full account. See also A. Carrington and W. J. Andrew, 'A Lancastrian raid in the wars of the roses', *Journal Derbs. Arch. and Nat. Hist. Soc.*, XXXIV (1912), 33-49; XXXV (1913), 207-44, both printing indictments from PRO, KB9/12. As R. L. Storey suggests, it is difficult to view these disturbances as anything but the product of local enmities; most of the participants, incidentally, were attached to the Staffords in the 1440s and 1450s (Rawcliffe, *Staffords*, pp. 223-5, 233, 239-40).

129 See above, pp. 717-18, for the extent of the king's recovery.

130 Above, p. 728.

131 Flenley, p. 141; *Foedera*, V, ii, 61. C. A. J. Armstrong, whose classic study 'Politics and the battle of St. Albans, 1455', *BIHR*, XXXIII (1960), 1-72, contains the fullest account of these months (8-26), unaccountably places the formal release on 4 February. See 'Benet's Chron.', p. 212.

132 *Foedera*, V, ii, 61; *CCR, 1454–61* p. 9, 44; *English Chron.*, p. 78. It was Buckingham, Wiltshire, and Roos who were said to have conducted Somerset from the Tower on 26 January.

133 'Benet's Chron.', p. 212.

134 Both Dudley and Beauchamp were paid a salary as councillors as from 21 February, whereas Salisbury and Worcester ceased to be paid on that day (PRO, E403/800 m. 11, 13; 817 m. 11).

135 *CPR, 1452–61*, p. 226; *Great Chron.*, p. 187; 'Benet's Chron.', p. 212.

136 *Foedera*, V, ii, 61-2; *CCR, 1454–61*, p. 49.

137 *Foedera*, V, ii, 62; G. L. Harriss, 'The struggle for Calais: an aspect of the rivalry between Lancaster and York', *EHR*, LXXV (1960), 39. The warrant states that York requested his own removal. The household peer Lord Stourton was still captain of Rysbank tower, and Somerset's lieutenants at Calais, Lords Rivers and Welles, had never been removed by York (ibid.; *CPR, 1452–61*, p. 209).

138 *HBC*, p. 85; 'Benet's Chron.', p. 212; Giles, p. 47.

139 *HBC*, p. 102.

140 *Foedera*, V, ii, 62; *CCR, 1454–61*, p. 13. Stafford had arrived at Pontefract by 28 March (StaffsRO, D1721/1/1 f. 396). Some doubt remains as to whether Exeter enjoyed complete freedom after his release from Pontefract (Storey, *End of Lancaster*, p. 253 n. 17). For the enmity noted between York and Buckingham at this time, see 'Benet's Chron.', p. 213. Giles, p. 47, is mistaken in stating that the earl of Devon was released at the same time (see Storey, *End of Lancaster*, pp. 253-4).

141 *CFR, 1452–61*, p. 119; *CPR, 1452–61*, pp. 217, 218. York had previously enjoyed the custody free of charge.

142 ibid., pp. 208, 217. See, by contrast, the appointment of two household servants to the charge of Exeter and Newcastle-upon-Tyne castles in April–May (*CPR, 1452–61*, pp. 227, 250).

143 'Benet's Chron.', p. 213; Giles, p. 47; Flenley, p. 108; *English Chron.*, p. 171.

144 Giles, p. 47; *Reg. Whetehamstede*, I, 164. The meeting at Leicester was arranged by 16 April, probably at a council held at Westminster during 15-18 April to which York, Salisbury, and Warwick were not invited (PRO, E403/801 m. 1; Virgoe *BIHR*, XLIII (1970), 152 n. 3; Armstrong, *BIHR*, XXXIII (1960), 14). C. A. J. Armstrong (ibid., 11-13) prefers to date the summoning of this council after the withdrawal of the Yorkist lords from the court: the matter is unclear.

145 ibid., 1-72.

146 ibid., 14-15. Though Rosenthal, 'Estates and finances of York', p. 199, says Sandal, the contemporary abbot of St Albans spoke of the north more generally (*Reg. Whetehamstede*, I, 164). Fabyan's belief that they went to Wales is unlikely to be correct (*Chronicle*, p. 629). It is possible that Warwick did not venture far from Warwick castle, where he is recorded on 12 April and 17 May 1455 (P. Chatwin, 'Documents of Warwick the kingmaker in the possession of St. Mary's church, Warwick' *Trans. and proc. Birmingham arch. soc.*, LIX [1938], 4-5; WorcsRO, 899: 95/Box 6/111 m. 2).

147 *RP*, V, 280-1.

148 Above, p. 694. To this end, York sought and received a papal dispensation from the oath he had sworn in March 1452 not to resort to force again (*Reg. Whetehamstede*, I, 163).

149 Armstrong, *BIHR*, XXXIII (1960), 12-13. For a convincing dismissal of military intent, see ibid., 13, 16, 23, 25.

150 There may have been an understandable reluctance on the king's part to summon a full parliament in the normal way, though that would probably have involved a delay. Hence the unusual summons to shire representatives.

151 ibid., 15-16; Giles, pp. 47-8; above, p. 726. See 'Benet's Chron.', p. 214, for the size of the Yorkist force.

152 Armstrong, *BIHR*, XXXIII (1960), 19, quoting PRO, C81/770/10,079. According to 'Benet's Chron.', p. 213, Lords Clinton (a Yorkshire magnate) and Powis (a marcher lord) were also in York's company.

153 Pembroke had sympathized with York in 1453–54; Devon had supported him before, Lord Fauconberg was Salisbury's brother, and Lord Berners was a moderate man and brother of Viscount Bourgchier. For the lords present, see Armstrong, *BIHR*, XXXIII (1960), 21, 24; and for the difference of opinion on tactics in the royal camp, Giles, pp. 47-8.

154 The letters are printed in *RP*, V, 280-1, and the second also in Gairdner, *PL*, III, 23-4. They were formally inserted on the parliament roll by the victorious Yorkists in order to vindicate their actions and demonstrate their goodwill under extreme provocation.

155 Armstrong, *BIHR*, XXXIII (1960), 26-39; Gairdner, *PL*, III, 26, partly reproduced in modernized English in *EHD*, IV, 275-6 (the pro-Yorkist 'Stow relation', whose reliability is discussed by Armstrong, *BIHR*, XXXIII [1960], 1-2); the so-called 'Dijon relation', an account written in England for the duke of Burgundy, is printed and commented on in ibid., pp. 63-5, 2-3, and translated by *EHD*, IV, 276-7.

156 Above, pp. 669ff; Gairdner, *PL*, III, 25, 27; *Reg. Whetehamstede*, I, 167. For the retainers of York and the Nevilles (the latter including Sir John Neville, Salisbury's son, and Sir Robert Ogle), see Armstrong, *BIHR*, XXXIII (1960), 27, 29; Pollard, *Northern Hist.*, XI (1976), 57, 68.

157 Armstrong, *BIHR*, XXXIII (1960), 26-8; to the estimates given there must be added the 7,000 noted in York's camp by 'Benet's Chron.', p. 214. Apart from the Nevilles, father and son, Lords Clinton, Powis, and Cobham and perhaps Viscount Bourgchier were with York, and Norfolk lay close at hand and sympathetic. For York's nervousness about delay, see Armstrong, *BIHR*, XXXIII (1960), 67.

158 Above, p. 717; Armstrong, *BIHR*, XXXIII (1960), 30, 33, 38-9. See the so-called 'Fastolf relation', written for Sir John Fastolf and remarkably objective in tone (ibid., 65-7, with comment on 3-5). Buckingham is portrayed as admitting to Mowbray herald that the king had not been shown York's letters. Norfolk was married to Buckingham's half-sister.

159 ibid., 34-7. The same strong suspicion falls on York's supposed address to his men before the fighting began.

160 ibid., 66 (the 'Fastolf' relation).

161 Armstrong, *BIHR*, XXXIII (1960), 40-50, with the known dead named on 67-72. A plan of the town in 1455 is in Ramsay, op. cit., II, 182, based on an earlier plan of 1700.

162 *EHD*, IV, 277, translated from the 'Dijon relation' in Armstrong, *BIHR*, XXXIII (1960), 64.

163 Below, p. 806.

164 Including some of Somerset's servants (e.g., Armstrong, *BIHR*, XXXIII (1960), 48 and n. 2). Wiltshire is said by one source to have been responsible for leaving the royal banner propped against a house before he fled (ibid., 43).

165 Gairdner, *PL*, III, 28-9, reproduced in modernized English in *EHD*, IV, 276. Cf. ibid., 277 (the 'Dijon relation').

166 The involvement of St Albans abbey in the events of that day is reflected in the long account in *Reg. Whetehamstede*, I, 171-3.

167 Armstrong, *BIHR*, XXXIII (1960), 49-50, 67-72. But the more recently discovered 'Benet's Chron.', p. 214, puts the dead at about 100.

168 Above, pp. 741-5.

169 Armstrong, *BIHR*, XXXIII (1960), 51; 'Benet's Chron.', p. 214; Flenley, pp. 108, 142; *Brut*, p. 522.

170 *RP*, V, 279.

171 The council expressed a certain nervousness about Exeter's detention because the duchess of Suffolk was constable of Wallingford (*PPC*, V, 245).

For uncertainty about the date of his confinement there, above, pp. 765-6.

172 Gairdner, *PL*, III, 44. Cromwell was relieved of the office of king's chamberlain in May 1455 or soon afterwards, presumably following the battle (Wedgwood, *Register*, xli-xlii).

173 'Benet's Chron.', p. 215; Armstrong, *BIHR*, XXXIII (1960), 56, 59-60.

174 Gairdner, *PL*, III, 44.

175 *RP*, V, 280-2. It seems that at first the blame was to be heaped on the dead Lord Clifford, Sir Ralph Percy and Thomas Tresham, as well as Thorp and Joseph (Armstrong, *BIHR*, XXXIII [1960], 57-8).

176 Gairdner, *PL*, III, 44. Of two other bills intended to victimize Thorp and Joseph further, only one passed all its stages in the second session of this parliament (12 November–13 December 1455) (Armstrong, *BIHR*, XXXIII [1960], 61 n. 5).

177 ibid., 61-2. The oath was recorded on the parliament roll and in 'the book of the council', and those who were not present on the 24th would swear when they arrived (*RP*, V, 282).

178 Gairdner, *PL*, III, 31. The appointments were officially recorded a little later (*HBC*, p. 102 [treasurer, 29 May]; Griffiths, *Principality of Wales*, pp. 202, 238 [Carmarthen and Aberystwyth, 2 June]; above, p. 735).

179 Harriss, *EHR*, LXXV (1960), 40-1; above, p. 732. Warwick's indenture was formally concluded at a great council on 4 August (*RP*, V, 309).

180 The appointment was made on 2 June, as from 22 May (Armstrong, *BIHR*, XXXIII [1960], 21 n. 1, 52). After the crown-wearing on 25 May, the king returned to Windsor, and then (by 7 June, not 7 July as in ibid., 54) to Hertford, with the queen and prince, until parliament opened on 9 July (PRO, E403/801 m. 4). It may be noted that Berners was one of those who stood surety for the duke of Exeter in January 1456 (Lander, *BJRL*, XLIII [1960–61], 54-5; *CCR, 1454–61*, p. 109). In the duchy of Lancaster, Warwick was appointed steward and constable of Monmouth and the Three Castles for life on 31 May, and Edward, son of Viscount Bourgchier, steward of Kidwelly for life a week later; but the new receiver- and attorney-general on 31 May, after the death of William Cotton at St Albans, was Nicholas Sharpe, a professional auditor in the service of the king and queen and a product of Eton and King's (Somerville, op. cit., pp. 640, 648, 399-400).

181 Bishop Boulers, the prior of the Hospital of St John of Jerusalem, the dean of St Seurin, Bishop Thomas Kemp of London, and Jasper Tudor, earl of Pembroke were at a council on 4 June (Virgoe, *BIHR*, XLIII [1970], 152 and n. 3). Lords Stourton and Sudeley, Bishop Kemp and Bishop Waynflete, were often summoned in the following months to council meetings (e.g., *PPC*, VI, 264ff). Boulers, incidentally, may have ingratiated himself with the new rulers, for during the parliament he and his cathedral were given special immunity from royal officers (*RP*, V, 304).

182 ibid., 342, 329; above, p. 699. Sir William Oldhall's attainder of 1453 was also reversed, though he was not an MP (*RP*, V, 451-2).

183 ibid., 335; *Reg. Whetehamstede*, I, 181. It was so proclaimed in London and elsewhere (Flenley, pp. 109, 142-3). C. A. J. Armstrong (*BIHR*, XXXIII [1960], 62) notes that Gloucester's former servant, Sir Roger Chamberlain, was an MP in 1455.

184 *PL*, II, 117-18, reprinted in Chrimes and Brown, op. cit, pp. 303-4;

Wedgwood, *Register*, p. 236. For Howard, see A. Crawford, 'The career of John Howard, duke of Norfolk, 1420–85' (London MPhil thesis, 1975)

185 *PPC*, VI, 246; *RP*, V, 450; Wedgwood, *Biographies*, pp. 521-2, 194-5. Clifton was treasurer of Calais at the time.

186 Wedgwood, *Register*, pp. 232-42. Five of Viscount Bourgchier's affinity were also returned (Woodger, thesis, p. 296).

187 *PL*, II, 120-1, reprinted in Chrimes and Brown, op. cit., p. 304. Most of the hereditary Howard lands in East Anglia were not held by John at this time (Crawford, thesis, p. 19).

188 Roskell, *Pub. Beds. Hist. Record Soc.*, XXXVIII (1958), 30-2; idem, *Speakers*, pp. 258-62. The reason for Wenlock's resignation from the queen's service is unknown.

189 *RP*, V, 333, 328, 332, 323, 326. More obvious, less controversial administrative abuses were dealt with. See Wedgwood, *Register*, pp. 212-21. The jingoism of the commons is reflected in an unsuccessful bill, introduced in the third session, that would have seriously restricted the activities of foreigners (*RP*, V, 334).

190 Roskell, *Pub. Beds. Hist. Record Soc.*, XXXVIII (1958), 32.

191 *RP*, V, 300-20. According to *Reg. Whetehamstede*, I, 249, the commons, after lengthy discussion, were unanimous in presenting the bill. Wedgwood, *Register*, p. 217, is mistaken in believing it to have been introduced in the third session; see Wolffe, *Royal demesne*, p. 138 and n. 53. But see below, p. 751 for its passage.

192 *RP*, V, 279-80. The new treasurer was probably responsible for the review of the realm's finances which was reported to parliament when it met (PRO, E403/801 m. 3, 5 [28 May, 15 July]). The lords' committee consisted of household officials led by Sir Thomas Stanley, the chamberlain, Lord Sudeley, the steward, and Lord Cromwell, lately chamberlain; the earl of Worcester, a former treasurer of England; Bishops Waynflete and Chedworth, and Viscount Beaumont.

193 Wolffe, *Royal demesne*, pp. 138-40. The numerous exemptions included the king's and other collegiate foundations, and many household officials; the presence of John Merston, cofferer of the household throughout the reign, and his wife, and Joan Asteley, Henry's old nurse, reflected the king's personal wishes (*RP*, V, 319).

194 B. P. Wolffe implies that it was introduced and accepted in the first session (*Royal demesne*, p. 138 and n. 53), but references to the prince of Wales, the protectorate, the earl of Douglas, Lord Stanley, and to Warwick as captain of Calais suggest that it was accepted at least a week after the opening of the second session (12 November). This need not preclude a few farsighted persons taking out new grants during November, to run from the previous Michaelmas (ibid., appendix C).

195 'Benet's Chron.', p. 216 (translated). The problem of the sheriff's farm had arisen not long before, when Sir John Tempest, sheriff of Lincs., had asked that he be charged not with the traditional farm but with a realistic sum of revenue; the problem seems to have been most serious in Lincs. (*PPC*, VI, 263; Jeffs, thesis, pp. 269-73). Cf. the pardon on 28 August 1455 to the late Sir Edward Hull, a former sheriff of Somerset–Dorset, for all his debts (*CPR, 1452–61*, p. 249).

196 *RP*, V, 320-1; *CPR, 1452–61*, pp. 295-8. This sum was augmented by £2,245, though not until July 1456. Wolffe, *Royal demesne*, p. 140 n. 62, gives a

total of £6,520, but he has included a few items twice and he implies that the whole was assigned to the household during the 1455–56 parliament. In fact, just over £6,000 was authorized at the exchequer for the treasurer of the household between Michaelmas 1455 and Michaelmas 1456 (PRO, E403/805-7 passim).

197 *RP*, V, 284-90, reprinted in Chrimes and Brown, op. cit., pp. 305-9. For Burley, see Roskell, *Trans. Salop Arch. Soc.*, LVI (1960), 263-72.

198 Above, p. 718. The king had been well enough to thank parliament in person when it adjourned on 31 July (*RP*, V, 283).

199 Lander, *BJRL*, XLIII (1960–61), 56; *RP*, V, 284; *CPR, 1452–61*, p. 273. York had not been present at this council.

200 Lander, *BJRL*, XLIII (1960–61), 57-9.

201 Storey, *End of Lancaster*, pp. 167-68.

202 ibid., pp. 166-71; Lander, *BJRL*, XLIII (1960–61), 60-3. Bonville's grandson was married to Salisbury's daughter, and on 12 November 1455 Bonville received a general pardon. See also G. H. Radford, 'The fight at Clyst in 1455', *TDA*, XLIV (1912), 252-65, based on PRO, KB9/16.

203 Nicholson, op. cit., pp. 370-3; Flenley, p. 142; *Three Chrons.*, p. 70. On 9 July the king congratulated the bishop of Durham, the earls of Northumberland and Westmorland, Lords FitzHugh and Scrope, and others for defending, victualling, and relieving Berwick by 3 July, and they were excused from attending parliament (*PPC*, VI, 247-9). James, earl of Douglas had earlier fled to England and surrendered his castle of Threave to Henry VI; though given a £500 annuity (which was exempt from resumption) on 4 August 1455, and other subventions from 15 July onwards, Threave could not be relieved (*CPR, 1452–61*, p. 245; PRO, E403/801 m. 6).

204 Stevenson, I, 319-22; Macrae, thesis cited, pp. 197-213. The exchequer made little cash available to the sentinels of the north after St Albans, though Northumberland at Berwick received £268 on 16 December (PRO, E403/805 m. 6).

205 Above, p. 751.

206 *RP*, V, 287. As far as the exchequer is concerned, the duke seems to have received none of this in 1455 or 1456 (PRO, E403/800-7 passim).

207 Above, p. 732; Harriss, *EHR*, LXXV (1960), 40-1.

208 ibid., 39-40; *PPC*, V, 187 (misdated to 1442); VI, 236. See Harriss, *HJ*, VI (1963), 4.

209 *RP*, V, 279.

210 Harriss, *EHR*, LXXV (1960), 40-3. Warwick was already exercising the powers of a captain: he had granted licences to fishermen before 22 November (*CPR, 1452–61*, p. 300).

211 It may be noted, too, that when sheriffs were chosen on 4 November, the number of household nominees had risen compared with 1454, whilst supporters of York and Salisbury had dwindled to one each (Sir Walter Devereux in Glos. and Sir Thomas Harrington in Yorks.). York may have needed to take an initiative to recover his position before it crumbled further (Jeffs, thesis, pp. 174ff).

212 Lander, *BJRL*, XLIII (1960–61), 63-5; Storey, *End of Lancaster*, pp. 171-3; *PPC*, VI, 267; Flenley, pp. 109-10. For angry exchanges on 22-23 November between Devon and Bonville, each accusing the other of outrages, see HL, Battle abbey, 32 no. 937/1-2.

213 *RP*, V, 290; cf. Roskell, *EHR*, LXVIII (1953), 226-7.

214 *RP*, V, 288-9; *CPR, 1452-61*, p. 273. See also *RP*, V, 293, 297, 302-3, 330. For arrangements to pay £1,000 a year to Edward and his servants until he was 8, transferring all other of his revenues and patronage to the king, in whose household he would reside until he was 14, see ibid., 290-3 (12 November).

215 Gairdner, *PL*, III, 75. Such qualities in the queen, coupled with her French birth and perhaps her antagonism to York, may have been responsible for the appearance of rumours during the winter of 1455–56 that Edward was not her son; an apprentice-at-law from Gray's Inn, John Helton, was executed on 23 February for distributing bills to this effect ('Benet's Chron.', p. 216). For her looks, see *CMilP*, I, 18-19 (1458).

216 Harriss, *EHR*, LXXV (1960), 43-5; *RP*, V, 341, 295-300; Wedgwood, *Register*, p. 218; Haward in *English trade*, p. 306.

217 Lander, *BJRL*, XLIII (1960), 64-5; Storey, *End of Lancaster*, p. 173; Gairdner, *PL*, 76 (for the quotation).

218 Above, p. 762; *PPC*, VI, 168; Emden, *Oxford*, II, 856-7 (Hals); II, 1347–49 (Neville). A number of the councillors of April 1454 were councillors in the winter of 1455–56 (above, p. 727).

219 Somerville, op. cit., p. 421.

220 'Benet's Chron.', p. 216; above, p. 751. The post-St Albans régime had not been able to attract significant loans, except from the treasurer, Viscount Bourgchier (£2,167), and Archbishop Bourgchier (£100), between 22 May 1455 and 25 February 1456 (PRO, E403/801 m. 4; 805 m. 1, 6; 806 m. 11). This was a measure of the régime's instability.

24   The Royalist Reaction, 1456–1460

A change of régime

English government in the late 1450s presents a curious aspect. The king and queen, their young son, and their court and advisers spent a good deal of their time far from London and Westminster. Between September 1456, when Henry took up residence in or around Coventry, and mid-July 1460, when he was escorted back to London virtually a prisoner, considerably more than half his time was passed in the midlands. Not since Henry V's day had the central executive been parted from its supreme head for so long a period.[1] It might be said that a king had much to gain from an extended acquaintance with parts of his realm which he rarely saw, but Henry VI undertook his lengthy provincial residence because he was more or less forced to do so by political tension in the country and growing tumult in London. At the same time, he was unable to maintain the firm grip on administration and policy-making that had been Henry V's *forte* even when he was campaigning abroad. Rather did the migration of the court to Coventry and its neighbourhood inaugurate a period of administrative difficulty, governmental paralysis, and intensified political faction, during which the king gradually lost a good deal of his authority to suppress disorder and preserve domestic peace.

During these years, the council appears to have shed much of its sense of corporate identity, partly because England was governed in practice from two widely separated centres, and partly because relations within the governing aristocratic élite were strained to breaking-point. Although York had been relieved of his office of protector on 25 February 1456, the councillors with whom he had co-operated during the previous six months continued to meet for a little while longer.[2] Nor was the duke rendered immediately powerless, for Henry at least valued his advice, even if the queen did not.[3] Thus, in May, by which time Margaret had taken her son on a tour of her midlands estates – even as far as Chester which would soon be part of Prince Edward's patrimony – York became involved on behalf of the king in a war of words with James II of Scotland.[4] While the duke was visiting his Yorkshire castle of Sandal, James repeated his threat of invasion by sending a provocative letter (dated 10 May) to Henry VI. It was York who replied on 26 July in Henry's name, recalling James to his traditional allegiance as a vassal in words reminiscent of Edward I and disdaining to take the threats seriously. He even sent a message of his own to the Scottish king toward the end of August, chiding him with cowardly tip-and-run raids across the border.[5] But already major changes were afoot which would drastically diminish whatever remained of York's influence with the king.

The summer vacation saw important changes in the personnel of the principal offices of state, and these were a prelude to a new direction in policy. Henry and his queen had been parted many times before and during the summer months it probably seemed a wise precaution to take the two-year-old prince away from the unhealthy capital. Margaret, moreover, was always a conscientious, even tenacious, landlord and may have welcomed the opportunity to inspect her dower possessions in central England.[6] The contemplated political changes could be fashioned more easily in the calmer atmosphere of a loyal provincial city than in the disorderly capital, and consequently Henry VI followed his wife to the midlands during late August 1456.[7] It was at Coventry that the new appointments were announced.

A suitable occasion presented itself with the illness – perhaps even the death – of the keeper of the privy seal, Thomas Liseux. On 24 September he was replaced by Lawrence Booth, his successor as dean of St Paul's. This cleric's early career owed everything to the queen's patronage; succeeding his elder brother as Margaret's chancellor on 7 March 1451, he was provided to the great see of Durham in September 1457.[8] His appointment as keeper of the privy seal set the tone for what followed. At a great council held in Coventry on 5 October, Viscount Bourgchier was replaced as treasurer of England by John Talbot, earl of Shrewsbury; though by no means a fervent partisan of the court (he had incidentally taken no part in the battle of St Albans), he was the brother-in-law of the earl of Wiltshire and at no time compromised his family's loyalty to the Lancastrians. A. J. Pollard regards him as 'a weak man content to follow where others led'.[9] Six days later, the king's confessor, Bishop Waynflete, took Archbishop Bourgchier's place as chancellor.[10]

If the Bourgchier brothers had indeed represented the spirit of accommodation between the Yorkist lords and the king's court, their moderation was now cast aside in favour of loyal and obedient servants securely attached to the king and queen. The invitation to Edmund, Lord Grey of Ruthin to join the council on 28 October enlisted an east-midlands lord whose attendance as a councillor during 1456–58 gave no hint that he would desert to the Yorkist side at Northampton in July 1460.[11] By the end of October 1456, therefore, those who supervised the realm's administration and advised the king were members of the late-Lancastrian court and had little or nothing in common with York or the Nevilles.

Communication between the departments of state and a peripatetic king presented its own problems. The royal messenger service was put under unwonted strain in conveying messages and instructions between the king and those of his ministers and councillors still in London, and in ensuring that adequate supplies of cash reached the royal household on its travels.[12] Council meetings continued to be held at Westminster, even though Henry and some of his advisers were in the midlands. On other occasions, councillors met in the king's presence wherever he might be and they then took decisions that had to be communicated to the officials at Westminster. Aside from the officers of state, relatively few lay lords (and no commoners) were among the king's more regular councillors in the late 1450s (as far as one can tell from the meagre surviving records): Wiltshire, who was as loyal a supporter of the Lancastrian crown as could be found; Lord Dudley, a senior household confidant; the dean of St Seurin, who was still in exile from Gascony; and the prior of the Hospital of St John of Jerusalem.[13] Others who were present less often included Bishop Chedworth of Lincoln, Viscount Beaumont, who was the queen's chief steward, and Lord Beauchamp of Powick, all three of whom were prominent courtiers.[14] By the autumn of 1456 a committed royalist régime was in being in which neither York, the Nevilles, nor the Bourgchiers had any part to play.[15] Even the duke of Buckingham was probably unhappy at recent events:

> ... it is seid the Duke of Bukyngham takith right straungely that bothe his brethren [the Bourgchiers] arn so sodeynly discharged from ther officez of Chauncellerie and Tresoryship, and that among othir causeth hym that his opynyon ys contrary to the Whenes [queen's] entent and many other also, as it is talked.[16]

According to one observer, '... the gret princes of the lond wer nat called to Counceil bot sett A-parte'.[17]

Yet even in these years, particularly urgent and serious problems dictated the summoning of larger, great councils to either Westminster or Coventry, and to these a wider range of lords was invited, including the Bourgchiers, the Nevilles, and the duke of York – and occasionally even representatives of the shires as an alternative to parliament.[18] To convene a full parliament at Westminster was unthinkable for the government in the late 1450s, for London's turbulence would have been accentuated by the arrival of lords, knights, and gentlemen with their retinues; in any case there was no guarantee that York would not be able to manipulate an assembly for his own purposes, or that the commons would not launch into a series of embarrassing proposals for reform, as they had done in 1455–56. Only when weighty matters of state, such as the peace of the realm, or aristocratic dissensions, or the pope's plans to stem the Turks in south-eastern Europe, needed to be discussed was the king prepared to consult more widely and even his critics and opponents.[19] Inevitably these meetings were far from amicable and often tense. At Coventry especially the king and his entourage were given to upbraiding the Yorkist lords for their lack of co-operation, accusing them of disloyalty. During the great council held there in October 1456, when the governmental changes were announced, it was reported that

> ... my lord of York hath be wyth the Kyng and is departed ageyn in right good conceyt wyth the Kyng, but not in gret conceyt wyth the Whene; and sum men sey ne hadde my lord of Bukyngham not haue letted it my lord of York had be distressed in his departyng.

At other times, the Yorkist lords refused to turn up at council meetings.[20] The failure of Henry VI and his court to show magnanimity and offer reconciliation, and their determination instead to leave London and humble the Yorkists by charging them with disloyalty and worse, provided the conditions in which personal relations ruptured and political life was irrevocably damaged.

The king and the queen

By 1456 Henry was a pathetic shadow of a king. His instinctive humanity caused him to strive intermittently for a reconciliation with his opponents, but at best his unsuccessful efforts were well-meaning; at worst they were impractical and theatrical, as witness the famous 'love-day' of March 1458.[21] By nature inclined to be generous and forgiving, his compassion and compelling desire to pardon became a pious obsession in the years following his breakdown.[22] Even after the battle of Ludford Bridge in October 1459, he was willing, out of reverence for God and St Edward the Confessor (whose translation feast fell on 13 October), to receive those who were prepared to submit to him.[23] Two months later, 'preferryng Mercy bifore Justice', he modified the effects of the act of attainder against the Yorkist lords so as to allow, amongst other things, a large annual pension of 1,000 marks to the duchess of York and her young children 'that have not offended ageynst us'.[24] He still cherished his favourite foundations of Eton and King's and made sure that grants and bequests to them were protected by parliamentary acts.[25] But his personal initiation of warrants was rare.[26]

Those who could observe Henry in these years were struck by his passivity in public. He seems to have taken no part in the various battles between 1455 and 1464 at which he was present. He appeared confused at St Albans in 1455, and on other occasions he fell easily and apparently without resistance into the hands of either his enemies, as at Northampton in July 1460, or his rescuers, as at St Albans a year later.[27] A contemporary poem about the battle of Northampton has Henry saying 'I folowed affter [the lords], I wist never why'.[28] It may be worth recalling at this point that the one quality which chroniclers writing after 1453 unanimously recognized in the king was his simplicity.[29] If the memory of octogenarians can be trusted, we have a vivid picture of him on several occasions towards the end of the 1450s when he visited Westminster abbey to discuss his tomb. Not yet forty years of age, he was morbidly anxious to prepare, not an imposing and defiant effigy such as the younger Richard II had commissioned about 1397, but rather a vault in which his body would soon be placed. One afternoon he measured with his own feet its dimensions, commanded a stone-mason to follow with a crowbar to mark the spot (and the scratches can still be seen on the floor of Edward the Confessor's chapel), and he leaned heavily on the shoulder of Sir Richard Tunstall, his chamberlain, when the discussions with the abbot became long and tiring.[30] Either because of bitter disillusion with the political world from which he could not escape, or through mental feebleness, or both, Henry VI was inclined to abandon his responsibilities, and his movements and actions were largely dictated by his wife.

Contemporary chroniclers give the impression that Margaret of Anjou's dominance of her husband was far more complete in the late 1450s than ever Suffolk's or Somerset's had been earlier. Even if the statement of one writer that by this time 'The quene with such as were of her affynyte rewled the reame as her lyked' and was trying to persuade Henry to abdicate in favour of Prince Edward, has in it a substantial element of slander injected by Yorkist propagandists, others were expressing not dissimilar opinions.[31] One Londoner acknowledged that Margaret was 'more wyttyer then the kynge, and [he added significantly] that apperythe by hys dedys'. Dr. Thomas Gascoigne, the embittered chancellor of Oxford university who was writing about 1457, noted with marked apprehension that after the king fell ill, Margaret became more prominent, proceeded to rule England, and was responsible for taking Henry and their son to Cheshire.[32] Contemporaries now found her a determined and ruthless woman, and one was moved to comment 'that euery lord in Englond at this tyme durst nat disobey the Quene, for she rewled pesibly al that was done About the Kyng, which was A gode, simple, and Innocent man. . . .'[33]

Not only were Henry's own perambulations in the midlands prompted by the queen, but the government of the realm and the management of his and the prince's households came increasingly under her masterful direction. This was easily achieved, for although the households of the king and queen were sometimes separately billeted in the midlands (the burden on a monastery, town, or castle would otherwise have been intolerable), they continued to share the services of a number of officials, as indeed they had done ever since Margaret's arrival in England.[34] This domestic situation had its problems, as John Holstun-liche, a clerk in Henry's kitchen, discovered after he accompanied Margaret and the prince to Tutbury in May 1456.[35] Despite repeated instructions that he should return to the king's service, Prince Edward's controller and chamberlain countermanded the orders so persistently at the queen's direction that Holstunliche, after nearly two years of a shuttlecock existence, 'of his sayd occupacion was discharged and anotherman pit on his place'.

Margaret's proposal that Lawrence Booth should become bishop of Durham after the death of Robert Neville on 8 July 1457 carried a similar authoritative tone. The king recommended his own chaplain and doctor, Master John Arundel, but by 22 August Booth had been provided to one of the most coveted bishoprics in England. It was not that Arundel was unacceptable to Margaret (for he soon received ecclesiastical patronage from her former chancellor and Lawrence's brother, Archbishop Booth of York); it was simply that Booth's claims as keeper of the privy seal and her chancellor were stronger on all grounds. Arundel eventually received promotion to the smaller see of Chichester in January 1459, probably with the queen's full backing.[36] Later that year, the queen's part in securing the see of Coventry and Lichfield for John Hals is reasonably clear. One of her chaplains since 1445, Hals was the queen's chancellor in 1457–59, and after his disappointment at Exeter in the closing weeks of York's second protectorate, she had sponsored his appointment as dean of Exeter cathedral in October–November 1457, 'considering the hearty and immutable desire that we have to our said clerk's preservation at this time'; his eventual provision to an English bishopric was assured.[37] It was Margaret, too, who had insisted on York's removal as protector in February 1456, even though the king was far less hostile to him, and it was she who forced the pace in 1459 at a council meeting at Coventry where the Yorkist lords were condemned.[38]

Coventry: government from the provinces

The choice of Coventry as the geographical focus of Lancastrian rule during 1456–60 had much to be said in its favour. According to historians' calculations, based on the poll-tax returns of 1377, the size of its population made it the third city in the realm; its prosperity was squarely based on the cloth trade, for which it acted as an important mart; and it lay nearer the heart of England than either Bristol or York, the two provincial cities that were larger.[39] Coventry's relationship with the royal family was a special one, for it had traditional links with the earls of Chester and the English princes of Wales, and as a consequence of Margaret of Anjou's frequent visits it became known as 'the queen's secret harbour'.[40] As recently as September 1451 it had capitalized on the king's presence in the city to petition for a new charter that would make Coventry a city and county like Bristol; after civic officials had travelled to London to work out the details, it acquired a new status and its own sheriff in November.[41] Coventry's citizens proved to be fiercely loyal to the Lancastrians, and most of its MPs in Henry VI's last years had some sort of link with either the king's household or the government departments at Westminster; doubtless it recognized the value of inviting well-connected officials to represent it in the commons. To take one example: John Brown, a local Warwickshire man, was also a senior exchequer official when he was elected to the successive parliaments of 1455–56 and 1459.[42] Several of the city's merchant houses would have been able to offer hospitality to the royal family, and Margaret stayed in Richard Wood's house in 1457 when she and her lords and ladies watched the famed Coventry plays, nibbling green ginger, oranges, apples, and other delicacies by the by.[43] There were also four religious houses in the city which could help to accommodate the court, and indeed when parliament met there in November 1459, the priory's chapter house hosted the meetings. A large carved figure of Henry VI, which probably originally stood in the house of the White Friars, is testimony to the affection in which the king was held in Coventry.[44]

The city's geographical position had much to commend it in 1456. It lay within convenient reach of a number of the queen's more valuable dower estates, especially those centred on Leicester, Tutbury, and Kenilworth, whose castles could be utilized by the royal households.[45] Formerly part of the duchy of Lancaster, they had accommodated kings and their entourages before and could do so again. Coventry also had good communications north-westwards to Chester and north Wales, and westward to the Welsh march, though access to the southern counties of the principality (Carmarthenshire and Cardiganshire) would be more difficult through the mountain passes of mid-Wales. It is significant that it was during the court's long sojourn at Coventry until October 1457 that Prince Edward was invested with his substantial patrimony, including the principality of Wales and the county palatine of Chester. The similarly autonomous franchise of Lancashire, which remained part of the duchy of Lancaster, lay immediately adjacent.

The royal family could feel secure in this part of the country, and Henry VI himself had his own boyhood memories of visits to Warwickshire in the care of his mentor, Richard Beauchamp.[46] The king and queen reposed a confidence in the gentry of this region which proved fully justified when they turned out in large numbers to protect their royal patrons.[47] After the manner of Richard II's plans in the 1390s, the Lancastrian court, under the direction of Margaret of Anjou, looked to Cheshire, Lancashire, and north Wales as a bastion of loyalist power and a reservoir of cash and retainers in the late 1450s. If their legendary pugnacity could be harnessed by the Lancastrian crown, then the courtship would have been well worth while.[48] The 1440s and 1450s saw north Wales, along with the county of Chester and to some extent Lancashire, fall under the tutelage of Cheshire landowners led by the Stanleys. Sir Thomas (Lord Stanley from 1455) was controller and then chamberlain of the king's household, and in 1437 he had acquired the small marcher lordships of Mold and Hawarden; his possession of the Isle of Man gave him regal status and even a kingly title, and it was a shrewd move to entrust him with the custody of the disgraced duchess of Gloucester after 1441. Stanley was justiciar of north Wales and Chester until his death in February 1459, whilst his kinsman John Stanley, usher of Henry's chamber, was constable of Caernarvon castle and sheriff of Anglesey for life.[49] Lord Sudeley was constable of Conway castle.[50] Thus, whereas close personal supervision of the community was often sacrificed to certain local interests, the Cheshiremen would find it relatively easy to exploit north Wales if required to do so, and hence these counties and the Cheshire plain were of crucial importance to the Lancastrians in the late 1450s. The significance of the household's grip on this area had been highlighted in 1450, when an attempt had been made to prevent York's arrival from Ireland.[51]

The southern counties of the principality offered a prospect that was not quite so promising. Although the justiciar of south Wales since 1447 was Lord Beauchamp of Powick, a number of Herefordshire men had long been installed in office there; in view of York's abundant estates in the southern marches, several of these officers were more sympathetic to him than to the Lancastrians, and were less likely to do the queen's bidding than their colleagues from Cheshire further north. Moreover, Somerset's hold on Aberystwyth and Carmarthen castles ended abruptly with his death at St Albans, and York promptly seized the constableships for himself.[52] Hence, when the court broke free from the second protectorate, and decided to move closer to the Welsh border, it appreciated that strenuous campaigning would be needed in south Wales in order to make it as dependable as the north.

Edmund Tudor, earl of Richmond and the elder of the king's half-brothers, was in south-west Wales by 30 November 1455, when he was staying at the Pembrokeshire palace at Lamphey of the bishop of St David's, John de la Bere, the king's almoner.[53] His mission was probably to reassert central authority in south Wales, where the independently-minded Gruffydd ap Nicholas was behaving as if he had unchallengeable powers.[54] Edmund remained in the area throughout the winter, close to the principality counties and his brother's lordship of Pembroke, for Gruffydd strongly resented such high-ranking interference in what he had grown to regard as his exclusive sphere of influence; still in June 1456 he and Edmund were reportedly 'at werre gretely in Wales'.[55] Gruffydd had occupied not only Carmarthen castle, but also the mountain fortress of Carreg Cennen and even the duchy of Lancaster's coastal castle at Kidwelly. But from the long struggle Edmund eventually emerged victorious, for by August 1456 he was in possession of Carmarthen. In the meantime, however, the political adjustments following the court's removal to Coventry had put a new complexion on his success. The constable of Carmarthen and Aberystwyth castles was none other than the duke of York and in August 1456 some of his Herefordshire and marcher tenantry and retainers moved swiftly to assert his authority there, regardless of the presence of the king's half-brother.

It was later alleged that on 10 August 1456 a force of about 2,000 men set out for west Wales under the command of Sir William Herbert of Raglan and Sir Walter Devereux of Weobley, his brother-in-law, both of whom were prominent retainers of the duke of York.[56] The force was well armed and well led by a leaven of substantial esquires and gentlemen of the Herbert–Devereux affinity from York's marcher estates. They seized Carmarthen castle, imprisoned Richmond, and pressed on to take Aberystwyth. They issued commissions and held sessions, posing as the rightful authority, presumably in the name of York. And even Gruffydd ap Nicholas seems to have been prepared 'to have the gode wille of Sir William Herbert yf he wold'.[57] Richmond was soon released – one could hardly keep the king's half-brother a captive for long! – but he died shortly afterwards at Carmarthen on 1 November; perhaps his recent experiences had shortened his life.[58]

Herbert and Devereux had meanwhile been summoned to the great council then meeting at Coventry; the latter was taken into custody and sent to Windsor castle, whereas Herbert, though committed to the Tower of London, secured bail and then fled to Wales.[59] He was at large by 25 October when, it was later alleged, he mustered men in the Neville and York lordships of Abergavenny, Usk, Caerleon, and Glamorgan. The queen turned with great speed to the general task of harnessing royal power in Wales; in particular, she travelled through the border counties, offering full pardon to Gruffydd ap Nicholas and his sons on 26 October in a successful bid to win their loyalty and isolate York's supporters, whom she resolved to bring to trial in the spring of 1457.[60] On 10 March a price (500 marks) was put on Herbert's head and the king and his entourage made their leisurely way to Hereford, via Evesham, to hold a commission of oyer and terminer in the first week of April.[61] A host of charges was laid against the Herbert–Devereux affinity for a catalogue of alleged offences that went back several years and had been committed throughout the southern marchland as well as in west Wales. In the event, the leaders were not treated with exceptional severity, perhaps because the aim of the court was to prise them from York's side rather than turn them into outlaws.[62] Herbert accordingly submitted to the king at Leicester and on 7 June 1457 received a general pardon; Devereux, who may have been the leading insurrectionist, was gaoled for a time and does not seem to have been freed until February 1458. The constableships of Carmarthen and Aberystwyth castles had been transferred from York to Jasper Tudor on 21 April 1457 in return for £40 *per annum* as compensation. In strategic terms it was a good bargain for the court and the queen at a moment when the prince's new council was embarking on an energetic campaign to assert its authority in the princely territories. As far as south Wales was concerned, the earl of Pembroke became henceforward the dynasty's lieutenant, mobilizing the region's resources on behalf of the court, promoting its security from his own extensive lordships in the south-west, and enjoying the support of the leading Welsh gentry. On 1 December 1457 Jasper authorized a major reconstruction of the defences of Tenby, where the massive stonework of the walls and gateways today are largely a legacy of his encouragement and partial financing.[63] On 1 March 1459 he headed a commission (including his father, Queen Katherine's husband) to arrest some Carmarthenshire men who had links with York; and at about the same time, he installed reinforcements in Carreg Cennen and Kidwelly castles after some of York's sympathizers had attacked them.[64] On 23 May Jasper was elected a knight of the garter: though this chivalric order had lost a certain amount of its military *cachet* during Henry VI's reign, its members still enjoyed great distinction and Jasper's election confirmed the high regard in which he was now held as a member of the royal family and its leading representative, under Prince Edward, in Wales.[65]

The presence of the household establishment in north Wales and north-west England had conferred considerable benefits on the Stanleys, had restricted the opportunities open to native-born Welshmen, and assured the king of a bastion of power in the late 1450s. Most of these officers managed to secure exemption from the acts of resumption or else, like Sir Thomas Stanley, were reinstated soon afterwards.[66] In the process, effective and efficient administration was seriously undermined and inadequate supervision led, in Merioneth above all other counties, to social anarchy. In the south, political rivalries among a largely absentee officialdom had encouraged enterprising Welsh gentlemen to seize what amounted to local independence.[67] Henry VI had neither the shrewdness nor (after 1453) the energy to remedy this state of affairs, and if Jasper Tudor and Prince Edward's council, directed from the midlands by the queen, showed a stronger will to exert a distant authority, it was only because they were anxious to enlist Wales and Cheshire in the service of the Lancastrian crown.

The prince's council was a powerful instrument in the queen's hands. She attempted to use it to establish her personal control over the principality and Cheshire, not to speak of more distant estates in the Cornish peninsula and elsewhere in England. Although nominally Prince Edward's advisers, the councillors who were appointed to manage his affairs on 28 January 1457 were under her thumb: decisions in his name were taken with their advice, but it was her assent that gave them force.[68] The men who were nominated to this council ensured her dominance. They included Archbishop Booth, a man of Cheshire origins who had been the queen's chancellor in the past; his younger brother Lawrence, keeper of the privy seal and Margaret's chancellor more recently; Bishop Waynflete, the king's confessor and chancellor of the realm; Bishop Boulers, whose household affiliations went back a long way and whose see coincided with many of the prince's and queen's properties; Bishop Stanbury of Hereford, formerly one of the king's chaplains, whose diocese was also close at hand; the duke of Buckingham's heir (who died in 1458), and the earl of Shrewsbury, treasurer of England, both of whom had vital interests in the marches; and the earl of Wiltshire, Viscount Beaumont, Lord Dudley, and Lord Stanley were four courtiers of the first rank. Within a further month the hereditary patrimony of the princes of Wales was assigned to them on behalf of young Edward, as from Michaelmas 1456; it was thenceforward their responsibility to manage his estates, supervise his officials, authorize his expenditure, collect his revenue, and file his archives. All but £863, which he was committed to pay annually to the king for his domestic expenses until he reached the age of eight, was now his – or rather at the disposal of 'our dearest mother the queen'.[69]

The prince's central officials brought to this essentially aristocratic council a mastery of the detailed management of his interests, and the most influential of them were seconded from the king's and queen's establishments. Robert Whittingham was made receiver-general as early as 26 September 1456, presumably in anticipation of the inheritance passing to Edward, for his appointment was formally announced within the first weeks of the court's residence at Coventry. A king's serjeant, usher of the chamber, and the son of a former treasurer of Calais, Robert was an experienced financier; he had also entered the queen's service, married one of her ladies-in-waiting, and later became keeper of her great wardrobe. Whittingham, therefore, afforded Margaret direct access to the prince's financial resources.[70] On 25 January 1457, Giles St Lo was appointed keeper of Edward's great wardrobe. A man who had grown old in Henry VI's service, St Lo was the queen's butler by 1446–47 and an usher of her chamber; he too had taken advantage of his position to court and then marry (as his third wife) one of the queen's ladies, and he was the messenger entrusted to convey the joyous news of the prince's birth to the city of London on 13 October 1453. The detailed running of the prince's household was therefore under the close scrutiny of one of Margaret's most trusted servants.[71] Edward's attorney-general, who was appointed on 20 February 1457, was Thomas Throckmorton. A Worcestershire lawyer whose family had served the Beauchamps faithfully, his connection with the queen seems less close: indeed, from 1451 he had been in the earl of Warwick's service, but what attracted the attention of the court was his proven expertise in legal and administrative matters gained in the employ of Westminster abbey on its Gloucestershire estates, the bishop of Worcester, and the abbot of Evesham. Throckmorton knew the west midlands like the back of his hand, and in any case he and his father were well known to a prominent courtier, Lord Sudeley.[72] Finally, the chief steward of Edward's newly-acquired lands was none other than Viscount Beaumont, councillor, courtier, formerly constable of England, and himself steward of the queen's lands ever since she had been granted them in 1445.[73]

Thus, the prince's council was dominated by the queen's men: nothing could be done without her permission, and the resources of his patrimony were directly open to exploitation by the Lancastrian court. The councillors soon set to their task of tightening control over the princely territories to the west and north. Some of them travelled widely to impose the reality of Lancastrian rule. In 1457 they consigned a number of lax officers in south Wales to gaol and in September 1458 visited Carmarthen to audit the accounts.[74] In August 1459 Robert Whittingham, accompanied by several of the prince's knights and gentlemen (perhaps for protection), was in north Wales holding judicial sessions at Beaumaris and Caernarvon; other councillors went on to Carmarthen and Cardigan the following month.[75] On yet other occasions, the major officials in Wales travelled to Coventry to report to Edward's council.[76]

No significant changes were required in the personnel of government in either Wales or Chester. Lord Stanley continued as justiciar and chamberlain of north Wales and justiciar of Chester until his death in February 1459, when he was succeeded as chamberlain by Lord Dudley and as justiciar of Chester by the earl of Shrewsbury. Lord Beauchamp was still justiciar of south Wales when Henry VI was deposed, though Lord Audley, who was chamberlain there, fell at Blore Heath in September 1459. At Chester, Sir Richard Tunstall, a Lancashireman who was one of the king's carvers and household officials, was appointed to the chamberlainship on 27 February 1457.[77]

Lancashire was under secure Stanley control in these years, and only when Thomas died in February 1459 was it really necessary to make important changes in order to safeguard Lancastrian influence. Richard Molyneux, Stanley's son-in-law, replaced him as escheator of Lancashire on 12 February and Sir Richard Tunstall as baron of the Lancaster exchequer and receiver of the palatinate.[78] Stanley's other important post was that of chief steward of the duchy estates south of the Trent; in 1459 that went to the earl of Wiltshire.[79] These appointments sustained the court's position in the north-west following Stanley's demise. That his son and heir, also called Thomas, was not given the royal confidence may be explained by his marriage to one of the earl of Salisbury's daughters; later in the year, indeed, he declined to oppose the earl at Blore Heath and only escaped attainder by the intervention of the king. Whether Lord Thomas inclined to the earl out of conviction and kinship or out of pique may never be known; but whatever attitude the court had adopted towards him it would have run the risk of losing his support.[80] The Lancastrian grip on the duchy of Lancaster was strengthened further after the attainder of the Yorkist lords in the Coventry parliament of November 1459. Those offices which Salisbury held for life were stripped from him: on 6 December, Viscount Beaumont ousted him from the chief stewardship of the northern estates of the duchy, and on 17 December, Shrewsbury succeeded him and his son Warwick as steward of the Yorkshire lordship of Pontefract and constable of its castle.[81] Thus, as with Wales and Chester, that part of the duchy that lay close to the midlands headquarters of the Lancastrian régime was delivered into the hands of courtiers and loyal servants obligated to the queen.

Outside these imposing royal franchises, the authority of the court was less direct. It depended on the good will and co-operation of the aristocracy, both lay and clerical, and especially on the magnates, and only the annual autumnal nomination of new sheriffs presented an opportunity to make congenial changes in shire administration. In terms of seignorial geography, the move to Coventry was inspired, for a notable number of courtier-magnates had estates in the west midlands that could be marshalled in ways not dissimilar to those applied in Wales, Cheshire, Lancashire, and the queen's territories. Maxstoke castle in north Warwickshire was a popular residence with the duke of Buckingham, who had numerous manors in the vicinity; Lord Sudeley's fine castle, rebuilt in the 1440s in the newest style, was situated in north Gloucestershire; Lord Beauchamp of Powick was a Warwickshire landowner and so was the earl of Wiltshire; and the earl of Shrewsbury had large estates on the Welsh border. The two Warwickshire manors of Solihull and Sheldon had been made over to the king's half-brothers in 1453 and at about the same time they acquired some valuable manors in Derbyshire and Nottinghamshire.[82] The gentry of Warwickshire may have been a proud and independent crew (in what county were they not?), but at Coleshill there resided the king's carver, Sir Edmund Mountford, who offered hospitality to the king and his entourage on at least one occasion in these years.[83] The dioceses of the region – Hereford, Worcester, and Coventry and Lichfield – were presided over by accommodating chaplains who owed their promotion to the king's patronage.[84]

The one striking exception to this pattern of aristocratic landownership was Richard Neville, earl of Warwick. The Beauchamp estates of his wife formed a wedge thrust into the heart of the Warwickshire countryside, but the earl spent most of his time at Calais from 1456 onwards and was never able to re-create the unchallengeable position of his father-in-law, Richard Beauchamp, in the area.[85] The court's presence at Coventry weighted the scales yet further against any likelihood of his reviving the influence of Warwick castle for the time being, and it is worth recalling that when the Yorkist lords discussed their plight and planned their strategy, they did so in their Yorkshire castles or at Ludlow. The Neville fortress at Warwick was only a few miles distant from Kenilworth, but in the late 1450s it was almost surrounded by the estates of the royal family and Lancastrian lords; it was effectively isolated from the Nevilles' Yorkshire lands and the duke of York's broad acres in the Welsh march.[86] As Salisbury discovered in September 1459, the court's dominance of the west midlands could successfully control communication between Yorkshire and the march. Warwickshire's administration was well nigh monopolized by household officials in the late 1450s, among them Henry Filongley, the sheriff appointed in November 1458 who had local connections and was keeper of the king's great wardrobe; and his successor as sheriff, Sir Edmund Mountford. Both he and George Ashby, clerk of the signet to both the king and the queen, were returned to parliament in 1459, the former for the county and the latter for the borough of Warwick.[87]

And yet the eyes of the court were raised to wider horizons as it made a concerted effort to insinuate its servants and sympathizers into more distant shrievalties. Since these offices were filled annually, it was a speedy and effective way of extending political influence into spheres of administration, finance, and justice, not to speak of parliamentary elections in 1459. An unusually high proportion of men with household connections were pricked as sheriffs during each of the four years 1456–59.[88] In addition, Buckingham's official, John Heton, was nominated in Bedfordshire–Buckinghamshire in 1458, and Hugh Egerton, another of his men, in Staffordshire in the same year.[89] By contrast, very few of the duke of York's associates became sheriff in these years: Sir John Barre in Gloucestershire (November 1456), Sir Thomas Green in Northamptonshire (1457), and Sir William Skipwith in Lincolnshire (1458) seem to stand alone. Not one of Salisbury's retainers appears on the list.[90]

The establishment of a provincial régime at Coventry during 1456–60, with an interval between November 1457 and April 1459 when the court returned to the south-east, should not therefore be regarded exclusively as a retreat from London but also as a political stratagem that conferred important benefits on the queen and her friends. It is ironic that Henry, devoted son of the church as he was, should have found himself in a city that had been the pre-eminent centre of lollardy in midland England earlier in his reign.[91]

Financing a provincial régime

The administrative complications of governing England from Coventry and the west midlands had a financial dimension. The wheels of the offices of state at Westminster could turn regardless of the king's perambulations, though major expenditure beyond the routine, and non-customary expedients of raising extra cash, could not be authorized without his or his council's knowledge. Although a provincial 'capital' offered better opportunities to tap the resources of the prince's patrimony, the queen's dower lands, and some of the duchy of Lancaster estates, the lengthy absence of the king and his court from the centre of government created obstacles to the smooth exploitation of the crown's resources and to ready access to the exchequer. In any case, despite the grant to the king for life of tunnage and poundage and the customs in 1453, the needs of the government and the household were already well beyond the financial resources available, and additional establishments for an adult queen with a mind of her own and a young prince made matters worse. Much of the surplus cash from Wales, Chester, and the duchy of Cornwall was devoted to Edward's household and council from 1456, whilst some of the richest properties in the duchy of Lancaster were in the queen's hands. The most recent parliament (1455–56) had made no new grants of taxation, and to judge from the mood of the commons it would have been mistaken to think that additional taxes could be imposed in the near future.[92]

The first concern of the king's advisers was Henry's own household. The question of its solvency had been viewed with growing alarm for ten years and more, and the successive bills of resumption since 1449 had been primarily designed to alleviate its indebtedness. Their success had been limited, as the continued complaints of creditors reminded royal officials. The move to the midlands in September 1456 raised new difficulties which the king's ministers strove to overcome.

On several occasions in the past, Henry VI had relied on his household establishment to organize certain exceptional enterprises which required the services of dependable agents and involved considerable financial outlay.[93] In 1456 his household servants were directly affected by the journey to Coventry and once again assumed the role of reliable agents to be employed as required. Yet on no occasion in the past had the household, through its treasurer, been assigned significant financial resources apart from the considerable sums pumped into the wardrobe and great wardrobe from the exchequer. Indeed, Westminster remained the principal paymaster of the household during the late 1450s, even though existing difficulties of obtaining regular supplies of cash were accentuated by newer problems of communication. On several occasions, messengers were sent to Westminster to bring cash from the treasury to supplement the all too uncertain collection of assigned revenues at source, whether it be customs duties at the ports or other monies, for tallies cut in favour of the household were just as prone to failure as anyone else's.[94]

Many of the household's debts to London merchants and financiers were now twenty years old, and in order to preserve confidence in the business world, these merchants were no longer issued with replacement tallies at the exchequer, which (experience taught them) were unlikely to be any more reliable than the original issue; instead, during 1456–59 the government offered a more formal guarantee of repayment by means of letters patent so that, for example, William Beaufitz, a prominent citizen, fishmonger, and broker, could recover £1,515.[95] The same device was employed to ensure that the household itself had a more secure income. On 21 June 1456 letters patent earmarked specific sources from which the treasurer of the household, John Brekenok, could be supplied with £2,588 as from Michaelmas 1455.[96] Moreover, as certain major prerogative items became available, so they were reserved for the household: £200 from the temporalities of the vacant bishopric of Durham, for instance, were assigned on 18 July 1457 to the treasurer of the king's chamber, William Grimesby, for Henry's personal use.[97] On 12 April 1458 Henry Filongley, the keeper of the great wardrobe, which organized the physical removals between Westminster and the midlands, was reserved as much as £2,000 from the prerogative sources – wardships, marriages, reliefs, and temporalities – in place of £2,619 which had been assigned him by letters patent on 20 October 1456 but which had not materialized.[98] If this was an attempt to assure the household a guaranteed income supplementary to subventions from the exchequer, it was by nature fortuitous and variable, and may not in fact have significantly increased the actual resources at the household's disposal.[99]

Distraint of knighthood, a money-raising expedient well known to Henry's ministers, was introduced once more to produce extra cash, not only for the repayment of the occasional loan, but also to provide John Brekenok with £667 for his expenses.[100] Indeed, distraint was employed during a three-year period (1457–59) in order to catch as many prosperous persons as possible in its net. The barons of the exchequer assembled the sheriffs' reports, but the cash that materialized from fines and pardons went straight to the household.[101]

The king's interest in the more fabulous methods of increasing wealth by transmutation of base metals had not flagged, for the naive monetary theory that 'Abundance of coinage genders universal prosperity' was powerfully attractive to a government in financial straits. Certain 'honest men' who had supposedly mastered this dubious art had come to the king's attention by May 1456, when a committee of London merchants was instructed to study their claims and credentials and report in haste by 1 July.[102] Others were authorized to study the writings and theories of 'wise ancients' and, if this proved productive, to go ahead and transmute metals, despite earlier statutes forbidding the practice.[103] The findings may have been sufficiently encouraging to warrant the appointment on 9 March 1457 of a more imposing commission of learned friars, clerks, and half-a-dozen London merchants to examine carefully how the king's debts could be paid off in good, new coin straight from the transmuter's furnace. It is either a sign of promising, preliminary results, or, more likely, increasing desperation on the part of the court after more than a year in the midlands that on 2 November 1457 a panel of even greater distinction was constituted to maintain the momentum of the investigations: four bishops and five abbots (who could provide the element of faith that was essential in dealing with this industry of illusion), and four lords and six judges.[104] One may safely assume that the king's household benefited not one groat from these quests among tricksters and the ancients.

Queen Margaret took advantage of her proximity to some of her dower estates to insist that her receivers bring as much hard cash to her coffers as possible rather than allow most of it to be expended on the internal costs of the estates themselves. Thus, even as early as 1451–52 she was receiving from the honour of Leicester three times the receipts of 1448–49 (£50), and the total crept higher until in 1458–59 alone it reached £221.[105] Even those estates nearer London were milked in the same way: her properties in Essex, Hertfordshire, and Middlesex produced a high cash return throughout the 1450s but especially during 1457–58 (£495).[106]

The prince's council adopted a similar attitude towards the principality and Cheshire. After years of neglect and government by absentee officials, the ability to realize the full financial potential of south and north Wales was seriously compromised. Thus, by 1457–58 there were no receipts at all from Aberystwyth and north Cardiganshire.[107] The councillors did their brisk best by means of personal intervention and a harsh exploitation of the prince's extensive judicial rights. During the 1440s and early 1450s there had been a marked decline in the size of the general fines imposed on the Cardiganshire and Carmarthenshire communities in return for prematurely dissolving the annual great sessions; by 1452 the Cardiganshire figure had fallen to as little as £100 and that of Carmarthenshire to £133 by May 1456, though that was a small price to pay for freedom from criminal investigation and trial. In 1458 both sums were doubled. Substantial recognisances for future good behaviour were extracted from prominent persons at Chester in November 1458, and these (amounting to about £2,200) may have been only part of what was demanded from the Cheshire gentry as a whole.[108] The visits paid to south Wales in 1457 and September 1458 by Edward's councillors were designed to improve financial administration: they supervised the annual audit, increased rents and farms, and sent defaulting officials to gaol.[109] The very creation of Edward as prince had produced its own financial windfall, for it enabled his advisers to cancel certain fees and annuities on the grounds that new warrants under Edward's seal had not yet been issued.[110] On 23 July 1459 the prince and his council were urged to keep up the pressure and 'to go to all such places in England and Wales and there stay as long and return as speedily as shall seem good for the increase of the revenue of the principality, duchy [of Cornwall] and the counties [of Chester and Flint]'.[111] The proceeds of this financial campaign were channelled to the prince's household and, of course, to the king's, where they were available to enlist liveried retainers in Cheshire and elsewhere in 1459.[112]

By the 1450s, the crown's credit with its wealthiest subjects was such that loans were few and far between. The quite small number that were forthcoming were offered repayment, not by exchequer tallies but by more authoritative letters patent.[113] The largest single group of loans came from the treasurer of England himself and may be regarded as an occupational hazard of office which grew larger as other loans disappeared. Shrewsbury lent £2,411 during his term in office (1456–58) and Wiltshire, his successor, £1,000 in February 1459. It must remain very doubtful that they were repaid before the collapse of the dynasty in 1461.[114]

The merchants of the Calais staple were practically deaf to appeals for further sums of money for the household when they were already underwriting the protection of Calais itself – certainly unless there were major trading concessions. The granting of licences to export up to 2,000 sacks of wool on behalf of the king was intended to provide the household with a proportion of the customs duties imposed at the ports.[115] The wool was destined for the Mediterranean, but it was strongly suspected in commercial circles that it did not always find its way through the straits of Morocco or across the Alps. Before the staplers would consent to a loan for Henry VI's household on 11 December 1458, these licences would have to be abandoned.[116] In return for £1,000 per quarter-year for the next four years, the staplers required an end to these licences and permission for themselves to recover their money by exporting wool to Calais free of duty. Even so, much of the loan was an illusion, for a high proportion of it – four-fifths after the first year – would be in the form of uncashed obligations which had been given to the staplers in exchange for earlier loans to the government. Thus, the staplers' investment in the Lancastrian régime in December 1458 was a modest one, especially in comparison with the prizes brought into Calais by the earl of Warwick's privateering and the merchants' payments to his soldiers.[117] It would have been unwise of the staplers to have rejected out of hand an appeal from the Lancastrian court, but they were not prepared to finance it to any substantial degree.

Their reluctance to do so was confirmed by the changes in financial administration that immediately preceded the agreement of 11 December. At the end of October 1458, when the court had temporarily returned to the south-east, changes were made in which political considerations were uppermost. On 30 October, Wiltshire replaced Shrewsbury as treasurer of England, and on or about the same day Sir Thomas Tuddenham, Suffolk's former friend of unsavoury reputation among the household entourage, replaced the skilled administrator John Brekenok as treasurer of the household.[118] Probably on the same occasion, John Wood, a former under-treasurer of England and exchequer official, was made keeper of the great wardrobe; his reputation too was tarnished, particularly in the eyes of the wool merchants, for in 1455 he was accused in parliament of embezzling £3,000 from the customs payable on wool shipped from London to ports other than Calais. To place him in charge of the great wardrobe, just when it may have been trying to acquire sources of income independent of the exchequer, was provocative to say the least.[119] These appointments, while they may have enhanced the court's (and the queen's) control of the financial departments of government, are unlikely to have inspired confidence in the king's creditors or encouraged the wool merchants to lend generously. As a result, the agreement with the latter shortly afterwards brought little practical comfort to the hard-pressed king and his household.[120] The court showed a monumental lack of political sensitivity and commonsense in this, as in other of its actions, in the late 1450s. In particular, its determination to rule through an unquestioningly loyal faction, preferably far from London, led to miscalculations that directly undermined its ultimate stability.

London and the crown

In the late 1450s the peace of London was shattered by a succession of riots and alarms that seriously prejudiced the stability of English society on a wider plane and fatally damaged relations between the capital and the government. News of tumults in London spread quickly – it certainly found a prominent place in all contemporary chronicles – and the climate of opinion in the city had a direct bearing on its readiness to aid the Lancastrian monarchy during its last years. One of the most prominent sources of unrest was the small community of alien merchants. By 1456 anti-foreign sentiment had a long and sorry history behind it, though it had rarely manifested itself with the violence that was to mark the years 1456–58. What is also noteworthy about the eruptions of these years is that they were directed exclusively against the Italians. On the surface this may appear surprising, for the Italian merchants were not as highly privileged as the Hansards, nor was the overall balance of their trade decisively in their favour. They were less well organized than the German and Baltic merchants, and therein may lie one of the reasons why the city's populace turned on the Venetians, Florentines, Lucchese, and, ultimately, the Genoese. Unlike the Hansards, who could shelter behind the walls of the Steelyard, the Italians had no real means of protecting themselves in their houses in Bread Street and Lombard Street; they had no organization to defend them or plead their cause before the courts; and there were few English merchants as yet trading in the Mediterranean against whom reprisals could be taken.[121] Significant, too, was the character of the Italians' commercial operations: their concentration on importing luxuries had for long given an impression that they were mercantile parasites; their role as bankers, brokers, and usurers aroused distrust and dislike; and the Calais merchants suspected, not without reason, that they were circumventing the staple's monopoly by trading with northern Europe under the guise of exporting wool to the Mediterranean. Moreover, by the mid-1450s, their loans to the Lancastrian crown (modest though they had recently been) were rewarded with special licences enabling some of them to despatch cargoes free of customs duty and even to dominate wool exports to southern Europe as the king's official factors.[122] Too many of the English mercantile community resented the role of Italians in English commercial and financial life, and the government's apparent readiness, because of its own needs, to tolerate it. As a letter to Cosimo de' Medici put it in February 1458, the 'Florentines are so much engaged in the wool trade that if the government should change hands it would harm them to please the city of London and the company of the staple'.[123]

These reasons, when placed in the context of a trade depression induced by war, disputes with the Hanse towns, and Burgundian hostility, explain the violence to which the Italians in London were subjected, particularly the Venetians, who were the pre-eminent purveyors of 'ifles and trifles', and the Florentines, the most experienced of financiers. Strange to tell, the Genoese, who were thicker on the ground in London (and Southampton too) than the traders of any other Italian city and imported more than they exported, were spared attack until 1458, perhaps because they were known to deal mainly in raw materials.[124]

The riots that occurred at the end of April 1456 were sudden and spontaneous, and owed much to the exuberance of young apprentices in the mercers' company; but in the following year, the anti-alien movement seems to have been better planned and its demonstrations more carefully executed; it expected and received sympathy from influential quarters, some of which may have been connected with the staplers.[125] The city authorities were hampered in the suppression of disorder by the withdrawal of the king and his court to the midlands in August 1456, largely because Henry VI, and more especially Queen Margaret, felt unsafe near the capital and had begun to distrust its inhabitants. This desertion (for so it must have seemed to the mayor, sheriffs, and aldermen, whose predecessors had witnessed something similar in 1450) undermined law and order and made it more difficult to obey royal instructions formulated at a distance. Moreover, the events culminating in the battle of St Albans, and the subsequent presence in London of magnates with unusually large retinues, not to speak of MPs, increased the uncertainty and apprehension. Deprived of the moral and practical authority of government, as represented by the king and his council, the city officials battled alone with the sources of disorder.

The parliament of 1455–56 had displayed the customary antagonism towards Italians. Criticism of their imports of cheap silk manufactures, which undermined the domestic manufacturing industry in the hands of women, had a sympathetic hearing from the government, which agreed to place an embargo on these imports for five years.[126] But an attempt to place tighter restrictions on aliens' movements and trade was resisted by the government. It was only a matter of weeks after parliament was dissolved on 12 March 1456 that the first serious outbreak of rioting occurred.

It sprang from a very minor incident indeed: a young Londoner relieved an Italian of his dagger and broke it over his head. Anxious to avoid dangerous reprisals, the city authorities next day arraigned the young man before the mayor and aldermen in the guildhall; they placed him in custody in the Contours prison. But he was not without friends and sympathizers, and when the mayor left the guildhall for dinner that evening, he was confronted in Cheapside by a large body of apprentice-mercers, stiffened by ruffians from the city; together they held the mayor and sheriffs at bay until they agreed to release their young hero.[127]

This incident served as a signal for more serious anti-alien protests, as rumours fanned the citizens' hostility to the Italians. That same evening, men from a number of crafts rampaged through London, robbing the homes of Italians in Bread Street. The mayor, sheriffs, and aldermen managed to disperse them, and a few were clapped in Newgate gaol; the young man whose escapade had started the rumpus sought sanctuary in Westminster abbey. Passions were such that King Henry decided to intervene, both personally and by appointing a commission of oyer and terminer to sit at the guildhall. On 30 April he was rowed by barge from Westminster and installed himself in the bishop of London's palace near St Paul's. Next day the commission began its hearings before the dukes of Buckingham and Exeter, the earls of Salisbury, Pembroke, and Stafford, the mayor of London, and several justices. But the mere presence of king and lords in their midst does not seem to have curbed the excitement of the Londoners, many of whom secretly armed themselves and prepared to raise the entire city by ringing Bow Bell. Though wiser counsels in fact prevailed, the commissioners concluded that caution was the better part of valour and for the moment withdrew from the sessions. They reassembled on 5 May, but without Salisbury, who may have felt somewhat ill at ease as a member of a court-dominated commission; the guildhall, where they sat, was surrounded by an ominous crowd of armed men. The mayor thereupon convened a common council of the city, to which the wardens of the various crafts were summoned to hear an exhortation to keep the peace. This done, suspects were presented to the commissioners and three were condemned to death for their part in the robberies; they were hanged on 8 May at Tyburn, amid noisy scenes of outrage.

Though strenuous efforts were made to restore the city to order and assure the Italians that they were safe, the atmosphere in London in the weeks that followed was very tense. The news from Southwark on 8 May was that

Myn Lord Bukingham rode on [5 May] to Writell [in Essex], noo thing weel plesid and sumwhat on-easid of herte to his purpose: for the Kyng hathe ley in London [30 April– 4 May], and Wednesday [5 May] remevid to Westminster ayen...The peas is weel kepte, but the straungiers ar soore a-dradde, and dar nought come on brode.

A week later,

there ar be this tyme proclamacions made, or shall be, thorwe London the pees to be kepte vp-on grete peynes, and the Lumbardes to occupie there merchaundizes as thei dide til the Counsail or Parlament haue otherwise determyned; . . . [128]

These disturbances in fact convinced King Henry that he would be wise to follow the queen and prince to the comparative calm and safety of Coventry.[129] From Lichfield on 3 September, Henry commanded the mayor to ensure order in the capital, allowing into the city only those with modest retinues appropriate to their station in life.[130] And in a further attempt to reassert lawful authority, particularly among the mercers and their apprentices, a prominent alderman and master of the mercers' company, William Cantelowe, was required to appear before the king and council at Coventry early in October, presumably to explain why he had failed to control his fellows; Lord Dudley took charge of him and put him in Dudley castle.[131]

The Italians took their own precautions. Although his merchants were at first spared the worst extremes of anti-alien violence, the doge of Genoa had become alarmed at the news from England by the beginning of April. After the riots a few weeks later, he expressed his concern to both Henry VI and the chancellor and demanded justice for Italians in London. On 14 June the Venetian senate authorized its citizens to leave the city if they wished.[132] Those who did so acted wisely, for further trouble was looming ahead. And this time, the movement, spearheaded once again by the mercers and staplers, was premeditated and more carefully organized. Towards the end of February 1457, a fleet of ships from Calais and Sandwich (which also hosted several Italian merchants) sailed into the Thames estuary and off Tilbury seized some Zeeland ships loaded with bales of wool belonging to Italian merchants. Though the exporters possessed a royal safe-conduct, the men from Calais and Sandwich (who must surely have represented the staplers' interests) may have believed that the Italians were about to ship their cargoes illegally to northern Europe without putting in at Calais. The mayor of London had so little success in pursuing the predators that twice during March the king, who was still at Coventry, ordered him to seek out and seize the ships responsible, and in the meanwhile to suppress any disorder that might occur in London, presumably directed against Italians.[133]

In mid-June a more serious threat to the foreigners arose. As a result of a plot hatched on 16 June in the Tower Royal hostelry with the intention of killing those Italians who lived in Lombard Street, a great carousing gathering assembled at Hoxton in Bishopswood, some 3 miles north of the city.[134] Many of those present (more than were willing to admit it at the subsequent inquiries!) swore an oath of solidarity and confidently expected widespread assistance, 'Inasmuche as myche people thenne hated dedely the saide marchantz estraungiers'. The week following, Thomas Graunt, one of the conspirators who had also been to the fore in the riots in 1456, collected a large quantity of staves at the Crown in Cheapside and distributed them with the rallying cry,

'Go we hens for ther is an Englishman sleyn by the lombardes in Lumbardstrete'. The mayor and city authorities on this occasion showed appropriate resolution: they threw an armed cordon round the guildhall to protect the city officials and the Italians were advised to stay barricaded in their homes. Some of the insurgents were arrested, a few were put in prison, while others fled to sanctuary at St Martin-le-Grand. On 1 August, Henry VI ordered twenty-eight mercers and apprentices to be confined in Windsor castle, where Lord Fauconberg, the constable, was to hold them in custody until they could be brought before the king himself. But this time serious damage had been done to relations between the government, the city, and the Italians.

These latest outrages, and the inability (or disinclination) of the city and royal authorities to afford them adequate protection, forced the Italians to take their own measures, which would provide them and their property with greater security and, at the same time, express their deep resentment at their treatment. On 22 June 1457, two delegates from each of the Venetian, Genoese, Florentine, and Lucchese communities in London met in conference to discuss their plight.[135] Under solemn oath and on pain of forfeiting £200, they each resolved that their fellow citizens would leave London for three years for Winchester or a comparable town beyond a 30-mile radius of the capital. The process of transferring their businesses would begin immediately and only the wine merchants were allowed as much as six months (to 1 January 1458) in which to dispose of their more perishable stock. They went even further and undertook to persuade all other Mediterranean merchants in London – Sicilians, Catalans, and Spaniards – to follow their example or else face the crippling sanction of having to find other than Italian ships to transport their cargoes. It was a momentous agreement, 'something hitherto unheard of in the annals of Italian political and economic history', and if fully implemented, it would have amounted to 'un véritable interdit lancé par les Italiens contre Londres'. It was ratified with great speed by the governing body of probably every parent city.[136]

The decaying town of Winchester, with its deserted houses and overgrown tenements, made ready to accommodate the visitors, but in the event the Italians never arrived in substantial numbers. They seem to have preferred Southampton, which enjoyed a deserved reputation for friendliness towards foreigners, and indeed the annual Venetian galley fleets were diverted there from October 1457.[137] For a year or two Southampton became the principal headquarters of all Italian shipping in England. The Venetians and Florentines joined the Genoese, the largest alien community in Southampton, to bring a singular increase in prosperity to the town for a short while. But before very long, the turbulence of London came to seem less of a deterrent than it had done, for anti-alien demonstrations flared up in Southampton with all the ferocity of those in London in 1456–57.

To date the Genoese had escaped lightly from anti-alien riots, but an incident far away in the Mediterranean in 1458 at last turned the wrath of Englishmen on them too. On its way back from an epoch-making voyage to the Levant, the flotilla of Robert Sturmy, a Bristolian whose enterprise had London backing, was attacked off Malta by Genoese pirates.[138] When the news reached England, it caused a renewed burst of anti-Italian demonstrations, this time with the Genoese as their main target. In London they were arrested and had their goods seized, and some of them were put in the Fleet prison until a demand for £6,000 in compensation was met. On this occasion, the king and the city authorities took action themselves by way of retribution.[139] The Genoese encountered similar treatment in Southampton, where Sturmy had been a familiar figure. A group of civic politicians, with close personal and commercial links with London, took advantage of the outcry to challenge the power of their rivals, who had constructed their authority in Southampton in part around a peaceful and profitable association with the foreign community. By cultivating the anti-alien prejudices of the townsmen in 1458 they were eventually able to seize control of Southampton's administration at the elections of 1460. As for the Italians, they found their proposed boycott of London undermined, and they had no alternative but to return to the capital.[140]

The attacks on the Italians during 1456–58 lay close to the heart of several of the fundamental problems faced by the late-Lancastrian monarchy. The foreigners themselves were valued by the government, and yet Henry VI's inability to afford them adequate protection at this time gave the Italians cause to reconsider whether their relationship with his régime was at all justified: certainly, they gave it no further loans in the late 1450s.[141] On the other hand, the way in which Henry's régime had attempted to protect the Italians by granting them preferential export licences and resisting the more extreme demands of the commons in parliament was a bitter pill for the London mercantile community to swallow and especially the merchants of the staple, who in the middle of the decade were advancing substantial sums to maintain the English hold on Calais and meet the wages of the garrison.[142] The task of preserving law and order in the city of London was not easy during the late-Lancastrian period, and the mounting violence of the anti-alien movement made it much more difficult; after the king and his court retired to the midlands in the summer of 1456, the city authorities could be pardoned for feeling deserted and their will to maintain urban peace faltered.[143] In all, the anti-Italian experience of these years brought nothing but discomfort to the Lancastrian régime, and its legacy of disorder in the capital soured the attitude of many prominent Londoners towards Henry VI and his ministers.

No less violent were the riots directed against the privileged but unprotected inns of the lawyers on the city's edge, near Fleet Street. Squabbles between the citizens and the inhabitants of the inns of court and chancery, which were closely associated with the king's courts at

Westminster, were not uncommon, but in the later 1450s they were especially vicious. On more than one occasion during the autumn of 1456, lawyers were responsible for affixing provocative verses to the standard and aqueduct in Fleet Street, most pointedly in front of the bishop of Salisbury's house when the duke of York was in residence. Although their content is unknown, one suspects that they were hostile to the duke at a time when his relations with the court were deteriorating sharply.[144]

A more violent episode occurred in 1458: a dog-fight took place between the lawyers and the men of Fleet Street in which the queen's attorney was among those killed. The earl of Warwick, who may have had soldiers available, was ordered to march through the streets fully armed and restore order.[145] But the worst disturbances of all were in 1459. On 19 April the lawyers seized the initiative and rose against the citizens who, when they tried to resist, were driven back to the aqueduct, where a scuffle lasted for an hour. The inhabitants of Fleet Street, accompanied by a troop of archers, retaliated by attacking the inns and pillaging the possessions of the lawyers, some of whom were pushed back even beyond the city walls. The struggle lasted for three hours until 6 p.m., and when it was all over, several lay wounded and a few were dead.

The lords who were then at Westminster, led by the officers of state and some of the councillors, intervened to calm the violence. They supported the city officials who threw a cordon round the Fleet Street area lest others attempt to aid the local citizenry. Shortly afterwards, twenty-four men from Fleet Street, including William Taylor, alderman of the ward, were arrested and sent under guard to Windsor; three of the lawyers' leaders were despatched to Hertford castle. There was no question in the mind of observers of the depth of hatred felt by the Londoners for the lawyers in their midst, and Clifford's inn and the Temple were thought to be in real danger of destruction. These severe disorders, of which that of 1459 was the most destructive, confirmed the court and the royal family in their distrust of the city of London, and in May the king threatened to suspend the city's franchises if the riots did not stop.[146]

The spectacle of Bishop Pecock's public abjuration of heresy at St Paul's in 1457 made its own distinctive contribution to the tense atmosphere in the city. For the first time, an English bishop was at the centre of a lollard scandal. Reginald, a gifted but vain Welshman, formerly bishop of St Asaph and, since 1450, bishop of Chichester, was accused of heresy at a great council at Westminster in October.[147] The abrasive bishop, whose *Reule of Crysten Religioun* and other works were designed to demonstrate by reasoned argument rather than unquestioning faith the falsity of lollard doctrine, found himself hoist with his own petard. He gave deep offence to more orthodox clerics, and the influential household magnate Viscount Beaumont intervened in June 1457 to bring the growing unease at Pecock's pronouncements to a head. He requested a formal examination of the bishop's teachings and his punishment if he were found to be in error. Pecock and the books he had written to confute lollard teaching were examined by assessors on more than one occasion during November, usually at Lambeth, until eventually on 28 November he appeared before a great council at Westminster in the presence of the king and Archbishop Bourgchier. Dr William Goddard, a distinguished cleric and provincial of the Grey Friars in England, read the appeal of heresy, after which Pecock agreed to recant.[148] The investigation was resumed at Lambeth on 3 December, when Pecock reappeared before the archbishop and a number of bishops, this time including Waynflete, the chancellor, and Bishop Lowe, a heresy-hunter of some renown, to reaffirm his abjuration. Next day, before St Paul's cross, he renounced any heresy that might be in his preaching and voluminous writings (in particular in his English translations from the scriptures) and a number of his books were burned to symbolize the cauterization of his heresy. In his abjuration, he affirmed:

> . . . Reynold Pekoke byschop of Chychester unworthy of myn own powere and fre wylle with owt any maner coarcyon' or drede confesse and knowleche that y here beforn thys tyme presumynge of my awyce Naturall' Wite and preferrynge the iugghement of naturall' resinz befor the holde and new testament and auctoryte and determinacyon' of owre moder holy chyrche, have holdyn' Wrytyn' and taught ortherwyse than the holy romayne and universal' chirche prechyth techeyth and obseruith . . .[149]

Pecock was induced to resign a year later and after a short period of close confinement in obscurity in Thorney abbey (Cambridgeshire), he died sometime in 1460 or 1461.[150]

The aristocracy and the court

The aristocracy – the lords and the greater magnates – were traditional pillars of the English monarchy. The patience of those who were not regularly welcomed to the late-Lancastrian court might be stretched by the queen's factional rule and the self-centred patronage which was its complement, but political or dynastic revolution by force scarcely entered their mind more than fleetingly – if at all – between 1456 and 1459.[151] It is true that York had special cause to resent the way in which Queen Margaret and her friends had once again undermined his standing with the king and neutralized his political influence in the realm beyond his own estates, for that had direct implications for his role in any future protectorate or regency that might be required during Henry VI's remaining years of uncertain health or during the minority of his son and

797

heir. It is true, also, that Salisbury and Warwick, primarily for their own reasons, had committed themselves wholeheartedly to York's side and showed no inclination to desert him after 1456; on the contrary, they protested vigorously at their own exclusion from power, and Warwick resisted successfully all attempts to deprive him of the captaincy of Calais. Yet, if York and the Nevilles received expressions of support from other lords, these are largely inaudible to the historian. Lords Clinton and Cobham had taken the field with them at St Albans in May 1455, and it is clear that Norfolk, who did not in fact arrive in time for the fighting, was widely considered to be sympathetic to the insurgents.[152] Worcester had established a *rapport* with York, and developed a respect for him, when he was treasurer of England during the first protectorate. But both Norfolk and Worcester had the good sense to make arrangements to leave England on pilgrimage when the political situation became dangerously unstable in the winter of 1457–58.[153]

Historians with an eagerness to identify the poles in politics have likewise proposed the existence of 'a middle party' between the Lancastrian court and the Yorkist lords, akin to that which was once thought to have stood between Edward II and his opponents a century and more before. Such ideas have little reality in the context of late-Lancastrian England, and those magnates who have been regarded as the most prominent of political moderates – the Bourgchiers and their relatives, the Staffords – hardly seem to possess the requisite qualifications. Viscount Bourgchier, Archbishop Bourgchier, and their brothers were inclined to prefer York's appointment as protector to a regency under Queen Margaret's control and therefore were unlikely to figure among the queen's advisers during the late 1450s; they did not compromise their loyalty to the crowned king by taking the Yorkist side openly at this juncture, but neither did they pose as reconcilers of divisions.[154] Buckingham and his son were even less likely to do so. Duke Humphrey may have been uneasy at some of the queen's more combative decisions, but he never faltered in his devotion to Henry VI, made no detectable effort to reconcile York with the court, and indeed was a consistently prominent member of the king's entourage in the midlands.[155]

Reconciliation was not a conviction that weighed heavily with the queen and her counsellors in the years following the second protectorate. The worst fears of York and the Nevilles were shown to be well justified, as the court determined to strip them of almost all public authority in the realm, starve them of lucrative royal patronage, and neutralize the local influence of their tenantry and retainers in the shires. This determination achieved such success that, as one chronicler suggests, it must have seemed only a matter of time before the queen would contemplate an indictment of treason as the final blow.[156] If the dynastic claims of himself and his lineage as members of the royal family were indelibly impressed on Duke Richard's mind, they were inevitably subordinated for the moment to the more basic instinct of self-preservation.

York was confirmed in office as lieutenant of Ireland when his current term approached its end in July 1457. This may have been in consolation for his loss of authority in Wales, the trial of his affinity at Hereford, and his exclusion from the ranks of the king's councillors; in any case, it may have been thought that Shrewsbury and Wiltshire, as major Irish landowners themselves, were well capable of countering the duke's influence.[157] In the event, this unique indulgence towards the duke proved a serious, not to say fatal, error, for he made good use of his powers in Ireland during 1459–60, preparatory to his return to England to claim the throne.[158] One may doubt whether in July 1457 it was hoped that he would remove himself from English politics and retire to Ireland; in fact, Richard preferred to remain in England, safely installed in his northern or western castles.[159] He also retained his position as JP in a large number of shires, but the crown's enormous debt to him, in particular his unpaid salary as protector and defender of the realm, was largely forgotten; only after the 'love-day' of March 1458 did he receive any new tallies from the exchequer – and they were worth little more than £450 and proved difficult to cash.[160]

Salisbury and Warwick fared no better. The steps that were taken to dislodge Warwick from Calais culminated in an unsuccessful attempt on his life in November 1458.[161] Meanwhile, he and his father were still joint-custodians of Carlisle and the west march, but, in contrast to Northumberland at Berwick, they were completely starved of exchequer funds until the summer of 1459.[162] Moreover, the rival senior branch of the Nevilles was advanced in the Yorkshire estates of the crown and, through Bishop Lawrence Booth, in Durham from 1457 onwards. The Percies, who already controlled the east march, were given further powers (in March 1457) in the northernmost shires which were nothing less than an insult to Warwick and his father.[163]

The earnest measures which the court took to humble its enemies and fortify its own position in the realm had their dangers. As far as most of the English aristocracy were concerned, the court managed to retain their loyalty, though with varying degrees of enthusiasm. But the queen and her advisers showed little circumspection and less tact in some of their dealings, and their treatment of the Yorkist lords amounted to victimization. Nothing was done to remove the bitter legacy of St Albans until it was too late, and whatever short-term success the court's administrative, governmental, and military arrangements brought, they signally failed to reconcile the régime's enemies and even alienated other important interests.

The disturbances in London from the spring of 1456 onwards, and the antagonisms in south-west Wales later that year were a potential threat to the authority of Henry's government and had their part to play in fuelling those aristocratic rivalries which the deaths at St Albans had already intensified. The king's abdication of his responsibility towards

799

the capital and the introduction of factional government at Coventry made it more likely that these conflicts would spread. The Yorkist lords sped to their estates or to Calais, but when they or their families appeared in London and Coventry, dangerous incidents took place, involving especially the young courtier-magnates.

Already, in November 1456, Thomas Percy, Lord Egremont had enlisted inside help to escape from Newgate gaol, where he had been incarcerated after his antics in Yorkshire. His flight seems to have been an encouragement to the rest of the inmates who, before the month was out, had climbed on to the roof of the prison's tower, seized the prison gate, and proceeded to hurl stones at passers-by.[164] In December, the duke of Somerset encountered Salisbury's son, Sir John Neville, in the city. A skirmish would have taken place in Cheapside had not the mayor, who was constantly on the alert for trouble, intervened to prevent it.[165] On two other occasions in 1458, when Warwick was paying brief visits from Calais, he was set upon and came within an ace of losing his life. The more serious attack occurred in November, when he arrived to attend a council meeting at Westminster. As he was preparing to take his barge at London for the royal palace, news of a plot by members of the household reached the ears of his friends, who were able to delay his journey by a day. As it was, a clash between the household men and some of Warwick's retinue led to cooks from the royal kitchen running out with pots and pestles to join in the scrimmage. Despite pressure on Henry VI to have the earl arrested and imprisoned in the Tower, Warwick secured the king's permission to retire from London; next day he bade farewell to his father and made his way back to the haven of Calais.[166] This incident, more than any other, was a foretaste of the complete breakdown in peaceful relations between the court and the Yorkists in the following year. Warwick was identified more closely than his father with the violence at St Albans, and the inability of the government to remove him from the captaincy of Calais was felt more keenly than probably anything else in these years.

The Yorkist lords were no safer at the court itself. Summoned to Coventry in the autumn of 1456, they faced a hostile queen who, had it not been for the more indulgent king, would probably have had them arrested. It was possibly on this occasion that they were verbally pilloried by the lords, led by Buckingham (if we may believe later Lancastrian propaganda):

And there and than the seid Duc of Bukyngham, and all other Lordes, knelyng on ther knees bisought You [Henry VI], seyng the grete Jupartie for youre moost noble persone, and also the Lordes so often charged, and inquietyng so often the grete parte of your Realme, that it shuld not lyke You to shewe the seid Duc of York, nor noon other hereafter grace, if they attempted eftsones to doo the contrary to youre Roiall estate, or inquietyng of youre Realme, and the Lordes therof, but to be punysshed after ther deserte . . . .[167]

Both York and Warwick swore an oath on the gospels, and gave a signed undertaking, that they would do nothing in the future to jeopardize the safety of the king or the stability of his realm. It is hardly surprising that they were disinclined to attend the council thereafter.[168]

There was a real danger that such discord involving the most important magnates in the kingdom would set a disastrous example to others and promote a spirit of lawlessness elsewhere. The court pursued constructive means of financing the stay of the king's entourage in the midlands, which it came to regard as an alternative citadel of power, and it took steps to attract most of the uncommitted magnates and assign them practical responsibility at least in the central shires of England, south of Cheshire and Yorkshire, west of East Anglia, and north of the lower Thames valley. It seemed to have some success, though judged on a longer perspective, its efforts were imperfectly conceived and poorly executed: without an effective grip on the law enforcement agencies in the realm at large, there was little hope of suppressing disorder permanently.

On 16 July 1457 a group of courtier-magnates received virtually military powers, in conjunction with the sheriffs who could summon the local posse, in the counties lying between Lincoln and Hereford, Nottingham and Bedford; the express purpose was to resist gatherings of men who might threaten the king or his government.[169] These commands were headed by Buckingham and his son, by Shrewsbury, Beaumont, Welles, Sudeley, Beauchamp, Rivers, and Grey of Ruthin.[170] The kind of resistance they anticipated arose from the unauthorized granting of livery and badges which was promoting commotions such as those for which York's retainers had been responsible in Wales and the borderland. That the court was actively engaged in creating its own affinity of retainers is shown by the fact that the liveries of the king and the prince could still be given for other than the customary purposes.[171]

A watchful eye could be kept on county society through the commission of the peace. During 1457–60 the court therefore introduced unquestionably loyal supporters to the bench of JPs, especially in midland England. A small corps of dependable bishops, magnates, and lawyers was appointed in counties where they had not previously or recently served, and a few were nominated in several shires.[172] It was a sound precaution to make available in counties close to the heartland of Lancastrian power major, loyal figures who could lead investigations and prosecutions of particularly serious crime. Bishop Waynflete was accordingly placed on the bench of no less than five additional shires between January 1458 and July 1459, all of them in the upper Thames valley. Viscount Beaumont was added to four others – covering much of eastern England, including East Anglia – between May 1458 and March 1460; and Richard Choke, a serjeant-at-law, was appointed between November 1457 and February 1459 to as many as seven benches whose jurisdiction was concentrated in the Welsh border-land.[173] By these means verdicts satisfactory to the court could be more reliably secured and activities considered especially threatening to the régime more swiftly punished. These two series of royalist commissions, one military and the other judicial, afforded Henry VI's government the means by which to maintain constant supervision of a region which the court had adopted as its power-base. The arrangements in the midlands complemented the achievement of the Tudors in Wales and the hegemony of the Stanleys in the north-west. London, Yorkshire and the north, and the southern littoral were comparatively neglected.[174]

The claustrophobic atmosphere of a court attended by compliant magnates is well conveyed by the series of aristocratic marriages that took place there between 1456 and 1460. Queen Margaret and the duke of Buckingham figured prominently in the arrangements, and it is highly significant that three of the matches were recorded in the register of Reginald Boulers, the faithful bishop of Coventry and Lichfield. The queen had the closest personal interest in the wedding in 1457 of her kinswoman, Marie, daughter of Charles, count of Maine, to Thomas Courtenay, the twenty-five-year-old son and heir of the earl of Devon.[175] Lord Bonville's success in ingratiating himself with the government during 1455 seems to have spurred Devon to seek closer links with the Lancastrian court with the waning of York's power during the first half of 1456; his future authority in the south-west demanded that he secure support from a more reliable source of patronage than that available to his rival.[176] This realignment of west-country interests for avowedly local reasons explains the marriage between the earl's heir and Marie of Maine, who had probably come to England in her aunt's train. From the court's point of view, it brought the earl into the royal circle and decisively ended his association with York. A pardon for Thomas Courtenay and his younger brother was sealed in November 1457 and it encompassed even the murder of Nicholas Radford; the earl himself had been reappointed to the commission of the peace in Devon on 12 September 1456.[177] Although the city of Exeter continued to be a focus of dispute and violence, the Devon–Bonville tensions gradually subsided; Bonville himself was now an old man and the earl died suddenly at Abingdon, on his way to the great council at Westminster, on 3 February 1458. The new earl and his French countess seem to have enjoyed some popularity in Exeter, and they were on good terms with the duke of Exeter, Henry Holand, whom they visited at Dartington during 1458.[178]

A second notable marriage was solemnized in 1457. Margaret Beaufort, countess of Richmond, whose husband Edmund Tudor had died on 1 November 1456, gave birth to Henry Tudor in Pembroke castle on 28 January 1457; nevertheless, she was quickly propelled to the altar for the third time in her young life (for she was still only fourteen!), this time to wed Henry Stafford, the second son of the duke of Buckingham.[179] Margaret was the wealthiest heiress in England and this new bond between the king's relations emphasized Lancastrian family solidarity at a time when the dynasty's survival rested squarely on the shoulders of Prince Edward alone.[180] Two further marriages in July 1458 had an associated significance. Buckingham's daughter Katherine was married to John Talbot, the son and heir of the earl of Shrewsbury, treasurer of England, and the duke's younger son John married Constancia, daughter of the wealthy Northamptonshire and Wiltshire landowner Henry Green.[181]

Nor did this infectious passion for matrimony stop there: Shrewsbury concluded a further agreement which enabled him to heal, at least temporarily, his family's long-standing feud with Lord Berkeley, for in 1457 the latter married the earl's sister, Joan, and at the same time became his retainer.[182] Two other unions bear mention, though the precise date at which they were arranged is regretably unknown. Shrewsbury's other sister, Eleanor, was married sometime between 1450 and 1460 to Thomas, the son and heir of Lord Sudeley, the king's chamberlain; and Edmund, Lord Grey of Ruthin, who had joined the Lancastrian council in October 1456, wedded Katherine, the daughter of the earl of Northumberland, well before January 1459.[183] Most of these marriages were probably arranged at court, and together they bound some of the principal magnate houses to the Lancastrian régime. Moreover, there were no matches of comparable significance contracted beyond the court circle, certainly none involving the offspring of the Yorkist lords.[184]

The king's patronage in these years was enjoyed by the same relatively restricted circle of household servants and magnates of the court. Among the latter, Viscount Beaumont was an exceptionally favoured individual, not only in the offices he accumulated but also in the wardships and marriages that were placed in his custody.[185] Others who were similarly treated included Lord Dudley, Bishop Booth, the more recently reconciled earl of Devon, and the duke of Exeter.[186] Among the household servants, the king's carvers did outstandingly well for themselves: Sir Richard Tunstall, even before he became Henry's chamberlain in 1459, acquired control of a number of heiresses and their estates, as well as the potentially lucrative office of master of the mints at the Tower and Calais in April 1459.[187] His colleagues as carvers, Sir Philip Wentworth and Sir Edmund Hungerford, were also recipients of valuable items from the store of crown patronage, Hungerford in particular acquiring properties in his native shire of Wiltshire.[188] Henry VI did not even forget his two old nurses, whose annuities had been cancelled by the act of resumption of 1455–56 but were restored in November 1458.[189]

The disposal of the considerable wealth of Edmund Tudor, earl of Richmond after his death in November 1456 reveals the motives that weighed most strongly with the king as patron in these years, even though he could not afford to relinquish entirely a major windfall like this inheritance. Nevertheless, much of it was granted to Henry's courtiers. Richmond's landed wealth was conservatively estimated at somewhat less than £600 a year, excluding the large inheritance of Margaret Beaufort, his widow.[190] Apart from the estates which he had held jointly with his brother, all of Edmund's properties escheated to the crown. Within a few days of the earl's death, the duke of Exeter leased the Cambridgeshire lands at a farm to be agreed with the exchequer, while on 15 April 1457 the widowed countess received £200 as her dower. The remaining income from the honour of Richmond derived from its Lincolnshire estates, and on 10 June 1457 these were leased for twenty years to Shrewsbury and Beaumont at an annual farm of £120 *per annum*. Other lands remained, however, but on 8 January 1458 Jasper Tudor and the earl of Shrewsbury were granted the wardship of the child-earl and custody of his remaining estates in England and Wales, at an annual farm which was later fixed at £74. The beneficiaries without exception seem to have obtained a good bargain, and the crown had therefore granted away badly needed sources of revenue to a small and highly favoured circle of magnates.

The court and the Yorkist lords

Aside from measures for its own security and survival, in the winter of 1457–58 the government embarked on an offensive campaign to bring London and the Yorkist lords to heal. The return of the court to Westminster in October 1457 was accompanied by most stringent security precautions which may have had a more sinister purpose. The king had taken up residence in his palace before the end of the month.[191] He and his ministers were well aware of the recent wave of anti-alien riots in the capital, and of the daring French attack on Sandwich two months earlier; and it could reasonably be anticipated that the public humiliation of Bishop Pecock would precipitate further disorder.[192] The piratical activities of men from Calais, particularly against foreign merchant shipping, roused suspicion that some of the staplers were involved, and this heightened the court's apprehension of the situation in London and its mistrust of Londoners. As might have been expected of divided counsels that oscillated between the king's compassion and generosity and the queen's harsh determination, the government's response was self-contradictory. It was Henry's earnest desire to reconcile conflicts, and yet the queen's attitude to the Yorkist lords was one of unforgiving severity, a sentiment which she shared with those younger magnates who had lost a father at St Albans.[193] Belligerence, rather than reconciliation, dictated the court's first actions after its return to the south-east.

For the first time since parliament in 1453–54 had authorized Henry VI to raise 13,000 archers in defence of the realm, various counties were required to produce contingents of soldiers for the king's service: during

October lords and others were commanded to assemble them at their own cost.[194] The fall of Normandy and the imminent collapse of Gascony had been justification enough for parliament's extraordinary grant. In October 1457, the lawlessness of London and the French raid on Sandwich could be pleaded as a comparable emergency; but there is a strong possibility that the court had a more specific purpose in mind, namely, to overawe the city and overcome the Yorkist lords. On 3–4 November the archers were deployed round London: some at Longfield park, between Haringay and Wheston, some at Hounslow heath, and, to guard London bridge, others at St George's fields in Southwark. As one London chronicler hinted, these armed companies were a threat to the commons of the city.[195] The citizens could hardly fail to mistake their purpose: the threat of force was being used to cow an unhappy capital and protect the court lodged in its suburbs.[196]

The mailed fist was accompanied by an olive branch, whose naivety and theatricality most likely sprang from King Henry's mind.[197] Soon after his return to Westminster, he presided over a great council that was designed to tackle the pressing political problems of the kingdom, and especially the alienation of the Yorkist lords. But on 29 November the meeting was adjourned before any solutions could be found, perhaps because of the tension which the presence of royal archers engendered. It was scheduled to reconvene on 27 January.[198] In the meantime, new authority was issued on 17 December to assemble the 13,000 archers, either to replace those who had already served during the autumn or else to extend their tour of duty.[199] If the king's advisers were bent on resolving the dangerous disputes among the aristocracy, force was evidently regarded as a necessary accompaniment of the formal arbitration and award which the king prepared to announce.

The aim of the king's award in the great council was to satisfy the craving of the younger magnates for revenge on those who had killed their fathers at St Albans in 1455 ('to eradicate the roots of rancour', as the king subsequently put it).[200] But that would barely touch the deeper and more significant issues of politics, power, and trust that lay at the heart of relations between the Lancastrian régime and the duke of York and his friends. Lords began arriving in London or its suburbs during the last week of January 1458, preparatory to the great council at Westminster.[201] The presence of most of the realm's magnates, each with his own retinue, was an unnerving prospect for the city authorities. York had arrived with 400 followers on 26 January and lodged at Baynard's Castle, his own house in the city. Salisbury was already there with an even larger force (estimated at 500) which accompanied him to the family inn, the Arbour beside the Thames.[202] The young dukes of Exeter and Somerset arrived a few days later with 800 men; and two weeks after that Northumberland, Clifford, Egremont, and Sir Ralph Percy put in an appearance with a truly substantial force that was thought to be in the region of 1,500.[203] Warwick was the last of the principals to come, on 14 February from Calais with about 600 retainers clad in red jackets with the earl's device of the ragged staff on front and back; they made for lodgings at the Grey Friars.[204]

The logistics of billeting these retinues and preventing clashes between them raised formidable problems. Strenuous efforts were made to keep them apart, the Yorkists inside the city walls and the Lancastrians outside to the west of Temple Bar and closer to Westminster, where the council was to be held. The Lancastrian lords were believed to be spoiling for a fight and for that reason alone were less welcome in the city than the Yorkist followers.[205] The mayor and sheriffs of London mounted a round-the-clock watch throughout the city, guarding the gates, forbidding the carrying of weapons, and despatching patrols of 5,000 men, led by men-at-arms, from Newgate to Holborn down Chancery Lane, along Fleet Street, and on to Ludgate, Thames Street, and the Tower in order to prevent fighting.[206] The Lancastrians were well placed to harry the Yorkists as they made their way to Westminster for the great council. On 1 March, Warwick was warned that Somerset and Northumberland planned to avenge St Albans there and then, but the earl refused to be deterred from attending the council meeting.[207] Some were evidently persuaded only with difficulty to await the king's award.

Henry VI arrived at Westminster from the country about the end of the first week in March, and during the weeks that followed he strove to bring the hostile parties to an agreement, though the presence of the queen and the archers is likely to have been more of a hindrance to him than a help.[208] The discussions were long and doubtless acrimonious, but eventually the king's hopes and prayers (and the hovering Lancastrian forces) produced an arbitration award that was announced on 24 March 1458 and was accepted by the Yorkists and the young Lancastrian lords. Following the example of extra-curial arbitrations and awards that had become increasingly common to compose violent noble quarrels, the king imposed a tariff of compensation for those lords who had lost a father at St Albans: accordingly, York promised to transfer tallies worth 5,000 marks to Somerset and his mother, Warwick 1,000 marks to Lord Clifford, and Salisbury and his sons agreed to forego the fines earlier imposed on Egremont and his brother; in addition, York and the two Neville earls agreed to endow the abbey at St Albans within two years with £45 *per annum* for masses to be sung in perpetuity for the souls of the dead killed in the battle.[209] A substantial bond of 4,000 marks was offered by Egremont that he would keep the peace towards the earl of Salisbury for ten years, but this was the only reciprocal undertaking entered into by the Lancastrian lords. That done, former bitter enemies took each other by the hand and went arm in arm to London. Later that some day, this great symbolic act of reconciliation was proclaimed throughout the city and the following day a solemn ceremony at St Paul's sealed the king's achievement. It was an astonishing spectacle: if elaborate ceremonial, royal prayer and example, monetary payments, and the holding of hands could banish the personal and political differences of a decade, then Henry VI's 'love-day' may be regarded as a resounding success.[210] The Yorkist lords had submitted to the king's arbitration, and apart from Egremont's promise all the concessions had been made by York, Salisbury, and Warwick. After a brief Easter visit to St Albans itself, which demonstrated that the site of the battle in which he had been wounded and his ministers slain no longer stirred fearful memories in his mind, Henry returned with his queen to London and its neighbourhood and there they stayed for the rest of the year. Celebrations continued during May with jousts and other festivities at the Tower and the queen's country house at Greenwich.[211] Yet subsequent events were soon to demonstrate how hollow the reconciliation was and how shabby the promises made at Westminster and St Paul's, not least by those in the king's entourage.

During 1456–59, the magnates who were in the court circle and associated with the queen had successfully isolated the Yorkist lords. Those who had confronted the king at St Albans in 1455 had been able to recruit no significant allies before Blore Heath and Ludford Bridge in 1459. Willingly or not, the aristocracy clung to their fundamental loyalty to the anointed king, whose security had been strengthened by practical measures based on the midlands. Yet these measures had been mainly extra-curial; they had not capitalized on men's respect for the law and the courts. Rather had the Lancastrians resorted to marriage alliances, martial law, arbitrations, monetary bonds, and sworn oaths. The procedures of the common law were admittedly slow, cumbrous, and unreliable, but the régime was content to ignore them rather than implement or improve them. Such a poor example was followed by lesser men, with the result that violence increased as the court narrowed the focus of its concerns. Bands of men roamed the country at will; although a few commissions were nominated to restrain and suppress them, especially in peripheral areas like the Welsh march, the far south-west, and Norfolk, the court's preoccupation with its own security limited their success in dealing with crime in the realm at large.[212] Therein lay the real threat to the house of Lancaster, for these areas were frequently dominated by the estates and retainers of the Yorkist lords.

The failure of the king's award in March 1458 to assuage magnate hostilities was assured as the court tightened its factional control of central and shire administration, and London grew ever more disorderly. During 1458 the lawyers' inns were attacked, Italians were persecuted, Calais seemed to be quite beyond the government's reach (and English envoys visiting the town in May 1458 heard alarming stories of treason), and in November Warwick was almost slain at Westminster.[213] The series of appointments made in the autumn of 1458 emphasized the pervasive influence of the queen and the household, whilst disorders in sensitive parts of the realm, including London, increased and French descents on the south coast demonstrated the régime's uncertain control – perhaps even its waning interest – in all but the heartland of England and Wales.[214] In May 1459, after eighteen months spent in the south-east, Henry and his queen returned to Coventry. Within a few months, the Yorkist lords were planning more concerted action to prevent by force a renewal of the military and civil campaign, by means of which a humiliating and, it seemed, a purposeless settlement was imposed on them. Calais became their base of operations.

When York's second protectorate came to a sudden end, he was well on the way to completing negotiations with the staple merchants and the garrison at Calais. The agreement he concluded was as reasonable a bargain as could be expected after years of difficult discussion and mistrust.[215] In the months that followed, York and the Nevilles continued to play a part in ruling England and therefore were able to ensure that the terms of the agreement were honoured. The soldiers were given a full pardon on 1 May 1456, a commission was appointed to settle all outstanding financial questions, the staplers were guaranteed repayment of their substantial loans from the customs imposed at English ports, and eventually, in July, Warwick was able to take possession of Calais as its captain.[216] From the Yorkist point of view, these delicately balanced arrangements came in the nick of time, for the queen had already retired to the midlands and within a few more months major governmental changes would be announced at Coventry. As it was, the staplers' company acquired an even greater interest in maintaining a flourishing wool trade and something of an investment in Warwick's captaincy of Calais.

The earl naturally took steps to strengthen his authority by establishing a loyal chain of command directly responsible to himself. Somerset's erstwhile lieutenants, Rivers, Welles, and Stourton, were relieved of their posts and Lord Fauconberg, the new captain's uncle, replaced them in practice (though not in name) as lieutenant of Calais. In fact, Warwick, perhaps because he intended spending a good deal of his time in Calais, assumed personal command of the colony and refrained from filling the captaincies of Calais castle and Rysbank tower.[217] He may also have realized that wholesale changes further down the scale might alienate some of the soldiers who, until quite recently, had been loyal to the late duke of Somerset and his lieutenants; indeed, several of the veterans could not bring themselves to fight against the king at Ludford Bridge in 1459.[218] Furthermore, Warwick would do well to remain on his guard against ill-disguised attempts by the Lancastrian court to dislodge him from the captaincy. In response to a privy seal letter instructing him to vacate the command, he is reported to have replied in a way that placed his captaincy on a par with York's second commission as protector of England: he had been appointed (he claimed, with scant respect for the truth) by authority of parliament and could not therefore be dismissed merely by an order under the privy seal.[219] This safeguard had not prevented York's resignation in February 1456, but at least with no parliament sitting between March 1456 and November 1459 (and the king's ministers understandably reluctant to summon one), Warwick felt relatively secure on this score. Other, more direct, methods were employed against him which were probably condoned by Henry's advisers. During the winter of 1457–58, when the Lancastrian court tried to overawe London by a show of force, an attempt was made to seize him while he was in the city. Early in November Exeter, Somerset, Shrewsbury, and Lord Roos, with an armed retinue 400-strong, planned to arrest him.[220] Some months later, when he arrived from Calais to attend the great council of reconciliation at Westminster, Somerset and Northumberland plotted against him, though once again he was warned in time and escaped.[221] Later in 1458, he came close to assassination at Westminster when a scuffle broke out between his men and members of the king's household; a plan to confine him in the Tower was foiled and he managed to slip away by barge to Calais.[222] The final resort was the formal appointment of Henry, duke of Somerset as his supplanter at Calais on 9 October 1459.[223] Although a parliament had still not met, by this stage the enormous advantage of Calais to the Yorkist lords was fully understood by the court.

Warwick put his stay at Calais to good use: he set out to win the loyalty of its garrison, boost its morale, and ensure that the soldiers received at least some recompense for their efforts.[224] His privateering exploits were conceived with these aims in mind. They sorely tried the patience of foreign powers whose treaties with England were being violated, but they inspired an emotional admiration in Englishmen, especially merchants, who savoured the news that foreign cargoes had been plundered and alien vessels captured. Attacks on Italian and Low Countries shipping in the Thames in February 1457 were launched by vessels from Calais and Sandwich which may have belonged to staple merchants; Andrew Trollope and other Calais men were responsible for several captures at sea; in May 1458 the great Hanseatic salt fleet from the bay of Biscay was attacked and dispersed with some slaughter; and in the summer of 1459 Warwick's spectacular encounter with a heavily-laden Spanish fleet brought him fame and popularity in the south-east of England and abroad.[225] These exploits produced booty for the Calais garrison at a time of declining customs revenue, on which the staplers (and through them the soldiers) relied, and meagre payments from the exchequer.[226]

The company of the staple found itself wedged with increasing discomfort between Warwick and his rogue command at Calais, where the staplers had their warehouses and conducted their trade with foreign merchants, and the Lancastrian government, to whom the company had advanced large sums of money that had not yet been repaid; in any case, the merchants bought their wool in England and exported it through London, Sandwich, and the east coast ports. On the other hand, the government had to preserve good relations with the staplers if there were to be any possibility of recovering control of Calais or of securing substantial loans for the royal household and the Calais garrison. The court's dilemma, then, was as stark as that of the staplers. At first, the king's advisers offered concessions to the company on the vexed question of licences, restricting the quantity of wool exported by privileged royal agents to 2,000 sacks a year, and then, when a major loan was being negotiated in December 1458, prohibiting them altogether for four years.[227] But after the agreement had been concluded, the government reverted to its old habits and in March 1459 issued more licences, though fewer of the recipients were the detested Italian creditors of the past.[228]

The outbreak of hostilities in England in September 1459 brought the day closer when relations between Warwick, the staplers, and the Lancastrian régime would reach breaking-point. The Coventry parliament suspended all trade with Calais and as a consequence committed Warwick and his men to seek a radical change of government. The staplers were instructed to conduct their trading operations elsewhere, but this was no easy task, for their investment in the Calais run was incalculable.[229] The embargo against Calais was extended on 11 December while parliament was still in session; the supply of all foodstuffs to the port was henceforward prohibited.[230] It would hardly be surprising, therefore, if certain individual merchants, perhaps with a heavy heart, were to contribute cash for a Yorkist invasion of England. Public, corporate support was out of the question, for that would invite retaliation against staple interests in London and the provinces. But, as K. B. McFarlane has concluded, 'It is becoming increasingly difficult to believe that the staplers did not finance the Yorkist expeditions from Calais to England both before and after the fiasco at Ludford in October 1459'.[231] Rather did Calais become for a brief while in the first half of 1460 'the seat of an alternative government' (to use G. L. Harriss's phrase), supported by staple merchants and aided by an agreement with the duke of Burgundy.[232] Just as the Lancastrians counted on Coventry and the resources of the midlands, Wales, and the north-west, so the Yorkist lords – Salisbury, Warwick, and March pre-eminently – were financed by the wool trade and relied on Calais's more experienced garrison for manpower. If bonds of loyalty tugged at a number of consciences at Ludford Bridge, these were soon afterwards loosened by the desertions to Warwick from Kent and the south-east of England, and the soldiers were induced to fight for their captain and his companions out of fear lest the wool trade be taken permanently away from Calais and their wages disappear with it.

The international dimension

The close interest shown by several foreign governments in England's domestic problems was ultimately to accentuate significantly the political instability of the kingdom and sharpen the dynastic disputes as they came to the fore. Even prior to the battles of 1459–61, the diplomacy of these governments, designed as it was to serve their own purposes, played an important part in hastening the outbreak of the 'Wars of the Roses'. It is paradoxical, in view of recent hostilities, that the France of Charles VII should have adopted a less mischievous role in English politics at this juncture than either the Scotland of James II or Burgundy under Philip the Good.

King James, whose distinctive red birth-mark seemed to contemporaries to reflect his fiery nature, was vigilant in his determination to capitalize on the weakness of his cousin, Henry VI. He regarded it as his kingly mission to restore the authority and prestige of the Scottish monarchy and, if possible, to extend them to those enclaves like Berwick and the Isle of Man to which the Scots had ancient claims. The situation in England in the late 1450s encouraged his ambitions, whilst more immediately incidents at sea and the Lancastrian reception of the fugitive earl of Douglas were regarded by the bellicose king as provocative.[233] Thus, from 1456 James embarked on a series of diplomatic exchanges that were designed to weave a web of international alliances directed against England, with the ultimate aim of launching a joint invasion by Frenchmen, Scots, and perhaps even the Irish. To this end, he made repeated requests to Charles VII for a formal alliance, diplomatic assistance, an army of invasion, or, at the very least, material aid. He sought, too, the co-operation of the duke of Milan and the king of Aragon–Naples; he contemplated composing his differences with Christian I of Denmark over sovereignty in the Outer Isles, and preserved good relations with Burgundy, whose dominions were vital to the continued health of Scottish trade. Yet James's explanations of his policy were hardly compelling: the English were denounced as 'the principal disturbers of the peace of all Christendom', a sentiment which might appeal to the crusade-conscious pope but could hardly be expected to galvanize hard-headed secular princes; whilst the French were offered a scenario in which an English threat to Scotland constituted an indirect threat to France itself.[234]

James's proposals must have bewildered Charles VII by their inconsistency, as James tried to react to the political changes in England during 1455–56. In November 1455, when York embarked on his second protectorate, the Scottish monarch urged a co-ordinated attack on Berwick and Calais as an expression of support for Henry VI against what appeared to James to be domestic rebellion. Early in 1456 he was even promoting the idea of a perpetual peace between the three kingdoms.[235] Yet by May 1456 he had decided to renounce unilaterally the Anglo-Scottish truce, and in a monumental miscalculation of the political situation at Westminster, in June he informed Charles VII that he was going to support York in his designs on the English throne which, James professed to believe, were patently justified.[236] Is it surprising that Charles should have been slow to respond to James's overtures?[237]

The energetic king could not contain himself sufficiently to await the fulfilment of his schemes, and in any case the English could not be relied on to refrain from cross-border raiding. Thus, the Scottish attack on Berwick in June 1455 was a failure, but after months spent improving Scotland's border defences, especially between Roxburgh and Berwick, James II renounced the truce on 10 May 1456 and launched another assault. He had already dusted off the Scottish claim to the Isle of Man, which was then held by Sir Thomas Stanley, Henry VI's chamberlain, and he resumed the campaign to eject the monks of Coldingham from Scottish soil – and not without success, for by 1461 there were only two left in the priory.[238]

Early in 1456 Roxburgh was invested by a Scottish force which shortly afterwards advanced into Northumberland, where the Scots burned and pillaged extensively for a week before withdrawing at the approach of an English army under the command of the duke of York.[239] This was a major rebuff for James, for whatever appeals York may have made to him in the past, in July 1456 the duke was still influential enough at Henry VI's court to lead the English expedition and to issue, in Henry's name, an outspoken condemnation of the Scottish king's action. James II had burned his fingers badly and his military offensive was therefore no more successful than his diplomatic manoeuvres.[240] By October he had concluded that it was wiser to negotiate a brief truce with the English during which he and his parliament could renew their defensive preparations on the border, confident in the belief that continued political animosities in England would make the enemy more vulnerable than ever.[241]

In February 1457 another attack was expected, this time against Berwick itself, but by 20 July a longer truce had been concluded. Margaret of Anjou may have taken a bold initiative to secure stability in the north by extending her domestic marriage diplomacy to Scotland; she proposed, probably in 1457, that James's sisters, Joan ('the dumb lady') and Annabelle, who were then in France, should marry the duke of Somerset's brothers. In the circumstances, James felt it wise to suspend open war with England (and the new truce was extended to 1468), though raiding and incidents at sea continued to cause strain between the two kingdoms.[242]

Henry VI's government was not deceived by James's willingness to ratify the truce of 1457; his inconstant behaviour alerted the Lancastrians to maintain a state of permanent preparedness in the north. Especially after the French descent on Sandwich in August 1457, the government took precautions lest James launch another attack.[243] Some effort was made during 1457–58 to provide Northumberland, as warden of the more vulnerable east march, with substantial sums of money, both to discharge his arrears and to sustain the defence of the frontier; the custodians of Roxburgh, Sir Ralph Grey and Sir Robert Ogle, were similarly treated.[244] On 20 November 1459, during the Coventry parliament, arrangements were made to pay Northumberland £16,985 of arrears by the following Whitsun.[245] Even Salisbury, the warden of the west march, was provided with £1,578 in June 1459, presumably in the belief that he (or his lieutenants) was more likely to defend the frontier for Lancaster than allow the detested Scots into the kingdom.[246] That such vigilance was necessary is indicated by the fact that judicial sessions that were scheduled to take place in Northumberland, Cumberland, and Westmorland in the late 1450s had to be abandoned because of the disturbed state of the countryside.[247]

These years of uneasy peace were employed by James II to strengthen his defences, pursue his hitherto unattainable alliances abroad, and twirl the muddied political waters in England. His encouragement of the manufacture of guns and mounted cannon ('cartis of weire') and of archery training among his subjects betrays his warlike intentions.[248] These acquired new purpose after the Yorkist lords were dispersed at Ludford Bridge in October 1459. James re-established communication with York himself, and sent emissaries to Ireland seemingly to discuss *inter alia* a marriage between one of the duke's sons and a daughter of the Scottish king. Indeed, by July 1460 it was being reported in Bruges that plans were afoot for a synchronized attack on England by the lords from Calais and James in the north. Yet despite the victory of the former at Northampton on 10 July, James persisted with his siege of Roxburgh later in the month.[249] There could be no clearer indication of his fundamental aim: the advantage of Scotland overrode every other consideration, even the undertakings given to kings and princes. Although James was killed at the siege when one of the great cannons exploded beside him, the Scots continued to invest Roxburgh castle in the presence of Queen Mary and several Scottish magnates; it surrendered within a week.[250]

James's manoeuvres were more irritating than dangerous, for there was a strict limit to what he could achieve by invading the northern shires. Moreover, his diplomatic negotiations did little more than encourage the domestic strife within the English realm; his major objective of an international assault on England never materialized. James's frequent missions to Charles VII, who was a sick man in the years immediately prior to his death in 1461, and the grandiose proposals they urged, were far from welcome at the Valois court. Relations between the two monarchs were somewhat strained by the supposed plot of Charles's Scots guard which was uncovered in August 1455; James took a keen interest in the trials that lasted even into 1457.[251] His claim that his sister Isabelle, dowager duchess of Brittany, and her two daughters were being wrongfully excluded from the Breton succession and kept in Brittany against their will was resented by the duchess herself, whilst James's request that Charles use his good offices in their behalf was inopportune.[252] His demand in 1458 for the county of Saintonge, in fulfilment of a promise by Charles to King James I thirty years before, in return for Scottish reinforcements for use against the victorious duke of Bedford, was astonishing, not least because the reinforcements had never arrived.[253] His requests for military aid and a joint invasion of England and Calais did not appeal to King Charles, who had his own domestic problems and was not inclined to offer open challenge to his niece, Margaret of Anjou, and her husband, Henry VI.[254] Charles, moreover, was not entirely happy with the Scottish king's friendly relations with Burgundy and with James's efforts to reconcile Charles with his estranged son, the Dauphin Louis, who was as welcome in Brussels in October 1456 'as was the Angel Gabriel to the Virgin Mary'.[255] As far as relations with Christian I of Denmark were concerned, James found it very difficult to come to terms which would not involve a heavy tribute to the Danish king; a proposed marriage alliance in 1460 found the Danes reluctant, and despite French mediation nothing came of it.[256]

Charles VII's suspicion of some of his own magnates, particularly the dauphin and the dukes of Alençon and Burgundy, largely determined the course of that king's international diplomacy in these years, and doubtless undermined his already failing health. He was therefore less anxious to join with James II in an invasion of England than to keep an eye on the Burgundians and their new allies, the Yorkist lords at Calais, and to deal vigorously with treason within France itself. As the Milanese ambassador reported from Lyons to Francesco Sforza on 7 December 1456,

> I therefore conclude that the French will have, in my opinion and that of everybody, so much trouble among themselves that they will forget about matters farther off.[257]

After his conquest of Normandy and Gascony in 1449–53, Charles was just as much afraid of a major retaliatory expedition from England, in alliance with dissident French noblemen, as the English were of a French invasion across the channel from a coastline that was now almost exclusively in enemy hands.[258] Disillusion with Valois rule, which implied the absorption of former English possessions in a French scheme of government, is likely to have surfaced within a year or two. As Charles VII explained to the Scottish king in January 1457,

> ... the English, having held the said country [of Normandy] for the space of twenty-two years, or more, know the landing places and all the condition of the country quite as well as those persons do who reside therein; nor, if we consider the long period that they have resided there, can it be otherwise than that they still have some adherents therein, upon whom it is always necessary to keep an eye. And as well from this reason, as also because only six hours of a favourable wind suffice to pass from England into the said country of Normandy, it is most requisite and necessary that the king continually place there a great power for the surety and defence of the country.

And as for the country of Guienne; every person knows that it has been English for the space of three hundred years, or thereabouts, and the people of the district are at heart entirely inclined to the English party; wherefore it is more necessary to be watchful over that than over any other of his lands . . . .

In like manner the duchy of Bretaigne and the country of Pontou and Xantoigne are continually in a state of fear in respect to the enemies, because they lie upon the sea-coast, where the enemy can make a descent any day.[259]

Even the spectacular French descent on Sandwich in August 1457 is unlikely to have been an attack on the English coast such as King James was urging; rather was it a bold stroke designed to locate and destroy some of those ships, perhaps owned by staple merchants, which were in Warwick's employ at Calais and were cruising the channel preying on French commerce.[260] Early in the morning of 28 August, the small port of Sandwich was beset by land and sea by men from a large French fleet out of Honfleur that had anchored in the Downs during the night. Under the command of Pierre de Brézé, seneschal of Normandy, Robert de Flocques, and Charles de Marais, captain of Dieppe, they put the town to the torch, killed many of the townsmen, and despoiled the houses of plate, gold, silver, and merchandise. Many prisoners were taken, though after Sir Thomas Kyriell had been able to rally a counter-attack, the French were driven back to their ships with the loss of about 120 drowned.[261] Rumours that Queen Margaret and her advisers had actually encouraged the raid on Sandwich by de Brézé, who was a confidant of both René of Anjou and Charles VII, were largely malicious or ill-founded, though they came near to reflecting the political situation in England and the anxiety of the French to strike a blow against Warwick, the staplers, and Calais, rather than against Henry VI and his queen.[262] Nevertheless, the attack caused consternation in all the Cinque ports, and at the end of August and during the whole of September, strenuous efforts were made to protect the south and south-east coasts and their main ports.[263]

The French attack gave the Lancastrians the opportunity to assemble those 13,000 archers whose recruitment had been authorized by parliament in 1453–54, though they were never used for coastal defence.[264] About the same time, Henry VI's régime installed dependable captains in certain strategic royal castles in the south-east. On 14 October 1457 Somerset was made custodian of Carisbrooke castle and appointed the king's lieutenant in the Isle of Wight, with a small royal garrison at his disposal.[265] Nicholas Carew was given charge of Southampton castle on 2 November for life, and Lord Rivers became constable of Rochester castle ten days later.[266] On 4 February following, Sir John Cheyne was installed in Queenborough castle, with a suite of rooms that implies that he was expected to be resident there.[267] Indeed, the English were perennially suspicious of what the French might plan across the channel, and after 1450 precautions were periodically taken, especially in the south-eastern shires and the Isle of Wight, to resist enemy marauders; the well-established system of muster, watch, and beacon was frequently activated. In April 1457, when James II was expected to attack Berwick, perhaps in alliance with the French, ships were commandeered in the south-eastern ports.[268] The French landing at Sandwich demonstrated that such measures were needed and they were intensified immediately afterwards. The English could be forgiven for assuming that invasion was the French king's intention.

In fact, Charles VII was unlikely to promote such ventures; booty and plunder might more easily be gained by individual corsairs. Nor was he eager to attack Calais, for that might bring him into dangerous confrontation with his over-mighty subject, Philip the Good. One may conclude, therefore, that political events in England, the French raid on Sandwich, and commercial piracy from Calais against Italian and other merchant ships led the Lancastrian régime to take these measures, not simply to protect the coast from possible invasion, but also to strengthen its grip on the south-east after its return from Coventry in August 1457.

The government's defensive measures continued during 1458 and the first half of 1459, though at a less intense pace. Men were arrayed from time to time in all the counties of the south and east, but especially in Kent, Sussex, and the Thames estuary. Before the court retired to the midlands for the second time in May 1459, it tried to secure the royal fortresses and manor houses in the Thames valley. By this stage, there can be little doubt about the nature of the threat: it would come not from Valois France but from Calais and the Burgundian allies whom the Yorkist lords had acquired, perhaps in league with James II, the arch-intriguer.[269] In this frame of mind, an embassy was sent to both Philip the Good and Charles VII in the autumn of 1458, armed with an important plan for peace; if implemented, it might have the effect of allaying English suspicions of the French and removing the dangerous Burgundian flirtation with Warwick and the Calais garrison. Led by Sir John Wenlock, the queen's former chamberlain, and Master Louis Galet, this embassy was charged with arranging a marriage settlement between the prince of Wales and the sons of York and Somerset, on the one hand, and either three princesses of Burgundian persuasion or else three Valois princesses. Charles VII seems to have been the more anxious to entertain these proposals, even to seal a truce, but nothing came of the mission, partly perhaps because Wenlock had committed himself irrevocably to the Burgundian interest by the time he returned to England early in 1459.[270]

The duke of Burgundy's vital commercial and strategic interest in Calais brought him into frequent contact with the new captain, Warwick. The Anglo-Burgundian truce was a cornerstone of the Anglo-Flemish textile trade, and breaches of its terms were periodically investigated at Calais and elsewhere by representatives of both sides.

Duke Philip was therefore wary of offending the English government, though his duchess, Isabelle of Portugal, and his eldest son, Charles, count of Charolais, seem to have been favourably impressed by the duke of York and the possibility of a marriage alliance with his house as early as 1453–54.[271] Yet after the flight of the dauphin to Burgundy in August 1456 and the deepening political divisions in England, the lines of communication between Calais and Duke Philip assumed greater significance. Moreover, as Henry VI is said to have admitted to the duke of Alençon's envoy early in 1456, the English could not forgive Philip the Good for his defection in 1435.[272] A conference between Warwick and the duke at Oye, not far from Calais, in July 1457 had little tangible result in terms of solving commercial disputes, but their meetings continued in a friendly atmosphere thereafter.[273].

The Lancastrian triumph

The reunion of the Yorkist lords and their retinues in the last week of September 1459 was well planned. York, Salisbury, and Warwick had probably resolved to act jointly after hearing of the robust measures taken by the court as it prepared to leave London once more for the midlands at the beginning of May. On 26 April the gentry of Norfolk (and doubtless other counties) were summoned by the king to join him at Leicester on 10 May 'wyth as many personys defensebylly arayid as they myte acordyng to her degre, and that they schuld bryng wyth hem for her expensys for ij. monythis'. These military preparations were menacing enough, but they were merely the backdrop for a great council which was held at Coventry towards the end of June. The queen and Prince Edward appear to have been present at this council, but York, the Nevilles, and a number of spiritual and temporal lords who were likely to be sympathetic to their predicament (Archbishop Bourgchier, Viscount Bourgchier, Bishop Neville of Exeter, Bishop Grey of Ely, and the earl of Arundel) either absented themselves or, more probably, were not invited. At the queen's insistence, the principal absentees were openly accused. This action is likely to have precipitated the armed clashes of 1459.[274]

Warwick arrived in London from Calais on 20 September, and after spending a night in the city, he and the several hundred men who were with him left next morning for his castle at Warwick.[275] His intention was to join his father and his uncle at Worcester a few days later. Salisbury, accompanied by his younger sons (Thomas and John) and his north-country retinue, may have had as many as 5,000 men at his back as he made his way from Middleham in Yorkshire in the direction of the Welsh border; this force is said to have excelled in experience, bravery, and discipline.[276] York had the shortest journey to make, from his castle of Ludlow.

The three magnates were determined to confront Henry VI. At the very least, noted a sympathetic chronicler, they intended to rebut the charges of disloyalty laid against them; but their purpose is certain to have been wider than that.[277] The so-called *English Chronicle* contains unrivalled knowledge of the movements of these lords during 1459–61, even to the extent of incorporating several documents that reflect their views and announce their intentions. Indeed, one may imagine that the author obtained his information from the Yorkist entourage that fled to Calais after the rout at Ludford Bridge. As a result, we have a clear indication of the purpose of the Worcester meeting:

> . . . an endenture sygned by oure handes in the churche Cathedralle of Worcestre comprehendyng the preef of the trouthe and dewte that, God knowethe, we bere to youre seyde estate [of king] and to the preemynence and prerogatif therof, we sent vn to youre good grace . . . .[278]

The contents of this indenture are regrettably lost, but their general character bears some of the hall-marks of those sworn indentures of brotherhood-in-arms which were not uncommon in England and France in the fourteenth and fifteenth centuries. At a solemn mass in Worcester cathedral, conducted by John de la Bere, bishop of St David's, 'sacred whereoponne, we and euery of vs deposyd for oure sayde trouthe and dewtee accordyng to the tenure of the seyde endenture'. Already kinsmen by blood, they now seem to have bound themselves by faith to aid and succour one another, saving as was customary their personal allegiance to the king.[279] They would thereby have undertaken military as well as civil obligations towards each other. A copy of the indenture was taken to the king by the prior of Worcester cathedral, Bishop de la Bere, and several other prominent theologians, not so much to threaten Henry as to warn him of the desperate measures the Yorkist lords were compelled to take for their own protection in the face of intense hostility from those who ruled the kingdom. These reputable ecclesiastics were persuaded to undertake this delicate mission by the scrupulously loyal declarations which the Yorkist lords were issuing at this time. The ills of the kingdom, which were laid at the door of the king's intimates, were catalogued – how respect for the law was undermined, the king's livelihood embezzled, and Henry himself deceived and ignored -- and the three lords announced their intention, in company with 'lords of lyke disposicion', of confronting the king and begging him for a remedy 'by thadvice of the grete lords of his blood'. York and the Nevilles respectfully offered their assistance and undertook to set aside personal grievances.[280]

This was the spirit in which they made a direct appeal to the king and 'the good and worthy lordes beyng aboute youre moste noble presence', both in writing and by a message carried by garter king-of-arms shortly after the indenture was sealed. A final appeal was sent to Henry after the Yorkist lords had withdrawn westwards to Ludlow and as the royal army was drawing close to Ludford Bridge. In a letter signed by the three magnates on 10 October, they offered to wait on the king personally (who was then at Leominster) to communicate their 'exclamacione and compleynt', provided their safety were guaranteed. This communication, preserved verbatim in the *English Chronicle*, expressed most clearly the aims of the three Yorkists at this juncture and the deep distrust they felt for those, apart from the king and 'worthy lordes', who had been pursuing them for the past three years. It was their belief (which York alone had held in 1450) that their enemies were about to attaint them and thereby strip them of their lands and inheritance and, in York's case, of any legal claim to pose as Henry VI's next adult heir (for an attainted person could hardly ascend the throne peacefully).[281]

> ... as entende of extreeme malyce to procede vnder shadow of youre hyghe myghte and presence to oure destruccione, for suche inordi-nate couetyse, ... as they haue to oure landes, offices, and goodes, ... nor nat hauyng regarde to theffusione of Crystyne blood, ne any tendrenesse to the noble blood of thys lond suche as serue to the tuicione and defens therof, ne nat weyng the losse of youre trew liegemenne of youre sayde reame, ... we here that we be proclamed and defamed in oure name vnryghtefully, vnlawfully, and sauyng youre hyghe reuerence, vntrewly, and otherwyse that God knowethe, then we haue yeue cause; knowyng certaynly that the blessed and noble entent of youre sayde goode grace and the ryghtwysnesse thereof ys, to take, repute, and accepte youre trew and lowly sugettys, and that it accordethe neyther with youre sayde entent, ne wythe youre wylle or pleasure, that we shuld be otherwyse take or reputed.

The lords accurately divined that whatever Henry VI's personal inclinations were – and the 'love-day' of March 1458 had probably reflected these – he was powerless in the hands of the queen and her advisers and that it was they who were pursuing the vendetta against York and his Neville allies. One final appeal over their heads to the king was the only course, short of rebellion, open to the embattled Yorkists to attain security, recover an honourable place in the kingdom, and, for York, recognition of the rights of lineage. The answer of the court to these approaches was to strive to overcome the dissident lords by force.

An attempt had already been made to prevent the junction of their retinues at Worcester. Forewarned of Salisbury's approach from the north, the queen and others urged that an army be sent to intercept him.[282] The king had already assembled men near Coventry and marched north-eastwards to Nottingham as if to do just this, but the earl had wheeled westward and the two forces never met. Instead, it was left to James, Lord Audley, at sixty-one years of age, to attempt to bar

Salisbury's path.[283] Audley had been an able soldier in his day, though his last expedition to France had taken place as long ago as 1431.[284] His Carmarthenshire estates made him an appropriate choice as justiciar of south Wales during 1423–38 and chamberlain there from 1439; despite an unimpressive record as a financial official, he was still in office twenty years later.[285] Most of Audley's estates lay in the west midlands (Staffordshire, Shropshire, and Cheshire), where they were a not insignificant element in the political dominance of the Lancastrian court in the late 1450s. His castle of Red Castle, at Hawstone in Shropshire, lay close to the route which Salisbury would follow from Yorkshire to Worcester in September 1459.[286] Audley was therefore well qualified to act as commander of the queen's forces in the Welsh borderland, not least because he could call on his own tenantry and retainers at relatively short notice; they doubtless formed part of the army which Margaret had recently been raising in the Cheshire region, nominally in her son's behalf, and to which she had been distributing the swan livery.[287] Audley also had a personal reason for relishing a confrontation with Salisbury. His second wife, Eleanor, was the illegitimate daughter of Edmund, earl of Kent and Constance, daughter of Edmund, duke of York; she had tried long ago in 1431 to prove her legitimacy and thereby claim her father's inheritance, which had meanwhile passed to co-heirs who included York and Salisbury.[288] If the stain on his wife's reputation still rankled with Audley in 1459, this was an additional reason for the Lancastrians to call on him to bar the Yorkist advance.

The Lancastrian army, which was much larger (perhaps even 10,000 strong) and more formidable in its cavalry contingent, halted Salisbury's march at Blore Heath, just south of Newcastle-under-Lyme. Audley was assisted in the command by Lord Dudley, whose own landed position in Staffordshire and Cheshire was akin to Audley's, and their army was mainly made up of men from Cheshire, Lancashire, Shropshire, and Derbyshire; the queen waited some 5 or 6 miles off at Eccleshall with a further force.[289] Lord Stanley, who had not been allowed to occupy all of his late father's influential offices in north Wales and north-west England, procrastinated and failed to answer summonses to join the royal retinue; he prevented levies from Wirral and Macclesfield from assembling, and sent his younger brother William to aid Salisbury while he himself with 2,000 men stood on the side-lines during the battle.[290] The two opposing forces met on Blore Heath on 23 September 1459.

The fighting lasted for about four hours, with Audley taking the offensive against the much smaller Yorkist force. During the fighting, Audley was slain by Sir Roger Kynaston of Hordley, one of York's Shropshire retainers who, after the battle, appropriated the Audley arms to his own; the body was taken for burial to Darley abbey, near the Audley residence at Markeston (Derbyshire).[291] Among the captured were Lord Dudley and about fifteen Lancastrian knights and other gentry.[292] In all, about 2,000 men were feared slain, including gentlemen who had only recently been prevailed upon by the court to become knights. The Cheshire contingents fared particularly badly, for members of the Venables, Dutton, Molyneux, Troutbeck, Legh, Egerton, Booth, Calverley, and Downes families were among the dead and wounded on the queen's side especially.[293] Nor did the Yorkist army escape lightly, for part of it decided to return home rather than press on to Worcester; on the way, Salisbury's two sons, Sir Thomas Harrington, and others were captured and locked in Chester castle.[294]

> ... the Erle of Saulysbury hadde ben i-take, save only a Fryer Austyn schot gonnys alle that nyght in a parke that was at the backe syde of the fylde, and by thys mene the erle come to Duke of Yorke. And in the morowe they founde nothyr man ne chylde in that parke but the fryer, and he sayde that for fere he a-bode in that parke alle that nyght.[295]

The magnitude of the death-toll was such that the site of the battle acquired in folk memory the unenviable description of 'Deadmen's Den'.[296] What the battle meant to the families of the fallen is graphically recorded by Margaret, widow of Sir William Troutbeck. A few months later, she catalogued her misfortunes: distraint of knighthood before the battle had cost her William dear; she and her four children faced a future without a husband and father; at Blore Heath her family had lost horses, harness, and other goods worth more than £500 (including perhaps the accoutrements of Troutbeck's retinue); and the wardship of her eldest son had recently cost her £100. In appealing to King Henry for relief, Margaret showed considerable courage, for her brother, William Stanley, had actually fought with Salisbury in the battle.[297]

The engagement at Blore Heath had taken place before Warwick arrived in the area, but a similar attempt to waylay him at Coleshill was mistimed and he was able to push on to Worcester, where he and his father were joined by Richard of York. The royalists' attempt to intercept Salisbury and Warwick had strengthened their collective resolve; hence the ceremony in Worcester cathedral and the final direct appeal to the king. The Lancastrian court was in no mood to parley, and despite the presence of Henry VI, there was evidently little inclination to heed the Yorkists' messages. The king's force at Nottingham had been in the saddle for several weeks, but it made its way back to the west midlands to join the queen and the remnant of Audley's discomforted company.[298] With an army about twice the size of that of the Yorkists, the king made for Worcester and from there pursued York and the Nevilles as they retreated before the superior forces southwards to Tewkesbury and then across country to Ludlow.[299] The combined Yorkist force was headed by York, accompanied by his two elder sons, March and Rutland, and the two Nevilles; the only other peers to join them were Clinton and Powis. Otherwise, the men were led by Salisbury's northern retinue, Warwick's Calais commanders, and the duke's own councillors and retainers, especially those from his marcher lordships.[300]

Henry VI responded to their Worcester appeal with the offer of a pardon signed by him personally and conveyed to the Yorkists by Bishop Beauchamp of Salisbury. It was offered to York and Warwick and their men provided they surrendered within six days; Salisbury may have been excluded because of the part he had played in the death of Lord Audley at Blore Heath. Such humiliating terms would hardly be acceptable to the Yorkist lords.[301] On the other hand, not only were York, Warwick, Salisbury, and their retinues wary of engaging a much larger royal force, but they were naturally reluctant to attack the king himself, whom they recognized to be well-intentioned and whose banner flew prominently over the tents of the royal army as it encamped near Ludford Bridge. Perhaps to forestall a further royal offer of pardon, rumours were circulated that Henry had died. But among the troops whom Warwick had brought from Calais were some who, like Andrew Trollope, had served under the duke of Somerset as captain of Calais and a few of these had already deserted to the king's camp, taking with them valuable intelligence of the size and disposition of the Yorkist army.[302] This was decisive in aborting the anticipated engagement. The lines of battle were drawn on 12 October at Ludford Bridge on the river Teme, just below the hill on which the town and castle of Ludlow stood. York decided to take the advice of his councillors, on whom he had relied heavily throughout his public life, and retired with the Nevilles during the night into Ludlow and thence abroad; they left their unsuspecting followers in their positions so that the Lancastrian army would not realize until morn that the birds had flown.[303] When day came, the leaderless men surrendered and most of them were pardoned. The fugitives took their separate ways.

York and his second son Rutland 'fledde fro place to place in Walys, and breke downe the bryggys aftyr hym that the kyngys mayny schulde not come aftyr hym. And he wente unto Irlonde', where the duke was still the king's lieutenant and refuge could be sought in his own lordships. Salisbury, Warwick, and York's eldest son March made for Calais, where Warwick's position as captain was still reasonably secure. Accompanied by Sir John Wenlock, they hired a ship in Devon through the good offices of John Dynham, and with a few servants they sailed to Guernsey and then Calais.[304] The court turned to demolish the foundations of York's influence in England. Immediately after the flight, the duke's tenantry were harried, their lands despoiled, and the duchess and her youngest children carefully watched.[305] The more permanent destruction of Yorkist power in England was reserved for the parliament which was due to meet at Coventry on 20 November.

The engagements at Blore Heath and Ludford Bridge were the culmination of three years of political and military planning by Queen Margaret and the court she dominated. Her burning desire to humble the Yorkist lords and ultimately treat them as rebels and traitors was about to be fulfilled. The confrontations of 1459 were the military expression of the Lancastrian court's attitude towards a man who, along with his allies, had attained power in preference to the queen and had claimed a special role in the English monarchy itself. To the Yorkist lords, the engagements signalled political bankruptcy: Duke Richard's periods of power had been short because they had depended solely on the temporary incapacity of the king, whilst the claims of his lineage were disputed by others, especially the queen. His last appeal to Henry VI had fallen on deaf ears and the events of September – October demonstrated that his position as premier duke – let alone as a duke with political or dynastic pretensions – could only be preserved either by mastering or destroying the king's ministers, or else by deposing King Henry himself. It is inconceivable that York failed to appreciate these stark alternatives as he contemplated his position in the safe haven of Ireland.[306]

Even before the confrontation at Ludford Bridge, the decision had been taken (on 9 October, when the king was on his way to Leominster) to summon a parliament to Coventry, the most loyalist of all English towns, on 20 November. It cannot seriously be doubted that its purpose was to proclaim York and his adherents traitors and attaint them.[307] Indeed, this was made clear immediately after the flight of the Yorkist lords from Ludlow when commissions were issued to confiscate their possessions as traitors.[308] On 30 October other commissions of oyer and terminer were issued in the west midlands and Welsh borderland for the arrest of all who had been implicated in their treason.[309] The stage was set for the attainder of the rebel leaders, the forfeiture of their lands, and the corruption of their blood.

Nothing was left to chance by the court to ensure that when the assembly met in St Mary's priory, Coventry, it would be a compliant body. The elections in late October and early November were carefully controlled. Most of the sheriffs who had been appointed in November 1458 were subservient gentlemen whom it was now convenient to retain as returning officers. In some instances, this meant extending their term beyond the statutory year and hence parliament authorized a bill of indemnity to remove the risk of prosecution and the danger that the validity of the returns might be challenged.[310] As far as the court was concerned, the sheriffs did their duty admirably and it is difficult to dispel the suspicion that they engineered the election of known loyalists. Accordingly, the new commons house proved staunchly Lancastrian in sympathy.[311] It is true that several of the actual returns do not survive (perhaps in a few cases none was sent in), but among the 169 members whose identity is reasonably certain (out of 260), one has to search long and hard to find a single servant of either York or the Nevilles. Even in Herefordshire, the Lancastrian knight Sir John Barre was elected, whilst the king's chamberlain, Sir Richard Tunstall, sat for Yorkshire.[312] In such an atmosphere of strident loyalty, it was a foregone conclusion that the new speaker, Thomas Tresham of Northamptonshire, should be one of Henry VI's household servants. Tresham had been introduced to the king's service as a boy by his father, and it is likely that by November 1459 he was controller of the household; under his guidance, the commons were certain to fall in with the government's proposals to attaint the Yorkists.[313]

The preparation of the bill of attainder seems to have been undertaken on behalf of the government by a select group of lawyers; it was later said that 'the parlyows writing and the myschevous inditing was ymaginid, contrivid, and vtterly concludid by here most vengeable labowr, etc., and here most malicyows conspiracye ayens the innocent lordys, knytis, gentilis, and comonys, and alle here issv perpetuel, etc.'[314] This small commission consisted of men well versed in the intricacies of civil and common law, and with a record of devotion to the Lancastrian dynasty; indeed, some of them were closely connected with the court's measures against York and his allies.[315] Thomas Daniel and John Heydon had made themselves notorious in Suffolk's company; Dr John Morton was a young and brilliant civil lawyer who was also chancellor of the prince of Wales; Sir John Fortescue was equally able and had been chief justice of king's bench since 1442; Dr Thomas Aleyn and Alexander Hody were also lawyers, and if the former had links with the house of York which he reforged later on, the latter displayed a loyalty to Queen Margaret which led to his death in battle; and finally Thomas Thorp, a lawyer who was baron of the exchequer and keeper of the privy wardrobe, had crossed York's path in the past and stood stolidly by Henry VI in 1459–60.[316] This group is likely to have been responsible for the detailed provisions of the bill of attainder, including the blatant propagandist tone of its preamble, whose Lancastrian view of recent political history emphasized York's accroachment of the royal prerogative since 1450. They set to their task with an eye on the rewards which might come their way for a job well done; Dr Aleyn was later overheard to say that

> yf the lordys that tyme reynyng and now [October 1460] discessid myte haf standyn in gouernauns, that [he and his colleagues] schuld be made for evir; and yf it turnyd to contrary wyse it schuld growe to here fynal confusyon and vttyr destruccyon.[317]

It is small wonder that once the Yorkists had secured control of the king and his government in July 1460, Warwick and Salisbury should have been intent on bringing these lawyers to book.

The attainder was the principal business of this month-long parliament (which was dissolved only five days before Christmas). Most other matters were set aside while the assembly 'abideth vpon the grete materes of atteyndre and forfeture'.[318] All the indications point to the court's determination that the condemnation of the Yorkists should be permanent. Though the king might reserve the right to show mercy to any who were named in the bill, the disposal of the property of the leaders demonstrates that the government had no intention of granting them a subsequent pardon.[319] York, his eldest sons, Salisbury, Warwick, Clinton, and the knights and gentlemen who had led Salisbury's and York's retinues were all attainted, together with Sir William Oldhall and Thomas Vaughan for their machinations in London. The countess of Salisbury was named too, for she was a rich heiress in her own right as the only daughter of the last Montague earl of Salisbury. The duke of Suffolk, who was married to York's daughter Elizabeth, was degraded to the rank of earl; not even the distinguished service of his father and mother to the house of Lancaster could protect him completely in the witchhunt of 1459.[320]

The king did extend his prerogative of mercy to Lord Powis, Walter Devereux, and Sir Henry Radford, for the bill's clause that deprived them of their lands was rejected by Henry, who granted each of them a general pardon.[321] The commons' wish to attaint Lord Stanley for his betrayal at Blore Heath was denied by the king, whose ministers doubtless realized the value of his co-operation in the north-west now that York had escaped to Ireland.[322] Towards the close of parliament, on 11 December, a solemn oath was sworn by the assembled lords in the presence of the king. Each of them acknowledged 'You moost high and myghty and moost Cristen Prynce Kyng Herry the VIth, to be my moost redoubted Soverayne Lord, and right-wesly by succession borne to reigne uppon one and all yure Liege people'. They further promised to preserve the queen and honour Prince Edward, whom they undertook to accept as king in due time.[323] The aristocracy of England thereby reaffirmed its allegiance to Henry VI and his line as the rightful inheritors of the throne. The possibility that York might now pursue his own claim to the crown was evidently in the court's mind and every lord at Coventry was made aware that the dynastic problems of the past two decades were coming to a head and polarizing on the royal diadem itself.

The act of attainder not only pronounced the legal death of Richard of York and his sons, but it brought into the king's hands forfeited estates of unprecedented extent. After three years mostly spent in ruling the country from the midlands, the court was in no hurry to return to Westminster after Ludford Bridge. Kent was known to admire the exploits of Warwick from Calais, and in October 1459 a preacher in London who denounced the Yorkist lords was ill received in the city.[324] On the other hand, the greater difficulty of administering the realm from Coventry and its neighbourhood, particularly in view of the increasingly precarious state of the royal finances, had been brought home to the court since 1456, when the Richmond estates fell to the crown.[325] Hence the careful consideration given to the disposal of Yorkist property between December 1459 and June 1460. The crown's interests demanded that it should not be dispersed in the form of ill-considered rewards to numerous supporters. Indeed, very few of the forfeited estates were granted away in fee tail or for life or even on leases for a term of years.[326] The vast bulk was assigned to royally-appointed stewards, receivers, and bailiffs who could exploit them for the crown's benefit and channel much of the income to the exchequer, or, more likely after the experience of 1456–59, directly to the king's coffers. That most of these officials were appointed for life indicates that the arrangements made by the government for the management of these properties were no temporary expedient but were designed to last for the foreseeable future. The York, Neville, and Clinton estates would be absorbed into the royal demesne.[327] As such, they were organized in stewardships and receiverships and although these generally preserved the administrative traditions of the former lords, in some cases a measure of rationalization was introduced so that (to take an example) the Suffolk and Essex lands of both York and Salisbury were put in the charge of Edmund Blake, an usher of the king's chamber, as steward and receiver.[328]

The new royal stewards were predominantly faithful courtiers like Beaumont, Pembroke, and Dudley, or else leading members of the household (the two carvers, Sir Philip Wentworth and Sir William Catesby, and the chamberlain, Sir Richard Tunstall, among them). The receivers were usually trusted household officials appointed to their new offices for life; if occasionally a York or Neville employee was allowed to stay in office – as was Sir William Herbert, John Milewater, and William Browning – their commissions were to last during the king's pleasure, presumably in the hope that they would be tempted to change their allegiance. Life-annuities which were drawn from these estates were strictly limited in number and size, and were granted mostly to magnates of the court, personal attendants of the king (including his stepfather, Owen Tudor, and his nurse) or participants in recent events (such as Thomas Thorp and Thomas Tresham).[329] Of the modest number of leases that were conceded (no more than twenty in all), most were for relatively short periods of less than a dozen years, and once again individuals with a special claim on the king's patronage were favoured (notably, the duchess of Somerset, Lord Dudley, and Sir Edmund Mountford).[330]

The Lancastrian monarchy had demonstrably learned much from its sojourn in the midlands and accordingly adapted current practices of estate management to ensure that the crown benefited most from the Yorkist forfeitures. It is likely that the estate-income was intended for the royal household, rather than the exchequer at Westminster; certainly the chamber had assumed greater prominence as an office of receipt while the court had resided at Coventry. Edwardian ideas about chamber finance and the organization of forfeited estates seem already to have been in the mind of Lancastrian administrators.[331] It was no imaginative leap for a monarchy that had organized expensive enterprises at home and abroad partly through the king's household to apply the same principle to the extensive properties that were forfeited in the Coventry parliament. In this respect, the court showed determination, foresight, and careful planning, but the days of the Lancastrian régime were numbered and its destruction on the field of Northampton (10 July 1460) preceded by several months the end of the financial year when the benefits of its landed arrangements could be expected to accrue.[332]

In dealing with the Yorkist lords themselves, the court was at a serious – and ultimately decisive – disadvantage. The fact that they had managed to reach Ireland and Calais unharmed presented the government with the very difficult task of defending the realm against attack from both quarters. Calais posed the graver threat, not least because of its garrison and the ships which Warwick could use for a descent on the south-east coast. Moreover, it was recognized that the loyalty of Kentishmen and the Londoners was uncertain, whereas Wales and Cheshire formed a Lancastrian *cordon sanitaire* between York in Ireland and his marcher estates in Wales. Calais, therefore, needed to be treated with greater urgency.

On 9 October, several weeks before parliament actually met, the duke of Somerset was appointed captain of Calais. His first priority was to give effect to his commission and dislodge Warwick. An expedition was quickly fitted out and later in the month he sailed for Calais, accompanied by Lord Roos, the new Lord Audley, and those Calais men who had defected to the king at Ludford Bridge.[333] Their entry to the port was blocked by the garrison, though a number (including Audley and certain captains) were forced by the weather to seek shelter there and were promptly seized. Roos seems to have made off in the direction of Flanders and later ignominiously returned to England. But the main force under Somerset landed at Scales Cliff and made for Guisnes, whence they proceeded to harass Warwick and his men in Calais.[334] Guisnes, in fact, became a strongly garrisoned fortress, geared for war under Somerset, Andrew Trollope, and several newly-appointed administrators who were in charge of its defence and victualling.[335] Their success was limited, and during the most violent skirmish with Warwick, Somerset's forces were routed at Newham bridge.[336] Moreover, during these months, increasing numbers of Englishmen crossed to Calais from Kent to reinforce Warwick and supply him with food and arms.[337] This apparent failure of the Lancastrian government to establish its authority over Calais focussed attention on the role of the staple when the Coventry parliament met. On 11 December restrictions were imposed on the despatch of supplies to relieve or victual the men at Calais, and it was also resolved to suspend trade with the port; although this latter directive was probably ignored by Warwick and the merchants who supported him (and the government may not have had the power to sever the link with London and Sandwich completely), it doubtless stiffened the resolve of the commercial community and therefore the will of the Calais garrison to hold out.[338]

The government was justified in fearing that Warwick might try to secure the ships that were at anchor in Sandwich's harbour, and on 6 December a commission, headed by Buckingham, was entrusted with the task of ensuring that they did not slip out at high tide.[339] Nevertheless, in January 1460 Warwick launched a spectacular raid on Sandwich to prevent the ships there being used to aid Somerset in Guisnes. Lord Rivers and his son, Anthony Woodville, and Lord Scales were charged with protecting the port and with leading an expedition to Guisnes. Before they could accomplish anything, they were attacked on 15 January by John Dynham, who had facilitated the escape of the Yorkist lords from Devon the previous October and now sailed into Sandwich with 800 men. Not only did he seize several ships and escort them to Calais, where they formed part of the invasion fleet in 1460, but he also had the good fortune to capture the Lancastrian lords in their beds.[340] Rivers, one chronicler wryly recorded, 'was commaundyd to have londyd at Calys by the kynge, but he was brought there sonner then hym lekyd'.[341] The jubilant Yorkists did not spare the unfortunate captives when they were paraded before them at Calais. Resentment at their own victimization led Salisbury, Warwick, and March to scorn and vilify Rivers in an outburst of aristocratic pride:

> ... my Lord Ryuers was brougth to Caleys, and by-for the lordys with viij[xx] torches, and there my lord of Salesbury reheted hym, callyng hym knaves son that he schuld be so rude to calle hym and these other lordys traytours, for they schull be found the Kyngys treue liege men whan he schuld be found a traytour, etc.. And my lord of Warrewyk reheted hym and seyd that his fader was but a squyer, and broute vp wyth Kyng Herry the V[te], and sethen hym-self made by maryage and also made lord, and that it was not his parte to have swyche langage of lordys beyng of the Kyngys blood. And my lord of Marche reheted hym in lyke wyse, ...[342]

The plan to winkle Warwick out of Calais and destroy his base of operations had signally failed.

Jasper Tudor was entrusted with the oversight of Wales and the subjugation of York's and Warwick's marcher lordships, particularly Denbigh, whose ready access to the sea had made it York's staging-post on the route to and from Ireland in the past.[343] Lord Stanley, master of the north-west, had been handled gently during the Coventry parliament, and in the south-east of Wales another olive-branch had been proffered to influential Yorkist retainers. Sir William Herbert, whose family had counselled York for two generations and dominated his (and Warwick's) southern lordships, was allowed to retain for life his offices in Glamorgan, Abergavenny, Usk, and Caerleon.[344] The government had also parried a commons' request that the royal officials in Wales and Cheshire should have their life commissions revoked so that they could be subjected to the law more easily. Most of these officials had been hand-picked and the more significant of them were now protected by the king, though sheriffs and escheators were required to provide bonds for their future good behaviour.[345]

On 5 January, Pembroke was appointed constable of Denbigh castle and steward and master forester of the lordship for life; a month later his father, Owen Tudor, also became an official of the lordship for life.[346] These appointments were a prelude to a full-scale siege. But Jasper asked for, and received, sweeping powers that extended far beyond Denbigh and made him a virtual royal recruiting officer in the west and south of Wales, where his own and the prince's territories could provide trustworthy retinues.[347] In the south-east, plans were laid to raise a security force to bring those York and Warwick lordships that were under Herbert's control firmly into the king's obedience.[348] At about the same time, on 4 February 1460, an extraordinarily powerful commission of oyer and terminer was issued to the prince, Buckingham, Pembroke, Shrewsbury, Viscount Beaumont, and a host of gentlemen and lawyers to inquire into all offences, particularly the granting of livery and unlawful assemblies, in the five royal counties of Wales, in Cheshire and Flint.[349] A month later (on 3 March), the same group was given authority to pardon any rebels in the Welsh castles, with the exception of those who had been attainted.[350] Once more, the government was prepared to temper its ruthlessness with conciliation: after all, the destruction of the Yorkist lords and their counsellors was the overriding goal, not the alienation of large numbers of lesser men. In mid-March, Jasper was granted 1,000 marks to finance the reduction not only of Denbigh but of the other castles in Wales that were still in the hands of Yorkist rebels.[351] Denbigh capitulated soon afterwards and by May, Jasper had travelled to Pembroke and was busily organizing the defence of the south coast; the arrest of enemy ships in Milford Sound, another obvious landing place from Ireland, was already in prospect.[352] His success in securing Wales for Lancaster was not inconsiderable, but as events in 1450 and 1460 demonstrated, it was an herculean task to watch every harbour and haven on the long, indented coast of Wales. The Lancastrians' crucial weakness was their failure to prevent their enemies from slipping through their fingers and finding refuge outside the kingdom and beyond reach. That being so, the king and his advisers could only take precautions and wait: the initiative lay with the Yorkists.

Notes

1 Henry VI's visit to France in 1430–32 may be ignored since he was only a child.
2 Virgoe, *BIHR*, XLIII (1970), 139, 153-4, 159-60. Few records of their activities survive beyond February 1456. However, even as late as 20 July Salisbury was being consulted, along with Archbishop Booth of York, Bishop Waynflete (the chancellor), Bishop William Grey, Bishop Lyhert, and Buckingham (PRO, E28/85/34).

3 See *PL*, II, 149 (7 June), 164 (16 October), for the mutual suspicion between Margaret and the duke.

4 ibid., 143, 148. The queen was at Tutbury by 8 May, though her household does not seem to have finally left Westminster until three days later (PRO, E101/410/15).

5 *PL*, II, 148; *Foedera*, V, ii, 69. Henry VI later appended a note to York's letter of 26 July, disclaiming its sentiments and accusing York of usurping the royal authority on several occasions in the past.

6 Above, p. 261; Myers, *BJRL*, XL (1957–58), 96-9.

7 By 18 August he was at Wycombe on his way to Kenilworth (which he had reached by the 24th), Lichfield, and Coventry (Gairdner, *PL*, I, 172). Christie, op. cit., pp. 387-8, has been misled by the dating of letters patent to put the move in the second half of September. The administrative changes may have been under consideration as early as 16 May, when a rumour was abroad that the earl of Wiltshire was to be appointed chancellor (*PL*, II, 144).

8 Liseux was dead by 13 October (C. N. L. Brooke, 'The deans of St Paul's, *c.* 1090–1499', *BIHR*, XXIX [1956], 243; *CPR, 1452–61*, p. 326). Booth succeeded him as dean of St Paul's on the 22nd of the month (Emden, *Cambridge*, pp. 78-9).

9 *HBC*, p. 103; above, pp. 742ff; Pollard, thesis, pp. 80-8 (with the quotation on 88).

10 *HBC*, p. 85; *PL*, II, 162. Both York and Archbishop Bourgchier at least were present at this great council (*CPR, 1452–61*, p. 360).

11 Virgoe, *BIHR*, XLIII (1970), 154 n. 2; Jack, thesis, pp. 63-6; PRO, E404/71/3/38.

12 e.g., PRO, E403/819 m. 4 (from certain councillors at Westminster to the king at Coventry); and for the transmission of cash from London to Chester, Coventry, and Kenilworth, ibid., 811 m. 2 (May 1457).

13 Virgoe, *BIHR*, XLIII (1970), 159-60. For payments to these councillors during 1456–59, see PRO, E403/811 m. 2; 814 m. 3; 817 m. 3. On 29 June 1459, the king replied to the Grand Master of Rhodes that he could not allow the prior of St John's to attend a chapter of their order on 1 October because he was old and sick and in any case was needed in England as a councillor (*PPC*, VI, 299-301).

14 PRO, E403/814 m. 3; 817 m. 4; 819 m. 2; above, p. 262.

15 Archbishop Bourgchier was last paid as a councillor on 2 July 1456, his brother, the viscount, on 17 July, Warwick at Eastertide, and John Say on 14 July (PRO, E403/807 m. 6, 7-10; 814 m. 2; 807 m. 9). By 28 October the earl of Salisbury had retired to Middleham (Yorks.) (ibid., 809 m. 3).

16 *PL*, II, 165 (16 October). But the duke never deserted the court and fell at Northampton in July 1460 (ibid., 172 [1 May 1457]).

17 *Brut*, p. 526.

18 For great councils, see PRO, E403/809 m. 2 (Coventry, October 1456); 812 m. 1, 3 (Westminster, October 1457); 817 m. 8 (Westminster, February 1459); *PPC*, VI, 297 (Westminster, October 1458), 290, 333, 339.

19 ibid., 293, 298, 333. So important was the proposed great council of 10 October 1458 considered to be that Henry VI apologized for summoning it during vacation (ibid., 297).

20 *PL*, II, 164 (for the quotation, 16 October); *RP*, V, 347-48 (c. 1458–59). The

earl of Arundel, too, failed initially to attend the great council in February
1458 (*PPC*, VI, 293).
21 Below, p. 806.
22 *CPR, 1452–61*, p. 500 (April 1459); and another pardon 'by word of mouth'
of the king, ibid., p. 591 (March 1460).
23 *RP*, V, 348.
24 ibid., 347, 350; *CPR, 1452–61*, p. 542; PRO, C81/777/10,706; J. R. Lander,
Crown and nobility, 1450–1509 (1976), p. 130; 'Gregory's Chron.', p. 206.
25 *RP*, V, 350, 363-4 (1459). See also *CPR, 1452–61*, p. 478, for building work
at King's.
26 *PPC*, VI, 290 (November 1456); *CCR, 1454–61*, p. 368 (November 1458);
PPC, VI, 297-8 (February 1459); *CCR, 1454–61* (October 1459).
27 Ramsay, op. cit., II, 229, 244-6, 303; above, p. 718.
28 Christie, op. cit., p. 308.
29 Above, pp. 2-5. Henry also seems to have been a man of few words after
1453 (Giles, p. 47; A. P. Stanley, *Historical memorials of Westminster
abbey* [2nd ed., 1868], p. 571).
30 Stanley, *Memorials*, pp. 570-9 (from depositions in the abbey's archives);
L. E. Tanner, *Recollections of a Westminster antiquary* (London, 1969),
pp. 110-11. Neither Henry IV (who was 47 when he died) nor Henry V went
to such lengths. On 20 November 1459 the king in parliament nominated
a new group of feoffees to implement his will; they were dominated by his
courtiers: *RP*, V, 352; Somerville, op. cit., p. 212 and n. 6.
31 *English Chron.*, p. 79 (reproduced in modernized English in *EHD*, IV, 282),
88. Cf. *Brut*, pp. 526-7 (dated after 1461): 'The gouernance of the Reame
stode moste by the Quene and hir Counsell'.
32 'Gregory's Chronicle', p. 209; Gascoigne, pp. 203-6; 'Benet's Chron.', p.
217. See also Rous, *Historia regum Angliae*, p. 210.
33 Gairdner, *PL*, III, 75; *Brut*, p. 527. For treasonable slanders against the
person and honour of the king, the queen, and the prince in Norfolk by May
1457, 'loose language' about the king and queen in London in March 1459,
and 'opprobrious words' and gossip about the king's person and dignity in
Yorks. later in 1459, see PRO, E403/811 m. 6; *CPR, 1452–61*, p. 400;
Guildhall, Journal VI, f. 117b; *CPR, 1452–61*, p. 518.
34 e.g., Master William Hatclyf, their doctor; John Turges, their harper; Giles
St Lo, a king's serjeant and usher of the queen's chamber; and William
Burton, yeoman of the king's chamber (*CPR, 1452–61*, pp. 195, 339, 458,
423, 288; PRO, DL29/58/1104). When the king and a considerable entourage
stayed at Evesham abbey in March 1457 the cost threw the account of the
abbey's receiver considerably into deficit (WorcsRO, 705: 56/33[iv]). And
for Henry's probable visits to Merevale and Winchcombe abbeys, see WA
MS 649, 3536 (1459).
35 PRO, SC1/57/98.
36 *HBC*, p. 221; *CFR, 1452–61*, p. 192; Emden, *Oxford*, I, 49-50.
37 ibid., II, 856-7; above, p. 757; *EHD*, IV, 280-1, from Exeter Cathedral MS
3498/22-23 (31 October–7 November 1457); PRO, DL29/58/1106-7. Bishop
Boulers had died about March–April 1459 and Hals was provided on 20
September (*HBC*, p. 234). Both the king and the queen were probably
content to support the candidature of John Hunden to the poor see of
Llandaff in June 1458; he was prior of the Dominican friary at King's
Langley (Herts.), near the royal manor house which had been closely

associated with the queens of England since its foundation in Edward I's reign (Emden, *Oxford*, III, 2184; *King's works*, I, 257-63; II, 970-7).

38 Gairdner, *PL*, III, 75; 'Benet's Chron.', p. 223.

39 *VCH, Warws.*, VIII, 3-4; M. D. Lobel (ed.), *Historic towns*, II (1975), section 3; C. Phythian-Adams, op. cit., pp. 19ff (with a map on p. 23).

40 Lobel, op. cit, p. 1.

41 *VCH, Warws.*, III, 248, 263-4; M. D. Harris (ed.), *The Coventry Leet book*, part II (EETS, 1908), pp. 265-6; *CChR, 1427–1516*, pp. 116-17. From 1451 it also returned its own MP. The campaign for a new charter had been under way since 1445.

42 VCH, Warws., III, 248. For Brown, see Wedgwood, *Biographies*, p. 120; and another example, William Elton, who was MP in 1453–54 and a household official, ibid., p. 299. Coventry was represented for the first time since 1315 in the parliament of 1450–51 (not that of 1453–54, as in idem, *Register*, p. 207).

43 *VCH, Warws.*, III, 214, from Harris, *Leet book*, p. 300.

44 *RP*, V, 345; *VCH, Warws.*, II, 438; III, 144. The figure, which was apparently affixed to Coventry cross after the Dissolution, is now in the city museumn (and I am grateful to the curator for supplying a photograph of it).

45 Above, p. 259. For a series of letters signed by the king and dated at Coventry, Kenilworth, and Leicester between December 1456 and June 1457, see Bodl, MS ch. England, 30-44.

46 Above, p. 57.

47 Below, p. 820.

48 For this subject, see Griffiths, 'Patronage, politics, and the principality of Wales', pp. 82-6, with further details in idem, *Principality of Wales*, passim.

49 Roskell, *Lancashire knights*, pp. 170-2; Bennett, unpublished paper, quoting J. R. Oliver (ed.), *Monumenta de Insula Manniae* (3 vols., Manx Soc., IV, VII, IX, 1860–€⁻ II, 235-46; III, 1-9.

50 Ralph Legh, who also hailed from Cheshire, was escheator of Merioneth from 1437 (*CPR, 1435–41*, p. 34; ibid., *1441–46*, pp. 22-3).

51 Above, p. 361.

52 Above, p. 748.

53 PRO, DL29/651/10533 m. 2.

54 Griffiths, *WHR*, II (1964–65), 223-5.

55 *PL*, II, 148.

56 PRO, KB9/35/24, 71. See Storey, *End of Lancaster*, p. 179; Griffiths, *WHR*, II (1964–65), 225. The indictments of April 1457 on which this account is based are fully analysed in Herbert, thesis cited, pp. 245-75; idem, in Griffiths, *Patronage, the crown and the provinces*, ch. 5. A number of those accompanying Herbert and Devereux were to become committed Yorkists later on: e. g., R. S. Thomas, thesis cited, pp. 168-70.

57 WA MS 5479x, for which see Griffiths, *WHR*, II (1964–65), 226 and n. 61.

58 Uncertainty about the date and place of his death and of his burial (in the Grey Friars at Carmarthen, whence the body was removed to St David's cathedral at the Dissolution), is now removed by R. S. Thomas, thesis p. 171 and n. 1.

59 *CCR, 1454–61*, p. 158; Storey, *End of Lancaster*, p. 180.

60 H. T. Evans, *Wales and the wars of the roses* (Cambridge, 1915), p. 96; *CPR, 1452–61*, p. 326.
61 For a record of the stay at Evesham abbey, see WorcsRO, 705: 56/33 (iv); Storey, *End of Lancaster*, p. 181, mistakenly places the sessions at the end of April.
62 Herbert, thesis, pp. 257-60; Storey, *End of Lancaster*, pp. 181-2.
63 R. S. Thomas, thesis, pp. 174-5; R. F. Walker, 'Jasper Tudor and the town of Tenby', *NLWJ*, XVI (1969), 1-22; idem, 'Tenby', in R. A. Griffiths (ed.), *Boroughs of medieval Wales* (Cardiff, 1979), pp. 295-6; E. Laws, 'Notes on the fortifications of medieval Tenby', *Arch. Camb.*, 5th ser., XIII (1896), 177-92, 273-90. For communications between Jasper at Tenby and Buckingham at Greenfield, near Newport, in 1456–57, see PRO, SC6/954/25 m. 11.
64 *CPR, 1452–61*, p. 494; PRO, SC6/584/9249 m. 2. For the Yorkist proclivities of the hunted men, see R. S. Thomas, thesis, p. 177; Evans, *Wales and the wars of the roses*, p. 95; Griffiths, *WHR*, II (1964–65), 227.
65 G. F. Beltz, *Memorials of the most noble order of the Garter* (London, 1841), p. clxii. Jasper took the place vacated by the death on 28 June 1458 of Alfonso V, king of Aragon.
66 Though required to resign as justiciar of north Wales and Chester, and chamberlain of north Wales by 17 October 1450, he was back in office by 14 July 1452 (*CPR, 1446–52*, pp. 403, 581).
67 Griffiths, *WHR*, II (1964-65), 213-31.
68 JRL Ch. 1366: a warrant of Prince Edward, issued on 19 November 1458 *cum advisamento dominorum de consilio nostro*, but with the assent *clarissime matris nostre Regine*. For references to similar warrants, see PRO, SC6/1217/3 m. 3-6.
69 *CPR, 1452–61*, pp. 357-8, 359; *Foedera*, V, ii, 70. Previously Edward had enjoyed the style and title of prince since 15 March 1456, and 1,000 marks for the expenses of his chamber, wardrobe, and servants from 20 July 1456.
70 *CPR, 1452–61*, pp. 323, 429; Wedgwood, *Biographies*, pp. 943-4; *CPR, 1446–52*, p. 410; Myers, *BJRL*, XL (1957-58), 405 n. 2. Whittingham had been captain of Caen at the time of its fall in 1450 (PRO, E404/66/80, 104).
71 *CPR, 1452–61*, p. 334; PRO, E404/46/211; 63/4; DL29/58/1104; Myers, *BJRL*, XL (1957–58), 405-6; Guildhall RO, Journal V f. 125b. See also Jeffs, thesis, p. 321.
72 *CPR, 1452–61*, p. 335; Wedgwood, *Biographies*, pp. 852-3; Carpenter, thesis, pp. 112, 114, 115; ShakesBT, Throgmorton MSS, Box 59/8; WorcsRO: 899/95/Box 6/110-13; 705: 56/33(iv); 009: 1/175/92483; WarwsRO, CR 623/Box 10 m. 4d, 6; GlosRO, D 1099/M 31/63.
73 *CPR, 1452–61*, pp. 338, 359; above, p. 262: PRO, DL29/212/3261, 3269.
74 PRO, SC6/1162/7, 8; 1168/8, 9.
75 ibid., 1217/3 m. 5; Griffiths, thesis, p. 549.
76 e.g., PRO, SC6/1217/3 m. 7 (December 1459).
77 Neither Stanley in north Wales nor Audley in south Wales seems to have been succeeded by a high-ranking official before March 1461 (Griffiths, *Principality of Wales*, pp. 185-6; *CPR, 1452–61*, p. 62). For Tunstall's appointment, see Wedgwood, *Biographies*, p. 882; PRO, E404/67/238; 68/104; and for Shrewsbury's, PRO, Chester 2/132 m. 6. This mastery of

the prince's affairs may have provided the basis for the rumour that Margaret was planning to induce Henry VI to abdicate in favour of Prince Edward (*English Chron.*, p. 80). Even if the events of 1327 could be used as a precedent, with Margaret taking the role of Queen Isabella, it is doubtful if the queen's position would have been made stronger with a young boy on the throne: a regency had been opposed by the lords in 1454 and York would still be able to forward a strong claim to be protector. It is safest to conclude that the suggestion is largely slanderous.

78 Somerville, op. cit., pp. 466, 498-9, 485, 494, 500; Wedgwood, *Biographies*, pp. 882-4. After Molyneux was killed at Blore Heath on 23 September 1459, he was replaced as escheator by William Tunstall, Sir Richard's son. Sir Richard Tunstall had been appointed receiver of the lordship of Tickhill on 28 September 1457 (Somerville, op. cit., p. 530).

79 ibid., p. 429. It is unnecessary to assume that Stanley could no longer be trusted by the court after his appointment as controller of the king's household and his elevation to the peerage in the months following St Albans, 1455 (as in Storey, *End of Lancaster*, p. 186): it is far from clear that the post-St Albans régime was decisively Yorkist in character (see above, p. 748). On the contrary, Stanley was not proceeded against by the queen and the court before his death in February 1459 and he retained all his offices in Chester, Wales, and the duchy of Lancaster. He is not certainly known to have been replaced as chamberlain of the household before his death: he is noted as chamberlain on 8 May and 22 October 1458 (BL, Cotton, Nero D VII f. 75-77; PRO, C53/190 m. 9-11), though a solitary reference to Sir Richard Tunstall as chamberlain occurs on 10 July (ibid.). This last reference I owe to Professor Storey.

80 Storey, *End of Lancaster*, p. 186n; Bennett, unpublished paper; *RP*, V, 369-70.

81 Somerville, op. cit., pp. 421, 514.

82 Carpenter, thesis, pp. 12-15; Rawcliffe, op. cit., passim (with a map on p. xiii); Pollard, thesis, passim; R. S. Thomas, thesis, pp. 113-14; *CPR, 1452–61*, pp. 116, 104; *CFR, 1452–61*, p. 30. On Earl Edmund's death in November 1456, the two manors became Jasper's alone; the Notts. and Derbs. lands were estimated to be worth £100 net in 1457.

83 *English Chron.* p. 80 (1459). See R. A. Griffiths, 'The hazards of civil war: the case of the Mountford family', *Midland Hist.*, V (1980), 1-19. For the queen's visit to Coleshill in 1457, see Harris, *Leet book*, p. 300.

84 Above, pp. 346, 351.

85 Carpenter, thesis, pp. 193ff.

86 York himself had little or no property between the marchland and his estates in eastern England, and hence in 1456–60 the kind of feverish communication that had stimulated risings in his behalf in 1452 was less practicable (Rosenthal, 'Estates and finances of York', pp. 194-6; above, p. 695).

87 Wedgwood, *Biographies*, pp. 325, 602-3, 21-2; Griffiths, *Midland Hist.*, V (1980), 1-6; Otway-Ruthven, *King's secretary*, pp. 158, 185. Ashby had Warws. origins and it is noteworthy that the court was careful to enlist household men with Warws. interests (but cf. Carpenter, thesis, pp. 179ff). The Coventry MP in 1459 was an exchequer official, also from Warws., John Brown, and Mountford's colleague representing the county was

Henry Everingham, an esquire of the household (Wedgwood, *Biographies*, pp. 120, 307; above, p. 370).

88 At least a dozen are known in 1456, 1458, and 1459, with rather fewer in 1457. These rough calculations are based on Jeffs, thesis, pp. 341-3; Wedgwood, *Biographies*, passim. Further research would probably reveal more. C. A. Robertson, 'Local government and the king's "affinity" in fifteenth-century Leicestershire and Warwickshire', *Trans. Leics. arch. and hist. soc.*, LII (1976-77), 41-2, supports this view.

89 Rawcliffe, op. cit., pp. 201, 222, 239; Wedgwood, *Biographies*, pp. 440-1.

90 ibid., p. 44; Rosenthal, 'Estates and finances of York', pp. 190, 176-7, 191 (though even Barre is a doubtful case since he deserted York after 1456: Herbert, thesis, pp. 50,258; below, p. 823). It may be noted, too, that whereas Viscount Bourgchier had always had several of his retainers returned to parliament in Henry VI's reign, there was none in 1459; despite Woodger, thesis, p. 296, it is likely that Sir Thomas Tyrell's household affiliations in 1459 were at least as strong as his ties with the Bourgchiers, for one day after his return to parliament for Essex on 13 November, he was made sheriff of the county (Wedgwood, *Register*, p. 257 and n. 8). For this parliament, see below, p. 823.

91 Thomson, op. cit., pp. 100-2; above, p. 131.

92 The idea may have been mooted, for in December 1458 a book detailing the imposition of a fifteenth and tenth on the laity in Henry V's reign, which had been borrowed by the treasurer, was then returned to the exchequer (PRO, E403/817 m. 8). This entire phase of government finance has not been thoroughly investigated, and one awaits the completion of the investigations of G. L. Harriss.

93 Above, pp. 359-62.

94 PRO, E403/807 m. 4 (November 1456); 811 m. 2 (May 1457). For the reliance of the great wardrobe on exchequer subventions in 1456–57, see PRO, E101/410/14, 19 (two separated sections of the same account). It is impossible to calculate the total payments to the treasurer of the household and the treasurer of the great wardrobe during 1457–60 because several issue rolls are missing, but it seems likely that the level of 1455 and 1456 was maintained at the very least (PRO, E403/807-19 passim).

95 *CPR, 1452–61*, p. 359 (30 May 1457); *CCR, 1454–61*, p. 165. For other London examples, see ibid., p. 468; *CPR, 1452–61*, p. 430.

96 ibid., p. 295. For Brekenok, who had supervised the financial arrangements of Queen Margaret's journey to England, see Wedgwood, *Biographies*, pp. 106-7 (which mistakenly refers to him as being appointed treasurer by York).

97 *CPR, 1452–61*, pp. 360, 367. On 16 August this was exchanged for a more dependable (and speedier) source, though when the new bishop of Durham, Lawrence Booth, eventually produced £710 from Durham in April 1458, he was warmly congratulated (PRO, E403/814 m. 1). For Grimesby's household service, see Wedgwood, *Biographies*, pp. 400-1.

98 *CPR, 1452–61*, pp. 418, 460.

99 If such sums did materialize, they would have increased the annual subventions to the great wardrobe several fold; there is no sign of them on the issue rolls, though they would represent a source of income for the household that was independent of the exchequer. The average exchequer

payment to the great wardrobe during 1455–57 was *c*. £750–£850 *per annum* (PRO, E403/800-11; E101/410/14).

100 *CPR, 1452–61*, p. 432 (12 May 1458). This decision of the council was reinforced, interestingly enough, by letters patent on 5 July.

101 *CCR, 1454–61*, pp. 205 (April 1457), 270 (April 1458); PRO, E403/812 m. 3 (October 1457); 817 m. 3 (November 1458). The clerks from the royal chapel were paid from the proceeds on 4 July 1459 (ibid., 819 m. 6). Those with £40 *per annum* in land and rents over a 3-year period were fined for distraint of knighthood or else required to purchase a pardon. By introducing the measure in 3 successive years, few could escape.

102 *CPR, 1452–61*, p. 286; above, p. 386.

103 *CPR, 1452–61*, p. 291 (31 May 1456). They included the king's physician, John Faceby, for whom see above, p. 717. For medieval writings on the subject, see Ogrine, *JMH*, V (1980), 104-23.

104 *CPR, 1452–61*, pp. 339, 390.

105 PRO, DL29/212/3261-69 (1445–59). Cash was transported from the honour of Leicester to Lichfield sometime after Michaelmas 1459, presumably to the queen's officials (ibid., 3269.).

106 ibid., 58/1103-7 (1453–59). The queen was rather less successful with more distant estates: the 'south parts' (scattered in several shires) showed stability in its cash deliveries between 1445 and 1458 (£140–£175 *per annum*), though Yarkhill manor in York-dominated Herefs. was conspicuous by its failure to achieve even this (PRO, SC6/1093/11-13; DL29/672/10815, 10818, 10820-22). This whole subject is being studied by J. G. Reid, to whom I am indebted for these references.

107 PRO, SC6/1162/8. See Griffiths, thesis, pp. 204, 419-20.

108 PRO, SC6/1224/1 m. 12; 1162/8 m. 5d, 6; 1168/8 m. 2; 9 m. 1d; ChesterRO, MB 5. f. 24-27. In addition, in May 1457 the 3 shires of north Wales offered a gift to Prince Edward of £12,667 payable over 6 years; many lords in late medieval England demanded such *mises* at their entry into their lordships in return for confirming charters and customs. The gift in north Wales was poorly paid (barely £58 in 1458–59) and none was forthcoming in the south. PRO, SC6/ 1217/3; Griffiths, thesis, p. 470. The subject is treated at length in ibid., pp. 462-76; Pugh, op. cit., pp. 145-7.

109 PRO, SC6/1168/8 m. 5; /9; 1162/7, 8, 9; above, p. 783.

110 Griffiths, thesis, p. 427.

111 *CPR. 1452–61*, p. 515. The result was impressive: whereas only £57 in cash was produced at the exchequer from north Wales in 1453–54, the figure for the prince in 1458–59 was £287 (PRO, SC6/1217/2-3).

112 *English Chron.*, pp. 79-80; below, p. 820.

113 e.g., the £700 loan of the London merchants, John Brown and John Poutrell, who had close links with the household; repayment was ordered from the proceeds of distraint of knighthood on 19 December 1457 (*CPR, 1452–61*, p. 397).

114 PRO, E403/811 m. 1, 6; 814 m. 2, 4; 817 m. 5, 8; Steel, op. cit., pp. 279-81. Shrewsbury was quick to exchange tallies (worth £372) issued on 30 May two days later. For loans by 2 other members of the Lancastrian court, Bishop Waynflete (£220, by November 1457) and Lord Stourton (by August 1459), see *CPR, 1452–61*, pp. 420, 511

115 *CCR, 1454–61*, pp. 173, 225, 227, 231, 233, 260, 266, 280, 299, 309; *CPR, 1452–61*, p. 329. These licences were issued to government creditors. Proof

and bonds were offered that the exports were legal. This cash would also go to the great wardrobe (see above, p. 835).

116 *CPR, 1452–61*, p. 500. They began to creep back in 1459 (below, p. 810; *CCR, 1454–61*, p. 414).

117 Haward, in *English trade*, pp. 313-14; Steel, op. cit., p. 282. Only modest sums were actually received at the exchequer.

118 *HBC*, pp. 102, 79; Storey, *BIHR*, XXXI (1956), 91.

119 Wood's appointment is first noticed on 30 March 1458 (PRO, E403/817 m. 5). He had been under-treasurer during Worcester's treasurership (1452–55) and at some point was Salisbury's servant; but the government's shielding him from attack in parliament in 1455 seems to have made him a willing servant of the court thereafter. See ibid., 807 m. 5; Roskell, *Speakers*, pp. 291-3; idem, 'Sir John Wood of Molesey', *Surrey Arch. Coll.*, LVI (1959), 15-28.

120 The appointments may have been the prelude to a demand for a fifteenth and tenth from the laity; if so, the prospect of summoning a parliament for this purpose probably caused its abandonment (above, n. 92). It is worth noting that in November 1457 York's former antagonist, Thomas Thorp, was appointed keeper of the privy wardrobe in the Tower for life, and in September 1458 he was reappointed baron of the exchequer (Roskell, *Speakers*, p. 366; *CPR, 1452–61*, p. 392).

121 Bolton, thesis, pp. 135-6, 169-70, 193-7. Only the Venetians had an English consul, though his powers were not great (*CVenP*, I, 84, 86).

122 Lloyd, op. cit., p. 276; Haward, in *English trade*, pp. 310-12; and above, p. 393 for their loans. Ordinances of 1421 and 1452 confining the brokerage business to Englishmen and resident Londoners were ineffective (Barron, thesis, p. 221).

123 Quoted in Bolton, thesis, p. 272.

124 ibid., pp. 169-70, 174; *Fabyan's Chron.*, p. 633. This demonstrates contemporaries' lack of understanding of ideas about the balance of trade. It may also be significant that the Genoese had recently, in February 1455, come to an agreement with the London authorities in their long-standing dispute about liability to the scavage (or foreign sales) tax (Barron, thesis, pp. 372-8). See also below, n. 126.

125 Below, pp. 792-5.

126 *RP*, V, 325; Flenley, p. 110 (mistakenly reporting the act to be operative for 7 years). The sheriffs of London were ordered on 16 March 1456 to proclaim the statute in the city. It is significant that Genoese silk was exempt.

127 *Brut*, pp. 522-3; *Great Chron.*, p. 188; *London Chrons.*, pp. 166-7; Flenley, pp. 143-4; *Three Chrons.*, p. 70; *Fabyan's Chron.*, pp. 630-1. Modern accounts of this riot appear in Flenley, *EHR*, XXV (1910), 650-2; Ruddock, *Italians in Southampton*, p. 163.

128 *PL*, II, 143-4.

129 The king was in the midlands by late August (Gairdner, *PL*, I, 172).

130 *Letter book K*, p. 377. The memory of large bands of seignorial retainers in the city was still fresh (above, p. 690).

131 Flenley, *EHR*, XXV (1910), 650-2. The council met at Coventry from 7 October 1456. For Cantelowe, see Thrupp, *Merchant class*, p. 328; Wedgwood, *Biographies*, pp. 152-3. He was knighted by Edward IV in 1461.

132 JRL, Latin 178 f. 138-39; *CVenP*, I, 81-2. The king accommodated the Italians by ordering the removal of the official wool scales to Winchelsea about 28 October (PRO, E403/809 m. 3).

133 *CCR, 1454–61*, pp. 192, 214; *Letter book K*, pp. 377-8; for this incident, see Flenley, *EHR*, XXV (1910), 652-3; Haward, in *English trade*, pp. 310-11. The recorder and aldermen of London travelled all the way to Kenilworth to assure the king of their continued loyalty, despite their inactivity.

134 *Three Chrons.*, p. 70; Flenley, pp. 110, 144; *Letter book* K, pp. 385-90 (misdated to 9 June). For modern accounts, see Flenley, *EHR*, XXV (1910), 653-4; Ruddock, *Italians in Southampton*, pp. 163-4.

135 C. S. Gutkind, *Cosimo de' Medici* (Oxford, 1938), pp. 188-9 (misdating it to July); J. Heers, 'Les Genois en Angleterre: la crise de 1458–1466', in *Studi in onore di Armando Sapori* (2 vols., Milan, 1957), I, 812, citing Florence, Arch. di stato, Filz Strozz., 249 cte, 138-9. See also L. Einstein, *The Italian renaissance in England* (New York, 1902), pp. 252-6. Only by mutual agreement could they return to London within the three years.

136 *CVenP*, I, 84-5 (by the Venetian senate, 23 August 1457); Heers, in *Studi*, p. 812 (by Genoa, 18 August 1457); and the fact that a copy of the agreement is still among the Florentine archives (above, n. 135) may indicate ratification there too. See Gutkind, op. cit., p. 188, and Heers, in *Studi*, I, 812, for the quotations.

137 Flenley, *EHR*, XXV (1910), 654-5; Ruddock, *Italians in Southampton*, pp. 66-8, 123, 165-73. The first known Venetian resident in Southampton can be detected in 1456.

138 Carus-Wilson, *Mediaeval merchant venturers*, pp. 66-73, first published in Power and Postan, *English trade* (1933), pp. 225-30; Ruddock, *Italians in Southampton*, pp. 173-6. It seems likely that the attackers were pirates, though they may have been encouraged by the French, who took Genoa under their protection in 1458 (Heers, in *Studi*, I, 810-13). That it was not an exclusively Bristol venture is indicated by the compensation payments to the merchants of Bristol and other towns in 1459 (*CPR, 1452–61*, p. 517).

139 *London Chrons.*, p. 169; *Great Chron.*, p. 190; Flenley, pp. 112, 161; *CPR, 1452–61*, pp. 488 (August–September 1458), 444; *CCR, 1454–61*, pp. 331, 363; *Fabyan's Chron.*, p. 633. The compensation was paid on 25 July 1459 (*CPR, 1452–61*, p. 517.) For the difficulty Italians had in securing just verdicts from jurors at this time, see Ruddock, *Italians in Southampton*, pp. 178-9, 185; and for restrictions in October 1458 on foreigners' use of other than the king's weights and measures, see *Letter book K*, p. 394.

140 Ruddock, *Italians in Southampton*, pp. 169-73, 176-7. The leader of the anti-alien movement in Southampton, John Payne, is dealt with in A. A. Ruddock, 'John Payne's persecution of foreigners in the town court of Southampton in the fifteenth century', *Trans. Hants. Arch. Soc. and Field Club*, XVI (1944), 23-37. The Florentine fleet of 1459-60 sailed to London (Mallett, *Florentine galleys*, p. 93), and the Genoese and Venetians also returned there (Heers, in *Studi*, I, 814; Flenley, *EHR*, XXV [1910], 655; *CVenP*, I, 87). Several Italians took the precaution of procuring letters of denization during 1459–61 (*CPR, 1452–61*, pp. 476, 579, 615, 641).

141 The Medici company in England was crippled by the events of 1456–58 (Gutkind, op. cit., p. 189), and the Genoese colony was much reduced by 1462–63 (Heers, in *Studi*, I, 814-15). T. H. Lloyd calculates (op. cit., p. 276)

that whereas total alien exports of wool from England between March 1455 and November 1457 were 5,062 sacks, during 1457–60 they amounted to only 1,168 sacks (with another 1,137 shipped by alien and denizen factors from Southampton in 1459–60).

142 Above, p. 790. Despite the arrest of the Genoese in 1458, an order (23 August) for the confiscation of all their merchandise in the city was countermanded (*CPR, 1452–61*, p. 444), and inquiries during 1459 into offences against commercial regulations often led to pardons for the Italians (Haward, in *English trade*, pp. 311-12).

143 It is worth noting that London's gifts and loans to Henry VI (including those of the staplers) in 1455–60 were little more than a quarter of those of 1450–55 (Barron, thesis, p. 612).

144 Flenley, p. 144; 'Benet's Chron.', p. 217.

145 Flenley, p. 146; *Brut*, p. 525; *Great Chron.*, p. 190; *London Chrons.*, p. 169.

146 'Benet's Chron.', pp. 222-3; *Chron. of London*, p. 140; *Three Chrons.*, p. 71; Flenley, pp. 113, 146. Waynflete, Booth, and Wiltshire, Beaumont and Sudeley, and the bishop of London, Lord Fauconberg, and the two archbishops were the lords who intervened. See Peake, thesis, pp. 125-6; Scofield, op. cit., I, 63 (misdating the king's threat to 1460).

147 All the contemporary chroniclers, but more particularly those writing in London, reported the episode ('Benet's Chron.', pp. 219-21; *Grey Friars Chron.*, p. 20; *English Chron.*, pp. 75-6; Flenley, p. 145; *Brut*, p. 525). See C. Babington (ed.), *The repressor of over much blaming of the clergy* (2 vols., RS, 1860), with his works listed vol. I, pp. lxi-lxxxiii, and his trial pp. xxxviff. Pecock's trial has attracted much attention from historians (e.g., Thomson, op. cit., pp. 215-17; E. F. Jacob, 'Reynold Pecock, bishop of Chichester', in idem, *Essays in later mediaeval history*, pp. 1-34 [first published in *PBA*, XXXVII (1951)]; V. H. H. Green, *Bishop Reginald Pecock* [Cambridge, 1945]; E. H. Emerson, 'Reginald Pecock: Christian rationalist', *Speculum*, XXXI [1956], 235-42).

148 Emden, *Oxford*, II, 776 (for Goddard); Jacob, *Essays in later mediaeval history*, pp. 21-2.

149 'Benet's Chron.', p. 219. For various versions of the abjuration, see ibid., p. 163; Jacob, *Essays in later mediaeval history*, p. 19 n. 2.

150 Emden, *Oxford*, III, 1447-9. For his resignation, rather than deprivation, see Jacob, *Essays in later mediaeval history*, pp. 21-2.

151 For recent studies of the nobility in the last years of Lancastrian rule, see C. F. Richmond, 'The nobility and the wars of the roses, 1459–61', *Nott. Med. St.*, XXI (1977), 71-86; Lander, *Crown and nobility*, pp. 301-6.

152 Above, p. 743. On balance, it seems unlikely that Viscount Bourgchier and his son were with York too (above, p. 766).

153 Above, p. 726; Mitchell, op. cit., ch. III; Lander, *Crown and nobility*, p. 301. Worcester certainly went abroad in the spring of 1458; it is unknown whether Norfolk did so, but by December 1459 he at least was not in rebellion with the Yorkist lords (*CPR, 1452–61*, p. 541).

154 Woodger, thesis, p. 48, is inclined to view the Bourgchiers as 'statesman-like' 'conciliators'. For the election to the garter of John Bourgchier, Lord Berners, in 1458–59, see Milner, thesis, p. 100.

155 The choicest piece of patronage – the marriage of Margaret Beaufort,

countess of Richmond – was granted to Buckingham's son in about 1459 (below, p. 802). But see Rawcliffe, op. cit., pp. 24-5.

156 'Benet's Chron., p. 217.
157 Otway-Ruthven, *Medieval Ireland*, p. 387; Storey, *End of Lancaster*, p. 182. Wiltshire was also earl of Ormond and Shrewsbury was chancellor of Ireland (above, p. 734).
158 Below, pp. 854-5.
159 For a sketchy itinerary of these years, see Rosenthal, 'Estates and finances of York', p. 199.
160 *CPR, 1452–61*, pp. 660-83; PRO, E403/814 m. 4, 6; 816 m. 2; 817 m. 9.
161 Below, p. 809.
162 Storey, *EHR*, LXXII (1957), 614; PRO, E403/807-19 passim. Northumberland was due to receive wartime rates of pay between 24 June 1455 and 6 July 1457.
163 Storey, *End of Lancaster*, pp. 182-3; Somerville, op. cit., p. 538. The earl of Westmorland's brother, John Neville, was raised to the peerage in 1459 (*GEC*, IX, 504).
164 'Benet's Chron.', p. 217; *Great Chron.*, p. 189; Flenley, p. 144; *Grey Friars Chron.*, p. 20. The prisoners were eventually subdued and put in irons. Egremont's escape so angered Salisbury and his sons that they contemplated taking legal action against the sheriffs of London (*Reg. Whetehamstede*, I, 304). It was a condition of the arbitration of March 1458 that their suits should be dropped.
165 Flenley, p. 159; *Great Chron.*, p. 189; *London Chrons.*, p. 167.
166 ibid.; Flenley, pp. 113, 146; *Brut*, p. 526; *Great Chron.*, p. 190.
167 ibid., p. 189; 'Benet's Chron.', p. 217; *Brut*, p. 523; *London Chrons.*, p. 167; *RP*, V, 348. The lords' criticism at a Coventry great council is undated, but C. L. Scofield (op. cit., I, 24) and R. L. Storey (*End of Lancaster*, pp. 180-1) plausibly assign it to the early part of 1457 or the autumn of 1456, when events in south-west Wales were causing tension between the duke of York and the court (above, p. 780). York is not known to have been at a Coventry great council after 1456–57 (Rosenthal, 'Estates and finances of York', p. 199).
168 Though their absence was not quite as total as Lancastrian propaganda claimed (below, pp. 805ff).
169 *CPR, 1452–61*, p. 370. For a special commission in Notts. against the Plumptons, see ibid. (13 August 1457).
170 Sir John Barre (in Herefs.) was the only non-aristocrat named, but for his recent royalist sympathies, see Wedgwood, *Biographies*, p. 44.
171 *CCR, 1454–61*, p. 205 (12 April 1457); Herbert, thesis, pp. 245ff; above, p. 780.
172 *CPR, 1452–61*, pp. 660-84.
173 For Choke, see E. Foss, *A biographical register of the judges of England* (1870), p. 164.
174 The south-west, however, was not neglected; in addition to the support it now received from the earls of Devon (father and son), the court appointed the duke of Exeter to the Devon bench in May 1457, to that of Cornwall in June 1457, Somerset in July 1457, and Dorset in November 1458; to Devon was added the earl of Wiltshire in July 1457 and Courtenay's councillor, William Boef, in June (*CPR, 1452–61*, pp. 662-76). The whole matter requires further study.

175 PRO, E101/410/19; DevonRO, CR 621; Bodl, MS. ch. England 30. Marie's wedding gowns were supplied by the king's great wardrobe in September. *GEC*, IV, 327, is mistaken in stating that Devon's heir died unmarried.

176 Storey, *End of Lancaster*, pp. 173-4.

177 *CPR, 1452–61*, pp. 393, 664; above, p. 753.

178 DevonRO, Exeter receiver's account 13; *GEC*, IV, 327. Exeter was another influential courtier. The slander in *English Chron.*, p. 75, that Queen Margaret poisoned the elder earl of Devon, is difficult to swallow.

179 LichRO, B/A/1/11 f. 87v. In March 1457 Margaret's brother-in-law, the earl of Pembroke, stayed with Buckingham at Greenfield in his lordship of Newport and met Margaret there (PRO, SC6/924/25 m. 11). Was the marriage already in prospect? The necessary dispensation was obtained from Bishop Boulers on 6 April (LichRO, B/A/1/11 f. 97d).

180 Griffiths, 'Sense of dynasty', pp. 22-3.

181 LichRO, B/A/1/11 f. 93v; Rawcliffe, op. cit., p. 21 n. 45. The indenture between Duke Humphrey and Henry Green was concluded on 19 January 1458 (ibid., p. 120, from NorthantsRO, SS 4254). The two ceremonies seem to have taken place simultaneously and were recorded in Bishop Boulers's register. Buckingham also had interests in Northants. and Wilts. (Rawcliffe, op. cit., pp. 51, 192-4).

182 Pollard, thesis, p. 49; above, p. 573. Soon afterwards, Berkeley and his new wife received a general pardon from the king (10 January 1458) and so did William, Lord Berkeley's son and heir (17 March 1458). See I. H. Jeayes, *A descriptive catalogue of the Berkeley muniments* (Bristol, 1892), nos. 603-4.

183 *GEC*, XII, i, 422; VII, 164-5: Kretschmer, dissertation, pp. 47ff, who established that Eleanor Talbot was the lady who was supposedly precontracted to Edward IV before 1464. Her husband had died in 1460–61.

184 If J. A. F. Thomson, 'John de la Pole, duke of Suffolk', *Speculum*, LIV (1979), 528-9, is followed, the marriage of Suffolk (b. 1442) to York's daughter, Elizabeth, in February 1458 would be an exception; they were certainly married at some point between 24 March 1453 (when John's marriage to Margaret Beaufort was annulled and his wardship granted to his mother, Alice Chaucer) and 1 February 1458 (when bonds were concluded by York consequent on the marriage). But would someone of Alice Chaucer's astuteness have arranged a Yorkist marriage as late as 1458 itself? R. S. Thomas, thesis, pp. 36-7; *CAD*, IV, 26-7. It is worth recalling two other family links among the courtier-magnates in the late 1450s: Buckingham's daughter Joan had married Viscount Beaumont's heir in 1452, and Shrewsbury himself was married to the earl of Wiltshire's sister (Rawcliffe, op. cit., p. 119; Pollard, thesis, p. 77). By contrast, Salisbury's third son married the daughter of a Cambs. knight, and three of his daughters married into the FitzHugh, Stanley, and Bonville houses in 1457–58 (*GEC*, IX, 92; V, 429; IV, 205; VI, 320).

185 *CPR, 1452–61*, pp. 324, 360 (with the earl of Shrewsbury); *CFR, 1452–61*, pp. 209, 240; above, p. 774.

186 e. g., *CPR, 1452–61*, pp. 508, 433, 362, 596; *CFR, 1452–61*, p. 182.

187 ibid., pp. 181, 229; *CPR, 1452–61*, pp. 335, 592, 533; *CCR, 1454–61*, p. 384.

188 *CPR, 1452–61*, pp. 592, 350; *CFR, 1452–61*, pp. 260, 177, 227, 240.

189 *CPR, 1452–61*, pp. 462-3 (Margaret Benet and Joan Asteley).
190 For what follows, see R. S. Thomas, thesis, ch. III (especially pp. 137-8). It is noteworthy that, with the exception of Frederick III of Germany, those elected to the garter in 1457–59 were all courtier-magnates (including Jasper Tudor) (Milner, thesis, pp. 93-100).
191 *EHD*, IV, 280-1 (by 31 October).
192 Above, pp. 793-7.
193 Above, p. 793.
194 PRO, E403/812 m. 3 (27 October 1457). This was probably pursuant to a commission of array issued on 26 September in the midland shires of England (*CPR, 1452–61*, pp. 402-3). Most of the leading commissioners were courtier-magnates like Shrewsbury, Buckingham, Beaumont, Rivers, Grey of Ruthin, and Dudley.
195 Flenley, p. 145.
196 Above, p. 804.
197 See *Reg. Whetehamstede*, I, 295-7, for the king's role, including a speech to the assembled lords that extolled the virtues of peace.
198 *PPC*, VI, 290, 293; *Reg Whetehamstede*, I, 296 (which erroneously says 26 January). 92 Lords were summoned to the reconvened meeting.
199 *CPR, 1452–61*, pp. 406-10. It is possible that the earlier array had not utilized the entire 13,000 authorized by the 1453–54 parliament (above, n. 194). London was instructed to produce its contingent of 1,137 archers a couple of weeks earlier than the rest, presumably because of the situation in the capital.
200 *Reg. Whetehamstede*, I, 300.
201 Flenley, pp. 111-12, 159-60.
202 ibid., p. 111; *Great Chron.*, pp. 189-190. *English Chron.*, p. 77, shows a distinct bias towards these two lords when it later reported that they had come to London peacefully, accompanied only by their household servants.
203 ibid., says that they, on the other hand, were likely to disrupt the peace.
204 Flenley, pp. 111, 159-60 (c. 2 and 18 February); *Great Chron.*, pp. 189-90.
205 *Brut*, p. 525; *London Chrons.*, p. 168; Flenley, p. 111.
206 ibid., pp. 111-12, 159; 'Benet's Chron.', p. 221; *Three Chrons.*, p. 71; *Brut*, p. 525; *London Chrons.*, p. 168; *English Chron.*, p. 77; *Chron. of London*, p. 139; *Grey Friars Chron.*, p. 20.
207 Flenley, pp. 159-60.
208 *Reg. Whetehamstede*, I, 295-308 (including a version of the eventual award). For contemporaries' differences of opinion about the date of the king's arrival, see 'Benet's Chron.' p. 221 (20 March); *Brut*, p. 525; *London Chrons.*, p. 168 (17 March); *Great Chron.*, pp. 189-90; *London Chrons.*, p. 168 (7 March); Flenley, pp. 159-60 (8 March). Henry was at Berkhamsted until at least 24 February (Christie, op. cit., p. 388) and he may have left London again during March while the negotiations were proceeding (*Reg. Whetehamstede*, I, 298).
209 No cash changed hands, only uncashed exchequer tallies, which may not have been particularly good currency at this juncture.
210 'Benet's Chron.', p. 221; Flenley, pp. 111-12, 159-60; *English Chron.*, p. 78; *Brut*, p. 525; *London Chrons.*, p. 168; *Great Chron.*, pp. 189-90. See Ramsay, op. cit., II, 208-9.

211 'Benet's Chron.', p. 221; Flenley, pp. 112, 160-1; *Great Chron.*, p. 190; *London Chrons.*, p. 168. Somerset and Lord Rivers were prominent in the jousts at Greenwich.

212 *CPR, 1452–61*, pp. 411, 440, 444, 491, 493, 516, 517, 518, 614 (January 1458–September 1459).

213 Above, pp. 795-6; 'Benet's Chron.', p. 222.

214 Above, pp. 778, 789; below, p. 815.

215 Above, p. 756.

216 Harris, *EHR*, LXXV (1960), 46; Haward, in *English trade*, p. 306.

217 Harriss, *EHR*, LXXV (1960), 47. Sir Thomas Findern was retained as captain of Guisnes, though as events would soon indicate, it might have been preferable if he too had been replaced in 1456 (below, p. 827; Wedgwood, *Biographies*, pp. 326-7).

218 Above, p. 756; below, p. 822. For confirmations of earlier appointments, see *CPR, 1452–61*, pp. 335, 423.

219 *English Chron.*, p. 78; Flenley, p. 112. Warwick had in fact been appointed on 4 August 1455 by an indenture with the king, and parliament was not then in session (though it had adjourned as recently as 31 July). For a discussion of this point, see J. W. McKenna, 'The myth of parliamentary sovereignty in late-mediaeval England', *EHR*, XCIV (1979), 493.

220 Flenley, p. 144. Soon after the court had moved to Coventry in the autumn of 1456, York, Salisbury, and Warwick are said to have been almost trapped there as a result of the queen's hatred for them ('Benet's Chron., p. 217; *Great Chron.*, p. 189; *Brut*, p. 523; *London Chrons.*, p. 167). Nevertheless, Lord Welles had been sent with reinforcements of 500 to Calais in October 1457 (PRO, E403/812 m. 3; *CPR, 1452–61*, p. 400).

221 Flenley, pp. 159-60.

222 *English Chron.*, p. 78 (9 November); above, p. 807.

223 Harriss, *EHR*, LXXV (1960), 48. Moves to have him removed from the captaincy were afoot by about January 1459 (Stevenson, II, 369 [misdated to November 1458]).

224 Harriss, *EHR*, LXXV (1960), 48.

225 Above, p. 793; *CPR, 1452–61*, pp. 344, 348, 437; Flenley, pp. 112-13, 147, 160-1; *Great Chron.*, p. 190; *English Chron.*, p. 84. Lord Fauconberg had been responsible for the capture of a Spanish ship in 1458 (*CPR, 1452–61*, p. 438).

226 No exchequer issues for Calais are recorded after July 1456, though a few issue rolls are missing (PRO, E403/807ff). See Harriss, *EHR*, LXXV (1960), 49, which records that the deficit on the treasurer of Calais's account in 1456–58 was more than £7,000 a year; by 1461 the soldiers' wages were again in arrears to the tune of £37,160.

227 Haward, in *English trade*, pp. 307-13; above, p. 789. The restriction on licences in November 1457 was stated to be 'for the weal of the land and especially for the weal of the Company of the Staple' (PRO, E159/234 m. 48; see *CPR, 1452–61*, p. 410).

228 Haward, in *English trade*, pp. 314-15. The loans seem to have quickly petered out (above, p. 789).

229 Haward, *in English trade*, pp. 316-17; Harriss, *EHR*, LXXV (1960), 49. Though compensation was offered in the form of a proportion of the customs in most ports, even on cargoes shipped in the king's name, according to *Fabyan's Chron.*, p. 636, the parliamentary act was ignored.

230 *CPR, 1452–61*, p. 556.
231 In a review of *CPapReg, 1471–84*, part i (especially pp. 209, 227-35, 241-2, 252-3), in *EHR*, LXXIII (1958), 679. The testimony of Richard Heron, a former staple merchant, maintained that he and others invested in Warwick's schemes reluctantly; in his vain pursuit of compensation, he took his case to Edward IV's council, the Bruges authorities, the duke of Burgundy, and ultimately, in 1476–77, to Pope Sixtus IV (hence the above record). Cf. *Fabyan's Chron.*, pp. 635, 652-3.
232 Harriss, *EHR*, LXXV (1960), 52. Warwick had negotiated with Philip the Good during 1457–58, and the duke had even visited Calais in June 1458; the purpose of these discussions, with the approval of the Lancastrian government, was to ease the staplers' commercial operations in the Burgundian territories, but they also led to a political understanding between Warwick and Philip to the detriment of Henry VI's régime (Haward, in *English trade*, pp. 313, 315, 317, 399 n. 72; below, p. 817). See Ferguson, op. cit., pp. 188-94.
233 Dunlop, op. cit., pp. 156-7, 207; Nicholson, op. cit., pp. 370-2, 392-3. Douglas had fled to England about April 1455 and received a substantial annuity of £500 on 4 August; this was reduced to £200 in November 1458, after the truce of June 1457 had been ratified (*Foedera*, V, ii, 63, 69; Stevenson, II, ii, 503; *CCR, 1454–61*, pp. 241, 325).
234 Dunlop, op. cit., pp. 163-4, 167 and n. 1, 195, 197-201; Nicholson, op. cit., pp. 393-4; Stevenson, I, 319-22. James had married Mary of Guelders in 1449, and his sister a member of the van Borselen family (which was intimately connected with the ducal house of Burgundy) in 1444. See Nicholson, op. cit., p. 347.
235 ibid., p. 394; Dunlop, op. cit., p. 164; Stevenson, I, 321-2.
236 Dunlop, op. cit., p. 167; Nicholson, op. cit., p. 394; Stevenson, I, 323-6 (*s. a.* 1460); *CMilP*, I, 27 (*s. a.* 1460). James's letters of 28 June have been assigned to both 1456 and 1460. Although the issue is not finally resolved (see Macrae, thesis, appendix 3), opinion inclines to 1456 (de Beaucourt, op. cit., VI, 140-1; Dunlop, op. cit., p. 167; Nicholson, op. cit., pp. 393-4). If this is so, York's appeal to King James for aid in his cause may refer to his determination to secure recognition as Henry VI's next adult heir rather than to seize the throne for himself (above, p. 811).
237 Dunlop, op. cit., pp. 164 n. 3, 169; Macrae, thesis, pp. 227-8; Stevenson, I, 328-31 (13, 20 October 1456).
238 Dunlop, op. cit., pp. 157-8, 176, 191, 165; Cardew, thesis, pp. 43-4, 204. The Coldingham question was even referred to the pope by James. His justification for renouncing the truce was the series of violations that had occurred recently (e.g., *HMC*, XIV, app. 3, p. 10 [April 1456]).
239 Dunlop, op. cit., pp. 168-9; Nicholson, op. cit., p. 372; 'Benet's Chron.', p. 217.
240 *Foedera*, V, ii, 69. On 24 August, York issued his own challenge to James II (Macrae, thesis, pp. 221-2; above, p. 773). Several Scots living in England hastened to reaffirm their allegiance to Henry VI in August and September 1456 (*CPR, 1452–61*, pp. 295, 323).
241 Cardew, thesis, p. 205; Macrae, thesis, pp. 223-5. This truce was to last until 2 February 1457.
242 Dunlop, op. cit., pp. 171, 203-5; Nicholson, op. cit., pp. 394-7; *CPR, 1452–61*, p. 346; Cardew, thesis, pp. 205-6, 263-6; *Foedera*, V, ii, 71, 75,

77, 78. For the marriage proposals, which had fallen through by early 1458, see d'Escouchy, II, 352-4; Dunlop, op. cit., pp. 172, 182; Stevenson, I, 352-3, 354-7. After this truce, the Douglas annuity was substantially reduced (above n. 233); for Stanley's retaliation in 1457 for the Scots attack on the Isle of Man, see Macrae, thesis, pp. 241-3, 250-1.

243 *CPR, 1452–61*, pp. 400, 405. Responsibility for aiding the northern wardens was placed on the counties north of the Trent.

244 PRO, E403/811 m. 2, 5, 7; 814 m. 3, 4; 817 m. 5, 11; 819 m. 3. In May 1457, just prior to the sealing of the truce, large sums were paid to Northumberland, who spent a good deal of his own money in the king's cause; licences enabled him to recover £6,000 from the customs (*CCR, 1454–61*, pp. 238, 310, 317; *PPC*, VI, 356). For the repair of Berwick's walls in May 1459, see *CCR, 1454–61*, p. 330; *CPR, 1452–61*, p. 498; and Newcastle-upon-Tyne in October 1458, ibid., p. 462.

245 ibid., p. 578; *CCR, 1454–61*, pp. 412-14. Northumberland became constable of Scarborough castle for life on 22 December 1459 (*CPR, 1452–61*, p. 594). On 4 October 1457, arrangements had been made to pay Roxburgh's custodians £4,109 of their arrears from the customs (*CCR, 1454–61*, p. 232).

246 PRO, E403/819 m. 4. Salisbury had received nothing in 1457 and 1458.

247 PRO, JI1/1546; 3/213.

248 Nicholson, op. cit., p. 396; Dunlop, op. cit., pp. 205-6.

249 ibid., pp. 205, 207; *CMilP*, I, 27; J. Gairdner (ed.), *Letters and papers illustrative of the reigns of Richard III and Henry VII*, vol. I (RS, 1861), 63. Earlier in the year, Scottish negotiations with Henry VI had also been proceeding, and the truce had been extended as recently as 12 September 1459 (*Foedera*, V, ii, 83-6).

250 Nicholson, op. cit., p. 396; Dunlop, op. cit., pp. 207-10. The castle was then dismantled.

251 De Beaucourt, op. cit., VI, 27-9; Stevenson, I, 332-51; Vale, *Charles VII*, p. 138. For Charles's worsening state of health from 1454, see ibid., pp. 172ff.

252 Dunlop, op. cit., pp. 147-8, 163, 180-2; Nicholson, op. cit., p. 393; Stevenson, I, 317-18. James hoped that with Charles's help he could become the guardian of his two nieces and thereby intervene in Breton affairs – something which Charles VII was unlikely to favour.

253 Nicholson, op. cit., p. 289; Dunlop, op. cit., p. 195 (8 November 1458).

254 Above, p. 811; Macrae, thesis, pp. 229-31 (January 1457).

255 Dunlop, op. cit., p. 169 (9 October 1456); Stevenson, I, 326-7; P. M. Kendall, *Louis XI* (1971), p. 83. Louis had fled north on 31 August 1456.

256 Dunlop, op. cit., pp. 197-201.

257 Ilardi and Kendall, op. cit., I, 244. Alençon was a member of the Burgundian order of the Golden Fleece (Vale, *Charles VII*, p. 160). For Charles VII's diplomatic efforts to isolate and harass Burgundy, see Vaughan, op. cit., pp. 347ff.

258 Stevenson, I, 332-51. For the king's well-known suspicions, see de Beaucourt, op. cit., VI, 260 (August 1458). If anything, he preferred an accommodation with England so as to leave him free to deal with Burgundy and the dauphin (Basin, II, 249; Ilardi and Kendall, op. cit., I, 244; Stevenson, I, 364). For Alençon's conspiracy, with accusations of collaboration with the English in an attack on Normandy in 1456, see de

Beaucourt, op. cit., VI, ch. IV; Ilardi and Kendall, op. cit., I, 198, 204; d'Escouchy, II, 319-22; Vale, *Charles VII*, pp. 154-62.

259 Stevenson, I, 342-3. Cf. the view of Normandy's weakness ascribed to the duke of Alençon in 1456 (Vale, *Charles VII*, pp. 157-8).

260 The duke of Burgundy certainly feared that the French fleet might harry his coast and took suitable precautions (de Beaucourt, op. cit., VI, 144-5, citing Archives du Nord, B 2026 f. 275*v*). The Castilians had negotiated a contribution to a French fleet as early as May 1457 in Lyons, so the Sandwich raid was probably part of a larger plan to establish French mastery of the channel (de Beaucourt, op. cit., VI, 132). For the staplers' increasing use of Sandwich to export wool from 1457 onwards, see Lloyd, op. cit., p. 277.

261 Flenley, pp. 110-11; 'Benet's Chron.', p. 218; *Three Chrons*, pp. 170-1; *Brut*, II, 524-5; *Grey Friars Chron.*, p. 20; *Great Chron.*, p. 189; *English Chron.*, p. 74. See de Beaucourt, op. cit., VI, 145-6, for booty worth £2-300,000.

262 D'Escouchy, II, 352-4. According to Chastellain, *Chroniques*, IV, 228, Margaret had been in touch with de Brézé *c.* 1455-56.

263 KentRO, NR/FAc 3 f. 33; *CPR, 1452–61*, pp. 371, 405, 400, 406 (29 August – 28 September). See Dunlop, op. cit., pp. 202-3. For a muster at Bridport (Dorset) on 1 September, with lists of weapons and equipment, see DorsetRO, B3/FG3.

264 Above, p. 805.

265 *CPR, 1452–61*, pp. 391, 405, 488; PRO, E403/819 m. 3, 5.

266 *CPR, 1452–61*, pp. 390, 394. Himself a king's serjeant, Carew's father (d. 1458) was a household servant connected with Henry, duke of Exeter (Wedgwood, *Biographies*, pp. 155-6; Jeffs, thesis, pp. 279-80).

267 *CPR, 1452–61*, p. 415. Victualler of Calais in 1452–59, Cheyne was also *persona grata* with the king's entourage (Wedgwood, *Biographies*, p. 181; Jeffs, thesis, pp. 282-3).

268 *CPR, 1452–61*, pp. 309, 307, 311, 344, 347, 348 (1456–57, from Cornwall to Suffolk); for the fleet, see ibid., p. 349.

269 ibid., pp. 411, 435, 436, 441, 488, 494, 496, 487; Stevenson, II, ii, 511. Sandwich not only repaired its walls in 1459 but inquired how many Scotsmen were in the town (KentRO, Sa/FAt 3).

270 De Beaucourt, op. cit., VI, 261-3; Thielemans, op. cit., p. 372; Stevenson, I, 361-77. For Wenlock's change of heart, see Roskell, *Beds. Hist. Record Soc. Publ.*, XXXVIII (1957), 33-4. On his return to England, Wenlock seems to have given the impression that the French, far from being amenable to a truce with England (as they were), were preparing to attack England; there is strong indication that Wenlock was playing the duke of Burgundy's part by February 1459 (Stevenson, I, 367, misdated to November 1458).

271 Thielemans, op. cit., pp. 161-3; Vaughan, op. cit., p. 342.

272 De Beaucourt, op. cit., VI, 137, quoting from BN, MS fr. 18, 441 f. 112*v*. The Dauphin Louis also formed good relations with the Yorkists as he did with Milan, partly as a counterpoise to the Angevin presence in England and Genoa (Kendall, *Louis XI*, pp. 97-8).

273 De Beaucourt, op. cit., VI, 124-5, 260 (1458), 270 and n. 3 (1459); Thielemans, op. cit., pp. 367-71; *Foedera*, V, ii, 80, 81, 82; Haward, in *English trade*, pp. 315-16. See Chastellain, *Chroniques*, III, 427-8, for

secret discussions between Warwick and Burgundy in 1458. For Warwick's gift of an Irish pony to the count of Charolais in 1457, see Vaughan, op. cit., p. 343.

274 Gairdner, *PL*, III, 139; 'Benet's Chron.', p. 223. Cf. *English Chron.*, p. 80; *Brut*, pp. 526-7; Storey, *End of Lancaster*, pp. 186-7. The king and his household appear to have reached Coventry by 9 May (PRO, E403/819 m. 3). Sir William Oldhall and Thomas Vaughan, two of York's councillors, may have been responsible for sending news of the council to Calais from London on 4 July (*RP*, V, 350).

275 Flenley, pp. 147-8; *Three Chrons.*, pp. 71-2; 'Benet's chron.', pp. 223-4. His retinue is variously put at 300 and 500 men.

276 As usual, contemporaries vary in their estimates of numbers (ibid., p. 224; Flenley, p. 147; *Reg. Whetehamstede*, I, 338; *Chron. of London*, p. 140 [3,000]; *Three Chrons.*, pp. 71-2 [4,000]; *English Chron.*, p. 80 [7,000]). The official Lancastrian estimate, which may be exaggerated, was at least 5,000 (*RP*, V, 348). See also *Great Chron.*, p. 191. For Salisbury's retinue, which included Sir Thomas Harrington, Sir John Conyers, Sir Thomas Parr, Thomas Mering, and John Saville (who was married to Harrington's daughter), see Pollard, *Northern Hist.*, XI (1976), 52, 67; Wedgwood, *Biographies*, p. 743.

277 *English Chron.*, pp. 80, 84.

278 This quotation is taken from the lords' letter of 10 October 1459 in *English Chron.*, pp. 81-3. For the authorship of the chronicle, see *EHL*, pp. 128-9.

279 *English Chron.*, p. 81, which is mistaken in stating that William Lyndwood (d. 1446) had presided at Worcester; his successor at St David's, John de la Bere, may be intended. The latter had been one of the king's intimates in the past, and it may have been fortuitous that he was in Worcester in 1459 (above, pp. 302-3). See M. H. Keen, 'Brotherhood in arms', *History*, XLVII (1962), 1-17 (esp. pp. 3-8, for the mass and indentures).

280 BL, Harleian MS 543 f. 164-65, a 16th-century copy in John Stow's handwriting of a manifesto issued by the Yorkist lords. There is no ground for Stow's assigning (followed by Scofield, op. cit., I, 33-4) of the authorship to Warwick, but he is right to date it before the battle of Ludford Bridge. It was almost certainly issued by all three lords (the 'we' of the document). Cf. Flenley, p. 147, which states that the lords wrote to the king to reveal the misgovernment of the realm.

281 *English Chron.*, pp. 81-3; *RDP*, IV, 940. For York's fear of attainder in 1450, see above, p. 687. For their sense that this was the only course of action open to them, see Flenley, p. 147; *Reg. Whetehamstede*, I, 341-2 (which contains a freer version of the lords' letter to the king).

282 *English Chron.*, p. 80. According to 'Gregory's Chron.', p. 204, it consisted of 'the Quenys galentys'; cf. 'Benet's Chron.', p. 224.

283 See ibid., p. 223; *RP*, V, 369, for the king at Nottingham.

284 *GEC*, I, 341; E. A. Thomas, 'The Lords Audley, 1391–1459' (Wales MA dissertation, 1976).

285 Griffiths, thesis, pp. 123-4, 204-5.

286 The ensuing engagement at Blore Heath is described most recently in E. A. Thomas, dissertation, pp. 14-20. See also F. R. Twemlow, *The battle of Blore Heath* (Wolverhampton, 1912); A. H. Burne, *More battlefields of*

England (1952), pp. 140-9; R. Brooke, *Visits to fields of battle in England in the fifteenth century* (1857), pp. 21-37.

287 *Reg. Whetehamstede*, I, 338; above, p. 779. A unique surviving swan in gold and ivory, which was perhaps akin to that distributed to the commanders of the queen's forces, was recently discovered at Dunstable, where her army halted in 1460; it is now in the BM.

288 *GEC*, VII, 162; *RP*, IV, 375.

289 'Benet's Chron.', p. 224 (8,000); *Reg. Whetehamstede*, I, 338 (10,000); Flenley, p. 147 (12,000); *Three Chrons.*, pp. 71-2; *Chron. of London*, p. 140 (14,000). 'Gregory's Chron.', p. 204, is likely to be mistaken in saying that the king was only 10 miles away.

290 *RP*, V, 369-70. Lord Stanley was soon to congratulate Salisbury, his father-in-law, on his success.

291 'Gregory's Chron.', p. 204; *GEC*, I, 341; E. A. Thomas, dissertation, p. 18. Salisbury seems to have tried to parley in an attempt to avoid battle ('Benet's Chron.', p. 224).

292 *Brut*, p. 601; Flenley, p. 147. For one of Dudley's retainers left for dead on the battlefield, see *CPR, 1452-61*, p. 595.

293 *Brut*, p. 601; *English Chron.*, p. 80; 'Gregory's Chron.', p. 204; *London Chrons.*, p. 169; *Great Chron.*, p. 19; Hall, *Chronicle*, f. xciv; Twemlow, op. cit., pp. 10-11. For distraint of knighthood, see above, p. 787. For Cheshire men killed on both sides, see the dramatic account of the Elizabethan writer Michael Drayton, himself a Warws. man who may have known of local traditions (J. T. Driver, *Cheshire in the later middle ages* [Chester, 1971], p. 18).

294 *English Chron.*, p. 80; 'Benet's Chron.', p. 224; *London Chrons.*, p. 169; *Great Chron.*, p. 19. According to 'Gregory's Chron.', p. 204, the controller of the prince's household was badly wounded. One of the king's household servants, Thomas Harper, was responsible for capturing some of the retreating Yorkists at Acton bridge (Cheshire) (*CPR, 1452-61*, p. 536).

295 'Gregory's Chron.', p. 204.

296 E. A. Thomas, dissertation, p. 19.

297 *CPR, 1452-61*, p. 582; *RP*, V, 348, 369-70. Margaret's letters patent are still in CheshRO, DDX 178/24(26 April).

298 *RP*, V, 348-9; 'Gregory's Chron.', p. 205. By the time the king's army reached Ludford Bridge, Henry was said to have been in the field for 30 days.

299 'Benet's Chron.', p. 224; Flenley, p. 147; *Three Chrons.*, pp. 71-2; *Chron. of London*, p. 140; *Reg. Whetehamstede*, I, 338; 'Gregory's Chron.', p. 205. The Yorkists are variously put at 20,000 and 25,000, and the royalists at over 30,000, 40,000, 50,000, and 60,000; the figures are exaggerated, but the implied relationship between the two armies is credible. The king's army had reached Leominster by 10 October (*RDP*, IV, 940). The city of Exeter sent a contingent to the king at Ludlow (DevonRO, Exeter receivers' account 13).

300 York's two nephews and annuitants, John and Edward Bourgchier, were present and so was his annuitant and the queen's former chamberlain, Sir John Wenlock (*RP*, V, 349; Rosenthal, 'Estates and finances of York', p. 191). Clinton was York's annuitant too (ibid., p. 191). Among his marcher retainers were Robert Bold, Roger Eyton, and Walter Devereux; for his councillors, John Clay and Thomas Colt, see ibid., pp. 177, 179, 180, 185.

Of Warwick's councillors, Walter Blount was present at Ludlow (Wedgwood, *Biographies*, p. 86).

301 *Reg. Whetehamstede*, I, 339-41. According to *RP*, V, 348-9, the pardon was conveyed by a herald of arms, but Beauchamp is said to have been employed because he was related to Warwick's wife (Emden, *Oxford*, I, 137-8). He was also chaplain to the order of the garter and as such could remind York of his obligations as a garter knight as opposed to a brother-in-arms of Warwick and Salisbury. One of Buckingham's marcher officials also seems to have taken messages between the court and York just before the engagement (NLW, Powis castle I/16733 m. 12d).

302 *Reg. Whetehamstede*, I, 343-4; 'Benet's Chron.', p. 224; *London Chrons.*, pp. 169-70; *Great Chron.*, p. 191; *Brut*, pp. 526-7; *RP*, V, 348-9. 'Gregory's Chron.', p. 205, puts Trollope's desertion some days earlier, but it is more likely to have occurred at Ludford Bridge.

303 *RP*, V, 348-9; *Brut*, pp. 526-7; *Great Chron.*, p. 191. Among those who surrendered were Lord Powis, Walter Devereux, and Sir Henry Radford (*RP*, V, 350).

304 'Benet's Chron.', p. 224; 'Gregory's Chron.', p. 205 (including the quotation); *Three Chrons.*, p. 72; *Great Chron.*, p. 191; *Brut*, pp. 526-7; *London Chrons.*, pp. 169-70; *Reg. Whetehamstede*, I, 345. They reached Calais on 2 November. For Wenlock's desertion of the queen, see above, p. 816. Dynham's mother was later rewarded for the aid which she and her tenants and servants had given to the fugitive lords (Scofield, op. cit., I, 41-2 [1461]).

305 'Benet's Chron.', p. 224; *Reg. Whetehamstede*, I, 345; *English Chron.*, pp. 83-4. Duchess Cecily and her younger children were placed in the charge of her sister, the duchess of Buckingham (*Brut*, p. 528). Scofield, op. cit., I, 37, is unduly sceptical in dismissing the evidence of harassment.

306 *Reg. Whetehamstede*, I, 337, gives expression to these attitudes in explaining the Yorkist lords' rising in September 1459.

307 See 'Benet's Chron.', p. 224, even though this was written a few years later.

308 *CPR, 1452-61*, pp. 561, 562, 564 (12, 14 October). Sir William Oldhall had evidently been captured after Ludford Bridge (Barron, thesis, p. 111; ct. Roskell, *Speakers*, p. 360).

309 *CPR, 1452-61*, p. 557. In view of the probable authorship of the bill of attainder, it should be noted that John Wyndham and John Heydon were said in October 1459 to be behind the commissions to arrest Yorkist supporters (*PL*, II, 184-5; below, p. 824).

310 Above, p. 785; *RP*, V, 367. The statute governing annual appointments was that of 1445-46. See Wedgwood, *Register*, p. 47. In the case of Derbs. and Surrey, the sheriffs of 1458-59 actually made the return even though they had been replaced. In 9 cases the appointment was delayed beyond the customary time until after the elections had been held. Moreover, the irregularity of the elections was partly due to the fact that writs of privy seal (rather than under the great seal) were sent to sheriffs (Roskell, *Speakers*, p. 263).

311 Wedgwood, *Register*, pp. 59-64. But see the disturbances among the students and townsmen of Cambridge at election time (ibid., p. 256; *PPC*, VI, 335, misdated to 13 November 1454). As a result, perhaps, no MPs were returned; the sheriff was Sir John Colville, who had Yorkist sympathies.

312 The MP for Shrewsbury was Edward Esthorpe, a king's serjeant. Some
returns may not have been made because of the hurried assembly of this
parliament. For Barre's desertion of York, see above, p. 840 n. 170.

313 Roskell, *Speakers*, pp. 263-6; idem, *Northants. Past and Present*, II, no. 6
(1959), 313-23. For a reward for his work at Coventry, see below, p. 826.

314 *PL*, II, 221 (24 October 1460).

315 Ibid., 210, 221.

316 Wedgwood, *Biographies*, pp. 253-5, 452-3, 6, 460-1, 849-51; Emden,
Oxford, II, 1318–20; above, pp. 585, 639, 723.

317 *PL*, II, 210, 221.

318 *PL*, II, 187 (7 December 1459); 'Benet's Chron.', p. 244. An associated bill
of resumption was enacted against all who had fought against Henry VI at
St Albans, Blore Heath, or Ludford Bridge (*RP*, V, 366).

319 For the bill as it was presented and approved, see *RP*, V, 349-50. The king's
personal intervention on the last day of parliament to assert his right of
pardon is recorded by *Reg. Whetehamstede*, I, 356. As in 1458, the king's
compassion was at odds with the court's relentlessness. Lists of the
attainted also appear in Stevenson, II, ii, [771] (copied from the 'great
book', which may refer to the parliament roll); *English Chron.*, pp. 83-4;
PL, II, 188.

320 'Benet's Chron.', p. 224; Thomson, *Speculum*, LIV (1979), 528-9.

321 *RP*, V, 350, 368; *CPR, 1452–61*, p. 536; Scofield, op. cit., I, 39. For other
pardons to more obscure rebels, including some from the Welsh border, see
ibid., 37 n.1; *CPR, 1452–61*, pp. 538, 529, 587 (4, 15 December). A general
pardon was issued in January 1460 (PRO, C67/43) and 342 are known to
have availed themselves of it (Storey, *End of Lancaster*, pp. 213, 216;
Scofield, op. cit., I, 39). J. P. Gilson, 'A defence of the proscription of the
Yorkists in 1459', *EHR*, XXVI (1911), 512-25, prints (from BL, Royal MS
17 D XV) an elaborate refutation in English, Latin, and French of the
wisdom of showing mercy to the Yorkist lords. It displays some knowledge
of the preamble of the bill of attainder and it was probably penned during
or soon after the Coventry parliament. Its author is likely to have been a
lawyer, perhaps one of those involved in drawing up the bill (though the
proposal that it was Fortescue is based on slim evidence); the suggestion
that the document was a polemic for circulation is less convincing in view
of the length and sophistication of its argument.

322 *RP*, V, 369; above, pp. 778, 781.

323 *RP*, V, 351-2. Lord Grey of Ruthin and Bishop Neville of Exeter declared
'them ful worshipfuly to the Kynges grete plesir' by 7 December (*PL*, II,
188).

324 Below, p. 857; *PL*, II, 184-5. Cf. ibid., p. 540, where it is reported that in
January 1460 the duchess of York 'ys stille ayen returned yn Kent'. One
may note that the Yorkists were not proclaimed in London as attainted until
21 January (Scofield, op. cit., I, 40, quoting *Three Chrons.*, p. 169).

325 For their disposal, see above, p. 834.

326 These sentences are based on *CPR, 1452–61*, pp. 526-97; *CCR, 1454–61*, pp.
405-18; *CFR, 1452–61*, pp. 261-75.

327 Though it is not mentioned in Wolffe, *Royal demesne*. Furthermore, on 1
December 1459 the master of the king's ordnance was commissioned to
survey their castles and towns and keep their fortifications in good repair
(*CPR, 1452–61*, p. 527).

328 ibid., p. 536 (6 December). Similarly, their Wilts. and Berks. estates were administered by one receiver, John Whityngton, who had been relied on by the Lancastrian régime before (ibid., p. 569 [5 April 1460], 175, 561). Some rearrangement took place after the initial crown organization; thus, the administration of York's Welsh and Yorks. estates was reordered (ibid., passim).

329 Most of these annuities were granted immediately, before parliament was dissolved; few were granted thereafter.

330 Perhaps the most generous lease was that to Northumberland of the Yorks., Derbs., and Cambs. estates of the earl of Salisbury for 12 years on 3 June 1460. The reason for this exceptional grant was probably the court's heavy reliance on the earl to maintain its authority in the north (*CFR, 1452–61,* p. 274; above, p. 812).

331 For Edward IV's ideas, see Wolffe, *Royal demesne,* ch. VI. This is the most recent statement of the author's views, which perhaps ascribe too much originality to the Yorkist kings. See also Ross, *Edward IV,* p. 376, for other criticisms of these views. For the use of a royal wardship to defray the great wardrobe's expenses in May 1460, see *CPR, 1452–61,* p. 596.

332 There were difficulties experienced in some areas in securing control of the Yorkist properties by the king's officials: e.g., on 5 February 1460 York's and Warwick's lordships in the southern marches were being 'forcibly and wrongfully kept from our possession . . . by the rebellion and disobedience of their followers' (NorthantsRO, Westmorland MSS, box 1, parcel 1, no. 3 [M]). Cf. below, p. 829. The commission of 27 January 1460 to resume York's possessions in Ireland had no chance of being implemented (*CPR, 1452–61,* p. 563). The entire matter of the disposal of these estates needs fuller investigation.

333 *Foedera,* V, ii, 90; *English Chron.,* pp. 78-9, 84; 'Benet's Chron., p. 224; *Brut,* p. 528. On 10 November, Somerset and Rivers were ordered to be paid £1,050 for raising 1,000 men, many of whom had been shipped to Calais with the duke (PRO, E404/71/4/18, printed in Stevenson, II, i, 512). On 13 December 1459 John, Lord Audley was allowed to enter his inheritance without the expense of an inquiry or payment of relief, and in recognition of his father's service at Blore Heath he was allowed the income from his estates from his father's death (*CPR, 1452–61,* p. 539).

334 *English Chron.,* p. 84; *London Chrons.,* pp. 169-71; 'Gregory's Chron.', p. 206; *Great Chron.,* pp. 191-2; *Brut,* p. 528; *Three Chrons.,* p. 72. *Reg. Whetehamstede,* I, 369-70, implies that Audley, accompanied by Humphrey Stafford, esquire, had been ordered to relieve Somerset at Guisnes. Those of the Lancastrian force who were captured by the Calais men were either disarmed and released, or (a few of them) beheaded. *Brut,* p. 528, claims that some surrendered because they preferred to serve Warwick. See Scofield, op. cit., I, 44 and n. 1.

335 *CPR, 1452–61,* pp. 545, 553, 581, 585, 608 (January–May 1460).

336 Stevenson, II, ii, [772] (23 April 1460). Somerset lost many men in this engagement. See also Harriss, *EHR,* LXXV (1960), 48-9, for the Lancastrian hold on Guisnes and Hammes, and some desertions from Rysbank and even Calais.

337 *Brut,* p. 528. In February 1460, one of the duke of Exeter's men arrested a member of the Temple and several vintners of London who were suspected of transporting bowstrings and arrowheads to Calais; they were

executed. *Three Chrons.*, p. 73; Stevenson, II, ii, [772]; Scofield, op. cit., I, 55.

338 *CPR, 1452–61*, p. 556; Haward, in *English trade*, pp. 316-17; *Fabyan's Chron.*, p. 633; above, p. 810. For breaches of the prohibition, see Scofield, op. cit., I, 48 and n. 1.

339 *CPR, 1452–61*, pp. 525, 526.

340 And Rivers's wife, the dowager duchess of Bedford ('Gregory's Chron.', p. 206). *Brut*, p. 528, makes it clear that many of the Lancastrian sailors were happy to defect to Warwick's side. See also *CPR, 1452–61*, p. 555; *Great Chron.*, pp. 191-2; *London Chrons.*, pp. 170-1; *English Chron.*, p. 84; Stevenson, II, ii, 772; *PL*, II, 540; *Reg. Whetehamstede*, I, 369. *Three Chrons.*, p. 72, says that the Woodvilles had a force of 400 with them. *Fabyan's Chron.*, pp. 635, 652, even claims that Dynham's expedition was financed by the staple merchants (Haward, in *English trade*, pp. 318-20; above, p. 816). See Scofield, op. cit., I, 51-2.

341 'Gregory's Chron.', p. 206. For men whom he had raised in the autumn for Calais, see above, n. 340.

342 *PL*, I, 162. This letter suggests that the attack on Sandwich took place just before 20 January; cf. Stevenson, II, ii, [772] (soon after Christmas). For the agitation in the south-east in the following weeks, see *CPR, 1452–61*, pp. 563, 604, 606.

343 Above, p. 686. Pembroke may have pursued York and Rutland through Wales after Ludford Bridge; his late arrival at the Coventry parliament with a large company was noted on 6 December (*PL*, II, 187-8). When the parliament granted Prince Edward full control of his inheritance, appointments to bishoprics and major offices in the principality and Cornwall were specifically reserved to the king, who therefore retained direct responsibility for their security (*RP*, V, 356).

344 Above, p. 825; *CPR, 1452–61*, pp. 549 (5 February 1460), 574. Herbert seems not to have been at Ludford Bridge. The proposition (in Evans, *Wales and the wars of the roses*, pp. 98-101, 109) that this grant strengthens the impression that Herbert had deserted York after 1457 is almost certainly erroneous (D. A. Thomas, thesis, pp. 38-45; Kent, thesis, pp. 20-3; *GCH*, III, 196-7).

345 *RP*, V, 366.

346 *CPR, 1452–61*, pp. 534, 547.

347 PRO, C49/32/12A is his (undated) petition; the king responded on 16 February (ibid., C81/1376/9, cited by Scofield, op. cit., I, 56). For the resultant letters patent, dated 22 February, see *CPR, 1452–61*, pp. 565, 550; *Foedera*, V, ii, 93.

348 *CPR, 1452–61*, p. 576 (5 February). The force would be financed from the revenue of the lordships themselves.

349 ibid., pp. 564-5.

350 ibid., p. 578; *Foedera*, V, ii, 93.

351 *CPR, 1452–61*, p. 574. The money was to be taken from the income of York's marcher estates, though great difficulty was encountered in securing control of them (see above, n. 332).

352 On 29 March, Jasper was probably still at Ruthin (Denbs.), whence he appealed to Lord Scales for money: PRO, SC1/51/86 (undated), cited in R. S. Thomas, thesis cited, p. 186 n. 5. But by 25 May he was at Pembroke calling on the assistance of his own townsmen at Tenby (CardiffCL, Pembs.

MS 42/1094). For the earl's movements at this time, see R. S. Thomas, thesis, pp. 179-87; Griffiths, thesis, pp. 549-51.

25 Lancastrian King and Yorkist Rule, 1460–1461

Yorkist plans, Lancastrian precautions

The duke of York's experiences during 1459–60 provided contemporaries with a classic demonstration of the extraordinary changes of fate signalized by the popular image of the wheel of fortune. A fugitive after Ludford Bridge, he at last became the acknowledged heir to Henry VI's crown before sinking once again to the depths of misfortune when, on 30 December 1460, he was slain at Wakefield by Lancastrian soldiers. With the aspirations of a decade all but realized, he was denied the opportunity to savour them.

The recovery of Yorkist fortunes after October 1459 depended on Ireland and Calais, where the exiles were reasonably secure, despite the vigorous Lancastrian efforts to dislodge them, at least from Calais. Henry VI's government was not able to contemplate an assault on Ireland, where York could rely on 'hys erles and homagers' and the enemies of the Butler earls of Ormond (and Wiltshire).[1] When he landed there with his second son Rutland, he was well received, and the decision on 4 December to replace him as lieutenant of Ireland by Wiltshire was unavailing; indeed, when Wiltshire's agent delivered an order for the duke's arrest, he was seized, speedily tried, and peremptorily executed.[2] Rather did the Lancastrians rely on Jasper Tudor in Wales and a prohibition on communication between England and Ireland to insulate the mainland from a Yorkist invasion.[3]

In his Irish sanctuary, York made preparations for his return to England. Envoys from James II of Scotland arrived with a proposal that one of his daughters should marry York's son, presumably the eldest boy, Edward of March.[4] At the same time, the duke tightened his control on the Irish administration by appointing the sixteen-year-old Rutland as chancellor and summoning a parliament to Drogheda; it met on 8 February and lasted, with an adjournment to Dublin, until late in July.[5] This assembly was of crucial importance to York and, indeed, of cardinal significance in subsequent Irish institutional history. Its busy meetings considered *inter alia* York's appeal to the Anglo-Irish nobility to acknowledge his authority in the lordship and support his return to England; the price was high in terms of the independent power which the parliament claimed for the administration at Dublin. As a result, York's lieutenancy was confirmed and the protection of the law of treason was extended to him as the king's representative; yet in taking these steps, the parliament was expressly exercising a legislative independence which enabled it to ignore Wiltshire's appointment and the attainder of York and his friends some months earlier. These and other claims, which denied the applicability of English law and custom in Ireland unless they had been specifically accepted by the Irish parliament, have rightly been regarded as a radical departure, though A. J. Otway-Ruthven's contention that they amounted to a 'frankly revolutionary programme' perhaps gives too little weight to demands that were already current, arising out of the frustrations of Irish disorder and political rivalries in England earlier in the reign, for a wider measure of independent rule. Nevertheless, the unequivocal declarations of 1460 were a decisive assertion of what had been voiced or discussed less formally in recent years. They could be made now because York needed shelter, an armed and mounted force of archers, and an act of resumption that could finance his régime.[6]

In this atmosphere, York was successful in commanding the loyalty of the Gaelic chieftains, who ignored Lancastrian summonses to reject the usurping lieutenant, and indeed the last session of the 1460 parliament extended a general authorization to any who wished to join the duke's enterprise in England.[7] Armed with these expressions of support and assured of Ireland's loyalty at his back, York appointed as his deputy the earl of Kildare, a Geraldine who had his own score to settle with Wiltshire and who had served the duke in the past; York's departure for England need not be delayed much longer.[8] The concessions he had had to make were substantial and amounted to the surrender of some of the authority of the very crown he was setting out to win. Later on, his son Edward would find himself in serious difficulties when he attempted to reassert royal authority in Ireland, and it was left to Henry VII to recover part of what York had yielded. But to Duke Richard, the needs of the moment had been paramount.[9] He may have imagined that as a major Irish landowner of popular reputation he was not prejudicing in practice the royal rights he hoped shortly to enjoy.

Before York arrived in England about 8 September 1460, there may have been widespread uncertainty about his intentions, even amongst his own sympathizers. The flight from Ludford Bridge had been hasty and had precluded any lengthy discussion of future strategy; in any case, not until the Yorkist lords had established bases in Calais and Ireland could the future be faced. However, in March 1460 the earl of Warwick sailed to Ireland to consult with York. He arrived in Waterford harbour on 16 March accompanied by 500 men and a fleet that included ships captured at Sandwich some months before. Contemporaries were well aware that the immediate purpose of their meeting was to discuss how best they could return to England.[10] To judge by events, they agreed on a co-ordinated invasion, initiated from Calais, with reasonable expectation of aid from Kent and the south-east; York and Rutland would sail from Ireland a little later, and it soon became known in Bruges that York was planning an invasion with Scottish aid.[11] Moreover, it is most likely that Warwick and York discussed their longer-term strategy, once they had established themselves on English soil; it is this aspect of their deliberations that is most obscure – and probably was kept strictly confidential at the time.

It is generally assumed that their agreed intention was once again to confront the king and secure the dismissal of his advisers. Yet their earlier attempts along these lines had been conspicuously unsuccessful and in any case by 1460 contemporaries had come to realize that the true fount of political power in England was Queen Margaret; to dispose of her as if she were a Suffolk or a Somerset or a Wiltshire would raise exceedingly daunting difficulties.[12] To judge by the speed with which March, Warwick, and Salisbury made for London after disembarking at Sandwich in the last week of June and then, after spending only two nights in the capital, marched northwards, they did not flinch from a confrontation with the king's forces which, after the events of 1459–60, was certain to end in violence. One may safely conclude that Warwick and York foresaw the possibility of a battle and the capture or even death of the king and his family.

The future rule of England had required consideration too. There were several alternatives open to York and his allies. First, they might be able to remove the king's advisers and dominate the government, though recent events indicated that this was not a satisfactory solution if the queen lived to intrigue and oppose, or if Prince Edward remained heir to the throne and under his mother's influence. Secondly (and more extremely), the Yorkists might be able to depose a captive king after the example of 1399 and disinherit his heir. Thirdly, the precedent of the treaty of Troyes (1420) might be followed, whereby the king could continue to reign for the rest of his life but the prince would be disinherited and his mother's influence correspondingly nullified. Finally, if Henry were to fall in battle, York would be most unlikely to tolerate the accession of his son if Queen Margaret were in the offing. From all but the first of these alternatives Duke Richard could draw hope that he and his line would eventually succeed to the English throne. Warwick, who can hardly have been unaware of the political courses open to him as York's ally, gave his assurance that England would be invaded from Calais sometime soon. It is tempting to suppose that York's regal demeanour in the weeks after his own landing and his determination to march towards the throne sprang from the meeting with Warwick in the previous March. This may be speculation, but it is certain that the eventual constitutional compromise was the least happy of outcomes: Henry VI was allowed to remain king for life and his progeny was disinherited; but Margaret and Prince Edward were still at large and resolutely opposed the Yorkist régime.

It was natural that the invaders from Calais in 1460 should claim that they simply wished to remove the king's disreputable ministers, for they dared not risk alienating popular opinion by openly advocating the deposition of an anointed king; moreover, most contemporary accounts eulogized Warwick, who could not be portrayed as a traitor or regicide.[13] Nor were the lords in England quite prepared to take the revolutionary (and, to their mind, unnecessary) step of dethroning the captive king. Even the Nevilles may have lost any enthusiasm they may have had for this course when Henry fell into their hands at Northampton; a change of dynasty suddenly seemed less relevant than strict control over an acknowledged monarch. York consequently found himself alone and exposed when he arrived at Westminster to claim the crown. Subsequent Yorkist commentators were not likely to express support for deposition when Henry and the Lancastrians could be convincingly blamed for the civil war in 1460–61 because of their faithless breach of the compromise between the king and York in October and their killing of York himself at Wakefield. It remains a distinct possibility, then, that Henry's deposition was discussed in Ireland, that dethronement was judged the best outcome of the Yorkist invasion, and that Warwick gave his support to this course of action. These speculations are worth keeping in mind, because the events of 1460 and the tainted character of the surviving evidence conspire to conceal from us the actual motives of the men in Ireland and Calais.

In the six months prior to the invasion, the Lancastrian government was permanently alert to the possibility of an attack, perhaps with Burgundian assistance and employing a foreign fleet as well as Warwick's ships.[14] It realized that the danger was greatest in the south and south-east, for at Calais the Yorkists had at their disposal a garrison to which growing numbers of disaffected Englishmen fled daily from Kent and nearby shires, and a fleet which was assembled from merchantmen belonging to the staplers and vessels seized in the daring raids on Sandwich in January and May 1460.[15] Moreover, London was much more vulnerable to an invasion from Calais, whereas Ireland was isolated to some extent by Lancastrian power in Wales, the midlands, and the north-west.

The first priority was to regain command of the channel by a series of patrols that would protect harbours and seafarers, facilitate the reinforcement of Guisnes and, perhaps, the recovery of Calais. To this end, several fleets were fitted out in succession between December and May. First, William Scot, a Kentish esquire who had been at sea before, was commissioned in December 1459, though his task was the modest one of protecting Winchelsea and its fishermen.[16] A larger naval squadron was assembled in February and the willing Devonshire sheriff Sir Baldwin Fulford was retained to seek out and destroy Warwick and the Yorkists; both Sir Baldwin, who volunteered as commander, and the government were incensed by the recent raid on Sandwich.[17] But the most energetic steps were taken at the end of March, when the duke of Exeter was engaged for three years with more than 3,500 men. His showing at sea was not impressive, and when Warwick's fleet hove into sight on the way back from Ireland, the loyalty of Exeter's force was so uncertain that he put into Dartmouth instead of engaging the enemy.[18] Moreover, although the Genoese had been induced on 13 February to make their vessels available for defence (and at least two were in Exeter's fleet), the Venetians were outraged at the proposal to commandeer their ships; some of them escaped just in time, leaving several Venetian merchants to be held to ransom by the thwarted government.[19] These naval measures did not prevent the raids on Sandwich or the Yorkist landing.

The Lancastrians were fully aware of the limitations of naval defence and channel patrols, and hence urgent attention was given to arraying land-based forces, especially in the south-east, at their own cost as an obligation on the king's subjects; the raid of January 1460 was a sharp reminder of the wisdom of such measures.[20] It was by this means that Henry VI was able to head a considerable army at Northampton on 10 July, though the rumour that levies from Lancashire and Cheshire had been promised plunder in the lusher south-eastern shires may simply be hostile Yorkist propaganda.[21] Steps were taken simultaneously to fortify vital castles and towns that were bound to play a part in deterring any invasion. Worcester had been the rendezvous for the Yorkist lords earlier in 1459; now, in late November, orders were given to strengthen its walls, bridges, and gates lest the enemy sweep down from neighbouring lordships.[22] In the following April, when the threat from Calais seemed more pressing, Winchelsea and Southampton were hastily fortified with cannon and their inhabitants alerted; the fear was that after fruitless operations at sea, shipping in their harbours might fall victim to the kind of lightning attack that Sandwich had suffered.[23] The master of the king's ordnance, John Judde, a London merchant, was kept busy transporting armaments, including guns, from the Tower arsenal to various royal fortresses, not least to Kenilworth which became the king's residence for a while before the battle of Northampton.[24] But among England's towns and cities, London was acknowledged to be the key to successful resistance to invaders from Calais; and the Lancastrians had good reason to be suspicious of the citizens' will to resist. They were ordered to suppress any risings and reject enemy overtures; but to ensure that these instructions were obeyed, a group of Lancastrian lords was despatched to hold the Tower and stiffen London's resolve. Lords Scales and Hungerford, with others, entered the fortress to the evident unease of the Londoners, who declared themselves well able to look after themselves.[25]

Apart from these precautions, the government had to contend with the threat of risings elsewhere in the realm, for hostile congregations might be turned into a rebellious movement. After the descent on Sandwich in January, commissions of oyer and terminer were nominated frequently and at large, but especially in the Thames valley and the southern counties; suspects were to be arrested, unauthorized assemblies banned, and treason rooted out.[26] In the last six months of Lancastrian rule, the southern part of the kingdom took on the aspect of an armed camp continuously on alert.

Yet, one may doubt whether such measures were at all effective after the stark polarization of opinion following the battles and attainders of 1459; and this polarization had a geographical dimension in which the south-east showed itself to be decidedly reluctant to obey a Lancastrian régime which had consolidated its authority in the midlands, Wales, and the north-west at the expense, to some degree, of its control elsewhere. The appeal for loans in March 1460 to finance the defence of the seas and the protection of the coast was disappointing, whilst the collection of customary taxes and subsidies may have encountered problems too; certainly the earl of Wiltshire, as treasurer, was bitterly denounced in the months preceding the Yorkist landing. The earl and his fund-raising expedients figured prominently in the propaganda which the invaders directed at those in the south-east who were already unwilling to support the beleaguered régime.[27] Even if these measures had been implemented to the letter, the Lancastrians would still have been at the mercy of the plotters in Ireland and Calais. The initiative lay with them so long as they received the support of the Anglo-Irish lords and the acquiescence of the Gaelic chiefs, and Somerset's men in Guisnes failed to overrun Calais. The Yorkist landing at Sandwich on 26 June was no surprise to the Lancastrians, but lack of enthusiasm for their cause made it impossible for them to halt the insurgents' march across north Kent towards the capital.

The Yorkist victory

The invasion of the earls of March, Warwick, and Salisbury was preceded by another attack on Sandwich. The Lancastrians had assembled several hundred soldiers there under Osbert Mundford, a distinguished captain of the French war whose orders were to succour Somerset's beleaguered force in Guisnes; impeccable Yorkist intelligence in Kent quickly made known these preparations in Calais. A strike force under Lord Fauconberg, Sir John Wenlock, and John Dynham entered the port, seized the armaments stored there, and captured a number of soldiers, including Mundford himself who was conveyed to Rysbank tower and beheaded; Dynham received a gunshot wound in his leg, but otherwise little else marred yet another daring sortie from Calais.[28]

This raid prefaced the main landing of the Yorkist lords a day or so later on 26 June; they encountered no resistance, for Fauconberg had stayed behind to hold Sandwich as a bridgehead. The three earls, along with Lord Audley, arrived in fine weather in accordance (one presumes) with the plan agreed in Ireland three months earlier.[29] The reception they received was encouraging, for whereas they may have brought only a small force with them, they soon attracted thousands of adherents from Kent, Surrey, and Sussex, including noble support in the person of Lord Cobham, York's companion at Dartford in 1452.[30] The indications of support which had reached Calais in recent weeks proved to be well founded.[31] The Londoners, though largely sympathetic, were naturally apprehensive at the approach of such a large body of men, and the city fathers, well aware of the chaos ten years before, were anxious to dissuade them from entering the city. Some urged the mayor to place guns on London bridge to deter the advancing Yorkists, and he seems to have been inclined to obey Henry VI's injunction to deny the king's enemies entry to the city. Even Archbishop Bourgchier and several bishops who were then in the city joined with the Lancastrians in the Tower to beg the Yorkists not to enter. But twelve of the aldermen took a different view, with the result that the Yorkist leaders were allowed into London on 2 July and took lodgings at the Grey Friars within Newgate; their host was encamped in the fields beyond Smithfield.[32] March, Warwick, and Salisbury made their way to St Paul's cathedral, where they were met by Archbishop Bourgchier and other bishops and by the mayor and aldermen. The winning of London and the submission of the authorities and part of the episcopate were crucial achievements, and these successes were consolidated by an important meeting on 3 July at which the Yorkists' demands were probably explained, and the indictment and imprisonment of certain Lancastrian sympathizers at the guildhall next day.[33] The common council was induced to provide horses and carts for the army and a modest loan of £1,000, whose payment was guaranteed by the Yorkist lords and Bishops Neville of Exeter and Grey of Ely. London had been reluctant to admit the Yorkists and eventually did so to avoid dissension in the city and possible bloodshed, but probably only after assurances had been given that the visitors would quickly leave on their journey north.[34]

The Yorkist aims had been publicized in south-eastern England even before the landing, for copies of a manifesto addressed to the archbishop and 'at large to the comunes of Engelond' were distributed from Calais. This was highly propagandist in tone, designed to win support from those who had been alienated by Lancastrian rule; though it need not reveal all that York and Warwick had discussed in Ireland.[35] The keynote of the manifesto, in the name of York and the three earls, was loyalty to the king and the need for a radical change in the nature of his government. Its complaints skilfully appealed to a variety of interests, both in the south-east and more generally: concern for the protection of the church would bring murmurs of approval from the archbishop and the clergy; the king's poverty and the oppressive actions of household purveyors would be familiar in Kent and the home counties; perversion of the law and the burdens of taxation, especially the recent expedients, would strike a chord practically everywhere; the archers authorized by parliament in 1453–54 had already threatened London and might do worse; the loss of France, the desertion of Calais, and the alleged encouragement of the Irish chieftains to overrun an Ireland under York's control were matters designed to stir Englishmen's pride and sense of patriotism; whilst the reputations of Henry V and the duke of Gloucester appeared in stark contrast to this squalid régime that seemed ready to submit the realm to foreign domination. The personal grievances of York and the earls seemed to exemplify these wider ills, not least by the vindictiveness of the Coventry parliament and the persecution of the Yorkists' tenants that followed. The manifesto came closest to articulating the duke of York's dynastic significance when the royal ministers were accused of plotting to destroy the duke 'and the yssew that it pleased God to sende me of the royalle blode'. Among the 'divers lordes' who were regarded as responsible, the earls of Shrewsbury and Wiltshire and Viscount Beaumont were singled out as 'hauyng the guydyng aboute the most noble persone of oure sayde souuerayn lorde, whos hyghenes they have restrayned and kept from the liberte and fredom that bylongethe to his seyde astate...' The proposed remedy was that advocated by York on several occasions since 1450, namely, to confront the king, assert the Yorkists' innocence, and to petition for an end to misrule. The only significant difference was the public appeal which York and his friends now made to the archbishop and the commonalty to assist them in their enterprise to ensure that their petition was acted upon. Couched in traditional language, the manifesto also hinted at the dynastic problem and recommended more forceful action than had been contemplated in the 1450s. This was doubtless the substance of the earl of Warwick's address to the assembled clergy and citizenry at St Paul's.[36] If York and Warwick had agreed to seize the crown itself as their best course, the earls from Calais had either changed their mind, or were biding their time, making conciliatory gestures until substantial support had gathered or the royal family was in their grasp.

To accompany this political campaign, informal propaganda was disseminated in Canterbury; but whereas those who read the ballads on the gates of the cathedral city might well appreciate the significance of such lines as

> Send hom, most gracious Lord Jhesu most benygne,
> Sende hoom thy trew blode vn to his propre veyne,
> Richard duk of York, Job thys seruaunt insygne, ...
> Edwarde Erle of Marche, whos fame the erthe shalle sprede,
> Richard Erle of Salisbury named prudence,
> Wythe that noble knyghte and floure of manhode
> Richard erle of Warrewyk sheelde of oure defence,
> Also lytelle Fauconbrege, a knyghte of grete reuerence; ....

the biblical imagery and Latin phraseology elsewhere in these verses were literary pretensions that probably sailed above the heads of most readers.[37]

On a more personal level, the Yorkist lords had in their company a distinct asset: Francesco Coppini, whose commission as papal legate instructed him to promote peace between the warring English factions in the interests of a crusade against the Turks. To Pope Pius's later regret, he exceeded his authority in attaching himself so firmly to the Yorkists' side, and then excommunicating the principal Lancastrian courtiers, including Shrewsbury, Wiltshire, and Beaumont.[38] On 5 July, Coppini accompanied the Yorkist host which then left London in two columns: the smaller under the command of Lord Fauconberg was followed by the main force under March and Warwick, who took with them Archbishop Bourgchier and Bishops Neville and Grey. Separate columns were advisable in order to prevent the king from reaching the comparative safety of the Isle of Ely, where it was proposed to make a stand, with the fenland and the coast affording a means of escape.[39] In the event, the two armies met in the fields near Delapré abbey, just outside the walls of Northampton, on 10 July.

The Yorkist army seems to have outnumbered the king's forces by a considerable margin; indeed, so alarmed were Bishop Waynflete (the chancellor) and Bishop Booth (the keeper of the privy seal) that they fled. So did the fainthearted Wiltshire, who hastened across country to Southampton and the galleys he had assembled there in March; he manned the ships, packed his treasure on board, and after some aimless cruising in the channel made for Holland.[40] Meanwhile, at Northampton the Yorkist lords tried to negotiate with the king, perhaps to induce him and his confidants to surrender; several ecclesiastics were charged with this mission, but they were rebuffed by Buckingham, who appears to have been the Lancastrian commander that day. On three separate occasions, the Yorkists sought to parley, but each time the king refused; one of the emissaries even defected to the Lancastrians and urged Henry to stand and fight.[41] The ensuing battle lasted barely an hour, for Lord Grey of Ruthin's desertion to the Yorkists was decisive; although some were drowned in the river Nene as they fled the field, the casualties were not high. The reason for this is the proclamation issued by March and Warwick on the battlefield itself that only the opposing lords and their retainers should be attacked and, as far as possible, the king and the commons spared; this adroit move reflected the Yorkists' declared aim of rescuing the king and kingdom from unworthy and oppressive rulers. The king's guns proved useless in the heavy rain, which turned the field into a quagmire.[42]

King Henry was taken in his tent, deserted by his advisers, many of whom – Buckingham, Shrewsbury, Beaumont, and Egremont among them – were dead. Compared with 1455, influential opinion on the issues that divided the court and the Yorkists had polarized sufficiently to enable the insurgents to take firm control of the king and the government of the realm. But it was their major misfortune that Queen Margaret and

Prince Edward had not been present at Northampton and therefore remained at liberty. Even if the Yorkists had now resolved to depose Henry VI in favour of Richard of York, they would not have been able to avoid the horrors of dynastic civil war. Thus, after Northampton, the Yorkist lords recoiled from revolution, pledged their loyalty to the king they now controlled, and led him in some state to London. All this had been achieved without the duke of York and therefore without his specific endorsement.[43]

In the months that followed, the victors established their mastery of the central government; as far as Westminster was concerned, the Lancastrian régime was at an end, even though Henry VI still wore the crown. As 'Gregory's Chronicle' puts it, after Northampton the Yorkist lords 'made newe offycers of the londe'. On 16 July, Henry and his escort reached London and the captive monarch was installed in the bishop of London's palace. A service at St Paul's celebrated the recent victory, though this was somewhat premature since the Lancastrian guns in the Tower could be heard outside. Salisbury had stayed in the capital when the other earls had marched towards Northampton primarily because Scales and Hungerford were holding out in the Tower. After the reception of the Yorkists in London, the Lancastrians began to strafe the city with cannon fire and did considerable damage, several Londoners dying in the bombardment.[44] This persuaded the city authorities to co-operate with Salisbury in a full-scale siege of the fortress: Lord Cobham and the sheriffs of London levelled their fire from the city, and Sir John Wenlock and John Harowe, a London mercer, concentrated their assault from St Catherine's. The Tower was thus effectively sealed, and no relief or food could be smuggled in. A short but destructive engagement took place, during which the Lancastrian guns set fire to houses and wounded men, women, and children in the streets. The citizens responded with their own cannon from across the river, with the aim of breaking down the stout walls of the fortress. The hopelessness of the Lancastrian position, especially when news filtered through that Henry VI had arrived in London a captive, was enough to shatter their morale. While negotiations for a surrender were proceeding, a mass escape was planned on 19 July. During the night, Scales and his companions tried to reach sanctuary at Westminster, but the former was recognized, pursued on the river, and eventually seized and slain near Southwark; others were captured and some killed in Holborn. A number were hauled before the Yorkist lords and the mayor in the guildhall and tried during the last week in July. Those who were condemned and beheaded at Tyburn were mostly minor servants of more distinguished Lancastrians.[45]

The question of the throne

The more important task of creating a Yorkist régime was much more difficult, for possession of the king and capital did not mean that the queen and her son would submit or that the provinces of the realm would be easily subdued. Still, the Yorkist lords could begin by restoring order in London and remodelling the central administration and the royal household. On 21 July, soon after the capitulation of the Tower, a proclamation was publicized by Warwick, who announced severe penalties for murderers, thieves, and others who prejudiced the re-establishment of good order. Meanwhile, the king set off on pilgrimage to Canterbury, where he had arrived by 1 August.[46] The Yorkists found Henry to be utterly pliable in their grasp. To Bishop Neville, who was admittedly speaking with bitterness after the king had slipped from Yorkist hands a few months later, he bore the outer trappings of kingship without its substance. This too was the impression conveyed by Coppini to Pope Pius II, who later described Henry as 'more timorous than a woman, utterly devoid of wit or spirit'.[47] The indications are that over the past few years Henry had progressively lost all strength of will and much of his mental alertness.

His household was already in process of being cleansed of its Lancastrian courtiers and servants, so that Henry eventually found himself surrounded by men whom he had not chosen, many of whom may not have been familiar to him, and who were intended to be his keepers rather than his companions. The household, therefore, was a Yorkist institution controlling a monarch who was completely in its power. Lord Beauchamp was allowed to retain his position as steward, but the new treasurer of the household was the Welsh marcher landowner Sir Walter Sculle, who remained in office under Edward IV; on 30 July, Salisbury himself was appointed the king's chamberlain in place of Sir Richard Tunstall.[48] Even more significant perhaps was the introduction to the household of serjeants, yeomen, esquires, and knights who had had no previous experience there because their loyalties were Yorkist ones, though they prospered thereafter in Edward IV's and Richard III's service. Thus, Robert Clavenger, who was made a yeoman of the chamber on 26 August, retained this position during the 1460s, and so did Nicholas Suthecotes, a serjeant-at-arms from 9 October.[49]

Yorkist control was no less complete over the offices of state. Very soon after Northampton, on 25 July, Bishop George Neville became chancellor of England; three days later, Viscount Bourgchier became the new treasurer and Robert Stillington, archdeacon of Wells, took charge of the privy seal.[50] But the recasting of the government, like that of the household, penetrated below the senior levels, for the appointment of men like Thomas Vaughan as master of the king's ordnance and Bishop Lowe as master of the mints assisted the consolidation of Yorkist power throughout the central administration.[51] The king's new council had an overwhelmingly Yorkist hue too, its principal members (aside from the officers) being Archbishop Bourgchier, Warwick, Salisbury, and Sir John Wenlock; among former Lancastrian councillors who continued to be consulted were the dean of St Seurin, the prior of the Hospital of St John of Jerusalem, and Lords Dudley, Stourton, and Beauchamp, who were evidently prepared to throw in their lot with Henry's new masters.[52]

Beyond the capital, the Yorkists were faced with the task of recovering property and positions forfeited at the time of the Coventry parliament and rewarding those who had aided their enterprise. At the same time, others had to be persuaded to accept the new order, preferably without violence, still less a civil war against Queen Margaret and her son. Moreover, the obligation lay heavy on these new rulers to restore English government to the condition from which the Lancastrians (it was alleged) had dragged it. The reversal of the Yorkists' attainder would have to wait until a new parliament had assembled and accordingly on 30 July writs announced that one would meet at Westminster on 7 October.[53] But the lords were impatient to get their hands on the estates and revenues they had once enjoyed, and probably before parliament had reversed his attainder, Salisbury's Yorkshire tenants were ordered to pay him their rent arrears.[54] The most important reward went to the staplers, without whose aid the invasion of 1460 would probably not have been successful; on 6 August they were assured that their debts would be repaid from the subsidy imposed in all but a few ports as from 1 January 1460, and extraordinary powers were conferred on the staplers to enable them to oversee the implementation of this grant.[55]

To impress Yorkist authority on the realm at large was a herculean task, for sympathy for the king was widespread and the machinations of the queen a major potential threat. Financial considerations alone suggested to the new treasurer in August that he replace all the controllers and collectors of the customs, and in an attempt to persuade suitable persons to become sheriffs in November, in more than half a dozen shires the prospective appointees were relieved from collecting the traditional (and partly unrealizable) revenues.[56] Warwick and Salisbury, who by their determination and daring had been the architects of the Yorkist triumph, sought their reward pre-eminently in the duchy of Lancaster. Warwick and his brother Thomas established their authority in the midlands estates of the duchy which had been such an asset to the Lancastrians in the late 1450s, and then on 1 December the earl and his father tightened their hold on the entire duchy by receiving, jointly and for life, the stewardships of both its northern and southern parts, as well as of Lancashire.[57] Yet the new government was prepared to conciliate when it seemed advisable. A few former household servants like John Penycock were pardoned, but the most generous treatment was reserved for the alien community, on whom the Yorkists might have to rely for loans in the future. Italians who had lately been denounced by the Lancastrian régime were pardoned on 25 August, and a number of foreigners received letters of denizenship in the months that followed.[58] In short, the Yorkist lords acted with calculated firmness, but with little sign of vindictiveness; their urgent responsibility, after all, was to restore peace to the shaken realm and confidence in its rulers.

One cannot be certain of Margaret's movements after the battle of Northampton. Precise intelligence about Lancastrian activities in the north and west was not readily or accurately available in the south and east, where rumour, false reports, and propaganda were an insidious encouragement to panic, discord, and uprisings. The Yorkist authorities were constantly on alert from August onwards to counteract rumours and prevent the dissemination of propaganda bills and letters.[59] It is likely, however, that the queen had retreated westwards, first to Lancashire and Cheshire, where she encountered a gang of thieves, and then to Wales, presumably in the hope of joining Jasper Tudor. York's arrival in September and his deliberate tour of his marcher lordships and the English borderland meant that a counter-attack from the loyal counties of the principality became distinctly hazardous. After retiring as far as Harlech castle with a small company, she therefore took ship for Scotland about the beginning of December (or even earlier) in order to appeal to her fellow queen, Mary of Guelders, who was regent for her young son.[60] The Scottish military menace had already receded. Although James II had been in touch with York in Ireland, he persisted in his siege of Roxburgh and Berwick castles after the battle of Northampton. Salisbury was accordingly commissioned to raise men to relieve the fortresses, but James's accidental death at Roxburgh on 3 August, followed by the withdrawal of the Scots soon afterwards, made it unnecessary to send to the northern border an army that might be required elsewhere.[61] Queen Margaret's arrival at the Scottish court revived the threat from that quarter.

In Wales, Earl Jasper had immense influence in the principality shires and his own lordships, and the Yorkists' attempts to command obedience from those who held York's own castles of Denbigh and Montgomery and others in north and north-east Wales encountered considerable opposition. Along the Welsh border, in south-west England, and in Yorkshire and the north, Lancastrian sympathies were strong and were encouraged by Margaret and the surviving Lancastrian lords, especially Somerset, who returned from Dieppe to Devon in October.[62] Somerset's landing emphasized the importance of patrolling the seas and guarding the coastline, responsibilities which were undertaken by Warwick, whose 'probity, loyalty, military skill, and prudence' and his highly successful naval enterprises from Calais were popularly admired. Towards the end of November, it was resolved to assemble a fleet under his command which would patrol the seas during the next six months. His indenture of service was concluded on 17 December and he was given full powers over his retinue and authority to punish pirates.[63]

The main features of Yorkist rule had been established well before the duke of York arrived at Westminster in October 1460. Whereas general strategy and aims may have been formulated in Ireland in March, the uncertainty of invasion and battle precluded any detailed consideration on that occasion of the practical policies to be followed by a new Yorkist régime. These were left to March, Warwick, and Salisbury to devise, and to judge by chroniclers' comments, it was pre-eminently Warwick who provided the leadership before York put in an appearance. The efforts of the earls had met with such success that it seemed less and less necessary (and certainly dangerously provocative) to unseat Henry VI. Neville ambitions at least could be realized without dynastic revolution, and the earl of March was not prepared to argue otherwise. York still held to other views. His arrival near Chester about 8 September threatened the achievement of the Yorkist earls and more than anything else – more even than the efforts of the queen and her followers – his claims precipitated the most bloody and decisive phase of the 'wars of the roses'.[64]

Only after news of the battle of Northampton and the capture of the king had reached Ireland did York make his final preparations to sail for England. His progress to Westminster may have been leisurely, but it gave him an opportunity to rally his supporters and to display the kingly state to which he unmistakably aspired. Either he was steadfastly adhering to an earlier agreement with Warwick or he had decided to regard the Yorkist victory as a prelude to his own enthronement. This stately progress across England contrasts starkly with the nature of the régime under construction at Westminster. Making his way southwards to Hereford, he posed as a king preparing for his crowning, disdaining to use Henry VI's regnal year in the indentures by which he retained marcher supporters from at least 13 September, displaying the arms of Lionel of Clarence, and unfurling as he approached London a banner with the arms of England undifferenced. As he neared the capital, his company, clad in Richard's white and blue livery with the fetterlock device, was met by the duchess of York, borne almost in triumph in a blue velvet chair to greet her husband. By the time he reached Westminster, his sword was being carried upright before him, and all the way from Abingdon trumpeters had heralded his approach. York went straight to the royal palace and took possession of it as if it were his own.[65]

He came well prepared. The duke probably had his claim to the crown ready when he attended parliament on 10 October, three days after it opened. On that day, he stalked into the chamber and made as if to take the king's place; when challenged by Archbishop Bourgchier as to whether he wished to see Henry or not, he replied haughtily that there was no one in the land with whom he should seek an interview. No longer was Richard content to fight for what he regarded as his rightful place as the king's next adult heir; he was insisting that the crown was and had been rightfully his.[66]

The lords who witnessed this spectacle were dismayed by his bold assertions and urged him to discuss his claims with the king. Regardless of whatever arrangements had been made in Ireland, regardless too of the duke's pretensions since his landing, to the lords in parliament this claim was embarrassing, unwelcome, and unacceptable. The deposition of Henry VI was inconceivable to them because it was unnecessary and irrelevant to all but the man who coveted the crown. After this rebuff, York seems to have retired with ill grace to contemplate his future tactics; he refused to vacate the royal palace, but equally he disdained to meet King Henry, whose natural timidity and alarm led him to avoid the duke in the corridors and suites of Westminster.[61] The Yorkist leaders were plunged into a crisis of the first magnitude and for the moment indecision reigned. The customary ceremonies on St Edward's day (13 October), when Henry VI was expected to wear his crown in procession to Westminster abbey, were cancelled; instead, the lords sat in permanent session at Black Friars grappling with this uniquely sensitive problem. Their discussions lasted until 25 October. To the superstitious, two incidents boded ill for the outcome: while the commons were discussing York's claim in the abbey, the crown that hung in the middle of their 'common house' fell down, and so (it was reported) did a crown perched on a tower at Dover castle.[68] York had misjudged the political climate, particularly among the lords, whose support was absolutely essential for a peaceful deposition, and there is no sign that the commons were ready to press the duke's case as they had done in 1455.[69] The months spent in relative isolation in Ireland, during which he was separated from his most experienced and influential allies and councillors – notably Salisbury, Oldhall, Herbert, and Devereux – may have misled him into believing that a personal challenge to the throne in an assembly summoned by Henry VI could be persuaded to endorse the king's deposition after the example of 1399. York's confidence was such that he even arranged for his own coronation to take place on 1 November.[70]

On 16 October, York's councillors presented a formal, detailed statement of his claim, supported by a lengthy pedigree which implied that the Lancastrians had been usurpers. After lengthy and difficult discussions lasting more than a week, a compromise emerged. At first, the lords had tried to flatter Henry VI into giving a judgement, 'in so moche as his seid highnes had seen and understonden many dyvers writyngs and cronicles'. The judges, the serjeants-at-law, and the king's attorney declined to comment on a matter which they maintained lay beyond their competence, and to the objections of the lords York produced cogent answers. The final accord adapted the provision of the treaty of Troyes whereby the dauphin had been disinherited and Henry V acknowledged as heir to the Valois throne; by the accord's terms, Henry V's grandson was disinherited and York and his offspring acknowledged as heirs to the Lancastrian throne.[11] It was an inspired solution to an intractable problem, though forty years after the treaty of Troyes it represented an ironic and painful humiliation for Henry VI and his dynasty. The wheel of fortune, as was its wont, was about to turn full circle. The accord was hardly satisfactory to the Lancastrians, though Henry VI was brought to accept it without undue resistance, and the prospect that York himself would succeed to the throne seemed rather remote, for he was ten years older than the king. It was the stubborn and outspoken opposition of the lords, including the Nevilles and even March, which dissuaded York from resorting to more violent action that would certainly have fractured the lords' ranks and encouraged retaliation from Queen Margaret. The situation was unstable enough without York risking a breach with magnates and others who had hitherto been prepared to accept the new régime. The agreement was accordingly accepted by the two royal cousins on 25 October 1460 and it was immediately authorized 'by thauctorite of this present parlement'.[72]

York had achieved more than he had ever done before, short of the crown itself. He was declared heir apparent and 10,000 marks were assigned him and his two eldest sons, March and Rutland. This sum was to be drawn from the principality of Wales and Chester, which meant that Edward of Lancaster was stripped of much of his inheritance as well as his status. Richard was also given powers to protect and defend the realm which he had enjoyed on two occasions earlier in the reign. All the assembled lords, both spiritual and temporal, swore a solemn oath to accept York as 'true heir to the kingdom' just as he was induced to acknowledge Henry VI as king for life.[73] This took place on 31 October and next day, to seal the agreement, Henry VI went crowned in possession to St Paul's cathedral, accompanied by dukes, earls, and other lords to demonstrate the amity among them.[74] A week later, the accord was publicly proclaimed in London and to meet York's wishes, parliament authorized its widespread publication; copies were sent to towns and cities so that the entire realm should understand the momentous dynastic adjustment that had been made.[75] It is likely that neither of the principals was entirely happy with its terms: it was a compromise imposed by lords, who were reluctant to depose a harmless monarch and yet viewed the accession of Prince Edward (and the restoration of his mother's influence) with deep distaste. It was a unique arrangement in English history, owing nothing to the precedents of 1327 or 1399. Its fundamental defect was that it did not take account of Queen Margaret or her son, who were made all the more determined to destroy those who held the king a prisoner.

The Lancastrian loyalists were rendered far from powerless by the constitutional arrangements extracted by York and his council from the hesitant lords at Westminster. Jasper Tudor retained a secure base in west Wales, Queen Margaret was busily pleading with the Scots for aid, and after Somerset landed in the west country, he joined forces with the earl of Devon. In the north of England, the Percies, Clifford, Dacre, Roos, and Lord Neville (of the Westmorland line) were equally devoted to Henry VI, whom they regarded as a prisoner acting under duress; and although FitzHugh and Greystoke had serious misgivings, they too swore to aid the queen. Few of these lords had been present at the parliament that had disinherited her son.[76] Sheer geography prevented a combined assault on the Yorkist régime, but Somerset, Devon, and Andrew Trollope succeeded in reaching Hull, where they assembled a considerable army in league with the northerners.[77] It was this dire threat which caused York, Salisbury, and Rutland early in December to lead an army northwards to Nottingham and on to Sandal castle, one of the duke's own fortresses in Yorkshire.[78]

The accord of 31 October had made it certain that sooner or later the dynastic dispute would be transferred to the battlefield. For the Lancastrians, there was no other way of annulling what Henry VI had been prevailed upon to accept; for the Yorkists there could be no assurance that the agreement would be implemented so long as large Lancastrian forces remained in being and attracted widespread support within the realm and beyond it. York's march northwards is therefore comprehensible, and in any case he and Salisbury were confident that they could count on men from their own estates to flock to their standard. And yet, York showed a degree of over-confidence which the Westminster accord did not warrant, and he might have foreseen that a northern Lancastrian army would be unlikely to gather recruits if it marched south of the Trent.[79] His actions after his arrival in Yorkshire confirm this lack of good sense. The massed Lancastrians under Somerset, Devon, and the northern lords were far more numerous than York's army, even though he had recruited supporters on the way and was followed by ordnance and cannon from the Tower.[80] On 30 December, while a number of his men were away in search of food and supplies, he unwisely ventured out of Sandal castle to attack the enemy whom he regarded as breaking the Christmastide truce by approaching surreptitiously in force. A battle took place near Wakefield during which York, Rutland, Sir Thomas Neville, and a large number of captains and retainers were slain. Salisbury was captured, and although Somerset seems to have been prepared to allow him to ransom himself, the commons of Pontefract so detested the earl that they seized him and cut off his head.[81] The heads of several leading Yorkists were placed on the gates of the city of York, the duke's mockingly adorned with a crown of paper and straw. In a single engagement, two of the arch-enemies of the queen and the Lancastrian court had been slain and the feud-like character of the political violence since 1455 had claimed new victims, though tradition alone is responsible for the assertion that Lord Clifford, whose father had fallen at St Albans, was responsible for the death of the young Rutland. The fighting at Wakefield was otherwise no turning-point in the civil war: Margaret and the Lancastrians had still to destroy the Yorkist establishment, for Henry VI was secure in Warwick's grasp in the south and by the Westminster accord Edward of March was his next heir. Those who had been party to that agreement were unlikely to lose their nerve when news of the disaster reached

London on 2 January, though the deaths at Wakefield significantly diminished Yorkist manpower.[82]

York's northern campaign was part of a larger strategy for the destruction of Lancastrian power before it could unravel the Westminster accord and prevent the Yorkist succession. Accordingly, in December, Edward, earl of March set off westward towards the wealthy Welsh marcher lordships which had been a refuge and a reservoir of men and money for his father on more than one occasion in the past. His intention was probably to prevent Jasper Tudor and his forces from joining the Lancastrians as they made their way from the north. He celebrated Christmas at Gloucester and seems to have toured his father's and Warwick's lordships recruiting as he went.[83] At the age of eighteen, Edward was embarking on his first independent campaign, though he would have had the support of York's senior councillors, among them Sir Walter Devereux, Sir William Herbert, and Sir John Wenlock. As he prepared to return to London after receiving, perhaps near Shrewsbury, news of his father's death, he was apprised of the approach of Jasper Tudor and the earl of Wiltshire from the west. They had brought together a mixed force of Welshmen from the southern counties of the principality and Pembrokeshire, reinforced by some Irish, Bretons, and French who may have been enlisted by Wiltshire.[84] A short distance from his own castle at Wigmore (Herefordshire), at a place known as Mortimer's Cross, Edward boldly threw himself on the Lancastrian army and thoroughly defeated it on 2 or 3 February.[85] Jasper and Wiltshire fled in disguise, many were slain, and others captured, including Owen Tudor. The widower of Queen Katherine and therefore step-father of the king, the father of Earl Jasper and grandfather of Henry Tudor, Owen's execution at Hereford a few days later went at least some distance towards avenging the death of York and Rutland at Wakefield.[86] Not until his very last moments did Owen comprehend that he was to be executed, and he went to the block murmuring

That hede shalle ly on the stocke that was wonte to ly on Quene Kateryns lappe . . . hys hedde [was] sette a-pone the hygheyste gryce of the market crosse, and a madde woman kembyd hys here and wysche a way the blode of hys face.[87]

Writing to some of the north Wales gentry three weeks after the battle, Jasper looked upon Mortimer's Cross as a 'great dishonour and rebuke that we and yee now late have by traytors Marche, Harbert and Dwnns, with their affinityes, as well in letting us of our Journey to the Kinge, as in putting my father your kinsman to the death'. Yet 'we purpose with the might of our Lord, and the assistance of you and other our kinsmen and frinds, within short time to avenge' the defeat.[88] Had Edward of March been worsted at Mortimer's Cross, it is likely that the Yorkist dynasty would never have occupied the English throne; as it was, the victory stiffened the resolve of the Yorkist establishment and brought closer a final test of strength with the Lancastrians in the north.

As soon as Queen Margaret heard of York's death early in January 1461, she hurried from Lincluden to place herself at the head of her victorious troops.[89] She recognized the military opportunity now open to her and the supreme advantage to be gained from marching quickly to the heart of the Yorkist régime, London. The depth of bitterness that the struggle had generated over the past year is reflected in the treatment accorded the estates of the Yorkist lords as she passed. The Lancastrian advance amounted to an organized harrying of the duke's property in particular; pillage and plunder were encouraged by the Lancastrian commanders, and towns situated close to York's lands in Nottingham-shire and Lincolnshire – for instance, Grantham and Stamford – suffered severely.[90] These outrages, however much they may have gratified the queen, proved a major blunder which Yorkist propaganda fully exploited to demonstrate what might happen if a northern Lancastrian army successfully established itself in the south.[91] At the Yorkist court of Henry VI and in London there was considerable alarm as Warwick, the only leading Yorkist available, prepared to face the enemy. From the last days of January, frantic efforts were made to array men and assemble provisions in south-east and eastern England to oppose the Lancastrians, and the brief session of parliament that lasted from 28 January to 3 February probably co-operated in the earl's strategy.[92] He planned a defensive operation to halt the advance until reinforcements arrived from the earl of March and the Welsh borderland. But his equipment and dispositions were unavailing. On 12 February he, Norfolk, Suffolk, and Arundel left London, taking with them the king in the hope that Lancastrians would not attack their own monarch. But Warwick's army, weakened by dissension and treachery, was outflanked on 17 February in the streets of St Albans and decisively beaten. The executions which were becoming an inevitable accompani-ment of these dynastic encounters carried off two prominent victims, Lord Bonville, who owed his peerage to the duke of Suffolk, and Sir Thomas Kyriell, a former Lancastrian soldier; Prince Edward stood watching as their heads were severed.[93] Warwick, Norfolk, and Arundel fled. Henry VI was so overjoyed that he proceeded to bless and knight his son, who thereupon knighted thirty others who had fought at St Albans.[94] But as an Italian in London ruefully observed on the eve of the battle, 'whoever conquers, the crown of England loses, which is a very great pity'.[95] What was of greatest significance was the fact that Henry had been seized from his Yorkist guardians and reunited with his wife and son. The Yorkist régime now had no king to call its own: the Westminster accord had been overtaken by events.

In two senses, the decisive point in the civil war had been reached: the Lancastrian king and queen were within reach of their capital and were about to demand entry; and the Yorkist lords were required to make a military, political, and constitutional decision about the crown of England. Had it not been for the speed and decisiveness of Edward of March, coupled with the Lancastrian reputation in London and the south-east, the Yorkists might have lost all in the last fortnight of February 1461. As soon as he heard of Warwick's defeat, Edward set off from the borderland on 19 February to return to London. He met Warwick *en route* about 23 February at either Chipping Norton or Burford in the Cotswolds, and doubtless both concluded that the only course open to them if they wished to pursue Yorkist aims was to march on London.[96] This meeting was even more crucial than that between Warwick and March's father less than a year before; on this occasion there was no question of divided or misunderstood counsels, and the Yorkist claimant played the leading role in implementing their decisions. Apart from military strategy, the two magnates must surely have discussed what should follow their arrival in the capital. They still had to take account of the Westminster accord which March had sworn to observe and the lords present (not all of them staunch Yorkists by any means) had accepted. If the throne were to be seized by force, then those who were now grappling with their consciences, and wriggling in a political situation from which they could not easily escape, needed to be offered a plausible justification for dynastic revolution. To meet this need, it was put about that Henry VI himself had broken the Westminster accord, though he had been a passive figure throughout.[97] Henry's personal involvement in the fighting at St Albans had been negligible (rumour had it that he 'was placed under a tree a mile away, where he laughed and sang'!), and all along most men had been reluctant to regard him as responsible for the actions of his ministers and his wife; but it was not unreasonable to consider his behaviour after St Albans as irrevocably breaching the agreement. In practice, no other conclusion was possible. It was unthinkable for March to accept Henry VI as king when he was in the clutches of his wife and her supporters, for that would simply restore the situation faced by March's father in the 1450s; it was just as inconceivable that Margaret should accept the earl of March as heir to the throne in place of her own son. Thus, after the battle of St Albans, Edward of March had no alternative but to seize the throne for himself and use Henry's rescue by the Lancastrians as evidence of the king's breaking of his sworn undertaking at Westminster.

The news that March and Warwick were approaching London, along with the Londoners' temporizing when presented with Lancastrian demands, persuaded Queen Margaret to abandon her advance and retire northwards.[98] In the short term, the queen had required supplies and money from London for her men as they lay near St Albans; in the longer term, she demanded the capital's submission. In the city 'the shops keep closed, and nothing is done either by the trades-people or by the merchants, and men do not stand in the streets or go far away from home'.[99] So nervous was the common council of a mass invasion of northern soldiery that the duchess of Buckingham (Anne Neville, Warwick's aunt), the duchess of Bedford, and Lady Scales (whose husband had been a loyal Lancastrian), together with a group of clergy, were despatched on behalf of the city to plead with the queen not to pillage London; they returned on 20 February reasonably reassured. A proclamation was even prepared announcing March to be a traitor. However, the queen's envoys at first returned empty-handed, though the mayor and aldermen agreed to admit four household knights and 400 men into London – but no more. When a delegation of aldermen and commoners made its way to Barnet on 22 February with food for the queen's army and to escort the Lancastrian contingent into the city, they were stopped by the citizens at Cripplegate.[100] The gates were slammed shut and barred against the Lancastrians in the hope that Edward of March would soon arrive. The fundamental lack of sympathy which the general populace of London had shown towards the Lancastrian court in the past surfaced once again to overrule the inclinations of the city fathers, who took a more pragmatic attitude to large forces in the neighbourhood.

In retrospect, these few days proved crucial for the Lancastrian monarchy and the enthronement of a new dynasty. Edward of March entered London on 27 February to a rapturous welcome from the citizens, to whom he appeared as a far more striking – indeed, royal – figure than Henry VI. During the next few days, his acclamation and accession as king were carefully orchestrated by means whose significance has been analysed by C. A. J. Armstrong. They included a declaration of his right title in terms that had been accepted by the lords in the previous October, and a denunciation of Henry's fitness to reign, partly because he had reneged on the Westminster accord. The proceedings culminated on 4 March with a service in St Paul's cathedral and a more secular ceremony later in the day in Westminster hall during which Edward took possession of his crown and kingdom.[101] The Yorkists' constitutional victory had been won. A decisive military engagement had been avoided so far and until it had been successfully fought, Edward could not feel politically secure on his throne or demonstrate to those of his subjects who were uncertain in their allegiance that he was likely to wear the crown unto death. Hurriedly raising money in London, he therefore sent Lord Fauconberg with an army in pursuit of the Lancastrians on 11 March; he himself followed two days later with the rest of his forces, encouraging others to join him as he marched north. The armies that confronted one another near Towton (Yorkshire) on 29 March were just about the largest to engage in the 'wars of the roses'. It was a bloody battle fought in bitterly cold weather and driving snow that seriously hampered the Lancastrian archers. Preliminary skirmishes the previous day had been indecisive. On Palm Sunday the main engagement lasted all day, accompanied by fearful slaughter and the death of a number of magnates, especially on the Lancastrian side (including Northumberland, Dacre, Welles, and Buckingham's son, as well as Andrew Trollope); after the fighting was done, Devon and Wiltshire were executed.[100] It was fortunate for

Henry VI, Queen Margaret, and Prince Edward that they had sat out the battle in York; they were able to evade capture and make for the Scottish border, where their situation could be reassessed.

Notes

1 *PL*, II, 540.
2 *English Chron.*, p. 83; *CCR, 1454–61*, p. 426; Curtis, *JRSAI*, LXII (1932),181. Wiltshire was optimistically appointed for 12 years, with deputies who included Archbishop May of Armagh. See Otway-Ruthven, *Medieval Ireland*, p. 386.
3 *CPR, 1452–61*, p. 602 (24 April 1460).
4 Above, p. 813; *CMilP*, I, 27-8; Dunlop, op. cit., pp. 205-7.
5 Scofield, op. cit., I, 45.
6 Curtis, *JRSAI*, LXII (1932), 181-3; Otway-Ruthven, *Medieval Ireland*, pp. 387-8; and more recently, Lydon, *Lordship of Ireland*, pp. 262-5. The decision to produce a new coinage not only reflected these political claims, but may have provided York with an immediate source of funds: see 'Gregory's Chron.', p. 205, for 'the newe gretys' (i.e., groats).
7 *English Chron.*, p. 83.
8 Wood, *PRIA*, XXXI, section C (1923–24), 236 (June 1460). Kildare was appointed justiciar of Ireland by the Yorkist-dominated régime in January 1461, following York's death (*HBC*, p. 154).
9 It is perhaps unlikely (as in Ross, *Edward IV*, p. 203) that York actually offered the concessions as an inducement to the Anglo-Irish lords in view of the latter's pre-existing demands.
10 Stevenson, II, ii, [772]; *Great Chron.*, pp. 191-2; *London Chrons.*, pp. 170-1; *Brut*, p. 529; Waurin, IV, 285-7. The Gascon, Gaillard de Durfort, lord of Duras, who had joined Charles VII after the fall of Bordeaux, was the fleet's commander and he seized several merchant vessels on his way to Ireland (Scofield, op. cit., I, 59; Vale, *English Gascony*, p. 221). For other communication between Ireland and Calais at this time, see Scofield, op. cit., I, 59.
11 *CMilP*, I, 27-8. See Griffiths, 'Sense of dynasty', p. 29.
12 *English Chron.*, p. 79.
13 See especially ibid., pp. 85ff; Waurin, V, 285ff.
14 *CPR, 1452–61*, pp. 563, 567, 602, 604-6, 609; *PL*, II, 334.
15 *English Chron.*, pp. 91-4; *CPR, 1452–61*, p. 554; above, p. 828.
16 *CPR, 1452–61*, p. 556.
17 ibid., pp. 563-4; *English Chron.*, p. 85; PRO, E404/71/4/28, 36; Stevenson, II, ii, 512-15 (reciting his indenture of 3 February); Scofield, op. cit., I, 53-4. His enthusiasm achieved little at considerable cost.
18 *CPR, 1452–61*, pp. 554, 566-7, 577, 602, 605; Scofield, op. cit., I, 60 (noting Exeter's indenture of 19 March), 64. Several chronicles record this ignominious incident ('Benet's Chron'., p. 225; Stevenson, II, ii, [772]; *Brut*, p. 529; *Great Chron.*, pp. 191-2; *London Chrons.*, pp. 170-1; Waurin, V, 287-90). The capital ship *Grace Dieu* had been made over to Exeter on 24 March (*CPR, 1452–61*, p. 577). Kelly, dissertation, pp. 35-6, has a useful discussion of the incident.

19 *CPR, 1452–61*, pp. 606, 591; *CVenP*, I, 88; Haward, in *English trade*, p. 317.

20 *CPR, 1452–61*, pp. 567, 561, 563-4, 602-6, 609, 611; *PL*, I, 162; *English Chron.*, pp. 90-1; Scofield, op. cit., I, 68-9.

21 *English Chron.*, p. 98.

22 *CPR, 1452–61*, p. 528; a similar order was issued on 27 March (ibid., p. 565).

23 ibid., p. 602; for precautions at Bristol, see ibid., p. 611 (26 February).

24 ibid., p. 605; 'Benet's Chron', p. 225. While on one of these missions, Judde was killed at St Albans on 22 June (*Three Chrons.*, p. 73; Flenley, p. 149).

25 ibid., pp. 149-50; *English Chron.*, pp. 95-6; 'Benet's Chron.', p. 225; Scofield, op. cit., I, 63.

26 *CPR, 1452–61*, pp. 565, 562-3, 604, 613, 607, 611, 609 (February–June 1460). For the ruthless persecution of York's tenantry at Newbury (Berks.), many of whom were imprisoned in Wallingford castle, see *English Chron.*, p. 90; *CPR, 1452–61*, pp. 648-9.

27 *English Chron.*, pp. 90-1; Scofield, op. cit., I, 57. Tunnage and poundage were devoted to sea-keeping by a council on 19 March (*CPR, 1452–61*, p. 554; *CCR, 1454–61*, p. 412; *CFR, 1452–61*, p. 258). For the failure to secure anticipated grants from convocation in May 1460, and the financial expedients in general, see Scofield, op. cit., I, 57-9.

28 *Brut*, p. 529; *Great Chron.*, p. 192; *London Chrons.*, pp. 141, 171; Flenley, p. 149; Stevenson, II, ii, [772]; *English Chron.*, pp. 85-6; *Three Chrons.*, p. 73. Mundford had been engaged on 23 May (*CPR, 1452–61*, pp. 607-9). See Scofield, op. cit., I, 65.

29 *Three Chrons.*, p. 73; 'Benet's Chron.' p. 225; *English Chron.*, p. 94. *Brut*, p. 529, says that they landed at Dover, but this is unlikely.

30 *English Chron.*, pp. 91-4; Stevenson, II, ii, [772]; Flenley, pp. 149-50; *London Chrons.*, p. 141; *Three Chrons.*, p. 73. There must be some doubt whether Archbishop Bourgchier met the insurgents at Sandwich and accompanied them to London with his cross held high before them (as in *English Chron.*, p. 94).

31 ibid., pp. 91-4; see also 'Gregory's Chron', p. 206. Fauconberg is said to have landed at Sandwich earlier in order to test the water.

32 Flenley, pp. 149-50; *English Chron.*, p. 94; *Three Chrons.*, pp. 73-4. The fullest account of London's cautious attitude is in Peake, thesis, ch. IV.

33 *Three Chrons.*, p. 74; Stevenson, II, ii, [773].

34 Peake, thesis, pp. 139-44; Scofield, op. cit., I, 80-1. Neville and Gray had been useful advocates of the Yorkist lords throughout the negotiations with the city authorities (Stevenson, II, ii, [772]).

35 'Gregory's Chron'., p. 206; *Brut*, p. 529. For a copy of the manifesto, see *English Chron.*, pp. 86-90. York contributed at least some of the material incorporated in it: witness his use of the first person and the specific reference to Ireland and his royal blood.

36 ibid., p. 95; see Waurin, V, 292-3.

37 *English Chron.*, pp. 91-4.

38 ibid., p. 94; 'Benet's Chron.', p. 225. See C. Head, 'Pope Pius II and the wars of the roses', *Archivum historiae pontificiae*, VIII (1970), 149-73; A Gottlob, 'Des Nuntius Franz Coppini antheil an der Entthronung des

Konigs Heinrich VI und seine Verurtheilung bei der romischen Curie', *Deutsche zeitschrift fur geschichtswissenschaft*, IV (1890), 75-111.

39 Flenley, pp. 150-1; *Three Chrons.*, p. 74. The Yorkist ranks also included Viscount Bourgchier, Lords Clinton, Audley, Abergavenny, Saye, and Scrope, the prior of the Hospital of St John of Jerusalem, and Bishops Beauchamp of Salisbury and Lowe of Rochester (*English Chron.*, pp. 95-6).

40 ibid., p. 90; 'Benet's Chron.', p. 226. According to the exaggerated estimate in Flenley, p. 151, the Yorkists had 160,000 (probably a mistake for 60,000 as in 'Benet's Chron.', p. 226, and *English Chron.*, p. 96) and the king only 20,000. 'Benet's Chron.', p. 226, has Fauconberg's column 10,000 strong followed by a larger force under March and Warwick.

41 Waurin, V, 297-9; *English Chron.*, pp. 96-7. At this point, the king's confessor, Bishop Stanbury of Hereford, also fled.

42 ibid., pp. 97-8. See R. I. Jack, 'A quincentenary: the battle of Northampton, July 10th, 1460', *Northants. Past and Present*, III (1960–65), 21-5, with a plan on 22. According to Flenley, p. 151, 50 of the king's men died and only 8 Yorkists; but 'Benet's Chron.', p. 226, puts the royal losses at 400, and Stevenson, II, ii, 773, at 300.

43 'Benet's Chron.', p. 226; *Three Chrons.*, p. 74; *English Chron.*, pp. 97-8 (including the speech of reassurance supposedly delivered to Henry in his tent by the Yorkist earls). The king was allowed to rest in Northampton for 3 days before journeying on to London.

44 ibid., pp. 95-6, 97-8; 'Benet's Chron.', p. 226; *Three Chrons.*, p. 74; Peake, thesis, pp. 143-5. Salisbury seems to have been given military command of London at this time, supported by Cobham and Wenlock; the Lancastrians in the Tower also included Lords Moleyns, Lovel, Vesci, and De la Warr, as well as household figures like Sir Edmund Hampden, Sir Thomas Browne, Sir Gervase Clifton, and Sir Thomas Tyrell.

45 *English Chron.*, p. 98; Stevenson, II, ii, [773]; Waurin, V, 302-4; 'Benet's Chron.', pp. 226-7 (for the trials between 23 July and 2 August, during which at least 7 were executed); *Three Chrons.*, pp. 74-5; Peake, thesis, pp. 146-9. See Williams, *BIHR*, I (1923–24), 72, citing PRO, KB27/805, 808; Scofield, op. cit., I, 89-92.

46 'Benet's Chron.', p. 227; *Three Chrons.*, pp. 74-5; Peake, thesis, p. 149 (dating the proclamation to 21 July); for a proclamation in similar vein to the authorities in Norfolk on 23 July, see Gairdner, *PL*, III, 221-2. Henry was still at Canterbury on 9 August (*PPC*, VI, 302).

47 *CMilP*, I, 61 (7 April 1461), 62 (where the translation of *idolo del re* as 'puppet' perhaps begs a question); Head, *Archivum historiae pontificiae*, VIII (1970), 145 (written after March 1461).

48 *HBC*, pp. 76, 79; Wedgwood, *Biographies*, pp. 773-4; Griffiths, *Principality of Wales*, p. 153. In addition, York's servant, Thomas Vaughan, was keeper of the great wardrobe by 1 September 1460 (*CPR, 1452–61*, p. 646); the king's new secretary by 20 August was James Goldwell, a Kentishman who was patronized by Archbishop Bourgchier (ibid., p. 599; Emden, *Oxford*, II, 783-6; Otway Ruthven, *King's secretary*, pp. 175-6). See also Morgan, *TRHS*, 5th ser., XXIII (1973), 6-7.

49 See *CPR, 1452–61*, passim, and *CCR, 1454–61*, passim; for the two mentioned, see ibid., pp. 464, 467; PRO, E404/72/4/79; 74/128. Control was established over the implementation of Henry's will when parliament in the

autumn added a number of staunch Yorkists to the panel of feoffees who administered a proportion of the duchy of Lancaster's revenue for this purpose (*RP*, V, 383-4).

50 Waurin, V, 301-2; *CCR, 1454–61*, p. 455; *PPC*, VI, 362; *HBC*, pp. 85, 92, 103. Bishop Neville received the great seal from Archbishop Bourgchier, who may have had temporary charge of it after the flight of Bishop Waynflete.

51 *CPR, 1452–61*, pp. 634, 644. Bishop Lowe was appointed the day after Northampton.

52 Virgoe, *BIHR*, XLIII (1970), 160; *PPC*, VI, 304-7, 310.

53 *CCR, 1454–61*, p. 462; *RP*, V, 373-4; below, p. 867.

54 *CPR, 1452–61*, p. 647 (8 October). The speaker was not chosen until 10 October. Cf. the treatment of Sir John Neville and his wife as early as 22 August (*PPC*, VI, 306; *RP*, V, 387-8).

55 *CCR, 1454–61*, p. 418; *RP*, V, 454. Only 4 ports were excepted. For an expression of support for the regularization of the wool trade, see *PL*, I, 259 (21 October).

56 *CPR, 1452–61*, pp. 589-90; *CFR, 1452–61*, pp. 253-60, 290-1, 294. For two of Warwick's nominees as customs collectors, see ibid., pp. 258, 283 (August, December 1460).

57 Somerville, op. cit., I, 421, 428-9, 492-3, 540, 564, 576, 583. Their appointments were for life. For Lord Stanley's nomination as receiver of Lancs. for life on 30 October, see ibid., pp. 492-3, 511, 540. For the Nevilles' unusual patronage, see also *CPR, 1452–61*, p. 589; *CFR, 1452–61*, pp. 275, 285, 287, 289. P. M. Kendall, *Warwick the kingmaker* (1957), strongly emphasizes the earl's role in 1460.

58 *CPR, 1452–61*, pp. 629, 598, 615, 634, 638, 641; *CCR, 1454–61*, p. 469. For the considerate treatment of the duchess of Buckingham and the countess of Shrewsbury (who took the veil), see *CPR, 1452–61*, pp. 639, 645, 635; *CFR, 1452–61*, pp. 284, 295.

59 *CPR, 1452–61*, pp. 608, 611, 612, 658, 647, 650, 651, 654, 659.

60 *English Chron.*, pp. 98-9; 'Gregory's Chron.', pp. 208-9; Stevenson, II, ii, 773. Margaret is said to have had 8 companions with her when she reached Harlech and had been relieved of goods worth 10,000 marks on the way; she may also have left some of her correspondence at Chirk castle (Denbs.) (Munroe, op. cit., pp. xiii-xviii). She was still thought on 12 October to be in Wales, where she had been joined by the duke of Exeter (*PL*, II, 216-17). For Margaret's arrival at Dumfries in December and her visit to the queen of Scotland at Lincluden, see Dunlop, op. cit., pp. 215-16.

61 *CPR, 1452–61*, pp. 589, 612; above, p. 813.

62 Ross, *Edward IV*, pp. 29-30; R. S. Thomas, thesis, pp. 187-8; *PPC*, VI, 302-5; 'Gregory's Chron.', p. 208; *English Chron.*, p. 99; *CPR, 1452–61*, pp. 607-8, 610, 612, 647, 649, 659. Somerset and his men had agreed to leave Guisnes and sought refuge in France (Stevenson, II, ii, [774]; Waurin, V, 306-8; *PL*, II, 216-17). For Yorkist precautions in the south-west from late November, see *CPR, 1452–61*, pp. 651, 653-4.

63 *CCR, 1454–61*, p. 474; *CPR, 1452–61*, pp. 642, 651. Tunnage and poundage would provide the requisite finance and so Warwick was authorized to appoint a customs collector in each port. For the safeguard of the Isle of Wight in December, see ibid., pp. 637-8.

64 Griffiths, 'Sense of dynasty', pp. 30-31; Ross, *Edward IV*, pp. 28ff;

Scofield, op. cit., I, ch. IV; Lander, *Crown and nobility*, pp. 101-2. For the popularity of Warwick in Norfolk, see *PL*, II, 210; I, 259 (October 1460).

65 'Gregory's Chron.', p. 208; Stevenson, II, ii, [774]; *Great Chron.*, p. 193; *London Chrons.*, p. 172; *English Chron.*, p. 99; *PL*, II, 216 (for the duchess's movements in September). See McFarlane, *PBA*, L (1964), 93-4; in the indentures the usual clause saving allegiance to the king was significantly omitted; York even promised William Stanley of Hooton the shrievalty of Cheshire when his indenture was concluded (PRO, Chester 2/135 m. 3*d*, ex irif. Miss D. J. Clayton). The account in Waurin, V, 308-12, is uncorroborated, though its general tenor is not significantly different from that of other writers.

66 *RP*, V, 375; 'Benet's Chron.', pp. 227-8; 'Gregory's Chron'., p. 208; *Brut*, p. 530; Stevenson, II, ii, [774]; *Reg. Whethamstede*, I, 376, reprinted in Chrimes and Brown, op. cit., pp. 312-13; *Chron. of London*, p. 141; *English Chron.*, pp. 99-100. For March's attempt to dissuade his father and brother from their course, see Waurin, V, 314-15.

67 *Three Chrons.*, p. 75; *Great Chron.*, p. 193; *London Chrons.*, p. 172; *English Chron.*, p. 99; *Reg. Whetehamstede*, I, 376.

68 *English Chron.*, p. 99; *Brut*, p. 530; *RP*, V, 375.

69 'Gregory's Chron.', p. 208; Stevenson, II, ii, [774]. The lords did not even include staunch Lancastrians (Lander, *Crown and nobility*, p. 103 n. 59). The speaker, John Green, was an Essex man who had links with Viscount Bourgchier, the new treasurer (*RP*, V, 373; Roskell, *Speakers*, pp. 267-9). Waurin, V, 313-17, stresses the disturbed state of London and the unwillingness of the populace to tolerate deposition.

70 *English Chron.*, p. 100; Waurin, V, 315-17.

71 Both York and the chancellor urged parliament to come to a quick decision (*RP*, V, 377).

72 *RP*, V, 375-83, reprinted in Chrimes and Brown, op. cit., pp. 313-18; Waurin, V, 313-15 (partly translated I, clxxvii-clxxviii), paints an interesting picture of Warwick and March remonstrating with York and Rutland about the claim. York and his sons swore to observe the accord provided Henry did so; the statute of treasons was extended to protect the duke and his family as members of the royal line. For comment on the constitutional significance of the reception of York's claim, see Chrimes, *Const. ideas*, pp. 23, 26-31; he points out that although the entire discussion had taken place in parliament and the subsequent arrangements were authorized there, the accord determining the succession was not enacted as a statute or act. His general views are reasserted in McKenna, *EHR*, XCIV (1979), 494-6, despite a revival of the 'parliamentary' or 'constitutional' view in W. H. Dunham and C. T. Wood, 'The right to rule in England: depositions and the kingdom's authority, 1327–1485', *American Hist. Rev.*, LXXXI (1976), 748-52.

73 'Benet's Chron', p. 228; Waurin, V, 317-18. The terms are reported fully in *English Chron.*, pp. 100-6 (which inaccurately states that York became prince of Wales, earl of Chester, and duke of Cornwall); see also *Great Chron.*, p. 193; *London Chrons.*, p. 172. Hall, *Chronicles*, p. 249, reprinted in Chrimes and Brown, op. cit., pp. 318-19, states that he was appointed protector.

74 *London Chrons.*, p. 172; *Great Chron.*, p. 193; Waurin, V, 317-18; McFarlane, *PBA*, L (1964), 93 n. 2. In the following weeks, Henry went

crowned to St Paul's on two other occasions, at Christmas and New Year's day (Flenley, p. 152).

75 *Great Chron.*, p. 193; *London Chrons.*, p. 172; 'Gregory's Chron.', p. 208. At Chester, the king's letters patent (8 November) ordering the proclamation was copied into the city's cartulary (ChesterRO, CHB/2 f. 51v-52v).

76 For the northern lords at Wakefield, see Flenley, p. 152; Stevenson, II, ii, [775]; 'Benet's Chron.', p. 228.

77 Somerset and Devon had 800 with them (*English Chron.*, pp. 106-7; 'Gregory's Chron', pp. 209-10). For their itinerary through Soms., Glos., and the midlands, see Stevenson, II, ii, [774].

78 Of the various dates given for their departure, 9 December is preferred ('Benet's Chron.', p. 228 and n. 281; 'Gregory's Chron.', p. 210; Flenley, pp. 151-2; *Great Chron.*, p. 193; *London Chrons.*, p. 172; Peake, thesis, pp. 151-2). On the previous day, they received a commission to investigate treasons and other offences in the east midlands and north (*CPR, 1452–61*, pp. 651, 653).

79 Below, p. 872; *PL*, I, 198.

80 Flenley, pp. 151-2; 'Benet's Chron.', p. 228 (which puts York's army at 12,000 and the Lancastrians at about 20,000); 'Gregory's Chron.', p. 210 (the Lancastrians at 15,000 at Hull); Stevenson, II, ii, [775] (the Yorkists at 6,000). See Scofield, op. cit., I, 120-2; Brooke, op. cit., pp. 53-65. York is said to have left London with only 300 men, and Salisbury with 100. His attempt to raise a force under Westmorland's son backfired, since Neville promptly went over to the Lancastrians (*English Chron.*, pp. 106-7, though the figure of 8,000 in his company is exaggerated).

81 Others killed included Sir Thomas Harrington, Edward Bourgchier, Sir Henry Radford, and (at Pontefract) John Harowe, the London merchant who had assisted in the siege of the Tower. See 'Benet's Chron.', p. 228 (which puts the dead at about 1,000); Stevenson, II, ii, [775] (2,000); *English Chron.*, pp. 106-7 (2,200); 'Gregory's Chron.', p. 210 (the Yorkists 2,500 and the Lancastrians 200); *Three Chrons.*, p. 76; Flenley, p. 167; *Brut*, p. 531; *CMilP*, I, 48, 57 (1,500 dead). See also *Great Chron.*, p. 193; *London Chrons.*, p. 172.

82 Flenley, p. 152, though Stevenson, II, ii, [775], says he stayed at a Salop friary. A fragmentary list (PRO, E163, unsorted) of lords, excluding committed Lancastrians and a few others who were not available, distinguishes between those who were committed Yorkists (21, led by Norfolk, Warwick, and March) and certain uncommitted (*newtri*) men (16, with Archibishop Bourgchier in both columns). It may refer to an assessment of attitude after York's death made about the time parliament reassembled on 28 January and Warwick was preparing to cope with Margaret's advance (*PPC*, VI, 307-10; 'Benet's Chron.', p. 229, which notes that Lords Montague and Scales, who appear in the list, were created peers in this session). I am grateful to Miss M. Condon and Professor C. D. Ross for making this list available to me.

83 Harvey, *Worcester's itineraries*, pp. 203-5; *Three Chrons.*, pp. 76-7 (which claims he raised 30,000 men). He even assembled loyal Yorkists from Kidwelly (Carms.), led by the Dwnns, and it is recorded that his father had granted the earldom of Chester to him, presumably to aid recruitment there (though it is doubtful if Chester could be alienated from the crown in this way) (R. S. Thomas, thesis, pp. 189-90; *RP*, V, 466). For repairs to the

defences of Shrewsbury in case the northern lords should advance there, see *CPR, 1452–61*, p. 657 (20 January).

84 *Brut*, p. 531; *Great Chron.*, p. 193; *London Chrons.*, p. 172; Stevenson, II, ii, [777]. March requested aid from the town of Shrewsbury immediately.

85 'Benet's Chron.', p. 229; *CMilP*, I, 57; Stevenson, II, ii, [776]. Little is known about this battle, but for modern accounts, see Evans, *Wars of the roses*, pp. 124-8 (with a plan); Ross, *Edward IV*, pp. 31-2; R. S. Thomas, thesis, pp. 188-91. Some chronicles give 3 February as the date of the encounter ('Benet's Chron.', p. 229; *English Chron.*, p. 110), but *Great Chron.*, p. 193; 'Gregory's Chron.', p. 211, and *London Chrons.*, p. 172, prefer 2 February.

86 *Brut*, p. 602. According to Flenley, pp. 76-7, and 'Gregory's Chron.', p. 211, 3,000 were slain and several Lancastrian captains beheaded; *English Chron.*, p. 110, says 4,000. L. T. Smith (ed.), *The maire of Bristowe is kalendar, by Robert Ricart* (Camden Soc., new ser., V [1872]), p. 42, places Owen's execution on 7 February.

87 Gregory's Chron.', p. 211. Owen's body was buried in the Grey Friars at Hereford. For discussion about his possible place of burial in the friary and excavation of skeletons there in 1933, see T. A. Jones, *Without my wig* (Liverpool, 2nd ed., 1945), pp. 19-20.

88 W. W. E. Wynne, 'Historical papers (Puleston)', *Arch. Camb.*, 1st ser., I(1846), 146, a letter written on 25 February to John Eyton and Roger Puleston, a kinsman of the Tudors and one of Earl Edmund's annuitants some years before. For Puleston, see R. S. Thomas, thesis, pp. 69, 192-3.

89 Stevenson, II, ii, [775]; Dunlop, op. cit., p. 217; Nicholson, op. cit., p. 400.

90 Flenley, p. 153; 'Benet's Chron.', p. 229; *English Chron.*, pp. 107-9 (which stresses Lancastrian desecration of churches); *Great Chron.*, p. 193; *London Chrons.*, p. 172; *Three Chrons.*, p. 76; *RP*, V, 462. The threat to Stamford was anticipated on 12 January (*CPR, 1452–61*, p. 657). The queen's men and the northern retinues bore the livery of the prince, as the Lancastrian heir, as well as their lord's or lady's ('Gregory's Chron.', p. 212).

91 Flenley, p. 167; *Brut*, p. 532. *English Chron.*, p. 108, and 'Gregory's Chron.', p. 212, mention that Bonville's execution was carried out by judgement of the prince, at the insistence of the queen, Exeter, and Devon, and despite Henry VI's assurance that he would be safe. See also *Brut*, p. 602; *Three Chrons.*, p. 76.

92 *PPC*, VI, 307; *CPR, 1452–61*, pp. 641, 656, 658-9. In this parliament the Yorkist nobility was augmented by the creation of Lords Montague, Scales, and Cromwell (Wedgwood, *Register*, p. 266 n. 2; 'Benet's Chron.', pp. 228-9). The recruitment of men from New Romney in February temporarily disrupted the town's administration (KentRO, NR/JB2 f. 57).

93 For the battle, see 'Gregory's Chron.', pp. 211-14 (an eyewitness who puts the death toll at 3,500); 'Benet's Chron.', p. 229 (4,000); Stevenson, II, ii, [776] (2,000); *English Chron.*, pp. 107-9 (1,916); *CMilP*, I, 61. Warwick's brother, Lord Montague, the king's chamberlain, was captured and lodged in York (*English Chron.*, pp. 107-9; *Brut*, p. 602). When the duchess of York heard of the defeat, she sent her younger sons, George and Richard, from London to the Low Countries (*Brut*, p. 602; *English Chron.*, p. 110; *Great*

Chron., p. 195; *London Chrons.*, p. 174). Others who fled were Philip Malpas, Thomas Vaughan, and Henry VI's doctor, William Hatclyf; the legate Coppini also retired to the continent on 10 February (above, pp. 626, 717; *Great Chron.*, p. 195; *Brut*, p. 532; *CMilP*, I, 53).

94 Great Chron., pp. 193-4; Stevenson, II, ii, [776]; *London Chrons.*, p. 173; 'Gregory's Chron.', p. 214. Robert Whittingham, Andrew Trollope, and Thomas Tresham were among the knighted. For the significance of the loss of the king, see Ross, *Edward IV*, pp. 32-3.

95 *CMilP*, I, 48 (14 February).

96 *Brut*, p. 531; Stevenson, II, ii, [777]; Ross, *Edward IV*, p. 32. 'Gregory's Chron.', p. 215, records that they discussed seizing the crown. March (with the title of duke of York) was authorized to array men in the border shires and the west country on 12 February, and some Bristolians appear to have joined him at this juncture (*CPR, 1452–61*, p. 659; BristRO, P/St. E/ChW 1 f. 38v).

97 *Brut*, p. 532; *Three Chrons.*, p. 76; *Great Chron.*, pp. 195-6; *CMilP*,I, 54-5 (for the ensuing quotation). Flenley, p. 167, loosely speaks of Henry contravening the decrees of parliament. It was officially recorded (*RP*, V, 466) that Henry VI had engineered Richard's death and had spoken openly of not intending to abide by the accord; but the evidence that was cited post-dated the battle of St Albans.

98 Dunstable was the furthest south they came (Stevenson, II, ii, [776]). True to form, the Lancastrians plundered as they retreated (*English Chron.*, p. 110).

99 *CMilP*, I, 48-9 (19 February).

100 'Benet's Chron.', p. 229; 'Gregory's Chron.', p. 214; Stevenson, II, ii, [776-7]; *London Chrons.*, p. 173; *English Chron.*, pp. 108-9; *Great Chron.*, pp. 193-4; *Brut*, p. 531; *CMilP*, I, 49-51; Peake, thesis, pp. 157-63; Scofield, op. cit., I, 145-7. The Lancastrian advance guard was also attacked and dispersed. Letters from the queen, Prince Edward, Jasper Tudor, and Northumberland to the city in the winter of 1460–61 elicited little sympathy (Peake, thesis, pp. 150-5; Scofield, op. cit., I, 136-7).

101 'Benet's Chron.', p. 230; *Three Chrons.*, p. 77; *Great Chron.*, pp. 194-6; Flenley, p. 161; Stevenson, II, ii, [777]; *London Chrons.*, pp. 173-5; 'Gregory's Chron.', p. 215. Edward IV's accession is discussed in Scofield, op. cit., I, 149-52, and Ross, *Edward IV*, pp. 33-4; see also C. A. J. Armstrong, 'The inauguration ceremonies of the Yorkist kings, and their title to the throne', *TRHS*, 4th ser., XXX (1948), 51-73. For the date of his arrival in London, see *CMilP*, I, 54.

102 'Benet's Chron.', pp. 230-1; 'Gregory's Chron.', pp. 216-17; *Chron. of London*, p. 141; *PL*, II, 229-30; *CMilP*, I, 61-2, 66, 68-9, 72-3, 76-8; Ross, *Edward IV*, pp. 34-8; Brooke, op. cit., pp. 81-129; Scofield, I, 159-66. For the slaughter, see accounts in Flenley, p. 167; *Brut*, p. 533 (30,000 Lancastrians); 'Benet's Chron.', p. 230 (30,000 Lancastrians and 5,000 Yorkists); *Three Chrons.*, pp. 77-8 (36,777); 'Gregory's Chron.', p. 217 (35,000 commoners); *PL*, I, 165 (20,000 Lancastrians), 166 (28,000); *CMilP*, I, 63-5 (28,000 northerners); but Stevenson, II, ii, [778] (over 9,000).

EPILOGUE
THE DESTRUCTION OF A DYNASTY

Epilogue: the Destruction
of a Dynasty

In 1461, for the first time since the Anglo-Saxon period, England had two rival monarchs, each of whom was in a position to appeal for the allegiance of Englishmen and command support within the realm. Although Edward of York had been acclaimed king on 4 March, Henry VI remained at liberty for a further four years, asserting the claims of Lancastrianism and acting as a focus for those who resisted the new dynasty. The civil war was about to enter its longest phase. Even after Henry was captured in Lancashire on 13 July 1465, Margaret of Anjou and Prince Edward were able to continue the struggle from their refuge in north-eastern France, and their intrigues were eventually rewarded by the second enthronement of Henry VI for a few months from 3 October 1470. But the Lancastrian tree was a delicate growth. Henry and Margaret had only one son, Henry himself had no brothers or sisters, and all of his uncles were dead and had left no legitimate heirs. Theirs was an impoverished line and never had the consequences of this fact appeared so damaging as in 1471, when Edward IV returned to reclaim his crown on 11 April, Prince Edward was killed at Tewkesbury on 4 May, and Henry VI was murdered in the Tower of London less than three weeks later (21 May). The Lancastrian dynasty in England was extinct. Margaret, who had fallen into Edward IV's clutches at Tewkesbury, was a prisoner until she was ransomed by King Louis XI. After her return to France in January 1476, she lived in obscurity until her death on 25 August 1482 at the age of fifty-three.[1]

Despite the outcome of the battle of Towton, Henry VI and his court did not regard the English throne as irrecoverable, for he, his queen, and Prince Edward were free to plan their counter-strokes.[2] They did so on two main fronts. On the one hand, there were many in England – followers of the Lancastrian lords, Exeter, Somerset, Wiltshire, and Oxford, as well as others in the principality of Wales and the north-west – who were but slowly reconciled to the new régime in 1461–62. Indeed, in Wales the fortress of Carreg Cennen (Carmarthenshire) held out until 1 May 1462 and that at Harlech (Merioneth) until 1468.[3] But it was in northern England that the Lancastrians concentrated their forces and, with anticipated Scottish aid, planned their strategy. Henry and Margaret had repaired to Scotland after Towton, and they were received in friendly fashion by the queen-regent, Mary of Guelders. Although the Scots had recently been at war with Lancastrian England, and Mary had strong links with Burgundy, the Yorkists' most dependable foreign ally, traditional political realities dictated that in 1461 the fugitive king and his company should be aided in their campaign against Edward IV. The price was high and damaging to Henry VI's reputation and credibility as king of England: in return for sanctuary and assistance, he surrendered Berwick to the Scots on 25 April and promised to hand over Carlisle too if it could be captured.[4] Henry and his lords, especially Dacre, Roos, and Rougemont-Grey, shortly to be reinforced by Somerset and others from Wales, were able to raid across the border into England on several occasions during the next two years. They occupied Bamburgh, Dunstanburgh, and Alnwick castles and besieged others at various times, and Henry himself appears to have spent almost as much time in the north-east borderland as he did in Scotland, reluctant to desert the kingdom he cherished.

On the other hand, Margaret was well placed to rally continental support for her husband's cause. She made contact with her relatives and friends in France, and with Charles VII, who had looked sympathetically on Henry as the Yorkist lords massed against him in Calais during 1460. But on 22 July 1461 Charles died and the accession of Louis XI, who as dauphin had sought refuge at the Burgundian court and had a representative in the Yorkist ranks at Towton, was a major blow to Margaret's hopes.[5] Her ally and advocate at the Valois court, Pierre de Brézé, was dismissed by Louis, and although Lancastrian envoys from Edinburgh were not molested in France, they failed to secure the men and money which Margaret craved; they were allowed to return to Scotland in October.[6] Of course, Louis's attitudes as king were bound to be rather different from those he had adopted as dauphin, and henceforward he viewed the English civil war with caution and calculation, always in the best interests of himself and France, rather than as a committed ally of the house of York. Indeed, despite any disquiet which they may have felt at the deposition of an anointed king, the rulers of western Europe, with the exception of Philip of Burgundy, soon came to regard Henry VI and his wife as diplomatic and military pawns, to be succoured or ignored as it suited Anglo-Scottish, Anglo-French, Anglo-Breton, Franco-Burgundian, Franco-Breton, even Franco-Spanish relations.

Margaret was tireless in her efforts on behalf of her husband and son; her determination and pride sustained her throughout the 1460s, despite periods that were undeniably dispiriting for the Lancastrian cause.[7] In the first months of exile, the prospects internationally were fairly hopeful, so that early in 1462 it was rumoured in London that a dynastic alliance was conspiring against Edward IV.[8] Jasper Tudor was visiting Brittany by 25 March with plans for an invasion of Wales which he laid before Duke Francis II; the latter listened sympathetically, for Brittany had been at war with England ever since the attack on Fougères in 1449.

A few weeks later, on 16 April, Margaret herself arrived in the duchy on her way to meet her father and Louis XI; she too was well received by Francis II and Louis entered into negotiations with her.[9] The kings of Castile and Portugal were descendants of John of Gaunt, and one purpose of the visit of Margaret's servant, Sir Edmund Hampden, to Bordeaux early in March 1462 may have been to appeal to their sense of dynastic solidarity.[10] This intense diplomatic activity caused considerable alarm in England and a large-scale invasion was thought to be imminent: Jasper Tudor and Exeter would land at Beaumaris; Somerset, Hungerford, and Margaret's brother, John of Calabria, would invade East Anglia with Spanish aid; and a Franco-Spanish force would arrive at Sandwich with Sir John Fortescue, Henry VI's chancellor-in-exile. This three-pronged attack would be followed by an invasion by the kings of Aragon, Portugal, France, and Denmark, and Duke René of Anjou.[11] At the centre of the plot in England was the earl of Oxford. Apprehension exaggerated both the magnitude of the threat and the size of the armies (in excess of 300,000 men, it was said), and the execution of Oxford and his son on 26 February 1462 seems to have destroyed all possibility that anything as serious would materialize.[12] Nevertheless, these rumours reflected the international vulnerability of the new Yorkist dynasty and Lancastrian optimism in the eighteen months or so after Towton.

Margaret's negotiations with Louis XI in the spring of 1462 led to a secret agreement at Chinon on 24 June and a public treaty of alliance four days later at Tours. A hundred-year truce, guaranteeing mutual assistance against the rebels of each side, was to be openly proclaimed, but the bargain struck at Chinon, whereby Margaret would receive a loan of 20,000 *livres tournois* on the security of Calais, was understandably concealed; it would certainly do Margaret's reputation in England and Calais no good if it became public knowledge, and Philip of Burgundy would not receive it kindly either. Louis, indeed, informed both Burgundy and Brittany of his Lancastrian alliance, but whereas Francis II, with Louis's encouragement, gave modest assistance to an expedition being prepared at Rouen, Duke Philip was far less co-operative.[13] In the event, Margaret returned to Scotland in October 1462 with resources and supplies that were quite inadequate.

This apparently impressive alliance of Scotland, France, and Brittany could not be maintained for long. Louis XI had good reason to suspect that Edward IV's overtures to the Spanish kingdoms might threaten his southern frontier and perhaps continued Valois occupation of Gascony. Francis II was no less concerned at indications that Louis was bent on asserting his sovereign rights in Brittany; whilst Edward IV had been in contact with dissident Scottish lords since 1461 and was angling for a truce that would deny the Lancastrians a refuge in the northern kingdom.[14] Thus, Lancastrian fortunes took a decisive turn for the worse during 1463. Louis opened negotiations with Edward IV in June, and Philip of Burgundy offered himself as mediator; despite Margaret's frantic diplomatic efforts, and her own visit to Flanders in August (in company with Prince Edward, who rarely left her side in these years), she could not prevent the sealing of an Anglo-French truce at Hesdin, near Calais, on 8 October; and both Brittany and Burgundy were invited to become parties to it.[15] The terms provided for a cessation of hostilities between England and France for one year, but from Margaret's point of view, the crucial clause bound each side not to assist the enemies of the other during that time. Meanwhile, Henry VI's position in Scotland was dangerously precarious. Edward IV's diplomatic offensive continued and in 1462 there were even rumours of a marriage proposal involving the royal families of England and Scotland. After the failure of a further Lancastrian invasion of northern England in the summer of 1463, news of the Anglo-French truce persuaded the Scots to open their own negotiations with Edward IV; by the truce of 9 December, the Scots undertook not to give further support to the Lancastrians for one year.[16]

Henry VI was thereupon forced to abandon his refuge and lead the life of a fugitive in northern England, principally in Bamburgh castle. His movements in these months hardly reveal him as a tenacious leader of devoted adherents, though the paucity of information about his activities in Scotland and the north makes it difficult to estimate his personal contribution to the Lancastrian cause. Nevertheless, he was not present on Hedgeley moor round about 25 April 1464, when Somerset, Roos, and Hungerford were routed; nor was he at the final battle of Hexham on 15 May, but rather awaited its outcome in Bywell castle not far away.[17] The king, in short, exhibited those qualities of ineffectualness and torpor which had characterized many of his actions since 1453. He spent the following year on the run in northern England, where he could keep beyond the arm of Edward IV and rely on sympathizers to give him shelter and protection. He was eventually captured in Lancashire on 13 July 1465 by several gentlemen who had earlier laid a trap for him at the Tempest family home near Bashall. Henry was brought to London and led to the Tower, securely bound to his saddle.[18]

Before the Anglo-French truce was concluded in 1463, Margaret of Anjou seems to have decided to devote her energies (taking her son with her) to the French diplomatic scene, where her family still had considerable influence and Louis XI might be prepared even now, for reasons of self-interest, to sustain her cause.[19] As early as July 1463, when she embarked for France, she had evidently decided to instal herself in one of her father's castles, at Koeur near St Mihiel-en-Bar. Certainly, a group of her chaplains, headed by Thomas Bird, an experienced diplomat who had been in Margaret's entourage on her journey to England in 1445 and was elected bishop of St Asaph in March 1450, were at Koeur preparing for her arrival.[20] Margaret's company at Koeur can hardly be dignified with the description of a 'court' for she had a very modest establishment of about fifty attendants, whose most

distinguished English members were Somerset, Exeter, and brothers of
the earls of Devon and Ormond; Sir John Fortescue, the former chief
justice who was the Lancastrian chancellor; several officials of Prince
Edward's household (including Sir Edmund Hampden, his chamberlain,
Dr John Morton, his chancellor, and Sir Robert Whittingham, his
receiver-general and also keeper of Margaret's great wardrobe); and a
number of former royal household knights and esquires who preferred
exile to risking all in Yorkist England (notably, Sir Edmund Mountford,
Sir William Vaux, William Grimesby, and William Joseph).[21] Jasper
Tudor may have been an occasional visitor, especially when he lived in
Paris in the winter of 1463–64 importuning Louis XI and Francis II for
aid.[22] Despite financial assistance from Duke René, the exiles lived 'in
grete proverte' (reported Fortescue in December 1464).

> . . . but yet the quene susteynethe us in mete and drinke, so as we
> buthe not in extreme necessite. Here hignesse may do no more to us
> thanne she dothe. Wherefore I counseille you [the earl of Ormond,
> who was then in Portugal] to spend sparely soche money as ye have,
> for whanne ye come hether ye shulle have nede of hit. And also here
> buthe maney that nede, and wolle desire to parte with you of youre
> aune money, and in all this contray is no manne that wolle or may lene
> you any money, have ye never so grete nede.[23]

In 1464 Margaret made contact with those rulers in western Europe who
had Lancastrian blood in their veins and who may have contemplated
assisting her and her husband in 1461–62: the kings of Portugal and
Castile, as well as the count of Charolais, who was a Lancastrian
through his mother, Isabelle of Portugal, and rarely saw eye to eye with
his father, Philip of Burgundy. It was desperate diplomacy, based on
dynastic sentiment and occasionally in ignorance of political realities –
as was made plain when Sir John Fortescue confessed that the
Lancastrians at Koeur could not remember the name of the Portuguese
king, Alfonso V, who had been on his throne since 1438. Taking
advantage of Ormond's presence in Portugal, Fortescue instructed him
to develop contacts made earlier by William Joseph to seek Alfonso's
aid in approaching other rulers, including his sister and her husband (the
empress and emperor of Germany), the pope and the cardinals.[24]

Margaret's diplomacy was singularly ineffective – until, that is,
extraneous factors gave her and her son a revived importance in
international affairs. Relations between Edward IV and the earl of
Warwick had begun to sour in the mid-1460s, and as their estrangement
became more obvious, particularly over Warwick's declared preference
for an alliance with France rather than with Burgundy, so Margaret and
her son acquired a renewed significance in Anglo-Franco-Burgundian
relations. As early as February 1465, she had tried to interest Louis XI
in exploiting the political rifts in England, but the civil war 'of the public
weal' between Louis and his princes put any foreign ventures out of the

question for the time being.[25] Later in the year (October), she was active in Paris trying to reconcile Louis and the princes (who included her brother, John of Calabria).[26] Soon afterwards, marriage negotiations took place between the count of Charolais, one of the leading French dissidents, and Edward IV on the basis that the former would marry Edward's sister; thus, whereas Margaret had expected and received much sympathy from Charolais in the past, the count's fear of Louis and Edward IV's preference for a Burgundian alliance encouraged the Lancastrian queen to pin more realistic hopes once again on Louis XI. The wily French monarch was now fully prepared to capitalize on the divisions in England, and it may have been he who conceived the idea of a reconciliation between Warwick and Margaret of Anjou, with the eventual possibility of restoring Henry VI to his throne.[27] This bold plan and the astonishing volte-face that it implied seems to have been discussed seriously for the first time in June 1467, when Warwick arrived in France on embassy from Edward IV; certainly, rumours of such a proposal were current in England by the autumn. At that time, Jasper Tudor was in Paris endeavouring to assemble men for another expedition to Wales, while Margaret maintained what pressure she could from Koeur to persuade Louis to give his assistance. His inclination to do so was fortified by Edward IV's alliances with both Burgundy and Brittany in February 1468.[28] When the final breach between Edward IV and Warwick came in 1469, the ground had been prepared for a diplomatic and dynastic revolution that promised to transform the fortunes of Margaret and her son – and even of Henry VI, who was still in the Tower.[29]

In May 1470 Warwick and Edward IV's feckless brother, George, duke of Clarence, arrived in France after their unsuccessful rebellion. Louis's plan could now be put into operation. For personal and dynastic reasons, it was going to be extraordinarily difficult to reconcile the Lancastrian queen with an earl who had done more than any other man to cast her from her throne, and a duke who was the brother of the man who had seized her husband's crown. Sir John Fortescue seems to have been a leading proponent of such an accommodation. Sometime during 1468–70 he submitted a series of memoranda to the French government which not only denounced the Yorkist claim to the English and French thrones, but outlined a way of forestalling the English invasion which Edward IV had announced in parliament in 1468. The proposals centred round Louis's espousal of the Lancastrian cause and ultimately his aid in restoring Henry VI; to this end, Fortescue proposed a marriage between Prince Edward and Warwick's daughter.[30] In 1470, therefore, Margaret was induced to travel – at Louis's expense – from Koeur to meet the English magnates, though Warwick and Clarence prudently withdrew while the king and the Lancastrian queen discussed the proposed *rapprochement* and marriage. After lengthy talks, in which Margaret proved 'very hard and difficult', a tense and embarrassed interview with Warwick took place at Angers on 22 July.

With great reverence Warwick went on his knees and asked her pardon for the injuries and wrongs done to her in the past. She graciously forgave him and he afterwards did homage and fealty there, swearing to be a faithful and loyal subject of the king, queen and prince as his liege lords unto death.[31]

A bargain was struck and sealed by the betrothal in Angers cathedral on 25 July of Edward and the fifteen-year-old Anne Neville; their marriage was probably celebrated at Amboise on 13 December.[32] At seventeen, Edward was a somewhat sanguinary youth. In 1467 it was said of him by the Milanese envoy in France that he

> already talks of nothing but of cutting off heads or making war, as if he had everything in his hands or was the god of battle or the peaceful occupant of that [English] throne.

His upbringing nurtured such traits in his character: not only had he witnessed the executions after the battle of St Albans in 1461, but

> as soon as he became grown up, [he] gave himself over entirely to martial exercises; and, seated on fierce and half-tamed steeds urged on by his spurs, he often delighted in attacking and assaulting the young companions attending him, sometimes with a lance, sometimes with a sword, sometimes with other weapons, in a warlike manner and in accordance with the rules of military discipline.[33]

It was as if Edward consciously strove to develop qualities that were diametrically opposed to those of his gentler father.

Warwick had meanwhile returned to England, and early in October 1470 he caused Edward IV to flee to the Low Countries. Henry VI was declared king again on 3 October.[34] Preparations were under way in France for the return of Queen Margaret and Prince Edward, and although they were ready to join the fleet at Honfleur by January, their departure was delayed by bad weather and especially by King Louis. Not until Warwick had fulfilled his promise to declare war on Burgundy in mid-February did Louis allow the Lancastrian party to leave. But this very declaration persuaded the Burgundians to support the exiled Edward IV, who was therefore himself enabled to return to England on 12 March. Louis's machinations had crippled the Lancastrian enterprise largely because he feared a Burgundian attack on France more than invasion from an England which was in the throes of renewed civil war.[35]

As Edward IV approached London in the first week of April, Warwick's brother, Archbishop Neville, accompanied Henry VI through the streets of London in an effort to rally support for the Lancastrian 'readeption'; but the appearance of the fifty-year-old king, who seems barely to have understood the significance of events about him and was dressed dowdily in a long, blue gown, served to blunt rather than excite the citizens' enthusiasm for their passive monarch.[36] When Edward arrived in the city on 11 April, he took Henry from the bishop of London's palace and returned him to the Tower. Two days later he was forced to accompany the Yorkist monarch to confront the Lancastrian forces at Barnet, doubtless in the hope that the sight of their king in Edward's hands would spread despondency through their ranks. After the Yorkist victory, Henry was taken once more to the Tower – and for the last time.

Oblivious of these events, Margaret and her son at last landed at Weymouth on 14 April. They made their way northwards through the west country to Bristol and the Severn valley beyond, hoping perhaps to meet up with Jasper Tudor and his forces from south Wales. At Tewkesbury on 4 May they were overtaken by Edward IV and in the battle that ensued Prince Edward was slain and Margaret captured. On the very night that Edward returned in triumph to London (21 May) Henry VI died in the Tower. There can be no reasonable doubt that he died violently, despite the claims of Yorkist propaganda, or even that his death was authorized by the king to remove once and for all (now that Prince Edward was dead) any possibility of a Lancastrian *coup* similar to the one that had humbled Edward IV the previous year.[37] Next evening, Henry's body was escorted from the Tower to St Paul's cathedral, where it lay overnight 'opyn vysagid, that he mygth be knowyn'; the following morning it was conveyed up river to Chertsey abbey for burial.[38] Queen Margaret was kept in strict confinement until ransom terms were agreed with Louis XI in 1475. Even then, care was taken to extract from her a renunciation of all interest in the crown of England and all claim to dower; in return, she could retire to France and Louis would pay a ransom of 50,000 crowns. But Margaret's final humiliation was yet to come.[39] After Louis's agents had received her at Rouen late in January 1476, the king required her (on 7 March) to surrender to him all her right in the inheritance of her father and mother, and thenceforward she lived an obscure existence as a minor pensioner of the French king until her death in penury on 25 August 1482.[40]

The Lancastrian royal line from Henry IV was extinct. Few appreciated the significance of Henry Tudor, grandson of Katherine of Valois (from whom no claim to the English throne could conceivably stem) and son of Margaret Beaufort, heiress of the formerly illegitimate offspring of John of Gaunt (whose claims may have been acknowledged earlier in the century but were not universally accepted). Philippe de Commynes, at the Burgundian court in 1465, believed the duke of Exeter to be 'next in line of succession to the Lancastrian family', but he was drowned in September 1475. A Yorkist writer could note in 1471: 'And so no one from that stock remained among the living who could now claim the crown'.[41] It was left to Henry VI himself now to embark on a vigorous posthumous career as the saintly king of England . . . .

Notes

1 Henry's later years are described in Scofield, op. cit., I, passim, and Margaret's fate in Bagley, op. cit., ch. IV-VI.

2 For the continued use of Henry's regnal year by the king himself and the earl of Ormond, see S. B. Chrimes (ed.), *Sir John Fortescue, De laudibus legum Anglie* (Cambridge, 1942), p. lxxiii; Richardson, *TRHS*, 4th ser., X (1927), 67-8; *Cal. Ormond deeds*, III, 189 (though Ormond was careful to use *anno domini* as well).

3 Ross, *Edward IV*, pp. 42-63 (for Lancastrian resistance in general during 1461–64); Griffiths, thesis, pp. 554-5 (for Carreg Cennen); R. S. Thomas, thesis, pp. 197ff (for Jasper Tudor's activities).

4 Nicholson, op. cit., pp. 397-405; Dunlop, op. cit., pp. 220ff; *CMilP*, I, 90, 93, 98; Kendall and Ilardi, op. cit., II, 368. James III was 9 in 1461; there may have been discussions about the possibility of his sister marrying Edward of Lancaster.

5 Above, p. 814; 'Gregory's Chron.', p. 216; Kendall and Ilardi, op. cit., II, 426. For Margaret's credence to Somerset and Lord Hungerford to go to Charles, dated at Edinburgh on the day the king died, see J. Calmette et G. Périnelle, *Louis XI et l'Angleterre, 1461–83* (Paris, 1930), p. 293 (misdated to 1463).

6 Kendall, *Louis XI*, pp. 111ff; *PL*, II, 252-3 (a letter from 2 of the envoys, Lord Hungerford and Robert Whittingham, to Margaret from Dieppe on 30 August). For a useful survey of the Lancastrians in exile, see C. J. M. McGovern, 'Lancastrian diplomacy and Queen Margaret's court in exile, 1461–1471' (Keele BA dissertation, 1973).

7 For these qualities in Margaret, see *CMilP*, I, 116 (6 February 1465).

8 *Three Chrons.*, p. 158; Scofield, op. cit., I, 23-33.

9 *CMilP*, I, 106-7; R. S. Thomas, thesis, pp. 200-1; Cottam, dissertation, pp. 43-4. Francis II had allowed Breton volunteers to join the Lancastrians at Mortimer's Cross in February 1461 (*Three Chrons.*, pp. 76-7).

10 Calmette et Périnelle, op. cit., p. 16 n. 4 (his pension from Louis XI); for Hampden, see above, p. 363.

11 Henry IV's daughter, Philippa, had married King Eric of Denmark in 1406 (Kirby, *Henry IV*, p. 252).

12 *PL*, II, 272-3; Ross, *Edward IV*, pp. 43-4. For other wild fears at the Yorkist court, see Ellis, *Original letters*, II, i, 126-31.

13 B. A. Pocquet du Haut-Jussé, *François II, duc de Bretagne et l'Angleterre* (Paris, 1929), pp. 49-51; Cottam, dissertation, pp. 43ff; Calmette et Périnelle, op. cit., pp. 19-21, 283-4; McGovern, dissertation, pp. 6-7.

14 Dom H. Morice, *Mémoires pour servir de preuves à l'histoire ecclésiastique et civile de Bretagne* (3 vols., Paris, 1742–46), III, 20, 35, 43-53, 63; Cottam, dissertation, pp. 53ff; Dunlop, op. cit., pp. 221ff. Burgundy had also tried to dissuade Mary of Guelders from giving refuge to Henry VI and Margaret of Anjou (Thielemans, op. cit., p. 386).

15 Ross, *Edward IV*, p. 56. Earlier in the year, Louis had been reluctant to receive Jasper Tudor, Exeter, and Fortescue when they arrived in April to seek aid for Henry VI (Thielemans, op. cit., p. 395).

16 Dunlop, op. cit., pp. 228-9, 238-40.

17 Ross, *Edward IV*, pp. 56-62; Scofield, op. cit., I, 329-30, 333-4. Somerset, Roos, and Hungerford were executed after Hexham. The Scots concluded a 15-year truce with Edward IV on 1 June 1464.

18 ibid., pp. 380-4; Ross, *Edward IV*, pp. 61-2 (for his movements and protectors). The captors rewarded later were Sir Thomas Talbot, Sir James Harrington, Sir John Tempest, and John Levesay, and this accords well with the chroniclers' accounts (PRO, E404/73/1/124B).

19 Jasper Tudor stayed with Louis for several months even after the Anglo-French truce; Louis acknowledged him to be his cousin germane and he received French and Breton assistance to return to Wales (R. S. Thomas, thesis, pp. 205-7, citing BN, f. fr. 6970 f. 501v; Chrimes, *Henry VII*, p. 14). At the end of 1463, Breton envoys visited Henry VI at Bamburgh and an agent of Louis XI arrived there early in 1464 (Pocquet du Haut-Jussé, op. cit., pp. 74-5; Ross, *Edward IV*, pp. 58-9).

20 McGovern, dissertation, ch. II, citing C. E. Dumont, *Histoire de la ville de Saint-Mihiel* (2 vols., Nancy, 1860–62), I, 177-9, based on the accounts of St Mihiel abbey. For Bird, who had been deprived of his see in January 1463, see Emden, *Oxford*, I, 191; above, p. 350. Margaret herself left Bruges for Koeur on 5 September (Thielemans, op. cit., p. 398 n. 180).

21 Wedgwood, *Biographies, s. n.*; above, pp. 824, 887. The Englishmen known to have been at Koeur are discussed in McGovern, dissertation, ch. III, IV. Morton was now keeper of Henry VI's privy seal.

22 Above, n. 19.

23 Chrimes, *De laudibus*, p. 145, from Lord Clermont (ed.), *The works of Sir John Fortescue*, I (1869), 23-5; the letter is now BN, f. fr. 4054 f. 176. For a comment on their destitution, see M. Jones (ed.), *Philippe de Commynes, Memoirs, 1461–1483* (1972), p. 180. Poverty was not a novel experience for the Lancastrians, for even in Scotland after 1461 they had found it difficult to make ends meet (Dunlop, op. cit., pp. 223, 231, 237). Both Margaret and Prince Edward were ill during 1464 and had to send for René's doctor (McGovern, dissertation, p. 14, citing Dumont, op. cit., I, 175).

24 McGovern, dissertation, pp. 16-19. Fortescue's letters probably never reached Ormond, for they are now BN, f. fr. 4054 f. 174, 176. Prince Edward sent an accompanying letter to Alfonso V, and another to Ormond in his own hand so that 'ye mey se how gode a wrytare I ame' (ibid., f. 172, 173). All the letters are published in Clermont, op. cit., I, 22-9. For Charolais's pension to Somerset and Exeter, see Ross, *Edward IV*, p. 106 n. 1.

25 *CMilP*, I, 116. Somerset had been with the king's enemies at the battle of Montlhéry on 16 July 1465 (Cottam, dissertation, p. 64).

26 Kendall, *Louis XI*, ch. 13, 14; Ross, *Edward IV*, p. 107.

27 ibid., ch. 6. For the estrangement between the new duke of Burgundy and Somerset at his court, see *PL*, I, 539 (July 1468).

28 *CVenP*, I, 119; *CMilP*, I, 120, 121, 125; Cottam, dissertation, pp. 65-70. For Jasper's landing in Wales in the summer and Margaret's abortive expedition from Harfleur in October, see R. S. Thomas, thesis, pp. 210-13; Ross, *Edward IV*, p. 113 and n. 4.

29 ibid., pp. 109, 118. For Henry's strict, though not uncomfortable, captivity during 1465–70, see Scofield, op. cit., I, 382-3. Jasper Tudor was in Louis's company from October 1469 to September 1470 and received a pension from him (R. S. Thomas, thesis, pp. 216-17).

30 The memoranda are analysed in a contemporary document in Calmette et Périnelle, op. cit., pp. 303-5, with a translation in McGovern, dissertation, pp. 59-60. On the other hand, staunch Lancastrians like Somerset and

Exeter were probably less enthusiastic about the Neville marriage, but they were in Burgundy by this time (ibid., pp. 52-3).

31 *CMilP*, I, 138-41. For a comment on the cynicism of this marriage, see *Commynes*, p. 184.

32 Scofield, op. cit., I, 527-33; Ross, *Edward IV*, p. 147 and n. 1 (though the ages of the couple are incorrectly given).

33 *CMilP*, I, 117; Chrimes, *De laudibus*, p. 3. For Edward's character, see Scofield, op. cit., I, 144.

34 For Henry VI's brief second reign, from 3 October 1470 to 11 April 1471, see Ross, *Edward IV*, pp. 154-60, and references cited there.

35 *CMilP*, I, 144-5, 149-50, 151; A. R. Myers, 'The outbreak of war between England and Burgundy in February 1471', *BIHR*, XXIII (1960), 114-15.

36 Much is made of *Great Chron.*, p. 215, which portrays a pathetic, ill-clad king, impressing London with his unkingly demeanour (Ross, *Edward IV*, pp. 166, 257). The king may also have grown a beard in his latter years, to judge by his tomb effigy and a representation of his second coronation (plate 000,; H. Cole, *The wars of the roses* [1973], p. 148).

37 Ross, *Edward IV*, pp. 169-75. For the battle of Tewkesbury, see Scofield, op. cit., I, ch. IX; J. D. Blyth, 'The battle of Tewkesbury', *TBGAS*, LXXX (1961), 99-120. For Henry's death, see *CMilP*, I, 157; above, p. 3.

38 *Great Chron.*, p. 220.

39 10,000 crowns were to be paid immediately and the remainder in four annual instalments (Ross, *Edward IV*, pp. 237-8). For Margaret's custody at Windsor until the end of 1461 and then at Wallingford in the charge of Alice, duchess of Suffolk, her old friend, see *PL*, I, 446; Metcalfe, dissertation, p. 43.

40 Calmette et Périnelle, op. cit., pp. 210-12; *CMilP*, I, 223. For Louis's determination to get her hounds, which seem to have been her only significant poseession by 1482, see Scofield, op, cit., II, 159.

41 *Commynes*, p. 108; Kelly, dissertation, pp. 47-8; *EHL*, p. 357 (for the quotation; cf. Ross, *Edward IV*, p. 175).

Table 1. The Lancastrian royal family

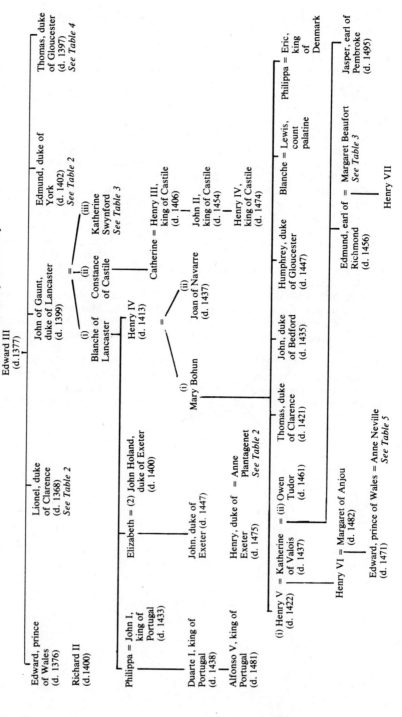

Table 2. The house of York

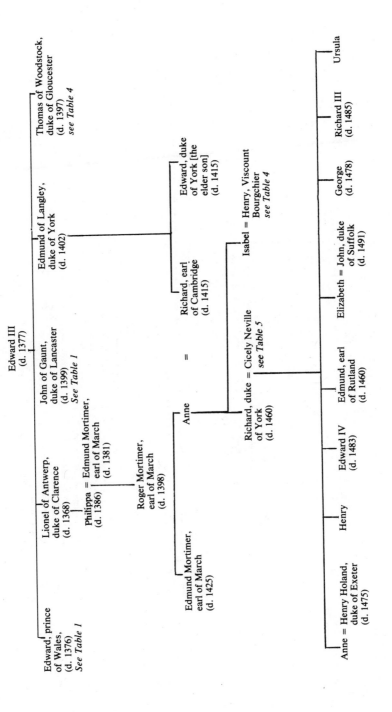

Edward III
(d. 1377)

Edward, prince
of Wales,
(d. 1376)
See Table 1

Lionel of Antwerp,
duke of Clarence
(d. 1368)

Philippa = Edmund Mortimer,
(d. 1386) | earl of March
(d. 1381)

Roger Mortimer,
earl of March
(d. 1398)

Edmund Mortimer,
earl of March
(d. 1425)

Anne =

John of Gaunt,
duke of Lancaster
(d. 1399)
See Table 1

Edmund of Langley,
duke of York
(d. 1402)

Richard, earl
of Cambridge
(d. 1415)

Edward, duke
of York [the
elder son]
(d. 1415)

Isabel = Henry, Viscount
Bourgchier
see Table 4

Thomas of Woodstock,
duke of Gloucester
(d. 1397)
see Table 4

Richard, duke = Cicely Neville
of York   *see Table 5*
(d. 1460)

Anne = Henry Holand,
duke of Exeter
(d. 1475)

Henry

Edward IV
(d. 1483)

Edmund, earl
of Rutland
(d. 1460)

Elizabeth = John, duke
of Suffolk
(d. 1491)

George
(d. 1478)

Richard III
(d. 1485)

Ursula

Table 3.   The Beaufort family

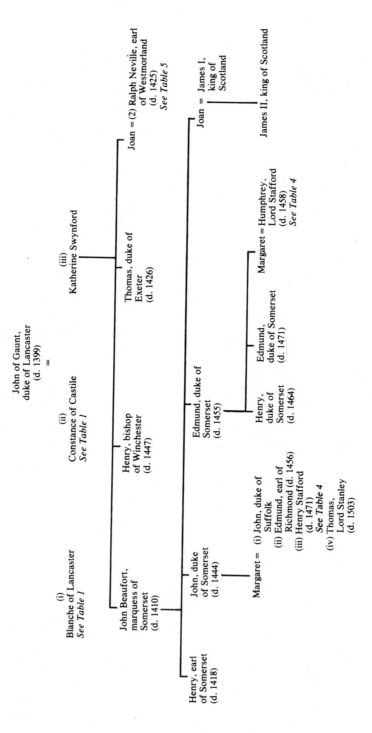

Table 4. The Stafford and Bourgchier families

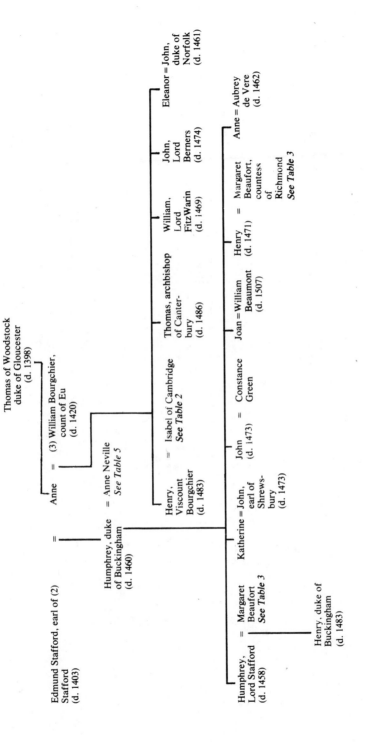

Thomas of Woodstock
duke of Gloucester
(d. 1398)

Edmund Stafford, earl of (2) = = Anne = (3) William Bourgchier,
Stafford   count of Eu
(d. 1403)   (d. 1420)

Humphrey, duke = Anne Neville
of Buckingham   *See Table 5*
(d. 1460)

Henry, = Isabel of Cambridge   Thomas, archbishop   William,   John,   Eleanor = John,
Viscount   *See Table 2*   of Canter-   Lord   Lord   duke of
Bourgchier   bury   FitzWarin   Berners   Norfolk
(d. 1483)   (d. 1486)   (d. 1469)   (d. 1474)   (d. 1461)

Katherine = John,   John   = Constance   Joan = William   Henry = Margaret   Anne = Aubrey
                earl of   (d. 1473)   Green   Beaumont   (d. 1471)   Beaufort,   de Vere
                Shrews-   (d. 1507)   countess   (d. 1462)
                bury   of
                (d. 1473)   Richmond
                                                                                                 See Table 3

Humphrey, = Margaret
Lord Stafford   Beaufort
(d. 1458)   *See Table 3*

Henry, duke of
Buckingham
(d. 1483)

Table 5. The Neville family and the Percy connection

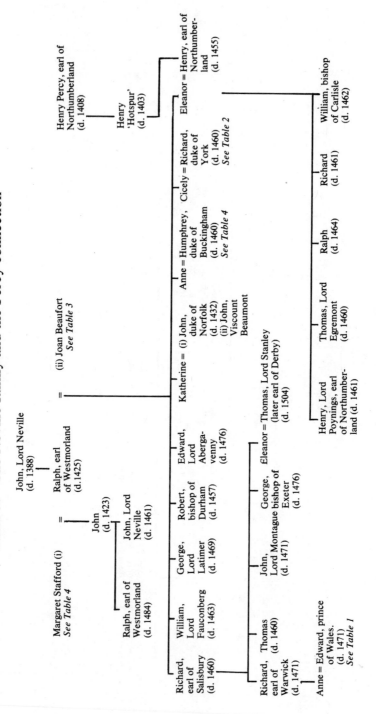

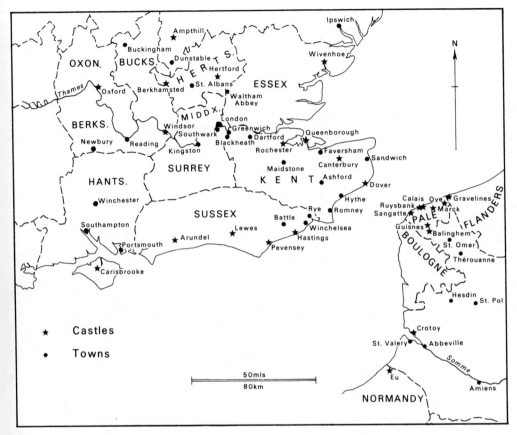

The Narrow Seas Region

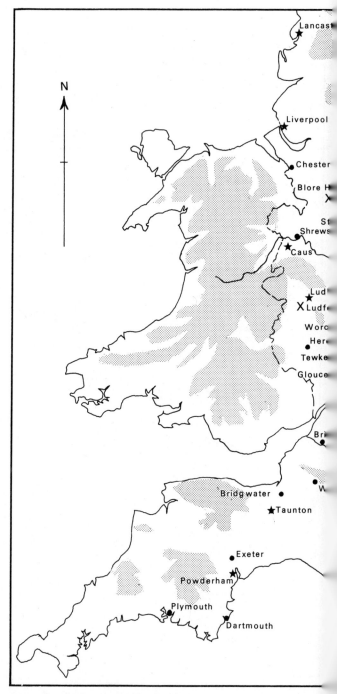

Central and Southern England

sborough
★ York
● York
Beverley
wton
X Hull
eld
X ★ Pontefract
★ Sandal
● Doncaster

Humber

Trent

Lincoln ●
Tattershall ★

Nottingham ●
by ● Grantham ●
Walsingham ●
Caister ★
Norwich ●

hfield
Leicester ● Stamford ●
Coleshill ●
Maxstoke
★ ● Coventry
★ Kenilworth
Warwick ●
Fotheringhay ★
Ely ●
Bury St. Edmunds ●
X Northampton
Bedford ● Cambridge ●
Framlingham ★
am
X
Edgecote

Dunstable ●
★ Hertford
Oxford ● X St. Albans
ames X Barnet
Wallingford ★ London ●
Windsor ● Rochester ★ Sandwich ●
Reading ● Canterbury ●
Dover ★

Salisbury
Southampton ■
Herstmonceux
★
Chichester ● Hastings
Portsmouth ● Pevensey ★

50mls
80km

Land over 200 metres ▒

Battles   X

Towns   ●

Castles   ★

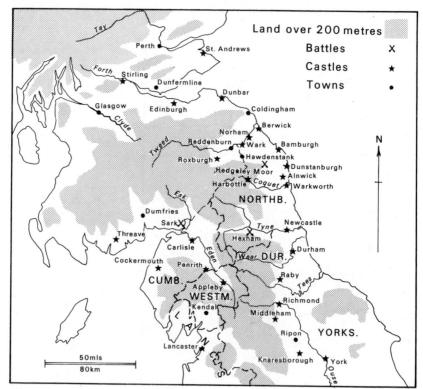

The Anglo-Scottish Borderland

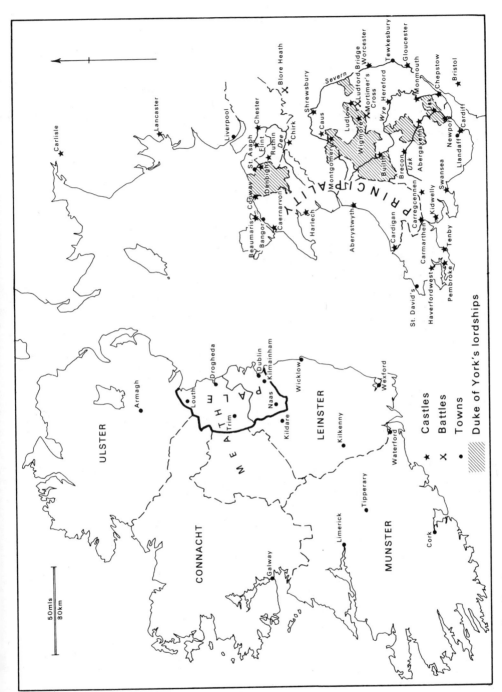

The Irish Sea Region

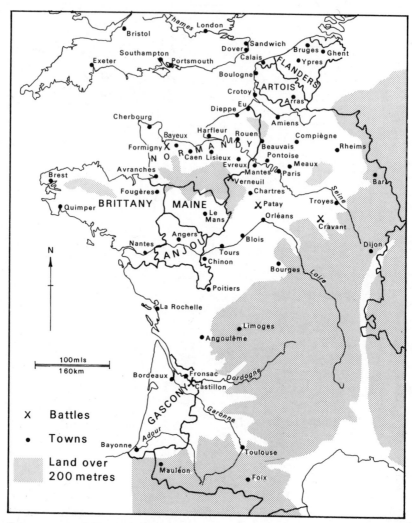

Lancaster and Valois in France

List of Authorities

This is a list of the authorities on which the book is based. Specific reference to documents in collections is given in the notes to each chapter. Recent comprehensive bibliographies of published work on the period appear in E. B. Graves (ed.), *A bibliography of English history to 1485* (Oxford, 1975); and DeLloyd J. Guth, *Late-mediaeval England, 1377–1485* (Cambridge, 1976), supplemented by his 'Fifteenth-century England: recent scholarship and future directions', *British studies monitor*, VII (1977), 3-50. Unless otherwise stated, the place of publication is London. The small number of abbreviations used is explained on pp. xv-xx.

A. Original Authorities: Unpublished

1 *Public record office, London*

CHANCERY
Early chancery proceedings (C1); Miscellanea (C47); Parliamentary and council proceedings (C49); Charter rolls (C53); Patent rolls (C66); Pardon rolls (67); Warrants for the great seal (C81)

DUCHY OF LANCASTER
Various accounts (DL28); Ministers' accounts (DL29)

EXCHEQUER
Treasury of receipt: Council and privy seal (E28);
King's remembrancer: Various accounts (E101); Memoranda rolls (E159); Miscellanea (E163); Parliamentary and council proceedings (E175).
Lord Treasurer's remembrancer: Foreign accounts (E364); Receipt rolls (E401); Issue rolls (E403); Writs and warrants for issues (E404)

INDEX ROLL 9995

JUSTICES ITINERANT
Assize rolls (JI1); Gaol delivery rolls (JI3)

KING'S BENCH
Ancient indictments (KB9); Plea rolls (KB27)

PALATINATE OF CHESTER
Enrolments (Chester 2)

PREROGATIVE COURT OF CANTERBURY WILLS (PCC)

PRIVY SEAL OFFICE
Series 1 (PSO1)
SPECIAL COLLECTIONS
Ancient correspondence (SC1); Minister's accounts (SC6); Ancient petitions (SC8); Rentals and surveys (SC11)

2 *British library, London*
Additional charters, Additional MSS, Cotton MSS, Egerton MSS, Egerton rolls, Harleian MSS, Royal MSS

3 *Bodleian library, Oxford*
Ashmole MSS, Bodleian MSS, Bodleian rolls, Carte MSS, Charters England, Charters Suffolk, Digby MSS, Don.e.120, England hist. MSS, Gough MSS, Jones MSS, Latin MSS, Rawlinson MSS, Tanner MSS

4 *Archives nationales, Paris:* K68

5 *Beverley corporation archives:* town 'chartulary'

6 *Birmingham public library:* Hagley Hall MSS, Hampton MSS

7 *Bibliothèque nationale, Paris:* fonds français, MSS français, nouvelles acquisitions françaises, nouvelles acquisitions latines, quittances

8 *Bristol record office:* Museum deeds, P/StE/ChW

9 *Cardiff central library:* Breconshire MSS, Pembrokeshire MSS

10 *Cheshire record office, Chester:* CHB; DDX

11 *Chester record office:* MB

12 *Chichester record office:* Ep 1/1, Winterton MSS catalogue

13 *Derbyshire record office, Matlock:* 410 M; 410/488, Vernon papers

14 *Devon record office, Exeter:* CR621; Exeter receivers' accounts

15 *Dorset record office, Dorchester:* B3/FG

16 *Eton college:* Henry V's will

17 *Folger Shakespeare Library, Washington, D.C.:* MSS 899.1; 1007.1

18 *Gloucestershire record office, Gloucester:* D1099/M31

19 *Henry E. Huntington library, San Marino:* Battle abbey MSS, Newhall MSS, Huntington MSS

20 *John Rylands library, Manchester:* Rylands charters, Latin MSS

21 *Kent record office, Maidstone:* Fa/LC; NR/FAc; NR/JB; Sa/AC; Sa/Fat.

22 *Leeds record office:* Plumpton coucher-book

23 *Leicestershire record office, Leicester:* DE221; DG5/857; 26 D53/47

24 *Lichfield record office:* B/A/1/11

25 *Lincolnshire record office, Lincoln:* Ancaster MSS

26 *Longleat, Wiltshire:* Miscellaneous MSS, MS 39886

27 *London, Guildhall record office:* Journal V, VI

28 *National library of Wales, Aberystwyth:* Powis castle MSS

29 *Northamptonshire record office, Northampton:* Brudenhall MSS, Fitz-William MSS, MSS 2049, 1102, SS 4254, Westmorland MSS

30 *Pierpoint Morgan Library, New York:* Autographs, RE

31 *Shakespeare birthplace trust, Stratford-upon-Avon:* DR98/477,497a, Throgmorton MSS, Willoughby MSS

32 *Somerset record office, Taunton:* DD/CC; DD/L

33 *Staffordshire record office, Stafford:* D1721/1/1

34 *Warwickshire record office, Warwick:* CR W1618; CR623/Box 10, Warwick castle MSS

35 *Westminster abbey muniments*

36 *Wiltshire record office, Trowbridge:* 192/55

37 *Worcestershire record office, Worcester:* Reg. Bourgchier, Reg. Polton, MS 009: 1/175/92483; MS 899: 95/Box 6/110-13; MS 705: 56/33(iv)
38 *Yale University Library:* MS 281

B. Original Authorities: Published

Allmand, C. T., 'Documents relating to the Anglo-French negotiations of 1439', in *Camden miscellany*, XXIV (Camden soc., 4th ser., IX, 1972), 79-149
Allmand, C. T. (ed.), *Society at war* (Edinburgh, 1973)
Amundesham, J., *Annales monasterii S. Albani*, ed. H. T. Riley (2 vols., RS, 1870-71)
Anstruther, R., *Prétensions des Anglois à la couronne de France* (Roxburghe club, 1847)
Arnold, R., *The customs of London* (1811)
Babington, C. (ed.), *The repressor of over much blaming of the clergy* (2 vols., RS, 1860)
Baildon, W. P. (ed.), *Select cases in chancery* (Selden soc., X, 1896)
Bain, J. (ed.), *Calendar of documents relating to Scotland preserved in the Public record office, London* (4 vols., Edinburgh, 1881-84)
Baldwin, J. F. (ed.), *Select cases before the king's council, 1243-1482* (Selden soc., XXXV, 1918)
Bannister, A. T. (ed.), *Registrum Thome Spofford episcopi Herefordensis* (Canterbury and York soc., 1919)
Basin, T., *Histoire des règnes de Charles VII et de Louis XI*, ed. J. E. J. Quicherat (4 vols., Paris, 1855-59)
Basin, T., *Histoire de Charles VII*, ed. C.Samaran (2 vols., Paris, 1933, 1944)
Bentley, S. (ed.), *Excerpta historica* (1831)
Blacman, J., *Henry the Sixth*, ed. M. R. James (Cambridge, 1919)
Blondell, R., *De reductione Normanniae*, in J. Stevenson (ed.), *Narratives of the expulsion of the English from Normandy* (RS, 1863), pp. 23-238
Bossuat, A., 'La littérature de propagande au XVe siècle: le mémoire de Jean de Rinel, secrétaire du roi d'Angleterre, contre le duc de Bourgogne (1435)', *Cahiers d'histoire*, I (1956), 129-46
Bowen, I., *Statutes of Wales* (1908)
Brie, F. W. D. (ed.), *The Brut, or the chronicles of England*, vol. II (EETS, CXXXVI, 1908)
Brown, C., 'Lydgate's verses on Queen Margaret's entry into London', *MLR*, VII (1912), 225-34
Brown, R. (ed.), *Calendar of state papers and manuscripts, Venice*, vol. I (1864)
Calendar of ancient deeds
Calendar of charter rolls
Calendar of close rolls
Calendar of fine rolls
Calendar of Ormond deeds
Calendar of papal registers
Calendar of patent rolls
Caxton, W., *The chronicles of England* (1st ed., 1480)
Champion, P., *Chronique Martiniane* (Paris, 1907)

Chartier, J., *Chronique*, ed. A. Vallet de Viriville (3 vols., Paris, 1858)

Chastellain, G., *Oeuvres*, ed. K. de Lettenhove (7 vols., Brussels, 1863–65)

Chatwin, P., 'Documents of Warwick the kingmaker in the possession of St Mary's church, Warwick', *Transactions and proceedings of Birmingham archaeological soc.*, LIX (1938), 2-8

Chesne, A. du, *Les oeuvres de M. Alain Chartier...* (Paris, 1617)

Chrimes, S. B. and Brown, A. L. (eds.), *Select documents of English constitutional history, 1307–1485* (1961)

Chronicles of the White rose of York, The (1845)

Clark, A. (ed.), *Lincoln diocese documents* (EETS, CXLIX, 1914)

Clermont, Lord (ed.), *The works of Sir John Fortescue*, vol. I (1869)

Clough, M. (ed.), *The book of Bartholomew Bolney* (Sussex record soc., LXIII, 1964)

Collier, J. P. (ed.), *Trevilian papers*, part 1 (Camden soc., old ser., LXVII, 1857)

Commynes, P. de, *Memoirs, 1461–1483*, ed. M. Jones (1972)

Cronne, H. A. and Hilton, R. H., 'The Beauchamp household book', *UBHJ*, II (1949–50), 208-18

Davies, J. S. (ed.), *An English chronicle of the reigns of Richard II, Henry IV, Henry V, and Henry VI* (Camden soc., old ser., LXIV, 1856)

Davis, N. (ed.), *Paston letters and papers of the fifteenth century* (2 vols., Oxford, 1971–76)

Deeds, C., 'Extracts from the episcopal register of Richard Praty', in *Sussex record soc.*, IV (1905), 85-214

Dilkes, T. B. (ed.), *Bridgwater borough archives, 1445–68* (Somerset record soc., 1945)

Dobson, R. B. (ed.), *York city chamberlains' account rolls, 1396–1500* (Surtees soc., CXCII, 1980)

Douët d'Arcq, L. (ed.), *La chronique d'Enguerran de Monstrelet... 1400–1444* (6 vols., Paris, 1857–62)

Du Boulay, F. R. H. (ed.), *Registrum Thome Bourgchier Cantuariensis archiepiscopi, A. D. 1454–1486* (Canterbury and York soc., LIV, 1957)

Dugdale, W., *Monasticon anglicanum* (6 vols., 1817–30)

Dunham, W. H., jnr., 'Notes from the parliament at Winchester, 1449', *Speculum*, XVII (1942), 402-15

Dunstan, G. R. (ed.),*The register of Edmund Lacy, bishop of Exeter, 1420–1455* (5 vols., Canterbury and York soc., 1963–72)

Ellis, H. (ed.), *Original letters illustrative of English history*, 1st ser. (3 vols., 1825); 2nd ser. (4 vols., 1827); 3rd ser. (4 vols., 1846)

Ellis, H. (ed.), *Three books of Polydore Vergil's English history* (Camden soc., old ser., XXIX, 1844)

Elmham, T. de, *Vita et gesta Henrici quinti Anglorum regis*, ed. T. Hearne (Oxford, 1727)

D'Escouchy, M., *Chronique*, ed. G. du Fresne de Beaucourt (3 vols., Paris, 1863–64)

Fabyan, R., *The new chronicles of England and France*, ed. H. Ellis (1811)

Fauquembergue, C. de, *Journal*, ed. A. Tuetey and H. Lacaille (3 vols., Paris, 1903–13)

Fenin, P. de, *Mémoires, 1407–27*, ed. L. M. E. Dupont (Paris, 1837)

Fleming, J. H. (ed.), *England under the Lancastrians* (1921)

Flenley, R. (ed.), *Six town chronicles* (Oxford, 1911).

Flügel, E., 'Eine Mittelenglische Claudian-Ubersetzung (1445)', *Anglia*, XXVIII (1905), 255-99, 421-38

Fordun, J., *Scotichronicon, cum supplementis et continuatione Walteri Bower*, ed. W. Goodall (2 vols., Edinburgh, 1775)

Fortescue, Sir J., *De laudibus legum Anglie*, ed. S. B. Chrimes (Cambridge, 1942)

Furnivall, F. J. (ed.), *Political, religious, and love poems* (EETS, old ser., XV, 1866)

Gairdner, J. (ed.), *Letters and papers illustrative of the reigns of Richard III and Henry VII*, vol. 1 (RS, 1861)

Gairdner, J. (ed.), *The historical collections of a citizen of London in the fifteenth century* (Camden soc., new ser., XVII, 1876)

Gairdner, J. (ed.), *Three fifteenth-century chronicles* (Camden soc., 3rd ser., XXVIII, 1880)

Gairdner, J. (ed.), *The Paston letters* (6 vols., Library ed., 1904)

Gascoigne, T., *Loci e libro veritatum*, ed. J. E. T. Rogers (Oxford, 1881)

Genet, J.-Ph. (ed.), *Four English political tracts of the later middle ages* (Camden soc., 4th ser., XVIII, 1977)

Giles, J. A. (ed.), *Incerti scriptoris chronicon Angliae de regnis . . . Henrici IV, Henrici V, et Henrici VI* (1848)

Gilson, J. P., 'A defence of the proscription of the Yorkists in 1459', *EHR*, XXVI (1911), 512-25

Graves, J. (ed.), *A roll of the proceedings of the king's council in Ireland* (RS, 1877)

Greatrex, J. (ed.), *The register of the common seal of the priory of St Swithin, Winchester, 1345-1497* (Hants. record ser., II, 1978)

Grosjean, P., *Henrici VI Angliae regis miracula postuma* (Brussels, 1935)

Gruel, G., *Chronique d'Arthur de Richemont*, ed. A. le Vavasseur (Paris, 1890)

Hall, E., *Chronicle*, ed. H. Ellis (1809)

Halliwell, J. O. (ed.), *A chronicle of the first thirteen years of the reign of King Edward the fourth by John Warkworth* (Camden soc., old ser., X, 1839)

Hardyng, J., *Chronicle*, ed. H. Ellis (1812)

Harris, M. D. (ed.), *The Coventry leet-book*, part II (EETS, 1908)

Harriss, G. L. and M. A. (eds.), 'John Benet's chronicle for the years 1400 to 1462', in *Camden miscellany*, XXIV (Camden soc., 4th ser., IX, 1972), 151-252

Harrod, H. D., 'A defence of the liberties of Chester, 1450', *Archaeologia*, LVII (1900), 71-86

Harvey, J. H. (ed.), *Itineraries of William Worcester* (Oxford, 1969)

Hearne, T. (ed.), *Vita Henrici quinti . . .* (Oxford, 1716)

Hinds, A. B. (ed.), *Calendar of state papers, Milan*, vol. I (1912)

Hingeston, F. C. (ed.), *John Capgrave, Liber de illustribus Henricis* (RS, 1858)

Historical manuscripts commission, vols. IV (1874); V (1876); VI (1877); VIII (1881); IX (1883); IX part 2 (1884); XIV part 3 (1894); Various collections I (1901); Rutland MSS IV (1905); Various collections IV (1907)

Holinshed, R., *Chronicles of England, Scotland and Ireland*, ed. H. Ellis (6 vols., 1807-08)

Jack, R. I. (ed.), *The Grey of Ruthin valor* (Sydney, 1965)

Jacob, E. F. (ed.), *The register of Henry Chichele, archbishop of Canterbury, 1414–43* (4 vols., Canterbury and York soc., 1938–47)

Jeayes, I. H., *A descriptive catalogue of the Berkeley muniments* (Bristol, 1892)

Kendall, P. M. and Ilardi, V. (eds.), *Dispatches, with related documents, of Milanese ambassadors in France and Burgundy, 1450–1483* (2 vols., Athens, Ohio, 1970–71)

Kingsford, C. L. (ed.), *The chronicles of London* (1905)

Kingsford, C. L. (ed.), *Survey of London by John Stow* (2 vols., Oxford, 1908)

Kingsford, C. L. (ed.), *The first English life of King Henry the fifth* (Oxford, 1911)

Kingsford, C. L. (ed.), 'The first version of Hardyng's chronicle', *EHR*, XXVII (1912), 462-80, 740-53

Kingsford, C. L., 'An historical collection of the fifteenth century', *EHR*, XXIX (1914), 505-15

Kingsford, C. L. (ed.), *The Stonor letters and papers, 1290–1483*, vol. I (Camden soc., 3rd ser., XXIX, 1919)

Klinefelter, R. A., 'The siege of Calais: a new text', *PMLAA*, LXVII (1952), 888-95

Klinefelter, R. A., 'A newly discovered fifteenth-century English manuscript', *Modern language quarterly*, XIV (1953), 3-6

Laidlaw, J. C. (ed.), *The poetical works of Alain Chartier* (Cambridge, 1974)

Le Bouvier, G., 'Recouvrement de Normandie', in J. Stevenson (ed.), *Narratives of the expulsion of the English from Normandy* (RS, 1863), pp. 245-376

Lodge, E. C. and Thornton, G. A. (eds.), *English constitutional documents, 1307–1485* (Cambridge, 1935)

Luce, S. (ed.), *Chronique du Mont-Saint-Michel, 1343–1468* (2 vols., Paris, 1879–83)

MacCracken, H. N., 'A new poem by Lydgate', *Anglia*, XXXIII (1910), 283-6

MacCracken, H. N. (ed.), *The minor poems of John Lydgate*, part 2 (EETS, 192, 1934)

Maxwell-Lyte, H. C. (ed.), *Register of Bishop Bekynton* (2 vols., Somerset record soc., XLIX, L, 1934–35)

Mollat, M. (ed.), *Les affaires de Jacques Coeur*, vol. I (Paris, 1952)

Moore, S. A. (ed.), *Letters and papers of John Shillingford, mayor of Exeter, 1447–50* (Camden soc., new ser., II, 1871)

Morice, Dom H., *Mémoires pour servir de preuves à l'histoire ecclesiastique et civile de Bretagne* (3 vols., Paris, 1742–46)

Munro, C. (ed.), *Letters of Queen Margaret of Anjou* (Camden soc., old ser., LXXXVI, 1863)

Myers, A. R., 'A parliamentary debate of the mid-fifteenth century', *BJRL*, XXII (1938), 388-404

Myers, A. R., 'The captivity of a royal witch: the household accounts of Queen Joan of Navarre, 1419-21', *BJRL*, XXIV (1940), 263-84; XXVI (1941), 82-100

Myers, A. R., 'Some household ordinances of Henry VI', *BJRL*, XXXVI (1954), 449-67

Myers, A. R., 'The household of Queen Margaret of Anjou, 1452–53', *BJRL*, XL (1957–58), 70-113, 391-431

Myers, A. R., 'The jewels of Queen Margaret of Anjou', *BJRL*, XLII (1959), 113-31

Myers, A. R., *The household of Edward IV* (Manchester, 1959)

Myers, A. R. (ed.), *English historical documents*, vol. IV: *1327–1485* (1969)

Myers, A. R., 'A parliamentary debate of 1449', *BIHR*, LI (1978), 78-83

Nichols, J. (ed.), *A collection of all the wills of the kings and queens of England, . . .* (1780)

Nichols, J. G. (ed.), *The chronicle of the Grey friars of London* (Camden soc., old ser., LIII, 1852)

Nichols, J. G. (ed.), *The boke of noblesse* (Roxburghe club, 1860)

Nicolas, N. H. (ed.), *A journal by one of the suite of Thomas Beckington . . .* (1828)

Nicolas, N. H. (ed.), *Proceedings and ordinances of the privy council of England* (7 vols., RC, 1834–37)

Nicolas, N. H. and Tyrell, E. (eds.), *A chronicle of London, 1189–1483* (1827)

Oliver, J. R. (ed.), *Monumenta de insula Manniae* (3 vols., Manx soc., IV, VII, IX, 1860–62)

Palgrave, F. (ed.), *The ancient kalendars and inventories of the treasurer of His Majesty's exchequer* (3 vols., RC, 1836)

Plummer, C. (ed.), *The governance of England* (1885)

Post, J. B., 'A fifteenth-century customary of the Southwark stews', *JSA*, V (1977), 418-28

Putnam, B. H. (ed.), *Proceedings before the justices of the peace in the fourteenth and fifteenth centuries, Edward III to Richard III* (1938)

Raine, J. (ed.), *The correspondence, etc. of Coldingham priory* (Surtees soc., XII, 1841)

Reports from the Lords' committees . . . touching the dignity of a peer (5 vols., 1820–29)

Reports of the deputy keeper of the public records, XLVIII (1887)

Rigg, A. G. (ed.), *A Glastonbury miscellany of the fifteenth century* (Oxford, 1968)

Riley, H. T. (ed.), *Ingulph's chronicle of the abbey of Croyland* (1854)

Riley, H. T. (ed.), *Registrum abbatiae Johannis Whethamstede* (2 vols., RS, 1872–73)

Robbins, R. H., 'A middle English diatribe against Philip of Burgundy', *Neophilologus*, XXXIX (1955), 131-46

Robbins, R. H., 'An epitaph for Duke Humphrey (1447)', *Neuphilologische Mitteilungen*, LVI (1955), 241-9

Robbins, R. H. (ed.), *Historical poems of the XIVth and XVth centuries* (New York, 1959)

Ropp, G. von der (ed.), *Hanserecesse, 1431–76* (7 vols., Leipzig, 1876–92)

Rous, J., *Historia regum Angliae*, ed. T. Hearne (Oxford, 1745)

Rotuli parliamentorum (7 vols., 1832)

Rymer, T. (ed.), *Foedera, conventiones, literae . . .* (3rd ed., 10 vols., The Hague, 1739–45)

Salter, H. E. (ed.), *Registrum cancellarii Oxon.*, vol. I (Oxford, 1930)

Sharpe, R. R. (ed.), *Calendar of the letter-books preserved among the archives of the corporation of the city of London: letter-book K* (1911)

Sheppard, J. (ed.), *Literae Cantuarienses*, vol. III (RS, 1889)

Shirley, J. (ed.), *A Parisian journal, 1405–1449* (Oxford, 1968)

Shirley, W. W. (ed.), *Fasciculi Zizaniorum* (RS, 1858)

Smith, L. T. (ed.), *The maire of Bristowe is kalendar, by Robert Ricart* (Camden soc., new ser., V, 1872)

Sotheby and co. catalogue of . . . W. W. Manning, esq., 24–25 January 1945

Sotheby and co. catalogue, 9 July 1973 (Westminster diocese manuscripts)

Sotheby and co. catalogue, 26 June 1974 (Phillipps manuscripts)

Sotheby and co. catalogue, 12 December 1976 (Lyttelton manuscripts)

Stapleton, T. (ed.), *The Plumpton correspondence* (Camden soc., old ser., IV, 1839)

Statutes of the realm (11 vols., 1810–28)

Stevenson, J. (ed.), *Narratives of the expulsion of the English from Normandy* (RS, 1863)

Stevenson, J. (ed.), *Letters and papers illustrative of the wars of the English in France during the reign of Henry the sixth, etc.* (2 vols. in 3, RS, 1861–64)

Stow, J., *The chronicles of England* (1580)

Stow, J., *Annales, or a generall chronicle of England* (1631)

Strong, P. and F., 'The last will and codicils of Henry V', *EHR*, XCVI (1981), 79-102

Taylor, F., 'The chronicle of John Strecche for the reign of Henry V (1414–1422)', *BJRL*, XVI 1932), 137-87

Taylor, F., 'Some manuscripts of the "Libelle of Englysche polycye"', *BJRL*, XXIV (1940), 376-418

Thielemans, M.-R., 'Une lettre missive inédite de Philippe le Bon concernant le siège de Calais', *Bulletin de la commission royale d'histoire*, CXV (1950), 285-96

Thomas, A. H. and Thornley, I. D. (eds.), *The great chronicle of London* (1938)

Thomson, T. (ed.), *The Auchinleck chronicle* (2 vols., Edinburgh, 1819, 1877)

Ullmann, W. (ed.), *Liber regie capelle* (Henry Bradshaw soc., XCII, 1961)

Veale, E. M. W. (ed.), *The great red book of Bristol* (5 vols., Bristol record soc., 1931–53)

Virgoe, R., 'Some ancient indictments in the king's bench referring to Kent, 1450–1452', in F. R. H. Du Boulay (ed.), *Kent records: documents illustrative of mediaeval Kentish society* (Kent record soc., 1964), pp. 214-65

Walsingham, T., *Historia anglicana, 1272–1422*, ed. H. T. Riley (2 vols., RS, 1863–64)

Warner, G. (ed.), *The libelle of Englysche polycye* (Oxford, 1926)

Watson, A. G., *Catalogue of dated and datable manuscripts, c. 700–1600, in the department of manuscripts, British Library* (2 vols., 1979)

Waurin, J. de, *Anchiennes cronicques d'Engleterre*, ed. E. Dupont (3 vols., Paris, 1858–63)

Waurin, J. de, *Recueil des croniques et anchiennes istories de la Grant Bretaigne*, ed. W. and E. L. C. P. Hardy (5 vols., RS, 1864–91)

Wilkins, D., *Concilia magnae Britanniae et Hiberniae, A. D. 466–1718* (4 vols., 1737)

Willard, C. C., 'The manuscripts of Jean Petit's justification: some Burgundian propaganda methods of the early fifteenth century', *Studi Francesi*, XII (1969), 271-80

Williams, G. (ed.), *Official correspondence of Thomas Bekynton* (2 vols., RS, 1872)

Withington, R., 'Queen Margaret's entry into London, 1445', *Mod. Philol.*, XIII (1915), 53-7

Worcestre, W., *The boke of noblesse*, ed. J. G. Nichols (1857)

Wright, T. (ed.), *A collection of political poems and songs relating to English history, from the accession of Edward III to the reign of Henry VIII* (2 vols., RS, 1859–61)

Wrottesley, G., 'Extracts from the plea rolls of the reign of . . . Henry VI . . .', *William Salt archaeological soc.*, XVII (1896), 87-153; new ser., III (1900), 123-9

C. Secondary Authorities

Adamson, J. W., 'The extent of literacy in England in the fifteenth and sixteenth centuries: notes and conjectures', *Library*, 4th ser., X (1929–30), 167-71

Allmand, C. T., 'The collection of Dom Lenoir and the English occupation of Normandy in the fifteenth century', *Archives*, VI (1963–64), 202-10

Allmand, C. T., 'The Anglo-French negotiations, 1439', *BIHR*, XL (1967), 1-33

Allmand, C. T., 'The Lancastrian land settlement in Normandy, 1417–50', *EconHR*, 2nd ser., XXI (1968), 461-79

Allmand, C. T., 'La Normandie devant l'opinion anglaise à la fin de la guerre de cent ans', *Bibliothèque de l'école de Chartes*, CXXVIII (1970), 345-68

Allmand, C. T. (ed.), *War, literature, and politics in the late middle ages* (Liverpool, 1976)

Allmand, C. T., 'The aftermath of war in fifteenth-century France', *History*, LXI (1976), 344-57

Anderson, R. C., 'The Grace Dieu of 1446–86', *EHR*, XXXIV (1919), 584-6

Armstrong, C. A. J., 'The inauguration ceremonies of the Yorkist kings, and their title to the throne', *TRHS*, 4th ser., XXX (1948), 51-73

Armstrong, C. A. J., 'Some examples of the distribution and speed of news in England at the time of the wars of the roses', in R. W. Hunt, W. A. Pantin, and R. W. Southern (eds.), *Essays in mediaeval history presented to F. M. Powicke* (Oxford, 1948), pp. 429-54

Armstrong, C. A. J., 'Politics and the battle of St Albans, 1455', *BIHR*, XXXIII (1960), 1-72

Armstrong, C. A. J., 'La double monarchie France-Angleterre et la maison de Bourgogne (1420–1435): le déclin d'une alliance', *Annales de Bourgogne*, XXXVII (1963), 81-112

Armstrong, C. A. J., 'La politique matrimoniale des ducs de Bourgogne de la maison de Valois', *Annales de Bourgogne*, XL (1968), 5-58, 89-139

Armstrong, C. A. J., 'The golden age of Burgundy', in A. G. Dickens (ed.), *The courts of Europe* (1977), pp. 55-75

Aston, M. E., 'Lollardy and sedition, 1381–1431', *Past and present*, XVII (1960), 1-44

Aston, M. E., 'Lollardy and literacy', *History*, LXII (1977), 347-71

Avery, M. E., 'The history of the equitable jurisdiction of chancery before 1460', *BIHR*, XLII (1969), 129-44

Aylmer, G. E. and Cant, R. (eds.), *A history of York minster* (Oxford, 1977)

Bagley, J. J., *Margaret of Anjou, queen of England* (n. d. [1948])

Baldwin, J. F., *The king's council in England during the middle ages* (Oxford, 1913)

Balfour-Melville, E. W. M., *James I, king of Scots, 1406–1437* (1936)

Barbé, L. A., *Margaret of Scotland and the Dauphin Louis* (1917)

Bartŏs, F. M., 'An English cardinal and the Hussite revolution', *Communio viatorum*, I (1963), 47-54

Bassett, M., 'Newgate prison in the middle ages', *Speculum*, XVIII (1943), 233-46

Baudier, M., *A history of the memorable and extraordinary calamities of Margaret of Anjou, queen of England* (1737)

Bean, J. M. W., *The estates of the Percy family, 1416–1537* (Oxford, 1958)

Beardwood, A., *Alien merchants in England, 1350 to 1377* (Cambridge, Mass., 1931)

Beaucourt, G. du Fresne de, *Histoire de Charles VII* (6 vols., Paris, 1881–91)

Beaurepaire, C. M. de Robillard de, *Les états de Normandie sous la domination anglaise* (Evreux, 1859)

Bellamy, J. G., *The law of treason in England in the later middle ages* (Cambridge, 1970)

Bellamy, J. G., *Crime and public order in England in the later middle ages* (1973)

Beltz, G. F., *Memorials of the most noble order of the garter* (1841)

Bennett, H. S., *Chaucer and the fifteenth century* (Oxford, 1947)

Bennett, H. S., *The Pastons and their England* (Cambridge, 1951)

Bennett, H. S., *Six mediaeval men and women* (Cambridge, 1955)

Bennett, J. W., 'The mediaeval love-day', *Speculum*, XXXIII (1958), 351-70

Bernard, J. H., 'Richard Talbot, archbishop and chancellor (1418–1449)', *PRIA*, XXXV, C (1918–20), 218-29

Betcherman, L. R., 'The making of bishops in the Lancastrian period', *Speculum*, XLI (1966), 397-419

Blake, W. J., 'Thomas Wetherby', *Norfolk archaeology*, XXXII (1961), 60-72

Blatcher, M., *The court of king's bench, 1450–1550* (1978)

Blyth, J. D., 'The battle of Tewkesbury', *TBGAS*, LXXX (1961), 99-120

Bond, S., 'The mediaeval constables of Windsor castle', *EHR*, LXXXII (1967), 225-49

Book of Hours, A (The Henry VI soc., n. d.)

Bossuat, A., *Perrinet Gressart et François de Surienne, agents d'Angleterre* (Paris, 1936)

Bourdeaut, A., 'Gilles de Bretagne entre la France et l'Angleterre', *Mémoires de la société d'histoire et d'archéologie de Bretagne*, I (1920), 53-145

Brill, R., 'The English preparations before the treaty of Arras: a new interpretation of Sir John Fastolf's "report", September 1435', *Studies in mediaeval and renaissance history*, VII (1970), 213-47

Brissaud, D., *Les anglais en Guyenne* (Paris, 1875)

Brockbank, J. P., 'The frame of disorder – *Henry VI*', in W. A. Armstrong (ed.), *Shakespeare's histories* (1972), pp. 92-122

Brooke, C. N. L., 'The deans of St Paul's, c. 1090–1499', *BIHR*, XXIX (1956), 231-44

Brooke, R., *Visits to fields of battle in England in the fifteenth century* (1857)

Brooke, R., *On the life and character of Margaret of Anjou* (Liverpool, 1859)

Brown, A., 'London and north-west Kent in the later middle ages: the development of a land market', *Arch. Cant.*, XCII (1976), 145-55

Brown, A. L., 'The commons and the council in the reign of Henry IV', *EHR*, LXXIX (1964), 1-30

Brown, A. L., 'The king's councillors in fifteenth-century England', *TRHS*, 5th ser., XIX (1969), 95-118

Brown, A. L., *The early history of the clerkship of the council* (Glasgow, 1969)

Burne, A. H., *More battlefields of England* (1952)

Calmette, J. et Périnelle, G., *Louis XI et l'Angleterre, 1461–83* (Paris, 1930)

Cambrian register, I (1795), 49-144

Camden, W., *Britannia*, ed. R. Gough (1789)

Campbell, L. B., 'Humphrey, duke of Gloucester and Elianor Cobham, his wife, in the "Mirror for Magistrates"', *HLQ*, V (1934), 119-55

Cameron, A., *Claudian: poetry and propaganda at the court of Honorius* (Oxford, 1970)

Carpenter, C., 'The Beauchamp affinity: a study of bastard feudalism at work', *EHR*, XCV (1980), 515-32

Carr, A. D., 'Sir Lewis John – a mediaeval London Welshman', *BBCS*, XXII (1967), 260-70

Carrington, A. and Andrew, W. J., 'A Lancastrian raid in the wars of the roses', *Journal of the Derbyshire archaeological and natural history soc.*, XXXIV (1912), 33-49; XXXV (1913), 207-44

Carus-Wilson, E. M., *The merchant adventurers of Bristol in the fifteenth century* (Bristol, 1962)

Carus-Wilson, E. M., *Mediaeval merchant venturers* (3rd ed., 1967)

Carus-Wilson, E. M. and Coleman, O. (eds.), *England's export trade, 1275–1547* (Oxford, 1963)

Chandler, R., *The life of William Waynflete* (1811)

Champion, P., *Vie de Charles d'Orléans* (2nd ed., Paris, 1969)

Cherry, M., 'The Courtenay earls of Devon: the formation and disintegration of a late mediaeval aristocratic affinity', *Southern history*, I (1979), 71-97

Cherry, M., 'The struggle for power in mid-fifteenth-century Devonshire', in R. A. Griffiths (ed.), *Patronage, the crown and the provinces in later medieval England* (Gloucester, 1981), ch. 6

Chrimes, S. B., 'The pretensions of the duke of Gloucester in 1422', *EHR*, XLV (1930), 101-3

Chrimes, S. B., '"House of Lords" and "House of Commons" in the fifteenth century', *EHR*, XLIX (1934), 494-7

Chrimes, S. B., *English constitutional ideas in the fifteenth century* (Cambridge, 1936)

Chrimes, S. B., *Lancastrians, Yorkists, and Henry VII* (2nd ed., 1966)

Chrimes, S. B., *Henry VII* (1972)

Chrimes, S. B., Ross, C. D., and Griffiths, R. A. (eds.), *Fifteenth-century England, 1399–1509* (Manchester, 1972)

Christie, M. E., *Henry VI* (1922)

Clarke, B., *Mental disorder in earlier Britain* (Cardiff, 1975)

Cobban, A. B., *The King's Hall within the University of Cambridge in the later middle ages* (Cambridge, 1969)

Cokayne, G. E., *The complete peerage of England, Scotland, Ireland, Great Britain and the United Kingdom . . .*, ed. V. Gibbs et al. (12 vols. in 13, 1910–59)

Cole, H., *The wars of the roses* (1973)

Colvin, H. M. (ed.), *The history of the king's works: the middle ages* (2 vols., 1 box, 1963)

Contamine, P., *Guerre, état, et société à la fin du moyen âge* (Paris, 1972)

Cooke, J. H., 'On the great Berkeley law-suit of the 15th and 16th centuries', *TBGAS*, III (1878–79), 305-24

Cooper, W. D., 'Participation of Sussex in Cade's rising, 1450', *Sussex archaeological collections*, XVIII (1866), 19-36

Cooper, W. D., 'John Cade's followers in Kent', *Arch. Cant.*, VII (1868), 233-71

Corbin, R., *Histoire de Pey Berland et du pays bordelais au XVᵉ siècle d'après les documents de l'époque* (Bordeaux, 1888)

Crawford, A., 'The King's burden – the consequences of royal marriage in fifteenth-century England', in Griffiths, *Patronage, the crown and the provinces*, ch. 2

Crosland, J., *Sir John Fastolfe* (1970)

Curtis, E., 'Richard, duke of York as viceroy of Ireland, 1447–1460', *JRSAI*, LXII (1932), 157-86

Davies, R. R., 'The survival of the blood feud in mediaeval Wales', *History*, LIV (1969), 338-57

Davies, R. R., *Lordship and society in the march of Wales, 1282–1400* (Oxford, 1978)

Davis, E. J. and Peake, M. I., 'Loans from the city of London to Henry VI, 1431–1449', *BIHR*, IV (1926–27), 165-72

Davis, J. F., 'Lollard survival and the textile industry in the south-east of England', *Studies in church history*, III (1960), 191-201

Denholm-Young, N., *Handwriting in England and Wales* (Cardiff, 1954)

Dicks, S. E., 'Henry VI and the daughters of Armagnac: a problem in mediaeval diplomacy', *Emporia State research papers*, 1967, pp. 5-12

Dickinson, J. G., 'The congress of Arras, 1435', *History*, new ser., XL (1955), 31-41

Dickinson, J. G., *The congress of Arras, 1435* (Oxford, 1955)

Dickinson, W. C., *Scotland from the earliest times to 1603*, ed. A. A. M. Duncan (Oxford, 1977)

Dictionary of national biography, The (63 vols., 1885–1900)

Dictionnaire de biographie française (Paris, 1933–)

Dobson, R. B., 'The last English monks on Scottish soil', *ScotHR*, XLVI (1967), 1-25

Dobson, R. B., *Durham priory, 1400–1450* (Cambridge, 1973)

Doucet, R., 'Les finances anglaises en France à la fin de la guerre de cent ans, 1413–35', *Le moyen âge*, XXXVI (1926), 265-332

Drake, H. E. (ed.), *Hasted's history of Kent*, part 1 (1886)

Driver, J. T., *Cheshire in the later middle ages* (Chester, 1971)

Du Boulay, F. R. H., 'The Pagham estates of the archbishopric of Canterbury during the fifteenth century', *History*, new ser., XXXVIII (1953), 201-18

Du Boulay, F. R. H., 'A rentier economy in the later middle ages: the archbishopric of Canterbury', *EconHR*, 2nd ser., XVI (1963–64), 427-38

Du Boulay, F. R. H., 'Who was farming the English demesnes at the end of the middle ages?', *EconHR*, 2nd ser., XVII (1964–65), 443-55

Du Boulay, F. R. H., 'The fifteenth century', in C. H. Lawrence (ed.), *The English church and the papacy in the middle ages* (New York, 1965), pp. 195-242

Du Boulay, F. R. H., *The lordship of Canterbury* (1966)

Du Boulay, F. R. H., *An age of ambition* (1970)

Dulley, A. J. F., 'Four Kent towns at the end of the middle ages', *Arch. Cant.*, LXXXI (1966), 95-108

Dumont, C. E., *Histoire de la ville de Saint-Mihiel* (2 vols., Nancy, 1860–62)

Dunham, W. H. and Wood, C. T., 'The right to rule in England: depositions and the kingdom's authority, 1327–1485', *American historical review*, LXXXI (1976), 738-61

Dunlop, A. I., *Scots abroad in the fifteenth century* (1942)

Dunning, R. W., 'Thomas, Lord Dacre and the west march towards Scotland, 1435', *BIHR*, XLI (1968), 95-9

Dupuy, P., *Traité de la majorité de nos rois, et des régences du royaume* (Paris, 1655)

Edwards, A. S. G., 'The influence of Lydgate's *Fall of Princes, c.* 1440–1559: a survey', *MedSt*, XXXIX (1977), 424-39

Edwards, J. G., *The principality of Wales, 1267–1967* (Caernarvon, 1969)

Edwards, J. G., 'The Huntingdonshire parliamentary election of 1450', in T. A. Sandquist and M. R. Powicke (eds.), *Essays in mediaeval history presented to Bertie Wilkinson* (Toronto, 1969), pp. 383-95

Edwards, J. G., *The second century of the English parliament* (Oxford, 1979)

Einstein, L., *The Italian renaissance in England* (New York, 1902)

Elton, G. R., 'Tudor government: the points of contact, III. The court', *TRHS*, 5th ser., XXVI (1976), 211-28

Emden, A. B., *A biographical register of the University of Oxford to A. D. 1500* (3 vols., Oxford, 1957–59)

Emden, A. B., *A biographical register of the University of Cambridge to A. D. 1500* (Cambridge, 1963)

Emerson, E. H., 'Reginald Pecock: Christian rationalist', *Speculum*, XXX (1956), 235-42

Emery, A., 'The development of Raglan castle and keeps in late mediaeval England', *AJ*, CXXXII (1975), 151-86

Empey, C. A. and Simms, K., 'The ordinances of the White Earl and the problem of coign in the later middle ages', *PRIA*, LXXV, C, no. 8 (1975), 161-87

Erlanger, P., *Marguérite d'Anjou et la guerre des deux roses* (Paris, 1928), translated as *Margaret of Anjou, queen of England* (1970)

Ettlinger, E., 'Notes on a woodcut depicting King Henry VI being invoked as a saint', *Folklore*, LXXXIV (1973), 115-19

Evans, H. T., *Wales and the wars of the roses* (Cambridge, 1915)

Ferguson, J., *English diplomacy, 1422–1461* (Oxford, 1972)

Fifteenth–century pilgrimage, A (The Henry VI soc., n. d.)

Flenley, R., 'London and foreign merchants in the reign of Henry VI', *EHR*, XXV (1910), 644-55

Fletcher, J., 'Tree ring dates from some panel paintings in England', *Burlington magazine*, CXVI (1974), 250-8

Foss, E., *A biographical register of the judges of England* (1870)

Gairdner, J., 'Jack Cade's rebellion', *Fortnightly review*, old ser., XIV (1870), 442-55

Gasquet, F. A., *The religious life of King Henry VI* (1923)

Gillespie, J. L., 'Richard, duke of York as king's lieutenant in Ireland', *The Ricardian*, V, no. 69 (1980), 194-201

Giraud, F. F., 'Faversham: regulations for the town porters', *Arch. Cant.*, XX (1893), 219-21

Giuseppi, M. S., 'Alien merchants in England in the fifteenth century', *TRHS*, new ser., IX (1895), 75-98

Gooder, A. (ed.), *The parliamentary representation of the county of York, 1258–1832*, vol. I (Yorkshire archaeological soc., XCI, 1935)

Gottlob, A., 'Des Nuntius Franz Coppini Antheil an der Entthronung des Konigs Heinrich VI und seine Verurtheilung bei der Romischen Curie', *Deutsche Zeitschrift für Geschichtswissenschaft*, IV (1890), 75-111

Gray, H. L., 'Incomes from land in England in 1436', *EHR*, XLIX (1934), 607-39

Green, V. H. H., *Bishop Reginald Pecock* (Cambridge, 1945)

Greenstreet, J., 'Jack Cade's rebellion', *The antiquarian magazine and bibliographer*, II (1883), 165-71

Griffith, M. C., 'The Talbot – Ormond struggle for control of the Anglo-Irish government, 1441–47', *IHS*, II (1940–41), 376-97

Griffiths, R. A., 'The rise of the Stradlings of St Donat's', *Transactions of the Glamorgan history soc.*, VII (1963), 15-47

Griffiths, R. A., 'Gruffydd ap Nicholas and the rise of the house of Dinefwr', *NLWJ*, XIII (1964), 256-68

Griffiths, R. A., 'Gruffydd ap Nicholas and the fall of the house of Lancaster', *WHR*, II (1965), 213-31

Griffiths, R. A., 'The rebellion of Owain Glyndŵr in north Wales through the eyes of an Englishman', *BBCS*, XXII (1967), 151-68

Griffiths, R. A., 'The trial of Eleanor Cobham: an episode in the fall of Duke Humphrey of Gloucester', *BJRL*, LI (1968–69), 381-99

Griffiths, R. A., *The principality of Wales in the later middle ages*, vol. I. *South Wales, 1277–1536* (Cardiff, 1972)

Griffiths, R. A., 'Patronage, politics, and the principality of Wales, 1413–1461', in H. Hearder and H. R. Loyn (eds.), *British government and administration: studies presented to S. B. Chrimes* (Cardiff, 1974)

Griffiths, R. A., 'Duke Richard of York's intentions in 1450 and the origins of the wars of the roses', *JMH*, I (1975), 187-209

Griffiths, R. A., 'Queen Katherine of Valois and a missing statute of the realm', *LQR*, XCIII (1977), 248-58

Griffiths, R. A., 'William Wawe and his gang, 1427', *Transactions of the Hampshire archaeological soc. and field club*, XXXIII (1977), 89-93

Griffiths, R. A., 'Un espion breton à Londres, 1425–29', *Annales de Bretagne et de l'Ouest*, LXXXVI (1979), 399-403

Griffiths, R. A., 'The Winchester session of the 1449 parliament: a further comment', *HLQ*, XLII (1979), 181-91

Griffiths, R. A. (ed.), *Boroughs of mediaeval Wales* (Cardiff, 1979)

Griffiths, R. A. (ed.), *Patronage, the crown and the provinces in later medieval England* (Gloucester, 1981)

Griffiths, R. A., 'The hazards of civil war: the case of the Mountford family', *Midland hist.*, V (1981), 1-19

Gupta, S. A., 'The substance of Shakespeare's "Histories"', in W. A. Armstrong (ed.), *Shakespeare's histories* (1972), pp. 60-91

Gutkind, C. S., *Cosimo de' Medici* (Oxford, 1938)

Haller, J., 'Piero da Monte, ein gelehrter und papstlicher Beamter des 15

Jahrhunderts, seine Briefsammlung', *Bibliothek des Deutschen historischen Instituts in Rom*, XLIX (Rome, 1941)

Hand, G. J., 'Aspects of alien status in mediaeval English law, with special reference to Ireland', in D. Jenkins (ed.), *Legal history studies, 1972* (Cardiff, 1975), pp. 129-35

Hand, G., 'The king's widow and the king's widows', *LQR*, XCIII (1977), 506-7

Hannawalt, B. A., 'Violent death in fourteenth- and early fifteenth-century England', *Comparative studies in society and history*, XVIII (1976), 297-320

Harcourt, L. W. V., 'The baga de secretis', *EHR*, XXIII (1908), 508-29

Harding, A., *The law courts of mediaeval England* (1973)

Harriss, G. L., 'Fictitious loans', *EconHR*, 2nd ser., VIII (1955–56), 187-99

Harriss, G. L., 'Preference at the mediaeval exchequer', *BIHR*, XXX (1957), 17-40

Harriss, G. L., 'The struggle for Calais: an aspect of the rivalry between Lancaster and York', *EHR*, LXXV (1960), 30-53

Harriss, G. L., 'Aids, loans, and benevolences', *HJ*, VI (1963), 1-19

Harriss, G. L., 'Cardinal Beaufort – patriot or usurer', *TRHS*, 5th ser., XX (1970), 129-48

Hasted, G., *The historical and topographical survey of the county of Kent* (new ed., 12 vols., Wakefield, 1972; original ed., 12 vols., Canterbury, 1797–1801)

Hastings, M., *The court of common pleas in fifteenth-century England* (Ithaca, N. Y., 1947)

Haswell, J., *The ardent queen: Margaret of Anjou and the Lancastrian heritage* (1976)

Hatcher, J., *Rural economy and society in the duchy of Cornwall, 1300–1500* (Cambridge, 1970)

Harvey, B., 'The leasing of the abbot of Westminster's demesnes in the later middle ages', *EconHR*, 2nd ser., XXII (1969), 17-27

Head, C., 'Pope Pius II and the wars of the roses', *Archivium historiae pontificiae*, VIII (1970), 149-73

Heers, J., 'Les Genois en Angleterre: la crise de 1458–1460', in *Studi in onore di Armando Sapori* (2 vols., Milan, 1957), vol. I, 507-32

Herbert, A., 'Herefordshire, 1413–61: some aspects of society and public order', in Griffiths, *Patronage, the crown and the provinces*, ch. 5

Holdsworth, W. S., *A history of English law*, vol. XIV (1964)

Hollaender, A. E. J. and Kellaway, W. (eds.), *Studies in London history presented to P. E. Jones* (1969)

Holmes, G. A., 'Florentine merchants in England, 1346–1436', *EconHR*, 2nd ser., XIII (1960), 193-208

Holmes, G. A., 'Cardinal Beaufort and the crusade against the Hussites', *EHR*, LXXXVIII (1973), 721-50

Holmes, G. A., *The good parliament* (Oxford, 1975)

Hookham, M. A., *Life and times of Margaret of Anjou* (2 vols., 1872)

Hughes, J. L. J. (ed.), *Patentee officers in Ireland, 1173–1826* (Dublin, 1960)

Hunnisett, R. F., 'Treason by words,' *Sussex notes and queries*, XIV (1954–57), 116-20

Jack, R. I., 'A quincentenary: the battle of Northampton, July 10th, 1460', *Northamptonshire past and present*, III (1960–65), 21-5

Jacob, E. F., 'Two lives of Archbishop Chichele', *BJRL*, XVI (1932), 428-68

Jacob, E. F., 'The building of All Souls College, 1438–1443', in J. G. Edwards, V. H. Galbraith, and E. F. Jacob (eds.), *Historical essays in honour of James Tait* (Manchester, 1933), pp. 121-43

Jacob, E. F., 'Reynold Pecock, bishop of Chichester', *PBA*, XXXVII (1951), 121-53

Jacob, E. F., *Henry Chichele and the ecclesiastical politics of his age* (1952)

Jacob, E. F., *The fifteenth century, 1399–1485* (Oxford, 1961)

Jacob, E. F., 'Thomas Brouns, bishop of Norwich, 1436–45', in H. R. Trevor-Roper (ed.), *Essays in British history presented to Sir K. Feiling* (1964), pp. 61-83

Jacob, E. F., *Essays in later mediaeval history* (Manchester, 1968)

Jalland, P., 'The influence of the aristocracy on shire elections in the north of England', *Speculum*, XLVII (1972), 483-507

James, M. K., *Studies in the mediaeval wine trade* (Oxford, 1971)

Jeffs, R. M., 'The Poynings–Percy dispute: an example of the interplay of open strife and legal action in the fifteenth century', *BIHR*, XXXIV (1961), 148-64

Johnston, C. E., 'Sir William Oldhall', *EHR*, XXV (1910), 715-22

Jones, E., '*Henry VI* and the spectre of strife', *Listener*, 7 July 1977, pp. 13-14

Jones, M., *Ducal Brittany, 1364–99* (Oxford, 1970)

Jones, M., 'John Beaufort, duke of Somerset and the French expedition of 1443', in Griffiths, *Patronage, the crown and the provinces*, ch. 4

Jones, T. A., *Without my wig* (2nd ed., Liverpool, 1945)

Judd, A., *The life of Thomas Bekynton* (Chichester, 1961)

Kantorowicz, E. H., *The king's two bodies* (Princeton, 1957)

Keen, M. H., 'Brotherhood in arms', *History*, XLVII (1962), 1-17

Keen, M. H., and Daniel, M. J., 'English diplomacy and the sack of Fougères in 1449', *History*, LIX (1974), 375-91

Kendall, P. M., *Warwick the kingmaker* (1957)

Kendall, P. M., *Louis XI* (1971)

Kerling, N. J. M., *Commercial relations of Holland and Zeeland with England from the late 13th century to the close of the middle ages* (Leiden, 1954)

Kerling, N. J. M., 'Aliens in the county of Norfolk, 1436–1485', *Norfolk archaeology*, XXXIII (1965), 200-12

Kimball, E. G., 'A bibliography of the printed records of the justices of the peace for counties', *University of Toronto law journal*, VI (1945–46), 401-13

Kingsford, C. L., *English historical literature in the fifteenth century* (Oxford, 1913)

Kingsford, C. L., 'Historical notes on mediaeval London houses', *London topographical record*, X (1916), 44-144; XI (1917), 28-81

Kingsford, C. L., *Prejudice and promise in fifteenth-century England* (Oxford, 1925)

Kirby, J. L., 'The financing of Calais under Henry V', *BIHR*, XXIII (1950), 165-77

Kirby, J. L., 'The issues of the Lancastrian exchequer and Lord Cromwell's estimates of 1433', *BIHR*, XXIV (1951), 121-51

Kirby, J. L., *Henry IV of England* (1970)

Knecht, R. J., 'The episcopate and the wars of the roses', *UBHJ*, VI (1957–58), 108-31

Knoop, D. and Jones, G. P., 'The building of Eton College, 1442–1460', *Transactions quatuor coronati lodge*, XLVI (1933), 70-114

Knoop, D. and Jones, G. P., *The mediaeval mason* (3rd ed., Manchester, 1967)

Knowles, M. D., *The religious orders in England*, vol. II (Cambridge, 1957)

Knowlson, G. A., *Jean V, duc de Bretagne, et l'Angleterre* (Rennes, 1964)

Knox, R. and Leslie, S. (eds.), *The miracles of King Henry VI* (Cambridge, 1923)

Kriehn, G., *The English rising in 1450* (Strassburg, 1892)

Lallemont, L, *Une héroine oubliée des biographes lorrains: Marguérite d'Anjou-Lorraine, reine d'Angleterre* (Nancy, 1855)

Lander, J. R., 'Henry VI and the duke of York's second protectorate, 1455 to 1456', *BJRL*, XLIII (1960), 46-69

Lander, J. R., *The wars of the roses* (1965)

Lander, J. R., *Conflict and stability in fifteenth-century England* (1st ed., 1969; 3rd ed., 1977)

Lander, J. R., *Crown and nobility, 1450–1509* (1976)

Laws, E., 'Notes on the fortifications of mediaeval Tenby', *Arch. Camb.*, 5th ser., XIII (1896), 177-92

Le Neve, J., *Fasti ecclesiae Anglicanae, 1300–1541*, ed. J. M. Horn *et al.* (12 vols., 1962–67)

LePatourel, J. H., 'Edward III and the kingdom of France', *History*, XLIII (1958), 173-89

Lewis, P. S., 'Sir John Fastolf's lawsuit over Titchwell, 1448–1455', *HJ*, I (1958), 1-20

Lewis, P. S., *Later mediaeval France* (1968)

List of Sheriffs for England and Wales (PRO, Lists and indexes, IX, 1898)

Lloyd, T. H., *The English wool trade in the middle ages* (Cambridge, 1977)

Lucas, P. J., 'John Capgrave, O. S. A. (1393–1464), scribe and "publisher"', *Transactions of the Cambridge bibliographical soc.*, V (1969–71), 1-35

Luce, S. (ed.), *Chronique du Mont-Saint-Michel, 1343–1468* (2 vols., Paris, 1879–83)

Lucie-Smith, E., *Joan of Arc* (1976)

Lydon, J. F., *The lordship of Ireland in the middle ages* (Dublin, 1972)

Lydon, J. F., *Ireland in the later middle ages* (Dublin, 1973)

Lyle, H. M., *The rebellion of Jack Cade, 1450* (Historical association, 1950)

MacCracken, H. M., 'An English friend of Charles of Orléans', *PMLAA*, XXVI (1911), 168-71

Macdougall, N. A. T., 'Foreign relations: England and France', in J. M. Brown (ed.), *Scottish society in the fifteenth century* (1977), pp. 101-11

McFarlane, K. B., 'Parliament and "bastard feudalism"', *TRHS*, 4th ser., XXVI (1944), 53-79

McFarlane, K. B., 'Loans to the Lancastrian kings: a problem of inducement', *CHJ*, IX (1947–49), 51-68

McFarlane, K. B., 'At the death-bed of Cardinal Beaufort', in R. W. Hunt, W. A. Pantin, and R. W. Southern (eds.), *Studies in mediaeval history presented to F. M. Powicke* (Oxford, 1948), pp. 405-28

McFarlane, K. B., 'The investment of Sir John Fastolf's profits of war', *TRHS*, 5th ser., VII (1957), 91-116

McFarlane, K. B., 'England and the hundred years' war', *Past and present*, XXII (1962), 3-18

McFarlane, K. B., 'The wars of the roses', *PBA*, L (1964), 87-119

McFarlane, K. B., *Lancastrian kings and lollard knights* (Oxford, 1972)

McFarlane, K. B., *The nobility of later mediaeval England* (Oxford, 1973)

McHardy, A. K., 'Some late-mediaeval Eton college wills', *JEccH*, XXVIII (1977), 387-95

McKenna, J. W., 'Henry VI of England and the dual monarchy: aspects of royal political propaganda, 1422-1432', *JWCI*, XXVIII (1965), 145-62

McKenna, J. W., 'The coronation oil of the Yorkist kings', *EHR*, LXXXII (1967), 102-4

McKenna, J. W., 'Piety and propaganda: the cult of King Henry VI', in B. Rowland (ed.), *Chaucer and middle English studies in honour of R. H. Robbins* (1974), pp. 72-88

McKenna, J. W., 'The myth of parliamentary sovereignty in late-mediaeval England', *EHR*, XCIV (1979), 481-506

MacKenzie, W. M., 'The debateable land', *ScotHR*, LII (1973), 1-29

McKisack, M., *The parliamentary representation of the English boroughs during the middle ages* (Oxford, 1932; reprinted 1962)

McKisack, M., *The fourteenth century, 1307-1399* (Oxford, 1959)

McLeod, E., *Charles of Orléans* (1969)

Macrae, C., 'The English council and Scotland in 1430', *EHR*, LIV (1939), 415-26

Madden, C., 'Royal treatment of feudal casualties in late-mediaeval Scotland', *ScotHR*, LV (1976), 172-94

Maitland, F. W., *The constitutional history of England* (Cambridge, 1909)

Mallett, M. E., *The florentine galleys in the fifteenth century* (Oxford, 1967)

Marche, Lecoy de la, *Le roi René* (2 vols., Paris, 1875)

Martindale, A. H. R., 'The early history of the choir of Eton College chapel', *Archaeologia*, CIII (1971), 179-98

Maxwell-Lyte, H. C., *A history of Eton College, 1440-1875* (1875; revised ed. 1889)

Maxwell-Lyte, H. C., *Historical notes on the use of the great seal of England* (1926)

Meekings, C. A. F., 'Thomas Kerver's case, 1444', *EHR*, XC (1975), 331-46

Mescal, J., *Henry VI* (1980)

Millar, E. G., *La miniature anglaise aux XIVe et XVe siècles* (Paris, 1928)

Mitchell, J., *Thomas Hoccleve* (Chicago, 1968)

Mitchell, R. J., *John Tiptoft, 1427-1470* (1938)

Monard, R., 'Le trésor monetaire du prieuré du Plessis-Grimoult: monnaies d'Henri VI roi de France et d'Angleterre', *Bulletin de la société française de numismatique*, IX (1969), 328-30

Morgan, D. A. L., 'The king's affinity in the polity of Yorkist England', *TRHS*, 5th ser., XXIII (1973), 1-22

Munro, J. H., 'The costs of Anglo-Burgundian interdependence', *Revue belge de philologie et d'histoire*, XLVI (1968), 1228-38

Munro, J. H., 'An economic aspect of the collapse of the Anglo-Burgundian alliance, 1428-1442', *EHR*, LXXXV (1970), 225-44

Munro, J. H., *Wool, cloth and gold* (Toronto, 1972)

Murray, A. L., 'The comptroller, 1424-1488', *ScotHR*, LII (1973), 1-29

Myers, A. R., 'The outbreak of war between England and Burgundy in February 1471', *BIHR*, XXIII (1960), 114-15

Newhall, R. A., *The English conquest of Normandy, 1416–1424* (New Haven, 1924)

Newhall, R. A., 'Henry V's policy of conciliation in Normandy, 1417–22', in C. A. Taylor (ed.), *Anniversary essays in mediaeval history . . . presented to C. H. Haskins* (Boston, 1929), pp. 205-29

Newhall, R. A., *Muster and review* (Cambridge, Mass., 1940)

Nicholls, K., *Gaelic and gaelicised Ireland in the middle ages* (Dublin, 1972)

Nicholson, R., *Scotland: the later middle ages* (Edinburgh, 1974)

Ogrine, W. H. L., 'Western society and alchemy from 1200 to 1500', *JMH*, V (1980), 103-32

Oman, C., *The great revolt of 1381* (2nd ed., Oxford, 1969)

Oppenheim, M., *A history of the administration of the royal navy and of merchant shipping . . .* (1896)

Orme, N., *English schools in the middle ages* (1973)

Orridge, B. B., *Illustrations of Jack Cade's rebellion* (1869)

Otway-Ruthven, A. J., *The king's secretary and the signet office in the XV century* (Cambridge, 1939)

Otway-Ruthven, A. J., *A history of medieval Ireland* (1st ed., 1968; 2nd ed., 1979)

Owen, H. and Blakeway, J. B., *A history of Shrewsbury* (2 vols., 1825)

Owst, G. R., *Preaching in mediaeval England* (Cambridge, 1926)

Petithuguenin, J., *La vie tragique de Marguérite d'Anjou* (Paris, 1928)

Peyrègne, A., 'Les émigrés gascons en Angleterre (1453–1485)', *Annales du midi*, LXVI (1954), 113-28

Phythian-Adams, C., *Desolation of a city* (Cambridge, 1979)

Pixérécourt, G. de, *Marguérite d'Anjou – mélodrame historique au trois actes, en prose* (2nd ed., Paris, 1810)

Platt, C., *Mediaeval Southampton* (1973)

Plucknett, T. F. T., 'The place of the council in the fifteenth century', *TRHS*, 4th ser., I (1918), 157-89

Plucknett, T. F. T., 'The impeachments of 1376', *TRHS*, 5th ser., I (1951), 153-64

Plucknett, T. F. T., 'State trials under Richard II', *TRHS*, 5th ser., II (1952), 159-71

Plucknett, T. F. T., 'Impeachment and attainder', *TRHS*, 5th ser., III (1953), 145-58

Pocquet du Haut-Jussé, B. A., *François II, duc de Bretagne et l'Angleterre* (Paris, 1929)

Pocquet du Haut-Jussé, B. A., 'Anne de Bourgogne et le testament de Bedford (1429)', *Bibliothèque de l'école des Chartes*, XCV (1934), 296-306

Pollard, A. J., 'The northern retainers of Richard Neville, earl of Salisbury', *Northern history*, XI (1976), 52-69

Postan, M. M., 'The costs of the hundred years' war', *Past and present*, XXVII (1964), 34-53

Postan, M. M., *Essays on mediaeval agriculture and general problems of the mediaeval economy* (Cambridge, 1973)

Postan, M. M., *Mediaeval trade and finance* (Cambridge, 1973)

Powell, J. E. and Wallis, K., *The house of lords in the middle ages* (1968)

Power, E. and Postan, M. M. (eds.), *Studies in English trade in the fifteenth century* (1933)

Powicke, F. M., *The thirteenth century* (Oxford, 1953)

Powicke, F. M., *King Henry III and the Lord Edward* (Oxford, 1966 ed.)

Powicke, F. M. and Fryde, E. B. (eds.), *The handbook of British chronology* (2nd ed., 1961)

Previté-Orton, C. W., and Brooke, Z. N. (eds.), *The Cambridge mediaeval history*, vol. VIII (Cambridge, 1936)

Prévost d'Exiles, A. F., *Histoire de Marguérite d'Anjou, reine d'Angleterre* (Amsterdam, 1740), translated as *The history of Margaret of Anjou, queen of England* (2 vols., 1755)

Probert, Y., 'Mathew Gough, 1390–1450', *Transactions of the honourable soc. of Cymmrodorion, 1961*, pp. 34-44

Pugh, R. B., *Imprisonment in mediaeval England* (Cambridge, 1968)

Pugh, T. B. (ed.), *The marcher lordships of south Wales, 1415–1536* (Cardiff, 1963)

Pugh, T. B. (ed.), *Glamorgan county history*, vol. III (Cardiff, 1971)

Radford, G. H., 'Nicholas Radford, 1385(?)–1455', *TDA*, XXXV (1903), 251-78

Radford, G. H., 'The field at Clyst in 1455', *TDA*, XLIV (1912), 252-65

Radford, L. B., *Henry Beaufort* (1908)

Raine, J., 'The Pudsays of Barford', *Archaeologia aeliana*, new ser., 11 (1858), 175-6

Ramsay, J. H., *Lancaster and York* (2 vols., 1892)

Rawcliffe, C., *The Staffords, earls of Stafford and dukes of Buckingham, 1394–1521* (Cambridge, 1978)

Reeves, A. C., 'William Booth, bishop of Coventry and Lichfield (1447–52)', *Midland hist.*, III (1974–75), 11-29

Richardson, H. G., 'Illustrations of English history in the mediaeval registers of the parlement of Paris', *TRHS*, 4th ser., X (1927), 55-85

Richardson, H. G. and Sayles, G. O., *The Irish parliament in the middle ages* (Philadelphia, 1952)

Richmond, C. F., 'The keeping of the seas during the hundred years' war, 1422–1440', *History*, XLIX (1964), 283-98

Richmond, C. F., 'English naval power in the fifteenth century', *History*, LII (1967), 1-15

Richmond, C. F., 'The nobility and the wars of the roses, 1459–61', *Nott. Med. St.*, XXI (1977), 71-86

Roake, M. and Rhyman, J. (eds.), *Essays in Kentish history* (1973)

Robertson, C. A., 'The tithe-heresy of Friar William Russell', *Albion*, VIII, no. 1 (1976), 1-16

Robertson, C. A., 'Local government and the king's "affinity" in fifteenth-century Leicestershire and Warwickshire', *Trans. Leics. arch. and hist. soc.*, LII (1976–77), 37-45

Romani, F., *Margerita d'Anjou – melodrame* (Milan, 1820, 1826)

Rosenthal, J. T., 'Richard, duke of York: a fifteenth-century layman and the church', *Catholic historical review*, L (1964), 171-87

Rosenthal, J. T., 'Fifteenth-century baronial incomes and Richard, duke of York', *BIHR*, XXXVII (1964), 233-40

Rosenthal, J. T., 'The estates and finances of Richard, duke of York (1411–60)', in *Studies in mediaeval and renaissance history*, II, ed. W. M. Bowsky (Lincoln, Nebraska, 1965), 115-204

Rosenthal, J. T., 'The training of an élite group: English bishops in the fifteenth century', *Transactions of the American philosophical soc.*, new ser., LX, part 5 (1970)

Rosenthal, J. T., *The purchase of paradise* (1972)

Roskell, J. S., *The knights of the shire for the county palatine of Lancaster, 1377–1460* (Chetham soc., new ser., XCVI, 1937)

Roskell, J. S., 'The office and dignity of protector of England, with special reference to its origins', *EHR*, LXVIII (1953), 193-231

Roskell, J. S., *The commons in the parliament of 1422* (Manchester, 1954)

Roskell, J. S., 'William Tresham of Bywell, speaker for the commons under Henry VI', *Northants. past and present*, II (1954–59), 189-203

Roskell, J. S., 'Sir Thomas Tresham, knight, speaker for the commons under Henry VI', *Northants. past and present*, II (1954–59), 313-23

Roskell, J. S., 'The problem of attendance of the lords in mediaeval parliaments', *BIHR*, XXIX (1956), 153-204

Roskell, J. S., 'Sir John Popham, knight banneret, of Charford', *Proceedings of the Hants. archaeological soc. and field club*, XXI (1958), 38-52

Roskell, J. S., 'John, Lord Wenlock of Someries', *Bedfordshire historical record soc.*, XXXVIII (1958), 12-48

Roskell, J. S., 'Sir James Strangeways of West Harsley and Whorlton, speaker in the parliament of 1461', *Yorkshire archaeological journal*, XXXIX (1958), 455-82

Roskell, J. S., 'Sir John Say of Broxbourne', *East Hertfordshire archaeological soc. transactions*, XIV, part 1 (1959), 20-41

Roskell, J. S., 'Three Wiltshire speakers', *Wiltshire archaeological and natural history magazine*, LVI (1956), 272-358

Roskell, J. S., 'Sir John Wood of Molesey', *Surrey archaeological collections*, LVI (1959), 15-28

Roskell, J. S., 'William Allington of Horseheath, speaker in the parliament of 1429–30', *Proceedings of the Cambridgeshire archaeological soc.*, LII (1959), 30-42

Roskell, J. S., 'William Catesby, counsellor to Richard III', *BJRL*, XLII (1959–60), 145-74

Roskell, J. S., 'William Burley of Broncroft, speaker for the commons in 1437 and 1445–6', *Transactions of the Shropshire archaeological soc.*, LVI (1960), 263-72

Roskell, J. S., 'Sir William Oldhall, speaker in the parliament of 1450–1', *Nott. Med. St.*, V (1961), 87-112

Roskell, J. S., 'Sir Richard Vernon of Haddon, speaker in the parliament of Leicester, 1426', *Derbyshire archaeological journal*, LXXXII (1962), 43-53

Roskell, J. S., 'Thomas Thorpe, speaker in the Reading parliament of 1453', *Nott. Med. St.*, VII (1963), 79-105

Roskell, J. S., *The commons and their speakers in English parliaments, 1376–1523* (Manchester, 1965)

Ross, C. D., 'The household accounts of Elizabeth Berkeley, countess of Warwick, 1420–1', *TBGAS*, LXX (1951), 81-105

Ross, C. D., *The estates and finances of Richard Beauchamp, earl of Warwick* (Dugdale occasional papers, XII, 1956)

Ross, C. D., 'The estates and finances of Richard, duke of York', *WHR*, II (1966–67), 299-302

Ross, C. D., *Edward IV* (1974)

Ross, C. D. (ed.), *Patronage, pedigree and power in later mediaeval England* (Gloucester, 1979)

Ross, C. D. and Pugh, T. B., 'The English baronage and the income tax of 1436', *BIHR*, XXV (1953), 1-28

Roy, J. T. E., *Histoire de Marguérite d'Anjou* (Tours, 1857)

Royal commission on historical monuments: Buckinghamshire, vol. I (1912); Cambridge, vol. I (1959)

Rowe. B. J. H., 'King Henry VI's claim to France in picture and poem', *Library*, 4th ser., XIII (1932–33), 77-88

Rowe, B. J. H., 'Notes on the Clovis miniature and the Bedford portrait in the Bedford book of hours', *JBAA*, 3rd ser., XXV (1962), 56-65

Ruddock, A. A., 'John Payne's persecution of foreigners in the town court of Southampton in the fifteenth century', *Transactions of the Hants. archaeological soc. and field club*, XVI (1944), 23-37

Ruddock, A. A., 'Alien hosting in Southampton in the fifteenth century', *EconHR*, XVI (1946), 30-7

Ruddock, A. A., 'Alien merchants in Southampton in the later middle ages', *EHR*, LXI (1946), 1-17

Ruddock, A. A., *Italian merchants and shipping in Southampton, 1270–1600* (Southampton, 1951)

Ruud, M. B., *Thomas Chaucer* (Minneapolis, 1926)

St John Hope, W. H., 'The discovery of the remains of King Henry VI in St George's chapel, Windsor castle', *Archaeologia*, 2nd ser., XII (1911), 533-42

Saltmarsh, J., 'The founder's statutes of King's college, Cambridge', in J. C. Davies (ed.), *Studies presented to Sir H. Jenkinson* (1957), pp. 337-60

Saltmarsh, J., *King Henry VI and the royal foundations* (Cambridge, 1972)

Sandquist, T. A., 'The holy oil of St. Thomas of Canterbury', in T. A. Sandquist and M. R. Powicke (eds.), *Essays in mediaeval history presented to Bertie Wilkinson* (Toronto, 1969), pp. 330-44

Sayles, G. O., 'The royal marriages act, 1428', *LQR*, XCIV (1978), 188-92

Scattergood, V. J., *Politics and poetry in the fifteenth century* (1972)

Schirmer, W. F., *John Lydgate* (1961)

Schmidt, K., *Margareta von Anjou vor unter bei Shakespeare* (Berlin, 1906)

Schofield, A. N. E. D., 'England and the council of Basel', *AHC*, V, no. 1 (1973), 1-117

Scofield, C. L., *The life and reign of Edward the fourth* (2 vols., 1923)

Searle, E., *Lordship and community* (Toronto, 1974)

Searle, W. G., *History of the Queen's College of Saint Margaret and Saint Bernard in the University of Cambridge, 1446–1560* (Cambridge, 1867)

Sharpe, R. R., *London and the kingdom* (3 vols., 1894–95)

Shakespeare, W., *Henry the sixth*, 3 parts

Smith, J. H., *Joan of Arc* (1973)

Smyth, J., *Lives of the Berkeleys*, ed. J. Maclean (2 vols., Gloucester, 1883)

Somerville, R., *History of the duchy of Lancaster*, vol. I (1953)

Spencer, B., 'King Henry of Windsor and the London pilgrim', in J. Bird, H. Chapman, and J. Clark (eds.), *Collectanea Londiniensia* (London and Middlesex archaeological soc., 1976)

Stanley, A. P., *Historical memorials of Westminster abbey* (2nd ed., 1868)

Steel, A., *Richard II* (Cambridge, 1940)

Steel, A., *The receipt of the exchequer, 1377–1485* (Cambridge, 1954)

Storey, R. L., 'Marmaduke Lumley, bishop of Carlisle, 1430–1450', *Transactions of the Cumberland and Westmorland antiquarian and archaeological soc.*, new ser., LV (1955), 112-31

Storey, R. L., 'The wardens of the marches of England towards Scotland, 1377–1489', *EHR*, LXXII (1957), 593-615

Storey, R. L., 'English officers of state, 1399–1485', *BIHR*, XXXI (1958), 84-92

Storey, R. L., *Thomas Langley and the bishopric of Durham, 1406–1437* (1961)

Storey, R. L., *The end of the house of Lancaster* (1966)

Storey, R. L., 'Lincolnshire and the wars of the roses', *Nott. Med. St.*, XIV (1970), 64-83

Strickland, A., *Lives of the queens of England*, vol. II (rev. ed., 1857)

Strong, R., *Tudor and Jacobean portraits* (2 vols., 1969)

Stubbs, W., *The constitutional history of England* (5th ed., 3 vols., Oxford, 1891–1903)

Talbot, C. H. and Hammond, E. A., *The medical practitioners of mediaeval England* (1965)

Tanner, L. E., *Recollections of a Westminster antiquary* (1969)

Taylor, J., 'The Plumpton letters, 1416–1552', *Northern history*, X (1975), 72-87

Thielemans, M.-R., *Bourgogne et Angleterre: relations politiques et economiques entre les Pays-Bas Bourguignons et l'Angleterre, 1435–1467* (Brussels, 1966)

Thomas, R. S., 'Geoffrey Pole: a Lancastrian servant in Wales', *NLWJ*, XVII (1972), 277-86

Thomson, J. A. F., 'A lollard rising in Kent: 1431 or 1438?', *BIHR*, XXXVII (1964), 100-2

Thomson, J. A. F., *The later lollards, 1414–1520* (Oxford, 1965)

Thomson, J. A. F., 'John de la Pole, duke of Suffolk', *Speculum*, LIV (1979), 528-42

Thrupp, S. L., 'A survey of the alien population of England in 1440', *Speculum* XXXII (1957), 262-73

Thrupp, S. L., *The merchant class of mediaeval London* (Chicago, 1948; reprinted Ann Arbor, 1962)

Thrupp, S. L., 'Aliens in and around London in the fifteenth century', in A. E. J. Hollaender and W. Kellaway (eds.), *Studies in London history presented to P. E. Jones* (1969), pp. 251-72

Thrupp, S. L., *Society and history* (Ann Arbor, 1977)

Tillyard, E. M. W., *Shakespeare's history plays* (1969)

Touchard, H., *Le commerce maritime breton à la fin du moyen âge* (Paris, 1967)

Tout, T. F., *Chapters in the administrative history of mediaeval England* (6 vols., Manchester, 1920–33)

Tout, T. F. and Broome, D. M., 'A national balance sheet for 1362-3 . . .', *EHR*, XXXIX (1924), 404-19

Tower, R., 'The family of Septvans', *Arch. Cant.*, XL (1928), 105-30

Tuck, A., *Richard II and the English nobility* (1973)

929

Turner, B. C., 'Southampton as a naval centre, 1414–1458', in J. B. Morgan and P. Peberdy (eds.), *Collected essays on Southampton* (Southampton, 1958)

Turner, G. J., 'The minority of Henry III', *TRHS*, new ser., XVIII (1904), 245-95; 3rd ser., I (1907), 205-62

Twemlow, F. R., *The battle of Blore heath* (Wolverhampton, 1912)

Tyas, G., *The battles of Wakefield* (1854)

Ullmann, W., 'Eugenius IV, Cardinal Kemp, and Archbishop Chichele', in J. W. Watt, J. B. Morrall, and F. X. Martin (eds.), *Mediaeval studies presented to A. Gwynn* (Dublin, 1961), pp. 359-83

Vale, M. G. A., 'The last years of English Gascony, 1451–1453', *TRHS*, 5th ser., XIX (1969), 119-38

Vale, M. G. A., 'Sir John Fastolf's "report" of 1435: a new interpretation reconsidered', *Nott. Med. St.*, XVII (1973), 78-84

Vale, M. G. A., *Charles VII* (1974)

Vallance, A., 'A curious case at Cranbrook in 1437', *Arch. Cant.*, XLIII (1931), 173-86

Vaughan, R., *Philip the Good* (1970)

Verger, J., 'The University of Paris at the end of the hundred years' war', in J. W. Baldwin and R. A. Goldthwaite (eds.), *Universities in politics* (Baltimore, 1972), pp. 47-78

Vickers, K. H., *Humphrey, duke of Gloucester* (1907)

Victoria history of England: county of Cambridge and the Isle of Ely, vol. III (1959); *county of Warwick*, vol. III (1945)

Virgoe, R., 'The death of William de la Pole, duke of Suffolk', *BJRL*, XLVII (1964–65), 489-502

Virgoe, R., 'The composition of the king's council, 1437–61', *BIHR*, XLIII (1970), 134-60

Virgoe, R., 'William Tailboys and Lord Cromwell: crime and politics in Lancastrian England', *BJRL*, LV (1973), 459-82

Virgoe, R., 'The Cambridgeshire election of 1439', *BIHR*, XLVI (1973), 95-101

Viriville, A. Vallet de, *Histoire de Charles VII et son époque* (3 vols., Paris, 1862–65)

Walker, R. F., 'Jasper Tudor and the town of Tenby', *NLWJ*, XVI (1969), 1-22

Wallenberg, J. K., *The place-names of Kent* (Uppsala, 1934)

Watson, A. G., *The library of Sir Simonds D'Ewes* (British Museum, 1966)

Watson, W. B., 'The structure of the Florentine galley trade with Flanders and England in the fifteenth century', *Revue belge de philologie et d'histoire*, XXXIX (1961), 1073–91; XL (1962), 317-47

Waugh, W. T., 'Joan of Arc in English sources of the fifteenth century', in J. G. Edwards, V. H. Galbraith, and E. F. Jacob (eds.), *Historical essays in honour of James Tait* (Manchester, 1933), pp. 387-98

Wedgwood, J. C., 'Staffordshire parliamentary history', *William Salt archaeological soc.* (3 vols. in 4, 1917–20), vol. I

Wedgwood, J. C., *History of parliament: biographies of the members of the commons house, 1439–1509* (1936)

Wedgwood, J. C., *History of Parliament: register of the ministers and of the members of both houses, 1439–1509* (1938)

Weiss, R., 'Henry VI and the library of All Souls College', *EHR*, LVII (1942), 102-5

Weiss, R., 'Humphrey, duke of Gloucester and Tito Livio Frulovisi', in D. J. Gordon (ed.), *Fritz Saxl, 1890–1948* (1957), pp. 218-27

Weiss, R., *Humanism in England during the fifteenth century* (Oxford, 1967)

Weisser, M. R., *Crime and punishment in early modern Europe* (Hassocks, Sussex, 1979)

Wickham, G., *Early English stages, 1300–1600* (2 vols., 1959)

Wilkinson, B., 'The duke of Gloucester and the council, 1422–8', *BIHR*, XXI (1958), 19-20

Wilkinson, B., *Constitutional history of England in the fifteenth century, 1399–1485* (1964)

Williams, C. H., 'Fifteenth century *coram rege* rolls', *BIHR*, I (1923–24), 69-72

Williams, E. C., *My lord of Bedford, 1389–1435* (1963)

Willis, R. and Clark, J. W., *The architectural history of the University of Cambridge and of the colleges of Cambridge and Eton* (4 vols., Cambridge, 1886)

Withington, R., *English pageantry: an historical outline* (2 vols., Cambridge, Mass., 1918)

Wolffe, B. P., 'Acts of resumption in the Lancastrian parliaments, 1399–1456', *EHR*, LXXIII (1958), 583-613

Wolffe, B. P., *The royal demesne in English history* (1971)

Wood, H., 'The office of chief governor of Ireland, 1172–1509', *PRIA*, XXXI, C (1923–24), 206-38

Wylie, J. H. and Waugh, W. T., *The reign of Henry V* (3 vols., 1914–29)

Wynne, W. W. E., 'Historical papers (Puleston)', *Arch. Camb.*, 1st ser., I (1846), 145-7

D. Unpublished Dissertations and Theses

Dissertations, as opposed to theses, are in partial fulfilment of the requirements for either the degree of BA or that of MA

Allmand, C. T., 'The relations between the English government, the higher clergy and the papacy in Normandy, 1417–50' (Oxford DPhil thesis, 1963)

Archer, R. E., 'The court party during the ascendancy of the duke of Suffolk, 1444–50' (Bristol BA dissertation, 1977)

Avery, M. E., 'Proceedings in the court of chancery up to *c.* 1460' (London MA thesis, 1958)

Avrutick, J. B., 'Commissions of oyer and terminer in fifteenth-century England' (London MPhil thesis, 1967)

Bennett, M. J., 'Late mediaeval society in north-west England: Cheshire and Lancashire, 1375–1425' (Lancaster PhD thesis, 1975)

Barron, C. M., 'The government of London and its relations with the crown, 1400–1450' (London PhD thesis, 1970)

Blatcher, M., 'The working of the court of king's bench in the fifteenth century' (London PhD thesis, 1936)

Bolton, J. L., 'Alien merchants in England in the reign of Henry VI, 1422–61' (Oxford Blitt thesis, 1971)

Bull, M.-L., 'Philip Morgan (d. 1435): ecclesiastic and statesman' (Wales [Swansea] MA dissertation, 1977)

Burney, E. M., 'The English rule of Normandy, 1435–50' (Oxford BLitt thesis, 1958)

Butt, G. E., 'The activities of household officials in the fifteenth century as illustrated by the Hatteclyff family' (London MA thesis, 1955)

Cardew, A. A., 'A study of society in the Anglo-Scottish borders, 1455–1502' (St Andrews PhD thesis, 1974)

Carpenter, M. C., 'Political society in Warwickshire, 1401–72' (Cambridge PhD thesis, 1976)

Chrimes S. B., 'John, first duke of Bedford' (London MA thesis, 1929)

Cottam, D. S., 'Anglo-Breton relations, 1435–91' (Wales [Swansea] MA dissertation, 1972)

Crawford, A., 'The career of John Howard, duke of Norfolk, 1420–85' (London MPhil thesis, 1975)

Davies, R. G., 'The episcopate of England and Wales, 1378–1443' (3 vols., Manchester PhD thesis, 1974)

Elder, A. J., 'A study of the Beauforts and their estates, 1399–1450' (Bryn Mawr PhD thesis, 1964)

Friedrichs, R. L., 'The career and influence of Ralph, Lord Cromwell, 1393–1456' (Columbia PhD thesis, 1974)

George, J. M., 'The English episcopate and the crown, 1437–50' (Columbia PhD thesis, 1976)

Griffith, M. C., 'The council in Ireland, 1399–1452' (Oxford BLitt thesis, 1935)

Griffiths, R. A., 'Royal government in the southern counties of the principality of Wales, 1422–85' (Bristol PhD thesis, 1962)

Gollancz, M., 'The system of gaol delivery as illustrated in the extant gaol delivery rolls of the fifteenth century' (London MA thesis, 1936)

Hare, J. N., 'Lords and tenants in Wiltshire, *c*. 1380-*c*. 1520' (London PhD thesis, 1975)

Hemmant, M., 'The exchequer chamber, being the assembly of all the judges of England for matters of law' (London PhD thesis, 1929)

Herbert, A., 'Public order and private violence in Herefordshire, 1413–61' (Wales [Swansea] MA thesis, 1978)

Huyler, D., 'The character and personality of King Henry VI as factors in the Lancastrian-Yorkist struggle' (Michigan State PhD thesis, 1964)

Jack, R. I., 'The Lords Grey of Ruthin, 1325–1490' (London PhD thesis, 1961)

Jeffs, R. M., 'The later mediaeval sheriff and the royal household' (Oxford DPhil thesis, 1960)

Jones, M. K., 'The new nobility, 1437–50' (Bristol BA dissertation, 1977)

Kelly, P., 'Henry Holand, duke of Exeter, 1430–75: a biography' (Keele BA dissertation, 1980)

Kent, G. H. R., 'The estates of the Herbert family in the mid-fifteenth century' (Keele PhD thesis, 1973)

Kightley, C., 'The early lollards: a survey of popular lollard activity in England, 1382–1428' (York PhD thesis, 1975)

Kirby, J. L., 'The Hungerford family in the later middle ages' (London MA thesis, 1939)

Kretschmer, R., 'Ralph Botiller, Lord Sudeley' (Keele BA dissertation, 1973)

McGovern, C. J. M., 'Lancastrian diplomacy and Queen Margaret's court in exile, 1461–1471' (Keele BA dissertation, 1973)

Macrae, C., 'Scotland and the wars of the roses' (Oxford DPhil thesis, 1939)

Marshall, A. E., 'The role of English war captains in England and Normandy, 1436–61' (Wales [Swansea] MA thesis, 1975)

Meehan, M. E., 'English piracy, 1450–1500' (Bristol MA thesis, 1971)

Metcalfe, C. A., 'Alice Chaucer, duchess of Suffolk, c. 1404–1475' (Keele BA dissertation, 1970)

Milner, J. D., 'The order of the garter in the reign of Henry VI, 1422–1461' (Manchester MA thesis, 1972)

Nigota, J. A., 'John Kempe: a political prelate of the fifteenth century' (Emory PhD thesis, 1973)

Oldfield, M., 'Parliament and convocation, with special reference to the pontificate of Henry Chichele, 1413–1443' (Manchester MA thesis, 1938)

Peake, M. I., 'London and the wars of the roses, 1445–61' (London MA thesis, 1925)

Pollard, A. J., 'The family of Talbot, Lords Talbot and earls of Shrewsbury in the fifteenth century' (2 vols., Bristol PhD thesis, 1968)

Price, E., 'Ralph, Lord Cromwell and his household' (London MA thesis, 1948)

Rawcliffe, C., 'The Staffords, earls of Stafford and dukes of Buckingham, 1394–1521' (Sheffield PhD thesis, 1974)

Rhydderch, A. E., 'Robert Mascall and John Stanbury: king's confessors and bishops of Hereford' (Wales [Swansea] MA dissertation, 1974)

Richmond, C. F., 'Royal administration and the keeping of the seas, 1422–1485' (Oxford DPhil thesis, 1962)

Rose, M. A., 'Petitions in parliament under the Lancastrians from, or relating to, towns' (London MA thesis, 1926)

Rose, S. P., 'The accounts of William Soper, clerk of the king's ships to Henry V and Henry VI for 1421–27' (London PhD thesis, 1974)

Ross, C. D., 'The Yorkshire baronage, 1399–1435' (Oxford DPhil thesis, 1951)

Smith, C. W., 'The register of Robert FitzHugh, bishop of London, 1431–36' (Ohio MA dissertation, 1979)

Thomas, D., 'The Herberts of Raglan as supporters of the house of York in the second half of the fifteenth century' (Wales [Cardiff] MA thesis, 1967)

Thomas, E. A., 'The Lords Audley, 1391–1459' (Wales [Swansea] MA dissertation, 1976)

Thomas, R. S., 'The political career, estates, and "connection" of Jasper Tudor, earl of Pembroke and duke of Bedford (d. 1495)' (Wales [Swansea] PhD thesis, 1971)

Virgoe, R., 'The parliament of 1449–50' (London PhD thesis, 1964)

Winkler, F. H., 'The making of king's knights in England, 1399–1461' (Yale PhD thesis, 1943)

Witchell, M., 'John Kempe (d. 1454): an ecclesiastic as statesman' (Wales [Swansea] MA thesis, 1979)

Woodger, L. S., 'Henry Bourgchier, earl of Essex and his family' (Oxford DPhil thesis, 1974)

Wright, F. M., 'The house of York, 1415–1450' (Johns Hopkins PhD thesis, 1959).

Index